IFIP Advances in Information and Communication Technology 336

IFIP – The International Federation for Information Processing

IFIP was founded in 1960 under the auspices of UNESCO, following the First World Computer Congress held in Paris the previous year. An umbrella organization for societies working in information processing, IFIP's aim is two-fold: to support information processing within its member countries and to encourage technology transfer to developing nations. As its mission statement clearly states,

> *IFIP's mission is to be the leading, truly international, apolitical organization which encourages and assists in the development, exploitation and application of information technology for the benefit of all people.*

IFIP is a non-profitmaking organization, run almost solely by 2500 volunteers. It operates through a number of technical committees, which organize events and publications. IFIP's events range from an international congress to local seminars, but the most important are:

- The IFIP World Computer Congress, held every second year;
- Open conferences;
- Working conferences.

The flagship event is the IFIP World Computer Congress, at which both invited and contributed papers are presented. Contributed papers are rigorously refereed and the rejection rate is high.

As with the Congress, participation in the open conferences is open to all and papers may be invited or submitted. Again, submitted papers are stringently refereed.

The working conferences are structured differently. They are usually run by a working group and attendance is small and by invitation only. Their purpose is to create an atmosphere conducive to innovation and development. Refereeing is less rigorous and papers are subjected to extensive group discussion.

Publications arising from IFIP events vary. The papers presented at the IFIP World Computer Congress and at open conferences are published as conference proceedings, while the results of the working conferences are often published as collections of selected and edited papers.

Any national society whose primary activity is in information may apply to become a full member of IFIP, although full membership is restricted to one society per country. Full members are entitled to vote at the annual General Assembly, National societies preferring a less committed involvement may apply for associate or corresponding membership. Associate members enjoy the same benefits as full members, but without voting rights. Corresponding members are not represented in IFIP bodies. Affiliated membership is open to non-national societies, and individual and honorary membership schemes are also offered.

Luis M. Camarinha-Matos Xavier Boucher
Hamideh Afsarmanesh (Eds.)

Collaborative Networks for a Sustainable World

11th IFIP WG 5.5 Working Conference
on Virtual Enterprises, PRO-VE 2010
St. Etienne, France, October 11-13, 2010
Proceedings

Springer

Volume Editors

Luis M. Camarinha-Matos
New University of Lisbon, Faculty of Sciences and Technology
Campus de Caparica, 2829-516 Monte Caparica, Portugal
E-mail: cam@uninova.pt

Xavier Boucher
Ecole Nationale Supérieure des Mines de Saint-Etienne (ENSMSE)
Centre G2I, Département OMSI
158 Cours Fauriel, 42023 Saint-Etienne Cedex, France
E-mail: boucher@emse.fr

Hamideh Afsarmanesh
University of Amsterdam, Computer Science Department
Science Park 107, 1098 XG Amsterdam, The Netherlands
E-mail: h.afsarmanesh@uva.nl

Library of Congress Control Number: 2010934859

CR Subject Classification (1998): H.5.3, C.2, H.4, J.1, D.2, H.5

ISSN	1868-4238
ISBN-10	3-642-15960-5 Springer Berlin Heidelberg New York
ISBN-13	978-3-642-15960-2 Springer Berlin Heidelberg New York

springer.com

Printed in Germany

Typesetting: Camera-ready by author, data conversion by Scientific Publishing Services, Chennai, India
Printed on acid-free paper 219/3180

Preface

Collaborative Networks for a Sustainable World

Aiming to reach a sustainable world calls for a wider collaboration among multiple stakeholders from different origins, as the changes needed for sustainability exceed the capacity and capability of any individual actor. In recent years there has been a growing awareness both in the political sphere and in civil society including the business sectors, on the importance of sustainability. Therefore, this is an important and timely research issue, not only in terms of systems design but also as an effort to borrow and integrate contributions from different disciplines when designing and/or governing those systems. The discipline of collaborative networks especially, which has already emerged in many application sectors, shall play a key role in the implementation of effective sustainability strategies.

PRO-VE 2010 focused on sharing knowledge and experiences as well as identifying directions for further research and development in this area. The conference addressed models, infrastructures, support tools, and governance principles developed for collaborative networks, as important resources to support multi-stakeholder sustainable developments. Furthermore, the challenges of this theme open new research directions for CNs.

PRO-VE 2010 held in St. Etienne, France, was the 11th event in a series of successful conferences, including PRO-VE 1999 (held in Porto, Portugal), PRO-VE 2000 (Florianopolis, Brazil), PRO-VE 2002 (Sesimbra, Portugal), PRO-VE 2003 (Lugano, Switzerland), PRO-VE 2004 (Toulouse, France), PRO-VE 2005 (Valencia, Spain), PRO-VE 2006 (Helsinki, Finland), PRO-VE 2007 (Guimarães, Portugal), PRO-VE 2008 (Poznan, Poland), and PRO-VE 2009 (Thessaloniki, Greece).

This book includes a number of selected papers from the PRO-VE 2010 Conference, providing a comprehensive overview of recent advances in various CN domains and their applications with a particular focus on sustainability issues. With this focus, this edition of the conference emphasized CN topics related to carbon-efficient value networks, active aging, management in humanitarian organizations, collaborative health networks, environment management, etc., but also including other important technical and scientific challenges in areas such as innovation networks, networking structures and consortia formation, competencies and trust management, service-orientation, collaborative process models, performance evaluation, collaborative work environments, virtual communities, inter-organizational information systems and interoperability, and game theory, among others.

Similar to previous editions of PRO-VE, the book itself is the result of cooperative and highly distributed work among the authors of the articles and the International Program Committee members who took part in paper evaluations. It therefore represents a valuable tool for those interested in innovation, emerging applications, research advances, and future challenges for R&D in collaborative networks. We would like to thank all the authors both from academia/research and industry for their contributions. We appreciate the dedication of the PRO-VE Program Committee members who helped with the selection of articles and contributed with their valuable comments to assisting authors in improving the quality of their work.

July 2010

Luis M. Camarinha-Matos
Xavier Boucher
Hamideh Afsarmanesh

PRO-VE 2010 – 11th IFIP Working Conference on VIRTUAL ENTERPRISES
St. Etienne, 11–13 October 2010

General Chair

Xavier Boucher (France)

Program Committee Chair

Luis M. Camarinha-Matos (Portugal)

Program Committee

Antonio Abreu (Portugal)
Hamideh Afsarmanesh (Netherlands)
Cesar Analide (Portugal)
Samuil Angelov (Netherlands)
Dario Antonelli (Italy)
Dimitris Apostolou (Greece)
Dimitris Assimakopoulos (France)
Vincent Augusto (France)
Corinne Autant-Bernard (France)
Américo Azevedo (Portugal)
Panagiotis Bamidis (Greece)
Ron Beckett (Australia)
Peter Bertok (Australia)
Béatrix Besombes (France)
Kirsimarja Blomqvist (Finland)
Xavier Boucher (France)
Jean Pierre Bourey (France)
Jeremy Bryans (UK)
Patrick Burlat (France)
Jorge Cardoso (Portugal)
Wojciech Cellary (Poland)
Aline Cuauvin (France)
Sophie D'Amours (Canada)
Alexandre Dolgui (France)
Rob Dekkers (UK)
Carine Dominguez (France)
Schahram Dustdar (Austria)
Jens Eschenbaecher (Germany)
Elsa Estevez (Argentina)
John Fitzgerald (UK)
Myrna Flores (Switzerland)
Rosanna Fornasiero (Italy)
Alexis Garapin (France)
Cesar Garita (Costa Rica)
Virginie Goepp (France)
Ted Goranson (USA)
Paul Grefen (Netherlands)
Jairo Gutierrez (New Zealand)
Tarek Hassan (UK)
Tomasz Janowski (Macau)
Toshiya Kaihara (Japan)
Eleni Kaldoudi (Greece)
Iris Karvonen (Finland)
Alexandra Klen (Brazil)
Bernhard Koelmel (Germany)
Kurt Kosanke (Germany)
Adamantios Koumpis (Greece)
George Kovacs (Hungary)
John Krogstie (Norway)
Andrew Kusiak (USA)
Daniel Llerena (France)
Éric Marcon (France)

Gregoris Mentzas (Greece)
István Mézgar (Hungary)
Arturo Molina (Mexico)
Gilles Neubert (France)
Roumen Nikolov (Bulgaria)
Ovidiu Noran (Australia)
Paulo Novais (Portugal)
Adegboyega Ojo (Macau)
Eugénio Oliveira (Portugal)
Angel Ortiz (Spain)
Martin Ollus (Finland)
Luis Osório (Portugal)
Hervé Panetto (France)
Iraklis Paraklakis (Greece)
Adam Pawlak (Poland)
Sophie Peillon (France)
Keith Phalp (UK)
Hervé Pingaud (France)
Willy Picard (Poland)
Goran Putnik (Portugal)
Michel Pouly (Switzerland)
Yacine Rezgui (UK)
Ricardo Rabelo (Brazil)
Raimar Scherer (Germany)
Hans Schaffers (Netherlands)
Waleed W. Smari (USA)
Weiming Shen (Canada)
Jorge P. Sousa (Portugal)
António L. Soares (Portugal)
Klaus-Dieter Thoben (Germany)
Volker Stich (Germany)
Chrysostomos Stylios (Greece)
Lorna Uden (UK)
Antonio Volpentesta (Italy)
Peter Weiß (Germany)
Lai Xu (UK)

Technical Sponsors

IFIP WG 5.5 COVE
Co-Operation infrastructure for Virtual Enterprises and electronic business

Society of Collaborative Networks

Other Sponsors

Organization Co-sponsors

Ecole Nationale Supérieure des Mines
SAINT-ETIENNE

New University of Lisbon

UNINOVA

University of Amsterdam

Université Jean Monnet SAINT-ETIENNE

Table of Contents

1. Introduction

2. Sustainability Cases – I

3. Sustainability Cases – II

4. Innovation Networks

5. Carbon Efficient Value Networks

6. Management of CNs in Humanitarian Organizations – I

7. Management of CNs in Humanitarian Organizations – II

8. Collaborative Networks Implementations

9. Collaborative Health Networks

10. Networking Structures

11. Partners Selection and VO Creation – I

12. Partners Selection and VO Creation – II

13. Modeling and Managing Competencies – I

14. Modeling and Managing Competencies – II

15. Trust and Information

19. Performance and Value – I

20. Performance and Value – II

21. Collaborative Work Environments

22. Learning and Collaboration

23. Virtual Communities and Teams

24. Inter-Organisational Information Systems for CNs – I

28. Game Theory for CN

The Role of Collaborative Networks in Sustainability

Luis M. Camarinha-Matos[1], Hamideh Afsarmanesh[2], and Xavier Boucher[3]

[1] Universidade Nova de Lisboa, Faculty of Sciences and Technology, Portugal
cam@uninova.pt
[2] University of Amsterdam, Netherlands
h.afsarmanesh@uva.nl
[3] Ecole Nationale Supérieure des Mines de St Etienne, France
boucher@emse.fr

Abstract. There is a great potential for mutual beneficial synergies between the two fields of Collaborative Networks and Sustainability science. This potential has in fact been recognized in many fields where these synergies are leading to novel approaches and solutions. It is particularly evident that the challenges of sustainability call for a wide collaboration among multiple stakeholders, as the needed changes exceed the capacity and capability of individual actors. With the purpose to illustrate the possible contribution and challenges for collaborative networks in sustainability, a number of relevant cases where examples of such synergies are already identified are briefly introduced.

Keywords: Collaborative Networks, Sustainability, Stability.

1 Introduction

The notion of sustainability is a subject of growing importance. It is present in most strategic and political agendas, being a prevalent issue in science and technology, and leading to related terms such as sustainable development [1] or even sustainability science. One important milestone was the UN's World Commission on Environment and Development report of 1987 [2], also known as the Brundtland report, which defined sustainability as:

> "*Meeting the needs of the present without compromising the ability of future generations to meet their own needs.*"

Environmental and ecological aspects have dominated the discussions on sustainability, which is natural since after all the environment is the elementary basis of life. Nevertheless, such perspective falls short if we do not pay attention to other aspects such as resource management, organizational forms of the society, cultural aspects, etc. Therefore, more recent discussions, as represented in the conclusions of the 2005 World Summit [3], [4], led to the identification of three main pillars of sustainability (Fig. 1):

- *Environmental* – aiming at maintaining a stable base of resources, preserving ecosystems and biodiversity, avoiding over-exploitation of renewable resources, safeguarding the quality of the atmosphere, recycling, etc.

L.M. Camarinha-Matos et al. (Eds.): PRO-VE 2010, IFIP AICT 336, pp. 1–16, 2010.

- *Economical* – focusing on the ability to generate wealth in the long term, namely producing goods and services, creating jobs and prosperity, pursuing efficiency, etc.
- *Social* – concerned with achieving equity, providing social services, guaranteeing social inclusion, preserving cultures, groups, places, and ensuring political accountability and participation (community).

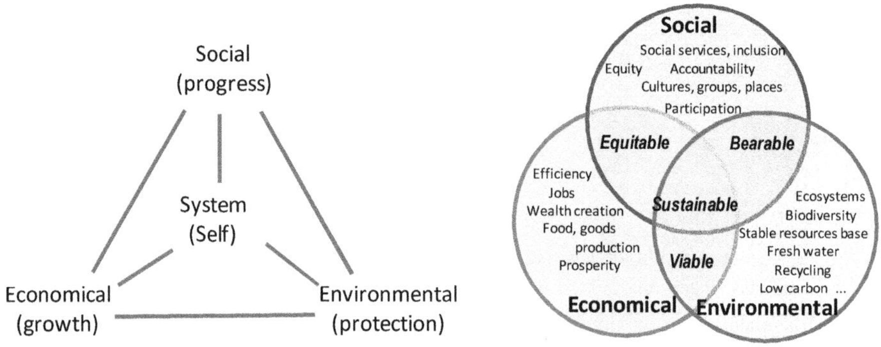

Fig. 1. Pillars of sustainability

Clearly, all these elements of sustainability, although an incomplete list of examples, introduce considerable complexity. Not only the goals expressed are clearly multi-dimensional but, additionally, they have to be coordinated within a long term vision of performance and development. Such complexity raises the issue of how to balance (sometimes incompatible) objectives and also how to measure the achievement level. Moreover, it is noticeable that new key actors, including the private sector, are now playing an increasingly constructive role. Due to the growing awareness among political sphere and in the civil society of the importance of sustainability, also the business sector starts to acknowledge that preserving the environment and the other inter-related pillars is both good business and a moral obligation. More strict regulations, consumers' demand for greener products, reduction of the carbon footprint, optimization of the usage of natural resources, more societal attention, and many other trends are triggers for the emergence of green, environmental-conscious, as well as social-oriented markets. At the academic and research level, the challenges of sustainability are becoming a key topic for various scientific communities and in some universities new focused units are being created.

Sustainability challenges clearly call for a wider collaboration as the needed changes exceed the capacity and capability of individual actors. The discipline of Collaborative Networks has certainly a key role to play, in the multi-stakeholder collaborative perspective which has to be now implemented.

2 Why Collaboration

Concepts, methods and tools developed in the area of Collaborative Networks (CNs) can facilitate the engagement and interplay of the multiple stakeholders which are participants needed in any effort towards sustainability. For instance:

- Basic infrastructures and collaboration tools – support interaction, information sharing and exchange (a basis for informed decision-making), coordination of potentially heterogeneous, distributed and autonomous entities.
- The notion of community, as implicit in the Virtual organization Breeding Environments (VBEs) or Professional Virtual Communities (PVCs), helps in building the perception of mutual dependency and co-responsibility for the stakeholders involved.
- What we have learned with studies on trust management, value systems, multi-cultural and multi-legal contexts for CNs can help in the development of better policies and governance methods for sustainable development projects. Sustainability is a global challenge and therefore it needs to be addressed at a planetary scale and with a multidimensional approach.

On the other hand, conceptual developments in CNs will also benefit as we gather deeper knowledge on the mechanisms involved in sustainability. One example is given by the emerging discipline of biomimicry or biomimetics, which studies Nature's best "ideas" in terms of models, systems, processes, and elements, and tries to imitate these designs and processes to solve human problems. The core assumption is that Nature has already solved many of the problems we are facing. This idea is also reflected in expressions such as "innovation inspired by nature" and has been, in fact, adopted by the collaborative networks research community. For instance, the notion of a business ecosystem, typically seen as a particular case of VBE, is an example of biomimicry, as it gets its inspiration from natural ecosystems.

But this analogy can be taken further. An ecosystem does not involve only collaboration but rather a complex interplay of collaboration and competition, producers, consumers, regulators, and support entities. Although a multiplicity of roles and even competition are present, there is some form of "survival instinct" and even shared vision that enables participants to align their investments and to find mutually supportive roles. Exploring these ideas will bring new insights on better governance principles that will likely help in reducing the percentage of failures and thus contributing to more sustainable business ecosystems. Even though lacking proper formalization, ideas such as business or organizational ecologies also touch on this issue. Other examples come from the so-called "bio-inspired" algorithms, e.g. swarm intelligence and genetic algorithms, which are progressively exploited to solve issues of self-organizing systems, distributed systems design, optimization and distributed scheduling, etc. In addition, sustainable development is not a fixed state of harmony, but rather a *process of change* in which the exploitation of resources, direction of investments, orientation of technological development and institutional changes need to be made consistent with present as well as future needs. This notion can also influence further research emphasis on dynamic models, networks evolution, and network-health supervision, which are subjects not yet well developed in CNs.

Therefore there is a great potential for mutual beneficial synergies between the two fields of Collaborative Networks and Sustainability Science. The following sections briefly introduce a number of relevant cases where examples of such synergies have already been identified.

3 Business Ecosystems

This is perhaps one of the most developed areas in Collaborative Networks. The advances in Information and Communication Technologies (ICT), especially the Internet and pervasive computing, have revolutionized virtual collaborations and enabled or induced the emergence of new paradigms such as extended enterprise, virtual enterprise (VE) / virtual organization (VO), and professional virtual community. All of these concepts represent the temporary alliances of entities that come together to share their skills, core competencies and resources in order to better respond to emerging business opportunities, and whose collaboration is supported by computer networks. In practice however, the rapid formation of a consortium to respond to a business opportunity, which is a major "selling point" for the VE/VO paradigm, faces many obstacles: notably the large heterogeneity of the autonomous participants involved (in terms of their technological infrastructures, business practices, culture, etc.), as well as the time needed to build trust. As a consequence, the concept of VO Breeding Environment (VBE) has emerged. A VBE is a long term association which aims at increasing the level of anticipatory preparedness of its members. This enables their more efficient integration and participation in temporary alliances, as triggered by emerging business opportunities [5]. This concept is a successor of earlier organizational structures such as industry clusters or industrial districts, but with better ICT support and more adequate governance models.

A business ecosystem, also known as digital business ecosystem, can be seen as a particular case of a VBE with, as its name implies, principles and mechanisms inspired from biological ecosystems. These ecosystems are frequently focused on one geographical region and try to involve the socio-economic *living forces* of that region. The industry cluster is one of the earliest forms of business ecosystems, consisting of a group of companies, typically located in the same geographic region and operating in a common business sector. Its function is to keep some long-term "binds" with each other in order to increase their general competitiveness in the larger region. These binds or agreements may include sharing some buyer-supplier relationships, common technologies and tools, common buyers, distribution channels or common labor pools, all contributing to some form of cooperation or collaboration when business opportunities arise. Earlier forms of clusters did not require a strong ICT infrastructure but more and more often, today's collaboration requires such support. The term industrial district, mostly used in Italy, represents a concept quite similar to an industry cluster. It can be focused on one single sector or cover a number of sectors in a given region. Another organizational structure that shares some characteristics with the above examples is the case of enterprise incubators. An incubator represents a pool of small companies in their early phase, co-located in the same geographical space, possibly covering different sectors. These start-ups share some basic infrastructures (communications and other generic services) as well as consultancy support in order to evolve towards mature organizations. However, traditional incubators are not yet real VBEs as they usually do not collaborate much in joint business opportunities. Nevertheless, it would be reasonable to imagine a next generation of incubators "absorbing" the goals, principles and mechanisms of a sustainability oriented VBE.

Besides the production and services industries, these organizational structures and related concepts are being adopted, although some times with different terminologies, in a growing variety of other domains such as: collaborative e-governments, education networks, remote assistance networks for the elderly, collaborative e-science and virtual laboratories, integrated transportation systems or environmental and disaster management systems, among many others. Related notions can also be found in some developments within the service oriented systems, such as the service parks and service ecologies.

4 Collaborative Agribusiness

Sustainable agriculture is understood as a way of raising food that is healthy for consumers and animals, does not harm the environment, is humane for workers, respects animals, provides a fair wage to the farmer, and supports and enhances rural communities. It thus addresses a number of key issues:

- Conservation and preservation of the environment,
- Support of biodiversity,
- Guarantee of animal welfare,
- Economic viability for farmers,
- Promotion of social justice for workers.

During the last decade the agribusiness industry has been forced to go through a major restructuring. The main driver has been economic, as a result of globalization and technological innovation. In addition, increased customer quality requirements, new environmental regulations, and the growing importance of "biological products", are playing a role in this process.

In order to survive, small producers need access to markets and to comply with increasingly tough regulations. This requires them to join efforts, e.g. by the formation of regional agribusiness clusters, where CNs can contribute. Needless to say, the survival of small producers is a fundamental element for the preservation of the culture and social cohesiveness in many regions. A survey of experiences in this direction in various European countries can be found in [6]. However, as for the agricultural and food industry, this shift towards virtual enterprises is somewhat under-developed. Nevertheless to the companies involved in food processing industry, it is becoming clear that a real competitive advantage can only be achieved and sustained through the creation of relationships, strong information links, and co-working among the enterprises along the various steps of the value chain. In our view, the creation of virtual enterprises is inevitable to efficiently utilize all of the relevant human, organizational, and business resources and to facilitate the necessary interdependencies between the suppliers (farmers and others), manufacturers, distributors, sellers as well as ultimately customers and consumer associations.

An interesting example of a collaborative network of agrifood SMEs and their client groups can be found in the Sibary region (Italy) as studied in [7]. Also in the production of canned tomato paste, enterprises which might work together to constitute a virtual enterprise include wholesalers and retailers, can producers and their supply chains, food processors and packers, farmers and fruit growers, transportation and delivery enterprises [8]. Such collaborative network would cover the set of all operations involved in the Agribusiness concept: production operations within the farm and storing, processing and distribution of all products and their derivatives. New regulations regarding traceability of food products also require new processes for information sharing and exchange. This again increases the need for greater communication and coordination among stakeholders involved in value-added partnerships.

In the same direction, the FORAGRO Position 2010 [9] identifies a number of mechanisms, e.g.:

- "*To promote a better integration between the public and the private sectors at all levels, as well as articulate public-private networks to make progress in the development of policies for innovation;*
- *To formalize alliances and mechanisms for the exchange of information and experiences;*
- *To promote mechanisms to facilitate access to new markets and decrease the risk for small- and family-scale agriculture;*
- *To strengthen consumer organizations and their participation in RDI processes;*
- *To agree on regulatory frameworks and others for the management of shared resources (water, basins, biodiversity, soils);*
- *Etc.* "

These could be greatly facilitated by a collaborative networks approach.

5 Collaborative Transportation Systems

The transportation / mobility sector is one of the most critical elements in sustainability, especially from the environmental and economic perspectives. Current development trends towards intelligent transport systems are leading to the progressive introduction of new technologies based on electronics, sensorial systems, and communication and information technologies. For instance, new road management policies, based on new user-paying models, and increasing concerns about traffic safety, establish requirements for a new family of emergent business services. A promising strategy to promote sustainable and safe mobility aims at offering new comprehensive service contracts integrating multiple possibilities of access to public transport systems, parking areas, subscription to innovative insurance policies, etc….

The next challenge is the development of a collaborative eco-driving environment, focused on effective support of integrated services targeting transportation energy efficiency, costs saving, and improvement of safety in mobility across Europe. There is an enormous potential for reducing accidents, optimizing mobility time, and improving energy efficiency. This requires enabling the vehicles and road infrastructures with a new generation of intelligent transportation systems. Furthermore, achieving such infrastructure on a large scale needs the currently fragmented scenarios of multiple stakeholders acting independently (and even in competition) to disappear and be replaced with a collaborative context promoting integrated services and service innovation.

The underlying assumption is that new business models and novel business entities will progressively emerge in the transportation domain. In the future eco-driving environment, Integrated Transportation Service Providers will act either as service brokers or integrators directly interacting with the end-users, providing them with a range of integrated services. All the while, the actual service providers and their transactions will become invisible for the individual drivers. Through a single contract, the driver is released from the burden details of dealing with separate business entities and, additionally, gains an advantage in reduced cost via subscribing to several services at once. Furthermore, providers incur lower service and administrative costs. The actual composition of elemental services into more complex (integrated) service-packs is built dynamically and depends only on the subscription options taken by each driver. For instance, one customer might be interested in the service for optimal routing and optimal parking, as well as navigational information. Such services are likely to involve a number of different actors, such as road and highway operators, city traffic controllers, parking lots and gas stations owners, payment clearance operators, etc., for which significant interoperability is required.

Some successful "specialized" examples have already started to emerge on the market, although still with much of an ad-hoc nature. Take for instance the case of the "Via-Verde" in Portugal. This integrated service offer extends the traditional electronic tolling service of motorways with covering the parking services, gas station payments, food in drive-in restaurants, etc. [10]. The growing success of this initiative clearly shows the potential for integrated transportation-related services, supported by a collaborative network of service providers. While challenging, it is therefore important to leverage these initial ideas through provision of systematic and comprehensive models and dedicated infrastructures. These will not only facilitate the addition of new services but also provide conditions and support for authorities to supervise, influence and improve the general mobility and transportation throughout their regions and areas, thus saving energy and costs as well as improving safety.

6 Smart (Energy) Grid

The so-called smart grid represents a move from a centralized, energy producer-controlled network to one less centralized and more consumer-interactive. Initially, it corresponds to an overlay of the energy distribution grid with an information and metering system. At the current stage, most efforts are very focused on infrastructure aspects [11], [12]. However, establishing a truly smart grid requires the participation of a large number of stakeholders, including producers, transmission and distribution operators, regulators, policymakers, and consumers. Thus, the next challenge is to adopt organizational models, governance structures, and develop advanced tools to support collaboration among these players.

A brief analysis of the main (desirable) features of a smart grid clearly shows the potential for CNs in this domain:

- Self-healing from power disturbance events – initially focused on sensors, acquisition of real-time information, monitoring, error detection, diagnosis and recovery, that is a typical classical intelligent supervision problem. When the scope becomes grid-wide we have to deal with a network of autonomous entities and the approach needs to be one of collaborative systems.

- Enabling active participation of consumers – in its essence, a smart grid attempts to change consumers' behavior via variable electric rates or to pay vastly increased rates for the privilege of reliable electrical service during high-demand. These grids include consumer equipments in an overall strategy of consumption optimization and are also related to intelligent buildings. The notion of shared responsibility implies that consumers be treated as partners, namely in terms of benefit sharing, and not just as simple customers.
- Operating resiliently against physical and cyber attack – as systems become more complex and ICT-based, resilient architectures design can benefit from a collaborative networks approach.
- Providing higher power quality – smart grids are expected to help achieving more stable power supply. One of the elements involved here is proper coordination of the various producers and distribution subsystems, which given the diversity and autonomy of such entities, requires more than a traditional control approach.
- Accommodating all generation and storage options – progressive addition of renewable energy sources, including micro-generation (e.g. solar panels at home), new energy harvesting methods, and options for energy storage, lead to a large pool of resources whose management can benefit from the resource sharing and management results from collaborative networks.
- Enabling new products, services, and markets – a variety of new services and more dynamic energy markets are likely to emerge, which also require proper treatment of issues being addressed by the CN community such as distribution of benefits, negotiation protocols and e-contracting, privacy and security.
- Optimizing assets and operating efficiently – better harmonization of local distribution with interregional energy flows, smooth integration of renewable energy resources, which are for the most part intermittent in nature, better-informed forecasting approaches, etc., are directions that could also benefit from a collaborative networks perspective.

One of the first works advocating the adoption of the virtual enterprise / collaborative networks paradigm to energy networks can be found in [13].

7 Water Management

Similarly to energy, water is one of the most important natural resources that need to be preserved and adequately managed. Since fresh water sustains life and is a finite and vulnerable resource, effective management of water resources demands a holistic approach, linking social and economic development with protection of natural ecosystems.

One particular aspect is the management of water distribution networks at regional level. In many cases those networks are managed by public entities, often associated with local city and town governments. In some countries, there is a trend to the privatization of these services. Then a new actor becomes critical, acting as the regulator or supervising authority. In addition, consumers are becoming more demanding, requiring from the water supply services very high levels of quality. Quality is not only related to the biological or physical-chemical factors, but also related to the continuity of the supply with adequate levels of pressure and flow. Therefore, the objectives of the water supply managers are not only to deliver water, but to distribute it with the lowest possible cost and within the currently accepted quality levels. In order to cope with variable demands, one water supplier might need to cooperate with neighboring suppliers.

Earlier developments in this area were focused on the development of some forms of intelligent supervision systems in order to reduce costs and guarantee proper quality of service but with an intra-organizational perspective [14]. The development of more advanced management systems however, shall consider an inter-organizational perspective to cope with the needed interactions among all stakeholders, e.g. water suppliers, distributors, regulators, local administration, consumers (people, industries), consumer associations, etc. Thus, collaborative networks may provide the adequate framework for this sector.

8 Biodiversity Infrastructures

Currently, a wide variety of stakeholder organizations involved in biodiversity activities, e.g. biodiversity data providers, laboratories, universities, conservation groups, etc., are increasingly participating in some form of networked interaction. However, all current networks are goal-oriented, as the main common reason for organizations to involve in their establishment is to share their competencies and resources as required to perform specific tasks which they cannot perform alone. In other words, current collaboration among the Bio-diversity organizations results from the need to obtain / share some resources available at other organizations, including physical resources (e.g. chemical processing machinery and equipments, specialized transportation means, or collected data and samples), human resources (e.g. specialists, researchers, knowledge workers), and/or technological resources (e.g. software systems, processing power), in order to achieve certain common goals. For example, in the collaboration scenario addressed in the FlySafe project [15] which is aimed at protecting airplanes from colliding with migrating birds, several regional Biodiversity-related Organizations which are involved in research on migrating birds, as well as a few external organizations involved in weather forecast, airport administration, etc. are co-working to jointly achieve the aim of reducing risks for the airplanes.

Nevertheless the future plans for Biodiversity virtual labs in Europe as well as worldwide, is stepping out of the current networking framework and aiming to support a distributed research infrastructure, well-equipped to explore, describe, predict and propose decisive actions, as well as impacting the state of biodiversity for the benefit of the society. To achieve these goals however, the pre-existence of a VBE, namely a *strategic collaborative biodiversity network* is the antecedent to: (i) the acquisition and management of the vast amount of existing and emergent dispersed data/information, (ii) the required diverse processing and integration of this data, as well as (iii) the development of new methods and software systems required for modelling the complexity, testing, and decision making. In this direction, the vision addressed within the LifeWatch European Infrastructure initiative [16], for instance, addresses the need for the development of global networks and infrastructures to support the activities of biodiversity stakeholders. To achieve this aim, all organizations active and/or related to different biodiversity domains shall participate in sustainable strategic networks, which will act as the Breeding environments for the formation of Temporary Collaborative Networks (BTCNs). The BTCNs are long term strategic virtual organizations, the so-called VBEs [17], which aim to equip and engage the entire biodiversity community in cooperating, co-working, and co-development. Once the BTCNs are established, goal-oriented Temporary Collaborative Networks (TCNs) may be configured to fulfil emerging society/market opportunities. With the support of their BTCNs, the TCNs embed the potential to cope with required unpredictable changes, as well as collaborating with other European and global initiatives.

The main potential benefits foreseen to be offered to the BOs through the BTCNs include: (i) Getting recognised as a stakeholder in the biodiversity domain, through the label of the corresponding BTCN community, (ii) Access to elements of the BTCN's Bag of Assets (e.g. shared data, pointers to relevant free software, some shared proprietary software, lessons learned, shared "procedures" to perform experiments, publication library), (iii) Benefiting from the BTCN branding, and public relation, and having a voice influencing policy makers, (iv) Provision of common effective ICT-infrastructures for interoperability and collaboration, (v) Increasing the chances of TCN involvement, even from remote geographic regions, through the BTCN management mechanisms, and (vi) Provision of mechanisms, guidelines, and assisting services to motivate/facilitate TCN establishment.

In order to comprehensively specify the BTCN characteristics for the biodiversity domain, the ARCON reference modelling framework for Collaborative Networks [5] is being applied in the LifeWatch initiative.

9 Collaborative Networks and Ageing

One important element of sustainability under the social pillar is the demographic dimension, leading to the term "demographic sustainability". This is usually understood as a constant population level related to an optimal growth rate of the population, corresponding to at least 2.1 fertility rate [18]. Another perspective of demographic sustainability is given by the relationship between working age and older population. Current demographic trends are leading to a growing unbalance, which has a large impact on the economic subsystem. Particularly, the ageing population increases the pressure on the state pension funds. In the design of most social security pension schemes pensioners' benefits are paid by those who are currently working. With relatively fewer people working and greater numbers claiming pensions, the long term sustainability of this "intergenerational contract" is in danger.

Recently there is a growing recognition that the elderly population should not be considered a burden on the society but instead an asset that needs to be properly considered. A critical challenge for the society [19] is to identify new organizational structures, approaches, and mechanisms so that elderly citizens do not feel excluded, and have the chance to use their knowledge and expertise in making valued contributions to the communities where they live. In particular the senior professionals / knowledge workers possess a number of skills and accumulated experience that need to be used better in value creation activities. As a support element, ICT, and particularly high-speed pervasive broadband connectivity and web-based technologies, offer new opportunities to create new ways of working, facilitate social interaction, and reduce limitations imposed by location and time, thus increasing personal control.

Currently, associations of retired professionals represent an important organizational structure supporting active ageing. It is however important to avoid that such associations turn into a ghetto for seniors. Their effective involvement in the socio-economic system needs to consider other stakeholders, namely intermediary entities and the recipients of the services provided by seniors. Some of these entities are also organized in some form of association e.g. associations of SMEs, enterprise incubators or science parks, networks of regional development agencies and associated private (small) consultancy companies. Therefore a tripartite network model (Fig. 2) for these collaborative networks [20] is a promising approach.

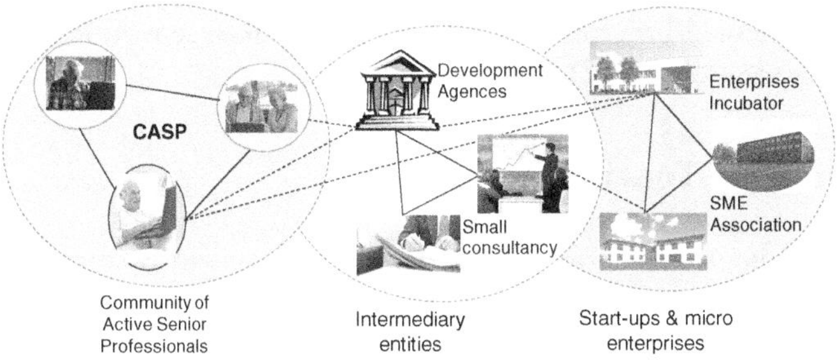

Fig. 2. Tri-partite networks in extending active professional life for seniors

Another case for the application of the CN approach is the provision of care for elderly. An integrated elderly care system consists of a number of organizations such as care centers, health care institutions, social security institutions, emergency services, and involves the collaboration of a number of different human actors e.g. social care assistants, health care professionals, the elderly people, and their relatives [21], [22].When based on computer networks and adequate supporting tools, collaboration among care institutions may be organized to operate as a long-term virtual organization and the various involved humans become part of a virtual community. In this direction, the ePAL and BRAID projects have been elaborating strategic research roadmaps for ICT and ageing.

10 Crime Networks

Criminal networks may constitute an important obstacle to sustainability, at least from the social pillar perspective. In some regions, there is even the risk of some countries being "taken over" and controlled by criminal networks.

Although this area of research is still at its early stages, as identified by Hernández [23], collaborative networks theory and models can be a useful instrument in refining the current understanding of criminal networks, helping to understanding their evolution, and ultimately providing hints regarding new approaches to fight them. For instance, in his pioneering work, Hernández uses the concepts of virtual organization and VO Breeding Environment to analyze Colombia's criminal networks. Approaches and mechanisms put forth by Social Network Analysis are also being used to analyze and visualize the structure of criminal networks, as in the work of Xu and Chen [24].

A complementary perspective in the area of criminality is to use network analysis to improve the performance of terrorism defense organizations. Policy chains constitute complex organizations having to coordinate one with another to develop, implement and administrate control public policies. Characterized by a large number of autonomous actors, policy chains often struggle with non-transparency among organizations (lack of overview on the actors involved, lack of information exchange, biases in the collaboration induced by relative power relationships, etc.) and, thus, with coordination weaknesses. To improve policy chain performance, Boorst & al [25] propose to use a network analysis method [26] to settle performance metrics adapted to terrorism defense organizations.

On the other hand, the study of these organizations, for instance understanding their resilience, could bring new insights for better management and the survival of business networks in times of market turbulence.

11 Sustainable Tourism

According to the World Tourism Organization, sustainable tourism development initiatives should meet the needs and interests of current tourists flowing within a country while at the same time ensuring the protection of the environment and enhancement of tourism opportunities for the future generations. Particularly, tourism in developing countries represents a unique case as it is suffering from a number of bottlenecks. For example [27]:

- excessive dependency on foreign investment and companies, contributing to a loss of local control over resources and substantial overseas leakage of tourism earnings;
- a lack of articulation between touristic enclaves and domestic economic sectors, producing low multiplier and spread effects;
- a large-scale environmental destruction, often involving nonrenewable resources and foundation assets;
- a rising alienation among the local population of host communities due to the unequal distribution of the costs and benefits of tourism and the perceived loss of cultural identity and social control to outsiders.

Such social as well as economic problems call for sustainable tourism initiatives, which stress on a wide-ranged involvement of tourism stakeholders, especially SMEs and government institutions, through collaborative networks. Early applications of collaborative networks to tourism (e.g. [28]), were mostly focused on the composition of multi-provider value-added services. More recent initiatives [29] address the role of CNs in the environmental governance for sustainable tourism. From a governance perspective two main types of networks are emerging [29]:

- Policy planning networks, which result from the need for cooperation and collaboration in tourism planning. Public institutions are the main players, as those defining priorities and policies. However, an increasing number of entities from the private sector are now being involved.
- Self-regulating action networks, based on action-oriented practices towards environment sustainability. Such networks involve distinct organizations sharing the same purposes, within the same territorial unit, including private businesses as well as non-governmental associations, aiming at creating mutual opportunities (a kind of business ecosystem).

For this sector, there is the need to manage all resources in such a way that economic, social and cultural needs can be fulfilled while maintaining cultural integrity, essential ecological processes, biological diversity, and life support systems. The complex interplay of the social, cultural and environmental dimensions of sustainable tourism requires a broad understanding and acceptance from different stakeholders, working directly and indirectly in the tourism sector. Therefore, the engagement of the key stakeholders e.g. accommodation providers, tour operators, leisure industry, catering companies, governmental and cultural entities, brokers and traveling agencies, etc., into a collaborative business ecosystem can create conditions for better sharing and more conscious use of resources.

12 Disaster Rescue Networks

Situations of disaster or crisis recovery constitute typical examples of complex collaborative networks which have been attracting increasing attention from the scientific community in the last few years [30], [31]. A crisis (being human induced or triggered by the forces of nature), is a complex and dynamic phenomenon, it is characterized by a high level of collective threat and risk, with a great need of reactivity throughout the crisis duration and a constant necessity of adaptation from the part of the recovery organisation. Such constraints, as well as the multiplicity of organisational and institutional actors to be coordinated during the management of a crisis, raise many challenges for collaboration. Efficacy and efficiency of collaborative crisis management require a sustainable approach: disaster events have a strong *social* impact and reducing this impact thanks to a very reactive response appears essential; in many cases, such crises have direct *environmental* consequences; the *economic* dimension is generally linked to management of the financial means allocated to disaster rescue. As a rather recent field of application for collaborative networks, this area of research quickly evolves both by integrating the theoretical knowledge now available on collaborative networks as well as by developing an in-depth analysis of the collaboration specificities in the context of crisis and disasters.

Lack of coordination and failures in collaboration and interoperability have often been pointed out as key issues to improve crisis management, in the case of humanitarian disasters [32] but also for other types of crisis [33]. Much research work is currently trying to provide a better understanding of the nature of coordination and collaboration in such contexts, as a first step before defining specifically adapted solutions. At a high level, collaboration starts with the coordination of intentionality among the various stakeholders. Organisational proximities integrate various notions of cognitive, social, cultural or institutional proximities which have to be considered as collaboration facilitators [34]. For instance, such factors can designate long-term humanitarian clusters, as means to improve the agile implementation of collaborative networks when a crisis occurs. This example puts forth that an in-depth knowledge on this specific context (i.e. organisational proximities) has to be developed before applying more generic concepts of collaborative science (i.e. Virtual Breeding Environment).

Heterogeneity among stakeholders' intentionality and rationality has significant impact on the coordination of decision processes. Performance management systems primarily based on improving coordination among stakeholders are a first way to increase decisional efficiency. Until now, for crises context, performance evaluation has been mainly used after crisis settlement, notably because of a lack of trustable indicators [35]. To make possible a broader use of performance management as a support of the crisis response process, specific performance indicators systems are required, to take into account the particularity of disaster contexts [36]. Typically, in the field of humanitarian supply chains, generic and reusable indicator systems are proposed as a reference to facilitate the development of more specific applications. If current advances already integrate the sociological and economic aspects of crisis management, the integration of environmental indicators is still a perspective for further works.

Disaster management, perhaps even more than any other type of virtual organisation, underlines the crucial information technology challenges to support collaboration. Crisis situations constitute strongly dynamic environments where the adaptability of information systems to the changes over time of the collaboration processes appears crucial [37]. Model-driven approaches for information system implementation provide a conceptual framework to support dynamic and adaptable collaborative information systems. For instance, considering crisis as an evolutionary process, the ISyCri project has developed a Mediation Information System to support the dynamic interoperability among changing stakeholders [33]. Supporting the evolutionary features of virtual recovery organisations with reactive information and decision systems remains a key challenge for future work.

13 Conclusions

Pursuing sustainable solutions is one of today's major challenges for the society. The need to consider the three main pillars of sustainability calls for both a more holistic perspective of the problems and a tighter collaboration among a wide range of stakeholders. Collaborative networks can bring a significant contribution to the better understanding of the stakes and paths towards potential solutions. As illustrated, there are already a large number of examples, in different domains, where CN contributions to the sustainability agenda are identified and new approaches are being tried. A continuation of this effort is likely to raise new research challenges and to ultimately help us building more sustainable systems.

Acknowledgments. Partial support for this work was given by the European Commission through the ePAL and BRAID projects.

References

1. Kates, R., Parris, T., Leiserowitz, A.: What is Sustainable Development? Environment 47(3), 8–21 (2005), http://www.hks.harvard.edu/sustsci/ists/docs/whatisSD_env_kates_0504.pdf
2. United Nations General Assembly: Report of the World Commission on Environment and Development: Our Common Future. Transmitted to the General Assembly as an Annex to document A/42/427 - Development and International Co-operation: Environment (1987), http://www.un-documents.net/wced-ocf.htm
3. United Nations General Assembly: 2005 World Summit Outcome, Resolution A/60/1, adopted by the General Assembly on September 15 (2005)
4. Adams, W.M.: The Future of Sustainability: Re-thinking Environment and Development in the Twenty-first Century. Report of the IUCN Renowned Thinkers Meeting, January 29-31 (2006), http://cmsdata.iucn.org/downloads/iucn_future_of_sustanability.pdf
5. Camarinha-Matos, L.M., Afsarmanesh, H.: Collaborative Networks: Reference Modeling. Springer, Heidelberg (2008)
6. Bojar, W.L., Drelichowski, L.: Analysis of tendencies in agribusiness networking coopetition in Poland and in the partner countries. Journal of Central European Agriculture 9(3), 445–456 (2008)
7. Volpentesta, A.P., Ammirato, S.: Networking agrifood SMEs and consumer groups in local agribusiness. In: Pervasive Collaborative Networks, pp. 33–40. Springer, Heidelberg (2008)
8. Camarinha-Matos, L.M., Carelli, R., Pellicer, J., Martin, M.: Towards the virtual enterprise in food industry. In: Re-Engineering for Sustainable Industrial Production, pp. 73–84. Chapman & Hall, Boca Raton (1997)
9. FORAGRO: Agriculture and rural prosperity from the perspective of technological research and innovation in LAC: FORAGRO Position 2010. Forum of the Americas for Agricultural Research and Technological Development (March 2010)
10. Osório, A.L., Camarinha-Matos, L.M., Gomes, J.S.: A collaborative case study: The extended "ViaVerde" toll payment system. In: Proceedings of PRO-VE 2005 – Collaborative Networks and their Breeding Environments, pp. 559–568. Springer, Heidelberg (2005)
11. Breuer, W., Povh, D., Retzmann, D., Urbanke, C., Weinhold, M.: Prospects of Smart Grid Technologies for a Sustainable and Secure Power Supply. In: 20th World Energy Congress, Rome, Italy, November 11-15 (2007)
12. Kok, J.K., Warmer, C.J., Karnouskos, S., Nestle, D., Dimeas, A., Weidlich, A., Strauss, P., Buchholz, B., Drenkard, S., Hatziargyriou, N., Lioliou, V.: Smart houses for a smart grid. In: 20th International Conference on Electricity Distribution, Prague, Czech Republic, June 8-11 (2009)
13. Allan, L., Menzel, K.: Virtual Enterprises for Integrated Energy Service Provision. In: Leveraging Knowledge for Innovation in Collaborative Networks, pp. 659–666. Springer, Heidelberg (2009)
14. Afsarmanesh, H., Camarinha-Matos, L.M.: Federated knowledge integration and machine learning in water distribution networks. In: Proc. ISIP 1997 Int. Conf. on Integrated and Sustainable Industrial Production, Re-Engineering for Sustainable Industrial Production, Lisbon, Portugal, pp. 121–140. Chapman & Hall, Boca Raton (May 1997)
15. FlySafe FP6 project, http://www.eu-flysafe.org/Project.html (viewed 2008-11-03)
16. LifeWatch – e-science and technology infrastructure for biodiversity data and observatories, http://www.lifewatch.eu/
17. Afsarmanesh, H., Camarinha-Matos, L.M.: A framework for management of virtual organizations breeding environments. In: Proceedings of 6th PRO-VE 2005 - Collaborative Networks and their Breeding Environments, pp. 35–48. Springer, Heidelberg (2005)

18. Roca, M.N.O., Leitão, N.: Demographic Sustainability In Portugal: Towards a Typology. In: 14th European Colloquium on Theoretical and Quantitative Geography, Tomar, Portugal (2005)
19. Camarinha-Matos, L.M., Afsarmanesh, H.: Collaborative mechanisms for a new perspective on active ageing. In: Proceedings of DEST 2009 - 3rd IEEE Int. Conference on Digital Ecosystems and Technologies, Istanbul, Turkey, June 1-3 (2009)
20. Camarinha-Matos, L.M., Afsarmanesh, H., Ferrada, F.: Collaborative Networks Approach to Active Ageing. In: Proc. of Pervasive Health 2010 / AGEmap workshop, Munich, Germany, March 22-25 (2010)
21. Camarinha-Matos, L.M., Afsarmanesh, H.: TeleCARE: Collaborative virtual elderly care support communities. The Journal on Information Technology in Healthcare 2(2), 73–86 (2004) ISSN 1479-649X
22. Camarinha-Matos, L.M., Afsarmanesh, H.: A multi-agent based infrastructure to support virtual communities in elderly care. Int. J. Networking and Virtual Organisations 2(3), 246–266 (2004) ISSN 1470-9503
23. Hernández, A.: Comparing Notes: Collaborative Networks, Breeding Environments, and Organized Crime. In: Leveraging Knowledge for Innovation in Collaborative Networks. IFIP AICT, vol. 307, pp. 87–95. Springer, Heidelberg (2009)
24. Xu, J., Chen, H.: Criminal Network Analysis and Visualization. Communications of the ACM 48(6), 101–107 (2005)
25. Baaijens, J.M.J., Lapré, L.J.: Network analysis of policy chains in the Netherlands. In: 20th EGOS Colloquium, Ljubljana (July 2004)
26. Borst, I., Baaijens, J.M.J., Meijer, G.R.: Network analysis of terrorism defense organizations – A network approach for developing performance indicators. In: Proceedings of PRO-VE 2005, Virtual Enterprise and Collaborative Network, Valencia, Spain, September 26-28, pp. 265–272 (2005)
27. Robertson, P.J.: An Assessment of Collaborative Governance in a Network for Sustainable Tourism: The Case of RedeTuris. In: 10th National Public Management Research Conference (2009)
28. Afsarmanesh, H., Camarinha-Matos, L.M.: Future smart organizations: A virtual tourism enterprise. In: Proceedings of WISE 2000 – 1st ACM/IEEE International Conference on Web Information Systems Engineering, June 19-20. Main Program, vol. 1, pp. 456–461. IEEE Computer Society Press, Hong Kong (2000)
29. Erkus-Ozturk, H., Eraydın, A.: Environmental governance for sustainable tourism development: Collaborative networks and organisation building in the Antalya tourism region. Tourism Management 31, 113–124 (2010)
30. Devlin, E.: Crisis Management Planning and Execution. Auerbach Publications (2006)
31. Kovács, G., Spens, K.: Humanitarian Logistics in Disaster Relief Operations. International Journal of Physical Distribution and Logistics Management 37, 99–114 (2007)
32. Beamon, B.M., Balcik, B.: Performance measurement in humanitarian relief chains. Int. J. Public Sect. Manag. 21(1), 4–25 (2008)
33. Truptil, S., Bénaben, F., Couget, P., Lauras, M., Chapurlat, V., Pingaud, H.: Interoperability of Information Systems in Crisis Management: Crisis Modeling and Metamodeling. In: IESA 2008. Springer, Germany (2008)
34. Hyypiä, M., Kautonen, M.: Dimensions of Proximity in Relationships between Knowledge Intensive Business Service Firms and Their Clients. In: Regional Studies Association International Conference on Regional Growth Agendas, Aalborg, May 28-31 (2005)
35. Kovács, G., Tatham, P.H.: What is special about a humanitarian logistician? A survey of logistic skills and performance. Supply Chain Forum – An International Journal (2004)
36. Balcik, B.: Relief chain planning and management: modeling and analyzing humanitarian logistic problems. PhD thesis, University of Washington (2008)
37. Oloruntoba, R., Gray, R.: Humanitarian aid: an agile supply chain? Supply Chain Management: An International Journal 11, 115–120 (2006)

Towards an Environmental Management Approach for Collaborative Networks

Ovidiu Noran

Griffith University, Australia
O.Noran@griffith.edu.au

Abstract. Environmental responsibility is evolving into a crucial aspect of strategic management as regulations are expected to tighten significantly in the near future following the need to mitigate the effects of climate change. Many businesses react to this challenge by implementing environmental reporting and management systems. However, often the environmental programme is not properly integrated in the overall business strategy and the management does not have timely access to appropriate environmental information. Moreover, within collaborative networks (CNs) the environmental management (EM) effort should be coordinated amid partners to achieve a much needed synergy and also enable prompt deployment of the required EM artefacts within the virtual organisations (VOs) created. This paper attempts to show a possible way to integrate environmental management (EM) into the VOs set up by the CN participants by using an Enterprise Architecture (EA) life cycle-based approach.

Keywords: Environmental management, enterprise architecture.

1 Introduction

The continued existence of businesses depends not only on their economic sustainability but also on their impact on the natural environment and on the way they treat their workers. This fact was emphasized by Elkington's [1] Triple Bottom Line (TBL) approach to business sustainability, stating that one must achieve not only economic bottom-line performance but also environmental / social accomplishment. Thus, Blackburn [2] compares economic sustainability to air and environmental and social sustainability to food: the first is more urgent however not more important than the second. The '2Rs' (Respect for humans and judicious Resource management) are another essential component of overall sustainability of a business. Hence, successful enterprises must take a whole-system approach to *sustainable development* (see [3]).

The above requirements add a new degree of complexity to the management of Collaborative Networks (CNs), which are typically formed so as allow their members to promptly create virtual organisations (VOs) that are able to bid for projects that go beyond the individual competencies of the CN participants [4].

This paper focuses on the challenges presented by the proper integration of the environmental sustainability aspect in the VOs created by a CNO and proposes a possible way to address these challenges based on an Enterprise Architecture (EA) approach.

L.M. Camarinha-Matos et al. (Eds.): PRO-VE 2010, IFIP AICT 336, pp. 17–24, 2010.

2 Environmental Management: Is There a Better Way?

Currently, EM efforts within many companies are fairly incoherent and often not properly supported by the ICT infrastructure. Thus, business units may approach environmental sustainability in different levels of detail and at a different pace producing a possible loss of *aggregate* capabilities; moreover, often the management cannot effectively use the information generated by the environmental reporting functions due to language, format, level of aggregation etc. Strategic EM integration requires prompt and effective access to environmental information facilitating the decision-making process [5, 6]. In the case of CNs, this challenge is complicated by the need to mediate between- and coordinate the EM approaches of the participants in order to promptly construct and deploy agreed-upon EM frameworks for the VOs created. An optimal way to solve this problem would be to set up an EM project with a) top-management support for the project champion(s), b) sufficient authority for the manager and appropriate human / infrastructure resources, c) a plan that is integrated in the general company strategic direction and d) a cross-departmental approach.

These requirements match to a good extent the scope of typical EA projects; it is therefore proposed here that EA could provide a solution to an integrated approach to the coordination of environmental aspects in the management and operation of the CN participants and especially their prompt introduction in the VOs created and operated by the CN. This is desirable because a company whose architecture includes EM competencies and responsibilities in an integrated fashion will have the necessary agility and preparedness required from CN participants and from the VO in particular.

3 Brief Review of Relevant Environmental Management Artefacts

Many companies address the need to introduce environmental responsibility in their business units by attempting to implement some type of environmental reporting and environmental management system (EMS).

While an EMS is a step in the right direction, when implemented in isolation it may not trigger the cultural change necessary to achieve permanent environmental responsibility. Thus, Coglianese and Nash [7] argue that the implementation of an EMS alone is irrelevant in the absence of genuine commitment to environmental improvements. It must be noted that relevant regulation such as ISO 14001:2004 [8] limits the constraints on an EMS to being designed such that companies can *work towards* the goal of regulatory compliance and *seek* to make improvements; it does not actually require achieving actual compliance with existing law.

Various reference models for EMS design and EMS alternatives have emerged. For example, Blackburn [2] proposes to rather build a 'Sustainability Operating System' - i.e. a management method to achieve sustainability based on the Brundtland report [3], the '2R's and the TBL approach applied to sustainability. Willard [9] recommends a TBL-based approach encompassing economy / profit, environment / planet and equity / people with obvious benefits: easier hiring and retention, increased productivity, reduced manufacturing / commercial site expenses, increased revenue / market share and reduced risk. Clayton and Redcliffe [10] advocate a systems approach towards the integration of sustainability aspects into the business and define the environmental quality as capital (and thus the viability of 'tradable pollution').

EM frameworks aim to provide a structured set of artefacts (methods, aspects, reference models, etc) specialised for the EM area. Some examples: The Natural Step (TNS) Framework, proposing a systems-based approach to organisational planning for sustainability [11], The Natural Edge Project [12] with a holistic approach taking into account system life cycle and the Life Cycle Management Framework for continuous environmental improvement [13]. Assessment and reporting frameworks aim to assist the measurement and reporting functions of the EMS. For example, the Life Cycle Assessment (LCA) method measures the environmental impacts of products or services relative to each other during their life cycles [14]. The Global Reporting Initiative's sustainability reporting framework [15] contains reporting principles and guidance potentially applicable to all types of businesses.

International Standards also cover the EM issue. ISO 14000:2004 is a set of reference models for EMS setup, life-cycle assessment, environmental auditing of processes and environmental labelling and performance evaluation. ISO 14001:2004 deals specifically with EMS-s, aiming to provide a framework for a holistic and strategic approach to the organization's environmental policy, plans and actions [8]. Standards provide a good starting point for design and assessment; unfortunately however, as mentioned current EM standards do not enforce EM performance levels.

As a conclusion, many of the above-mentioned artefacts recognize the need to analyse the life cycle of the products. However, in reality it is often required to also take into account other life cycles as well. For example in a scenario of a VO created by a CN one must consider the life cycles of the CN participants, of the VO, of the project to create the VO's EMS and of course the life cycle of the EMS itself. It is also necessary to analyse the interactions between these entities in that context. The proposed approach involves life cycle architectures elements that describe systems during their entire life and thus allow identifying potential problems and aspects that may not be otherwise obvious in a snapshot-type representation.

4 Tools Used in the Proposed Approach

In this research we have selected a reference architecture framework (AF) obtained by generalising several other AFs and thus potentially expressive enough to contain all the elements necessary to achieve EM integration using EA artefacts. This AF is GERAM (Generalised Enterprise Reference Architecture and Methodology), described in ISO 15704:2005 [16]. Among others, GERAM has been used in practice to guide EA projects [17], assess other enterprise AFs [18-20] and build a structured repository of AF elements for a project management decision support system [21].

The main component of the reference architecture of GERAM (called GERA) is a MF containing an extensive set of aspects including life cycle, management, organisation, human and decision, corresponding to various stakeholder concerns [22]. A subset of GERA has been used as a modelling formalism in the creation of a life cycle-based business model as subsequently shown in this paper. For more details on GERAM and GERA see [16].

The paper argues that EA can provide an overarching and life cycle-based approach in setting up and operating an EM project aiming to produce an EMS in an integrated and coherent manner in relation to the host organisation (VO), CN participants and other relevant external entities. To illustrate this approach, the researcher has used a meta-methodology, or a 'method to build methods' applicable for specific types of EA tasks (projects), based on an original approach abiding by EA principles. The meta-methodology, tested in several case studies [21, 23, 24] employs a set of steps and sub-steps. In the first step, the user is prompted to create a list containing entities of interest to the project in question, including project participants, target entities (e.g. the organisations / systems being created) and importantly, the project itself. The second step comprises the creation of business models showing the relations between the previously listed entities *in the context of their lifecycles*, i.e. illustrating how entities influence each other within each life cycle phase. The third step assists the user to infer the set of project activities by reading and interpreting the previous representations for each life cycle phase of the project and other target entities. The resulting activities are then decomposed to a level deemed suitable for the intended audience. Due to its scope and to space limitations, the paper will cover only the first and second meta-methodology steps, focusing in particular on the benefits of creating a business model in the context of the life cycles of all relevant participant entities. For more details on all the meta-methodology steps see [24].

5 Application to the Environmental Management Project

In this case, the meta-methodology deliverables are various models of the EM project and the EMS, created in a life cycle context. The CN participants, the VO, and other relevant entities (e.g. organisations, agencies, laws etc) that need to be involved in the EM project and/or influence the resulting EMS are to be included in the entity list (first step of the meta-methodology). Thus, their influence will be taken into account *throughout the life cycles* of the EM project and the EMS. An important prerequisite for EM integration into the organisation is thus fulfilled. The meta-methodology assists in creating new knowledge (in this case, how to go about setting up and operating the EM project and the EMS) based on 'context expertise', i.e. the know-how of running the businesses including corporate culture, relations with suppliers, clients, authorities etc, typically available at middle and top management levels. The involvement of these roles in the methodology creation process establishes the conditions for management buy-in, support for the upcoming EM project and for the early involvement of the EA approach and department (if present) in the EM project. This will create the best conditions for the integrated development of the EMS.

Proposed members in the entity list (the first step) are the CN participants, the VO set up by the CN, the VO's EMS, the EM project (to build that EMS), environmental reports, NGOs, the government, Environmental Protection Agency (EPA), EM principles (e.g. 2R, TBL), EM laws, EM standards, EM frameworks, assessment and reporting frameworks, social responsibility standards, Quality Standards and EM consultants. As mentioned, the MF of GERA is adopted here as the most suitable to provide a formalism for the (mandatory) life cycle and other selected aspects.

In this case, the future (TO-BE) state is incremental and based on the present (AS-IS) state – i.e. no radical redesign is recommended when setting up an EMS. This requires the AS-IS state to be represented for all aspects. While there is no tangible advantage in showing separate AS-IS and TO-BE states in the business model, it is useful to do so in the decisional / organisational structure. This is because here it is imperative to clearly show where and how the functions of the EMS interact with the existing system so as to ascertain the degree of integration and effects of the EMS on the decisional and organisational structure of the VO. Separate TO-BE decisional / organisational models also help define various future scenarios.

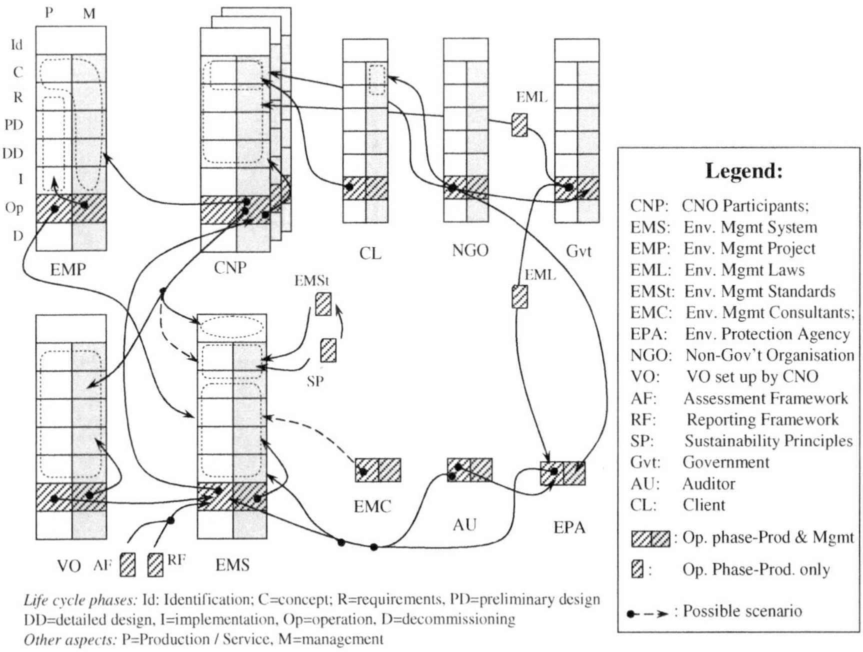

Fig. 1. Business model showing relations of relevant entities in the context of their life cycles

The business model is constructed (in step two) based on context knowledge (often tacit and requiring eliciting by the meta-methodology facilitator) owned by stakeholders, i.e. CxO, enterprise architect, top management, etc. A possible result is shown in Fig. 1. As can be seen, the relations between the relevant entities can be explicitly represented at each life cycle phase. Note that some entities' life cycle representation has been reduced to the phase(s) relevant for the EM project and the EMS. For example, we are only interested in the Operation life cycle phase of Auditors, EM assessment / reporting frameworks, EM consultants. The figure shows the relations between the CN participants, the VO, the EM project and the VO's future EMS, thus facilitating a common understanding, building consensus and representing what needs to be done, step by step, first at a high level and then more detailed as necessary.

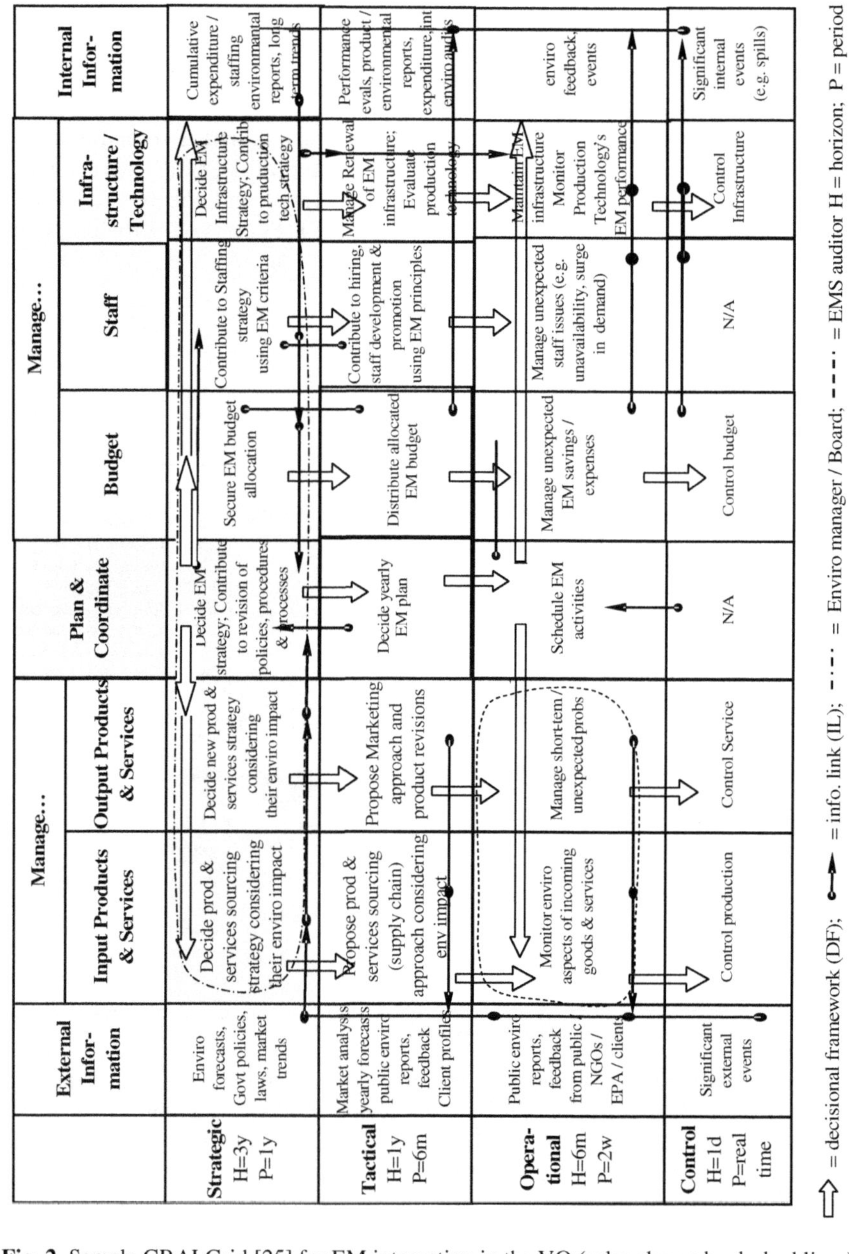

Fig. 2. Sample GRAI Grid [25] for EM integration in the VO (roles shown by dashed lines)

For example, the EMS is built by the EM project (EMP), with the possible involvement of consultants (EMC). The CN participants are lobbied by NGOs and must abide by EM laws (EML). Auditors (AU) perform certification audits (during the design of the EMS) or surveillance audits (to check if the EMS is still compliant). The EPA looks into the EMS operation / receives information from external auditors.

Importantly, the EMS should be able to redesign itself (arrow from its Mgmt operation to its other life cycles) to a certain extent and thus remain agile in the face of moderate EM regulation and market changes. Reaction to major changes will however be delegated to the upper company management via an EM project (EMP) (arrows from CN participants (CNP) management operation to EMP and from EMP operation to EMS life cycles). The arrow from the operation management side of the EMS to CNP management reflects the requirement to integrate (e.g. via partial re-design / co-design) CN participants' management to the VO's EMS functions. Such inter-relations are detailed in the next meta-methodology steps as controls and inputs to activities, decision frameworks, etc.

The influences of other entities on the EMS and the EMP can also be interpreted as stakeholder concerns that translate in particular areas of interest being modelled and addressed. For example, the client may want to know how the mission and vision of the CN participants (the Concept area of CNP in Fig. 1) address its environmental concerns, and the government (Gvt) will want to ensure that the Company abides by the public environmental concerns expressed in EM laws.

Note that in order to limit the complexity of the figure, relations between entities that are not relevant to the task at hand have been omitted (e.g. the general setup of the VO by the CNO, or most relations between government, auditors and EPA, etc).

Models of the AS-IS and several potential TO-BE decisional and organisational aspects have also been constructed. For example, Fig. 2 shows in a simplified form (using the GRAI-Grid [25] formalism) a possible TO-BE decisional / organisational structure of an EMS seen as an *integrated* add-on of the VO management system. This approach enables the organisation to manage, benchmark and improve its environmental performance in an integrated manner (i.e. taking into account all relevant areas in a cross-departmental approach).

The space available for this paper does not allow a detailed presentation. In-depth descriptions and additional models (including activity models of the third meta-methodology step) are available in [26].

6 Conclusions and Further Work

Currently, businesses (including those participating in CNs) do not appear to achieve the maximum benefits from implementing and operating an EMS internally and/or in the VOs they create. Firstly, there seems to be a lack of integration of the EM initiative with the business, especially at the strategic level. Thus, the management cannot take full advantage of the knowledge present in the environmental reporting mainly due to wrong format and/or level of aggregation. Secondly, an EMS needs to be driven internally and permeate all business areas in a consistent manner in order to produce organisational culture change, hence lasting effects. This paper has argued for and tried to show (at high level due to space limitations) that such needs are best addressed from an EA perspective. Thus it appears that EA can provide the necessary artefacts and the prerequisites for a coherent, cross-departmental and culture-changing approach. This promises business sustainability and profitability in the long term for CN members but also agility and competiveness for the VOs created by CNs.

References

1. Elkington, J.: Cannibals with Forks: The Triple Bottom Line of 21st Century Business (1998)
2. Blackburn, W.R.: The Sustainability Handbook. EarthScan Publishers, Cornwall (2007)
3. UN World Commission on Environment and Development. Our Common Future (Brundtland Report). Oxford University Press, Oxford (1987)
4. Camarinha-Matos, L., et al.: Collaborative networked organizations - Concepts and practice in manufacturing enterprises. Computers and Industrial Engineering 57(1), 46–60 (2009)
5. Nilsson, I.: Integrating Environmental Management to Improve Strategic Decision-Making. Chalmers University of Technology, Götteborg (2001)
6. Molloy, I.: Environmental Mgmt Systems and Info Mgmt, Strategic-Systematical Integration of Green Value Added. In: Gómez, J.M., et al. (eds.) ITEE 2007 - (3rd Int. ICSC Symp.) (2007)
7. Coglianese, C., Nash, J. (eds.): Regulating from the Inside: Can Environmental Management Systems Achieve Policy Goals? RFF Press (2001)
8. ISO, ISO 14001: Environmental management systems - Requirements with guidance for use. International Standards Organisation (2004)
9. Willard, B.: The Sustainability Advantage: Seven Business Case benefits of a Triple Bottom Line. New Society Publishers, Gabriola Island (2002)
10. Clayton, A., Redcliffe, N.: Sustainability - A Systems Approach. Earthscan Ltd. (1998)
11. Upham, P.: An assessment of the Natural Step theory of sustainability. Journal of Cleaner Production 8(6), 445–454 (2000)
12. TNEP: The Engineering Sustainable Solutions Program Whole Systems Design Suite. The Natural Edge Project, TNEP (2007)
13. Hunkeler, D. (ed.): Life-cycle Management. Society of Environmental Toxicology etc. (2004)
14. EPA: Management Tools. Environmental Protection Agency, South Australia (2008)
15. GRI: Sustainability Reporting Guidelines, in Sustainability Reporting Framework. Global Reporting Initiative (ed.): Global Reporting Initiative (2002)
16. ISO/IEC: Annex C: GERAM, in ISO/IS 15704:2000/Amd1: 2005: Industrial automation systems - Requirements for enterprise-reference architectures and methodologies (2005)
17. Bernus, P., Noran, O., Riedlinger, J.: Using the Globemen Reference Model for Virtual Enterprise Design in After Sales Service, in Globemen. In: Karvoinen, I., et al. (eds.) VTT Symposium, vol. 224. Helsinki, Finland, pp. 71–90 (2002)
18. Noran, O.: A Mapping of Individual Architecture Frameworks on GERAM. In: Bernus, P., Nemes, L., Schmidt, G. (eds.) Handbook of Enterprise Architecture, pp. 65–210. Springer, Heidelberg (2003)
19. Noran, O.: An Analytical Mapping of the C4ISR Architecture Framework onto ISO15704 Annex A (GERAM). Computers in Industry 56(5), 407–427 (2005)
20. Saha, P.: A Synergistic Assessment of the FEAF against GERAM (ISO15704:2000 Annex A). In: Saha, P. (ed.) Enterprise Systems Architecture in Practice, pp. 1–17. IDEA Group, USA (2007)
21. Noran, O.: Discovering and modelling Enterprise Engineering Project Processes. In: Saha, P. (ed.) Enterprise Systems Architecture in Practice, pp. 39–61. IDEA Group, USA (2007)
22. ISO/IEC: ISO/IEC 42010:2007: Recommended Practice for Architecture Description of Software-Intensive Systems (2007)
23. Noran, O.: Using Reference Models in Enterprise Architecture: An Example. In: Fettke, P., Loos, P. (eds.) Reference Modeling for Business Systems Analysis, pp. 141–165. Idea Group, Hershey (2006)
24. Noran, O.: A Meta-methodology for Collaborative Networked Organisations: Creating Directly Applicable Methods for Enterprise Engineering Projects. VDM, Saarbrücken (2008)
25. Doumeingts, G., Vallespir, B., Chen, D.: GRAI Grid Decisional Modelling. In: Bernus, P., Mertins, K., Schmidt, G. (eds.) Handbook on Archs of IS, pp. 313–339. Springer, Heidelberg (1998)
26. Noran, O.: Engineering the Sustainable Business: An Enterprise Architecture Approach. In: Doucet, G., Gotze, J., Saha, P. (eds.) Coherency Management: Architecting the Enterprise for Alignment, Agility, and Assurance, Int. Enterprise Architecture Institute, pp. 179–210 (2009)

Green Virtual Enterprises and Their Breeding Environments

David Romero and Arturo Molina

Tecnológico de Monterrey, Campus Monterrey & Ciudad de México, México
david.romero.diaz@gmail.com, armolina@itesm.mx

Abstract. The Industrial Ecology (IE) is a new interdisciplinary field focused on sustainable development. IE aims to the shifting of industrial processes from open-loop systems where different resources move through a system to become wastes to a closed-loop system where wastes become inputs for new processes. This paper introduces a Green Virtual Enterprise (GVE) model as an emerging sustainable manufacturing and logistics mode focused on offering, delivering and recovering green products to/from the market, under a lifecycle thinking and supported by its source network. GVEs creation is considered within a GVE breeding environment context, which acts as a long-term collaborative network aimed at offering the conditions to efficiently promote the sharing and recycling of resources such as: information, materials, water, energy and/or infrastructure with the intention of increasing economic gains and achieving sustainable development.

Keywords: Collaborative Networked Organisations, Green Virtual Enterprises, Breeding Environments, Industrial Ecology, Industrial Symbiosis, Sustainable Industrial Development.

1 Introduction

The *Industrial Ecology (IE)* stands for an important strategy to promote sustainable industrial development for enterprises and their related support institutions by providing a unique collaboration opportunity, with a "business sense", to integrate ecological, economic and social considerations into the creation and operation/ evolution of new or existing industrial networks (e.g. industry clusters, industrial districts, eco-industrial parks). IE attempts to understand the potential improvement of industrial networks using an analogy between natural *ecosystems* and *industrial* systems. IE aims to the shifting of industrial production systems from open-loop systems to closed-loop systems, evolving from a linear to a cycle production approach, in order to reduce wastes and pollution and efficiently share and recycle resources within an *industrial ecosystem* towards increasing economic gains and achieving sustainable development [1].

Collaborative Networked Organisations (CNOs) represent a promising paradigm in manufacturing and service industries to help organisations to cope with the challenges of turbulent market conditions in the context of ecological, economic and social pressures on the global industry. CNOs show a high potential as drivers of sustainable industrial development by joining of complementary capabilities and capacities for creating products that are non-polluting, conserve energy and natural resources, and that are economically viable and socially rewarding for all stakeholders involved [2].

L.M. Camarinha-Matos et al. (Eds.): PRO-VE 2010, IFIP AICT 336, pp. 25–35, 2010.

Both scientific disciplines can provide together a new interdisciplinary approach for enterprises to improve their competitive and environmental performance in terms of better managing their skills or core-competencies and resources (e.g. information, materials, energy, waste, infrastructure) to realise sustainable industrial collaborative networks and pursue new green business opportunities. In this sense, *collaboration* is presented as a challenge and at the same time as an opportunity for enterprises to re-engineer their production processes and/or networks in order to eliminate/recycle their wastes to maximise returns per unit of resource consumed, share/reduce their costs over limited natural resources (e.g. raw materials) and supporting infrastructure, and increase their business opportunities and profit by establishing long- and short-term strategic coalitions to develop new competitive advantages (e.g. green products and processes) without compromising critical resources for the future.

2 Green Virtual Enterprises and Their Breeding Environments

Green Virtual Enterprise Breeding Environments (GVBEs), also known as virtual eco-industrial collaborative networks, are long-term strategic alliances of green enterprises [1] and their related support institutions aimed at offering the necessary conditions to support the rapid and fluid configuration of Green Virtual Enterprises. GVBEs, as source networks focus on traditional bases on creating an adequate environment for the establishment of cooperation agreements, common operation principles, common interoperable infrastructures, common ontologies, and mutual trust among others, with the objective of preparing their members to collaborate in potential GVEs that will be established when a green business opportunity arises or is identified by a GVBE member acting as a broker [adapted from 3] [see also 4].

On more innovative bases, GVBEs focus on bringing together a variety of green enterprises into a business ecosystem that aims to mimic the relationships between different species in a natural ecosystem and establish symbiotic mechanisms to create synergies towards an optimal production level and ecological balance in a virtual eco-industrial collaborative network. GVBEs concentrate on bringing their business ecosystems as close as possible to being a closed-loop system by keeping a close interaction of material, energy, information and technology among their members towards a near complete recycle or sharing of resources for producing and delivering green products with sustainable manufacturing and logistics practices through GVEs creation, and by recruiting new GVBE members (green enterprises) that can enhance the network capabilities and capacities to grasp new green business opportunities in time and taking into account environmental impact and resources utility.

These last aims are what differentiate traditional VBEs from the novel GVBEs in where collaboration targets the creation of economies of scale in a recycling and shared sustainable engineering efficiency strategy. As a result, GVBEs aim to offer their members and to the market and society a sustainable industrial development model characterised by an economic growth together with a low environmental impact in comparison with other traditional industrial development models.

---

[1] A *Green Enterprise* is an enterprise that strives to meet the triple bottom line by ensuring that all products, processes and manufacturing activities in its business operation address the sustainable principles: economic-equitable, environmental-viable, and social-bearable.

Green Virtual Enterprises (GVEs) are short-term and dynamic coalitions of green enterprises that may be tailored within a GVBE to respond to a single collaboration opportunity, through integrating the green technology (skills or core-competencies and resources) required to meet or exceed the quality, time and cost frames expected by the customer with a low ecological footprint, and that dissolve once their mission/goal has been accomplished, and whose cooperation is supported through computer networks [adapted from 3].

Furthermore, GVEs as goal-oriented collaborative networks can be designed within a GVBE with two different aims, on the one hand to become *dynamic forward supply networks* for delivering new green products to the market, and on the other hand to become *dynamic reverse supply networks* for recovering the products sold under the GVBE brand (product stewardship) for direct-use, repair, re-manufacture, recycle or safe disposal (see Fig. 1).

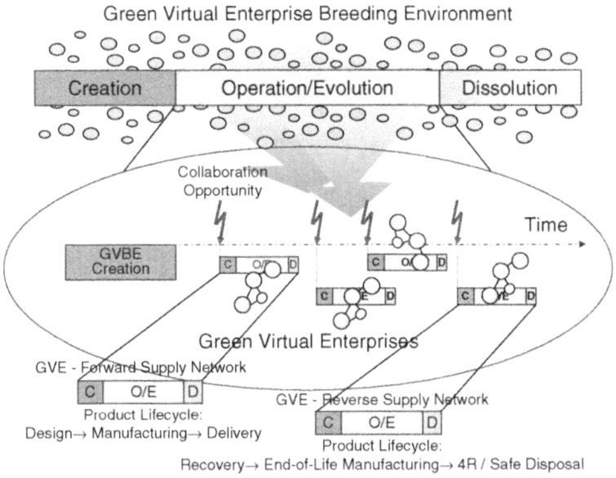

Fig. 1. GVEs creation (both modalities) within GVBE lifecycle

3 Green Virtual Enterprises Characterisation

GVEs represent an emerging sustainable manufacturing and logistics mode focused on offering, delivering and recovering green products to/from the market, under a lifecycle thinking and supported by their source networks. GVEs focus on adopting lean-agile manufacturing and other sustainable engineering and logistics principles in order to enhance production, reduce wastes and improve their management, decrease energy consumption, achieve logistics efficiency and consequently reduce production and logistics costs and environmental impact.

In this paper, two GVE modalities are introduced as a response to the difficulties of creating and managing integrated and stable forward & reverse supply networks, better known as closed-loop supply networks, to address the market dynamic changes (e.g. shortened product lifecycles) in a sustainable way, in where enterprises normally focus on their traditional forward supply networks and outsource their reverse supply networks to third-parties.

The two GVE modalities proposed will be crafted within a GVBE in where green enterprises will be prepared and ready to participate in dynamic forward and reverse supply networks created according to the needs and opportunities of the market and remain operational as long as these opportunities persist, offering in this way an assertive approach towards the market dynamicity and true sustainability.

3.1 Green Virtual Enterprises as Dynamic Forward Supply Networks

GVEs as dynamic forward supply networks (F-GVEs) are temporary alliances of green enterprises that come together in order to better respond the market demands through the most efficient use of their complementary skills or core-competences and shared resources, for developing and delivering in a sustainable way new products (goods and services) to the customer with a minimal environmental impact.

GVEs lifecycle in their dynamic forward supply networks modality will go through the following stages: During its *creation,* (a) a new green business opportunity will be identified (e.g. new product developments) and will trigger the F-GVE formation; (b) the green business opportunity will be characterised in order to detail its competency requirements in terms of green design, green materials, green processes, green manufacturing, green packaging and green logistics needed to later on look for the F-GVE partners that posses these green competencies [2], and for drafting the F-GVE rough plan (e.g. work-breakdown-structure) to schedule, assign and locate activities, tasks and resources to be performed/used by the potential F-GVE partners during the F-GVE operation; (c) F-GVE partners will be searched, assessed and primarily selected from the pool of GVBE members available and in case there is a lack of competencies inside the GVBE, F-GVE partners can be recruited from outside, based on their green degree level [3] and other key performance indicators (e.g. price, delivery date, quality level, etc.) to respond to the competency requirements and constrains of the green business opportunity; (d) the selected F-GVE partners will negotiate to reach agreements and align needs with offers towards the F-GVE final configuration, following the triple bottom line sustainability principles (economic-equitable, environmental-viable, social-bearable); (e) a detailed F-GVE planning (e.g. working structure) with roles and responsibilities assigned to the F-GVE partners will be defined; and lastly (f) the F-GVE collaboration will be formalised in a contract and the F-GVE will be launched [adapted from 5] (see Fig. 2).

Furthermore, during the *operation stage,* the F-GVE most perform in an agile, green and optimal way following sustainable engineering, manufacturing and logistics principles in order to offer and deliver green products with the required quality and within the required time and cost frame needed to meet or exceed the customer expectations and environmental regulations [adapted from 6] (see Fig. 2).

Finally, during the F-GVE *dissolution,* since the F-GVE was created within a GVBE, any surplus and/or abandoned resources/scrap should be placed in the GVBE bag of assets [4] for its direct-use (re-use), repair, re-manufacture, recycle and/or safe disposal

---

[2] *Green competencies* are those environmentally conscious business practices and strategies such as: Design for the Environment (DFE), Product Lifecycle Management (PLM) and Lifecycle Analysis, Lean Manufacturing, Total Quality Environmental Management (TQEM), Environmental Management Systems (EMS), Green Supply Chain Management (G-SCM), Green Logistics, ISO14000 series' requirements, etc. [*Focus on Forward Supply Networks*].

[3] *Green degree level* is the outcome of using quantitative and qualitative metrics to scale and provide a meaningful evaluation of the green capabilities and capacities of an enterprise.

[4] A *GVBE bag of assets* is a common virtual and physical warehouse to make easier the share of tangible and intangible assets between the GVBE members for different purposes.

as part of the GVBE sustainable strategy, and of course the GVE product will be delivered to the customer using optimised/green logistics [adapted from 7] (see Fig. 2 & 3).

3.2 GVE Modality: Dynamic Reverse Supply Networks

GVEs as dynamic reverse supply networks (R-GVEs) are temporary alliances of green enterprises that come together in order to better respond a business opportunity based on a sustainable reverse logistics and end-of-life manufacturing approach for recovering products, parts, subassemblies and/or scrap through the most efficient use of their complementary skills or core-competences and shared resources for their direct-use (re-use), repair, re-manufacture, recycle or safe disposal - within a GVBE.

GVEs lifecycle in their dynamic reverse supply networks modality will go through the following stages: During its *creation,* (a) a new green business opportunity will be identified (e.g. products or scrap recovery) and will trigger the R-GVE formation; (b) the green business opportunity will be characterised in order to detail its competency requirements in terms of direct-use (re-use), repair, re-manufacturing, recycling and/or safe disposal approaches needed for managing certain products or scrap in their end-of-life to later on look for the R-GVE partners that posses these green competencies [5], and for drafting the R-GVE rough plan to be carried-out by the potential R-GVE partners during the R-GVE operation; (c) R-GVE partners will be searched, assessed and selected based on their green degree level and other key performance indicators to respond to the competency requirements and constrains of the green business opportunity, (d) the selected R-GVE partners will negotiate to reach agreements towards the R-GVE final configuration, following the triple bottom line sustainability principles, (e) a detailed R-GVE planning with roles and responsibilities assigned to the R-GVE partners will be defined, and (f) lastly the R-GVE collaboration will be formalised in a contract and the R-GVE will be launched (see Fig. 2).

Furthermore, during the *operation stage,* the R-GVE most perform in an agile, green and optimal way following sustainable logistics, end-of-life manufacturing and safe disposal principles in order to re-use (e.g. deal with the direct-use of product components as spare parts), re-manufacture (e.g. restoring and rebuilding products), recycle (e.g. reclaim raw materials) and/or safe disposal (e.g. hazardous wastes management) of products and their scrap always respecting the environmental regulations (see Fig. 2).

Finally, during the R-GVE *dissolution,* outputs may take two paths: (a) the outputs of the end-of-life manufacturing processes that were selected for direct-use (re-use) re-manufacturing and/or recycling will be returned immediately, if possible, as inputs to active forward supply networks (F-GVEs) within the GVBE or will be placed in the GVBE bag of assets as inputs for future F-GVEs, and/or (b) those outputs selected for safe disposal may trigger a new GVE formation specialised in hazardous wastes disposal practices (see Fig. 2 & 3).

---

[5] Green competencies are those environmentally conscious business practices and strategies for dealing with the end-of-life of products such as: inspection, diagnostic and recondition techniques to obtain the most value from a recovered product through a re-use (e.g. spare parts), refurbish (e.g. repair or re-manufacturing), recycling (e.g. scrap) and/or safe disposal (e.g. hazardous wastes treatments) strategy [*Focus on Reverse Supply Networks*].

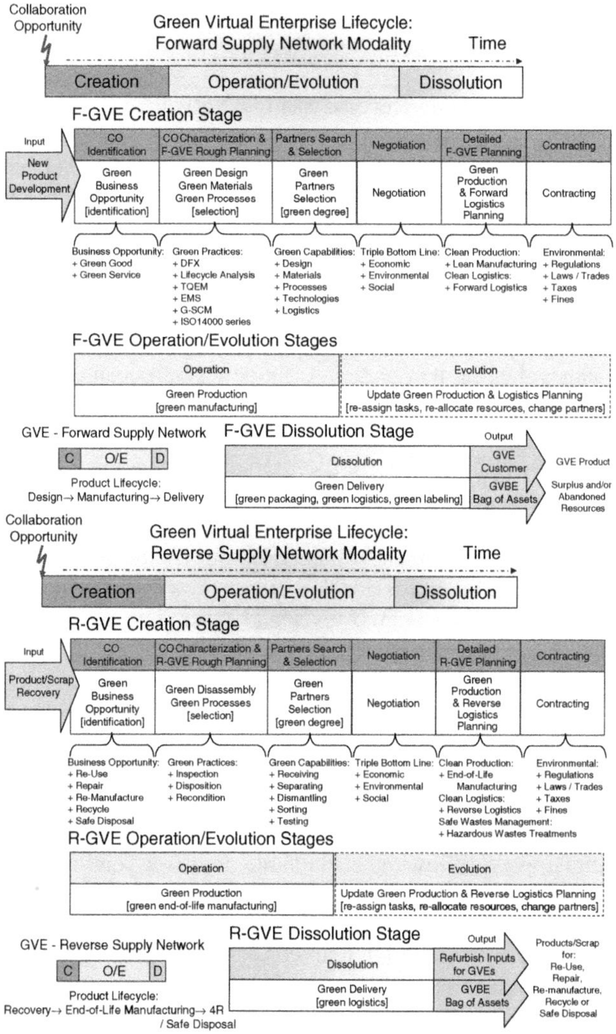

Fig. 2. GVE Modalities (top – F-GVE || bottom – R-GVE) Lifecycle, Methods & Tools

4 GVE Breeding Environments: Industrial Symbiosis

Industrial Symbiosis (IS) can be defined as an industrial ecology strategy, based on collaboration and synergetic possibilities, aimed at sharing/exchanging information, materials, water, energy and/or infrastructure (e.g. services) among industrial actors in order to increase economic gains and achieve sustainable development in a eco-industrial network [8]. IS systems like GVBEs, offer their members the opportunity to collaboratively optimise resources utility at efficiencies beyond those achievable by any single enterprise and at the same time open new possibilities to access/explore green business opportunities in the global marketplace that would not be possible, or would have a higher cost, if attempted individually.

In this paper, GVBEs are introduced as virtual eco-industrial collaborative networks with the capabilities and capacities to deploy innovative, cost-effective and green technologies and practices to promote sustainable industrial development through F-GVEs and R-GVEs creation, operation and dissolution. GVBEs have as their main goal becoming intelligent networks for resources management (GVBE bag of assets) in order to match GVEs inputs and outputs (match-making) to maximise resources utility towards achieving industrial symbiosis.

In Fig. 3 a generic GVBE industrial symbiosis scenario is presented, in this setting when a F-GVE is created: [a] some inputs can be collected from the GVBE bag of assets, [b] some others can be provided by running GVEs acting as green suppliers, and [c] if necessary, missing inputs within the GVBE bag of assets can be purchased outside of the virtual eco-industrial network. Furthermore, F-GVEs outputs such as surplus and/or abandoned resources: [d] will be placed in the GVBE bag of assets for its later use or [e] will be immediately incorporated as inputs for other active GVEs within the GVBE. On the other hand, in the R-GVE case, inputs may come from: [f] products/scrap recovered from GVBE inside (bag of assets warehouse) as a result of an endogenous green business opportunity (e.g. 4R[6] or safe disposal strategy) that can be announced inside the GVBE by its manager and simply GVBE members will organise to respond to it (GVE creation), or [g] products/scrap can be recovered from GVBE outside (marketplace) as an exogenous green business opportunity that can be detected by a GVBE member playing the role of a broker and GVBE members will be selected to become the R-GVE partners. Moreover, R-GVEs outputs similar to F-GVEs outputs can be [h] placed in the GVBE bag of assets for its later use or [i] can be immediately incorporated as inputs for other active GVEs within the GVBE.

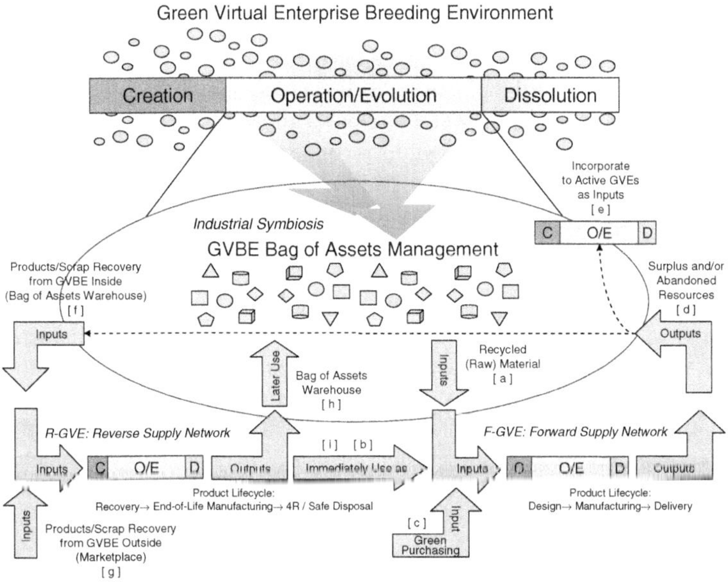

Fig. 3. GVBE Industrial Symbiosis

[6] 4R strategy stands for repair, re-manufacture, recycle and re-use green strategies.

In general, GVBEs industrial symbiosis and other collaboration strategies can increase green enterprises' competitive and environmental performance by becoming GVBE members and participating in GVEs. Some industrial symbiosis benefits/ reasons for green enterprises to join a GVBE can be to reduce natural resources consumption, improve approaches for sustainable business operations, reduce (raw) materials costs, reduce treatment and disposal costs, etc. to meet economic gains by saving money and protecting the environment. While some collaboration benefits for green enterprises in a "business sense" can be to access/explore emerging green markets, increase activities/profit in a sustainable way, copying with market green trends and environmental regulations, joint purchasing (better negotiation power), joint promotion (eco-branding/marketing), social and environmental responsibility prestige/reputation, sustainable innovation as differentiator, among others; and in a more "technical sense", GVBEs collaboration benefits offer possibilities for shared commuting and shipping, alternative (green) packing, integrated (green) logistics, common environmental information systems, (green) production technology sharing and integration, etc. [see 2] [see 9].

5 Discussion and Reflexions

In the past, some eco-industrial collaborative models (e.g. eco-industry clusters/parks) bounded to their geographical proximity have improved their members competitive and environmental performance through different collaboration strategies (e.g. industrial symbiosis), which have resulted in economic benefits for the enterprises and their support institutions, and in environmental care and social welfare for their localities.

Nevertheless, with the advances in information and communication technologies and new environmental-friendly transportation vehicles/systems (e.g. hybrids), novel *virtual* eco-industrial collaborative models [10] such as the GVEs and their GVBEs are gradually emerging in the global industrial landscape, making (green) enterprises step beyond their geographical regions in order to access new complementary green competencies, and market and symbiosis opportunities. As such, nowadays eco-industrial collaborative models do not have to be bounded anymore by their members' geographical closeness and can use collaborative business infrastructures [11] playing the intermediary role as the enablers of interoperation among enterprises to support their coordination and cooperation mechanisms (e.g. design, manufacturing, logistics, warehousing) towards sustainable operations and therefore development.

Geographical proximity vs. virtuality can be a debate for the eco-industry clusters establishment; however researchers and industrial practitioners have to consider that "it is possible", as proved by the *Collaborative Networks* scientific discipline, for not physically co-located enterprises to create economics of scale and cost effective support for information, materials, water and/or energy exchanges across distance using collaborative logistics networks [12] and collaborative business ICT infrastructures [11] [see also 13].

As any strategy for an eco-industry cluster establishment, traditional eco-industry clusters (e.g. eco-industrial parks) vs. virtual eco-industry clusters (e.g. GVBEs) have their advantages and disadvantages and these tradeoffs are briefly depicted in Table 1.

Table 1. Traditional Eco-Industry Clusters vs. Virtual Eco-Industry Clusters

Eco-Industrial Parks (EIPs)	GVE Breeding Environments (GVBEs)
Involve a strong investment and high environmental impact with a physical location construction and/or the re-development of an exiting one.	Do not involve an investment in a physical location construction, but require a moderate investment in a collaborative business ICT infrastructure, which represents a lower environmental impact.
EIPs most suitable members need to be collocated in a certain geographic location in order to participate in the industrial symbiosis and other collaboration opportunities, incurring in the costs associated and environmental impact to re-setup a green enterprise in a new location. Also potential EIP members will be limited to geography proximity.	GVBEs most suitable members do not need to be collocated in the same place to participate in the industrial symbiosis and other collaboration opportunities, just need to create virtual linkages supported by computer networks without any geographic barriers that could limit the best green enterprises recruitment scope.
Recruiting new EIP members in order to enhance the eco-industrial park capabilities and capacities can be extremely difficult because of the green enterprise reallocation.	Recruiting new GVBE members in order to enhance the breeding environment capabilities and capacities can be very easy thanks to a GVBE membership management system.
In an EIP more materials, water, energy and/or other waste exchanges seem to be possible in comparison to GVBEs, but this exchanges as well as enterprises skills and resources sharing are limited to the ones available in the geographical proximity.	In a GVBE perhaps less materials, water, energy and/or other waste exchanges seem to be possible because of geographic distance, but more enterprises skills and resources sharing can take place by being able to have a large number of GVBE members.

6 Emerging Eco-Industry Clusters: Typology and Examples

As discussed in the previous section, geographical proximity vs. virtuality can offer different advantages and disadvantages towards traditional and/or virtual eco-industry clusters establishment. Nevertheless, as depicted in Fig. 4, different models for eco-industry clusters exist, from traditional eco-industrial parks with enterprises located at the same site to geographically distributed enterprises creating virtual linkages, in opposition to co-location, to form virtual eco-industry clusters. Each of these sustainable industrial development models or combinations of them are characterised by different activities and uses, including green manufacturing (e.g. producing green products), closed-loop manufacturing (e.g. zero-emissions), by-product exchange (e.g. using by-products rather than disposing them as wastes), renewable energy, resource recovery (e.g. 4R strategy), green infrastructure (e.g. landscaping), green building design, cleaner production, pollution prevention, energy efficiency, and partnerships between green enterprises and their related support institutions [14].

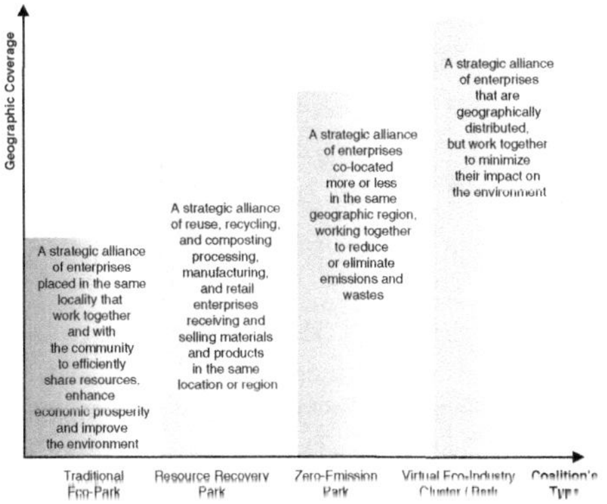

Fig. 4. Eco-Industry Clusters Typology [14]

Most famous and first eco-industrial park, which has been the reference model for today's eco-industry clusters, is *Industrial Symbiosis* at Kalundborg, Denmark, where different industrial firms have been working together for more than 30 years exchanging waste materials and energy, and sharing resources [8]. Moreover, the first virtual eco-industry cluster was established at *Brownsville, Texas* (1996) as a regional approach to exchange materials and by-products across the USA-Mexican boarder [14], which has been followed by other virtual initiatives such as the *Karlsruhe* virtual eco-industrial park (1998), where different enterprises exchange organic and mineral by-products, share information and focus on dematerialisation chains, and the *Bioenergie und Rohstoffzentrum Dormagen* virtual eco-industrial park (1999), where companies focus on by-product exchanges and energy cascades, information sharing and extended collaboration with universities and public entities, both at Germany [15].

Nowadays, different eco-industrial park projects can be found around the World, for some relevant case studies in America, Europe and Asia [see 15].

7 Conclusions and Further Research

The materialisation of a potential synergy between IE and CNOs scientific disciplines requires a further research on understanding these possible synergies and underlying principles for better GVEs and their GVBEs creation and management as sustainable industrial collaborative networks. Nevertheless, significant progress is already available in terms of conceptual frameworks and models [3] [4], methods and processes [13], and software tools and systems [5] [6] in CNOs scientific discipline, and perhaps is just a matter of bringing from IE scientific discipline the sustainability element as a main driving force behind the future success of sustainable collaborative networks.

Future looks for more "green" enterprises and sustainable industrial development models, and the proposed approach based on GVEs and their GVBEs appears to be well-suited to cope with emerging socio-economic and environmental challenges of the global industrial landscape.

Acknowledgments. The research presented in this document is a contribution for the ECOLEAD Project (FP6 IP 506958), for the S-MC-S Project (FP7 NMP-ICT-FoF 260090), and for the ITESM, Campus MTY & CCM, Research Chairs.

References

1. Chertow, M.R.: The Eco-Industrial Park Model Reconsidered. Journal of Industrial Ecology 2(3), 8–16 (1998)
2. Camarinha-Matos, L.M., Afsarmanesh, H.: Collaborative Networks: Value Creation in a Knowledge Society. In: Knowledge Enterprise. IFIP, vol. 207, pp. 26–40. Springer, NY (2006)
3. Camarinha-Matos, L.M., Afsarmanesh, H.: A Framework for VO Creation in a Breeding Environment. Annual Reviews in Control 31(1), 119–135 (2007)
4. Romero, D., Molina, A.: Virtual Organisation Breeding Environments Toolkit: Reference Model, Management Framework and Instantiation Methodology. Journal of Production Planning & Control 21(2), 181–217 (2009)
5. Camarinha-Matos, L.M., et al.: A Framework for Computer-assisted Creation of Dynamic Virtual Organisations. International Journal of Production Research 47(17), 4661–4690 (2009)

6. Negretto, U., et al.: VO Management Solutions. In: Methods and Tools for Collaborative Networked Organizations, pp. 257–274. Springer, NY (2008)
7. Karvonen, I., Salkari, L., Ollus, M.: Identification of Forms and Components of VO Inheritance. In: Establishing the Foundation of Collaborative Networks. IFIP, vol. 243, pp. 253–262. Springer, NY (2007)
8. Chertow, M.R.: Industrial Symbiosis: Literature and Taxonomy. Annual Review of Energy and the Environment 25, 313–337 (2000)
9. Cohen-Rosenthal, E.: Handbook on Codes, Covenants, Conditions, and Restrictions for Eco-Industrial Parks. Cornell Center for the Environment, Work & Environment Initiative, NY (1999)
10. Ausubel, J.H.: The Virtual Ecology of Industry. Journal of Industrial Ecology 1(1), 10–11 (1997)
11. Rabelo, R.J., Gusmeroli, S.: The ECOLEAD Collaborative Business Infrastructure for Networked Organizations. In: Pervasive Collaborative Networks. IFIP, vol. 283, pp. 451–462. Springer, NY (2008)
12. Langley, J.: Seven Immutable Laws of Collaborative Logistics. NISTEVO Consulting (2000)
13. Romero, D., Molina, A.: VO Breeding Environments & Virtual Organizations Integral Business Process Management Framework. Journal of Information Systems Frontiers 11(5), 569–597 (2009)
14. PCSD: Eco-Industrial Park Workshop Proceedings (1996), http://clinton2.nara.gov/PCSD/index.html
15. Fleig, A.: ECO-Industrial Parks: A Strategy towards Industrial Ecology in Developing and Newly Industrialised Countries, Deutsche Gesellschaft für Technische Zusammenarbeit (GTZ) GmbH (2000)

Collaborative Networks for Biodiversity Domain Organizations

Ekaterina Ermilova and Hamideh Afsarmanesh

University of Amsterdam, FCN group,
Science Park 107, 1098 XG Amsterdam, The Netherlands
{e.ermilova,h.afsarmanesh}@uva.nl

Abstract. European scientific research and development organizations, operating in the domains of biology, ecology, and biodiversity, strongly need to cooperate/collaborate with other centers. Unavailability of interoperation infrastructure as well as the needed collaboration environment among research organizations restricts their exchange of research results and efficient launching of co-working/co-development R&D initiatives. This paper proposes the pre-establishment of a long term strategic Collaborative Network called BTCN (Breeding environment for Temporary Collaborative Networks) for these organizations based on a survey of this environment. BTCN supports in a cost/time effective manner the formation and creation of potential future collaboration sub-networks addressing different R&D opportunities.

Keywords: Biodiversity, Collaborative Network, Breeding environment for Temporary Collaborative Networks.

1 Introduction

Organizations involved in biodiversity domain, e.g. data providers, research laboratories, universities, conservation groups, etc., referred to in this paper as BOs (Biodiversity-domain Organizations), are increasingly involved in collaborative activities with some other BOs as well as with some organizations outside the biodiversity domain, referred to here as EOs (External Organizations). For example, the collaboration scenario addressed in the FlySafe project [1], that is aimed at protection of airplanes from colliding with birds, identifies the co-working among several regional BOs involved in birds-related research, as well as a few EOs involved in weather forecast, airport administration, etc. Typically, such collaboration aims at supporting BOs with sharing their competencies and resources in order to together perform some monitoring, research, analysis, or development tasks at the level of a specific region, a country, or entire continent [2] [3]. The co-working and co-development approaches among BOs are increasingly growing in time as the proportion of complexity and demand of market / society opportunities in relation to existing resources and competencies and reaching beyond what single organizations can effectively support. Therefore, in order for BOs to increase their chances of involvement in emerging opportunities within the biodiversity domain, they need to

L.M. Camarinha-Matos et al. (Eds.): PRO-VE 2010, IFIP AICT 336, pp. 36–45, 2010.

get organized and supported by a special form of Collaborative Network (CN), which is referred to in this paper as the **Breeding environment for Temporary Collaborative Networks (BTCN)**. The definition of BTCN is rooted in [4]:

> *BTCN is a "strategic" alliance of Biodiversity Organizations (BOs), and External Organizations (EOs), which adhere to a base long term cooperation agreement, and adopt common operating principles and infrastructures, with the main goal of increasing the preparedness and their chances for participating in potential goal-oriented collaboration with others within Temporary Collaborative Networks (TCNs).*

The main objective of the research addressed in this paper is both: (i) the study and characterization of existing forms of collaboration identified between European BOs, such as the networks of excellence and national research networks (as addressed in section 3), and (ii) the identification of new suitable forms of collaboration providing advanced support mechanisms to improve the efficiency of collaboration among the BOs (as addressed in section 4).

The research presented in this paper is partially performed within the FP7 project **LifeWatch**. This project aims at development of an e-Science & Technology Infrastructure for Biodiversity Research, in which support of collaboration among biodiversity domain organizations is important task. More details about the research presented in this paper are addressed in a LifeWatch report [5].

2 Study of Related Research on Collaborative Networks

The research, presented in this paper, uses the main R&D results in the area of Collaborative Networks (CNs) as the primary input. Particularly, it applies: (1) the base concepts of Collaborative Networks, including the types and forms of CNs as well as the identified actors and their roles in long-term CNs, and (2) the ARCON modelling framework elements and the ARCON reference model for CNs. Below this section briefly addresses the CN classification and ARCON models.

The **classification of CNs** is addressed by the CN taxonomy introduced in [6]. In this taxonomy, all CNs are first divided into organized CNs that are called collaborative networked organizations, and the ad-hoc CNs. The collaborative networked organizations are further divided into two groups depending on their purpose and duration, namely divided into long-term strategic alliances and Goal-oriented networks. The long-term strategic alliances typically exist for indefinite time and aim at preparation of their members for future collaboration activities. The goal-oriented networks are created for a specific goal and exist until that goal is achieved. These networks are also further divided into two groups, by the type of their goals, namely into grasping-opportunity-driven-networks and continuous activity driven networks. The networks from the first group are formed on demand, when a new opportunity appears in the market or society. The networks from the second group have a longer term specific goal. Then, collaborative networked organizations are also divided by the types of their members, that can be either organizations or people. The long-term strategic alliances of organisation are called virtual organizations breeding environments (VBEs). Namely they represent breeding environments for formation and establishment the grasping-opportunity-driven-networks of organizations, which are called virtual organizations. The long-term strategic alliances of people are called professional virtual communities. In their turn they represent breeding environments for the grasping-opportunity-driven-networks of people, which are called virtual teams.

The **ARCON (A Reference model for COllaborative Networks)** [7] is developed as an evolving system, constituting: (1) ARCON reference modeling framework, and (2) a set of ARCON reference models generated within this framework each representing one specific kind of CN, for instance the virtual organizations breeding environments, virtual organizations, virtual teams, etc.

The ARCON framework comprehensively addresses the heterogeneous elements of different CN environments. In this model, the CN elements are grouped into two "subspaces" (as addressed in Fig. 1). The "*CN Endogenous Elements*" subspace represents all elements and components inside the CN, while the "*CN Exogenous Interactions*" subspace represents all elements and components outside the CN. Each subspace is divided into four different "dimensions" (i.e. the *structural, componential, functional* and *behavioural* dimensions for the "CN Endogenous Elements" subspace, and the *market, support, societal* and *constituency* dimensions for the "CN Exogenous Interactions" subspace). These two subspaces and their dimensions together represent the CN environment characteristics.

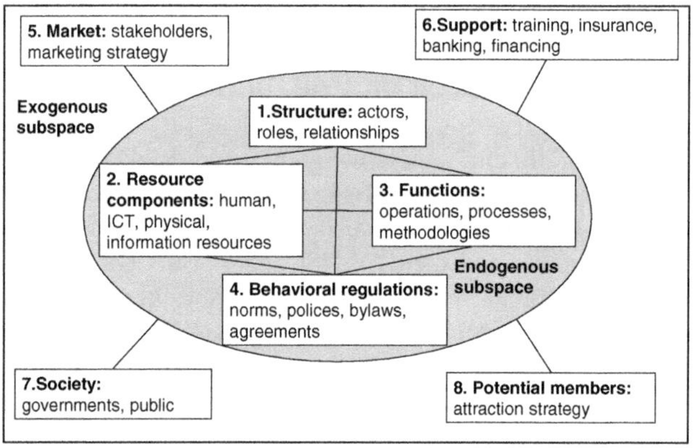

Fig. 1. Subspaces and dimensions in the ARCON reference framework

The above aspects of the CN are applied to the conduction of case studies and define the steps of our research on existing collaboration forms in the LifeWatch biodiversity domain (presented in section 3). Firstly, through applying the CN classification to our case study we have identified two specific types of CNs for which their 1st generation currently exist in the biodiversity domain. Secondly, using the ARCON reference model for CNs we have both: (1) characterised those existing CNs, specifying their main elements (e.g. actors and their roles, resources, regulation documents, etc.), as well as (2) identified the requirements for their specific aspects, mechanisms, and tools that are needed to be supported for the LifeWatch CNs.

3 Case Study of Existing Collaboration Forms

In order to study the current forms of collaboration among BOs, a questionnaire titled "Collaboration requirements of Biodiversity Organizations", is prepared and distributed among the biodiversity organizations participating in LifeWatch project.

The two main objectives of the study conducted through this questionnaire are addressed below:

Objective 1: *Characterisation of the existing collaboration among different European BOs and other related EOs, as well as the identification of the current forms of these collaborations.* To achieve this first objective, we specifically aimed at discovering whether the forms of collaboration, existing within the biodiversity domain, match one (or more) of the advanced forms currently defined CNs taxonomy, namely the CNO, long-term strategic alliance, goal-oriented network, virtual organization breeding environment, professional virtual community, virtual organization, or virtual team.

Objective 2: *Identification of both the drawbacks/weaknesses of these current forms of collaboration, as well as the so far identified needs/requirements in these networks to improve the collaboration among BOs and other related EOs in Europe.* To achieve this second objective, we were specifically aiming at understanding whether the European BOs have currently identified either some problems or some needs for improvements, related to current collaboration stage among different biodiversity centres, or the lack of it.

The participants at this case study represent more than ten major research organizations (BOs) from nine European countries involved in the LifeWatch consortium, including universities, large institutes, and research centres.

3.1 Observations on Identified Collaboration Forms

As addressed by the related research on Collaborative Networks, different forms of collaboration can be established among the organizations working in the biodiversity domain. All responders to the above questionnaire have indicated that they do regularly participate in some form of research related collaboration with other organizations, to enhance their effectiveness in their daily activities. This section further represents the main conclusions deduced related to different forms of existing biodiversity collaboration, involving European BOs. For better processing purposes, the main observations gathered through the questionnaire are categorised into the following five categories:

- **Actors in collaboration.** Currently the number of partners associated to a specific BO is directly proportional to the size of BO. Particularly, small BOs have far less chances to participate in cooperation and collaboration activities with others, and thus need more support for that. Also, currently while some organization types are strongly involved in collaboration with some types of BOs (e.g. data providers, research organizations, governmental organizations, etc.), there is a lack of collaboration with other organization types, such as organizations from industry, commercial/profit organizations, political organizations, and service (e.g. ICT-service) providers, while

BOs express their interest in such collaborations. It means that current BOs are currently not benefiting from: (1) those opportunities that are associated with these organizations and (2) the support that these organizations can provide. For example, BOs currently lack the support that can be provided by ICT support providers. BOs are also lacking the opportunities to start new initiatives, e.g. an R&D projects, involving commercial companies and industry.

- **Existing forms of collaboration.** There are currently two main forms of collaboration identified: *goal-oriented networks* that mainly represent Virtual Organizations with some elements of virtual teams. These alliances are named in this document as **Temporary Collaborative Networks (TCNs)**. *Long-term strategic alliances* that mainly represent virtual organization breeding environments with some elements of professional virtual communities. These alliances are named in this document as **Breeding Environment for Temporary Collaborative Networks (BTCNs)**. Other observations in this area are addressed in Table 1.

Table 1. Some observations about existing forms of collaboration

Main reasons for existence of current long-term strategic alliances: They include: homogenization of potential partners, accessing common infrastructure and assets, and funding new projects.
Characterization of members in long-term strategic alliances and goal-oriented networks: Currently, the partners of goal-oriented networks for the responders mainly overlap with their partners in alliances, but there can be also some other external partners appearing for specific projects. It means that responders state that current members of the long-term strategic alliances are not always enough for addressing opportunities, namely they might not have enough possibilities to serve as breeding environments for goal-oriented networks. The respondents to the questionnaire find it beneficial to extend the alliances to larger networks of different organizations that can be potentially useful for collaboration, so that they can search and select potential partners in these networks.
Early forms of long-term strategic alliances: Networks of excellence in biodiversity, such as ALTER-net [8] and MARBEF [9] are referred to as early forms of long-term strategic alliances.
Main reasons for existence of current goal-oriented networks: They include: initiating and performing projects and delivering assigned tasks, among others.
Main members' roles in long-term strategic alliances / goal-oriented networks: The specific roles that members play in networks mainly represent the roles of regular actors and coordination/administration actors. Some other roles are also weakly represented, such as Broker of new opportunities, Customer, Support provider (e.g. training), Advisor or expert, Supplier, and Competitor. This means that the identified CNs might lack the support role for BOs to improve themselves, for example training. Also, lacking the role of Broker in long-term strategic alliances currently can result to absence of dynamism in finding and addressing new opportunities.

- **Collaboration opportunities.** Currently, collaborative opportunities are understood by BOs as opportunities to collectively conduct research projects by a number of partners. Furthermore, these opportunities are typically brokered by scientific institutions and governments-related organizations. There is no mentioning of opportunities brokered by other organization types, e.g. commercial companies or industry. This is a serious limitation for current BOs activities and research results transfer and dissemination. Current long-term strategic alliances cannot address some emerged collaborative opportunities and form goal-oriented networks. Thus they need some support for becoming strong breeding environments for goal-oriented networks.
- **Benefits of collaboration.** The main benefit for collaboration among BOs is currently to pursue their "mission", namely performing research in the biodiversity area and achieving substantial result. Thus, this benefit constitutes the base for the

BOs' value system. Consequently, measurement of research result achievement is the base for measurement of performance in biodiversity networks.

- **Support for collaboration.** Currently, to support remote collaboration, BOs use only basic ICT tools such as wiki, e-mail, web-sites. There is a lack of specific ICT tools supporting remote cooperation and collaboration (e.g. ontology management, performance measurement, etc.). Existing ICT tools represents only tools for storage, exchange and analysis of domain-related biodiversity data. Among the human resources, there are jobs (e.g. coordination, consultation, and technical jobs) that specially support collaboration. Among physical resources, there are recourses (e.g. ships and measurement devises) that are shared during collaboration activities.

3.2 Analysis of Responses – Identified Requirements

A main part of this case study also focused on investigating and identifying which support systems, tools, and functionalities are needed to be provided by long-term strategic alliances both to support their BO members as well as to support the administration of the networks. The supporting means and functionalities, as mainly addressed by their functional dimension of the ARCON reference model, are divided here into two groups, namely: (i) ICT support and background management activities and functionalities needed for long-term strategic alliances, and (ii) support tools and systems for dynamic creation of goal-oriented networks.

The conclusions in relation to these two groups are described below. For every support functionality, the percentage of responders who specified needing this functionality is also addressed below.

Main conclusions about requirements for **ICT support and background management activities for long-term strategic alliances** are addressed in Table 2:

Table 2. Requirements for ICT support and background activities for long-term strategic alliances

Common ICT infrastructure: Currently, the need for developing specialized ICT infrastructure to support cooperation and collaboration among the BOs is identified by 100% of responders. This is mainly maintained as required for cooperation among Biodiversity Organizations and with less necessity for supporting cooperation between the BOs and External Organizations such as government-related organizations and public sector.
Governance system: Improving the governance system of current long-term strategic alliances is needed, as addressed by 70% of the responders.
Support-providers: Support-providing organizations are needed to be added within the long-term strategic alliances, as addressed by 55% of responders.
Bag of assets: A common "bag of assets" is needed to be established and properly managed by the long-term strategic alliances, as addressed by 100% of responders.
Competency management: Management of BO's competency is required by the long-term strategic alliances, as addressed by 75% of responders.
Trust management: Trust establishment among BOs and its management is strongly needed within the long-term strategic alliances, as addressed by 100% of responders.
Common understanding: Increasing the common understanding of the general concepts of long-term strategic alliances as well as of the biodiversity domain concepts is required by the members of long-term strategic alliances, as addressed by 85% of responders.

Main conclusions about ICT requirements for the dynamic creation of **goal-oriented networks** within their breeding environments are addressed in Table 3.

Table 3. ICT requirements for the dynamic creation of goal-oriented networks

Need to support dynamic creation of goal-oriented networks: BOs do not have so far enough experience and/or knowledge about the CN and the possibilities for dynamic creation of goal-oriented networks within long-term strategic alliances. Therefore they currently create goal-oriented networks mainly in the traditional way. Namely, from the open universe of organizations and individuals, but primarily with those BOs with which they have past experiences. The support for dynamic creation of goal-oriented networks is stated to be needed by all types of national and international partner organizations, except for forming a new goal-oriented network with BOs that have a long history of collaboration in the past.
Agility in creation: BOs would like to see an increase in agility of creation of goal-oriented networks, as indicated by the responders.
Size of goal-oriented networks: BOs also find it useful to support acquiring a larger size (through formation of goal-oriented networks) responding to bids for most projects.
Chances for involvement: BOs indicated the need to increase their chances for involvement into goal-oriented networks.
Creation risks for goal-oriented networks: BOs indicated the need for, to the extent possible, decreasing the potential of risks in creation of goal-oriented networks especially for larger networks.

3.3 Conclusions on Restrictions for Existing Cooperation/Collaboration among BOs

The main conclusions reached from our case study are summarised below.

1_ **Lack of homogeneity in chances for BOs.** The responders have indicated that there is no uniformity between different BOs, which in turn strongly affects their chances for collaboration. Namely the identified heterogeneity includes:

- **Size of BOs** (that ranges from 5 to 300 employees) that usually proportionally affects their resource capacity (e.g. amount of human or machinery recourses) as well as their lists of contacts/partners. Namely, small organizations do not have much recourses and contacts with other organizations. It means that even if small BOs are competent in performing some specific tasks, since they do not have enough resource capacities, they have difficulties for involvement into collaboration with others. Similarly, if they have a small number of contacts, currently it is difficult to get involved in TCN partnership that gets established to address an emerged opportunity.
- **Locality of partners** (that ranges from dominated by local partners to wide variety of local and international partners) that also affects their chances of collaboration involvement. Organizations which (due to some reasons, e.g. tradition of the geographic location) can only collaborate nationally, miss those benefits that can be provided by international collaboration.
- **Range of partner types** (that ranges from partners in a similar area of activity to partners from multiple areas of activity) affects the capabilities within the collaboration projects. For example, the BOs who collaborate only with those BOs which have the same area of activity (e.g. marine biology) do not have opportunity to address collaborative opportunities requiring a merge of capabilities.
- **Age of organizations** (that ranges from decades to centuries) that directly affects the number of currently established relationships with other organizations. Older

organizations have longer and larger partnerships with others, thus for them it is easier to find trustworthy partners to address collaborative opportunities.

- **Expertise in the area of CNs** (that ranges from medium to high) that affects the smoothness of both the collaboration as well as the adoption of new CN approaches for biodiversity domain. For example, the organization that have a high expertise in the area of CNs are able to adopt new developed CN related approaches, and be a part of more advanced collaborative consortiums.

Therefore, some approaches and mechanisms developed within the CN discipline shall be applied to homogenize all BOs representation within BTCNs, homogenizing their chances for involvement into collaboration with others in potential TCNs.

2_ Limitation of fulfilling possibilities and lack of dynamism in creation of TCNs. The responders have indicated existence of a number of goal-oriented networks for biodiversity domain that constitute: a number of BOs, their related EOs, and a number of individual experts working together on a specific project. Earlier on, we introduced **Temporary Collaborative Networks (TCN)** referring to this kind of goal-oriented networks for the LifeWatch collaboration infrastructure. Current TCNs mainly represent projects aimed at specific research opportunities. The partners of TCNs are often selected among those which had some collaboration or cooperation experience in the past. However there are a large number of BOs that are at disadvantage, since they are not well-connected through any long-term strategic relationships. Furthermore, the current set of the Collaboration Networks are set statically, consequently posing a great obstacle for creation of time/cost effective and competitive dynamic TCN that require the pre-existence of a large strategic-alliance. The responses to questions about the requirements for dynamic TCN creation have indicated that BOs do not form TCNs dynamically, but rather traditionally, on the "friends of friends" basis, and therefore for this approach almost 40% of the responders indicated that currently there is no use for dynamic TCNs creation. However dynamism in TCN creation facilitates addressing more opportunities that are missed today due to the limitation of negotiation power, capabilities, etc. that are symptomatic of the existing closed long-term strategic alliances. Facilitating dynamic TCN creation shall therefore be studied and supported for future LifeWatch collaboration infrastructures.

3_ Small or loosely administrated 1st generation BTCNs. Some *early forms* of breeding environment for TCNs (BTCN) have been identified through the study. Specifically two types of BTCNs are identified through our study. *First type* of BTCNs represents alliances of partners with long-term and well established relationships. Typically they include national partners or some organizations of the same type. Currently, most such BTCNs are small, and thus they are not always of a large enough size to address collaborative opportunities only through their members, and therefore loose those opportunities. The *second type* of BTCNs includes a set of partners, who had some experience of both working together within past TCNs or past bilateral cooperation through which they have got to know each other. Examples of such BTCNs include networks of excellence in biodiversity. These BTCNs are typically large but the relationships between their members are loose and they lack the needed facilitating management functionalities of long-term strategic alliances. Consequently, these provide obstacles for effective joining of BOs competencies and for dynamically addressing collaborative opportunities. New generation of BTCNs should be established to support both better cooperation among a variety of members and better management of the BTCN, increasing possibilities of dynamic creation of TCNs.

4_ **Lack of ICT collaboration support.** While there ICT is currently used to support research in TCNs, e.g. many software tools, databases, etc., there is a lack of specialised ICT to support biodiversity collaboration infrastructure, e.g. negotiation support, partners' profiles and competencies management, common bag of assets management, trust management, etc.

5_ **Heterogeneity of requirements to improve collaboration.** Every responder identifies certain requirements as the "main" current obstacle in its way to effective collaboration, which is mostly unique and very different than other responses, as it represents the typical wide range of complexity to be addressed by the CN paradigm. These requirements depending on the BO and its location, widely varies and may range from the need to increase the number of partners with which to collaborate to the provision of lacking ICT support, or even establishing trust. While this observation indicates that there is no homogeneity between European BOs in relation to their situation and requirements for collaboration, on average more than 70% of responders have stated that they find the CN-related support "very useful" for their collaboration activities.

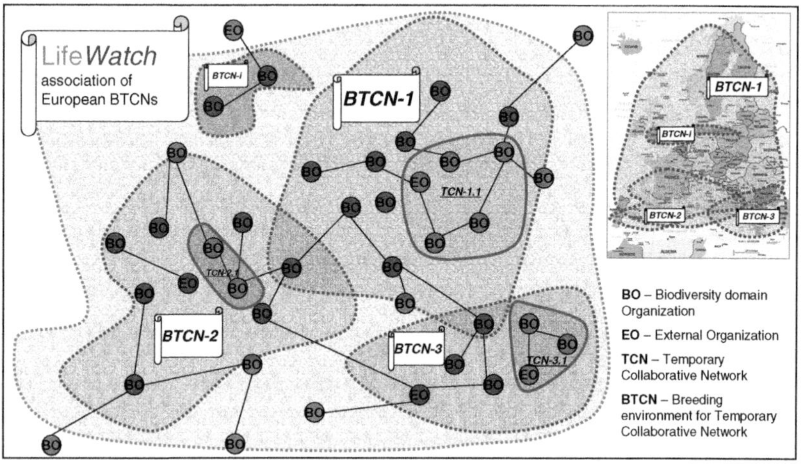

Fig. 2. LifeWatch association of European BTCNs

4 Suggested Approach

To address all requirements addressed in the previous sections, the new generation of BTCNs for this domain should be modelled, specified, and established. The 2nd generation BTCNs shall strengthen relationships among their members that will support both: better cooperation among the members as well as better conditions for dynamic creation of TCNs. For the biodiversity domain, the BTCNs can be established either based on their geographical location, or based on their specialization area (e.g.

for the marine domain, flora domain, weather domain under the aegis of the LifeWatch project, thus constructing the: "**LifeWatch's association of European BTCNs**", as illustrated in Fig. 2.

Furthermore, there are a number of questions that needs to be answered before specification and establishment of the 2nd generation BTCNs, e.g.: *What are the specific principles for clustering of BOs, EOs, and individual experts within BTCNs (BTCN typology)? How to attract BOs to join BTCNs and keep them interested and active? How should BTCNs be instantiated, organized, and coordinated?* These questions will be further addressed in forthcoming papers.

5 Conclusions

This paper aims at addressing and applying the new developments and experiences achieved in the area of Collaborative Networks as potential solutions for establishing an effective collaboration infrastructure and for the European network of biodiversity research.

To achieve its aim, the paper presents: (i) study of the existing collaboration forms among European Biodiversity Organizations (BOs), (ii) identification of their types and complexities according to the existing CN's taxonomy and reference model, (iii) identification of main requirements for improvement of BOs' collaboration, and (iv) suggestion of an effective and most suitable collaboration form for BOs' networks. The paper also suggests establishment of a long-term strategic network of BOs end their related external (non-biodiversity) organizations, which is called the BTCN (Breeding environment for Temporary Collaborative Networks).

References

1. FlySafe FP6 project, `http://www.eu-flysafe.org/Project.html`
2. Westley, F., Vredenburg, H.: Interorganizational Collaboration and the Preservation of Global Biodiversity. Organization Science 8(4), 381–403 (1997)
3. Guralnick, R.P., Hill, A.W., Lane, M.: Towards a collaborative, global infrastructure for biodiversity assessment. Ecology Letters 10(8), 663–672 (2007)
4. Afsarmanesh, H., Camarinha-Matos, L.M.: A framework for management of virtual organizations breeding environments. In: Collaborative networks and their breeding environments, pp. 35–48. Springer, Heidelberg (2005)
5. Ermilova, E., Afsarmanesh, A., Msanjila, M.: D5.2.a - Virtual Collaborative networks supporting LifeWatch R&D infrastructure in biodiversity domain. Lifewatch (2009)
6. Camarinha-Matos, L.M., Afsarmanesh, H.: Collaboration forms. In: Collaborative networks reference modeling, pp. 51–66. Springer, New York (2008) ISBN: 978-0-387-79425-9
7. Camarinha-Matos, L.M., Afsarmanesh, H.: The ARCON modeling framework. In: Collaborative networks reference modeling, pp. 67–82. Springer, New York (2008) ISBN: 978-0-387-79425-9
8. ALTER-net - A Long-Term Biodiversity, Ecosystem and Awareness Research Network, http://www.alter-net.info
9. MARBEF - Marine Biodiversity and Ecosystem Functioning EU Network of Excellence, `http://www.marbef.org`

Active Ageing Roadmap – A Collaborative Networks Contribution to Demographic Sustainability

Luis M. Camarinha-Matos[1] and Hamideh Afsarmanesh[2]

[1] Universidade Nova de Lisboa, Faculty of Sciences and Technology, Portugal
cam@uninova.pt
[2] University of Amsterdam, Netherlands
h.afsarmanesh@uva.nl

Abstract. The application of the collaborative networks paradigm, and a new generation of collaboration-support platforms and tools, is a promising approach to supporting active ageing, and facilitating better use of the talents and potential of retired or retiring senior professionals. As such, collaborative networks can contribute to demographic sustainability. This paper introduces the results of a roadmapping initiative addressing the implementation of a new vision for extending professional active life. To support this vision, a strategic research plan for the development of a new digital ecosystem, covering the social, organizational, and technological perspectives, is proposed. A large number of stakeholders coming from different backgrounds contributed to the design and validation of this roadmap.

Keywords: Collaborative networks, active ageing, roadmap.

1 Introduction

Sustainability is currently a major challenge for the society. The usual notion of sustainability focuses on keeping, in the long run, a balanced system of environmental, economic, and social interacting dimensions or sub-systems. Achieving the optimal functioning of this system requires the contribution of many stakeholders which can be facilitated by a collaborative networks approach.

One important element of sustainability under the social sub-system is the demographic dimension, which leads to the term "demographic sustainability", usually understood as a constant population level related to an optimal growth rate of the population, corresponding to at least 2.1 fertility rate [1]. Another perspective of demographic sustainability is given by the relationship between working age and old population. Current demographic trends lead to a growing unbalance under this dimension, which has large impacts on the economic subsystem. In fact, as the proportion of older people in the population increases, it influences consumer patterns, business systems and capital markets, and put a considerable pressure on the social security systems. Particularly the ageing population increases the pressure on the state pension funds. Most pension schemas are designed so that pensioners' benefits are paid by those who are currently working. With relatively fewer people

L.M. Camarinha-Matos et al. (Eds.): PRO-VE 2010, IFIP AICT 336, pp. 46–59, 2010.

working and greater numbers claiming pensions, the long term sustainability of this "intergenerational contract" is in danger.

With the increase in both the percentage of senior citizens and expectation of life, it is timely to reassess the understanding of ageing and retirement, and questioning elderly's work, happiness, leisure, community involvement etc. and their inter-relationships with respect to old age. Many elderly citizens, following retirement, quickly become marginalized and considered as a cost burden rather than a resource that is capable of "value creation" in the society [2, 3]. This feeling of exclusion and isolation creates a vacuum in the life of the elderly citizens which in turn affects their health and well being.

More recently there is a growing recognition that the elderly population should not be considered a burden on the society but instead an asset that needs to be properly considered. A critical challenge for the society in respect to the "**active ageing / ageing well**" process [4] is to identify new organizational structures, approaches, and mechanisms so that elderly citizens do not feel excluded, and have the chance to use their knowledge and expertise in making valued contributions to the communities where they live. In particular the senior professionals / knowledge workers possess a number of skills and accumulated experience that need to be better used in value creation activities.

On the other hand, as the older population increases and the growth in the middle-aged population slows down, older adults are becoming an increasingly important labour source. They typically bring maturity, dependability, and years of relevant experience to the workplace. Nowadays with more people remaining in good health at older ages and increasingly more jobs not involving physical strength, more old adults are able to continue working than ever before. Furthermore, active ageing, through a balanced combination of leisure, social interaction, and continued work involvement, is central to meeting citizen expectations and maintaining mental and physical health [5]. Retirement does not necessarily need to represent the end of the working period, but rather a career and lifestyle transition, where the retiree in principle has multiple options -- such as continuing to work (though perhaps at a different pace), returning to school for additional training or education, changing career, venturing into entrepreneurship, becoming more involved in volunteer work, or simply enjoying leisure and travel possibilities -- thus a mix of working, learning, relaxing, and trying new things can be foreseen as a desirable scenario.

ICT, and particularly high-speed pervasive broadband connectivity and web-based technologies, offer new opportunities to create new ways of working, facilitate social interaction, and reduce limitations imposed by location and time, thus increasing personal control. Nevertheless the sensitivity of the area, the dependency on the "parallel" introduction of new organizational models and creation of a new culture in society, the lessons learned with the limited success of existing associations of senior professionals, the risk of continuously developing technology that is not taken-up by target users, among others suggest the need for a careful analysis and a better planned approach towards what concerns new developments. In this context, roadmapping plays a fundamental role in the identification of a strategic research agenda and prioritization of needed actions.

In order to elaborate a strategic RTD plan in this direction a 27-month European initiative – ePAL (extending Professional Active Life) project – was launched in 2008 [6].

ePAL aimed to explore innovative ways to best facilitate and support active ageing and ensure a balanced and inclusive post-retirement lifestyle. A major hypothesis followed in ePAL is that ICT and particularly collaborative networks can provide an adequate framework for the implementation of effective support to active ageing [6].

2 Organizational Forms

In addition to the traditional initiatives focused only on socialization and entertainment activities for elderly, a number of other organizational forms and mechanisms, already existing or emerging, are focused on providing ways to help seniors remain professionally active after their retirement. In fact, as a response to the active ageing challenges, in recent years we can observe the emergence of a growing number of associations of senior professionals. Although bringing some benefits to their members, namely in the scope of socialization, the current model of these associations may lead to some form of "organized ghettos" for seniors with little inter-generational interaction. In order to guarantee a more holistic integration, the different socio-economic stakeholders must develop a whole series of business and behavioral models of varied structure, composition and characteristics to allow a variety of alternatives for the integration of senior professionals.

Nevertheless, associations of retired professionals represent an important organizational structure supporting active ageing. Therefore, ePAL conducted a survey on 29 of those associations in Europe and outside Europe in order to get a consolidated view of their practices. The main conclusion is that these organizational forms exist due to the fact that retired people refuse to accept the retirement as the end of a professional life, claiming instead for remaining professionally active. The aim of these associations is essentially to provide assistance to organizations and people that cannot afford market prices for such services, or assistance to organizations located in developing countries. Offered services are basically business consultancy and mentoring. The majority of them work on a voluntary basis sustaining themselves through membership fees and/or private or public funding and sponsorship. In terms of ICT, the majority of these organizations only use basic tools; nevertheless they are willing to use new and modern tools to help in their daily activities.

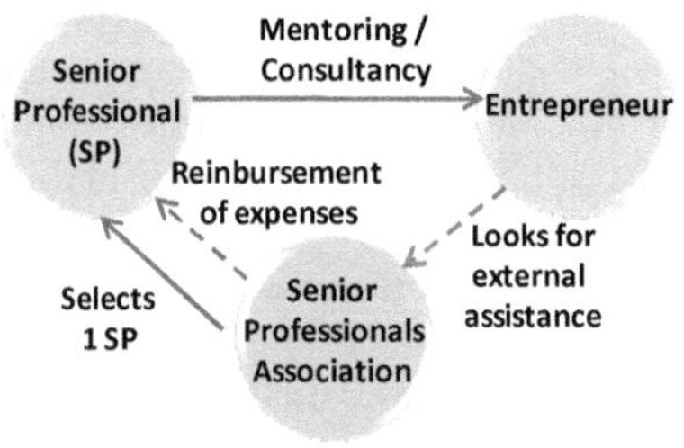

Fig. 1. Existing intermediation model

One example of operation is illustrated in Fig. 1. In this case an entrepreneur typically needs consultancy services in order to get a company project off the ground but cannot afford these services at market rates. The senior professionals association acts as an intermediary and selects the senior that best fits the needs of the entrepreneur from among its members. Typically, besides reimbursement of expenses, the senior professional does not receive remuneration from the entrepreneur although he/she might benefit from the association in other ways (e.g. prestige, experience with new methods, infrastructures, etc.).

A more complex example is represented by Fig. 2. In this case it is assumed that a Governmental Institution has created a consultancy program for SMEs, with financial support from a Regional Government. However, different from the previous case, the consultancy services are delivered by a virtual team supported by an ICT platform, which is provided by some ICT company. The association is in charge of assigning the work to a team of its members and putting them in contact with the recipient SME, in order to provide their consultancy services. For this collaboration the association receives some monetary remuneration. In order to offer the SME a high quality service, the Team of Senior Professionals includes experts in different areas (e.g. marketing, finance, management strategy, etc.) which jointly provide integrated mentoring and consultancy services. Senior professionals receive some reward (monetary or other).

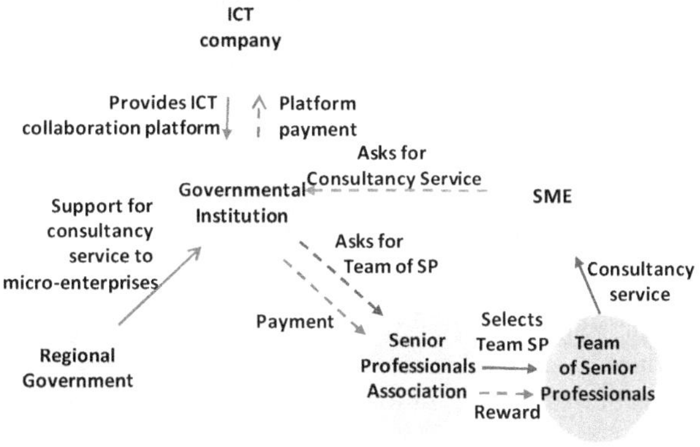

Fig. 2. Existing complex model

Currently this case in which tasks are carried out by teams of senior professionals is quite rare. In most cases only one senior is involved in each task.

The existing associations are mostly composed of a "professional elite" i.e. people with high education and who had high positions in the socio-economic system before retirement. In most cases, these people have reasonable pensions, although varying from region to region, and therefore can afford to do voluntary (unpaid) activities. However, the number of people involved in such networks is not very high and many contacted seniors claim that it would be reasonable to receive some compensation for their contribution to value creation.

As illustrated in the above example, the effective involvement of seniors in the socio-economic system needs to consider other stakeholders, namely intermediary entities and the recipients of the services provided by seniors. Some of these entities are also organized in some form of association e.g. associations of SMEs, enterprise incubators or science parks, networks of regional

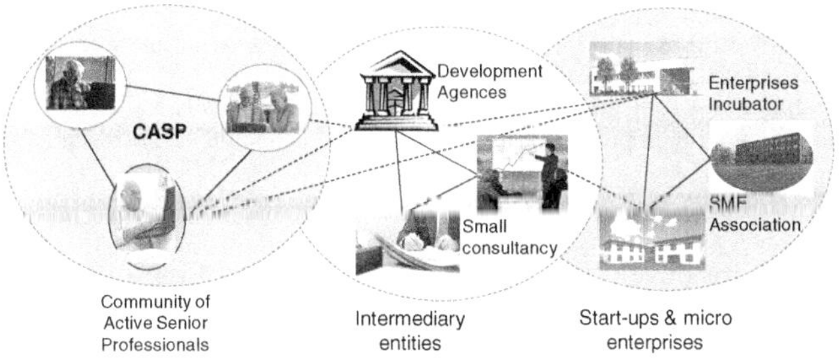

Fig. 3. Tri-partite networks

development agencies and associated private (small) consultancy companies. Therefore ePAL proposes a tri-partite network model (Fig. 3) for these collaborative networks.

In recent years a considerable amount of tools have been developed in what concerns web-technologies, social networks and collaborative networks (see [7], for instance). Nevertheless new specialized platforms and support tools are needed specifically focused on the needs of seniors and considering the suggested tri-partite model.

3 A Vision for a Desirable Future

The application of *visioning* in defining and shaping the future direction of an organization or a society is increasingly becoming popular in today's world. A vision defines *a desired future,* while strongly interconnected with the framework that underlies the organizations or societies [8]. It is a deeply held picture of where a person, a group of people, an organization, or a society, wants to reach in the future. We create meaning in our lives by pursuing our future visions, and we refine our visions based on the meaning and trends we are discovering through our experience. A vision is the most inspiring future the society can imagine. Because of this ambitious prospect, the society can never truly achieve its vision. It rather works toward that vision.

Table 1. General vision statement of ePAL

Core ideology:
Building strong and cohesive societies across Europe that embrace active senior professionals to create value for individuals, communities and the economy
Envisioned future:
In the coming decade, a comprehensive paradigm will emerge in response to the challenges of demographic shift in Europe that enables a balanced active life for senior professionals, regardless of gender, capitalising on their talents and expertise, and facilitating value creation for the benefit of the individual, the economy and European society as a whole.

Main desired facets:
- **V1**. Well founded reference model of the environment, specifying its: endogenous *(structural, componential, functional, and behavioural)* and exogenous *(market, support, societal, constituency)* elements, and their interlinks
- **V2**. Well established technological infrastructure, support tools/services
- **V3**. Policies promoting changes in societal perceptions of age and support mechanisms to motivate and empower seniors, taking account of cultural differences, giving them the choice to continue their professional active life
- **V4**. Established organizational infrastructures that support the interaction between senior professionals and other actors in the socio-economic system, facilitating value creation
- **V5**. Established policies, legal frameworks and ethical principles – regionally, nationally and across Europe - that motivate and support senior professionals and other socio-economic actors and regulate their interactions

A fundamental prerequisite for developing a vision for the desired future for active ageing is to identify both: the key drivers (i.e. the main driving forces in the market and society) and their related trends regarding the ePAL environment. A well-conceived vision consists of two major components, namely, the ***core ideology*** and the ***envisioned future*** [9]. *Core ideology* is the first primary component of the vision framework which consists of two parts: ***core values*** and ***core purpose***. *Core values* are the essential and enduring tenets of an organization or society. Core values have intrinsic value and importance to those inside the organization or society. *Core purpose* however points to certain fundamental reason for society to exist. *Envisioned future* is the second primary component of the vision framework which consists of 2 parts: a ***long-term audacious goal*** and a ***vivid description*** **or desired facets** of what it will be like when goals are achieved.

In this research, to comprehensively cover the most important aspects related to a desired vision for ePAL, three main perspectives that are required to be addressed were identified. Namely, the vision of a desired future for active ageing shall cover its social perspective, its organizational perspective and its technological perspective. Tables 2, 3 and 4 show the instantiation of the vision according to these perspectives.

Table 2. Vision - social perspective

In the coming decade, extending active professional life will be a high priority strategy across Europe. European societies will mature to accommodate demographic shift through supporting and empowering senior professionals to fulfil their potential as active participants in the economy. Attitudes amongst individuals and organisations will evolve to embrace senior professionals as a value-creating pool of talent, thereby supporting and promoting equal opportunities in active aging. Both senior and young professionals will derive greater benefit from the exchange of knowledge and experience. As the social environment evolves, new support mechanisms will arise to sustain an aging but more active and inclusive population.

Main desired facets:

VS1. New mechanisms to enhance positive understanding and perception in society regarding the value of the abilities, skills and experience of individual senior professionals in the economy, taking account of gender

VS2. Mechanisms to build awareness, and to motivate senior professionals to join communities of active senior professionals

VS3. Mechanisms to support cross-cultural interactions among senior professionals as well as to the active labour force addressing barriers to communication

VS4. Mechanisms to support a balanced economic benefits sharing among the entire society including senior professionals

VS5. New mechanisms to help articulate the collective needs of seniors across national boundaries

VS6. Mechanisms to support cross generational interaction between seniors and younger citizens; fomenting inter-generational solidarity and understanding within the EU

VS7. Mechanisms to capitalize on the increased sense of trust and understanding which comes through leveraging seniors' social capital

Table 3. Vision - organizational perspective

In the coming decade, the primary organisational stakeholders – governments, intermediaries, businesses and unions – will adopt positive, proactive and coordinated policies and approaches that enable seniors to choose to continue their professional active life. As a consequence, senior professionals will enjoy new opportunities and a new market space of senior skills will be created, benefiting businesses and strengthening the wider European economy.

Table 3. (*continued*)

Main desired facets:

VO1. Employment and retirement policies will change to provide greater flexibility for seniors to choose to continue as active economic participants

VO2. Regulations and policies will change to encourage businesses to collaborate with senior professionals, taking account of fair competition

VO3. The knowledge and skills of seniors will be harnessed to generate value and stimulate innovation amongst European businesses

VO4. New forms of intermediate organizations will provide highly efficient brokerage that will create opportunities in line with market needs and that help seniors engage with businesses nationally and across Europe

VO5. There will be sustainable funding models – from both public and private sectors - and the political drive to support new forms of senior associations and other intermediate brokers

VO6. All stakeholders will have access to the relevant training and other support services to facilitate the seniors' transition between working life and active retirement

VO7. New organizational cultures will positively embrace relationships between senior professionals and pre-retired (active) professionals

Table 4. Vision - technological perspective

In the coming decade, technology will facilitate and enable the continued active involvement of senior professionals in the socio-economic system. Through engagement with end-users, novel ICT collaboration platforms and tools will be developed that catalyse the creation of new organisational forms that connect and empower all stakeholders and facilitate the interaction between them. This technology will be accessible to all, 'senior friendly' and will enable seniors to expand their capabilities, leave a legacy and create value.

Main desired facets:

VT1. Advanced collaboration support services, including (virtual) teams' formation and management

VT2. Development of collaboration ontology supporting variety of stakeholders

VT3. Support for user-generated knowledge assets

VT4. "Configure yourself "based philosophy infrastructure

VT5. Easily adaptable and customizable user interfaces

VT6. Affective computing and context aware enriched environments

VT7. Support for establishment of trust among stakeholders

VT8. Tools supporting the process of value creation

VT9. Novel contractual and cooperation agreements, including negotiation support

VT10. Advanced marketing and brokerage services

VT11. New networking models for elderly communities' involvement with the socio-economic system

VT12. Security and ethical / privacy support.

4 Strategic Actions Plan

The elaboration of a plan of strategic actions is a fundamental step in roadmapping. Such actions, when successfully implemented, shall take the society from its current situation to a desirable future, as stated in the proposed vision [10]. The process of formulating such actions starts with an intense brainstorming activity within a small group of experts. The gap analysis, i.e. the identification of the "distance" between the current situation and the desired future, is an important element in this process [11]. In this formulation some base principles were followed:

– Consider the needs according to the social, organizational, and technological perspectives of analysis and thus identify suitable actions for each of these areas.
– Keep the number of actions in each focus area relatively small (up to 6) in order to facilitate focused discussion.
– Ensure that the proposed actions cover all stated facets of the vision.
– Propose actions that although ambitious, are feasible considering the current situation (baseline) and trends, and that take into account the results of the gap analysis.

The following tables introduce the proposed set of strategic R&D actions [10] that resulted from the roadmapping process conducted within the ePAL consortium and the extensive discussions held with stakeholders during several regional Consensus Building Events. The actions shown below reflect already the extensive feedback received in those events.

Considering the need to address technological developments within a socio-organizational context, similarly to the vision statement, the proposed actions are grouped into three major areas: social perspective actions, organizational perspective actions, and finally technological perspective actions.

Table 5. Proposed actions under the social perspective

S1: Value identification and communication. Promote socio-economic studies that identify the unique value senior workers bring to the workplace (experience, compensation flexibility, etc.) as well as their motivation and value systems, investigate new ways of senior workers interacting with the socio-economic system and communicate findings to seniors, employers, unions and to the society as a whole.
S2: Leveraging skills and talents. Design/develop mechanisms for skills/talent identification, categorization and improvement that assess acquired experience, provide career transition advice and support skills-enhancement to maximize the potential of seniors.
S3: European Senior Space facilitation. Promote dialogue and consensus around issues of technology, culture and socio-economic participation, creating links between existing and emerging senior associations and groups to develop a single, powerful voice for senior professionals across Europe.
S4: Facilitating inter-generational interaction. Investigate the barriers and potentials for cross generational interaction and collaboration between senior professionals and younger people, and fund/promote programmes and technology development that support and facilitate this interaction/collaboration.
S5: Improving working practices. Investigate new models of working practices and related reward and taxation models for senior professionals, taking account of issues of work-life balance, aging well and gender, and promote the findings in order to positively influence societal perception of older workers.
S6: Developing training and awareness. Design / develop ICT and collaboration training programs for seniors, and promote awareness and usage of collaboration technologies.

Table 6. Proposed actions under the organizational perspective

O1: Enhancing policy and legislation. Identify and assess current national and European policy, legislation and incentives relevant to active participation of seniors in the socio-economic system and recommend new approaches that lower barriers and promote and support active aging.

O2: Keeping links. Investigate new mechanisms that forge mutually beneficial relationships between seniors and their former employers

O3: Creating organizational structures. Investigate and promote new roles, governance rules and organizational forms for communities of active senior professionals to enhance inter- and intra-community collaboration and to create new opportunities for member engagement.

O4: Improving mediation and brokerage. Characterize and design new roles and modes of operation for intermediate organizations, both public and private, that provide brokerage and assistance to better facilitate integration and collaboration between senior professionals and the socio-economic system.

O5: Guiding career transition. Define new programmes and realistic practices that prepare for and guide the successful transition of senior professionals from full employment to active retirement, taking account of issues of gender, profession and local context.

O6: Meeting and creating market demand. Explore the best fit between capabilities of senior professionals and market demand and identify new channels to harness these resources and potentials in order to generate value and stimulate innovation amongst European businesses, thus supporting the economy.

Table 7. Proposed actions under the technological perspective

T1: Developing conceptual models. Establish formal conceptual models for people's professional life cycle and the support environment for active ageing.

T1.1 - Establish a reference model for extension of professional active life and active ageing.
T1.2 - Elaborate common ontologies for communities of senior professionals.
T1.3 - Develop contractual and business models for communities of senior professionals.

T2: Generating adaptive solutions. Develop and integrate self-adaptive and configurable technology solutions in ICT collaboration environments facilitating technology acceptance and enabling customization for/by seniors.

T2.1 - Develop self-adaptive interface systems.
T2.2 - Develop self-customizable collaboration environments empowering seniors to better use ICT.
T2.3 - Develop technology assistance wizards.
T2.4 – Increase involvement of seniors in the design of new technologies for seniors.

T3: Building collaboration platforms. Develop open ICT collaboration platforms for communities of senior professionals that promote human interaction and socialization and are enhanced by affective computing, context awareness, and trust establishment.

T3.1 - Develop advanced functionalities and systems for management of communities of senior professionals.
T3.2 - Develop affections / emotions management systems for communities of senior professionals.
T3.3 – Design and support governance systems for communities of senior professionals.
T3.4 - Develop trust building management systems for communities of senior professionals.

T4: Building collaboration tools. Design and develop collaboration support tools and systems to facilitate value creation, considering the specific needs of senior professionals.

Table 7. (*continued*)

T4.1 – Develop marketing and brokerage support tools for communities of senior professionals.
T4.2 - Develop tools for virtual team creation, negotiation and e-contracting.
T4.3 - Develop tools for virtual team management and collaborative problem solving support.
T4.4 - Develop models and tools for management of Intellectual Property and performance.

T5: Leveraging legacy. Develop environments that empower seniors to leave a legacy capitalizing on their valuable and transferable personal / professional experience.

T5.1 – Define conceptual models of talents and develop user-centred knowledge acquisition tools .
T5.2 - Create reward mechanisms (system of incentives) to attract user-generated knowledge.
T5.3 – Develop knowledge assets assessment and intellectual property models.
T5.4 - Mechanisms to promote inter-generational inheritance.

T6: Elaborating behavioural models. Develop approaches that discover patterns and model "the evolution of senior professionals' interests and their involvement in the socio-economic system" and "the behaviour and emotional health of senior professional networks".

T6.1 – Develop a conceptual base for behavioural modelling.
T6.2 - Develop data-mining / machine learning approaches for behavioural patterns discovery.
T6.3 - Develop forecasts and simulation methods and tools for behavioural analysis.
T6.4 - Develop models and tools for emotional health management.

As previously mentioned, an important assumption in this roadmapping initiative is that the collaborative networks paradigm provides a useful context for more effective active ageing support and thus contributing to demographic sustainability. Therefore, the development of reference models, collaboration platforms, and collaboration support tools specifically oriented towards the facilitation of the continuation of the involvement of senior professionals in the socio-economic system is a major goal.

Certainly considerable progress has been made in recent years in the area of collaborative networks, accompanied by rapid developments in computer networks and web-based technologies. Thus the proposed actions for the technological perspective take account of these trends, and focus on the specificity of active ageing and particularly on support to the extension of active professional life.

As the main focus of ePAL is on a roadmap for ICT development, the actions under the technological perspective (Table 7) are more detailed than the actions under the other perspectives.

The following diagrams show the proposed time sequence for the implementation of the actions.

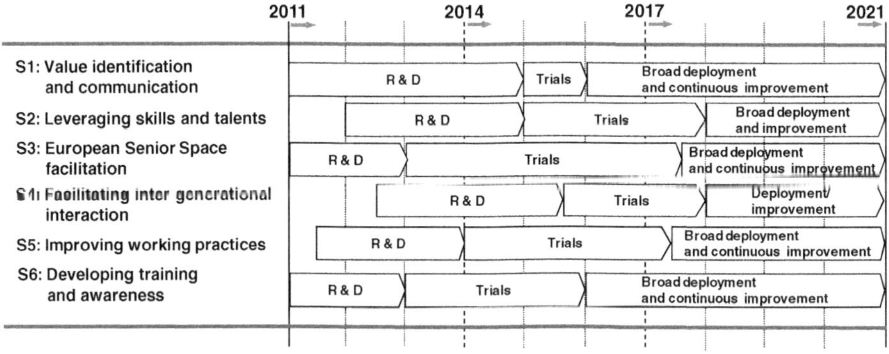

Fig. 4. Time sequence for actions under the social perspective

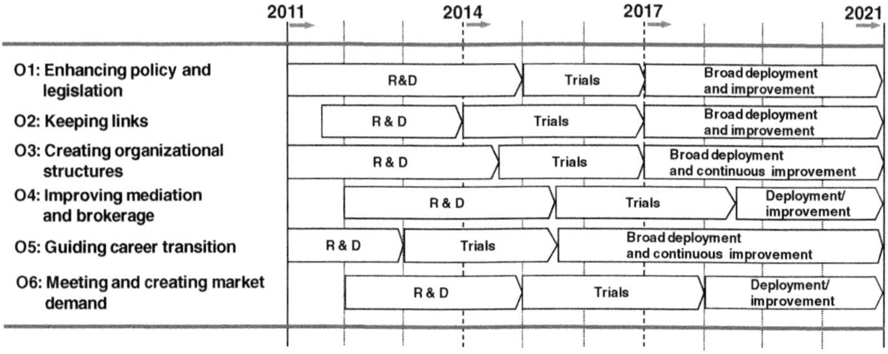

Fig. 5. Time sequence for actions under the organizational perspective

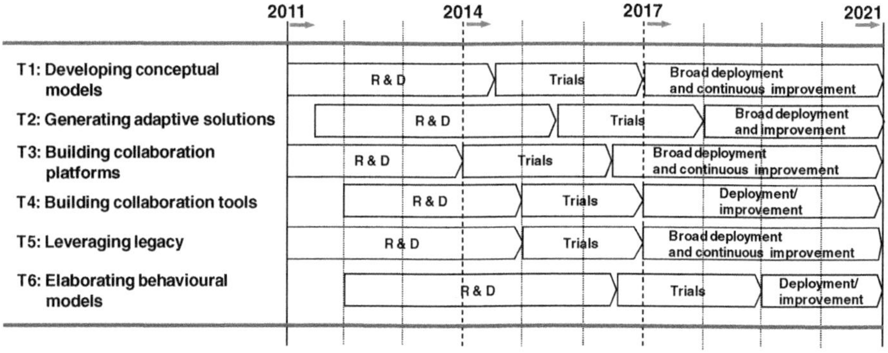

Fig. 6. Time sequence for actions under the technological perspective

In the above diagrams three modalities of implementation are considered:

- R&D – focusing on fundamental research and prototype development / proof of concept, aimed at addressing longer term challenges.
- Trials – oriented towards the development of pilots and validation scenarios that allow verification and refinement of the results of previous phase with the objective of facilitating the development of innovative products and services.
- Broad deployment and continuous improvement – aiming at large scale validation – large pilots – of new technologies and services, as a mechanism to facilitate their take-up by society.

5 Roadmap Validation

The proposed vision statements and strategic actions plan resulted from a multi-stage construction and validation process. An initial formulation was prepared by the ePAL consortium following a series of consultation workshops and brainstorming sessions. Once a set of strategic actions emerged as a result of the brainstorming exercise, it was then necessary to proceed with a verification of those actions. The adopted verification process, at this stage of the roadmapping process, comprised two main activities: (i) Verify that the set of proposed actions adequately cover all stated facets of the vision. (ii) Assess the feasibility of each action considering the results of the gap analysis. Figure 7 illustrates the first step of validating the roadmap results for the action T5 under the technological perspective.

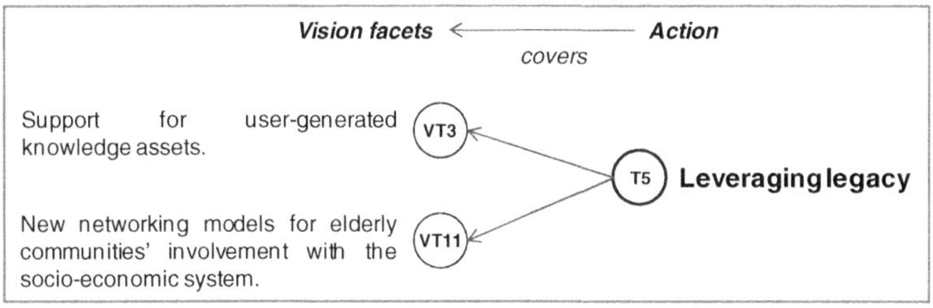

Fig. 7. Covering the vision facets – organizational perspective

Regarding the second step of validation, related to feasibility, the adopted approach was to consider how the strengths and limitations at European level identified in the gap analysis facilitate or make difficult the implementation of each action. Fig. 8 shows the result. This verification needed to be conducted by experts and depends on the perception of each individual according to his/her background knowledge. Therefore a qualitative scale (scale: Moderate, Hard, Very Hard) was adopted.

Social perspective		Organisational perspective		Technological perspective	
S1	Moderate	O1	Hard	T1	Very hard
S2	Hard	O2	Moderate	T2	Very hard
S3	Hard	O3	Moderate	T3	Moderate
S4	Moderate	O4	Very hard	T4	Hard
S5	Very hard	O5	Hard	T5	Very hard
S6	Moderate	O6	Very hard	T6	Very hard

Fig. 8. Feasibility assessment

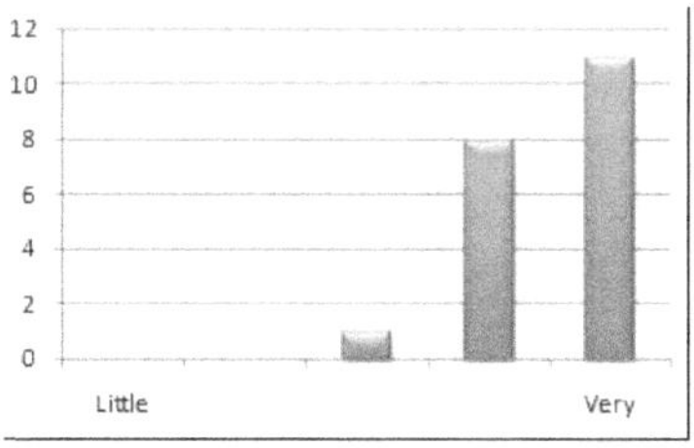

Fig. 9. Example of agreement with ePAL vision

The last phase of the project was focused on the refinement and consensus-building among relevant stakeholders. For this purpose, a number of *Consensus Building Events* were organized in different regions of Europe, namely Porto, Seville, London, Madrid, Maastricht, Lisbon, and Thessaloniki, involving more than 170 experts from different fields.

Fig. 9 illustrates the level of agreement with ePAL vision as voted by participants in one of these events. Fig. 10 shows the level of prioritization of actions as a result of voting by the consulted stakeholders.

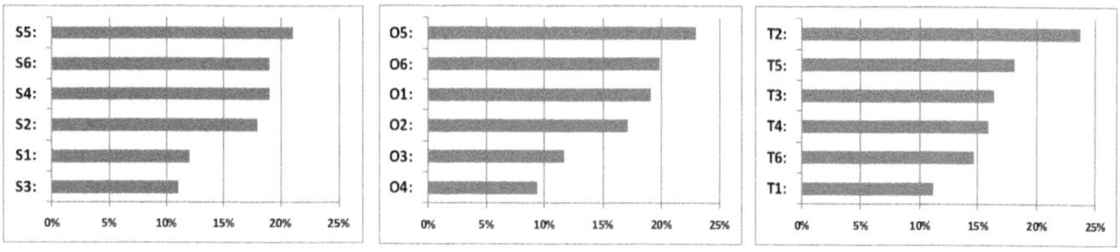

Fig. 10. Prioritization of actions

This prioritization, combined with the expected difficulty identified in the feasibility assessment, can give decision makers important elements when deciding on research resources allocation.

6 Conclusion

Increase in aged population is a critical issue in sustainability. As the expectancy of a longer and healthy life increases, the issue of extending the active professional life of senior people becomes an important topic. Such extension, if properly balanced with leisure and social activities, is likely to: (i) Facilitate active ageing, keeping seniors involved in, and contributing to, society; (ii) Generate additional income to help them maintain their standard of living and to support the wider economy, thus responding to the demographic sustainability challenges.

In this process, avoiding isolation and loneliness or even the creation of "elderly ghettos" is a major concern. ICT can be an important enabler in facilitating the creation of collaborative networks involving not only communities of seniors, but also potential recipients of their services and intermediary entities in a multi-level network. The collaborative networks paradigm supported by relevant technologies can also facilitate inter-generational interactions and thus contribute to the avoidance of ghettos.

The systematic roadmapping process behind the proposed research agenda as well as the extensive validation process involving a large community of stakeholders, are important factors for providing confidence in the adequacy of the proposed roadmap. Nevertheless, as normal in any "futures planning" initiative and taking into account the impossibility of adequately foreseeing the future, a roadmap is a dynamic construct that needs to be periodically revised alongside its implementation, taking into account new trends as they inevitably emerge.

Acknowledgements

This work was funded in part be the European Commission through the ePAL project. The authors also thank the contribution of their partners in the ePAL project as well as the multiple stakeholders involved in the consensus building workshops. This work is now being continued in the scope of the BRAID project, also funded by EC.

References

1. Roca, M.N.O., Leitão, N.: Demographic Sustainability In Portugal: Towards a Typology. In: 14th European Colloquium on Theoretical and Quantitative Geography, Tomar, Portugal (2005)
2. HSBC Insurance: The future of retirement – The new old age (May 2007), http://www.hsbc.com/1/PA_1_1_S5/content/assets/retirement/gender_perspective_eurasia_africa_1.pdf
3. WHO: Active Aging: A Policy Framework, WHO/NMH/NPH/02.8, World Health Organisation report 2002 (2002)
4. Camarinha-Matos, L.M., Afsarmanesh, H.: Collaborative mechanisms for a new perspective on active ageing. In: Proceedings of DEST 2009 - 3rd IEEE Int. Conference on Digital Ecosystems and Technologies, Istanbul, Turkey, June 1-3 (2009)
5. Wilson, P., Johnson, K., Buller, W.: Ageing well in a connected world: Smarter care, smarter participation. CISCO Internet Business Solutions Group (December 2008)
6. Camarinha-Matos, L.M., Afsarmanesh, H.: The Need for a Strategic R&D Roadmap for Active Ageing. In: Leveraging knowledge for innovation in Collaborative Networks, pp. 669–680. Springer, Heidelberg (2009)
7. Camarinha-Matos, L.M., Afsarmanesh, H., Ollus, M. (eds.): Methods and tools for Collaborative Networked Organizations. Springer, Heidelberg (2008)
8. Afsarmanesh, H., Camarinha-Matos, L.M., Msanjila, S.: A Well-conceived Vision for Extending Professional Life of Seniors. In: Camarinha-Matos, L.M., Paraskakis, I., Afsarmanesh, H. (eds.) Leveraging knowledge for innovation in Collaborative Networks, pp. 681–692. Springer, Heidelberg (2009)
9. Cummings, T.G.: Organization Development and Change. Thomson South-Western (2005)
10. Camarinha-Matos, L.M., Afsarmanesh, H., del Cura, A., Playfoot, J.: ePAL Roadmap for Active Ageing - A Collaborative Networks Approach to Extending Professional Life. In: Proceedings of AGEmap Workshop / Pervasive Health 2010 conference, Munich, Germany, March 22 (2010)
11. Leonard, W., Afsarmanesh, H., Msanjila, S., Playfoot, J.: Exploring the Gap for Effective Extension of Professional Active Life in Europe. In: Camarinha-Matos, L.M., Paraskakis, I., Afsarmanesh, H. (eds.) Leveraging knowledge for innovation in Collaborative Networks. Springer, Heidelberg (2009)

ePAL Vision 2020 for Active Ageing of Senior Professionals

Hamideh Afsarmanesh[1] and Simon S. Msanjila[2]

[1] Informatics Institute, University of Amsterdam, Science Park 107, 1098 XG, Amsterdam, The Netherlands
h.afsarmanesh@uva.nl

[2] Faculty of Science and Technology, Mzumbe University, P.O. Box 1, Mzumbe-Morogoro, Tanzania
smsanjila@mzumbe.ac.tz

Abstract. In order to enhance the active life of senior professionals, one fundamental challenge is to identify ways to assist promoting the role of elder people within the continuously ageing European society. This paper proposes a vision for establishing required support environment for communities of active senior professionals, and provision of fundamental ICT tools for senior professionals to continue delivering professional services to the society, but in a balanced manner and not as regular workers. For smooth establishment and operation of such communities, a well conceived vision must be established to guide this process towards achieving its desired goals. This paper presents the vision statement developed in the EC funded ePAL project for enhancing the active life of senior professionals in Europe, as well as its instantiation into three orthogonal perspectives of technological, societal, and organizational.

Keywords: Visioning, Multi-perspective vision, Professional active life.

1 Introduction

It is estimated that by 2050, the number of people over 60 in Europe will have doubled to 40% of the total population, or 60% of the working age population [Jeavans, C, 2004]. Over the next few decades, the "baby boomers", the largest generation, born in the 1950s and 1960s, will start to retire. The situation will be exacerbated by the very different expectations as well as life expectancy when compared to their parents and grandparents. This new scenario, while creating new opportunities, is mostly a cause of concern for societal systems which find it challenging to cope. This large group of retirees will need healthcare, pensions, housing, and community care - on much greater scale than before. As the Europe's population ages the number of those who are of working age (defined as 15-64) becomes smaller, when compared with those of 'non-working' age, also referred to as economic "dependants" [Stranges, 2008].

The paper focuses on developing a vision suitable for supporting the senior (retired and/or retiring) professionals to remain active in professional and daily activities. As such the paper studies and focuses on communities of senior professionals that can be

L.M. Camarinha-Matos et al. (Eds.): PRO-VE 2010, IFIP AICT 336, pp. 60–72, 2010.

established on the basis of concepts related to collaborative networks. While characterizing the collaboration among senior professionals we have introduced the following terms related to collaborative networks of senior professionals to support characterization of these communities [Afsarmanesh, et al, 2009].

CASP (Community of Active Senior Professional) constitutes an association of senior professional individuals that are largely autonomous, geographically distributed, and potentially heterogeneous in terms of their: capabilities, offered capacities, culture, system of values, etc., but sharing their main compatible and/or common goals of increasing their active professional life in the society and/or market, through co-working with others in Teams of Senior Professionals supported by computer networks, under the slogan of: "Together Everyone Achieves More!".

TSP (Team of Senior Professionals) is a collaborative network of individuals configured and established within the CASP in response to opportunities in the society and market that are in need of their wisdom and/or knowledge assets that they can offer, which as a consequence supports the retired professionals remaining professionally active.

SP (Senior Professional) is a retired professional who becomes a member of CASP in order to increase his/her chances of staying active and involved in the socio-economic system, and perhaps also through getting involved in potential TSPs established through the CASP.

2 Base Concepts Related to Vision and Visioning

Visioning is an important aspect for leadership, strategy implementation and change for the better [Laubacher & Malone, 1997].. A vision defines a *desired future*, while strongly interconnected with the present framework that underlies the organizations or societies [Collins & Porras, 1998]. It is a deeply held picture of where a group of people in an organization or society, wishes to reach in the future. Therefore, a vision is the most inspiring future that the society can imagine, and thus creates meaning and purpose which catapults the individuals aim at high levels of achievement [Donald, 2003]. Namely, A vision for a society shall provide: (1) Compelling image of the future, (2) Credible and attractive view of what is potentially feasible to achieve for the society, (3) Unifying guides to what the society wishes to and can become, and (4) Inspirational focal point for the spirit of the society and its members.

A well-conceived vision [Cummings, 2005] consists of two major components, namely the core ideology and the envisioned future. ***Core ideology*** *is the 1st primary component of the vision framework which consists of two parts: core values and core purpose. The Core values are the essential and enduring tenets of an organization or a society - a small set of timeless guiding principles that require no external justification. Core values have intrinsic value and importance to those inside the organization or society. The Core purpose however points to certain fundamental reason for society to exist. An effective purpose reflects the importance that people attach to daily activities of the organization or society.* ***Envisioned future*** *is the 2nd primary component of the vision framework which consists of two parts: a long-term audacious goal and a vivid description of what it will be like when goals are achieved.*

The visioning process is one of the least straightforward, yet most important, concepts that enable influencing the future, and building successful organizations and societies. The cornerstone of a vision is a clear image of how the society will satisfy important stakeholders' needs. It is important that the vision is built from what stakeholders perceive to satisfy their needs and not what the providers (government, non-government organizations, regulatory bodies, etc.) think will satisfy them. This requires an extensive interaction with all stakeholders in the society in order to perceive the needs from stakeholders' perspective. Nevertheless, while formulating a vision and when it is needed to estimate the possible future situation forecasting can be used as a tool in the visioning process, such as in understanding the societal drivers and trends as well as for designing possible future scenarios.

3 Potential Vision Requirements and Indicators for Ageing Society

Any change within a society or a specific established community such as CASP starts with establishment of requirements and indicators on why changes are needed. Vision tends to guide the needed changes that require to be gradually and systematically implemented towards realizing the expected future. Below we describe some indicators that may trigger the reformulation of a vision of a society which also apply for specific established communities such as CASPs:

- **Reasons for existence:** Analysis of the present situation is essential as it provides the true picture of today from where we shall begin our efforts towards a better future. The next question is whether the developed vision is well-conceived, and can guide a specific society or community towards its desired future, considering its present situation; and hence validating the need and the reason for developing and existence of the vision in the community/society.
- **Values:** Values are traits or qualities that are considered worthwhile. They represent a society's highest priorities and deeply held driving forces. Values define how the society wants to behave or what it wants to achieve in future. Effective societies or communities identify and develop a clear and concise meaning of values/beliefs, and priorities so that everyone understands and can contribute to it. Once defined, values impact every aspect of the society.
- **Strategies:** Strategy is a plan, method, or series of maneuvers for obtaining a specific goal or result. Strategies are established by communities or societies to guide them define the kind of activities that shall be implemented towards achieving the planned objectives. Strategies are usually aligned to the vision.
- **Picture of preferred future:** Here the society is trying to project what it wishes to become in its future. The vision promotes trust and trust is the foundation of any successful society. It is this trust that can build successful teams and team work within the environment.

4 The Need for Strategic R&D Roadmap for Active Ageing in Europe

There is a growing recognition that the elderly population should not be seen as a burden on the society but instead an asset that needs to be properly considered [HSBC insurance, 2007]. In particular the senior professionals possess a number of skills and accumulated experience that need to be better used in value creation activities. And yet the way society is organized does not offer many opportunities to older people.

Recognizing this situation, the World Health Organization has been advocating the need for proactive strategies for the ageing population. Kofi Annan, while secretary-general of the United Nations, stated that: "By promoting older persons' active participation in society and development, we can ensure that their invaluable gifts and experience are put to good use". "Older persons who can work and want to work should have the opportunity to do so" [Camarinha-Matos & Afsarmanesh, 2009]. It is also well known that by keeping an active life people can remain healthier. As such, the concept of active ageing was developed.

The critical challenge for the society in respect to the "active ageing / ageing well" process [Camarinha-Matos & Afsarmanesh, 2009a] is to identify new organizational structures, approaches, and support mechanisms and tools, so that elderly citizens do not feel excluded, and have the chance to use their knowledge and expertise to contribute to the communities where they live.

On the other hand, as the older population increases while the growth in the middle-aged population slows down, older adults are becoming an increasingly important labour source. They typically bring maturity, dependability, and years of relevant experience to the workplace. Nowadays with more people remaining in good health at older ages and increasingly more jobs not involving physical strength, more old adults than before are able to continue working. Retirement will indeed no longer represent the end of the working period, but rather a career and lifestyle transition, where the retiree in principle has multiple options -- such as continuing to work (though perhaps at a different pace), returning to school for additional training or education, changing career, venturing into entrepreneurship, becoming more involved in volunteer work, or simply enjoying leisure and travel possibilities – thus a mix of working, learning, relaxing, and trying new things can be foreseen.

In addition to the traditional initiatives focused mostly on socializing and entertainment activities for elderly, a number of new organizational forms and mechanisms are emerging, focused on providing ways to help senior professionals remaining active, in professional terms, after retirement. Although with different involvement and commitment levels from retirees, such initiatives try to make use of their valuable knowledge, wisdom, and experience, namely through consulting and mentoring activities. ICT and particularly collaborative technologies can play an important facilitating role in this area. There is a need to provide support in the form of "ready-made 2nd generation affective and socio-economically integrated communities" to which the elderly professional can join. Moreover, there is a need to provide the opportunity for elderly professionals to choose a balanced proportion between their value creating and the leisure activities, as well as the opportunity to modify the balance in their portfolio of activities over time. To elaborate a strategic R&D plan in this direction we have developed a vision for extending Professional Active Life of seniors [Camarinha-Matos & Afsarmanesh, 2009].

5 The Need for Visioning for European ePAL Environments

Any Initiative aiming to support the extension of professional active life of elder people in Europe is affected by a number of external factors in the market and society, which have the potential to either positively and negatively influence it. Current practices indicate that the European society, while started to act on this subject, is still slow to recognize the rationale behind and the importance of fully supporting the extension of active professional life of seniors. The actions being taken are mostly done in an ad hoc manner and without clear vision of the future of the European society. This is because there is no common vision on what the Europeans need to achieve regarding the extension of professional active life of seniors.

Similarly, the capacity of the societies and the service sector to fully support the involvement of seniors in economical activities is at present limited, given the huge number of these seniors in different countries which need to be mobilized. In brief the following factors indicate the need to formulate a well conceived vision for the European society regarding ageing well.

- *Ageing of the European population and economic difficulties*: The population of the European society is ageing fast and its consequence is that the ratio of work force to economically dependent people is decreasing. Traditionally, the life of elder people is supported through pension systems, which relied on the taxes paid by the active workers. Today, but even more steeply in the coming decades, the **pension systems are becoming overloaded**, as on one hand the number of people who shall receive benefits increases, while on the other hand the labour force and thus the number of tax payers gradually decreases. Severe economical difficulties will rise for the pension system in Europe, in relation to supporting the life of this increasing group of retired people. Another form of support at elder age is needed which could be a **secondary financial income in addition to the pension system**. Establishment of policies to support secondary financial sources for elder professionals need to be harmonized across Europe for which a vision at the European level can play this harmonization role.
- *Lack of human resources*: In the same line of argument the availability of qualified experts in different working domains is gradually decreasing. Harsh economical challenges will be faced increasingly at the workplace by the lack of qualified human resources, since every year a very large group of the ageing population retires. One recent promising approach to address the challenge of dealing with the ageing population in Europe looks into the possibility of **extending the involvement of senior professionals** who are willing to do so in the on-going activities in market and society.

6 Applied Approach for Building Visions for ePAL Communities

We have applied a systematic approach for building the ePAL vision which supports the involvement of multiple stakeholders at different stages. This approach provides a generic step-wise guidance for the process of building a vision for an organization or a society. To enhance the clarity of presentation of the proposed approach below in some steps we provide examples related to vision construction for ePAL environment. The approach has five steps as shown in Table 1, namely: *(1) Discussion and generation of visionary ideas for the environment, (2) Elaboration of 1st vision, (3) Testing and validating the elaborated vision, (4) Consensus building through consulting and workshop, (5) Documenting and finalizing the vision.* The focus and

Table 1. Steps of the applied approach for visioning

<table>
<tr><th>Step name</th><th>Main activities and focus</th></tr>
<tr><td colspan="2">Step 1: Discussion and generation of visionary ideas
This step starts when the need for building a vision is realized and that some aspects of the society require systematic changes to reflect on the future life of the society. For example, this step is triggered by identification of a crisis or immediate need in the society and where its possible solutions demand changes within the society. The main focuses of this step are:
• Identification of input materials: Refer to existing materials that can be sources of fundamental ideas related to the ePAL vision such as state of the art in literature, results of related projects, related vision and mission statements,
• Identification of constraints: Refer to practices that are relevant to the ePAL environment in the European society which unless properly considered and addressed by the vision may have the potential to prevent, restrict, or dictate the actions that may need to be taken to realize the vision such as laws, rules and regulations; society indicators, etc.
• Establishment of resources and mechanisms: Refer to the available knowledge, competencies and capabilities that can be applied to generate, analyze, and organize vision's ideas for ePAL environment.</td></tr>
<tr><td colspan="2">Step 2: Elaboration of 1st vision
In this step the aim is the identification and generation of the main elements related to the vision statement for the environment, based on the knowledge and experience available/gained within the ePAL consortium, the acquired understanding of the baseline and the visionary ideas generated in Step 1. This phase is extremely important - where the 1st vision statement is established based on the analysis of the main drivers and trends, and through developing and analysing a number of scenarios. The two main focuses of this step are:
• Establishing drivers and trends: Drivers refer to the main influences (driving forces) which guide the running and changes of the society. Trends refer to the main happenings related to each driver. Trends indicate how each driver will influence the changes in the market or society. The analysis of drivers and trends enables the visionaries and researchers to identify fundamental areas or perspectives that need to be properly covered by the vision.
• Establishing scenarios: Building scenarios serves as a tool to provide actors with essential understanding, orientation, context, direction, and some degree of consensus in planning research developments and implementations. In relation to ePAL's vision for future, scenarios are used to support understanding of different future possibilities regarding the enhancing of active life of senior professionals, as well as possible actions to take and which events are probable to occur in future.</td></tr>
<tr><td colspan="2">Step 3: Testing and validating the elaborated vision
Validating the vision is an important step focused on making sure that the society will be moving in the right direction once it implements this vision. In this step, representatives from each group of stakeholders must be involved in assessing the vision and providing improvement and extension suggestions. The focus is analyzing whether the vision is: (1) capturing the current objectives of the society, (2) properly addressing future potential objectives of the society, and (3) feasible for the society to achieve such future objectives, considering current trends, drivers and strategies.</td></tr>
<tr><td colspan="2">Step 4: Consensus building through consulting and workshop
It is a decision making process that includes all stakeholders to together make a general agreement and commitment on a joint initiative. It is the most powerful decision process as stakeholders together agree to the final decision. In order for the vision to get full support from stakeholders in the society it first needs their acceptance. Building consensus on the proposed vision can apply the following approaches: (1) organizing workshops of representatives of stakeholders' groups, (2) generating questionnaires and other kind of surveys, (3) arranging round tables involving decision makers, and (4) performing online discussions and forums.</td></tr>
<tr><td colspan="2">Step 5: Documenting and finalizing the vision
This step focuses on improving the vision statement by applying and incorporating feedbacks from the consensus building actions (Step 4). The final vision statement is documented to be ready for directing research regarding the gap analysis and defining actions for their realization and implementation in the society.</td></tr>
</table>

main activities of these steps are summarized in the Table 1. The full description of this approach is presented in [Afsarmanesh, et al 2009].

7 Drivers, Trends, and Scenarios

As a fundamental prerequisite for developing the vision both its key drivers/perspectives (i.e. its main driving forces in the market/society) and their related trends (i.e. their main related happenings in the market/society) are identified. These are achieved through extensive survey of existing practices related to active ageing and ageing well. The survey was done following the steps of our developed approach as introduced in Section 6 and further addressed in [Afsarmanesh et al 2009]. Three complementary drivers, namely the technological, social, and organizational perspectives and their sub-drivers, decompose detailed characterization of ePAL's vision. The identified trends and drivers are summarized in Figure 1.

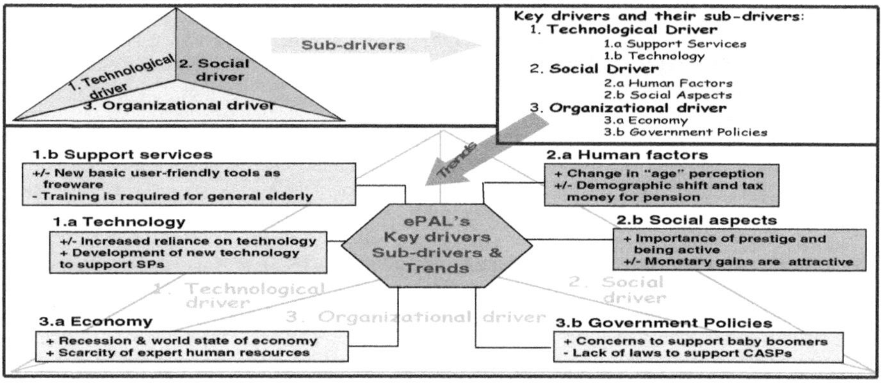

Fig. 1. Drivers and trends for ePAL environments

From the results of the two processes - identification of the drivers and trends related to the ePAL vision, and building of scenarios for potential cases, both the potential of the ePAL as well as its main constituents and limitations become evident. Table 2 summarizes example scenarios established for the ePAL environment.

Table 2. Example scenarios for ePAL environment

Scenario Category	Main focus
Associations of retired professionals: voluntary work	Focusing on the need for communities of active senior professionals to enhance chances of the involvement of senior professionals in daily activities as volunteers within their own societies or in other regions. These scenarios address the establishment, management and operation of the elderly communities. They also characterize the nature of activities of the communities and roles of senior professionals in performing those activities.

Table 2. (*continued*)

Scenario Category	Main focus
Associations of retired professionals: brokerage and launching	Focusing on the role of brokerage of opportunities that can be responded by senior professionals either individually or through communities of active senior professionals. These scenarios characterize the roles related to brokering of opportunities, namely: direct brokerage where senior professionals are involved in capturing an opportunity or indirect brokerage where a third party is involved in capturing an opportunity.
Service markets	Focusing on potential markets, mostly technology enabled markets, which are typically feasible for senior professionals to deliver their services. These scenarios also address the categorization of clients into those who can pay and those who cannot pay for the services provided by seniors.
Tri-partite collaboration forms	Focusing on different roles that need to be performed by different parties to realize the establishment and operation of communities of active senior professionals. As such these scenarios first characterize different stakeholders of the ePAL and then define the roles of each category of actors.
Keeping the link to former employer	Focusing on existing practices regarding keeping communication with the former employers and how it enhances the professional activeness of senior professionals.
Second job	Focusing on the need for establishing some form of payments for the involvement of senior professionals in market and society activities.

8 Proposed ePAL Vision 2020 for European Society

A number of initiatives such as research projects have been carried out in Europe addressing different aspects related to ageing well. Most of these initiatives see the SPs (Senior Professionals) as the recipient of services from the market and ineligible to continue participating in societal activities. As a result, there is a lack of models or regulations guiding elders' participation in value creation activities.

Consequently, the European society has been loosing or misusing the massive knowledge and experience possessed by these elders especially those who were involved in professional employments. Furthermore, after retirement most SPs feel lonely, isolated and useless to the society although they are sure that they possess both the knowledge and experience that their society is in need. Senior professionals have been trying to remain active in the European society by volunteering to perform certain activities. Such volunteering has been realized either by individual initiatives or through certain associations of senior professionals. At present, a number of associations are established for senior professionals in some regions of Europe [Afsarmanesh, et al 2009]. They aim at supporting individuals and teams of individuals either to provide services which are lacking in the market or to address specific beneficiaries not dealt with by normal market actors, and thus there is no competition or conflict with business organizations. They also aim at providing services to some categories of organizations, e.g. those that cannot afford buying such services in the market. Based on the study of ePAL drivers and their trends, the development of a number of representative scenarios for the ePAL environment has revealed different desired future possibilities for "extending professionals active life".

Vision 2020 for ePAL is then deduced from the above elements, while following the Cummings's [Cummings, 2005] definition of a well-conceived vision, it is specified by its core ideology (i.e. core purpose and values) and envisioned future (i.e. long-term audacious goal and vivid description) elements, as shown in Figure 2.

The ePAL's vision statement provides a direction where the European society shall strive to follow, in order to achieve a balanced life for senior professionals who either need or desire to remain active in the society. It addresses providing opportunities and support for senior professionals who are willing to get involved in socio-economic activities. On the other hand, it suggests the main areas needing attention from other stakeholders in order to reach this desired state, such as: (1) research institutions to provide innovative and new ideas in areas which require more R&D, (2) regulatory bodies (e.g. governments, law chambers, judiciaries) to provide a regulatory and legal infrastructure for the involvement of senior professionals in markets, (3) intermediaries (e.g. non-profit organizations, etc.) to support the brokerage of opportunities for senior professionals, etc.

Clearly enough, the creation of a desired vision for ePAL for the next decade is not a one shot action rather it is a live and interactive process. To develop the vision statement for the ePAL environment we have followed a systematic approach, as presented throughout this paper. In the same manner, for the challenging task of defining the vision statement itself, we applied the classification proposed by Cummings [Cummings, 2005] for defining a well-conceived vision. We therefore piece by piece define the needed conceptual elements for the well-conceived vision for ePAL environment.

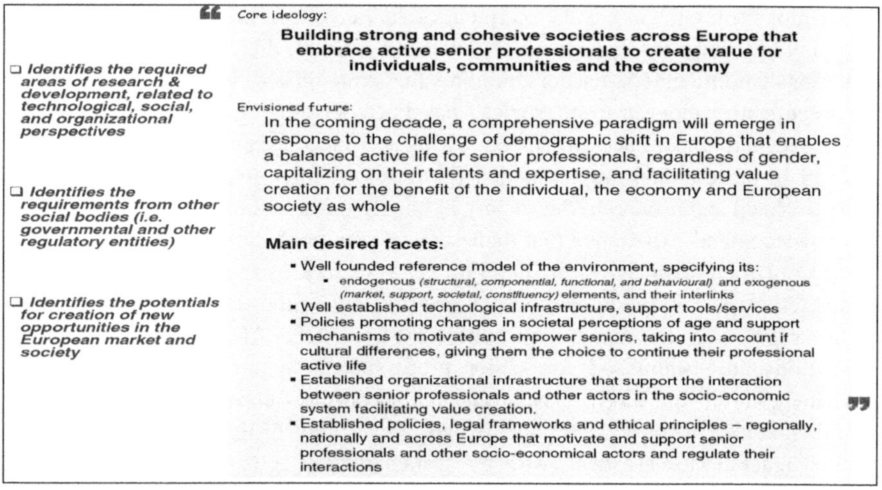

Fig. 2. Desired ePAL vision 2020 for European society

Below first each such element of this vision is defined and then they are integrated to form the "vision statement for the ePAL environment for Active Ageing Society", as shown in Figure 2. The vision elements are presented in Table 3.

Table 3. A well-conceived ePAL vision 2020 and its core components

Core ideology:
Building strong and cohesive societies across Europe that embraces active senior professionals to create value for individuals, communities and the economy

Envisioned future:
In the coming decade, a comprehensive paradigm will emerge in response to the challenges of demographic shift in Europe that enables a balanced active life for senior professionals, regardless of gender, capitalising on their talents and expertise, and facilitating value creation for the benefit of the individual, the economy and European society as a whole.

Main desired facets:

V1. Well founded reference model of the environment, specifying its: endogenous *(structural, componential, functional, and behavioural) and exogenous (market, support, societal, constituency) elements, and their interlinks*

V2. Well established technological infrastructure, support tools/services

V3. Policies promoting changes in societal perceptions of age and support mechanisms to motivate and empower seniors, taking account of cultural differences, giving them the choice to continue their professional active life

V4. Established organizational infrastructures that support the interaction between senior professionals and other actors in the socio-economic system, facilitating value creation

V5. Established policies, legal frameworks and ethical principles – regionally, nationally and across Europe - that motivate and support senior professionals and other socio-economic actors and regulate their interactions

9 Instantiation of the Vision into Its Multi-perspectives

In order to address all relevant aspects of the vision that we develop for extending the professional active life of seniors, the definition of this vision is instantiated into several orthogonal perspectives. This instantiation approach has its roots in the visioning methodology introduced in VOmap project [Camarinha-Matos & Afsarmanesh, 2003], which suggests to not overload one vision statement with too many relevant details. Rather, it suggest to first identify the main influencing perspectives in the environment, which can comprehensively capture all important aspects related to the desired vision, and as a second step instantiate the vision into these perspectives. Therefore, the main perspectives for the ePAL vision are first identified. Namely, the vision of a desired future for active ageing shall cover its social perspective, its organizational perspective, and its technological perspective. As such, through this multi-perspective instantiation, the formulated vision for ePAL only contains its common aspects, shared by the above three perspectives. Furthermore, the three vision instantiations complimentarily capture its fundamental technological, societal, and organizational aspects. Tables 4, 5 and 6 show the instantiation of the ePAL vision according to these three perspectives.

Table 4. ePAL Vision 2020 - Social Perspective

In the coming decade, extending active professional life will be a high priority strategy across Europe. European societies will mature to accommodate demographic shift through supporting and empowering senior professionals to fulfil their potential as active participants in the economy. Attitudes amongst individuals and organisations will evolve to embrace senior professionals as a value-creating pool of talent, thereby supporting and promoting equal opportunities in active aging. Both senior and young professionals will derive greater benefit from the exchange of knowledge and experience. As the social environment evolves, new support mechanisms will arise to sustain an aging but more active and inclusive population. ***Main desired facets:***
VS1. New mechanisms to enhance positive understanding and perception in society regarding the value of the abilities, skills and experience of individual senior professionals in the economy, taking account of gender **VS2.** Mechanisms to build awareness, and to motivate senior professionals to join communities of active senior professionals **VS3.** Mechanisms to support cross-cultural interactions among senior professionals as well as to the active labour force addressing barriers to communication **VS4.** Mechanisms to support a balanced economic benefits sharing among the entire society including senior professionals **VS5.** New mechanisms to help articulate the collective needs of seniors across national boundaries **VS6.** Mechanisms to support cross generational interaction between seniors and younger citizens; fomenting inter-generational solidarity and understanding within the EU **VS7.** Mechanisms to capitalize on the increased sense of trust and understanding which comes through leveraging seniors' social capital

Table 5. ePAL Vision 2020 - Organizational Perspective

In the coming decade, the primary organisational stakeholders – governments, intermediaries, businesses and unions – will adopt positive, proactive and coordinated policies and approaches that enable seniors to choose to continue their professional active life. As a consequence, senior professionals will enjoy new opportunities and a new market space of senior skills will be created, benefiting businesses and strengthening the wider European economy. ***Main desired facets:***
VO1. Employment and retirement policies will change to provide greater flexibility for seniors to choose to continue as active economic participants **VO2.** Regulations and policies will change to encourage businesses to collaborate with senior professionals, taking account of fair competition **VO3.** The knowledge and skills of seniors will be harnessed to generate value and stimulate innovation amongst European businesses **VO4.** New forms of intermediate organizations will provide highly efficient brokerage that will create opportunities in line with market needs and that help seniors engage with businesses nationally and across Europe. **VO5.** There will be sustainable funding models – from both public and private sectors - and the political drive to support new forms of senior associations and other intermediate brokers **VO6.** All stakeholders will have access to the relevant training and other support services to facilitate the seniors' transition between working life and active retirement **VO7.** New organizational cultures will positively embrace relationships between senior professionals and pre-retired (active) professionals.

Table 6. ePAL Vision 2020 - Technological Perspective

In the coming decade, technology will facilitate and enable the continued active involvement of senior professionals in the socio-economic system. Through engagement with end-users, novel ICT collaboration platforms and tools will be developed that catalyse the creation of new organisational forms that connect and empower all stakeholders and facilitate the interaction between them. This technology will be accessible to all, 'senior friendly' and will enable seniors to expand their capabilities, leave a legacy and create value. ***Main desired facets:***
VT1. Advanced collaboration support services, including teams' formation and management **VT2.** Development of collaboration ontology supporting variety of stakeholders **VT3.** Support for user-generated knowledge assets **VT4.** "Configure yourself "based philosophy infrastructure **VT5.** Easily adaptable and customizable user interfaces **VT6.** Affective computing and context aware enriched environments **VT7.** Support for establishment of trust among stakeholders **VT8.** Tools supporting the process of value creation **VT9.** Novel contractual and cooperation agreements, including negotiation support **VT10.** Advanced marketing and brokerage services **VT11.** New networking models for elderly communities' involvement with the socio-economic system **VT12.** Security and ethical / privacy support.

10 Conclusion

We have emphasized the need for systematic formulation of a vision for the ePAL environment, together with all types of its stakeholders, involved in different activities. Applying the proposed approach, a final vision statement for ePAL environment is developed. The vision mainly focuses on technological, societal and organizational perspectives. For the proposed vision to be realized, a main requirement is related to the design and development of senior- friendly collaborative ICT services and infrastructures, to facilitate both their usage by seniors as well as supporting the interactions between seniors and other stakeholders. In relation to the societal aspects, there is a need to enhance the positive perception of the society towards elder people to view them not as a socio-economical burden but as wells of knowledge and experience of great value and needed in the society. In a similar manner, organizationally, there is a need for reformulating regulations and organizational models to provide opportunities to senior professionals to remain involved and active as other actors in the market.

For the realization of the proposed vision in the society or communities across different socio-cultural contexts in Europe a detailed set of implementation actions and models are required. The ePAL project has thoroughly addressed these aspects in details presented in [Camarinha-Matos & Afsarmanesh, 2009]. This work is now being continued in the scope of another project (BRAID).

Acknowledgement. This work was supported in part by the ePAL and BRAID projects funded by the European Commission.

References

Afsarmanesh, H., Camarinha-Matos, L.M., Msanjila, S.S.: A well-conceived vision for extending professional life of seniors. In: Proceedings of PRO-VE 2009 Conference, pp. 682–695. Springer, Thessalonica (2009)

Afsarmanesh, H., Camarinha-Matos, L.M.: Towards Modeling a Collaborative Environment for Extension of Professional Active Life. In: Proceedings of PRO-VE 2009 Conference, pp. 721–732. Springer, Thessaloniki (2009)

Camarinha-Matos, L.M., Afsarmanesh, H.: The Need for a Strategic R&D Roadmap for Active Ageing. In: The Proceedings of PRO-VE (2009)

Camarinha-Matos, L.M., Afsarmanesh, H.: Collaborative mechanisms for a new perspective on active ageing. In: Proceedings of DEST 2009 - 3rd IEEE Int. Conference on Digital Ecosystems and Technologies, Istanbul, Turkey (2009a)

Camarinha-Matos, L.M., Afsarmanesh, H.: A roadmap for strategic research on virtual organizations. In: Proceedings of PRO-VE 2003 – Processes and Foundations for virtual organizations. Kluwer Academic Publishers, Dodrecht (2003)

Collins, J.C., Porras, J.I.: Organizational vision and visionary organizations. In: Leading organizations – Perspectives for a new era, pp. 234–249. SAGE, London (1998)

Cummings, T.G.: Organization development and change. Thomson South-Western (2005)

Donald, E.H.: Building leadership vision. Eleven strategic challenges for higher education. The EDUCAUSE review, 25–34 (2003)

HSBC Insurance: The future of retirement – The new old age (May 2007), http://hsbc.com/1/PA_1_1_S5/content/assets/retirement/gender_perspective_eurasia_africa_1.pdf

Jeavans, C.: Will we still be working at 70? (2004), http://news.bbc.co.uk/2/hi/uk_news/4016969.stm

Laubacher, R.J., Malone, T.W.: Two scenarios for 21st century organizations: shifting networks of small firms or all-encompassing "virtual countries"? A working paper. MIT, USA (1997)

Senge, P., Keliner, A., Roberts, C., Ross, R., Smit, B.: The fifth discipline fieldbook – strategies and tools for building a learning organizations. Doubleday Publishing (1994)

Stranges, M.: Immigration As a Remedy for Population Decline? An Overview of the European Countries. In: European papers on the new welfare, Special issue on the counter ageing society, paper no. 8 (2008)

A Network of Complementary SMEs for a Global Infrastructure for Services: The Example of Environmental Urban Services

Alan Lelah[1], Fabrice Mathieux[1], Daniel Brissaud[1], and Lucien Vincent[2]

[1] Grenoble University, G-SCOP, 46 av Félix Viallet,
38000 Grenoble, France
alan.lelah@g-scop.grenoble-inp.fr
[2] ENSM SE, département G2I/OMSI, 158 cours Fauriel,
42023 Saint Etienne Cedex2, France

Abstract. High-technology SMEs have shown their capacity for creating and developing innovative services. Reduced size often confines them to vertical applications and limits possibilities for broader development. Network strategies are possible but may need a strong leader to ensure credibility. On the other hand, large operators cannot be proficient in all the necessary domains, particularly when applications move very fast. Therefore they very much need the diversity and the dynamics of SMEs to provide service packages within a global infrastructure. Bringing together different SME actors behind a telecom provider is a challenge displaying good promises if the links between the different services are correctly identified and modelled.

Keywords: network of SMEs, PSS, service delivery.

1 Introduction

SMEs play an important role in European industry [1]. Small high-technology firms have often proved their capacity for creating innovative services. Their small, flexible structures are well-adapted for converting new ideas into tangible projects that they can deploy rapidly in changing markets. They have core-skills that make them very competitive in specific areas. However they often lack the scale needed to introduce their new technologies and small size can be a handicap for developing complex systems requiring complementary know-how. It is not always easy for them to enter public markets [2]. Cities, for example, often unite to form communities of agglomerations or other structures that deal with such services of common interest and they have often already piled up many technologies and show reluctance to introduce new systems especially when they are proposed by small firms.

On the other hand, large operators cannot be proficient in all the different fields that they need to cover in a rapidly changing world. High-technology applications can move too fast for their slowly matured replies. They need to integrate the diversity and the dynamics of smaller firms if they want to provide novel service packages within a global infrastructure that would be the heart of their know-how.

L.M. Camarinha-Matos et al. (Eds.): PRO-VE 2010, IFIP AICT 336, pp. 73–80, 2010.

Bringing together complementary SMEs into a network to build a complex system will combine market-positioning with adaptable and innovative approaches [3-5]. The driving force of a big operator, capable of gaining the confidence of local authorities and guaranteeing QoS, is a natural leader for such a network [2]. However to succeed it is important that the links between the different service providers and the underlying technical structures be correctly identified, described and understood.

This article takes the case of a network of complementary SMEs behind a telecom operator that seeks to build a telecom backbone for urban services. It will study how service-oriented architecture could help to clarify relations between the partners as they move from vertical applications to the global infrastructure.

2 A Network of SMEs with a Global Infrastructure for Services

2.1 An M2M Enhanced Service from a Single SME

M2M Systems

In Machine-to-Machine (M2M) communication networks, machines exchange data with other machines taking decisions without human intervention [6]. Basically networks of sensors gather information from the outside world and dispatch them towards more powerful machines. These could be service platforms capable of processing data and providing services that can be directly used by human-beings. Potential applications cover areas like environment, safety, public transport and health [7]. One particular application is waste glass collection, experimented in 2006 by the telecom operator Orange/France [8], while a similar, but full-scale, commercial offer, is already proposed by the French SME, BH Technologies [9].

Basic Waste Glass Collection

A service-oriented architecture is used to describe the basic urban waste glass collection service in figure 1.

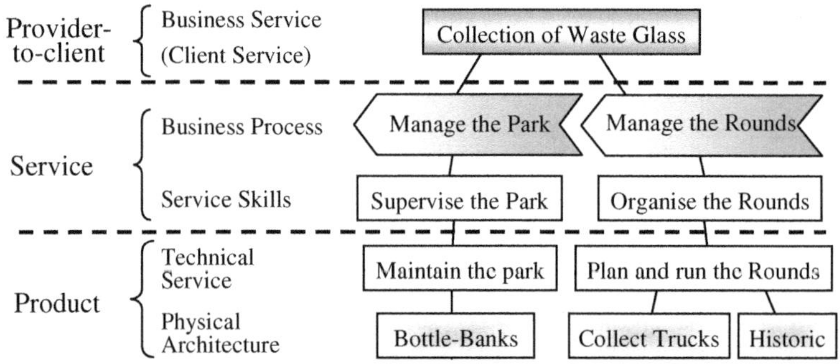

Fig. 1. In the basic waste glass collection service the provider is the waste collection company and the clients are the city and its residents

Cities provide waste banks to residents for disposal of waste glass. The glass is discarded in bins and collected by dedicated trucks doing regular rounds. In the basic service the truck-driver systematically checks the glass-level in each bin and empties the bin if it is at least half-full. Otherwise he would skip the bin and drive to the next bank.

The figure shows how the service is organized. At the top level, the service is represented on a provider-to-client point of view. The clients are the residents and the service rendered is the collection of waste glass. The service is operated by a private waste collection company or by the local authorities. On the service level, two business processes are operated: managing the waste-bank park and managing the rounds. The first concerns supervision of the park and that basically means adding new bins and up-keeping the banks. The second deals with the organization of the rounds by planning and allocating trucks. This is generally done on statistical (historic) basis combined with the experience of the truck driver. A third level shows the technical services and structure used by the service.

The M2M-Enhanced Vertical Application

Starting with this basic scenario, the collect can be optimized if the driver knows ahead which bottle-banks must be emptied. This is possible with sensors in an M2M network [8]. It is a vertical application because it supports only one specific service.

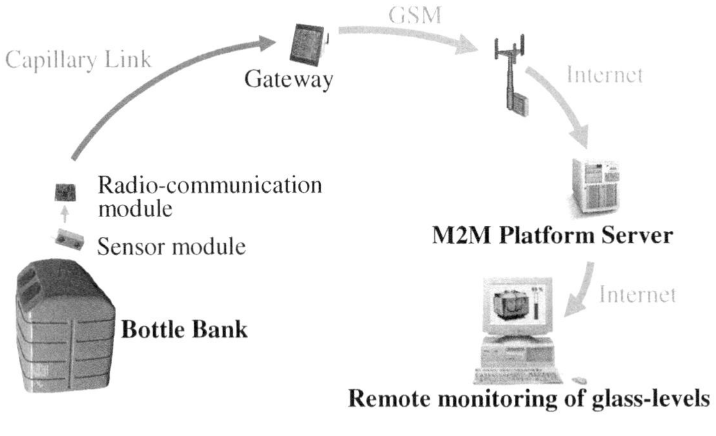

Fig. 2. A vertical service for waste glass collection

The principals can be seen in figure 2. In the bottle-banks, to measure the glass-level, bins are equipped with ultrasound sensors. Communication modules link them to gateways placed not too far away. The entire park is covered in this way and the data collected is relayed through the telecom network to an urban service platform. Here the information is aggregated and processed to optimize the collect rounds. The results can be seen by the waste collection company. The service is run by one SME deploying the sensors and running the network alone. The firm will simultaneously operate the urban service platform, collect data and optimize rounds. Organization is straightforward and the data belongs to one company.

Figure 3 shows how the M2M service (shaded) is solicited by the initial service. Only the telecom service (not shown) between the gateways and the urban service platform is not directly under the control of the SME.

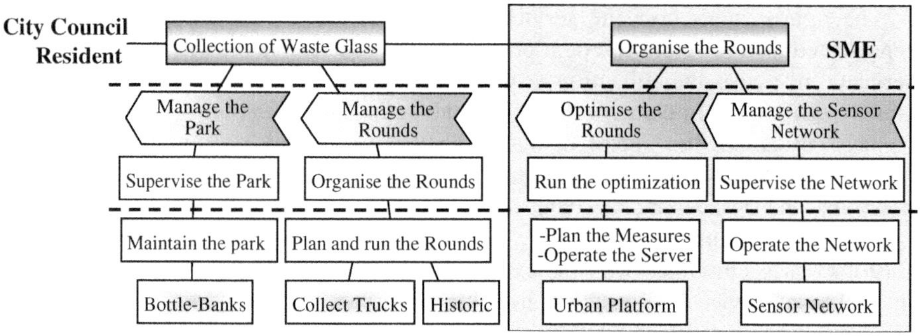

Fig. 3. A new service is provided by the *SME* to the waste collection company

To optimize the rounds it is necessary to specify what data is needed. The glass-levels must be monitored. Technically it is necessary to plan the measures and collect the data on the urban service platform. Server operation and support also have to be insured. The management of the sensor network requires identification and supervision of the network devices. They must be installed, maintained and operated.

2.2 A Global Urban M2M Infrastructure

An Urban M2M Infrastructure

The vertical organization described above is not optimal in terms of resources. The service provider must run everything alone. Also it must use the telecom network as a client and has no way to insure continuity and security of data in case of network failure. It is proposed to build an infrastructure capable of supporting different services. The services will cover a coherent field of activities, such as city community-services. The glass collection example will be just one of them. The overall architecture of the system is illustrated in figure 4.

In the figure, data is collected on the left. Sensors are positioned in the city to meet service-requirements. Basically the system is the same as before, but this time, before sending information to the service platforms (for each service), a distinct urban collect and command platform must deal with data confidentiality and brokerage. The infrastructure has to know who is allowed to access what data. Additionally, the platform will deal with issues like device-managing, and for example, instructions can be relayed to the sensors to modify measuring times. Detection of new installations will also be done.

Services are deployed on the right. The urban collect and command platform organises the data and safeguards. It takes care of legal issues like access to data, security and privacy. Service-provider platforms are connected to the collect and command platform via internet and pilot different service-offers including web services or SMS alerts. The information is made available to local administrations and residents.

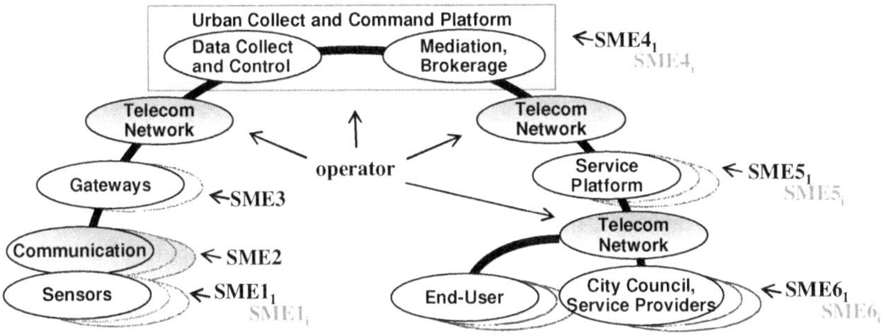

Fig. 4. M2M services with a common infrastructure. The SMEs participating at each level are represented (*SME1₁, SME1ᵢ, SME2 …*).

Service-Oriented Network

To clarify complex relations between partners, the infrastructure can be understood as B2B services interlinked together.

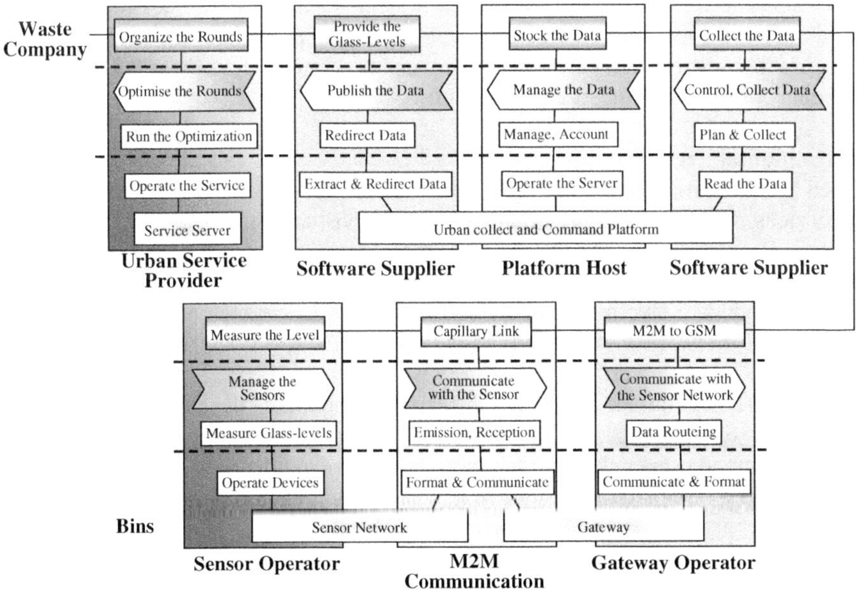

Fig. 5. Simplified diagram of the complementary M2M service with a common infrastructure

Figure 5 shows the supply chain in the case of waste glass collection. The diagram starts with the waste collection company addressed by the M2M service. The main service provided by the first SME deals with the organization of the collection rounds. To obtain data for optimization, the SME must acquire the glass-levels published by the urban collect and command platform. Within the platform, data must be managed to know who can receive what information and an account of exchanges must be kept for records and billing. And so on, down to the last service that is the measure of glass-levels in the bins.

It should be noted that any one SME can cover multiple services in the supply chain. For instance, the service provider could own and operate the corresponding sensors. Although some of the actors of the chain are more product-oriented they must at the least ensure upgrading for technical, legal or other necessary evolutions.

Of course the full process is more complicated and the schema has been simplified in order to get an overall view. For example, the service provider must exchange information with the system concerning sensor-management, particularly for security and ownership issues, but also when new sensors are added or resets are required.

3 Opportunities and Limits of a Network of Enterprises Providing Environmental Urban Services

Vertical services cannot be considered as optimal from an environmental perspective. This section will discuss some of the implications of the passage from single business vertical applications to a common infrastructure for city services as seen by the project SensCity [10]. This French funded project seeks to build a network of SMEs behind a telecom operator, Orange/France, with the support of university laboratories. Its goal is to construct an M2M backbone capable of supporting a variety of services using data collected through a city-wide sensor network [11].

Environmental Pressure

Pressed by the European Commission, governments and public opinion, new products and services developed today should integrate environmental concerns. As a major operator, Orange cannot ignore the environmental impacts of new services. Its' president-general director stressed "in effect it is essential to review in depth our economic models to favour sustainable modes of production and consumption" [12].

Within the network Orange will incite the SMEs to review their products and services in a move towards eco-design. The SMEs are very receptive to this, and some, like BH and Azimut - two French service companies - have already moved this way at their own initiative. Conditions are good so that mutual stimulation will enhance this trend especially from the more environmentally conscientious partners. It is nonetheless a large step to take with new skills to gain and coaching from Orange and the university partners in the network is much expected.

Optimal Size

From the point of view of the operator, Orange is too big to develop all the applications necessary to invest new markets like M2M. It obviously cannot pretend, for example, that it will develop solutions internally to resolve the optimization of waste glass collection. Orange has become more and more dependant on its supply chains. It needs some insurance that suppliers meet certain standards and it must have a view of future trends in the telecom network. The success of the network of SMEs would allow Orange to create the conditions for a solid infrastructure capable of quickly adapting to changing markets. In return, the SMEs are capable of rapidly integrating new tools even if their small size does not allow them to penetrate the market alone. They also have a lot to gain in credibility if the project succeeds.

Delegation
When entering the M2M consortium the SME concedes parts of its service to other specialized companies. Instead of having to deal with all the aspects it can concentrate on the real added value of its core skills. For example, communication will be advantageously covered by specialized SMEs. They would be more capable of upgrading to national and international standards and normalizations and ensure long term competitiveness. Issues of security, communication and other such tasks would be assumed by the best partners.

The advantages to be gained by all are evident, but the system has limits that must not be ignored. Dependence on other SMEs is not without risk, for example, communication protocols and technologies may fail to meet expectations. Another point is that large firms like Orange can be long in taking decisions and tend to ignore the imperatives of the smaller partners. There is a large gap between an experimental project and a serious business offer and the small SMEs must take care and continue developing their own markets not to end up trapped by the operator's hesitations.

Territorial Advantages
Instead of continuously piling up new vertical services, each with a new infrastructure, a backbone capable of supporting multiple services could certainly improve environmental performances of cities. When an operator like Orange makes an offer to a town or agglomeration it means that a complete network can be adapted to the city. New services could be added without rebuilding the infrastructure, and that potentially means environmental advantages from sharing facilities. Equipment doesn't necessarily have to be duplicated and catering for many applications simultaneously would be advantageous. Human resources can be engaged when a critical size is reached, allowing for professional intervention for installation, maintenance and end-of-life treatment. Finally the service rendered to its' residents would be both better and more environmentally efficient.

4 Conclusions and Perspectives

A service-oriented architecture for a network of SMEs behind a larger-sized operator has been studied. It helps clarifying the passage from vertical M2M services to an infrastructure for environmental services in the city and was applied to the case of the French project SensCity. The main consequences of the infrastructure were identified and examined for different points: environmental pressure; optimal size; delegation and territorial advantages.

The advantages of the infrastructure could easily be extended to other waste collection schemes. Organised collection of carton and paper, metal or organic waste could be promising. Other environmental services like public lighting, pollution and noise measurement are also concerned. The list of potential environment-friendly applications is long.

Future work should explore the mechanism of the transformation that the SMEs providing such services must go through. It should determine to what extent it would be a necessary evolution for sustainable high-technology environmental city-services and whether it could be a key for successful innovation in other domains as well. In parallel the conditions for obtaining real environmental gains must be pursued.

Acknowledgements

The authors would like to thank Xavier Boucher, ENSM SE, and Claude Pellegrin, COACTIS, and the other participants of the GOSPI cluster, Rhone-Alps, France [13] for the interesting debates that clarified the service relations described in this article.

References

1. Study on the Competitiveness of the EU eco-industry, ENTR/06/054, p. 156 (2009)
2. Attali, J.: Rapport de la Commission pour la libération de la croissance française, XO Éditions, La Documentation française, p. 16, 47, 52 (2008)
3. Brass, D.J., Galaskiewicz, J., Greve, H.R., Tsai, W.: Taking stock of networks and organizations: A multilevel perspective. Academy of Management Journal 47, 795–817 (2004)
4. Provan, K., Kenis, P.: Modes of Network Governance: Structure, Management, and Effectiveness. Journal of Public Administration Research and Theory 18(2), 229–252 (2008)
5. Borgatti, S., Foster, P.: The network paradigm in organizational research: A review and typology review and analyze the emerging network paradigm. Journal of management (2003)
6. Orange, FING, Syntec Informatique: White paper Machine To Machine, stakes and prospects (2006)
7. Bonneau, V.: Strong Growth of Wireless M2M and Impact of RFID, M36105-2005 Edition IDATE DigiWorld (2005)
8. Houang, T., Lelah, A., Mathieux, F., Brissaud, D., Gimeno, V.: Environmental Evaluation of Machine-to-Machine Services: the case of Glass Waste Collection. In: Proceedings of the 2nd CIRP IPS^2 Conference, Linköping, pp. 75–82 (2010)
9. BH Technologies, http://www.bh-environnement.com/
10. SensCity, http://senscity.minalogic.net
11. Lelah, A., Mathieux, F., Brissaud, D., Gimeno, V.: SensCity: a new project opening the way for sustainable services in the city based on a mutualised M2M infrastructure. In: Proceedings of the 2nd CIRP IPS^2 Conference, Linköping, pp. 99–106 (2010)
12. Orange, Report on Corporate Social Responsibility 2008, p. 1 (2008), http://www.orange.com/fr_FR/responsabilite/att00012430/Rapport_RSE_090904.pdf
13. GOSPI, http://www.cluster-gospi.fr

A Framework for Maintaining Socio-technical Balance during the Evolution of Complex Systems

Igor Hawryszkiewycz

School of Systems, Management and Leadership
University of Technology, Australia
igorh@it.uts.edu.au

Abstract. Distributed systems are growing increasingly complex in the sense that they need to reorganize on a regular basis to respond to external opportunities. At the same time research has shown that performance is improved where technology support is aligned to people's activities within the system. This paper provides a framework for ensuring that such alignment is maintained during system evolution. The paper first defines the nature of change using complexity theory as the foundation for defining the nature of change. It then builds on the idea of socio-technical gaps to identify the gaps created by a change. The changes are then outlined in terms of perspectives to provide a systematic basis for managing change. To do this change is expressed in terms of the perspectives to provide a meaningful way to respond to change.

Keywords: Complexity theory, System evolution, Social factors.

1 Introduction

Business trends as outlined by McAfee [1] are towards what is called Enterprise 2.0, which focuses on obtaining competitive advantage through networking and collaboration. This when combined with Web 2.0 provides the infrastructure for a more collaborative business environment. Typical developments here are process ecosystems [2], where process owners create independent processes, a service oriented environment where systems must continually respond to changing customer needs; greater client involvement in design as described by Cova and Salle [3], and new forms of collaborative supply chains, where services are negotiated jointly at each interface during the operation of the supply chain. Rye [4] proposes that knowledge be shared at each supply chain transition to continually adjust the process as requirements change.

These systems are dynamic in nature and differ from the predominantly deterministic systems. Many design processes, however, still use methods that support deterministic processes. This paper focuses on ways to design dynamic systems. It proposes that complexity theory can provide a systematic way to support evolution. It also has the additional goal of ensuring that any change is implemented in ways that maintain system balance during the change. The paper follows the approach shown in Figure 1 and described following:

L.M. Camarinha-Matos et al. (Eds.): PRO-VE 2010, IFIP AICT 336, pp. 81–87, 2010.

- The paper first describes the socio-technical framework that provides a systematic method for identifying imbalances in a system and ways to identify and correct any imbalances that may arise during system evolution.
- This is followed by an outline of complexity theory and the criteria it provides to information system design especially as a way of defining system evolution in terms of a complete set of change
- The paper then describes a way to manage complexity by describing systems from different perspectives,
- The paper then provides a way to identify the potential impact of change or evolution in terms of different perspectives, in particular, the business activity, the social network and the knowledge flows.

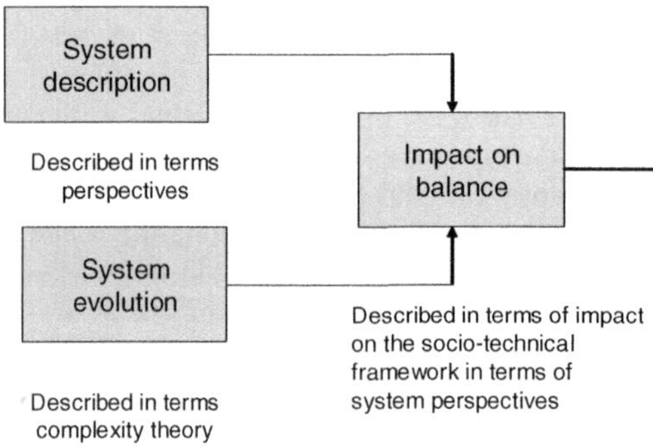

Fig. 1. Managing Change

2 Socio-technical Framework

This paper uses the idea of gaps based on the structure introduced by Leavitt [5] and illustrated in Figure 2.

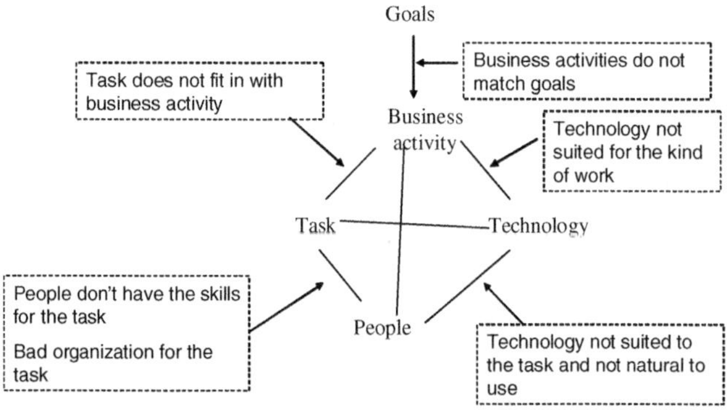

Fig. 2. Defining socio-technical gaps

Figure 2 shows the major concepts that make up a system, namely, business activity, task, people and technology. The system is driven by goals and business activities must be designed to realize the goals. The goal of design is to have the concepts designed in such a way that there are no "gaps" in system operation. Thus business activities must be chosen to realize the goals. Other gaps may be that the people are assigned to tasks without necessary skills needed for the task; or that the technology does not match people's work practices.

3 Defining Criteria of Change from Complexity Theory

Knowledge workers should be able to quickly comprehend how to adopt any new technology, and assimilate it in their work [6]. The suggestion here is that IS system design no longer focus on the design of deterministic systems that attempt to reduce complexity through structure but on systems that support evolution and change. The paper suggests that the foundation for such systems comes from complexity theory.

There is now an emerging body of knowledge that sees close correspondence to complexity theory and the emerging information system environment. The major contribution is to use complexity theory to define a generic framework for system evolution and then show that a number of perspectives are needed to address evolution in a systematic manner. It draws on work such as that of Merali [7] or McElroy [8], who see information systems now becoming more complex and suggest that designers draw on the principles of complex systems when designing new information systems. This implies a change of emphasis in design. Instead of top down development of systems that follow predefined processes, what are now needed are systems that support change. McElroy describes this as a change from complexity reduction through the top-down creation of deterministic systems to designing systems that are designed to support change. The paper introduces the idea of perspectives that can be used to respond to change.

4 System Perspectives

Managing system evolution requires cognitive abilities to understand the impact of change on different system components. The proposal here is to view components of information systems as different perspectives that go across functions. Such perspectives are system wide rather than focused on each individual functions thus providing a holistic view of change. In summary, the perspectives proposed here are:

- The **business activities** and their actions and outcomes,
- The **process workflow** or sequence of activities and the interdependence between activities,
- The **social structure**, which is seen as a critical element (Pralahad and Krishnan, 2008), that describes roles and their responsibilities and the assignment of roles to individuals and the relationships between them. This is critical in the design of the collaborative infrastructure as it defines the specific collaboration
- The **knowledge** created and used during the activities,

- The **organizational perspective** in the kinds of teams support or leadership provided to support collaboration and innovation,
- The **technology** to support the collaboration, which is needed to share and create knowledge.

Another view of perspectives is as components of an information system. A working system should maintain good working relationships between these components.

System Evolution expressed in Terms of Perspectives

The structural dimensions are derived from the foundation to provide a meaningful way to talk about change in terms understood by system designers. These include:

Table 1. Structure change and perspectives

Structural Change	Effect on perspectives
Ability to self-organize at local levels in response to wide variety of external change.	This kind of results in an impact social structure in terms of business activities. It often requires new viewpoints on decision making by bringing in new expertise and the need for new knowledge from existing systems.
Quick establishment of self-contained units that address w ell-defined parts of the environment.	This often implies the creation of a new business activity. This in turn calls for new responsibilities and resulting changes to the social structure.
Loose connections between system elements and a way to reorganize the structure to respond to external change.	This often requires the injection of an innovative social structure to maintain brokering arrangements between existing processes.
Ability to organize connections into larger components with consequent changes to connections and interactivity	The initial impact here is on social structure and knowledge requirements. Generally access to knowledge is provided to a wider set of activities although the activities themselves do not change.
Aggregation of smaller units into larger components	The initial impact here is on social structure and knowledge requirements. It generally requires a consolidation of knowledge requirements and providing access to a wider set of roles.

5 Combining Perspectives and the Socio-technical Framework

Change can then be expressed by identifying the primary reason for the change and then following through the links in the socio-technical framework in terms of the perspectives. For example a change of goal can be seen to first impact on the business activity, then on the tasks, the people and social structures needed and the technology. The relationships between perspectives shown in Figure 3 provide the necessary rules for mapping between the perspectives. For example:

Change of goal → Impact on business activity → change in task --.> change of social structure → change in technology.

These changes are then expressed in terms of the perspectives. Often as shown in Figure 5 a different perspective can be used in reducing each gap.

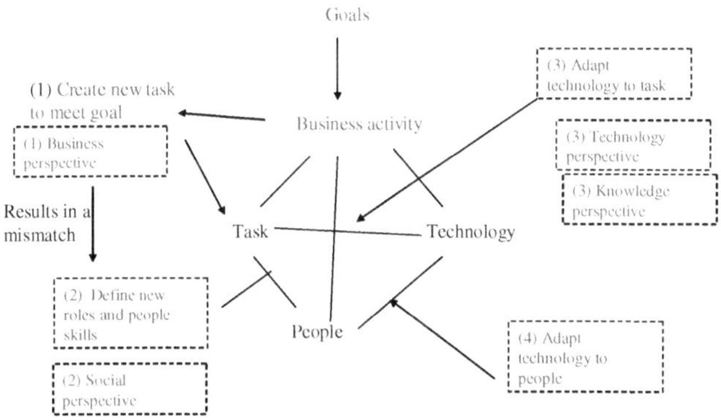

Fig. 3. Mapping change to the socio-technical framework

Support for such can be provided through agents. To do this requires some guidelines and rules that can be used by agents to support evolution. These guidelines must express the relationships ion Figure 3 in more detail. Typical rules can be

- A change in business activity where a new expert opinion is needed result is a social change where a new innovative social structure is inserted into an activity.
- A problem has arisen in a supply chain requires the creation of a new team structure linked to an existing activity as for example [9] system problems that require a software provider to resolve software issues in a service provision.

6 The Architecture for Alignment

One question not addressed so far is who manages system changes to respond to the evolution in the business environment. The standard approach has been for information technology (IT) specialists to implement changes to supporting technologies. In the more dynamic environments now found in industry the response times may not be adequate.

The paper suggests the architectural structure shown in Figure 4. It separates the more traditional applications based on ERP systems from the more dynamic requirements of knowledge workers. The analytical work support requires support for creation new social structures and providing them with abilities to access information in the ERP systems.

Workspaces for the more analytical work should provide the ability to change the social structure as new knowledge needs arise or new business relationships are established. Workspaces can contain commands that can be used to make the kind of changes described in Table 1. The goal is to extend workspaces by providing supporting agent use the relationships described in Figure 3 to guide users through making these changes.

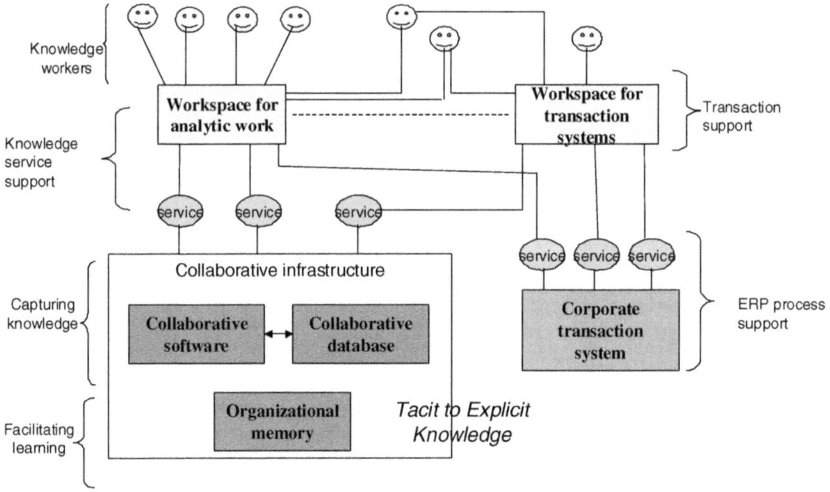

Fig. 4. Combining explicit and tacit

7 Summary

The paper proposed a systematic way of managing change within evolving information systems. It combined the idea of change as defined by complexity theory with a socio-technical framework using the idea of system perspectives. Change was described in terms of the perspectives, which then indicated a systematic way of adjusting other perspectives. Future work is focusing on defining the relationships between perspectives in more detail with the goal of identifying ways to assist knowledge workers to change the system themselves.

References

1. McAfee, A.P.: Enterprise 2.0: The Dawn of Emergent Collaboration. MIT Sloan Management Review, 21–28 (2006)
2. Vidgen, R., Wang, X.: From business process management to business process ecosystem. Journal of Information Technology 21, 262–271 (2006)
3. Cova, B., Salle, R.: Marketing solutions in accordance with S-D logic: Co-creating value with customer network actors. Industrial Marketing Management 37, 270–277 (2008)
4. Rye, K., Lee, S., Choi, H.: Modularization of web-based collaboration systems for manufacturing Innovation. In: Proceedings of the Tenth International Conference on Enterprise Information systems, Barcelona, June 12-16, pp. 174–177 (2008)
5. Leavitt, H.J.: Applied Organizational Change in Industry: Structural, technical and humanistic approaches. In: March, J.G. (ed.) Handbook of Organization, pp. 1144–1170. Rand-McNally, Chicago (1965)
6. Davenport, T.: Thinking for a Living. Harvard Business School Press, Boston (2005)
7. Merali, J.: Complexity and Information Systems: the emergent domain. Journal of Information Technology 21(4), 216–233 (2006)
8. McElroy, M.W.: Integrating Complexity theory, knowledge management and organizational learning. Journal of Knowledge Management 4(3), 195–203 (2000)
9. Hawryszkiewycz, I.T.: Lightweight Technologies for Knowledge Based Collaborative Applications. In: Proceedings of the IEEE CEC/EEE2007 Conference on E-Commerce Technology, Tokyo, pp. 255–264 (July 2007)

Adoption and Diffusion of m-Government: Challenges and Future Directions for Research

Ahmed Al-Hadidi[1] and Yacine Rezgui[2]

[1] School of Engineering, Cardiff University, Queen's Buildings, The Parade, Cardiff CF24 3AA, Wales, UK
Al-HadidiA@cardiff.ac.uk

[2] School of Engineering, Cardiff University, Queen's Buildings, The Parade, Cardiff CF24 3AA, Wales, UK
RezguiY@cardiff.ac.uk

Abstract. The paper reviews mobile government (m-Government) adoption and diffusion factors in developed and developing economies. m-Government is viewed as a class of e-Government applications and refers to any transaction via mobile technologies, such as laptops, phones or personal digital assistants (PDAs). The most significant features of mobile technology include mobility and portability. The ubiquitous dimension of mobile technologies provides means of accessing services anywhere, anytime, and on the move, thanks to advanced wireless interface technologies. The paper examines the literature base in respect of known obstacles to the adoption and diffusion of m-Government, drawing the distinction between technical and non-technical barriers. Furthermore, the paper discusses the economic impacts achieved by e-Government in many countries following the transfer of public services to electronic services; some examples are given from the developed and developing countries.

Keywords: e-Government, m-Government, technical barriers, non-technical barriers.

1 Introduction

E-Government relies on the availability of computer hardware and software, and a favourable citizen predisposition towards the use of electronic communication. Unfortunately, such assumptions about the affluence of individuals, a country's level of technological development, and the predisposition of its citizens towards electronic communication, may not be legitimate, and even some advanced nations are struggling to increase their citizens' adoption of e-Government initiatives [9]. With respect to developing and transitional countries, a survey revealed that 35% of e-Government projects were total failures, 50% were partial failures, and only 15% were successful [7]. M-Government exploits the large adoption of mobile phone technology by citizens to achieve the goal of e-Government. In fact, mobile phones have a much wider dissemination than computers. In 2002, the number of mobile subscribers surpassed that of fixed-line subscribers in 97 countries [10], and by the

L.M. Camarinha-Matos et al. (Eds.): PRO-VE 2010, IFIP AICT 336, pp. 88–94, 2010.

end of 2004, that number had almost doubled to 171, while the number of mobile subscriptions had increased to 1.8 billion. This take-up of mobile technology is an encouragement for governments seeking to develop their channels of communication with citizens and organisations [12].

Following the introduction, the paper discusses the relationship between m-Government and e-Government and introduces the main category of barriers facing the adoption of m-Government service. This is followed by the economic impact of e-Government and m-Government in developed and developing countries. Discussion of the study and conclusion are offered.

2 The Relationship between e-Government and m-Government

E-Government is defined variously, and the vast majority of definitions focus on the role of information and communication technologies (ICTs) in facilitating the delivery of public services to the government, companies and citizens [6; 16]. However, [5] define m-Government as the use of all kinds of wireless and mobile technologies, applications and devices for improving services delivery to the parties involved in e-Government including citizens, businesses and all government units.

From the above, it was established that m-Government is a complimentary sub-set of e-Government [13]. Furthermore, most researchers believe that e-Government is the cornerstone for m-Government [9; 18]. Therefore, the real differences between these two deliveries of public services as noted by [13] relate to the mean of access and delivery. E-Government provides services through wired networks with interactive and relatively intelligent web applications. However, the value of m-Government comes from the capabilities of applications supporting mobility of the citizens, businesses and internal operations of the governments. Furthermore, some of the typical challenges and barriers for e-Government are naturally shared by the m-Government efforts [13]. Further details on e-Government and m-Government technologies can be found in [1].

3 Barriers facing the Adoption and Diffusion of m-Government

Data communications, however, is now becoming very attractive to many consumers and business users [13]. That said, despite the fact that ICT systems are valuable communication tools, they also bring many technological and cultural concerns. In this respect, [9] have observed that "it is ironic that Information Technology (IT) is currently serving as both a facilitator of the global economy and as a potential impediment to its advancement". This section reviews the technical and non-technical barriers faced by many countries when attempting to adopt m-Government systems.

3.1 Technical Barriers

The most common technical barriers to m-Government development and dissemination involve a lack of infrastructure [13; 9; 2] and this is a particular problem in developing countries. According to [13], m-Government infrastructure is comprised of wireless networks and mobile access devices (e.g. mobile phones, laptops, PDAs), and accessing software services. Another technical barrier is identified as security [14]. In the US, for example, [20] noted the many challenges confronting federal agency web managers, such as the need to remove sensitive information that may be useful to terrorists, the need to take steps to prevent hacking, and the need to maintain privacy. According to [2], security of m-Government applications is considered the hallmark of a successful initiative. In this respect, [9] recommends the fundamental standards of wireless network security in order to secure controlled and managed access to services. And yet another barrier is the potential lack of compatibility between mobile systems and existing e-Government systems, a problem which as noted by [15], may escalate where government offices have legacy systems which may not be easy to integrate both in terms of functionalities and data administration.

3.2 Non-technical Barriers

Non-technical impediments are generally found in relation to those who develop, manage and/or use an e-Government system, and the environment that hosts the system. The literature highlighted culture as a non-technical barrier for the adoption of e-Government and m-Government a belief that is echoed in the literature by such scholars [9; 15]. Reference [21] investigating the tendencies of Chinese people in relation to e-commerce, found that rely on the use of cash, whereas e-payment operates on the basis of credit cards, hence their predisposition to engage in online shopping is less than other nations. Other cultural factors that are known to impact upon the adoption and dissemination of m-Government are: trust, language, resistance to change, management support, and users' expectations [15].

Privacy and security are also raised by [15; 12] who suggest that these issues are the most significant concerns citizens have about m-Government. The fear is that their opinions will never be anonymous because government will be able to trace their mobile numbers when they communicate. Another major problem of a non-technical nature, is people's resistance to change, which occurs generally because offear of the unknown, or an inability to deal with uncertainty [15].

Furthermore, another barrier in some countries, as identified by [13], is the lack of data protection legislation, which articulates the rights of data subjects (citizens) and the responsibilities of the data holders (government). In some cases the law of a country does not recognise mobile documents and transactions, there is no clear legal status for government online publications, no regulations for online filings, online signings, and on online taxable transactions. In discussing resistance to change, the [16] notes that this may lead to other barriers to the adoption and dissemination of e-Government, such as poor project management, technology failure, lack of funding, and high political demands and expectations. It is imperative to remove any such obstacles to implementation, since it has been documented [7] that about 60% of e-Government initiatives fail due to: lack of high-level officials' commitments; funding; and project control.

Reference [5] classify the lack of IT skills as another barrier that confronts some hard challenges relating to government's ability to provide e-Government and m-Government services. Reference [13] comment that accessibility is key for the success of m-Government, but factors such as income, education level, gender, age, handicap, language differences and regional discrepancies affect accessibility, and hence citizens' attitudes towards m-Government initiatives. Clearly, the cost issue is one that applies to populations in all countries, and as [13] have pointed out, the cost of owning mobile devices and of accessing services should be affordable, and low.

4 The Economic Impact of e-Government and m-Government

In spite of such failures and barriers, however, efforts towards providing government services in the electronic environment, and establishing e-Government projects are growing rapidly and today billions of dollars worldwide are spent in this way. However, as e-Government and m-Government are still in their infancy [20; 6], effective implementation cannot be taken for granted, and financial, organisational and cultural issues represent the potential for serious obstacles in this respect. Today, governments are trying to reshape their citizens' old perceptions of long queues, cumbersome processes [18] and corruption. Therefore, some examples are given in the following sub-sections, which also identify the benefit to both developed and developing countries from moving towards the e-Government model.

4.1 Developed Countries

According to [4] State governments in the US are saving up to 70% by moving services online, compared to the cost of providing the same services over the counter. For example, online license renewal in the state of Arizona costs $2 per transaction, versus $7 over the counter. Furthermore, In Washington State, government e-procurement systems are saving an average of 10-20% in terms of material and purchase costs as well as In Alaska, online vehicle registration costs have dropped from $7.75 to only $0.91 using an online system. Furthermore, according to [15], that Australian e-Government providing services to over 6 million people. It has launched an online system at a cost of AU$600 thousand in 2001 to facilitate communication with users. The system is convenient and time saving for its clients and the agency's transaction savings over a three-year period totalled AU$5 million. In addition, E-tax (ato.gov.au) was launched by the Australian Taxation Office (ATO) in 1997 to help taxpayers to prepare and lodge their income tax returns. The initiative has helped to reduce the ATO's processing time from eight weeks to two, and reduced overall costs by a AU$1 million, per year for five years.

4.2 Developing Countries

According to [4] eight out of ten Brazilians are filing their income tax forms online. The government of Brazil saved $10 million when eleven million people paid their income taxes online. In addition, the use of Internet in Chile to schedule tax payments, check accuracy, and refer back for full tax history has reduced both time and error. Therefore, the Chilean government is expected to save $200 million, from a total of $4 billion in bids tendered annually, after the introduction of a procurement website. Another example form the developing country, that Singapore's e-citizen initiative is achieving an annual saving of $14.5 million to the government and through the portal, the government was able to offer 92% of its services online by the end of 2001 [11]. According to [4] the integration of databases of the Moroccan Ministries of Finance and Planning has cut in half the preparation time of the national budget. Also, the use of Internet by the Dubai Ports and Customs Authority allows thousands of freight transport companies to reduce time and costs with 24-hour access to customs clearance services. Therefore, the overhaul of government services offered to businesses and individuals in Dubai is estimated to have reduced administrative costs by at least 10%.

5 Discussion

Undoubtedly, the development of an integrated infrastructure, suitable hardware and software that provides full security is crucial, as is the creation of appropriate legal apparatus to facilitate the easy and secure use of electronic transactions. Significantly, the development of an e-culture will be of tremendous value in preparing a society for the adoption of m-Government. Important also, is the need for governments to ensure their e-Government and m-Government services are properly developed and that serious consideration is given to the types of service to be offered. Public/user opinion should be canvassed and user-friendly interfaces are imperative, since these actions will promote successful user experiences and help to reduce negative predispositions towards the change. Furthermore, as we mention above that in developed and developing countries it is clear that implementation of e-Government and m-Government in these countries and Arab world creates opportunities to save money and facilitate transaction in public and private sector. Also, m-Government initiatives will help give opportunities to increase transparency and reduce corruption, in particular in developing economies. Therefore, the international society need to consider these impacts of economics in m-Government projects to help adoption and diffusion of m-Government project around the world in developed and developing countries.

The finding of this paper can lead to the following future researches. Firstly, the barriers proposed from this paper will lead to further research to suggest a contingent approach for evaluating m-Government services and a mix of technical and non technical approaches for the evaluation. Secondly, this paper demonstrates that lack of infrastructure and security represents the main challenge in developed and developing countries. As well, factors such as culture, trust, privacy, lack of funding, People's resistance, their education level, and Internet cost, are the main challenges facing the adoption of e-Government and m-Government projects. Future work may investigate these challenges in more the detail in the context of the intention to adopt m-Government services both in developed and developing countries or the Arab countries in general. It is important to identify the level of significance and interdependence of each challenge in order to secure successful implementation of m-Government projects.

6 Conclusion

M-Government cannot be seen as replacing e-Government, so in many cases it will be complementary to e-Government efforts. The conventional e-Government efforts provide services through wired networks and the value of m-Government comes from the capabilities of applications supporting mobility. In addition, this paper has grouped the barriers into two categories, technical aspects, and non-technical aspects. In terms of technical aspects, the development of infrastructure and the need to ensure compatibility with already-existing provision, are paramount, and this requires much co-ordination with many different agencies. In respect of non-technical aspects, the human factor is crucial since without commitment from those in leadership positions, adequate funding for the long term is not likely to be allocated, and a poor system will result. Consequently, the range of problems that cause citizens not to want to engage with e/m-Government occur, such as mistrust of the system, will ensue. Above all, an e/m-Government service must be accessible and affordable, and citizens must have the intellectual capability to use it. Hence, barriers include a variety of elements relating to citizens' socio-economic and cultural background. Without attention to these, the willingness among citizens to engage with electronic government will be minimal. Overall, the research provides a better understanding of the complex environment in which e/m-Government is deployed, including the drivers and barriers to adoption. The authors are currently conducting a comprehensive fieldwork study in a developing country to explore government services adoption patterns by citizens. This will be reported in future publications.

References

1. Al-Hadidi, A., Rezgui, Y.: Barriers Facing the Adoption and Diffusion of m-Government: Literature Review. In: 7th Eastern European e|Gov Days: (eee|Gov Days (2009), Prague, Czech Republic, pp. 456–466 (2009) ISBN 978-3-85403-255-7
2. Al-khamayseh, S., Lawrence, E., Zmijewska, A.: Towards Understanding Success Factors in Interactive Mobile Government (2007), `http://www.mgovernment.org/resurces/euromgvo2006/PDF/2_Al-Khamayseh.pdf` (accessed March 21, 2008)
3. Antovski, L., Gusev, M.: M-Government Framework. In: EURO mGOV 2005, Brighton, UK, pp. 36–44 (2005)
4. Atallah, S.: E-Government Considerations for Arab States SURF-AS [Internet] (2001), http://www.surf-as.org/Papers/e-gov-english.PDF (accessed March 6, 2008)
5. Bassara, A., Wisniewski, M., Zebrowski, P.: USE-ME.GOV- Usability-driven open platform for mobile government. In: Proc. Business Information Systems (BIS 2005), Poznan, Poland, pp. 193–202 (2005)
6. Choudrie, Jyoti, Ghinea, Gheorgite: Evaluating global e-Government sites: a view using web diagnostic tools. Electronic Journal of e-Government 2(2), 105–114 (2004), http://ejeg.com/volume-2/volume2-.pdf
7. Commonwealth Telecommunications Organisation: E-Government for Development Information Exchange Project Website [Internet] (2002), http://www.egov4dev.org (accessed March 22, 2008)
8. Foghlú, M.Ó.: Infrastructures for Mobile Government Services. In: EURO Mgov 2005, Brighton, UK, pp. 192–199 (2005)
9. Goldstuck, A.: Government Unplugged - Mobile and Wireless Technologies in the Public Sector, Centre of Public Service Innovation, Tshwane, South Africa (2003)
10. ITU, International Telecommunication Union: The E-Government Hand book for Developing Countries (2002)

11. Ke, W., Wei, K.K.: Successful e-Government in Singapore. Communication of the ACM 47(6), 95–99 (2004)
12. Kushchu, I., Borucki, C.: A Mobility Response Model for Government (2004), http://www.mgovlab.org/library/mgovlab/mgovlab_ikcb.pdf (accessd March 14, 2008)
13. Kushchu, I., Kuscu, H.: From E-Government to M-Government: Facing the Inevitable? In: The Proceeding of European Conference on E-Government (ECEG 2003), Trinity College (2003)
14. Lambrinoudakis, C., Gritzalis, S., et al.: Security requirements for e-Government services: a methodological approach for developing a common PKI-based security policy. Computer Communications 26(16), 1873–1883 (2003)
15. NOIE: Improving Confidence, Trust and Security [Internet] (2002), http://www.noie.gov.au/projects/confidence/Improving/index.htm (accessed May 2, 2008)
16. OECD: The e-Government Imperative. OECD publications, France (2003)
17. Rezgui, Y.: Exploring virtual team-working effectiveness in the construction sector. Interacting with Computers 19(1), 96–112 (2007)
18. Scholl, H.J.J.: The Mobility Paradigm in Government Theory and Practice: A Strategic Framework. In: EURO mGOV 2005, Brighton, UK, pp. 377–385 (2005)
19. Silcock: Institute of Public Administration and Management. University of Liverpool, Liverpool (2001)
20. Stowers, G.N.L.: The State of Federal Websites: The Pursuit of Excellence. In: Abramson, M.A., Morin, T.L. (eds.) E-Government 2003. Rowman & Littlefield Publishers Inc., USA (2003)
21. Stylianou, A.C., Robbin, S.S., Jackson, P.: Perceptions and attitudes about e-commerce development in China: An exploratory study. Journal of Global Information Management 11(2), 31 (2003)
22. United Nations Development Program UNDP (2003), http://www.undp.org (accessed February 8, 2008)
23. World Bank (2004), http://www.wordbank.org (accessed March 4, 2008)
24. Zálešák, M.: M-Government: more than a mobilized government (2003), http://www.developmentgateway.org/download/218309/mGov.doc (accessed March 27, 2008)

Support for Innovation Processes in Collaborative Networks

Heiko Duin[1], Manuel Fradinho[2], Marcus Seifert[1], and Klaus-Dieter Thoben[1]

[1] BIBA – Bremer Institut für Produktion und Logistik GmbH, Hochschulring 20, D-28359 Bremen, Germany
{du,sf,tho}@biba.uni-bremen.de
[2] Cyntelix Corporation Ltd., Dublin, Ireland

Abstract. Effective innovation is the key challenge for European manufacturing enterprises in the global market. New approaches such as Open Innovation combined with the Extended Product paradigm are currently heavily under discussion among practitioners as well as scientists. This paper provides a discussion of the processes and challenges in the early phase of innovation, i.e. the idea seeding, ideation and evaluation phases which take place before formally structured processes like stage-gate approaches are applied. Special attention is paid to learning and knowledge creation aspects. Additionally, aspects concerning further research directions are discussed.

Keywords: Innovation, Collaborative Innovation.

1 Introduction

In the global market, with the emergent economies, European enterprises have serious difficulties in surviving, let alone excelling, unless they are capable to leverage successfully their capacity to innovate. Enterprises in almost all sectors are forced to develop innovative products in shorter cycles due to market constraints. In this context, Wang and Ahmed [1] describe the market situation as dominated by hyper-dynamics, uncertainty and chaos.

The innovation statistics carried out with European enterprises demonstrates a paradox in Europe of having good research activities, but with poor impact concerning innovation and global competitiveness [2]. The problem is not necessarily lack of funding, with the EU RTD program totaling 229 billion Euros in 2007, neither is it lack of engagement of enterprises in innovation (with exception of France), with 41.2% in industry and 36% in services [3]. However, the reality demonstrates that a total 85% of product development resources are wasted on products and services that never reach the market, which is compounded by the fact that only 18% of those products reaching the market actually prove successful [4,5]. In addition, the distribution of innovation across Europe is uneven, with Sweden, Finland, Germany, Denmark and the UK considered as innovation leaders in the European Innovation Scoreboard (EIS) in 2008 [2].

L.M. Camarinha-Matos et al. (Eds.): PRO-VE 2010, IFIP AICT 336, pp. 95–102, 2010.

In response to the pressures resulting from competing in a global market, enterprises follow two major trends: Open Innovation and Extended Products.

1.1 Open Innovation

The limitations of the internally focused innovation are summarily captured in the simple simulation of Red Queen Effect [6] applied to product development. The simulation indicates that a 10% decrease in product life cycle would require a company to double the introduction of new sustainable products each year, which implies significant increases in innovation funding just to maintain for the company to keep its market position. This is a simple simulation based on shrinkage of the product lifecycle. If one considers the globalization phenomenon, then it is unthinkable to keep the closed innovation model. Consequently, organizations have been compelled to reach out beyond their boundaries to engage with others in the attempt of maximizing the efficiency of their innovation processes by collaborating with others. The realization that the world no longer allows for companies functioning in isolation has led to the establishment of a networked fabric composed of enterprises collaborating with one another based on a platform of trust – Collaborative Networked Organizations [7].

1.2 Extended Products

Facilitated by a paradigm of sustainable development in the vision of Adams [8], enterprises have realized that their customers are more interested in solutions to a need, rather than a packaged product. This introduces the concept of extended products, where a product is enriched with services and the business model is focused on what needs are addressed by the combined solution (e.g. [9]). So for example, one may consider that car manufacturers are moving away from providing a simple car towards providing a solution for mobility.

1.3 Implications and Chances

These trends have a significant impact on the way innovation has been traditionally viewed and dealt with by enterprises, which no longer consider it viable to harness alone the necessary creativity power within their corporate boundaries to excel. Consequently, the barriers of closed innovation have been torn down and the new paradigm of open innovation [10] has been adopted, where multiple parties are engaged thus increasing the creativity potential. Initially the paradigm of open innovation was applied solely to the enterprises, but the open innovation movement has gone even further than organizational boundaries reaching out towards individuals, realizing that the global connectivity provided by the Internet has created a Global Brain. This has led to the notions of crowd sourcing and the existence of a global brain, but there are multiple challenges towards harnessing successfully the power of the masses and the success cases are still more anecdotal rather than systematic.

A harsh reality concerning innovation is the low success rate of transforming ideas into sustainable business models, and in response, the Living Lab paradigm [11] has emerged where the creation process is not only open involving multiple innovators, but places the customer at the centre of the innovation process, actively taking part of the creation of products and services at every step. However, the novelty of Living Labs implies that there are serious challenges for individuals and organizations to adopt the paradigm to produce successful outcomes.

2 Innovation

Innovation in public is often seen as the invention of something groundbreaking new. Innovation isn't solely concerned with the generation of new ideas but also with making an economical effort out of them. Innovation encompasses the entire process from the generation of an idea – the invention or the combination of known objects – to the penetration of the market with a economically successful implementation of the idea – as much for products as for processes or services [12].

The innovation process therefore represents all phases from idea generation to marketing and sales. The diagram in Fig. 1 reflects the innovation from seeding of the idea until the new product development, which then leads to the operations.

A new concept is introduced by Henry Chesbrough [10]: Open Innovation. The central idea of Open Innovation is that in a world consisting of widely distributed knowledge, organizations like enterprises cannot afford to rely entirely on their own research. Instead they should buy or license processes or inventions (e.g. patents) from other companies. In addition, internal inventions which are not used in business could be taken outside the enterprise (e.g. by licensing or joint ventures). On the other hand side collaboration in the critical phase of product innovation conducts the reduction of the in-house production depth and leads to the dependency of external partners.

Another solution or a concept enhancing the open innovation idea is the concept of European Living Labs. These offer a unique opportunity for organizations to include end-users and other stakeholders in new product development or other innovation processes. This enables the user to be a co-creator in the innovation process [11].

These approaches have the early stage of innovation in focus. The early stage of innovation is characterized by high uncertainties and the constant generation of new and relevant knowledge [13]. The knowledge is generated and immediately used in non linear work steps. The complexity of these work processes cannot be described appropriate in a quantifiable model [14]. This is taken into account as today's attempts do not have the pretence to describe the early stage processes in a whole within methods or best practice examples [15].

Within the early stage of innovation up to 70 % of all follow up costs are determined [16]. Taken into account the high development cost in the automotive sector the understanding and the successful support of the early stage of innovation becomes indispensible for economical success.

2.1 Ideation

Ideation is a concept that is generally not understood well in depth. In many organizations ideation is viewed similar to creating ideas. However, creating ideas is only the very initial seed for the ideation process. Recent empirical studies have

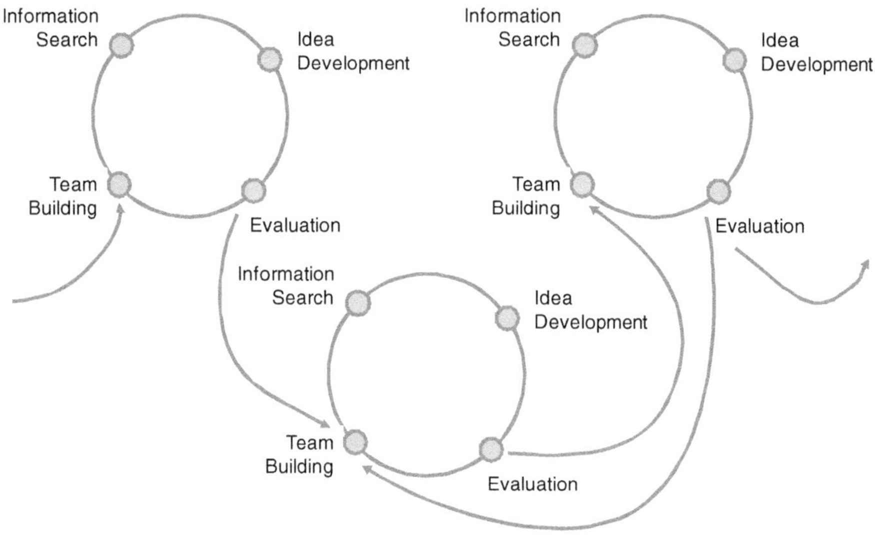

Fig. 2. Ideation process

revealed that the process of generating ideas is not considered as a problem in industrial organizations – the perceived problem is the continuing idea development process – the ideation process [17].

Ideation is basically a circular process (as shown in Fig. 2) that differs significantly from the sequential process approach that most people are trained in [18]. Furthermore, ideation is an inter-disciplinary and cross-organizational process that requires a certain degree of common language. Due to the inter-disciplinary nature the common language additionally has to be neutral [19].

Traditionally, problems have been seen as complicated challenges that should be solved through breaking them down into smaller and smaller chunks. However, most modern problems – and ideation problems in particular – are complex rather than complicated. Complex problems are messier and more ambiguous in nature; they are more connected to other and often very different problems; more likely to react in unpredictable non-linear ways; and more likely to produce unintended consequences.

The perception and response to complex issues are dependent on the nature of the sense-making process. The sense-making process, on the other hand, is dependent on the perceived nature of the problem.

2.2 Connectivity

The advent of Web 2.0 [20] concepts and technologies not only fostered users' active participation to content creation, and therefore transforming knowledge consumers into 'prosumers', but also boosted the collective creation of knowledge and made users keep active control on the kind of knowledge and information produced and diffused and on its quantity and quality too (e.g. Wikipedia). This new perspective [21] brought new life to innovation and, of course, to its creative component, as Web

2.0 clearly supported the so called 'knowledge fusion' process that characterizes the knowledge creation emerging from combining, adapting and improving different knowledge components developed in different contexts as now commonly happens in diverse and dispersed professional environments.

McAfee [22] translated the Web 2.0 into the SLATES paradigm in order to bring it into the corporate (and more in general, organizational) environment by labeling it as ENTERPRISE 2.0. Therefore, by introducing ENTERPRISE 2.0-inspired tools in the work routine knowledge workers find in their organization the Web 2.0 social and collaborative tools they are already accustomed to. Moreover, in the Open Innovation perspective, the emergence of workers belonging to virtual communities not only within the organization itself, but also, extended beyond or, even completely external to it, can be not only tolerated, but even encouraged. A key point, as [23] pointed out, is related to the fact that in the cooperative creation process people like to ask for advice to, and receiving it from, their peers or the ones who are reputed being experts in some domains of knowledge. The explanation relies on the "emotional, psychological and social needs of individuals" that have to be fulfilled [24]. Therefore, it becomes apparent how sharing content and being part of virtual communities in blogs or in online video sharing websites or contributing to wiki projects and the use of any other Web 2.0 tool increase people feelings of self recognition, of reputation in the community, of being connected to other people which is one of the basic needs of individuals experience [25].

2.3 Evaluation

Evaluation is a general technique, which is applied in several domains, but in the particular domain of innovation, it has been mostly applied to product development where each process is completed by running evaluations against the objectives of the phase [26]. These objectives shift from phase to phase, for example form the completeness of requirements in the requirement phase, to feasibility in the design phase, or functioning in the implementation phase. In any case these evaluations are focused on technical criteria [27], which are categorized in groups of overall aims, such as manufacturability, assembly, ecology, maintenance, safety and others as design-for-X sets of constraints. Such evaluations are typically undertaken by test engineers in the development departments. It is recognized that such technical approach often leads to good but expensive solutions, which is overcome by adding a separate value analysis evaluation with cost/benefit measurements, often through a separate department and initially in a late design phase.

Evaluation draws on another source of quality management, risk management and project management, where the focus is more on identifying the potential impact of events on the development, production and delivery process. A well known example is the Fish-bone diagram [28], which relates possible product failures to its consequences, so that corrective actions can be taken already in the early design phases. Such evaluations are typically undertaken by dedicated risk / project / quality management departments following their own standard operation procedures.

A third evaluation perspective is a more recent, advanced-state-of-the-art financial and entrepreneurial perspective that is implemented in business idea competitions and business plan competitions [29]. Rather than an internal perspective on the product or the organization of its development, the focus of this evaluation is on its outside validity with questions like: will there be enough financial, personal and knowledge resources to complete the project? Will the result be acceptable to its users, and who are the users [30]? How likely is it that the idea under consideration will prevail over its contenders? Such evaluations are organizationally not yet well placed and are undertaken by associations and (ad hoc) board within the innovation ecosystem.

4 Living Labs

The initiative of Living Labs came up in the early nineties and the term Living Lab was firstly proposed by Lasher, Ives and Jarvenpaa [31] to the academic community. In Europe, Living labs gained more attention during the European test bed discussion from 2000 to 2004. Living Labs can be viewed as a method in the innovation process to integrate users. Simplified, Living Labs reverse the idea of product development to some extent. In this concept, consumers are involved in the innovation process from the inception of ideas thus they can directly influence the innovation process instead of being just customers of a pre-developed product.

Furthermore, a rather medium- and long-term time frame for conducted Living Lab studies is stated by common literature on Living Labs. In terms of the number of participants in Living Lab studies, there seems to be a slight change over the last years. Whereas at the beginning of Living Lab studies, the number of participants involved was rather small, nowadays the possibility of big user groups in Living Lab environments is rising [32].

As bottom line Folstad [33, p. 116] defines Living Labs as follows: "Living Labs are environments for innovation and development where users are exposed to new ICT solutions in (semi)realistic contexts, as part of medium- and long-term studies targeting evaluation of new ICT solutions and discovery of innovation opportunities".

5 Conclusions and Research Directions

The key challenge with innovation is to understand that it is more than the acts of inventing something new, in fact, the processes supporting innovation are quite complex and change as an idea is seeded until it reaches the market as a product or service. In particular, the following research topics are relevant:

- **Global Brain.** The ultimate instantiation of the open innovation model is captured with the imagery of the global brain, where it is necessary to research technology and processes that enable manufacturing enterprises to engage with the collective intelligence of all individuals within the global reach of the internet and across cultural barriers.
- **Learn to Innovate.** The ability to create has long been regarded as an innate attribute of an individual, but it is a cognitive ability and consequently it is feasible for individuals to improve. However, the development of innovation capability also applies to organizations as they distil best practice and mature their processes. It is necessary to research new approaches to competence

development that target the associated competences in ever smaller time-to-competence time slots.

- **Go Green.** Rather than regarding sustainability as an impending hurdle with legal and regularity entanglements, enterprises can embrace it as an opportunity for change and become first movers into new markets. The challenge is to research new frameworks that address the challenges of manufacturing enterprises to adopt sustainability as a means to become competitive.
- **Living Labs.** The potential of involving the consumer in the innovation process from its inception holds enticing promises, from achieving higher success in innovation outcomes to creating a market ready to consumer the resulting invention. The living labs movement is relatively new, requiring further research into facilitating the implementing and transferring knowledge concerning living labs paradigm to manufacturing enterprises.
- **Risk Management.** The complexity of reality with its multi-faceted social dependencies makes randomness difficult to predict with a model, thus it is necessary to research new ways of coping and attenuating risks of low probability but with high impact.

References

1. Wang, C.L., Ahmed, P.K.: Organisational Learning: A Critical Review. The Learning Organization 10, 8–17 (2003)
2. EIS: European Innovation Scoreboard 2008. Comparative Analysis of Innovation Performance. European Commission - Enterprise and Industry, Luxemburg (2009)
3. Parvan, S.: Quality in the Focus of Innovation. Eurostat. Statistics in Focus, 1–8 (2009)
4. Bauer, R.: Kein Bedarf für Plastikräder. Freitag, 43 (2005)
5. INA: Innovation Network Austria Study (2005)
6. Bayless, D.: Innovation, Clockspeed and the Red Queen Effect, `http://www.evergreenip.com/presentations/redqueen/redqueen.html`
7. Camarinha-Matos, L.M.: Advances in Collaborative Networked Organisations. In: Azevedo, AmericoInnovation in Manufacturing Networks, pp. 3–16. Springer, New York (2008)
8. Adams, W.M.: The Future of Sustainability: Re-thinking Environment and Development in the Twenty-first Cenury, `http://cmsdata.iucn.org/downloads/iucn_future_of_sustanability.pdf`
9. Jansson, K., Thoben, K.-D.: The Extended Products Paradigm, An Introduction. In: Arai, E., Kimura, F., Goossenaerts, J., Shirase, K. (eds.) Knowledge and Skill Chains in Engineering and Manufacturing. Information Infrastructure in the Era of Global Communications, pp. 39–47. Springer, New York (2005)
10. Chesbrough, H.W.: Open Innovation. Harvard Business School Press, Boston (2003)
11. Schumacher, J., Niitamo, V.-P.: European Living Labs A New Approach for Human Centric Regional Innovation. wvb (2008)
12. Baldwin, J., Hanel, P.: Innovation and Knowledge Creation in an Open Economy. Cambridge University Press, Cambridge (2003)
13. Klünder, P.: Planbarer Brückenschlag. Design Report (2006)
14. Akin: An Exploration of the Design Process. Design Methods and Theories (1979)
15. Bauer, B.: Design und Methoden. Design Report (2006)

16. Gebhard, A.: Rapid Prototyping: Werkzeuge für die schnelle Produktentwicklung. Hanser Fachbuchverlag, Munich (2000)
17. Bessant, J., Stamm, B.v: Twelve Search Strategies that Colud Save your Organisation. Executive Briefing Advanced Institute of Management Research, London (2007)
18. Leifer, R.: Radical Innovation – How Mature Companies can Outsmart Upstarts. Harvard Business School Press, Boston (2000)
19. Hansen, P.K., Mabogunje, A., Moeller Haase, L.: Get a Grip on Sense Making and Exploration. In: Proceedings of the IEEM 2009, Hong Kong (2009)
20. O'Reilly, T.: What Is Web 2.0. Design Patterns and Business Models for the Next Generation of Software, http://www.oreillynet.com/pub/a/oreilly/tim/news/2005/09/30/what-is-web-20.html
21. Sigala, M.: Integrating web 2.0 in e-learning environments: A socio-technical approach. International Journal of Knowledge and Learning 3, 628–648 (2007)
22. McAfee, A.P.: Enterprise 2.0: The dawn of emergent collaboration. MIT Sloan Management Review 47, 21–28 (2006)
23. Angehrn, A.A., Maxwell, A., Sereno, B.: Enhancing social interaction in competence development networks: A conceptual framework. International Journal of Learning Technology 3, 424–442 (2008)
24. Angehrn, A.A., Maxwell, A.: TENTube: A video-based connection tool supporting competence development. International Journal of Emerging Technologies in Learning 3, 29–37 (2008)
25. Maslow, A.H.: Motivation and Personality. Harper & Row, New York (1987)
26. Kerzner, H.: Project Management - A Systems Approach to Planning, Scheduling and Controlling. John Wiley & Sons, New Jersey (2009)
27. Kahn, K.B.: New Product Forecasting - An Applied Approach, New York (2006)
28. Brussee, W.: Statistics for SixSigma made Easy, New York (2004)
29. Hitt, M.A., Ireland, R.D., Hoskisson, R.E.: Strategic Management - Concept and Cases: Competitiveness and Globalization, Marson (2007)
30. Exner, K.: Controlling in der New Economy - Herausforderungen, Aufgaben, Instrumente, Vienna (2002)
31. Lasher, D.R., Ives, B., Jarvenpaa, S.L.: USAA-IBM Partnerships in Information Technology: Managing the Image Project. MIS-Quarterly 15, 551–565 (1991)
32. Eriksson, M., Niitamo, V.-P., Kulkki, S., Hribernik, K.A.: Living Labs as a Multi-Contextual R&D Methodology. In: The 12th International Conference on Concurrent Enterprising: Innovative Products and Services through Collaborative Networks, ICE 2006 (2006)
33. Folstad, A.: Living Labs for Innovation and Development of Information and Communication Technology: A Literature Review. The Electronic Journal for Virtual Organizations and Networks, 99–131 (2008)

The Role of Collaborative Networks in Business Model Innovation

Joseba Arana and Eduardo Castellano

IKERLAN Technological Research Centre, PºJ.M. Arizmendiarrieta 2,
20500 Arrasate-Mondragón, Basque Country
{jmarana,ecastellano}@ikerlan.es

Abstract. It seems clear that innovation is a key factor in increasing competitiveness of European enterprises in a global market with new players from developing countries. It also seems clear that innovation in organizations must necessarily be based on an open concept that allows them to take advantage of ideas, competences and external resources, hence the concept of Collaborative Networks. Among the different types of innovation that are likely to be addressed within the concept of collaboration it is worth emphasizing what is known as Business Model Innovation. This kind of innovation aims to analyze and assess the logic of the business and establish new requirements for improving it, or changing it. This paper, based on several empirical research studies developed by the authors, describes the role that Collaborative Networks can play in the Business Model Innovation process.

Keywords: Collaborative Networks, Business Model, Innovation.

1 Introduction

It seems clear that innovation is one of the fundamental engines for improving the competitiveness of European companies, which are facing major threats posed by the entry onto the market of enterprises from new developing countries with lower production costs. On the other hand, it also seems understandable that approaching innovation in isolation is not a very viable alternative for many SMEs within this highly competitive environment. So, such organizations should consider an open innovation, and an open business model approach, to take advantage of ideas, competences and resources external to them. From the needs stated, during the last few years, the interest, both from the academic and business environment, in developing and applying the concept of Collaborative Networks for innovation development, as well as Business Model Innovation, has risen significantly [1][2].

Linking both stated topics seems to be an interesting issue to investigate. And this is what the research developed for this paper has focused on: the analysis of the role that Collaborative Networks can play in the process to specify and implement an Innovative Business Model.

L.M. Camarinha-Matos et al. (Eds.): PRO-VE 2010, IFIP AICT 336, pp. 103–109, 2010.

2 Literature Review

The concept of innovation networks, although appearing in the literature in the late 80s [3], did not began to be researched extensively until the last decade. Rothwell [4], in his work on innovation models, already pointed to the fact that the nature of the innovation process evolves towards more interactive models, both on the intra- and inter-organizational levels. From the perspective of innovation networks design and management, the literature includes many approaches, although they are sometimes more conceptual and descriptive in nature [5][6][7] rather than experience based [8][9].

More recently, Chesbrough [10] extended the innovation networks vision through the term Open Innovation, characterized by the cooperation for innovation within wide horizontal and vertical networks of customers, start-ups, suppliers, and competitors. According to the Open Innovation paradigm, companies can and should use external ideas as well as those from their own R&D departments, and both internal and external paths to the market, in order to advance their technology and processes. Along with this line of argument, co-creation with customers/users as well as crowdsourcing have been particularly stressed [11][12].

As regards business models, both the definition of what a business model is, as well as what its key building blocks should be, have been topics for debate in the last few years [2][13][14][15][16][17].

However, there are few articles in the reviewed literature that specifically relate the concept of business models with the one of Collaborative Networks. In fact, those few references that link these two fields are mainly narrowly focused on just identifying the specific place collaborative networks should occupy in the business model framework, but not so much on a broader level related to studying the potential collaborative networks could have in order to redefine the business model itself. The work presented in this paper aims to shed some light on the latter aspect, based on the analysis of nine empirical case studies developed by the authors.

3 Methodology

The research conducted is based on nine application research experiences developed by the authors. These experiences, structured in the form of case studies, were developed following an action research approach. The research methodology adopted can be classified, therefore, as a qualitative research methodology, where case studies are frequently used for exploratory and theory building research [18]. In this research, based on the analysis developed, a set of enablers and inhibitors have been identified in order to foster collaborative business model innovation.

The application research experiences presented belong to different industries, and will be denoted with acronyms in compliance with confidentiality requirements: HINCO (office furniture fittings and hinge systems for automotive and white appliances industry), CARCO (automotive components), VALCO (valve manufacturer), ELCO (elevation systems components), LIFTCO (elevation systems), MACHCO (machining supplier), COOLCO (refrigerators), COACHCO (luxury coaches), and RAILCO (railways).

In order to structure the insights derived from the empirical research developed, Osterwalder's business model framework has been used [2]. According to this framework: (1) The business model of a company is a simplified representation of its business logic, and; (2) The business model consists of four main areas (customer interface, value proposition, infrastructure management and profit equation) composed of nine basic business model building blocks that describe all the aspects of the business logic (see Fig. 1).

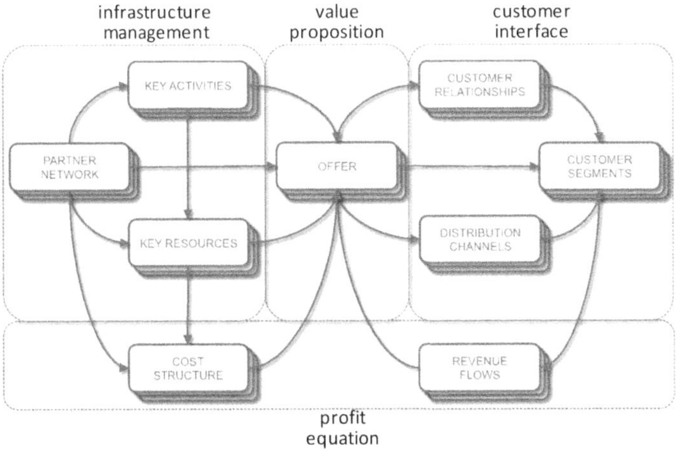

Fig. 1. Four main areas and building blocks of a business model. Source: Osterwalder [2]

4 Collaborative Business Model Innovation: Discussion

In this section, taking the empirical research developed as the basis, some insights on the potential that collaborative networks could play in order to redefine the business model itself are discussed. The presentation of these insights, in the form of benefits and risks, has been structured covering the four main areas of a business model (see Fig. 1). Also, the insights presented are supported by the cases developed and analyzed in the empirical research (see Table 1).

The first area to discuss is the Customer Interface one. In the innovation process of a business model the area relating to customers is crucial. Identifying target customer segments, the relationship to be established with them, and channels to be used, are primary factors of the new business model that drive the contents of the other areas.

The analysis of the Customer Interface, when approached from the limited perspective of a single organization, usually leads to significant inaccuracies: (1) It reduces the range of potential customers to those segments with which the organization currently works; (2) It segments customers based on criteria related to the current value propositions; (3) It reduces the needs of each customer segment to those directly related to products and services currently offered; (4) It reduces the identification of needs and opportunities to one of the stages in the product life cycle, and; (5) It does not take into account the possibility of induced needs derived from other value propositions based on technologies, provision of services, or new forms of communication and distribution.

From the viewpoint of coming up with a new business model, this is perhaps one of the areas where the contribution of the partners in a Collaborative Network is most needed. In general, the analysis of the segments, needs and related opportunities, should be established with an approach not restricted to current existing products and services, but with a broader customer-related issues approach. Addressing the analysis from this perspective allows other partners to interact and create a wider vision which results in an improved identification of opportunities (see Case 1 in Table 1). However, the analysis of uncovered needs should also consider, not only the final use stage of the value proposition, but also an analysis, in collaboration with other partners, of the other value proposition life cycle stages, since failure to meet the needs of some of the stakeholders in any phase of the product life cycle might jeopardize final market success (see Case 2 in Table 1). Moreover, successful innovations origins are not so much related with collecting explicit needs expressed by the customers, but more from providing product features, accessories or services that customers had not even thought about. So, working in a network with technology partners and service providers in the same market segment can catalyze the generation of successful innovation ideas (see Case 3 in Table 1).

The second area for discussion is the Value Proposition one, which focuses on specifying the value propositions to cover the identified needs and opportunities. In line with what has been noted before, specifying the value propositions from the perspective of a single organization can lead to some inaccuracies: (1) Specifying value propositions that just cover only part of the customer's needs and consequently not having the necessary appeal to capture its buying decision; (2) Missing other potential value propositions that go beyond the current skills of the organization; (3) Not visualizing correctly the form of value proposition that customers want to perceive, or; (4) Not taking into account value propositions coming from the supply chain processes.

The specification of value propositions to serve the customer segments should be a compromise between market-related issues and those related to technology, as well as skills and the production processes domain. So it requires the participation of partners with different perspectives to offer appropriate products and services. Along the same lines, the participation of different stakeholders providing a functional vision throughout the life cycle, plus partners that could provide the necessary competences to develop the potential value propositions, should make up a discussion forum from which the final value proposition map would emerge (see Case 4 in Table 1). Within this collaboration relationship, it is necessary to make special mention of the participation of customers and users as well as key suppliers that add remarkably high value technology, components or functions to the products and services that make up the value proposition. Regarding the latter, in some cases, this collaboration might be reciprocal (see Case 5 in Table 1). Also, when specifying new value propositions, another point that should not be forgotten is that the value perceived by the customer not only comes from the functionalities provided by products and services, but can also come from substantial changes in the supply chain in the form of more agile and profitable channels for communication or distribution (see Case 6 in Table 1).

The third area to discuss is Infrastructure Management. Identifying value propositions and customer interfaces within a collaborative network is an essential practice for creating an innovative business model. However, the business model specification also requires the consideration of the activities, resources and partnerships required for the creation-communication-delivery of the value proposition. In this sense, the analysis of the Infrastructure area without members of the network entails the following hazards: (1) Establishing requirements related to activities and/or resources that are impossible to deploy; (2) Specifying activities for outsourcing without the necessary contrast and level of commitment; (3) Specifying activities without the necessary sense of integration in the business; (4) Establishing activities and milestones without the required resources, or; (5) Not having the required visualization of the necessary and available partners for the implementation of activities or for complementing resources/capabilities.

The involvement of the network in the process of infrastructure specification for the new business is essential, and the participation of experts in the key processes needed for the creation, supply, and distribution of value propositions should be taken into account (see Case 7 and Case 8 in Table 1). Moreover, the need for outsourcing some of the activities and resources required implies seeking partners in a variety of activities and knowledge areas. These extra competences are not always to be found in what the network's partners can contribute. So another advantage of having a collaborative network is the potential it has for drawing on existing partners as antennas for search, referral and even for managing external networks with the necessary skills (see Case 9 in Table 1).

Finally, the fourth area for discussion is the Profit Equation one. It is always important to remember that the goal of any business is to offer value propositions by reaching an appropriate balance of the profit equation between the revenue streams and cost structure. The specification of a new business model within a collaborative network raises new questions that are different from those usually addressed in the case of a single organization. In this sense, not addressing this issue collaboratively, and therefore not establishing clear criteria of value contribution / return for each partner, can produce the following undesirable effects: (1) Disappointment regarding the return expectations of the network partners; (2) Underestimation of some proposals that may not generate direct income, or; (3) Specification of a model of revenue streams not commensurate with the cost structures of the partners.

In order to clarify the profit equation from a collaborative network context viewpoint, three complementary practices have been identified as highly relevant: (1) The establishing of channels to collect full information about the revenue generated; (2) The validation that the business is sustainable, and; (3) The creation of mechanisms for ensuring that the different partners achieve their return expectations (see Case 10 and Case 11 in Table 1).

Table 1. Case studies

Case	Area	Description
Case 1	Customer Interface	COOLCO, when using functional analysis to identify customer needs, starts from the "preserving food" concept, instead of the usual "refrigerator as machine" concept, and includes several partners of its value network related to the distribution of food.
Case 2	Customer Interface	In its analysis of customers needs, HINCO includes assembly, distribution, exhibition-sale and end users partners.
Case 3	Customer Interface	LIFTCO, incorporates into its innovation network technology centers and universities in order to identify new potential needs derived from the state-of-the-art technology.
Case 4	Value Proposition	CARCO, when addressing the business opportunities arising from the introduction of the electric car, incorporates within its value proposition specification process, customers and users, as well as partners from the insurance industry and charging stations.
Case 5	Value Proposition	HINCO is involved as a partner in the innovation network of its oven manufacturer customer, providing innovative solutions for the opening mechanism. In turn, the oven manufacturer participates in the innovation process of HINCO incorporating into the process a functional vision from the field of home appliances.
Case 6	Value Proposition	The introduction of a commercial product-service configurator, and the implementation of a production monitoring open system with its mold automotive supplier customers, allowed MACHCO, to greatly revalue its offer.
Case 7	Infrastructure Management	The commitment to offer a value proposition based on customization and highly flexible production systems has conditioned the participation of partners with high competences in the adaptation of production systems for mass customization during the business model innovation process of HINCO.
Case 8	Infrastructure Management	Committing oneself to, and launching a product that incorporates high-performance technology, requires the participation of technology centers and universities within the specification of resources in the new business model of RAILCO. The role in this network is twofold, the estimation of resources and time involved, as well the development of new product technology.
Case 9	Infrastructure Management	The need for advanced technical materials knowledge in the design of steel structures for COACHCO has been routed through one of the technology centers in its network. The role of this partner is the identification and management of new external partners not directly involved in the core group of the network.
Case 10	Profit Equation	VALCO, has the support of several technology centers for the task of specifying a new business model based on maintenance and remote diagnosis. Neither of these partners expects to have a stake in the new business.
Case 11	Profit Equation	LIFTCO, has based its new product development strategy on a long-term agreement with universities and technology centers. These partners do not benefit from the exploitation results of their technical developments. By contrast, within the same network, ELCO, manufacturer of elevation systems components, has an agreement with LIFTCO for sharing business results.

5 Conclusions

The results emerging out of the analysis of the empirical research cases developed and presented above, highlight the important role that collaborative networks can play in the process of business model innovation.

The findings presented could certainly help many organizations, especially those devoted to a systemic innovation approach, to set up collaborative networks to support their business model innovation process.

The development of general conceptual frameworks, methodologies and ICT tools that support a continuous process of opportunity discovery, innovation and implementation of new business models based on the collaboration among partners, is envisaged as a major challenge for future research.

References

1. Camarinha-Matos, L.M., Afsarmanesh, H., Ollus, M. (eds.): Methods and Tools for Collaborative Networked Organizations. Springer, New York (2008)
2. Osterwalder, A., Pigneur, Y.: Business Model Generation (2009) ISBN: 978-2-8399-0580-0
3. Freeman, C.: Networks of innovators: a synthesis of research issues. Research Policy 20(5) (1991)
4. Rothwell, R.: Successful industrial innovation: critical factors for the 1990s. R&D Management 22(3), 221–239 (1992)
5. Conway, S., Steward, F.: Managing and Shaping Innovation. Oxford Univ. Press, Oxford (2009)
6. Radjou, N.: Innovation Networks. A New Market Structure Will Revitalize Invention-To-Innovation Cycles. Forrester Research, June 17 (2004)
7. Dilk, C., Gleich, R., Wald, A.: State and development of innovation networks. Management decision 46(5), 691–701 (2008)
8. Arana, J., Berasategi, L., Aranburu, I.: Collaborative Innovation Networks Management in the Elevation Sector. In: eChallenges Conference, The Hague (2007)
9. Berasategi, L., Arana, J., Castellano, E.: Networked Innovation in Innovation Networks: A Home Appliances Case Study. In: 10th IFIP WG5.5 Working Conference on Virtual Enterprises, PRO-VE, Thessaloniki, pp. 3–12. Springer, Heidelberg (2009)
10. Chesbrough, H.: Open Innovation: The New Imperative for Creating and Profiting from Technology. Harvard Business School Press, Boston (2003)
11. Surowiecki, J.: The Wisdom of Crowds. Doubleday, Anchor (2004)
12. von Hippel, E.: Democratizing innovation. MIT Press, Cambridge (2005)
13. Hamel, G.: Leading the revolution. Harvard Business School Press, Boston (2000)
14. Mahadevan, B.: Business Models for Internet-based e-Commerce: An anatomy. California Management Review 42(4), 55–69 (2000)
15. Amit, R., Zott, C.: Value creation in e-business. Strategic Management Journal 22(6-7), 493–520 (2001)
16. Chesbrough, H., Rosenbloom, R.S.: The role of the business model in capturing value from innovation: evidence from Xerox Corporation's technology spin-off companies. Industrial and Corporate Change 11(3), 529–555 (2002)
17. Magretta, J.: Why Business Models Matter. Harvard Business Review 80(5), 86–92 (2002)
18. Yin, R.K.: Case Study Research, Design and Methods, 3rd edn. Sage Publications, Newbury Park (2002)

Stakeholder Analysis of a Platform and Ecosystem for Open Innovation in SMEs

Jan Zibuschka, Uwe Laufs, and Wolf Engelbach

Fraunhofer IAO,
Nobelstr. 12,
70569 Stuttgart, Germany
firstname.lastname@iao.fraunhofer.de

Abstract. In today's globalized economy, innovations become more and more crucial for the success of enterprises on the global markets. This article presents a reference architecture for an intermediary platform - and surrounding ecosystem - supporting the Open Innovation process in a network of SMEs and related stakeholders. Its main aim is to foster stakeholder dialogue in networked innovation management, but it also offers technical measures for data acquisition. We demonstrate business viability of the platform based on an analysis of involved stakeholders and their requirements.

Keywords: Intermediation, Open Innovation, Stakeholder Analysis, Platform.

1 Introduction

Innovations are becoming more and more crucial to the success of an enterprise due to the increasing competitiveness of the globalised economy. The development of new technologies, products and services offers an effective means to differentiate against competitors. However, to avoid leapfrogging and imitation, innovative enterprises need to be agile and flexible in bringing innovations to the market [1]. In the EU, SMEs' contribution to employment growth between 2002 and 2007 (84%) has been much larger than could be expected from their share in total employment (67%) [2]. Open Innovation [3] has been presented as a key paradigm to achieve a more agile innovation process. However, while the adoption of Open Innovation practices in SMEs is growing, it is much lower than in larger enterprises [4], depriving them of a central strategy for increased growth and competitiveness.

We aim to support SMEs by offering a platform enabling stakeholder dialogue and helping identify scenarios where coopetition or value network approaches involving several SMEs can lead to sustainable win-win situations [5]. In addition to innovative SMEs, the platform also addresses investors and innovation integrators.

The following section will give related work. Section 3 presents the overall approach and architecture of the platform, followed by a stakeholder analysis showing elicited requirements and how they are met by the platform design in section 4. Section 5 discusses advantages of our proposed architecture.

L.M. Camarinha-Matos et al. (Eds.): PRO-VE 2010, IFIP AICT 336, pp. 110–116, 2010.

2 Related Work

There have been several papers investigating the deployment of Web 2.0 technologies in the context of innovative SMEs and SME networks, such as the ones by Lindermann et al [6] as well as Blinn et al [7]. Those papers offer a requirements analysis and first steps in a design science approach, but no resulting artifact has been presented yet. Duin et al [8] present components for such a system, but do not integrate them or discuss their business value. We are not the first to use ontologies in innovation management; similar approaches are presented by Li et al [9].

We use a combination of social and semantic web to mitigate the chicken-egg effect. This is discussed in much more detail in [10]; however, we introduce it to innovation management and illustrate its value in this use case.

While existing approaches focus either on the participating SMEs, and supporting communications between them, capturing the knowledge of the non-executive workers, or capturing the users' knowledge, our approach integrates a wider set of stakeholders, discusses their requirements and presents a fitting reference architecture.

3 Architecture

Intermediaries in open innovation settings have several advantages, specifically for SMEs [11]. They have the potential to aggregate common and field-specific knowledge bases, as well as acceleration and standardization of innovation-related information exchange, and support in the formation of temporary virtual organizations [12]. Additionally, the hosted application service provider paradigm also shared by our web based intermediary platform is the most viable means of engaging SMEs in complex e-business activities in the area of innovation [13].

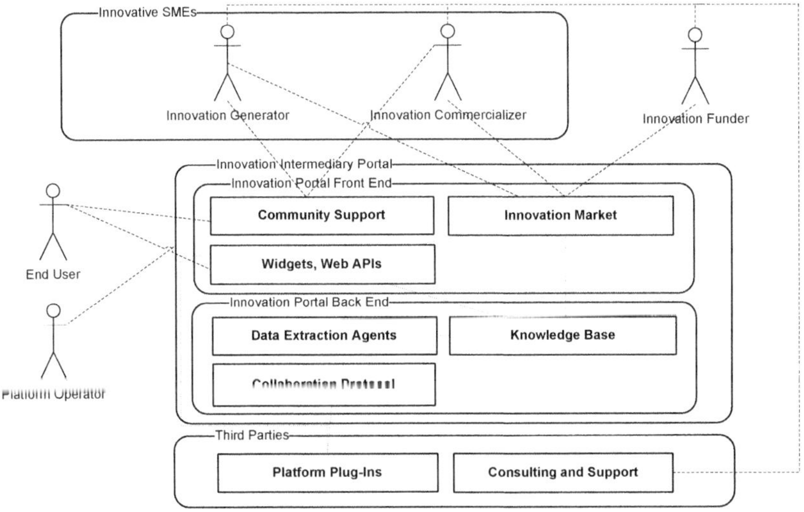

Fig. 1. Overview of System Structure and Stakeholders

An overview of the overall proposed architecture, data flows (dotted lines) and stakeholder involvement in use cases (dashed lines) is given in Figure 1. The main components of the envisioned core innovation intermediary platform are:

- A community portal, acting as the entry point, hosting **community support** services, such as discussion boards.
- A set of **agents** extracting information from available external data sources on the WWW or semantic web, such as software agents extracting information from publication databases, technology blogs, or semantic services on the internet of knowledge.
- Semantic **Knowledge Base** aggregating information from agents, user feedback, experiences from previous projects and data mining. This data will be the base for e.g. technology forecasting and decision support in different phases of network-centric innovation processes.
- **Widgets and Web APIs** around innovation management, such as feedback mechanisms for new or emerging products or innovative enterprises. Those components are the main source of input to the system besides the agents, are often based on earlier agent input, and provide feedback from users to fine-tune the system. Offering tools to users to motivate them to contribute in open innovation processes is discussed in some detail in [14].
- A **collaboration protocol** definition allowing collaboration tools implementing it to be able to become part of a temporary network of businesses or individuals within or beyond the platform. The portal-mode is aimed at small SMEs, leveraging a Software as a Service approach to lower the barriers they are facing when entering enterprise collaboration systems [13].
- The Web APIs, along with the collaboration protocol, form the basis for the extensible plug-in system enabling an ecosystem of **third party plug-ins** that may be integrated in the platform.

4 Stakeholder Analysis

Stakeholder analysis is widely used as a tool for gathering and evaluating comprehensive requirements in information system design [15]. The stakeholder analysis presented here is the result of interviews with representatives of all the identified stakeholder groups involved in the platform. It includes feedback from several SME, research institute and large industry partners commonly involved in Open Innovation processes. We followed the research paradigm of design science, seeing the design of the platform as a search process, which we steered be eliciting stakeholder feedback on designs early on. Several iterations of the design were presented to the stakeholders, and their feedback integrated. The design presented here can be seen as the core, which holds the main business value, and prevailed across all application fields.

We mainly base on stakeholder roles identified in [3], but also including users (customers, lead users and domain experts from the broader web population), as well as the platform operator of the intermediary design presented here, leading to the following roles: **Innovation Commercializer**, **Innovation Funder**, **Innovation**

Generator, **End User**, and **Platform Operator**. We note that roles are not exclusive, for example it is very viable that the platform operator is as well an Innovation Architect and an Innovation Commercializer. This is in line with the definition of the roles given in [3].

For our analysis, we use the stakeholder requirements dimensions identified by Kafenzis et al in their analysis of knowledge marketplaces [16], namely: A viable **revenue model** for the involved stakeholders, mitigation of the **chicken-egg problem** of getting all stakeholder groups to adopt the multi-sided platform at the same time, and **risk/trust** requirements related to the disclosure of potentially valuable intellectual property in the platform.

Each of these requirements dimensions will be discussed for every stakeholder, illustrating how concerns are addressed and value is created within the platform.

4.1 Innovation Commercializers

Innovation Commercializers are defined as innovation marketers or one-stop centres in [3]. Their main role is to act as middlemen in the commercialization of innovation, mediating between end users and innovation generators.

- **Revenue Model:** Innovation Commercializers benefit from participation in the platform by being able to pick and match innovation, while also having the opportunity to evaluate potentials of technologies due to the user feedback aggregated within the platform.
- **Chicken-Egg Problems:** Innovation Commercializers will be able to directly benefit from the platform, even if no innovation explorers are present, due to the semantic agents aggregating information on innovations from the web, providing information relevant in the commercialization process, such as extracted capabilities of innovative technologies.
- **Risk/Trust:** Innovation Commercializers need to make sure that the technologies or products the innovation generators are supplying meet their requirements. This is usually realized in the form of service level agreements, contractual obligations negotiated between the parties.

4.2 Innovation Generators

Innovation Generators are defined as innovation explorers, merchants, architects or missionaries in [3]. Their role is to provide innovations, and they are one of the main sources of innovations processed within the platform.

- **Revenue Model:** Innovation Generators can benefit from using the platform to identify uses for their innovations and commercialize them in cooperation with Innovation Commerzializers and Funders. Explorers and merchants are mainly supplying their innovative solutions, while architects can offer services to identify and integrate innovations made available to them by other participating enterprises via the platform. Missionaries can use the platform to influence product development to more closely match their vision.

- **Chicken-Egg Problems:** Innovation Generators are not dependent on other parties to benefit from the platform, as the coordination the platform offers between innovation generators in different fields and between explorers and architects creates value through product and service innovation. Depending on the quality of available information in the specific innovation domain, a certain amount of other interested users or own configuration will be necessary to leverage the platform.
- **Risk/Trust:** Innovation Generators need to protect their innovative intellectual property, and thus cannot accept an unregulated presentation of their ideas on the platform. The platform will offer processes that disclose relevant innovation generators to interested parties, but does not disclose the relevant innovations.

4.3 Innovation Funders

Are defined in [3] as either innovation investors or benefactors. They provide funding for innovative project, enabling other platform participants to e.g. spin out their innovations or acquire additional venture capital.

- **Revenue Model:** Innovation funders benefit from participation in the platform due to the combination of innovations with relevant user feedback supplied by the idea marketplace by being able to more precisely ex-ante valuate the innovations they are investing in.
- **Chicken-Egg Problems:** Innovation Funders will be able to directly benefit from the platform, even if no innovation explorers are present, due to the semantic agents aggregating information on innovations from the web, providing information that can already be used for technology forecasting and ex-ante evaluation of investments they may make outside of the platform.
- **Risk/Trust:** Of course, funding innovations is, as any venture funding, inherently risky. Beyond the aforementioned information, the platform itself can hardly mitigate this risk. It is expected that the platform will only be used for match-making between innovation funders and Innovation Generators or Commercializers, and not for e.g. an actual transfer of funds.

4.4 End Users

The main user groups that are expected to participate in the intermediary are early adopters/lead users of the relevant technologies providing feedback on their expectations and experiences, as well as domain experts offering their expertise in the ideas market.

- **Revenue Model:** End users are empowered to influence the development of new products and services. In addition, idea marketplaces often contain challenges where marketplace participants such as innovation commercializers offer rewards for the successful solving of specific problems. Also, innovation architects or commercializers may provide incentives such as coupons or early access to products to users providing valuable feedback.
- **Chicken-Egg Problems:** Attracting users is central to the success of the platform, and several measures have been taken to appeal to relevant user groups. The platform provides widgets that are directed at the users, helping them in visualizing

innovation-relevant facts while at the same time collecting their feedback. This measure also is aimed at multiplicators like technology blogs, which may employ such a widget to e.g. host a survey considering a specific innovation.
- **Risk/Trust:** A user providing an idea may want to protect it against misuse, such as by an enterprise not paying for his idea and not using it officially, but still acting on it. While this problem cannot be easily solved technologically, the platform should not encourage such behaviour.

4.5 Platform Operator

The platform operator may be a SME in one of the Open Innovation-related roles from [3], or an independent entity, e.g. a provider of a commercial idea marketplace.

- **Revenue Model:** The Platform Operator has several possibilities to monetarize the platform. He may offer advanced premium services to paying customers. He may present advertising to and data-mine the non-paying customers, especially in the context of the widget toolkits, but also in the context of the internal innovation management process, which may in turn form the basis for further decision support services offered to premium users. He may also offer consultancy to third parties developing services for the ecosystem.
- **Chicken-Egg Problems:** The platform provider is aided in the typical chicken-egg problem by the semantic technology. Of course, he still needs to find interested parties. Promoting the tool in SME networks (via individualized deployments) and multiplicators [17] (via widgets) is essential. To this end, several implementations in SME networks are planned.
- **Risk/Trust:** The platform operator needs to be a trusted partner for the participating SMEs. It should be made very clear what data is mined (e.g. data related to assessment of innovations) and what data isn't (e.g. information from specific innovation projects). If the Platform Operator is an involved SME itself, it needs to be trusted by its partners, and may want to consider a more federated deployment of the platform.

5 Conclusion

We presented an innovation intermediary platform design meeting elicited stakeholder requirements. Building on this, we demonstrated viable incentives and revenue models for all participants using a stakeholder analysis based on interviews and stakeholder interactions with prototypical components. We addressed the chicken-egg problem often troubling multi-sided platforms by employing a combination of semantic technologies and stakeholder feedback, providing some information as a working basis right away, allowing for involvement of all stakeholders in the fine-tuning of aggregated information, and generally meeting business requirements of Open Innovation stakeholders, specifically in the areas of instant usefulness of the platform and revenue opportunities.

References

1. Horii, R., Iwaisako, T.: Economic Growth with Imperfect Protection of Intellectual Property Rights. Journal of Economics 90, 45–85 (2007)
2. European Commission: First Section of the Annual Report on EU Small and Medium-sized Enterprises (2008)
3. Chesbrough, H.W.: The Era of Open Innovation. MIT Sloan management review 44, 35–41 (2003)
4. van de Vrande, V., de Jong, J.P., Vanhaverbeke, W., de Rochemont, M.: Open innovation in SMEs: Trends, motives and management challenges. Technovation 29, 423–437 (2009)
5. Hearn, G., Roodhouse, S., Blakey, J.: From value chain to value creating ecology. International Journal of Cultural Policy 13, 419–436 (2007)
6. Lindermann, N., Valcárcel, S., Schaarschmidt, M., von Kortzfleisch, H.: SME 2.0: Roadmap towards Web 2.0-Based Open Innovation in SME-Networks. In: Creativity and Innovation in Small and Medium-Sized Enterprises, pp. 28–41 (2009)
7. Blinn, N., Lindermann, N., Fäcks, K., Nüttgens, M.: Web 2.0 in SME Networks - A Design Science Approach Considering Multi-perspective Requirements. Value Creation in E-Business Management, 271–283 (2009).
8. Duin, H., Geven, A., Dittenberger, S., Tscheligi, M., Hesmer, A., Thoben, K.D.: A Toolset to Support the Early Stage of Innovation. Towards new challenges for Innovative management practices 2, 111–118 (2008)
9. Li, Y., Wang, J., Li, X., Zhao, W.: Design creativity in product innovation. The International Journal of Advanced Manufacturing Technology 33, 213–222 (2007)
10. Ankolekar, A., Krötzsch, M., Tran, T., Vrandecic, D.: The two cultures: Mashing up Web 2.0 and the Semantic Web. Web Semantics: Science, Services and Agents on the World Wide Web 6, 70–75 (2008)
11. Lichtenthaler, U., Ernst, H.: Intermediary Services in the Markets for Technology: Organizational Antecedents and Performance Consequences. Organization Studies 29, 1003–1035 (2008)
12. Carlsson, S., Corvello, V., Migliarese, P.: Enabling open innovation: Proposal of a framework supporting ICT and KMS implementation in web-based intermediaries. In: 17th European Conference on Information Systems, Verona, Italy, pp. 2218–2230 (2009)
13. Brown, D.H., Lockett, N.: E-business, innovation and SMEs: the significance of hosted services and firm aggregations. International Journal of Entrepreneurship and Innovation Management 7, 92–112 (2007)
14. von Hippel, E., Katz, R.: Shifting Innovation to Users via Toolkits. Management Science 48, 821–833 (2002)
15. Pouloudi, A.: Aspects of the stakeholder concept and their implications for information systems development. In: Proceedings of the 32nd Annual Hawaii International Conference on System Sciences, 1999, HICSS-32, p. 7030 (1999)
16. Kafentzis, K., Apostolou, D., Mentzas, G., Georgolios, P.: A Framework for Analysis and a Review of Knowledge Asset Marketplaces. Practical Aspects of Knowledge Management, 301–313 (2002)
17. Goldenberg, J., Han, S., Lehmann, D.R., Hong, J.W.: The Role of Hubs in the Adoption Process. Journal of Marketing 73, 1–13 (2009)

Linking Carbon Performance and Effectiveness of Supply Chains

Anicia Jaegler[1,2] and Patrick Burlat[1]

[1] Division Manufacturing and Computer Sciences, Ecole Nationale Supérieure des Mines de Saint-Etienne, 158 cours Fauriel, 42023 Cedex, Saint-Etienne, France
[2] Idrac Center of Applied Research, IDRAC International School of Management 47 rue Sergent Berthet, CP 607, 69258 Lyon Cedex, France
lagier-jaegler@emse.fr, anicia.jaegler@idraclyon.com, burlat@emse.fr

Abstract. Rendering the supply chain more eco-friendly is an innovative idea progressively adopted by industry. Consequently, our research focuses on the CO2 emissions along the supply chain due to freight energy use and storage. A supply chain approach by using a discrete event model was developed. Our proposed tool is able to model Re Order Point production management policy (ROP) and the main demand response strategy Make To Stock (MTS). In addition, the Overall Equipment Effectiveness indicator (OEE), the location of the firms and their types of products are modeled. This method is applied to mechanical and textile industries. The principle objectives of the study are twofold: develop a supply chain simulation benchmark and conduct pertinent experiments to improve green supply chain.

Keywords: simulation, carbon emissions, supply chain.

1 Introduction

Companies have been interested in supply chain management since the 1980s because of the benefit when collaborating downstream with suppliers and upstream with customers all along a chain. In 1987, the Bruntland report incorporated the definition of "development that meets the needs of present without compromising the ability of future generations to meet their own needs"[1]. This concept has begun to be adopted among many companies during the last few decades. Moreover, sustainability has become a way in which organizations distance themselves from the pack, with the resulting improvement in environmental and social factors and the advantage of reducing cost or even increasing competitiveness. The comprehensive and efficient design of supply chain still lacks some conceptual tools to understand the complex ties between industrial indicators (mostly inventory and delay) on one side, and the environmental impact of meeting their day to day needs on the other. For instance, Carrier (UTC group), a large cooler manufacturer, currently has dealt with a challenging design problem with some success. In another sector, textile, Zannier Group also looks for methodologies to design green supply chains. Roughly, their main problem is how to select suppliers so as to lessen environmental impact without adversely affecting industrial efficiency.

L.M. Camarinha-Matos et al. (Eds.): PRO-VE 2010, IFIP AICT 336, pp. 117–124, 2010.

To address part of these concrete issues, our paper studies how localization of suppliers influences both industrial and environmental performance within a supply chain. While inspired by these two real life industrial cases, our model encompasses other settings as well. It consists of three manufacturers operating along the same value stream, and addressing a final market. With this, three tier supply chains can be evaluated in term of CO_2 emissions. Different scenarios can be generated to compare these emissions. One of the objectives is to determine best practices to balance green performance and supply chain efficiency. To do so, discrete event simulation is used to benchmark supply chains composed of firms with various levels of efficiency, two types of products (depending on weight and bulk) and four different locales. We evaluate their resulting performances in terms of inventory levels, customer service, and CO_2 emissions due to storage and transportation.

The remainder of this paper is organized as follows: section 2 presents a brief state of the art on green supply chain modeling and simulation. Section 3 suggests a supply chain model. Section 4 explains the way an enterprise library of standard cases has been built to support the model. Section 5 discusses the configuration and the calibration of the simulator and explains the experimental approach. Section 6 shows the main results. Section 7 goes into further detail on these results and provides some managerial insights. Finally, the conclusion provides some perspectives on possible future research.

2 Green Supply Chain Modeling and Simulation: State of the Art

Increasingly, firms are pushed by their customers, shareholders and governments to adopt environmental measures. In addition, several authors show empirically that environmental and financial performances have a positive relationship [2]. Many papers have also indicated that it is financially beneficial for companies to adopt a green supply chain [3]. In addition, other articles also establish a link between green initiatives and increased competitiveness, but do not always have enough evidence to measure the importance [4].To assess performance, green indicators have been studied [5-7]. Several authors have selected relevant indicators [8]. Examples of indicators and their use in research are given in [9]. They agglomerate them in six groups according to activity in the supply chain. On top of that, an eco-efficiency analysis has been conducted [10]. In their study, the societal weighting factors used indicate that emissions, energy and raw materials consumption are the three principal factors (approximately 20% each). Additionally, air pollution emission accounts for 50% of all emissions. As most are aware, the greenhouse gas CO_2 is the measurement of reference. Furthermore, according to the Intergovernmental Panel on Climate Change (IPCC) the most important problem facing our planet is global warming with the resulting increase of CO_2 [11]. Based on the aforementioned literature, our research focuses on the CO_2 emissions along the supply chain.

One of the results of a survey was that supply chain availability, quality, and lower level of greenhouse gas emission (mostly CO2 emissions) are positively linked [12]. An article based on an analytical hierarchy process (AHP) proposed to evaluate a supply chain of an environmental point of view through a Delphi group of environmental experts [13]. But the AHP seems to have some drawbacks: there is no single hierarchy for most criteria, and human trials may bias the results. Another approach used a model called Interactive Selection Model which systemizes the processing steps before the implementation of AHP [14]. But all these studies rely on statistical analysis based on collected data. This restricts the cases and requires data of high quality. These limitations motivated us to propose another methodological approach based on a discrete event simulation model.

Simulation methods are gaining more and more importance both in research and industrial practices. Indeed, making it possible to explore policies and operating procedures is one of the greatest advantages of simulation [15]. This ability to evaluate "what if" scenarios with a variety of inputs makes simulation a useful technique for analyzing supply chains [16]. Some authors argue that the increasing popularity of simulation as a tool in supply chain management is due to its excellent capacity to evaluate system variation and interdependencies [17]. This enables a decision-maker to assess changes in part of the supply chain and visualize the impact of those changes on the other parts of the system, and ultimately on the efficiency of the entire supply chain. A recent study used the simulation to create a green supply chain [18]. The study is based on ideal conditions and the authors underlined that it could be interesting to make it more realistic.

Therefore studying a CO_2 indicator throughout a supply chain and demonstrating the changes with different management choices seems relevant. With these aims in mind, a data driven supply chain model is proposed here to analyze supply chains which differs by the choice of location of product of the players involved.

3 Supply Chain Conceptual Model

The proposed model consists in a raw material supplier, a supply chain composed of three enterprises, and a final customer. The raw material supplier is considered to have an infinite supply of stock. The final customer orders according to a stochastic external demand.

Between each enterprise, a delivery module will simulate transport and buffer storage due to delivery time amongst firms. It is composed of a transportation resource to be chosen and downstream and upstream inventory buffers that will be sized according to the frequency of delivery. A CO_2 Data collector is attached to the delivery modules.

Each enterprise is comprised of a Planning and Control System to manage procurements with a reorder point (ROP) rule, and synchronize the flows according to a Make to Stock (MTS) policy. The physical system is made of a reception module and two serial processes, transforming raw material (RM) into semi-finished goods (SFG) and SFG into finished goods (FG). These production processes are transfer lines where two product flows are simultaneously treated.

4 Enterprise Instance Collection

A library of enterprises has been built to provide the three tiers within the supply chain model. A consistent way to construct a realistic library was to utilize real manufacturing data to categorize production systems. In this article, the data came from the two industrial cases: Carrier and Zannier groups. More generally, in the model manufacturers have been classified according to three main attributes: Overall Equipment Effectiveness (OEE), localization and type of product.

4.1 Overall Equipment Effectiveness

An effectiveness level is used in the model as a metric to categorize the manufacturing systems. OEE is defined as follows: OEE = Availability × Performance × Quality. Availability is measured in amount of downtime. Performance is assessed in losses of speed. Finally, Quality is gauged by percentage of defects. The OEE indicator is widespread, easy to calculate for firms and offers a comprehensive evaluation of a production process. Furthermore, OEE can be embodied quite easily within simulation parameters like cadences, breakdowns, scrap rates and set up times. Many studies have provided OEE levels in various industrial sectors [19-20]. The typical world class manufacturing target tends to be approximately 90 % (data of Carrier).

4.2 Plant Locations and Types of Products

Shipment of raw materials, parts, and finished goods from one location to the next in a supply chain happens by truck, boat or plane. To calculate the CO_2 emissions, we need to model the shipping distance between two companies as well as estimate the weight and bulk of the manufactured product. Transport pollution types and levels are dependent on cargo weight, mode of transportation and distance travelled. Indeed, the unit of the CO_2 emissions is calculated in g per m² or ton-km.

First, the plant locations are defined by four areas representing the distance between two successive echelons of the supply chain: local (50km), regional (500km), continental (1600km) and global (8000km). In the transportation module, in case of delays, a speedy transportation mode is modeled. A standard or express transportation is automatically chosen whether the expected delivery date is attainable (including the transport time). Here, discrete event simulation provides a powerful tool to dynamically calculate the delays and trigger express transports with respect to the manufacturing parameters (set up, breakdowns, scraps items and inventory buffers).

Second, we have categorized products into four types according to the following attributes: heavy/light and bulky/small. Only the two extremes are studied: bulky/heavy and small/light. The others are linear combinations of the other two. Configuration 1 is typical of the mechanical industry, and will be illustrated by data from Carrier. The data of the product 1 are: 8,44 tones and 53,93 m². Configuration 2 is widespread in the textile industry and will be instanced with data from Zannier group. The data of product 2 are: 0,0002 tones and 0,0005 m².

For freight energy use, only the weight of the product and the number of kilometers between two firms are used. The French Agency of the Environment and the Energy Mastery (ADEME) provides the figures of CO_2 emissions per ton-km. Table 1 indicates the number of CO_2 emissions in gCO_2 equivalent per ton-km according to the transportation. For the local, regional and continental loci trucks are often used. Worldwide delivery employs container shipping. To explain more fully the figures from table 1 it is important to know that for local transportation, the trucks used are smaller than for the regional or continental shipping so the CO_2 emissions are higher per kg.km. When time is of the essence, planes are used and they emit more CO_2 during take-offs and landings than during the flight itself. Therefore, emissions per km are significantly higher for medium haul than long haul. The warehouse is considered as an industrial shed.

Table 1. CO_2 emissions due to the transportation according to the location and storage (uncertainty)

Location	gCO_2 equivalent per ton-km/ per m^2
Local (l)	145,10 (10%)
Regional (r) or Continental (c)	74,90 (10%)
Global (g)	37.68 (10%)
Express continental air freight	570 (20%)
Express global air freight	320 (20%)
Industrial shed	75 000 (50%)

5 Simulation Model and Calibration

5.1 Configuring Simulation

Before the start of the simulation, the supply chain needs to be configured. Adding a manufacturer type to the library entails (i) opting a locale (l, r, c and g), (ii) choosing a type of product (product classes 1 or 2). Therefore, the three tiers may have different profiles. These are picked up from the library. Then, the model is automatically formed. ARENA simulation software is used.

5.2 Simulation Characteristics

Final customers are modeled with a normal stochastic distribution with an average of 50 units, a standard deviation of 5 at an arrival frequency of once a day. Customer requests are directly transformed into delivery orders at the finished goods, following a Make To Stock policy. If enough finish goods are available, then delivery proceeds from stock. Otherwise, a delay is recorded in the case for local or regional destinations. If the order date is overdue, an express transportation is effectuated in the case for continental or global shipping. A buffer stock due to the delay of transportation is forecasted and another buffer is required for the lead-time between two transportations departures.

Production processes, set up and changeover times have been modeled using stochastic triangular distributions with variability. Availability is adjusted via breakdowns modeled by exponential functions representing mean times among failures and repairs and set up times. Performance is set via machines cadences. All these parameters are fixed to meet effectiveness target values, and correspond to average measures from our case studies. After having set these variables in an enterprise profile, command variables such as replenishment reorder points and batch sizes are calibrated. In our approach, the command variables have been calibrated so that the supply chains always meet the final demand without any delay. This means that extra inventory buffers have been sized to compensate for the distance between firms in the case of regional, continental and global locations. This calibration makes it possible to compare supply chains offering identical customers' performance, and to focus on CO_2 emissions.

Twenty simulation runs of 10 000 hours were performed for each configuration. Simulation campaigns are sufficiently numerous and long-term to overcome the system's transitional phase and seem to take account the possibility of most random phenomena.

6 Results of Simulation

128 configurations can be simulated because two types of product can be chosen and four locations can be designated. Discrete Mobile Centers method is used to categorize the locations with both transport and storage CO_2 emissions. Six classes were obtained (table 2).

Table 2. Location according to classes

class 1	**rgr, grl, glr, cgr, gll, ggr, lgl, grr, ggl, rcl**
class 2	rrg, gcg, cgg, grg, ggg, glg, lgg, llg, ccg, rgg
class 3	rcc, crc, clg, ccc, glc, lgc, grc, lcg, crg, rgc, llc, clc, rlc, lcc, lrc, rlg, rrc, rcg, lrg, gcc, cgc, ggc
class 4	rcr, gcl, cgl, grc, crr, ccl, rgl, lgr, cll, lcl, clr, lcr, crl, ccr
class 5	rrl, rlr, rrr, llr, rll, lrl, lrr
class 6	Lll

Figure 1 shows the distribution of 6 classes. Class 2 has the highest level for emissions due to storage and transportation. We find Xgg, gXg and XXg configuration for product 1. Class 3 presents fewer emissions than Class 2 and is composed of Xcc, cXc. Class 6 has the lowest level for both emissions with the 3 local configurations. Class 5 emits more according to storage than class 6 and is composed of configurations which are combinations of regional and local. The other classes 1, 4 are concentrated and are composed of regional or local in the last tier. If an analysis of product 2 were to be presented the same classification would be found with a decrease of an average of 10^5. The results of the products 3 and 4 are obtained with linear combinations.

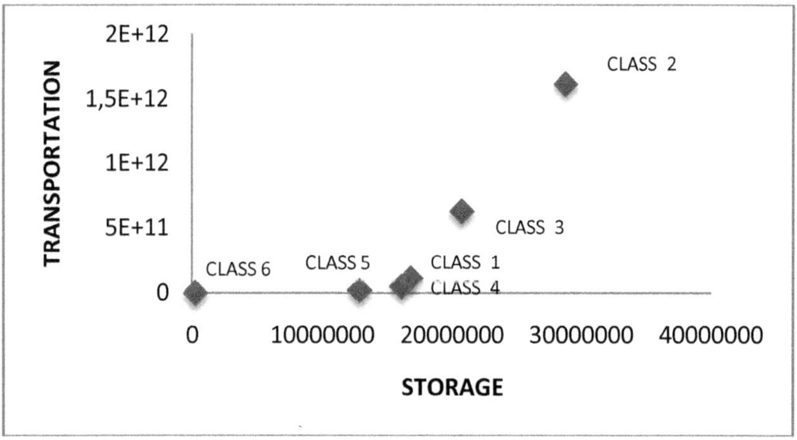

Fig. 1. Distribution of classes according to CO_2 emissions due to storage and transportation in kg CO_2 equivalent

7 Discussion and Managerial Implications

Simulation results highlight the following findings: according to the type of product, the CO_2 emissions could increase of a factor of 10^5 for storage and 10^4 for transportation. When the supply chain is homogeneous, the CO_2 emissions logically increase is in the order of 3 local, 3 regional, 3 continental, 3 global. If the supply chain is very heterogeneous (containing local and global locations), then the green performance degrades as the global locations are located further downstream the supply chain. Indeed, the second and also the last tier have to absorb the delays and so on of the upstream tier. Therefore there is more transportation required at the end of the supply chain as well as more express transportation. Generally, when the arrangement is heterogeneous, the more distant the location is downstream the more their CO_2 emissions increase: llr, llc, llg are emitting more CO_2 than lrl, lcl, lgl and than rll, cll, gll.

The results provide a basic guide for logistics partner selection helping to choose their supplier to optimize their green supply chain. While not obvious at first glance, it is crucial to pay attention to the position of the farthest link in the chain. Even if the first two locations are quite close, farther the end producer is from the final customer more the emissions increase.

8 Conclusion and Perspectives

In this paper a supply chain model is developed, implemented and assessed. Simulation is used to evaluate a wide variety of supply chain scenarios. This simulation tool has been tested in the case of a supply chain in a make to stock environment to produce two flows of products with two types of products and with four locations choices (local, regional, continental and global). Types of products affected the CO_2 emissions considerably. The effect was linear. Unexpectedly, last tier's locations have significantly influenced simulation results with global locales being the worst choice.

This brings an irksome question: in a green supply chain, would it be better in term of CO_2 emissions to have in place a local supplier with poor production management and high stocks, or a global supplier with world class results and lean inventories? Future work may focus on this question by decreasing the OEE performance of some tiers and fine tuning consequently the simulation parameters. A more complete view of the ecological performance of enterprises could be simulated.

References

1 Bruntland, G.: http://www.ecoresponsabilite.environnement.gouv.fr (05/26/2009)
2 King, A., Lenox, M.: Does it really pay to be green? An empirical study of firm environnmental and financial performance. The Journal of Industrial Ecology (2001)
3 Porter, M.E., Van der Linde, C.: Green and competitive: ending the stalemate. Harvard Business Review 73, 120 (1995)

4 Rao, P., Holt, D.: Do green supply chains lead to competitiveness and economic performance? International Journal of Operations & Production Management 25(9), 898–916 (2005)
5 Brent, A.C., Visser, J.K.: An environmental performance resource impact indicator for life cycle management in the manufacturing industry. Journal of Cleaner Production 13(6), 557–565 (2005)
6 Siracusa, G., Sterlini, S.E.: A new methodology to calculate the environnemental protection index. A case study applied to a company producing composite materials. Journal of Environmental Management 73, 275–284 (2004)
7 Srivastava, S.K.: Green supply-chain management: A state-of-the-art literature review. International Journal of Management Reviews 9(1), 53 (2007)
8 Scherpereel, C., et al.: Selecting Environmental Performance Indicators. Greener Management International (33), 97 (2001)
9 Tsoulfas, G.T., Pappis, C.P.: A model for supply chains environmental performance analysis and decision making. Journal of Cleaner Production 16(15), 1647–1657 (2008)
10 Saling, P., et al.: Eco-efficience analysis by BASF: the method. The International Journal of Life Cycle Assessment 7(4), 203–218 (2002)
11 Soytas, U., Sari, R.: Energy consumption, economic growth, and carbon emissions: Challenges faced by an EU candidate member. Ecological Economics 68(6), 1667–1675 (2009)
12 Vachon, S., Mao, Z.: Linking supply chain strength to sustainable development: a country-level analysis. Journal of Cleaner Production 16(15), 1552–1560 (2008)
13 Handfield, R., et al.: Applying environmental criteria to supplier assessment: A study in the application of the Analytical Hierarchy Process. European Journal of Operational Research 141(1), 70–87 (2002)
14 Kannan, G., et al.: Analysis and selection of green suppliers using interpretative structural modelling and analytic hierarchy process. International Journal of Management & Decision Making 9(2), 1 (2008)
15 Banks, J.: Handbook of Simulation: Principles, Methodology, Advances, Applications, and Pratice. John Wiley, New York (1998)
16 Hellström, J., Johnsson, M.: Using discrete-event simulation in supply chain planning. In: The 14th Annual Conference for NRL (2002)
17 Wyland, B., Buxton, K., Fuqua, B.: Simulating the supply chain. IIE Solutions 32(1), 37 (2000)
18 Hui, K., Spedding, T.A., Bainbridge, I., Taplin, D.M.: Creating a green supply chain: a simulation and a modeling approach. In: Sarkis, J. (ed.) Greening the supply chain, pp. 341–363. Springer, London (2006)
19 Ahmad, M.M., Dhafr, N.: Establishing and improving manufacturing performance measures. Robotics & Computer-Integrated Manufacturing 18, 171 (2002)
20 Muchiri, P., Pintelon, L.: Performance measurement using overall equipment effectiveness (OEE): literature review and practical application discussion. International Journal of Production Research 46(13), 3517–3535 (2008)

Methodology for Carbon Footprint in Forestry Findings and Ways of Improvement

Gabriel Chauvet[1,3], Jean-Luc Paris[1,2], Olivier Devise[1,2], and André Charles[4]

[1] CNRS – UMR 6158, LIMOS, F-63173 Aubière
firstname.name@ifma.fr
[2] Clermont Université – Institut Français de Mécanique Avancée, LIMOS, BP 10448, F-63000 Clermont-Ferrand
[3] CCI Tulle, Immeuble Consulaire du Puy-Pinçon, Av Dr Schweitzer, BP 30, F-19000 Tulle
[4] DRAAF Auvergne, Site de Marmilhat, F-63370 Lempdes

Abstract. Classic methodologies for carbon footprint are made for conventional companies or territories. None is well adapted for entire sectors or parts of sectors, which usually contain numerous and very different companies, such in the forestry. In this work, we proposed a methodology to count GHG emissions for forestry in a region, from harvest preparation to the entrance of industries. We divided forestry in three steps: harvesting, forwarding and transport, for which we listed each GHG emitting process. Then, we applied this methodology in the Auvergne region (FR) and estimated GHG emissions to bring one cubic meter of wood to the industry to an average of 4.7 kgCe; with each step (harvesting, forwarding and transport) causing around a third of it. We also estimated related emissions for different types of wood (timber, industrial wood and fuelwood) and finally, we proposed 32 recommendations to reduce GHG emissions in forestry.

Keywords: forestry, GHG, emissions, carbon, footprint, wood, forest.

1 Introduction

For many years, the Greenhouse effect has become one of the favorite talking points. Human used the Earth for ages, and now he starts to think about consequences. Many authorities already set objectives to reduce Greenhouse gases (GHG) emissions and every sector has to take actions for that. The work we present here, for the Auvergne (FR) DRAAF (Regional Management for Alimentation, Agriculture and Forest), consisted in adapting a Carbon Footprint method to a whole sector — the forestry — and to suggest different ways of reduction for its GHG emissions. We will first describe the context of the study, then the methodology we used to collect data and finally the results in Auvergne and the list of propositions we made.

L.M. Camarinha-Matos et al. (Eds.): PRO-VE 2010, IFIP AICT 336, pp. 125–132, 2010.

2 The Subject

2.1 The Context

The goal of this study was to propose a methodology to realize carbon footprints for forestry on a region scale. Thus, along financial and social considerations, the market would use the environmental factor to compare projects. To develop our approach, we took inspiration from the ADEME (French Environment and Energy Management Agency) methodology: the Bilan Carbone®. Unfortunately, the Bilan Carbone® is only adapted for conventional companies or territories, not for larger entities like the forestry in a region. We needed thereby to propose a methodology adapted to a whole sector, containing numerous and different companies. After having delimitated geographical and structural frames, we had to gather raw data and change it into carbon equivalent. Like in most of carbon footprint methodologies, we decided to estimate GHG emissions over one year of activity; in our application case it was 2008.

2.2 Bibliography

A lot of studies focus on carbon sequestration in the wood — e.g. the Carbofor project [1] in France — but much fewer deal with GHG emissions in forestry. However, several significant works have been carried out in some of the main forested countries (Sweden, Finland, Canada and the USA). For instance, Dimitris Athanassiadis worked on GHG emissions due to mechanized harvest in Sweden [2] and GHG emissions resulting from the manufacture of a forwarder [3]. There have been other studies on the subject; some were general [4] or more specific to one species or area [5-7]; but none really took in account all GHG emissions we wanted to study here (e.g. those of woodcutters using motor saw). Our work took up with listing each emitting activity, from harvest preparation to the entrance of industries (paper mills, sawmills, etc.). We proposed a generic method and applied it to the Auvergne region.

3 Methodology

3.1 Different Sectors

Some data on the forest were available at region organizations but, because of the parceling of the forest between owners, it was almost impossible to gather statistics over the whole forest using owners' data. Then, we decided to base our methodology on forestry companies, which are much fewer than forest owners and better referenced in institutions [8]. For commodity with statistics, instead of dealing with companies working in a region, we decided to deal with companies based in that region.

To ease data gathering and processing, we divided forestry in three sectors: (1) wood harvesting (mechanized or manual), (2) wood forwarding and (3) wood transport. Then, in each sector we listed every emitting activity:

Table 1. Emitting activities for each forestry sector

Mechanized harvesting/forwarding	Manual harvesting
Car use	Car use
Motor saws consumption	Motor saws consumption
Motor saws amortization[1]	Motor saws amortization
Others (computers, services, etc.)	Others (computers, services, etc.)
Machines consumption	
Machines amortization	**Transport**
Transport truck use	Truck consumption
Transport truck amortization	Truck amortization

Three different machines are used in forestry: the harvester (for harvesting), the forwarder (for forwarding) and the skidder (for forwarding). GHG emissions for these machines are the same type so we treated them the same way. We also included fuel consumption for cranes to (un)load logs on working sites. Concerning the transport part, a rough estimation stated besides emissions (e.g. for non-driver employees) as 25-30 times less important than trucks emissions, thus we neglected it. In this model, emissions from logging facilities are neglected as well, because they are frequently included in ETF[2] personal buildings, and so cannot be included in forestry emissions.

3.2 Data Gathering

The wood transport is different from other types of transport because there is usually no return load[3]: trucks are adapted to shapes and dimensions of wood pieces. Thus, general statistics on transport were useless and, to gather data, we used a note from FCBA (Forest, Cellulose, Construction-wood, Furniture) [9] and a recent national report [10] to get information on wood transport (type of trucks, GVWR[4], fuel consumption, use, etc.). For harvesting and forwarding, we based our statistics on two sources. Firstly, we used a survey on mechanization in Auvergne forestry [11], which gives us the annual mean time of utilization per type of machine. These values include

---

[1] The amortization of a product represents emissions due to its manufacture divided by the number of years it will last.

[2] ETF (Entrepeneurs de Travaux Forestiers) are, literally, "forestry contractors". They are self-employed workers who carry out forestry works (harvesting, forwarding, etc.) and usually work alone or in a small group of associates.

[3] In our case, we used a 60 % loaded rate, as logistics optimize routes.

[4] GVWR stands for Gross Vehicle Weight Rating.

all machines activities. Secondly, we collected data from different forestry professionals, forestry machines manufacturers and ETF's, including their machines ranges of work and productivities.

3.3 Emissions Factors

Once we had gathered data on all the emitting activities (productivity, loads, etc.), we needed to "turn them" into emissions. Moreover, as we decided to obtain simple and comparable results, it was necessary to express results with only one unit.

Consequently, as it is the most commonly accepted unit — notably in the Bilan Carbone® — we decided to use the kgCe, which stands for kilogram "Carbon equivalent". Using that, all GHG emissions would be expressed the same way.

In order to change raw data, such as fuel consumption, into kgCe emissions, we used values called emissions factors, which turn raw data into the GHG emissions they lead to. Most of the emissions factors we used were taken from the Emissions Factors Guide [12]; the others were adapted from IPCC (Intergovernmental Panel on Climate Change) issues. Here are the emissions factors (EF) we used the most:

Table 2. Most used emissions factors during the study

EF diesel oil	0.804 kgCe/l	EF various services	0.03 kgCe/€
EF premium gasoline	0.774 kgCe/l	EF machine manufacture	1.5 kgCe/kg
EF oil	0.82 kgCe/l	EF computer manufacture	350 kgCe/unit
EF car (with amort.)	58 gCe/km	EF institution employee	1.14 tCe/year

4 Findings

We decided to express emissions for each type of wood (industrial wood, timber, fuelwood) and the average wood in Auvergne (which was called "general"). Values varied with the proportion of mechanized harvest; the proportion of forwarding done with forwarders; the transport distance and the wood density. The harvesting/ forwarding information was adapted from the survey on mechanization in Auvergne forestry [8]. Table 3 presents the results.

We can notice that the distribution of emissions between sectors is clearly defined. Harvesting, forwarding and transport count for almost a third each, and the rest of it goes to cooperatives and institutions for which we used a single emission factor: the emissions per employee and per year. The harvesting proportion is a little less important than the two others because a large part of it is manual in the Auvergne region. It should be noted that we voluntarily excluded the emissions from roads construction because of its allocation particularities, but a rough estimation showed that they could represent substantial values for this type of activity.

Table 3. Estimation of emissions for each part of forestry, depending on the use of the wood and expressed in kgCe per cubic meter of wood

Sector	Wood	Type	Per m³ (kgCe)	%
Harvesting	General	Mean	1.178	24.9
	Industrial	57 % mechanized	1.204	22.6
	Timber	64 % mechanized	1.277	28.6
	Fuelwood	10 % mechanized	0.6797	20.6
Forwarding	General	Mean	1.675	35.4
	Industrial	81 % with forwarder	1.550	29.1
	Timber	20 % with forwarder	1.787	40.1
	Fuelwood	80 % with forwarder [5]	1.555	47.1
Transport	General	75 km	1.760	38.4
	Industrial	127.5 km	2.510	47.1
	Timber	70 km	1.333	29.9
	Fuelwood	30 km	1.003	30.4
Other (institutions, cooperatives)	General	/	0.0627	1.3
	Industrial	/	0.0627	1.2
	Timber	/	0.0627	1.4
	Fuelwood	/	0.0627	1.9
Total	General	/	**4.676**	100
	Industrial	/	**5.327**	100
	Timber	/	**4.460**	100
	Fuelwood	/	**3.300**	100

5 Ways of Improvement

Since GHG emissions are a recent issue, there haven't been a lot of actions already taken in this area. However, in the forestry sector, the ecological optimization is also economical (more than 75 % of emissions are due to fuel consumption by cars/trucks/machines); so some actions have been done to reduce emissions, but indirectly.

Several studies were conducted to determine if one action or another was ecologically relevant [13-16]. The Canadian organization FPInnovation worked on numerous possibilities to improve wood transport [17-22] and the AFOCEL (Forest Cellulose Association), in France, created several notes suggesting improvements in forestry. Based on these works and personal observations, we listed 32 propositions to reduce GHG emissions in forestry and we classified them according to their reduction potential and applicability.

[5] The rest is done with tractors. To estimate tractors emissions and productivity, we used skidders data which, considering the influence on results, can be assimilated to tractors ones.

Table 4. List of suggestions to reduce GHG emissions in forestry, and the relevance of their realization (+++ stands for the most relevant suggestions)

Suggestion	Relevance
Cable-forwarding in plain	++
Use of biofuels	+++
Piggy-back or fluvial transport	++
Transport of drier wood	++
Auto-inflating for tires	++
Better aerodynamic for trucks	+
Eco-drive for truck drivers	++
Use of larger forwarders for large operations	++
Centralizing for logistics	+++
Cooperative for trucking companies	+++
Give priority to depot on the bottom of sloping working sites	++
Use of hybrid or electric machines	++
Use of hybrid or electric trucks	++
Use of larger trucks	+++
Use of GPS to optimize machines moves	++
Adapting logging trucks to other freight	+++
Limit the crane transport on logging trucks	++
Change of machines to reduce consumption	++
Drive the machines on the road to reduce their transport	+++
Limit road transport by lengthening forwarding distances	+++
Create straighter forest roads	++
Give priority to specialized logging trucks	++
Limit the use of air-conditioner	+
Lower the size of trucks engines	+
Reduce trucks tare weight	+
Fuel-saving tires	++
Encourage industries to use wood closer to their site	+++
Encourage industries to hire ETF closer to forest sites	+
Grouping for manual ETF	+
Use the alternative methods for forwarding	+
Give priority to manual harvest	++
Use harwarders (harvester/forwarder)	+++

We can notice that the most important suggestions usually concern the transport or forestry as a whole. Finally, when we add all suggestions "realizable" on a close future, we can hope to cut emissions by 15 %. On a longer scale (several years), we can estimate reductions to be up to 25-30 % if professionals follow these suggestions.

6 Conclusion

Studies on carbon balances are more and more important in all types of activity. Unfortunately, some sectors cannot really carry out a carbon footprint because there isn't any adapted methodology yet. That is the case in forestry. In this article, we presented a simple methodology to obtain GHG emissions data for the process of a cubic meter of wood, depending on several parameters (transport distances, mechanized proportion, etc.).

Our methodology, by dividing steps and emitting activities in forestry, saves us from meeting the usual problems when the sector is fragmented. Our approach, by presenting results per cubic meter of wood, makes the comparisons easier. This study also led to 32 suggestions to reduce GHG emissions in forestry. Applied to the Auvergne region, this work estimated emissions due to forestry to an average of 4.7 kgCe per cubic meter, with each step (harvesting, forwarding and transport) causing around a third of it. We also could evaluate possible reductions in a close future to 15 %, and up to 30 % in several years if professionals follow our propositions.

References

1. Lousteau, D.: Séquestration de carbone dans les grands ecosystems forestiers en France. Quantification, spacialisation et impacts de différents scenarios climatiques et sylvicoles. INRA (2004)
2. Athanassiadis, D.: Energy consumption and exhaust emissions in mechanized timber harvesting operations in Sweden. In: The Science of the Total Environment (2000)
3. Athanassiadis, D., Lidestav, G., Nordfjell, T.: Energy use and emissions due to the manufacture of a forwarder. In: Resources, conservation and recycling (2001)
4. Lindholm, E.-L.: Energy use in Swedish Forestry an its Environmental impact. Licentiate thesis (2006)
5. Gaboury, S.: Evaluation du Bilan Carbone du boisement en épinettes noires de territories denudes québécois (2006)
6. Sonne E.: Greenhouse Gas Emissions from Forestry Operations: A life Cycle Assessment. Journal of Environmental Quality (2006)
7. Valleix B.: Exploitation forestière et sciage en Auvergne. DRAAF Auvergne (2006)
8. White, M.K., Gower, S.T., Ahl, D.E.: Life cycle inventories of roundwood production in northern Wisconsin: Inputs into an industrial forest carbon budget. In: Forest Ecology Management (2005)
9. Forcet M.: Emissions de CO_2 des poids lourds de transport de bois résultant de la poursuite des objectifs du Grenelle de l'Environnement. In: FCBA (2008)
10. Bourcet J., Bourget C., Danguy des Deserts, D.: Le transport du bois et sa logistique. MAP-MEEDAT (2008)
11. Promobois, A.: Enquete sur la mécanisation du secteur de l'exploitation forestière en Auvergne (2009)
12. ADEME: Emission Factors Guide. Version 5.0 (2007)
13. De Paul, M.-A., Bailly, M.: Le débardage par téléphérage est-il vraiment trop coûteux ? In: Forêt Wallone, vol. (84) (2006)
14. Fryk, J.: Swedish Forest Operation R&D for Maintained Competitiveness. Skogforsk (2004)

15. Nordfjell T., Athanassiadis D., Talbot B.: Fuel Consumption In Forwarders. International Journal of Forest Engineering 14(2) (2003)
16. Suvinen, A.: Economic Comparison of the Use of Tyres, Wheels Chains and Bogie Tracks for Timber Extraction. Croatian Journal of Forest Engineering (2006)
17. FPInnovation: Pneus à gonflages automatiques. In: Etudes de cas de transport de merchandises, vol. (25). FERIC (2006)
18. FPInnovation: Transporter plus en consommant moins, comparaison de la performance de deux moteurs de cylindrées différentes. FERIC (2006)
19. FPInnovation: Essais d'évaluation de measures visant à réduire la trainee aérodynamique. FERIC (2008)
20. FPInnovation: Des matériaux legers pour l'efficacité du carburant. Bulletin d'efficacité énergétique. FERIC (2008)
21. FPInnovation: Pneus économiseurs de carburant. Bulletin d'efficacité énergétique. FERIC (2008)
22. FPInnovation: Prochaine campagne Energotest^{MC}. FERIC (2009)

How IS Contribute to the Development of a Sustainable Procurement Policy

Oihab Allal-Chérif

Professor at BEM Bordeaux Management School France
680 Cours de le Liberation 33400 Talence France
oihab@bem.edu

Abstract. Sustainability has become a central corporate concern as well as a key factor of success in terms of both image and productivity. In turn, the procurement function is crucial to the definition and implementation of a sustainability policy. It drives a company's sourcing activities and connects its other functions (i.e. internal customers) to external suppliers and providers. IS, which have come under heavy criticism due to their negative environmental effects, can provide support services while also stimulating and disseminating sustainable purchase policies. The present study combines a literature review with a qualitative study to illustrate this emergence and show how IS can and will contribute to the development of corporate sustainable procurement policies. Using an exploratory approach and constructivist positioning, a "business forecasting" method is implemented to suggest a possible future for sustainable procurement management, along with a new role for IS. Towards this end, a scenario is co-constructed by 12 procurement function experts responding to questions about their customs and practices and talking about their experiences, the effects of the rising wave of environmentalism, the problems they face in implementing and optimizing IS and their professional. They also offer a few predictions and suggest new methods and modes of coordination. Procurement functions and IS departments work together to reduce the environmental footprint of technology and to exert greater influence on collaboration and teamwork by building an economic environment that is more viable and livable and also fairer.

Keywords: Procurement, IS, sustainability, collaboration, forecasting.

1 Introduction

The rapid generalization of management IS (IS) can be partially explained by such systems' ability to improve organizational performance, particularly as regards productivity. Inter alia, IS enable a leaner management of flows by reducing delays and errors, increasing reliability and responsiveness, eliminating undesirable tasks, optimizing resources and facilitating decision-making. Information and communications technology (ICT) is a pillar of corporate activity because it (1) embodies competitive advantage in and of itself thanks to its optimization of processes, introduction of a high-performance technological watch function and improvement in knowledge management, while also (2) contributing as a tool that creates indirect competitive advantage through, for instance, the development of new

L.M. Camarinha-Matos et al. (Eds.): PRO-VE 2010, IFIP AICT 336, pp. 133–141, 2010.

killer technologies. Professionals try to achieve savings at both the design and utilization levels. IS' sustainable performance is more than ever a challenge and an opportunity for IS departments. Yet sustainable performance must also overcome a number of hurdles, like how to ensure that IS that are increasingly complex, open and interdependent can function sustainably and provide top performance, or how to take advantage of innovations and new kinds of usage to create sustainable performance and value. The idea here is that the procurement function plays has a particularly significant role to play since it transforms intra-organizational IS into integrated management programs while using the Internet and inter-organizational tools as platforms for managing supply chains and supplier relationships. The present study therefore focuses on procurement functions' management and use of IS for sustainability purposes. The first section construes procurement management as a paragon of sustainability since it is this function that wields the action lever that is paramount in environmental, social and societal performance terms. A literature review then highlights procurement IS' role in improving performance. The second section describes a research protocol based on exploratory and constructivist approaches associating "business forecasting" and scenario methods. 12 business experts are interviewed according to a precise interview format and asked to differentiate between good and bad practice. The third section presents a number of predictions grounded in literature and discussions with experts.

2 IS Serving the Sustainable Procurement Function

Procurement management and IS management both play highly strategic roles in modern companies, particularly large multinationals. Thus, associating these two functions creates a powerful internal coalition capable of developing tools that will advance the cause of sustainability in its economic, ecological and social dimensions.

2.1 Procurement Mutates from Cost-Killing to Sustainable Value Creation

Little by little, large, vertical and very hierarchical firms have been replaced by horizontal organizations that concentrate on what they view as their core business. In turn, this has meant growing reliance on market-based actions [1]. The procurement function has developed naturally, with each outsourced activity giving birth to one or several new procurement portfolios. Relying on external providers for increasingly strategic tasks has created a need for highly qualified and specialized purchasers. The fact that the procurement functions are starting to account for a rising percentage of total corporate revenues has underpinned their growth and given them considerable power since each procurement decision can have major financial consequences [7]. The current crisis has further amplified this phenomenon. At the same time, it appears that after a period during which Procurement frantically sought to cut costs and rationalize processes, it now concentrates on things like technological watch, innovation, sustainability and global B2B marketing.

The emergence of networked companies has led to a redefinition of firms' relationship to their territories [16]. Right-sourcing and in-sourcing have started to replace outsourcing. As a solution, cooperative management of the procurement function is a budding success that very few companies had thought about before the crisis but which suddenly became much more popular afterwards. A cooperative management of the procurement function can only be found in a few very mature pioneering companies such as Schneider Electric, IBM or Nestlé. This method has gained many fans since the outbreak of the economic crisis and is being applied to both internal and external collaborations. Internally, it can materialize in the form of (1) synergies between Procurement and other functions such as Research and Development or Marketing, (2) decisions taken jointly by different hierarchical levels, and (3) cross-departmental project management run by procurement professionals. Externally, the main forms of a cooperative management of procurement are (1) the technological co-development or co-design of products in conjunction with suppliers, (2) innovation sponsoring, (3) the assisted piloting of production (4) the integration of IS, (5) the automation or externalization of some purchases, and (6) collaborative strategic management [2].

2.2 Inter-Organizational IS (IOIS) Serving the Procurement Function

Networks enable members to concentrate on their core business and externalize the rest of their activities. They organize interdependency relationships between multitudes of firms coordinate physical, financial and information flows and establish standards [4]. An e-procurement IS constitutes a platform that is specific to a network of purchasers and suppliers, enabling them to communicate and collaborate. It is a "virtual" and "decentralized" website where companies can meet and interact with one another and with partners such as IT service providers, consultants, banks, insurance companies or marketing firms. Unlike traditional markets, electronic markets make massive usage of ICT. They are more transparent, making it easier to create relationships among a large number of actors found anywhere in the world and helping people to obtain information more easily about companies, products, technologies or legislation.

Procurement IS are a response to researchers' "premonitions" or efforts to anticipate both changes in the relationships between actors operating in one and the same market as well as their strategic moves. Four criteria can be used to distinguish corporate networks: whether they have a high or low degree of specificity; and whether their logic is additive or complementary. In particular, additive logic consists of creating new competencies and resources by exploiting the competencies or resources of other companies cooperating within the same network. It is this pooling of complementary activities that helps to bolster the value chain of companies in a transactional network.

2.3 Procurement IS: Disputed Tools in the Service of Sustainability

ICT plays an increasingly important role in relationship between business and the ecosystem, or the human, social, geographic, urban and rural environment. IS departments can innovate and offer proposals that are decisive for the conservation of natural spaces while limiting consumption of energy or other resources and helping in the battle against global warming. More specifically, just measuring the "sustainability" of an economic activity requires very reliable and high performance IT tools. IS make it possible, for example, to find ways of measuring a product's pollutant substances or contribution to global warming in CO2 equivalency terms. This carbon footprint can be analyzed and lowered by means of an IS that will compare the company's environmental performances to current standards.

Above and beyond the purely financial dimension of cost-cutting facilitated by procurement IS, such IS also feature a very strong social dimension insofar as they help many employees to link up via a single platform where they can exchange information, conduct negotiations, share resources and collaborate on projects. This means that economic relations cannot be dissociated from social relations, some of whose components - particularly trust - influence commercial mechanisms and embody the principle that economic activities are first and foremost comprised of social activities and networks [9]. For companies to be able to work together, it is indispensable that the individuals representing them agree about the conditions of their collaboration and learn to know and trust one another.

3 "Business Forecasting" Associated with the Scenarios Method

To apprehend the future of procurement functions and discover how they might use IS to go green; it is worth scrutinizing the expectations and forecasts of the actors working in this function. The purpose here is to adopt a "global, rational and appropriation-oriented approach" that is action-oriented. After all, procurement function management should be part of a long-term vision based on a precise and subtle perception of weak signals announcing future developments, detected by persons immerged in the procurement sphere but who want to have some influence on and control over their business.

3.1 Exploratory Constructivist and Qualitative Methodology

Procurement IS are relatively new tools that have generated a more or less limited number of studies. Hence the idea of exploring such virtual technologies and their universe to try and deduce theories and predictions can be useful for the future. A polemic tone is adopted in the style of an appeal to researchers that they find a different way of conducting scientific research [6]. This can be contrasted with the hypothetical-deductive method where researchers explain phenomena based on postulates. In the present study, the starting point is the sum total of practices used by actors-experts offering their vision of a preferable future path for procurement IS. Grounded theory derives from an immersion in the empirical data that is associated with the theories covering the phenomena being observed. These are "new theories" that supplement existing theory and explain new situations.

Epistemological positioning has had a major influence on the way in which this study was run and on its findings. It is therefore important to clarify this positioning to justify the method chosen, validate the knowledge produced and legitimize the results obtained. A choice had to be made between the three epistemological stances proposed in literature: positivism; interpretivism; and constructivism [17]. More specifically, constructivism focuses on social interactions and processes as modes for explaining a reality [5] that is produced by the logical individual actors who are participating in it and which therefore undergoes permanent reconstruction. It is the rationality of action manifested by each of the actors involved in particular decisions - in this case, procurement processes - that will determine the reality of the situations in which they find themselves [8]. Individuals make constructions and are constructed by engaging in interactional phenomena together with other individuals, in a particular environment and using certain tools that force them to make choices.

3.2 Procurement Forecasts: Towards Structural and Functional Anticipation

The purpose of this article is to co-construct, according to rigorous principles, a shared representation of procurement IS' utilization within a procurement function management framework, thanks to viewpoints expressed by the dozen actor-experts whom we interviewed. Environmental changes can to some extent be predicted and even partially controlled. The desire to adopt a proactive attitude towards sustainability, i.e. to avoid being overwhelmed by rising environmentalism, is also an argument in favor of using business forecasting within this kind of framework. Prepared adaptation will always be much more effective than simply reacting to the unexpected.

The scenarios method is a good way of stimulating the imagination and reflection of selected experts since they are supposed to envision how the procurement function - construed as a complex set of professions, relationships and tools – might evolve towards a possible future. The role that IS play in the changing management of the procurement function, plus their role as levers of sustainable action will emerge naturally through these scenarios. The procurement professionals we interviewed accepted to co-construct a new profession for purchasers, based on virtual purchasers born out of the changes in their old profession and its convergence with others, characterized by new qualifications and kinds of expertise; new tools; and a markedly different behavior towards their organizations and the environment.

3.3 Selection of Business Experts and Interview Protocol

For this study, 12 purchasers and procurement managers were chosen from companies of varying sizes and different sectors. This diversity allowed for a sufficient heterogeneity of viewpoints to cover the lion's share of competencies, activities and responsibilities associated with the kinds of purchasers who were the object of analysis.

Table 1. Presentation of panel of procurement manager interviewees

Code	Function	Staff	Revenues	Sector
A1	Procurement Manager	400,000	€104 billion	IT
A2	Procurement Manager	270,000	€75 billion	Food
A3	IS/Procurement Manager	200,000	€19 billion	Electricity
A4	Procurement Director	120,000	€180 billion	Energy
A5	Procurement Manager	100,000	€40 billion	Machines
A6	Purchaser	70,000	€20 billion	Cosmetics
A7	Procurement Manager	55,000	€10 billion	Distribution
A8	Procurement Director	9,000	€5,1 billion	Telecoms
A9	Procurement Director	8,000	€2,5 billion	Textiles
A10	Procurement Director	1,400	€800 millions	Healthcare
A11	Managing Director	47	€200 millions	Equipment
A12	Managing Director	20	€50 millions	IT

To minimize subjectivity and interpretation effects, only half of these experts were previously known to the interviewers. The project's exploratory status and focus on the future was coherent with this approach since the business experts being interviewed would talk about their experiences, answer one another and communicate specific experiences relating to the themes in question. Thus, it is a whole research universe that was reconstructed, with the singularity of each background and viewpoint considered crucial in evaluating lines of questioning and potential hypotheses [15].

4 New Tools for a New Sustainable Procurement Policy

Since the 1990s, purchasers have often been assimilated with cost-killers. However, given the extreme pressure on prices and suppliers, what came out of this has been un-fair trade characterized by destabilization maneuvers and bargaining practices, along with highly compartmentalized management focused on independent profit centers and short-term profitability objectives.

4.1 The Rise of Sustainable e-Procurement: Managing Relations with Suppliers

As explained by A5, "In our business, the integration of suppliers has become fundamental. We must be humble and accept that our suppliers have business expertise that we lack. Our roadmap reprises our suppliers' roadmaps. Our future depends on them and our success depends on their success". In some sectors like automobiles, IT or aeronautics, the integration of suppliers is a key strategic axis for companies. The advent of concepts such as integrated SRM supplier relationship management and CRM customer relationship management illustrate this evolution. According to A2, "We understood that we could not make profits on our suppliers' backs but that we had to consider them as extensions of ourselves and treat them more fairly by valuing their talents". This has led to the advent of new and more cooperative or integrated forms of subcontracting featuring joint objectives and the pooling of knowledge, competencies and resources in a bid to achieve success through collective endeavor.

Thus, organizational proximity can be supplemented by electronic proximity in a way that cumulates or replaces inter-firm geographic proximity and helps companies to access their collective strengths and overcome individual weaknesses. As A8 says, purchasers "need to travel less but is completely utopian to imagine that they won't have to travel at all simply because they use IT. Clearly, this would be fantastic from a green perspective but the best thing in business is always a good handshake. We need to see our contacts otherwise than through the deformed prism of a webcam". Sustainable, responsible and ethical procurement will also become a standard applied to all sourcing activities, i.e. it will no longer be viewed as a more or less marginal aspect of procurement. Rather than economic calculation, it is the stability of partnerships, the stimulation of innovation and the development of new projects that become the priority. Unilateral decisions are no longer taken in the exclusive interest of one stage in the supply chain – what happens instead are joint decisions that help to consolidate the overall structure.

4.2 IS as Tools for Measuring, Analyzing and Aiding Sustainable Decisions

As a purchaser specialized in energy in a company that sells energy, A4 explains: "Energy is a question of who has the strongest nerves! We see sustainability as a key issue for both customers and suppliers, even as we try to act as trailblazers in this area to avoid being victimized by a green dictatorship. We have carried out an in-depth modification of our practices, products and internal and external relationships while also perfecting our measurement tools to achieve a broader and more precise vision of our environment". All of the purchasers interviewed in the present study were aware of very sudden changes that will occur over the next few years and sought to be the actors of this evolution rather than the victims.

Ecological performance contrasts with economic performance for most of the experts-actors we interviewed. A2 said, "We have signed the UN Global Compact and got all our suppliers to sign it but the day when I presented plans for auditing and supporting all of these suppliers in a sustainability drive, I was told that it costs too much so we didn't do anything concrete". Geographic IS (GIS) are a crucial issue in purchasers' decision-making and in the advent of a future-oriented vision of the markets. Such IS are currently evolving from production-related IT to collaborative information sharing IT used to manage communitarian projects and redevelop the territories where companies operate. More complete, transparent and higher quality information helps to rapidly raise awareness of problems associated with sustainability and enables an informed decision that should increase the effectiveness of the policies being implemented. For some purchasers, GIS are indispensable. A1 uses them every day to compare sites and markets worldwide, explaining that, "Without geographic tools, I couldn't do my work – almost nothing! All of my decisions are based on data that has been collected and analyzed by digital intelligence of this kind. Geographic IS help me to assess opportunities and risks and engage in impact studies, in particular in the sustainability arena". GIS also play an increasingly crucial role in choices about transportation, the localization of new structures and sourcing from new emerging country suppliers.

4.3 Re-establishing Customers and Partners' Trust in Procurement IS

The advent of sustainability in companies, materializing in ethical, fair and ecological trade, has changed the world and led to an in-depth modification of purchasers' behavior. The procurement function would appear to be a particularly apt area for applying the rules of sustainability, given its openness and actions on the external environment, and because of its interactions with other corporate functions. IS are used to optimize costs more than resources, and also to organize radical competition between suppliers instead of integrating them. As such, IS provoke mistrust and are associated with purchasers' destructive practices. According to A11, "When we suggest to our suppliers that they collaborate on new IT tools, how do you think that they are going to react? They'll be afraid! They don't want to be controlled by us and be subject to even more pressure than they already are". Companies are not credible when they pretend that they would like to collaborate. Indeed, the last five years have even seen a marked deterioration in trust levels.

With procurement IS, each firm can provide very specific know-how and make this available to other firms doing the same. The approach is the same as in a community of practices where everyone contributes to other members' wealth. At the same time, individuals are reluctant to share the things that create value for them without being guaranteed compensation that is at least equivalent. Power relationships are more accentuated in procurement IS than in traditional markets since perceptions of interactions are amplified by the virtual modes of communication that have replaced geographic proximity. Power wielded by some leads to domination over others who must then adopt a defensive posture and reject the tool that they sense their partners want to impose on them. The collective choice of a reliable IS reduces suspicion of partners who do not play by the rules and try to hide their failings by falsifying data. Securing information and ensuring its tracability is crucial in this respect.

5 Conclusion

People rely on procurement IS to construct, disseminate and pilot sustainable procurement policies and improve performance. Products and services that are labeled and have been guaranteed in codes of conduct can cost between 0 and 10% more. Purchasers are prepared to pay this to contribute to their company's good image, especially since such goods often offer better value for money than their more standard counterparts do. Green products remain harder to access, although depending on the sector in question, the relevant branches are becoming more identifiable. Among other tasks, purchasers must ensure that suppliers adhere to an industrial policy that is compatible with sustainability principles. For this, they increasingly rely on different sorts of procurement IS. The awareness is rising that collaboration comprises a major strategic issue enabling people to capitalize upon knowledge, ascertain joint projects and guarantee the financial viability of all commercial partners. Sustainable development has become a major organizational performance criterion, an indicator of the procurement function's maturity and a broadening of the concept of total quality. It involves the development of new digital collaborative platforms enabling practices that are more in line with the green mindset with which companies would like to associate their image.

References

1. Allal-Chérif, O.: An Economic Model for Electronic Marketplaces, Ph.D in Management Sciences (Mai 2007)
2. Allal-Chérif, O., Poissonnier, H., Maira, S.: Prospective du management de la fonction Achats: vers l'Acheteur Collaboratif. In: 10eme colloque prospective des métiers: le Management de Demain, Mars 16, ESSEC, Paris, Mars 16 (2010)
3. Allemand, S.: Le développement durable: au regard de la prospective du présent. L'Harmattan, Paris (2006)
4. Barringer, B., Harrisson, J.S.: Walking a tightrope: creating value through interorganizational relationships. Journal of Management 26(3) (2000)
5. Berger, P.L., Luckmann, T.: The social construction of reality. A treatise in the sociology of knowledge, Doubleday, New York (1966)

6. Dey, I.: Grounding Grounded Theory: Guidelines for Qualitative Inquiry. Kluwer, San Diego (1999)
7. Emiliani, M.L.: Business-to-business online auctions: key issues for procurement process improvement. Supply Chain Management 5(4) (2000)
8. Girin, J.: L'analyse empirique des situations de gestion. In: Martinet, A.C. (ed.), Épistémologies et Sciences de Gestion, Paris, Economica, pp. 141–182 (1990)
9. Granovetter, M.: Economic Action and Social Structure: the Concept of Embeddedness. American Journal of Sociology 91(3), 481–510 (1985)
10. Hamel, G., Prahalad, C.K.: The core competences of the corporation. In: Montgomery, C.A., Porter, M.E. (eds.) Strategy: seeking and securing a competitive advantage, pp. 277–299. Harvard Business School Press, Boston (1991)
11. Jarrosson, B.: Vers l'économie 2.0: du boulon au photon, Eyrolles (2009)
12. Miles, M.B., Huberman, A.M.: Analyse des données qualitatives, Éditions De Boeck (2003)
13. Miles, R.E., Snow, C.C.: Causes of Failure in Network Organizations. California Management Review 34(4), 53–72 (Summer 1992)
14. Quairel, F., Auberger, M.-N.: Management responsable et PME: Une relecture du concept de responsabilité sociétale de l'entreprise. La Revue des Sciences de Gestion, Direction et Gestion (211-212), 111–126 (2005)
15. Rogers, C.: The non directive method as a technic for social research. American Journal of Sociology 50(4), 279–283 (1945)
16. Veltz, P.: La mondialisation, villes et territoires, Puf, Paris (1996)
17. Wacheux, D.: Méthodes Qualitatives et Recherche en Gestion, Economica (1996)

Promoting Sustainability Awareness through Energy Engaged Virtual Communities of Construction Stakeholders

Yacine Rezgui, Ian E. Wilson, and Haijiang Li

School of Engineering, Cardiff University, Queen's Buildings, The Parade, CARDIFF, CF24 3AA, Wales, UK
RezguiY@cf.ac.uk, WilsonI@cf.ac.uk, LiH@cf.ac.uk

Abstract. Sustainability requires the engagement of every single constituent of the "building" product supply chain, from concept design to operation. The research explores ways of creating circles of impacts that bind building professionals, energy administrations, and citizens in a shared low carbon experience through a "one-stop-shop" Sustainable Construction Service Platform. The paper discusses awareness raising, stakeholders' engagement, technical requirements, and adoption and diffusion factors related to the platform. The research identifies the need to use advanced knowledge management functionality to leverage the value dimension of the proposed "one-stop-shop" service platform initiative.

Keywords: Sustainability, Construction, Awareness Raising, Communities of interest, Knowledge Management.

1 Introduction

Construction stakeholders involved in new or refurbishment projects are faced with: (a) complex legislation related to low carbon buildings, (b) a plethora of overlapping commercial tools supporting the process of delivering low carbon buildings, (c) numerous guidelines and documentation related to low carbon buildings, (d) an increasingly rigorous energy certification process, and (e) lack of clarity on types of financial assistance and eligibility criteria [1]. Furthermore, while a great deal of expertise already exists in detailing and constructing low-energy buildings, much of this expertise is fragmented and exists in various forms, with no real systematic means or mechanisms to assist construction stakeholders in their low carbon decision-making [2]. In this context, it is imperative to make building energy expertise widely available; in particular during the early design stages of a project, when most of the key decisions that impact on energy are made.

Existing knowledge on sustainability is multi-disciplinary (i.e. concerns various specialties, including Architecture, Heating, Ventilation, Air conditioning, Electricity, Plumbing). It involves architectural and engineering sciences applied to the lifecycle of a building project from concept design to demolition. Sustainability knowledge is available in the form of, and embedded in, text documents, spreadsheets, drawings,

L.M. Camarinha-Matos et al. (Eds.): PRO-VE 2010, IFIP AICT 336, pp. 142–148, 2010.

images, video, and in some cases, relational databases (e.g. product libraries). It has a strong "tacit" dimension. It can be nurtured (shared, enhanced, and transferred) through discussion forums, story telling, or simple knowledge enrichment techniques such as annotation. In fact, sustainability goals can only be achieved if shared and value-added relevant resources of knowledge and expertise inform construction activities.

The paper describes research conducted in the context of the SCrIPt project that aims to assist and improve the capacity of building professionals to offer effective energy and low carbon solutions and increase the demand for such solutions, while at the same time adopting energy reducing use patterns in buildings. This has the potential to pave the way to better educated, more engaged and energy responsible/responsive building professionals and citizens. The paper summarizes the methodology that underpins the research, followed by a review of related work. The 'Sustainable Building Portal' prototype demonstrator is then briefly discussed, followed by key recommendations that emerged from consultation. Finally, the paper concludes with directions for future work.

2 Methodology

The research is exploratory in nature; the overall aim is to answer the following research question: *Would construction stakeholders, organized into virtual communities, adopt and promote sustainability practices in projects by nurturing (sharing, creating, enriching, and transferring) sustainability knowledge through a Sustainable Construction Service Platform?*

The project first developed a prototype demonstrator that was then used as a guide to gather consensus on the requirements for such a "one-stop-shop" platform.

The industry consultation involved three workshops; the first two (Initial Scoping Workshop and Consensus Building Workshop) were hosted by the project partners. The third was hosted by the Low/Zero Carbon Hub in Wales (Wales LZC Hub) and was attended by the project partners. The Wales LZC Hub is a coalition that is supported by the Welsh Assembly Government (WAG), the building industry, housing, and voluntary sectors, to help meet WAG's target of making new buildings zero carbon from 2011 and to help Wales meet its goal of reducing carbon dioxide emissions by three per cent a year from 2011.

The findings from these workshops fed forward to a series of interviews and also to the recommendations for the proposed "one-stop-shop" Sustainable Construction Service Platform. The combined results from these methodological elements allowed the formulation of key recommendations for the full development of the platform.

3 Related Work

The construction sector is complex and is characterized by a culture and organizational environment that differentiate it from many other industrial sectors [3,4,5]. As reported in [6,7], many KM initiatives in construction have failed because they: (a) relied on employees' willingness to share knowledge, (b) completely overlooked the social dimension of KM, and (c) could not make sense of much of the data and information produced and managed by legacy software applications. The low take up and use of advanced ICT solutions for KM and information sharing in general are due to various issues including:

- Problems of technology adoption can have a negative effect on individual satisfaction with the team experience and performance. Conversely, when team members are able to deal with technology related challenges, high trust develops, which promotes a culture of knowledge sharing.
- Rather than widely sharing valuable knowledge, much of which is tacit and nurtured in small social networks, cultural restraints engender "silos" of isolated knowledge.
- Lack of awareness about the value in sharing knowledge and experiences.
- Off-the-shelf commercial solutions often fail to deliver as they tend neither to accommodate existing practices, nor to build on existing corporate solutions.
- KM solutions tend to lack flexibility and scalability as the needs of the organization and users evolve.
- A lack of shared language holding a common understanding of concepts across disciplines prevents effective communication and experience sharing.
- Access to knowledge from construction sites is essential, but restricted by technical limitations.
- Employees and organizations feel reluctant to share knowledge when security, confidentiality, and IPR concerns are not properly addressed.

These issues engender reluctance and a resistance to adopt technology [5], and hence access useful information and knowledge available electronically. Difficulty of use and lack of perceived usefulness of ICT solutions are also due to limited search facilities, information overload, etc., and, crucially, lack of structure in existing documents.

The authors analysed a number of relevant web sites to look at the nature of their content, including "sustainability", and ways to access the information. The chosen sites cover the construction sector, sustainable building, and/or low carbon issues [6].

Overall, whilst there is a plethora of information available regarding sustainable construction, there is no central location that appears to be authoritative and comprehensive. Also, the various portals operate on an "information push" basis and there is little or no attempt to capture the user experience. Moreover, on viewing these various sites in the process of searching for sustainable construction information there is a feeling of confusion and uncertainty in what constitutes the best and particularly the most important information.

4 The Sustainable Building Portal Demonstrator

The Sustainable Building Portal demonstrator, which takes a 'top-down' approach to information provision, aims at facilitating and structuring access to existing (codified and available in electronic form) sustainability knowledge. The portal aims to be

"Wales' official guide to help the construction industry minimize the impact of buildings on the environment" and to become the primary source of reference for sustainable construction. It comprises ten main sections covering: Sustainable Design; Costs & Financial Support; Legislation & Policy; Guides, Codes & Articles; Wales LZC Hub; Project Team; Training & Skills; Buildings & Infrastructure; Materials & Products; Research & Development.

A solution such as the Sustainable Building Portal, provided that it is widely used (becoming a pervasive process), constitutes a starting point for centralized information sharing, but much of the information required by many practitioners is either unavailable to them because they do not have the correct technical services – which may be due to cost limitations, inadequate ICT literacy, lack of training, etc. – or perhaps is buried in documents that, due to a lack of contextualization, do not appear to be relevant to them.

5 Results from the Consultation

The consultation confirmed the fact that sustainability knowledge in construction is fragmented, diverse, embedded in various documents, and developed in a non-concerted and integrated way across stakeholders, localities, regions, and countries. It also highlighted a number of issues related to the Sustainable Building Portal demonstrator, including:

- Lack of sharing, exploitation, and reuse of isolated sustainable practices and principles acquired through practice across the industry.
- Lack of education and awareness across key construction stakeholders and building end-users.
- Lack of easy access to structured sustainability information and knowledge.
- Unclear links between sustainability principles and current construction regulations and standards. In fact, there is no explicit statutory requirement that the Building Regulations should cover sustainability, even though many of the approved documents already do so. This is a substantial statutory barrier to progress on the sustainability of buildings.
- Uncertainty about the cost of sustainable solutions / technologies.

The notion of creating a "Map of Everything" emerged from the Wales LZC Hub workshop and was the most highly weighted issue of immediate concern to the delegates. The Sustainable Building Portal is perceived as a starting point for centralized information sharing, but what is required is a more complete KM solution, which incorporates a 'bottom-up' approach to sustainable construction information and thereby its transformation to knowledge.

The major themes that emerge from the fieldwork may be summarized according to three categories that inform recommendations for a fully workable solution: Information Requirements; Functionality/Services; Development and Management. These recommendations to ensure a feasible solution, and which will need to be addressed in a follow-up to this study, are as follows:

5.1 Information Requirements

- *Categorize information*: various different information types and topics need to be catered for, including regulations, legislation, research and innovation, etc.;
- *Cultivate and promote a shared perception of sustainable construction*: there is need for a consistent 'message' to mitigate uncertainty and to ensure that all stakeholders (including end users and consumers) are in concord;
- *Provide a reliable and verified repository of 'basics' information*: possibly the 'top 10 most important documents' to alleviate current misconceptions;
- *Dedicated and focused best practice information*: currently much of this information is very 'high level'; consider inclusion of (anonymous) failures;
- *Information and knowledge management and sharing*: there is a need to transform 'information' into knowledge, which requires advanced content management, and contextualization of new concepts;
- *Real data provision*: there is currently a lack of empirical data for Wales, including costs data, which need to be collected/disseminated across the sector;
- *Provide avenues of marketing, or connectors*: data and information regarding supply chain, products, etc. are required;
- *"Map of Everything"*: include this result from the Wales LZC Hub once it is completed, or a clearly visible link to it.

5.2 Functionality/Services

- *Smart Searching Facilities*: current searching methods are unsatisfactory and limited, treating documents as 'black boxes' and lacking filtering mechanisms.
- *Create and implement a Sustainable Construction Ontology*: this will act as the kernel of the portal and will support smarter functionality, including search engine;
- *User Profiling*: this service will enrich users' experiences, and will increase user adoption and participation;
- *News Service(s)*: including filtering, searching capabilities, and optional automatic news 'push' (notification) for key developments that are of direct interest to a particular user, with timely delivery. This will rely on both the Ontology and User Profiling;
- *Bi-directional channels for information sharing and enrichment*: incorporating wiki concepts and e-Forums. This will rely on both the Ontology and User Profiling;
- *Interface for shared tools/services*: free to use tools and potential for paid tools possibly on a rental basis. Also potentially include a tools register and/or tools market watch;
- *CPD facilities*: to potentially include educational tools such as live and/or interactive case studies, and with clear information on access to skills training programmes, educational courses, etc.
- *Value added tools and services*: "one-stop-shop" access to energy tools and related services, including Energy compliance checking tools.

5.3 Development and Management

- *Focus and scope*: the area under investigation is vast, and therefore requires a clear agreement of the ultimate aims and objectives, starting from an initial focus for concentration of development covering a manageable scope;
- *Iterative and Incremental Development*: a clear 'project plan' will be required to ensure that development proceeds according to a realistic timeframe. Initially doing one thing really well and subjecting it to testing and validation will ensure 'proof of concept' before proceeding to expand the platform. Requirements and functionality will almost inevitably change, but it is important to stick to the remit;
- *Continual consultation*: end-users should be involved in the development process from the beginning; industry consultation will provide real-world feedback;
- *Partners*: a broad spectrum of partners (whether 'full' partners or consultation partners) should be agreed as soon as possible. The full proposed platform will need expertise from various disciplines;
- *Define ownership*: this includes who pays for maintenance of the developed solution, and also addressing IPR issues;
- *Management team*: to manage information quality; moderation (e.g. on forums); continual management of information content to ensure accuracy, trustworthiness, and consistency;
- *Management plan*: to manage resources and financing; costs have to be addressed for maintenance of the platform after development and implementation – it may cost at least as much per year to run as to build, and it is essential that it is kept up to the minute to maintain credibility;
- *Marketing and Dissemination*: plans need to be implemented to ensure wide awareness raising and acceptance and use of the developed solution;
- *Involve intermediaries*: e.g. builders merchants and other communities of interest for those who do not frequently use/have access to the internet.

6 Conclusion

Several construction-related information portals have been commissioned and developed by various institutions at a UK (including Wales) and European level. The information published by these portals is in many cases redundant, overlapping, specialized, and not easy to locate and access [6]. Furthermore, these portals do not provide user friendly and effective knowledge management functionality, including smart search facilities, which results in low adoption from construction stakeholders.

Moreover, the research highlighted the fact that existing sustainability knowledge suffers from a number of problems, and that sustainability goals can only be achieved if shared and value-added relevant resources of knowledge and expertise inform construction activities. The research has clearly established the need for a number of requirements and user-centred services that can enhance the current Sustainable Building Portal. The Authors believe that the development of these services, in line with the industry consultation results, clearly defines the need for a fully workable version of the Sustainable Building Portal that can be developed using state-of-the-art Web 2.0 technologies, using a web service approach [9] underpinned by a low carbon ontology. A consortium has been put together, involving the Wales LZC Hub, BRE Wales, and Constructing Excellence in Wales, and a number of industrial organizations that took part in the consultation, to deliver the above upgraded version of the Sustainable Building Portal. This will be reported in follow-on publications.

References

[1] Rezgui, Y., Miles, J.C.: Exploring the potential of SME alliances in the construction sector, Construction Engineering and Management. Journal of the American Society of Civil Engineering (2010), 10.1061/(ASCE)CO.1943-7862.0000150

[2] Rezgui, Y.: Knowledge systems and value creation: An action research investigation. Industrial Management & Data Systems 107(2), 166–182 (2007)

[3] Wetherill, M., Rezgui, Y., Boddy, S., Cooper, G.S.: Intra- and interorganizational knowledge services to promote informed sustainability practices. Journal of Computing in Civil Engineering 21(2), 78–89 (2007)

[4] Boddy, S., Rezgui, Y., Cooper, G., Wetherill, M.: Computer integrated construction: A review and proposals for future directions. Advances in Engineering Software 38(10) (2007)

[5] Rezgui, Y.: Exploring Virtual Team-Working Effectiveness in the Construction Sector. Interacting with Computers 19(1), 96–112 (2007)

[6] Rezgui, Y., Wilson, I., Miles, J.C., Hopfe, C.J.: Federating information portals through an ontology-centered approach: A feasibility study. Advanced Engineering Informatics (2010), 10.1016/j.aei.2010.02.001

[7] Rezgui, Y., Hopfe, C.J., Vorakulpipat, C.: Generations of knowledge management in the architecture, engineering and construction industry: An evolutionary perspective. Advanced Engineering Informatics (Elsevier) (2010) 10.1016/j.aei.2009.12.001

[8] Vorakulpipat, C., Rezgui, Y., Hopfe, C.J.: Value Creating Construction Virtual Teams:A Case Study in the Construction Sector, Automation in Construction (Elsevier) (2009), 10.1016/j.autcon.2009.11.016

[9] Rezgui, Y.: Role-based service-oriented implementation of a virtual enterprise: A case study in the construction sector. Computers in Industry 58(1), 74–86 (2007)

Conceptualising Inventory Prepositioning in the Humanitarian Sector

Delia Richardson, Sander de Leeuw, and Iris F.A.Vis

VU University Amsterdam, De Boelelaan 1105, 1081HV Amsterdam, The Netherlands
drichardson@feweb.vu.nl

Abstract. Improved responsiveness to natural and man-made disasters is critical to saving lives and alleviating the suffering caused by such disasters. Emphasis on the design of the relief chain to reduce delivery time of relief inventory improves responsiveness. This is the essence of inventory pre-positioning (IPP). IPP is yet to be clearly defined; and the main factors affecting IPP decision-making need to be further discussed in the humanitarian literature. Quantitative factors such as costs usually take precedence over qualitative factors such as collaboration, infrastructure and others that can substantially impact IPP decisions. This can lead to ineffective decision-making in humanitarian organizations. This paper provides a definition of IPP by reviewing relevant literatures; and a conceptual framework of the main factors affecting IPP decision-making specific to the humanitarian sector, developed through desk reviews and observations.

Keywords: humanitarian logistics, inventory prepositioning, collaboration.

1 Introduction

Disasters destroy the very infrastructure of the country, affecting the social, financial, economic and physical structure of the society and can be triggered by natural, political and economic events (Whybark 2007). The least developed countries are very vulnerable to disasters (Kovacs and Spens 2007). The overarching aim of the humanitarian sector is to save lives, meet the basic needs of people and alleviate suffering (Van Wassenhove 2006), which is partly contingent on the speed of humanitarian response (Campbell et al 2008). Emphasis is in the humanitarian literature is often placed on response to disasters (Barbarosoglu et al 2004, Sheu 2007) however, effectiveness and efficiency of humanitarian logistics is improved with focus on preparative activities (Tomasini and Van Wassenhove 2009). Increasing the effectiveness of response is possible through positioning inventory in preparation for disasters, to reduce the procurement and transportation phase in response to disasters (Duran et al 2007). Stocks are strategically placed that when disasters occur the time between getting goods to the disaster area is greatly reduced (Duran et al 2007, Balcik and Beamon 2008). The positioning of inventory for relief purposes is termed inventory pre-positioning (IPP). IPP is also identified as improving the cost effectiveness of the relief chain (Balcik and Beamon 2008).

L.M. Camarinha-Matos et al. (Eds.): PRO-VE 2010, IFIP AICT 336, pp. 149–156, 2010.

IPP is yet to be consistently defined in the humanitarian literature. Duran et al (2007) argue that IPP consists of facility locations, inventory management and network design decisions, while Balcik and Beamon (2008) consider that IPP consists of facility location and inventory management decisions. Factors considered in IPP decisions are incomplete. Reference is often made to quantitative factors such as inventory, transportation and other costs (Barbarosoglu et al 2004), with very little attention being paid to qualitative issues such as difficulty with customs clearance, the impact of collaboration and coordination or unrest (Duran et al 2007). Thus the aim of this paper is to describe IPP which is done in two parts. First a definition of IPP encompassing key IPP decisions is presented, which lends to the second part, the development of a conceptual framework of the factors that affect these IPP decisions. Given the far reaching implications of collaboration on IPP special emphasis is placed on this as impacting the IPP decision. A desk review of the business and humanitarian literature forms the basis of the definition and decisions of IPP while the desk review of the humanitarian literature forms the basis of the framework of factors that affect IPP. The structure of the paper is such that section two provides a definition and description of IPP along with the key IPP decisions that need to be taken. Sections three discusses that factors that affect the IPP decisions as identified in section two. Section four concludes the article and discusses opportunities for further research.

2 Defining IPP in the Humanitarian Sector

There are three decisions commonly treated in studies related to IPP. These include facility location, identifying the most suitable place for inventory in the relief network; inventory management concerned with inventory policy decisions; and transportation decisions to transport inventory to where it is needed. These decisions are very often treated independently in the humanitarian literature (Jia et al 2007, Kapucu et al 2007, Barbarosoglu et al 2004). However, Balcik and Beamon (2008) and Duran et al (2007) in integrating facility location and inventory policy decisions showed improvements in the responsiveness of the relief supply chain, with a reduction in some associated costs. However, facility location, inventory management and transportation decisions all need to be integrated for the relief network to be truly effective and efficient, as transportation decisions at the strategic level directly affects facility location, facility capacity, and inventory policy decisions (Crainic et al 1997). Additionally, Balcik and Beamon (2008) and Duran et al (2007) did not consider factors deemed to be significant to any network design exercise such as operating costs (Chopra and Meindl 2004) and factors significant to the humanitarian sector such as the effect of customs regulations, road damage, collaboration and coordination in their model. We contend that these factors need to be considered in the design of effective and efficient relief networks. Below we present a working definition of IPP before briefly discussing the decisions that need to be integrated to realise improvements in disaster relief network. IPP is defined as:

> 'The strategic positioning of inventory in the relief network in preparation for disasters, through the integration of facility location, inventory management and transportation decisions, while taking into account the key factors affecting it, to improve the response and efficiency of the relief network.'

In *facility location* decisions (Table 1) the business literature considers the number, location, size and capacity of each facility in the network (Simchi-Levi et al 2008). These basic facility location decisions which are also applicable to the humanitarian sector need to be taken simultaneously. For example, the number of facilities impacts the spatial arrangement of facilities in the network, such that the greater the number of facilities the closer the facilities will be located. This in turn impacts on the capacity requirement of each facility, such that the greater the number of facilities the smaller the capacity of each facility. The location of each facility impacts on the distribution centre to be allocated to each facility.

Table 1. Facility location decisions

Decision	Description	Source
Number of facilities	The number of facilities in the network	Simchi-Levi et al 2008
Facility points	The location of each of the facilities	Jayaraman 1998
Capacity of facility	The available capacity of the facility	Chopra & Meindl 2004
Allocation	Allocating demand to facility locations	Chopra & Meindl 2004

In the business literature *inventory management decisions* (Table 2) include decisions on the type of inventory and inventory policy decisions (Zipkin 2000). The disaster for which the organisation is being prepared influences the choice of and the amount of inventory to be stored at each facility and the inventory policy. For instance, preparing for a cholera outbreak will require different inventory than preparing for and earthquake or storm which in turn impacts on inventory policy decisions.

Table 2. Inventory Management Decisions

Decision	Description	Source
Inventory types	Related to customer order decoupling point, and what inventory to store at each facility.	Hoekstra, S. and Romme 1992
Inventory policy	The target inventory levels; minimum and maximum inventory levels; stock replenishment policy; order quantity; safety stock levels; review policy; out of stock policy; shelf life policy	Zipkin 2000

Transportation decisions (Table 3) address transportation policy decisions of mode, route planning, scheduling and resource repositioning decisions (Crainic et al 1997).

Table 3. Transportation Decisions

Decision	Description	Source
Transportation policy	The number of vehicles, route planning, transportation mode, vehicle scheduling, resource repositioning	Crainic et al 1997, Melo et al 2009

The facility location, inventory management and transportation decisions discussed in this section are not unfamiliar to the decisions that need to be made in the business sector. In fact, this is the lens through which we view the relevant decisions in the humanitarian sector. The added value is in relating these decisions to the humanitarian sector to establish a definition of IPP and to further analyse the factors that affect IPP, the topic of discussion in the following section.

3 Framework of Factors Affecting Inventory Pre-positioning

The decisions that need to be made in IPP as presented in section two form the basis on which we develop the framework of factors that affect IPP decisions. Many factors can affect the design of a network (Schmidt and Wilhelm 2000), however, not many authors present a comprehensive framework taking into consideration quantitative as well as qualitative factors in their network design decisions (Schmidt and Wilhelm 2000, Candas and Kutanoglu 2001). This necessitates the development of a framework of factors specific to the humanitarian sector to facilitate sound IPP decision-making. Please refer to Figure 1 below for this framework.

Balcik and Beamon (2008) argue that the lack of financial resources inhibits organisations in pursuing the option of IPP and thus impacts on the *number of facilities* an organisation can have in its network. This also implies that logistics and facility costs can affect the number of facilities to be in the relief network, as financial resources are required to cover these costs. With demand forecasting, the more uncertain demand is, the greater the need to pool resources. This tends to reduce the number of facilities to be located in the relief network (Whybark 2007).

Several factors affect where to locate the facility, referred to here as *facility points*. According to Whybark (2007) determining facility points in the humanitarian sector can be influenced by logistics costs and the political environment. High transportation, warehousing and other overhead costs may make locating facilities in certain areas unattractive, whereas low facility costs tends to increase the attractiveness of certain locations. Some organisations choose certain facility points as they are rent free, sometimes to the neglect of additional transportation costs. Opportunities for collaboration and coordination amongst relief organisations counteracts high logistics costs (Balcik et al 2010) making it attractive for organisations to position inventory in close proximity to each other. Political factors such as conflicts, deteriorating security and piracy (Ashagabley 2006) can make certain areas unattractive as facility points due to the risk of imminent danger and theft. Forecasting demand affects the location of relief inventory, not solely because of the need to know where to locate inventory (Chang et al 2007), but also for the removal or rotation of supplies if disasters do not occur (Whybark 2007). Infrastructure includes easy access to major roads, other transportation infrastructure and ports (Jia et al 2009). Poor infrastructure signals difficulty in transportation and accessibility to the facility, reducing the attraction to that facility point. Macro-economic factors, such as high taxes at boarder crossing in Africa (Camm et al 1997) and high tariff barriers to products from Asia to Africa (Broadman 2007) can dissuade organisations from locating in such areas.

Available funds and logistics costs are limiting factors in the design of the relief network (Balcik and Beamon 2008) and thus can impact the *capacity of the facility*, as the organisation may not be able to afford a large facility. The ability to forecast demand allows for the synchronisation of supply and demand. The inability to achieve this synchronisation may necessitate having a larger facility as the organisation is unsure of inventory requirements and thus will keep more inventory in stock. Physical characteristics of inventory impact the capacity of the facility such that bulky products require larger facilities.

Collaboration and coordination amongst relief organisations is important to the *allocation* decision to avoid overlaps or gaps in response to disasters. The quality of infrastructure also affects allocation such that poor transport infrastructure between a facility and distribution centre may impact on the transportation mode. If the road access is poor then an organisation may opt to use air transport, a more costly, unattractive option for a high volume distribution centre, thus resulting in the facility being allocated to a different facility. The ability to forecast demand allows organisations to determine which facilities will be able to satisfy the need of each distribution centre.

The *inventory type* refers to whether the make to stock order is centrally or locally located, which is contingent on the strategy of the organisation. An organisation may decide to store generic, inexpensive inventory in its local facilities, placing the customer order decoupling point (CODP) closer to the beneficiary and it may decide to store more expensive inventory in a central facility, placing the CODP further upstream the relief supply chain.

For *inventory policy* decisions, demand forecasting and financial resources have been briefly addressed in the literature. Lodree and Taskin (2008) showed in their study of inventory policy for an imminent hurricane, that the inability to forecast demand directly impacts inventory policy as it is difficult to estimate inventory requirements due to the disaster. Balcik and Beamon (2008) showed that a larger pre-disaster budget allowed for the storage of more relief inventory, which improved the responsiveness of the relief supply chain. Greater supply lead times may encourage facilities to opt for ordering smaller batches of inventory at more frequent intervals to have more inventory in the pipeline or at the facility, thus affecting the inventory policy. Product characteristics such as the shelf life affect how long a product can be stored and the policy for disposal if it becomes obsolete.

Transportation policy is affected by the availability and quality of ports, roads, other major thoroughfares (Kapucu et al 2007), and bureaucratic customs procedures (Ashagbley 2006) as these impact on the transportation mode of choice, thus also impacting routing and scheduling decisions. Collaboration and coordination amongst organisations in sharing distribution resources also impacts the transportation policy as organisations pool resources (Balcik 2010). Available financial resources impact the decision to outsource distribution and also vehicular fleet composition. Duran et al (2007) showed that a lack of financial resources caused CARE to use third party logistics providers for goods distribution. The availability of vehicles in the fleet impacts resource positioning and vehicle scheduling decisions. The uncertainty of demand creates problems in scheduling, routing and the use or resources as the need for inventory is unknown (Chang et al 2007). Conflicts, piracy and general safety (Ashagabley 2006) impacts the mode of transportation and route planning, as organisaions may not use routes that are deemed unsafe. The physical characteristics of inventory affect the mode of transportation, for example it may be more effective to ship rather than air freight bulky products.

Decisions	Factors affecting the decision
Number of facilities	• Logistics and facility costs • Availability of financial resources • Potential to accurately forecast demand
Facility points	• Potential for collaboration and coordination • Political environment (safety and security) • Quality of infrastructure • Logistics and facility costs • Impact of macro-economic factors • Potential to accurately forecast demand
Capacity of facility	• Logistics and facility costs • Availability of financial resources • Potential to accurately forecast demand • Supply lead time • Product characteristics
Allocation	• Potential for collaboration and coordination • Quality of infrastructure • Logistics and facility costs • Potential to accurately forecast demand
Inventory type	• Strategic
Inventory policy	• Availability of financial resources • Potential to accurately forecast demand • Supply lead time • Product characteristics
Transportation policy	• Quality of infrastructure • Potential for collaboration and coordination • Political environment (safety and security) • Logistics and facility costs • Availability of financial resources • Potential to accurately forecast demand • Physical characteristics

Fig. 1. Conceptual Framework of factors affecting IPP decisions

This discussion has identified various factors that affect decisions relevant to IPP. Some factors have shown to have a greater range of influence than others, influencing more decisions than other factors. We also envisage that some factors are able to influence a range of factors which in turn affects a range of decisions. One such factor is the potential for collaboration and coordination, which has the potential to impact factors such as logistics and facility costs, financial resources, the impact of macro-economic factors, supply lead time, the quality of infrastructure as well as the safety and security of personnel and inventory. Relief organisations that collaborate can do so in the context of warehousing, transportation and inventory. According to Balcik et al (2010) organisations that collaborate can share transportation resources leading to reduced transportation cost; and procure jointly, facilitating a reduction in the cost of inventory with the purchase of larger quantities. They further argue that collaborating on long-haul shipments allows for reductions in freight costs and time savings in handling customs procedures. Shared warehousing also has the potential to improve inventory turnover. In the context of the factors that affect IPP decisions it is evident that collaboration among relief organisations reduces the negative effect of the majority of the factors that affect IPP. These include reducing logistics and facility costs, while simultaneously reducing the need for financial resources and reducing supply lead times as a result of the collaborative power of the various organisations working together. Collaboration and coordination also extends to pooled warehousing in locations that are probably less likely to be affected by poor infrastructure, safety and security issues, high taxes or problems at border crossings as experienced in some areas in Africa.

4 Conclusion

The overarching objective of the paper was to give form to inventory pre-positioning in the humanitarian literature through providing a definition of IPP and identifying and discussing the factors that affect these decisions in the humanitarian sector. In section two we formulated this definition and identified that these decisions must be considered in an integrated manner to increase the effectiveness and efficiency of the relief supply chain. The factors that affect these decisions were identified and discussed in section three, emphasizing the potential to collaborate as impacting on many of the other factors which affect IPP decisions. The culmination of the paper is the framework of decisions in IPP and the factors that affect IPP, which can be directly applied in the process of making IPP decisions.

Avenues of further research include the empirical validation of the definition of IPP through the validation of the decisions that need to be taken in IPP; the validation of the factors identified as affecting IPP decisions, through the use of case studies and expert interviews. The research can then be extended to investigate the relationships that exist amongst the various factors affecting IPP, paying particular attention to the impact of potential to collaborate on the other factors as previously discussed. Additionally, now that this paper has positioned the view point of the definition of IPP and the factors that affect it elements of the framework once further validated can be used to develop solution approaches appropriate to deal with these factors.

References

1. Ashagbley, V.: Robust Supply Chains for Humanitarian Aid in Africa. Zaragoza Logistics Center, Zaragoza (2006)
2. Balcik, B., Beamon, B.M.: Facility Location in Humanitarian Relief. Int. J. of Logistics Research and Application 11(2), 101–121 (2008)
3. Barbarosoglu, G., Arda, A.: A Two-stage stochastic programming framework for transportation planning in disaster response. Journal of Operations Research Society 55, 43–53 (2004)
4. Balcik, B., Beamon, B.M., Krejci, C.C., Muramatsu, K.M., Ramirez, M.: Coordination in humanitarian relief chains:Practices, challenges and opportunities. International Journal Production Economics 126, 22–34 (2010)

5. Broadman, H.G.: Africa's Silk Road. The World Bank, Washington (2007)
6. Camm, J.D., Chorman, T.E., Dull, F.A., Evans, J.R., Sweeney, D.J., Wegryn, G.W.: Blending OR/MS, Judgement, and GIS: Restructuring P&G's Supply Chain. Interfaces 27(1), 128–142 (1997)
7. Campbell, A.M., Vanderbussche, D., Hermann, W.: Routing for Relief Efforts. Transportation Science 42(2), 127–145 (2008)
8. Candas, M.F., Kutanoglu, E.: Benefits of considering inventory in service parts logistics network design problems with time-based service constraints. IIE Transactions 39, 159–176 (2007)
9. Chang, M., Tseng, Y., Chen, J.: A scenario planning approach for the flood emergency logistics preparation problem under uncertainty. Transportation Research Part E 43, 737–754 (2007)
10. Chopra, S., Meindl, P.: Supply Chain Management, Strategy, Planning, and Operations, 2nd edn. Pearson Education International, USA (2004)
11. Crainic, T.G., Laporte, G.: Planning models for freight transportation. European Journal of Operational Research 97, 409–438 (1997)
12. Duran, S., Guiterrez, M., Keskinocak, P.: Pre-Positioning of Emergency Items Worldwide for CARE International. In: INFORMS annual meeting, USA (2007)
13. Hoekstra, S., Romme, J.: Integral logistic structures - developing customer-oriented goods flow. McGraw Hill, London (1992)
14. Jayaraman, V.: Transportation, facility location and inventory issues in distribution network design An investigation. International Journal of Operations & Production Management 18(5), 471–494 (1998)
15. Jia, H., Ordonez, F., Dessouky, M.: A Modeling Framework for Facility Location of Medical Services for Large-Scale Emergencies. IIE Transactions 39(1), 41–55 (2007)
16. Kapucu, N., Lawther, W., Pattison, S.: Logistics and Staging Areas in Managing Disasters and Emergencies. Journal of Homeland Security and Emergency Management 4(2-3) (2007)
17. Kovacs, G., Spens, K.: Humanitarian logistics in disaster relief operations. International Journal of Physical Distribution & Logistics Management 37(2), 99–114 (2007)
18. Lodree, E.J., Taskin, S.: An insurance risk management framework for disaster relief & supply chain disruption inventory planning. Journal of the Operational Research Society 59(5), 674–684 (2008)
19. Melo, M.T., Nickel, S.: Saldanha-da-Gama: Facility location and supply chain management – A review. European Journal of Operational Research 196(2), 401–412 (2008)
20. Schimdt, G., Wilhelm, W.: Strategic, tactical and operational decisions in multi-national logistics networks: a review and discussion of modelling issues. International Journal of Production Research 38(7), 1501–1523 (2000)
21. Sheu, J.: An emergency logistics distribution approach for quick response to urgent demand in disasters. Transportation Research Part E 43, 687–709 (2007)
22. Simchi-Levi, D., Kaminsky, P., Simchi-Levi, E.: Designing and Managing the Supply Chain Concepts, Strategies and Case Studies, 3rd edn. McGraw Hill, USA (2008)
23. Tomasini, R., Van Wassenhove, L.: Humanitarian Logistics. Palgrave Macmillian, UK (2009)
24. Van Wassenhove, L.: Blackett Memorial Lecture: Humanitarian aid logistics: supply chain management in high gear. Journal of the Operational Research Society 57, 475–489 (2006)
25. Whybark, D.C.: Issues in managing disaster relief inventories. International Journal of Production Economics 108, 228–235 (2007)
26. Zipkin, P.: Foundation of Inventory Management. McGraw Hill, USA (2000)

Collaboration Networks Involving Humanitarian Organisations – Particular Problems for a Particular Sector

Aurélie Charles[1], Matthieu Lauras[1,2], and Rolando Tomasini[3]

[1] Université de Toulouse – Mine Albi, Campus Jarlard, Route de Teillet, 81013 Albi CT Cedex 09, France
[2] Toulouse Business School, 20, Bd Lascrosses - BP 7010 - 31068 Toulouse Cedex 7, France
[3] INSEAD, Bd de Constance, 77300 Fontainebleau, France
{aurelie.charles,matthieu.lauras}@mines-albi.fr,
rolando.tomasini@insead.edu

Abstract. There is no relief operation similar to another. Nature, number and incentives of stakeholders vary tremendously from one operation to another, and so do the collaboration modes. One thing is always true thought: for each disaster, collaboration networks are implemented on both global and local levels. Yet, lack of collaboration is often underlined as a major weakness of humanitarians. Practitioners have therefore recently focused on this issue in order to find improvement paths. This paper, using a review of existing academic literature as well as reports published by practitioners, illustrates how collaborative networks are designed in the humanitarian sector. A panorama of existing collaboration networks during and in-between relief operations is presented. Barriers and enablers to implement them are made explicit. Two frameworks are finally proposed to better understand collaboration modes at a local level on one hand, and collaboration protocols at a global level on the other hand.

Keywords: Humanitarian, Disaster Relief, Collaborative Networks, Collaboration, Coordination.

1 Introduction

Every year, disasters are impacting more than 210 million people, and year after year, their frequency increases. So is the number of Non Governmental Organizations (NGOs) created to help those in need before or after a disaster. Ten years ago, most of the time, humanitarian actors in the field had a really limited knowledge of what others were doing. This kind of knowledge is still very difficult to gather and spread, especially because there are so many stakeholders involved. Yet, many improvements have been made recently, driven both by field necessities and by humanitarian organizations' professionalization. This article aims at illustrating and analysing the collaboration networks that are implemented in the context of humanitarian aid. As humanitarian organisation work as well between disasters than on the field, during relief operations, we will also illustrate and analyse the collaboration networks that are build on a global, long term perspective. This picture of the actual situation is a first, but needed step

L.M. Camarinha-Matos et al. (Eds.): PRO-VE 2010, IFIP AICT 336, pp. 157–165, 2010.

before any proposal of improvement. It complements the recent research applications in the humanitarian sector, which usually give priority to more technical approaches, without much consideration of their applicability. [1] Various factors, such as local capacity or nature and number of stakeholders involved are influencing the design of collaboration networks in such a difficult context. Concretely, the paper proposes an overview of practices in terms of collaboration networks in a context of relief operations, both at local and global levels. For each level, a framework is developed in order to classify collaboration modes, means and applicability.

2 Collaboration Networks on a Local Level in the Context of Relief Operations

2.1 Overview of Existing Modes

On a local level, we call collaboration network "the system-wide structure of inter-organisational coordination during humanitarian operations."[2] Donini [3] has identified three categories of collaboration in the context of relief operations:

- *Coordination by command* where there is central coordination; agreement on responsibilities and objectives; and common territorial areas of responsibility.
- *Coordination by consensus* where organizations have access to compatible or shared communications equipment, liaison and interagency meetings and pre-mission assessments.
- *Coordination by default* includes routine contact between desk officers and civil military operations centers.

We will use those definitions, but detail the conditions under which they can be implemented or not. Figure 1 shows a simplified picture of usual collaboration modes. Many stakeholders with various incentives are involved in operations (see figure 2). And the bigger the disaster, the bigger the number of NGOs that will have sufficient funding to participate to the humanitarian response... and the more difficult coordination will be. The 2004 Indian Ocean Tsunami is one example of the chaos that can happen when auto-regulation does not take place. Many factors, from the magnitude of the disaster to the presence of many tourists "generated massive media attention which in turn prompted an inordinate public response to donate money as people felt a moral obligation to help. There was also an unprecedented wave of governments' attention which was not necessarily free of a political agenda." [4]

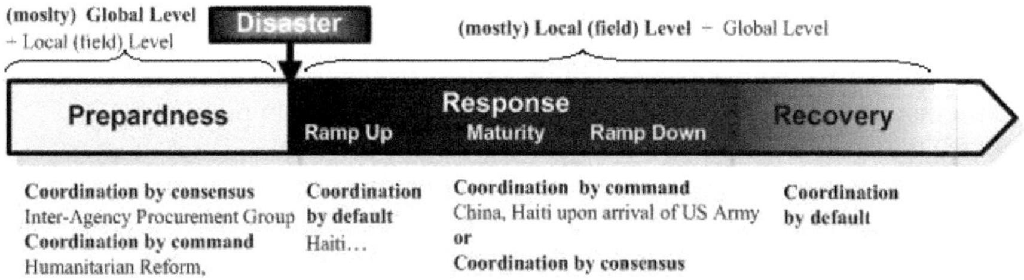

Fig. 1. Disaster phases and collaboration modes (Inspired by [5] and [3])

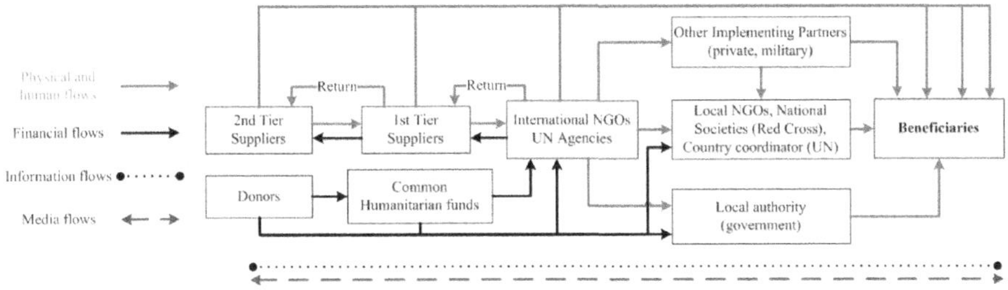

Fig. 2. Stakeholders involved in global relief efforts

"Due to the lack of adequate regulation and the presence of too many players, chaos ensued in Sumatra after the tsunami." [4] The presence of a local authority able and willing to act as *central coordinator* is a first element that shapes the relief operations. The presence of the army, local or not, also impacts the collaboration networks. They often act as central coordinator and therefore impose a coordination by command (see figure 3). Pettit and Beresford [6] have detailed the relations between military and humanitarian organizations. UN agencies also sometimes act as such. See [7]; [8] and [9] for details of centralized coordination around a UN Agency. Recent publications have applied "organizational design" best practices to humanitarian relief, thought they focus on a specific country and study only the response phase, like [10] and [11].

Thus, the diversity of stakeholders and the variability of their presence and strength from one disaster to another makes it really difficult sometimes to find and implement the appropriate collaboration network. Even usual humanitarian organisations, though they share the same humanitarian principles, may be reluctant to partner each other. The neutrality and impartiality imposed by the humanitarian space has already made MSF (among others) refuse to work with some governments, and sometimes also UN agencies. It is therefore difficult, if not impossible for NGOs to have formal coordination processes with hierarchical links that would make them report to governmental agencies or other humanitarian stakeholders. Similar issues can also be faced between actors, that would not appear much different at first glance. The French Red Cross and IFRC, for example, share the same name, but that doesn't mean that they accept clear reporting lines.

Fortunately, if we consider only humanitarian organizations offering the same range of products and services and having a shared initial intent, collaboration is more frequent. They realize that "in a world of scarce resources, although humanitarian action has no price, it obviously has a cost, and an improved management of this cost has an influence on the ability to send relief to a varying number of operation sites. Among possible savings, the best logistical coordination plays a significant part, for example in trying to avoid useless equipment or food redundancies in one place when a few miles further, both are sorely lacking."[12] Such successful collaboration networks on local level often include local partners. Because they know the local customs and networks, because they are really useful to capture knowledge of the local environment, locals are in a position to complement international staff. Those implementing partners can be local NGOs or local companies with an existing network and trained resources. During the 2006 Lebanon conflict, Agility, a logistics company, has been a major stakeholder. "We had decided that we were going to provide in-kind services in the form of transportation and warehousing, and also offer the expertise of some experienced operational managers to humanitarian organisations, since we knew that the logistics landscape of Syria and Lebanon would be unfamiliar to many humanitarian actors." [13] In such environments, local knowledge is essential. "The minute something happens, you see, you listen… you are used to working with difficult, uncertain and constantly changing conditions" [13] With a turnover of 80% per year, international NGOs have limited trained resources. Local implementing partners are therefore often really useful. Yet, their presence and strength vary from one disaster to another. Collaboration networks vary accordingly. The Table 1 summarizes the main barriers and enablers to implement collaboration networks involving humanitarian organizations on a local level.

Table 1. Barriers and enablers to implement collaboration networks involving humanitarian organizations on a local level, inspired from [14] [5] [15] and [16]

Barriers	Enablers
In-country NGOs vary widely in their ability and willingness to partner UN or International NGO bodies	Most organisations are connected to one another in principle through their desire to provide aid effectively
Most organisations are tied to each other only episodically	General awareness of the aims and competencies of principals actors
Accurate data, for need assessment, logistics management and many other critical part of operations is vital but typically difficult to obtain	Specific shared IT tools are developed to improve data capture and analysis
All humanitarian organisations are poor in lessons learnt and need structure to prepare knowhow, knowledge rules/pools, to clarify what they need in specific fields	Score Cards are under development in most major International NGOs
The humanitarian community has many serious weaknesses in managing human resources, from recruitment to training to appraisal	

2.2 Proposition to Support the Collaboration on a Local Level

"Each State has the responsibility first and foremost to take care of the victims of natural disasters and other emergencies occurring on its territory. Hence, the affected State has the primary role in the initiation, organization, coordination, and implementation of humanitarian assistance within its territory." [17] In the field, after a disaster, collaboration networks involving humanitarian organisations have to include local governments. It is their ability and willingness to take the lead or not, that shape the global humanitarian relief effort. [14] [17] Then, the strength of the local capacity comes into consideration. "If trained resources and adequate means of actions are already ready to be deployed, they should be and usually are involved from the beginning."[14] Local collaboration networks involving humanitarian organizations can therefore take many forms, depending on the nature, number and incentives of stakeholders involved. The selection of the most appropriate collaboration mode is never easy, particularly in a context of humanitarian crisis. We have drawn up a brief panorama of various existing collaboration modes and their applicability on a local level, stressing the diverse barriers and enablers to set them up. Based on those elements, we propose a framework that explains the different steps which enable, in a given situation, to choose the appropriate collaborative mode on local level (see Figure 3).

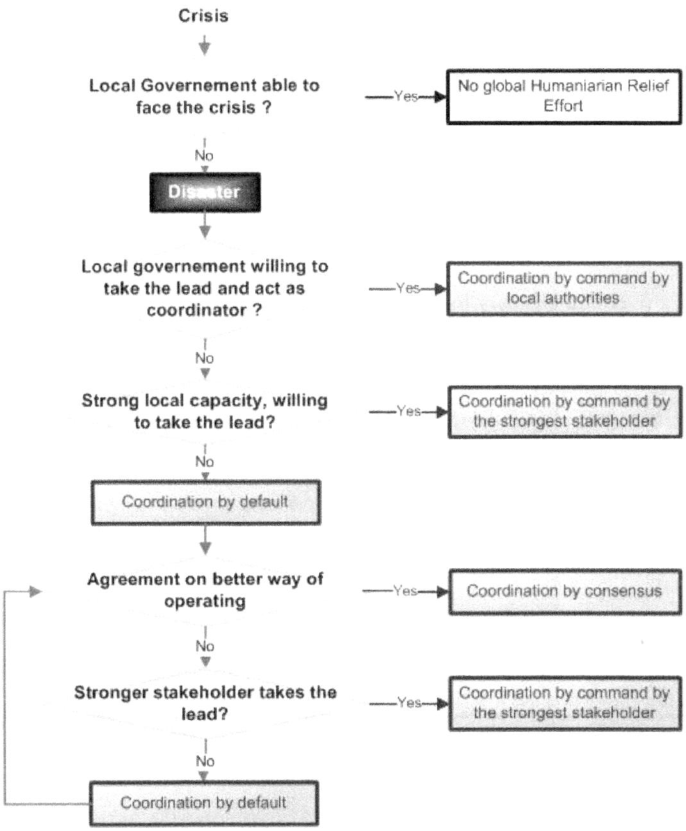

Fig. 3. Choice of local level collaboration modes during the response phase

3 Collaboration Networks on a Global Level

3.1 Overview of Existing Modes

More and more stand alone initiatives are giving birth to global collaboration networks. The Global Humanitarian Platform, for example, has been created in 2006 to strengthen partnership between humanitarian actors. The red cross and red crescent movement, NGOs and UN agencies are thus meeting once a year to increase their *transparency and complementarities*. We can also add more dedicated group meetings, like the Inter-Agency Procurement Group or the Fleet Forum. Those gather practitioners to share best practices and align on key improvement areas, like procurement or fleet management. There again, academics working on those specific subjects could be much helpful. Indeed, some partnership with private companies are already under development. Many case studies illustrated such successful approaches. See [13][18][19]and [5] among others. More recently, partnerships have begun to include other humanitarian actors, such as governmental agencies like the Centre National d'Etudes Spatiales (CNES) and also academic partners. One of those public-private partnership is Huma-Nav. It aims at developing a dedicated service for humanitarian fleet management, enabling to share information on mutual experiences and existing initiatives[20]. Those are a few chosen examples of collaboration networks involving humanitarian organizations. Many others exist, including other actors like donors or suppliers. "Such partnerships are interesting, challenging and rewarding… but really difficult sometimes. It is essential to choose the right partners and find the optimal number of actors"[14]. Table 2 summarizes the major barriers and enablers to implement such collaboration networks.

Table 2. Barriers and enablers to implement collaboration networks involving humanitarian organizations on a global level, inspired from [5] [21] and [20]

Barriers	Enablers
Lack of mutual understanding due the diversity of actors	Choice of the right ecosystem of actors
Lack of transparency and accountability	Incentives for shared information on mutual experiences and existing initiatives
Insufficient commitment on all levels	Involvement of key actors of the value chain
Lack of clarity on roles and responsibilities	Develop clear and jointly agreed roles and responsibilities to encourage commitment of actors
Lack of change management	Participatory approach
Lack of funding for activities that have no direct, visible and dedicated field application	Support of adequate Information Management tools and services

3.2 Particular Case: The Humanitarian Reform

In 2005, The United Nations Emergency Relief Coordinator, Jan Egeland asked four independent consultants to identify the factors that have hindered the speed and effectiveness of humanitarian response in the past and to propose appropriate steps to improve the timeliness and impact of future humanitarian interventions. [22] This has lead to the 2005 Humanitarian Reform. Its aims are as follow:

- Strengthening of the response capacity: the Cluster Approach

The response is organized per sector or area of activity (Camp Coordination, Logistics, but also Education, etc.) Each sector has its *cluster leads* well identified on a global level. Then, for each emergency, different local clusters leads are chosen.

- Better Humanitarian Financing: the Central Emergency Response Fund (CERF).

It is a *cash-flow mechanism*, loaned to enable quick access to funds and a stand-by fund, granted for rapid response and under-funded emergencies (response only).

- Strengthening of the Humanitarian Coordination System

The aim is the creation of a *poll of human resources equipped* with the right skills and experience and the development of a Score-Card. It is still under development.

Most of the UN community agrees that its implementation constitutes an improvement, but many others consider that there are many challenges remaining. The competitive funding environment, focused on the response phase instead of long-term, more sustainable improvements remains a major issue [23]. The use of local NGOs and cluster partners is also far from systematic [24] and therefore remains a challenge. Change management is never easy, and in this case, many NGOs, local or international felt disregarded or decided to by-pass this new organization proposed by the United Nations. And those who accepted this reform still lack a rationalized coordination structure. "Clusters were hampered by a lack of full attendance at meetings and problems with, for example, operational/field staff located at hub clusters while decision-makers, such as heads of agencies in Islamabad, a problem compounded by communication problems between hubs and clusters."[25] Best practices exist, but the management of this knowledge is still dependant on the presence and training of local capacity. "In Union of Myanmar, a dedicated Information Manager has been appointed and a web based information management system has been developed, enabling agencies to search and access relevant information for the response, including digitalized maps showing operational agencies by geographical area."[21] Yet, many reports for other emergencies pinpoint the "need for adequate IM tools and services to support the approach."[24] Those are areas that research on collaboration networks could focus on.

3.3 Proposition to Support the Collaboration on a Global Level

The two previous parts clearly illustrated the difficulty to have a pre-defined response model to implement no matter where and what the disaster is. To become more effective and more efficient in their response, humanitarians seem to want to develop a kind of *collaborative protocol* at a global level (see the UN experience). Our purpose is to propose a framework that should be considered as a first step to support the different stakeholders in designing such a protocol.

First, as we have described before, humanitarian organizations have to control globally their operations. But because they are under-resourced, they have to define priorities in order to dispatch properly funds and, of course, human resources. This is a problem of *balancing* of mobilization and affectation activities. Secondly, because a humanitarian supply chain is made up of several partners (private companies, army, humanitarians…), the coordinator (see part 2.) has to guarantee the coherence and efficiency of the network. Each stakeholder must synchronize its actions in order to be more effective and reactive. Globally, this is a problem of *synchronization*. The last thing that appears in the previous literature review is that the two precedent components do not relate to the preparedness phase of the lifecycle (see Figure 1). Actually, during the preparedness phase, all humanitarian stakeholders should capitalize and share on their past experiences in order to define best practices in terms of supplier selections, business processes, skill management, etc. Collaboration at a global level could enable a cross-learning between stakeholders and ensure the use of best practices during future operations. Globally, this is a problem of *training*.

To summarize, the design of a collaborative protocol at a global level seems to include three major components:

1. Balancing: mobilize and affect properly funds and skills for on-going crises;
2. Synchronization: guarantee coherence and efficiency on a relief operation;
3. Training: facilitate cross-learning between network members and implementation of best practices.

4 Conclusion and Future Works

This paper has detailed various collaborations modes and their applicability in the context of disaster management. It has illustrated the particularities of the humanitarian sector and the specific problems they create. Our approach is a first step aiming at a better understanding of those particularities by proposing two frameworks for supporting collaboration at a local level and global level. It sets the basis for successful applications of research works on collaboration network in this sector.

References

1. Schmenner, R.W., Wassenhove, L.V., Ketokivi, M., Heyl, J., Lusch, R.F.: Too much theory, not enough understanding. J. Oper. Manage. 27, 339–343 (2009)
2. Moore, S., Eng, E., Daniel, M.: Spencer, International NGOs and the Role of Network Centrality in Humanitarian Aid Operations: A Case Study of Coordination During the 2000 Mozambique Floods. Disasters 27, 305–318 (2003)
3. Donini, A.: The policies of mercy: UN coordination in Afghanistan, Mozambique and Rwanda (1996)
4. Tomasini, R., Van Wassenhove, L.N.: Humanitarian Logistics. PalgraveMacmillan, Oxford (2009)
5. Van Wassenhove, L.N.: Humanitarian aid logistics: supply chain management in high gear. Journal of the Operational Research Society 57, 475–489 (2006)
6. Pettit, S.J., Beresford, A.K.C.: Emergency relief logistics: an evaluation of military, non-military and composite response models. Int. J. of Logistics: Res. App. 8, 313–331 (2005)
7. Kent, R.C.: The United Nations' Humanitarian Pillar: Refocusing the UN's Disaster and Emergency Roles and Responsibilities. Disasters 28, 216–233 (2004)
8. De Mul, E.: Coordination of humanitarian aid-a UN perspective. The Lancet 360 (2002)
9. Van Wassenhove, L.N., Samii, R.: The United Nations Joint Logistics Centre (UNJLC): the genesis of a humanitarian relief coordination platform. INSEAD Case Study (2003)
10. Benini, A.A.: Network Without Centre? A Case Study of an Organizational Network Responding to an Earthquake. Journal of Contingencies Crisis Management 7, 38 (1999)
11. Stephenson, M.: Making humanitarian relief networks more effective: operational coordination, trust and sense making. Disasters 29, 337–350 (2005)
12. Chandes, J., Paché, G.: Investigating humanitarian logistics issues: from operations management to strategic action. J. of Manuf. Technol. Manage. 21, 320–340 (2010)
13. Tomasini, R.M., Hanson, M., Van Wassenhove, L.N.: Agility: A Global Logistics Company and Local Humanitarian Partner. INSEAD Case Study (2008)
14. Humanitarian Workers Interviews (2010)
15. Stephenson, M.: Toward a Descriptive Model of Humanitarian Assistance Coordination. Voluntas: Int. J. of Voluntary and Nonprofit Organizations 17, 40–56 (2006)

16. ICVA The Evolving UN Cluster Approach in the Aftermath of the Pakistan Earthquake: An NGO Perpective, http://www.icva.ch/doc00001756.html
17. United Nations, Strengthening of the coordination of humanitarian emergency assistance of the United Nations, General Assembly Resolution 46/182. In: 78th plenary meeting (1991)
18. Tomasini, R.M., Van Wassenhove, L.N.: Logistics firms and relief agencies: learning from each other. INSEAD Quaterly 14 (2005)
19. Van Wassenhove, L.N.: Fleet forum: rethinking humanitarian vehicle management (2006)
20. Faucher, P.: Space-based applications for development, disaster management, emergency response, humanitarian action. In: Third Int. UN-SPIDER Workshop, Bonn (2009)
21. Boughen, L., LeTurque, H.: Implementation of the WASH Cluster Approach (2008)
22. UNOCHA: Humanitarian Response Review (2005), http://www.reliefweb.int
23. Jahre, M., Heigh, I.: Does failure to fund preparedness mean donors must prepare to fund failure in humanitarian supply chains? NOFOMA, Helsinki (2008)
24. UNOCHA: Building a Stronger, More Predictable Humanitarian Response System (2005)
25. ActionAid International: The Evolving UN Cluster Approach in the Aftermath of the Pakistan Earthquake: An NGO perpective (2006), http://www.icva.ch/doc00001756.html

What Really Matters in Locating Shared Humanitarian Stockpiles: Evidence from the WASH Cluster

Sander de Leeuw[1], Laura Rock Kopczak[2], and Martijn Blansjaar[3]

[1] VU University Amsterdam, Faculty of Economics & Business Administration, De Boelelaan 1105, 1081 HV Amsterdam, Netherlands
sleeuw@feweb.vu.nl

[2] Zaragoza Logistics Center, Edificio Náyade 5, C/Bari 55 - PLAZA, 50197 Zaragoza, Spain
kopczak@stanfordalumni.org

[3] Oxfam GB, Oxfam House, John Smith Drive, Cowley, Oxford OX4 2JY, UK
MBlansjaar@Oxfam.org.uk

Abstract. Through a case study of locating shared stockpiles at the United Nations Water Sanitation and Health (WASH) cluster, we contribute to literature by characterizing the real overriding complexities that impact location of shared humanitarian stockpiles. We find that unique complexities related to 1) demand patterns/projections, 2) charter and commercial transport rate structures and uncertainties, 3) interagency supply and dispatch networks, 4) how programs and donors define service requirements and provide direction, and 5) in-kind service donations, all come into play and materially affect the analysis. We recommend that further research be done in these areas.

Keywords: collaboration, humanitarian logistics, supply chain design.

1 Introduction

It is generally understood that stockpiling items is necessary to provide timely and cost effective response to disasters [1]. Locating these stockpiles in humanitarian supply chains is receiving increasing attention, particularly in the OR domain [2-4]. Typically, several aspects encountered in practice are not modeled. For example, no model accounts for response tactics of organisations. Some organisations may only provide specialised activities that are not always necessary (e.g. search and rescue) whereas others provide broad cover. Context influences response tactics; few response models for rural areas are transferable to urban settings. Needs vary by disaster type [5]: disasters always require a form of water supply to people in need but earthquakes necessitate trucking of water as the water piping system will be deteriorated; if local water supply is still operational, water purification equipment may suffice. Supply aspects are furthermore not taken into account explicitly; stockpile strategies differ dependent on local or global sourcing of supplies. Last, models all take the perspective of one organisation.

Under the umbrella of the clusters formed by the United Nations in 2005, organisations have started to cooperate in responding to disasters. Through a case

L.M. Camarinha-Matos et al. (Eds.): PRO-VE 2010, IFIP AICT 336, pp. 166–172, 2010.

study of locating shared stockpiles at the United Nations Water Sanitation and Health (WASH) cluster we contribute to literature by eliciting and characterizing the real overriding complexities that impact location of shared humanitarian stockpiles.

2 The WASH Stockpile Project[1]

In 2005, the UN established nine (later eleven) collaborative platforms of humanitarian activity (referred to as "clusters")[2] to address the problem of coordination among agencies. One of these clusters is the Water Sanitation and Hygiene (WASH) cluster, for which UNICEF has been appointed as lead agency and a global cluster working group created[3]. Water is one of the dearest items after disaster strikes and crucial to survival. Availability of WASH materials and equipment is essential to any humanitarian response. Yet, for beneficiaries access to water and provision of sanitation in the aftermath of a disaster is often problematic.

WASH materials and equipment can be divided into 6 categories based on intended use, of which three – water treatment, trucking and storage & distribution make use of water related materials and equipment (e.g. bladder tanks, pipes, tanks, pumps and water purification items). The other are sanitation (e.g. latrine slabs, potties), hygiene (e.g. hygiene kits or soap) and "other" (e.g. reference books). The WASH stockpile project is one of several WASH cluster projects that are being pursued to support the cluster objective of having greater preparedness within the sector for response to emergencies. Phase I concluded that timely availability of appropriate WASH related materials and equipment on the ground after an emergency was limited in some cases because agencies with capacity on the ground did not have materials. To address this gap, Phase I recommended a comprehensive programmatic solution consisting of a shared stockpile of WASH items that would:

- Stock and deploy a pre-defined standardized set of WASH materials organized in six modules with quantities to support 50,000 beneficiaries and response capability to address a single large emergency (50,000) or multiple smaller emergencies; and
- Be deployed by the WASH cluster and delivered within one week after activation of the WASH cluster to one or more implementing agencies in country that have capacity on the ground to respond.
- Be in addition to existing agency stocks.
- Be pre-funded for multiple years including cost of dispatch and stock replenishment after use.

---

[1] This is project 5 of the WASH cluster. Project documents for Phase I and Phase II of this project can be found on http://www.humanitarianreform.org/Default.aspx?tabid=345

[2] The other clusters are agriculture, camp coordination and management, early recovery, education, emergency shelter, emergency telecom, health, logistics, nutrition, and protection.

[3] Current active members of the working group include: Action Contre la Faim (ACF), CARE, Center for Disease Control (CDC), Concern, Catholic Relief Services (CRS), InterAction, International Center for Health and Migration (ICHM), International Federation of Red Cross and Red Crescent Societies (IFRC), International Rescue Committee (IRC), MercyCorps, Norwegian Church Aid (NCA), Oxfam, REDR-IHE, TearFund, UNHCR, UNRWA, WHO and World Vision International (WVI).

2.1 Project Approach for Phase II

This paper focuses on Phase II of the project, which was managed by Martijn Blansjaar of Oxfam GB with the two other authors acting as consultants to develop the solution. Phase II investigated the design of the supply chain and selection of supply chain partners together, acknowledging that different sets of partners would offer different supply chain options with different potential for performance. Furthermore, the project sought to make maximum use of existing agency capacity in designing supply chain options, thereby minimising set-up and operating expenditure and delay. The WASH cluster thus focused on the logistics departments of WASH cluster member agencies as potential partners; eight agencies that had expressed interest in participating were considered. Logistics service providers were considered only to the extent that the agencies being considered were using them. The intent was to select agencies and design a collaborative supply chain to be implemented once funding was obtained in a two-year pilot, after which an evaluation and potential adjustment would be made.

The project ran from August to December 2009. During that time, the consultants developed supply chain alternatives, evaluation criteria and interview scripts which were then agreed upon by the steering committee (a sub-section of the working group). Based on initial agency interviews with the eight agencies, a short list of four supply chain alternatives with participating agencies was decided upon. The pre-defined evaluation criteria were used twice – once to narrow the list of agencies/supply chains and a second time to compare the short-listed options.

A demand and stock location/allocation analysis was conducted in parallel with agency interviews and site visits. A workshop was held in Geneva in late September 2009 to solicit agency input. Site visits were made to the procurement/supply chain department offices of the short listed agencies in Bicester (UK), Geneva, and Oslo, to UNICEF (the cluster lead) in Copenhagen, and to dispatch warehouses in Bicester (UK), Kuala Lumpur and Dubai. Design reviews were conducted to understand overlap of current materials and suppliers with WASH stockpile items. Finally, recommendations were presented to and agreed upon by the steering group.

2.2 Analyzing Potential Stockpile Locations for a Given Set of Agencies

WASH Cluster members discussed and agreed on items and related specifications and packaging for six modules as described in section 2 above, with the intent that the six modules would be deployed together for a comprehensive solution in sets to fulfill needs of 5,000 beneficiaries, with a minimum deployment quantity for 10,000 and a maximum deployment for 50,000 beneficiaries. It was estimated that a set of the six modules to support 10,000 beneficiaries would cost roughly USD $200,000, weigh 28,000 kilograms and occupy roughly 150 cubic meters. This load could fit well in the commonly used IL76 rear loading charter aircraft or similar.

Four alternative supply chain concepts with varying agency participation were analyzed using a spreadsheet. The analysis looked at (among other things) transport costs for different stockpile locations, stock allocation, and transport options, for a given demand scenario. The recommended supply chain was the Oxfam-IFRC supply chain with additional potential to leverage UNICEF transport contracts and ability to receive goods in country (as a diplomatic entity). The analysis was based on the related supply chain design and considered existing locations and current transport approaches of the three agencies as shown in the table below. Using current processes will ease implementation of the pilot. Interested readers are referred to the project documents mentioned above in footnote 1.

Table 1. Supply chain design

Anticipated location of source of supply	Existing dispatch warehouse locations	Current transport approaches
Water modules: complete modules from UK suppliers through Oxfam	IFRC: Dubai, Kuala Lumpur, Panama City, Gran Canarias	IFRC: Charter/scheduled air cargo, ocean depending on origin-destination pair
	Oxfam: Bicester	Oxfam: Commercial air
Sanitation, hygiene and reference modules: from Asian or regional suppliers	UNICEF: Copenhagen, Dubai	UNICEF: Charter/ commercial air depending on origin-destination pair

2.3 Findings from Demand Analysis and Service Requirements Workshop

A demand analysis was done in an effort to better project the location, timing and size of needs that will potentially be addressed by dispatching from the stockpile. With help from Oxfam GB WASH engineers, we analysed publicly available data on flash appeals to determine for which of these past emergencies WASH modules would have been deployed and in what quantities.[4] It was determined that if a stockpile had been in place, modules would have been deployed for 17 of the 50 flash appeals during that time.[5] The resulting annual demand scenario is shown below:

- 1 big emergency (deployment of modules to support 50,000 people)
  > Location: 50% chance in Africa and 50% in Asia
  > Timing: May hit anytime throughout the year
- 3-4 small/medium emergencies (total deployment to support 45,000 people)
  > Location: 2 in Africa, 1 in Asia, 1.5 in Latin America
  > Timing: Roughly 75% of this demand would occur during the peak season (July-December).

This analysis is limited by the fact that data on flash appeals only covers the years 2005-2009. It appeared from this limited data set that if a large emergency occurs

[4] "A Flash Appeal is the way that the many agencies responding to a sudden humanitarian crisis coordinate their response and present a unified set of needs to donors. It provides a concise overview of urgent life-saving needs and a plan to address acute needs for up to six months based on the best available information at the time of writing. A Flash Appeal may be developed into a Consolidated Appeal if the emergency continues beyond six months. All implementing agencies, ranging from UN agencies, international organisations, the Red Cross Movement, and NGOs, are encouraged to list their humanitarian projects in a joint Appeal." http://ocha.unog.ch/ets/Default.aspx?ContentType=FixedContent&ContentID=3.

[5] The hygiene promotion kit (printed materials) alone would have been deployed for an additional 6 of the 50 flash appeals.

(or two in a year, as with the tsunami and Pakistan earthquake), agencies might respond to fewer or no small to medium-size emergencies that year. We chose not to reflect this as an either/or situation in the demand scenario. From the flash appeal data (and discussions with WASH experts) we concluded that Latin America is typically hit by disasters requiring a small response (for 10,000 beneficiaries); nevertheless in early 2010 Haiti was hit by an earthquake that would be considered a big emergency.

In the September 2009 workshop, consultants led a discussion among WASH engineers and logisticians that defined a service requirement for dispatch speed (dispatch warehouse to receipt in country) of 48 hours to 7 days and a service requirement for replenishment time (stock dispatched to stock received) of 60 days.

2.4 Findings from Analysis of Stockpile Location/Allocation

In keeping with the collaborative approach to the stockpile and the idea of leveraging existing agency capacity, we used existing response approaches and networks of individual agencies as a starting point. Using a spreadsheet we analysed where to hold stock and how to allocate the 50,000 unit stockpile and a possible 10,000 additional units during peak season among potential locations (Dubai, Kuala Lumpur, Panama City, Las Palmas, Bicester) to respond to the demand scenario. All locations have good access to airports and flight times are less than 12 hours different.

The analysis approach taken was to obtain indicative charter airfares from UNICEF and IFRC for transport from warehouses indicated to sample destinations represented in our demand analysis.[6] In analyzing each stockpile option, we used the indicative transport rates to decide from which stockpile location each destination would be served. We then calculated a projected annual transport cost for the demand scenario, weighing the cost of responding to large and small emergencies equally.

We found that looking solely at charter air transport cost led to a *narrow* analysis, with few factors considered. Even so, while some insights were gained, the results were inconclusive because the indicative transport rates obtained from the multiple agencies varied so dramatically that the order of preference of stockpile locations and the value of holding additional 10,000 units of stock during the peak season changed dependent on whether UNICEF or IFRC transport rates were used. UNICEF rates were relatively more favorable for "*northern*" origins such as Bicester; IFRC rates were relatively more favorable for IFRC *regional hub locations* in KL and Panama City.[7] Indicative charter transport costs for an IL76 charter are roughly equal to the item cost for a quantity of 10,000 but potentially 2 to 3 times that cost on particular origin-destination pairs. We also found that charter air rates for some lanes (e.g. Panama City to African destinations) were asymmetric due to unbalanced flows. What we could conclude from the analysis was that a single location strategy is very expensive for serving small disasters in the regions – apart from the question of whether it is a good idea to do so – and that keeping a significant amount of stock in Europe and in Panama City would be very expensive because large disasters are not very likely to occur there. (In contrast, one stockpile in Dubai would serve large disasters well because it is well positioned for both Africa and Asia.) To carry

[6] Pakistan, Haiti, Zimbabwe, Philippines, Burkina Faso, Uganda, Mozambique.

[7] This could be due, for example, to relative volumes for the two agencies on particular lanes or focus of their freight forwarders with respect to lanes.

forward this narrow analysis, we would have to work further to understand the differences in UNICEF and IFRC rates.

Additional factors that would come into play in a broader analysis include:

- A solution in which, for example, some stock is held by Oxfam in Bicester and some by IFRC in Dubai and Panama City, seems attractive, particularly as Oxfam engineers would have stock close by that could be examined should engineering issues arise. However, physical, financial and information processes would be more complex and deciding from which stockpile to deploy (commercial from Bicester vs. commercial/charter from elsewhere) could become an issue.
- Some donors may prefer to see stock in particular locations or held by particular agencies.
- Variability in charter air rates / plane availability over time is not well understood.
- Possibilities for use of scheduled commercial flights and for donated space on these flights should be investigated further. A quick look suggested that scheduled cargo rates may be as low as one tenth of charter rates, but require a trade-off between cost and response time that would have to be made by WASH cluster programs. Donated space occurs typically as ad hoc offers for flights from "northern" origins.

3 Discussion

Three major aspects made it difficult to develop a conclusive design. First, it is necessary to understand the demand and desired response to a disaster. Understanding the demand side was not seen as a necessary first step by the agencies involved. It is fairly typical for the current humanitarian supply chain literature to state that demand is "...unpredictable regarding timing, location and scale" [6] without further detailed analysis. Our analysis – though not complete and in need of further work – shows that natural disaster occurrence is not that unpredictable as typically understood. Discussions with programs on required responsiveness in the supply chain were inconclusive: trading off speed in delivery with costs of that delivery (including costs of capacity on the ground to set up the operation) was not seen as an input to design; instead, programs just set response times irrespective of potential cost impact.

The input to the project was a requested stock level to serve 50,000 beneficiaries. Such a requirement may be a simple statement used for a donor but in reality it is unclear what it implies. Does this mean that stock for 50,000 people is required at all times? If so, peak stock levels (order-up-to points) may need to be higher. Discussions about this with the programs were inconclusive.

Our results are inconclusive because of uncertainty in transport costs. Transport costs are asymmetric along lanes and are influenced by aircraft availability and choice for chartered vs. commercial air cargo. It is clear that inclusion of transport cost in any location analysis is crucial due to the level of costs, unlike e.g. Duran et al. [3] who do not take operating costs into account. Research – including ours – often assumes that aircraft is the typical mode of response for disasters but that is not the only option for response, c.f. Pettit and Beresford [1]. Response by truck or ship may be equally well possible. Also, we found that an apparently growing volume of governments and corporations offer of in-kind service support (e.g. free warehouse space in the Humanitarian City in Dubai, free air-cargo transport offered by scheduled freight carriers) can potentially reduce operating costs, but may increase coordination needs or limit flexibility.

Last, the set up of a shared stockpile poses several challenges that interact with the outcome of a location analysis. The preferred scenarios seemed to be influenced by respective transport rate tables. Therefore, one needs to decide who will do the contracting and whose transport rates will be used. This is not a matter of simply selecting the cheapest overall due to the fact that both quotes showed different preferred scenarios though total lowest costs were roughly similar. This implies one needs to think of a transport strategy first: will we rely on chartered aircraft for response or will we also use commercial air? Discussions with donors also showed that they sometimes have preferences that influence the design; donors may make their funding dependent on the use of certain locations or suppliers.

4 Conclusion and Future Research

In this article we have identified the real complexities and practical challenges that humanitarian agencies face when designing a shared stockpile. Additional research is needed to understand and characterise demand as input for location analysis, to incorporate transport rate complexity and uncertainty, to investigate the size and impact of in-kind service donations, to investigate interagency coordination problems, particularly in the area of contracting, and to research the role of programmes and donors in providing directives for the humanitarian supply chain.

References

1. Pettit, S., Beresford, A.: Critical success factors in the context of humanitarian aid supply chains. Int. J. Phys. Distrib. 39(6), 450–468 (2009)
2. Balcik, B., Beamon, B.: Facility location in humanitarian relief. Facility location in humanitarian relief 11(2), 101–121 (2008)
3. Duran, S., Gutierrez, M.A., Keskinocak, P.: Pre-Positioning of Emergency Items Worldwide for CARE International. In: INFORMS, USA (2007)
4. Rawls, C.G., Turnquist, M.A.: Pre-positioning of emergency supplies for disaster response. Transp. Res. B 44, 521–534 (2010)
5. Tomasini, R.M., Van Wassenhove, L.N.: From preparedness to partnerships: case study research on humanitarian logistics. Int. Trans. Oper. Res. 16(5), 549–559 (2009)
6. Kovacs, G., Spens, K.M.: Humanitarian logistics in disaster relief operations. Int. J. Phys. Distrib. 37(2), 99–114 (2007)

A Mediation Information System to Help to Coordinate the Response to a Crisis

Sébastien Truptil, Frédérick Bénaben, and Hervé Pingaud

Université de Toulouse – Mines Albi, France
{truptil,benaben,pingaud}@mines-albi.fr

Abstract. In a crisis situation, several heterogeneous actors have to work together in a hurry to solve or at least reduce the crisis. Their coordination and the transfer of information between them in such context are a crucial point. Unfortunately, lacks of coordination and collaboration have often been underlined as a major weakness of humanitarian crisis response. To help the whole of actors to work together, The ISyCri project aims to provide an information system. This system must be in charge of (i) information exchange, (ii) services sharing and (iii) behavior orchestration. Nevertheless, a crisis is by definition an evolutionary phenomenon. So a panel control is presented to help to detect when it is necessary to change the system because of the evolution of the situation. This paper aims to present, through an example, the approach of system creation and the control panel.

Keywords: interoperability, crisis management, evolution, information systems.

1 Introduction

According to [1], [2] and [3], a crisis is an abnormal situation which occurs suddenly and impacts a subpart of the world with unacceptable consequences. Such a break into the continuous state of the considered subpart of the world implies to deal with the crisis management through a dedicated set of stakeholders in charge of the crisis response. According to [2], [4], [5], crisis management is divided in four main parts:

1. Mitigation: this step aims at addressing the proactive social component of emergencies. This includes laws and mechanisms that reduce the vulnerability of the population and increases their resilience.
2. Preparedness: this step aims at defining the actors' abilities and preparing the means for crisis response. The definition of actors' abilities is made thanks to the analysis of past experience.
3. Response: once the crisis appears, several heterogeneous actors have to work simultaneously in a hurry with the global aim of crisis reduction.
4. Rehabilitation: this step aims to restore the (eco)system after the crisis. For example, rebuild buildings, schools…

The ISyCri project [6] focuses only on the response step of crisis management. Indeed, the global objective of the project is to help the whole heads of organizations

L.M. Camarinha-Matos et al. (Eds.): PRO-VE 2010, IFIP AICT 336, pp. 173–180, 2010.

in charge of the situation (in the following, we will use the terms: crisis cell), to deduce, on the base of preparedness results, a crisis response.

The crisis response concerns two kinds of actors. First, there are actors on the field, using their specific abilities (to perform activities such as evacuating injured persons, fixing a road, etc.). Second, there are heads of these actors on the field. Each head is in charge of, first the activities of operational actors on the field, and second, the exchange of information between the field and the crisis cell (report and instructions). Furthermore, even if actors share the same global goal, they do not tackle the same issue. The result of this point is the following: As explained in [7], the communication and the exchange of information inside the crisis cell is not sufficient enough to give each member the global view of the crisis and to help them to coordinate their activities. Nowadays, this lack of coordination and collaboration has been underlined as a major weakness of crisis response. This is why the ISyCri project focuses on the crisis cell and on the question of coordination and exchange of information between the stakeholders, inside the crisis cell.

The point is the following: considering that the stakeholders of the crisis response have the competences and the procedures to deal with their own mission, how is it possible to help to manage, to coordinate and to synchronize this set of operational experts of the crisis cell? Then this article aims at presenting the MIS deduction approach through an example. This approach is used to (help to) define, at the beginning of the crisis, the appropriate collaborative behavior through a collaborative process model. Nevertheless, because crisis is by definition a dynamic phenomenon, the crisis response has to be flexible. So the last part of this article aims at presenting the modification of the MIS according to the evolutions.

2 Overview of ISyCri Project

When a crisis occurs, several stakeholders are involved simultaneously to solve (or at least to control) the situation. The question is then: "How to provide this set of heterogeneous actors with the ability to organize and coordinate their actions in an optimal manner". Depending on the type, the size and the location of the crisis, this organization may be more or less formalized. The first hypothesis of this research work is that this collaborative organization is based on a crisis management cell, which may be seen as a decision center. The question then becomes: "how to provide the crisis cell with the ability to organize and coordinate the actions of heterogeneous stakeholders in an optimal manner".

Interoperability is defined in [8] by the European network of excellence InterOp as "the ability of a system or a product to work with other systems or products without special effort from the customer or user". It is also defined in [9] as "the ability of systems, natively independent, to interact in order to build harmonious and intentional collaborative behaviors without modifying deeply their individual structure or behavior". Considering these definitions we propose to consider that the previous main question is, at this point, the following: "how to support the interoperability of actors into the crisis cell".

2.1 Ideas and Tracks to Answer the Main Question

An important point is that the members of the crisis cell have to communicate with their operational resources on the crisis field through their own channels. Another assumption of this article is that members of the crisis cell are able to use these specific means of communication to receive incoming reports and to send outgoing instructions. However, the central issue is that the members of the crisis cell are not used to exchange information between each other. If they expect to organize and coordinate their actions, they need to find a way to support their exchange of information into the crisis cell. This characteristic matches the framework proposed in [10] and so the proposed conceptual solution could be a Mediation Information System (MIS) dedicated to support interoperability.

To be useful for the crisis response, the MIS has to be perfectly relevant for the situation. That is why, the MIS deduction approach, start by deducing a collaborative process from the crisis information and the description of each stakeholder.

2.2 Overview of MIS Deduction Approach

The MIS deduction approach is divided into three main steps, corresponding exactly with the model-driven architecture defined by OMG [12]. First, a collaborative process deduction, explained in [13], from the crisis information and the stakeholders' information provides the representation of the coordination between the several stakeholders. This collaborative process is the CIM (computer independent model) of this approach. Second, a logical architecture of MIS, corresponding to the PIM (platform independent model), is build thanks to a transformation described in [14]. Third, another transformation is used to configure the technical deployment of MIS, corresponding to the PSM (platform specific model).

The collaborative process represents the collaboration while the last two steps of this approach are automatically executed. Consequently, we choose to illustrate only the first step through an example based on an exercise of crisis management realized by French authorities. This example was chosen because we witnessed the whole exercise, but this approach is also experimented in humanitarian crisis context.

The scenario is the following: "Policemen were informed that an accident occurred between a tanker and a train. A cloud of escaping products was created and people of railway station felt sick."

The model, represented by figure 1, is the crisis model of this example that summarizes all the information of the crisis, as the "collision" event, the risks of explosion and contamination, the fact that some people felt sick.

Once this knowledge gathered, it is injected into an ontology already embedding information concerning partners' abilities. Then deduction rules, explained in [13] are executed to extract the stakeholders' abilities, which could be used to reduce one (or several) problem(s) of the crisis. Then to deduce the order of stakeholders' abilities execution, people in charge of crisis management must answer provide two choices: The priority ranking of identified problems and their selection among the set of selected abilities. In this example, the priority ranking is the following: (1) Explosion risk, (2) Contamination risk, (3) Sick people, (4) Panic risk.

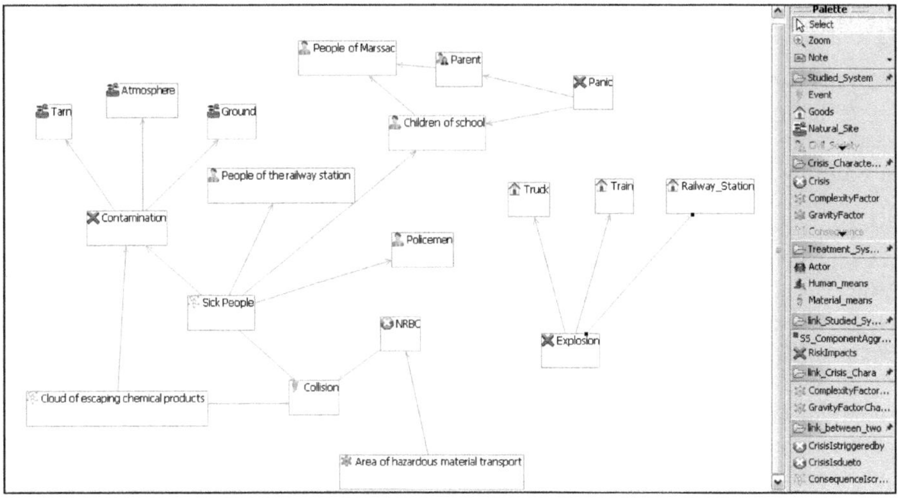

Fig. 1. Example of crisis model

Then abilities are selected (the partner in charge of the service is in brackets):

- *Explosion risk*: FightExplosion (Firemen), SetSecurityPerimeter (Policemen).
- *Contamination risk*: RescuePeople (Firemen), MaintainPerimeter (Policemen), SetMedicalPost (Red Cross).
- *Sick people*: BringPeopleToMedicalPost (Red Cross).
- *Panic risk*: Care People (EMS).

This set of services and the priority ranking of problems are the basic elements of the collaborative process deduction (figure 2) as explained in [13].

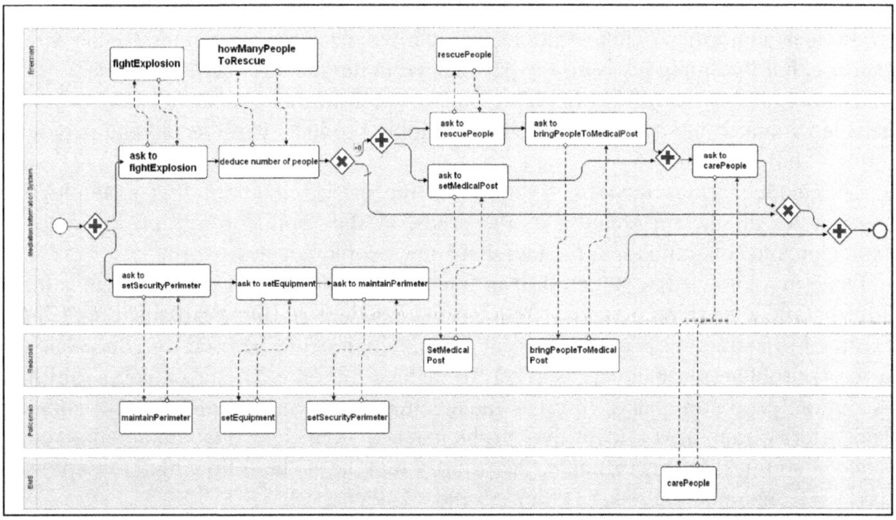

Fig. 2. Collaborative process

3 Limits of This Approach in Humanitarian Crisis

In humanitarian crisis situation, the crisis cell is generally geographically disseminated. Consequently, the creation of an overall view, represented by the crisis model needs a tool to help the set of stakeholders to build it together. This tool has to collect all the information about the situation and then modify the crisis model according to them. We are currently working on tools, dedicated to the stakeholders IS, to transfer such modification. At this point, just one tool has been built to ensure the collect of information: EarlyWarning. This is a specific service that was build to collect information about the situation. For this, each stakeholder has its own interface of EarlyWarning that allows it to share information. Depending on this information, the crisis model is modified either with the creation or deletion of problems.

At any moment, the design approach, explained in section 2, can be executed to build a MIS adapted to the crisis model and the stakeholders' abilities. Unfortunately, new information about the situation and/or stakeholders could feasibly render MIS obsolete at any moment. So in our work we believe that it is a better way to build a MIS and then modify it than to wait after the whole information about the situation. This point of view implies that the MIS has to evolve according to the situation. In the following part of this article, we explain how our tool allows to detect and take into account the potential evolutions of the situation.

3.1 Possible Evolutions and Their Impacts on MIS Deduction Approach

Crisis situation is by definition an evolutionary phenomenon. So, the crisis response has to be able to adapt depending on evolutions. In [9], the author proposes a classification of evolutions, which can occur in context of collaboration between several heterogeneous organizations. In crisis management context, this classification can be adapted as follows: (i) the crisis itself changes (several earthquakes successively), (ii) the set of organizations in charge of crisis response evolves during the response (an organization quits the crisis field) (iii) dysfunction can append during the crisis response (restarting of a fire).

MIS, and collaborative process has to be maintained in order to correspond exactly to the situation, depending on the kind of evolutions. Indeed, (i) if the crisis itself evolves, then the collaborative process is out-of-date, whereas, (ii) if the crisis situation does not evolve but the whole of stakeholders changes, then, the collaborative process may just need a small adaptation, (iii) finally, if a dysfunction happens during the crisis response, the collaborative process may be partially re-executed, but the situation or the set of stakeholders may also require an adaptation.

Therefore, when an evolution occurs, the MIS design process can be restarted at several levels to obtain a MIS, specifically dedicated to the current situation. Nevertheless, it is necessary to ensure that what has already been done is taken into account. For this, another tool has been added: mediation services.

At the beginning, this tool was created to realize information's transformations from one service of a stakeholder to another. Consequently, before each service, a data transformation is realized, currently based on a static correspondence table. By this way, we obtained a new functionality, which send the state of the service (waiting, started, finished or execution fault). This functionality allows to follow the collaborative process and to know status of any service at any time.

In crisis context, we believe that it is not possible to automatically decide if MIS has to be modified. So, we try to help the crisis cell to take that decision by providing, a control panel. It aggregates all the information send by EarlyWarning and mediation services and helps the crisis cell to detect evolutions.

3.2 How to Detect the Several Kinds of Evolutions

In this part, a control panel is proposed to help to detect the evolutions. This control panel, represented in figure 3, is composed of four tables. The two upper tables refer to risks (potential problem) and consequences (actual problem), of the crisis. The others refer to the crisis response (Actors state and Services state).

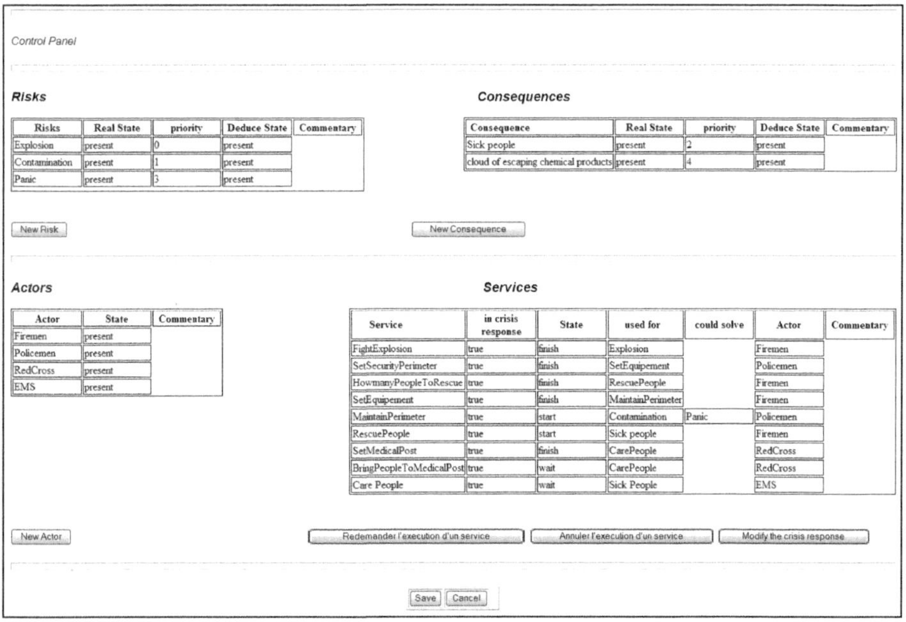

Fig. 3. Panel control uses to detect the evolutions

The two first tables have the same use. They summarize the whole of characteristics of the crisis and their treatment priority. They inform on the difference between the real state and the deduced state of crisis characteristics. The real state corresponds to the real situation thanks to information coming from the field. The deduced state is inferred from the progress of the crisis response. When all the services that have been specifically chosen to reduce the crisis characteristic A have been executed, the deduced state of that characteristic A is turn into solved.

The two others tables (Actors and Services) are used to draw an overview of the crisis response and to detect dysfunctions or changes into the crisis cell composition. Indeed, the service table inform on the collaborative process execution, especially on the service state (waiting, started, finished or execution fault) whereas the actor table inform on the crisis cell composition, and each partner's state (present, wait, leave).

Based on the supervision of these tables, four kinds of reaction are available:

- If a new information appears in one of the two first tables (Risk and Consequence), the crisis cell has to change the crisis model and launch again the whole MIS deduction approach (because a critical evolution of the situation has just appeared).
- If there is a difference between the deduced state and the real state of one risk or consequence, the crisis cell has to change the crisis response and the MIS because at least one dysfunction occurred. In this case, the crisis cell has several choices: (i) restart a service. (ii) Launch again the MIS deduction approach with the same crisis model, with other ranking choices or service affectation choices.
- If there is a problem during the execution of service (service state = fault), the crisis cell has to change the crisis response according to the same options than the ones presented at the last point.
- If the state of a partner changes, because it quits or joins, the crisis cell may also have to change the response according to the same options than the ones presented at the last point.

4 Conclusion and Future Work

The presented works aims at providing a mediation information system able to support the interoperability between information systems in a crisis context. The design of the MIS is based on the following assumptions: (i) the crisis management is assumed by a crisis cell, (ii) each stakeholder of the crisis cell is able to ensure the communication with its own resources on the operational field and finally, (iii) each stakeholder of the crisis cell is able to propose a set of services reflecting its concrete operational abilities. The two first ones could not be changed for the moment, but concerning the third one an interesting perspective may be the support of service design. This track concerns the assisted conception of technical services, according to interfaces patterns and business services analysis.

One obvious weak point of this work concerns the fact that a single collaborative process may be a too poor model to describe the crisis response. It could be better to get several processes, which could cover several levels of process (decisional, operational and support).

Finally the use of the panel control provides the crisis cell with an overview of the crisis response and a way to detect the possible evolutions. Today, on the occurrence of any evolution, the crisis cell modifies on its own the crisis response (process and/or activities). Thus, automatic modifications can be deduced from specific events. These automatic modifications could be a strong improvement for the crisis cell management.

References

1. Devlin, E.: Crisis Management Planning And Execution, p. 528 (2006)
2. Tomasini, R.: Van Wassenhove, L.: Humanitarian logistics INSEAD (2009)

3. Lagadec, P.: La gestion des crises. In: Ediscience International, p. 326 (1992)
4. Atlay, N., Green, W.: OR/MS research in disaster operations management. European Journal of Operational Research 175, 175–475 (2005)
5. Beamon, B.M., Kotleba, S.A.: Inventory modelling for complex emergencies in humanitarian relief operations. International Journal of Logistics: Research and Applications 9, 1–18
6. Truptil, S., Bénaben, F., Couget, P., Lauras, M., Chapurlat, V., Pingaud, H.: Interoperability of Information Systems in Crisis Management: Crisis Modeling and Metamodeling. In: IESA 2008. Springer, Germany (2008)
7. Hansen-Glize, C.: de la maîtrise des crises. Techniques de l'ingénieur, France (2008)
8. Konstantas, D., Bourrières, J.P., Léonard, M., Boudjlida, N.: Interoperability of Entreprise Software and Applications. Springer, Genoa (2005)
9. Pingaud, H.: Rationalité du développement de l'interopérabilité dans les organisations. In: Management des technologies organisationnelles, pp. 19–30. Presses de l'Ecole des Mines de Paris, France (2009)
10. Wiederhold, G., Genesereth, M.: The conceptual basis for mediation services. IEEE Expert: Intelligent Systems and their Applications 12(5), 38–47 (1997)
11. Benguria, G., Larrucea, X., Elveseater, B., Neple, T., Beardsmore, A., Friess, M.: A Platform Independent Model for Service Oriented Architectures. In: IESA 2006, Bordeaux, France, pp. 407–416. Springer, Heidelberg (2006)
12. OMG, MDA Guide Version 1.0.1, omg/2003-06-01 (2003)
13. Truptil, S., Bénaben, F., Pingaud, H.: Collaborative process deduction to help the crisis cell emerging ecosystem to coordinate the crisis response. In: IEEE DEST 2010, Dubai (2010) (accepted paper to be published)
14. Touzi, J., Bénaben, F., Pingaud, H., Lorré, J.P.: A Model-Driven approach for Collaborative Service-Oriented Architecture design. International Journal of Production Economics 121(1), 5–20 (2009)

Towards a Reference Mission Map for Performance Measurement in Humanitarian Supply Chains

Sander de Leeuw

VU University Amsterdam, Faculty of Economics & Business Administration,
De Boelelaan 1105, 1081 HV Amsterdam, Netherlands
sleeuw@feweb.vu.nl

Abstract. Research on performance measurement in humanitarian supply chains is scant. Experiences with developing performance measures in commercial environments show that it is particularly important to understand linkages between higher level goals and performance measurement, for example through using strategy maps in for-profit organisations or mission maps in non-profit organisations. In this article, we use literature and four mini-case studies in humanitarian organisations to develop a reference mission map for a humanitarian supply chain. This reference mission map may be used by humanitarian organisations to develop an organisation specific mission map for their supply chain.

Keywords: Performance measurement, humanitarian supply chain management, humanitarian logistics, mission maps, balanced scorecard.

1 Introduction

It has been widely recognised that there is a need for performance measurement in humanitarian supply chains [1-4]. Recently, several publications have paid attention to the development of performance metrics [5-8] and conditions for success of performance measurement in humanitarian supply chains [9]. However, to date, performance measurement has not been developed and implemented systematically in the relief sector [3, 6]. Performance measurement systems currently known have typically been developed for business organisations and not for non-profit organisations such as humanitarian organisations. Although many aspects of commercial supply chains may be similar to their humanitarian counterpart, the direct transfer of findings will be challenging [2]. However, profit sector based performance measurement frameworks are a useful starting point for the non-profit sector [10].

The most common performance measurement framework in the profit sector is the Balanced Score Card [11]. Also in the relief sector, the Balanced Score Card (BSC) has been applied [8]. We therefore take the BSC as a starting point for our discussion on developing performance measurement in humanitarian supply chains. When implementing and using the BSC in industry, executives identified a missing link between performance metrics and strategy [12]. To cope with this "... the main constituencies of the [performance measurement] model and the cause and effect

L.M. Camarinha-Matos et al. (Eds.): PRO-VE 2010, IFIP AICT 336, pp. 181–188, 2010.

relations between them should be identified" [13]. Kaplan and Norton developed the concept of a strategy map to fill this gap. Such a strategy map – or mission map in non-profit organisations – shows the cause-and-effect links by means of which specific improvements in areas created desired outcomes [12]. We aim to apply the concept of strategy maps as developed by Kaplan and Norton [12] in a humanitarian environment. Developing such a mission map compels non-profit organisations to set measurable and mission-oriented goals and to assess the progress of their operations towards these goals. These goals can then be used for systematic development of performance measures.

In this article, we set out to construct a reference mission map for a humanitarian supply chain. This map may be used to pick and choose themes from for making an organisation-specific mission map. We do not discuss the variety of performance measurement approaches, as there are several excellent overviews available that discuss this [cf. 14, 15]. We deploy an exploratory research design to increase our understanding of aspects to include in such a mission map, as there is no research available into humanitarian mission maps. Four different humanitarian organisations participated; they desired to remain anonymous for confidentiality reasons. Organisation A is a relatively small humanitarian organisation that mainly focuses on development activities; B is one of the largest non-governmental organisations (NGO) in the world with a broad scope of relief activities, and C is a large international NGO that mainly focuses on medical support. Organisation D is part of an inter-governmental organisation. For exploratory and theory-building research, case studies are often recommended [16, 17]. Although there are limitations to using case studies, we have followed methodological guidelines [16, 17] to increase the validity of our findings. We focused on a variety of organisations and developed an outline of a humanitarian mission map using literature; this map has been verified and expanded by means of interviews with managers responsible for supply chain processes in the four humanitarian organisations using a script; we have transcribed the interviews to increase content validity and respondents have reviewed interview records.

Below we review humanitarian supply chain literature. We discuss empirical data from four case studies in humanitarian organisations to develop a reference humanitarian mission map that can be used for designing performance measures. Last we provide conclusions and recommendations.

2 Four Perspectives

A balanced scorecard (BSC) contains four perspectives: a financial perspective, customer perspective, internal perspective, and a learning and growth perspective [12, 18]. The customer perspective deals with the question "how do customers see us". The internal perspective of the BSC provides an answer to the question "what must we excel at". The learning & growth perspective covers an answer to the question "how can we continue to improve and create value" and the financial perspective deals with improving the bottom-line of an organisation. In order to develop a humanitarian mission map, we investigated humanitarian supply chain literature on each of the four perspectives using the strategy maps framework of Kaplan and Norton [12, 18] as a reference. Table 1 provides a brief overview of literature from the humanitarian sector on each of the four perspectives, which we only provide in summary. Consecutively, we used the results of the four case studies to develop a reference mission map for humanitarian supply chain management. Below, we will first discuss the case study input on each of the four perspectives. The reference mission map is we developed based on this input is discussed afterwards.

Table 1. Literature overview balanced scorecard perspectives in the humanitarian supply chain

Perspective	Content [12, 18]	Humanitarian sector examples
Customer	Product and service attributes	Right supplies at the right place and time for those who need it most [19]; speed of delivery [1, 20]
	Customer relationships	There are different customers in a supply chain simultaneously with different requirements [21]
	Image	Branding conflicts with ideals of voluntarism, altruism and democracy connected to humanitarian agencies [22]
Internal	Operations management	Provide excellence from field needs assessment to delivery in the field [23]
	Customer management	Donors want to know their money is used well [24]; need to manage a diversity of customers [21]
	Innovation	Need for flexible technology solutions [25]
	Regulation & social	Focus on environmental issues [25] Employment of locals [26] Comply with government regulations [26]
Learning & Growth	Human capital	Appropriate logistics knowledge required and not available [2, 21]; manage high field personnel turnover [25, 27]
	Information capital	Create visibility and foster transparency required [28]; good information management is critical [2, 20]
	Organisational capital	Profit incentives to perform certain actions are not like private companies [19]
Financial	Manage revenue	Ensure sufficient and timely donor funding [20, 21]
	Manage costs	Track spending of money [20]; focus on efficiency [29]

2.1 Case Study Results: Customer Perspective

With regard to product and service attributes, all agreed that for beneficiaries, quality, availability and speed are key attributes. Organisation C mentioned that efficiency is relevant as donors pay attention to this. Organisation B indicated that reliability of delivery needs to be included. They indicated that unreliable deliveries of supplies to camps may lead to unrest. Organisations B and D furthermore argued that relevance is a key attribute. Organisation D quoted an example where shelter was provided to people who did not accept shelter because of their religious backgrounds.

The interviewees argued that there are three kinds of key customers: donors, intermediaries such as government or implementing partners, and beneficiaries. All indicated that donors request insight into the costs of the project and expect efficient and effective operations – although organisation D added that donors often do not have good means to measure that. In terms of building customer relationships, interviewees were focusing on donors, though that depended on strategy.

Organisation B did not invest much in donor relationships as they focus on smaller (private) donors, which was different from the other organisations interviewed.

With regard to corporate image, all four organisations argued that trustworthiness and reliability are key aspects of their image. Organisation D furthermore indicated that they strive for a sustainable supply chain, minimising environmental impact.

2.2 Case Study Results: Internal Perspective

All interviewees agree that operations management processes entail activities from needs assessment to final delivery and that operational excellence in these processes is a prerequisite for success in a supply chain. The agencies interviewed used different strategies to target, acquire and manage donors. Organisation A rather keeps few large donor organisations instead of many small to keep time and effort needed for donor management reasonable and to manage the substantial influence that donors typically have on the execution of the processes because of their special demands. Organisation B indicated that they focus on private non-institutional donors; they are then more independent to take their own decisions as funds are typically not earmarked. All considered feedback to donors about field performance essential. Organisation D added that donors often do not have the capacity or interest to check supply chain related aspects such as the performance of the supply chain towards beneficiaries.

Organisation A always sets up a partnership with the central or local government of a country as the support and the activities of the humanitarian organisation need to be in line with the political objectives of a government. Organisation C tries to stay as independent as possible and therefore does not see the government as a key partner. They may sign an agreement with a government but that is only to grant admission to an area. Organisation D quoted one example of an ambulance that was shipped and got lost in the customs clearance process. Only through using contacts within government it was possible to trace back the vehicle quickly. Organisation D indicated that there are many different intermediary parties to manage and the targeting, acquisition and building of partnerships with them is key. Typically, they work with partners to perform final delivery to beneficiaries. In some countries they run operations with one partner while in others with tens of different partners.

Innovation is gaining attention among the organisations interviewed. Organisation A focused on process innovation, e.g. by having more beneficiaries involved in support processes from an early stage of the operation onwards. Organisation D indicated they are active in the development of more durable tents and that they are starting to use GPS technology to map refugee camps and trace vehicles. Organisation C quoted an example of service innovation: they use identity cards with chips for beneficiaries in refugee camps. Through these cards refugees can be recognized fast and be supplied with exactly the products and services they need.

All organisations interviewed argued that regulatory and social processes are key aspects to account for. Organisation C indicated they more and more depend on permissions of governments to perform their work. They have to stick to labour laws and they need a high community acceptance. To be able to deal with local cultural issues two interviewees argued that it is advisable to engage an anthropologist who can recommend solutions about how to deal with local cultural challenges. Such action could lead to more and faster community acceptance and avoid issues as quoted by organisation D that e.g. tents supplied to refugees were not accepted because of religious beliefs. Organisation A focused on involving local people to support the people who live in refugee camp. For specific jobs, they only hired locals, e.g. for installing water pumps. One aspect that also requires attention is the environmental impact. Organisation D indicated that their suppliers more and more are judged on sustainability aspects and that they would like relief activities be more focused on sustainability as well, e.g. by mainly using fuel efficient vehicles in areas where four-wheel-drives are not really necessary (such as cities).

2.3 Case Study Results: Learning and Growth Perspective

All organisations acknowledged the need for logistics training and a focus on managing high turnover of functions in the field. They argued more attention should be given to developing and expanding skills and to keeping skills and capabilities in-house. Organisation A for example installed explicit requirements for the level of training of their local employees and organisation D was in the process of developing standard job descriptions. All interviewees agree that within learning and growth the human capital is by far the most important element.

All interviewees also identified that information capital is crucial and not developed significantly in humanitarian supply chains. Organisation A argued that information is mostly shared with other people in meetings instead of using computers and information systems. Organisations B, C and D already use standard logistical information systems covering a large part of their supply chain. Supply chain information such as inventory levels is becoming available but is not complete yet. However, organisation D argued that particularly the adherence to procedures is a big issue in information management, e.g. stock is booked in the system incorrectly.

All organisations argued that fostering a culture of teamwork within the organisation and with partners is key to humanitarian aid. Organisation A furthermore added that in many cases international expat employees are flown in at decision-making positions. However, since they often do not stay long in country it is crucial to develop local leadership capacity. If a humanitarian organisation then leaves a country local workers have the capabilities to take over and continue activities.

2.4 Case Study Results: Financial Perspective

The four organisations all manage the financial perspective - managing funding, budgets and costs - differently. Organisation A uses a plan of activities to ensure steady donations from institutional parties. Typically, they will not deviate much from plans. Organisation B and Organisation C make a yearly budget for all ambitions of the organisation and then identify required funds. Organisation B has few large donors in order to spend budgets as independent from donors as possible. Organisation D has a budgeting procedure for regular support activities and an emergency procedure to obtain extra funds from institutional donors in case disaster strikes. All organisations tightly monitor costs.

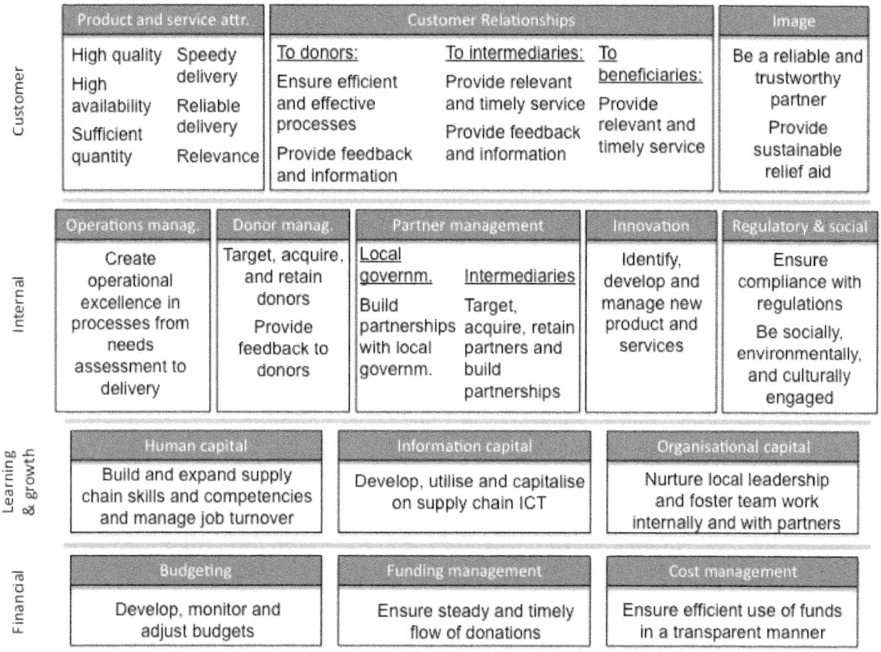

Fig. 1. Reference mission map for humanitarian supply chain management

3 Discussion, Conclusions and Future Research

Based on the above, we have compiled a reference mission map in Fig. 1. Compared to the Kaplan and Norton framework there are a few aspects that stand out in a humanitarian supply chain. In the customer perspective, there are different relationships with different customers simultaneously, cf. Oloruntoba and Gray [21]: not only beneficiaries but also donors and intermediary parties are customers in the supply chain at the same time. For all these customers, relevancy of products and services stands out; beneficiaries are not really demanding voices contrary to customers in commercial transactions; in fact, they have little choice [27].

The internal perspective deals first with donor management, focusing on excellence in selecting, acquiring, retaining and collaborating with donors to ensure and grow funding. Secondly, agencies need to manage partners. Humanitarian organisations work with many players and these relations often turn out to be unsatisfactory [21] and thus require close attention. Partner management deals with local government of the host country - good relationships with government are essential to get shipments into a country without delay. It also deals with intermediaries in delivery of aid to beneficiaries – whether it is other NGO-s or for example a third party logistics service provider. Though deemed important, innovation - both in products and services - will continue to be a challenge since typically there is little time and money for being prepared [1, 19]. Last, like in the commercial world, it is becoming more and more important for agencies to take account of the environment as well as social impact.

Humanitarian organisations therefore need to account for sustainability, e.g. in their sourcing activities, and increasingly involve local people (e.g. by sourcing more products locally).

The learning and growth perspective is not unlike its commercial counterpart. Humanitarian agencies have challenges in managing human capital [2, 27] and in information systems deployment [19]. The financial perspective focuses mainly on funding management (which would be the revenue aspect in a commercial BSC). Many agencies do not have the means to provide services without first obtaining the necessary donor funds [25, 29]. Particularly receiving funding for preparatory activities instead of direct funding of disaster operations is difficult to achieve [25]. If funding depends on many (small) private donors, the execution of a supply chain strategy that focuses on preparation instead of mainly response is typically easier.

Performance measurement in humanitarian supply chains is in a nascent stage. We presented a development approach based on a method that is popular in industry. There are other approaches, e.g. based on service quality management, that may provide interesting avenues for further research. An interesting research direction is to support mission maps with quantifiable cause-and-effect relations, along the lines of the study by Santos et al. [30], who used system dynamics models. This enables identification of strengths in cause-and-effect relations between aspects of a mission map. With the wealth of research on performance measurement in commercial settings it is furthermore interesting to understand where and how performance measurement implementation and use is different from the commercial world. An improved understanding of how to design, implement and use humanitarian supply chain performance measurement is a key lever for improving performance.

Acknowledgments. Thanks to Tom Bouwman for supporting the empirical research.

References

1. Tomasini, R., Van Wassenhove, L.: Humanitarian logistics. Palgrave MacMillan, Basingstoke (2009)
2. Pettit, S., Beresford, A.: Critical success factors in the context of humanitarian aid supply chains. Int. J. Phys. Distrib. 39(6), 450–468 (2009)
3. Altay, N., Green, W.G.: OR/MS research in disaster operations management. Eur. J. Oper. Res. 175(1), 475–493 (2006)
4. Kovacs, G., Spens, K.M.: Humanitarian logistics in disaster relief operations. Int. J. Phys. Distrib. 37(2), 99–114 (2007)
5. Davidson, A.L.: Key performance indicators in humanitarian logistics, Institution. Cambridge, Master of Engineering in Logistics (2006)
6. Beamon, B.M., Balcik, B.: Performance measurement in humanitarian relief chains. Int. J. Public Sect. Maneg. 21(1), 4–25 (2008)
7. Moe, T.L., Gehbauer, F., Senitz, S., Mueller, M.: Balanced scorecard for natural disaster management projects. Disaster Prev. Manag. 16(5), 785–806 (2007)
8. Schulz, S.F., Heigh, I.: Logistics performance management in action within a humanitarian organization. Manage. Res. News 32 (2009)
9. Van der Laan, E.A., De Brito, M.P., Vergunst, D.A.: Performance measurement in humanitarian supply chains. Int. J. Risk Assessm. Manage. 13(1), 22–45 (2009)
10. Moxham, C.: Performance measurement: Examining the applicability of the existing body of knowledge to nonprofit organisations. Int. J. Oper. Prod. Man. 29 (2009)

11. Neely, A.: The evolution of performance measurement research. Int. J. Oper. Prod. Man. 25(12), 1264–1277 (2005)
12. Kaplan, R.S., Norton, D.P.: Strategy maps: Converting intangible assets into tangible outcomes. Harvard Business School Press, Boston (2004)
13. Micheli, P., Kennerley, M.: Performance measurement frameworks in public and non-profit sectors. Prod. Plan. Control 16(2), 125–134 (2005)
14. Gunasekaran, A., Kobu, B.: Performance measures and metrics in logistics and supply chain management: a review of recent literature (1995-2004) for research and applications. Int. J. Prod. Res. 45(12), 2819–2840 (2007)
15. Akyuz, G.A., Erkan, T.E.: Supply chain performance measurement: a literature review. Int. J. Prod. Res., (first published: August 25, 2009), iFirst (2009)
16. Eisenhardt, K.M.: Building Theory from Case Study Research. Acad. Manage. Rev. 14(4), 532–550 (1989)
17. Voss, C., Tsikriktsis, N., Frohlich, M.: Case research in operations management. Int. J. Oper. Prod. Man. 22(2), 195–219 (2002)
18. Kaplan, R.S., Norton, D.P.: The Balanced Scorecard. Harvard Bus. Rev., 134–137 (September-October 1993)
19. Tomasini, R.M., Van Wassenhove, L.N.: From preparedness to partnerships: case study research on humanitarian logistics. Int. Trans. Oper. Res. 16(5), 549–559 (2009)
20. Van Wassenhove, L.N.: Humanitarian aid logistics: supply chain management in high gear. J. Oper. Res. Soc. 57(5), 475–489 (2006)
21. Oloruntoba, R., Gray, R.: Customer service in emergency relief chains. Int. J. Phys. Distrib. 39(6), 486–505 (2009)
22. Vestergaard, A.: Humanitarian branding and the media: The case of Amnesty International. J. Lang. Polit. 7(3), 471–493 (2008)
23. Blecken, A., Hellingrath, B., Dangelmaier, W., Schulz, S.F.: A humanitarian supply chain process reference model. Int. J. Ser. Technol. Manage. 12(4), 391–413 (2009)
24. Oloruntoba, R., Gray, R.: Humanitarian aid: an agile supply chain? Supply Chain Manag. (2005)
25. Thomas, A.S., Kopczak, L.R.: From logistics to supply chain management: The path forward in the humanitarian sector. Fritz Institute, San Francisco (2005)
26. Perry, M.: Natural disaster management planning. Int. J. Phys. Distrib. 37(5), 409 (2007)
27. Fritz: Lessons Learned: recipient perceptions of aid effectiveness: rescue, relief and rehabilitation in tsunami affected Indonesia, India and Sri Lanka. Frits Institute, San Francisco (2005)
28. Van der Laan, E.A., De Brito, M.P., Van Fenema, P.C., Vermaesen, S.C.: Managing information cycles for intra-organisational coordination of humanitarian logistics. Int. J. Ser. Technol. Manage. 12(4), 362–390 (2009)
29. Balcik, B., Beamon, B.M., Krejci, C.C., Muramatsu, K.M., Ramirez, M.: Coordination in humanitarian relief chains: Practices, challenges and opportunities. Int. J. Prod. Econ. (2009)
30. Santos, S.P., Belton, V., Howick, S.: Adding value to performance measurement by using system dynamics and multicriteria analysis. Int. J. Oper. Prod. Man. 22(11), 1246–1272 (2002)

Towards a Performance Measurement System to Control Disaster Response

Carine Rongier, Didier Gourc, Matthieu Lauras, and François Galasso

Université de Toulouse, Mines Albi, Centre Génie Industriel,
Route de Teillet, 81000 Albi, France
carine.rongier@mines-albi.fr, didier.gourc@mines-albi.fr,
matthieu.lauras@mines-albi.fr, francois.galasso@mines-albi.fr

Abstract. During a crisis, the main goal for decision-makers consists in restoring a stabilized nominal mode. The stakeholders have to face an important pressure and drastic constraints of response time and coordination. This study proposes a method assisting these stakeholders in their choices while carrying out a performance evaluation of the activities run during the crisis response process. Currently, in crises, the performance evaluation is only used subsequently due to difficulties in gathering and aggregating information into trustable performance indicators. The interest of this paper is to present this method which permits to obtain a relevant decision support system. Decision-makers will use it to resolve the crisis based on performance assessment. A case study about crisis management within the French Red Cross non-governmental organization is developed in order to explain how performance indicators can on the one hand support crisis response management and on the other hand improve the collaboration of stakeholders.

Keywords: disaster management, performance assessment, humanitarian organization process, indicators.

1 Introduction

The topic of this paper is disaster management and in particular response to disaster. This issue, whatever the kind of crises, is topical. For example, "the increased frequency and scale of disasters, scarce resources, funding competition, and the need for accountability require more efficient, effective and transparent relief operations" [1]. During a crisis, the system leaves its nominal mode and the goal for the actors is to restore it. So stakeholders have to react quickly and have to deal with an important pressure and constraints of coordination from the stakeholders. It seems important to use tools to help the control to guide decision-makers in this phase. Currently, the actors implement a process of response with actions mainly based on their experience. Particularly in the case of humanitarian organizations intervening in disasters, best practices are developed from the report of results drawn up after each crisis. Thus, it enables them to elaborate a response to the crisis. This technique, which is based on experience feedback, is important because it is known that whatever the situation is, the capitalization of the data is useful. However, it does not enable a control of the

L.M. Camarinha-Matos et al. (Eds.): PRO-VE 2010, IFIP AICT 336, pp. 189–196, 2010.

response and has the following limits: it is not possible to make improvements to the response process in real time because the actors assess the performance of their response process once the crisis is solved and enacting collaboration is difficult for the stakeholders due to the lack of formalization of the actions.

The reasoning suggested in this paper aims to guide the actors during the response. This paper presents a method which permits to create a Performance Measurement System (PMS) which will be used during the crisis. This new method, combined with the actors' expertise, helps the resolution of a crisis.

Firstly, section 2 presents a state of the art on performance assessment. Then, section 3 deals with the improvement of the control of the response to a crisis considering the performance assessment, lastly a case study will be exposed.

2 Literature Review and Problem Statements

This section explains the performance assessment, and especially the implementation of indicators in time of crisis. That is why a short state of the art about the PMS is defined to see which are the methods used in this domain. The purpose of this paper consists in proposing a method to design PMS to support the management of the response in case of crisis. PMS are defined by a set of metrics and performance ratios, used to quantify both the efficiency and the effectiveness of actions [2].

2.1 Process Oriented PMS

In the literature several methods to create indicators are proposed. The mostly known are :

- The Activity Based Costing (ABC) method assigns costs to activities on the basis of their use of resources and then allocates costs to products according to their ratio of activity consumptions.
- The Holistic Process Performance Measurement System [3], or the Fraunhofer approach [4] develop the idea of PMS design based on business processes at the scale of an enterprise. Pertinence of Key Performance Indicators (KPI) is enhanced by the knowledge captured in process representation.
- The SCOR model [5] provides a unified representation of supply chains with five general processes: Plan, Source, Make, Deliver and Return. Each process can be refined in sub-processes, which are themselves decomposed into sub-sub processes. Three categories of KPIs are proposed in the SCOR model dashboard [6] depending on what they are related to: customers; internal processes and shareholders.
- The Balanced Scorecard where the indicators are given following four defined axes of performance: customer, finance, internal processes and growth.

According to these methods, the element which is interesting to retain is the cutting of the system in several axes and the creation of specific indicators for each axis.

So, it is necessary to determine on which level the assessment is made, i.e. to identify the several business processes which have to be monitored. (problem statement 1).

2.2 Performance and Decision-Making Processes

A large number of PMS's methods link performance to decisions. We can quote for instance the Strategic Performance Measurement System [7], the Performance Measurement Questionnaire [4]; [8], the Strategic Measurement Analysis and Reporting Technique system [9] or the Cambridge University's PMS method [4]. They insist on the need to split decisions into many levels depending on their weight on the organization and their time effect. They also look for the sensitivity between KPI variations and alternative decisions by direct investigation. But if information on performance is condensed in KPIs, it is also possible to synthesize information on decision using the well known performance determinant, a concept first introduced by the Balanced Scorecard method (BS) [10]. The performance determinants have been natively defined as a control variable because one of the main criteria to select them is a sensitivity evaluation of their influence on the system. BS focuses on strategic management, and even if a reference to internal processes is proposed as an improvement policy, there is very little information about the method to do it. As previously said it is capital to set up KPIs to help actors concerning the most difficult decisions, *i.e.*. the most critical ones. So it is necessary to identify the most critical activities among all the activities of the system.

Thus we can wonder how to make this classification of the activities (problem statement 2).

2.3 Key Performance Indicators

Lorino [11] defines the performance indicator as an 'information that can help an actor, individual or more generally collective, to lead action towards the realization of an objective or can permit to evaluate the result of it'.

According to [12], [13], [14] and [15] the performance is the conjunction of several dimensions: relevance, efficiency, effectiveness, effectivity, responsiveness, flexibility and resilience. These dimensions constitute the key components upon which the subsystems of the organization in crisis shall be evaluated. According to the situation, several dimensions can have more importance.

So, in case of disaster, it is useful to determine the dimensions which will predominate (problem statement 3).

Once the indicators are created, it is necessary to begin the measurement process at a defined frequency. The performance measurement is an observation of the state of a system. It is the reflection of the real state of the system, given by indicators [16]. Once the measurements are made, they are compared with the objectives to obtain the performance assessment. After the assessment, improvements can be made if the performance is not satisfactory.

3 Designing the Crisis PMS

The meaning of the word *crisis* differs from a field to another. In the literature, two words are used to describe this concept: crisis and disaster. "Usually, crisis is considered as man made and a disaster as a natural phenomenon" [17]. In this paper these two words are used equally, in general context. However, during the description of the case study, the term disaster is used.

A crisis can be defined as a complex and dynamic phenomenon, which constitutes a threat for the survival of an organization and its members, which gives short time to react and which leads to an adaptation of the system [18]. This definition underlines the fact that it is necessary to make decisions in emergency. However, it introduces a new element: the dynamic aspect of a crisis. A crisis situation is rarely fixed, it changes all the time. Obviously, its management is made more difficult. This study is focused on sudden crises, *i.e.* we do not deal with pandemic or durable economic crises, for example.

Based on Alexander's cycle management [19] and on literature review, the disaster management cycle is composed of: prevention, preparation, response and recovery. Our study concentrates on the third phase: the *response.* It integrates all the actions to be carried out as fast as possible after an impact such as for example the release of the emergency plan or the evacuation of a threatened population. At this level, the main aim is to set up actions acting on the system in crisis in order to bring it back to a normal situation as soon as possible.

The goal of this study is to implement a method during this phase, which will help the decision-makers in their management, based on PMS. This method will permit to make readjustments in real time in the management of the response.

The method is then detailed, to answer the three principal problem statements evoked previously. It is composed of three steps.

3.1 Step 1: On Which Level Is the Assessment Made?

The creation of indicators of performance implies an analysis of the organization to determine on which part the assessment must focus. Each group of response's actors has its own objectives and thus it is necessary for them to have specific indicators. So that our method can apply to various types of crises, a 'standard' cutting of the organization which manages the response is chosen. Based on the generic structure described by [20], generic business processes concerning the response phase has been defined. In fact, some domains, specific to crisis management, have been added or adapted to the Porter's structure, based on NGO reports. Thus a map for the response process has been defined (see figure 1).

To model the different parts of the response system, we have used the Business Process Management concept, according to the rules of standard ISO 9000 – 2000.

The map in figure 1 shows three levels of processes:

- *1st level: operational*:

In this level, the *evaluation* takes place at the beginning of the response. There are processes for the preparation and processes for the field.

- *2nd level: management:*

The *study* permits to validate the importance to start an intervention. Then there is a process which describes the field management and another which explains the preparation management. There is also a unit to coordinate these ones and to manage collaboration with other stakeholders. At least, a process is devoted to the *a posteriori* performance assessment, which permits to draw up reports on response and make feedback.

- *3rd level: supporting*:

Human and material resources and information systems are put at disposal. There are also financial aspects and activities of communication.

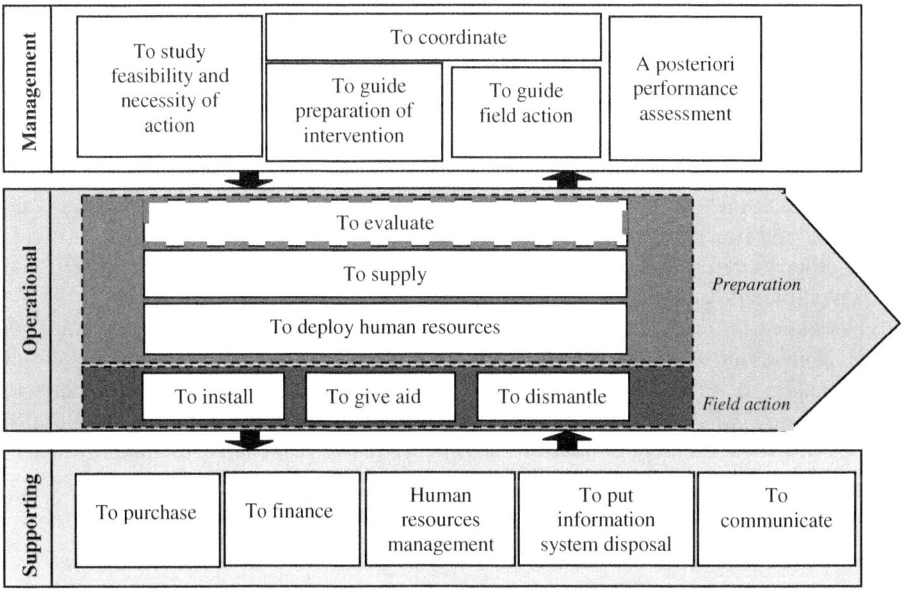

Fig. 1. Map of response process

The highest decisional level: the strategic level, is thus divided in three main domains (i.e. Supporting, Operational and Management). Each domain is composed of processes which represent the tactical decisional level and finally each process is made up of activities, not detailed at this stage, which are the operational level. Thus according to the decisional level at which the user wants to place himself he will choose to install indicators for the domains, the processes or the activities.

We depicted at which place the indicators could be positioned. Let us now explain how the most important processes which have to be monitored are selected.

3.2 Step 2: Selection of Processes Thanks to a Risk Analysis

Our study is led in a context of crisis, the time factor is thus essential, so it is necessary to limit the critical activities which could slow down the progression of the response, directly by causing a waste of time or indirectly by generating errors whose resolution would mobilize too many resources. That is why it seems more relevant to put indicators on the less reliable parts of the system. Thus, we will propose a risk analysis, based on the FMEAC method, in order to index the most critical processes and to supervise their realization with the indicators. This method consists in defining the causes and the consequences of a studied risk while calculating its *criticity* which is the product of *gravity* by *detectability* by *occurrence*. If the result exceeds a given threshold, the risk is considered as critical. According to the kind of crisis it is possible to attach more importance to one of the criteria, for example gravity for a natural disaster. The goal is to determine the most critical activities to treat them in priority. This stage is important because the indicators which will not be positioned on tactical places will not be useful. Moreover it is important to keep only the most critical risks in order not to have too many indicators to manage.

3.3 Step 3: The Creation of Key Performance Indicators

For each critical activity, it is necessary to determine one or more indicators of performance. These indicators are characterized by a name which describes what the indicator measures, by a formulation which shows the calculation to be done to obtain the result and finally by a class.

In order to define indicators, the stakeholders use their expertise and international organization's database.

The indicators created are selected and indexed in a summary table (see example in table 1) in order to facilitate their use. The classes are the different dimensions of performance, described in section 2.3. Each indicator is associated with a class in order to know what component of performance the indicator is measured. In case of disaster the most frequent dimensions are effectiveness, responsiveness and resilience.

4 Case Study

The case study chosen is an earthquake. The method seen before has been implemented on the case of this disaster. Our study has been focused on the humanitarian organization's response phase.

For this paper, a focus is made on *evaluation* process (see details in figure 2).

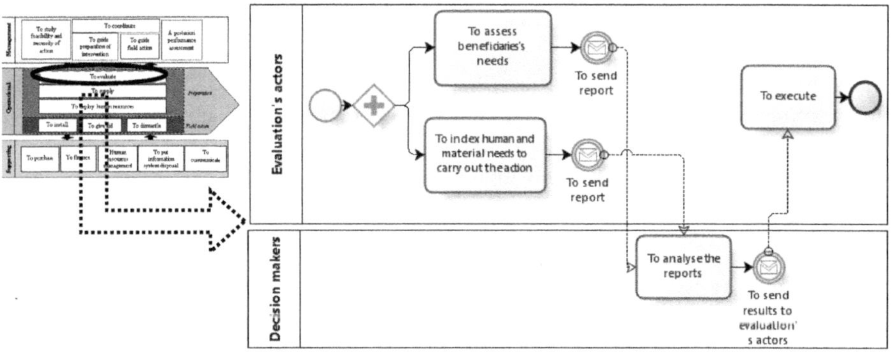

Fig. 2. Process: evaluation of means

Two kinds of evaluations must be differentiated:

- the evaluation of means consists in determining the human and material resources that are necessary in the place of the disaster and in which quantity,

- the determination of the suitable kind of response: this assessment is made once the accessibility of the place is determined. It consists in defining which are the means usable for the procurement and movement to the place of the disaster and their quantity.

In this paper only the results for the process *evaluation of means* are detailed (see table 1). According to the method, once processes are defined it is necessary to carry out a risk analysis. The scale of points used for the criticity runs from 1 to 9 and the threshold is 100 points. If a risk obtains more points: it is critical so an indicator has to be set up on the process concerned. This work is summarized in table 1.

Table 1. Results obtained for *evaluation of means*

Process: Evaluation of means						
Risks				KPI		
Names	**Causes**	**Consequences**	**Criticity** D x G x O	**Name**	**Formulation**	**Classes**
Slow evaluation	Bad organization of estimation	Waste of time	6 x 9 x 3 = 162	Cycle time	1-Days between the beginning of crisis and appeal	Responsiveness
Error on the assessment of needs	Pessimistic estimation: too many means requested	Waste of means	6 x 9 x3 = 162	Coherence between orders and needs	2-Number of items asked (order)/number of items requested (crisis area)	Effectiveness
					2.2-Ref. asked (order)/ref. requested (crisis area)	Effectiveness
	Optimistic estimation: not enough means requested	Lack of means	9 x 9 x3 = 243		2.3-Number of means asked (order)/number of means requested (crisis area)	Effectiveness

The evaluation is essential. It should not take too much time as the response process would be slowed down. However it must be carried out seriously because errors of estimation can have serious consequences on the continuation and reduce the effectiveness of the response, in particular as regards supply chain.

5 Conclusion

Because of the increase of crises, it is necessary to have tools to manage a crisis response as correctly as possible. This paper presents a method which gives an assistance to crisis management. It shows how to control the phase of response to a crisis by the performance. Thus, after a state of the art on crisis management and performance assessment, we have presented a modeling of the response process for a crisis. According to this method, to carry out a performance assessment, it is necessary (1) to know what has to be evaluated *i.e.* on which processes the indicators will be set up, (2) how the processes to monitor are selected and (3) how the key performance indicators are defined. The method has been applied to a case study: the humanitarian organization's response to give an example of key performance indicators which can be defined thanks to our method.

The main perspective is the implementation, on the field, of tools to apply this method at the strategic, tactical and operational levels of a humanitarian organization. The French Red Cross organization has been already contacted in order to validate the relevance of this method.

Then, the second field that will be investigated is an extension of this tools to industrial sectors.

References

1. Balcik, B.: Relief chain planning and management: modeling and analyzing humanitarian logistic problems. PhD thesis, Université de Washington (2008)
2. Neely, A.D., Mills, J., Platts, K., Gregory, M., Richards, H.: Performance measurement system design: should process based approach be adopted? International Journal of Production Economics (1996)
3. Kueng, P.: Process performance measurement system: a tool to support process-based organizations. Total Quality Management (2000)
4. Bourne, M., Neely, A., Mills, J., Platts, K.: Implementing performance measurement systems literature review. International Journal of Business Performance Management (2003)
5. S.C.C. Supply Chain Council: Supply Chain Operations reference-models – SCOR version 6.0, Edition Supply Chain Council, 278p (2003)
6. Bolstorff, P.: How does SCOR measure up? In: Supply Chain Technology news, pp. 22–25 (2002), http://www.totalsupplychain.com
7. Vitale, M., Mavrinac, S.C., Hauser, M.: New process/financial scorecard : a strategic performance measurement system. Planning Review 22(4), 12–16 (1994)
8. Chan, F.T.S., Chan, H.K., Qi, H.J.: A review of performance measurement systems for supply chain management. International Journal of Business Performance Management 8(2-3), 110–131 (2006)
9. Cross and Lynch (1989)
10. Kaplan, R.S., Norton, D.P.: The Balanced Scorecard: translating strategy into action. Harvard Business School Press, Boston (1996)
11. Lorino, P.: Méthodes et pratiques de la performance. Editions d'Organisation (2003)
12. Marcon, E., Sénéchal, O., Burlat, P.: Evaluation des performances des systèmes de production, sous la direction de Tahon, C. Hermès. In: Concepts pour la performance des systèmes de production (2003)
13. Humez, V.: Proposition d'un outil d'aide à la décision pour la gestion des commandes en cas de pénurie: une approche par la performance. PhD thesis, INP Toulouse (2008)
14. Durieux-Paris S., Genin, P. and Thierry, C.: document de synthèse du projet. GdR Macs, Prise de décision dans la chaîne logistique en monde incertain (2007)
15. Tang, C.S.: Perspectives in supply chain risk management. International Journal of Production Economics 103, 451–488 (2006)
16. Gunasekaran, A., Bulent, K.: Performance measures and metrics in logistics and supply chain management: a review of recent literature (1995-2004) for research and applications. International Journal of Production Research (2007)
17. Mukhopadhyay, A.K.: Crisis and disaster management turbulence and aftermath. New Age International (2005)
18. Jacques, J.M., Gatot, L.: De l'incident à la catastrophe: un modèle organisationnel (1996)
19. Alexander, A.O., Coppola, D. P.: Introduction to international disaster management. Butterworth-Heinemann, Butterworths (2002)
20. Porter, M.: Competitive advantage. The free press, New York (1985)

A Structured Approach for Implementing Virtual Organization Breeding Environments in the Mold and Die Sector – A Brazilian Case Study

Fabiano Baldo[1] and Ricardo J. Rabelo[2]

[1] Department of Computer Science, Santa Catarina State University, Zip Code 89223-100, Joinville, Brazil
[2] Department of Automation and Systems, Federal University of Santa Catarina, P.O. Box 476, Zip Code 88040-970, Florianópolis, Brazil
baldo@joinville.udesc.br, rabelo@das.ufsc.br

Abstract. This paper contributes with the general problem of how transforming classical industry clusters in Virtual Organization Breeding Environments (VBEs). Having into account reference frameworks and models, a structured approach for implementing VBEs has been proposed and its preliminary results are presented here. This approach has been preliminarily tested in a cluster of moulds and dies industries from Brazil where the main VBE's characteristics have been found. In the future, it is intended to use this structured approach as a concrete mean to systematize the implementation of any type of VBE.

Keywords: Virtual Organization Breeding Environment, Members Preparedness, Virtual Organization, VBE Implementation Methodology.

1 Introduction

Since late 1990s, Brazilian industry clusters started to create a more advanced strategic alliance over the country based on a so-called local productive arrangement concept. Despite of the benefits of this initiative, it has been realized that this form of alliance is limited to face some new business requirements, as volatility of economics, commercial barriers, global competition and innovation needs [1]. New forms of alliances have been recently arisen under the scope of the new organization paradigm called Collaborative Network Organizations (CNO).

Actually, there are several types of CNO manifestations. Considering the set of new requirements and taking the original goals of local productive arrangements into account, VBE has been seen as its natural evolution. Among other advantages, the transformation of local productive arrangements to VBEs has the potential to enhance knowledge sharing, to decrease costs and risks, and to augment competitiveness to reach new markets.

The establishment of VBEs is a very complex task, regarding the number of technical and non-technical aspects to embrace. Recently, a first attempt to answer this question has been proposed by Romero et al. [2]. They have devised a generic

L.M. Camarinha-Matos et al. (Eds.): PRO-VE 2010, IFIP AICT 336, pp. 197–203, 2010.

methodology to create VBEs based on a CNOs' reference model. However, it requires a derivation process when very particular VBE is desired to be built. Besides that, this work does not take into consideration VBE member candidates' preparedness. As stated by Afsarmanesh et al. [3], members' preparedness is crucial for the successful creation of VBEs. So, the problem is how to create VBE implementation methodologies that consider candidate members' preparedness in their specification?

This is the underlying research question of this paper, assuming a hypothesis that a more correct identification of preparedness aspects not only speed up the VBE creation process and decrease launching costs, but also create more confidence in the process by members and more correct preparation. In this sense, this paper presents a structured approach used for a more proper members' preparedness identification and then for further better VBE implementation methodology specification.

In this paper, section 2 presents the approach for implementing VBEs. Section 3 describes the VBE model specified to the cluster. Section 4 depicts characteristics for assessing cluster's members. Section 5 presents directives to create questionnaires. Section 6 shows the evaluation of cluster's members. Section 7 specifies the VBE implementation methodology. Section 8 presents some conclusions and future work.

2 Structured Approach towards VBE Implementation

This section presents the structured approach designed for implementing VBEs. This approach has been developed based on studies performed into a cluster of mould and die producers (see section 3). The approach is composed of the following steps:

1. VBE specification. In this step is specified the VBE model that represents every key-element to be considered when implementing a VBE for a particular cluster. The VBE model specification should be supported by a reference framework selected after a comprehensive literature review. This representation aim at providing a better understanding of all elements involved in the VBE.
2. Assessment description. Based on the model specified in step 1, this step envisages to describe the important characteristics that should be considered when assessing actual organizations' preparedness against VBE creation requirements. These characteristics should be classified according to some predefined perspectives.
3. Preparedness pre-evaluation. This step performs a preliminary evaluation of how prepared the cluster's members are to support the characteristics described in step 2. This activity mainly consists in the specification of assessment questionnaires to evaluate the organizations' preparedness degree.
4. Preparedness analysis. Having an individual mapping of the main weakness and strengths of each organization, this step compiles a comprehensive and precise view about the candidates' global needs that is going to be used to specify a more tuned VBE implementation methodology.
5. Methodology instantiation. This step is devoted to specify the methodology for implementing the VBE regarding the previously assessed group of organizations. This methodology identifies the activities, their relationships and the actors involved in the VBE implementation.

Next sections detail these steps.

3 VBE Specification

In order to better understand the whole set of characteristics involved in the construction of a VBE it is necessary to model this VBE using a reference framework. Several works have addressed the problem related to model CNOs. A comprehensive review of the state-of-the-art about such subject is found in Baldo and Rabelo [4]. In this work, the authors state that ARCON modeling framework is suitable enough to model VBEs and can be used to model a VBE for an industrial clusters. ARCON (*A Reference Model for Collaborative Networks*) [5] brings the possibility to model abstract representations for understanding the involved CNO's entities and the relationship among them. ARCON intends to be used as the basis for deriving models for any manifestations of CNOs. In general terms, this is made applying three inter-related perspectives: Life Cycle; Environment Characteristics; and Model Intents.

Having selected the reference framework used to model the VBE, it is necessary to collect information for modeling the specific VBE. For the NuFerJ particular case, it has been used information collected mainly from the cluster itself and from an educational institution that has performed some studies inside NuFerJ. Concerning NuFerJ characterization, it can be said that NuFerJ (*Group of Moulds and Dies Industries of Joinville*) is a cluster founded in 1993 that has about 50 members. Several members are competitors with each other and their main customers are automobile and household appliance companies. Moulds and dies are very unique parts that are produced only once and each one of them uses to be very complex to manufacture [6]. Considering the increasing and extreme hard world-wide competition, NuFerJ has been looking for an alternative model which allows its members to better and more effectively prepare themselves for the new reality.

Taking into account ARCON modeling framework, a NuFerJ VBE Model has been created. This model classifies every element necessary to design the NuFerJ VBE, which in turn will guide the work towards its implementation. Baldo and Rabelo [4] presents the VBE model created specifically for NuFerJ, considering all involved elements in the Endogenous and Exogenous ARCON's subspaces [7].

4 Assessment Description

Taking into account that to implement a VBE it is necessary to know quite well the target cluster and its members, a way to perform such recognition is doing an assessment of the cluster members. This assessment evaluates the cluster members' preparedness to be part of a VBE. Conceive assessment strategies, e.g. questionnaires, base of the information available at the VBE model is to complex due to its broad coverage. So, to overcome this obstacle it is proposed to extract from the VBE model the relevant characteristics and to organize them into perspectives of assessment. Table 1 shows a sample of the identified characteristics. It is important to highlight that to assess the actual industries' preparedness degree is crucial because best practices showed in the literature stated that one of the main fails of VBEs is caused by industries not prepared in terms of: culture, governance, interoperation, etc.

Table 1. Perspectives and Characteristics for NuFerJ Members' Assessment

Perspective	Characteristic
Business Process	- Production planning process - Production control process and performance data collection - Purchase process
Organizational Structure	- Departments well-defined and structured - Functions and responsibilities defined - Low accumulation of functions per employee
Resources (human and ICT)	- High utilization of ICT - Enterprise resource planning system - Collaborative systems utilization (e-mail, chat, wflow, forum, etc.)
Organizational Culture	- Resource utilization optimization - Quality prioritization - Standards and norms utilization (technology and process models)
Market	- Target market well-defined - Customer interaction (post-sales) - Long-term planning

5 Preparedness Pre-evaluation

The characteristics contained in those perspectives mentioned in section 4 can be used as guideline to specify questions for evaluating how prepared an industry is to be part of a VBE. Thus, each identified characteristic, where a sample of them can be seen in Table 1, has been written as a question in order to ask for each candidate if it presents or not such VBE requirement. However, when appropriated, some characteristics have been combined into a single question due to their intrinsic correlation. The final version of such questionnaire has 45 questions divided among the five perspectives as follows:

- **Business Process**: 9 questions;
- **Organizational Structure**: 4 questions;
- **Resources (human and ICT)**: 14 questions;
- **Organizational Culture**: 13 questions;
- **Market**: 5 questions.

Each question on the questionnaire was conceived in a way to estimate the level of preparation of an industry concerning a specific characteristic. This level is estimated through a scale of possible values on which the industries should fit in one of them. This scale is composed of the following values: excellent, good, not good and bad. Besides that, each question has two verification options containing yes and no values, respectively. These options are necessaries in situations where a question is not applied for a specific industry or the industry does not have any manifestation of such characteristic stated in the question.

6 Preparedness Analysis

Having the questionnaire prepared it is time to start the interviews. The questionnaire has been applied to six industries that participating in the NuFerJ cluster. The selection of those six has been supported by a senior manager that knows pretty well most of the industries. During the selection, it has been chosen medium size industries with high automation and organizational degree, as well as small size industries with low automation and organizational degree.

The results obtained through the interviews have been first charted and afterwards analyzed and graphically plotted. In order to chart the obtained data the scale presented in the questionnaire (see section 5) has been converted as follows: "excellent" → 4; "good" → 3; "not good" → 2; "bad" → 1; "no" → 0.

Considering the business process perspective, in general terms the industries are not much prepared reaching 2.28 as average. It means that they do not have a good systematization of daily performed business processes. This has a direct impact in the VBE implementation process. Concerning the organizational structure, the industries have gotten a better level of preparation, reaching an average of 2.63. This result has been obtained because most of the industries are well-structured in departments physically separated, and their employees have well-defined functions. This characteristic is essential for industries that want to be part of a VBE because it supports the inter-organizational communication. Regarding the human and ICT resources, it can be verified that the industries utilize them in an moderated way, reaching 2.38 as average. However, assessing each industry separately it could be verified that there is a considerable difference among them, where some of them are highly automated while others are poorly automated. This discrepancy impacts negatively in the VBE implementation process because everyone needs to have a minimal ICT bases to collaborate. Considering the organizational culture, it could be observed that most of the industries do not stimulate neither internal nor external collaboration. This low preparedness, with 2.15 of average, represents the main problem to implement the VBE for NuFerJ because to slight improve this perspective it is necessary a deep change in institutional and organizational principles, and this takes time. About the market, this perspective reached the lowest average among all the perspectives evaluated, which is 1.87. This has been caused mainly because the industries are not habituated to make strategic planning. For instance, several industries do not have budget planning longer that one year. It is strong recommended to improve this aspect before allowing an industry to be part of a VBE.

7 Methodology Instantiation

The last step of the structured approach is to design the VBE implementation methodology. This methodology aims at identifying all the activities, as well as the sequence of their execution, necessary to cope with the main aspects modeled in the NuFerJ VBE Model. The activities' position inside the methodology is guided by the preparedness assessment done previously (see section 6). The methodology specified identifies which steps should be done within each VBE life cycle phase [3]. Next paragraphs detail the proposed methodology.

VBE Creation (*Foundation*): This phase is mainly devoted to define the VBE mission and goals, its strategies in terms of marketing, political, economical issues, and the operating rules and duties. Although it may vary, a VBE usually begins with the so-called strategic members, whose selection can be accomplished by a sort of commission. Business processes, ICT infrastructure and governance structure definitions complete the list of activities in this phase. Considering industries' market preparedness assessment done before, it can be noted that the definition of market and economical strategies will be the bottleneck.

VBE Creation (*Initiation & Recruiting*): This phase is concerned to recruiting the VBE members (the industries themselves) and the VBE supporting institutions (e.g. educational, financial, R&D institutions). Considering the VBE members, the envisaged competences should be firstly specified in order to invite the right members. Every candidate should be empowered with basis knowledge on how to work in a VBE, which includes the aspect of trust, governance, etc. Once the industry is ready, its ICT infrastructure is prepared. Having all this prepared, the VBE can be launched. Based on the organization culture preparedness it can be identified that the establishment of trust will take time.

VBE Operation (VBE management): VBE management comprises the activities related to full the operation of the VBE and its main business processes. In NuFerJ the processes of Membership management and ICT infrastructure management should be firstly introduced. Profile and Competence Management activity comes after that and includes the deployment of a system to register and maintain the information related to VBE members. A number of activities can start in parallel after this: Financial, Marketing, Performance, Acquisition, Trust, VE inheritance and Customer Relationship. Considering the resource assessment done previously, acquisition management is critical for NuFerJ because it has a tremendous impact on the final cost of the mould, so it can represent to win or lose the business.

VBE Operation (VE creation): VE creation encompasses activities devoted to the creation and initiation of new VEs. The Opportunity Identification is the first one to be deployed. This seems natural as it is responsible for brokering business. The Opportunity Quotation is the next one to be deployed. Based in the business process assessment, this is another critical task that must be paid attention because wrong quotations can imply on high financial losses. To deploy the partners selection it is necessary first the deployment of performance and trust management. The remaining activities are deployed in sequence: Contract Negotiation (among VE members), VE Planning (to specify which partners will do what and when), VE Registration (to prepare the VBE's repositories to store VE's information), and Launching management (to coordinate the VE starting).

8 Conclusions

This paper presents a structured approach devised to implement VBEs for mould and die industry sector. Its main contribution is to systematize the whole process that concerns the implementation of a VBE. Besides that, it also presents the first results of an ongoing research, which has been based on a case study where the devised approach is being applied for more than one year.

This work is essentially based on the ARCON reference model, applying a top-down approach to derive comprehensive instances of VBEs. This modeling of VBE not only facilitates the VBE scalability and change management, but also supports the

VBE implementation methodology specification as the model considers most of the possible elements involved in the VBE.

Even being a concrete methodology, the implementation itself of its several structured steps naturally depends on the particularities and preparedness level of the involved cluster's members. This means that such steps can present different complexity and take different times to be implemented.

Next steps are concerned to a deeper evaluation of the approach considering a larger number of NuFerJ's members as well as its further validation as long as the process of VBE creation proceeds.

Acknowledgements. This work has been partially supported by Brazilian Council for Scientific and Technological Development – CNPq. The authors thank NuferJ's managers, in particular Mr. Alexandre Wanzuita and Mr. Christian Dihlmann.

References

1. Vallejos, R.V., Lima, C.P., Varvakis, G.: Towards the development of a framework to create a virtual organisation breeding environment in the mould and die sector. Journal of Intelligent Manufacturing 18(5), 587–597 (2007)
2. Romero, D., Galeano, N., Molina, A.: A Virtual Breeding Environment Reference Model and its Instantiation Methodology. In: Ninth IFIP Working Conference on Virtual Enterprises. Springer, Poznan (2008)
3. Afsarmanesh, H., Camarinha-Matos, L.M.: A Framework for Management of Virtual Organization Breeding Environments. In: Collaborative Networks and their Breeding Environments, Valencia, Spain, pp. 35–48. Springer, Heidelberg, September 26-28 (2005)
4. Baldo, F., Rabelo, R.J.: For a Methodology to Implement Virtual Breeding Environments – A Case Study in the Mold and Die Sector in Brazil. In: Tenth IFIP Working Conference on Virtual Enterprises. Springer, Thessaloniki (2009)
5. Camarinha-Matos, L.M., Afsarmanesh, H.: The ARCON Modeling Framework. In: Camarinha-Matos, L.M., Afsarmanesh, H. (eds.) Collaborative Networks: Reference Modeling, pp. 67–82. Springer, New York (2008)
6. SOCIESC: Projeto Pesquisa de Mercado Interno para o APL Metalmecânico de Joinville, p. 57. SOCIESC - Educational Society of Santa Catarina, Joinville (2007)
7. Camarinha-Matos, L.M., et al.: ARCON Reference Models for Collaborative Networks. In: Camarinha-Matos, L.M., Afsarmanesh, H. (eds.) Collaborative Networks: Reference Modeling, pp. 83–112. Springer, New York (2008)

An Innovative Framework Supporting SME Networks for Complex Product Manufacturing

Luis Maia Carneiro[1], Ricardo Almeida[1,2], Américo Lopes Azevedo[1,2], Timo Kankaanpaa[3], and A.H.M. Shamsuzzoha[3]

[1] INESC Porto, Portugal
[2] FEUP, Portugal
[3] University of Vaasa, Finland
luis.carneiro@inescporto.pt, timo.kankaanpaa@uwasa.fi, ahsh@uwasa.fi

Abstract. Current market dynamics require European SME's to focus on complex products manufacturing and to build non-hierarchical business networks, to assure competitiveness and sustainability. Such trend demands appropriate methods for network formation and management, including reference collaboration processes and supporting ICT tools. This paper presents a framework to support SME's in the creation and management of non-hierarchical networks designed and developed within the European RTD project Net-Challenge. This framework includes methodologies, processes and ICT decision support tools aiming at the efficient creation and management of these networks assuring quick response times and competitive and differentiated offerings.

Keywords: complex manufacturing, dynamic networks, non-hierarchical business networks, sustainability.

1 Introduction

In the context of today's complex product manufacturing, SMEs will have to adopt new business models and to establish dynamic and non-hierarchical networks to respond to market opportunities, assuring quick response, fast time to market, differentiated offerings and competitive prices. Sustainability for SMEs will be found in high-variety low-volume businesses, related with complex products manufacturing [1], [2], [3].

The major problems when dealing with complex products in traditional manufacturing environments are usually the long lead times that require long planning horizons and the multiplicative effects of dependent demands of product components. Small disturbances on higher level components can lead to major problems in the supply network (i.e. the "whip effect" can have even more impact). Furthermore, high variety and low volume requirements can considerably increase the complexity of planning and imply the need for highly flexible resource configurations.

This environment where dynamic networks of SMEs emerge to respond to market opportunities will only work in practice if companies are provided with appropriate methods for network formation and management, reference collaboration processes and

L.M. Camarinha-Matos et al. (Eds.): PRO-VE 2010, IFIP AICT 336, pp. 204–211, 2010.

supporting ICT tools. However, there were no proven and effective methodologies, approaches or tools to support SMEs in creating, managing and dissolving this type of dynamic and non-hierarchical networks for complex products manufacturing.

This study presents a framework being designed and developed by the European RTD project NET-Challenge - Innovative networks of SMEs for complex products manufacturing that aims to fill this gap with the design of effective methodologies, processes and IT decision support tools. It presents an innovative architecture to ensure communication and operational management between companies included on non-hierarchical business networks, heading to achieve the needed flexibility, agility and sustainability.

2 The Net-Challenge Project

Temporary networks or Virtual Organizations (VO) are usually set up to dynamically respond to emerging market opportunities. The way companies react to these opportunities is critical to their performance in different phases of the network life-cycle (creating, managing and dissolving).

Net-Challenge is a European research project in the area of collaborative business networks; whose objective is to design, develop, validate and disseminate an integrated framework to support SMEs in creating, managing and dissolving dynamic and non-hierarchical networks for complex products manufacturing. This framework includes the following main components:

- A methodology to help SMEs in partner qualification, formation and operation of dynamic networks (able to quickly respond to market opportunities characterized by low volume, high variety and customer centered products);
- Reference collaboration processes for non-hierarchical networks, to be used to promote and facilitate real collaborative business processes;
- Distributed decision support tools to help companies to manage manufacturing and logistics processes, including: aggregate collaborative planning with dynamic capacity management and real-time order promising; real-time monitoring integrated with event management and performance management.

3 Business Requirements

3.1 Scope

Business requirements define the high-level needs and features, by focusing on the capabilities needed by the stakeholders and key-users. This chapter aims to define the major needs to promote collaboration in non hierarchical networks for complex products manufacturing.

To ensure a user driven approach, three Business Cases of non-hierarchical business networks aiming at the design and manufacturing of complex products were defined within the project. The business cases were selected to be representative of a large variety of industries and include the following sectors: textile, apparel and wearable technologies (Portugal), customized footwear (Italy) and machine tools (Spain). In each business field it was selected two case companies, acting in the same network. These companies played a key role in requirements analysis and will test and demonstrate the final results. The relations of these companies with their business partners was analyzed in detail, in order to deeply understand the present and potential future business networks these companies can promote [5].

3.2 Approach to Requirements Analysis

The approach used for this study (presented on Figure 1) was based, initially, on a research for current trends related with business collaboration and respective support tools, in order to define a target domain.

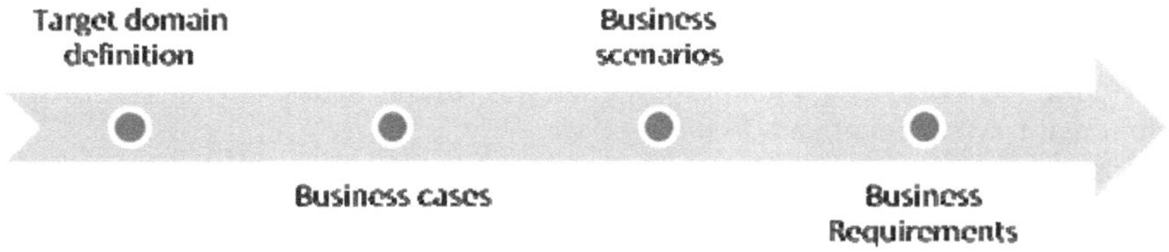

Fig. 1. Approach to requirements analysis

The second step was the detailed analysis of the case companies and the Business cases pilot networks. This was done through detailed interviews with key persons in the case companies and some of their business partners, following structured and detailed interview guidelines. The study was conducted through multiple case study approach, gathering and comparing retrieved information, and sharing the initial findings of the case companies.

The following step included the definition and discussion of future scenarios related with the creation and management of business networks. These future scenarios are like "short stories", easily understood and discussed with companies for a complete validation. Meetings with companies were organized to build and validate the respective scenarios and Skype meetings with RTD partners from the different countries were organized to harmonize and define integrated scenarios.

The analysis of the companies and respective networks and the analysis of the defined future scenarios were done to define the requirements for the Net-Challenge Framework.

3.3 Business Requirements

As an output from business scenarios and case company analysis, it was developed a single requirements list, which was submitted to a classification stage. The main objective was to identify the most important requirements for companies. Figure 2 presents a summary of the identified requirements.

Fig. 2. Business requirements

The requirements were then prioritized with the case companies by clarifying the main focus of the requirement. The case companies gave the highest priority to the following requirements (in the order of importance): 1) Updating production statuses, 2) Selection of partners for a specific business opportunity, 3) Lead-time calculation of a business opportunity, 4) Setup and enlargement of the business community, 5) Standardize and improve communication with the partners.

4 Proposed Framework

4.1 Concept

Innovative methods and collaborative processes are specifically designed for complex and customized products because they address very important market segments for European SMEs´ differentiation and sustainability.

The proposed approach assumes that the relations between participating companies are non-hierarchical and the decision making processes are decentralized. Individual companies must be able to find and receive the commitment of the required partner companies (in terms of competencies and available capacity) to respond to all potentially interesting market opportunities they are aware of in real time. SMEs will only be able to assure differentiation and long term sustainably through the ability to efficiently and effectively form these dynamic networks.

The vision defines the development of regional or sectorial Business Communities, where trust can be built and communication streamlined, as critical for the fast and efficient creation of these business networks.

The proposed framework is composed of three main components: **a Methodology, reference business processes and IT decision support tools**.

The proposed approach defines 5 main phases for the successful implementation of non-hierarchical networks of SMEs for high-variety, low-volume and complex products manufacturing, which are identified in the Methodology phases below.

4.2 The Net-Challenge Methodology

The proposed Methodology is structured in the main five phases of the Framework which are linked with the lifecycle of these networks.

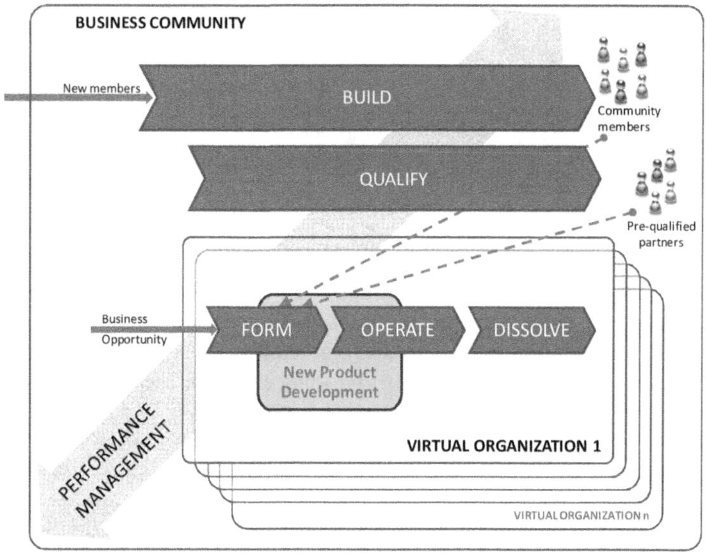

Fig. 3. The Methodology high-level structure

Phase 1: Build and develop a Business Community

The establishment of dynamic Business Communities is an important pre-requisite for the fast and efficient formation of temporary Virtual Organizations able to successfully respond to specific market opportunities. In this sense, the Building of Business Communities is seen as a crucial enabler for collaboration.

These Business Communities are business environments that comprise a significant number of organizations (mostly SMEs) where trust is developed and communication mechanisms are established. There should be easy mechanisms for finding business partners. This phase specifies the life-cycle of a Business Community and the needed activities and initiatives that need to be implemented to assure its desired performance [4], [6], [7]. Market research activities and sharing of business opportunities is promoted. Social networking and knowledge sharing is supported by relevant ICT tools.

Phase 2: Qualify

During all phases of non-hierarchical networks' lifecycle (and all phases of the Methodology) information about each company participating in the business community is collected and stored. This information will be stored in suitable information systems and a profile of each community member will be created and enriched over time.

For some critical business lines and/or operations community members need to ensure and develop the competencies and capabilities of potential partners. In other words, they need an innovative and collaborative qualification of potential partners. In those cases, companies will only consider qualified partners, instead of working with any member of the Business Community.

Phase 3: Form

The Form phase is responsible for the creation of a Virtual Organization to respond to a specific market opportunity. In the Form phase a group of partners are interactively selected to collaborate in order to develop and produce a product or collection of products [4], [8]. For complex products the collaborative product design activities assume a very important role. In the innovative approach designed, the product concept is defined in the Form phase to allow the rough plan of the VO and cost estimation. The detail engineering is carried out in the Operate phase.

For complex products manufacturing two complementary scenarios were defined:

(i) One-of-a-kind custom made products that are handled by an ETO (Engineer to Order) strategy.

(ii) Customized products, where a product platform is defined and the requirements from different customers are solved by ATO (Assemble to Order) strategies. The platform enables the customers to specify their needs based on the parameters and options available (customization). The routing and the bill-of-material (BOM) are generated automatically based on the customer selections.

Phase 4: Operate

The Operate phase is related with the execution of the planned operations to respond to a specific market opportunity.

The approach for Operation is different for the scenarios defined for one-of-a-kind and customized products. Operation starts by the detailed product engineering on the first case and with the engineering of the product platform on the second case.

On the first case, a detailed plan is defined, executed and monitored. On the second case different customers can place orders over time, which are individually planned and executed. In this second case the VO is kept active until there is sufficient demand for the designed product platform. In both cases unforeseen events are monitored and handled.

Phase 5: Dissolve

Virtual Organizations are created to accomplish a mission and not to operate forever. This mission is linked to responding to a Business Opportunity and should be included in the contract signed by partners when forming the VO. Therefore, this contract should also define when the VO will be dissolved as well as the strategies to follow in case other reasons provoke a premature dissolution. In this phase it is of paramount importance the activities related with performance evaluation and sharing of the knowledge accumulated.

4.3 Reference Collaboration Processes

Reference collaboration processes are defined for non-hierarchical business networks, promoting and facilitating real collaborative business processes, supporting the high level phases defined in the Methodology.

These reference collaboration processes are designed to allow an easy adaptation to each specific business network. The following areas are covered: Building and managing Business Communities (activities related with creating the business community, membership and profile management, knowledge management); Partner qualification (collaborative assessment and continuous improvement); VO Formation (activities related with product concept definition, technical validation of partner's capabilities and VO's rough plan); Order management and planning processes (activities which include order deployment, collaborative fine planning, monitoring production status); Event management (classification of events, procedures to be performed, handling of unexpected events) and Performance management (aiming at strategic and operational business alignment and continuous improvement).

4.4 IT Decision Support Tools

The proposed system architecture includes 4 major areas: Business Community management and integration infrastructure, Aggregate Collaborative Planning (ability of all partners to share and provide a common answer concerning production planning issues), Real Time Monitoring and Event Handling (accurate control of production status and event management, to promote quick answer to unexpected events) and Performance Management (which will constantly update network and partner's performance, for feedback purposes and future analysis, improvement and partner qualification).

For the management of the Business Community, the system concept includes social networking and knowledge management platforms. It supports the management of the community, including membership and profile management.

Taking into account this particular environment, the proposed Decision Support Tools need to be distributed. Each company will be provided with the set of key ICT tools to manage its collaborative activities, to integrate with traditional legacy systems, to interface with business partners and to support decision making. For company a rough capacity model is defined and updated in real time, to enable the real time information on available capacity.

The system architecture is defined to be simple and affordable, and applicable to most European SMEs. Available standards and interoperability frameworks are proposed, such as *TexWeave* and *Shoenet* data models, SOA and the *ebXML* (Electronic Business XML–defined by United Nations and OASIS) framework.

5 Conclusions and Future Developments

Dynamic and non-hierarchical business networks for complex products design and manufacturing is proposed as the key for European SMEs sustainability.

This paper presents the framework being designed and developed by the Net-Challenge European project, including effective methodologies, processes and ICT decision support tools, aiming at the successful and efficient implementation of such networks. It includes the development of an innovative architecture to ensure communication and operational management between companies included on non-hierarchical business networks, heading to achieve the needed flexibility and agility to company's sustainability.

This study relies on the conceptual framework of the Net-Challenge project, following the identified specific requirements for complex and customized products.

This project aims to apply their study results on real business scenarios; therefore, it's expected to validate the proposed methodologies, processes and ICT solutions on pilot companies, in order to evaluate an effective application.

Acknowledgements

The authors would like to acknowledge the co-funding of the European Commission within NMP priority of the Seventh RTD Framework Programme (2007-13) for the Net Challenge project (Innovative Networks of SMEs for Complex Products Manufacturing), Ref. CP-FP 229287-2. The authors also extend their acknowledgments to anonymous reviewers for their helpful comments and support.

References

1. Gunasekaran, A., Lai, K.-H., Cheng, E.: Responsive supply chain: A competitive strategy in a networked economy. Omega 36(4), 549–564 (2008)
2. Görlitz, O., Neubert, R., Benn, W.: Co-operation Formation in Nonhierarchical Production Networks. In: Proceedings of the eBusiness and eWork Conference (2004)
3. Myers, J.: Future Value Systems: Next Generation Economic Growth Engines & Manufacturing. In: Proceedings of the IMS Vision Forum 2006, Seoul, Korea, pp. 30–47 (2006)
4. Camarinha-Matos, L.M., Afsarmanesh, H., Ollus, M.: Ecolead and CNO Base Concepts. In: Methods and Tools for Collaborative Networked Organizations. Springer Science+Business Media, LLC 2008, Heidelberg (2008)
5. Carneiro, L., Kankaanpää, T., Almeida, R., Ferreira, P., Loichate, M., Pecina, M., Fornasiero, R., Zaniacomi, A., Chiodi, A., Rymaszewska, A.: Specification of Business Cases. Delivery D1.2. NetChallenge Project (2009)
6. Julka, N., Baines, T., Tjahono, B., et al.: A review of multi-factor capacity expansion models for manufacturing plants. Int. J. Prod. Econ. 106(2), 607–621 (2007)
7. Van Mieghem, J.A.: Capacity management, investment, and hedging: Review and recent developments. Manuf. Serv. Oper. Manag. 5(4), 269–302 (2003)
8. Chen, Q.X., Chen, X., Lee, W.B.: Qualitative search algorithms for partner selection and task allocation in the formulation of virtual enterprise. International Journal of Computer Integrated Manufacturing 2(20) (2007)

The Implications of the 4 C's of Supply Chain Network Interaction Strategies for Cost Information Visibility and Network Profitability – An Integrative Model

Jyotirmoyee Bhattacharjya[1,*], David Walters[1], and Charlotte Newton[2]

[1] Institute of Transport and Logistics Studies, The University of Sydney, Newtown Campus, 144 Burren Street, Newtown, NSW 2042, Australia
[2] Northeast Europe IBM Basel
{jyotirmoyee.bhattacharjya,david.walters}@sydney.edu.au, charlotte.newton@uk.ibm.com

Abstract. The globalization of supply and demand has resulted in increasingly complex supply chain interaction strategies across different industries. Since the different interaction strategies are associated with different types of interdependence between partners, the impact of these strategies on cost information visibility across a supply chain network merits further investigation. The importance of cost information visibility lies in the fact that a firm's internal costs can often depend on the business processes of other members within their network. The paper uses a multi-theoretical perspective to develop an integrative model of the impact of the different dimensions of interaction strategies on cost information visibility and profitability in supply chain networks.

Keywords: Coordination, collaboration, interdependence, cost information visibility, profitability.

1 Introduction

Organizations increasingly operate within globally distributed complex supply chain networks and employ different interaction strategies due to their interdependence on other members. The configurations for these interaction strategies have been described by 4 C's: communicative, coordinated, collaborative, co-opetitive [7]. Although these 4 C's have been defined variously in the literature, but their underlying concept of interdependence, can potentially have a significant impact on cost information visibility for members in a supply chain network. Many business decision-makers struggle with limited supply chain cost visibility and an understanding of how the costs of other members in their network affect their own costs [45]. While information technologies has been shown to positively influence general information visibility in a supply chain [e.g., 48] the relational factors that

* Corresponding author.

L.M. Camarinha-Matos et al. (Eds.): PRO-VE 2010, IFIP AICT 336, pp. 212–218, 2010.

specifically influence cost information visibility need further investigation. This paper attempts to provide some insight in this context.

2 Theoretical Background

The interactions between companies in a supply chain network are complex and may involve the flow of physical goods [2], finances [3] and information [4] across organizational boundaries. A number of issues add to the complexity of these interactions and pose challenges for researchers: time, interdependence, relativity, jointness and subjective interpretation [1]. The nature of interactions between companies at a given time may be an outcome of their previous interactions, current interactions with others and anticipation of future interactions.

2.1 The 4 C's of Configuration in Network Based Interaction Strategies

Fiske [5] identified four relational forms as fundamental to most forms of social interactions: market pricing, authority ranking, equality matching and communal sharing. The market pricing relational form is one based on socially meaningful rates such as prices, wages and rents. Authority ranking relationships involve people in asymmetric positions in a hierarchy. Equality matching relationships are those in which people keep track of the emerging difference between participants and what is required to restore the balance. Communal sharing involves people treating a group as equivalent to the given domain. Building on this conceptualization of relational forms [5], Sheppard and Sherman [6] identified four forms of interdependence based on depth (i.e., intensity) and form (i.e., the directionality of dependence): shallow dependence, deep dependence, shallow interdependence and deep interdependence. The term dependence implies that the nature of dependency is unidirectional. Shallow dependence involves a transfer of responsibility from one party to another and relates to Fiske's market pricing relational form. Shallow interdependence involves parties coordinating their behavior in order to achieve their objectives and is associated with the equality matching relational form. Deep dependence relates to the authority ranking relational form and involves a principal-agent type of relationship with knowledge based asymmetry. Deep interdependence involves parties having a greater and wider-ranging reliance on each other and is associated with the communal sharing relational form. Based on these ideas of relational form and depth and form of interdependence, Lejeune and Yakova [7] distinguished between four types of supply chain configurations. The four configurations are as follows:

- *Communicative* - This type of configuration ([7],[8],[9],[10]) is related to the market pricing relational form and characterized by shallow dependence. Collaboration only takes place at an inter-functional level within each company in the network.
- *Coordinated* - This configuration ([7],[13],[14],[15]) is related to the authority ranking relational form and characterized by deep dependence. These types of supply chain networks are dominated by a lead organization ([11],[12],[16],[17]) and exhibit a combination of both reliability and deterrent-based trust [7].

- *Collaborative*: This configuration relates to the equality matching relational form and is characterized by shallow interdependence. Trust in this context is reliability, competency and goodwill (openness) based [8] and the decision-making process is dyadic, parity-based and centralized ([18],[19]).
- *Co-opetitive*: This configuration ([20],[21],[24],[25]) relates to the communal sharing relational form and is marked by deep interdependence. It is viewed as an example of lateral collaboration in which competitors share resources and private information [22]. Trust in co-opetitive supply chains is based on reliability, competency and goodwill (openness and benevolence). Unlike collaborative supply chains co-opetitive ones exhibit both components of goodwill trust - openness and benevolence ([23],[9]).

This classification of configurations, though insightful, does not explicitly take into account the evolving nature of relationships in the network over time and the dynamic nature of resources and capabilities which form the basis of interdependence as suggested by [1]. Resource dependency theory and the relational view provide some insight in this context.

2.2 Resources and Capabilities in Supply Chain Networks

Relational View. This perspective [26] extended the arguments presented by the resource based view of the firm ([27], [28], [29]) to introduce the notion that the critical resources of a firm may lie beyond organizational boundaries and may be embedded in interorganizational routines and resources. Some potential sources of interorganizational competitive advantage are identified by this view: relation-specific assets, knowledge sharing routines, complementary resources/capabilities and effective governance [26]. Time can play an important role in the context of these sources of relational rent. Supply chain members can combine capabilities or resources which then coevolve over time and become difficult to imitate, thus becoming a source of competitive advantage. Informal safeguards, such as goodwill trust and reputation may also take considerable time to develop and are also subject to opportunity for abuse [30].

Resource Dependency Perspective. This view focuses on how organizations acquire resources and thereby affect their power relationships with other firms ([31], [32]). It is based on three assumptions [33]. Firstly, organizations are assumed to comprise of external and internal coalitions arising from social exchanges which are designed to influence behavior [32]. Secondly, the environment contains critical resources and poses variability and complexity during acquisition from other firms [34] which can be reduced by forming different types of linkages [33]. Thirdly, organizations work towards acquiring control over resources that minimize their dependence on other firms and maximize the dependence of other firms on themselves and attaining either objective could affect an organization's power [31]. For example, Millenium Pharmaceuticals, a company that had in the past relied quite heavily on partnerships, began to undertake acquisitions in the late 1990's in order to expand its downstream presence [35] but was subsequently acquired by the Takeda Group in 2008 [36]. This third assumption, therefore, points towards the dynamic nature of configuration in supply chain network interaction strategies.

3 Antecedents and Outcomes of Cost Information Visibility – An Emergent Model

Total Productivity and Profitability. The term productivity means different things to different people. This paper adopts the definition suggested by Craig and Harris [37]. According to this definition, the total productivity of a firm is the ratio of the total output in dollars and the sum of the labor input, capital input, raw material and purchased parts and other miscellaneous goods and services (also in dollars). Productivity is positively related to the profitability of a firm ([38],[39]) and has been measure in terms of return on equity (ROE), the ratio of a firm's net income and the shareholders' total equity [39]. While the literature suggests that the business landscape is one of networks competing against each other (e.g. [40]), there is little attempt to describe profitability from a network perspective. In attempting to address this issue, this paper defines network profitability as an index which is *the sum of ROE's of all firms in the supply chain network for a given configuration at a given time*.

Cost Information Visibility. The issue of cost information visibility poses many challenges in a supply chain context, including supplier guile and the lack of managerial experience in sharing sensitive cost information with other supply chain members [41]. Use of archaic cost allocation processes [42], different definitions of overhead costs [43], managerial awareness of weakness in internal cost systems, perception of cost management as an internal affair, lack of agreement amongst supply chain members regarding which costs to report, levels of dependence and trust [44] have all been argued to inhibit cost transparency. The visibility of cost information across a firm's supply chain network can provide opportunities for driving cost reductions and enabling higher performance as many internal costs of a firm can result from the business practices and behavior of other members of the supply chain network [45]. Such improvement in performance could be manifested as higher productivity and profitability for an organization. The model in Figure 1 considers *both a buyer's perception of a supplier's cost visibility and vice versa.*

Dimensions of Network Interaction Strategy. The four types of network configurations (communicative, coordinated, collaborative and co-opetitive) have been differentiated in the literature in terms of form (trust and decision-making) and depth (information sharing and goal congruence) of interdependence [7]. It has also been suggested that practitioners may have a different perspective on interorganizational relationships than researchers [46,47] and network members may themselves subjectively interpret the actions of other members [1]. Given the dynamic and complex nature of interfirm relationships, different configurations may even co-exist within the same network and the distinction between the configurations may not be as clear. Therefore, rather than focusing on the specific configurations, the model in Figure 1 considers the *perceived overall nature* of the two dimensions (*form of interdependence and depth of interdependence*) based on which these configurations are distinguished and their influence on cost visibility. It also assumes that there may be differences in perceptions between buyers and suppliers with regards to both form and depth of interdependence.

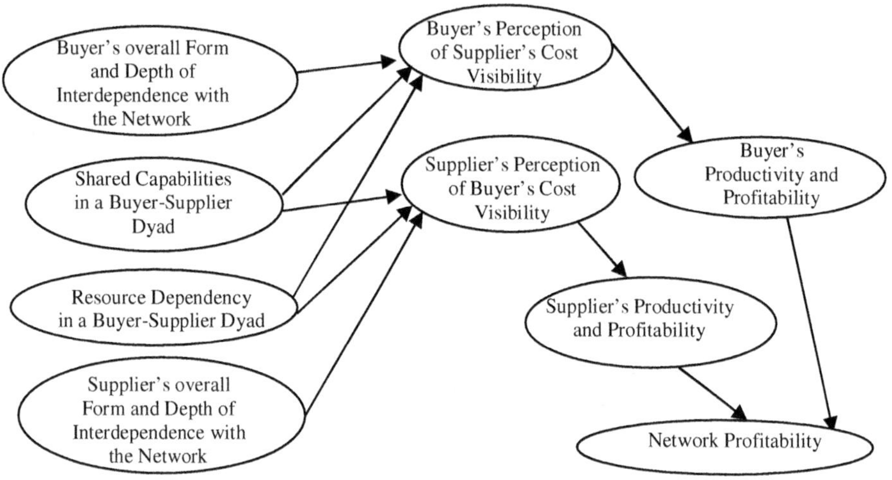

Fig. 1. The Influence of Network and Dyad Level Interdependencies on Perceived Cost Information Visibility and Profitability

Capabilities and Resources in Relationships. Interdependence in interorganizational relationships generally arises from different firms combining their resources and capabilities [26] or from the dependency of one firm on the resources of another ([31], [32]). These bonds evolve over time and may impact upon the perceived cost information visibility. The integrative model is illustrated in Figure 1.

4 Discussion

The paper presents an integrative model of the antecedents and outcomes of cost information visibility in a supply chain network. The model is in early stages of development and does not incorporate broader environmental factors like national cultures and regulatory requirements which could vary across a global supply chain network. It also does not include intra-organizational factors such as leadership that might have significant influence on supply chain decisions. It should also be noted that theory often lags business practice and misses the organic nature of change in the business landscape. These issues suggest that the model could be further refined based on input from supply chain practitioners and future research could identify how cost information visibility evolves over time based on changing antecedents and verify the impact of improved cost information visibility on firm and network profitability.

References

1. Ford, D., Håkansson, H.: The Idea of Business Interaction. The IMP J. 1, 4–20 (2005)
2. Stevens, G.C.: Successful Supply Chain Management. Management Decision 28, 25–30 (1990)

3. Mabert, V.A., Venkatraman, M.A.: Special Research Focus on Supply Chain Linkages: Challenges for Design and Management in the 21st Century. Decision Sciences 29, 537–550 (1998)
4. Lee, H.L., Padmanabhan, V., Whang, S.: Information Distortion in Supply Chain: The Bullwhip Effect. Management Science 43, 546–558 (1997)
5. Fiske, A.P.: Relativity within Moose ("Mossi") culture: four incommensurable models for social relationships. Ethos 18, 180–204 (1990)
6. Sheppard, B.H., Tuchinsky, M.: Interfirm relationships: a grammar of pairs. In: Cummings, L.L., Staw, B.M. (eds.) Research in Organizational Behavior, vol. 18, pp. 331–373. JAI Press, Greenwich (1996)
7. Lejeune, M.A., Yakova, N.: On characterizing the 4 C's in supply chain management. Journal of Operations Management 23, 81–100 (2005)
8. Handfield, R.B., Nichols Jr., E.L.: Introduction to Supply Chain Management. Prentice-Hall, Upper Saddle River (1999)
9. Stuart, F.I., McCutcheon, D.M.: The manager's guide to supply chain management. Business Horizons 43, 23–44 (2001)
10. Villa, A.: Introducing some supply chain management problems. International Journal of Production Economics 73, 1–4 (2001)
11. Alvarado, U.Y., Kotzab, H.: Supply chain management: the integration of logistics in marketing. Industrial Marketing Management 30, 183–198 (2001)
12. García-Dastugue, S.J., Lambert, D.M.: Internet-enabled coordination in the supply chain. Industrial Marketing Management 32, 251–263 (2003)
13. Käser, P.A.W., Miles, R.E.: Understanding knowledge activists' successes and failures. Long Range Planning 35, 9–28 (2002)
14. Cox, A., Sanderson, J., Watson, G.: Supply chains and power regimes: toward an analytic framework for managing extended networks of buyer and supplier relationships. Journal of Supply Chain Management 37, 28–35 (2001)
15. Kelley, H.H., Thibaut, J.W.: Interpersonal Relations: A Theory of Interdependence. Wiley, New York (1978)
16. Dyer, D.H., Ouchi, W.G.: Japanese-style partnerships: giving companies a competitive edge. Sloan Management Review, 51–63 (1993)
17. Fung, V.K., Fung, W.K., Wind, Y.: Competing in a Flat World: Building Enterprises for a Borderless World. Wharton School Publishing, Upper Saddle River (2008)
18. Grandori, A., Soda, G.: Inter-firm networks: antecedents, mechanisms and forms. Organization Studies 16, 183–214 (1995)
19. Clark, T.H., Lee, H.G.: Electronic commerce and supply chain management. Information Technology and Management 1, 85–105 (2000)
20. Brandenburger, A.M., Nalebuff, B.J.: Co-opetition. Doubleday, New York (1996)
21. Bengtsson, M., Kock, S.: "Coopetition" in business networks – to compete and cooperate simultaneously. Industrial Marketing Management 29, 411–426 (2000)
22. Simatupang, T.M., Sridharan, R.: The collaborative supply chain. International Journal of Logistics Management 13, 15–30 (2002)
23. Strickland, L.H.: Surveillance and trust. Journal of Personality 26, 200–215 (1958)
24. Grahovac, J., Chakravarty, A.: Sharing and lateral transshipment of inventory in a supply chain with expensive low-demand items. Management Science 47, 579–594 (2001)
25. Greis, N.P., Kasarda, J.D.: Enterprise logistics in the information era. California Management Review 39, 55–78 (1997)
26. Dyer, J.H., Singh, H.: The Relational View: Cooperative Strategy and Sources of Interorganizational Competitive Advantage. Academy of Management Review 23, 660–679 (1998)

27. Barney, J.: Firm resources and sustained competitive advantage. Journal of Management 17, 99–120 (1991)
28. Rumelt, R.P.: How much does industry matter? Strategic Management Journal 12, 167–185 (1991)
29. Wernerfelt, B.: A resource-based view of the firm. Strategic Management Journal 5, 171–180 (1984)
30. Granovetter, M.: Economic action and social structure: The problem of embeddedness. American Journal of Sociology 91, 481–510 (1985)
31. Pfeffer, J.: Power in organizations. Pitman, Marshfield (1981)
32. Pfeffer, J., Salancik, G.: The external control of organizations. Harper and Row, New York (1978)
33. Ulrich, D., Barney, J.B.: Perspectives in organizations: Resource dependence, efficiency, and population. Academy of Management Review 9, 471–481 (1984)
34. Pfeffer, J.: The micropolitics of organizations. In: Meyer, M.W., Associates (eds.) Environments and organizations, pp. 29–50. Jossey-Bass, San Francisco (1978)
35. Champion, D.: Mastering the Value Chain - An Interview with Mark Levin of Millennium Pharmaceuticals. Harvard Business Review, 108–115 (2001)
36. Takeda Pharmaceutical Company Limited, Takeda Completes Acquisition of Millennium (2008), http://www.takeda.com/press/article_29939.html
37. Craig, C.E., Harris, R.C.: Total Productivity Measurement at the Firm Level. Sloan Management Review 14, 13–29 (1973)
38. Anderson, E.W., Fornell, C., Rust, R.T.: Consumer satisfaction, productivity, and profitability: Differences between goods and services. Marketing Science 16, 311–329 (1997)
39. He, Y.-Q., Chan, L.-K., Wu, M.-L.: Balancing productivity and consumer satisfaction for profitability: Statistical and fuzzy regression analysis. European Journal of Operations Research 176, 252–263 (2007)
40. Lambert, D.M., Cooper, M.C.: Issues in supply chain management. Industrial Marketing Management 29, 65–83 (2000)
41. Lamming, R., Jones, O., Nicol, D.: Transparency in the Value Stream from Open-Book Negotiation to Cost Transparency. In: Hines, R., Lamming, R., Jones, D., Cousins, P., Rich, N. (eds.) Value Stream Management. Pearson Education Limited, Harlow (2000)
42. Cokins, G.: Activity-Based Cost Management: An Executive's Guide. John Wiley & Sons, New York (2001)
43. Munday, M.: Buyer-Supplier Partnerships and Cost Data Disclosure. Management Accounting 70, 28–35 (1992)
44. Kajuter, P., Kulmala, H.I.: Open-Book Accounting in Networks - Potential Achievements and Reasons for Failures. Management Accounting Research 16 (2005)
45. Pohlen, T.L., Klammer, T.P., Cokins, G.: The Handbook of Supply Chain Costing. Council of Supply Chain Management Professionals, Lombard, Illinois (2009)
46. Porac, J.F., Thomas, H., Baden-Fuller, C.: Competitive groups as cognitive communities: the case of Scottish knitwear manufacturers. Journal of Management Studies 26, 397–415 (1989)
47. Reger, R.K., Huff, A.: Strategic groups: a cognitive perspective. Strategic Management Journal 14, 103–123 (1993)
48. Wang, E.T.G., Wei, H.-L.: Interorganizational Governance Value Creation: Coordinating for Information Visibility and Flexibility in Supply Chains. Decision Sciences 38, 647–674 (2007)

Idioms for Collaborative Government Networks – Conceptualization and Applications to Seamless Services

Elsa Estevez[1,2], Adegboyega Ojo[1], and Tomasz Janowski[1]

[1] United Nations University – International Institute for Software Technology
Center for Electronic Governance
P.O. Box 3058, Macao SAR, China
[2] National University of the South, Department of Computer Science and Engineering
{elsa,ao,tj}@iist.unu.edu

Abstract. We examine the nature of Collaborative Networked Organizations in Government (CNO-G) and identify three core capabilities characterising such organizations - Partnership, Coordination and Integration. By considering these capabilities as idioms for the CNO-G domain, we define a conceptual model that expresses such capabilities using modeling abstractions provided by ARCON (A Reference Model for Collaborative Networks). Finally, we illustrate the resulting domain-specific modelling framework through the example of a concrete CNO-G aimed at delivering a seamless public service.

Keywords: Modeling Collaborative Networked Organizations, Idioms for Collaborative Government Networks, Seamless Public Services.

1 Introduction

e-Government is defined as the use of Information and Communication Technologies (ICT) to achieve better government [1]: to provide customer-focused, efficient and reliable access to public services; to engage citizens in two-ways interactions with government; to support internal government operations; to enable cross-agency public services, etc. e-Government development increasingly aims at enabling collaboration and networking between agencies, with its highest maturity level - Seamless Government reached when strong collaboration leads to the whole public administration behaving as a single organization.

Seamless Government [2] promotes technology-enabled improvement through collaboration in government: between agencies from different levels and functions of government; between public, private and voluntary sectors; and between public administration systems. Collaboration in government offers clear benefits: better sharing of information by agencies, higher utilization of resources, more engaged policy-making, delivery of Seamless Public Services, etc. The latter, accessed through one-stop portals and organized into clusters, allow customers to specify their needs – life situations for citizens or business episodes for businesses, and obtain services to fulfill such needs, unaware which agency or government level should be contacted.

L.M. Camarinha-Matos et al. (Eds.): PRO-VE 2010, IFIP AICT 336, pp. 219–226, 2010.

However, a transition from the operations carried out by a single agency to the operations by several collaborating agencies is difficult. What an agency is able to achieve on its own, considering existing legal frameworks, financial arrangements, working culture, organizational structure and technological preparation may be difficult to scale up to the cross-agency context. Building Collaborative Networked Organizations in Government (CNO-G) is challenging. The aim of this paper is to enable design and development of such networks through domain-specific modeling.

A number of frameworks exist to model Collaborative Networked Organizations (CNO) in general [3] including the Zachman's Frameworks, GERAM - Generalized Enterprise Reference Architecture, and ARCON - A Reference Model for Collaborative Networks. In particular, ARCON consolidates existing frameworks through generic abstractions to model basic elements of CNO [3][4]. It defines three modeling perspectives and three levels of abstraction to describe CNOs, covering both domain-independent and domain-specific aspects of such organizations.

This paper provides a domain-specific modeling framework of CNO-G based on ARCON, expressing CNO-G models as ARCON idioms for the e-Government domain, and demonstrating the application of the framework through a case study involving the delivery of a seamless public service by a concrete CNO-G. The paper makes three contributions: (1) it validates the applicability of ARCON for modeling CNO at the specific and implementation levels; (2) it provides rigorous descriptions of the core CNO-G concepts based on ARCON; and (3) it provides prescriptive models to guide the design and development of CNO-G.

The rest of the paper is organized as follows. Sections 2 and 3 outline CNO-G and the ARCON modeling framework respectively. Section 4 carries out domain-specific modeling for CNO-G based on ARCON: general representations (Section 4.1); specific models of the partnership, integration and coordination idioms (Section 4.2); and an implementation model for a CNO-G that delivers a seamless public service (Section 4.3). Section 5 outlines conclusions and directions for future work.

2 Collaborative Government Networks

Organizations today are faced with rapidly changing environments that require flexible structures and fast responses to emerging needs and opportunities. Networked organizations, characterized by team-based structures and highly decentralized control [5] emerged from hierarchical organizations in response to such changes.

In government, the adoption of networked organizations has been influenced by policy formation through interactions between the actors with different interests and goals [6], the need for individual agencies to overcome asymmetries [7], etc. The adoption was reinforced by the practices of [8]: the use of external entities to deliver services and fulfill policy goals; many agencies at different government levels providing integrated services; provisioning of customized services to respond to increasing customer demands for more choices; and acquisition of IT infrastructures that enable real-time collaboration with external partners. In response, different network patterns have emerged [9][8]: joined-up government, whole-of-government, public-private partnerships, etc. leading to the benefits of: higher performance, innovation in policy making, and stability of relationships allowing network actors to combine their knowledge, experience and resources in new and productive ways [7].

Two types of collaboration are carried out within government networks - vertical and horizontal [10]. The former involves collaboration across levels of government and includes (1) information seeking and (2) adjustment seeking. The latter involves actors at the same level of authority and includes: (3) policy making and strategy making, (4) resource exchange and (5) project-based work. See Table 1.

Table 1. CNO-G collaboration types

NO	TYPE	EXAMPLE
1	Information seeking	interpretation of standards and rules
2	Adjustment seeking	policy changes
3	Policy and strategy making	engaging in policy making
4	Resource exchange	seeking financial resources or incentives
5	Project-based work	partnership for projects and seeking resources

The structure of government networks plays a major role in attaining the desired goals, including a system of authority that determines how the partners coordinate their actions and use resources to achieve their goals [11]. In general, coordination is deployed to ensure that the network's functional and organizational resources create the maximum value, implemented through structural decisions related to control and oversight [5][11][12]. Control mechanisms are: (1) providing the context for action, (2) providing advice and information to support action and (3) authorization or direct supervision over action execution [6]. In addition, control can take place within an overall coordination context; from direct supervision; through standardization of work processes, outputs and skills; to mutual adjustment by network partners [6]. Specific instruments for coordination and control are budget-making and oversight processes to fund network initiatives.

Guided by collaboration goals and activity types, the CNO-G design fundamentally relies on: (1) the partnership configuration required for the collaboration activity; (2) the integration through shared functions implemented as services and processes, and supporting shared resources; and (3) the overall coordination mechanism to optimize the structure, function and network resources towards achieving collaboration goals.

3 Modeling CNO in ARCON

The ARCON modeling framework includes abstractions to capture CNO entities and their relationships [3]. The framework defines three modeling perspectives: (1) life cycle stages, (2) environment characteristics and (3) modeling intents. The first comprises: creation, operation, evolution, metamorphosis and dissolution. The second identifies internal aspects of the CNO (endogenous elements) and interactions with the environment (exogenous interactions). The third defines modeling layers: general representation, specific modeling, and implementation modeling. See Fig. 1.

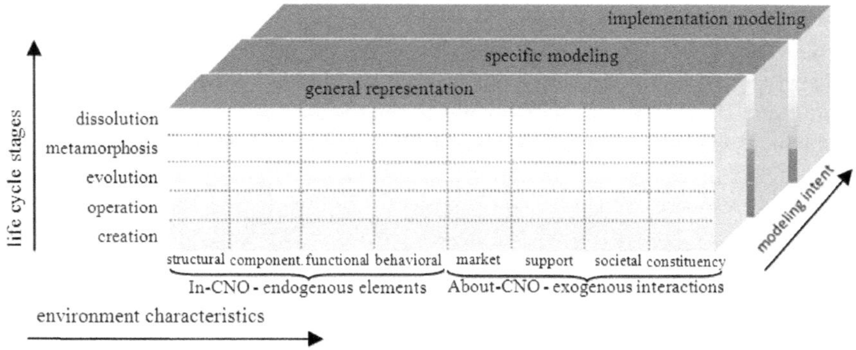

Fig. 1. ARCON Reference Model

The environmental aspects are divided into: endogenous elements - structural, componential, functional and behavioral (In-CNO); and exogenous interactions - market, support, societal and constituency (About-CNO). In the following, we focus on the In-CNO subspace as relevant to CNO-G. The subspace includes four types of endogenous elements: (1) Structural – identifies the constituting elements of CNO like members and their relationships and roles, and other member- and network-related attributes; (2) Componential – tangible and intangible resources of CNO such as hardware and software, human resources, information and knowledge resources, and meta-data repositories owned by CNO; (3) Functional – the elements that enable the operations of CNO, such as processes and methodologies; and (4) Behavioral – the elements that drive or constraint the behavior of CNO members, for example the elements specifying prescriptive and mandatory behaviors, constraints and conditions, and contracts and cooperation agreements.

4 Modeling CNO-G Based on ARCON

This section shows how the structural, componential, functional and behavioral aspects of CNO-G and their collaboration goals (Section 2) can be captured by three domain-specific concepts – partnership, integration and coordination, treated as idioms for the application of ARCON (Section 3) to the e-Government domain.

4.1 General Representation

In order to achieve collaboration goals, CNO-G members create partnerships to identify the members involved in collaboration and their roles, and integrate processes to enable the execution of multi-organizational processes as part of Seamless Government. Partnership and Integration extend Structural and Functional dimensions of ARCON respectively. Both dimensions match: structures are defined to fulfill processes, processes are assigned to members, and both support members to achieve collaboration goals. Integration is defined by extending Componential aspects and integrated resources are supplied to execute integrated functions. Coordination is required to shape Partnership and guide Integration, but the type of Partnership influences the way Coordination is performed; Coordination is modeled using the Behavioral dimension of ARCON. The model is depicted on the left side of Figure 2, with the corresponding UML Class Diagram on the right. The latter includes: CNO-G Collaboration Goal is implemented through Partnership, Integration and Coordination; Partnership contributes to Integration; Coordination governs Partnership and Integration; all apply ARCON interfaces - Partnership (Structural), Integration (Componential and Functional) and Coordination (Behavioral).

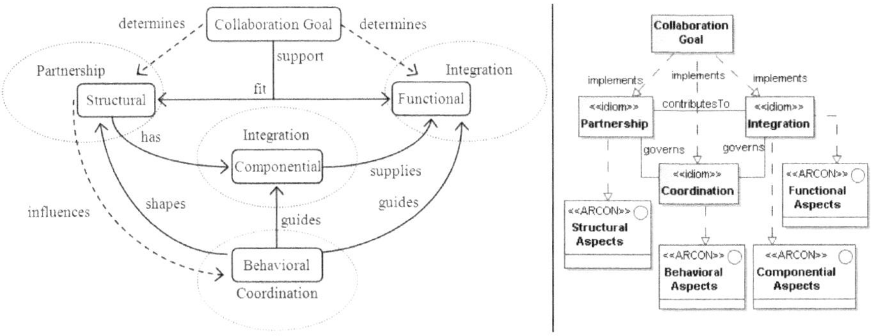

Fig. 2. CNO-G Capabilities - ARCON Meta-Model and its Formalization

4.2 Specific Modeling

At a lower level of abstraction, corresponding to the ARCON specific modeling level, the Partnership, Integration and Coordination capabilities are modeled using UML Class Diagrams, with the corresponding idioms depicted in Figures 3, 4 and 5.

Partnership consists of Partners, each determining other Partners, having Partner Role and Partner Responsibility, and contributing to Shared Resources and Shared Functions (part of Integration). Partner is ARCON Actor and Partner Role is ARCON Role. Partnership has different types (Partnership Type): Public-Private Partnership, Inter-Agency Collaboration and Multi-Stakeholder Partnership. See Figure 3.

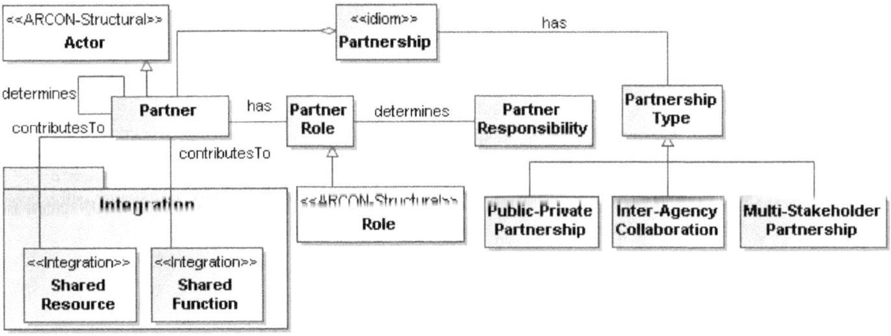

Fig. 3. CNO-G Modeling – Partnership Idiom

According to Figure 4, Integration produces Shared Resources and Shared Functions. Generalizing ARCON elements, Shared Resources may be Technological - Hardware and Software; Human - Human Resources; or Informational - Data, Information and Ontology. Shared Functions are executed by Shared Processes which can be Core or Auxiliary, both subtypes of the corresponding ARCON elements. Finally, Integration applies Integration Methods as a kind of ARCON Methodology.

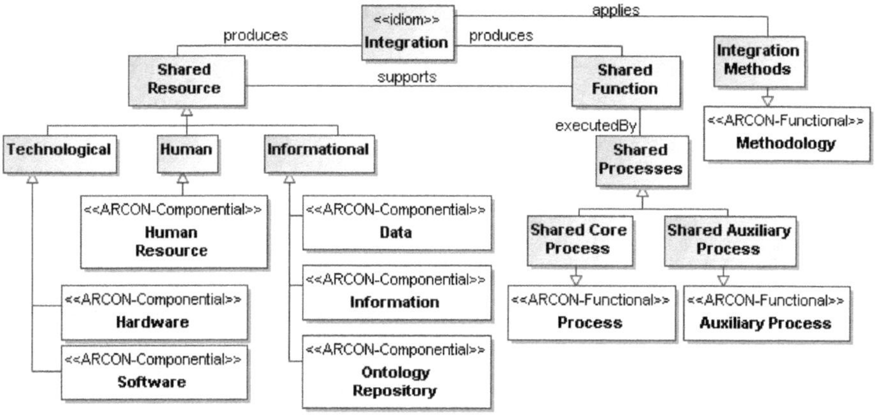

Fig. 4. CNO-G Modeling – Integration Idiom

According to Figure 5, Coordination is carried out by a Central Unit which is of two possible types: Organizational Structure – created as a government agency, or Committee – group of top-level decision makers. Both are ARCON Actors. A Central Unit issues Recommendations, enforces Standards and Guidelines, and defines Collaboration Frameworks. Recommendations are a sub-type of ARCON Prescriptive Behavior, Standards and Guidelines are subtypes of ARCON Obligatory Behavior, while Collaboration Frameworks is a subtype of ARCON Cooperation Agreement.

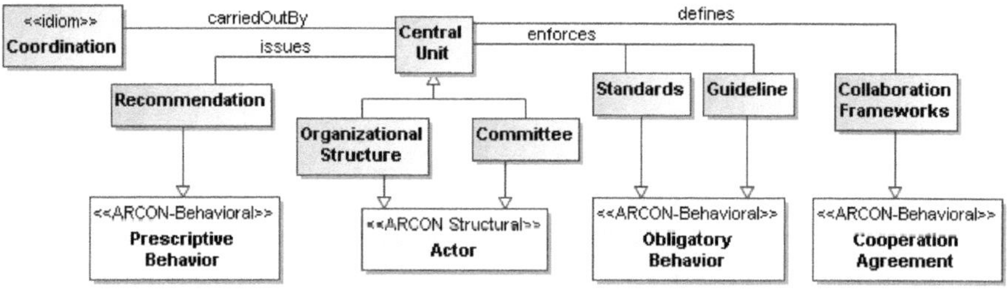

Fig. 5. CNO-G Modeling – Coordination Idiom

4.3 Implementation Modeling

As an implementation model, we present a real-life CNO-G comprising a set of agencies of the Government of Macao SAR, jointly issuing business licenses for running food and beverage establishments. The Civic and Municipal Affairs Bureau (IACM) is responsible for issuing such licenses, relying on other agencies to carry out inspections, provide technical opinions, and check conformance to relevant laws. Depicted in Figure 6, the application process comprises [14]: (1) Submission - an applicant submits an application form and supporting documents; (2) Completeness Assessment – IACM checks completeness of the application and notifies the applicant about any missing parts; (3) Evaluation – IACM requests opinions from: Labor Bureau about safety of the working environment, Public Works Bureau about construction plans, Cultural Affairs Bureau about outdoor landscaping for cultural heritage, Fire Brigade about fire prevention and Health Bureau about sanitary conditions; (4) Decision Making - IACM makes a decision based on the opinions; and (5) Follow-up – IACM notifies the applicant and issues the license if granted.

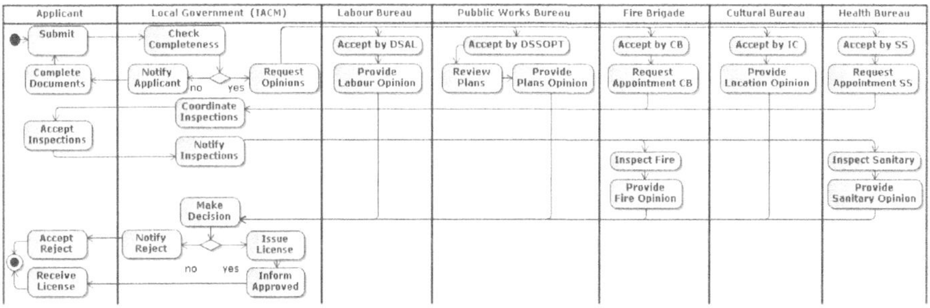

Fig. 6. Implementation Modeling - Licensing Service Workflow

Based on this example, the implementation model for Partnership is presented as a UML Object Diagram in Figure 7. Partnership (Inter-Agency Collaboration type) comprises: IACM, LabourBureau, PublicWorksBureau, FireBrigade, CulturalBureau and HealthBureau. IACM plays the role of licensingAgency and is responsible for issuingLicense. LabourBureau and CulturalBureau play the role of technicalAdvisor, responsible for revising TechnicalDocument and providingOpinion. Shared functions include issuing TechnicalOpinion by PublicWorksBureau, and controlFirePreventions by FireBrigade. Building inspectors are shared resources by PublicWorksBureau.

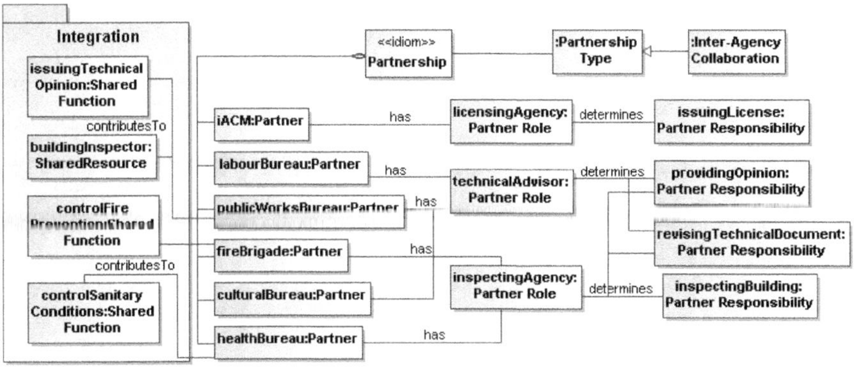

Fig. 7. Implementation Modeling – Partnership for Licensing CNO-G

5 Conclusions

We introduced Collaborative Networked Organizations in Government (CNO-G) as a kind of Collaborative Networked Organizations (CNO); identified a set of capabilities characterising them – partnership, integration and coordination; defined them as idioms for the CNO-G domain; and modeled them based on ARCON. The main contributions of this work are: (1) validating ARCON in a specific domain; (2) modeling CNO-G capabilities based on ARCON's three abstraction layers; and (3) providing three idioms as prescriptive models for CNO-G design and development. We argue that the model is valid independent of the government structure involved - the case study does not depend on the level of government and the agencies could be replaced by other kinds of organizations. In the future, we plan to identify and specify additional idioms for CNO-G, focusing on the exogenous interactions of the About-CNO sub-space, and validating these idioms for different CNO-G collaboration goals.

References

1. Field, T., Muller, E., Law, E.: The e-Government Imperative. Organization for Economic Co-operation and Development (2003) ISBN 92-64-10117-9
2. Office of Public Service, Merit and Equity, Queensland Government. Seamless Government: Improving Outcomes for Queenslanders (2004), http://www.opsc.qldgov.au/library/docs/resources/publications/Notices/SeamlessGovernment.pdf
3. Camarinha-Matos, L.M., Afsarmanesh, H.: On reference models for collaborative networked organizations. Int. J. Production Research 46(9), 2453–2469 (2008)
4. Camarinha-Matos, L.M., Afsarmanesh, H. (eds.): Collaborative Networks: Reference Modeling. Springer, Heidelberg (2008) ISBN 978-0-387-79425-9
5. Ahuja, M., Carley, K.: Network Structure in Virtual Organizations. Organization Science 10(6), 741–757 (1999)
6. Klijn, E.: Networks and Interorganizational Management – Challenging, Steering, Evaluation, and the Role of Public Actors in Public Management. In: Ferlie, E., et al. (eds.) The Oxford Handbook of Public Management. Oxford University Press, Oxford (2005)
7. Fountain, J.E.: Building the Virtual State – Information Technology and Institutional Change. Brookings Institution Press, Washington (2001)
8. Goldsmith, S., Eggers, W.: Governing by Network – The New Shape of the Public Sector. The Brookings Institution Press, Washington (2004)
9. Christensen, T., Laegreid, P.: The Whole-of-Government Approach to Public Sector Reform. Public Administration Review (November/December 2007)
10. Agranoff, R., McGuire, M.: Collaborative Public Management – New Strategies for Local Governments. Georgetown University Press, Washington (2003)
11. Jones, G.R.: Organizational Theory – Text and Cases. Prentice-Hall Inc., NJ (2001)
12. Powell, W.: Neither Market nor Hierarchy: Network Forms of Organization. Research in Organizational Behaviour 12, 295–336
13. Camarinha-Matos, L.M., Afsarmanesh, H.: A comprehensive modeling framework for collaborative networked organizations. Journal of Intelligent Manufacturing 18(5), 527–615 (2007)
14. Instituto para os Assuntos Civicos e Municipais (IACM), One-Stop Licensing Service for Food and Beverage Establishments, IACM, Macao SAR Government, China (2004)

A System Architecture Supporting the Agile Coordination of Homecare Services

Elyes Lamine[1], Sabrina Zefouni[1,2], Rémi Bastide[2], and Hervé Pingaud[1]

[1] Université de Toulouse, EMAC, CGI, Campus Jarlard, 81013 Albi Cedex 09, France
{Elyes.lamine,Herve.pingaud}@mines-albi.fr
[2] Université de Toulouse, IRIT, CUFR J.F. Champollion, ISIS, Avenue George Pompidou, 81104 Castres, France
{sabrina.zefouni,remi.bastide}@univ-jfc.fr

Abstract. Dependent people (especially the elderly) are nowadays surrounded by various health services, as well as by social and multi-technology monitoring devices. The PASPORD research project focuses on improving the management of processes involved in home care. These processes are known to be collaborative: their activities spread over different organizations, are carried out by diverse health or logistical actors. These activities must be coordinated by an integrated system, which is the purpose of the present project. However, the deployment of such a process takes place in a very dynamic and uncertain environment. In this paper, we seek to characterize and model this complex process. On the basis of its features, we define the principles of a system architecture to support the collaboration between the stakeholders and provide agility to overcome difficulties induced by its specificity.

Keywords: Homecare ecosystem, collaborative process, workflow, information system, eHealth.

1 Introduction

Given the increase of 'fragile' persons who require monitoring and care management on a long-term basis, and with the aim of reducing costs of health care, home care is becoming an increasingly common in healthcare delivery. However, in a current trend of increased numbers of elderly persons in need of home cares and shrinking resources within the healthcare sector, these home care providers are facing management challenges in terms of coordination and follow up of activities [1].

It is well-recognized that the establishment of an information system is a major asset to guaranty continuity of care and to enhance its quality. In addition, many reports have underlined that the use of information and communication technologies (ICT) in the performance and management of the health sector is essential for improving the global efficiency of healthcare systems. Therefore, the field of eHealth is currently the subject of intense research projects and commercial development, whose main objective is to design new products or new services to enrich the offer of ICT Health [2-5].

L.M. Camarinha-Matos et al. (Eds.): PRO-VE 2010, IFIP AICT 336, pp. 227–234, 2010.

However, as concluded in reports on the home healthcare field [1][3-4], today there is not, to our knowledge, a single "killer application" or work addressing the definition of a generic system architecture to support the home care process and allow easy integration of existing ICT health devices or services.

Within this context and in order to provide some answers to the definition of an open and interoperable technology architecture specific to the home care process, the research project PASPORD has been developed. This project, supported by the French region Midi-Pyrénées, aims to define a system architecture supporting the agile coordination of homecare services [8]. It will be experimented across the French region Midi-Pyrénées.

The remaining of this paper is structured in three parts. The first one is focused on a description of the homecare process and its ecosystem. In the second part, the system architecture that we propose to improve is shown. We then present a case study on the use of the proposed system concerning the detection and monitoring of malnutrition in the elderly.

2 Analysis of Homecare Process and Its Ecosystem

2.1 The Organizational Point of View

Home care includes all health services (medical and para-medical) and social services (cooking, cleaning) provided for the needs of the patient to allow him/her to continue living at home, regardless of age or disability. It is a complex process which represents the chain of various activities achieved by several stakeholder trades (nurse, physician, professional caregivers, etc.) which follow the patient's evolution and needs at home.

Fig.1 shows the ecosystem of the home care process which involves many stakeholders. As shown, multiple exchanges are required to mange and follow up this home care process.

The stakeholders in the homecare process differ widely in terms of their organizational structure, responsibility and technical ability [8]:

- Most of the medical staff involved in homecare in France (doctors, nurses) is self-employed (liberal profession): they have no hierarchic dependency on the organization that manages the overall homecare process. They usually possess their own information system support, albeit very limited (agenda management, paper or digital patient records, etc).
- Social service (house cleaning and meal delivery) is usually performed by staff that has little computer literacy and are often reluctant to use a computer-based system in their daily work.
- The elderly's relatives often live far away, paying him/her irregular visits. However, they wish to keep in touch with their parent via telephone and be kept informed on his/her health state.
- Finally, the homecare system is funded by regional public units, which are billed for the work of the various stakeholders. These units need to be reliably informed of the actual work that has been performed, time spent at home by the various stakeholders, etc.

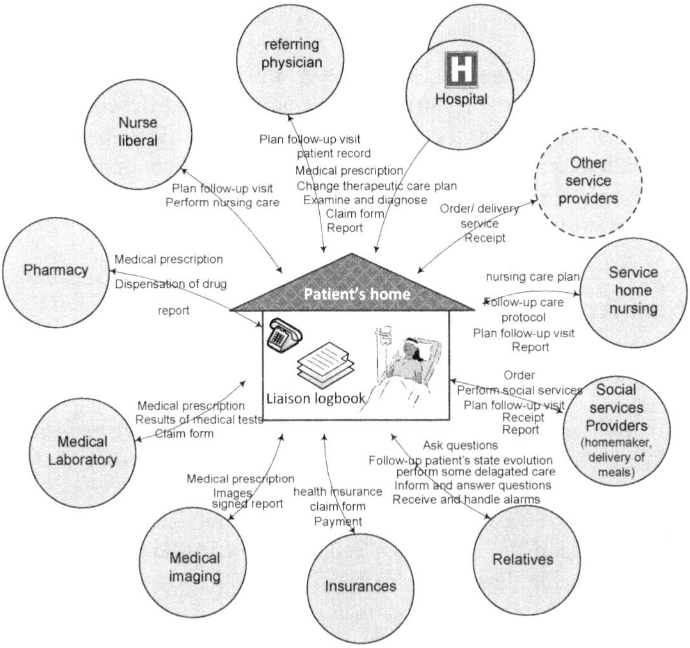

Fig. 1. Home care ecosystem

In France, homecare is mainly managed by regional associations that coordinate the activity of all the stakeholders involved (doctors, nurses, meal delivery, etc.).

2.2 Informational Point of View

The coordination of these numerous stakeholders with heterogeneous profiles and trades is definitely required to assure the quality and the continuity of care. Two levels of coordination in the homecare are notable:

- Internal coordination between stakeholders from the same organization or the same service. They use a shared Information System (IS) and act towards the same goal.
- External coordination requires interacting and coordinating actors and heterogeneous IS belonging to the various organizations involved in the homecare. Several upcoming services such as future electronic medical record will be required to interact with the systems already in place.

Currently, the activity of all these persons is mainly managed manually, using a so-called 'liaison logbook'. It is generally an unstructured, physical notebook that is kept at the elder's home and used for communication between the family and the various stakeholders, as well as between stakeholders. Each stakeholder notes the date of the visit, the operations performed, recommendations or any other form of comment. Fig.1 illustrates the central role played by the liaison logbook in the various processes of care at home. The logbook is the primary means of communication between different stakeholders.

It is noteworthy that the liaison logbook contains very useful data, underused in the homecare process. Indeed, it stores information of different types: logistical information which helps for the coordination of activities, medical information, general information on the patient, any information which may help improve the quality of the homecare and possibly the detection of the patient's health change via an intelligent monitoring system [8].

3 Proposed Architecture System

3.1 Screening Relevant Elements to Be Considered

Currently, the home care ecosystem is still in a primary stage of maturity with a lack of adequate access to information and of communication between stakeholders which hampers the management and the follow up of the home care process.

This gap results in a weak use of the ICT tools and services and an insufficient interoperability between these services and the information system of the different stakeholders. The idea is thus not to develop new ICT products, but to think how to make them useful and integrate them in a consistent common scenario covering a wide range of home care situations. This is the main purpose of the research project PASPORD.

In order to target and facilitate the identification of components of our proposed architecture, two major findings are pointed out:

- Even though the patient in home care receives daily visits from the different stakeholders, it sometimes occurs that he/she spends a long time without being visited by any of them. This could be problematic especially in the case of elderly patients who are subject to falls, discomfort and many serious domestic incidents. It is obvious that improving homecare implies a better detection and prevention of incidents or of the degradation of the elder's health.
- In order to assure the quality of care, relevant information such as alerts, personal to-do list, incident reports, organization requests, update of the patient's plan care or records, etc., should be accessible to the most appropriate actor of the home care circuit (doctor, nurse, emergency service, neighborhood, relatives, etc.) at the right time. This implies improved means of communication and coordination of stakeholders to overcome the limitations of the current liaison logbook.

3.2 Target Architecture

In order to achieve the two objectives mentioned above, we propose as shown in Fig. 2, an architecture that includes a surveillance system in order to detect dangerous situations, combined with an agile system of automatic exchange of information to coordinate the different performances. The whole is supported by multi-modal communication systems, such as a combination between personal digital assistants (PDA) and tablet PCs).

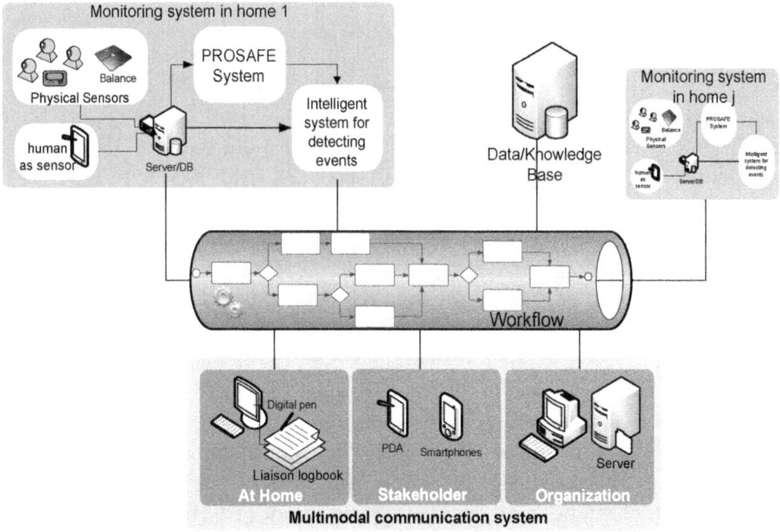

Fig. 2. Overall Architecture of the PASPORD project

The architecture of choice that we propose here, is composed of:

1. PROSAFE which consists of a monitoring system for dependent people. It was designed in the laboratory LAAS in Toulouse, one of the project partners. This system has been tested on several sites such as a retirement home and an apartment. This system can warn of certain dangers in real time (fall, fugue, etc.), based on the learning habits of the person under surveillance [10].
2. An intelligent system for detection of relevant events using Multi-Agent System (MAS), an organized set of agents [11]. An agent is a software entity or person, which are assigned a certain task that they can perform independently and in cooperation with other agents. The purpose of this multi-agent system is to prevent, on the long-term, degradation of the patient's status. This is based on a classification made by agents regarding the parameters monitored.
3. The database saves patient information as it does at present, in addition to actimetry information provided by the monitoring equipment installed at home (e.g. stirring overnight, movement speed, etc.), and transmissions made between different stakeholders, in order to track them easily at any time.
4. The workflow engine [9][12] based on the WfMC (Workflow Management Coalition Specification) is the automation process in which documents, information and tasks move from one part to another according to a set of rules. In other words, it consists of a system that allows the coordination of work among several participants following a predefined process model. Its role is to coordinate the work involved by transmitting the necessary information and tasks to different stakeholders, depending on the condition of the patient's treatment plan and the role of the interveners.

4 Case Study

We propose a case study on the detection and monitoring of malnutrition for the elderly. According to a study conducted by the French HAS (Haute Autorité de Santé: High Health Authority) in 2007, cases of malnutrition were observed in 350 000 to 500 000 elderly people living at home and at least between 100 000 and 200 000 living in institutions [15]. These numbers will tend to grow as the population continues to age. Malnutrition among the elderly has dramatic consequences –the risk of death is two to four times higher. Malnutrition exacerbates the health problems of the elderly person and increases the risk of falls, dehydration, mental disorders, and time required for healing. In addition, it generates enormous healthcare costs at the expense of the whole society. According to the causes of undernutrition, the treatment plan is different. This means that according to the patient's status the process should be adapted differently.

The best way to combat malnutrition is to detect it as early as possible. This can be done by early detection before it has negative consequences on the health of the elderly or even by avoiding people at risk. There are simple ways to detect malnutrition. Most studies and general practitioners [13-16] agree on screening for malnutrition based on some criteria such as: the change in weight over time, body mass index, the MNA test result [16], etc.

In the table 1, largely inspired by that of the HAS[13], We present the different thresholds for alerting undernutrition, distinguishing two types of malnutrition: undernutrition and the severe malnutrition that requiring medical intervention.

Table 1. Characterization of under nutrition and malnutrition

Under nutrition	Severe malnutrition
Weight loss of 5% in a month or 10% in 6 months	Weight Loss: ≥ 10% in a month or ≥ 15% in 6 months
Body Mass Index <21	BMI <18
Albumin <35g / l	Albumin <30g / l
Cholesterol <1.6 g / l	
17<MNA Global <23,5	MNA Global < 17

The system proposed in the PASPORD project helps detecting malnutrition as soon as possible:

- Preventing measures can be taken by informing family members of a potential risk of malnutrition and by displaying the evolution of weight and body mass index to nurses visiting the patient.
- In other cases, through automatic monitoring of weight, an alert will be triggered whenever there would be an indication of malnutrition. This warning will trigger the appropriate process to the origins of the problem and how to treat it. The process of screening and treatment of malnutrition in the elderly is shown in Fig.3.

We chose to model this process with BPMN (Business Process Modeling Notation). Five pools represent five different categories of actors involved in the process: the monitoring system that triggers the alarm as the system environment.

The nurses' aide, coordinator and family as business actors, and a central line (workflow) which represents the sequence of activities in the process of screening and treatment of malnutrition.

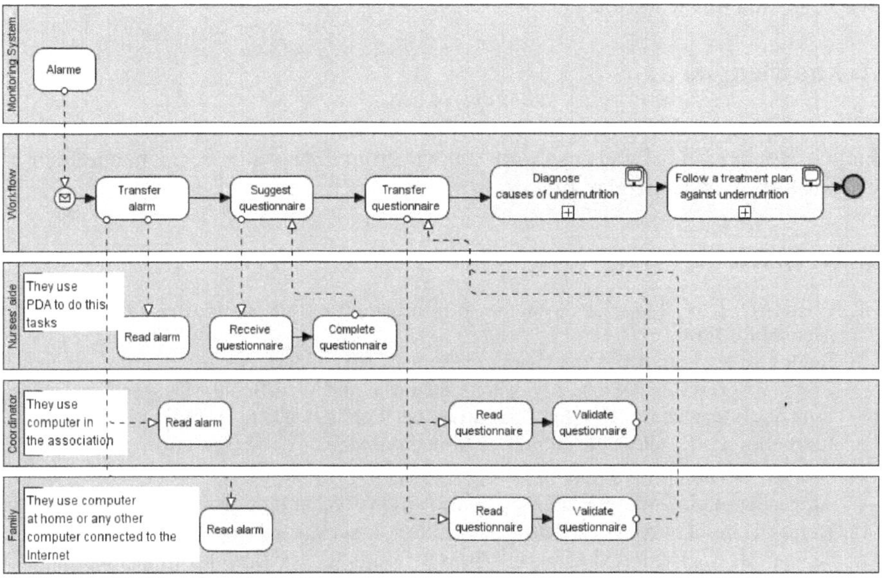

Fig. 3. Overall process management of malnutrition

In summary, the process of screening and treatment of malnutrition follow these steps:

1. Detecting malnutrition: when the person is weighed, compare his current weight with his past weight record of the previous period. Trigger an alarm if malnutrition is suspected.
2. Preventing medical staff and family: alert stakeholders of the malnutrition problem.
3. Diagnose the cause of weight loss: diagnosis begins with a questionnaire that helps fill nursing and will be forwarded to the nurse coordinator. The family then decides to inform the treating physician.
4. After the intervention of a doctor and discussion between the family and the nurse coordinator, a new treatment plan will be implemented to allow the resumption of weight lost.

5 Conclusion

In this paper we present an overall architecture of a collaborative system to improve homecare. This architecture is a coupling system of monitoring and coordination system which helps to ensure the safety of the elderly and facilitates coordination among stakeholders. The innovative idea is the use of human actors as sensors that transmit information on the status of the elderly. This information feeds the progress of the workflow and helps prevent some deterioration in the elderly's condition. The next step in our work is the implementation of a flexible and adaptive inter-organizational workflow in which we will define connections between the business process of homecare and this workflow.

Acknowledgment

The work presented here, as well as the PhD. of Sabrina Zefouni, is mainly funded by French Region Midi-Pyrénées, with support from University J.F. Champollion and Castres Syndicate for Higher Education and Research.

References

1. FNEHAD: Livre blanc des systèmes d'information en hospitalisation à domicile, white paper (Juin 2009)
2. Boulos, M.K., Lou, R.C., Anastasiou, A., Nugent, C.D., Alexandersson, J., Zimmermann, G., Cortes, U., Casas, R.: Connectivity for Healthcare and Well-Being Management: Examples from Six European Projects. Int. J. Environ. Res. Public Health 6(7), 1947–1971 (2009)
3. Lasbordes, P.: La télésanté: un nouvel atout au service de notre bien-être
4. Gartner: eHealth for a Healthier Europe (Juin 2009)
5. Alexander, G.L., Wakefield, D.S.: Information Technology Sophistication in Nursing Homes. Journal of American Medical Directors Association 10(6), 398–407 (2009)
6. Guinet, A., Ladet, P., Marcon, E.: 2HM: Hospitalisation Hors les Murs. Journées STP d'Aix en Provence, CNRS (2007)
7. Liu, C., Li, Q., Zhao, X.: Challenges and opportunities in collaborative business process management: Overview of recent advances and introduction to the special issue. Springer Science and Business Media, LLC, Heidelberg (2008)
8. Bastide R., Zefouni S., Lamine E.: The Homecare Digital Ecosystem: an Information System Support Architecture. In: IEEE DEST 2010, Dubai, EAU (2010)
9. Van der Aalst, W.M.P., Jablonski, S.: Dealing with Workflow Change: Identification of issues and solutions. International Journal of Computer Systems, Science, and Engineering (2000)
10. Bonhomme, S., Campo, E., Esteve, D., Guennec, J.: PROSAFE-extended, a telemedicine platform to contribute to medical diagnosis. Journal of Telemedicine and Telecare 14(3) (May 2007)
11. Rammal, A., Trouilhet, S., Singer, N., Pecatte, J-M. : An Adaptive System for Home Monitoring Using a Multiagent Classification of Patterns. International Journal of Telemedicine and Applications (2008)
12. Hollingsworth, D.: TheWorkflow Reference Model, Technical report wfmctc- 1003, Workflow Management Coalition (1995)
13. HAS: Stratégie de prise en charge en cas de dénutrition protéino-énergétique chez la personne âgée (2007), http://www.has-sante.fr/portail/jcms/c_546549/malnutrition-in-the-elderly-nutritional-support-strategy
14. Pirlich, M., Lochs, H.: Nutrition in the elderly. Best Practice & Research Clinical Gastroenterology, 868–884 (2001)
15. David, B., Reuben, M.D.: Quality Indicators for the Care of Undernutrition in Vulnerable Elders. Jags 55(S2) (October 2007)
16. Guigoz, Y., Vellas, B.: The Mini Nutrition Assessment (MNA) for grading the nutritional state of elderly patients: presentation of the MNA, history and validation. In: Nestlé nutrition workshop series clinical & performance, vol. 1, pp. 3–12 (1999)

Care Network Coordination for Chemotherapy at Home: A Case Study

Tian Zhang[1], Eric Marcon[1], and Maria Di Mascolo[2]

[1] Laboratoire d'Analyse des Signaux et des Processus Industriels, IUT de Roanne, Université Jean Monnet St-Etienne, 20, av. de Paris
42300 Roanne, France
{tian.zhang,marcon}@univ-st-etienne.fr
[2] Laboratoire G-SCOP (Grenoble – Science pour la Conception, l'Optimisation et la Production), UMR5772 CNRS, Grenoble INP, UJF, 46, av. Félix Viallet
38031 Grenoble, France
Maria.di-mascolo@g-scop.grenoble-inp.fr

Abstract. This paper deals with a system of chemotherapy at home which is managed by a Home Care Services (HCS) structure. The main role of this HCS structure is to coordinate care actors for a smooth organization of chemotherapy at home. In this work, we model a real system of chemotherapy at home managed by a HCS structure, and simulate its behaviour. The objective is to evaluate the relevance of such a system for current activities of the HCS structure, and to propose solutions for improving the optimal coordination of the care network for chemotherapy at home.

Keywords: Care network coordination, Home Care Services, Cancer chemotherapy at home, Process modelling, Discrete event simulation.

1 Introduction

The increased aging population is an important pressure to hospitals, which are heavily constrained by their resources to meet growing patient demands, especially for patients with severe acute illness and chronic conditions. The fact becomes a main motivation and explains the speed development of the Home Care Services (HCS) in France. The cancer chemotherapy at home occupies 15.6% of stays in HCS in 2006.

In this paper, we focus on cancer chemotherapy at home process by referring a real-word case study, which can be considered as a care network managed by a coordination center. The management performance depends greatly on quality and effectiveness of coordination. Therefore, we aim above all to understand the chemotherapy at home process and to identify the care actors' responsibility using process modelling method; and then to evaluate quality of coordination of the system using discrete event simulation. Based on previous results, we propose two improvement procedures, which are simulated. The simulation results are used for a comparative analysis.

The remainder of the article is organized as follows: In section 2, we give general information on the cancer chemotherapy at home. Section 3 describes the studied

L.M. Camarinha-Matos et al. (Eds.): PRO-VE 2010, IFIP AICT 336, pp. 235–242, 2010.

system of chemotherapy at home using process modelling method. Section 4 presents the simulation approach with three scenarios; the results of the study are also discussed. The article ends with a conclusion of our work.

2 Development of Cancer Chemotherapy at Home

The French government encourages the development of chemotherapy at home in regarding it as one of the objectives of the Cancer Plan and the reorganization of oncology care (Urban, 2006).

Some existing research works [Dahan & al., 2007] [Boothroyd & al., 2004] show that chemotherapy at home is feasible, not only in terms of quality and safety of care, but also in terms of patients and their family satisfaction. Urban (2003) points that chemotherapy at home only suits valid patients, who are informed and integrated in a care program, and who are treated in a suitable family environment. Gorski & al. (2008) survey chemotherapy at home and other infusion therapies being realized at home; they indicate more clearly the advantages and disadvantages of these treatments, especially some critical success factors of their realization at home. Chahed & al. (2008) are interested in a drugs delivery problem for a chemotherapy at home system. Collomp & al. (2008) propose to use new technologies to facilitate the traceability management of products and care actors' activities in order to improve quality of care for chemotherapy at home. Some other researchers [HAS, 2005] [Launois, 1996] analyze the economic aspect of the chemotherapy at home and show that chemotherapy at home does not seem more expensive than its implementation in conventional hospitalization.

However practices of chemotherapy at home are not much in France, the same for research works surveying chemotherapy at home organization process. Our work helps to fill this gap.

3 Chemotherapy at Home Process Modeling: A Case Study

In this work, we present a real world case study of the chemotherapy at home. The studied system is implemented by a HCS structure situated in the Rhône-Alpes province of France. The HCS structure exists for more than thirty years. Today, it treats about 250 patients per day, and its operation areas extend across the Rhône department and part of the Isere department. They began the chemotherapy at home activity in the early 90's. This activity represents nowadays 3% of the admissions of the studied HCS structure.

Using process modelling method, we analyze the system in detail and divide the process into three phases: patient admission phase, home care preparation phase and cure realization phase. We present here only the realization phase of chemotherapy at home because that is the focus of the whole system. At this stage, we can see different internal and external actors really involved for delivering cares or services for patients.

The realization process of chemotherapy at home takes here three days; the most important activities are only concentrated in the first two days. The last day is used for the follow-up post chemotherapy that could be usually carried out by a coordinator nurse by phone, or occasionally by a private nurse with a home visit if necessary. A simplified model of the process is shown in Figure 1. We simulated the studied system based on this model for evaluating system performance. The simulation approach and results will be discussed in the next section.

3.1 Realization Process for Chemotherapy at Home

The first day of the realization process is devoted to chemotherapy cure validation and drugs preparation. Above all, patient's blood sample has to be analyzed; blood sample could be taken by a private nurse or by a city biological laboratory, at patient's home or in the laboratory. And then, the city biological laboratory ensures blood analysis and transfers the results to the HCS structure, patient's family doctor and his hospital. The family doctor plays a role of evaluator by understanding the results and permitting or not chemotherapy cure realization. If results are normal, the family doctor visits the patient at his home and gives chemotherapy validation in signing a written order depending on patient's physical conditions. The validated written order is named "Clinical Green Light" (CGL) and will be transmitted to the HCS structure by fax. It is received by a coordinator nurse, especially allocated for the chemotherapy at home activity. The coordinator nurse shows the CGL to a coordinator doctor in order to obtain the final validation of the cure at home, named "Final Green Light" (FGL). The FGL is then transferred to the pharmacy of the HCS structure and verified by a pharmacist in terms of chemotherapy drugs dosage. The pharmacist gives his agreement for drugs preparation by fax with the signed FGL to a contracted hospital pharmacy which will prepare chemotherapy drugs corresponding to the defined dosage. Simultaneously, pharmacy of the HCS structure ensures other necessary medicines preparation. Ideally, chemotherapy drugs production should be finished in the first day in late afternoon; in cases of delays, this production must be performed in emergency on second day of the process in early morning.

During the second day of program, a staff delivery person of the HCS structure takes firstly the necessary medicines prepared by the HCS structure's pharmacy, then chemotherapy drugs at the hospital pharmacy, and transports them together to patient's home. Delivery verification will be done by an assigned private nurse after his arrival at patient's home. He hereafter prepares the patient for treatments and administrates chemotherapy drugs one by one. Treatment durations vary according to prescribed chemotherapy protocols. At the end of the cure, the private nurse stays with patient for a certain period of time for surveillance.

3.2 Coordination Design Presentation

By looking at the simplified model illustrated in Figure 1, we can observe that coordination is necessary all around the realization process. It is ensured by a coordinator doctor and a coordinator nurse belonging to the studied HCS structure. The coordinator doctor plays here just a role of supervisor, by overseeing medical operations and chemotherapy protocols performance. However, the coordination tasks done by the coordinator nurse are very significant for the quality assurance of the realization process; she links the different actors (HCS structure, private nurse, city biological laboratory, family doctor, hospital pharmacy, ...) delivering cares or services to a patient, and follows the accomplishment of their activity, accelerating them in case of forgetfulness, mistakes and delays.

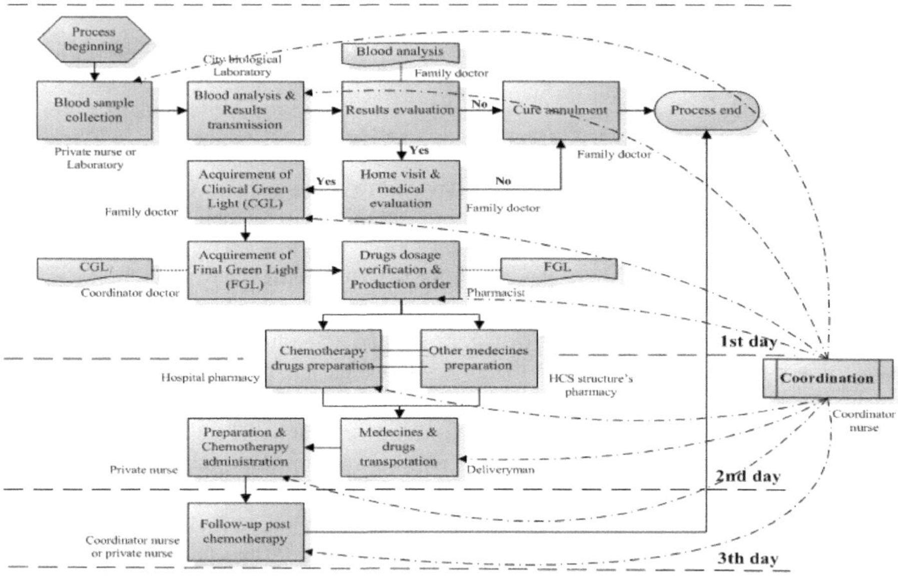

Fig. 1. Realization process of chemotherapy at home of the studied HCS structure

Obviously, the coordinator nurse is deemed as core of the chemotherapy at home system, especially for the first two days of the realization process, during which various activities must be achieved by different external actors, within a limited time. The coordinator nurse must ensure a good sequence for these activities, and an efficient communication.

In the studied system, the main activities are carried out by external actors, but coordination is principally guaranteed by a staff nurse of the HCS structure. We thus define this system as chemotherapy at home system managed by a coordination center.

4 Simulation Approach and Results

Discrete event simulation is a good method for resolving performance evaluation and coordination problems. Using this method, we evaluate in this section the studied system's performance, and propose improvement procedures.

The presented chemotherapy at home system, managed by a coordination center, seems flexible and simple to pilot, but the system performance depends hardly on the quality of coordination. Our aim here is to use simulation in order to evaluate firstly the quality of coordination for a real system; results are then compared to those of two proposed improved scenarios. We restrict our simulations to the first two days of the realization process, because they need more coordination tasks, due to the presence of concentrated activities.

4.1 Experiment Configuration and Validation

The proposed simulation model, built basing on the realization process of chemotherapy at home (Figure 1), includes not only the different necessary activities for chemotherapy at home realization, the coordination tasks being ensured by the coordinator nurse, but also the uncertainty on the accomplishment dates for some activities and decision-making fulfilled by external actors. Data used for building simulation model are collected and calculated from direct field observation and interviews with care actors.

The entities are created according to an analysis of a six months' patient treatment program. Seven chemotherapy protocols are considered. Two hospital pharmacies are available for chemotherapy drugs preparation, and one ensures more activities than the other. Patients' homes are dispersed in an area of 80 km around the studied HCS structure.

Performance indicators chosen for the evaluation of coordination quality are the coordination time spent by coordinator nurse and the effect of the coordination design on chemotherapy at home organization.

The experiment period is fixed to three months, and we use a 95% confidence interval to validate the relevance of the simulation model. Operation durations of key activities are seen as validation factors. Taking into account the stochastic aspects related to distribution laws, the simulation model is validated with 30 replications for offering reliable results.

4.2 Simulation Scenarios Description

The first simulation scenario concerns actual chemotherapy at home system of the studied HCS structure (***Scenario 1***), in which different external actors ensure only their activities for chemotherapy at home realization, but not the communication with the HCS structure. Coordination is initialized by coordinator nurse who follows activities' progress and accelerates external actors if necessary, usually by phone. The coordination design is supported by a manual way.

The first improvement solution we propose (***Scenario 2***) consists in modifying the coordination design by redefining actors' responsibility and eliminating superfluous tasks. On the one hand, all the external actors participate to coordination tasks; they should inform achievement of their activities to coordinator nurse on their own initiative. Instead of verifying, informing and accelerating external actors, the coordinator nurse ensures nothing more than information reception and transmission by phone or fax. On the other hand, we notice in the actual model (Figure 1), that some tasks are performed twice successively, by two competent actors: chemotherapy at home cure is validated by both, the family doctor and the coordinator doctor; chemotherapy drugs dosage is verified by the pharmacist of the HCS structure and then by hospital pharmacy. We propose here to keep only one actor for each task: family doctor for cure validation and hospital pharmacy for drugs dosage verification.

In the ***Scenario 3***, we recommend the use of new information and communication technologies (NICT) to replace the manual way of coordination. Applications of NICT in the home care domain are already approved by the literature [Koch, 2006] [Collomp & al., 2008] [Tan & al., 2002] [Maglaveras & al., 2002]. In this second improvement procedure, we propose a framework of a traceability management of actors' activities, in which several actors are connected by cable network and others by mobile network. Patient records are stored in a central server and could be shared between different care actors. Information transfers become automatic, accompanied by an alert to recipient. The HCS structure, city biological laboratory and hospital pharmacy are connected to central server by cable network. A mini pocket pc should be assigned to each patient across mobile network. The validation tasks could be done by electronic signature that permits the automatic transfer of the necessary information to the predetermined recipient. For private nurse and family doctor, their electric signatures could be done using the pocket pc assigned to patient. Thus, patient has the responsibility to carry the pocket pc always with him for the treatments and to provide it to certain care actors (i.e. private nurse, family doctor) if necessary.

4.3 Results Analysis

In this subsection, we present the results obtained thanks to the simulation of the three scenarios described above. A comparative analysis enables to determine the most optimal coordination design. The used comparison indicators are coordination time spent by coordinator nurse during experiment period for each patient, realization time used by each external actor for achieving his activity, and delay ratio depending on realization time constraint. For laboratory and family doctor, the realization time is composed by an operation time and a variable waiting time before activity execution. Results of comparative analysis are showed in Table 1 and Table 2.

Table 1. Comparative analysis in terms of coordination time between 3 scenarios

Scenario	Number of patient	Coordination time per patient
Scenario 1	60	47 minutes
Scenario 2	66	32 minutes
Scenario 3	63	18 minutes

In Scenario 1, 60 patients are treated by the system during the experiment period; coordination nurse devotes 47 minutes per patient for coordination tasks. The realization time of each external actor is respectively 175 minutes for private nurse, 169 minutes for city biological laboratory, 253 minutes for family doctor and 22 minutes for hospital pharmacy. Ordinarily, family doctor should give the CGL before five o'clock p.m. in the first day of the process, but in 27% of cases, this deadline is not respected, which results in delay of chemotherapy drugs preparation in 28% of cases.

66 patients are received in Scenario 2. The coordination time per patient reduces to 32 minutes. There is no great difference compared with Scenario 1, in terms of realization time for most external actors, such as private nurse, city biological laboratory and hospital pharmacy. But family doctor uses less time: 187 minutes here against 253 minutes in Scenario 1, to fulfill his activity thanks to the first improvement solution. In the same way, the delay ratio drops from 27% to 5% for giving the CGL by family doctor, and from 28% to 5% for preparing chemotherapy drugs by hospital pharmacy.

For scenario 3, the system treats 63 patients during the experiment period. The coordination time drops to 18 minutes per patient. Thanks to an automatic communication way, the waiting time for information transmission is almost eliminated; the quality of coordination is thus improved. This way, for two external actors mostly concerned by

Table 2. Comparative analysis actors between 3 scenarios in terms of realization of external actors' activities

Actors	Activities realization	Scenario		
		Scenario 1	*Scenario 2*	*Scenario 3*
Private nurse	Realization time	175 minutes	136 minutes	135 minutes
	Delays (%)	0%	0%	0%
Labora-tory	Realization time	169 minutes	165 minutes	55 minutes
	Delays (%)	0%	0%	0%
Family doctor	Realization time	253 minutes	187 minutes	97 minutes
	Delays (%)	27%	5%	0%
Hospital pharmacy	Realization time	22 minutes	21 minutes	21 minutes
	Delays (%)	28%	5%	0%

information transfers, namely the city biological laboratory and the family doctor, we can observe a reduction of time: 55 minutes only for the first, and 97 minutes for the second. The delays observed previously disappear here completely.

To sum up, the current system is not optimal, coordination time is long and delays are important. Responsibility redefinition, accompanied with redundant tasks elimination, causes quality improvement of coordination and delay reduction for certain external actors. As expected, the implementation of a traceability management system of actors' activities permits an optimal coordination and eliminates all the delays. Though decline of the delay ratio between Scenario 2 and Scenario 3 is not significant (5%), the latter could reduce potential incidents caused by human with automatic information transfers; the quality of coordination is more secure, especially against a growth of activity in the future. However, other aspects should be designed before the system implementation, such as economic aspect and technical aspect, which requires further studies.

5 Conclusion

In this work, we are interested in chemotherapy at home system implemented by a HCS structure in France. A staff nurse is assigned especially for coordination task to ensure a smooth organization. We model and simulate the system to evaluate its performance.

An optimal coordination design permits less coordination time, which is not actually the case for the studied system. We therefore propose to redefine its coordination design in the first place and secondly to implement a traceability management system of actors' activities. According to comparative analysis of results, the latter leads the most optimal coordination.

References

1. Anderson, H., Addington-Hall, J.M., Peake, M.D., McKendrik, J., Keane, K., Thatcher, N.: Domiciliary chemotherapy with gemcitabine is safe and acceptable to advanced non-small-cell lung cancer patients: results of a feasibility study. British Journal of Cancer 89, 2190–2196 (2003)

2. Chahed, S., Marcon, E., Sahin, E., Dallery, Y.: Home care planning decisions: bibliography and case study. In: ORAH 2008 (2008)
3. Collomp, R., Mirfendereski, N., Gaziello, M.C., Ruitort, S., Housseman, S., Verdeaux, S., Lapeyre, B., Mallea, P., Mousnier, A.: Sécurisation du processus chimiothérapie : quelles attentes vis-à-vis des nouvelles technologies. In: GISEH 2008 (2008)
4. Dahan, M., Paule, B., Vordos, D., Larre, S., Salomon, L., Yiou, R., Hoznek, A., Abbou, C., De La Taille, A.: Hospitalisation à domicile en onco-urologie : bilan des 5 premières années et enquête de satisfaction. Progrès en Urologie 17, 855–859 (2007)
5. HAS: Service évaluation medico-économique et santé publique. Analyse comparée de la chimiothérapie anticancéreuse administrée à l'hôpital ou prise en charge à domicile : aspects économiques et organisationnels, 92pages (Juin 2005)
6. Koch, S.: Home telehealth – Current state and future trends. International Journal of Medical Informatics, 565–576 (2006)
7. Launois, R.: Chimiothérapie ambulatoire : les enjeux économiques. Bulletin du Cancer 83(12), 974–976 (1996)
8. Maglaveras, N., Koutkiasa, V., Chouvardaa, I., Goulisb, D.G., Avramidesb, A., Adamidisc, D., Louridasc, G., Balas, E.A.: Home care delivery through the mobile telecommunications platforme : the Citizen Health System (CHS) perspective. International Journal of Medical Informatics, 99–111 (2002)
9. Tan, K.C., Khor, E.F., Cai, J., Heng, C.M., Lee, T.H.: Automating the drug scheduling of cancer chemotherapy via evolutionary computation. Artificial Intelligence in Medicine, 169–185 (2002)
10. Urban, T.: Département de Pneumologie de CHU Angers, Réorganisation des Soins en cancérologie et chimiothérapie au domicile. Revue des Maladies Respiratoires 20(5-C1), 659–661 (2003)
11. Urban, T.: Comité de coordination de Cancérologie et Pôle Thorax Vaisseaux, CHU Angers, La chimiothérapie au domicile en cancérologie thoracique. Revue des Maladies Respiratoires 23(3), 207–208 (2006)

Strategic and Tactical Hospital Bed Management in Belgium and in France

D. Gossart[1], N. Meskens[1,*], and A. Guinet[2]

[1] UcLouvain - Louvain School of Management – Campus Mons
Management department
Chaussée de Binche 151 - 7000 Mons - Belgium
Tel.: +32 65 32 33 50
gossartd@fucam.ac.be, meskens@fucam.ac.be
[2] INSA – Lyon, France
alain.guinet@insa-lyon.fr

Abstract. Nowadays, lots of healthcare establishments decide to integrate a hospital bed management department, while taking into account the financial impact on the budget, the disruptions and factors influencing the bed planning as e.g. the type of care units management and the existing networks between hospitals and satellite structures. Lots of constraints will also have an impact while optimizing the available resources: accepting the emergency case and therefore delaying the planned patient, adding additional beds within a care unit and studying at the same time the collateral costs, opening or closing beds related to a specialty, etc.

Keywords: hospital bed management, strategic and tactical management, collaborative networks, mono site hospital, multi-site hospital.

1 Introduction

Nowadays, the hospital management takes place in an increasingly competitive environment and it is therefore essential to focus on delivering high quality care to patients. Lots of healthcare establishments have decided to center the organization on the hospital bed management while stimulating changes and systems improvements.

The aim of the hospital bed management is to allocate beds to elective and non-elective patients while taking into account several constraints. This task is very complex. These difficulties come from on one hand, the uncertainty related to the length of stay, the arrival of emergencies and on the other hand from an important number of constraints: single-sex rooms, the nursing staff competencies, the notion of asepsis, the social or medical isolations and of course the patient's preferences in terms of room type. Moreover, the type of care units organization and also the existence and the form of the collaborative networks can have an impact on bed

* This research is financed by the Interuniversity Attraction Poles Program - Belgian State - Belgian Science Policy.

L.M. Camarinha-Matos et al. (Eds.): PRO-VE 2010, IFIP AICT 336, pp. 243–250, 2010.

management. In the current economic context, collaborative networks appear to be a good compromise to reduce costs and to improve healthcare delivery. Hospital bed management has a crucial impact on the hospital financing and on the care units occupancy rates all along the patient's pathway.

This research will focus on the strategic and tactical levels due to the fact that it is crucial to achieve the long-term objectives, while developing plans and allocating as best as possible the existing resources. A strategic type of management consists in determining on the long run a number of rooms and a bed capacity in function of one or more future evolution axis of the healthcare establishment. From a tactical point of view, it focuses on pre-planning admissions, on forecasting demand, on human and material resources needed in function of seasonal effect, while measuring the impact that emergencies would have on this planning.

This paper will be structured into five parts: after the introduction, the hospital bed management will be tackled as well as the factors influencing bed management with a special focus on the influence of the collaborative networks. The third part will then expose the encountered issues linked to bed management within the framework of the visited hospitals. The fourth section will go back over the reformulation proposition of the problems. Finally, the conclusion will then sum up few avenues that undoubtedly have to be explored and courses of improving that could be realized in further stages of this research.

2 Hospital Bed Management

As an optimal bed management is nowadays becoming crucial for hospitals, it is important to highlight factors influencing the bed management. To realize this, we used two methods. On one hand, we made a short literature review and on the other hand, we visited eighteen Belgian and French hospitals whereas people occupying different functions were interviewed. An overview of these visits is presented in the following section.

Different compulsory factors complicate and impact on the bed management e.g. uncertainty related to the length of stay and uncertainty related to the number of emergency cases. Other elements also need to be taken into account in order to build up beds planning: single-sex rooms, the importance of putting a pathology in the appropriate care unit, the notion of asepsis, the social or medical isolations, the patient's preferences in terms of room type, etc. These are key elements that bed managers have to keep in mind. In the literature, some authors approached these elements.

In a strategic point of view, Nguyen et al. [1] used an average duration of stay to determine the necessary bed capacity. In a tactical point of view, Cochran and Roche [2] used a methodology also based on queuing network in order to improve the capacity of emergency service according to patients' type, the random entrances, etc. Wang [3] studied the bed resources allocation taking into account hospitalization demands, bed capacity and incomes coming from the activity, while optimizing the incomes and minimizing of additional beds. In an operational point of view, Vassilacopoulos [4] used a simulation model in order to improve the bed utilization while taking into account specific operational constraints (level of emergency, bed occupancy and length of waiting list). Furthermore, Walczak et al. [5] used the neural network theory to estimate the duration of stay of each patient coming from the emergency room. This developed resource permits to physicians and staff people allocating beds in function of estimated length of stay.

Moreover, two main factors influence the hospital bed management: the type of care units organization, explained hereunder and the collaborations existing between hospitals and their environment.

Three main ways of care units management need to be distinguished (Ben Bachouch et al., [6]): management by specialty (coded as S in Tables 1 and 2), management by length of stay (coded as LOS) and management by groups of specialties (coded as GS).

The other important factor in terms of hospital bed management is linked to the different networks that mainly exist between hospitals (i.e. multi-site architecture or not) and between a hospital and satellite structures as rest homes or rehabilitation centres. A collaborative network is expressed as links between several organisations, whereas members have a key role, in order to achieve and solve goals. Axelrod [7] said that "trust and reciprocity are the shadow of the future: the more trust and reciprocity in the network, the greater the ability of the network to accomplish shared goals." According to Milward and Provan [8], four types of management network exist: *service implementation network* based on joint production of services, *information diffusion network* sharing information across organizations, *problem solving network* and *community capital network* building social relationships and capital across members. The important element to take into account is the way of evolving and thus the created dynamic around the network. According to the majority of bed managers we met, it is essential to develop new competencies, to enhance cohesion between all members and to induce over and over again new connexions and exchanges. Data integration is therefore a crucial element due to the importance of having a general view on functioning. Indeed, collaborations within the healthcare environment mainly permit collecting data about patients and exchanging clinical data.

3 Overview of Visited Healthcare Establishments

In order to better analyze the current situation in Belgium and in France, fourteen Belgian hospitals and four French hospitals have been visited from end 2009 to beginning 2010. The aim was to diversify as much as possible the visits in order to get a picture of the different hospitals in terms of size (number of beds), organization (multi or mono site) and type (university hospital or not). The aims of these visits were to clearly understand how the hospital beds are managed and what kind of issues they encounter every single day.

Tables 1 and 2 below indicate the principal characteristics of visited hospitals, respectively regarding mono site and multi-site hospitals. Healthcare establishments can be categorized according to their size: "Big" means that the size is superior to 500 beds, "Average" stands for a structure containing between 200 to 500 beds while hospitals with less than 200 beds are characterized as "Small". Hospitals can also be categorized as multi-site or mono site (i.e. built up on one site or laid out in different sites). The fourth column presents the different types of hospitals. Three types of hospitals mainly exist in Belgium: "G" stands for general hospitals, "U" for university hospitals and "GCU" for general hospital with university characters. In France, the main types are: "CH" stands for hospital centres, "CHU" for university hospitals and

"CHR" for regional hospital centres. Finally, the fifth column goes back over the type(s) of management existing in the care units.

In order to better visualize the daily problems encountered by each visited hospitals, Tables 1 and 2 below sum up the following issues:

a) if the patient is not in the appropriate care unit related to his pathology, it implies an organizational problem regarding the physicians' visits, a problem related to the nursing staff competencies, not always used to care specific pathologies and also problems regarding his internal transfer that can be costly, especially in terms of stretch-bearing activities, administration, etc.
b) it is not always possible to give the type of room that the patient wanted (especially private rooms). Indeed, the bed allocation needs to take into account different elements: length of stay that must be estimated and that are not always known before the beginning of the hospitalization, the patient's age, single-sex rooms, the nursing staff competencies, the notion of asepsis and isolation and of course the patient's preferences in terms of room type. It is thus not always easy to give a private room when other elements need to be taken into account uppermost. Indeed, some visited hospitals consider this patient's preference as the most/least important element and will prioritize or not this criteria in comparison with other factors.
c) patients sometimes stay more than twenty-four hours in the temporary emergency service. Indeed, lots of hospitals must welcome a huge number of emergencies, disrupting the original planning. Generally, hospitals have a temporary emergency service, coupled with the emergency department, that allows welcoming patients for maximum twenty-four hours when no other beds are available in the appropriate medical service. Nevertheless, it happens that patients stay for longer than one day due to the lack of beds in the care units, consequently implying an obstruction in the process of hospitalization.
d) it happens to transfer externally patients to other hospitals. Therefore, it implies a loss of patients. In the worst case, if no bed (even additional bed added for a short-term period) can be found inside the hospital or in another site belonging to the same structure, an external transfer must be planned, even if this transfer means a possible escape of patients in favor of other establishments. Indeed, it goes further than a loss of one hospitalization: it also means a loss of one or more consultations after the hospitalization and even a possible patient loyalty to a physician working in another healthcare establishment.

Find hereunder a quick reminder in order to facilitate the reading of these Tables:

- issue a) is related to a patient who is not in the appropriate care unit,
- issue b) stands for the inadequacy between the room type that the patient initially wanted and what he received,
- issue c) is linked to a stay, longer than twenty-four hours, in the temporary emergency service,
- issue d) is related to the external transfers that are done.

Majority of problems, presented in Tables 1 and 2, can be differently considered according to the different decisional levels. All situations can be categorized as

Table 1. Characteristics of hospitals and sum-up of the main encountered issues (mono site)

Hospital	Country	Size	Type	Mgt type	Strategic/tactical/ operational			
					a)	b)	c)	d)
1	B	Big	U	S, GS	X			
2	B	Big	G	S, GS		X	X	
3	B	Average	G	S, LOS	X	X	X	
4	B	Average	G	S, GS, LOS	X	X		
5	B	Small	U	S	X			X
6	B	Average	U	GS, LOS	X	X		
7	Fr	Average	CH	S, GS, LOS		X		X
8	Fr	Average	CH	S, GS				
9	Fr	Big	CHU	LOS	X	X	X	
Number of occurrences					6	6	3	2

Table 2. Characteristics of hospitals and sum-up of the main encountered issues (multi-site)

Hospital	Country	Size	Type	Mgt type	Strategic/tactical/ operational			
					a)	b)	c)	d)
10	B	Big	GCU	S, GS	X		X	
11	B	Big	G	S, GS, LOS		X	X	
12	B	Big	G	S, GS, LOS	X		X	
13	B	Big	U	S, GS	X		X	
14	B	Average	G	GS, LOS	X			
15	B	Average	G	LOS	X	X		
16	B	Average	G	S, GS	X		X	X
17	B	Big	G	GS	X	X		
18	Fr	Big	CHU	GS, LOS	X	X		
Number of occurrences					8	4	5	1

belonging to operational problems. Nevertheless, as these issues appear frequently, it is also possible to study them in the long-term i.e. to a strategic or tactical level. Additionally, hospitals were asked to precise which networks were existing inside their structures. Consequently, we mainly observed four main collaborations along the eighteen visited hospitals: multi-site structure, collaboration between two hospitals from different networks, collaboration with other structures and collaboration between two cross-border hospitals.

Some healthcare establishments are organized in a multi-site architecture. This permits a joint management and harmonizes the patients' flows when needed. Indeed, when the occupation rate is pretty high, patients can be welcomed in another site thanks to an internal transfer between both establishments. This naturally implies a surplus of work in terms of administration and stretcher-bearing activities. However, this has an impact on the care accessibilities when they are only provided on one site, especially regarding care units with a huge activity e.g. paediatrics, maternity service, emergency service and cardiology.

As part of collaborations between two hospitals from different networks, some agreements are set up in order to ensure the continued good management in terms of financing and medical activity. It is also the case when one establishment cannot offer a specific treatment to patients e.g. cardiac coronagraph. The hospital sends thus its patients to another structure able to do the radiological exam. Collaborative networks between the hospital and other structures also exist. Some revalidation centres or rest homes sometimes have specific collaborations with hospitals.

Let us also note that collaboration between healthcare establishments and GP's from the area is sometimes set up. Indeed, some hospital software's allow general practitioners to have a look at patients' data, radiotherapy reports, etc. in order to better understand patients' medical history.

Collaborations between two countries also have an important impact on hospitals located near the border. As the financing is based on the activity rate, Belgium and France are desirous to welcome international patients.

4 Reformulation of the Problem

All problems explained in the previous section need to be reformulated. Indeed, all of them can be linked to an objective function with different aims: to maximize the profit in terms activity volume and if we welcome more patients, to maximize patients' satisfaction and finally to minimize the logistic costs and the waste of time.

As all encountered issues can be easily linked to the Figure 1, the objective function that will be calculated, will permit taking into account all the statements of facts. It will also be interesting to calculate this objective function and conclude if and how these problems can be resolved thanks to the creation of networks and collaborations between hospitals. Based on that, few examples of strategies can be foreseen and will be further explored: if there is no available bed, what is the best solution: to transfer in another hospital or cancel a planned hospitalization while it can

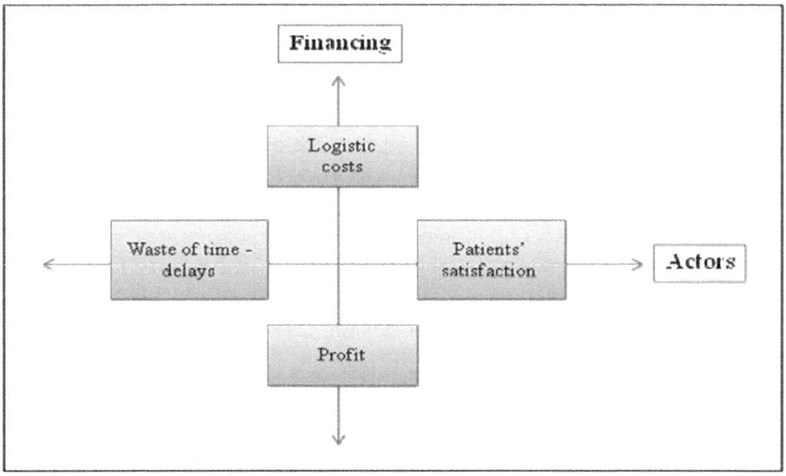

Fig. 1. Reformulation of the different issues

damage the qualitative brand image of the hospital and cause an additional stress for the patient? In the same context, what would be the impact of the creation of a multi-pathologies temporary service if this temporary department is between the emergency room and the care units? In the same way, what would be the financial impact if all beds from different hospitals were grouped together and would thus accept patients from another site but directly in the appropriate care unit? The creation of networks between healthcare establishments lets us think about the interest of creating more collaborations with rehabilitation centers and rest homes, and even about the opportunity of studying the return-on-investment in case of building an additional unit dedicated to geriatrics or rehabilitation. It could be also interesting to study the impact of external, internal and intra-units transfers in terms of costs and patients' satisfaction, especially in the case of multi sites establishments. The impact of a duty period for different emergency rooms from different hospitals could also be interesting to study in the context of networks and especially in terms of financial impact and good patients' allocation in the appropriate care units.

However, started research will mainly concern the necessary of having a good vision in real time of the occupation rates, especially when the structure is laid out in several sites. The current idea is to further develop a patient's satisfaction survey, to cross findings with findings found thanks to the different visits and to analyze, in different angles, the added-value, strengths and weaknesses of these ideas.

5 Conclusion and Perspectives

Lots of elements and disruptions need to be taken into account when a bed planning is put in place, without forgetting the impact that it will have on the budget. Therefore, studying the encountered issues based on the structure type (mono site versus multi-site) is crucial, especially regarding the strategic management and the routes of improvement that will be proposed in the future research.

Started research will thus work on one or few compromises evaluated on different criterions, quantitative (e.g. financial) or qualitative (patients' satisfaction). This satisfaction can be studied for example via a questionnaire oriented "managing/planning of hospital beds" related to the whole hospitalization process while bringing to light the different stages of the patients' stay. It is therefore important to also get the patients' opinion about the main encountered issues related to hospital bed management. Within the framework of a multi-site structure, it could be interesting to compare the efficiency and costs of a bed manager for one or several structures versus the advantages linked to a subcontract, outside the healthcare establishments. Lots of constraints will also have an impact while optimizing the available resources: accepting the emergency case and therefore delaying the planned patient, adding additional beds within a care unit and studying at the same time the collateral costs, opening or closing beds related to a specialty, etc. Although this research is at its first stages, several avenues are still to be explored and courses of improving remain open.

References

[1] Nguyen, M., Six, P., Antonioli, D., Glemain, P., Potel, G., Lombrail, P., Le Beux, P.: A simple method to optimize hospital beds capacity. International Journal of Medical Informatics 74(1), 39–49 (2005)
[2] Cochran, J.K., Roche, K.T.: A multi-class queuing network analysis methodology for improving hospital emergency department performance. Computers & Operations Research 36(5), 1497–1512 (2009)
[3] Wang, T., Guinet, A., Besombes, B.: A sizing tool for allocation planning of hospital bed resources. In: Intelligent patient Management. SCI, vol. 189, pp. 113–125 (2009)
[4] Vassilacopoulos, G.: A simulation model for bed allocation to hospital inpatient departments. Simulation 45, 233–241 (1985)
[5] Walczak, S., Pofahl, W.E., Scorpio, R.J.: A decision support tool for allocating hospital bed resources and determining required acuity of care. Decision Support Systems 34, 445–456 (2002)
[6] Ben Bachouch, R., Guinet, A., Hajrj-Gabouj, S.: Gestion des lits mutualisés d'un établissement hospitalier. In: 7e Congrès international de génie industriel, Trois-Rivières, Québec, Juin 5-8 (2007)
[7] Axelrod, R.: The evolution of cooperation. Basic books, New York (1984)
[8] Milward, H., Provan, K.: A manager's guide to choosing and using collaborative networks. IBM center for the business of governmment (2006)

From Clinical Practice Guideline to Clinical Pathway – Issues of Reference Model-Based Approach

Hannes Schlieter and Werner Esswein

Department of Business Management and Economics, Chair for Information Systems, esp. ystems Engineering, Münchner Platz 3, 01062 Dresden, Germany
{Hannes.Schlieter,Werner.Esswein}@tu-dresden.de

Abstract. Health care systems are facing new challenges such as the aging population, the increasing amount of chronicle diseases and the rapid development of medical technologies. The increasing of the related health care costs lead to the limits of affordability of health care systems. Building Health networks and standardization of clinical processes are the main trend facing these challenges. Actually, the main instrument for documentation and managing of clinical processes are Clinical Pathways (CPs). They allow to transfer evident knowledge in practice and they are the central point of clinical quality management. In contrast, Clinical Practice Guidelines (CPGs) aggregate the evident medical knowledge in a compact form to support physicians in their practice. In the paper analyze the model-driven development of CP for a health network. Therefore, we work out problems of integration. Finally, the paper shows aspect for a model-based integration of CPGs in CPs. These findings are proofed with the help of the documentation of the regional stroke-network called SOS-NET.

Keywords: Process Model, Clinical Practice Guidelines, Clinical Pathways.

1 Introduction

Hospitals in Europe especially in Germany are exposed a more competitive business environment as a result of variegated political- and judicial changes. Furthermore the modern media like internet-technologies promote the emancipation of patients. It enables a more competitive situation between hospitals. So, the objectives of care providers concentrate increasingly on the assurance of efficient care on a high level of quality. Consequently, more and more modern economical concepts like process orientated business structures and management are applied in health care sectors.

In this context CPs were established as an instrument for the standardization of clinical business and care processes [1]. Furthermore CPGs were developed by medical associations to aggregate evident knowledge and best practice [2]. CPGs are used to reduce inappropriate variations in practice and to promote the delivery of high quality, evidence-based health care [3].

Different approaches for integration of the content of CPGs in CPs exist (section 4). One of them is the reference model-based approach. Reference models (RM) are special kinds of conceptual models. Conceptual models can be understood as the result of

L.M. Camarinha-Matos et al. (Eds.): PRO-VE 2010, IFIP AICT 336, pp. 251 – 258, 2010.

a construction "... done by a modeler, who examines the elements of a system for a specific purpose..." [4]. In the information systems discipline, models are used to redesign organizations or to develop software systems [5, 6]. Therefore, graphical models have been established as "...a medium to foster communication with prospective users..." [7]. RMs are used to communicate best practice, common practice or normative rules [8] (chapter 3).

The present study exhibits the basic idea of the development of RMs, which link CPGs and CPs. Problems are identified with the help of case study, which arise for the RM-based approach. For that case scenarios serve the CPs of the regionally stroke network (SOS-NET), the internal CPGs of SOS-NET as well as the external CPGs of "*European Stroke Organization*" (ESO) and of the "*Deutsche Gesellschaft für Neurologie*" (DSG).

The motivation of our research is to analyze methodical ways of integration CP based on the CPG with the use of RM. The motivation of that paper follows the state of Campbell et al. who characterize as one aim of CPs as: "They can provide a link between the establishment of clinical guidelines and their use." [9]. Two scenarios should clarify aspects of connection of CPs to CPGs.

Scenario I: Implementation of CPs is a huge organizational process. To guarantee a high quality care they need to be developed systematically. A derivation of CP from the CPG would help to reduce manual work. There is always an element of risk associate with such manual procedures.

Scenario II: Since CPs guide evident clinical care, they need to be on the top of medical state of the art. Kaveh et al. showed in their study that CPG are permanent under revision [10]. Due to no real integration especially the alignment of models as well as other CP documents is a complex manual task. Goals for integration are making the process of alignment more efficient. It would also be helpful to check existing CPs due to their compliance.

The present paper dealing with the research question (RQ):

RQ 1 What are the upcoming problems during the development of CP for the network based on the CPGs?

The study is organized in 6 sections. After case scenario was introduced in section 1.1, the concept of CP and of CPG are introduced based on the literature mentioned in section 2. In section 3 we analyze the status quo of the CPG-integration in CP. In this section we build the fundamentals for the following analysis. In section 4 the concepts of CP and of CPG are compared to identify similarities, which would help to integrate them. In section 5 the results of the comparison are used to indentify issues, which challenge the RM-based approach. The paper ends with conclusions and suggestions for further research (section 6).

1.1 Project Background – The SOS-Net

In industrialized countries is the stroke the third major frequent cause of death and the most frequent reason of lasting physical handicaps [11]. In the acute stroke care the capabilities of therapy worsen with each minute, in which the stroke is not diagnosed and not treated accordingly. Immediately a medical intervention is necessary to avoid consequential damage.

That effort has to be done especially for the radiological findings. Further characteristics for the acute stroke are short delay for decision-making, limited possibility local transfer and difficulty diagnosable symptoms. In 2007, the SOS-NET was founded to build a telemedical infrastructure for regional stroke care. Goal of the network is to treat all stroke patients independent from of the distance to next stroke expert over the whole region on the same level. Within two years the SOS-NET is growing to an important stroke care in Saxony (Germany). At present, twelve hospitals are part of the network (05/2010).

The different suspension of employees and the differences of the technical infrastructure necessitate a defined responsibilities and process within the network. Therefore the stroke center as core of network allocates CPG for the partners of the network (stroke units). A meta-analysis of 17 high quality studies finds that CPs seem to be effective especially for invasive care like stroke care [1]. The CPGs (internal) are used to transfer best practice to the partners, who implement them in CPs, which are used in clinical every day life. Additionally they serve the definition of works principles of the network.

Figure 1 depicts the state-of-the-art of different documentations of clinical processes like they are in stroke care in general (layer 0 - 1) and in the SOS-NET in detail (layer 2 - 3). Conceptual models are used only in the documents of the layers 0 and 1.

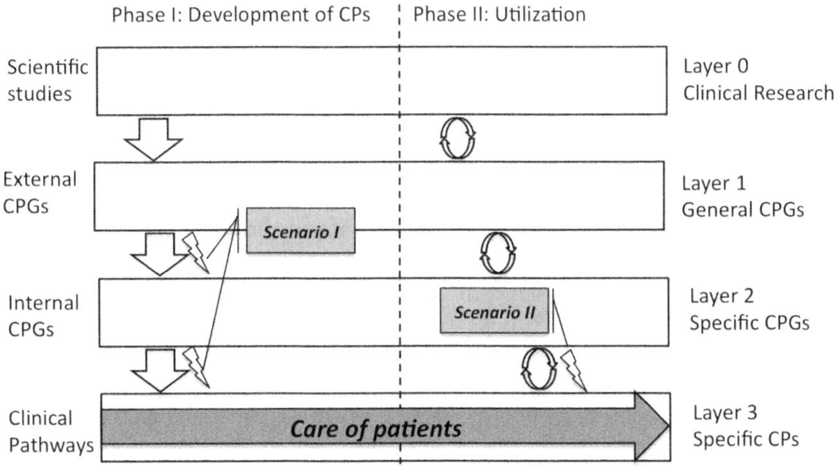

Fig. 1. As-Is-Situation of clinical documentation

2 Theoretical Foundations

2.1 The Clinical Pathway

CPs are a fundament in process management to achieve economical and qualitative objectives of hospitals [1]. The European Pathway Association defines a CPs as: "Clinical pathways are a methodology for the mutual decision making and organization of care for a well-defined group of patients during a well-defined period. Characteristics of care pathways are: "An explicit statement of the goals and key elements of care based on evidence, best practice, and patient expectations; The facilitation of the communication, coordination of roles, and sequencing the activities of the multidisciplinary care team, patients and their relatives; The documentation, monitoring, and evaluation of variances and outcomes; And the identification of the appropriate resources" [12]. The aim of a care pathway is to enhance the quality of care by improving patient outcomes, and promoting patient safety, increasing patient satisfaction, and optimizing the use of resources. The terms *Critical Pathway*, *Clinical Pathway* or *Integrated Care* Pathway are used for this concept synonymously. Some authors try to define them differently [12, 13]. But until now, no real consensus was found in the scientific community.

2.2 The Clinical Practice Guideline

CPGs are defined "as systematically developed statements to assist practitioner and patient decisions about appropriate health care for specific clinical circumstances" [2]. Furthermore, the role of economic statements within the CPG is discussed widely. For example, Priori et al. discuss the impact between economic statements versus the quality of the CPG. They conclude that CPGs should be produced with the primary aim of assessing the quality of science and the strength of evidence of clinical studies [14]. Wollersheim et al. characterize the content and contribution of CPG in the: inclusion of specific recommendations, sufficient supporting evidence, a clear structure and an attractive lay out [15]. The term CPG is used differently and is often not clearly disconnected from related concepts like medical protocol, standard operation procedure or CP. CPG can be developed either locally (internal guidelines) or regionally or nationally (external guidelines) [3]. Hence, several CPGs for same clinical case with different designs and representations exist.

3 Status Quo of CPG-Integration in Clinical Pathways

Several methodological approaches for the development of CPs based on the CPGs exist [13, 16-18]. One approach is to formalize the CPG in a computer-interpretable (CI) form [19, 20]. Arden-Syntax or XML are markup languages to prepare the narrative CPGs in a CI format. The aim of this approach is to transfer the non-formal rule-system (*clinical algorithm*, section 4) of the CPG in decision support systems (DSS) [19]. The DDS supplements the CPs within a hospital [21, 22]. Therefore the hospital information systems (HIS) have to be able to interpret the formal language and combine it to the specific state of patient documented in electronic health record (EHR). The approach of that transformation of CPG in CI structures is thus rather an extension of the paths than a methodology of the systematic transfer and organizational implementation.

A further approach to take CPGs into account of CPs is the inclusion of CPGs-analysis in its research phase during early project stage. Therefore, project members need to analysis the existing literature. This is a highly manual task with no methodical support [20]. The results of the analysis depend on the expertise of the single project member. In order to ensure a high quality of the analysis results several iterations are necessary.

Another approach, which represents an intermediate way between the formal procedure of CI transformation and not a systematic literature review, is the model-based methodology to transfer CPG-knowledge in CPs. Jacobs et al. present this idea for implementation of CPs in treatment of breast cancer [16]. The central element of their idea is the RM, which was used as instrument to structure and transfer the CPGs content. The purpose of RMs usage is the reduction of development costs and of development time and furthermore the alignment of model construction to common practice or best practice solutions [23]. A further aim is to specify rules and standards that guarantee the compliance to adaptability of a standardized application system or the compliance to organizational rules. The advantage of this approach is that the reference model can be reused. Thus the RM is an adequate instrument around the implementation of CPGs in clinical practice. On the one hand these support the CP creator in the adaptation by construction techniques. On the other hand RMs leave sufficient freedom for the CP-development. Actually, no RM, which includes construction techniques are added to the CPGs. Such construction techniques contain the definition and integration of rules for derivation of specific models. These represent rule sets that define the way of reusing model content and their adaptation and extension [24]. The development of the RM is a cost-intensive process. In contrast are the savings, which can be obtained by the employment of RMs. Due to the multiple applications, in network organization like SOS-NET, RMs can be used to guide best practice for network member. For them conceptual models are taken to communicate best-clinical practice of stroke care. The current models of SOS-NET do not support the adaptation of specific models.

4 Comparison of Clinical Practice Guideline and Clinical Pathway

The evaluation criteria that are used based on the concept definition. These are the aim, user groups, type of dissemination, general and specific design characteristics. The major similarity is the approach of each concept. Both purpose a standardization of medical care processes to improve clinical care. In addition to reach a high quality of care, CPs are also focused economic dimension. These derive typically from the formal organizational objectives. CPGs are not as focused on economical aspect as the CPs do [13].

he user groups of the concepts are heterogeneous. The key users of both instruments are the physicians. Patients are the second user group, especially for the CPGs. Additionally, CPs are used by the clinical management and controlling.

Dissemination means the mechanism how clinical knowledge implemented in the clinical practice. CPGs are developed in a general form. That means the physicians have to search actively in databases to CPG. Thus the type of dissemination is passive. CPs are developed in project teams by the care-provider themselves. The process of implementation is a common project step of CPs development. The dissemination of CPs is active. The concepts describe similarity as like as different aspects. CP contain beside clinical content administrative or fosterage services. Moreover, CPs include the entire range of the care process. The level of detail of CPs is on a constant level. These are not selected due to the importance in the care process. The level of abstraction varies according to the importance for the respective medical case. Combinations of prose and tabular form, protocol charts, lists as well as conceptual models are used to describe a step-per-step procedure for solving a clinical problem in both concepts. These procedures are defined as clinical algorithm [25]. They are subjected to both concepts like a skeleton. The clinical algorithm is an important similarity, which can help to integrate both concepts.

5 Issues of Development

According to the approach of Jacobs et al. the present analysis (scenario I) follows based on the main steps: Preparation of the CP project, Modeling of the CPGs, if it were not made with the CPGs development, Implementation of construction techniques (placeholders, configuration and construction advises) of RMs, Adaptation of RM by the specification of RM to a CP model, Dissemination of CP within the hospital. The task of preparation phase is the determination of CPGs, which are associated for the CP. The relation between CPGs and CP is not similar and is not defined by any institution. The relation between sections of the CP and of the CPGs has to be organized. In case of the SOS-NET, we have five relevant CPGs, which need to be taken in account. Different recommendations, which have to be integrated, exist. Thus it is required to have modular components, which compose these recommendations. The next step (step 2) of the procedure can be skipped, if the CPG as conceptual model exists already, and if they have the same format. Otherwise, the clinical algorithm of the guideline has to be extracted and modeled. The possible languages are Standard Nomenclature of MDM [25], Flowchart or Business Process Modeling Notation (BPMN) or Activity Chart of Unified Modeling Language (UML).

Due to the multiple relations between the concepts different CPGs have to be considered for CP. The kind of the composition cannot be pre-defined, since they find in each case in differently contexts application. Consequently, integrations of the conceptual models are necessary. CPGs lay on level of abstraction layer. The so-called problem of horizontal integration is mentioned in previous literature [26]. If it is necessary to model the CPGs again, additionally an integrated model of the CPG has to be developed. Otherwise the different languages have to be adapted. In the third step, the model of the CPGs is transferred a reference model. Up-to-date no standardized reference model language is accepted. Exemplarily, the ARIS method (architecture of integrated information systems) often used the event-controlled process chain (EPC) as well as the entity relationship model (ERM) [27]. In stroke care external CPGs are in prose. The solution of the SOS-NET is to describe the CPG with the help of Flowcharts. In addition, migration schemata, which allow transforming the flowchart to another type of process model, are published. We used the Flowchart because it is widely accepted, easily to understand. To enrich the clinical content of the CPG with administrative process aspects we add to the CPG model additional content of the stroke center. Furthermore, we implement placeholder at position, which need to specify while adaptation.

In the fourth step, the RM is adapted to a specific model. Therefore the path team implements the CPs with help of the construction techniques. An important fact, which has to be taken into account, is that if the goal modeling language of the CP deviates itself from the reference model language, the adapted model has to migrate in the right modeling language. In contrast to CPGs, CPs describe all activities of clinical care. For the adaptation of CP that means that additional aspect like administrative processes need to be create. Due to the indispensable fact that the CPGs are more general and the CPs are more detailed no aspects are found.

6 Conclusion and Further Research

In that paper the different concepts of CPG and CP are presented. With the method of case study the situation in SOS-NET was analyzed. The CPG and CP were compared on a conceptual level and similarities and differences were observed. The comparison of the CPGs and CPs shows that the clinical algorithm is an important similarity, which could be used to link the concepts. In the state-of-the-art we showed that the RM-based approach is one possible way to integrate both concepts. The identified problems are the relation between the concepts, the different aspects and the not standardized design. Furthermore the RM as technique itself raises problems like the missing tool support and evaluated RM-languages. Finally, the study shows that a methodical RM-based development of CP based on CPG can be built. One of the main deficits is the missing standardization for design of CPGs and CPs. Especially, CPGs should be published in combination with a RM and a description how to use it. That would be help to assure a constant quality of dissemination. Further research is need on detailed method of implementation and on a method for utilization and for half-automatic alignment of CP. Moreover, the alignment as instrument of clinical process quality should be investigated. An empirical validation of the case study results is also necessary.

References

1. Rotter, T., Kugler, J., Koch, R., Gothe, H., Twork, S., van Oostrum, J., Steyerberg, E.: A systematic review and meta-analysis of the effects of clinical pathways on length of stay, hospital costs and patient outcomes. BMC Health Services Research 8, 265 (2008)
2. Field, M.J., Lohr, K.N.: Clinical practice guidelines: directions for a new program. National Academies Press, Washington (1990)
3. Thomas, L.: Clinical practice guidelines. Evidence Based Nursing 2, 38–39 (1999)
4. Schuette, R., Rotthowe, T.: The Guidelines of Modeling - An Approach to Enhance the Quality in Information Models. In: Ling, T.-W., Ram, S., Li Lee, M. (eds.) ER 1998. LNCS, vol. 1507, pp. 240–254. Springer, Heidelberg (1998)
5. Fettke, P., Loos, P.: Klassifikation von informationsmodellen-nutzenpotenziale, methode und anwendung am beispiel von referenzmodellen. In: Working Paper of the Research Group Information Systems & Management, Universität Mainz, vol. 9 (2002)
6. Rosemann, M., Schwegmann, A., Delfmann, P.: Vorbereitung der Prozessmodellierung. In: Prozessmanagement, pp. S45–S103. Springer, Berlin (2002)
7. Frank, U.: Conceptual modelling as the core of the information systems discipline perspectives and epistemological challenges. In: Proceedings of the Fifth Americas Conference on Information Systems (AMCIS 1999), pp. S13–S15 (August 1999)
8. Becker, J., Delfmann, P., Ralf, K.: Konstruktion von Referenzmodellierungssprachen - Ein Ordnungsrahmen zur Spezifikation von Adaptionsmechanismen für Informationsmodelle, pp. 251–264 (2004)
9. Campbell, H., Hotchkiss, R., Bradshaw, N., Porteous, M.: Integrated care pathways. BMJ, 133–137 (1998)

10. Kaveh, D., Shojania, M., Ansari, M., Ji, J., Doucette, S., Moher, D.: How quickly do systematic reviews go out of date? A Survival Analysis. Anal. of Internal Medicine 147, 224–233 (2007)
11. Kolominsky-R., P.L., Heuschmann, P.U., Marschall, D., Emmert, M., Baltzer, N.: Lifetime Cost of Ischemic Stroke in Germany: Results and National Projections From a Population-Based Stroke Registry. Stroke 37, 1179–1183 (2006)
12. De Bleser, L., Depreitere, R., De Waele, K., Vanhaecht, K., Vlayen, J., Sermeus, W.: Defining pathways. Journal of Nursing Management 14, 553–563 (2006)
13. Greiling, M., Rudloff, B.: Klinische Pfade optimal gestalten. Baumann Fachzeitschriften Verlag, Berlin (2005)
14. Priori, S.G., Klein, W., Bassand, J.P.: Medical Practice Guidelines: separating science from economics. European heart journal 24, 1962 (2003)
15. Wollersheim, H., Burgers, J., Grol, R.: Clinical guidelines to improve patient care. The Netherlands Journal of Medicine 63, 188–192 (2005)
16. Jacobs, B., Oberhoff, C., Stausberg, J.: Ableitung von Klinischen Pfaden aus evidenzbasierten Leitlinien am Beispiel der Behandlung des Mammakarzinoms der Frau, `http://www.egms.de/static/de/journals/mibe/2007-3/mibe000057.shtml`
17. Hellmann, W.: Praxis Klinischer Pfade: Viele Wege führen zum Ziel. Ecomed. (2003).
18. Schluechter, D., Conen, T., Holler, T., Müller, H., Schmid, K.: Pfad-Controlling im Modell integrierter Patientenpfade - ein neues, innovatives Prozesscontrolling-Instrument. Gesundheitsökonomie & Qualitätsmanagement 8, 355–362 (2003)
19. Peleg, M., Tu, S., Bury, J., Ciccarese, P., Fox, J., Greenes, R.A., Hall, R., Johnson, P.D.: Comparing Computer-interpretable Guideline Models: A Case-study Approach. Journal of the American Medical Informatics Association 10, 52–68 (2003)
20. Kaiser, K., Akkaya, C., Miksch, S.: How can information extraction ease formalizing treatment processes in clinical practice guidelines? Artif. Intell. Med. 39, 151–163 (2007)
21. Arden Syntax, `http://www.hl7.org/implement/standards/ardensyntax.cfm`
22. ASTM E2210 -06 Standard Specification for Guideline Elements Model version 2, `http://www.astm.org/Standards/E2210.htm`
23. Schütte, R.: Grundsätze ordnungsmäßiger Referenzmodellierung. Gabler (1998)
24. vom Brocke, J., Buddendick, C.: Referenzmodellierung: Grundlagen, Techniken und domänenbezogene Anwendung. Physica-Verlag, Heidelberg (2007)
25. Barak, N., Margolis, C., Gottlieb, L.: Proposal for Clinical Algorithm Standards: Society for Medical Decision Making Committee on Standardization of Clinical Algorithms. Medical Decision Making 12, 149–154 (1992)
26. Rosemann, M.: Komplexitätsmanagement in Prozeßmodellen. Gabler, Wiesbaden (2002)
27. Scheer, A.: ARIS–business process frameworks. Springer, Heidelberg (1999)

Implementing Self-organising Virtual Enterprises Using Social Behaviour Nets

Ping Jiang[1], Quentin Mair[2], and Mingwei Yuan[3]

[1] Department of Computing, The University of Bradford, Bradford BD7 1DP, UK
[2] School of Engineering and Computing, Glasgow Caledonian University, Glasgow G4 0BA, UK
[3] Department of Information and Control, Tongji University, Shanghai 200092, China
qma@gcal.ac.uk

Abstract. Frameworks to support Internet-based virtual enterprises are currently characterised as having fixed process models, fixed meta-data models and a fixed set of users at project inception. This paper proposes the SoBeNet architecture to support a highly dynamic, self-organised, Internet-based approach based on social interaction. The architecture is based on a multi-agent approach, Internet communication being achieved through RSS feeds. RSS conveys state changes by carrying data defined in a common ontology. Each agent assesses state changes using a virtual sensor by calculating the semantic distance between the change and its own interests. Each agent also contains a behaviour network which uses an activation spreading paradigm to react to a combination of its own goals and state changes. The SoBeNet test-bed is based on the Java JADE environment.

Keywords: multi-agent, behaviour network, ontology, virtual organization.

1 Introduction

Social interaction is a dynamic, changing sequence of social actions between individuals (or groups) who try to affect or take account of each others' subjective experiences or intentions. Today the Internet has augmented the traditional methods of social interaction. According to the UK Office of National Statistics there are now around 15 million households in Britain alone with Internet access. As a result the Internet has become an important tool for social interaction supporting activities such as chatting, shopping, dating and information exchange. An Internet-based virtual organisation (VO) will provide a set of tools to support the creation and operation of an organisation of *ad-hoc* partners who have come together for a cooperative project. The Internet supports individuals who may want to work together across organisational boundaries but who do not have much prior knowledge on which to base relations. VOs are highly dynamic and their operation unpredictable. Therefore a key aspect of social interaction in VOs to study is how to organise independent individuals with a limited understanding of each other. It is also necessary to address how to exchange local information and orchestrate local processes together. These characteristics reflect the *ad hoc opportunistic* nature of a VO [1][2].

L.M. Camarinha-Matos et al. (Eds.): PRO-VE 2010, IFIP AICT 336, pp. 259–266, 2010.

Research into the support necessary to implement social interaction in a VO has been widely carried out in different areas such as: virtual enterprises [3], e-business [4], professional virtual communities (PVCs) [5] and grid computing; common requirements have been identified [6][7][8]. These include: the ability to assign job priorities through collaborative shared goals, coordinated and controlled access to shared resources, delegation, discovery services and collaborative processes. Two general approaches can be taken to implement a VO: transaction-oriented layer-based and as a distributed multi-agent system [3]. The transaction-oriented layer-based approach usually applies a top-down design approach to specify goals and subgoals. A protocol for interaction is defined beforehand by a consortium or standards body as a reference model, including meta-data and process models, and is subsequently deployed by customising the cooperation layer of an existing IT infrastructure. This produces a structurally static VO. Examples of this approach can be seen in the ARPA NIIIP (National Industrial Information Infrastructure Protocols) and the EU DIECoM (Distributed Integrated Environment for Configuration Management) projects. However it has been found that this approach is deficient in open and dynamic environments due to its inflexibility and operational inefficiency [3]. The next generation of VOs are faced with a more dynamic environment, requiring user functionality akin to that found in current Web 2.0 applications: RSS feeds, WIKI, Blogs, Social Book Mark, FaceBook, Podcast etc. Such VOs will be required to be able to provide flexible and fast responses to changing information and goals during operation. In comparison to the transaction-oriented layer-based approach we propose that multi-agent based approaches [1][8][9][10] are more suitable to support the next generation of VOs. These may offer a better approach to support the lifecycle of VOs from partnership seeking, partnership configuration, partnership execution to partnership dissolution. An agent can be viewed as perceiving its environment through sensors and acting upon that environment through actuators [11]. Whilst RSS feeds in the Internet provide almost instant awareness of information updates, software agents could help Internet users conduct real-time and automatic interaction with others. Although general frameworks to support distributed agent-based VOs have been developed, e.g. mobile-agent based architectures [1], the required intelligent mechanisms and techniques have not been well studied to support such social interaction.

In this paper we propose a novel synthesis of approaches to deal with a dynamic and partially observable VO for social interaction in the Internet. We propose a **Social Behaviour Network** (SoBeNet) i.e. a distributed behaviour network-based approach organised in a more dynamic, loosely coupled and self-organisational way than that previously attempted in VOs. Our behaviour net concept is based on the goal-driven behaviour nets first proposed by Maes [12]. A SoBeNet is a distributed multi-agent system which uses the Internet. An agent in a SoBeNet senses RSS updates of other agents via virtual sensors and feeds these to a virtual controller. The virtual controller manages a behaviour net fragment, execution of the behaviour only taking place when it has enough activation energy from its goal or from state changes detected through RSS. After the agent executes a state change it will update its RSS documents and cause activation energy to be spread to other behaviour nets. Hence distributed agents interact with each other in a spontaneous way and can form a VO with diverse local goals/missions.

The rest of this paper is structured as follows. Section 2 presents a high-level overview of our SoBeNet system. Section 3 focuses on our main contribution in this paper – the adaptation of Maes behaviour networks to the SoBeNet system. Section 4 discusses the implementation of a SoBeNet software platform built on the Java Agent Development Environment (JADE). Section 5 discusses a case study validation scenario. Finally Section 6 presents conclusion and future work.

2 SoBeNet Architecture

A SoBeNet is composed of distributed agents supporting the whole lifecycle of social interaction in the Internet but without a predefined process model. Multiple agents work towards diverse local goals but are self-organised into a cooperative social behaviour network. The interaction between agents takes place spontaneously through RSS feeds which allow changes of web content to be monitored. The schematic diagram of a SoBeNet is shown in Fig.1:

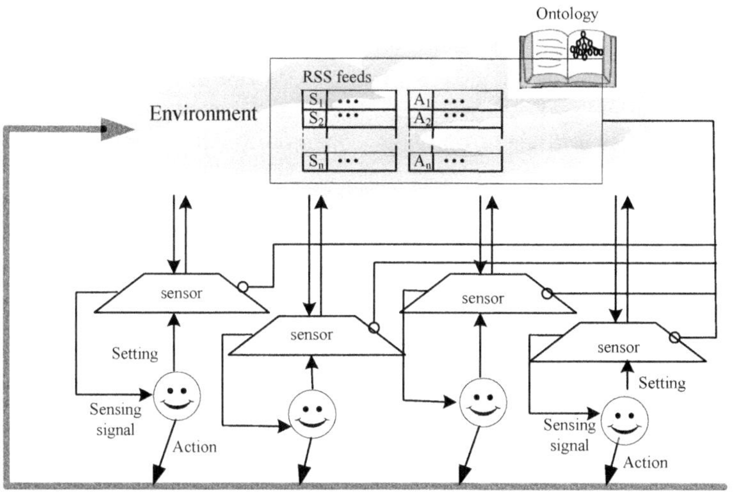

Fig. 1. Architecture of a SoBeNet

An ontology allows rich semantics to be carried via RSS as OWL documents. These collectively constitute the virtual state space of the SoBeNet. To avoid an extremely complicated and large state space only the relevant aspects of a set of tasks are modelled in an ontology. The RSS documents in the state space change dynamically. The use of an ontology enables agents to understand the meaning of RSS feeds from other agents. This functionality is implemented by virtual sensors.

The structure of our proposed agents is shown in Fig.2. Each agent in a SoBeNet has several virtual sensors. A virtual sensor can perceive and reason about changes in RSS feeds and acts as a text mining agent for the semantic retrieval of RSS documents. It serves two purposes. Firstly it allows behaviour net fragments to detect relevant changes in the state space and goals i.e. detect events for behaviour activation.

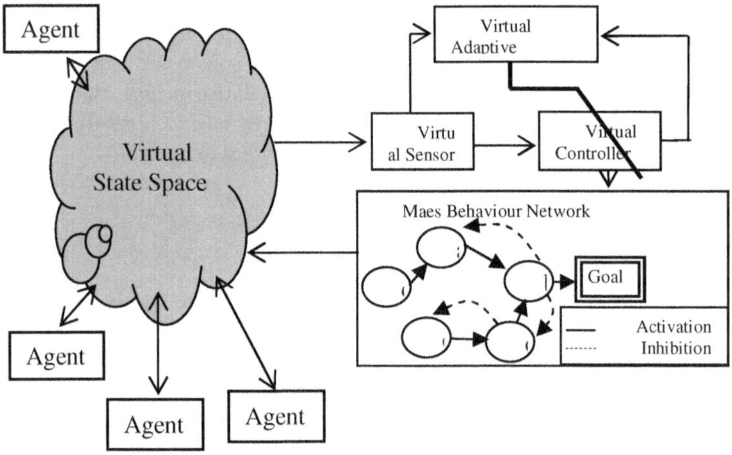

Fig. 2. SoBeNet agent structure diagram

Secondly, for interpretation of RSS documents, it facilitates fuzzy matchmaking between the expected criteria for interaction and the received RSS feeds from candidates. A virtual sensor conducts logic-based binary assessment about the executability of a behaviour and is also able to provide a measure of the semantic closeness between two RSS documents.

Each agent (Fig. 2) contains a local Maes behaviour network which is governed by a virtual controller. The virtual controller selects reasonable actions according to activation/inhibition energies induced from the virtual sensors and local goal, which will be presented in section 3. The social interaction in the VO is thus driven by goals and the state of artefacts in the virtual state space but without an explicit cooperation model.

In a SoBeNet each virtual sensor perceives the state changes of other agents from RSS feeds. To define the semantic data content of RSS feeds for a specific domain, we define an ontology for the data source. This is defined in OWL. We use a semantic distance measure to evaluate the relevance of RSS feed changes together with a hierarchical clustering analysis approach. In this paper, for brevity, we do discuss this further but the interested reader is referred to our other work in [13].

In addition each agent maintains a virtual adaptive machine to provide the virtual controller with learning and predictive capability. This maintains a belief model about the VO-based on historical experience and predicts other agents' future behaviour patterns. An agent is thus able to reason on the suitability of other agents to take part in collaboration for achieving its goal.

3 An Energy Driven Social Behaviour Network

A behaviour network can be represented as a three-layer network as shown in Fig.3: sensor layer, behaviour layer and goal layer. The virtual sensors are located in the sensor layer. A user can set goals or sub-goals at the goal layer. The behaviour layer includes behaviour modules linked by activation or inhibition channels for energy spreading. A behaviour network can be formalised as a tuple (G, M, Π), where G is a

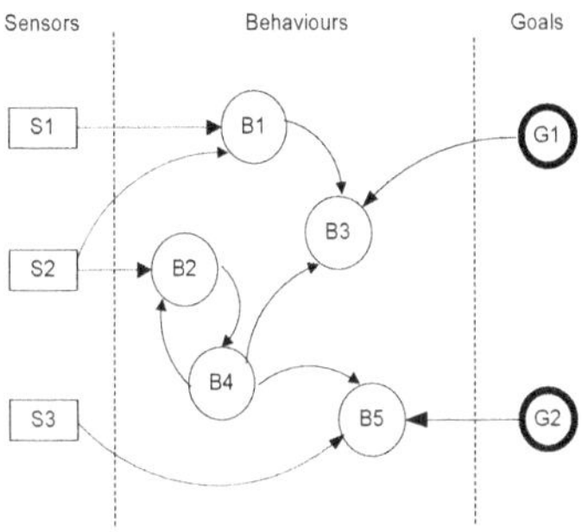

Fig. 3. A behaviour network

set of goals; M is a set of behaviour modules and Π is a set of parameters that control the energy spreading. An agent executes a behaviour module in M when its activation energy level exceeds an activation threshold defined in Π.

Energy control parameters defined in Π are normalised into [0,1] following [15], which includes:

$\gamma \in [0,1]$ activation parameter of module
$\delta \in [0,1]$ inhibition parameter of module
$\beta \in [0,1]$ inertia parameter of activation
$\phi \in [0,1]$ activation parameter of state
$a \in [0, \hat{a}]$ activation threshold,with $\hat{a}$ the upper bound
η normalisation constant

The energy control parameters affect the performance of a behaviour network. Their values can be set by users from their own experience or set through a machine learning process.

Each behaviour module M_i in M can be defined by another tuple (p_i, b_i, Eff_i, h_i, r_i) in which b_i represents a functional behaviour. p_i represents a precondition list to be satisfied in order to activate b_i, and r_i is the desired resolution of a virtual sensor. Taking p_i as the subscriber interest, the virtual sensor receives a RSS stream s and generates the degree of behaviour executability, denoted as $\tau(p_i,s)$. A higher resolution expects a more precise check of executability but a lower resolution means a fuzzier condition. Eff_i:={eff^+, eff^-} defines a set of effects after execution of the behaviour b_i with eff^+ representing the positive effects and eff^- representing the negative effects, $eff^+ \cap eff^- = \phi$. Exp(eff^+) and Exp(eff^-) denote the expectations of energy injection from eff^+ and eff^- to a linked behaviour respectively. The value h_i denotes the activation energy level of b_i, accumulated from goals or other modules. When the activation energy level exceeds the activation threshold $a_i \in \Pi$, the behaviour can be activated. Energy flows through links between behaviour modules. Consider a link from behaviour A to behaviour B. B is called a successor of A if A has a positive effect (eff^+) in the proposition of B's precondition, whilst A is called a predecessor of B. There is a conflicting link from A to B if A has a negative effect (eff^-) in the proposition of B's precondition. A behaviour module can take energy from current states and final goals directly or indirectly. A direct acquisition means energy obtained from the current sensors and goals; an indirect acquisition means energy obtained from other behaviour modules.

Execution of a behaviour network is carried out by repeatedly scanning activation energy in individual behaviour modules. For each step only the behaviour with the highest energy level will be activated.

A key characteristic of behaviour networks is that the behaviours that currently cannot be executed spread activation energy backwards to predecessor behaviours. This allows sub-goals to be addressed. As this can be applied iteratively it facilitates a VO to be self-organising.

4 SoBeNet Implementation

A SoBeNet test-bed has been developed using JADE (Java Agent Development Framework). JADE was developed by Telecom Italia Lab in compliance with FIPA (Foundation for Intelligent Physical Agents) specifications. As the JADE architecture is based on Java this allows us to easily extend the architecture to incorporate our SoBeNet functionality. JADE is also open source. It is efficient and scalable for large multi-agent systems [14] and flexible enough to be deployed in fixed and mobile environments [15]. JADE provides support for automatic document exchange in XML and RDF [15].

Each running instance of JADE is a container which could include one or more agents. The set of active containers constitutes a platform in which only a single main container need be active for administration and coordination purposes, i.e. the main container contains the JADE AMS (Agent Management System) and DF (Directory Facilitator) components. Distributed agents can communicate with each other through asynchronous messages defined in ACL (Agent Communication Language). The main container includes a blackboard agent in addition to the AMS and DF components. This provides the virtual state space describing the environment and the information sources monitored by the virtual sensors. The blackboard agent receives RSS feeds subscribed to by user agents and provides a common space for information exchange between agents. This information includes RSS data, domain ontology, agent IDs and a message routing table. Each container representing a user includes a sensor agent S_i and a controller agent C_i. The sensor agent implements the proposed virtual sensor. A user is allowed to subscribe to RSS feeds, define interests and configure sensor parameters, e.g. resolution. The controller agent maintains a set of behaviour modules. Each extends the JADE behaviour class to implement in code a local behaviour network. Each behaviour module is activated by energy from virtual sensors and other behaviours. The user is allowed to configure the controller agent, e.g. energy spreading parameters and activation threshold. Note that each user can also receive RSS feeds from its sensor agent and publish a RSS information update using its controller agent directly rather than via the Blackboard agent. Due to the current lack of websites allowing bi-directional and interactive RSS information exchange, we use the blackboard agent as a common information pool for carrying out interactive RSS information exchange.

5 Case Study Validation Scenario

We have validated the work by creating a virtual organisation for a new product development as a simulation scenario. Given 20 SoBeNet agents which are either job-hunters or development leaders, we attempt to show that a hierarchical virtual organisation can be organised automatically. The information sources come from RSS feeds including websites at Yahoo Hotjobs, UK Academic Jobs, and CareerBuilder. Because no RSS feeds are available today to announce personal abilities, a simulated RSS source is created in the blackboard agent. This is obtained by inserting bindings of user names to job descriptions received from job advertisement websites.

An agent will publish a job description in RSS and wait for applications. Once a competent applicant appears it will notify the user and the development leader will confirm if the job should be offered. The social interaction for organising a development team is completed automatically by generated events; from virtual sensors, timers and user input.

The role of a user is not fixed; conceivably a user can take the role of a job-hunter for the overall task and then decompose the job into subtasks and then become a development leader for the purposes of subcontracting. Thus a hierarchical VO can be formed. The goal here is to subcontract to others the development of new hardware with an embedded software element. After execution of the publish-job behaviour the job specification is added and the "match-candidates" behaviour is activated. The virtual sensor detects the top 3 candidates as Agents A, B and C. Agent A is identified as the best matched. Agent A then divides the job into subtasks and becomes the development leader for the hardware development and software development subtasks. The candidates with highest similarity, Agents B and C, are selected by the "Match-job" behaviour and invited to join the team. Agent C refused the invitation for "hardware development" and Agent B with the second highest similarity was recruited into the team. This task reallocation process is repeated until no further subcontracting is possible.

The simulation shows that each agent does not know the other agents in advance and executes independently according to sensed information. Social interaction happens naturally by activating distributed local behaviours. This is more suitable for interaction in dynamic and uncertain environments than traditional process model-based approaches.

6 Conclusions

Social interactions in the Internet are often characterised by a set of organisations or individuals who come together to perform an intellectually focussed project over some period of time. Such virtual organisations may exhibit unpredictable events and operate with previously unknown participants. It is often difficult to adapt traditional process model-based approaches especially if a reorganisation or problem arises mid-project. In a SoBeNet each person is aided by a software agent which embeds semantic sensors and a behaviour network, taking RSS feeds as the information source. The behaviour nets manage all agent actions enabling them to achieve individual goals concurrently. This ability allows them to react to changes in the Internet e.g. the alteration of a behaviour mid-project or the replacement of a project partner. Social interaction is thus spontaneous. A SoBeNet test-bed was developed using the Java-based JADE toolkit and validated with a new product development scenario.

References

1. Aerts, A.T.M., Szirbik, N.B., Goossenaerts, J.B.M.: A flexible, agent-based ICT architecture for virtual enterprises. Computers in Industry 49, 311–327 (2002)
2. Martinez, M.T., Park, K.H., Favrel, J.: Virtual enterprise: organisation, evolution and control. Int. J. Production Economics 74, 225–238 (2001)
3. Camarinha-Matos, L.M., Afsarmanesh, H.: Elements of a base VE infrastructure. Computers in Industry 51, 139–163 (2003)
4. Burn, J., Marshall, P., Barnett, M.: E-business Strategies for Virtual Organizations. Elsevier, Kent (2002)
5. Santoro, R., Bifulco, A.: PVC Reference Framework. In: European Society of Concurrent Engineering – Net (2008), http://www.ami-communities.eu/
6. EC DataGrid, VOMS vs EDG security requirements, Work Package 6 (2002)
7. EC ECOLEAD, Challenges in virtual organisations management, D32.1, Work Package 3 (2004)
8. Norman, T.J., Preece, A., et al.: Agent-based formation of virtual organizations. Knowledge-Based Systems 17, 103–111 (2004)
9. Goldman, C.V., Rosenschein, J.S.: Evolutionary patterns of agent organizations. IEEE Trans. Systems, Man, and Cybernetics—Part A 32, 135–148 (2002)
10. Subbu, R., Sanderson, A.C.: Network-based distributed planning using coevolutionary agents: architecture and evaluation. IEEE Trans. Systems, Man, and Cybernetics—Part A 34, 257–269 (2004)
11. Russell, S., Norvig, P.: Artificial Intelligence: A Modern Approach, 2nd edn. Prentice Hall, Upper Saddle River (2003)
12. Maes, P.: Situated agents can have goals. Robotics and Autonomous Systems 6, 49–70 (1990)
13. Jiang, P., Mair, Q., Feng, Z.: Agent alliance formation using ART-networks as agent belief models. Journal of Intelligent Manufacturing 18(3), 433–448 (2007)
14. Chmiel, K., Gawinecki, M., Kaczmarek, P., Szymczak, M., Paprzycki, M.: Efficiency of JADE agent platform. Scientific Programming 13, 1–14 (2005)
15. Bellifemine, F., Caire, G., Poggi, A., Rimassa, G.: JADE: a white paper. EXP 3(3), 6–19 (2003)

Network Structures in the International Clothing Industry

B.L. MacCarthy and P.G.S.A. Jayarathne

Nottingham University Business School,
Jubilee Campus, Nottingham, NG8 1BB, UK
bart.maccarthy@nottingham.ac.uk

Abstract. The structure and operation of supply networks have received considerable attention from both the business community and academic researchers in the last two decades as the pace of globalisation has accelerated. Supply networks in the international clothing industry have developed and evolved significantly over that period. This paper reviews different ways to categorise supply networks and notes their limitations in providing insights on the structure and operation of networks in the contemporary global clothing industry. Leading retailers and major clothing brand owners influence strongly how such networks operate. Given the limitations of existing generic classifications, a new classification of clothing supply networks is presented based on extensive empirical evidence from the Sri Lankan clothing industry. The relevance of the findings for network design and management are noted. This study of supply networks in the international clothing industry provides much potential for further research, particularly in globally dispersed industries.

Keywords: goal-oriented supply network structures, global clothing industry, classification.

1 Introduction

The structure and management of supply networks have received considerable attention from both the business community and academic researchers in the last two decades as the pace of globalisation has accelerated and supply networks have become increasingly globally dispersed. The clothing industry is known to be one of the most global, mobile and dynamic industries in the world [20] and contributes significantly to the world economy. The international export trade in clothing increased by over 100% in the period 1990 – 2003 [27].

Over the last two decades, complex global supply networks have emerged to supply garments to world markets with different network structures, strategies and practices. Although different ways of categorizing supply networks have been discussed in the literature, they are very limited in providing insights on global apparel supply networks. International clothing supply networks are driven primarily by retailers that exert significant power and control. The work presented here is part of a study that seeks to *(1)identify the different supply network structures that operate in the international clothing industry* and *(2) examine how such structures are developed and managed according to the goals of different retailers.*

L.M. Camarinha-Matos et al. (Eds.): PRO-VE 2010, IFIP AICT 336, pp. 267–278, 2010.

The paper first provides a brief overview of different ways of categorizing supply networks from the existing literature, highlighting some of their limitations. Then, the nature of international clothing supply networks and the role of retailers within such networks are discussed. A case study of a major supply network is used to illustrate the complexity of such networks and the influence of retailer goals on network structure, policies and operation. A new way of classifying networks is described. The differences between the supply networks of major reputable retailers and supermarket clothing retailers are highlighted.

2 Supply Network Structures

The term 'supply network' has been defined in different ways. Harland (1996) defines it as a set of supply chains describing the flow of goods and services from original sources to end customers [11]. Harland and Knight (2001) define a supply network as a system comprising of actors, resources and activities and their connections related to transforming inputs into products and services [12]. Harland et al. (2004) describe supply networks as being nested within wider inter-organizational networks and consisting of inter-connected entities whose primary purpose is the procurement, use and transformation of resources to provide packages of goods and services [13]. Christopher (2005) defines a supply network as "a network of connected and interdependent organizations mutually and co-operatively working together to control, manage and improve the flow of materials and information from suppliers to end users" [3]. Here we use the definition given by Harland and Knight (2001).

Different perspectives have been used to classify supply networks. Hinterhuber and Levin (1994) have categorized networks into four classes with respect to direction and network orientation - internal, vertical, horizontal and diagonal [15]. Some 'vertical' networks operate in the clothing industry. For instance, Zara manages its globally dispersed supply networks as essentially a vertically integrated network. However, not all apparel supply networks operate in a 'vertical' mode [19]. Cravens et al (1996) categorize supply networks into four clusters - flexible, hollow, virtual, and value-added. Although 'flexible' and 'virtual' networks may appear in apparel networks, one can be contained in the other [4]. In particular, virtual networks provide a strategic perspective in which a flexible network can operate at the operational level.

Nassimbeni (1998) identifies three main supply network categories - 'supply network', 'agreements and joint ventures', and 'regional industrial systems' [21]. However, many different types of clothing supply networks can be put into one category – 'supply networks'. Lamming et al. (2000) categorize supply networks based on two dimensions – product innovation and uniqueness ('innovative-unique' products against 'functional' products), and product complexity (high against low) [17]. However, such categories do not discriminate well between different clothing products, as will be noted later. Ernst and Kamrad (2000) identify four types of supply networks - rigid, flexible, modularized and postponed [6]. Among these, only 'flexible' and 'postponed' structures have clear implications for the apparel industry and not all clothing networks can be categorized into these two types.

Harland et al. in 2001 discuss four types of supply networks based on two dimensions – whether they are routinized or dynamic and the degree of influence of the focal firm (high or low) [14]. This classification is empirically based and, compared to other classifications, provides more detail on operational strategies of relevance in the apparel industry. However, the identification of the 'focal firm' may be problematic in applying this classification. Lee (2002) classifies supply network types into four, based on their supply and demand characteristics and the strategy that should be deployed - efficient supply chains, risk-hedging supply chains, responsive supply chains, and agile supply chains [18]. Almost all clothing supply networks need to be responsive in today's world. Hence, sub categories within the responsive category need to be identified with relevance to the apparel industry.

Verwaal and Hesselmas (2004) use two dimensions in their classification of supply networks – interdependence of organizational activities and asset specificity [29]. They identify two network types - 'equal-partner network' and 'dominated network'. International clothing supply networks can be identified as dominated networks as they are typically controlled by powerful retailers. However, although this is generally true, the way retailers exercise their power differs depending on their goals. This is discussed further in section 5 below.

Other supply network classification perspectives reported include: whether the network is formalized or not and whether it is centralized or parity-based [10]; different types of industrial clusters [22]; hard and soft networks [23]; and a classification based on manufacturing flexibility characteristics [8].

Most of the identified classifications are very general and fail to discriminate clearly or provide significant explanatory power when examining the detailed structure and operation of many real supply networks. In particular they are weak in explaining the nature and characteristics of supply networks in the contemporary international clothing industry. This paper presents a new approach to the classification of supply networks in this sector.

3 International Clothing Supply Networks

3.1 The Global Clothing Industry

The global clothing industry is important for both developed and developing countries. For instance, the apparel industry in Sri Lanka is the main foreign exchange income source, contributing 56% of its industrial export income and 43% of its total export income in 2008 [2]. In the EU, over 2 million people were employed in the textile and apparel industry in 2006 (Euratex, 2006 – cited from [5]). In the US, the sector currently employs over four hundred thousand workers [28].

Although the US and the EU are major clothing markets, apparel manufacturing has migrated in the last three decades to newly industrialized countries, developing countries and under-developed countries [27]. Deregulation and the abolition of quotas, in particular abolition of the Multi Fibre Agreement (MFA) at the end of 2004 has accelerated the mobility of this industry. Some countries have benefited whilst others have lost out. China and India have shown very strong growth after 2004 [1]. However, Sri Lanka with a long tradition of apparel manufacturing has seen its clothing industry decline from 71% of its total industrial exports in 2004 to 56% in 2008 [2] with the abolition of the MFA. These phenomena are important in understanding the types of supply networks that have emerged in the international clothing industry.

3.2 Retailer-Driven International Clothing Supply Networks

In addition to the dispersal of clothing manufacturing activities, the industry has changed tremendously during the last two decades owing to the dynamics in apparel demand and supply. Today's apparel demand is more fragmented with an increasing fashion influence across all product categories [16]. Both product variety and new product introduction have been accelerating in 'basic garments' as well as 'fashion garments' [24]. A fashion element has now developed in many 'basic garments', typically classed as volume or commodity products [19], [24], [25]. Traditional apparel markets with two fixed seasons per year have given way to frequent refreshes within a season. Competitive retailers focus on replenishment of the specific styles, designs and colours that are selling well, whilst reducing or abandoning those that turn out to be less popular than forecast [7], [19], [25]. Importantly, the trends of compressing new product introduction time, multiple refreshes per season and very quick response from suppliers, need to be achieved at low cost [19], [25].

Retailers and major brand owners are the most powerful players in the apparel supply network. Gereffi (1999) and Tyler et al (2006) highlight how current international clothing supply networks are buyer-driven in contrast to producer-driven supply networks [9], [26]. Gereffi (1999) notes that buyer-driven clothing supply networks are often characterized by loose and dynamic couplings linking production mainly in developing countries with fashion demand in developed countries [9]. Hence, they rely on global sourcing strategies to meet demand. Profit is generated from design, sales, marketing and services that link globally spread production plants with consumer markets [26].

Apparel supply networks may contain many entities including designers, merchandisers, yarn producers, fabric producers, trims producers, garment manufacturers, distributors, logistics and warehouse companies, and retailers [30]. Retailers use different supply network members to cope with dynamic demand in apparel markets. Further, because of raw material and capacity availability, cost advantages, and other factors such as trade policies, clothing supply networks tend to be dispersed internationally and may become highly complex, long and heterogeneous.

Most of the powerful apparel retailers are based in the developed countries mainly in the US and in EU. Some of these retailers are noted brand owners (e.g. M&S, Next, Zara, Nike, Victoria Secret) whilst others are supermarket brands (e.g.: Asda, Tesco, Sainsbury, and Wal-Mart). In the UK, the supermarket brands now account for a significant proportion of the apparel sales per year. Apparel manufacturers in developing countries supply both types of retailers. A question considered here is whether these two types of apparel retailer use different supply networks and whether they operate them differently.

The Sri Lankan clothing industry has evolved during the last three decades as the most important industrial sector in the economy in terms of production, employment, and foreign income generation. It has developed a reputation as a niche supplier of intimate apparel. Sri Lankan apparel manufacturers supply high quality value-added garments to leading retailers in EU and in the USA, including many well known international brands such as Gap, Liz, Claiborne, Next, Tommy Hilfiger, Victoria Secrets, Nike, and M & S [27]. They also supply garments for supermarket brands such as Asda, Tesco, and Wal-Mart. Thus Sri Lanka provides an opportunity to examine different types of clothing supply networks and how they operate in the global context.

4 Methodology

The goal of the work is to understand the structure, operation and policies of different supply networks in the international clothing industry. The field work for this research has been conducted in a non-contrived setting – the Sri Lankan apparel industry. The unit of analysis is a specific apparel supply network. Several research methods and data collection instruments have been used. Both primary and secondary data have been collected. The study was cross-sectional in the time horizon as data have been collected over a specific period of time.

Thirty case companies were selected from the Sri Lankan apparel industry, including all of the major producers in the country, each of which has significant manufacturing networks. In-depth interviews were carried out with strategic and operational level managers to gain detailed information on the structure and operation of different supply networks. Strategic level managers were interviewed to investigate the goals, motives and policies of different retailers. Typically such managers had worked closely with retailers for a long time. Operational level managers were interviewed to investigate the operational aspects of the supply networks. In addition, observations were made by the researcher on each organisation to add to the primary data. Interviews were also conducted with relevant government bodies and agencies to provide context and understanding of the international dimensions of the industry.

Secondary data sources used include literature resources, reports and publications from government authorities and from selected apparel manufacturers. Together the different sources have provided rich information for analysis and mapping of a large number of supply networks. The multiple methods and sources used, including in-depth interviews, company documents, government publications and observations, have enabled triangulation of research findings to increase validity and reliability.

5 Findings and Discussion

We illustrate the complexity of international supply networks in clothing and the need for a new classification scheme with an example from the field work.

5.1 Case Study

Company SLX (note: company identities have been anonymised) is a leading established Sri Lankan apparel company and a major supplier to a range of well known retailers, garment brand owners and supermarkets including M&S, Tommy Hilfiger, Liz Claiborne, Nike, Victoria's Secret, Polo, Bhs, Tesco and Asda. As a group its overall manufacturing capacity is in excess of 3 million garments per month. It has three main local manufacturing clusters including woven and knit and maintains strategic alliances with international factories in Bangladesh and Vietnam. Currently it operates with an integrated manufacturing structure that includes factories, designing capabilities, product development, printing, embroidery and washing facilities. SLX's entire network, including the major material and information flows and quality processes of for all its customers, is highly complex. Space limitations preclude us depicting the entire network here. Figures 1 and 2 illustrate how Company SLX operates for two different types of retailer.

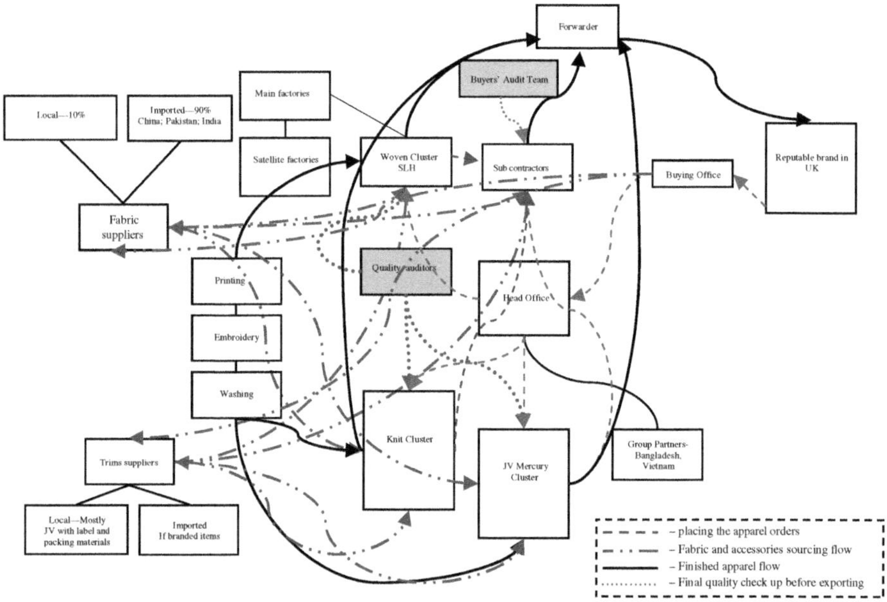

Fig. 1. Supply Network for a Leading Retailer

Figure 1 depicts the supply network for a leading retailer producing both simple and complicated garments. The retailer designs the styles using the services of garment designers and fashion houses. They then request the manufacturer to develop samples accordingly. Once the samples are approved by the buying team at the retailer they place orders with agreed colours, volume, sizes, delivery dates, etc (note: sample development consists of several steps not discussed in this paper). These orders are then placed with an appropriate production cluster according to the request of the retailer or its agent while considering the cluster's competency. It is important to note that fabric and accessory sourcing decisions including material specification and supplier selection are done mostly on the recommendation of the retailer or its buying office. Mostly, the retailer has already developed the fabrics at the product development stage itself. Sometimes the retailer may place only part of the order in Sri Lanka, placing the rest in another country to minimize risk. In that case, all the suppliers, including those in Sri Lanka, need to source from the same fabric suppliers to maintain quality and consistency. The agent of the retailer closely monitors the entire process in order to ensure garments are produced according to their standards and on time. Then, a final quality audit is carried out mostly by the buyer appointed by quality auditors collaborating with the buying office. Finally, the approved garments are first sent to the buyer's stores in Sri Lanka and then exported to the retail stores via a forwarding company recommended by the retailer.

Figure 2 depicts the supply network of a major supermarket. Unlike the network in Figure 1, the design is a more collaborative activity with the supplier. The manufacturer may design the garments alone and present them as 'story boards' from which the buying team at the supermarket selects certain designs and then proceeds with sample development. Garment designers are employed in the company for such designing purposes. Sometimes the manufacturers provide the design or the supermarket may provide ideas or samples for the manufacturer to develop a design. In such cases, a supermarket may use the service of garment designers. After sample approval, orders are placed including details of colours, volume, sizes, delivery dates, etc. These orders are then placed to the respective cluster according to their production competency. Fabric and accessory sourcing decisions including material specification and supplier selection are mostly made by the respective production clusters, unlike the case of a leading retailer's network. The company needs to get the quality of all fabric and accessories approved by the supermarket in advance and then they can source from any suppliers that provide such approved standards. The final quality audit is also carried out by the manufacturing company itself. Finally, the approved garments are first sent to the stores of such supermarket brands in Sri Lanka and then exported to the buyer via the forwarder recommended by the supermarket retailer.

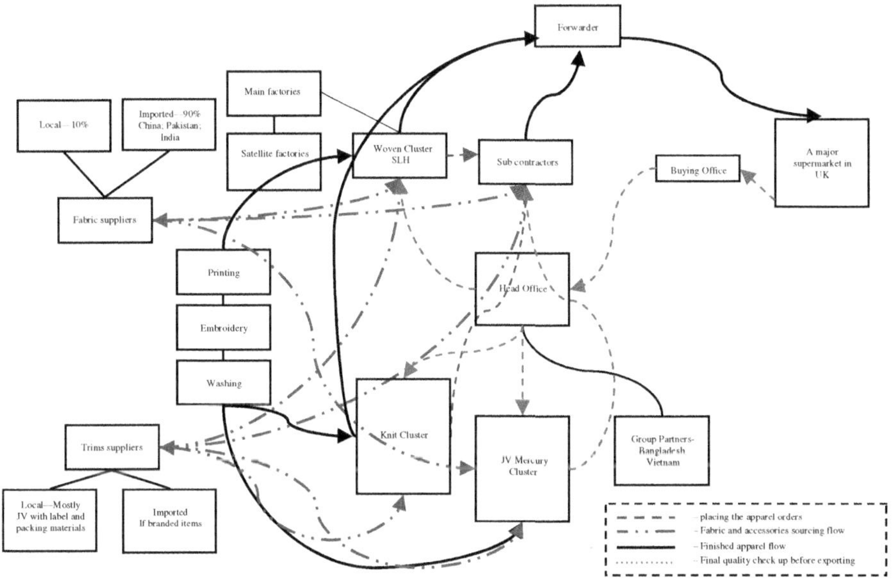

Fig. 2. Supply Network for a Major Supermarket

5.2 A New Classification for Supply Networks in the International Clothing Industry

As noted earlier the supply network categorizations in the literature provide only limited insights into the structure and operation of international clothing supply networks. Based on an analysis across all the thirty case companies studied in this research, a new classification is being developed from the retailer's perspective (including both the leading retailers and supermarkets). The perspective of the new scheme is to provide insights into how the apparel retailer governs the supply to meet anticipated demand from their customers. The principles of this classification are described briefly here. The classification is based on four dimensions:

1. *Direct or indirect retailer control*: considers whether retailers use agents (buying offices) as intermediaries when dealing with manufacturers or whether they deal directly with manufacturers.
2. *Control of sourcing*: considers which entity controls the sourcing of fabrics and in some cases trims – the retailer, the manufacturer or through collaborative sourcing. Fabric sourcing practices have mainly been considered as it is the most important sourcing decision in garment production.
3. *Garment complexity*: two types of garments are considered - complicated designs and simple designs. Garments with complicated structures and/or embellishments (e.g. embroidery, washing) are considered as complicated designs whereas garments with basic structures and/or without embellishments are simple designs. This dimension is more specifically relevant to the contemporary apparel industry than a 'functional' or 'innovative' product differentiation as advocated in some generic classifications.
4. *Direct or indirect retailer involvement in quality assurance:* this relates to the presence or absence of a retailer's involvement in the final quality assurance procedures.

These four dimensions have been derived from a two stage analysis. Initially the dimensions used in literature classifications were analysed to examine their applicability to contemporary clothing supply networks. The results showed that none could be applied to generate strong insights on the observed networks. The above dimensions were derived in the second stage of the analysis from in-depth interviews with key participants and detailed offline analysis of the observed networks.

The classification approach generates twenty four types of clothing networks in which Sri Lankan apparel manufacturers operate, as shown in Table 1. Existing classifications in the literature would typically place all of these network structures in a single category (e.g. 'virtual networks', Cravens et al 1996 [4]; 'flexible networks' by Cravens et al in 1996 [4] and by Ernst & Kamrad in 2000 [6]; 'responsive networks' by Lee in 2002 [18]; 'dominated networks' by Verwaal & Hesselmas in 2004 [29]; 'dynamic/high degree of focal firm influence' by Harland et al in 2001 [14]). The identification of twenty four types of clothing supply networks provides clearer and deeper insights and understanding on network structure and operation.

Table 1. Clothing Supply Network Classification

		Work directly with the manufacturers			Work with the manufacturers via an agent		
		Retailer Sourcing	Manufac-turer Sourcing	Collaborative Sourcing	Retailer Sourcing	Manufacturer Sourcing	Collaborative Sourcing
Simple Designs	DIQA	Type 1 C20NW1	Type 2 C21NW1 C28NW3	Type 3 C4NW3 C4NW4	Type 4 C4NW2A C12NW1 C25NW1 C29NW1 C13NW1 C14NW1 C26NW1 C28NW1 C19NW1 C19NW2	Type 5 C25NW3 C29NW1 C26NW3 C28NW2	Type 6
	NDIQA	Type 7 C6NW2 C7NW3	Type 8 C7NW1 C17NW1 C17NW4 C24NW2	Type 9 C1N4 C8NW3 C6NW2 C17NW5 C8NW1 C8NW2	Type 10 C1N2	Type 11 C4NW2B C22NW1A C24NW2 C26NW2	Type 12 C1N3
Complicated Designs	DIQA	Type 13 C2N2 C11NW1 C27NW1	Type 14 C3NW1 C21NW1 C27NW1 C28NW3	Type 15 C23NW2	Type 16 C29NW1 C7NW2A C14NW1 C26NW1 C1N1 C15NW2A C16NW1 C27NW1 C2N1 C17NW2 C18NW1B C28NW1 C4NW2A C19NW1 C19NW2 C6NW1 C22NW1B C25NW1	Type 17 C25NW3 C29NW1 C26NW3 C27NW1 C28NW2 C7NW2B	Type 18 C6NW1 C9NW1 C15NW1A C23NW1
	NDIQA	Type 19 C7NW3 C16NW2	Type 20 C10NW1 C18NW2 C24NW2	Type 21 C8NW1 C8NW2 C8NW3	Type 22 C15NW2B C18NW1A C22NW3	Type 23 C10NW2 C24NW1 C25NW2 C26NW2	Type 24 C15NW1B C17NW3 C18NW3

Note: The codes refer to supply networks in which apparel manufacturers operate. Identification codes are given for twenty nine companies although thirty companies have been studied. That is because C3NW represents two selected companies.

A significant finding is that apparel manufacturers frequently operate within more than one type of supply network. For instance company 1 operates in four types of supply networks, namely type 16, type 10, type 12, type 9. Also in many cases, the same network physical structures have been shown to operate under different policies and hence are classified differently. For instance, C6NMW2, C28NW3, C24NW2, C27NW1. In most of the cases, the same physical network has been noted in two different types of network categories as it produces both complicated and simple designs for the same retailer under the same practices (e.g. C6NW2, C8NW1). Some networks appear in more than two categories (e.g. C24NW1, C27NW1) as they deal directly and indirectly with different retailers and produce garments both with and without embellishments for different retailers. Also control of fabric sourcing may vary between retailers and manufactures in some cases.

From the in-depth interviews with strategic level managers, the different motives and goals of retailers dictate how their supply networks are coordinated and managed. Consequently, major apparel manufacturers have to operate within different types of networks simultaneously, given that they may deal with different retailers and brand owners. This study shows how the different goals of the retailers result in different supply networks being developed and operated differently.

Two contributions are derived from this study. Firstly, different types of supply network structures operating in the international clothing industry are identified. These different types of network can be identified specifically by considering the four dimensions discussed above instead of considering only two dimensions used by previously reported generic supply network classifications. Secondly, it is clear that different types of network are governed by the different goals of the retailers in the clothing industry. Discussion on how such goals influence the development and management of supply networks has further added to the contribution.

We believe the study reported here and the classification developed has relevance for network design, management and improvement. Retailers need to understand the pressures being placed on their supply networks and how best to optimise performance for different classes of garments and different types of demand. Suppliers need to understand the strategies and policies of different retailers and how they can best position themselves to supply different retailer customers.

6 Conclusions

The design, operation and control of supply networks have become very important in many globally dispersed industries. The apparel industry is one of the most globalized and dynamic industries in the world and thus the structure, operation and control of its supply networks are important to investigate.

In this paper the nature of global supply networks in clothing has been discussed. The literature on supply network classification is limited in providing detailed understanding or insights on the structure and operation of such networks. The significance of retailers and their influencing power on the development and operation of global clothing supply networks has been noted. Due to the limitations in existing generic classifications, a new classification of clothing supply networks has been presented using evidence from a large scale study. This will be subjected to further analysis and development. The study here provides much potential for further research. In particular, the concepts and classification presented should provide valuable lines of enquiry for supply networks in other globally dispersed industries.

References

1. Audet, D.: Smooth as silk? A first look at the post MFA textiles and Clothing landscape. Journal of International Economic Law 10(2), 267–284 (2007)
2. CBARSL – Central Bank Annual Report Sri Lanka, several issues
3. Christopher, M.: Logistics and Supply Chain Management: Creating Value-Adding Networks, 3rd edn. Prentice Hall, Englewood Cliffs (2005)
4. Cravens, D.W., Piercy, N.F., Shipp, S.H.: New Organizational Forms for Competing in Highly Dynamic Environments: the Network Paradigm. British Journal of Management 7, 203–218 (1996)
5. EMCC – European Monitoring Centre on Change: Trends and drivers of change in the European textiles and clothing sector: mapping report. European Foundation for the Improvement of Living and Working Conditions Report (google accessed on December 18, 2008)
6. Ernst, R., Kamrad, B.: Evaluation of Supply Chain Structures Through Modularization and Postponement. European Journal of Operational Research 124, 495–510 (2000)
7. Ferdows, K., Lewis, M.A., Machuca, J.A.D.: Rapid-fire Fulfilment. Harvard Business Review, 104–110 (2004)
8. Garavelli, A.C.: Flexibility Configurations for the Supply Chain Management. International Journal of Production Economics 85, 141–153 (2003)
9. Gereffi, G.: International Trade and Industrial Upgrading in the Apparel Commodity Chain. Journal of International Economics 48(1), 37–70 (1999)
10. Grandori, A., Soda, G.: Iner-Firm Networks: Antecedents, Mechanisms and Forms. Organization Studies 16(2), 183–214 (1995)
11. Harland, C.M.: Supply Chain Management Relationships, Chains and Networks. British Journal of Management 7, S63–S81 (1996) (special issue)
12. Harland, C.M., Knight, L.A.: Supply Network Strategy: Role and Competence Requirements. Int. Journal of Operations and Production Management 27(4), 476–489 (2001)
13. Harland, C., Zheng, J., Johnsen, T., Lamming, R.: A Conceptual Model for Researching the Creation and Operation of Supply Networks. British Journal of Management 15, 1–21 (2004)
14. Harland, C.M., Lamming, R.C., Zheng, J., Johnsen, T.E.: A Taxonomy of Supply Networks. Journal of Supply Chain Management 37(7), 21–27 (Fall 2001)
15. Hinterhuber, H.H., Levin, B.M.: Strategic Networks – The Organization of the Future. Long Range Planning 27(3), 43–53 (1994)
16. Hunter, A., King, R., Lowson, R.H.: The Textile/Clothing Pipeline and Quick Response Management, The Textile Institute (2002)
17. Lamming, R., Johnson, T., Zheng, J., Harland, C.: An Initial Classification of Supply Networks. Int. Journal of Operations and Production Management 20(6), 675–691 (2000)
18. Lee, H.L.: Aligning Supply Chain Strategies with Product Uncertainties. California Management Review Reprint Series 44(6), 106–119 (2002)
19. MacCarthy, B.L., Jayarathne, A.: Fast Fashion: Achieving Global Quick Response (GQR) in the Internationally Dispersed Clothing Industry. In: Cheng, E., Choi, J. (eds.) Springer Handbook on Innovative Quick Response Programs in Logistics and Supply Chain Management, ch. 3. Springer, Heidelberg (2010)
20. Martin, M.F.: US clothing and textile trade with china and the world: trends since the end of quotas. CRS report for congress, A report prepared for members and committees of congress on July 10 2007, Order Code RL34106 (2007), `http://www.fas.org/sgp/crs/row/RL34106.pdf` (accessed October 18, 2008)

21. Nassimbeni, G.: Network Structures and Co-ordination Mechanisms: A taxonomy. International Journal of Operations and Production Management 18(6), 538–554 (1998)
22. Robertson, P.L., Langlois, R.N.: Innovation, networks, and vertical integration. Research Policy 24, 543–562 (1995)
23. Rosenfeld, S.A.: Does Cooperation Enhance Competitiveness? Assessing the Impacts of Inter-Firm Collaboration. Research Policy 25, 247–263 (1996)
24. Sen, A.: The US Fashion Industry: A Supply Chain Review. International Journal of Production Economics 114(2), 571–593 (2008)
25. Tokatli, N.: Global Sourcing: Insights from the Global Clothing Industry-The Case of Zara, A Fast Fashion Retailer. Journal of Economic Geography (Advance Access Published in October 23, 2007)
26. Tyler, D., Heeley, J., Bhamra, T.: Supply Chain Influences on New Product Development in Fashion Clothing. Journal of Fashion Marketing and Management 10(3), 316–328 (2006)
27. UNCTAD Current Studies on FDI and Development: TNCs and the Removal of Textiles and Clothing Quotas, The United Nations (2005), http://www.unctad.org/en/docs/iteiia20051_en.pdf
28. US department of labour, http://www.bls.gov (accessed on March 15, 2010)
29. Verwaal, E., Hesselmans, M.: Drivers of Supply Network Governance: An Explorative Study of the Dutch Chemical Industry. European Management Journal 22(4), 442–451 (2004)
30. Wadhwa, S., Saxenay, A., Chanz, F.T.S.: Framework for Flexibility in dynamic supply chain management. International Journal of Production Research 46(6), 1373–1404 (2008)

Discerning Industrial Networks, Clusters and Competences – An Alternative View Using Web Mining Techniques

John R. Williams[1] and Dimitris Assimakopoulos[2]

[1] Director, Fabriam Ltd,, United Kingdom
jrw@fabriam.com, J.Williams@ncl.ac.uk
[2] Professor and Director of Doctoral Programs, Grenoble Ecole de Management, Europole, 12 rue Pierre Semard, BP127, 38003 Grenoble, France
dimitris.assimakopoulos@grenoble-em.com

Abstract. This short extract is part of a wider study into the use of the web for research into the presence and structure of industrial clusters and is concerned here with the discernment of networks of firms and the presence of commonalities of competence amongst firms within the identified networks.

The research shows that the information that can be extracted using web based methods is sufficiently informative to gain a wide and detailed picture of industrial activity in the locale under study. In addition to finding evidence of industry clusters and networking activity hidden by company list based investigations the methodology developed has shown that for the region studied, we are looking not so much at the clustering of artefacts *per se* but the clustering of 'competencies' in a wide range of sectors that share both common antecedents and current practice in engineering skills for the design and manufacture of large structures that operate in difficult or even hostile environments.

1 Introduction

In recent years the notion of industrial clustering has been the subject of much research and investigation and the number of available publications on the subject is significant. Much of this research activity stems from the part that industrial clusters are thought to play in the competitiveness of defined areas, such concepts having being promoted on a world stage by prominent authors of whom Porter (1998a)(1998b)(2000) is perhaps the best known.

A good definition of clustering in an industrial context is from (Van den Berg, Braun and van Winden 2001):

"The popular term cluster is most closely related to this local or regional dimension of networks. Most definitions share the notion of clusters as localised networks of specialised organisations, whose production processes are closely linked through the exchange of goods, services and/or knowledge".

However it has been observed that many of the tools and data available to those engaged in cluster research have known shortcomings particularly related to descriptive data on firm activity and a number of commentators have given the opinion that such

L.M. Camarinha-Matos et al. (Eds.): PRO-VE 2010, IFIP AICT 336, pp. 279–286, 2010.

deficiencies can lead ultimately to significant errors and omissions related to the discernment of clustering activity (Feldman, Francis and Bercovitz 2005) and particularly by (Porter 1998c) when he complained, in relation to cluster boundaries, that they:

"rarely conform to standard industry classification systems [SIC] which fail to capture many important actors in competition as well as linkages across industries ...Because parts of a cluster often fall within different traditional industrial or service categories, significant clusters may be obscured or even go unrecognised".

2 Problem Statement

In the introduction we briefly outlined the difficulties and now postulate that the Web as a vast and powerful information source could provide some additional insights into the basic description of individual firms that go to make up sectors, industries, networks and clusters. In this context the research question becomes:

'Can the use of the internet and the world wide web as an information resource add anything useful to more conventional methods of researching industrial clusters and networks?'

3 Towards a Web Based Methodology

The basic principle was to submit a database of regional company URLs to a spider[1] to extract relevant text present on each company website. This sounds a simple task but the presence of large amounts of irrelevant noise makes the task less straightforward. Even a simple excursion into the web using URLs for say a group of industrial companies shows that the above approach is fraught with problems due to the mass of 'messy' text and other data including hidden programming instructions that characterise most web pages. The result of this is that some way has to be found to deal with the type of information that obscures 'relevant' data or text in the search to find information that helps the objective of describing the firm and its activities.

In the event and after some considerable development and test a proprietary program (http://www.phantomsearch.com) written initially to spider large single sites proved effective and this was used in all subsequent tests.

In designing the test the following boundary conditions were adopted:

1. The catchment area would be the North East of England. This is the smallest of the English RDA[2] regions having in 2007 about 42000 VAT[3] registered companies and a long tail of micro firms falling below this VAT threshold.
2. The number of companies scanned should be sufficient to give confidence in the robustness of any comparisons.

---

[1] A spider can be thought of a web crawler with some inherent capability that allows it to act in the manner of an intelligent agent operating to a specific set of instructions.
[2] Regional Development Agency.
[3] Value Added Tax. In the UK at the time this was £57000 of company turnover.

The next stage therefore involved acquiring the URLs of as many regional firms and other relevant organisations as was reasonably practical. No single database existed of all companies and in the records obtainable from many of the most prominent data providers the URL was often absent as a field in the company record. The basic method of approach was to acquire as many URLs from regional organisations as possible from a credit rating agency followed by further company data obtained from trade associations, the regional Chamber of Commerce, other membership organisations and trade directories. The net result of the whole exercise was that the list of what appeared to be valid URLs numbered 14000.

We were now in a position to submit these URLs to the spider program with the aim of acquiring text from all text, html, word documents and translated pdf files to be placed into a suitable database which was then fully indexed.

The metrics for this database when complete were:

- File size 60.81Mb
- Number of unique keywords 177432 with 231 noise words (not indexed)

What this means is that we now have, fully indexed the collective text from almost 14000 websites in the region. It is fully acknowledged that at this stage, any biases within the collected seed URLs will be similarly reflected in the keyword database.

The final stage in this part of the research was to undertake a comparison between the information coming out of the keyword database and that which could be elicited regarding company activity from the same set of firms but using SIC derived activity. The keyword database program has the ability to choose one or more or indeed all of the datasets noted above. The most robust of the datasets in terms of quality of the data (when checked independently by sample) was the DNB company credit rating derived dataset numbering some 8518 records. It was thus possible to search for certain types of industry keywords known to be present in regional industry. Examples such as 'engineering' could be refined by Boolean operators to find such specialism's as 'precision engineering'.

A short test was set up using the 8518 records to find companies by (a) SIC and (b) SIC accompanying text description and then by submitting activity descriptors to the keyword database. It is known that some industrial activities are hard to find in an SIC based system, for example 'motorsport' (Pinch and Henry 1999) and a number of these were chosen for the test. The results of the comparison between the Keyword System and the SIC based system yielded Table 1 - Test of keyword frequency by number of firms.

Whilst this exercise is relatively simplistic compared with the more elegant and focussed route taken by for example (Hajlaoui and Boucher 2009) the conclusion here is that not surprisingly, a search system based on whole text searching in a closed set of websites is far superior for finding activity than by searching on SIC based activity alone. This can be seen in the right hand column where the number of firms found against each activity word is sometimes as much as an order of magnitude greater than the SIC based columns.

This result indicates that the basic methodology of finding firms engaged in some nominated activity using only the Web does work within limitations. The methodology does however require the user to input various supposed activities or groups of activities that may be prominent in the region under study. It does not of itself find

Table 1. Test of keyword frequency by number of firms

Word	Count by DNB 'Main Activity'	Count by any DNB 'SIC text'	Count by Keyword
Motorsport	0	0	11
Motor racing	0	0	9
Motorcycle	3	24	38
Automotive	10	8	104
Defence	0	0	48
Military	2	0	25
Offshore	5	0	105
Subsea	1	0	15
Yacht	2	0	13
Sail	1	0	9
boat	6	8	36
TOTALS	30	40	413

clusters in the same way that a study based on location quotients does but on the other hand it does find activities that are often hidden to more conventional methods of discerning firm activity.

Various other searches of the Keyword database were tried exploring the industrial make up of the region and in particular that associated with a sub-sea 'cluster'. It had been known from other studies (Siedlock and Andriani 2006) that this type of activity was prominent amongst the region's offshore and engineering firms but an SIC based search yielded little evidence of this. This is because the firms involved do not put 'sub-sea' down as their primary or even secondary activity, they regard themselves as being in various kinds of engineering. However many of these same firms have the word 'sub-sea' somewhere on their website and this is picked up in the keyword database. Additionally such searches do not limit the scope to companies as often educational establishments, quality assurance organisations, specialist law firms and a whole raft of supporting organisations also appear and this sort of thing helps to gain a wider understanding of the potential cluster effect.

4 Finding Industrial Networks

Here with regard to finding linkages between organisations either as a buyer, or as a supplier or for knowledge exchange we have made the assumptions that a link exists if, on a company website:

(i) a firm puts a reference to another organisation on its own website as a clickable link (found by a short search program)

(ii) there are visual clues to other organisations on a company website e.g a client list (carried out by inspection)

(iii) an external firm references the URL being looked at, so called in-links (using an in-link finder such as www.linkpopularity.com)

For comparison purposes we used the list of firms noted above in the 'subsea' cluster. This corpus was derived from the first part of the research and comprised firms and other organisations with the words 'sub-sea' somewhere on the firm's website and in addition the firms identified by (Siedlock and Andriani 2006) in their snowball sampling based study were also added.

The only limitation applied was that as we were seeking evidence of activity on a closed geographical basis then any connection found should be to another regionally based entity.

When all these three types of link were merged, for each of the organisations in the subsea cohort it became possible to discern some interesting patterns of connectivity within the cohort. For the combined dataset of 282 nodes (organisations), website searching found 394 intraregional links.

5 Analysis of Firm Linkages

The linkages have been drawn and analysed using UCINET (Borgatti, Everett and Freeman 2005) and also VISONE (www.visone.info). These are simple links and say nothing about strength although direction can be inferred. The overall network of the subsea cohort is as shown in Figure 1 and it is of course possible to carry out all manner of analyses regarding the metrics of the network.

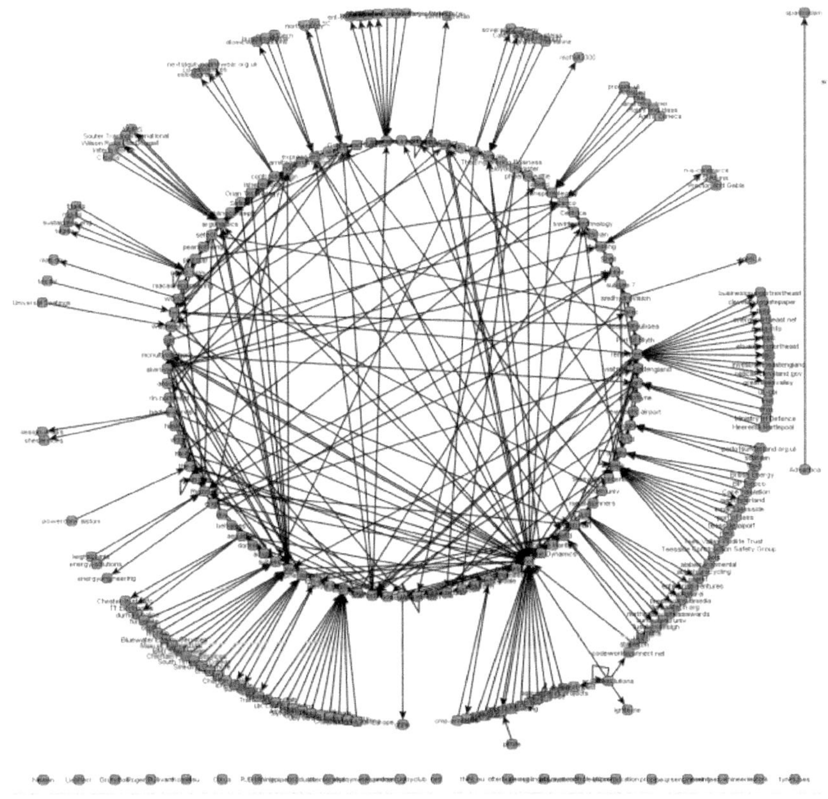

Fig. 1. Subsea Network in the N.E. of England (circular representation)

6 Overlaps between Clusters

In the work looking at the activity of clustered groups of firms it was observed that many firms had 'membership' of more than a single grouping i.e. they used their expertise to address a variety of market segments. To test the extent to which such overlaps took place a test was set up to track the activities of a nominated group with respect to its activities in one or more other clusters. The groups chosen were Marine Engineering, Environmental technologies, Offshore Oil and Gas, Subsea and Defence as these groups had shown up strongly in the wider study of the region as distinct groupings although whether they could each be regarded as a Porter type cluster is open to discussion.

As a result of this exercise it was possible to draw Table 2 which shows the extent to which firms in main or primary cluster are also engaged in other clusters.

Table 2. Degree of Involvement by Firms in other Sectors

	Main Sector					
	Marine	Envir	O'shore	Subsea	Defence	Totals
Populations	199	386	344	283	290	1502
Firms in other sectors	49	45	40	11	123	268
% 'hits'	25%	12%	12%	4%	42%	18%
Sector by sector detail:						
Marine		22	4	1	30	
Env	1		1	3	29	
Offshore	29	15		6	38	
Subsea	18	8	31		26	
Defence	1	0	4	1		
TOTALS	49	45	40	11	123	268

Of the 1502 firms in Table 2, it was noted that 140 had a presence in another grouping in addition to their 'main' activity, 47 had a presence in 2, 10 in 3 groups and 1 firm had a presence in 4 in addition to their own. When we looked in detail at the capability of these organisations it was possible to discern from their websites that they have a combined capability in supporting engineering manufacture of medium and large sized artefacts such as for example ships, armaments, rigs and subsea ploughs.

7 Discussion and Concluding Remarks

At this stage of the research we are firstly seeking to establish a methodology rather than a comprehensive picture of industry in a specified locale. The URLs used in this research are but a sample of commerce and industry in the region under scrutiny and a complete or near complete set would be required to have complete confidence that we would have a comprehensive database of all the activities being undertaken. Secondly, initial attempts to use the keyword database for discerning clusters free from the known constraints of an SIC based system clearly have some limitations. What the keyword database does is find activity by firm and in considerable detail. It does not of itself find clusters although in conjunction with other methods as noted earlier it may help to find the presence of firms and supporting organisations to feed into a database of candidate firms for more conventional cluster analyses.

In the research into linkages it is fully acknowledged that to discern networks we are using the presence of links on (or into) a site as evidence of some form of collaboration or of economic dependency or some measure of esteem. Whilst this may be true for some firms, for many others with all manner of networks of their own, no such relationships at all are inferred on their own websites. It was observed that the system works better for smaller firms as their websites tend to have more regional linkages. For example the corporate website of a very large offshore operator who had commissioned a multi-million dollar rig project in the region would be unlikely to have links back to the yard and main contractors who built the rig. Conversely the many smaller companies who had contributed to that project, even in a small way, put a link on their sites citing the corporate as a prestigious client. Many links that might have been gleaned by snowball sampling or other practical means are thus missed by the web based methods described here. However on-the-ground sampling methods are far from perfect and it is perhaps salutary to note that the internet derived links were greater in number than those from the practical observations cited. The links as shown in Figure 1 are also useful for determining the presence of 'key nodes' i.e. those organisations that are 'important' in network terms as they are gatekeepers of knowledge or of trade within the network as shown. Further, the phenomena known as 'the strength of weak links' becomes evident (Granovetter 1973) and that is the ability of one dense network to be joined to another remote network by a small number of individual links but the important part played by these 'connectors' was out of proportion to the actual number of occurrences.

A key question when looking at web derived networks is do such gatekeepers appear because they put lots of links on their sites and they are then similarly reinforced by external sites through in-links and thus are they really economically important in the cluster of activity? Comparison with networks derived by sampling would indicate about a 50% match in terms of indentifying 'important' nodes. However as with the first part of the research in finding firms, the web based system found networks and sub-nets not found by manual sampling and vice versa. The two methods in combination therefore helped to discern a much richer network of industrial interactions than either method in isolation.

Although the example of the subsea cluster given here has been used partly because of the opportunity for comparison it should be noted that in many sectors it is almost impossible to carry out any form of a snowball sampling exercise because of suspicion over commercial confidentiality from individual firms. In such cases the 'hands off' methodology shown here may be the only option for finding the presence of interconnectedness.

Spidering whole text from organisational websites frees the researcher from the constraints imposed by an SIC based system and one of the advantages is that it is possible to look at firms' capabilities or competences rather than looking simply by aggregated sector or product. SIC based systems cannot easily cater for this type of search as they are based only on a main and a small number of secondary activities. In the work on overlaps therefore it was possible to find firms that could sell into different sectors and markets because of the range of their competences as noted on their own websites. In the region studied and with the sample database used some 198 organisations were identified that when examined had competencies in engineering design and manufacture for medium complex engineering artefacts often designed for harsh environments. This outcome probably has much to do with the history of the North East of England and the region's traditions in shipbuilding, mining machinery and offshore rig building. The same skills and competencies however are now being deployed in advanced subsea operations and offshore wind technologies. This plays well with the notion of 'related variety' (Boschma 2008) in that competences established either as part of a cluster or trading network in one sector can be transposed to new markets and technologies and the ability to see this amongst the admittedly engineering related groups used was one of the unexpected results of this research.

This has been an attempt at using the web to try and discern the presence of agglomerations of connected industrial activity within a regional boundary. At the present stage of research it is considered that the methodology developed shows promise but that it clearly needs more work to improve the confidence in the results found. As web tools develop and as commerce and industry generally further embrace web based promotion and trading such progress will help to strengthen the possibilities for developing a robust web based methodology as outlined above.

References

Barabasi, A.B.: Linked - How everything is connected to Everything Else and what it means for Business, Science and Everyday Life. Penguin Books (2003)

Borgatti, S.P., Everett, M.G., Freeman, L.C.: Ucinet for Windows: Software for Social Network Analysis, vol. 6, p. 181. Analytic Technologies, Harvard (2005)

Boschma, R.: Constructing Regional Advantage: related variety and regional innovation policy. Report for the Dutch Scientific Council for Government Policy. University of Utrecht (2008)

Feldman, M.P., Francis, J., Bercovitz, J.: Creating a Cluster While Building a Firm: Entrepreneurs and the Formation of Industrial Clusters. Regional Studies 39(1), 131,139 (2005)

Granovetter, M.S.: The Strength of Weak Ties. American Journal of Sociology 78, 1360–1380 (1973)

Hajlaoui, K., Boucher, X.: Neural Network Based Text Mining to Discover Enterprise Networks. In: Proceedings of th 13th IFAC Symposium on Information Control Problems in Manufacturing, Moscow (2009)

Pinch, S., Henry, N.: Paul Krugman's Geographical Economics, Industrial Clustering and the British Motor Sport Industry. Regional Studies 33(9), 815–827 (1999)

Porter, M.E.: On Competition. Harvard Business School Press, Boston (1998a)

Porter, M.E.: Location, Clusters and the 'New' Microeconomics of Competition. Business Economics 33(1), 7–17 (1998b)

Porter, M.E.: Clusters and the New Economics of Competitiveness. Harvard Business Review, 77–90 (December 1998c)

Porter, M.E.: Locations, Clusters and Company Strategy. In: Clark, G.L., Feldman, M., Gertler, M. (eds.) Handbook of Economic Geography, pp. 253–274. Oxford University Press, Oxford (2000)

Siedlock, F., Andriani, P.: The emergence of the sub-sea technology clusters in the North-East of England: Some evolutionary considerations and implications for cluster policy. In: Conference on 'The Organising Society'. EGOS Bergen (2006), http://www.egosnet.org

Van den Berg, L., Braun, E., van Winden, W.: Growth Clusters in European Cities: An Integral Approach. Urban Studies 38(1), 187 (2001)

A Multi-layer Framework for Virtual Organizations Creation in Breeding Environment

Khouloud Boukadi[1], Lucien Vincent[2], and Chirine Ghedira[3]

[1] LIMOS laboratory, University of Blaise Pascal, Clermont-Ferrand, France
[2] Industrial Engineering and Computer Sciences, ENSM, Saint-Etienne, France
[3]LIRIS Laboratory, Claude Bernard Lyon 1 University, Lyon, France
Boukadi@isima.fr, Vincent@emse.fr, cghedira@liris.cnrs.fr

Abstract. Nowadays collaboration among organizations in the so called Virtual Organizations (VOs) is the most advanced form to make business. Their emergence and growing are closely related to integrated information and communication technology (ICT). One of the promising approaches to carry out the agility and flexibility in VO creation is defined under the assumption of a VO Breeding Environment (VBE). To support such agile organizations, an efficient IT system and methodologies should be set in order to facilitate their daily management activities. Service-oriented software technologies provide promising means to regulate and enforce coordination of cross-organisational business services interactions but lack organizational abstractions and methodology. This paper proposes a framework for collaborative network coordination in the VBEs's context. The proposed framework satisfies flexibility and agility requirements of virtual organization using a multi layer approach combining VBE management systems layer that assist flexible VO creation, a semantic interoperability layer essential for promoting integration on the basis of common language that describe VO concepts and inherent dependencies, and a service oriented layer that introduces the concept of service domain that encapsulates business processes fitting VO requirements.

Keywords: Virtual Organizations, VO Breeding Environment.

1 Introduction

In response to global competition, rapid changes in market conditions, increased customer selectivity on prices, many companies are restructuring their organizations to achieve more flexibility. Organizations migrate to inter-organizational relationships and especially to collaborative networks as a way to adapt to their new environment, to increase their efficiency, and to gain competitive advantages.

The concept of virtual organization (VO) represents one of the most discussed examples of collaborative networks [1], that is centered on the realization of specific product types and consisting of a possibly large number of autonomous organizations. The virtual organization form is nowadays receiving ample attention [2]. There are a number of different definitions and uses for the VO concept. Our definition follows the one proposed by [3]: ''VO is an association of (legally) independent organizations

L.M. Camarinha-Matos et al. (Eds.): PRO-VE 2010, IFIP AICT 336, pp. 287 – 296, 2010.

(VO partners) that come together and share resources and skills to achieve common goals, such as acquiring and responding to a market/society opportunity''.

Both research and practice have shown that dynamic creation of VOs, driven by the emergence of new opportunities, faces a large number of challenges. For example, finding the right partners and establishing on demand collaborative business process have proved to be costly in terms of time and effort [2]. Other barriers include lack of information, lack of common collaboration infrastructure and heterogeneity of potential partners (e.g. in ICT infrastructures, culture and business practices).

The concept of Virtual Organizations Breeding Environment (VBE) is therefore introduced to address many challenges involved in the establishment and management of these VO. The VBE is not a new concept as a large number of related initiatives have emerged during the last decades, and a set of various case studies are presented (e.g. Virtuelle Fabrik, Switzerland; IECOS, Mexico; CeBeNetwork, Germany; etc.). However, these cases use little support from ICT tools and are governed by a limited conceptual framework. Consequently, a growing number of works has being published that present new models and conceptual frameworks for VBEs as well as for dynamic creation of VOs within the VBEs.

We consider that overcoming the VO obstacles within the VBE context forces organizations to abandon traditional modes to design business processes to embrace an entirely new paradigm based on service oriented vision. Service-oriented software technologies provide promising means to regulate and enforce coordination of cross-organisational business services interactions but lack organizational abstractions and methodology. Hence a comprehensive framework to guide and manage organizations within a VBE, considering business services as a first building block for collaborative business process, is still missing.

For this reason, we propose in this paper a framework that satisfies flexibility and agility requirements of VO using a multi layer approach combing VBE management systems layer that assist flexible VO creation, a semantic interoperability layer essential for promoting integration on the basis of common language that describe VO concepts and inherent dependencies, and a service oriented layer that introduces the concept of service domain that encapsulates business processes fitting VO requirements.

The remainder of this paper is organized as follows. In section 2, we describe briefly the VO breeding environment, the service oriented architecture and the semantic interoperability and ontology. Section 3 presents the proposed layered framework with more stress on layer's functionalities. Finally, some concluding remarks and future research directions are presented.

2 Background

2.1 Virtual organizations Breeding Environment

A Virtual organization Breeding Environment (VBE) is defined by [5], [6] as "an association of organizations and their related supporting institutions, adhering to a base long-term cooperation agreement, and adoption of common operating principles and infrastructures, with the main goal of increasing both their chances and their preparedness towards collaboration in potential Virtual Organizations".

A diversity of roles can be achieved by actors in the VBE, where an actor represents either a VBE member organization or an individual representing a VBE member organization [8],[9]. The same organization may undertake different roles, e.g. acting as a VO participant, a VO broker, etc. where each role requires assigning different rights/responsibilities within the VBE.

2.2 Service Oriented Architecture (SOA)

A Service-Oriented Architecture (SOA) is an architectural style that proposes a set of patterns and guidelines for creating loosely coupled, business-aligned services [10]. Service oriented architecture plays an ever more important role in modern networked economies. SOA can reinforce business aspects with a flexible infrastructure thanks to independent, reusable automated business process called services. This trend is leading paradigm shift in enterprise structure from the traditional single entity to a collaboration of services. So from this perspective, the goal of the SOA is to allow autonomous partners to advertise their terms and capabilities, to engage in peer-to-peer interactions with any other partners and to enable on demand computing through composition and outsourcing [12] [13]. SOA addresses the requirements of loosely coupled, standard-based, and protocol-independent distributed computing.

2.3 Semantic Interoperability and Ontology

Semantic interoperability is a crucial issue for the successful development and further growth of VO paradigm. Within the VO, different and independent organizations need to cooperate and share heterogeneous information resources. Accessing heterogeneous and distributed informational resources requires appropriate semantic interoperability techniques [14]. These techniques target to enable a seamless access and retrieval of the right information resources. Semantic interoperability and its content description standards are based on ontologies and their inherent rules. There are several ontology definitions that have evolved in the last decades. However, there is a consensus among the ontology community of researchers about their role: they provide a common understanding regarding domain knowledge. In the context of VBE, we consider ontologies as an essential tool for allowing communication and knowledge sharing among distributed organizations, by providing a semantically rich description and a common understanding of a domain of interest [15].

3 Multi-layer Framework for Virtual Organizations Creation

In this section, the multi-level framework that supports and facilitates the operation and management of a VBE is exposed. This framework is presented in terms of concepts, duties per layer, and components specifications (Figure 1).

3.1 The Management System Layer

This layer's objective is to assist VBE members with a fluid creation of VOs that correspond to business opportunities. The main elements of the management system level include: Reputation Manager, Community Manager, Resources Manager and Business decision making manager. These managers are implemented as services, that we call management system services.

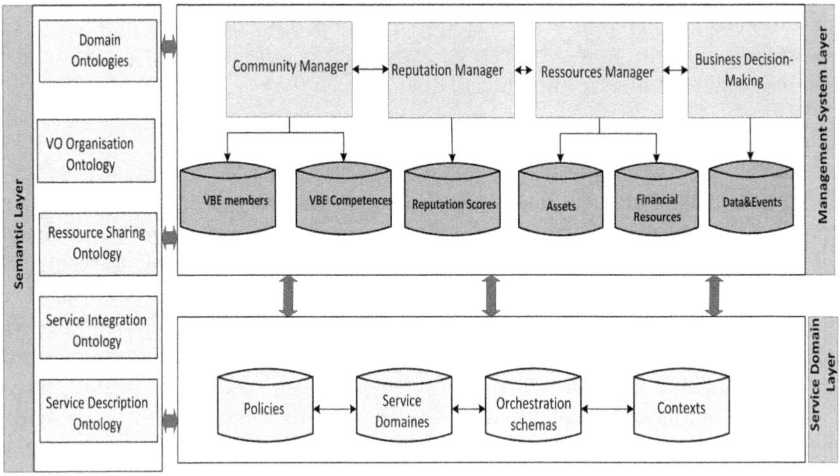

Fig. 1. The proposed framework for VO creation

3.2 The Community Manager

Our approach for VO creation within the VBE context is based on the concept of community. Organizations belonging to communities can participate in VBEs initiated by other organizations. However, their membership in the community does not impose their participation in collaborative scenarios. A community groups organizations with the same kind of activity. Its establishment is designer-driven and starts as follows. Initially, the community administrator defines the functionality like "Automobile Assembling" of a community. Afterwards, he deploys the community manager that will lead this community. This manager undertakes many functions that we can classify into three categories: community management functions, organization attraction and retention functions, and organizations nomination and selection functions for participation in on demand collaborative business processes.

Once the community is created, the community manager is responsible for inviting organizations to sign up in this community and checking their credentials. In addition, it proposes functionalities to store, access, delete, and modify the member's company and contact information.

Besides, the community manager is responsible for attracting new organizations to the community and retaining existing one. Attracting new organizations makes the community manager regularly consult web pages and portals looking for new members. Moreover, organizing and managing of member profiles and competences is a key activity of the community manager. The need for management of profiles is an important issue especially in medium-size and large-size VBEs, where typically the member organizations do not have the chance of getting to know all others directly. In our approach, member profile consists of descriptive information about the business. This would include information such as name and descriptions, contact information and classification information. This information is essential to analyze the suitability of each organization for involvement in a VO creation. VBE member organizations competencies are divided into two categories: core organizational values which describe the essential managerial competencies for the organization and the technical and functional competencies for the organization described through the list of service domains proposed by the organization. Service domains are composite structure used as major building block for implementing on demand VO. In the following we describe the service domain concept and the rationale behind using this service for VO creation.

Dismantling a community is designer-driven as well and happens upon request from the community manager. The community manager monitors all events happening in a community such as the arrival of new organizations, departure of existing ones, identification of organisation'services to be part of collaborative business processes, and imposing sanctions on organizations in case of misbehavior. If the community manager notices that (i) the number of organizations in the community is less than a certain threshold and (ii) the number of participation requests in VO creation over a certain period of time is less than another threshold, then the community will be dismantled. Both thresholds are predetermined by the designer.

3.3 The Reputation Manager

With an increasing number of organizations providing similar services and products, more emphasis is being placed on how to find the organization that best fits the VO's requirements. There are functional requirements that are, what the organizations services or products can do, and non-functional requirements, such as the price and quality of service or product guaranteed by an organization. The problem, however, is that the advertised quality information relating to an organization is not always trustworthy. When it comes to services for example, a service provider may publish inaccurate quality information to attract more customers, or the published quality information may be out of date.

Reputation, besides other selection criteria, has been widely used for evaluating and ranking organizations. Reputation is defined as "the opinion of the public toward a person, a group of people, or an organization. It is an important factor in many fields, such as business, online communities or social status" (Wikipedia Online Dictionary).

Organization reputation can be considered as an aggregation of service ratings for a service from VBE members over a specific period of time. Allowing VBE member to rate the quality they receive from a member's service, and making these ratings public, can provide new VBE members with valuable information on how to choose services. This provides also a general and overall estimate of the reliability of a VBE member offering the service. With organization reputation taken into consideration, the probability of finding the best service to respond to a business opportunity can be increased.

In the proposed framework service reputation is handled by the reputation manager. Reputation score is calculated based on feedback by service consumers. We assume that service consumers provide a rating indicating the level of satisfaction with a service belonging to the VBE. A rating is an integer ranging from 1 to 10, where 10 denotes extreme satisfaction, 5 denotes average satisfaction and 1 denotes extreme dissatisfaction.

The reputation manager is responsible for collecting the data from service consumers, processing the data, and then updating the reputation score for related service providers. In order to encourage consumers to provide ratings of a service to the reputation manager, a bonus point system may be introduced to award consumers for their feedback.

The computation of reputation score is based on previous work [16],[17] in which a reputation score (RS) of a service belonging to an organization is computed as the weighted average of all ratings the service received from customers, where an inclusion factor is the weight attached to each of the ratings for the service. The ratings of services by consumers are stored in the reputation manager's local database.

3.4 The Resource Manager

In the proposed framework, resource manager supports the management of resources including tangible assets, financial resources, materials, and human resources in the VBE. These resources are of common interest and useful for VBE members. Besides, the resource manager purpose is to facilitate the flow of information between all VBE members. By focusing on managing sharable information or data and lessons learned, many opportunities for reuse of functionality will arise, resulting in more efficient use of existing resources. Many researchers in literature are interested in studying the issue of managing resources in virtual organization context [18], [19].

3.5 The Business Decision Making Manager

Decision-making is a crucial issue for a successful establishment of a VBE. In the proposed framework, the business decision making manager helps to make information clearer and better analyzed by VBE member. To accomplish its mission, business decision making manager collect, store and manage large volumes of variant, mostly time-series data. Besides, it defines sophisticated events that occur within a VBE; alerts are triggered when those events fall outside of predefined parameters and are delivered to desktop or handheld devices, enabling rapid decision making and crisis management. Examples of these events can be the performance of member organizations in the VBE and sends warning message to the community manager when and if the performance of some VBE member organization falls below certain threshold.

In addition, the business decision making manager has a market and customer oriented role. It observes the needed competencies in the market, which are frequently required by the collaboration opportunities, and compare them with those available within the VBE through its member organizations. Once a gap is detected, an alert will be sent to the community manager in order to take appropriate action (e.g., encourage organizations with the required competencies to join the VBE).

3.6 Service Layer

This layer presents business services exposed by VBE members within a community. Business services correspond to a functional representation of a real world business activity having a meaningful effect to the end-user. The business services can be atomic services called functional or composite services called service domains. Functional services are fine grained services exposing a set of business activities. They are identified when analyzing enterprise business processes. Business activities within a process can be easily identified as belonging to the potential logic that should be encapsulated by a functional service.

Service domain orchestrates a set of functional services and it is used as major building block for implementing on demand VO. The rationale of the service domain concept is to abstract at a higher-level the integration of a large number of functional services. A service domain is built upon (in fact, it uses existing standards such as WSDL, SOAP, and UDDI) and enhances the Web service concept. It does not define new application programming interfaces or standards, but hides the complexity of this exercise by facilitating service deployment and self-management.

Besides, in order to ensure that organization can easily adapt to context changes, business services must be more than functions provided through the Web. Indeed, business services must have the capacity to adapt their own behavior by configuring appropriately to the situation in which they evolve. The adaptability of business services within a VO context was the object of our research project in [20], so further details are provided there.

To correspond to VO creation needs and requirements, services domains are governed by a set of policies. Policies might be imposed by different types of initiators like the service itself, the VBE member exposing the service, and the VBE member who plans to use the service. In this paper, we suggest the two types based on some of our previous works [13], [21]:

– Business policy defines the constraints that restrict the completion of a service domain and determines how this service should be executed according VBE member' requirements and VO' internal regulations.

– Behavior policy supports the decisions that a service domain has to make when it receives a request from a VBE member to be part of VO creation. Examples of behaviors can be permission, dispensation, and restriction.

3.7 Semantic Layer

Our proposed framework for the VBE management addresses the heterogeneity problems between the VBE members by providing an ontology-driven integration solution. This solution is based on a set of mediation ontologies which are orthogonal to the two other layers (the service and the management system layers) and aim to extend service and management layer with a semantic that enhance service mediation in the context of a VBE. The main proposed ontologies are: service integration ontology, resource sharing ontology, VO Organization ontology and Domain ontologies. These ontologies are described in detail in the following.

3.8 The Service Integration Ontology

The aim of the service integration ontology is to perform mediation processes in order to resolve mainly the semantic heterogeneity problem between services participating in a VO. In our proposal, we use the hybrid approach to perform service integration. The rationale behind this choice is that in the context of a VBE the definition of a single set of ontology standards that are suitable for all the VBE member is nearly impossible. The service integration ontology is based on a set of modules that perform the matching or resolution of semantic heterogeneity between services [22]. These modules are based on ontology mapping. The mapping is the process whereby two or more ontologies are semantically related at conceptual level. According to the semantic relations defined in the mappings, source ontology instances can then be transformed into target ones [22].

3.9 The Resource Sharing Ontology

In order to support the discovery of relevant information in the context of a VO creation, information resources need to be described in a way that is understandable and usable by the VBE members. To this end, each member should provide an ontological description of its information resources, according to a Semantic Web-compatible language for its specification (e.g., OWL [23]). In order to describe the resources in an ontology language-independent way, we refer to a reference ontology model, in terms of concepts, properties and semantic relations between concepts. A concept is characterized by a name and a set of properties that represents its features. We distinguish between strong and weak properties, to denote mandatory properties and optional properties, respectively. Each property is associated with a name and a value, which can be a datatype or a reference to another concept. Semantic relations are defined between concepts, to express the most appropriate relations existing between them.

3.10 The VO Organization Ontology

We consider VO organization ontology to be a set of constraints on the activities performed by VBE members. In particular, VO organization consists of a set of divisions and subdivisions, a set of organization-members (which are the members of a division of the organization), a set of roles that the members play in the organization, and an organization-goal tree that specifies the goals (and their decomposition into subgoals) the VO try to achieve.

3.11 The Domain Ontologies

Domain ontologies are required to help in the collaborative work and ensure that organizations are negotiating about the same good/product/service. Organization may use different ontologies to represent their view of a domain. Each domain may be specified in many different ways, and this ontology mismatch is a question under intensive research. For example, a domain expert may derive a domain-specific ontology that describes the vocabularies for concept used within a sector. In our work, we adopt the domain ontologies specification as the one reported in [22].

4 Related Work

There are many ongoing research efforts related to the VO creation framework within a VO Breeding Environment context. The most relevant work in this area is proposed by Camarinah-Matos et al. within the ECOLEAD project [1]. This work characterizes a first attempt to the definition of a reference framework for VO creation that addresses the fundamental elements of the VBEs. The proposed framework presents a detailed process covering a number of steps from the identification of the collaboration opportunity till the lunching of the VO. Besides, the framework is validated through empirical studies relating to international industry based VBE involved in the ECOLEAD project.

In a recent work, the authors present an excellent approach for the establishment and management of 2nd generation VBEs and fluid formation and creation of VOs [24].

The key aspects of the approach are: a reference framework, value systems and trust management, a VBE management system and contract negotiation wizard.

Zirpins et al. in [26] introduce a SOA model for virtual service enterprises. In particular, the authors propose an UML-based SOA metamodel for realisation of services that represent virtual service processes. However, the proposed approach doesn't include any facility to manage the virtual services within a VO context.

While most of the previous endeavors have been focused on particular aspects namely on the VBE management system, partners' selection and VO creation process, one of the innovative contributions of this work is the consideration of a holistic approach covering VBE management system, interoperability issues and service domain adapted to enterprise collaboration.

5 Conclusion

The VO Breeding Environment enables dynamic and fluid establishment of potential opportunity-based virtual organizations. However, its implementation in a real organization context is more challenging and requires a particular attention, a comprehensive guiding framework and strong engineering principles. In this paper we have proposed a three layered framework combining VBE management systems layer that assist flexible VO creation, a semantic interoperability layer essential for promoting integration on the basis of comment language that describe VO concepts and inherent dependencies, and a service oriented layer that introduces the concept of service domain that encapsulates business processes fitting VO requirements.

As to future work, an empirical study to validate and test the proposed approach will be at the centre of ongoing research. For other related endeavors, modeling the inter-organizational trust and management of performance measurements appear to be a promising path as well.

References

1. Camarinha-Matos, L.M., Afsarmanesh, H.: A framework for virtual organization creation in a breeding environment. Annual Reviews in Control 31(1), 119–135 (2007)
2. Grefen, P., Mehandjiev, N., Kouvas, G., et al.: Dynamic business network process management in instant virtual enterprises. Computers in Industry 60(2), 86–103 (2009)
3. Camarinha-Matos, L.M., Afsarmanesh, H., Ollus, M.: Virtual organizations: Systems and practices (2005)
4. Chiu, D.K.W., Kafeza, E., Kafeza, I.: View-based contracts in an e-service crossorganizational workflow environment. In: Casati, F., Georgakopoulos, D., Shan, M.-C. (eds.) TES 2001. LNCS, vol. 2193, p. 74. Springer, Heidelberg (2001)
5. Afsarmanesh, H., Camarinha-Matos, L.M.: A framework for management of virtual organization breeding environments. In: Collaborative Networks and their Breeding Environments. Springer, Boston (2007)
6. Afsarmanesh, H., Camarinha-Matos, L.M.: Towards a semi-typology for virtual organization breeding environments. In: 8th IFAC symposium on cost-oriented automation (2007)
7. Smith, R.V.: Industry cluster analysis: Inspiring a common strategy for community development. Central Pennsylvania Workforce Development Corporation Report (2003)

8. Angelov, S., Grefen, P.: The 4W framework for B2B e-contracting. International Journal of Networking and Virtual Organizations 2(1), 78–97 (2003)
9. Afsarmanesh, H., Camarinha-Matos, L.: Future smart organizations: A virtual tourism enterprise. In: Proceedings of WISE 2000-First ACM/IEEE international conference on web information systems engineering, pp. 456–461 (2000)
10. Khouloud, B., Lucien, V., Patrick, B.: Modelling adaptable business service for enterprise collaboration. In: PROVE 2009 (2009)
11. Gorton, S., Montangero, C., Reiff-Marganiec, S., et al.: StPowla: SOA, Policies and Workflows. In: Di Nitto, E., Ripeanu, M. (eds.) ICSOC 2007. LNCS, vol. 4907, pp. 351–362. Springer, Heidelberg (2009)
12. Boukadi, K., Ghedira, C., Vincent, L.: An Aspect Oriented Approach for Context-Aware Service Domain Adapted to E-Business
13. Boukadi, K., Ghedira, C., Lucien, V., et al.: The Contextual Service Oriented Analysis and Design. The special issue on Service Intelligence: The next wave of Service Computing, IJOCI (2010)
14. Gomez-Perez, A., Corcho, O.: Ontology Languages for the Semantic Web. IEEE Intelligent Systems 17(1), 54–60 (2002)
15. Afsarmanesh, H., Ermilova, E.: Management of ontology in VO breeding environments Domain. International Journal of Services and Operations Management (IJSOM), the special issue on Modelling and Management of Knowledge in Collaborative Networks (2009) (in press)
16. Khouloud, B.: Coopération interentreprises: une approche flexible à base de services adaptables. Ecole Nationale Supérieur des Mines de Saint Etienne, France (2009)
17. Xu, Z., Martin, P., Powley, W., et al.: Reputation-Enhanced QoS-based Web Services Discovery. In: IEEE International Conference on Web Services (ICWS 2007), pp. 9–13 (2007)
18. Romero, D., Galeano, N., Molina, A.: Virtual organisation breeding environments value system and its elements. Journal of Intelligent Manufacturing (2008)
19. Romero, D., Galeano, N., Molina, A.: Mechanisms for assessing and enhancing organisations' readiness for collaboration in collaborative networks. International Journal of Production Research 47(17), 4691–4710 (2008)
20. Boukadi, K., Ghedira, C., Chaari, S., et al.: CWSC4EC: How to Employ Context, Web Service, and Community in Enterprise Collaboration
21. Boukadi, K., Ghedira, C., Maamar, Z., et al.: Context-Aware Data & IT Services Collaboration in E-Business. Transactions on Large Scale Data and Knowledge Centered Systems 1(5740), 91–115 (2010)
22. Izza, S., Vincent, L., Burlat, P.: Framework for Semantic Enterprise Integration, pp. 78–89
23. Dean, M., Connolly, D., Harmelen, F.v., et al.: Web Ontology Language (OWL) W3C Reference version 1.0 (2003), `http://www.w3.org/TR/2002/WD-owl-ref-20021112`
24. Afsarmanesh, H., Camarinha-Matos, L.M., Msanjila, S.S.: On management of 2nd generation Virtual Organizations Breeding Environments. Annual Reviews in Control 33(2), 209–219 (2009)
25. Benatallah, B., Medjahed, B., Bouguettaya, A., et al.: Composing and Maintaining Web-based Virtual Enterprises. In: TES 2000, pp. 155–174 (2000)
26. Zirpins, C., Emmerich, W.: Pattern-based e-service modelling for virtual service enterprises. Service Oriented Computing and Applications 3(1), 65–98 (2009)

Autonomic Approach to Planning and Scheduling in Networked Small Factories

Flavio Bonfatti[1], Luca Martinelli[1], and Paola Daniela Monari[2]

[1] DII, University of Modena and Reggio Emilia,Via Vignolese 905, 41125 Modena, Italy
[2] SATA srl,Via Notari 103, 41126 Modena, Italy
flavio.bonfatti@unimore.it, p.monari@satanet.it, luca.martinelli@unimore.it

Abstract. The paper considers the complex behavior of a small company in a business ecosystem, time by time leader or supplier or both in one or more supply chains, and points out the data exchange and processing problems it must face for reacting fast to customer requests. Then the paper suggests that in order to meet these requirements it is convenient to provide every company with proper automatic functions, covering its distributed planning, resource scheduling and exception handling needs, whose policies can be fully customised by the company itself to mirror its specific intentions: in short, a practical implementation of the autonomic model.

Keywords: autonomic approach, small company, distributed planning, resource scheduling, self-configuration, self-optimization, self-healing.

1 Introduction

The paper aims at showing how the autonomic approach is suited to solve the planning and scheduling problem in factories constituted by networked small companies. The focus is put on small companies (less than 50 employees) since they represent the great majority of companies and in spite of this they are normally disregarded by the offer of advanced yet affordable ICT solutions [1].

Networked small factories are normally organised into regional and/or sectoral business ecosystems (or breeding environments), thus sharing habits, tacit knowledge and informal relations. In general they follow co-evolutionary models showing the autonomous development of the involved parties [2] and need communication and collaboration supports to efficiently share their production resources [3].

Small distributed factories reach high levels of effectiveness. They innovate products by adapting fast to the changing market demand, their products are of good quality, and a significant percentage of their production is sold in other countries thus showing the attitude to be active in the global market. However, while effectiveness is already there what is actually missing is a reasonable level of efficiency.

Efficiency relates to a number of aspects such as (a) fast response time to requests for quotation and customer orders, (b) ability to establish more dynamic relations with suppliers and subcontractors, (c) better allocation of internal resources and monitoring

L.M. Camarinha-Matos et al. (Eds.): PRO-VE 2010, IFIP AICT 336, pp. 297 – 303, 2010.

of their behavior, (d) better logistics to minimise transport costs of worked materials, (e) strict collaboration with partners to damp down exceptions and perturbations. In short: higher productivity and competitiveness.

The vision is for a manufacturing environment where every small factory has access to a suite of autonomic ICT functions relating it, on the one side, with its customers and, on the other side, with its suppliers and subcontractors, and supporting both distributed planning and scheduling of internal resources.

While processes are completely automated, each company remains autonomous and has the right to customize the policies of its automatic behavior. The solution must be scalable, easy to access and use, actually customisable, cheap and not diverting company resources from the core business.

The following of this paper is made of four main sections. Section 2 briefly presents the collaboration scenario constituting the operational context for the proposed approach. Section 3 recalls the functions of the autonomic model and maps them onto the main collaboration steps. Section 4 examines the recursive network planning procedure needed to instantiate the supply chain for the fulfillment of a customer order. Finally, Section 5 examines the internal resource scheduling task that every supplier must carry out to answer the supply chain leader invitation.

2 Collaboration Scenario

Imagine a business ecosystem grouping small companies that are specialized in complementary manufacturing activities as producers, subcontractors or suppliers and are used to participate in several supply chains. Imagine now that one of them is reached by a customer order (similarly for a request for quotation). This event will trigger a succession of consequent actions that is worth recalling here briefly:

- The receiving company must activate its supply chain, if any, as leader (see Figure 1 left). To this purpose it will carry out a planning activity to decide which tasks are better performed internally, which are conveniently assigned to partners and which are the preferred partners in those specific cases.
- According to this plan the leader company will communicate the assigned task to each of the involved partners. If one partner is leading in turn a supply chain it will carry out a similar planning activity with the involvement of further partners to fulfill the received task (see Figure 1 right).
- The result of this distributed planning process is the configuration of the working supply chain for that customer order. The configuration will be static if partners are predefined for every task to assign; it will be dynamic if partners are selected within constellations of competing companies [4].
- As last step each involved company, including leaders, will undertake a scheduling activity for the tasks to perform internally in order to allocate and book the required resources on routings and phases. This is also the step for each company to determine lead time and cost of the assigned task.

The propagation of the distributed planning process across the ecosystem is intended to select the suited supply chain members to fulfill that specific customer order and commit them to participate in the forthcoming execution of the planned and scheduled tasks. The process will end when all the devised activities will be successfully

Fig. 1. A company in the business ecosystem is reached by a customer order. As a consequence it activates its supply chain (left) by sending the proper requests to its members. Every member with its own supply chain will activate it in turn (right).

covered and this will produce proper changes on the work calendars of the allocated internal resources at each selected partner.

Later, during order execution, the distributed plan will be put in action and the tasks progressively carried out by the selected companies. Transports will be performed whenever the materials need to be worked in different locations. Should a task be affected by problems (delay, loss of materials) this will trigger a replanning effort for damping down the perturbation while propagating it to the other partners.

3 The Autonomic Model

The Autonomic Computing Initiative (ACI) was launched by IBM in 2001 [5] as a self-management capability for facing the rapidly growing complexity of distributed computing. The essence of autonomic computing is automating low-level management tasks. The adjective is taken from the autonomic nervous system of the human body that controls important functions without any conscious intervention.

More recently, the Autonomic Network Architecture (ANA) integrated project co-funded by the European Commission [6] moved the focus to network organization based on the application of the autonomic principle. The ultimate goal was the dynamic adaptation and re-organization of the network according to the working, economical and social needs of the users. The project results confirmed the application potential of such novel network architecture.

In an autonomic system the human operator takes on a new role: he does not control the system directly, instead he defines general policies and rules that serve as an input for the self-management process. For this process the ACI defines the following four functional areas:

- Self-Configuration. This means automatic configuration of a subset of nodes in a certain zone of the network. This function is then strongly localized and includes the addition of nodes as well as the creation and cancellation of relations between nodes in order to meet the defined requirements.
- Self-Optimization. This means automatic allocation of resources in the single node to ensure an optimal functioning with respect its expected behaviour. The

optimization algorithm is driven by performance objectives set during the self-configuration phase and by policies set by the node responsible.

- Self-Healing. This means automatic discovery and correction of faults. Self-healing methods are triggered by events or exceptions occurring in a single node or by changing requirements. Normally self-healing propagates through the network and impacts on configuration and optimization.
- Self-Protection. This means proactive identification of and protection from defaulting conditions or intentional attacks. Since in networked small factories the main cause of faults is the negative behaviour of certain nodes, self-protection is mostly based on evaluation of past performances.

The adaptation of the autonomic model to the approach proposed by this paper establishes the following relations: self-configuration for distributed planning, self-optimization for internal resource scheduling, self-healing for (distributed and internal) exception handling. Self-protection affects the previous functions with performance indicators derived by off-line functions.

Every company is subject in principle to a double autonomic process, respectively as leader of the supply chain and as subcontractor (Figure 2). If leader it will be provided with self-configuration and self-healing functions allowing automatic reaction to customer orders and automatic propagation of purchase orders to suppliers. If supplier, possibly of itself, it will automatically manage the internal scheduling phase and face possible exception coming from the shop-floor.

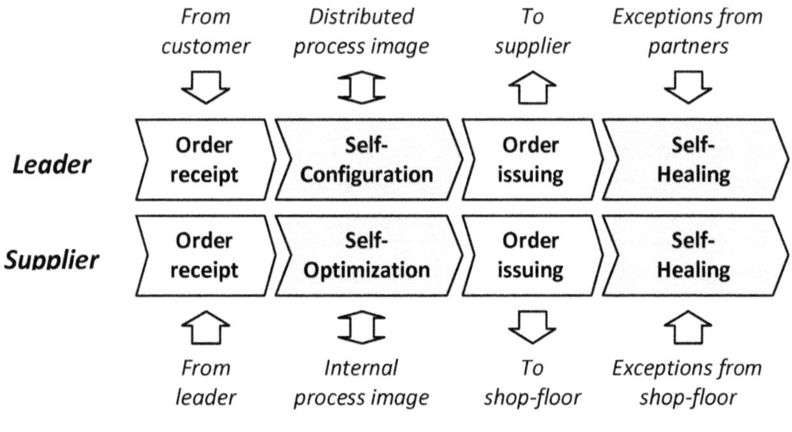

Fig. 2. The full autonomic process is triggered by the receipt of a customer order and leads to planning the supply chain, issuing purchase orders and scheduling the internal resources.

4 Distributed Planning

Instantiating the supply chain to fulfill the operational needs triggered by a customer request is a complex task to which much research effort has been devoted in the last years from the methodological [7] and implementation [8] viewpoints. Our approach exploits the autonomic concept and model with the ultimate aim of relieving small companies from repeatedly planning tasks and negotiations with partners.

To this purpose it is worth analyzing what happens when a customer order for the supply of a certain quantity of product X reaches that company. In general, the process P(X) for manufacturing product X includes a number of activities linked to each other by sequence, parallelism and alternative relations (Figure 3).

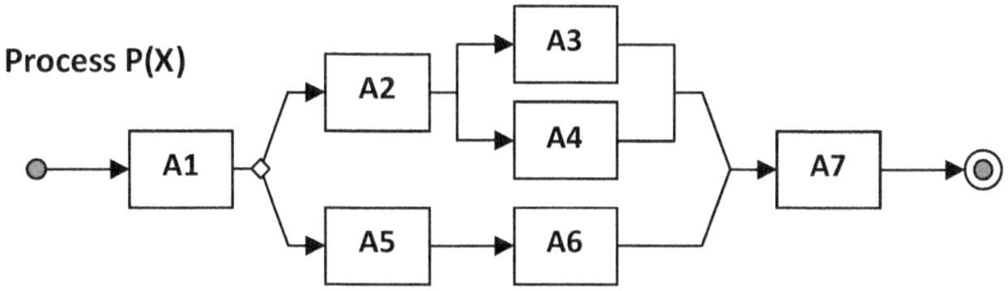

Fig. 3. Example of distributed manufacturing process. It includes seven activities where A3 and A4 are executed in parallel while the A2 and A5 braches correspond to alternative paths.

- Scan process P(X) left to right and identify A1 as first activity. Since A1 devises one or more candidate suppliers Sj, possibly including the "make" option, each of them will be informed of the possible involvement in A1 starting from time T1 and asked to foresee its respective lead time T1j and cost C1j.
- Consider now the upper branch and its first activity A2. Having in turn one or more candidate suppliers Sk, every pair (Sj, Sk) must be considered in order to estimate time Tjk and cost Cjk for moving materials (if any) from the one to the other. The starting time T2 for activity A2 is then given by T1+T1j+Tjk.
- With the following parallel activities A3 and A4 the number of combinations increases further but the procedure does not change: each candidate supplier of every activity is informed of the estimated start time for that activity and is asked to foresee time and cost of its possible contribution to process P(X).
- At the end of this procedure the algorithm has available a complete estimation of all the feasible process instantiations for that order, and detailed measures of intermediate and final lead times and costs. It can then choose the best one according to the established policy (e.g. the fastest, the cheapest, etc.).

The algorithm can be simplified to reduce the number of combinations to consider. To this purpose the policy could include some heuristics for the early selection of candidate suppliers or choice among alternative paths. In any case, reaching the optimal or suboptimal solution requires an intense message traffic with candidate suppliers that is hardly managed in a small company by means of not automatic tools.

This problem is technically overcome by providing every company with automatic self-configuration and self-healing functions based on the described planning algorithm. The human intervention remains to identify interesting partners and define the policy that such a company intends to autonomously apply for driving the process instantiation phase and the exception handling phase. The benefits are important:

- No resource must be diverted from the company core business to manage real-time interactions with partners.

- The final response to the customer and the assignment of tasks to the selected partners are fast and accurate.
- The reaction to exceptions is also computed accurately, in a very short time and with minimal consequences.

It is worth observing that these benefits are particularly important to small companies, while larger ones are normally provided with resources letting them manage more easily the process configuration and re-planning phases. In other words, the smaller is a company the greater can be its advantage in adopting a full autonomic solution. Of course, other problems arise e.g. the need to build confidence towards an approach that apparently subtracts the operation control to them.

5 Resource Scheduling

The last critical aspect of a full autonomic solution is the support that must be assured to each small company behaving as supplier in the supply chain. To this purpose let us analyze what happens when the supply chain leader proposes to this company to perform activity Ai belonging to process P(X). Normally the execution model of Ai is represented in form of a routing made by a sequence of operational phases.

A phase is intended by the shop-floor as an individual operation to be carried out by a certain type of resource team. The resource team type is composed by a combination of primary and secondary resources (persons, machines, equipment, etc.) for each of which the company has available one or more instances. Scheduling the execution of activity Ai means allocating the resource instances able to perform the phases of the relative routing. More precisely:

- The routing is scanned one phase at a time. The first phase is expected to start as soon as possible after the established start time Ti for activity Ai. In practice it will start when an instance of the required resource team can be organized and allocated to it, taking into account the engagements of resource instances.
- To this purpose the work calendars of the proper resource instances are examined and one or more combinations are identified with the constraint to involve them for the estimated duration of that phase. The choice of the best combination will be based on the policy established by that company.
- After scheduling the resources allocated to the first phase it is possible to derive its cost and the delivery time of the worked materials. The latter is the reference start time for the next phase, with possible positive or negative slacks.
- At the end of the entire scheduling procedure the total activity cost and the total lead time are finally known and can be communicated to the leader company for feeding its planning decisions.
- Later, during task execution, exceptions can occur e.g. because of delayed operations, missing resource instances, loss of materials. The schedule must be modified in such a way to solve them and, if this is not sufficient, they must be communicated to the supply chain leader for higher-level intervention.

Although not so complex like the planning algorithm, the scheduling algorithm must however consider a large number of variables and conditions, and apply a policy that can be in turn quite complex. This calls again for an automated solution under the condition that it leaves wide margins for the definition of autonomous policies.

6 Conclusions

Small companies behaving as nodes of networked factories, with both leader and supplier roles, must increase their efficiency or risk to be left aside of the increasingly competitive global market. Being provided with limited resources that they cannot divert from the core business, it is fundamental for them to adopt strongly automated planning, scheduling and exception handling solutions under the condition to maintain wide margins for policy customization.

This can effectively be done by autonomic functions for dynamic configuration of the networked factory, optimization of resource allocation within every node, automation of healing reactions to exceptions, policy enrichment with node performance indicators. The paper has shown the way to realize this solution starting from an analysis of the collaboration scenario representing the intended behaviors.

The autonomic functions for a networked small factory are presently studied and developed in the frame of the EU co-funded FP7-Capacities-SME 243554 eBEST project [9] with special attention to the subcontracting sector. The new ICT solution will be subject to validation by networks established in six European regions, namely Belgium, Greece, Hungary, Italy, Slovakia and Spain.

References

1. e-Business Watch: An Economic Assessment of ICT-related Industrial Policy (2009), http://www.ebusiness-watch.org/studies/special_topics/2009/ICT_policy.htm
2. Dekkers, R.: Distributed Manufacturing as Co-evolutionary System. International Journal of Production Research 47(8) (2009)
3. Noori, H., Lee, W.B.: Dispersed Network Manufacturing: an Emerging Form of Collaborative Networks. In: Dekkers, R. (ed.) Dispersed Manufacturing Networks: Challenges for Research and Practice. Springer, Heidelberg (2009)
4. Camarinha-Matos, L.M., Afsarmanesh, H.: A framework for virtual organization creation in a breeding environment. Journal Annual Reviews in Control 31(1), 119–135 (2007)
5. IBM Autonomic Computing Initiative, http://www-01.ibm.com/software/tivoli/autonomic/ (visited March 2010)
6. Rodriguez-Fernandez, D., et al.: Demonstrating Autonomic On-demand Content Delivery. In: Mauthe, A., Zeadally, S., Cerqueira, E., Curado, M. (eds.) FMN 2009. LNCS, vol. 5630, pp. 206–211. Springer, Heidelberg (2009)
7. Romero, D., et al.: A Virtual Breeding Environment Reference Model and its Instantiation Methodology. In: Proceedings of PRO-VE 2008, Poznan (2008)
8. Ignatiadis, I., et al.: Panda – a Virtual Breeding Environment for SMEs in the ERP/CRM Industry Using a Service Oriented Approach. World review of Science, Technology and Sustainable Development 7, 1–2 (2010)
9. The eBEST project, http://www.ebest.eu

An Approach to Select Suppliers for Sustainable Collaborative Networks

María José Verdecho, Juan José Alfaro-Saiz, and Raúl Rodríguez-Rodríguez

Department of Business Organization, CIGIP (Research Centre on Production Management and Engineering), Universidad Politécnica de Valencia, Camino de Vera, s/n, 46022, Valencia, Spain
{mverdecho,jalfaro,raurodro}@cigip.upv.es

Abstract. Supplier selection is an important decision-making process within supply chain management that involves qualitative and quantitative factors. This process is even more complex if different partners that are already collaborating desire to choose a partner for enhancing the sustainability of their collaborative network. Sustainability literature supports the need to consider three main types of sustainability factors: environmental, social, and economic factors. In addition, the management of collaborative networks is better done using a performance management framework/system that allows managing performance under various performance perspectives or dimensions in a structured manner. This paper proposes a novel approach to select suppliers for sustainable collaborative networks using a performance management framework. With this approach, enterprises that are collaborating (or desire to do it) will have a tool to select suppliers aligned with their strategy and the sustainability of their collaborative network, and therefore, improving the supplier selection process and their competitiveness.

Keywords: performance measurement, collaborative networks, sustainability, supplier selection.

1 Introduction

Supplier selection is one of the decision-making processes that organizations perform in order to achieve/maintain a competitive position. This task is even more complex if it involves different partners that are already collaborating and desire to choose a partner for enhancing the sustainability of their collaborative supply chain/ network. Supplier involvement in early and extensive stages has many beneficial results for supply chain management: faster development process, reduced costs, reduced inventory, etc. [1-3]. Thus, selecting suppliers becomes a crucial process for manufacturers.

The academic literature about collaborative relationships points out the importance of considering the performance measurement of the entire supply chain in order to provide products and services that meet the expectations of end customers and promote improvement and innovation of the whole processes [4-6]. For that reason, it is important to define common performance indicators for all the enterprises that are

L.M. Camarinha-Matos et al. (Eds.): PRO-VE 2010, IFIP AICT 336, pp. 304–311, 2010.

collaborating as they will aid to focus their efforts towards strategic aspects of their business [7-9]. In fact, in order to provide a general overview of their performance status, those enterprises should define and use a structured performance measurement framework that allows managing performance under various performance perspectives or dimensions. One of the most important performance measurement frameworks is the Balanced ScoreCard (BSC) [10]. The BSC was initially developed for managing performance of individual enterprises and has been extended by different authors for interorganizational performance management such as the frameworks proposed by [11-14].

In addition, there is an increasing interest in improving the sustainability of collaborative supply chains/networks. In [15], the main pressures and incentives for sustainability within these contexts are identified: legal demands/regulations, customer demands, response to stakeholders, competitive advantage, environmental and social pressure groups and reputation loss. Literature supports the need to consider three main types of sustainability factors or criteria: environmental, social, and economic factors [16-17]. Therefore, in order to support the sustainability of the collaborative network, suppliers should be evaluated regarding these three types of criteria and selecting suppliers can be defined as a multi-criteria decision-making (MCDM) problem involving both qualitative and quantitative factors.

Thus, there are two main interrelated inputs that influence the supplier selection problem: performance of the enterprises that are collaborating and sustainability criteria. On the one hand, the enterprises that are collaborating pursue the improvement of the overall system. For that purpose, they should define performance elements (such as performance objectives, performance indicators, etc.) for the whole interorganizational context and select the new supplier that better match those performance elements. On the other hand, enterprises need to identify relevant criteria for sustainability assessment of suppliers regarding a specific collaborative context. In addition, both performance elements and sustainability criteria are interrelated. For example, if one of the sustainability criteria to assess suppliers is "environmental practices", this criterion will influence the outcome of some performance elements such as those related to brand image and process performance of the collaborative network. Similarly, some performance elements may affect the supplier outcome on some criteria. For example, the improvement of waste disposal on the network may improve the environmental practices of the supplier.

Despite the importance of these aspects, the approaches found in the literature for supplier selection do not integrate all these aspects: performance measurement framework of the collaborative enterprises, sustainability criteria and interrelationships among them. The purpose of this paper is to propose an approach that aids to select suppliers that fills this research gap. With this approach, enterprises that are collaborating and have defined a BSC framework (or desire to do it) will have a tool to select suppliers aligned to their common strategy and improving the sustainability of the whole enterprise association.

The structure of this paper is as follows. First, a literature review of MCDM applied for supplier selection is presented focusing attention on the Analytic Network Process (ANP) method. Then, the approach to select suppliers is described and a case study within the automotive industry is presented. Finally, conclusions are exposed.

2 Background

MCDM approaches consists of a set of concepts, methods and techniques that aim to aid individuals or groups to make decisions that imply various criteria or trade-offs and multiple agents. Several methods have been proposed for solving the supplier selection problem such as vendor profile analysis (VPA), multi-objective programming (MOP), data envelopment analysis (DEA), analytic hierarchy process (AHP) and analytic network process (ANP). The ANP method developed by Saaty [18] allows solving problems that involve both quantitative and qualitative criteria as well as considering interdependence and feedback among these criteria. For that reason, ANP is a useful method for modeling and solving the problem of this paper while the other approaches assume the independence among their elements without a clear distinction if they can be generalized to model interdependence without compromising their theoretical foundations.

In addition, ANP has been recently used for supplier selection. In [19], a model to select suppliers depending on different levels of cooperation is defined. In [20], an ANP model to select members for an agile virtual enterprise is presented. In [21], an ANP model to select suppliers to establish strategic alliances is developed. Other models are specifically developed for selecting suppliers within specific industries such as pharmaceutical industry [22]. In addition, in the literature, few ANP models are encountered that consider sustainability factors. In [23], it is presented a strategic decision framework for green supplier management that integrates the economic and environmental dimensions of sustainability. This framework has been lately extended including the social dimension by [24]. However, there is not a specific model developed for selecting suppliers that integrates sustainability factors and the overall system performance. For this reason, the purpose of the remaining of this paper is to present an ANP model for supplier selection that solves this research issue.

3 The Supplier Selection Approach

An approach to select suppliers has been developed in order to integrate under a unique model both types of aspects: performance of collaborating enterprises and supplier sustainability criteria. This approach has been modeled using ANP as it allows considering: qualitative and quantitative criteria as well as interdependences and feedback among the model elements. The approach comprises eight phases and should be developed by a group of experts from all the collaborative enterprises. It is recommended that an internal or external person to the enterprises acts as a consultant to aid in the approach application.

Phase 1: The first phase aims at describing the specific supplier selection problem having as main goal the selection of the best supplier that better match the performance objectives of the collaborative network as well as sustainability criteria.

Phase 2: In this phase, performance elements (objectives and key indicators) are defined for the whole collaborative network according to the four performance perspectives of the BSC [10]: financial, customer, internal business process and innovation & learning perspectives. In addition, it is important that objectives and indicators are coherently defined from the strategic mission and vision of the collaborative association. For that purpose, it is possible to use benchmarking or standard indicators such as the ones described in the SCOR model. Once established, periodical reviews (normally annual reviews) are to be made by managers of all the collaborative enterprises to verify the relevance of the performance elements and decide if they are to be updated.

Phase 3: Potential suppliers that are to be considered in the decision-making problem are determined.

Phase 4: In this phase, sustainability criteria to assess the different suppliers are defined. These criteria are clustered according to the three sustainability dimensions: business, environmental and social dimensions. It has to be noted that the economic dimension has been renamed to business dimension in order to reflect not only the economical aspect of the suppliers but also other important supplier characteristics such as their product, the relationship with the members of the network given by their trust, commitment, cooperation, conflict management techniques, etc. Environmental criteria comprise two types of sub-criteria. On the one hand, environmental practices such as pollution controls and prevention, and environmental management. On the other hand, environmental performance includes indicators for measuring resource consumption and pollution production. The social dimension involves employment practices, health & safety and stakeholders influence.

Phase 5: The ANP model is built. The ANP model consists of a set of elements (criteria and performance elements) grouped into clusters. A cluster was defined for each type of performance perspective or criteria as clusters are groups of elements with a common characteristic [18]. The different interdependences and feedback between elements of the clusters are defined according to the experience of the group of experts. For modeling and solving the problem, *Superdecisions* software was used.

Phase 6: At this phase, the local priorities among elements are calculated. For that purpose, pairwise comparison matrices among elements are fulfilled by managers of all the collaborative enterprises. In order to fill the pairwise comparison matrices in, the fundamental scale is used which ranges from 1/9 to 9 [25]. In addition, consistency ratio is checked in order to avoid including inconsistent judgments.

Phase 7: This phase comprises obtaining different supermatrices. First, the unweighted supermatrix is composed. This matrix represents the relative influences among all the elements that are formed by introducing the local priorities previously calculated in the columns of the matrix. Then, the eigenvectors of the cluster matrix are calculated in order to prioritize the importance of the different model clusters following a similar procedure to the one explained in phase 6. For that purpose, pairwise comparison matrices among clusters of elements are done and consistency checked. Then, the weighted supermatrix is calculated by multiplying the unweighted supermatrix by the priority weights of the clusters. Thus, the weighted supermatrix gets stochastic which will derive meaningful limiting priorities.

Phase 8: Finally, the limit matrix is calculated raising the weighted supermatrix to powers until all the columns remain with the same values. The values in the columns are the global/limit priorities or influences of each element. The supplier that rates the higher value is selected.

4 Case Study

The ANP-based approach to select suppliers has been applied to a collaborative enterprise network belonging to the automotive industry in Spain. The supplier selection problem aims at selecting the best supplier of one high-volume subassembly. Managing directors of purchasing and R&D departments were in charge of the assessment of the suppliers. The three suppliers currently delivering the subassembly have the capability and know-how to manufacture the component and, therefore, are potential candidates for the selection. Thus, the problem is to select the best supplier as single source. Fig. 1 shows the ANP model. The model consists of eight clusters. Four clusters correspond to the four perspectives of the BSC: financial, customer, process and innovation & learning. Specifically, the elements within the clusters are the key performance indicators (KPI) for the collaborative enterprise network. These KPIs have been defined from the specific performance objectives identified for each perspective that were established by consensus by all the members participating in the collaborative enterprise network in order to manage the enterprise network at a global level. Although consensus demands discussion and agreement that takes some time to achieve, the strategic nature of the issues approached justify its application. Reaching consensus may be complicated in some cases. The consultant person should have the role to moderate and organize the meetings in order to develop all the phases successfully.

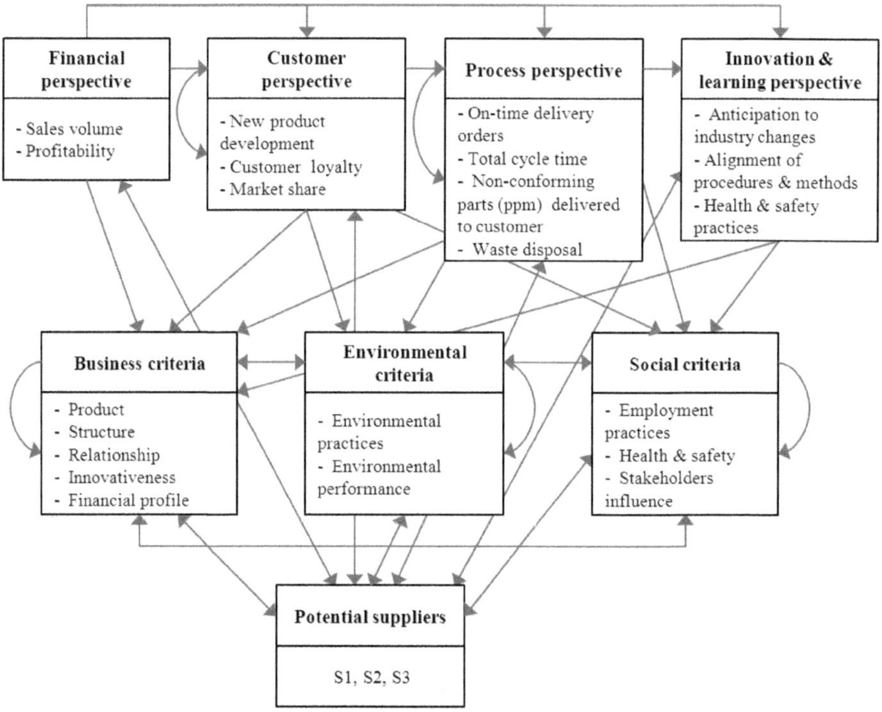

Fig. 1. ANP model for supplier selection

The arrows among the clusters represent the relationships among the elements within the clusters. Thus, interdependences among performance clusters show the relationships among KPIs of the different clusters (outer dependence). Similarly, there are some performance clusters whose elements present inner dependence such as the case of the customer cluster. For example, the success in the development of new products affects the market share and the customer loyalty. This is reflected by an arc on the customer cluster. Regarding sustainability criteria, they were identified from different frameworks [26-30]. All three sustainability clusters present interrelationships among them. In addition, criteria within each cluster also present inner dependences (reflected by an arc). Finally, the cluster of potential suppliers presents interdependence with the rest of clusters, as suppliers will be evaluated regarding the global KPIs and the sustainability criteria.

Once the ANP model is composed, pairwise comparison matrices were fulfilled by using the ANP method [18]. Table 1 shows the pairwise comparison matrix of the KPIs within the customer perspective with respect to the profitability KPI. As can be observed, local priorities are 0.1047 (new product development), 0.2583 (customer loyalty), 0.6370 (market share). Consistency ratio is 0.037 which is acceptable [18].

After all local priorities are calculated, unweighted supermatrix, weighted supermatrix and limit supermatrix are obtained. Limit priorities suggest that supplier 2 is the best. It has to be said that results show that supplier 2 is outstanding for the business and environmental dimensions, which are the two most important dimensions for the group of experts. These results were validated by the decision makers of the collaborative enterprise network so that supplier 2 was selected.

Table 1. Pairwise comparison of customer perspective KPIs with respect to profitability KPI

	New Prod. Dev.	Cust. loyalty	Market share	Priorities
New Prod. Dev.	1	3	5	0.1047
Cust. loyalty	1/3	1	3	0.2583
Market share	1/5	1/3	1	0.6370
			C.R.	0.037

5 Conclusions and Further Research

This paper introduces a multi-criteria approach to select suppliers for sustainable collaborative relationships based on two interrelated inputs: supplier sustainability criteria and performance of the collaborating enterprises. The novelty of this approach is that the supplier assessment attributes are the elements within the BSC of the whole collaborative enterprises as well as supplier sustainability criteria. Therefore, the supplier selected is the one that best performs at both aspects while considering interdependence and feedback among them. The main contribution of our approach is the link between supplier sustainability criteria and the common performance indicators defined by all the enterprises that are collaborating. The approach is applicable to all types of inter-enterprise associations taking into account that the performance elements definition will change depending on the specific context analyzed. In addition, some specific collaborative relationships may consider other factors, e.g. industry specific factors. Modification and adaptations to be performed for these two reasons will enable to use this approach in other collaborative relationships.

Research implications are also noted. We are developing further a BSC for the whole collaborating enterprises that allows integrating sustainability indicators coherently to increase the traceability among the supplier sustainability criteria and the collaborative enterprise performance framework.

Acknowledgments. This work has been developed within the framework of a research project funded by the Polytechnic University of Valencia, titled "Design and Implementation of Performance Measurement Systems within Collaborative Contexts for aiding the Decision-making Process", reference PAID-06-08-3206.

References

1. Mentzer, J.: Managing Supply Chain Collaboration. In: Supply Chain Management. Sage Publications, Inc., Thousand Oaks (2001)
2. Petersen, K.J., Handfield, R.B., Ragatz, G.L.: Supplier integration into new product development: coordinating product, process and supply chain design. Journal of Operations Management 23, 371–388 (2005)
3. Fawcett, S.E., Osterhaus, P., Magnan, G.M., Brau, J.C., McCarter, M.W.: Information sharing and supply chain performance: the role of connectivity and willingness. Supply Chain Management: An International Journal 12(5), 358–368 (2007)
4. Beamon, B.M.: Measuring supply chain performance. International Journal of Operations and Production Management 19, 275–292 (1999)
5. Gunasekaran, A., Patel, C., Tirtiroglu, E.: Performance measures and metrics in a supply chain environment. International Journal of Operations and Production Management 21(1-2), 71–87 (2001)
6. Romero, D., Galeano, N., Molina, A.: A conceptual Model for Virtual Breeding Environments Value System. In: Camarihna-Matos, L., Afsarmanesh, H., Novais, P., Analide, C. (eds.) Establishing the Foundation of Collaborative Networks. Springer, Boston (2007)
7. Bititci, U.S., Carrie, A.S., McDevitt, L.: Integrated performance measurement systems: a development guide. International Journal of Operations and Production Management 17, 522–534 (1997)
8. Pun, K.F., White, A.S.: A performance measurement paradigm for integrating strategy formulation: a review of systems and framewors. International Journal of Management Reviews 7(1), 49–71 (2005)
9. Alfaro, J.J., Rodríguez, R., Verdecho, M.J., Ortiz, A.: Business process interoperability and collaborative performance measurement. International Journal of Computer Integrated Manufacturing 22(9), 877–889 (2009)
10. Kaplan, R.S., Norton, D.P.: The balanced scorecard – measures that drive performance. Harvard Business Review 70(1), 71–79 (1992)
11. Brewer, P.C., Speh, T.W.: Using the Balanced ScoreCard to measure supply chain performance. Journal of Business Logistics 21(1), 75–93 (2000)
12. Bititci, U.S., Mendibil, K., Martinez, V., Albores, P.: Measuring and managing performance in extended enterprises. International Journal of Operations & Production Management 25(4), 333–353 (2005)
13. Folan, P., Browne, J.: Development of an Extended Enterprise Performance Measurement System. Production Planning and Control 16(6), 531–544 (2005)

14. Alfaro, J.J., Ortiz, A., Rodríguez, R.: Performance measurement system for Enterprise Networks. International Journal of Productivity and Performance Management 56(4), 305–334 (2007)
15. Seuring, S., Müller, M.: From a literature review to a conceptual framework for sustainable supply chain management. Journal of Cleaner Production 16, 1699–1710 (2008)
16. Robins, F.: The challenge of TBL: a responsibility to whom? Business and Society Review 111(1), 1–14 (2006)
17. Presley, A., Meade, L., Sarkis, J.: A strategic sustainability justification methodology for organisational decisions: a reverse logistics illustration. International Journal of Production Research 45(18/19), 4595–4620 (2007)
18. Saaty, T.L.: The Analytic Network Process: Decision Making with Dependence and Feedback. RWS Publications, Pittsburgh (1996)
19. Cheng, E.W.L., Li, H.: Application of ANP in process models: An example of strategic partnering. Building and Environment 42, 278–287 (2007)
20. Sarkis, J., Talluri, S., Gunasekaran, A.: A strategic model for agile virtual enterprise partner selection. International Journal of Operations & Production Management 27(11), 1213–1234 (2007)
21. Chen, S.H., Lee, H.T., Wu, Y.F.: Applying ANP approach to partner selection for strategic alliance. Management Decision 46(3), 449–465 (2008)
22. Kirytopoulos, K., Leopoulos, V., Voulgaridou, D.: Supplier selection in pharmaceutical industry An analytic network process approach. Benchmarking: An International Journal 15(4), 494–516 (2008)
23. Sarkis, J.: A strategic decision framework for green supply chain management. Journal of Cleaner Production 11, 397–409 (2003)
24. Parks, L., Karpak, B.: Sustainable supply chain: a modification suggestion to an existing strategic framework. In: 10th International Symposium on the Analytic Network Process, Creative Decisions, Pittsburgh (2009)
25. Saaty, T.L.: The Analytic Hierarchy Process. McGraw-Hill, New York (1980)
26. Croom, S.R.: The dyadic capabilities concept: examining the processes of key supplier involvement in collaborative product development. European Journal of Purchasing & Supply Management 7, 29–37 (2001)
27. Akarte, M.M., Surendra, N.V., Ravi, B., Rangaraj, N.: Web based casting supplier evaluation using analytical hierarchy process. Journal of the Operational Research Society 52, 511–522 (2001)
28. Kahraman, C., Cebeci, U., Ulukan, Z.: Multi-criteria supplier selection using fuzzy AHP. Logistics Information Management 16(6), 382–394 (2003)
29. Bai, C., Sarkis, J.: Integrating sustainability into supplier selection with grey system and rough set methodologies. Int. J. Production Economics 124, 252–264 (2010)
30. Dou, Y., Sarkis, J.: A joint location and outsourcing sustainability analysis for a strategic offshoring decision. International Journal of Production Research 48(2), 567–592 (2010)

Evaluating How Potential Pool of Partners Can Join Together in Different Types of Long Term Collaborative Networked Organizations

Andrea Cardoni[1], Stefano Saetta[2], and Lorenzo Tiacci[2]

[1] Università degli Studi di Perugia - Dipartimento di Discipline Giuridiche e Aziendali
Via Pascoli, 20 – 06123 Perugia, Italy
[2] Università degli Studi di Perugia - Dipartimento di Ingegneria Industriale
Via Duranti, 67 – 06125 Perugia, Italy
{acardoni,stefano.saetta,lorenzo.tiacci}@unipg.it

Abstract. The considerable benefits brought up by strategic alliances and diverse types of long term Collaborative Networked Organizations (CNOs) are nowadays widely recognized. There is an increasing demand in the industrial world for concretely implement new forms of collaborations. For example, demand often comes from pre-existent form of clusters or local productive arrangements, that want to evolve to more efficient forms of collaboration, or from small and medium enterprises that are facing a crisis, and look at collaboration with other enterprises as almost the last chance to survive. In general, variety of motivations in collaborating implies variety of missions of potential collaborations, that in turn requires the choice of an appropriate form of Collaborative Network aligned to the mission statement. This paper addresses the problem to define a methodology for analyzing potential pool of partners and for identifing the mission, the form, the governance structure and the value drivers of long term strategic alliance that would bring highest benefits to the partners. Three different forms of CNOs are considered: the Virtual organizations Breeding Environment (VBE), the Virtual Development Office (VDO) and the T-Holding.

Keywords: Network Mission, CNs creation, VBE, VDO, T-Holding.

1 Introduction

In recent years the economy have developed a deep changes involving the increasing importance of the knowledge in the economic and social development. This has significantly altered the paradigm of industrial development, based on the traditional division between labor and capital factors, identifying a new category of assets attributable to cognitive and relationship attitudes and skills.

In this context the traditional market and business structures that had supported the industrial development for the last two centuries have shown some limits to control efficiently the new form of coordination and the new challenges emerging from the so-called "knowledge economy"[1][2][3]. The creation of the hybrid form of coordination [4] able to combine all the benefits deriving form the competitive

L.M. Camarinha-Matos et al. (Eds.): PRO-VE 2010, IFIP AICT 336, pp. 312–321, 2010.

transactions with the stability and the performance control of the organization has been indicated as the right strategy to adapt the business structure to the main features of the knowledge economy (positive externalities, increasing productivity and the market failures) introducing the background framework for what is possible to define the "network vision".

The economic literature has followed this evolutionary process by providing ample evidence of the importance of knowledge and intangible assets and the same policies developed by the Community authorities have set a strategic goal of making Europe "the knowledge-based economy more competitive and dynamic world" (Lisbon strategy), highlighting the need of a hybrid form of organization between market and hierarchies.

From different perspectives also the industrial and management literature increasingly highlights the need to promote the networked organization developing a broad interdisciplinary approach to deepen the strategic and operational issues [5][6][7][8]. Developments in Collaborative Networks have benefited from contributions of multiple disciplines, namely computer science, computer engineering, communications and networking, management, economy, social sciences, law and ethics, etc. [9]. Referring to particular economic context characterized by the presence of SMEs, many important contributes also found that the network strategy has particular importance for small and medium-sized businesses [10][11][12] and entrepreneurial business [13], allowing them to activate the processes of growth and globalization that are necessary for the acquisition and the preservation of competitive advantage in the knowledge economy.

Although from existent literature the network vision appears as a consolidated way to face the new market challenges, and different cooperative networks structures have been proposed, it has been assumed that, for each type of theses, a specific collaborative mission has already been defined. However it can be highlighted the importance to investigate the conceptual steps that lead to the choice of the most appropriate strategic mission (and consequently the associated type of collaborative network), based on the characteristics of a potential pool of partners (see Fig. 1).

Fig. 1. The missing conceptual steps that link a network vision to a network mission definition

Putting these theoretical references as fundamental assumptions, the present paper is intended to focus attention on the process that guides a group of companies with a "network vision" to define the strategic mission of a networked organization project. The work is inspired by a real case: a study commissioned by the ICE (the Italian Institute for Foreign Trade) and by a local industrial association (Confartigianato Terni) to the University of Perugia, in order to investigate how the companies belonging to an industrial cluster of the metal-mechanic industry in Italy could be aggregated in an innovative way. The study is still in progress, and the present work just intends to illustrate the conceptual steps that are needed to approach the problem in order to define a framework that will be validated through the implementation of the case study.

The study follows a deductive interdisciplinary approach based on the rich literature about networked organization and presents the main conceptual steps to move a group of companies from the network vision to the definition of a strategic network mission. Firstly our analysis will describe three types of collaborative networks and combinations, that are characterized by different degree of business and process integration, namely: VBE, VDO e T-HOLDING. Secondly the strategic goals on which aggregation and collaboration forms can be based are identified and classified; the three above mentioned forms are then assessed on the basis of their capability to be aligned with the different strategic goals. Finally the analytical tools that allow to evaluate which strategic goals are attainable by a potential pool of companies are identified. On the basis of this results, the collaborative strategic network mission can be defined, and in turn the most appropriate collaborative form can be chosen.

Note that the procedure presented here in has been developed considering three possible collaborative network forms, taken as representative of long term collaboration forms with different integration degree. However, the methodology is generalizable and can be extended to include other forms of collaborative networks.

2 Three Possible Ways of Collaboration/Aggregation

VBE (Virtual Organizations Breeding Environment). VBE is a strategic association/alliance of organizations and the related supporting institutions, adhering to a base long term cooperation agreement and adoption of common operating principles and infrastructures, with the main goal of increasing their preparedness towards collaboration in potential Virtual Organizations [14]. That is, when an opportunity of business is identified by one of the members (what it acts as broker), a subset of the organizations of the VBE can be selected to form a VO / VE (Virtual Organization / Virtual Enterprise). A VO "is an association of (legally) independent organizations (VO partners) that came together and share resource and skills to achieve common goals, such as acquiring and responding to a market/society opportunity" [15].

The VBE maintains and manages well classified repositories/catalogs of information regarding the profile, competence, resource, production, service, ect. about its member organizations. Different member of the VBE, depending on their role/right, can have access to and use this information, e.g. for a broker to react on new business opportunities, for a VO coordinator to replace a failing partner in the VO, etc. In addition, the VBE results to be an innovative model as is offers an infrastructure base common ITC to facilitate the formation and the collaboration of the Virtual Organizations [16]. The VBE is an ampler concept of industry cluster, industry district, business echo system, virtual laboratories and crises management that operates only to regional level and they is essentially focused on a product / service. It is a more recent term that was coined to cover these cases and clearly extends their scope to both regional and global coverage, single and multi-specialty sector, and for-profit/ non profit organizations [17].

Romero and Molina [18] provide a framework that describes a set of process models that depict what happens during each VBE and VO management processes, to provide rationale of activities that should be carried out by a set of VBE actors to achieve the expected business process results.

VDO (Virtual Development Office). VDO organizational model has been developed inside of the MIGEN research project [18]. The model provides a central entity, namely the Virtual Development Office (VDO), which has tasks of creation, coordination and management of the network of enterprises, supplying some interface with the market and guaranteeing the consolidation of relations of mutual confidence between the actors of the community in an optical of strategic alliance of long period. The VDO acts as unique interlocutor toward the ecosystem of Business, it favours both the wish of cooperation and to the collaboration every time that introduces a Collaboration Opportunity.

The former definition is [20]: "VDO is a network entity with the aim to identify competitive positioning of the network enterprise and to promote, within the network, business missions". This definition clarifies what is a VDO, the entity introduced to manage the Collaborative Network, but does not clearly explain the role of the Network if compared to the VBE. In this sense it can be possible to formulate a new definition, based on the VBE one, that clarifies the VDO network model as "A strategic association/alliance of organizations and the related supporting institutions, adhering to a base long term cooperation agreement and adoption of common operating principles and infrastructures, with the main goal to create innovative BOs. This goals is accomplished by introducing a new for-profit company, the VDO, operating as a permanent network management/coordination entity. In pursuing these business opportunities the VDO realizes VOs and VEEs of network members and/or external partners". From this definition it is noteworthy that VDO is similar to VBE but it focused in particular on innovative businesses. VDO promotes research, marketing and innovation and is continuously looking for Business Opportunities. In this sense it acts as a permanent broker. VDO members focus on their core business keeping traditional activities and independence, but they can increase their competitiveness thanks to the activities of the VDO, which is always searching for innovative BOs. With VEE, VDO addresses explicitly the fact that it can include external partners.

If we make a comparison between VDO and VBE it can be observed a higher degree of coordination because of the VDO entity presence. VDO is also proactive because it promotes research, innovation, marketing within the network, due to its nature of for profit company and the connected need to reach a profitable dynamic. VDO does not wait for a BO from the single members but it is itself the proactive broker. Also, VDO always plays the role of VO/VEE planner and coordinator.

T-Holding. T-Holding is an aggregation model that represents the result of a collaboration project between the University of Perugia and "Piccola Industria", which is the branch dedicated to SMEs of the principal Italian industrial association, "Confindustria". Founded in 1910 Confindustria is the leading organization representing the manufacturing, construction, energy, transportation, ICT, tourism and services industries in Italy. The model has been officially presented during the XI Forum of "Piccola Industria" in Mantova (Italy) (23-24 October 2009), and attracted the national press and media attention thanks to the high potential impact of its application on the Italian industrial structure, impact that has been simulated through a scenario analysis.

The letter "T" stands for 'protection' (from the Italian word "Tutela") of small and medium enterprises that risk to lose their capacity of maintaining competitiveness and profitability in the new economic scenario. The basic idea is to avoid the collapse and the disappearance of these companies in crisis thanks to a strong push to the aggregation: for example, a number of companies in crisis could considerate the possibility of aggregation through the formation of a new company (namely the T-Holding). This new company should be in a position able to guarantee the industrial continuity and consequently to safeguard the industrial, entrepreneurial, financial and occupational patrimonies otherwise destined to a destruction process. The T-Holding should be born from an aggregation that involves a consistent number of firms belonging to compatible market sectors or supply chains.

The model was originally created in order to be applied to SMEs that are facing a deep financial and economic crisis. However, the model can be utilised also to aggregate companies that not necessarily are facing a crisis, and can be viewed as the model with the stronger degree of integration with respect to the others two models, the VBE and the VDO (Figure 1). The mechanism is the following: the entrepreneur transfers the ownership of its own firm (both tangible and intangible assets) to the T-Holding and becomes shareholder of this new company, acquiring a number of shares (or stocks) on the base of the assets value that are brought to the newco. The entrepreneur can also assume an operative role (partner-entrepreneur), for example being responsible for the production function of the plant. In other cases the entrepreneur could just participate as a financial partner, without executive responsibilities. The strategic and operative Governance is assigned to an "Industrial Manager", that is responsible for the industrial strategy and for the general management, while a "Financial Manager" is responsible for the financial and economical planning. This aggregation is based on the strategic principles of acquisition of the competitive advantage through the careful analysis of needs, and the development of innovative products obtained implementing high value added processes. These objectives become feasible through the sharing of:

- existing markets, controlled by the companies participating in the aggregation;
- plants and technology, with the ability to optimize their use, by reducing, if necessary, the production sites;
- competences and business skills, both those ones related to production processes and those ones related to the resources that are responsible of the managerial leadership of the new company;
- administrative and financial structures, to allow the reduction of overhead costs, to limit the financial debt and to renegotiate the account payable to suppliers and banks;
- commercial organizations, to rationalize market penetration policies;
- supply units, to allow the reduction of raw materials and services purchasing costs.

3 Strategic Goals Identification

The first step that links the network vision to the network mission definition is the strategic goals identification (see Fig. 2). The study and the experimentation on corporate networks have identified a number of strategic goals on which you can build an aggregation. The main reasons why firms aim to start an alliance of long period, of different sizes and with different integration degrees (ranging from a "soft" to a "strong" integration) should be referred to a combination of 'Primary' and 'Secondary' strategic goals.

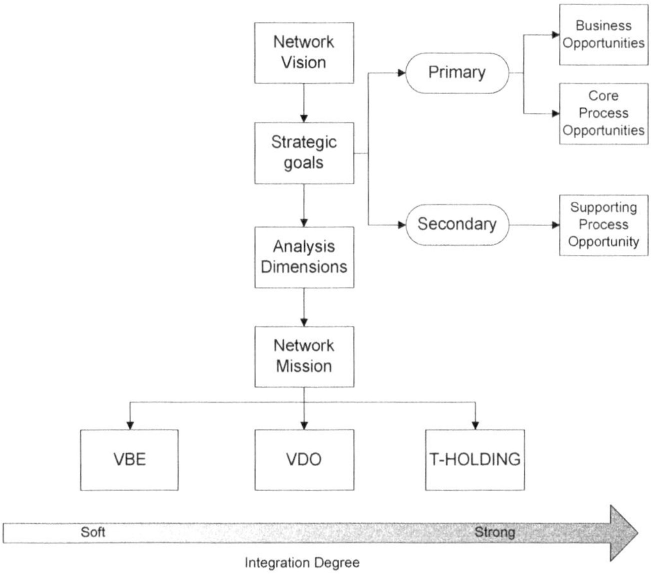

Fig. 2. The steps that link the network vision to the network mission definition, and the choice of the appropriate aggregation form.

The strategic goals of Primary type represents the ability of the network to permanently increase the value added related to its business core competencies. To achieve these goals it is necessary that the alliance is able to create new Business Opportunities (BOs) and Core Process Opportunities (CPOs):

- Business Opportunities: are related to new markets and new products development, able to increase the network turnover;
- Core Process Opportunities: are related to the increase of effectiveness and efficiency of the core operational activities, able to reduce the network costs.

In the strategic goals of Secondary type we can include all the other synergies that brings to new Supporting Process Opportunities, that are related to increase the efficiency and effectiveness of all the supporting activities, such as finance, control, quality, research, administration, education, etc., that are able to emphasize the benefits of Primary type.

Each kind of strategic goal (BOs, CPOs, SPOs) can be achieved in a stable or occasional manner, depending on the persistence and the intensity of the network effect. Table 1 shows that each one of the three aggregation form analysed is based on the three strategic goals that we have defined. However the identification of the different impact on each of the strategic goal can support the choice for the most appropriate network model and the related strategic mission.

If the opportunities tends to be occasional, due for example to high market instability or hard processes integration, it is undesirable to introduce a new for-profit company (the VDO). In this case the VBE seems to be the best model to maximize the cooperation benefits. On the contrary, when the companies are able to share in a persistent way the stable benefits of cooperation, the VDO and T-Holding models are more

Table 1. New Business and Process Opportunities in each of the three types of aggregation considered.

		VBE	VDO	T-Holding
Business Opportunities	Stable	+	+++	++
	Occasional	++	+	+
Core Process Opportunities	Stable	+	++	+++
	Occasional	++	+	+
Supporting Process Opportunities	Stable	+++	+	+++
	Occasional	+++	++	+

valuable models, with a preference for the first model when the network shows the potential to strongly increase new Business Opportunities, and for the second one when the combination of the business structures allow to maximize processes synergies.

4 Analysis Dimensions

In this step we identify which are the analysis dimensions through which assess a potential pool of companies in order to evaluate the possibility that their aggregation brings to new Business Opportunities, Core Process Opportunities and Supporting Process Opportunities, that is, to fulfill the strategic goals that have been defined in the previous step. Firstly it is necessary to identify and assess the business model of each company included in the pool of potential partners using an appropriate framework of analysis. We propose to focus on two main perspectives represented by the strategic business in which the company operates and the processes implemented to plan and manage the operations. From the theoretical view the analysis of strategic business of the company could be obtained by using the Abell [22] definition of Segments of Business: "A business may be defined in three dimensions. Customer groups describe categories of customers, or *who* is being satisfied. Customer functions describe customer needs, or *what* is being satisfied. Technologies describe the way, or *how* customer needs are satisfied" . Thus with the Abell analysis the business model is represented through the use of this three dimensions, and in particular:

- Served Customer Group concerns the customer segments that can be interested to the products or to the services of the enterprise;
- Served customer function is finalized to underline the needs that the enterprise intends to satisfy;
- Technologies utilized suggest the alternative ways in which the need can be satisfied.

In order to evaluate the process capabilities we suggest the Porter's [21] value chain approach, which is based on the identification and evaluation of 'primary' and 'supporting' activities. The first ones are directly involved in the logistics and operations flow, and are:

- Inbound Logistics: includes receiving, storing, inventory control, transportation scheduling.
- Operations: includes machining, packaging, assembly, equipment maintenance, testing and all other value-creating activities that transform the inputs into the final product.
- Outbound Logistics: the activities required to get the finished product to the customers: warehousing, order fulfillment, transportation, distribution management.
- Marketing and Sales: The activities associated with getting buyers to purchase the product including channel selection, advertising, promotion, selling, pricing, retail management, etc.
- Service: the activities that maintain and enhance the product's value, including customer support, repair services, installation, training, spare parts management, upgrading, etc.

The second ones facilitate the primary activities, and are represented by:

- Procurement: procurement of raw materials, servicing, spare parts, buildings, machines, etc.
- Technology Development: includes technology development to support the value chain activities, such as Research and Development, Process automation, design, redesign.
- Human Resource Management: the activities associated with recruiting, development (education), retention and compensation of employees and managers.
- Firm Infrastructure: includes general management, planning management, legal, finance, accounting, public affairs, quality management. etc.

The results of the analysis conducted thorough the above mentioned models has to be integrated by the assessment of the critical resources hold by each company, following the resource based view [23]. According to this view, firms resources "include all assets, capabilities, organizational processes, firms attributes, information, knowledge, etc.; controlled by a firm that enable the firm to conceive of and implement strategies that improve its efficiency and effectiveness" [24].

Finally the evaluation process on a single firm basis should be completed with a financial statement analysis in order to measure the economic performance and appraise the financial position of the company.

Evaluating and consolidating all the information gathered in a network perspective will allow to define the types of occasional/stable Business/Process Opportunities that in turn allow to identify the most appropriate strategic mission for the collaborative network. Particularly the strategic business analysis will be implemented on a network basis to assess the capability of a pool of companies to generate new Business Opportunities and to understand how potential partner compete each other and complement each other.

On the other side, the identification of the business processes and the critical resources of the companies together with the performance measurement will allow to assess the capabilities to obtain new Process Opportunities and to understand how competent and competitive is each firm in terms of cost and delivery. It is noteworthy that our definition of Supporting Process Opportunities is based on a concept of supporting activities that matches with the Porter's definition of Firm Infrastructure supporting activity. As far as the other Porter's supporting activities are concerned, it is necessary a further investigation to asses if they could bring to Core Process Opportunities or just Supporting Process Opportunities, depending on the type of synergy that the network could allow. For example, the Procurement activity in a network organization may not be considered just as a supporting activity, due to its high potential of increase the economic value added (as in the case of an extended Collaborative Procurement agreement between companies).

5 Conclusions

In the paper, we presented a general framework to investigate the missing conceptual steps that link the network vision to the definition of a strategic network mission. The choice of the strategic goals for the collaborative network is a crucial analytical phase that determines the most appropriate form of alliance. In general, when analyzing a pool of company that wants to collaborate, strategic network goals are not defined 'a priori', but should be the result of an assessment of the possible opportunities deriving from the collaboration. Firstly we identified a different level of possible strategic goals, Primary and Secondary on the basis of the different impact on value added creation. Primary strategic goals can be achieved through the turnover increase generated by new products and market developments (new Business Opportunities), as well as through an operative cost decrease obtainable through the increase of the effectiveness of the core operational activities (Core Process Opportunities). Secondary strategic goals are obtained through the benefits deriving from the collaborative implementation of supporting activities.

The impact and the persistence (stable/occasional) of these opportunities influence the choice of the most appropriate collaborative network form. To asses the opportunities that can potentially arise from an aggregation of a pool of partner a general framework is identified. This framework will be further developed in more detail and tested on real case study, arising from a project commissioned to the University of Perugia, concerning a pool of companies belonging to an industrial cluster of the metal-mechanic industry in Italy.

References

1. Vitro, R.A. (ed.): The knowledge economy in development: perspectives for effective partnerships, Washington, D.C (2005)
2. Cowan, R., Foray, D.: The Economics of Codification and the Diffusion of Knowledge. Industrial and Corporate Change 6(3), 595–622 (1997)
3. Mokyr, J.: The Gifts of Athena: Historical Origins of the Knowledge Economy. Princeton University Press, Princeton (2002)
4. Williamson, O.E.: Markets and Hierarchies. Free Press, New York (1975)
5. Jack, S.L.: Approaches to studying networks: Implications and outcomes. Journal of Business Venturing 25, 120–137 (2010)
6. Ricciardi, A.: Le reti di imprese. Vantaggi competitivi e pianificazione strategica. Franco Angeli, Milano (2003)

7. Antonelli, V., et al.: Le coalizioni aziendali. Caratteri del fenomeno e forme relazionali, Giappichelli, Torino (2008)
8. Bastia, P.: Gli accordi tra imprese. Fondamenti economici e strumenti informativi. CLUEB, Bologna (1989)
9. Camarinha-Matos, L.M., Afsarmanesh, H.: Collaborative networks: a new scientific discipline. Journal of Intelligent Manufacturing 16, 439–452 (2005)
10. Lewis, D.J.: Partnership for profit: structuring and managing strategic alliances. The Free Press, New York (1990)
11. Donkels, R., Lambrecht, J.: Networks and small business growth: an explanatory model. Small Business Economics 7, 273–289 (1995)
12. Macpherson, A., Holt, R.: Knowledge, learning and small firm growth: A systematic review of the evidence. Research Policy 36, 172–192 (2007)
13. Parker, S.C.: The economics of formal business networks. Journal of Business Venturing 23, 627–640 (2008)
14. Camarinha-Matos, L.M.: Collaborative Networked Organizations: Status and trends in manufacturing. Annual Reviews in Control 33, 199–208 (2009)
15. Afsarmanesh, H., Camarinha-Matos, L.M., Msanjila, S.S.: On management of 2nd generation Virtual Organizations Breeding Enviornments. Annual Reviews in Control 22, 209–219 (2009)
16. Afsarmanesh, H., Galeano, N., Camainha-Matos, L.M.: Characterization of key components, features, and operating principles of the Virtual Breeding Environment. Deliverable 21.1. ECOLEAD (2004)
17. Camarinha-Matos, L.M., Afsarmanesh, H., Galeano, N., Molina, A.: Collaborative networked organizations – Concepts and practice in manufacturing enterprises. Computers & Industrial Engineering 57, 46–60 (2009)
18. Romero, D., Molina, A.: VO breeding environments & virtual organizations integral business process management framework. Information Systems Frontiers 11, 569–597 (2009)
19. Lunghi, P., Tonelli, F., Rinaldi, R., et al.: MIGEN: Modelli e Strumenti Innovativi per la Gestione dei Network di imprse, Edizioni Anteo, Perugia, Italy (2008)
20. Botarelli, M., Taticchi, P., Cagnazzo, L.: The Virtual Development Office Framework for Business Networks: a Case Study from the Umbrian Packaging District. In: PRO-VE 2008, Poznan (September 2008)
21. Porter, M.: Competitive Advantage: creating and sustaining superior Performance. Free Press, New York (1985)
22. Abell, D.F.: Defining the business: the starting point of strategic planning. Prentice Hall, Englewood Cliffs (1980)
23. Birger, W.: A resource based view of the firm. Strategic Management Journal 5(2), 171–180 (1984)
24. Daft, R.L.: Organization theory and design. West Pub. Co., St.Paul (1983)

Creation of Dynamic Virtual Organizations for Child Abuse Prevention in the VO Breeding Environment Context

Pedro Sanz Angulo* and Juan José de Benito Martín

University of Valladolid, Industrial Engineering School.
Paseo del Cauce, 59. 47011 Valladolid, Spain
{psangulo,debenito}@eis.uva.es

Abstract. Child abuse is a serious problem in our society. In order to provide an adequate response, all the entities involved in its prevention, detection and intervention should work in collaborative networks. In this sense, our labor aims at facilitating the creation of DVOs adapted to the different abuse situations. To that end, we are working to define both a VBE in the Castilla y Leon region (Spain) and a multi-agent expert system able to facilitate the selection of partners.

Keywords: Child Abuse Prevention, Dynamic Virtual Organization, VO Breeding Environments, Partner Selection, Multi-Agent and Expert Systems.

1 Introduction

Child abuse is a universal phenomenon that our society must try to completely eradicate as soon as possible. This goal, undoubtedly ambitious, requires an intensive work in the education of every individual and, of course, in the recognition of the children's rights.

Although in recent years significant progresses have been made in this sense, our efforts must continue in order to protect children, i.e., to respond promptly and in a personalized way to each abuse situation. For this purpose, we must employ all the available resources and search for new solutions and tools.

Furthermore, all stakeholders (both entities and people) in the prevention and solution of child abuse must work together creating collaborative networks and providing to the group what they do best, i.e., their *core business*.

This need leads us to consider the formation of Dynamic Virtual Organizations (DVO) tailored to each particular abuse situation. However, the efficient creation of DVOs only is possible within the VO Breeding Environment (VBE) context.

Based on these ideas, our current work is focused both on the definition of a VBE for our region (Castilla y Leon - Spain) and on the development of a multi-agent expert software tool able to support the selection process in an efficient way.

* This work is derived from the participation of the authors in a research project financed by the Castilla y Leon region (Spain), with reference number VA009A09, entitled "Information and Communication Technologies in the Creation of Organizational Networks: Application in the Field of Child Abuse Prevention."

L.M. Camarinha-Matos et al. (Eds.): PRO-VE 2010, IFIP AICT 336, pp. 322–328, 2010.

The introduction of the VBE concept in conjunction with the use of software agents whose behavior is guided by an expert system is a novelty in the field of child abuse prevention. This combination will allow us optimizing the use of resources and facilitating communication between institutions and professionals, making possible a more agile response of the DVO created ad hoc for the abuse problem.

This document aims, first, at justifying the use of DVO-VBE concepts for the child abuse problem and, second, at presenting the tool we are developing for the selection of partners in these sceneries, the VCAP platform.

2 The Context: Child Abuse Problem and Networking

The United Nations Convention on the Rights of the Child 1989 defines child abuse as [1] "all forms of physical or mental violence, injury or abuse, neglect or negligent treatment, maltreatment or exploitation, including sexual abuse, while in the care of parent(s), legal guardian(s) or any other person who has the care of the child." In short, we can say that there is child abuse if children's rights are not respected and there is not a response to their needs [2]; we cannot forget that abuse is, primarily, the lack of good treatment.

There is a great variety of abuse types according to its forms (physical, sexual, psychological, neglect, etc.), the place, the involved actors, the degree of intensity, and so on. Each abuse situation is unique and requires, of course, a different approach: an appropriate response must be designed to each particular case. In this sense, prevention is the best possible approximation to the problem.

Prevention may take place at three different levels: a) *primary prevention* aims to decrease the incidence or onset of abuse cases, through child advocacy and special attention to their needs, b) *secondary prevention* is addressed to social groups, families or individuals classified as "high risk" to avoid some situations that end up in abuse, and finally, c) *tertiary prevention* tries to reduce the duration and severity of the consequences of the problem (stage of rehabilitation or cure). As we will see, our work can be perfectly included in the latter two levels of prevention, and especially in the tertiary one.

Networking is, clearly, the best way for creating a collaborative workspace where to achieve the pursued goals. It is based on the communication of the agents and institutions, so an optimum exchange of information, both qualitative and quantitative, must exist between them.

The originators of the sociotherapeutic networking were Speck and Attneave [3]. They created therapeutic teams to intervene in families in crisis, in the United States, in order to break destructive patterns of family relationships and provide support for alternative options. Several years later, in the eighties, Elkaim [4] carried out the first practice at European level in deprived areas of Belgium. Since then, the networking experiences have evolved and multiplied.

In our country, Spain, we find the networking pilot program of Burlada (Pamplona). Its promoters recognize that one of the challenges of any network program is to provide a process able to organize the different institutional levels and professional resources, in order to ensure the creativity and competence of each one of these instances [5].

These and other works, experiences and projects emphasize the need of networking as a means to achieve the ultimate goal of prevention and resolution of child abuse, establishing guidelines and procedures that normally are constructed ad hoc. However, they do not possess software tools capable of solving the different problems of such relationships, e.g. the need for a rapid intervention.

3 Justification of Our Work

Network collaboration must face several challenges to become a truly effective instrument to combat the child abuse problem. Every abuse case is unique, so networks must involve different components in each new situation, and even these components can vary during the performance. It is necessary, therefore, a dynamic and flexible networking model that allows the continuing evolution of resources and services, as well as the incorporation of new ones.

These inter-collaborative problems in child abuse domain are difficult to solve without considering the new organizational models and the Information and Communication Technologies (ICT) that make them possible. In this way, the DVOs are, probably, the best response to the problem.

In a DVO a set of business partners come together dynamically, on demand, and in accordance with the requirements and needs [6] of the problem, disappearing when those needs have been met. DVOs are rapid creation and fast dissolution organizations [7], constructed ad hoc the opportunity of collaboration.

However, the effective creation of a DVO only is possible in the context of what Afsarmanesh and Camarinha-Matos [8] have called Virtual Organization Breeding Environments. The VBEs are clubs of organizations prepared to work in long term relations and from which temporary coalitions emerge able to respond dynamically to the different business opportunities [9].

Obviously, there are several similarities between networking that a child abuse situation requires and the networking of the DVOs. We can start, for example, talking about the VBE. In the child abuse domain it is obvious that the VBE would be constituted by any entity or person involved in the solution: schools, social services, health centers, youth services, law enforcement agencies, state security bodies, and so on. All of them bring to the partnership their core business, what they do best, so the VBE contains all necessary processes that the abuse situation requires. In addition, these entities are required to share certain culture of work, ICT infrastructure, etc., to achieve the highest possible performance.

After identifying a new case of abuse (either in the school, or in a health center, or through a complaint at the police station or in the child line, etc.), it is time to go to the VBE and select the set of institutions and/or persons that are the best prepared to respond to the particular problem.

The union of the selected entities configures, ultimately, the DVO responsible for providing the personalized answer to the child abuse situation. Naturally, different DVOs can arise from the breeding environment to provide this response, although the selection of the best one depends both on the requirements and needs of the particular situation of abuse and on the features and capacities of the partners.

After the selection process, partners need to work together and coordinate their actions in order to find an efficient and agile solution to the problem. This operation phase lasts until an adequate response to the initial problem has been provided. That moment coincides, precisely, with the dissolution of the DVO.

In addition, whenever it is necessary, more partners can be searched, or even their number can be reduced, according to the changes of each abuse case. In short, during the operation of the DVO a reconfiguration phase can take place.

Finally, we must also notice that the entities of a particular DVO can be partners of another consortium which tries to response to a different abuse case.

4 The VCAP Multi-agent Expert Platform

Our fundamental objective is to enhance and develop a networking model through the creation of DVOs capable of facing child abuse problems in an agile and efficient way. For this purpose, it is necessary to align the VBE and DVO concepts to the child abuse domain and provide efficient tools to support its formation and operation.

In this paper we propose a multi-agent approach to support the selection process in this context. This technology provides several advantages over other proposed methods, especially for its ability to manage complex and distributed problems. But in addition, our agents have an intelligent behavior through a rule-based Expert System (ES) implemented in their decision module.

Through this platform the best combination of partners is defined dynamically, in real time, based on the system state, the predefined objectives and the features both of the problem and of the stakeholders. The identification and assignment of partners emerge from the interaction between agents, through different negotiation mechanisms. In this sense, we can introduce the Virtual Child Abuse Prevention (VCAP) concept.

4.1 Analysis of the VCAP Multi-agent Expert System

The analysis of the platform has been made following the steps defined by Nikraz, Caire and Bahri [10]. Thus, we have identified the different types of agents and users in the system, along with their responsibilities and the acquaintance relationships that exist between them. The result is the agent diagram shown in Fig. 1.

Taking into account the agent container architecture of JADE (Java Agent Development Environment), we have defined the distributed structure of the Fig. 2. As seen in this figure, there is a main container on the manager server in which the VCAP Management Agent resides, in addition to the Information Provider Agent, the Yellow Pages Agent (where the Resource Agents register their services) and the rest of agents responsible for the management of the Jade platform.

Also there are multiple remote containers: specifically, so many remote containers as institutions and professionals the breeding environment has. In each of these containers we can identify the VBE Member Agent (associated to the different actors involved in the solution) and an Access Agent for security issues.

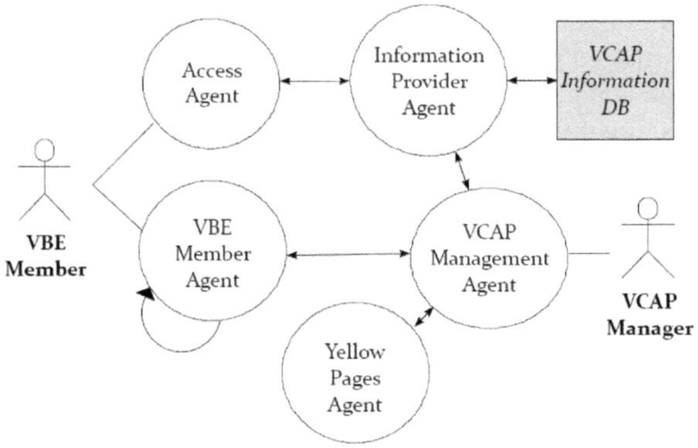

Fig. 1. Agent diagram for the VCAP platform

We have considered that all of these entities can provide their core business and, at the same time, be the promoters of the DVO formation process. It is also possible that a third entity or person starts the process, but for now we just consider that the system is open only to the VBE members. Perhaps in the future the platform can be open to everyone, but previously it is necessary to solve different security problems.

The union of these remote containers with the main container results into the distributed agent platform shown in the Fig. 2.

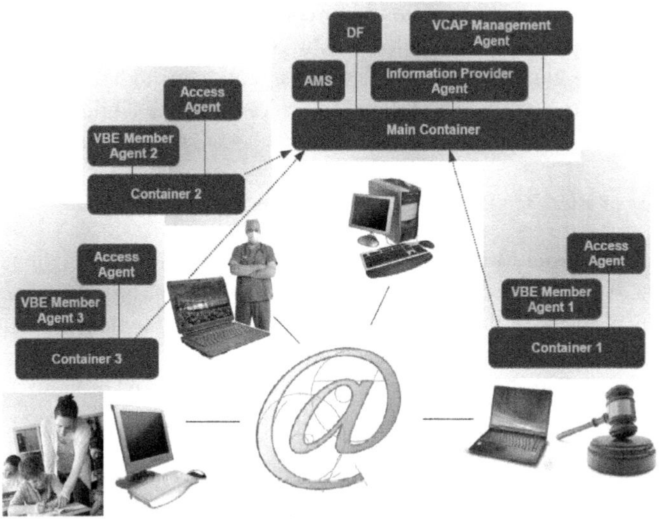

Fig. 2. Distributed structure of the VCAP platform

4.2 Current Development of the VCAP Platform

The current development of the VCAP platform is possible thanks to our experience in the creation of the DVEBreeder tool (see Fig. 3), a multi-agent expert platform developed to support the selection of partners in the enterprise domain [11].

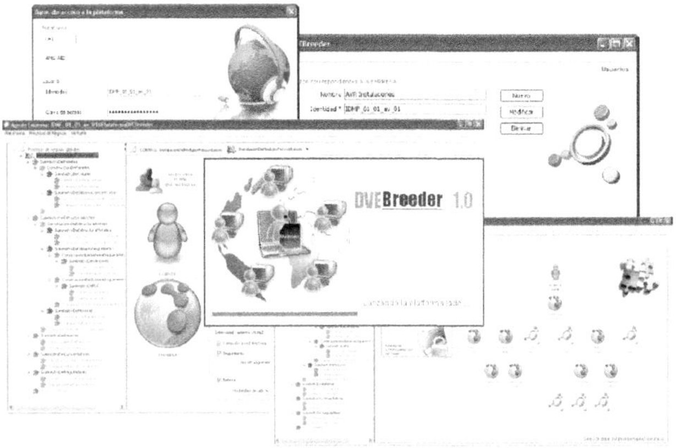

Fig. 3. Some snapshots of the DVEBreeder platform

The VCAP platform inherits many of the features of its predecessor: the integration of multi-agent and expert system technologies; the identification of the intelligent agents is made through an multi-approach model that takes into account the VBE concept; the negotiation between autonomous agents is based on the knowledge embodied in its decision modules; the communication between agents is quite simple thanks to the platform used in the MAS development (Jade); the behavior of agents is quite similar to the behavior that a human expert can have thanks to JESS, the rule-based expert system; it is flexible, dynamic and scalable; FIPA standards are met; the interface is intuitive and the code reuse is simple thanks to its open structure, etc.

In summary, VCAP is an innovative tool able to solve the CAP problem in an agile and efficient way. Fig. 4 shows a simplified scheme of the platform performance in the application domain.

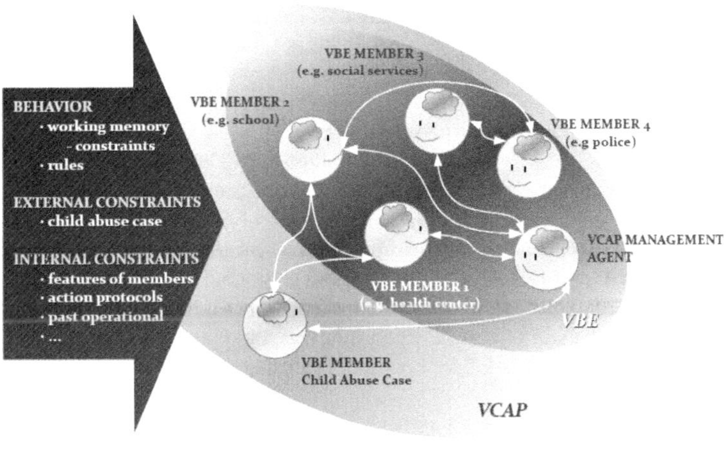

Fig. 4. Simplified scheme of the VCAP platform performance

5 Conclusions

In this article we have tried to justify the use of DVO and VBE concepts in the child abuse domain. In this sense, we also have presented a multi-agent expert solution in which DVOs emerge from the VBE context. After having done the planning and analysis, we are currently working in the design and implementation phases. To do this, we need to define some elements of the platform as e.g. the application domain ontology, service descriptions, agent decision modules, etc. Others, such as the agent interactions, message templates, interaction protocols or the ontologies for the management of the platform, are very similar to those established in the DVEBreeder tool, what will greatly facilitate the final implementation of the platform.

Acknowledgments. We would like to express our gratitude to the managers and members of REA, the Association for the Children and Youth Defense of Castilla y León, and, in particular, to Ms Mª Elena Villa Ceinos.

References

1. United Nations - Office of the High Commissioner of Human Rights. Convention on the Rights of the Child, resolution 44/25 of November 20 (1989), `http://www2.ohchr.org/english/law/crc.htm` (Last visit in February 2010)
2. Sanz, P., Villa, M.E., Manso, M.A., De Benito, J.J.: Aplicación de la Tecnología Multiagente y los Sistemas Expertos al trabajo en Red para la Prevención del Maltrato Infantil. In: IX Congreso Estatal de Infancia Maltratada, Valladolid, Spain (2008)
3. Speck, R., Attneave, C.: Redes Familiares. Amorrortu Editores, Buenos Aires (1974)
4. Elkaïm, M.: Las prácticas de la terapia de red. Gedisa, Barcelona (1989)
5. De Miguel, M., Fernández, M.: Detección precoz del maltrato infantil. Programa piloto de trabajo en red. Anales del Sistema Sanitario de Navarra 25(2), 25–34 (2002)
6. Ouzounis, E.K.: An Agent-Based Platform for the Management of Dynamic Virtual Enterprises. PhD thesis. University of Berlin (2001)
7. Browne, J., Zhang, J.: Extended and Virtual Enterprises - Similarities and Differences. International Journal of Agile Management Systems 1(1), 30–36 (1999)
8. Afsarmanesh, H., Camarinha-Matos, L.M.: A Framework for Management of Virtual Organization Breeding Environments. In: Collaborative Networks and their Breeding Environments, pp. 35–48. Springer, Boston (2005)
9. Camarinha-Matos, L.M., Afsarmanesh, H., Ollus, M.: ECOLEAD: a Holistic Approach to Creation and Management of Dynamic Virtual Organizations. In: Collaborative Networks and their Breeding Environments, pp. 3–16. Springer, Boston (2005)
10. Nikraz, M., Caire, G., Bahri, P.A.: A Methodology for the Analysis and Design of Multi-Agent Systems Using JADE. Int. J. of Computer Systems Science and Engineering (2006)
11. Sanz, P., De Benito, J.J.: Design and Implementation of a Multi-agent Framework for the Selection of Partners in Dynamic VEs. In: Leveraging Knowledge for Innovation in Collaborative Networks, pp. 341–348. Springer, Heidelberg (2009)

MAPSS, a *M*ulti-*A*spect *P*artner and *S*ervice *S*election Method

Zbigniew Paszkiewicz and Willy Picard

Department of Information Technology, Poznań University of Economics
ul. Mansfelda 4, 60-854 Poznań, Poland
{zpasz,picard}@kti.ue.poznan.pl

Abstract. In Service-Oriented Virtual Organization Breeding Environments (SOVOBEs), services performed by people, organizations and information systems are composed in potentially complex business processes performed by a set of partners. In a SOVOBE, the success of a virtual organization depends largely on the partner and service selection process, which determines the composition of services performed by the VO partners. In this paper requirements for a partner and service selection method for SOVOBEs are defined and a novel *M*ulti-*A*spect *P*artner and *S*ervice *S*election method, *MAPSS*, is presented. The MAPSS method allows a VO planner to select appropriate services and partners based on their competences and their relations with other services/partners. The MAPSS method relies on a genetic algorithm to select the most appropriate set of partners and services.

Keywords: partner selection, service selection, virtual organization creation, competence description, social requirement, genetic algorithm.

1 Introduction

A *Virtual Organization* (VO) is an operational structure consisting of different organizational entities and created for a specific business purpose, to address a specific business opportunity. The success of a VO strongly depends on all participating organizations being capable of cooperating as a single unit, which usually implies an appropriate choice of partners.

The concept of *Virtual Organization Breeding Environment* (VOBE, sometimes referred in the literature as VBE) has been proposed to facilitate, among others, the VO creation process. A VOBE is "an association of organizations with the main goal of increasing preparedness of its members towards collaboration in potential virtual organizations" [1]. A VOBE provides a set of tools and data sources that may be used in partner and service selection process, including competence repositories, negotiation tools, history of collaboration etc.

As a valuable approach for the architecture and implementations of VOBEs and integration of cooperating organizations, the Service-Oriented Architecture (SOA) [2] has been suggested [3]. In this paper, only *Service-oriented Virtual Organization Breeding Environments* (SOVOBEs) are taken into account. In a SOVOBE, VOBE

L.M. Camarinha-Matos et al. (Eds.): PRO-VE 2010, IFIP AICT 336, pp. 329–337, 2010.

and VO operations are based on services performed by people, organizations and information systems, composed in potentially complex business processes.

Selection of services is usually separated from the concept of selection of partners. While service selection is a concept investigated by the distributed systems community (especially in terms of SOA), partner selection is a subject of interest of mainly the collaborative networked organization (CNOs) community. Nevertheless, in most methods presented in the works from both communities, it is possible to distinguish two elements: first, an *information model* captures and structures information about artifacts based on which the selection is performed. Second, various *selection techniques* have been proposed, focusing on the selection context, scope of the selection and selection strategy.

Partner selection is strongly connected with the idea of competence modelling [4]. The research works on competence modelling aim at providing a structural description of organizations with a special emphasis on competences, profiles, capacities, resources etc. [5, 6]. The concept of competence modelling is now developing rapidly and some works referring to partner selection based on organization profiles have been published [6, 7]. In a competence-based approach, inclusion of service characteristics is marginal [5] or not present at all [6].

In [8, 9], the *selection of services* is based on an information model consisting of service descriptions. A service description usually includes a wide range of technical, functional, non-functional and business characteristics of a given service [10]. In [11, 12] opinions concerning services and user feedback are taken into account. However, these works do not take advantage of the concepts elaborated in the area of competence modelling so proposed descriptions of service providers are often not structured, consisting of a simple list of attributes. Moreover, while the importance of social aspects in SOA has been noted recently [13, 14, 15], existing approaches are not mature and models for social relations and modelling requirements based on these relations are still to be developed. As a example, Ding and al. [16] have proposed a simulation-optimization approach using genetic search for supplier selection, integrating performance estimation, social aspects and genetic algorithm. However, the social relation model encompasses only a simple social model for supply chains limited to only one relation type, i.e. customer-supplier.

A number of selection strategies have been proposed for partner selection. The conclusion of the comparison of various popular approaches presented in [8] and [17] is that genetic algorithms are the most popular approach.

The main contribution of this paper is *MAPSS*, a novel method for *M*ulti-*A*spect *P*artner and *S*ervice *S*election in SOVOBEs supporting social aspects, competences of VO participants and performance characteristic. The proposed method has been implemented in the *ErGo* system within the ITSOA project [18].

This paper is organized as follows. In Section 2, basic notions related with collaboration in SOVOBEs are presented. In Section 3, the main requirements for the selection method are presented. In Section 4, a general outline of the method is described. The proposed information model is shortly described in Section 5 while the selection technique is the subject of Section 6. Finally, Section 7 concludes the paper.

2 Basic Notions

A business process is "a set of one or more linked procedures or activities which collectively realise a business objective or policy goal, normally within the context of an organisational structure defining functional roles and relationships" [19].

A *business process definition* consists traditionally of "a network of activities and their relationships, criteria to indicate the start and termination of the process, and information about the individual activities, such as participants, associated IT applications and data, etc." [19]. The set of activities and their relations is referred to as *business process structure*. An aim of each partner and service selection method for VOs is to identify process participants and services that can perform activities identified in a process structure. In the presented approach, each activity is performed by a *process participant* consuming a *service* provided by a *service provider*. A *process element* may refer to a process participant, a service or a service provider. Process participants and service providers are called *partners*. A *role* is a set of requirements that a potential partner or service has to satisfy to be assigned to a particular process element. Roles are in M:N relation with process elements.

Among requirements defining a role, social requirements concern relations with other roles. Examples of relations are past cooperation, recognition, former financial exchange, etc. The set of roles assigned to process elements and the relations among these roles are referred as a *social network schema*. A *social protocol* is a business process structure supplemented with social network schema.

3 Requirements for a Partner and Service Selection Method in SOVOBEs

The following requirements have been defined for a partner and service selection method:

- human control over the process – in context of complex business processes selection can hardly be fully automated;
- support for social aspects,
- support for competence descriptions,
- requirement-based approach – verification of social and non-social requirements coming from multiple sources (SOVOBE, VO planner, potential VO customers, etc.) defined for various elements of VO (process, partner, etc.)
- definition of VO planner's preferences,
- multi-variant analysis – evaluation of various partner and service compositions to maximize requirements satisfaction;
- indicator-based verification of VO network structure and performance characteristics, following a reference model proposed in [20].

4 Overview of the *MAPSS* Method

The *MAPSS* method consists in five phases and follows the general selection method guidelines presented in [21]:

1. definition of VO specification – definition of requirements and associated preferences (importance, acceptable level of satisfaction etc.);
2. selection of partners and services for roles – selection of candidate elements; the output of this phase is a set of partners or services for each role defined in the social protocol;
3. VO variant generation – optimization of elements composition according to some fitness criteria defined by VO planner, this phase includes comparison of best possible VO variants; as an output a sorted set of variants is generated – a level of requirements satisfaction according to VO planner preferences is used as a sorting criteria;
4. performance evaluation – assignment of selected elements to process activities and validation of performance requirements;
5. VO inception – registration of the new VO in competence and service repository.

In every phase, human action may lead to requirements redefinition, preference modification, repetition of a steps, and reconfiguration of used supporting tools.

5 MAPSS Information Model

5.1 Competence and Service Description Modules

In the *MAPSS* method, the description of services is extended with additional information concerning the organization providing these services (service providers). The additional description concerning the service providers takes the form of a competence description, based on the 4-C model [5], based on four key concepts: competence, capability, cost, and conspicuity. The competence and service description modules provide the following features used by *MAPSS*:

- structured description of organization competences and services,
- competence-based search of organizations based on submitted criteria consisting in required competences or other aspects described in model,
- evaluation of the conformance of an organization to a set of defined competence-based requirements,
- service description search based on submitted criteria consisting of required values of fields in service description,
- evaluation of the conformance of a service to a set of service description requirements.

5.2 Social Network Module

A social network is implemented as a graph of *nodes*, which may be connected by *relations*. The social network module provides information about the existence of relations among organizations and services registered in a SOVOBE. Relations in a social network are typed and contain a set of attributes. The social network module provides the functionality of verification of relations among organization. The module validates the level of conformance of a set of organizations to a set of social requirements.

5.3 Indicator Module

In SOVOBEs, various services, provided either by the SOVOBE itself or SOVOBE members, may be considered as data sources which may be aggregated into indicators [20]. Indicators may allow a VO planner for definition of complex requirements involving various aspects, e.g. competences and social relations, of the planned VO in a single indicator. An important application of indicators is the verification of information from one data source by other data sources, e.g. information provided by organization in competence description may be confronted with the collaboration history stored in SOVOBE bag of assets. The indicator module provides the functionality of indicator definition, storage and reuse.

5.4 Monitoring Module

The *MAPSS* method is accompanied by a monitoring mechanism. The monitoring mechanism is based on the *Observer* design pattern [22]. A VO planner, being the Observer, may define indicators referring to objects (i.e. competence) and values (i.e. resource amount) existing in SOVOBE or events (i.e. registration of new organization with particular competence, update of service parameters, changes in the social network). When events or changes concerning objects or values occur, indicators are recalculated. If the indicator reaches a predefined alarm level, the VO planner is informed and may potentially change the set of services that has already been selected.

6 *MAPSS* Selection Technique

The *MAPSS* selection technique consists of 5 phases as presented in Section 4.

Phase 1: Definition of VO specification

A *virtual organization specification* consists of:

- a set of *requirements* concerning various *aspects* of the virtual organization;
- *preferences* – optimal, reject values and weights referring to requirements defined for selection process;
- *fitness functions* – global fitness functions, and multi-attribute utility functions used in the second and third phase;
- acceptable requirement conformance levels to limit the size of various sets of process elements generated during the execution of *MAPSS*.

Aspects of VO specification include: process elements, process, subsets of partners and subsets of services. It is possible to distinguish three types of requirements:

- *roles* referring to elements, e.g. localization, required set of competences, level of available resources, response time of a service, cost of the service; requirements are based on the competence and service description model;
- *social requirements* referring to structure of relations among organizations and services, e.g. past cooperation, recognition, use of service, recommendation; the main source of social requirements is a social network schema, but indicators may also provide the VO planner with means to define social requirements.

- *performance requirements* referring to evaluation of composition of partners and services in a process in terms of performance, e.g. maximum time of process duration or maximum time of sub-process response time.

Table 1 presents the structure of VO specification and the potential use of different requirements types in various phases of MAPSS.

Table 1. VO specification structure

Aspects	Roles	Social req.	Performance req.
Partner	Phase 2	-	-
Service	Phase 2	-	-
Subset of partners	-	Phase 3	-
Subset of services	-	Phase 3	Phase 4
Process	-	-	Phase 4

Phase 2: Selection of partners and services for roles
Based on role requirements, a set of services or organizations are selected for each role. Identified elements may be sorted and filtered out according to the level of conformance to the associated role requirements.

Phase 3: Generation of VO variants
The number of potential VOs that may be constituted with services and organizations identified in phase 2 is usually high. The goal of the third phase is to search in the usually large domain of potential VOs a sorted list of VO *variants* ranked according to a *fitness function.* A VO variant is a set of services and organizations assigned to the roles defined in phase 1 of the *MAPSS* method.

In phase 3, a genetic algorithm is used for the determination of the best fitted VO variants, as illustrated in Figure13. The genome *g* is an array of N items, *N* being the number of roles. Genes *re* are sets of partners or services selected in phase 2 and assigned to roles *r* from the genome *g*.

The crossover operator is the standard two-point crossover, while the mutation operator randomly selects a role (a position in the genome) and randomly replaces the corresponding partner or service with another one among those available from the set of elements assigned to this role. In this way the genetic algorithm creates many VO variants. Each variant is evaluated with the use of the fitness function defined by VO planner in VO specification. The *fitness function* used in this phase estimates the level of satisfaction of social requirements. The result of this phase is a sorted set of VO variants. The value of the fitness function calculated for each VO variant is used as sorting criteria. A *threshold value* defined with the VO planner in phase 1 is used to filter out the VO variants: VO variants for which the value of the fitness function is below the threshold value are not passed to phase 4.

Phase 4: Performance evaluation
The goal of phase 4 is to establish a *ranking* of VO variants selected in phase 3 according to a *fitness performance function.* The fitness performance function is defined by the VO planner, based on the performance requirements defined in phase 1. A fitness performance function may take into account various performance aspects,

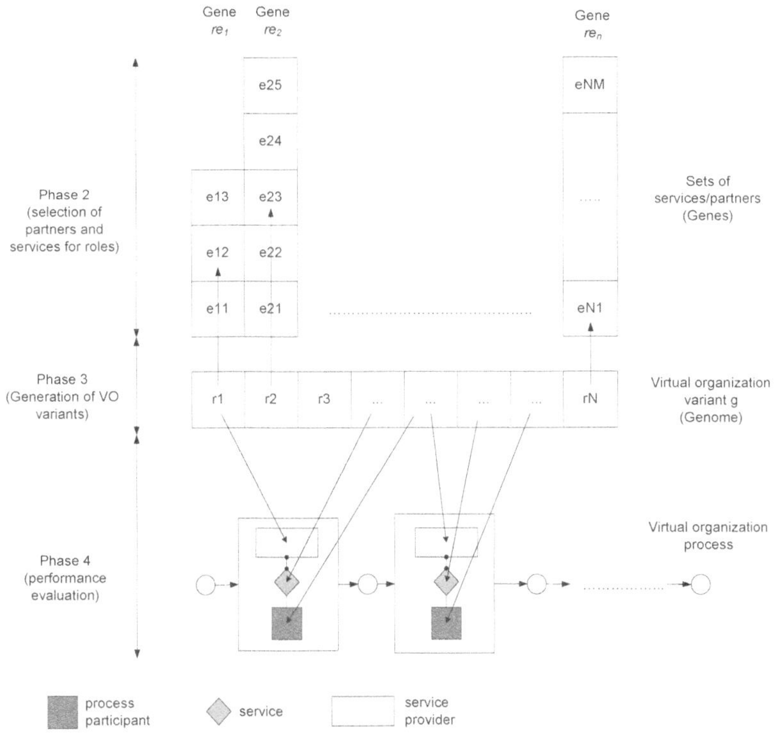

Fig. 1. Phases 2-4 of MAPSS

including operational performance, effectiveness, responsiveness, cost, social relations among VO elements.

The values of a fitness performance function may be vectors, where each vector component is associated with the evaluation of a particular performance aspect. A *ranking function* is responsible for sorting the values of the fitness performance function for the VO variants. As a consequence, various performance evaluations may be performed on a given set of VO variants, either with different fitness performance functions, or with difference ranking functions.

Phase 5: VO continuance

The VO variant proposed as the best ranked in phase 4 is registered as a VO in the SOVOBE, i.e. the VO is registered in the competence description module as a new organization in SOVOBE, having non-empty set of competences and non-empty set of services.

Technical implementation

The *MAPSS* method has been implemented as part of the *ErGo* system developed within the ITSOA project [18], in the Java programming language. The functionality provided by the *MAPSS* modules is exposed as OSGi services [23] within the Equinox container [24] and can be externalized as SOAP web services. Modularity of the system supports exchange of system modules, e.g. other implementation of competence and service description, and social network modules can be used.

7 Conclusions

The main contribution presented in this paper is a novel method for multi-aspect service selection, integrating competencies, social aspects and performance. While each of these topics have already been studied, the novelty of the proposed method lays in their combination.

The method proposes a structured approach to requirement definition in a form of VO specification. This approach distinguishes different requirement types, method phases for their use and selection technique for verification of their satisfaction. In particular social requirements are considered.

The potential involvement of the VO planner at various steps of the proposed method, combined with the possibility to loop back to formerly performed steps, meets the complex, often iterative, nature of partner and service selection. However, it results in a potentially undetermined duration of the method execution.

The important issue of privacy related with information about SOVOBE members is not taken into account in the proposed method. As a consequence, it is assumed that all information related with competencies, social relations and performance are publicly available, which is usually not wanted in real cases.

The method was implemented as a part of the *ErGo* system.

Among future works, the *MAPSS* method should be extended to encompass the collaborative nature of the partner and service selection process. In its current form, the *MAPSS* method is based on the assumption that a VO planner is the only responsible person/organization for the selection process.

Within the IT-SOA project [18], further development of the proposed method and its verification is planned with a pilot application in the construction sector.

Acknowledgments. This work has been partially supported by the Polish Ministry of Science and Higher Education within the European Regional Development Fund, Grant No. POIG.01.03.01-00-008/08.

References

1. Camarinha-Matos, L.M., Afsarmanesh, H., Ollus, M.: ECOLEAD and CNO Base Concepts. In: Methods and Tools for Collaborative Networked Organizations, pp. 3–32. Springer, US (2008)
2. OASIS: OASIS Reference Architecture Foundation for Service Oriented Architecture 1.0. Committee Draft 02 (2009), `http://docs.oasis-open.org/soa-rm/soa-ra/v1.0/soa-ra-cd-02.pdf`
3. Rabelo, R., Gusmeroli, S.: The ECOLEAD Collaborative Business Infrastructure for Networked Organizations. In: Camarinha-Matos, L.M., Picard, W. (eds.) Pervasive Collaborative Networks, PRO-VE 2008, pp. 451–462. Springer, Heidelberg (2008)
4. Gallon, M., Stillman, H., Coates, D.: Putting Core Competency Thinking Into Practice. Research Technology Management 38(3), 20–29 (1995)

5. Ermilova, E., Afsarmanesh, H.: Competency Modeling Targeted on Boosting Configuration of Virtual Organizations. Production planning and control. The management of operation 21(2), 103–118 (2010) (special issue)
6. Pepiot, G., Cheikhrouhou, N., Furbringer, J.M., Glardon, R.: UECML: Unified Enterprise Competence Modelling Language. Computers in Industry 58, 130–142 (2007), `http://www.sciencedirects.com`
7. Ermilova, E., Afsarmanesh, H.: Competency and Profiling Management in Virtual Organization Breeding Environments. In: Camarinha Network-Centric Collaboration and Supporting Frameworks, pp. 131–142. Springer, Heidelberg (2007)
8. Canfora, G., Di Penta, M., Esposito, R., Villani, M.L.: An Approach for QoS-aware Service Composition Based on Genetic Algorithms. In: Proceedings of the 2005 conference on Genetic and evolutionary computation, pp. 1069–1075 (2005)
9. Mueller, E.: Production Planning and Operation in Competence-Cell Based Networks. Production Planning and Control 17(2), 99–112 (2006)
10. The Open Group: TOGAF version 9. Enterprise Edition (2009), `http://www.opengroup.org/togaf/`
11. Claro, D.B., Albers, P., Hao, J.K.: Selecting Web Services for Optimal Composition. In: International Workshop on Semantic and Dynamic Web Processes (ICWS) (2005)
12. Jaeger, M.C., Mühl, G.: QoS-based Selection of Services: The Implementation of a Genetic Algorithm. In: KiVS 2007 Workshop: Service-Oriented Architectures und ServiceOriented Computing (SOA/SOC) (2007)
13. Jarimo, T., Salo, A.: - Multicriteria Partner Selection in Virtual Organizations With Transportation Costs and Other Network Interdependencies. IEEE Transactions on systems, man, and cybernetics—part C: Applications and reviews 39(1), 124–129 (2009)
14. Świerzowicz, J., Picard, W.: Social Requirements for Virtual Organization Breeding Environments. In: Leveraging Knowledge for Innovation in Collaborative Networks, PRO-VE 2009, pp. 614–622. Springer, Heidelberg (2009)
15. Picard, W.: Social Protocols for Agile Virtual Teams. In: Leveraging Knowledge for Innovation in Collaborative Networks, PRO-VE 2009, pp. 168–176. Springer, Heidelberg (2009)
16. Ding, H., Benyoucef, L., Xie, X.: A Simulation-Optimization Approach Using Genetic Search for Supplier Selection. In: Proceed. 2003 Winter Simulation Conf. (2003)
17. Crispim, J.A., Sousa, J.P.: Multiple Criteria Partner Selection in Virtual Enterprises. In: Establishing the Foundation of Collaborative Networks, pp. 197–206. Springer, Heidelberg (2007)
18. ITSOA project, `http://www.soa.edu.pl`
19. Workflow Management Coalition: The Workflow Management Coalition Specification Terminology & Glossary, Doc. Nr. WFMC-TC-1011, Doc. Status - Issue 3.0 (February 1999)
20. Paszkiewicz, Z., Picard, W.: Reference Model for Performance Management in Service-Oriented Virtual Organization Breeding Environments. In: Leveraging Knowledge for Innovation in Collaborative Networks, PRO-VE 2009, pp. 505–513. Springer, Heidelberg (2009)
21. Camarinha-Matos, L.M., Oliveira, A.I., Ratti, R., Demsar, D., Baldo, F., Jarimo, T.: A Computer-Assisted VO Creation Framework. In: Establishing the Foundation of Collaborative Networks, pp. 165–178. Springer, Heidelberg (2007)
22. Gamma, E., Helm, R., Johnson, R., Vlissides, J.: Design Patterns: Elements of Reusable Object-Oriented Software. Addison Wesley Professional, Reading (1994)
23. OSGi - The Dynamic Module System for Java, `http://www.osgi.org/`
24. Equinox, `http://www.eclipse.org/equinox/`

Managing the Competencies of Team Members in Design Projects through Multi-period Task Assignment

Onanong Hlaoittinun, Eric Bonjour, and Maryvonne Dulmet

Institute FEMTO-ST UMR CNRS 6174, Department AS2M
24, Rue Alain Savary, 25000 Besançon, France
{onanong.hlaoittinun,eric.bonjour,maryvonne.dulmet}@ens2m.fr

Abstract. Product design projects involve multiple team members with various knowledge and competencies that have to evolve with time, due to rapid organizational, technological and marketing changes. Project managers require management methods to optimize the assignment of tasks to human resources according to their competency levels and the need for competency evolution. In this paper, we tackle this optimization problem in the context of multiple design projects and multiple periods. The model we propose seeks to minimize two function objectives: (i) minimize the supplementary salary cost due to the extended task duration when using under-competent employees and (ii) minimize the financial penalties when the competency goals have not been reached. This problem has been solved by means of a simulated annealing -based optimization algorithm.

Keywords: Project management, Design project, Task assignment, Multi-skilled Resource allocation, Competency modeling.

1 Introduction

In product development projects, project managers face highly complex situations in which they have to deal with a great number of components with their interactions, a multiplicity of design tasks with their interdependencies, and a great number of team members with their evolution in competencies. They have to make difficult decisions concerning the allocation of numerous team members to design tasks.

The rapid evolution of technology in product design and business process re-engineering often results in a change in the definition of design tasks. Consequently, R&D departments can suffer from a lack of competencies and may be unable to design future innovative products. In this paper, we are interested in tackling the problem of managing the team members' competencies and their evolution during the execution of design projects. This issue becomes one of the greatest concerns of project managers.

It has been commonly accepted that an appropriate task assignment can either maintain or improve the competency level of the team member assigned to the corresponding task. So project managers need methods to help them to optimize task assignments and to ensure that the evolution of team members' competencies is relevant to the objectives of future projects.

L.M. Camarinha-Matos et al. (Eds.): PRO-VE 2010, IFIP AICT 336, pp. 338–345, 2010.

Research works concerning task assignment problem can be classified according to two criteria: "single-period" or "multi-period" task assignment and "static" or "dynamic" competency modeling. "Single-period" task assignment refers to the situation in which all tasks are considered as a single group, in other words, when time constraints between tasks have not been taken into account. "Multi-period" task assignment concerns the situation in which precedence constraints have been considered. "Static" competency modeling represents the situation in which the levels of competency for each actor are unchanged during the execution of tasks. "Dynamic" competency modeling aims at representing and simulating the evolution of the competency level for each actor during the execution of tasks.

These criteria, when combined, help us to divide related works into four categories.

The first category concerns "mono-period" task assignment with "static" modeling of competency. This is the easiest case because there is a single group of tasks to be assigned and competency levels are unvaried during the task execution.

The second category concerns "mono-period" task assignment with "dynamic" competency modeling [1]. This category concerns the evolution of competency levels but these competency levels are measured and followed during only one period (at the beginning and at the end). So, this task assignment model is not aimed to plan competency levels of actors in the long term. However, it needs incorporating learning and forgetting curves in the decision model.

The third category deals with "multi-period" task assignment with "static" competency modeling [2-3]. In project scheduling problems, this problem is called MSPSP which stands for Multi-skill Project Scheduling Problem. For instance, Bellenguez-Morineau [2] proposes a method that solves the MSPSP problem and ensures that the assigned actors are competent enough to carry out project tasks. This method seeks to minimize the total completion time of the project (Cmax).

The fourth category concerns "multi-period" task assignment with "dynamic" competency modeling [4-5]. The authors propose a model that optimizes the long term resource allocation. The evolution of competency (learning effect and knowledge depreciation) is also considered. The authors assume that the competency level of the assigned person will increase in accordance to the number of periods he/she activates this competency and his/her learning rate. Similarly, the competency level of a particular actor will decline in accordance to a knowledge depreciation rate if this actor has not been assigned to tasks corresponding to this competency. However, the authors have not modeled design project environments [4] or they have not focused on competency-based objectives [5].

Because of the increasing importance of competency evolution in the field of project management and due to a lack of research works concerning this issue, we are interested, in this paper, in dealing with the latter type of problem described above.

In competency modeling, Harzallah et al. suggests the CRAI model (Competency, Resource, Aspect, Individual), associated with axioms based on set theory [6]. Competencies are characterized by sets of knowledge, know-how and behavior associated to a context and linked to individual actors. Based on a classical evaluation of the "knowledge", "know-how" and "behavior" characteristics, a mathematical aggregation is suggested to provide a quantitative evaluation of competencies. Boucher et al. [7] propose a literature review of competency management from a performance point of view. They underline that the characterization of competency is a first step for modeling the development of competency and improving goals of competency management.

Different attributes of competency have been used in the field of team formation to model competency, such as qualification (0 or 1) [8], technical knowledge, skills and know-how [9-10], psycho-sociological capacities or personal traits [11]. In the rest of this paper, to simplify the terminology, the concept of knowledge will cover all these attributes.

The organization of this paper is as follows: Section 2 presents the main steps of the task assignment modeling we propose. Section 3 outlines the mathematical formulation and the optimization approach for the considered problem. To illustrate the interests of this approach, simulation results are presented and shortly discussed in section 4. Section 5 sums up the paper and opens new directions of research.

2 Proposition for Modeling Multi-period Task Assignment

The method we propose is decomposed into four main stages of modeling that will be shortly outlined in this part.

2.1 Identifying Relevant Knowledge to Characterize Tasks and Actors

We define a generic set of tasks, indexed by i (i=1,…,M), a set of projects, indexed by l (l = 1, ..., P), a set of periods, indexed by k, (k = 1, ..., K), a set of actors, indexed by j (j = 1, ..., N) and a set of knowledge, indexed by c, (c = 1, ..., C).

We can classify two types of tasks used in multi-period task planning: generic and specific tasks. Each generic task T_i corresponds to one competency and covers a class of specific tasks $T_i^{k,l}$ sharing the same knowledge but with different performance levels, depending on period k and project l.

Task characterization. Performance levels concerning a task can be characterized by two types of expertise levels: competency level and knowledge level. The variable $rq_i^{k,l}$ represents the competency level required by specific task $T_i^{k,l}$. The variable $r1_{i,c}^{k,l}$ represents the performance level in knowledge c required by specific task $T_i^{k,l}$. We assume that $r1_{i,c}^{k,l} = rq_i^{k,l} \times r1_{i,c}$, where $r1_{i,c}$ is the performance level in knowledge c required by the generic task i.

Actor characterization. The variable $r2_{c,j}^{k}$ represents the performance level in knowledge c that is acquired by actor j in period k. We assume that the performance levels in knowledge c evolve during the task execution and depend on period k.

2.2 Calculating the "A priori" Compatibility Level and the Work Efficiency

The compatibility level aims at estimating the similarity between specific task $T_i^{k,l}$ and actor j before the assignment of tasks in period k. This similarity is computed for each actor j by penalizing his/her insufficient performance level for each type of knowledge according to the performance level required by $T_i^{k,l}$ (Equation 1). This indicator has been presented in detail in [12]. The value of this indicator is included between 0 and 1.

$$v3_{i,j}^{k,l} = r1_{i,\bullet}^{k,l} \circ r2_{\bullet,j}^{k-1} = 1 - \frac{\sum_{c=1}^{O} \max(0, r1_{i,c}^{k,l} - r2_{c,j}^{k-1})}{\sum_{c=1}^{O} r1_{i,c}^{k,l}}, 0 \le v3_{i,j}^{k,l} \le 1. \quad (1)$$

The compatibility level helps to select the appropriate actor for the kth assignment by turning it into the coefficient of work efficiency. We suppose that the time spent on a task has to be adjusted according to the "a priori" compatibility level $v3_{i,j}^{k,l}$. Therefore, there will be additional costs due to the assignment of specific task $T_i^{k,l}$ to under-competent actor *j*. We introduce the coefficient of work efficiency $\gamma_{i,j}^{k,l}$ (Equation 2 - note that $\gamma_{i,j}^{k,l}=1$ if $v3_{i,j}^{k,l}=1$, that is, if the actor is competent). Then this coefficient is used to compute the actual execution time of specific task $T_i^{k,l}$ for actor *j*: $\gamma_{i,j}^{k,l} \times L_i^{k,l}$, where the theoretical time $L_i^{k,l}$ is given. This indicator is explained in detail in [13].

$$\gamma_{i,j}^{k,l} = 2 - v3_{i,j}^{k,l}. \quad (2)$$

2.3 Propagating the Evolution of Competency after Each Period of Task Assignment

We assume that if actor A_j is allocated to task $T_i^{k,l}$ (that is, $x_{i,j}^{k,l}>0$), this actor either maintains his/her performance level in knowledge *c* if $r1_{i,c}^{k,l} \ge r2_{c,j}^{k}$ or develops this performance level in knowledge *c* if $r1_{i,c}^{k,l} < r2_{c,j}^{k}$. If actor *j* is not allocated to task $T_i^{k,l}$ (that is, $x_{i,j}^{k,l} = 0$), his/her performance level in knowledge *c* will decrease. To shorten this paper, we have not presented in detail how we have modeled the competency evolution.

2.4 Calculating the "A posteriori" Compatibility Level (Competency Level)

The variable $r3_{i,j}^{k}$ estimates the competency level of actor *j* for generic task T_i (that is, the compatibility between actor *j* and generic task T_i). This variable is calculated at the end of period *k* when actor *j* has carried out the tasks he/she has been responsible for.

$$r3_{i,j}^{k} = r1_{i,\bullet} \circ r2_{\bullet,j}^{k} = 1 - \frac{\sum_{c=1}^{O} \max(0, r1_{i,c} - r2_{c,j}^{k})}{\sum_{c=1}^{O} r1_{i,c}}, 0 \le r3_{i,j}^{k} \le 1. \quad (3)$$

3 Mathematical Formulation for the Task Assignment Problem

The proposed model is based on the following assumptions:

- An under-competent actor could be assigned to a task but he/she will be accompanied by a trainer (or teaching tutor), which will generate additional costs to the project.
- Each assigned task is supposed to be carried out with success.

- There is no load constraint for tutors
- The actor's capacity can be estimated in any time unit (day, month, etc). This capacity is supposed to exclude all the absence time due to the unavailability of employees (planned/unplanned absence, legal and social constraints, etc.)

The overall objective function, the cost functions and the constraints that are used in the proposed task assignment model are described as follows:

$$\text{Min}\left\{\left[\sum_{k=1}^{K}\sum_{l=1}^{P}\sum_{i=1}^{M}\sum_{j=1}^{N}\left[(\gamma_{i,j}^{k,l}\times L_i^{k,l})\times S_j+(\gamma_{i,j}^{k,l}-1)\times L_i^{k,l}\times ST\right]x_{i,j}^{k,l}\right]+\sum_{i=1}^{M}\varphi_i(O_i-R_i)\right\}. \quad (4)$$

$$\sum_{j=1}^{N}x_{i,j}^{k,l}=1 \quad ,\forall i=1,...M,\forall l=1,...,P,\forall k=1,...,K \quad (5)$$

$$\sum_{i=1}^{M}\sum_{l=1}^{P}\gamma_{i,j}^{k,l}L_i^{k,l}x_{i,j}^{k,l}\le LM_{j,k},\forall j=1,...N,\forall k=1,...K \quad (6)$$

$$0\le x_{i,j}^{k,l}\le 1,\forall i,j,k,l;\quad x_{i,j}^{k,l}\in R^{+} \quad (7)$$

The optimization of the assignment problem aims at minimizing the total project costs by determining the best assignment of tasks to actors. The overall objective function is split up into three criteria (or kinds of cost): the actors' salary, the tutors' salary and the financial penalties due to a lack of competent actors at the end of the horizon.

Criterion related to actors' salary $[(\gamma_{i,j}^{k,l}\times L_i^{k,l})\times S_j]$ This criterion relates to the competency level of employees concerning the assigned tasks. It is calculated from their salary rates and their estimated work duration (based on the coefficient of work efficiency). The product of the coefficient of work efficiency and the theoretical work duration ($\gamma_{i,j}^{k,l}\times L_i^{k,l}$) represents an estimated work duration for specific task $T_i^{k,l}$ of actor *j*. This duration is longer than the theoretical work duration ($L_i^{k,l}$) if the person is under competent ($\gamma_{i,j}^{k,l}>1$) for specific tasks.

Criterion related to tutors' salary $[(\gamma_{i,j}^{k,l}-1)\times L_i^{k,l}\times ST]$ This criterion is derived from the case when tutors have to help the under-competent actor to accomplish the assigned tasks. This cost is based on the tutoring duration (calculated from the coefficient of work efficiency) and the salary rate of tutors.

Criterion related to financial penalties $\sum_{i=1}^{M}\varphi_i(O_i-R_i)$ These penalties are explained as lost incomes that companies could have if their competency objectives have not been reached. Competency objectives O_i (i = 1,..., M) are used to describe the number of expected competent actors, required by generic tasks. To determine whether a person is competent, we define required performance thresholds, called $thres_i$ (i = 1,..., M). Actor *j* is judged competent for task *i* if $r3_{i,j}^{k}\ge thres_i$. At the end of the horizon of task assignment (*k*= K), we have obtained the number of competent actors R_i for each task *i* (*i*= 1, ..., M): $R_i=\sum_{j=1}^{N}\max(0;E[r3_{i,j}^{K}-thres_i+1])$. The penalty rate for each missing competent actor is defined by constant φ_i.

Two types of constraints are used in this model.

Workload constraint (Equation 4) This constraint aims at ensuring that each task is completely assigned.

Resource load constraint (Equation 5) This constraint aims at ensuring that the total assigned load concerning an actor does not exceed his/her capacity.

To solve this problem, we have to face two difficulties: the non-linearity in competency evolution and the objectives in competency development at the end of the horizon of task assignment. To deal with these difficulties, this N-P hard problem can not be solved by the known exact optimization methods. Therefore, we develop a meta-heuristic approach to solve the problem. Simulated annealing (SA) is a generic probabilistic meta-algorithm for the overall optimization problem, namely locating a good approximation to the minimum of a given function in a large search space [14-15].

The choice of using the simulated annealing is justified by the fact that we are able to find an initial solution to the global problem and to generate neighbors. The initial solution of this task assignment problem is found by considering k sub-problem separately (for each period k). The optimal solution of each sub-problem is found by using the linear programming successively for each period k and by propagating the evolution of competency (the algorithm starts from k=1,..., K). The parameter setting of SA (such as neighbor function, acceptance probabilities, annealing schedule) is described in detail in [13]. When the SA algorithm reaches the stop condition, it returns the final assignment solution.

4 Computational Results

The case study concerned two projects that have been planned over three periods. The lists of 15 generic tasks, 20 actors and 23 types of knowledge have been generated. The performance levels in knowledge have been defined for each task and each actor. The project managers are in charge of defining these data for their projects. To shorten this paper, we sum up the results according to two viewpoints: competency-based aspect and financial aspect. For more information, please see [13].

4.1 Competency-Based Viewpoint

Figure 1-(1) shows the variation of performance levels in knowledge acquired by actor N°1 after 3 periods of assignment (initial period, $k = 0$; last period, $k = 3$). Figure 1-(2) shows the variation of competency levels (concerning generic tasks) acquired by actor N°1 after each period. These results confirm that knowledge and competencies that have been activated to carry out tasks have been developed. The performance levels in knowledge that have not been mobilized in order to carry out tasks have declined.

4.2 Financial Viewpoint

By using the simulated annealing based algorithm, the total cost obtained by the partial optimization of the k sub-problems has been decreased about 3%. The variation of the total cost is presented by the first graph in Figure 2, and the variation of three sub-costs is presented by the other graphs. Concerning the financial penalty, we found that, before task assignment (k=0), 9 competent actors were missing. At the end of the horizon, the number of competent actors was increased and only 5 competent actors were still missing.

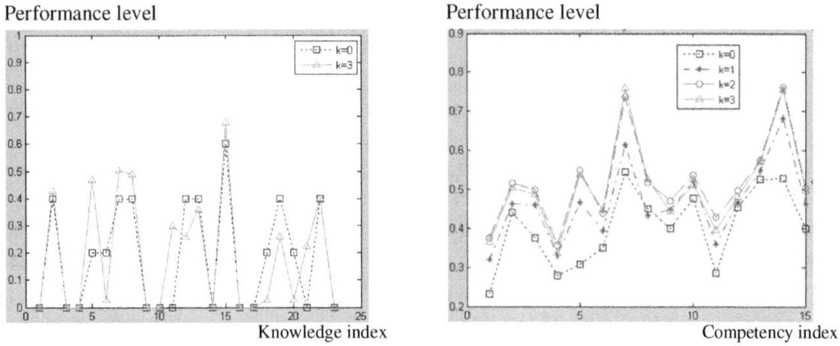

(1) (2)

Fig. 1. Evolutions of the performance levels in knowledge and in competency

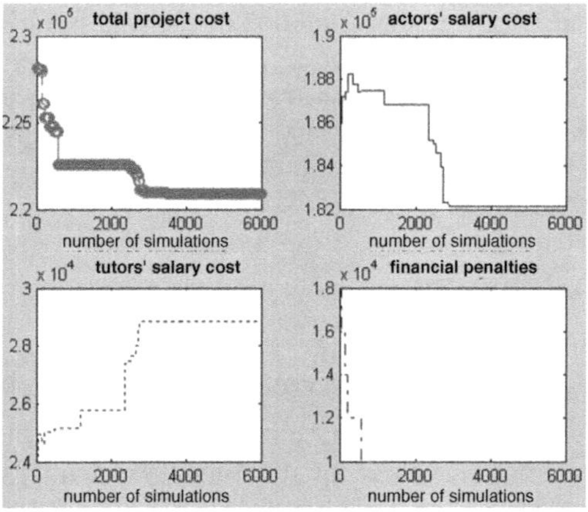

Fig. 2. Financial viewpoint

5 Conclusion

In this article, we have proposed a model of the multi-period task assignment problem with the modeling of the evolution of competencies. The short literature review that we have presented reveals that this problem has been rarely studied. This NP-hard problem has been solved by a simulated annealing -based optimization algorithm. The main assumption of this model is justified by psychological studies: an actor develops his/her knowledge when he/she has to carry out the task that activates this knowledge. Two types of tasks have been defined: generic tasks for modeling competencies and specific tasks for modeling their occurrences. Tasks have been characterized according to two levels: performance level in knowledge and competency level. A compatibility indicator between tasks and actors has also been proposed in order to calculate the coefficient of work efficiency that is used to penalize under-competent actors in the assignment problem.

The obtained results confirm that this method is convincing from the financial and competency-based viewpoints. Globally, we decreased the project costs, even if this decrease seems to be rather low. On the one hand, this can be explained by the fact that this decrease depends on how we fix the penalty rate. On the other hand, the initial solution (obtained by linear programming) is a good solution. From the competency-based viewpoint, the increase in the number of competent actors after the horizon of task assignment has proved that the proposed algorithm tried to reach the objectives of competency development.

Further work will concern the sensitivity analysis of the proposed algorithm. Project managers' estimations concerning the performance level in knowledge and the competency level that is required by a specific task may be imprecise. Due to the way of computing the compatibility level (Equation 1), we have good reasons to assume that the proposed method is few sensitive. Other experimentations will be led to prove this point.

References

1. Sayin, S., Karabati, S.: Assigning cross-trained workers to departments: A two-stage optimization model to maximize utility and skill improvement. European Journal of Operational Research 176(3), 1643–1658 (2007)
2. Bellenguez, O., Néron, E.: Lower Bounds for the Multi-Skill Project Scheduling Problem with Hierarchical Levels of Skill. In: Burke, E.K., Trick, M.A. (eds.) PATAT 2004. LNCS, vol. 3616, pp. 229–243. Springer, Heidelberg (2005)
3. Corominas, A., Pastor, R., Rodrıguez, E.: Rotational allocation of tasks to multifunctional workers in a service industry. International Journal of Production Economics 103, 3–9 (2006)
4. Gutjahr, W.J., Katzensteiner, S., Reiter, P., Stummer, C., Denk, M.: Competence-driven project portfolio selection, scheduling and staff assignment. Central European Journal of Operations Research 16(3), 281–306 (2008)
5. Fowler, J.W., Wirojanagud, P., Gel, E.S.: Heuristics for workforce planning with worker differences. European Journal of Operational Research 190, 724–740 (2008)
6. Harzallah, M., Berio, G., Vernadat, F.: Analysis and modeling of individual competencies: toward better management of human resources. IEEE Transactions on Systems, man, and Cybernetics-PART A: Systems and Humans 36(1) (2006)
7. Boucher, X., Bonjour, E., Grabot, B.: Formalisation and use of competencies for industrial performance optimisation: a survey. Computers in industry 58(2), 98–117 (2007)
8. Caron, G., Hansen, P., Jaumard, B.: The assignment problem with seniority and job priority constraints. Operations Research 47(3), 449–454 (1999)
9. Tseng, T.L., Huang, C.C., Chu, H.W., Gung, R.R.: Novel approach to multi-functional project team formation. International Journal of Project Management 22, 147–159 (2004)
10. Hadj-Hamou, K., Caillaud, E.: Cooperative design-A framework for a competency-based approach. In: 5th International Conference on IDMME (2004)
11. Fitzpatrick, E.L., Askin, R.G.: Forming effective worker teams with multi-functional skill requirements. Journal of Computers & Industrial Engineering 48, 593–608 (2005)
12. Hlaoittinun, O., Bonjour, E., Dulmet, M.: A multidisciplinary team building method based on competency modeling in design project management. International Journal of Management Science and Engineering Management 3(3), 163–175 (2008)
13. Hlaoittinun, O.: Contribution à la constitution d'équipes de conception couplant la structuration du projet et le pilotage des compétences. PhD. Thesis, Université de Franche-Comté, France (2009)
14. Kirkpatrick, S., Gelatt, C.D., Vecchi, M.P.: Optimization by simulated annealing. Science 220(4598), 671–680 (1983)
15. Suman, B., Kumar, P.: A survey of simulated annealing as a tool for single and multiobjective optimization. Journal of the Operational Research Society 57(10), 1143–1160 (2006)

Aided Virtual Team Building System: Zooming in on Web 2.0 Tools and Competence Management

Marinita Schumacher[1], Marc Diviné[2], Julie Stal-Le Cardinal, and Jean-Claude Bocquet[1]

[1] Ecole Centrale Paris, Industrial Engineering Department, Grande Voie des Vignes, 92295 Chatenay Malabry Cedex, France
{marinita.schumacher,julie.le-cardinal,jean-claude.bocquet}@ecp.fr
[2] IAE-Paris, University Paris1 Panthéon-Sorbonne, 21, rue Broca - 75005 Paris, France
divine.iae@univ-paris1.fr

Abstract. Our paper responds to the need of an Aided Virtual Team Building System (Aided VTB System). It focuses on virtual teams that are active in virtual design projects in the area of New Product Development (NPD). An extract of requirements of this Aided VTB System is presented that is based on the idea of Quality Function Development and its tool "house of quality". The fulfillment of the demand of the requirements by appropriate relevant and recent concepts and techniques as solutions is discussed with help of a sample survey of 34 virtual team leaders. One of the outcomes of the Aided VTB System is to provide recommendations, guidelines and even best practices to take a choice of web 2.0 tools and concepts and techniques in the domain of competence management.

Keywords: Aided VTB System, virtual teams, competence management, web 2.0 tools, sample survey, house of quality.

1 Introduction

Even if virtual collaborative environments and platforms are getting more and more popular in various domains such as New Product Development (NPD), R&D, customer services etc. there is still a weak support of the human dimension for virtual teams [1, 2]. Empirically-based prescriptions, guidelines and best practices for a system for virtual team building that considers aspects of competence management are often missing. The changing nature of teams and its rising complexity has brought on a need to implement an **Aided** Virtual Team Building **System** (Aided VTB System). The Aided VTB System functions as tool kit that features recommendations, guidelines and best practices for virtual team building adapted to the requirements of each specific organization. Many authors have provided their own definition of virtual teams and the concept of virtual team lacks a universally accepted definition [3, 4, 5, 6]. We consider that a virtual team consists of individuals that are geographically and temporally dispersed and act interdependently through technology to achieve a common goal. The purpose is to demonstrate an extract of the Aided VTB System that considers the technical dimension in form of web 2.0 tools and concepts and techniques in the domain of virtual project management as well as the human dimension

L.M. Camarinha-Matos et al. (Eds.): PRO-VE 2010, IFIP AICT 336, pp. 346–355, 2010.

with focus of concepts and techniques in the domain of competence management and virtual team building. In this work we focus especially on concepts and techniques of the domain of web 2.0 tools and competence management.

Secondly, to broaden our results, we present a sample survey that devotes on the part of the web 2.0 tools of the Aided VTB System. It shows the interrelation between four types of value for each web 2.0 tool. These values have been calculated by an extract of the Aided VTB System, its requirements the fulfillment of their demand by concepts and techniques that are considered as most famous virtual team practices in the literature. The sample survey helps us to compare an extract of the results of the Aided VTB System designed with those virtual team practices as described in the literature with the actual use of the tools in the industrial practice. This will help to find out strengths and weaknesses of the extract of existent concepts and techniques due to the demand of the requirements that could be adapted easily to the Aided VTB System. In addition, the Aided VTB System will show correlations between respective concepts and techniques that have a specific rapport among each other. Furthermore, through this approach we get information about those requirements whose demands are not achieved by existent concepts and techniques. We finish in a last step with our concluding remarks and some perspectives for future work. Building on the extract of the Aided VTB System and the comparison with the survey sample makes it possible for us to give guidelines and recommendations for further research to implement a system like ours in industry.

2 Positioning of the Aided VTB System

In this work we bring the purpose on virtual design project teams in the domain of NPD. This is why the Aided VTB System has next to the domain of competence management also to consider concepts and techniques of the field of virtual project management, virtual team building and web 2.0. Virtual teams are more complex than traditional teams and have specific characteristics related to the fact that they cross boundaries concerning time, geographical distance and organisations. They use web 2.0 tools to communicate and share information and collaborate to achieve a common goal. The web 2.0 tools are considered as a series of tools which allow interaction between internauts with web sites and other web connected devices [7].

Before presenting the approach of our study we give an overview of the positioning of the Aided VTB System. Due to the systemic approach that we pursued in our previous work [8, 9] the domains competence management, virtual project management, virtual team building, and web 2.0 tools are considered as systems that are in interrelation with the Aided VTB System. The Virtual Teams which we handle are active in virtual design projects in the area of NPD. The value of virtual teams in NPD is undeniable. In our work we are considering the virtual aspect in NPD processes that claim other demands than traditional design projects in the domain of project management. The Aided VTB System handles the domain of NPD as context. It is evident, that virtual teams generally face greater project management challenges than traditional face-to-face teams. The aspect of project management is considered as kind of organisation of our work. An overview of the positioning of the Aided VTB System is given in figure 1.

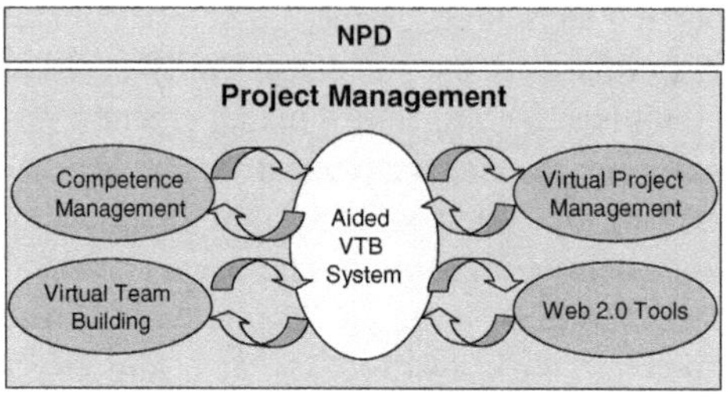

Fig. 1. Positioning of the Aided VTB System

Figure 1 highlights that all four systems are integrated as subsystems in the domain of project management that functions as organisation sector and is canopied by the context of the NPD.

To explain the arrows it is to say that the Aided VTB System functions as method that supports the four respective subsystems to create virtual teams by giving best practices, guidelines and recommendations. On the other hand the experience of those four subsystems can enhance the Aided VTB System by giving recommendations. This is important for the functioning of the project management and thereby as well for the NPD.

3 Approach of Our Study

In the first step of our study requirements of the presented Aided VTB System are defined and the fulfillment of their demand by appropriate relevant and recent concepts and techniques as solutions discussed on the basis of a graphic tool called house of quality. In the second step we broaden the results gained by the extract of the Aided VTB System with help of a sample survey.

3.1 House of Quality

The approach of the house of quality is based on the Quality Function Deployment (QFD) method, which was introduced by Akao [10] in the shipbuilding industry in the 1970s. It has been used successfully for many years as a quality assurance methodology. The house of quality helps to translate customer requirements into a pertinent number of quality characteristics [10, 11]. In the approach we describe the underlying customer requirements describe the demand of the Aided VTB System. The quality characteristics are in our case detected solutions, concepts and techniques in the domain of competence management (CM), virtual project management (VPM) and virtual team building (VTB), as well as web 2.0 tools (WEB).

The house of quality helps to define not only the relationship between customer requirements describing the Aided VTB System and quality characteristics. It analyses also the correlation between the individual quality characteristics. The basic construction of the house of quality is made up of four major building blocks that compose the form of a house [10]. These include customer requirements, quality characteristics, a relationship matrix, and a correlation matrix. An overview of the basic structure of the house of quality is presented in figure 2.

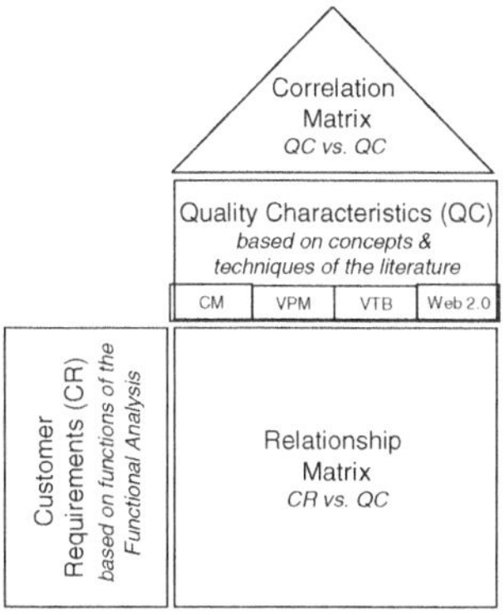

Fig. 2. Scheme of House of Quality due to the Aided VTB System

A table with customer requirements on the left and quality characteristics on the top is shown in figure 2. The roof is composed as diagonal matrix of quality characteristics. The body of the house of quality builds a relationship matrix of customer requirements versus quality characteristics. It helps to draw conclusions in which degree the proposed quality characteristics respond to the demand of the customer requirements.

3.1.1 Customer Requirements

The customer requirements are based on the functional analysis that has been performed in our previous work [4, 5]. The functional analysis is the tool that we use to be as objective, generic and exhaustive as possible [12]. It helps us to understand the complexity of the Aided VTB System from a systemic point of view. It is considered as a system that is described by functions. The functions describe the optimum behavior of the system and its terms of usability. They are considered as customer requirements in the house of quality. The following listing gives two examples of those functions.

FT19 The system should make competencies accessible and useable for organisations.

FC29 The system should allow distance reduction and easy socialization in trustworthy virtual environment.

3.1.2 Quality Characteristics

While customer requirements describe *what* should be implemented, quality characteristics are focused on the way *how* those requirements should be implemented and give precise recommendations. For reasons of visualisation table 1 shows only a brief extract of the eight quality characteristics due to the domains of competence management and web 2.0 tools that are considered in this study.

3.2 Sample Survey

In the second part of our study we compare the theoretical results of the presented extract of the Aided VTB System gained by the approach of house of quality with the industrial reality. With the help of a sample survey based on interviews with 34 participants we aim to provide proposition due to the Aided VTB System. We verify

Table 1. Quality characteristics due to the domains of competence management and web 2.0

Competence Management (CM)	
CM1	Access to a global network of experts, providers and partners [13]
CM2	On demand weak to strong ties processes [14]
CM3	People experience and competencies profile data base [14]
CM4	Interdisciplinary teams of excellence consisting of experts from different areas [15]
CM5	Process-oriented human resources planning [16]
CM6	Systematic identification, assessment & assignment of competence requirements of projects [17]
CM7	Projects' associated competencies ontology [16]
CM8	Repeatedly analyses of partial tasks to determine changed requirements for competencies during the process [17]
Web 2.0 (WEB)	
WEB1	Chat: Instant written conversation area, where the real-time dialog appears line by line as in a book's people dialog.
WEB2	Forum (Fm): Area opened by a moderator who suggests specific topics and invites members to post messages and comments.
WEB3	Web Conferencing: Live meeting combining voice on the phone and onscreen presentations by a speaker.
WEB4	Blog: Personal web site where owner post messages and invite people to post comments.
WEB5	Wiki: Web site which pages can be created and modified by visitors.
WEB6	Posting & Sharing (P.S.): Ability given to visitors to upload & to modify documents located in a web site area.
WEB7	Commenting, Rating, Polling (C.R.P.): Add a written remark, evaluate content & survey participants' opinion with online questionnaires
WEB8	Social Network (S.N.): A site where community members post in a personal area their profile, photo, interest and links with other persons

whether the selection of tools deducted from the requirements of the Aided VTB System and the concepts and techniques is the same as the tools in use or the tools best rated in interest. The choice of the interviewees of the sample survey is based on organisations that employ over 5000 employees worldwide. The interviewees work in marketing departments as manager and are involved in virtual teams in mid or long term interdisciplinary NPD projects. They are based in France in order to limit cultural differences. The number of the 34 organisations with over 5000 employees worldwide that intervened can be compared with the number of organisations with over 5000 employees in France that is in total 82. This deduces that the sample survey reaches a very significant proportion of 36%. Furthermore, out of the 34 organisations, 16.37% belong to the Stock French Index CAC40.

The interview took about an hour. It was structured in three parts and started with an introduction part about 20 existing web 2.0 tools definitions to get to a common understanding. The second part focused the question if each respective tool was used by the virtual teams in which the interviewees are involved. We considered also the question if other web interaction tools are used apart from the 20 listed. In the third part of the interview the interviewee was asked to evaluate the interest of the use of the tool within the project teams.

4 Results

Before going into detail of purposes of our work we present with figure 3 the extract of the house of quality that builds the basis of our results.

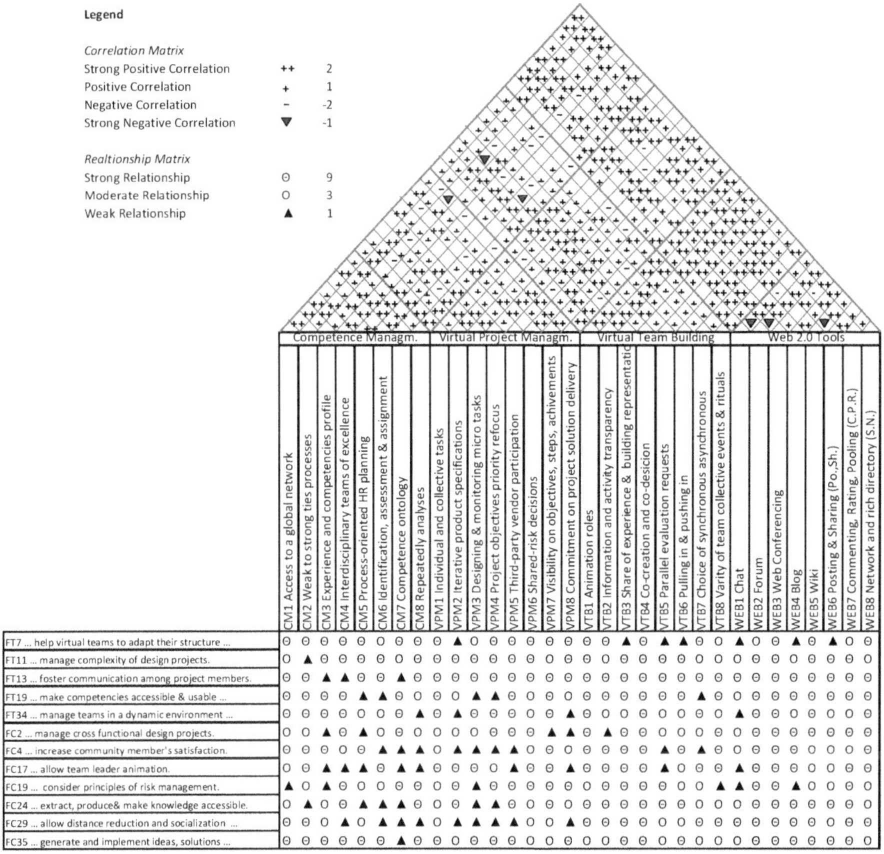

Fig. 3. Extract of the Aided VTB System due to the house of quality

The results of the house of quality are extremely rich and there is much potential of interpretation depending on the respective point of view on the work. In this study we concentrate on two aspects. Our first purpose is set on the functions and represents how well they are satisfied by the extract of 24 quality characteristics as well which quality characteristics in the domain of competence management and web 2.0 satisfied the best most of the functions. The second focus is set exclusively on the web 2.0 tools to put our theoretical results in relation with the sample survey of the industrial practice.

4.1 Results due to the House of Quality

By establishing a relation between the customer requirements and the quality characteristics we get information about if concepts and techniques match the demand of the functions and in what degree. The results of the analysis of the relationship matrix are shown in table 2.

Table 2. Analysis of relationship matrix according to the extract of the Aided VTB System

Customer Requirements The system should...	**QC: all** **Total**	 **Index**	**QC: WEB** **Total**	 **Index**	**QC: CM** **Total**	 **Index**
FT7 ... help virtual teams to adapt their structure to the objectives to the requirements by agility.	166	**1.16**	36	**0.65**	66	**1.48**
FT11 ... help to manage the complexity of design projects with variable. rich requirements.	172	**1.2**	51	**0.93**	52	**1.18**
FT13 ... foster communication among project members.	192	**1.34**	72	**1.3**	48	**1.08**
FT19 ... make competencies accessible and useable for organisations.	146	**1.06**	66	**1.2**	66	**1.48**
FT34 ... manage virtual teams in a dynamic environment that is described by fluid boundaries and fluid team memberships.	144	**1.01**	46	**0.84**	52	**1.18**
FC2 ... help to manage cross functional design projects.	116	**0.8**	66	**1.2**	32	**0.72**
FC4 ... increase project member's satisfaction.	120	**0.84**	48	**0.87**	45	**1.02**
FC17 ... allow team leader animation.	134	**0.94**	52	**0.94**	26	**0.59**
FC19 ... consider principles of risk management.	142	**0.99**	38	**0.69**	38	**0.86**
FC24 ... extract. produce and make knowledge accessible.	126	**0.88**	60	**1.09**	29	**0.66**
FC29 ... allow distance reduction and easy socialization in trustworthy virtual environment.	102	**0.71**	66	**1.2**	29	**0.66**
FC35 ... generate and implement ideas. solutions and improvements.	157	**1.1**	60	**1.09**	64	**0.66**
Ø	143.08	1	55.08	1	44.25	1

Next to the simple additions of the total, indexes are calculated by division with the mean values to allow direct comparison. Table 2 is rich on information. We set the focus on the customer requirements. As example, we devote to the beforehand presented functions FT19 *"The system should make competencies accessible and useable for organisations"* and FC29 *"The system should allow distance reduction and easy socialization in trustworthy virtual environment"*. Regarding all quality characteristics of the four different domains (QC:all) FC29 shows an index of 0.71, while FT19 is better replied by this extract of concepts and techniques with an index of 1.06. Concentrating on how the respective quality characteristics of the web 2.0 tools (QC:WEB) respond to the demand shows for FT 19 an index of 1.2. The index of the quality characteristics of competence management (QC:CM) is 1.48. As function FT19 considers competencies as focus, it is evident that the QC:CM respond on the demand. Interestingly, also the QC:WEB satisfies its demand significantly which seems to be based on the access of competencies that provides web 2.0 tools.

In contrast, FC29 is well satisfied by QC:WEB (index: 1.2) but less by QC:CM (index: 0.66). Regarding the index of QC:all (0.71) highlights that the web 2.0 tools respond the best to this requirement.

4.2 Results due to the Sample Survey

In a second step we concentrate on the quality characteristics. That gives insights about the relationship matrix from another point of view. To give an example, we point on the respective QC:WEB considering also the beforehand presented sample survey to compare the theoretical results of this extract of the Aided VTB System with the industrial reality. The analysis of web 2.0 tools is shown in table 3.

Table 3. Valuing web 2.0 tools due to the house of quality and the sample survey

House of Quality	Chat	Fm	Conf	Blog	Wiki	P.S.	C.P.R.	S.N.	Ø
A. Relation to customer requirements	40	102	108	80	108	70	90	84	85.3
Index A	**0.47**	**1.20**	**1.27**	**0.94**	**1.27**	**0.82**	**1.06**	**0.99**	**1.00**
B. Correlation to the quality characteristics of all three domains: CM. VPM. VTB	19	35	39	18	35	34	35	28	30.4
Index B	**0.63**	**1.15**	**1.28**	**0.59**	**1.15**	**1.12**	**1.15**	**0.92**	**1.00**
C. Correlation to the quality characteristics of the domain CM	3	10	10	7	11	7	12	11	8.9
Index C	**0.34**	**1.12**	**1.12**	**0.79**	**1.24**	**0.79**	**1.35**	**1.24**	**1.00**
Sample Survey									
% of use in the sample survey	1.38	0.83	1.20	0.53	0.43	1.49	0.88	1.26	1.00
Interest rate in the sample survey	1.01	0.95	1.32	0.82	0.78	1.29	0.93	0.89	1.00

Index A highlights how the concepts and techniques of the domain of web 2.0 tools answer to the need of the customer requirements. While the web 2.0 tools web conferencing (1.27) and wiki (1.27) satisfy the best the demand, chat (0.47) does hardly respond to the customer requirements.

Index B focuses on the correlation matrix of the house of quality. Blog (0.59) and chat (0.63) show the less correlation with the quality characteristics of the three other domains. Web conferencing (1.28) shows the highest correlation with the other quality characteristics. The correlation matrix is important to analyse which quality characteristics are compatible to provide the Aided VTB System.

Index C presents the correlation between each respective web 2.0 tool and the quality characteristics in the domain of competence management. While chat (0.34) shows again the less correlation commenting, rating, polling (1.35) show the highest one.

In the second part of table 3, the sample survey highlights that the web 2.0 tool chat (1.38 and 1.01) is overused compared to its actual use and its interest estimation. On the opposite, the web 2.0 tools blog (0.53 and 0.82) wiki (0.43 and 0.78) show an interest at a higher level than their actual use.

5 Conclusion and Future Work

Care must be taken in generalizing our results, however given the small sample survey size. The size of the sample survey and the extract of the Aided VTB System trigger an uncertainty level which has to be taken into account in our conclusions. More than to generalize the results of this study, we intended to represent our approach of the Aided VTB System to make future choices of web 2.0 tools based on a robust basis. We are aware that the small extract that we have given as example is not significant but it gives sophisticated insights of how the Aided VTB System may function in future. Nevertheless, we would like to give some recommendations due to our results.

- To implement an Aided VTB System quality characteristics which are in high correlation with forums and wikis should be fostered. For example "CM8 Repeatedly analysis of partial tasks to determine changed requirements for competencies during the process" that deepens the debate with structured and collective tools.

- Virtual team leader should discourage the use of the chat as soon as team members' conversation deals with their project and encourage forum, wiki, commenting, pooling and rating. Those tools are under used and rated according to their respond to the demand of the customer requirements and the value provided by their correlation to the three other types of quality characteristics in the domain of competence management, virtual project management, and virtual team building.
- To respond to the demand of FC29 virtual team leaders could compensate the distance with "physical" meeting at specific occasions, particularly at project kick off meeting and in the end of phases.
- The quality characteristics in the domain of competence management have been presented as human dimension of the Aided VTB System. Interestingly, is that the web 2.0 tools respond also to human demands (FT19) and the correlation between some of the web 2.0 tools and the quality characteristics in the domain of competence management is much higher than expected. Future work should consider the human side of technical dimensions.

In future research we are concentrating on customer requirements that are not satisfied because there are solutions missing in the literature. In this case it will be purpose to propose concepts and techniques that answer as quality characteristics to the need of the customer requirements. Additionally, we aim to provide an interrogation platform in form of the house of quality where concepts and techniques of already well-developed methodologies could be consolidated. This permits us to be as inclusive as possible also in all four domains of competence management, virtual project management, virtual team building, and web 2.0 tools. The fast development of use web 2.0 tools and the regular arrival of new tools make necessary to reevaluate the use and the perceptions. The list of these tools increases quickly, so that the understanding and the choice of them becomes a managerial issue.

References

1. Horvarth, L., Tobin, T.J.: Twenty-first century teamwork: Defining competencies for virtual teams. Virtual teams 8, 239–258 (2001)
2. Picard, W.: Social Protocols for Agile Virtual Teams, PRO-VE 2009 – 10th IFIP – International Federation for Information Proceeding – Working Conference on Virtual Enterprises, Thessaloniki (October 2009); In: Luis M. Camarinha-Matos, Iraklis Paraskasis and Hamideh Afsarmanesh (Eds.) Levering Knowledge for Innovation in Collaborative Networks, pp. 169-178. Springer, Heidelberg (2009)
3. Griffith, T.L., Sawyer, J.E., Neale, M.A.: Virtualness and Knowledge in Teams: Managing the Love Triangle in Organizations, Individuals, and Information technology. MIS Quarterly (27), 265–287 (2003)
4. Schmidt, J.B., Montoya-Weiss, M.M., Massey, A.P.: New Product Development Decision-Making Effectivness: Comparing Individuals, Face-To-Face Teams, and Virtual Teams. Decision Science 32(4), 575–601 (2001)
5. McDonough, E.F., Kahn, K.B., Barczak, G.: An investigation of the use of global, virtual, and colocated new product development team. Journal of Product Innovation Management 18(2), 110–120 (2001)

6. Rezgui, Y.: Exploring virtual team-working effectiveness in the construction sector. Interacting with Computers (19), 96–112 (2007)
7. DiNucci, D.: Fragmented Future. Print 53(4), 2–32 (1999)
8. Schumacher, M., Stal-Le Cardinal, J., Mekhilef, M.: A competence management methodology for virtual teams – A systemic approach to support innovation processes in SME's. In: International Design Conference – Design 2008, Dubrovnik (2008)
9. Schumacher, M., Stal-Le Cardinal, J., Bocquet, J.C.: Towards a methodology for managing competencies in virtual teams – A systemic approach, PRO-VE 2009 – 10th IFIP – International Federation for Information Proceeding – Working Conference on Virtual Enterprises, Thessaloniki (October 2009); In: Luis M. Camarinha-Matos, Iraklis Paraskasis and Hamideh Afsarmanesh (Eds.) Levering Knowledge for Innovation in Collaborative Networks, pp. 235–244. Springer, Heidelberg (2009)
10. Akao, Y.: Quality Function Deployment. Productivity Press, Portland (1990)
11. Hauser, J., Clausing, D.: House of Quality. Harvard Business Review (2009)
12. Le Moigne, J.L.: La théorie du système général, Théorie de la modélisation. Presses Universitaires de France, Col. Systèmes-Décisions, Paris (1977)
13. Marion, J.T., Schumacher, M.: Moving New Venture New Product Development from Information Push to Pull Using Web 2.0. In: International Conference on Engineering Design, ICED 2009, Stanford (2009)
14. Edmondson, A.C., Nembhard, I.M.: Product Development and learning in Project Teams: The Challenges Are tge Benefits. Journal of Product Innovation Management (26), 123–138 (2009)
15. Kjellberg, A.: Teams- What's Next? From Fragmentation and Consciousness to Responsiveness by Competence Management for Modular Manufacturing Learning. Annals of the CIRP 48(2), 599–609 (1999)
16. Berio, G., Hazallah, M.: Towards an integrating architecture for competence management. Computer in Industry 58, 199–209 (2007)
17. Shpitalni, M., Guttmann, G., Bossin, D.: Creation of project teams in networks of excellence. In: 2nd German-Israeli Symposium on Design and Manufacture, Advances in Methods and Systems for the development of Products and Processes, Production Technology Center, Berlin, Germany, pp. 3–12. Fraunhofer IRB Verlag (2005)

A New Approach to Competence-Based Business Partner Profiles for Collaborative Business Process Management

Thomas Schuster and Peter Weiß

FZI Forschungszentrum Informatik, Haid-und-Neu-Straße 10-14,
76131 Karlsruhe, Germany
{weiss,schuster}@fzi.de

Abstract. In this paper a novel approach and thinking to foster the derivation of competence and skill requirements by business process models is presented. Management of intra- and inter-organizational business processes is a significant issue that influences a company's success. A multitude of competence models, standards and frameworks exist. Furthermore, current resource models in business process management solutions are not sophisticated and adequately reflecting the needs of collaborative resource planning and competence management. Our research activities yielded a meta model which tends to overcome existing shortfalls. In this article we present an extensible resource meta-model that allows the modeling of resources including their competences, skills and knowledge. Furthermore we demonstrate the aggregation of competence concepts to business partner profiles in collaborative networks.

Keywords: Collaborative Resource Management, Competence, Business Process Management, Ressource Allocation.

1 Introduction

The selection of business partners can be identified as key to success and key capability for the realization of collaborative networks in near future [15, 14]. Against this background the paper looks at competence management and related models in the context of business process engineering. In particular our approach fosters the alignment of business process modeling and human resource planning. Previous research has already motivated the debate to link competence theory and business processes [12]. While it is worthwhile to look at competence models and business processes from a single company perspective, the added value from an inter-company perspective shows to be even higher. The remainder of the paper is structured as follows: first the current state of the art and basic concepts are introduced. Consecutively an extensible resource meta-model comprising subsets of meta models (workflow systems, human resources and competence) is presented. Competence-based and resource-based views in the organization are motivated and an example for collaborative competence-modeling is presented to illustrate how the model shall be applied. Finally, we summarize the achievement and provide an outlook on next steps and future research.

L.M. Camarinha-Matos et al. (Eds.): PRO-VE 2010, IFIP AICT 336, pp. 356–363, 2010.

2 Collaborative Networks and Business Process Management

In the past, research made a clear distinction of business process perspective and competence-based management views. Whereas, workflow management rather relates to the operational and functional view, competence management is hitherto associated with the HR domain and recruitment processes. Collaborative networks comprises a interdisciplinary research community which has elaborated in the meanwhile a comprehensive knowledge base encompassing theoretical foundations, services, collaboration and innovation environment, and last but not least the analysis of the impact collaborative networks have on daily life and economy [15]. Competence management and a resource-based view on collaborative networks get popular and subject of related research [12,15]. The selection of business partners is considered as a key to success for the realization of collaborative networks in near future. Assessment of competences can be seen as integral part of partner selection processes and partnership formation.

"*An allocation relates tasks, resource classes, case attributes, and resources to each other*" [13, p. 81]. In this context a collaborative resource management formulates and analyses preconditions of allocation policies, which can become highly complex. Therefore a formal approach and machine readable format is required. Resources available in a collaborative network to carry out the workflow typically are classified and decoupled from specific employees. Today resource classification is realized solely based upon two dimensions: role models and organization chart. The latter contains organizational units and hierarchical structure. Role models are in most cases derived from the functional structure of an organization [13, p.77]. Most workflow management systems provide graphical resource classification tooling [13, p.153].

In this paper, we propose a novel approach to classify resources based on business partner profiles (BPP) [15] extended through role profiles. The latter include qualifications and capabilities a resource may require to perform an activity in expected quality and time. BPP represent information required to discover, select, and integrate business partners into emerging or existing value chains [15,14]. Job profiles are built according to specific company and work place needs. A job profile can be specified by a set of competences and related descriptors for skills, knowledge and attitude. Descriptors relate to an internal or external skill framework. To specify and store job profiles standards such as [11,4,5] may be used. Resource classes are allocated to workflows through analysis of the characteristics and requirements of an activity in relation to a specific case [13, p.80]. In our approach information stored in job profiles is used in addition to enhance the allocation of resources to specific cases. On one hand it is necessary to extract requirements of business partners' competences (from strategic to individual levels such as performance levels, proficiency levels, qualification and training) from the business processes, on the other hand metrics that allow for the matchmaking or alignment of these requirements with available roles or job profiles of companies are needed. In this way, workflow management can profit from sophisticated software services allowing job profile aggregation, comparison and alignment to specific tasks. Within companies, the recruiting process usually involves at least three interested parties [11]: line management, HR department, and potential applicants (internal or external to the company), all of them need to clearly understand the specification of the job, the company, compensation and, benefits. In collaborative networks those functions may be as well broken down into tasks and distributed between network nodes and resources. These tasks can be again aggregated to respective collaborative processes. Facilitating communication between these three functions is a key issue in the effectiveness and success of the recruitment process [11]. A meta model of competences is a prerequisite to allow inter-company interaction and information exchange.

3 Analysis and Design of Proposed Solution

In this section we illustrate requirements and the derived conceptual design of the proposed solution. Consequently we outline a meta model for competences. Furthermore we strive to reveal relationships of competence models [16] (in a HR resource view) and resource models (a workflow management view). Supplementary existing standards that have influenced the conceptual model (such as the European e-Competence Framework (e-CF) and HR-XML) are pointed out. Our conceptual model [7] is based on a MOF-compliant meta-model [9] that is built on three parts, the resource meta-model (RMM – containing general aspects of resources such as allocation state, current location etc., nevertheless details of the RMM will not be covered in this paper), the human resource meta-model (HRMM) and the competence meta-model (COMM).

Figure 1 illustrates details of the human resource meta-model (HRMM). HRMM combines common resource meta-models as known in workflow management [13,12] with competence descriptions. The meta-model allows precise definitions of organizational aspects and hierarchies, furthermore it enables an explicit by descriptions of competences. Competences can be modeled independently and may be reused for further specifications of roles and human resources. The specification of competences is covered by the competence meta-model (COMM). As a key part of HRMM the human resource (`HumanResource`) depicts manpower. In order to represent the

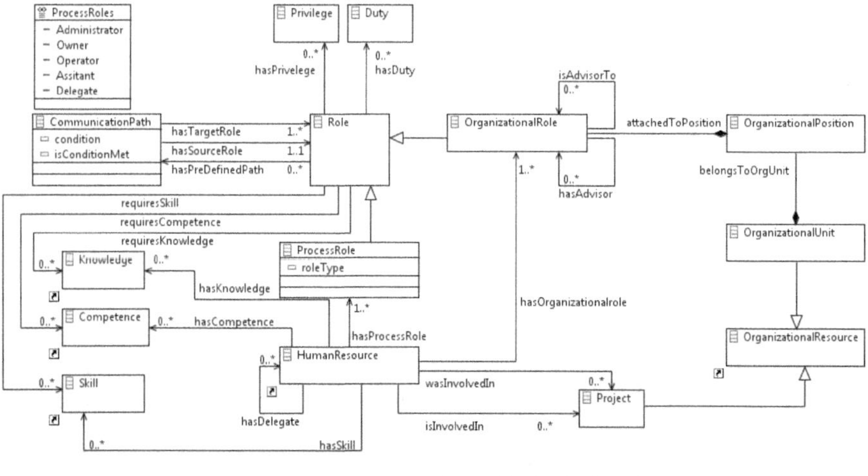

Fig. 1. Human Ressource Meta Model (HRMM)

organizational structures a human resource can be associated to an organizational role (OrganizationalRole) [3,12], furthermore in a business process context an association to a process role (ProcessRole) [3] is possible. Organizational hierarchies are reflected by OganizationPosition, OrganizationalUnit and the relations hasAdvisor and isAdvisorTo. The business process-related role (ProcessRole and the accordant enumeration ProcessRoles) is used to describe the relationship between human resources and assigned tasks [10,12]. Organization-related roles can be used to determine appropriate resources for task execution. Both role types share properties of their super class Role. These properties are rights (Privilege), obligations (Duty) and defined communication channels (CommunicationPath), e.g. for reporting or escalation mechanisms [13,6]. The model elements OganizationPosition and OrganizationalUnit substantiate organizational role descriptions of the type OrganizationalResource, referenced directly from the RMM part.

The details of HRMM stated above enclosed organization-, project- and process-related data, these aspects are covered by most common resource models in workflow management [3]. Furthermore a number of studies state that roles [13,12] and human resources also include specific competences [11,4], however these are not modeled explicitly so far. HRMM integrates competence descriptions and associates them to roles and human resources in order to tackle this concern. These descriptions are represented by the model elements Competence, Skill and Knowledge, that are reused elements specified by the competence meta-model outlined below. Clearly this bridges the gap between business process management and human resource management by a precise and formal connection mechanism. In consequence this mechanism does not only reveal details about the modeled resources and their competences, but also enables decision support for a multitude of questions. Decisions that may be supported by this modeling technique are: (1) matching between resources and roles with sound decisions for the allocation of new or idle roles; (2) allocation of resources to tasks in business processes, not only role based but also competence driven assignments; allowing enhanced scheduling mechanisms compared to role based scheduling. The utilization of competences to assign resources to tasks may restrict or extend the selection of acceptable resources. (3) Identification of core competences, driven by analysis of competences needed to execute the business processes. (4) Identification of additional competences needed to perform business goals, either resulting in recruitment of new resources, engagement of subcontractors or further education of resources. As previously discussed, competence models are mainly used by HR to accompany recruitment processes, thus being completely separated from business process modeling. RMM tackles this issue, since it is designed to integrate both model types thereby exploiting potential synergies. Besides the reuse of competence models in business process modeling, derived requirements from business process models may be included in competence models vice versa, thereby improving correlative HR competence profiles with enhanced accuracy. The competence meta-model (COMM) as depicted in Figure 2 specifies competence [16] concepts and relationships. COMM was influenced by several competence standards, such as HR-XML [4], the e-CF [11] and eCCO [2].

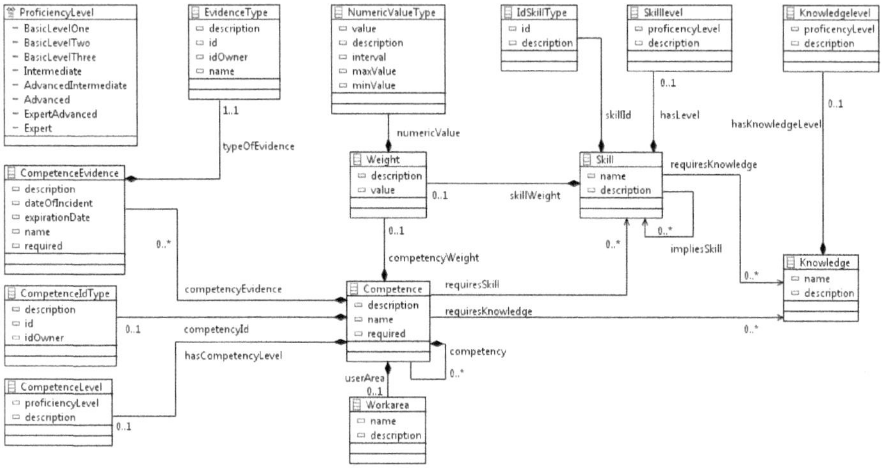

Fig. 2. Competence Meta-Model (COMM)

The basis was derived from HR-XML, since this is not only widespread, but also defines a precise model through the usage of XML schema. Existing HR-XML descriptions may be the input of transformations to create COMM-based models. Additionally the integration of other standards allows a transformation of those descriptions, as we will demonstrate in our use case. The essential elements of COMM are `Competence`, `Skill` and `Knowledge`. According to COMM a competence may imply further competences, require various skills (`requiresSkills`) and knowledge (`requiresKnowledge`). This relationship between competences, skills and knowledge is an extension to HR-XML according to [2]. In COMM each of these concepts has attached level descriptions that describe the degree of proficiency (`proficiencyLevel`). Furthermore a competence can be valid in a particular context (`Workarea`) only, in turn it is invalid in other areas. Additionally competences can be associated with a proof of evidence (`CompetenceEvidence`). The evidence states dates of achievement, duration of validity and a general description for characterization. Finally, the association of weights to competences and skills is used to measure their importance for an enterprise or a business process. The extensible meta-model design allows to add furthers means for measurement of different aspects in the future (e.g. for scheduling).

4 Collaborative Competence Modeling

In order to exemplify the practical relevance of this approach, we present a recruitment process in collaborative scenario. In Figure 3 distinct Conversations between collaborating participants (`Consignee; HR department; IT department; Personnel Consultant; Advertising Agency; Career Platform; Job Candidate`) of the recruitment process in a partner network are depicted by a BPMN 2.0 Conversation diagram [8].

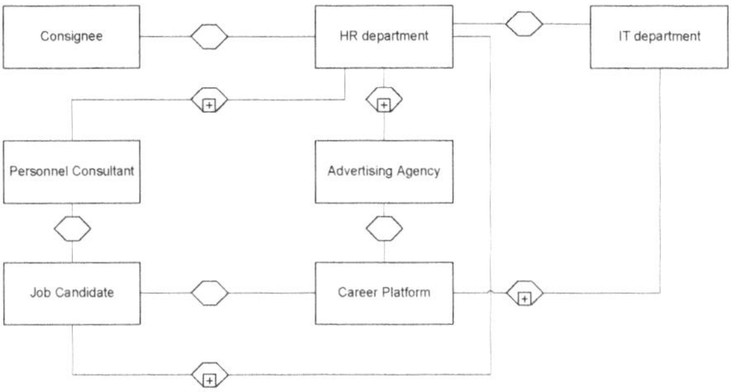

Fig. 3. Conversational Overview Recruitment Process

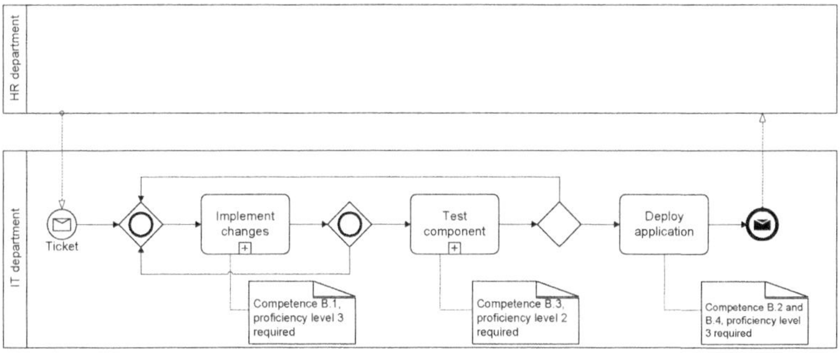

Fig. 4. Example Process - Ticket Processing

At this level competence profiles can be added to the participants. In order to exemplify how these can be aggregated, we will first step into process details by examination of a Collaboration between the `HR department` and the `IT department` (Figure 4). In this case the Collaboration is defined as the handling of service tickets, which may lead to changes in a system used by HR to generate adverts in a career platform. The Collaboration (the `IT department`'s view) is quite simple, changes are implemented according to incoming tickets. In a sequential order changes are tested and afterwards made available to the user by redeployment of the application. Development will be continued, if testing fails or further changes need to be implemented, otherwise the ticket processing is completed by sending a message to the issuing partner (`HR department`). The Collaboration in Figure 4 is extended by the annotation of competences and proficiency levels, these are competence descriptions given by e-CF. The tasks may be assigned to employees from the IT department (specific roles are not defined in this example), the assignment is constrained by the annotated competences. Thus only employees with according competences may execute the tasks.

In Figure 5 a) an organizational description is given as HRMM model with annotated competences, in Figure 5 b) the competence `Testing` is exemplified as COMM diagram. The skills and knowledge in Figure 5 b) are defined additionally to e-CF. In the COMM diagram the proficiency level is mapped to an attribute of the competences. Thus HR competence definitions may be reused in business process

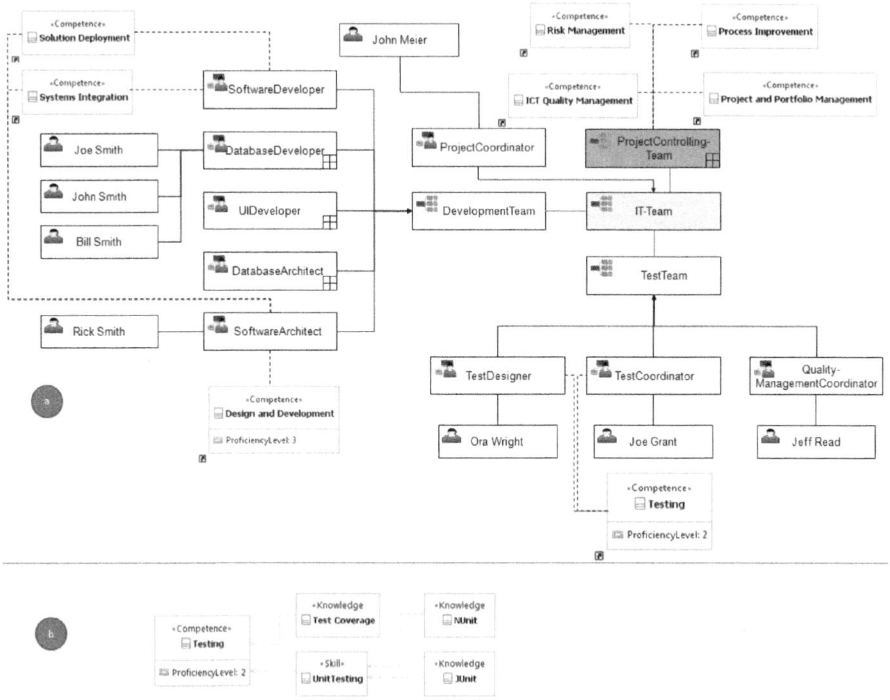

Fig. 5. a) IT-Team as HRMM Model b) Competence B.3 as COMM Model

models, in particular this information may now be used for scheduling. In order to generate partner profiles the competences from the Collaboration level may be aggregated on the Conversation level. If competences do occur repeatedly in Collaborations, the highest proficiency level has to be integrated in the partner profile.

5 Summary and Outlook

In collaborative networks data exchange between several IS and the challenge to map available data and information concerning job roles and profiles comes to the fore. Standards to ensure exchange competence requirements and definitions between network companies are needed. On basis of the presented meta-model interoperable resource profiles can be described. Effects of this analysis can be plentiful. We outlined aspects of resource and business process modeling associations between both modeling disciplines. The presented resource meta-model demonstrates the potential of the combination and extension of known concepts in resource modeling, competence modeling and business process management. Competence and resource models of human resource departments can be re-used for the modeling of business process relevant resources. Furthermore existing competence models can be adapted to the actual needs of the business processes. These adapted competence models can in turn be used to improve recruitment of new employees or to set up measures for further education of existing personnel. To extend concepts outlined in this paper, we plan to develop mechanisms for competence gap analysis and automatic aggregation of competence profiles. In addition, we plan to enhance our meta-model by industry-sector-specific features. Finally we strive to generate resource models automatically by the usage of transformations to combine information provided by directory services with existing competence models.

References

1. Camarinha-Matos, L.M., Paraskakis, I., Afsarmanesh, H. (eds.) Leveraging Knowledge for Innovation in Collaborative Networks, Proceedings of 10th IFIP WG 5.5 Working Conference on Virtual Enterprises, PRO-VE 2009, Thessaloniki, Greece, October 7-9, p. 307. Springer, Heidelberg (2009)
2. eCCO: A European e-Skills Meta-Framework. Draft Proposal. AICA, Federcomin, Fondazione Politecnico di Milano (2005)
3. Hollingsworth, D.: The Workflow Reference Model: 10 Years On, Workflow Management Coalition (WfMC) (2005)
4. HR-XML Consortium: Competencies (2007/2009), `http://www.hr-xml.org/`
5. IEEE Learning Technology Standards Committee: RCD: Draft standard for Reusable Competency Definitions (RCD) (March 2006)
6. OASIS: OASIS WS-BPEL Extension for People (BPEL4People) Technical Committee; Version 1.0 (2007)
7. Oberweis, A., Schuster, T.: A meta-model based approach to the description of resources and skills. Appears in 16th Americas Conference on Information Systems, AMCIS 2010 Proceedings (2010)
8. Object Management Group: Business Process Model and Notation (BPMN) Specification Version 2.0 Beta 1 (2009)
9. Object Management Group: Meta Object Facility (MOF) Core Specification OMG Available Specification Version 2.0 (2006)
10. Russell, N., van der Aalst, W.M.: Work Distribution and Resource Management in BPEL4People: Capabilities and Opportunities. In: Bellahsène, Z., Léonard, M. (eds.) CAiSE 2008. LNCS, vol. 5074, pp. 94–108. Springer, Heidelberg (2008)
11. The European e-Competence Framework, CEN Workshop Agreement (CWA 15893 (part 1 & 2), CEN (November 2008), `http://www.ecompetences.eu/` (visited 17.03.2010)
12. van der Aalst, W.M.P., Kumar, A., Verbeek, H.M.W.: Organizational modeling in UML and XML in the context of workflow systems. In: Proceedings of the 2003 ACM symposium on Applied computing, Melbourne, Florida, pp. S603–S608 (2003)
13. Van der Aalst, W., Van Hee, K.: Workflow Management: Models, Methods, and Systems. MIT Press, Cambridge (2004)
14. Weiß, P., Klink, S.: Collaborative services to maintain electronic business relationsships Establishing the Foundation of Collaborative Networks. In: Establishing The Foundation of Collaborative Networks, Eighth IFIP Working Conference on Virtual Enterprises, Guimarães, Portugal, September 10-12, vol. 243, pp. 435–442. Springer, Heidelberg (2007)
15. Weiß, P., Klink, S.: Social Impact of Collaborative Services to Maintain Electronic Business Relationships. In: Cruz-Cunha, Oliveira, Tavares & Ferreira (eds.) Handbook of Research on Social Dimensions of Semantic Technologies and Web Services, XXXII, vol. 1, pp. 643–674. IGI Global (2009)
16. Winterton, J., Delamare- Le Deist, F., Stringfellow, E.: Typology of knowledge, skills and competences: clarification of the concept and prototype. In: Cedefop 2005 (2005)

Pattern-Based Competence Management: On the Gap between Intentions and Reality

Ralf Klamma and Zinayida Petrushyna

Information Systems and Databases, RWTH Aachen University,
Ahornstrasse 55, 52056, Aachen, Germany
{klamma,petrushyna}@dbis.rwth-aachen.de

Abstract. Competence management in collaborative networks depends on the identification of gaps between the actual performance and the desired behavior. Therefore, collaborative networks need means to express their goals and intentions as well as to measure this against their own performance. In this paper, we present the i*-based modeling framework for agent-oriented elicitation of dependencies and goal-orientation in collaborative networks. Moreover, we sketch a method to translate the resulting models into a pattern-oriented analysis framework, which allows to compare the models with social network analysis results on real media traces left by the networks while collaborating using social software. This results in the identification of hidden or missing competences within a network. We will illustrate the approach with examples from ongoing project work. Finally, we discuss a collection of collaborative patterns indicating which (meta-)competences can be acquired.

Keywords: competence, collaborative networks, agents, i* modeling, social network analysis, patterns.

1 Introduction

The gap between reality and intentions points out what fails in the reality to come to the intention state. Competences fulfill the goals by performing actions with the purpose to achieve results. As soon as we identify the gap, we can define what actions should be performed to achieve the goal, thus we can say what competences fails and should be applied. The question we aim to answer in this paper is how to generate models of collaborative networks that reflect intentions and reality.

In the next section we describe how competences, competence management (CM) and development are defined in the scope of this paper. Afterward, we explain what are the patterns appropriate for and what social network analysis patterns can reveal. In Section 4 we introduce the basics of Actor Network Theory, Community of Practice (CoP) and we precisely describe agent-based i* modeling framework. In Section 5 we describe the model of one of test-bed scenarios representing collaborative networks in a university. Later we combine the model with the pattern oriented framework. Thus we extend the model with patterns extracted using social network analysis and present some examples of competences management and development that can be draw out from the model. The paper is finished with discussions where we reveal some related works and conclusions.

L.M. Camarinha-Matos et al. (Eds.): PRO-VE 2010, IFIP AICT 336, pp. 364–371, 2010.

2 Preliminaries

Before we start to model collaborative networks (CN) and consider competences in models, we introduce some terms important in this work. The term *competence* stems from Latin *competentia* that means *agreement* or *conjunction*. Actual definition of competence is often used within working associations to form quality standards [3].

Although numerous definitions for *competence* exist, many scholars agree that the term is associated with skills and abilities that people currently hold and may acquire in the future [10]. Competences allow an individual to perform an organizational or a personal task. For example, social competences like socializing, team working and social thinking are abilities that a manager should have.

CM stands for the identification of competences and the optimization in fitting persons with according competence profiles to appropriate tasks. *Competence development* and *learning* or *advanced training* can be used synonymously as it is connected with the process of *knowledge acquisition*. The development of competences is based on extending or acquiring expertise.

3 Management and Development of Competences Using SNA Patterns

Both, management and development of competences depend on the actual status of competences in an environment, which we can extract by precisely analyzing the environment. The activities, that repeat periodically in the environment, e.g., people wake-up, eat, work, have meetings and reports, are called patterns. Pattern analysis bears on the real situation of the environment. It can advise what competences are presented or needed currently in the environment.

Pattern analysis was firstly introduced by [1]. A pattern consists of a description of a problem, a context where it is applied, forces, which are influencing appearance of the problem, and possible solutions to the problem Moreover patterns can be stimulations to change the current situation [11]. The purpose of patterns is not only to analyze the reality but as well to give advice or enable people to figure out how to proceed in the current situation. We choose social network analysis (SNA) to identify patterns of CNs.

3.1 SNA Applications

SNA technique reveals hidden roles and goals of workers, which are not highlighted by applying other analysis [9]. Above all, the characteristics of networks and their nodes indicate persons with the biggest and smallest social capital and the highest reputation. It has been proved that the centrality of a node in a student network influences onto students' performance, team outcomes and satisfaction from learning [2]. Moreover, using SNA one can calculate the frequency of collaborations and consensus degree in a network.

In any case, the information SNA gives us must be interpreted and further steps must be inferred. If a network is not dense enough and clusters of the network do not communicate with each other, this can be a reason why the network is not productive enough because teams (clusters) are not communicating with each other or only through one channel. We name the pattern for the described problem *silent collaboration.* It is clear that in the case of *silent collaboration* no or few team members possess social competences. Thus, a competence manager infers why the productivity is not high and can enhance the situation by organizing an event where isolated teams get to know each other.

3.2 Pattern Analysis Oriented Framework

In our past work we created a framework that uses SNA technique for discovering patterns in digital media communities [7]. We defined the rules of communications within CNs and the *spammer*, the *troll*, the *answering person*, the *questioner*, the *communicator,* and some other patterns were defined using the rules. For example, the *troll* is a person who interacts within a thread/topic that he was initiating and there are no more threads/topics where the *troll* contributes to but not a thread/topic initiator.

In our experiments with communities in digital media, mailing lists in our case, we defined the following patterns: *unluckily initiators, reply senders, reply receivers, communicators* and *cross-users.* We notice that in threads with many *reply senders* (the outcoming degree of links is higher than average), which are answering the questions, *posemo* [1] and *negemo* [2] words are used. In such a case we can infer that people have longtime or personal contact with each other and can freely express themselves.

3.3 Contribution to Competence Management

The application of SNA contributes to evaluation of competences of CNs members as the rating of social skills is possible using SNA measures. Considering activities of the members in the past and evolution of their positions in CNs we can find which activities infer which competences. Scrutinizing goals of CNs and their members, the appropriate activities can be proposed for acquiring required competences.

4 Agent-Based Modeling of Collaborative Networks

4.1 Agents of Collaborative Networks

Before retrieving patterns of CNs we want to conceptualize the structure of the networks and their environments. That is why we refer to Actor Network Theory (ANT) presented by [4]. He claims that any object in a system is an actor, be it a human or not. Therefore, a system is represented as a set of actors that are depending on each other. Further, we consider a CN as a network of actors connected to each other thus depend on each other.

Figure 1 depicts the basic idea of *Actor Network.* Any thing is an *Actor.* In previous work [6] we defined that the *Actor Network* of CNs in digital environments includes *Process, Media, Community, Artefact,* and *Agent* actors.

---

[1] Agree, improve, support.

[2] Contend, protest, decline.

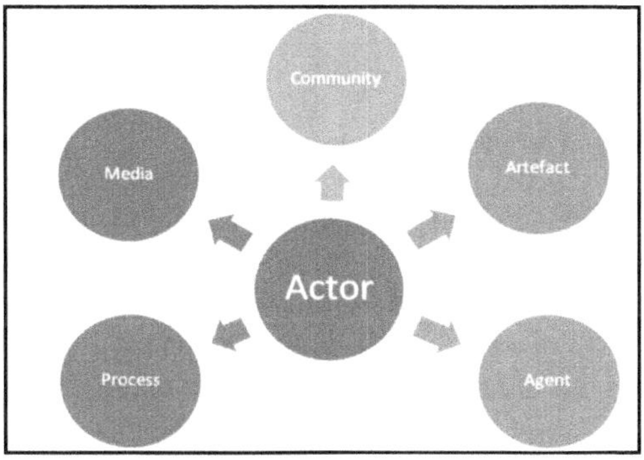

Fig. 1. Actors of digital collaborative network

We consider digital environments as *Media* actors, e.g., a digital learning environment, forums, virtual classrooms. *Artefact* actors are bits of *Media*, e.g., a course, a forum post, a video lecture. *Agent* actors correspond to persons in a CN. *Community* actors are sets of *Agent* actors that collaborate using *Media* and communicate operating *Artefact* actors. *Processes* are mostly initiated by actor's activities, e.g., using *Media* and operating *Artefact* actors.

Latour emphasizes that any actor is influenced by another one. Thus, we need to define the dependencies of actors. That is why we appeal to sociology and consider Communities of Practice.

4.2 Community of Practice

The concept of CoP was precisely described by Wenger [12]. The author postulates that some communities are organized because the members of the communities are interested or evolved in the same practices. Moreover, Wenger states that a CoP has three dimensions that define it. These are *joint enterprises* (JE), *mutual engagement* (ME) and *shared repertoire* (SR). JEss are *policies* and *rules* which all members follow, MEs correspond to members' *collaborations* and the SR is the *knowledge repository* formed by information possessed by a community.

Considering the described dimensions we can determine how *Actors* depend on each other: *communities* depend on *Media* as the latter is liable to provide an environment for collaborations (ME); *Media* and *Artefacts* depend on *Processes* as without *Processes* it is impossible to create, extend or change *Artefacts* and attach them to *Media* (JE); *Processes* depend on *Communities* and *Agents*, which initiate activities (JE); *Agent* depends on *Communities* as the latter identifies the role of *Agent* in *Community* based on his knowledge and his collaborations (SR, ME). We can mention some more of the possible dependencies but abstain from it for the sake of brevity.

Considering dimensions of CoP and agent-based nature of CNs we can conceptualize CNs in general and adopt the model of CNs to our test-bed scenarios. An appropriate modeling technique that satisfies our requirements must be found. First of all, the technique must be agent-oriented, as we consider a CN as a set of agents. Secondly, it must be possible to explicitly define dependencies between actors. Thirdly, we require the consideration of social characteristics to discover competences of CNs.

Finally, models must be extendable so that we can include facts from reality in the form of patterns.

4.3 i* Agent-Oriented Modeling Technique

The i* language is an agent-oriented high-level modeling approach [13]. It was developed for the design of business processes on a strategic level. The core of i* models are motives, interests, options and constraints of agents in a business process. Cooperation among agents is needed for fulfillment of common goals. Due to dependencies between goals, tasks, resources and the agents themselves, agents become also vulnerable. In i* we find the following premises: agents act intentionally, because they are following their goals, have beliefs, competences, commitments, needs and desires. Agents are strategic actors, because they have to proceed according to their plans. Intentional dependencies can be made explicit with i* to disclose the reasons behind observable processes. Questions to an i* model are: Who is deciding what? Which options does an agent have? How can I reduce critical dependencies?

In i* we use the strategic-dependency-model (SDM) with a focus on the intentions of agents so that it perfectly fits the requirements of communities. It serves as an abstract view on the external relations of an agent. It delivers very concrete models, e.g., if information is delivered from agent A to agent B but never the other way around, agent B is depending on agent A but not vice versa.

Here we present a short description of conceptual modeling components in i* and use it later in Figure 2 and 3 A so-called *dependee* is an agent that influences other agents' performance, e.g., *Website of the course* in Figure 5.1. The depending agents are *dependers*, e.g., *Learner*. The object through which the dependency is defined is called *dependum*, e.g., *announcements*. The dependencies can be one of the following four types - *resource dependency, task dependency, goal dependency* and *softgoal dependency*. A *resource dependency* like *announcements* exists in case a target *Website of the course* provides a resource to a source *Learner*. There is a *task dependency* such as *create/find/reuse* when a source *Artefact* expects a target *Learner* to execute a task and *goal dependency* indicates the case when a source *Artefact* expects that a target *Teacher* achieves a goal, e.g., *Evaluation*. The *softgoal dependency* like *to focus on professional competences* in Figure 5.2 is used when the goal cannot be described clearly, although a dependency exists.

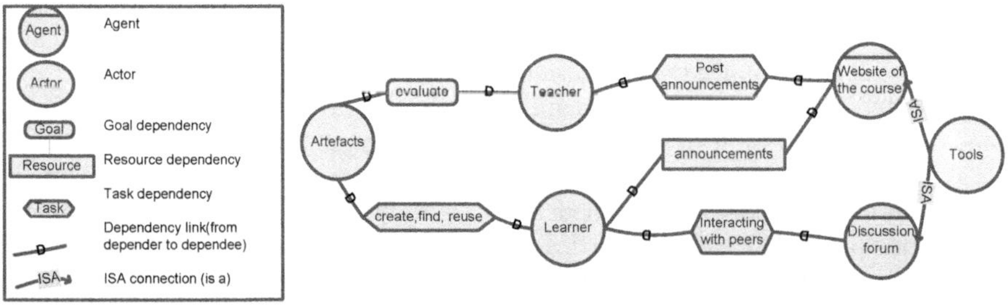

Fig. 2. Model of a collaborative network within a university course

Although i* is already helpful, it does not solve the problem how to manage competences in CNs. We need to extend it for accomplishing our needs. We propose to combine the modeling framework with the SNA pattern-based framework (PBF) and describe all the working procedures of the SNA PBF. On the preparation phase of the framework, we examine CNs and model them. Based on SNA patterns, models can be extended with additional information. Then the gap between imagined scenario *how it is intended to be* and real scenario *how it is in reality* can be filled, considerately existed and missing competences of CNs are defined.

In the following, we present the outcome of our SNA PBF for CM cooperating with i* modeling framework. The presented scenario is taken from a real university course of one of the test-bed partners in EU IP ROLE.

5 University Collaboration Scenario

Courses in universities are constructed in such way that they require a lot of team work. Universities pursuit of letting students to acquire both professional and social competences. On the Figure 2 we consider the university course that utilizes Web technologies for some of its tasks. It provides possibilities for collaborations and awareness, such as *Discussion forum* and *Website of the course.*

In order to apply the methods of the SNA PBF we need to define collaboration networks that exist in the scenario. There are at least two types of CNs possible: *Learner-Learner* CNs and *Learner-Teacher* CNs. With the help of the framework we can identify a learner network characteristics in *Learner-Learner* CNs, in *Learner-Teacher* CN and a teacher network characteristics in *Learner-Teacher* CN. Based on numerous network characteristics it is possible to answer whether the learner's status in *Learner-Teacher* or the status in *Learner-Learner* CNs correlate with the learner's marks. As a result it can be discovered that the learner is too communicative (*degree/betweenness/closeness centralities* of the learner) but pays not enough attention to managing learning material (*create/find/reuse* task for *Artefact*).

The person responsible for CM and development (the course manager or the teacher of the course) can help the learner to focus on *professional competences* so that the learner can better succeed in the course. The learner can be asked to handle more often with *Artefacts,* e.g., to create a knowledge map about a topic from the

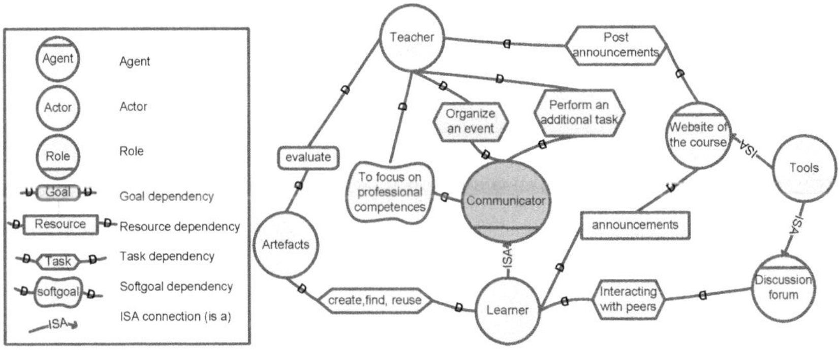

Fig. 3. Model of a CN using i*modeling framework and SNA pattern-oriented framework

course. Afterwards, the learner can discuss his *Artefact* in a *Discussion Forum* as according to the *communicator* pattern, it is the part of learning he enjoys. While this is a *competence development* application, the next scenario is an example of *CM*.

On the other hand, if the teacher of the course needs to organize an event for the students of the course, the learner is the right person for the task.

The result of the application of the SNA PBF is depicted in Figure 3 Here we use the *Role* i* notation for illustrating the *communicator* pattern.

6 Related Work

The i* modeling framework we used here proposes an ostensive type of modeling as the framework aims to express the goals the agents of the systems want to achieve. Another type of modeling is performative modeling, which depicts collaborations as it happens in reality (Feldman and Pentland, 2003). Even goal-oriented modeling (i*) describes how collaborations are expected to be, the combination of i* modeling with the pattern-oriented framework makes the models both reflect *the reality* of a CN and the goals of actors, *the intensions*. However, the latest elaborated survey on modeling [9] distinguishes only between ostensive and performative modeling techniques[3] for collaborative technologies.

The model of collaborations using the concept of patterns was recently published by [8]. The work describes capturing and reusing recurring segments of work or parts of collaborations. Patterns are identified through analysis of actions of users in a system.

Another approach for CM applies a competence performance approach [5]. The authors collect information about competences needed for task performance and based on the information and competence profiles of workers appropriate tasks are assigned to suitable workers. If workers do not have required competences appropriate courses are assigned to workers.

7 Conclusion

We introduced the notions of patterns and competences and showed how competences can be managed and developed using patterns. We particularly consider social network analysis techniques to identify patterns. Moreover, we applied the i* modeling technique that allows us to conceptualize one of our test-bed scenarios of CNs. We considered Actor Network Theory and Communities of Practice in our model. Finally, we propose the SNA pattern based framework that extend the goal-oriented i* model with facts from reality extracted using SNA patterns. We show how such models support competence development and management tasks.

Acknowledgments. The research leading to these results has received funding from the European Community's Seventh Framework Programme (FP7/2007-2013) under grant agreement no 231396 (ROLE project).

---

[3] UML models, workflow, coordination theory, Grounded theory, temporal models (rhytms), social network models or language action perspective.

References

1. Alexander, C.: A Pattern Language: Towns, Buildings, Construction. Center for Environmental Structure Series. Oxford University Press, New York (1978)
2. Baldwin, T.T., Bedell, M.D., Johnson, J.L.: The Social Fabric of a Team-Based M.B.A. Program: Network Effects on Student Satisfaction and Performance. The Academy of Management Journal 40(6), 1369–1397 (1997)
3. Cheetham, G., Chivers, G.E.: Professions, competence and informal learning. Edward Elgar Pub. (2005)
4. Latour, B.: On Recalling {ANT}. In: Law, J., Hassard, J. (eds.) Actor-Network Theory and After, Oxford, pp. 15–25 (1999)
5. Ley, T., Lindstaedt, S., Albert, D.: Supporting Competency Development in Informal Workplace Learning. In: Althoff, K.-D., Dengel, A.R., Bergmann, R., Nick, M., Roth-Berghofer, T.R. (eds.) PWM 2005. LNCS (LNAI), vol. 3782, pp. 189–202. Springer, Heidelberg (2005)
6. Klamma, R., Petrushyna, Z.: The Troll Under the Bridge: Data Management for Huge Web Science Mediabases. In: Proc. Informatik 2008 Band 2 - Workshop Digital Social Networks, pp. 923–928. Gesellschaft für Informatik (2008)
7. Klamma, R., Spaniol, M., Denev, D.: {PALADIN}: A Pattern Based Approach to Knowledge Discovery in Digital Social Networks. In: Tochtermann, K., Maurer, H. (eds.) Proceedings of I-KNOW 2006, 6th International Conference on Knowledge Management, Graz, Austria, September 6 - 8, pp. 457–464. Springer, Heidelberg (2006); J.UCS (Journal of Universal Computer Science)
8. Papageorgiou, N., Verginadis, Y., Apostolou, D., Mentzas, G.: A collaboration pattern model for virtual organizations. In: Leveraging Knowledge for Innovation in Collaborative Networks. IFIP Advances in Information and Communication Technology, vol. 307, pp. 61–68. Springer, Heidelberg (2009)
9. Poltrock, S.E., Handel, M.: Modeling Collaborative Behavior: Foundations for Collaboration Technologies. In: HICSS, pp. 1–10. IEEE Computer Society, Los Alamitos (2009)
10. Sampson, D., Fytros, D.: Handbook on Information Technologies for Education and Training, Berlin, Heidelberg, pp. 155–177 (2008)
11. Schuler, D.: Liberating Voices: A Pattern Language for Communication Revolution, p. 504. MIT Press, Cambridge (2008)
12. Wenger, E.: Communities of Practice: Learning, Meaning, and Identity. Cambridge University Press, Cambridge (1998)
13. Yu, E.S., Mylopoulos, J.: Towards Modelling Strategic Actor Relationships for Information Systems Development – With Examples from Business Process Reengineering. In: Proceedings of the 4th Workshop on Information Technologies and Systems, Vancouver, B.C., Canada, December 17-18, pp. 21–28 (1994)

Reasoning about Skills and Competencies

Maryam Fazel-Zarandi[1] and Mark S. Fox[2]

[1] Department of Computer Science,
[2] Department of Mechanical and Industrial Engineering,
University of Toronto, Toronto, Canada
mfazel@cs.toronto.edu, msf@eil.utoronto.ca

Abstract. Human Resources Management (HRM) is the strategic management of the employees, who individually and collectively contribute to the achievement of the strategic goals of an organization. Most HRM tasks are based on acquiring the right information and reasoning about skills and competencies of individuals. In this paper we present a formal ontology for competency management and consider three reasoning problems related to HRM, namely, determining the set of skills of an individual, conducting competency gap analysis, and determining whether an individual satisfies a set of requirements.

Keywords: Competency management, Skills ontology.

1 Introduction

In today's competitive business environment, companies need to accurately grasp the competency of their human resources in order to be successful. This is particularly important for organizations that engage with multiple and changing clients such as consulting firms and software development companies since these organizations need to be able to flexibly respond to internal and external demands for skills and competencies. As such, proper and flexible human resources management (HRM) and competency management approaches for more effective resource allocation, human resource hiring, knowledge management, learning support, and human resource development are of outmost importance to the survival of these companies.

In order to facilitate the management of available human resources' competencies, provide a global view of competencies available at the organizational level, and perform qualitative and quantitative reasoning about available and required skills, the use of formal ontologies has been suggested in previous research. In almost all the existing systems and approaches, however, the focus has been either on building and maintaining ontology-based skill catalogs [e.g. 1, 2, 5, 6], or searching for individuals that match certain requirements [e.g. 2, 3, 10, 11, 12]. As such, the reasoning has been limited to subsumption checking. Furthermore, existing approaches have mainly focused on binary matching and do not take into account the cases where skills do not completely match existing requirements.

In this paper, we attempt to extend existing ontologies to address other interesting HR-related problems in addition to determining whether an individual satisfies a set of requirements. These problems include: 1) determining the set of skills of an

L.M. Camarinha-Matos et al. (Eds.): PRO-VE 2010, IFIP AICT 336, pp. 372–379, 2010.

individual and 2) conducting competency gap analysis to determine who to train and what training program to offer. Note that in this paper we are not addressing the concerns raised about incorporating the human and judgmental aspects of HR.

2 Motivating Use-Cases

Following the ontology development methodology of Gruninger and Fox [8], we first identify the problems the ontology is going to address. The following examples from two different perspectives motivate and illustrate the need for the skills ontology.

- *Example 1*: A HR manager working at a high tech firm is responsible for suggesting individuals for a team to work on a specific software development project. To do her job well, she needs to know the competencies of available human resources to match them with existing requirements, to determine the training and development needs of employees, and to determine if the company suffers from a shortage of competency. As such, she has asked all the employees to state their skills based on an existing skills taxonomy which consists of technical computer skills related to all aspects of software design and development. However, since self declarations of skills and competencies can be inaccurate or insufficient, she wants to be able to distinguish between proposed and demonstrated skills of an individual and detect the competencies that were not explicitly mentioned but the individual may have. In addition, she wants to determine the gaps that may exist between the skills of an individual and a set of requirements and use this information to suggest under-qualified matches when qualified ones cannot be found or to suggest training opportunities.
- *Example 2*: A software engineer with previous work experience working at two high tech firms is looking for a software development position that includes some managerial elements. He has a degree in computer science and has taken some management courses. To make a decision, he needs to find out which job postings he is currently qualified for, what are the requirements of the position he wants, and what training is required for him to qualify for that particular job.

Using these examples we can define the ontologies' requirements in the form of questions that it must be able to answer. We divide these questions into those that previous research has been able to address, and those that it does not address.

- *Questions addressed by previous research*: What are the credentials and previous work experience of an individual? Who are the individuals that satisfy a particular requirement? What are the proposed skills of an individual? Which skills are required for a particular job? Who are the qualified matches for a job posting? Which job postings is an individual qualified for?
- *Questions not addressed by previous research*: What are the demonstrated skills of an individual? What are the skills that an individual has which were not explicitly mentioned? Who are the individuals that *may* have a particular skill? Does the company suffer a shortage of a competency? If qualified matches cannot be found, who are the next best choices? If an individual does not qualify for a particular job, what training is required?

3 The Skills Ontology

In this section we briefly present the ontology we developed to answer the questions posed in section 2[1]. We use first-order logic (FOL) as the basis for the ontology because of its expressive and declarative capability. With the ontology being defined in FOL and applied in a theorem prover, the ontology will have the deductive capability to answer queries. In particular, our ontology is an extension of the Process Specification Language (PSL) [9], a first-order language for modeling processes.

3.1 Skill

There are several definitions of competency present in the literature [4]. The definition we assume is the one given by the HR-XML Consortium work group (http://hr-xml.org): "a specific, identifiable, definable, and measurable knowledge, skill, ability and/or other deployment-related characteristic (e.g. attitude, behavior, physical ability) which a human resource may posses and which is necessary for, or material to, the performance of an activity within a specific business context." We adopt this definition for its emphasis on measurable knowledge and skills and the connection between competencies and activity performance. Hereafter, we focus on measurable skills possessed by human resources and use skill instead of competency.

We assume skills in a specific domain of interest and distinguish between demonstrated and proposed skills. Demonstrated skills are those related to previous performed activities. Proposed skills are either based on self-declarations of expertise or the skills that an individual may posses after completing a learning activity.

As stated earlier, a skill suggests the possibility of performing an activity. In the formal PSL ontology, the notion of activity is a basic construct, which corresponds intuitively to a kind of activity. An activity may have associated *occurrences*, which correspond to individual instances or executions (from start to finish) of the activity[2]. We represent the relation between a skill and an activity using the *enables* predicate:

$$\ldots s\ \mathrm{Skill}(s) \equiv |\, a\ \mathrm{Activity}(a)\ .\ \mathrm{enables}(s, a) \qquad (1)$$

We define specific tools or technologies as resources in PSL and associate them with activities using the *requires* relation. For example, in "object-oriented coding in Java", "object-oriented coding" is the activity which requires "Java". We also define the *related-to* relation between two skills indicating that they are highly related to each other in the domain of interest (i.e., having one usually implies having the other). For example, software development skills are *related-to* programming skills. Put formally, two skills are related if they enable the same activity, or if they enable subactivities of the same activity:

$$\begin{aligned}\ldots s1, s2\ &\text{related-to}(s_1, s_2) \equiv |\, a\ \mathrm{Activity}(a)\ .\ [(\mathrm{enables}(s_1, a)\ .\\ &\mathrm{enables}(s_2, a)) - (|\, a_1, a_2\ \mathrm{Activity}(a_1)\ .\ \mathrm{Activity}(a_2)\ .\ \mathrm{subactivity}(a_1, a)\ .\\ &\mathrm{subactivity}(a_2, a)\ .\ \mathrm{enables}(s_1, a_1)\ .\ \mathrm{enables}(s_2, a_2))]\end{aligned} \qquad (2)$$

[1] For brevity, not all axioms of the ontology are included in this paper. The interested reader is referred to http://www.cs.toronto.edu/~mfazel/publications/mfz_fox_pro-ve_extended.pdf .

[2] In PSL an activity is not a class or type with occurrences as members; rather, an activity is an object, and occurrences are related to this object by the binary predicate *occurrence-of.*

3.2 Learning Activity and Work Experience

A learning activity (LA) is an activity that has one or more *learning outcomes* associated with it and occurs within a particular context [7]. A learning outcome is what the learners should be able to do after completing the LA. Currently we only consider formal learning activities which occur as a result of instructor-led programs within the curricula of educational institutions or the courses or workshops offered by different agencies [15]. Formal learning activities can have a set of skills at a particular knowledge level (beginner, intermediate, advanced, expert) as required preconditions (*has-precondition*), but must have at least one proposed skill at a particular knowledge level as outcome (*has-outcome*).

$$\ldots x\ \text{FormalLearningActivity}(x) \equiv \text{Activity}(x)\ .\ \mid y, z\ \text{has-outcome}(x, y, z) \tag{3}$$

An individual has taken a learning activity if and only if an occurrence of that activity exists in which she has participated in:

$$\ldots x, y, t, e\ \text{has-taken}(x, y, t, e) \equiv (\text{Person}(x)\ .\ \text{FormalLearningActivity}(y)\ .\ \mid o\ \text{occurrence-of}(o, y)\ .\ \text{participates-in}(x, o)\ .\ \text{beginof}(o) = t\ .\ \text{endof}(o) = e\ .\ \text{legal}(o)) \tag{4}$$

Having the definition for formal learning activity, we can define a degree in a field of study as a program that requires a set of formal learning activities (*requires-fla*), is offered by some organization (*offered-by*), and has a starting and ending time point. If an individual has a degree then it must be the case that she has completed all the formal learning activities required for the degree.

Work experience indicates past performed activities at a particular organization. We associate these activities to positions the experience refers to using the *includes-activity* relation. We define the *has-experience* predicate between a person, a position, an organization, and a starting and ending time point. If an individual has a previous work experience then she has participated in an occurrence of all the activities associated with the position that experience refers to:

$$\ldots x, y, p, t, e\ \text{has-experience}(x, p, y, t, e)\ \theta\ (\text{Person}(x)\ .\ \text{Position}(p)\ .\ \text{Organization}(y)\ .\ (\ldots a\ \text{includes-activity}(p, a)\ \theta\ (\mid o\ \text{occurrence-of}(o, a)\ .\ \text{participates-in}(x, o)\ .\ \text{legal}(o)))) \tag{5}$$

We also define *has-experience-in* between a person, a skill, and a positive integer to denote the years of experience the individual has with respect to a skill. For brevity we omit the axioms related this predicate.

3.3 Job Posting

We define a job posting as a set of requirements in terms of job related descriptions and constraints on skills. Every job posting has a description (*has-description*), a set of skill requirements (*has-requirement*), and zero or more degree requirements (*has-degree-requirement*). Skill requirements can either be must-have or nice-to-have constraints.

$$\ldots j \text{ JobPosting}(j) \equiv \,|\, d, r, z \text{ has-description}(j, d) \,.\, \text{Requirement}(r) \,.\, \text{has-requirement}(j, r, z) \,.\, (z = \text{must-have} - z = \text{nice-to-have}) \tag{6}$$

Requirements are constraints on proposed or demonstrated skills. Every requirement refers to only one skill. It is possible to defined requirements by adding constraints on minimum required years of experience performing activities related to a skill (*requires-experience*), required knowledge level (*requires-knowledge*), or required tool or technology (*requires-use*). For example, a resource requirement requires the use of one or more tools or technologies.

The description consists of a title (*has-title*), a position (*has-position*) including the specific activities that the individual holding the job needs to perform, a brief description in free text format (*has-brief-description*), and a category (*has-category*).

4 Additional Axioms

4.1 Determining the Set of Skills

Using the HR-XML definition, having a particular skill becomes tightly bound to the evidence that suggests one has a certain skill at a particular level of proficiency. The evidence also helps in understanding how a skill can be achieved, which is especially useful for arranging training programs. To detect whether an individual has a skill, we also need to determine the particular level of proficiency which may depend on different factors such as the span of the activities one can perform, how much experience one has in performing an activity, how well an activity is performed, what others think about how an activity was performed, etc. Different quantitative and qualitative measurement scales exist for evaluating an individual against a skill. Rating scales are the most popular and consist of a numeric scale with a brief description of each number's corresponding meaning. The disadvantage of these scales, however, lies in their inconsistent interpretations across users of a scale [13]. To overcome this problem, we distinguish between skills enabling two different types of activities: 1) activities which successfully performing them confirms proficiency in a skill (e.g., brain surgery); and 2) activities which the outcome does not necessarily confirm proficiency (e.g., having programmed once does not mean one is a programmer). We focus only on the first type for demonstrated skills and plan on addressing the second type in future by considering social networks and peer reviews.

To determine the skill set of an individual, we use learning activities and experiences related to the workplace and consider demonstrated and proposed skills. We define three relations: *has-skill, has-proposed-skill*, and *may-have-skill.*

If an individual can perform all the activities which a skill enables, then it is the case that she has that skill:

$$\ldots x, y \text{ has-skill}(x, y) \equiv (\text{Person}(x) \,.\, \text{DemonstratedSkill}(y) \,.\, (\ldots a \text{ enables}(y,a) \;\theta\; |\, o \text{ occurrence-of}(o, a) \,.\, \text{participates-in}(x, o) \,.\, \text{legal}(o))) \tag{7}$$

Considering learning activities, if a person has taken a formal learning activity and a proposed skill is a precondition or outcome of it, then it is proposed that the person has that skill:

$$\ldots x, y, t, e, z, k\ \text{has-taken}(x, y, t, e).\ [\text{has-outcome}(y,z,k) - \text{has-precondition}(y, z, k)]\ \theta\ \text{has-proposed-skill}(x, z, k) \tag{8}$$

If an individual has participated in an occurrence of an activity which required a particular resource (tool or technology), then it might be the case that she can perform other activities which require the same resource. For example, if an individual has experience plotting graphs in Microsoft Excel, then she might also be able to do macro programming in Excel.

$$\ldots a, a', r\ \text{requires}(a, r)\ .\ \text{requires}(a', r)\ \theta\ (((\mid o\ \text{occurrence-of}(o, a)\ .\ \text{participates-in}(x, o)\ .\ \text{legal}(o))\ .\ (\neg \mid o'\ \text{occurrence-of}(o', a')\ .\ \text{participates-in}(x, o')\ .\ \text{legal}(o')))\ \theta\ \text{may-perform}(x, a')) \tag{9}$$

and as such have the skills that enable those activities:

$$\ldots x, y\ \text{Person}(x)\ .\ \text{Skill}(y)\ .\ (\mid a\ \text{enables}(y, a)\ .\ \text{may-perform}(x, a))\ \theta\ ((\ldots z\ \text{enables}(y, z)\ \theta\ ((\mid o\ \text{occurrence-of}(o, z)\ .\ \text{participates-in}(x, o)\ .\ \text{legal}(o)) - \text{may-perform}(x, z)))\ \theta\ \text{may-have-skill}(x, y)) \tag{10}$$

We can also consider highly related skills in the domain of interest. For example, software development skills are related-to programming skills, and having one may suggest having the other.

$$\ldots x,y,z\ \text{has-skill}(x,y).\neg\text{has-skill}(x,z)\theta(\text{related-to}(y,z)\theta\text{may-have-skill}(x,z)) \tag{11}$$

4.2 Gap Analysis

Competency gap analysis serves two purposes in HRM. First, in real world situations, it is rarely the case that individuals satisfy all the requirements of a job posting. Second, competency gap analysis is beneficial for understanding whether the company suffers from a shortage of knowledge or skill in a particular area, and for finding suitable learning opportunities and arranging training programs [14]. To this end, we need to calculate the gap between the set of requirements and the set of skills of an individual. We consider two types of gap: competency gap and proficiency gap. A *competency gap* refers to the absence of a skill in the individual's profile.

$$\ldots p, s, k\ \text{has-competency-gap}(p, s) \equiv (\neg\text{has-skill}(p, s)\ .\ \neg\text{has-proposed-skill}(p, s, k)\ .\ \neg\text{may-have-skill}\ (p, s)) \tag{12}$$

A *proficiency gap*, on the other hand, refers to the difference in proficiency levels of a skill requirement and a skill statement. To determine proficiency gap for demonstrated skills, we focus on metrics such as years of experience and activities that an individual can perform. It is possible to define domain-specific metrics, such as the number of bugs found in a code for a programmer, or the number of failed projects for a contractor, etc. For example, a proficiency gap based on years of experience can be determined as follows:

$$\ldots p, r, s, m, e\ \text{Person}(p)\ .\ \text{Requirement}(r)\ .\ \text{refers-to}(r, s)\ .\ \text{requires-experience}(r, m)\ .\ \text{has-experience-in}(p, s, e)\ .\ e < m\ \theta\ \text{has-proficiency-gap}(p, r) \tag{13}$$

4.3 Skills-Requirements Matchmaking

In skills-requirements matchmaking, we are interested in determining whether or not an individual satisfies a set of requirements. An individual satisfies a requirement if and only if 1) when the requirement requires experience greater than zero, then she has demonstrated that skill for the require time period; otherwise, 2) she has the proposed skill.

$$\ldots p, r, s, m, e \text{ satisfies}(p, r) \equiv \text{refers-to}(r, s) \;.\; \text{requires-experience}(r, m) \;.\\ ((m = 0 \;\theta\; \text{has-proposed-skill}(p, s)) - (m \;\gamma\; 0 \;\theta\; \text{has-experience-in}(p, s, e))) \tag{14}$$

For a job posting *j*, a *qualified* match denotes that an individual satisfies all its degree and skill requirements.

$$\ldots j, p\; ((\ldots t, f \text{ has-degree-requirement}(j, t, f) \;\theta\; \exists d \text{ has-degree}(p, d) \;.\\ \text{has-degree-title}(d, t) \;.\; \text{has-study-field}(d, f)) \;.\\ (\ldots r \text{ has-requirement}(j, r, \text{must-have}) \;.\; \text{satisfies}(p, r))) \;\theta\\ \text{qualified-match}(j, p) \tag{15}$$

In real world situations, however, it rarely happens that applications match all the requirements specified in a job posting. For this, in addition to the qualified match, we consider different types of under-qualified matches. For one type of under-qualified match, we relax the required proficiency level constraints. In this case, an application is considered to be *proficiency-under-qualified* match for a job posting if and only if a proficiency gap exists for one or more of the required skills. Another type of under-qualified match, *competency-under-qualified* match, takes competency gaps into account and considers all individuals who satisfy a subset of the required skills.

5 Conclusions and Future Directions

This paper presented a formal ontology for competency management and considered three problems related to HRM, namely, determining the set of skills of an individual, conducting competency gap analysis, and determining whether an individual satisfies a set of requirements. The main evaluation criterion for the development of the ontology was competency, the capability of a representation to support the use-cases for which it is designed. An interesting topic of future research would be to evaluate the ontology according to knowledge representation criteria such as consistency and completeness, as well as systems performance criteria like efficiency and scalability.

In addition to satisfying advertised job requirements, other factors such as job seekers' and recruiters' preferences, cultural fit, and ability to adapt to the company's marketplace play an important part in selecting employees. Furthermore, when considering individuals for teams, complexities may arise due to fitness between an individual and other team members. It would be interesting to see how these complexities can be supported by automated techniques.

Acknowledgments. The authors gratefully acknowledge the constructive comments and helpful advice of Professor Michael Gruninger. This research is supported, in part, by the Natural Science and Engineering Research Council of Canada.

References

1. Biesalski, E., Abecker, A.: Human Resource Management with Ontologies. In: Althoff, K.-D., Dengel, A.R., Bergmann, R., Nick, M., Roth-Berghofer, T.R. (eds.) WM 2005. LNCS (LNAI), vol. 3782, pp. 499–507. Springer, Heidelberg (2005)
2. Bizer, C., Heese, R., Mochol, M., Oldakowski, R., Tolksdorf, R., Eckstein, R.: The Impact of Semantic Web Technologies on Job Recruitment Processes. In: Proceedings of the 7th International Conference Wirtschaftsinformatik (2005)
3. Colucci, S., Di Noia, T., Di Sciascio, E., Donini, F.M., Mongiello, M., Mottola, M.: A Formal Approach to Ontology-Based Semantic Match for Skills Descriptions. Journal of Universal Computer Science 9(12), 1437–1454 (2003)
4. De Coi, J., Herder, E., Koesling, A., Lofi, C., Olmedilla, D., Papatreou, O., Siberski, W.: A Model for Competence Gap Analysis. In: Proceedings of 3rd International Conference on Web Information Systems and Technologies (WEBIST) (2007)
5. Dittmann, L.: Towards Ontology-based Skill Management, Projektbericht zum Verbundprojekt KOWIEN, Universität Duisburg-Essen (2003)
6. Gomez-Perez, A., Ramirez, J., Villazon-Terrazas, B.: Reusing Human Resources Management Standards for Employment Services. In: Proceedings of the Workshop on the First Industrial Results of Semantic Technologies at ISWC/ASWC, pp. 28–41 (2007)
7. Gráinne, C., Fill, K.: A Learning Design Toolkit to Create Pedagogically Effective Learning Activities. Journal of Interactive Media in Education 8 (2005)
8. Gruninger, M., Fox, M.S.: The Design and Evaluation of Ontologies for Enterprise Engineering. In: Workshop on Implemented Ontologies, European Conference on Artificial Intelligence (ECAI 1994), Amsterdam, NL (1994)
9. Gruninger, M., Menzel, C.: Process specification language: Theory and applications. AI Magazine 24, 63–74 (2003)
10. Lau, T., Sure, Y.: Introducing Ontology-Based Skills Management at a Large Insurance Company. In: Proceedings of the Modellierung, pp. 123–134 (2002)
11. Liu, P., Dew, P.: Using Semantic Web Technologies to Improve expertise Matching within Academia. In: Proceedings of I-KNOW 2004, pp. 370–378 (2004)
12. Mochol, M., Wache, H., Nixon, L.: Improving the Accuracy of Job Search with Semantic Techniques. In: Abramowicz, W. (ed.) BIS 2007. LNCS, vol. 4439, pp. 301–313. Springer, Heidelberg (2007)
13. Moyer, R.: Defining and Measuring Competencies: An Overview of Approaches. Click2learn Inc. (2001)
14. Schmidt, A., Kunzmann, C.: Towards a Human Resource Development Ontology for Combining Competence Management and Technology-Enhanced Workplace Learning. In: Meersman, R., Tari, Z., Herrero, P. (eds.) OTM 2006 Workshops. LNCS, vol. 4278, pp. 1078–1087. Springer, Heidelberg (2006)
15. Schugurensky, D.: The Forms of Informal Learning: Towards a Conceptualization of the Field, NALL Working Paper No. 19 (2000)

A Competence-Based Collaborative Network: The West Midlands Collaborative Commerce Marketplace

Yen Cheung[1], Helana Scheepers[2], Mark Swift[3], Vincent Lee[1], and Jay Bal[3]

[1] Clayton School of IT, Monash University, Victoria 3800, Australia
[2]Swinburne University, Victoria 3122, Australia
[3] WMG, University of Warwick, Coventry, CV4 7AL, UK
ycheung@infotech.monash.edu.au, HSCHEEPERS@groupwise.swin.edu.au, Mark.Swift@warwick.ac.uk, Jay.Bal@warwick.ac.uk, vincent.lee@infotech.monash.edu.au

Abstract. We present a competence-based collaborative network, the West Midlands Collaborative Commerce Marketplace (WMCCM) that was successfully employed to gain new business opportunities for SMEs in the West Midlands region of the UK. The competence profiling methodology employed places an emphasis on what SMEs are capable of doing rather than what products they make. This generates an increased number and wider range of enquiries to the SME. Further, a combination of tender feeds classified by semantic analysis of the tender requirements matched to the SME capability with a novel partnership formation function generates higher level systems type opportunities for these SMEs, which they would have been unable to undertake on their own. The paper discusses the functionality of the WMCCM using a case study to demonstrate its functionalities with reference to the I-BPM framework from the ECOLEAD project. It also highlights the roles in managing competence exchanges in collaborative networks as well as providing a common infrastructure for businesses to launch and operate their virtual organizations.

Keywords: collaborative network, competence, profiling, tender.

1 Introduction

The introduction of Internet technology and electronic communication in the mid 1990s, have created expectations about how businesses could benefit from this new electronic environment i.e. electronic marketplaces (eMarketplaces) and how they could have access to global economy [1]. However despite rapid developments and implementation of eMarketplaces, there is only a modest uptake of this technology with many cases of failure to deliver promises being reported in the literature [2]. Hence to date, there has been a limited acceptance of eMarketplace models that has given investors confidence in their long-term financial viability as independent businesses. The main reason for such failures is the lack of robust models and understanding in the structure and complexities of interactions (or collaborations) amongst the various entities in eMarketplaces. Although collaborations bring huge benefits for the

L.M. Camarinha-Matos et al. (Eds.): PRO-VE 2010, IFIP AICT 336, pp. 380–387, 2010.

stakeholders, a high failure rate among collaborative organisations is reported in the literature [3]. In the case of eMarketplaces, both benefits of collaboration and the potential of the Internet should lead to even more benefits for organisations. However as discussed above, this is not the case as their development and deployment has been rather ad hoc. Indeed various projects around the world (e.g. ALIVE, GENESIS, ATHENA and ECOLEAD to name a few), are working to provide solutions to the challenges of the emerging discipline of collaborative networks of which eMarketplaces are an example.

Triggered by opportunities provided by eMarketplaces, distributed global eBusiness collaborations have given rise to virtual enterprises (VEs), where autonomous organisations collaborate primarily over the Internet to achieve a common goal. These VEs are said to operate in collaborative-networked breeding environments. This area of research in Internet enabled collaborative systems is generally known as collaborative networks (CNs) [4]. For example, in Europe, ECOLEAD (European Collaborative networked Organizations LEADership Initiative) addresses the areas of CNs such as a framework to form the basis for dynamic and sustainable-networked organisations.

In this paper, a practical and successful example of a virtual organisation breeding environment (VBE), the WMCCM is presented as a competence-based collaborative network. The design and functionalities of the WMCCM is described using the reference framework of ECOLEAD.

The structure of the paper is as follows: in the following section we provide background on CN frameworks as suggested by ECOLEAD, followed by a description of the West Midlands Collaborative Marketplace (WMCCM), its design and functionalities such as the competence profiling methodology. This is followed by a section presenting the outcomes of the system i.e. providing improved access to existing and new market opportunities as well as enhancing collaboration amongst stakeholders to generate new opportunities. In the conclusion we summarise our findings and articulate some directions for further research.

2 Collaborative Networks

A comprehensive CN framework called the Integral business process management framework (I-BPM) has been developed by Romero and Molina [5] based on the ECOLEAD project [4]. The I-BPM takes a holistic view of CNs and includes the creation as well as ongoing management of virtual organisations (VOs) and virtual breeding environments (VBEs). A VBE is a pool of organisations and their related supporting institutions that have both the potential and interest to cooperate [6]. A subset of this pool is a VO that can be formed on a short term (a dynamic virtual organisation) or long term (a permanent structure such as a cluster) basis.

The I-BPM consists of the following five process groups:

- VBE actor management – creation and update of information about members, VBE structure and member competence profiles;
- VO creation – identification of business opportunities, initial VO planning, partner search and the development of partner agreement;
- VO Management - management of VOs from their initialization through to their demise;

- VBE General management – management of the overall activities of the VBE for example strategic and marketing management and ICT management;
- VBE horizontal management – management of the processes that cuts across the VBE such as trust management, performance management and innovation management.

The following section presents the design and functionalities of the WMCCM as a CN that includes some of the major processes of the I-BPM framework.

3 The WMCCM

The goal of the WMCCM was to address a critical need of SMEs in the West Midlands. Like the rest of the UK, the West Midlands has a large number of SMEs. In the UK, overall SMEs make up the majority of businesses with a total of 4.3 million enterprises employing 22 million people [7]. Their inherent size means that many operate within limited financial resources, skills and competences resulting in limited economies of scale and scope and an inability to react quickly to these pressures and demands [8]. West Midlands UK research however showed that for SMEs supplying the automotive sector, on average just under 50% of their turnover is derived from that sector [9]. It would therefore be impractical for a small business firm to sign up to these vertical online e-marketplaces, each with its own unique protocols, procedures, practices and ultimately costs. To participate in e-commerce via the many eMarketplaces that exist is not viable for SMEs with limited funds and technical capability.

The WMCCM is a specific case study to test and validate the regional marketplace model. It is a six-year, €5.2 million regional ICT initiative, funded under the European Regional Development Fund to support the economic and social conversion of industrial areas that face structural difficulties.

3.1 WMCCM Workflow

WMCCM is designed to support the following key workflow processes as shown in Figure 1. The workflow, as illustrated from left to right in Figure 1, are described below:

1. Sourcing new business from varied e-tender external online sources including a range of both public and private sector contracts. Firms can also generate tenders for their own needs.
2. Competence Profiling of SMEs. This is a structured process that measures capability within firms using a standardised formal questionnaire with the objective of generating trust and giving easily comparable information. The focus of the questionnaire is to discover what the firm can do, rather than what they are doing currently. The competence profile also captures a range of hard and soft factors so that firms with similar cultures can be identified when trying to form effective collaborations and virtual organisations. The competence profile of each company is indexed against a common system ontology.
3. The classification of tender requirements and SME capability uses the same common ontology. The daily tenders listing each day (200+ tenders) is semantically analysed and the tender requirements are automatically classified by

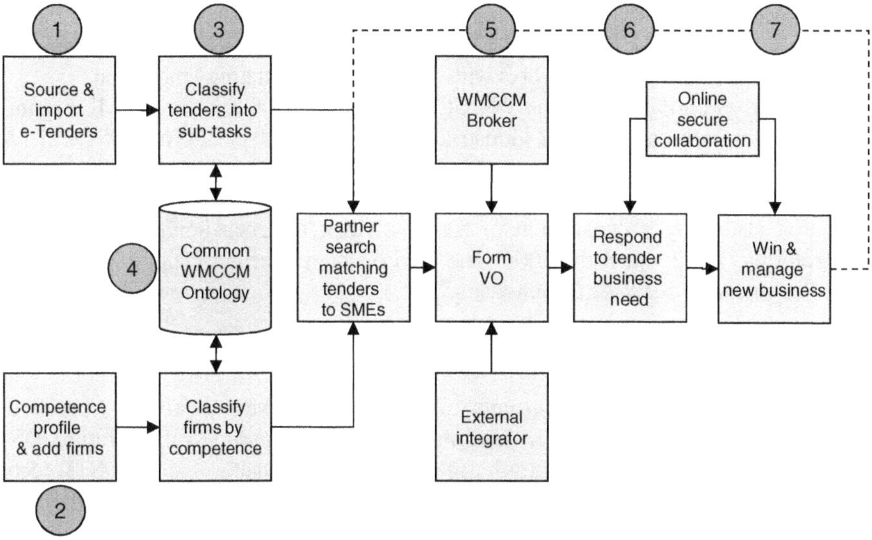

Fig. 1. The WMCCM workflow

process capability required, skill need, location and quality standards by the WMCCM system.

4. Match tender to individual or group of SMEs using WMCCM online Partner Search System. The Partnership Search system is used when a tender requires a competence, which SMEs cannot fully cater for. This is a common situation since the tenders are higher value "systems" type tenders. It is a two-stage search process. The first stage matches against an absolute need or hard factors such a capability in networks, injection moulding, metal spinning etc. The second stage is a preference or soft factor scoring process to generate a partnership which has common cultural elements and is more likely to be able to work together. These relate to industry knowledge, size, quality standards, location etc. The system scores marks for each eligible company and then suggests a best-fit partnership based on the highest matched scores. The SME's are automatically alerted by a daily email giving detail about the tender opportunity.
5. The results of the partner search suggest an initial best fit grouping of SMEs who collectively have the potential capability to bid for the tender contract. At this stage the VO starts to take shape as members undergo a stage of team forming through a number of initial face-to-face meetings. WMCCM provides secure on-line collaboration spaces to facilitate this.
6. To respond to tender (business need) and collaborate online in secure project spaces. Default functionality includes document storage, simple project and task allocation management and discussion forums with associated knowledge management tools.
7. If the bid is successful and the contract won, further collaboration tools can be used such as an integrated supply chain visibility facility.

In summary, rather than just measuring current operational capability, competence profiling seeks to determine transferable capability. SMEs who are competence profiled are matched against a dynamic ontology, which allows their capabilities to be matched against the tasks of any online tender. This is the matching of tasks (tender requests) with resources (the SMEs capability) with the view of stimulating innovation.

As of early February 2010, the WMCCM had over 9,000 registered SME organisations, covering a broad range of industrial competence. Over 350 of WMCCM SME members have been competence profiled. The following section provides the SME Military Tender case study that was a result of a competitive tender procurement invitation issued by a department of the UK MoD, Defence Scientific Technology Laboratories (DSTL) in April 2006. The goal of the tender is to supply complex and varied engineering services for ten years.

3.2 A Case Study: SME Military Tender

The DSTL tender was an opportunity to apply automotive industry best practice to form a VO, comprising of multi-disciplinary SMEs in order to meet future DSTL engineering requirements. Due to the scale and complex nature of the DSTL technical requirements and scale of the contract value at over €15m, it was accepted that a typical engineering SME within the West Midlands, UK could not provide the wide range of competencies nor realistically expect to navigate the intricate tendering procedures independently.

Thus a collaborative VO was established through utilising the WMCCM to address the specific requirements of the DSTL contract. Aspîre Consulting, a Defence based SME and WMCCM member, was used to act as a conduit between the automotive and military industry sectors, to facilitate the long and intricate DSTL procurement process and in the future to act as a potential prime contractor.

When the DSTL tender was received by WMCCM, it was automatically processed by the in-built dynamic ontology, which splits the tender into a number of sub-tasks including industrial market, technical skill and geographic location.

The online partner search selection tool was run to identify a short list of potential consortium members covering each area of technical expertise. This matching of capability is a key part of grouping potential members, in order to build a dynamic VO. Each company was then contacted and invited to form part of the collaborative consortia, attending a number of face-to-face briefing sessions. The VO structure of the DSTL bid can be seen in Figure 2.

The collaborative bid aimed to provide DSTL with a "one-stop-shop" for all of the engineering service disciplines detailed in its competitive tender call. In addition to the membership of WMCCM and its approach seeks to give a number of further benefits:

- The ability to address all of DSTL's needs both from a capability and capacity perspective without any additional investment in tooling, machinery and software.
- The ability to offer additional services from other SME members of WMCCM to meet DSTL additional service options. WMCCM has a wider membership of 4,000 SMEs, each with a brief business or detailed competence profile. Consequently if the combined capability and capacity of the companies identified in this proposal are unable to meet the task requirements set by DSTL then within a short time period an alternative supplier can be identified from the WMCCM membership to join the team.

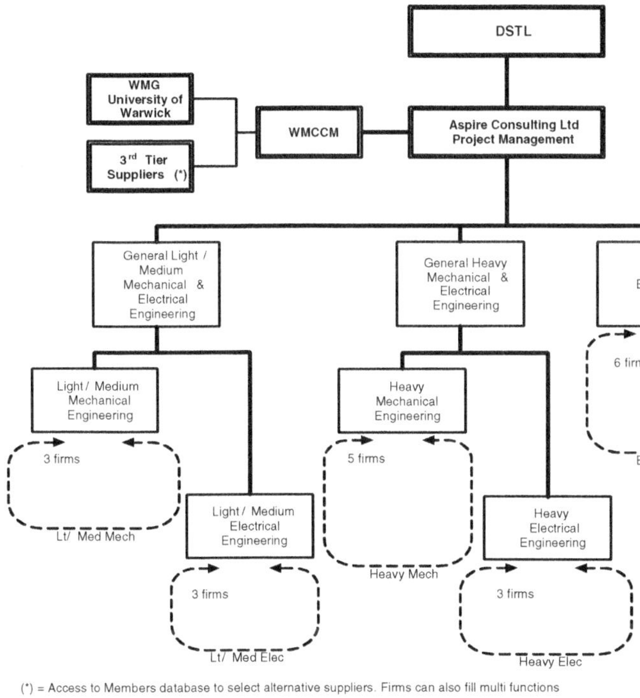

Fig. 2. Proposed DSTL response VO structure

4 Discussion

WMCCM incorporates aspects of the business process groups of the I-BPM framework such as VBE actor management, VO creation and limited aspects of VBE horizontal management. The workflow of the WMCCM as shown in Figure 1 will be compared with the business processes of the I-BPM framework as shown in Table 1.

The competence profile of SMEs is performed by the WMCCM team, which visits those SMEs that wish to be competence profiled to extract their capabilities (such as unique metal turning capability). The identified capabilities are classified using the common ontology (process 4 in Figure 1) within the WMCCM. The conduct of the competence profiling is process 2 as shown in Figure 1. Companies that do not wish to be competence profiled can simply register with the WMCCM to use the features of the system such as browsing through the marketplace or search for partners to form teams for collaborative projects. The main difference between profiled and non- profiled members is that profiled members have a higher visibility on the Internet in terms of their capabilities. So far, successful cases in the WMCCM mainly came from those SMEs that have been competence profiled. SMEs when participating in a CN organise the projects themselves and hence, no functionality exist in WMCCM to identify and manage the roles of VO. Online collaborative project spaces are available within the WMCCM should the teams decide to use this facility (processes 5, 6 and 7). However processes 1 and 3, initiates collaboration opportunities for members through the matching of tenders to individuals or groups. The system functions like a

Table 1. Comparison between I-BPM processes and WMCCM processes

I-BPM framework process	WMCCM process
VBE Actor Management	(2) Competence Profiling
• Membership and structure management	Registered (not competence profiled) and Competence Profiled members
• Profiling and Competence Management	Update and maintain competence profiles
VO Creation	
• Collaboration opportunity identification	(1) (3) Source and import eTenders, classify tenders
• Initial VO Planning	Not supported
• Partner Search and Selection	(4) Partner search matching tenders to SMEs
• Agreement or contract negotiation	Not supported
VO Management	Not supported
VBE General Management	Not supported
VBE horizontal Management	In general it is not supported, except for trust management

'match-making' facility linking capabilities with requirements and any agreement or contract negotiations between partners are handled outside the WMCCM system.

A factor that distinguishes WMCCM from other proprietary CN systems is that the developers of the WMCCM operate in a trust worthy environment. Experts within the Warwick Manufacturing Group (WMG) at the University of Warwick (UK) capture competence profiles and WMG is seen as a respected impartial organisation. The WMCCM provide a trustworthy environment within which activities takes place.

5 Conclusion

WMCCM is a free market model, empowering and encouraging SMEs to dynamically form VOs driven by business needs from the prospect of gaining new work from online tender requests. It is one of the first empirical examples of a VBE for SMEs. WMCCM is a practical implementation of the VO creation framework of the I-BPM framework. At the same time, it also supports other business processes of the I-BPM framework. Further work involves expanding the model to link up other regions of the world such as Australia, which has a similar SME profile.

References

1. Mehler, M.J., Worthington, R., Fife, E., Pereira, F.: The Internet a la Fin de Siecle: The prospect for Internet commerce Centre for telecommunications management. University of Southern California, Los Angeles (1997)

2. Fisher, J., Craig, A.: Developing business community portals for SMEs: Issues of design, development and sustainability. Electronic Markets 15(2), 136–145 (2005)
3. Chituc, C.M., Azevedo, A., Toscano, C.: A Framework Proposal for Seamless Interoperability in a Collaborative-Networked Environment. Computers in Industry 60, 317–338 (2009)
4. Camarinha-Matos, L.M., Afsarmanesh, H.: Virtual Enterprises and Collaborative Networks. In: 18th IFIP World Computer Congress, pp. 3–16. Kluwer Academic Publisher, Dordrecht (2004)
5. Romero, D., Molina, A.: VO breeding environments & Virtual Organisations in Integral Business Process Management Framework. Inf. Syst. Front 11, 569–597 (2009)
6. Kürümlüoglu, M., NØstal, R., Karvonen, I.: Base Concepts. In: Camarinha-Matos, L., Luis, M. (eds.) Virtual Organisations: System and Practices, pp. 11–28 (2005)
7. National Statistics, Press release, Small Business Service website, http://ww.sbs.gov.uk/SBS_Gov_files/researchandstats/SMEstats2005pr.pdf
8. Sunday Times: Skills shortage holding back e-business innovation says SMEs, Sunday Times, February 1 (2000)
9. Szczygiel, M.: AutoLean II – Project. Summary Report, Accelerate Partnership (November 2000)

UNICOMP: Identification of Enterprise Competencies to Build Collaborative Networks

Kafil Hajlaoui[1], Xavier Boucher[2], and Omar Boussaid[1]

[1] Université de Lyon (ERIC Lyon 2)
5 Avenue Pierre Mendès-France, 69676 Bron, France
{kafil.hajlaoui,omar.boussaid}@univ-lyon2.fr
[2] Ecole des Mines de Saint Etienne
158 cours Fauriel, centre G2I, 42023 Saint Etienne, France
boucher@emse.fr

Abstract. In a context of decision-aid to support the identification of collaborative networks, this paper focuses on extracting essential facets of firm competencies. Due to the complexity of the notion of competence, this contribution is based on a semantic representation of information using semantic ontology, bonds and a linguistic treatment based on the utilization of syntactic patterns. To identify enterprise competencies, the UNICOMP system uses company web sites as information source, as well as a general ontology of competencies as semantic resource.

Keywords: information extraction, ontology, patterns, enterprise networks.

1 Introduction

The approach presented below is part of a research to provide a decision support to support the identification of potential Virtual Breeding Environments (VBE). This work takes as a hypothesis the existence of an "open universe" of potential partners to build VBEs where any company can participate. Typically, this issue often appears when one has to analyse a regional business area to identify potential collaborative networks among firms. As a consequence, the identification of potential collaborative partners will be based on the use of public available information.

The web is considered as the fist information on business partners. In previous publications [1] [2], the authors explained the decision aid approach based on the extraction and use of key characteristic information on companies, concerning their activity fields and internal competencies. This information on company competencies will be further used, at a second stage, to generate new knowledge on the potential structure of VBEs. This assumption induces the use of specific information extraction mechanisms. The objective of this paper is to present an information extraction approach to extract company competence traces, through the utilization of public information available on company websites.

Some research on competencies identification techniques are based on the analysis of texts presenting rather homogeneous and structured data. In such approaches, the characterisation of competencies requires private information provided by the

L.M. Camarinha-Matos et al. (Eds.): PRO-VE 2010, IFIP AICT 336, pp. 388–395, 2010.

companies [3] [4]. Non structured documents, like interviews on competence description realized with company experts can be analyzed to further generate a structured description of company competencies. Other authors identify company competencies by inferring expert rules. [5] and [6] employ "expert rules" based on similarities among individual competencies to generate a systematic identification of available competencies. [7] applies other kinds "of expert rules" to individual competencies, based on deductive relationship and not similarity. Another example is provided by [8] where the semantic annotation is also employed on the documents produced by the employees. This competence identification technique is primarily based on rules manually made by an expert of the domain.

However, such approaches can not be applied to our context where, by hypothesis, only non-structured public information on companies is available. The basic information to characterize competencies is available through company public websites: this assumption induces the use of specific information extraction mechanisms, requiring to cope with difficult semantic issues.

Section 2 presents the extraction approach based on the use of ontology and lexical patterns. Since the ontology has been presented in previous works [1], the paper focuses on the formalisation of lexical patterns (section 3). Section 4 describes the implementation of the extraction system and discusses the performance results, followed by conclusion in section 5.

2 Competence Identification: Use of Ontology and Lexical Patterns

Due to the complexity of the notion of competence, the identification of competencies through website information requires implementing semantic mechanisms [2]. The approach presented here uses ontology and lexical patterns applied to the specific area of mechanical industry. The ontology provides a generic description of this domain and the projection of patterns on the corpus is used to activate the ontology classes for each company, thus providing a company competence trace.

The formalization of the ontology has been described in [1] [2]. Consequently, we just provide here a brief summary and the rest of the paper focuses on formalization and use of patterns for competence identification.

The ontology requires rigorous conceptualization of the notions related to firm competencies. ARCHONTE ontology building methodology [9] was chosen, because it defines precise cognitive principles and mechanisms for each step of ontology formalization. This method makes possible a good semantic representation of the conceptual network of the ontology through a « semantic normalisation » mechanism.

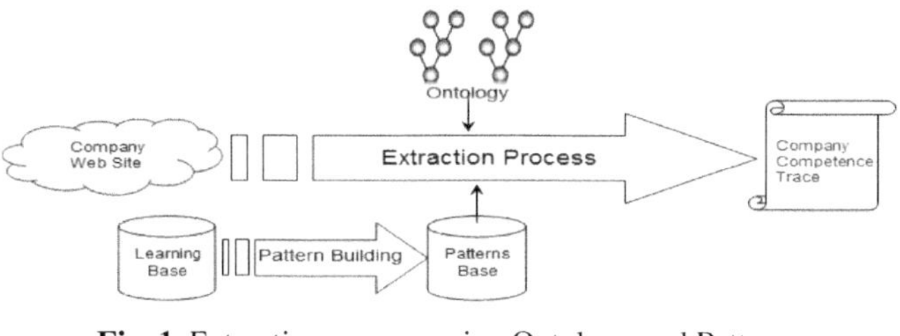

Fig. 1. Extraction process using Ontology and Patterns

From a company website, it is often impossible to extract a weel structured and exhaustive identification of firm competencies. However it remains possible to extract a sufficient set of competence "traces", which makes possible to assess with a good degree of precision an indicia of competence similarity among firms. To implement the extraction mechanism, an ontology of "competence traces" has been formalized. This ontology is composed of two sub-ontologies: a *generic ontology* and a *domain ontology*. The former provides a very generic conceptual model of "competence traces", which is independent of any business sector. However because of this high generality level, the generic ontology is not directly applicable for information extraction. Then, it is complemented by a *domain ontology*, which constitutes an extension of the generic ontology, specific to some selected business sector (mechanical industry in our case). The "competence traces" concepts of this domain ontology are directly linked to the applied field of the mechanical industry. Furthermore, at the lower level of the domain ontology, each ontological concept is associated to specific terms of the domain, further used in the extraction mechanism as "competence trace *identifiers*". The *identifiers* will be used to detect the presence of a competence trace concept within document corpora (extracted from company websites). This detection of "competence traces" is called the activation process applied to the ontology conceptual classes.

To fulfill the objective of extraction information, the direct detection of terms in a corpus is not a sufficient condition. To confirm the presence of an ontology concept (associated to one or several *identifiers*) in the corpus, we have to cope with context-dependent linguistic phenomena which can change the semantic of the *identifiers*: synonyms, antonyms and, more generally, semantic similarity among terms make necessary to use specific semantic techniques. To deal with such ambiguity phenomena we propose the use of linguistic patterns.

3 Lexical Patterns

Lexical patterns aim at formalising a contextual signature of an expression (*identifiers* in our case). Patterns are based on principles of distributive semantics which states that the meaning of a word is strongly correlated to its context. More formally, lexical patterns identify and formalize linguistic relationships, by defining syntactic constraints on the context of the terms [10]. Patterns are built by schematizing the lexical and syntactic context which appears common to several text fragments (corresponding to various occurrences of the linguistic relationship considered). This scheme constitutes the lexical pattern, which can be used to extract other text fragments from a textual corpus [11]. In linguistics approaches for information extraction, patterns are used to reduce ambiguity, when associating structural regularities with semantic information.

In our case, the patterns generalize expressions identified in the texts and provide a generic formalization of particular lexical relations identified in the corpora between the *identifiers* of the "competence traces" ontology and additional contextual terms. For each lexical relation, several occurrences from the corpora are analyzed, to build a generic abstraction, at the linguistic level. Later on, the objective is to re-use these patterns to extract new occurrences of the identifiers from new corpora without semantic ambiguity. In fact, the lexical patterns are built to deal with identified situations of semantic ambiguity linked to the *identifiers* of the domain ontology.

The 3 phases below briefly describe the procedure followed to identify and formalize patterns.

3.1 Corpus Normalization and Filtering of Relevant Sentences

The corpora considered is constituted by text extracted from websites. This first stage consists in normalizing the corpora by substituting some domain expressions (with several semantically equivalent alternatives) by a normalized term. This normalization makes easier later linguistic treatments. For example, the identification of a company can be expressed by various terms: "our company", "our corporation", "we", "the name of the company", etc. These expressions are replaced by the normalized expression "Company Represent". Two brief examples are illustrated below (original expression then normalization):

ATTAX designs, industrializes and markets fastenings for all industries.
<Company Represent> designs, industrializes and markets fastenings for all industries
MECADEX Company is specialized in the undercutting of precision.
<Company Represent> is specialized in the undercutting of precision.

During the normalization stage, the *identifiers* of the domain ontology are also identified in the corpora. In the examples, the identifiers "Design" and "specialized" are identified using an automatic search of their lemma. For instance the lemma <specialize> recognizes all words including "specialize" in their canonic form.

After this normalization and *identifiers* localization, human experts are necessary to filter some relevant text fragments (sentences) linked to the *identifiers*, which appear relevant to identify and to formalize semantic patterns as shown in the two following steps.

3.2 Identification of Representative and Relevant Examples

This second step consists in using the relevant text fragments previously filtered to identify semantic ambiguity situations linked to the *identifiers*. Then, examples of representative syntagms are associated with each ambiguity situation. They can help understanding the relevant meaning. Such syntagms are linguistic expressions which can and/or must be correlated with the identifier to define a relevant semantic interpretation. Only the expert is able to select and evaluate the relevance of a syntagm. Example of ambiguity recorded in the corpora:

<Company Represent> industry, based in Genas (Lyon France), is specialized in the **design and the realization of assembly machines**.

One of the main activities of *<Company Represent>* is the **design and the manufacture of telpher carriers**.

Ambiguity: how to distinguish between the design of final mechanical product and the design production equipments? When identifying firm competence traces, 2 different semantic orientations have to be considered linked to 2 distinct ontology classes.

When such ambiguity is identified for a concept, the expert extracts from the text fragments several expressions using this concept without ambiguity. As a result of this second step, each *identifier* is characterized by a set of structural linguistic diagrams, aiming at dealing with semantic ambiguity.

3.3 Pattern Generation

In this 3rd step, the examples of syntagms associated to ambiguity concerning the *identifiers* are used to generate generic linguistic structures (patterns) semantically equivalent to the syntagms examples. This formalization stage is based on the expertise of a cognitive engineer, and the patterns are expressed in a formal language for further use. The application to the case study (corpora from mechanical industry) generated 35 patterns dealing with ambiguity, complemented with 100 simple patterns (no ambiguity). Below we underline 3 typical use cases of patterns for information extraction:

Simple detection of a concept: patterns constituted by a simple expression used to confirm the presence of an *identifier*. This pattern category is only applied for *identifiers* without ambiguity.

Semantic clarification of a concept: this type of pattern is constituted by a more complex linguistic scheme. The linguistic scheme makes possible to deal with ambiguity situations by checking contextual information which confirms the semantic interpretation of a text fragment.

Extraction of additional information attached to a concept: some patterns are used to extract additional relevant information linked to an *identifier*. For instance, with the *identifier* "specialization", we need to extract the speciality of the company and not only to detect that the company has a speciality.

As explained in section 4, these 135 patterns are first used to confirm the presence of *identifiers* (even in ambiguity situations) throughout the corpora extracted from a company website. Then, depending on the detected *identifiers*, an activation procedure will confirm or not the activation of classes of the "competence traces" ontology. This competence traces will characterise a company.

4 UNICOMP System, for Competence Identification

4.1 Architecture of the System

UNICOMP system is the implementation of our approach which aims at extracting company competence traces, using public information available on websites. It is constituted of four modules.

Pre-Processing: The pre-processing module extracts text from HTML pages constituting the company websites and realises a first filtering and cleaning of the text obtained. This pre-treatment has been explained in [12].

Acquisition and transcription of patterns: As described in section 3, the patterns are generated through various steps (normalisation, filtering, identification of examples and the pattern formalisation). Then, the semi-formal patterns are transformed into automatic comprehensible formal diagrams, which can be formally manipulated by a pattern matching system called UNITEX. The result of this transformation is a set of syntactic graphs (see example on the annex), constituting the pattern base associated to the identifiers, and later use to extract information on competencies.

Pattern localization: In this step UNITEX[1] is utilized to locate occurrences of patterns throughout the corpora constituted by the company websites. The result of the pattern projection on the company text is a set of occurrences. An occurrence is a valid syntactic diagram, which will be further use to validate the presence of an elaborate competence *identifier*, correlated with relevant information. However, a single pattern is not sufficient alone to confirm an *identifier* as underlined below.

Class activation: the module of class activation uses the various occurrences of patterns, located by the precedent module, to validate or not the presence of identifiers from the "competence traces" ontology. This validation called "activation" is realised by the algorithm PCA (Pattern and Classes Activation) which uses a specific protocol presented in [2]. Each class activation is generally based on the use of several patterns identified previously. The algorithm PCA exploits deterministic rules defined to confirm the effective activation of some classes depending on all the patterns identified.

The current version of UNITEX system generates syntactic patterns, via a semi-automated procedure, still requiring an expert contribution. It would be interesting to build a fully-automated method, making possible to generate patterns related to every identifier linked to the ontology concepts.

4.2 Results of the Competencies Extraction

Applying pattern localization and class activation, several terminal classes of the domain ontology will be considered activated by a company website. An activated class corresponds to a competence concept, the presence of which has been confirmed by the patterns. The result of the full activation process constitutes a "company competence trace" constituted by a sub-ontological tree. Fig. 2 provides an example of a competence trace structure. This figure provides a schematic representation of a part of the whole competence trace ontology. Each conceptual class is only represented by a circle. The activated conceptual classes are shown with black circles and the non-activated with white circles. The ontology has 4 conceptual levels, among which the 2 last ones (3rd and 4th) correspond to the domain ontology. The activation process, based on pattern localization (with patterns linked to the *identifiers*), activates the terminal classes situated on the bottom levels of the ontology (domain ontology). Then the activation is propagated upwards in the tree (each node is linked to its children by an "OR" activation link: the activation of 1 child class is sufficient to activate the parent class).

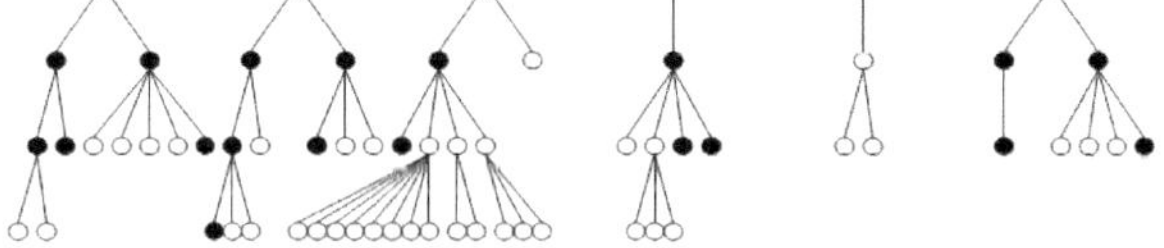

Fig. 2. Competence trace : an ontological sub-tree

[1] Unitex is an application which uses a set of software to treat texts in natural language by using linguistic tools.

4.3 UNICOMP Performances

The performance evaluation of UNICOMP system is based on a comparison of the performance of the system with regards to the competence identification realized by a human expert. The human expert provides a reference of the expected result, and this reference makes possible to define the two indicators *precision* and *recall* (table 1). These 2 indicators are very common to evaluate information extraction mechanisms. Precision is defined by the capacity of the system to exclude the non-relevant classes. Recall is defined by the capacity of the system to activate the relevant classes The test was realized on a sub-collection composed by 10 companies in the mechanical industry domain.

Table 1. Indicators of precision and recall obtained by UNICOMP

Companies	Precision	Recall
E1	0,81	0,56
E2	0,92	0,7
E3	0,87	0,5
E4	1	0,66
E5	0,75	0,54
E6	*1*	0,7
E7	*0,76*	0,83
E8	*0,8*	0,66
E9	*0,87*	0,77
E10	*0,88*	0,57
Average	***0,87***	**0,64**

The precision and the recall indicators show a good performance of UNICOMP system. They validate the pertinence of the current pattern base and ontology. However, these performances could still be improved both by a more exhaustive ontology and by a larger pattern base. A more exhaustive ontology would increase the representativity of the extraction process and thus ameliorate the recall. A higher number of linguistic patterns would improve ambiguity treatment and thus increase the precision.

5 Conclusion and Perspectives

The identification of company competencies is a key factor for a decision support to build collaborative networks. The competence extraction approach adopted in this paper is based on a complex process of information extraction, using ontology and semantic patterns. This contribution has been implemented by the system UNICOMP, the performances of which have been studied. The coupling between ontology and patterns present a real added-value for the richness of information extraction. This research has already been further developed to integrate these results in a Decision Support System for collaboration Network Building using competence similarities measures [12]. As a perspective, an automatic or semi-automatic enrichment of the ontology and the pattern base, using case-learning techniques would be able to increase the overall performance of the system.

References

1. Hajlaoui, K., Boucher, X., Beigbeder, M.: Construction et usage d'une ontologie de compétences pour l'identification de réseaux collaboratifs d'entreprises. In: Nurcan, S., Benali, K., Pingaud, H. (eds.) Special issue, Ingénierie d'entreprise et des systèmes d'information of the review ISI (Ingénierie des Systèmes d'Information), vol. 15(4) (Juillet-août 2010)
2. Hajlaoui, K., Boucher, X., Girardot, J.J.: Competency ontology for network building. In: 10th IFIP Working Conf. on V. E (PRO-VE 2009), Thessaloniki, Greece (2009)
3. Ermilova, E., Afsarmanesh, H.: Modeling and management of profiles and competencies in VBEs. Journal of Intelligent Manufacturing 18, 561–586 (2007)
4. Vanderhaegen, Loos: Distributed model management platform for cross-enterprise business process management in virtual enterprise networks. JIM 18, 553–559 (2007)
5. Blanchard, E., Harzallah, M.: Reasoning on competence management. In: Workshop on Knowledge Management and Organizational Memories of the 16th European conference on Artificial Intelligence (ECAI 2004), Valence 22-27 août (2004)
6. Laukkanen, M., Helin, H.: Competence management within and between organizations. In: Proceeding of the CAISE 2005 Workshops, Enterprise Modelling and Ontologies for Interoperability Workshop, Porto, Portugal, June 13-17, vol. 2, pp. 359–362 (2005)
7. Sure, Y., Maedche, A., Staab, S.: Leveraging corporate skill knowledge: from ProPer to OntoProPer. In: Proceedings of the 3rd International Conference P.A.K.M., Switzerland (2000)
8. Corby, O., Dieng-Kuntz, R., Faron-Zucker, C.: Querying the Semantic Web with the CORESE search engine. In: Lopez de Mantaras, R., Saitta, L. (eds.) Proceedings of the 16th European Conference on Artificial Intelligence (ECAI 2004), subconference PAIS 2004, Valencia, Spain, pp. 705–709. IOS Press, Amsterdam (2004)
9. Bachimont, B., Issac, A., Troncy, R.: Semantic commitment for designing ontologies. In: Gómez-Pérez, A., Benjamins, V.R. (eds.) EKAW 2002. LNCS (LNAI), vol. 2473, pp. 114–121. Springer, Heidelberg (2002)
10. Grabar, N., Hamon, T.: Les relations dans les terminologies structurées: de la théorie à la pratique. Revue d'intelligence artificielle 18(1), 57–85 (2004)
11. Hearst, M.A.: Automatic acquisition of hyponyms from large text corpora. In: Zampolli, A. (ed.) Computational Linguistics (CoLing 1992), Nantes, France, pp. 539–545 (1992)
12. Hajlaoui, K.: Thèse, Dispositifs de recherche et de traitement de l'information en vue d'une aide à la constitution de réseaux d'entreprises. EMSE Saint Etienne, France (December 2009)

The Role of Organizational Competences in the Evolution of Business Models

Matheus Pinotti Moreira[1], Sophie D'Amours[1],
Robert Beauregard[1,2], and Riadh Azouzi[1,3]

[1] Forac Research Consortium, Dept. of Mechanical Engineering, Pav. Adrien-Pouliot, Université Laval, G1V 0A6, Québec, QC, Canada
[2] Dept. of Forestry and Wood Sciences, Pav. Abitibi-Price, Université Laval, G1V 0A6, Québec, QC, Canada
[3] CRIQ (Québec Industrial Research Centre), 333 Rue Franquet, G1P 4C7, Québec, QC, Canada
{Matheus.PinottiMoreira,Sophie.Damours}@cirrelt.ca
{Robert.Beauregard,Riadh.Azouzi}@cirrelt.ca

Abstract. This paper presents the use of a conceptual framework designed for the management of organizational competences to contribute to the evolution of the business model of an enterprise. The framework, developed based on a detailed review of the history of the car manufacturer Toyota, was used for a Delphi study and an action-research applied in the furniture industry. The results suggest that it is applicable for ex-post analysis of organizational changes, as well as a strategy planning tool.

Keywords: Organizational competences, business model, competitive advantage, competence management, organizational change.

1 Background

Competence-based theory explains the competitiveness of an enterprise based on its internal characteristics, inspired from the resource-based view of the firm [1], [2], [3]. An organizational competence (OC) is the deployment, combination and coordination of a firm's resources, knowledge and individual competences along different value streams to attain strategic objectives [4], [5]. An OC is not located in a single resource or person, but in the interaction of several of them.

OCs are dependent on the level of dynamism of the environment, with stable contexts calling for a different set of OCs than highly dynamic environments [6], [7]. An OC can be evaluated according to characteristics like its perceived value, rareness, imitability, substitutability and applicability to different markets [8], [9]. These characteristics allow categorizing the competences as operational or dynamic [10], [11] and also as core, specific or basic [12], bringing different levels of competitive advantage for the company [13].

The management of OCs is a responsibility of top and functional managers [14]. It consists in developing new OCs and improving or replicating existing ones, as well as preventing them from becoming core rigidities [12], [15]. This development can be

L.M. Camarinha-Matos et al. (Eds.): PRO-VE 2010, IFIP AICT 336, pp. 396–403, 2010.

accomplished through different mechanisms, such as hiring, on-the-job training, job rotation, external and internal formation, intensive and extensive training, partnerships, R&D, benchmarking, technological innovation, mergers and acquisitions, utilization of a knowledge referential, and participation in communities of practice [16], [17], [18]. The complete lifecycle of an OC can be divided in four phases: founding, development, maturity and selection, when it can be renewed, redeployed to other markets and functions, or retired [15]. It is usually measured in an ascendant five interval scale [18], [19].

1.1 Business Model

The objective of the concept of business model (BM) is to help understand, analyze, manage and prospect new and evolutionary business logics for a company [20]. It corresponds to an intermediary level of analysis, linking strategic issues of profit strategy, revenue and cost structures, to functional decisions [21].

The first occurrences of the term BM in academic research appeared at the end of the 1990's, in studies about digital and virtual companies using new ICT for e-commerce and e-business. Since then, several frameworks to define a BM and its main components have been published [22]. The BM approach used in this study is an adaptation of the works of Boyer and Freyssenet [23] at the GERPISA (Permanent group for the study of the automobile industry and its employees), chosen because of its academic origin and simplicity. A BM is then defined as the representation of a company's strategy, processes and people under specific environmental conditions.

As these components are interrelated, changing one of them may impact the others, causing potential conflicts and achieving unpredictable results [23]. However, in evolving or dynamic environments, these changes become necessary and vital to the survival of a business. The sustainability of a company is dependent on the coherence of the three main components of its BM with the environment.

We propose that the management of OCs can help achieve this coherence on a regular basis, and a framework to do so is presented. The following section explains the research methodology. Section 3 presents the framework and Section 4 exemplifies its usage with two examples. Section 5 closes the paper with some conclusions and identification of future researches.

2 Methodology

This research focused on defining what the roles of OCs and their management are for the evolution of the BM of an extended enterprise. To develop and propose a conceptual and referential framework useful for both research and practice, three methods were used: (1) literature review, (2) a Delphi study, and (3) action-research (Figure 1). The choice and application of these methods was guided by a longitudinal and contextual view of organizational change, linking the context, the content and the process of change [24].

The literature review was based on a detailed codification and analysis of the evolution of the Japanese car manufacturer Toyota, a typical example of extended enterprise. The reasons for this choice were the sustained competitiveness and profitability of this company until 2005, combined with a vast bibliography available on the subject. The codification strategy was made in three steps: the first was the description of

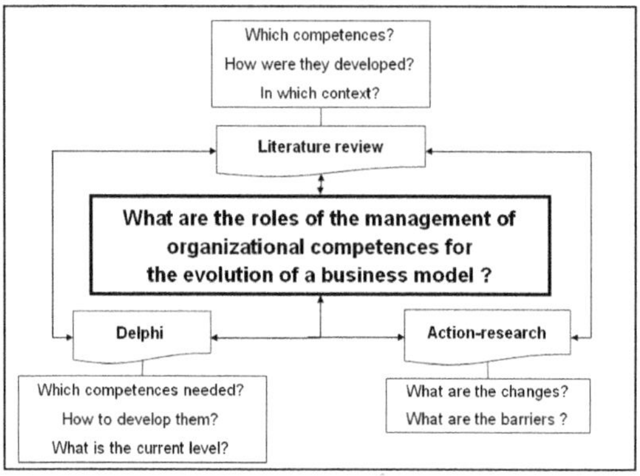

Fig. 1. Methodological framework

the socio-economical environment in six 10-year periods, from 1940 to 2000. The second step was the identification of OCs and the development mechanisms utilized by the company in each period. The third step consisted in establishing the relationship between each OC identified with a specific BM component. Triangulation with the Delphi and action-research methods explained below, were used to enrich the results of the literature review, thus increasing the robustness of the conceptual framework.

To be able to transpose, adapt and adequately apply the learning from the literature review to a specific context, a Delphi study with expert researchers was conducted. Delphi is a sequential group communication technique used to obtain consensus through several feedbacks to and from the participants, who do not need to be together. After each communication round, each participant receives a synthesis and a statistical analysis of the group's responses, being then asked to change his opinion or to explain the reasons for not changing it. The iterations are conducted until an acceptable consensus level is achieved.

To identify specific difficulties and barriers to implement and sustain an organizational change from an enterprise's point of view, an action-research was conducted in a company under real change. This method is characterized by a collaborative problem-solving relationship between company professionals and researchers to solve real problems and to generate new knowledge.

3 Conceptual Framework

The codification and analysis of the evolution of Toyota from OC and BM points of view led to the following observations:

- There was a gradual change in strategy, starting from the just-in-time upon foundation, then complemented by a constant cost reduction strategy in the 1950's, the identification of value from the client standpoint in the 1970's and more recently technological innovation for hybrid engines;
- These strategy changes were translated into a gradual development of OCs, starting with production, a culture of incremental improvements and human capital

management, then expanding to supply, sales & marketing and product development, reaching its main suppliers and dealerships;
- The main development mechanisms used were benchmarking, internal and extensive on-the-job training, partnerships, R&D and the utilization of a structured scientific method for learning (kaizen and plan-do-check-act).

It is then possible to propose two cornerstones for a successful change of a BM by the management of OCs:

a. The management of OCs is a strategic process, under the responsibility of top and functional managers.
b. It is cyclical and iterative, dependent on the evolution of internal and external environments. A new competence is added to a set of competences already in place, which are rarely abandoned, but improved.

As a strategic process, the development of OCs requires formulation and implementation phases. The formulation phase proposed has two steps, and the implementation phase has one. The three steps are described below with actors and actions, and a graphical representation is presented in Figure 2.

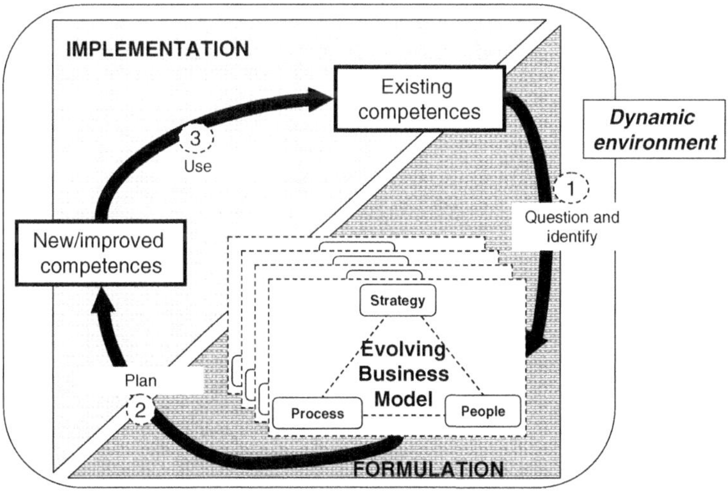

Fig. 2. Conceptual framework

1) Top and functional managers question and evaluate the already existing OCs, the level of competitive advantage brought by them, and the components of the BM based on the environment situation. It is then possible to identify misalignments and translate them into OC gaps;
2) The next step is to plan the development and improvement of OCs identified in the previous step, taking into consideration the different development mechanisms available. As in any good planning approach, risk analysis, prioritization, drawing roadmaps and defining milestones are useful practices;
3) At the third step, the managers implement the plan and actively use the new OCs so they become effective and enter the set of existing OCs of the enterprise. The cycle can then restart to evaluate the competitiveness of both the recently developed and previously acquired OCs.

This framework represents a dynamic OC, leading to the evolution of operational OCs aligned with specific components of the BM. As so, it is supported by specific learning mechanisms [25]:

- Experience accumulation (behavioral approach) : it is an iterative process, allowing the adoption of routines by the individuals based on trial and error and selection of sucessful past behaviors;
- Knowledge articulation (cognitive approach) : it proposes a formal process of collective discussion about the main elements of the enterprise, guiding constructive dialogues between different business functions;
- Knowledge codification (explicit knowledge) : the framework gives origin to an action plan for the development of Ocs, which is a codification process.

Another important issue is the payoff of implementing such a framework in an enterprise. Based on criteria such as the level of dynamism of the environement, the size of the enterprise and the economical importance of the elements questioned [25, 26, 27], the framework would bring bigger gains for medium to large extended enterprises, working in dynamic environments. The integration of the concept of BM assures that the most important elements are always questioned.

Even if the recent recalls impacted considerably the image and the performance of Toyota, we consider that the results are still valid for two major reasons. First, the observations are based on data and information up to the year 2000, excluding therefore the events and actions that led to the current crisis. Second, in taking the latest 10-years period, we see a major strategy change, focusing more on becoming the world's biggest manufacturer than on gradual and sustainable growth. In the next section, applications of this framework for strategy formulation and change explanation are presented.

4 Applications

4.1 Delphi

In this first application of the framework, a two-round Delphi study was organized with expert researchers and expert service providers from the furniture industry in the Canadian province of Quebec, which needed to identify and implement innovative BMs to assure its sustainability in a different economic context than in the 1990's. Mass customization had been identified previous to the survey as a strategy that could potentially re-establish the competitiveness of the sector [28].

The objectives of the survey were the identification of (1) the OCs needed to succeed with a mass customization strategy, (2) the level of competitiveness brought by them, (3) their current level of maturity in the industry and (4) the best mechanisms to develop them, covering steps 1 and 2 of the framework [29].

The metaphor of a house was used to represent the results of the survey, expliciting the strategic objectives of the organization as the roof, the core OCs bringing sustainable competitive advantage as the pillars, and the basic OCs bringing competitive parity, as the foundation of the house (Figure 3). The human capital elements are

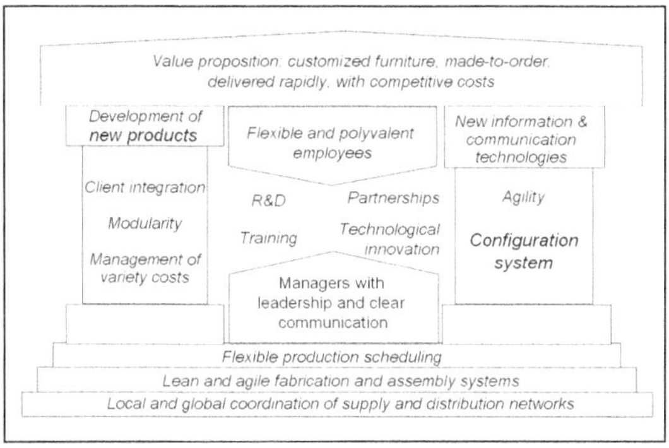

Fig. 3. Organizational competences for the furniture industry

found in the centre with the selected development mechanisms. A replication of the research is planned for 2011 to evalute the progress accomplished.

4.2 Action-Research

The action-research took place during a period of 18 months in two plants of a company engaged in a change process, which had started before the proposal of Figure 3. The required OCs had been identified previously by the managers (Step 1) as related to the concept-to-launch and order-to-delivery processes. Their development was planned and they were implemented during or slightly before the action-research period (Steps 2 and 3).

By applying Step 1 of the framework for a second cycle, this time as part of the action-research, a major gap was identified regarding the sales-to-order process. This urgent need to develop new OCs may have resulted from an incomplete environmental analysis done by the managers at the first cycle. One year after, the company ceased its operations.

As the framework was derived by induction from the analysis of the history of Toyota, there may be a possibility that cultural differences between East and West play some role in this failure. However, western enterprises have already proved that they can improve tremendously their performance in a sustainable way [30]. Easier travelling, distance learning and virtual social networks are also helping to reduce the cultural boundaries, making adaptation and adoption of different methods easier, and that on both senses. With this in mind, we suggest that the discussion of failures should be held rather on an enterprise culture level than on a national culture level.

To create a dynamic capability, an enterprise needs to have an organized team with some type of leadership to act jointly, as well as a central objective and a cyclical learning mental model [15]. Therefore, it is the lack of one of these pre-requisites that will more probably dictate the success of founding such a dynamic OC.

5 Conclusions

This paper proposed and exemplified the use of a conceptual framework defining the role of OCs and their management for the evolution of the BM of an extended enterprise. It proposes the management of OCs as a way to bridge the gap between changes in the environment and business sustainability. The framework is a cyclical process composed of three steps under the responsibility of the top and functional managers, supported by key organizational learning mechanisms.

The framework integrates the concept of business model with the theories of competence-based management and organizational learning, increasing the focus of these last. Even though a BM approach with three main components was used in the framework, its applicability to other BM approaches can be studied in future research.

Testing and adaptation to other types of collaborative networks, including the definition of BM for collaborative networks, is another potential field of research.

From a practical point of view, the framework presented a good potential for ex-ante strategy formulation and ex-post strategy explanation, as shown by the applications. Issues of enterprise culture may play a major role for a successful development of the framework in an enterprise. Research on the best development mechanisms for such a dynamic OC is therefore important, integrating "soft" concepts such as leadership, ownership and mental models.

References

1. Penrose, E.: The theory of the growth of the firm. ME Sharpe White Plains, New York (1959)
2. Barney, J.B.: Firm Resources and Sustained Competitive Advantage. Journal of Management 17, 99–120 (1991)
3. Grant, R.M.: The resource-based theory of competitive advantage: implications for strategy formulation. California Management Review, 114–135 (Spring 1991)
4. Sanchez, R., Thomas, H.: Strategic goals. In: Sanchez, R., Heene, A., Thomas, H. (eds.) Dynamics of competence-based competition: theory and practice in the new strategic management, pp. 63–84. Elsevier, London (1996)
5. St-Amant, G.E., Renard, L.: Aspects théoriques d'un cadre de développement des capacités organisationnelles. Cahier de recherche 03-2004, École des sciences de la gestion, Université du Québec à Montréal (2004)
6. Eisenhardt, K.M., Martin, J.A.: Dynamic capabilities: What are they? Strategic Management Journal 21(10/11), 1105–1121 (2000)
7. Sanchez, R.: Understanding competence-based management: Identifying and managing five modes of competence. Journal of Business Research 57, 518–532 (2004)
8. Prahalad, C., Hamel, G.: The core competence of the corporation. Harvard Business Review, 79–91 (May-June 1990)
9. Peteraf, M.A.: The cornerstones of competitive advantage: a resource-based view. Strategic Management Journal 14(3), 179–191 (1993)
10. Collis, D.J.: How valuable are organizational capabilites? Strategic Management Journal 15, 143–152 (Winter 1994)
11. Teece, D.J., Pisano, G.: The dynamic capabilities of firms: an introduction. Industrial and corporate change 3(3), 537–556 (1994)
12. Leonard-Barton, D.: Wellsprings of knowledge: building and sustaining the sources of innovation. Harvard Business School Press, Boston (1995)
13. Barney, J.B.: Integrating organizational behaviour and strategy formulation research: resource based analysis. In: Advances in Strategic Management, vol. 15, pp. 39–61. JAI Press, Greenwich (1992)

14. Brown, S., Bessant, J.: The manufacturing strategy-capabilities links in mass customization and agile manufacturing – an exploratory study. International Journal of Operations & Production Management 23(7), 707–730 (2003)
15. Helfat, C.E., Peteraf, M.A.: The dynamic resource-based view: capability lifecycles. Strategic Management Journal 24, 997–1010 (2003)
16. Hamel, G., Heene, A.: Competence-based competition. Wiley, New York (1994)
17. Sydänmaanlakka, P.: An intelligent organization, Oxford, Capstone (2002)
18. St-Amant, G.E., Renard, L.: Développement des capacités ou compétences organisationnelles: quels liens avec les compétences individuelles. Cahier de recherche 14-2006, École des sciences de la gestion, Université du Québec à Montréal (2006)
19. Drejer, A.: How can we define and understand competencies and their development? Technovation 21, 135–146 (2001)
20. Osterwalder, A., Pigneur, Y., Tucci, C.L.: Clarifying BMs: origins, present, and future of the concept. Communications of the Association for Information Systems 15 (2005)
21. Warnier, V., Lecocq, X., Demil, B.: Le BM: l'oublié de la stratégie? In: 13e Conférence de l'AIMS. Normandie, Valée de la Seine (Juin 2004)
22. Moreira, M.P., D'Amours, S., Azouzi, R., Beauregard, R.: L'évolution du modèle d'affaires par le management des capacités organisationnelles. 5e Colloque management des capacités organisationnelles, 77e Congrès de l'Acfas, Ottawa (2009)
23. Boyer, R., Freyssenet, M.: Les modèles productifs, Paris, La Découverte (2000)
24. Pettigrew, A.M.: Longitudinal field research on change: theory and practice. Organizational science 1(3), 267–292 (1990)
25. Zollo, M., Winter, S.G.: Deliberate learning and the evolution of dynamic capabilities. Organization science 13(3), 339–351 (2002)
26. Winter, S.G.: Understanding dynamic capabilities. Strategic Management Journal 24(10), 991–995 (2003)
27. Bradford, J., Childe, S.J.: A non-linear redesign methodology for manufacturing systems in SMEs. Computers in Industry 49, 9–23 (2002)
28. Lihra, T., Buehlmann, U., Beauregard, R.: Mass customisation of wood furniture as a competitive strategy. International Journal of Mass Customization 2(3/4), 200–215 (2008)
29. Moreira, M.P., Azouzi, R., D'Amours, S., Beauregard, R.: Organizational competencies and competitive advantage: a mass customization strategy for the furniture industry. In: International Conference on Industrial Engineering and Systems Management, Montréal (2009)
30. Collins, J.: Good to great. Collins business (2001)

The Variable Nature of Trust in Sustainable Collaborative Ventures

Ronald C. Beckett[1] and Michael Jones[2]

[1] Centre for Industry and Innovation Studies, University of Western Sydney, Australia
rcb@reinvent.net.au
[2] School of Management and Marketing University of Wollongong, Australia
mjones@uow.edu.au

Abstract. We observe that trust is context sensitive: actors that may trust each other in one situation may not display the same level of trust in other situations, for example when different competencies are required. It is broadly agreed that trust is important in relation to collaborative ventures. In this paper we use the ARCON reference model as a framework to consider endogenous and exogenous aspects of trust important in the establishment, operation and dissolution of collaborative ventures. Some comments are made about the use of the model and some possible shortcomings are noted.

Keywords: Trust, Collaboration.

1 Introduction

The focus of collaboration activities is changing and there is an expectation of increasing levels of collaboration [1]. In 2004 a review of ten years of European collaboration research [2] noted changes in collaboration focus, seeing movements away from a supply chain focus to a customized products orientation. In addition, as a result of advances in information and communication technologies (ICT), the study predicted further evolution in the area of collaboration with an increased focus on sustainable collaboration, managing and taking advantage of complexity, and inter-enterprise creation and innovation. New ways of doing business may require new forms of collaboration that may introduce unique interdependencies between the collaborators. As a result there is now increased emphasis on trust and the important role it plays in ensuring collaboration success. Trust, in its various permutations, (trust in the product, trust in the enterprise, trust in the people, trust in ICT) impacts on how disparate business practices make sense to collaborating firms [3].

While trust may be important in facilitating the endogenous workings of collaboration, we observe there are some exogenous interactions relating to trust in and by a collaborative network organization (CNO). This is what we are exploring in this paper. Our research approach draws on our own case study material accumulated over many years. These studies are combined with similar research projects taken from extant literature. Combined, these data will illustrate the variable nature of trust as it occurs in different collaborative environments. The paper will reference findings and proposals according to a comprehensively researched virtual enterprise reference

L.M. Camarinha-Matos et al. (Eds.): PRO-VE 2010, IFIP AICT 336, pp. 404–411, 2010.

model, ARCON [4]. The paper will discuss the utility of ARCON from a trust perspective, and will present a number of issues for future consideration.

2 The Context-Dependent Nature of Trust: Some Illustrative Cases

2.1 Trust in Cooperative Marketing

2.1.1 Austmine [5]

Austmine was established in the early 1990's as a virtual enterprise to assist in accessing export markets. The collaboration comprises around 80 member companies each with a diverse range of specialities focusing on the provision of equipment and services to the mining industry. Members are relatively small by international standards, typically ranging in size from around ten employees to a few hundred. The collaboration has established competence-based trust [6] which revolves around the equity endowed in the Austmine brand. Austmine provides a central point of contact, and then contract negotiations are between the client and the individual member firm. The focus of trust in this case is on the CNO.

2.1.2 TIFA Aerospace [5]

TIFA Aerospace was established in 2002/03. The original collaboration comprised three focal firms (each with many years experience making tooling for the Australian Aerospace industry) and an industry association, potentially involving up to 60 small firms. The collaboration was intended to expand business opportunities with overseas aircraft manufacturers. After business links had been established, the three focal firms promoted themselves separately, and the collaboration fell apart. This case demonstrates failure based on poor economic trust. TIFA Aerospace operated in the style of a short-term opportunity-driven network.

2.1.3 Nepean IT [5]

Nepean IT was established to create a business network that would assist a large telecommunications company (Telstra) in fulfilling its clients' needs by providing an extended range of combined information and communication technology services. A group of firms decided to form a virtual company and a participant code of behaviour was agreed. The project was championed by the CEO of a regional development organisation. Eventually the strategic partner, Telstra, withdrew from the collaboration which led to a reduction in business referrals from that source. Some participants dropped out when they could not meet the performance standards required by the group, leading one of them to comment that they should have learned more about each other before committing to work together. Nepean IT operates as a virtual enterprise impacted by both external market conditions that diminished the need to collaborate, and issues of internal competency-based trust [6].

2.2 Trust in the Supply Chain

2.2.1 Nielsen et al [8]

Nielsen et al [8] compared two enterprises that sought to get their suppliers involved in innovation initiatives. They observed an interplay between power, trust and politics at different levels (personal and departmental) within and between the cooperating enterprises that in turn led to different levels of commitment, openness and participation. In some cases, a change in the individuals involved was (or could have been) beneficial. The supplier firms were collaborating to support their customer, but parts of the customer organization were not comfortable with collaborative arrangements.

2.2.2 TAAG (Tooling Australia Automotive Group) [9]

TAAG (Tooling Australia Automotive Group) [9] formation was stimulated by some collaborations being explored by other members of their industry association. Impressive brochures describing the combined capabilities of firms in plastic mold-making were produced, and the group started to work with the engineering departments of new international clients, establishing significant levels of goodwill and competency-based trust. However, once a level of competency had been verified, the client firm purchasing departments were only interested in price. In one instance, the purchasing department was given a directive to buy everything from China. This discounted the value of any goodwill trust that had been established.

2.2.3 A Japanese Manufacturer-Supplier Study [10]

This study investigated collaborative buyer-supplier relationships from the perspective of a Japanese manufacturer. Feedback was obtained from 117 Japanese manufacturers and structural equation modelling was used to assess relationships and antecedent interactions between the firms and the roles of three attributes of customer trust (contractual, competence and goodwill trust). It was found that four forms of interaction supported all three trust attributes. These were:

- Task compliance and competency demonstrated over time
- Responding behaviour – the actions a supplier undertakes to satisfactorily accommodate a customer's requests, or operational and/or strategic 'needs'
- Alerting behaviour – the actions a supplier engages in to alert a customer, at the earliest point, of any possible supply problem that affects the customer's sourcing operation in order to allow the customer to make, in advance, necessary adjustments in the exchange and
- Initiating behaviour – the initiative a supplier takes in realising a customer's operational and/or strategic 'wants'.

2.3 Trust in Inter-organisation Innovation

2.3.1 An Agricultural Network

Kilpatrick and Bell [11] have observed the evolution of small business networks of farmers in regional Australia. A community of practice was formed to help make changes in the operations of participating firms to improve business outcomes. A series of network "chapters" were formed in a number of geographical centres, and members were required, as a prerequisite, to complete a farm management training course. This provided them with some common experiences and a common language. It also provided a foundation for building trust. The CNOs operated in the style of a professional virtual community with external training support. This type of trust is similar to the behavioural perspective from Ratnasingam (2005) where trust is developed through normative influences deriving from common experiences and values, and through shared competencies.

2.3.2 An Innovation Incubator

Burnett & McMurray [12] studied the experience of twelve start-up entrepreneurial firms supported by a business incubator. The incubator provided space, access to business services and networks, mentoring and regular performance reviews. Analysis of interview data showed that trust and networking were the two dominant themes supporting success, particular that of trust between mentor and mentee. The most valued external networks were entrepreneurial networks that may stimulate new linkages and business opportunities, and linkages with other family businesses. The incubators established a form of 'breeding environment' CNO. Trust in an intermediary was a feature of this case. This is similar to affective trust (Huang and Wilkinson [13]).

2.3.3 An Aerospace Design and Development Network [14]

A number of one-to-one strategic alliances evolved over time, and exhibited high levels of trust between collaborators. This allowed the alliance to operate in the style of an extended enterprise when required. After a period of time discussions took place regarding the extension of relationships into a multi-partner network that would offer a wider range of services. Despite the well-established history of working together, which generally supported positive responses to the new network, most participants wanted to address new issues of potential risk. Some only wanted an associate relationship and wanted to offer services on the historical project-by-project basis, as they saw a risk that any other arrangement might be regarded by other stakeholders in their business as some form of exclusivity (response – too risky, so withdraw). Some were concerned about protecting any intellectual property that might be shared, and wanted to set up a contractual framework for further development of the concept (response – enhance situational control, focus on contract based trust). Others wanted to have a meeting to clarify goals and practices and to meet some of the people that would be the "organizational influencers" (response – try and initially assess trust at a personal level by establishing the extent of goodwill). In this case, the additional risk altered the trust relationships creating a range of reactions. However, all of these reactions were based around Huang and Wilkinson's [13] concept of calculative and affective trust.

2.4 Trust in e-collaboration

2.4.1 Promoting e-collaboration

Three established cluster groups were encouraged to enhance their collaborative relationships through the use of e-collaboration [15]. E-collaboration approaches the formation and maintenance of cooperative enterprises through the introduction of electronic communication tools to facilitate collaboration. With e-collaboration the interface between firms changes and can take a multitude of forms. The Internet and email are two forms most commonly used. A focus group approach involving about 70 business owner-managers in groups of 8 - 10 was used to identify perceived barriers. Four distinct aspects of trust emerged: individual (interpersonal) trust [7], economic trust [7], system trust [16], and technology trust [7]. We observed that all four aspects had to be addressed before e-collaboration could proceed. Of these, individual (interpersonal) trust was considered the most important, leading to the suggestions for face-to-face networking events. However, consistent with other research [17], it was thought that such trust would take some time to develop, depending on the nature of antecedent linkages between the parties.

3 Characterizing Collaborations

3.1 The ARCON Model

The ARCON model [4] was constructed to provide a framework that helps capture the multi-dimensional complexity of Collaborative Networked Organization (CNO). Aspects of the social networks and technology networks that support CNO operations are inter-woven in the model. At the highest level there are seen to be three interacting perspectives: life-cycle stages, environment characteristics and modelling intents. CNOs are seen to have both internal (endogenous) and external (exogenous) environment interactions. The ARCON model defines three levels of detail in each category. The modelling intent may be to identify general concepts and relationships in a particular instance of a CNO, or to more specifically identify how it is to operate, or at a finer level of detail, define how operations are implemented. In this paper, we are only concerned with the general conceptual level.

3.2 Trust and the ARCON Model

Taking the view of Sako and Helper [6], there are elements of contract, competence and goodwill trust evident in B2B relationships. We identify aspects of trust embedded in the ARCON model at the third level of detail.

3.2.1. Endogenous Interactions in relation to trust were seen as:

- Relationship - trust between actors (goodwill)
- Knowledge resources - profile and competency (competency)
- Network management, operational competencies and approach (competency)
- Functional processes - trust management (goodwill)
- Functional processes - risk management (contract/competency/goodwill)
- Prescriptive behaviour - general principles (contract)
- Contract/Agreement constraints and conditions (contract)

3.2.2. Exogenous Interactions in relation to trust were seen as:

- Market - Network identity - references and testimonials, interaction parties: customers and suppliers (contract and competency), Interactions: advertising and customer/supplier-oriented transactions (goodwill)
- Support - Network identity: social aspect e.g. not-for-profit (goodwill), Interaction parties: certification entities, coaching entities and training entities (competency),
- Societal - Network identity: values and principles (goodwill)
- Constituency - Network identity: inclusiveness of external members (goodwill)

To summarize; there are elements related to trust *within* the network and elements related to trust *of* the network. Not surprisingly, contract trust has an endogenous inter-enterprise focus and an exogenous supply chain focus. Competence trust has an endogenous focus on both capabilities to contribute to the goal of the CNO and collaboration capabilities, whilst the exogenous focus is on the supply chain and external certification. The goodwill trust endogenous elements are relatively simply represented in the model as various forms of rules and procedures. The exogenous elements are focused on network identity and seen as more complex due to the variety of stakeholder perspectives that may have to be addressed.

4 Some Observations from Our Case Studies

We tabulated the main focus of exogenous trust from each case in terms of their ARCON market, support, societal and constituency interactions. This simplified view of the cases indicated that some of the collaborations presented may not have a direct link with markets, but when they do, the objective is to establish network identity trust in a CNO brand or via the reputation of the participants. The other market approach is to establish trust in the CNO by direct interaction with specific customers. Customers may not choose to contract through the CNO, and may exercise power in constructive or destructive ways. Notions of 'economic trust' came up in some cases, and this will be discussed later.

Support may be provided through government agencies in a policy context, through industry associations pursuing industry objectives, through academia in an action research context, through training organizations or through mentors. Here the CNO has to have trust in the support agency. Trust in the CNO can be enhanced by interaction with certification entities. The e-collaboration cases raise questions about trust in the internet, and other ICT, as an external logistics entity.

Societal interactions in all of the cases related to economic sustainability values supporting growth or competitiveness for both the benefit of the CNO members and their broader stakeholder community, and this is linked to government support. The focus is on trust in the network entity.

Constituency interactions varied, but none were completely open. Some were restricted by the establishment of a CNO company, some by a pre-requisite membership of an industry association or regional group, and others by some form of competency test. These are matters of trust in the network entity, and bear further consideration from a social capital perspective.

Doing things together was a recurring theme in building trust within a CNO. However, this might draw on external resources.

5 Concluding Remarks

Our first comment relates to working with the ARCON reference modelling framework using some pre-conceived aspects of trust (contract-based, competency-based, goodwill-based trust) and a comprehensive (60 page) description of the framework [4]. We selected items within the model that we thought could impact on the assignment or development of trust. All of these items were found at least somewhere in our case study set, implying that the ARCON framework can be used in a variety of circumstances. Reversing the position and using a high level view of the ARCON framework to characterize our cases provided an interesting overview.

Our second comment relates to context. Some of the cases illustrate that trust developed in one context does not necessarily translate to the same level of trust in another context. The ARCON framework presents some internal and external views of CNO context. Endogenous elements we identified were relationship structures, competencies, some functional processes (e.g. trust management) and contract-driven behaviour. This presented as a structural view, whereas much of the literature on trust takes an agency view. From a trust perspective, the ARCON framework generally views exogenous interactions in the context of trust *in* the CNO as an entity. Our case studies suggest that exogenous factors also impact on trust within the CNO - if the original CNO objectives are compromised, if a client, a sponsor or the community introduce some 'rules' or behaviours that cause conflict, or if some form of support is not effective.

Our third comment relates to things that we did not perceive to be part of the ARCON framework - matters of agency related to the constructive or destructive use of power, to the role of interpersonal trust amongst key internal or external supporters of a CNO.

Our final comment relates to trust and the CNO life-cycle. An initial quantum of trust has to be assigned by the participants to get a CNO started. This may be based on prior relationships or some past performance data [18]. But trust must be built as the CNO evolves for it to operate effectively. This did not happen in some of our cases, sometimes due to internal factors, sometimes due to external factors. Trust and related aspects of power may have their own life-cycle [11, 13], which may or may not synchronise well with the CNO life-cycle.

References

1. EC: Reinvent Europe from a knowledge society to an innovation society through innovation (2009), `http://ec.europa.eu/enterprise/policies/innovation/files/panel_report_en.pdf` (last accessed February 25, 2010)
2. Bacquet, J., Fatelnig, P., Villasante, J., Zwegers, A.: An outlook of future research needs on networked organizations. In: Camharinha-Matos, L.M. (ed.) Virtual Enterprises and Collaborative Networks, pp. 17–24. Kluwer Academic Publishers, Boston (2004) ISBN 1-4020-8138-3
3. Chi, L., Holsapple, C.: Understanding computer-meditated interorganisational collaboration: a model and framework. Journal of Knowledge Management 9(1), 53–75 (2005)
4. Camarinha-Matos, L.M., Afsarmanesh, H.: On reference models for collaborative networked organizations. International Journal Production Research 46(9), 2453–2469 (2008)
5. Beckett, R.C.: Marketing capabilities under a collective brand - three longitudinal case studies of Australian SME experience. Small Business Research 16(2), 21–31 (2008)
6. Sako, M., Helper, S.: Determinants of trust in supplier relations: Evidence from the automotive industry in Japan and the United States. Journal of Economic Behaviour and Organisations 34, 387–417 (1998)
7. Ratnasingam, P.: Trust in inter-organisational exchanges: a case study in business to business electronic commerce. Decision Support Systems 39, 525–544 (2005)
8. Nielsen, J.S., Boer, H., Gertsen, F., Kaltoft, R.: The influence of power, trust and political behaviour in the process of collaborative improvement. In: 5th CINet Conference, Sydney, Australia (2004)
9. Beckett, R.C.: Mobilizing Minnows – Small Firms Striving for Global Leadership. In: International Manufacturing Leaders Forum (IMLF 2006), Taiwan (October 2006)
10. Miyamoto, T., Nexhimi, R., Grainger, R.: The Antecedent and Roles of Three Attributes of Customer Trust in Japanese Manufacturer – Supplier Relationships. In: IMP Group Conference – Culture and Collaboration in Distribution Networks, Perth, Australia, December 11-13 (2002) ISBN 1 74067 186 4
11. Kilpatrick, S.: How Social Capital Facilitates Learning Outcomes for Small Business, Paper D8/1999, Centre for Research and Learning in Regional Australia, University of Tasmania (1999)

12. Burnett, H.H.M., Murray, A.J.: Exploring business incubation from a family perspective: How startup family firms experience the incubation process in two Australian incubators. Small Enterprise Research 16(2), 60–75 (2008)
13. Huang, Y., Wilkinson, I.F.: Understanding power and trust in inter-firm relationships: a dynamic perspective. In: Proc. IMP Conference, Milan (2006)
14. Beckett, R.C.: Collaboration is now a strategic necessity. In: Handbook of Business Strategy, pp. 327–332. Emerald Group Publishing (2005) ISSN 0849-4318
15. Burgess, L., Jones, M.: Exploring the Determinants and Dimensionality of SME e-Collaboration Trust. In: Asia-Pacific Researchers in Organization Studies 2009, Conference, Monterey, Mexico, December 6-9 (2009)
16. Brunetto, Y., Farr-Wharton, R.: The Moderating Role of Trust in SME Owner/Managers' Decision-Making about Collaborating. Journal of Small Business Management 45(3), 362–387 (2007)
17. Abdul –Rahman, A., Hailes, S.: Supporting trust in virtual communities. In: Proceedings of the Hawaii International Conference on System Sciences, Maui, Hawaii, January 4-7 (2000)
18. Msanjila, S.S., Afarmanesh, H.: On hard and soft models to analyze trust life cycle for mediating collaboration. In: Camarinha-Matos, L.M., et al. (eds.) PRO-VE 2009. IFIP AICT, vol. 307, pp. 381–392 (2009) ISBN10-3-642-04567-7

Informedness in Collaborative Networks through Active Information Provisioning

Heiko Thimm[1] and Karsten Boye Rasmussen[2]

[1] Pforzheim University, School of Engineering, Tiefenbronner Str. 65
D-75015 Pforzheim, Germany
heiko.thimm@hs-pforzheim.de
[2] University of Southern Denmark, Department Marketing and Management, Campusvej 55
DK-5230 Odense, Denmark
kbr@sam.sdu.dk

Abstract. Successful collaboration in business networks calls for well-informed network participants. Members who know about the many aspects of the network are an effective vehicle to promote trust within the network, successfully resolve conflicts, and build a prospering collaboration climate. The importance of well-informed network participants has lead to our concept of network participant informedness which is derived from existing theories and concepts for firm informedness. Through a specialized IT based active information provisioning service it is possible to effectively obtain well informed network participants. A corresponding modeling framework and a rule based approach for the needed active system capabilities are presented.

Keywords: Collaborative Networks, Information Provisioning, Knowledge Management, Rule Based Information Management, Active Database Systems.

1 Introduction

Companies seek to improve their competitive position by collaborating with other companies in *collaborative networks* [2] that are expected to provide many potential benefits. The benefits include: reduction of costs due to economy of scale effects [8], access to new markets and extra resources [5], better access to partner expertise, faster collaboration forming [16], and creation of new business opportunities [6].

There exist different kinds of collaborative networks where the members collaborate in different areas such as knowledge sharing and joint product development [1]. It also can be observed in the networking practice that network members collaborate on the operational level [18]. That is, several members of a network jointly process business transactions such as inquiries and orders from the market. The joined customer order fulfillment processes of collaborative networks typically deliver a composite product or service for which the involved members contribute individual parts and services. The collaborative provisioning of composite products and services, can lead to cross-organizational processes with high complexity [14]. The subset of network members that participate in these processes for a specific business opportunity form a temporary

L.M. Camarinha-Matos et al. (Eds.): PRO-VE 2010, IFIP AICT 336, pp. 412–419, 2010.

alliance referred to as *Virtual Enterprise (VE)* [2]. A VE is terminated in a controlled way when the order or project resulting from the business opportunity is completed.

Successful collaboration in collaborative networks calls for network participants who are well-informed about the many aspects of the network [9]. Well-informed network participants can promote trust within the network, successfully resolve conflicts, and build a prospering collaboration climate.

Without an appropriate level of informedness, a network can be threatened by distrust between the participating members and distrust to the idea and outcome of the network. So far in the research literature on building and promoting trust in networks [11, 13] the role of informed network participants has not been studied extensively. The fact that modern companies are more often participating in business networks has only recently been addressed in theories on firm informedness [9]. Thus, there still exist numerous research questions in this particular area of collaborative networks. In our work we are addressing some of these issues with the goal to define a foundation for an active information provisioning service in collaborative networks. We in the current stage of our research consider especially the type of collaborative networks where the completion of customer orders implies joint order fulfillment processes by a subset of network members. For example, the members being selected to work together in a VE fulfill complementary parts of the order such as production steps. As a further characteristic of the focused network type we assume that the network is managed by a central management instance such as a human moderator [19]. Our proposed service is not intended to substitute such a moderator. Instead it is the objective of the service to free the moderator from routine information dissemination tasks. The example cases presented in the article will illustrate this specific type of collaborative networks.

By active information provisioning we mean a service that automates a continuous and asynchronous delivery of information about the many networking aspects according to the individual network participant's needs. The automated information provisioning through an IT support service will reduce the influence of time constraints on the informedness of network members. We propose the concept of *network participant informedness* as a theoretical basis for such a service as a novel addition to our earlier work on active information provisioning in collaborative networks [20]. In this article we will discuss central aspects and possible generic solutions for the service. This includes a specialized modeling framework for information provisioning and an approach for the needed active system capabilities. We propose the use of an Event-Condition-Action rule formalism [15]. Through this approach it is possible to couple the active provisioning of tailored information to temporal events and conditions that refer to network indicators and states of business processes that are simultaneously executed in the network.

Following this introduction we introduce the concept of network participant informedness in section two. Section three and four give an overview of our modeling framework and our rule based approach for active provisioning. An outlook for our future work and concluding remarks are contained in section five.

2 Firm Informedness in Collaborative Networks

It is a generally accepted fact that information is a source of competitive advantage for firms [3]. For example, the use of information with or without IT can lead to both improved business capabilities but also to new business capabilities [10, 12]. By improving the availability of information a possibility is created for firms and customers to achieve a new level of informedness. Clemons [4] defines *consumer informedness* as the degree to which consumers know the products or services, and their precise attributes and prices that are available in the market. Kauffman's firm informedness theory [9] extends this consumer informedness theory to include both consumer informedness and firm informedness.

On the grounds of these theories we are suggesting the concept of *network participant informedness.* In general, we refer by this concept to firms as members of a collaborative network and especially their knowledge about the many aspects of the network. Similar to the informedness theory of Kauffman [9] we first of all require informed network participants to know about resources, competences, and the value of other participants in co-production. The knowledge about the participants' value in co-production concerns both shared and private high quality information about the network strategy, the current network status, and also the business processes that are cooperatively executed within the network. In addition to knowing isolated details of these information categories well-informed network participants also understand the semantic relations between the different information items. That is, they have a broad understanding of the structure of the network and its business capabilities.

A high level of network participant informedness can be achieved with and without IT. If information availability for network participants is not based on IT still a high level of network participant informedness can occur. The intrinsic motivation of the participants to be well-informed about what is going on in the network can lead to an appropriate level of informedness. However, aiming at an appropriate level of informedness without use of IT support will usually require substantial time efforts and lead to high information acquisition cost.

For that reason, our research targets a flexible information provisioning service to automate information provisioning to the network participants. The system will be presenting tailored content about the above mentioned network aspects in the form of reports frequently delivered by the service. User-defined provisioning schemes will determine at what exact instances of time reports are to be delivered.

Table 1 contains an illustration of a sample report prepared for a network member Metal Gurus. This report informs about an ongoing inquiry handling business process for a customer Volcano ships. The details of this sample report are as follows. Information specific to the inquiry received is contained in row 1. Row 2 describes the fulfillment steps (called request elements denoted by RE_u(< *a textual description* >), u=1,...,k needed to complete a corresponding order. Row 3 contains the VE (i.e. Virtual Enterprise) in charge of the inquiry with details about the corresponding request elements and the assigned network members denoted by M_v, v=1,...,l. Information about the quotation issued and the corresponding response received from the inquiring shipyard are contained in row 4 and 5, respectively. Row 6 provides information about the resulting order received by the network.

Table 1. Sample report informing about an ongoing inquiry handling process

Report-ID: 161109-091624, Generation Date: 2009-11-16, Prepared for: Metal Gurus		
	Caption	**Content**
1	New inquiry received:	Inquiry ID: 210409-1654-59, Date received: 2009-04-21, Inquiring company: Volcano Ships, Inquiry description: 400 seats (Ocean Convenience) with final assembly at customer's site, Demanded delivery: 2009-12-30
2	Request elements:	RE_1 *(provision of metal seat frame)*, RE_2 *(provision of seat upholsteries)*, RE_3 *(provision of circuit systems)*, RE_4 *(provision of monitors)*, RE_5 *(provision of harnesses)*, RE_6 *(final assembly of seat)*
3	VE in charge of inquiry:	$RE_1[M_3]$, $RE_2[M_6]$, $RE_3[M_9]$, $RE_4[M_9]$, $RE_5[M_{13}]$, $RE_6[M_7]$,
4	Quotation issued to customer:	Quote ID: 260409-1332-16, Date issued: 2009-04-26, Quote Description: Offer for 400 standard seats (Ocean Convenience) with final assembly at customer's site, Offered Price: 880K€
5	Quotation result received:	Quote ID: 260409-1332-16, Date received: 2009-05-02, Quote result: positive, Response of customer: Offer accepted without changes; will sign contract
6	Order received:	Order ID: 080509-0918-34, Date received: 2009-05-08, Quote ID: 260409-1332-16

3 Modeling Framework for Information Provisioning

In this section we propose a modeling framework for flexible information provisioning in collaborative networks. Our framework consists of an extensible set of predefined information object types that belong to the information object categories *State Object Type* and *Process Object Type*.

In general *State Object Types* (SOT) correspond to network indicators that refer to network state information. Table 2 contains the skeletons of four examples. Each predefined object type is given an identifying and unique object type name such as Inquiries Received SOT. It is first explained in Table 2 what specific indicators the individual objects of the given types represent. Then, the *base content* and *complementary content* of each object type is described. These two concepts are similar to properties in object-oriented modeling [17]. The *base content* specifies the information content provided by the object by default. From a semantic point of view the base content primarily refers to aggregated information about the entire network. For example, objects of type Inquiries Received SOT by default provide the number of external inquiries received by the network together with related statistical information. The *complementary content* corresponds to further complementary information from the analytical context of the object's base content. In contrast to the base content, the complementary content provides information that is specific to the own company. For example, while the base content of objects of type Inquiries Received SOT will provide the number of inquiries received by the entire network, the complementary content will provide the number of received inquiries where the own company has been a supplier.

Table 2. Skeletons of four sample State Object Types

Inquiries Received SOT	Quotations Given SOT	Orders Received SOT	VEs Formed SOT
Individual object represents the set of ...			
external inquiries received	quotations given to customers	received orders	formed VEs
Base content concerns number(s) and detailed statistical information about ...			
inquiries received by network	quotations issued to customers	orders received	VEs formed
Complementary content concerns number(s) and detailed statistical information about ...			
inquiries where own company is demanded as a supplier	quotations where own company is considered as a supplier	orders where own company is considered as a supplier	formed VEs with participation by own company

Table 3. Skeletons of two sample Process Object Types

Inquiry Handling POT	Order Fulfillment POT
Individual object represents a concrete ...	
inquiry handling process	order fulfillment process
Processing states and corresponding base content (BC) and complementary content (CC)	
1. Inquiry Received	1. Order Received
Who issued inquiry? (BC) What product/service is demanded? (BC) Has the own company been requested as supplier? (CC)	To what offer is referred? (BC)
	2. Suborders Issued
2. Inquiry Decomposed	Which suborders have been issued? (BC) What are the details of the suborder issued to own company? (CC)
What are the elements of the inquiry? (BC)	
3. VE Configured	3. Suborders Completed
Which partners are assigned to the inquiry? (BC) What are the VE configuration details of the own company? (CC)	When were all suborders completed? (BC) What are the completion details of the suborder of the own company? (CC)
4. Quotation Issued	4. Order Completed
...	...

In general *Process Object Types* (POT) correspond to information about the execution of business processes within the network such as inquiry handling, order fulfillment, and marketing campaign planning. The individual objects of these types can be regarded as proxy objects that represent real world business processes executed within the network. Table 3 contains the skeletons of two examples which have the unique object type names Inquiry Handling POT and Order Fulfillment POT. Each type's sequence of potential processing states which are of interest to network members is specified. Note that in Table 3 the state sequences and state descriptions are not fully defined. The description of each state consists of a state number and a unique state name such as 1. Inquiry Received. Furthermore, a set of questions is given for each state. These questions describe the specific information items available in the given and also all following states. The information items that refer to the business process from the global view of the entire network are referred to as the *base content* of the object which is specified by the acronym BC in the state descriptions of Table 3. The company specific process information items are referred as *complementary content* of the object (specified by CC).

Based on our modeling framework it is possible to create and maintain an appropriate level of network participant informedness by a frequent information provisioning. The information provisioning operations can be described in terms of the information objects to be retrieved and the further information processing operations required to prepare informative reports as described above. The preparations can consist of calculations performed with the retrieved information items and also the completion of layout and formatting operations. Note, however, since we aim on a reoccurring provisioning of similar information items, a generic description of the relevant information objects and preparation operations is needed. This approach is similar to the popular generic forms of information systems. We refer to these generic descriptions in our framework by *report templates.*

4 Rule Based Information Provisioning

Active information provisioning in our research means that if certain expected events occur information is provided to users (subscribers) based on a push rather than a pull mechanism. Not only what information is to be prepared but also when the information preparation has to be performed should be as much as possible under control of the users. For this reason we support user defined *information provisioning schemes* which are associated with corresponding report templates.

In the following we describe our rule based approach for provisioning schemes. The approach is based on the ECA model which is the most popular model for the specification of rules in active database systems [15]. The ECA model defines a rule to consist of three parts, event, condition, and action. The semantic is that whenever the event happens, the condition is evaluated, and if satisfied then the action is taken.

We first of all assume a database that stores general information about the network and its members. The user defined report templates are also stored in this database. Furthermore, the database stores information about the current status of the network represented as a corresponding set of SOT objects. Information about currently executing and also already completed business processes in the network are administered in the database, too. This process information is represented as POT objects. Assuming the use of relational database technology the data are stored in flat tables for every defined SOT and POT type. Another separate table is kept for each of the defined set of a process's states in order to administer process state information.

Given the above outlined database the three components of ECA rules can be generally described as in Table 4. We divide the set of relevant events into four sub-sets. The first subset of events refers to value changes of network indicators. The second subset refers to the registration of new business processes and the third subset reflects state changes of business processes. The fourth subset of events is different from the previous events. This subset represents time controlled events where the level of time granularity here is restricted to a calendar day. In the condition part of our rules it is referred to values of network indicators and values related to business processes. In particular, conditions are described that imply the usual comparison operations of numeric values. The conditions can be very short and only consist of a single comparison operation. But it is also possible to specify complex condition statements by combining several single comparison operations by the logical binary operators. This approach for our conditions is described in Table 4 in the popular EBNF notation [7]. As actions of our rules we consider the orchestration of information reports according to user defined report templates and the provisioning of the reports to the corresponding users.

Table 4. Using the ECA rule model for Active Information Provisioning

E	Update of SOT object	Creation of new POT object	State Update of POT object	Switch into next calendar day
C	Given the database state at time t_i referred to by DB_{t_i} and given any pair of object items $OI_l, OI_k \in DB_{t_i}$ which are data values of SOT objects or POT objects, then a condition $cond$ is $cond = (cond_{single} \mid cond_{composite})$ with $cond_{single} = OI_l(= \mid \neq \mid \leq \mid \geq)(OI_k \mid C) with\ C \in \mathbb{R}_0$ and $cond_{composite} = cond_{single}\{(\wedge \mid \vee)\ cond_{single}\}_1$			
A	Generation of individual report according to a referred user-defined report template and provision to user			

5 Outlook and Conclusions

Based on the concepts introduced in this paper a first "light-weight" prototype for an active information provision service has been specified. Through experiments with the prototype we expect to gain further insights especially concerning the active system capabilities and the modeling framework. Among others, the results of the experiments will lead to both an extension and refinement of the predefined object types. Through the prototype we will also obtain requirements for the functionality that the service needs to offer to the various user types. For example, this includes functionality for the extension of the predefined object types by the system administrator. This also includes functionality for the specification of report templates and provisioning schemes by the users of the service. Through manual data entry activities our prototype is provided with information about executing business processes. We will extend this approach by a corresponding data interface so that process information can be exchanged with a business process monitoring environment.

For our proposed service approach several implementation barriers are to be considered. There is first of all the requirement that the relevant information objects and processes of the network need to be defined, analyzed, and mapped to our modeling framework. This can require a substantial amount of work and especially group negotiations and decision processes in order to obtain globally agreed process definitions. Furthermore, the technical integration of the various pre-existing systems with our service can lead to complicated integration problems due to the expected heterogeneity of the involved systems.

References

1. Braha, D., Bar-Yam, Y.: Information flow structure in large-scale product development organizational networks. J. of Information Technology 19(4), 244–253 (2004)
2. Camarinha-Matos, L.M., Afsarmanesh, H.: Collaborative networks: a new scientific discipline. J. of Intelligent Manufacturing 16, 439–452 (2005)
3. Clemons, E.K., Row, M.C.: Sustaining IT advantage: the role of structural differences. MIS Quarterly 15(3), 275–292 (1991)
4. Clemons, E.K.: How information changes consumer behavior and consumer behavior determines corporate strategy. J. Mgmt. Information Systems 25(2), 13–40 (2008)
5. Davidow, W.H., Malone, M.S.: The Virtual Corporation. Harper Business, New York (1993)
6. van Heck, E., Vervest, P.: Smart business networks: how the network wins. CACM 50(6), 28–37 (2007)
7. ISO/IEC 14977: ISO Standard for the EBNF (1996)
8. Jarillo, J.C.: Strategic Networks: Creating the Borderless Organization. Butterworth-Heinemann, Oxford (1993)
9. Kauffman, R., Li, T., van Heck, E.: A Theory of Informedness and Business Network Co-Production. In: Proceedings Hawaii Int. Conf. System Sciences, p. 1–10 (2010)
10. Kohli, R., Grover, V.: Business value of IT: an essay for expanding research directions to keep up with the times. J. Association Information Systems 9(1), 23–29 (2008)
11. Kumar, K., Diesel, H.G.: Sustainable Collaboration: Managing Conflict and Cooperation in Interorganizational Systems. MIS Quarterly 20(3), 279–300 (1996)
12. Li, T.: Informedness and Customer-Centric Revenue Management. Thesis, Erasmus Univ., Netherlands (2009)
13. Msanjila, S.S., Afsarmanesh, A.: A Multi-Model Approach to Analyze Inter-organizational Trust. In: Collaborative Networks reference modeling, pp. 195–216. Springer, New York (2008)
14. Mulder, W., Meijer, G.T.: Distributed Information Services Supporting Collaborative Network Management. In: Network-Centric Collaboration and Supporting Frameworks, pp. 491–498. Springer, Boston (2006)
15. Paton, N., Diaz, O.: Active Database Systems. ACM Computing Surveys 31(1) (1999)
16. Österle, H., Fleisch, E., Alt, R.: Business Networking - Shaping Collaboration Between Enterprises. Springer, Berlin (2001)
17. Rumbaugh, J., et al.: Object-Oriented Modeling and Design. Prentice Hall, Englewood Cliffs (1991)
18. Saxena, K.B.: Business Process Management in a Smart Business Network Environment. In: Vervest, et al. (eds.) The Network Experience, pp. 69–81. Springer, Berlin (2009)
19. Thimm, H., Rasmussen, K.B.: An Information Support Service for Moderators of SME Company Networks. Management Research News 32(9), 846–857 (2009)
20. Thimm, H., Rasmussen, K.B.: An Active Information Provisioning Service for Collaborative Networks. In: Proceedings IADIS Int. Conf. on e-Society, Porto, pp. 282–290 (2010)

Integration of Business and Industrial Knowledge on Services to Set Trusted Business Communities of Organisations

Frédérique Biennier, Régis Aubry, and Mathieu Maranzana

INSA Lyon, LIESP, 69621 Villeurbanne Cedex, France
{frederique.biennier,regis.aubry,mathieu.maranzana}@insa-lyon.fr

Abstract. To fit the globalized economical environment, more and more SMEs have to develop networked and collaborative strategies. Such collaborative networks are mostly based on trusted and well known networks. At the international level, the European Union promotes clearly internet of services based solutions to support innovative business communities of organisations. The results accumulated by various projects provide a consistent environment (including methods, design tools and ESB-based developments) to support, at a technological level, Business Service oriented organizations. Nevertheless, these visions are mostly technology oriented and lack of taking into account industrial characteristics. To overcome this limit, we aim at integrating industrial functional and non functional business and industrial properties (including management strategy, quality, process maturity…) in service registries. This improves service selection and composition to set consistent dynamic collaborative organizations based on trusted business communities of organisations.

Keywords: Service Oriented Enterprise, non functional properties, industrial services, business governance, trust community of organisations.

1 Introduction

The increased calls for mass customization and for integrating sustainable constraints in production organization raised interest in product/service management, leading to the emergence of ecosystem of services allowing to build dynamically "product-service chains" to anticipate consumer needs. These new business conditions induce significant **organizational changes within enterprises**, such as focusing on their core business and developing new collaborative strategies, calling for agility and new business strategies [9]. Setting collaborative processes between enterprises and especially among SMEs is a promising approach to industrial competitiveness and is expected to generate substantial savings, expand market positions or develop new opportunities for the participants. Within inter-firm collaborations, participants undertake joint business activities that may include co-design, co-marketing, co-production, co-development, sharing resources. This involves (1) reorganizing the enterprise according to the business services it can propose and publish, (2) being able to select the convenient partners, and (3) being able to orchestrate its activity according to these business services among different business areas to provide an end-to-end business

L.M. Camarinha-Matos et al. (Eds.): PRO-VE 2010, IFIP AICT 336, pp. 420–426, 2010.

value-added service chain to the customer. **By this way, industrial networks can emerge leading to new business opportunities and new management rules.** Nevertheless, the development of large-scale collaborative organizations is by now limited due to geographic constraints or lack of trust between partners.

Such distributed and collaborative organizations make heavy use of ICT technologies [4] requiring more and more IT inter-operability and agility. Unfortunately, as different software environments are used to support different business areas, the global information system often lacks consistency, interoperability and agility. Moreover, web-economy oriented collaborative frameworks are devoted to commercial relationships, and do not integrate any industrial constraints nor business related knowledge. This can lead to inconsistent industrial collaborative organization, decreasing the global efficiency and increasing waste rate due to non value-added activities.

To overcome these limits, business service ecosystems have to integrate various constraints (as industrial ones) to define extended business service models, paying a particular attention on "functional" properties (describing what the service can do) and "non functional" properties (as security, quality of service, industrial reliability…) in order to improve services discovery and CNO enactment. In this paper, after describing the context and the state of the art (section 2), we introduce our industrial service architecture (section 3), focusing mostly on the governance tools to support trusted-community of organisations management features.

2 Context and State of the Art

Developing large scale networked and collaborative strategies involves improving the potential partner selection process and increasing the IT support agility and interoperability. At the international level, the European Union clearly promotes solutions to support and favour innovative business networks on the basis of an internet of services in the FP7 work program. Nevertheless, this vision focuses mostly on the IT support stakes (syntactic and semantic interoperability, collaborative work space organization, process formalization…) but does not take into account neither the industrial constraints (production or purchase management, industrial process organization…) nor the way partners are identified and selected (face to face contact, cooptation…). Moreover, integrating sustainable constraints involves focusing on the "delivered product" lifecycle, adding value-added services, leading to Product-Service Systems. These product-Service Systems have been pointed out since the beginning of the 2000s [11] and have been classified by [20] depending on the tangible/intangible parts (from a product oriented organisation to a result oriented organisation). These different models lead to a product-service taxonomy based on the product identification and ownership but they lack taking into account the global product service supply-chain organization, and the way partners can be selected. Only few works pay attention on the way services are created, selected and composed [15] and collaborations are set to support the global product life-cycle [14]. Nevertheless, this service-based approach is limited by the way partners can be discovered and selected.

To improve at a large-scale partner discovery and selection, services must be published widely. This is partly done at the IT level by enriching SOA-based registries with semantic annotation that are used to discover more efficiently potential partners fitting the requirements. Nevertheless, discovering services is not enough to set a collaborative organization: a particular attention must be paid on trust level between partners [8]. Different criteria can be used to define this trust level: objective value of non functional properties (as cost, delay…) related to the service [18], security policy implementation [5], a mix of criteria including human relationships [10], or other cultural criteria [6]... All these approaches bring to light that non functional properties must be described and managed. As proposed in different enterprises Architecture Level, supervision and governance functions are split between the business and the technological levels. Works developed at a technological service level entail a dynamic monitoring system, taking into account several Service Level Agreements (SLAs). As several services, suppliers and technologies are involved in a complex service chain, the global management is rather complex. On one hand it requires online computing of Quality of Service (QoS) levels. On the other hand, Business Activity Monitoring systems lack of connections between the collaborative process organization, performance indicators and SLAs. To overcome this limit, the OASIS WS-Quality Management proposal [12] establishes a first link between these basic SLAs and Business Level Agreements (BLA) but it lacks of defining strategies to combine agreements. This requires setting a Business Level Agreement (BLA) composition mechanism and a BLA based supervision console to improve the agreement negotiation process [13].

To overcome these limits (namely lack of industrial constraints in service definition and limited partners selection), hybrid approaches mixing industrial engineering, IT components and virtual networks' management skills must be set.

3 Industrial Services Registry Organization

To meet the large-scale collaborative organization challenge, we propose to organize an industrial service infrastructure taking advantage of the cloud technology development and extending the breeding virtual organization proposed by [1]. Instead of setting groups of trusted partners waiting for a collaboration opportunity, we propose to organise an open publication of industrial services and second to support an open cooptation mechanism thanks to a multi-level governance toolsets in order to manage trust-oriented parameters. Each potential partner sets and manages its own registry to publish its offers / demands. Identified business communities of organisations (breeding virtual organisation) also set their own registries and / or federate their members own registries. A distributed federation manager is implemented on each node managing a registry (1) to discover other registries, and (2) manage trust relationships within new potential partners (fig 1). This industrial service infrastructure relies on two challenges (1) the industrial multi-dimensional description and (2) the organization of a distributed governance environment able to manage the different parameters used to establish trusted relationships.

Our industrial Semantic Web Service takes into account the industrial functional properties (describing the "business related" competencies) and non functional properties (describing the industrial quality of service as well as security). By this way, a qualitative management process can be supported [7]. This business dimension goes beyond semantic annotation of services. It describes the operational part, the business rules and the organizational constraints related to services. Each service is described according to 2 main dimensions:

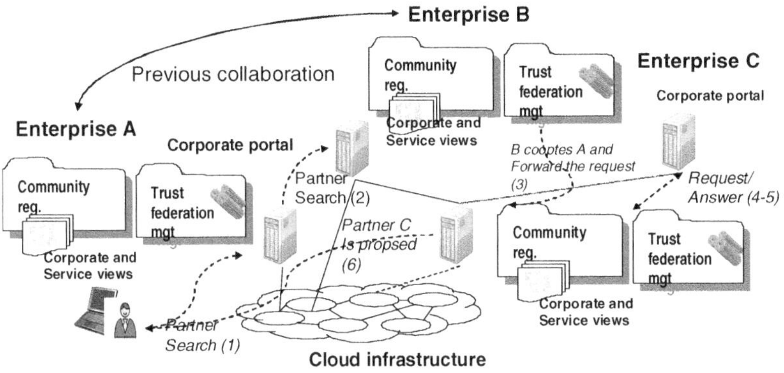

Fig. 1. Industrial registry organization

Each partner manages its own service registry. The trust federation manager is used to interconnect these registries, and manages cooptation rules. For example, A looks for a partner, due to a previous collaboration, B coopts A to its community of organisations so that A can discover enterprise C.

- *Corporate dimension*: It is divided four axis:
  - **Partner administrative properties**: it includes both partner identification and location information. This last information can be fruitfully used to improve the delivery process.
  - **Collaboration-oriented properties**: it refers to other partners with whom collaborative organizations are / have been sets. This can be seen either as "references" to be selected for a new collaborative organization or as basic network building mechanisms.
  - **Maturity property**: it refers to the enterprise organization so that potential partners can identify if the process / service is well formalized, documented, and consequently can be associated to certification process. To the end, we use the Capability Maturity Model Integration classification first defined in the software development context and adapted to other production contexts including service environment [17].
  - **IT support properties**: it describes optionally the current ICT tools and means that are commonly used by the partner. This information is used to manage the technological interoperability objective.
- *Service dimension*: it includes 2 axis:
  - **Functional properties**: It refers to product / service industrial description:
    - *Competencies description* is related to business area and is detailed according to a specialized ontology in order to describe what is offered by the partner. It includes production machines and tools, material and product / service identification.
    - *Production strategy description* : It refers to the Production management part of the ISA S95 ontology, this description is used to set a consistent industrial collaborative organization (depending on production management strategy and its related "configuration parameters").

- **Non functional properties**: They describe how the product / service could be achieved and are used to establish trusted relationships between partners. They includes different parameters (as security, process maturity, quality of service) describing for each parameter both a pledge part (what can be promised and integrated in a BLA) and a control part (in order to check if the pledge is fulfilled or not):
  - *Security properties*: In order to fit the dynamic environment, different security policies are defined as semantic annotations referring to a perceived risk and counter-measures [16]. The convenient policy is selected according to the current context and is used to conclude the related Quality of protection agreement.
  - *Quality of Service properties*: They refer to the service "environmental" interface, paying attention on the industrial performance indicator associated to the requested good (product and / or service). It includes (but it is not limited to):
    - Reliability: Associated to a particular good, it assessesz the partner confidence of being able to deliver the good according to the request. This indicator is coupled to the monitoring system (so that experiences can be capitalized), storing different values: mean, standard deviation and current offer.
    - Delay: It describes the potential delay necessary to provide the good and is also associated to different values: mean, standard deviation and current offer.
    - Configuration ability: It defines if the good can be tuned according to given patterns or not.
    - Adaptation level: It defines if the good production process can be adapted or not.
    - Global quality: Based on business-area certification classification, it assesses the production quality and focuses on reporting abilities.
    - Cost and financial characteristics: It includes current cost value, payment facilities…
    - Sustainable growth characteristics: material certification, CO2 evaluation…

All these properties are defined as semantic annotation on the service. To overcome the limit due to the single reference ontology involved in SAWSDL, YASA4WSDL [3] refers to different ontologies within the annotations. By this way, we define different onologies related to the industrial service dimensions to enrich the service description with the convenient WSDL semantic annotation. This multiple description technique improves the semantic matching used to discover and select services fitting the best functional and non functional requirements.

Built upon the existing JONES platform, our industrial registry infrastructure is organized in a distributed way. This architecture allows us to take advantage of the semantic and service layer governance toolsets provided by PEtALS[1] (SOA monitoring features),

[1] PEtALS is an open source ESB supported by the JONES platform. Documentation and downloads are available at: petals.ow2.org

DRAGON[2] (distributed registry, SLA and contract management) and SemEUsE[3] (semantic registry, semantic probes and late binding features) to manage, discover, compose and monitor industrial services. It also allows establishing the related BLA and SLA thanks to adapted monitoring features [2]. Using the federation registry manager, this tool will be enriched to assess trust levels and control its evolution while exchanging information with other registries, taking advantage of our previous works in real-time system QoS management [19].

4 Conclusion

Due to increased customization in a globalized economy and to the development of "Service Oriented Products," enterprises have to adapt their organizational and business strategy, enhancing their own agility, reducing waste (non value-added activity) and focusing on their core-business. Setting collaborative processes between enterprises and especially among SMEs is a promising approach to industrial competitiveness, and is expected to generate substantial savings, expand market positions and / or develop new opportunities for the participants. To develop large-scale collaborative organization, we propose a distributed industrial service registry that enriches the SemEUsE architecture with different industry related ontologies and business level monitoring abilities.

Acknowledgments. This work has been partly supported by the ANR SemEUsE project under grant 2007TECLOG017 and by the Rhône-Alpes area council via the Cluster GOSPI SIMSYPROD project.

References

1. Afsarmanesh, H., Camarinha-Matos, L.M.: A framework for management of virtual organizations breeding environments. In: Proceedings of PRO-VE 2005 - Collaborative networks and their breeding environments, September 26-28, pp. 35–48. Springer, Valencia (2005)
2. Alhalabi, F., Narkoy, B., Aubry, R., Maranzana, M., Morel, L., Sourrouille, J.L.: Centralized vs decentralized QoS management policy. In: 3rd International Conference on Information and Communication Technologies: From Theory to Applications (ICTTA 2008), April 7-11, pp. 1–6. IEEE Press, Los Alamitos (2008)
3. Chabeb, Y., Tata, S.: Yet Another Semantic Annotation for WSDL. In: IADIS International Conference WWW/Internet 2008, pp. 437–441 (2008)
4. DeVor, R., Graves, R., Mills, J.J.: Agile manufacturing research: accomplishments and opportunities. IIE Transactions 29, 813–823 (1997)
5. Garcia, D.G., Felgar de Toledo, M.B.: An approach for establishing trust relationships in the web service technology. Pervasive collaborative networks. In: Camarinha-Matos, L.M., Picard, W. (eds.) Proceedings of PRO-VE 2008, pp. 509–516 (2008)

---

[2] Dragon is an open source SOA governance toolset including a syntactic registry manager, a SLA manager and a policy manager. Information and downloads are available at: dragon.ow2.org

[3] SemEUsE is a semantic extension of PEtALS currently under development via the ANR 2007TecLog017 project. Information and demos are available at: www.semeuse.org

6. Grudzewski, W.M., Hejduk, I.K., Wantuchowicz, M.: Cultural determinants of creating modern organizations – The role of trust. Pervasive collaborative networks. In: Camarinha-Matos, L.M., Picard, W. (eds.) Proceedings of PRO-VE 2008, pp. 323–332 (2008)
7. Karvonen, I., Ollus, M., Uoti, M.: Qualitative monitoring to support pro-active virtual organization management. Pervasive collaborative networks. In: Camarinha-Matos, L.M., Picard, W. (eds.) Proceedings of PRO-VE 2008, pp. 185–192 (2008)
8. Laaksonen, T., Kulmala, H.I.: Coordinating supplier relations: the role of interorganizational trust and interdependencies. Network-centric collaboration and supporting frameworks. In: Camarinha-Matos, L., Afsarmanesh, H., Ollus, M. (eds.) Proceedings of PRO-VE 2006, pp. 191–198 (2006)
9. Lee, H.L.: The Triple A Supply Chain. Harvard Business Review, 102–112 (October 2004)
10. Mezgar, I.: Trust building for enhancing collaboration in virtual organization. Network-centric collaboration and supporting frameworks. In: Camarinha-Matos, L., Afsarmanesh, H., Ollus, M. (eds.) Proceedings of PRO-VE 2006, pp. 173–180 (2006)
11. Mont, O.: Product-service systems: panacea or myth? PhD Dissertation, Lund University, p. 25 (2004)
12. OASIS: Web Services Quality Model v1.0 (2007), http://www.oasis-open.org/committees/download.php/26678/wsqm-ws_quality_model-wd-v1.0-r04.doc
13. Oliveira, A.I., Camarinha-Matos, L.M., Pouly, M.: Agreement negotiation support in virtual organization creation. Pervasive collaborative networks. In: Camarinha-Matos, L.M., Picard, W. (eds.) Proceedings of PRO-VE 2008, pp. 107–118 (2008)
14. Salkari, L., Hytönen, H.: Challenges of lifecycle service business for virtual organizations. Network-centric collaboration and supporting frameworks. In: Camarinha-Matos, L., Afsarmanesh, H., Ollus, M. (eds.) Proceedings of PRO-VE 2006, pp. 443–452 (2006)
15. Schuh, G., Dirlenbach, H., Georgi, L.: Service development in virtual enterprises. Network-centric collaboration and supporting frameworks. In: Camarinha-Matos, L., Afsarmanesh, H., Ollus, M. (eds.) Proceedings of PRO-VE 2006, pp. 527–534 (2006)
16. Sliman, L., Biennier, F., Badr, Y.: A security policy framework for context-aware and user preferences in e-services. Journal of Systems Architecture Journal of Systems Architecture 55(4), 275–288 (2009)
17. Software Engineering Institute: CMMI for Services, version 1.2. Carnegie Mellon University Technical Report, February 2009. p. 545 (2009), http://www.sei.cmu.edu/publications/documents/09.reports/09tr001.html
18. Urze, P.: Industrial networks trust bonds: a sociological perspective. Network-centric collaboration and supporting frameworks. In: Camarinha-Matos, L., Afsarmanesh, H., Ollus, M. (eds.) Proceedings of PRO-VE 2006, pp. 199–210 (2006)
19. Vienne, P., Sourrouille, J.L., Maranzana, M.: Modeling distributed applications for QoS management. In: Gschwind, T., Mascolo, C. (eds.) SEM 2004. LNCS, vol. 3437, pp. 170–184. Springer, Heidelberg (2005)
20. Yang, X., Moore, P., Pu, J.S., Wong, C.B.: A practical methodology for realizing product service systems for consumer products. Computers and Industrial Engineering 56, 224–235 (2009)

Social Service Brokerage Based on UDDI and Social Requirements

Jan Świerzowicz and Willy Picard

Department of Information Technology, Poznan University of Economics, Mansfelda 4, 60-854 Poznań, Poland
{jswierz,picard}@kti.ue.poznan.pl

Abstract. The choice of a suitable service provider is an important issue often overlooked in existing architectures. Current systems focus mostly on the service itself, paying little (if at all) attention to the service provider. In the Service Oriented Architecture (SOA), Universal Description, Discovery and Integration (UDDI) registries have been proposed as a way to publish and find information about available services. These registries have been criticized for not being completely trustworthy. In this paper, an enhancement of existing mechanisms for finding services is proposed. The concept of Social Service Broker addressing both service and social requirements is proposed. While UDDI registries still provide information about available services, methods from Social Network Analysis are proposed as a way to evaluate and rank the services proposed by a UDDI registry in social terms.

Keywords: Service Brokerage, UDDI, Social Network Analysis, Social Requirements, Service Oriented Architecture.

1 Introduction

The Service Oriented Architecture (SOA) has been defined by OASIS (Organization for the Advancement of Structured Information Standards) as a "paradigm for organizing and utilizing distributed capabilities that may be under the control of different ownership domains" [1].

According to OASIS, the main idea underlying SOA is to help needs to be satisfied by services performed by entities having capabilities. An important issue in SOA is therefore the identification of services fulfilling the requirements of the needy actor. A widely accepted solution to the service search issue is the use of a service broker: in this approach, the needy actor sends its requirements to the service broker who seeks next for a service fulfilling the needed requirements. When such a service has been identified, the service broker informs the needy actor about the service(s) that satisfying the requirements, as presented in Figure 1.

The service broker approach is a common approach in distributed systems, with applications e.g. in the Java world with RMI [2] or in Common Object Request Broker Architecture (CORBA) [3] In SOA, and more precisely in its most common implementation technologies, i.e. Web Services, the service broker approach is based on the concept of UDDI registry in which descriptions of services and their providers are stored.

L.M. Camarinha-Matos et al. (Eds.): PRO-VE 2010, IFIP AICT 336, pp. 427–434, 2010.

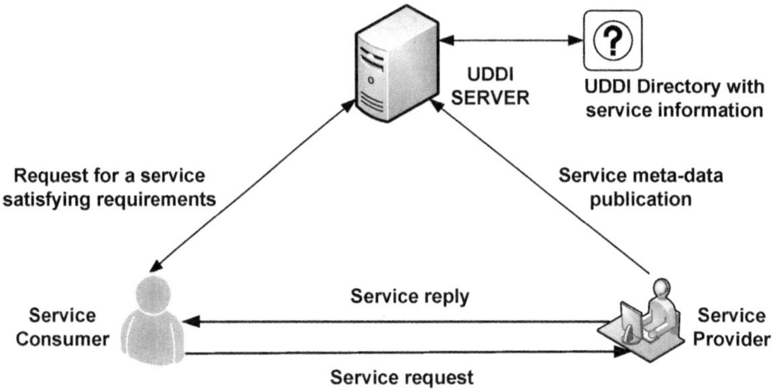

Fig. 1. Looking up service using UDDI (adapted from [9])

UDDI, which stands for *Universal Description, Discovery and Integration*, consists of a set of web-services providing access to information about a business or other entity and its technical interfaces (or APIs). UDDI registries are run by Operator Sites. UDDI registries may be used to publish and find information about one or more businesses or entities. As a consequence, UDDI registries allow service consumers to discover available services fulfilling given requirements, with the specification of the technical programming interfaces, usually written in the Web Services Description Language (WSDL) [4].

Lately UDDI has been criticized primarily because of its *decentralized* approach. Service providers are responsible for managing the contents of UDDI registries. UDDI operators do not monitor the entries in their UDDI registries. As a consequence, many entries concern companies that no longer exist, or provide imprecise information about organizations. As a consequence, UDDI registries have not been endorsed massively as foreseen in the first years of 2000's, leading to Microsoft, IBM and SAP discontinuing their UDDI Business Registry (UBR) project for Web services [5].

As a consequence of the decentralized approach of UDDI registries and the strong focus on services, "social" aspects, such as reputation, trust, and previous collaboration history of service providers, are not supported by UDDI registries. However, there is a need, not only for efficient mechanisms for the search of services satisfying a set of functional requirements (as provided by UDDI registries), but also for an evaluation of found services in social terms (answering questions such as "is a service satisfying my functional requirements trustworthy).

The purpose of this paper is to propose a solution for enhanced Service Provider selection taking into consideration social aspects. The concept of *Social Service Broker* is introduced as an intermediary between Service Consumer and Service Provider. The solution proposed in this paper is based on UDDI backed by Social Network Analysis, which addresses abovementioned social aspects. To our best knowledge, no such solution was proposed earlier.

The paper is organized as follows. In section 2, the features of UDDI registries are briefly introduced. In Section 3, Social Network Analysis and the idea of Social Requirements are presented. In section 4, the concept of Social Service Broker is detailed. Next, a short example illustrating a potential use of a Social Service Broker is given. Finally, Section 6 concludes the paper.

2 UDDI

UDDI registries implement the UDDI standard [6], providing transactional access to search and update registry entries. UDDI enables organizations, *service providers*, to publish information about their companies and services. These services and their technical details may then be discovered by other potential trading partners, *service consumers*. Once a service is chosen, the trading partners can exchange request/response messages and thus integrate with each other, potentially realizing extended enterprise solutions in Web services frameworks, allowing heterogeneous platforms and applications to discover and interoperate with existing applications [7].

2.1 UDDI Components

The information that a service provider can register encompasses various information “areas”, providing answers to the questions "who, what, where and how" about services.

In UDDI, the familiar metaphor of telephone directories is applied to Web services registries: UDDI registries contain White Pages, Yellow Pages and Green entries [7, 8]. UDDI Components are as follows:

White Pages
Contain basic contact data of the service provider (name, address, phone, Web site URL, and description of the organization.

Yellow Pages
A set of categories and taxonomies that classify services and service providers

Green Pages
Contain technical information about services- details about their location and the way they should be invoked

2.2 UDDI Registry Data Structures

In the UDDI API Schema [4], a set of UDDI data structures has been specified: business entities, business services, and binding templates.

The *business entity* is the top level UDDI element and represents the organization that is publishing its services. This element contains basic information about organization; i.e. name, business description, contact information, identifiers and classifications for an organization entity and a description of the services the organization is offering.

Each business entity contains a number of *business services*. A business service has a name, description, and categorizations. So by using business services, a business entity can organize its services.

Each service contains a number of *binding templates* that specify where the service is located and how to invoke it. Each binding template contains a set of keys that link the binding template to more detailed technical specifications ("*tModels*") which in turn contain more detailed technical information about the services. tModels can be regarded as "reference standards" and may be re-used by several different business entities [7, 8].

3 SNA and Social Requirements

3.1 Social Network Analysis

A social network is a graph of nodes (sometimes referred as actors), which may be connected by relations (sometimes referred as ties, links, or edges). Social Network Analysis (SNA) is the study of these relations[10].

An important aspect of SNA is the fact that it focused on the how the structure of relationships affects actors, instead of treating actors as the discrete units of analysis. SNA is backed by social sciences and strong mathematical theories like graph theory and matrix algebra [11] , which makes it applicable to analytical approaches and empirical methods. SNA uses various concepts to evaluate different network properties.

Recently, numerous networking tools have been made available to individuals and organizations mainly to help establishing and maintaining virtual communities. The common characteristic to all of them is that members build and maintain their own social networks, which are, then, connected to other networks through hubs (individuals that are members of two or more networks) [12].

3.2 Social Requirements

Social Network Analysis may be used to examine a given network by evaluating its properties. Social requirements may be considered as the reverse approach: using social requirements, properties of a network and their associated expected values are defined. One may then check if an existing network satisfies these social requirements. It should be noticed that social requirements are usually at a higher level of abstraction than SNA metrics, and therefore, a "translation" phase between social requirements and SNA metrics is usually required. [13]

3.3 Finding Services with Social Requirements

Social Network Analysis may also be used to find a service provider to fulfill the need. Unlike using UDDI registries, provider's selection may be enhanced with the issues of trust and previous collaboration while using SNA and social requirements. Unfortunately, such searching is time consuming because one needs to browse whole social network structure and check if a given actor 1) provides a required service 2) meets social requirements.

4 Social Service Broker

The concept of Social Service Broker is proposed in this paper as a combination of the two approaches – UDDI registries and Social Network Analysis. Comparing the search for a service with a Social Service Broker to the search for a service in a human society:

- UDDI registries are similar to phone books that may be consult to find information about companies providing a given service, e.g. plumbing;
- SNA methods may lead to ranking of available services, similarly to the opinion of friends about a given service provider, e.g. "is John Smith a good plumber".

Therefore, combination of UDDI registries and SNA methods is similar to the case when a list of service providers coming from a phone book is then ranked based on the opinion of friends.

In the proposed approach, the Social Service Broker is responsible for both aspects, i.e. retrieving the list of service providers satisfying the requirements of the service consumer, as well as ranking the results from the UDDI registry according to a set of social requirements.

In Figure 2, the processing of a request sent by the Service Consumer to the Social Service Broker is illustrated. In this process, seven steps may be distinguished:

1. Both service and social requirements are specified and sent out by the Service Consumer to the Social Service Broker.
2. Service specifications are sent by the Service Broker to a UDDI registry, which seeks entries in yellow and green pages and generates the list of services satisfying the received requirements

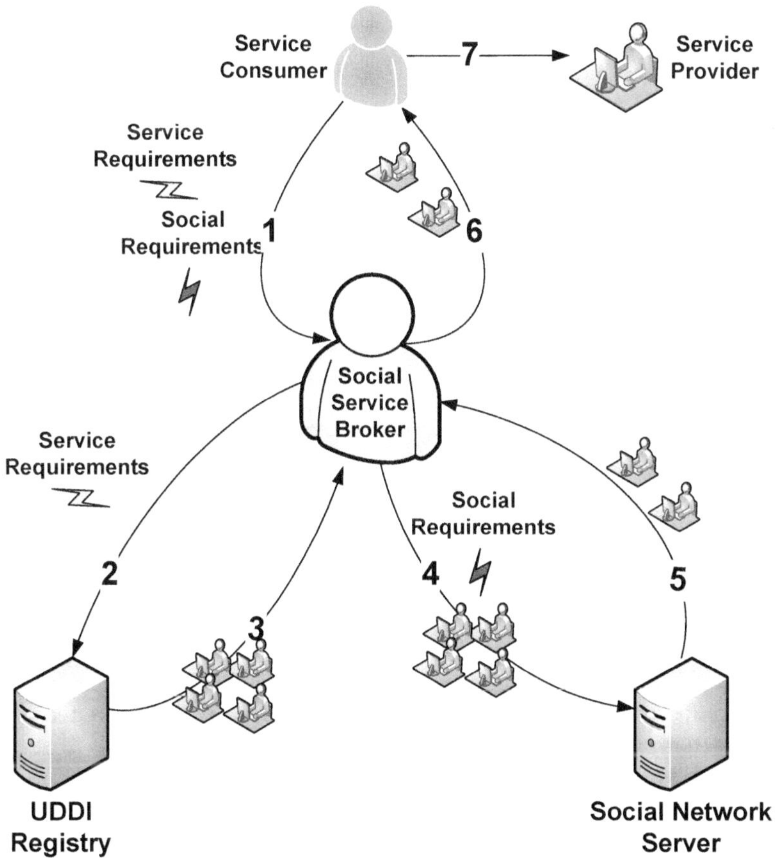

Fig. 2. Social Service Brokerage

3. Meta-data from the white pages about the providers of services satisfying the received requirements are sent back to the Social Service Broker by the UDDI registry.
4. The Social Service Broker sends a list of service providers from the white pages meta-data sent by the UDDI registry, together with the set of social requirements sent by the Service Consumer to the Social Network Server.
5. The Social Network Server evaluates the list of service providers as regards the social requirements, and sends back the results of its evaluation to the Social Service Broker.
6. The Social Service Broker sends a ranked set of service providers to the Service Consumer.
7. Based on the ranking of found service providers, the Service Consumer makes a choice of the most suitable service provider and sends him a request to perform the required service.

It should be noted that set of services that satisfies requirements may be empty (if the requirements are too strict); on the other hand it may contain many solutions (if the requirements are too vague).

5 Example

To illustrate the concepts presented in the former section, let's assume that the partnerships of an organization (A) with other organizations are modeled as the social network presented in Figure 3. Two organizations are or were partners if an edge between these organizations exists in the social network presented in Figure 3.

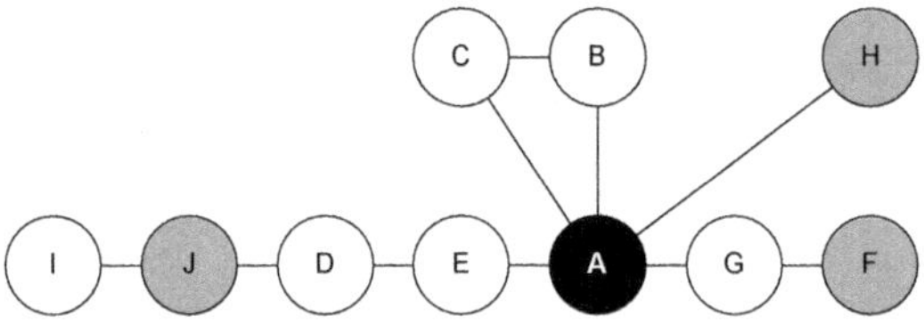

Fig. 3. Social Network of Organization A

The organization A has a given **need**, such as the writing of a performance report concerning a new product to highlight new features in an advertisement campaign. Company A sends its social and service requirements to a Social Service Broker. Afterwards the Social Service Broker forwards the service requirements to a UDDI registry and the result is that such report (**a capability to fulfill the need**) can be written by actors F, H, and J.

Along with service requirement, the following social requirement was also specified: a service provider must be a company that either company A or a direct partner of company A has already collaborated with.

As it can be seen from Figure 3, only actors H (direct collaborator) and F (collaboration through actor G) meet the social requirements. However, actor H should be ranked higher than actor F, as actor H was/is a direct collaborator while the collaboration with

F took/takes place via the actor G. Therefore, the Social Service Broker should send back a list of two service providers, i.e. companies G and H, satisfying both the service and social requirements, together with the appropriate ranking, i.e. actor H is ranked higher than actor F.

6 Conclusions

UDDI registries have been under a lot of criticism lately, partly because UDDI registries do not support social aspects related with the choice of appropriate services and service providers. The main contribution in this paper is the concept of Social Service Broker. To our best knowledge, the integration of Social Network Analysis/Social Requirements with UDDI is a novel approach to service brokerage.

Thanks to the proposed Social Service Broker, actors with **needs** may more easily find actors who have **capabilities to fulfill these needs in a socially satisfying manner,** with support both for efficient search (provided by UDDI registries) and social issues (modeled as social requirements).

Among future works, the concepts presented in this paper should be formally defined. Mechanisms to evaluate the relevance of social properties of the collaborative partners are still to be proposed. Additionally, within the context of the IT-SOA project [14], a prototype implementing the concept of Social Service Broker is currently under development. The project will gather companies from the construction sector in the Great Poland region. During the IT-SOA project, the Social Service Broker is planned to be a core element of the Service-Oriented infrastructure that construction companies will use to integrate their processes, leading to an evaluation of the proposed Social Service Broker concept in a real business environment.

References

1. OASIS SOA Reference Model, http://www.oasis-open.org/committees/tc_home.php?wg_abbrev=soa-rm (retrieved 05/2010)
2. Wollrath, A., Riggs, R., Waldo, J.: Distributed Object Model for the Java System. In: USENIX 1996, Conference on Object-Oriented Technologies, Toronto, Ontario, Canada (June 1996)
3. Object Management Group: Common Object Request Broker Architecture: Core Specification, http://www.omg.org/docs/formal/04-03-12.pdf (retrieved 05/2010)
4. UDDI Committee Specification (July 19, 2002), http://uddi.org/pubs/ProgrammersAPI-V2.04-Published-20020719.htm (retrieved 05/2010)
5. Skowroński, Z.: UDDI is (not) dead, http://devlicio.us/blogs/ziemowit_skowronski/archive/2007/11/15/uddi-is-not-dead.aspx (retrieved 05/2010)
6. UDDI Technical White Paper, http://www.uddi.org/pubs/Iru_UDDI_Technical_White_Paper.pdf (retrieved 05/2010)
7. Khoshafian, S.: Service Oriented Enterprises. Auerbach Publications (2007)
8. GovDex: Introduction to UDDI, https://www.govdex.gov.au/confluence/display/GTM/Introduction+to+UDDI (retrieved 05/2010)
9. Larsson, C., Wedi, N., Thiemann, H.: PRISM System Specification Handbook, http://www.prism.enes.org/Software/WSS/arcdi/index.html (retrieved 05/2010)

10. Baroudi, B., Olson, M., Ives, J.: An Empirical Study of the Impact of User Involvement on System Usage and Information Satisfaction. CACM 29(3), 232–238 (1986)
11. Borgatti, S.: What is social network analysis, `http://www.analytictech.com/networks/whatis.htm` (retrieved 05/2010)
12. Lavrac, N., Ljubic, P., Urbancic, T., Papa, G., Jermol, M., Bollhalter, S.: Trust Modeling for Networked Organizations Using Reputation and Collaboration Estimates (2007)
13. Świerzowicz, J., Picard, W.: Social Requirements for Virtual Organization Breeding Environments. In: Leveraging Knowledge for Innovation in Collaborative Networks, PRO-VE 2009, pp. 614–622. Springer, Heidelberg (2009)
14. IT-SOA, `https://www.soa.edu.pl/` (retrieved 05/2010)

Conceptual Design of Service Procurement for Collaborative Service Networks

Maik Herfurth and Peter Weiß

FZI Forschungszentrum Informatik, Haid-und Neu-Str. 10-14,
76131 Karlsruhe, Germany
{herfurth,weiss}fzi.de

Abstract. In this paper we propose a conceptual model for e-procurement solutions for industrial services. Product-related services are of particular interest of companies and should be supported through an appropriate network strategy. However, in the service field, e-business solutions and current standards are still not or only partially considering specifications and related variables of services. We make an approach to develop a conceptual model which allows analyzing existing systems and to specify requirements by distinguishing four system levels. Services can be classified using criteria such as degree of tradeability, intangibility, degree of labor intensity or interaction, etc. In the context of collaborative networks and professional services another common variable is the level of customer contacts or interactions. Services looked at in this paper require close buyer-supplier relationships in nature, and motivate to apply collaborative networks as a strategy, as trust between buyer and seller can be seen as a central focus.

Keywords: Service procurement, e-business, collaborative networks, e-catalogues, service descriptions, product classification.

1 Introduction

Collaborative networks are emerging in service industries since many years [17]. Customers integrate service providers and suppliers through implementing appropriate collaborative strategies. The aim is the better integration of service suppliers into their business processes and information systems. Purchasing of services in real business practice still causes many problems.. Classification of services can be realized either from a customer or service provider perspective and can be done by applying top-down or bottom-up approach [3]. Hence, there is a need to develop electronic data transfer models and standards to foster the development and application of web-based information systems during a service negotiation and buying process between companies and their suppliers [5]. Service procurement is gaining more and more importance in industry. However, purchasing expends too much time and routine administrative work on the procurement of services [16].

2 Collaborative Networks and Services

Service procurement processes are still a source of high costs to companies, and due to its complex and heterogeneous purchasing processes. Large companies typically support

L.M. Camarinha-Matos et al. (Eds.): PRO-VE 2010, IFIP AICT 336, pp. 435–442, 2010.

up to now have tried to support those processes via the application of individual web-based information systems [5], [16]. In the context of collaborative networks and professional services another common variable is the level of customer contacts or interactions. Services looked at in this paper require close buyer-supplier relationships in nature, and motivate to apply collaborative networks as a strategy, as trust between buyer and seller can be seen as a central focus. "*Industrial services have typically been divided into two broad categories: (1) maintenance and repair services, e.g., equipment repair, janitorial services, usually supplied under contract; and (2) business advisor services, e.g., legal, accounting, advertising, management consulting, typically new task-buying situations*" [2]. In the remainder we focus solely on category (1). Complexity refers to the "level of technical training and difficulty associated with providing the service to the customer" [2]. "*Elementary services are those related to products that are purchased frequently, are not essential to the industrial consumers primary functions, have low complexity, and do not require formalized service providers"*. [2]. Personal delivery describes "whether the service has to be delivered in-person by the service provider, whereas credence properties "refers to characteristics of the industrial product or service that makes it difficult to evaluate or understand" [2]. Thus, confidence in the service provider is essential "*because the higher the credence properties of the service, the less likely the customer will understand or make an objective assessment of the quality of the service delivered*" [2]. Tradeability of services depends on various other variables. Based on variables [3] classify services with regard to their appropriateness to be purchased and delivered online. Six service groups could be defined: (1) mass services, (2) professional services, (3) intellectual services, (4) credit services, (5) support services, (6) facility services. Three principal components to characterize service could be derived based on variables (shown in Table 1). Most variables describe the characteristics of the customer/provider relationship which is referred to as (A) "intimacy between service providers and customers". Further factors are: (B) "customer involvement on service good transactions" and (C) "importance of offline factors in the provision of service online goods". Whereby, C depends on "features of search goods" and "necessity of offline", B depends on "criticality for customer" and "necessity of membership relation". The emerging of e-catalog standards the product search can be used in a very different and improved matter [4]. Searching and purchasing of services necessitates the provision of electronic service descriptions and specifications, however, today it is still an unsolved problem for complex service. Complex services are offered and delivered in facility-oriented and product-related service industries such as maintenance, repair, disposal, etc. Services of this type have intangible and tangible elements and are typically exchanged in interaction processes where buyers and sellers are closely integrated [3]. Interactions include problem analysis and diagnosis to configure required services. To facilitate buying of services electronically requires product catalogues to find, compare, select, order and invoice complex services. Today, those systems are supporting mainly simple services with more tangible than intangible nature of service act. Customization and service packages are seen as adequate means to overcome current limitations of collaborative systems. Variables can be grouped into traditional service variables, online goods variables and variables relevant to both. "*Necessity of membership relation*" can be seen of high relevance in the context of collaborative networks. It signifies customer expectations as to the type of relationship with the service organization, "*e.g. whether it is involves a membership relationship or not*" [3].

Table 1. Variables for classification [3]

Traditional service variables	- Criticality for customer - Importance of professional knowledge - Degree of labor intensity - Degree of interaction - Degree of customer contact - Necessity of membership relation
Online goods variables	- Frequency to purchase - Features of search goods - Price
Variables relevant to both	- Degree of customization - Necessity of offline

Collaborative networks would allow decreasing transaction costs and agreeing on common standards and collaborative processes by fostering trust and quality of relational ties [2]. Configuration of collaborative processes depend on nature of rendered services (characterized through variables as shown in table 2 as well as quality of network ties and relationship. Latter are supposed to have strong influence on required interaction processes and transaction costs. Services offered or delivered electronically require specific characteristics. Services appropriate for e-commerce need to be standardized to provide them online. Thus, service industries are starting to offer more and more services electronically, which in turn requires implementing appropriate strategies [3]. Strategies depend on the type of service offerings.

3 Conceptual Model for Service Procurement

In our paper we specifically look at the procurement of industrial professional Services in Collaborative Networks. Procurement processes are defined by specific transaction phases which are looked into in the remainder. Especially, decision and control processes are related to procurement of direct material. This has negative effects on process costs, which increases through increased interactions e.g. manual clarification of identified differences verifying invoice of service suppliers against invoice, or invoice against delivery note and against order. In the context of procurement of industrial professional services new business documents and transactions logics are required. Delivery note for example is replaced by the bill of quantities and approval protocol. Collaborative service networks require reference models and standardized transaction documents to reduce costs and to internalize supplier services. Long procurement times and above related inefficiencies and problems have the effect that purchasing of services is often bypassing official purchasing process through so called "maverick buying". It causes greater capital commitment and low transparency of sales volumes and spending [16]. We present a *conceptual model for service procurement in collaborative networks*. Our model (figure 1) describes four different abstract layers to comprise service procurement in collaborative networks. The highest *level A* of the model is defined as the *business operational view level* to describe and define requirements for the organization and business for service procurement between clients and service providers.

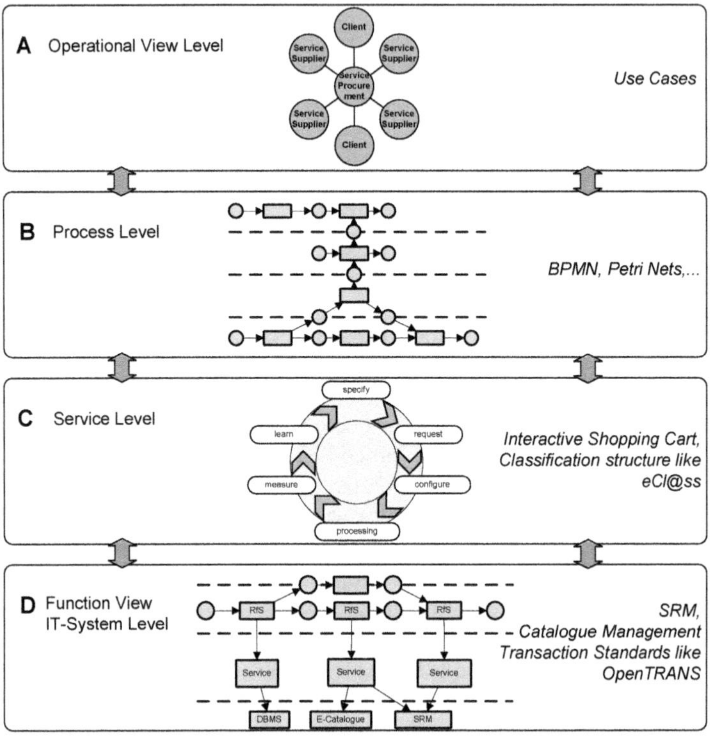

Fig. 1. Conceptual Model for Service Procurement

It defines the business model and the relationship between participating actors in the collaborative network. Therefore it can be defined by use case to identify the reality of e-procurement for services. The next *level B* is called *process level.* Business processes for service procurement are represented. It defines the alignment of processes and reference process models with the functional perspective and the use cases can be mapped on business processes. An implementation of the process level could be the use of formal modeling languages. The *level C* is called *service level.* The service level defines phase-oriented persistent states transition types of a service. The different state transitions are *request*, *specify*, *configure*, *processing*, *measure* and *learn*. The status request describes the definition of the service. While the specification of the service, the service will be in the specification status. The negotiating of the service defines the configure status. The execution of the service formulates the processing status. The status after the processing will be the measurement status. The learn status saves the final status. The saved status of a service can be used for following transactions and serves as a frozen status to draw experiences for this service type. The status types are following a continuous cycle along a service transaction process and oriented at transaction phases aligned with the eight phases service transaction model. The state transition types define the status of a service at different stages. The interactive shopping cart [13] could be an implementation of this level. *Level D* is the system level and describes the software system functionality view of different enterprise software systems. On the system level, we build up different business software system like SRM or catalogue management systems. The conceptual model for service procurement allows us to structure service procurement in different perspectives and views. The conceptual model for service procurement is a holistic model for service e-procurement. The different levels are influencing each other and are dependant. Requirements are defined on level A and will have an influence on the other levels. With this model, we are able to structure service procurement and assign terms and definitions. An important issue is the allocation of standards. By using our conceptual model, we are able to assign important procurement standards and demonstrate the influence of these standards. In Fig. 1, we are giving examples of elements in the different phases.

Additionally transaction phases of service differ from material process phases. This is another specific characteristic of service processes and important for the electronic transaction of services. Interfaces within phases are collaborative interfaces between actors. These interfaces are needed for interaction and information exchange. The corporate interfaces are decisive for efficiency, effectiveness and performance of the collaboration and interaction between actors. Theses interfaces are missing harmonization and standardization which leads to problems for the whole transaction process. Besides these corporate interfaces, interfaces between transaction phases are existing. These interfaces can be internal or corporate interfaces. Information is exchanged within companies by internal interfaces.

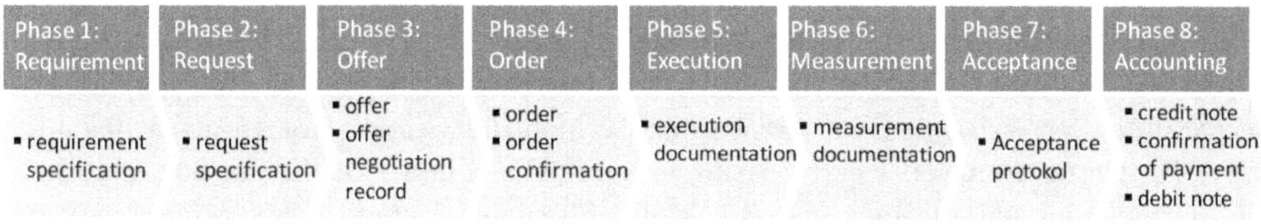

Fig. 2. Eight Phases Service Transaction Model

Corporate interfaces between transaction phases are result-oriented. At the end of every transaction will be a phase-oriented result by which the phase can be defined as concluded. The eight phases service transaction model defines typified properties of service processes. Fig. 2 shows the eight phases service transaction model with the specific service phases. The phase-related results are listed. The results document each phase and are exchanged between the actors.

4 Description of Services

For transaction in the content of e-Business a unique description of services is required. The description of service can be defined on level B of the conceptual model (Fig. 1). In service networks, different companies collaborate in order to transact services. The eight phases transaction model defines the structure of the transaction of services. Within collaborative service networks, also called value added networks, the collaboration occurs on a *n:m*-relationship: several service providers interact together with several service requesters. In [11], [12], [13] we presented a Meta model for the description of services. For our conceptual approach, we use an XML-based description of services.

Additionally, material positions like commodities and durables or tools are assigned. Also materials are assigned to service positions. Therefore this shows the typical characteristic of industrial services. Service units can be used to describe and define specific service-oriented business document types. Service units can be cumulatively represented in *service specifications.*

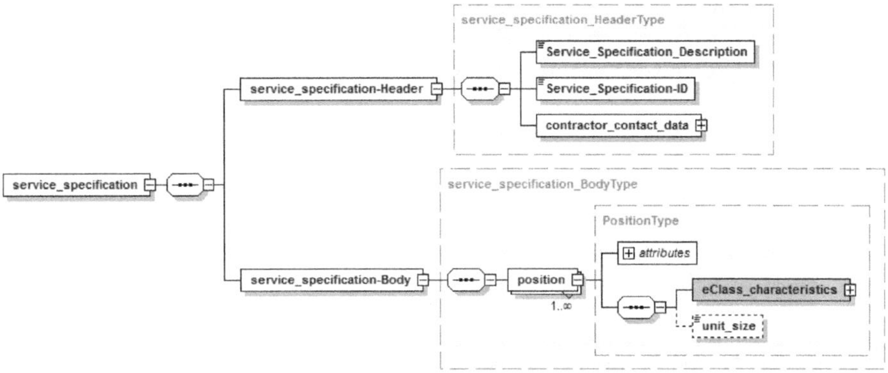

Fig. 3. Service Specification Structure

Service specifications are contract-based collections of service units as a base of businesses between clients and contractors and define individual sub positions of service units. Service specifications can be defined individually for an order or on the basis of a frame contract. Figure 3 shows the XML scheme of the service specification. The header part defines specific Meta information about the service specification, a unique ID of the service specification and related information about the contract partner. In the body part, the description of services is defined. The element type *position* defines services.

5 Transaction Standards for Service Procurement

Transaction standards can be used for the specification of business documents for e-commerce. Out of different data types, business transaction documents can be defined. Many transaction standards are based on the principle of core components technical specification (CCTS[1,2]). The CCTS approach shall improve the interoperability between e-business applications and business partners. The use of Core Components in

[1] Core Components are a library of basic atomic or composed data types with a unique description and are defined by UN/CEFACT. Core Components are modules for the development of semantic correct and significant packages for the exchange of business information. Different organizations are standardizing Core Components explicitly or they are implicitly part of transaction standards. The standardization organization OASIS is maintaining the ebXML Core Components Technical Specification (CCTS).

[2] The specification ISO/TS 15000-5 ebXML (Electronic Business Extensible Markup Language) Core Component Technical Specification, Version 2.01 (ebCCTS) was published in September 2005 as an ISO standard.

a specific business context, it is called Business Information Entities (BIE). For the electronic description and transaction, a specific description and transaction format is needed. Service-oriented business document transaction types have to be supported. The description of single services (service objects) should be based on a classification structure for a unique identification of services to use the advantages of classification systems. In our conceptual model of service procurement, transaction standards can be classified on level D. Existing transaction standards are the Universal Business Language (UBL) [15], openTRANS [8], GS1-XML [10], GAEB DA XML [9] and myOpenFactory [16].

Table 2. Comparison of Transaction Standards

Document types	**Transaction Standards**					
	UBL	***open-TRANS***	***GS1-XML***	***open-Factory***	***GAEB XML***	***ebus XML***
service specification					√	√
e-catalogue structure		√				√
request	√	√		√	√	√
offer	√	√		√	√	√
frame contract						√
order	√	√	√	√	√	√
order confirmation		√	√	√	√	√
measurement document						√
acceptance protocol						√
debit note	√	√		√	√	√
payment confirmation						√
credit note	√					√

We compared these transaction standards and we develop a new approach based on the requirements for the electronic transaction of industrial services. In Table 2, the analyzed transaction standards are compared. None of these standards defines all document types needed for the electronic data exchange of the transaction of industrial services. The structure of all standards differs. By the orientation on existing standards, we try to establish a solution with a high acceptance on the market which aims to be standardized. Our approach is compatible towards the existing presented transaction standards and can be transferred by XML converters.

6 Results

In this paper we presented a new holistic approach by a conceptual model of service procurement. The model provides a comprehensive view on service procurement. Finally identified terms and definitions can be described by this model and be assigned on the different levels. Based on this model, we provided solution approaches for the different levels and demonstrated the dependent elements of services procurement. For the electronic procurement of services, the specification of services has to be formally be defined. We proposed a structure for the specification based on XML. Transaction standards describe important business document types. Depending on the requirements for service procurement, we defined a new proposal for a transaction with service-specified document types. Transaction standards and business processes are related. In service procurement, transaction processes and business documents are interweaved by a choreography of processes based on service-specific business document types.

References

1. ECl@ss: International Standard for the Classification and Description of Products and Services (2009), http://www.eclass.eu/
2. Boyt, T., Harvey, M.: Classification of Industrial Services: A Model with Strategic Implications. Industrial Marketing Management 26, 291–300 (1997)
3. Lee, S., Park, Y.: The classification and strategic management of services in e-commerce: Development of service taxonomy based on customer perception. Expert Systems with Applications 36, 9618–9624 (2009)
4. Döring, S., et al.: Evaluation and optimization of the catalog search process of e-procurement platforms. Electronic Commerce Research and Applications 5, 44–56 (2006)
5. Gomes Campelo Filho, E.: Analysis of Current Supplier Relationship Management Practices: A Solution Proposal, Dissertation University of Karlsruhe (2009)
6. Meier, A., Stormer, H.: eBusiness & eCommerce: Management der digitalen Wertschöpfungskette. Springer, Berlin (2009)
7. BMEcat eBusiness Standardization Committee: BMEcat 1.2 (2005), http://www.bmecat.org
8. eBusiness Standardization Committee: openTRANS 2.1 (2009), http://www.opentrans.org
9. Bundesamt für Bauwesen und Raumordnung, DIN: GAEB DA XML 3.1 (2009), http://www.gaeb.de/produkte505.php
10. GS1 Germany: GS1 XML-Standards 2.7 (2009), http://www.gs1-germany.de/content/standards/ebusiness/gs1_xml/index_ger.html
11. Herfurth, M., Meinhardt, A., Schumacher, J., Weiß, P.: eProcurement for Industrial Maintenance Services. IFIP Advances in Information and Communication Technology, vol. 307. Springer, Boston (2009)
12. Herfurth, M., Weiß, P.: E-Procurement for Industrial Maintenance Services. In: eChallenges 2009, Istambul/Turkey (2009)
13. Herfurth, M., Kern, R., Rudolf, C., Weiß, P.: Reducing the complexity of Services: a new Approach to Service e-Procurement. In: Proceedings of the Multikonferenz Wirtschaftsinformatik MKWI 2010, Göttingen/Germany, (2010)
14. Benz, J., Höflinger, M.: Logistikprozesse mit SAP. 2. Auflage. Vieweg (2008)
15. OASIS: Universal Business Language (UBL) v2.0 (2006), http://docs.oasis-open.org/ubl/os-UBL-2.0/UBL-2.0.html
16. myOpenFactory, DIN PAS 1074: myOpenFactory 4.0 (2009), http://myopenfactory.com/products-myopenfactory.html
17. Camarinha-Matos, L.M., Paraskakis, I., Afsarmanesh, H. (eds.): Leveraging Knowledge for Innovation in Collaborative Networks, 10th IFIP WG 5.5 Working Conference on Virtual Enterprises, PRO-VE 2009, Thessaloniki, Greece, October 7-9 (2009)

Applying e-Service Model in Assessment and Comparison of Services

Egidijus Ostasius and Zivile Petraviciute

Vilnius Gediminas Technical University, Department of Fundamental Sciences, Sauletekio ave. 11, LT-10223 Vilnius, Lithuania
EgidijusOstasius@gama.vtu.lt, Zivile.Petraviciute@vgtu.lt

Abstract. The varying complexity, different maturity and rapid growth of the number of new e-services promote the assessment and their comparison with each other. This paper presents the application of e-service model in assessment and comparison of services in public sector. The model will assist the authorities to evaluate the maturity and complexity of the e-services they provide, and the systems that support these services. It could be helpful in comparing of e-services with other e-services provided by other authorities in the country and/or with other countries. The e-service model is based on the Reference Model for Service Oriented Architecture. A list of evaluation criteria that are based on the model is presented.

Keywords: e-government, e-service model, evaluation criteria, complexity, maturity.

1 Introduction

Aspirations of citizens, private sector, communities place new demands on governments for performance and efficiency and renewed focus on delivering better services. This forces trends towards reforming the public sector. It may move from traditional service delivery to the services in electronic domain or from the e-services in some sophistication (or maturity) level to the higher level. There is a need of measuring tools to show their respective areas of strengths and weaknesses with the e-government readiness domain, to have possibilities for a comparative assessment of the e-services provided by the administrations or to transform their governments by using ICT to deliver e-services to their citizens and to monitor the advancement of governments in implementing e-government services.

Some studies with their methodologies of measuring sophistication level applied were conducted and they have ranked countries for e-government implementation. e-Europe benchmarking [1] methodology essentially is based on online availability and ranking of e-services by the level of sophistication – five-stage maturity model: 1) *Information*: information necessary to start the procedure to obtain the service available on the web. 2) *One way interaction*: downloadable or printable form to start the procedure to obtain the service on the web. 3) *Two-way interaction*: electronic forms to start the procedure to obtain the service on the web. 4) *Transaction*: full electronic case handling of the procedure by the service provider. 5) *Targetisation*:

L.M. Camarinha-Matos et al. (Eds.): PRO-VE 2010, IFIP AICT 336, pp. 443–450, 2010.

proactive, automated service delivery. It was defined an initial set of 20 e-services and the existence and maturity levels of these services in EU member countries were assessed.

One of three main measures of the method of the UN study [2] - the Web Measure Index was based upon another five stage model of sophistication: 1) *Emerging*: a government's online presence is mainly comprised of a web page and/or an official website. 2) *Enhanced*: governments provide more information on public policy and governance. 3) *Interactive*: governments deliver online services such as downloadable forms. 4) *Transactional*: governments begin to transform themselves by introducing two-way interactions between 'citizen and government'. 5) *Connected*: governments transform themselves into a connected entity that responds to the needs of its citizens by developing an integrated back office infrastructure. This is the most sophisticated level of online e-government initiatives.

There were more methods and models presented (e.g. [3], [4], [5] and [6] - these methods are well discussed in [7]; [8]) that measure the sophistication level for e-services: they bear the basic features in common and are based on the stage models of sophistication. The stages in these models are not as distinct from each other as they need to be. The assessments using these methods are not sufficient: borders between stages are unclear and not distinguishable from each other on the criteria given in the model [7]. The new, more precise approaches and measures are needed for such an evaluation.

We suggest to evaluate and to separate e-services from each other in a more detailed way by seeking to identify the main aspects of the e-service characteristics. This paper provides an alternative model for e-service evaluation and presents an approach that could provide more comprehensive assessment for maturity and complexity of e-services and the systems that provide them. It also could fill the gap of the lack of self-evaluation methodology or comparison of e-service maturity, complexity in more detailed aspects for the purposes of the enhancement of e-services.

The presented evaluation model is based on evaluation criteria that are used to assess the sophistication level of e-service. Taking into consideration that the higher sophistication level means the higher maturity of the e-service the higher sophistication level causes the higher service level. Assuming that technology and service levels are intimately interwoven factors the complexity is higher when the service level is higher for the system that provides the e-service. Defining e-services as the result of automation, enhancement and integration of the business processes of the traditional services that are moving towards the e-services *on demand* [8] the higher service level means the more complex system providing the e-service. And contrary – the higher sophistication level means the simpler e-service from the user point of view (at least it should happen if the automation level is high enough). So the evaluation of the e-service maturity means also the evaluation of the system complexity.

2 Constructing Evaluation Criteria

The selection of the criteria was in accordance with the principles: 1) the importance and informativeness of the criteria, 2) the specific technological nature of the elements of e-services, and 3) the possibility to measure these criteria in practice.

For the construction of the evaluation criteria we used different elements of service models that are important for the assessment in our context: the entities of Reference Model (RM) for Service-oriented Architecture [9], the service categorization according the model presented in the paper [7], and the elements of the e-service model [10] that is graphically presented in Fig. 1. We grouped the evaluation criteria in the hierarchical tree that represents a decomposition of attributes of criteria of different levels.

First group of attributes is related with the *visibility* of the e-service [9]. *Visibility* means that service provider and consumer to interact with each other they have to be able to 'see' each other. One of the entities that visibility is based is *awareness*. *Awareness* means that both service provider and the service consumer must have information that would lead them to know of the other's existence. The information about the e-service may be presented as *electronic description* and *policy* including it in a service directory or broadcasting it to all service consumers. There must be sufficient information about the e-service and the method for the consumer to interact with the service in such a manner and form that a potential consumer is aware of existence and capabilities of the e-service. It is also desirable if an *on-line demo* version for the e-service is available where customers could look and test the e-service on their own before they use it. Another entity that *visibility* is based is *reachability* that means that service participants must be able to communicate with each other. If there is no communication between the consumer and provider then the service is not visible to the consumer and he/she cannot use it. As *reachability* means the possibility to communicate there are different options of means for the electronic communication. Most usable is public *internet* but there are more *others communication means* as well.

Second group of attributes is related with the *identification of user* (customer) of the e-service. *Public services* (C1) [7] are limited to services that need no identification of the users (customers) as they are publicly available to all citizens in a continuum of increasing interaction possibilities limited by the absent need for identifying the user (customer) in any degree at all. Services under this category do not involve the secure identification of the user (customer). *Directed (or individualized) services* (C2) are built up from services that need the user to be indirectly identified; it means that identification is carried out in automatic way using non-secured – semi personalized means for identification (e.g. e-mail address). *Restricted services* (C3) are based upon the need for a securely identified user in services that transfer information that is of no interest and that should not be accessible to people other than the user (customer) himself. This category requires secured means for user identification (e.g. eID) and has subcategories accordingly that are related with the option how customer identification is handled:

- *outside information system (IS) initiation* (SC1) means user identification outside the scope of information system: identification is carried out via the traditional signed document manually or in automatic way using electronic means of the third party;
- *inside IS initiation* (SC2) means user identification inside the scope of information system: identification is carried out in automatic way using secured – fully personalized means for identification.

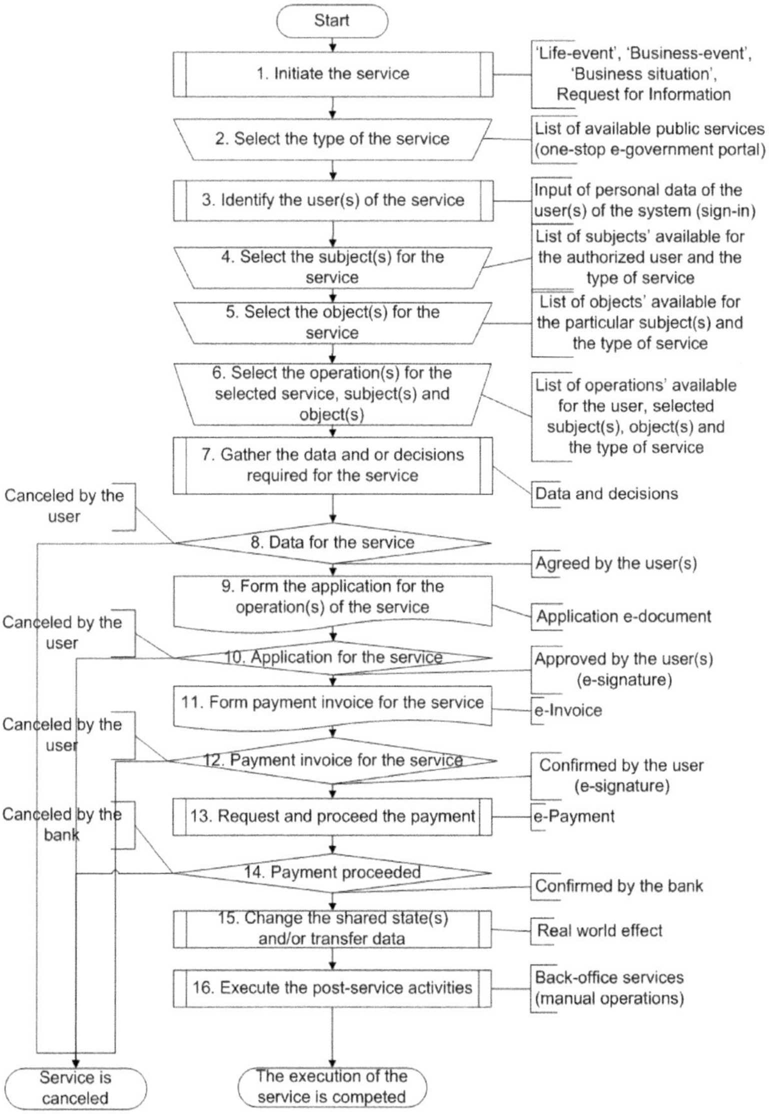

Fig. 1. E-service model [10]

User identification (Fig. 1, 3rd step) [10] starts from authentication activity where the identity of the person accessing services is executed and continues with authorization – the activity that allows the access to the services that are conditioned by the individual's access level and his *role*. The user who will be using the services offered can possess one or a combination of the following roles: *individual* (user as the customer of the service), *agent* or *organizational representative* (user represents the customer).

Third group of attributes is related with the e-service *case handling* that means data collection (all the data that are required for the service should be collected) and decisions to be taken (internal approvals or rejections that are required for the service) (Fig. 1, 7th step) [10]. All the data if they are accessed electronically should be collected in automatic way. Other required data that cannot be accessed electronically or not available in electronic form should be entered *manually*. Next subcategories are related with this group. *Manual case process* (SC3) [7] means that handling and decision will be taken by a handling officer in the agency. Depending on the specific of data and the decision to be made it could be done in several ways: by the customer himself or entered by the agent or the organizational representative of the organization that provide the service or from the external organization according to the contents of the data sources - documents provided by the customer or organization. In all these cases the agent or the organizational representative has to approve electronically the certainty of the entered data that are based on the original documents that were presented or of the decisions that are based on obligations that the agent or the organizational representative possesses.

This subcategory may be characterized by next attributes:

1. The use of an *interactive form* in on-line processing. That means the user (customer) fills an electronic forms interactively.
2. The use of a *non-interactive form*. That means the electronic form can be downloaded, filled with data and uploaded or sent by the user (customer).
3. The *electronic approval* of data. It may be required in this case that data and/or decision must be approved by the user (customer) electronically.

Automated case process (SC4) means that data collection and/or the decisions in certain cases will be conducted in automatic way by programmed rules in an information system and no manual actions are needed for e-service case handling. The possibility of *electronic notification* allows monitor the progress of the e-service process.

Fourth group of attributes is related with the e-service *document handling*. After the data and/or decisions are collected and confirmed an *electronic application* (*service contract*) for the service may to be formed (Fig. 1, 9th step) [10]. It is optional depending on the specific of the service and is formed according to the selections, decisions and data collected. It is an option to use *electronic document* here or to add some *attachments* (e.g. documents, pictures) in electronic form to the application if it is necessary for the e-service. There may be other type of documents required that depend on the specific of the service in electronic or non-electronic form. Any electronic document may be *authenticated* by the user (customer) using electronic signature if it is required and if there are means for this action.

Fifth group of attributes is related with the *payment handling*. Direct payment for the e-service is optional and consists of two types: using *internet banking* or *other electronic payment* methods if such means are available (e.g. Credit/Debit cards).

Sixth group of attributes is an *integration of services* (C4) category that covers integration of government-to-government and other third party services for the e-service. This category has several subcategories.

1. *Joint web production* (SC5) subcategory bridges borders between government agencies and other organizations. In our case it covers common horizontal services such as electronic identification, electronic signature, electronic payment or other electronic services that are provided by other agencies and/or third parties.
2. *Info or decision provision* (SC6) required where an agency can be relying on input information or a decision from another agency or third party organization in order to be able to take a decision in a case relating the specific customer and/or

service. The particular e-services may be controlled by one or several *electronic restrictions* that are originated in other agencies or third parties. There also may be an option for the *electronic approval of the decisions* from other agency or third party organization during the e-service procedure if it is necessary.
3. *Database access* (SC7) subcategory is needed for accessing a database in another agency or third party organization for receiving a piece of information needed for the e-service or decision to be taken in a certain case. There are options when the information is requested from *registers* or *other electronic data sources*.
4. *Transparency* in processes of several independent decisions (SC8) is when certain decisions need to be taken independently by several agencies or departments in order for the case process to be completed.

Seventh group of attributes covers *post-service activities* processes that are *manual* or *not automated* and they are needed for the completion of e-service process. The system may *request* for the human interaction to proceed some activities (e.g. logistics, printing certificates, non-electronic delivering of e-service results). It is optional when the completion of the e-service may be finalized by the automatic forming and *electronic delivery* of the e-service results: *electronic certificates*, *electronic invoices* or *other results* that can be delivered electronically if it is requested by the user (customer).

According to RM [9] the consequence of the *service* is a realization of one or more *real world effects*. These effects may include information returned in response to a request for that information or a change to the *shared state* of defined entities, or some combination of both. *Real world effect* means that the goal of the service consumer can often be expressed as ‘trying to get the service to do something’. Eighth group of criteria covers the *real world effect*: return of the requested *information* and change of *shared state* of the defined entity of the e-service – object or subject.

Table 1. The hierarchical tree of criteria to be used for the e-service evaluation

E-service evaluation criteria	
1- Visibility	Visibility of the e-service
-- Awareness	Information about the e-service
---- e-Description	Electronic description and policy of the e-service
---- On-line demo	Existence of an on-line demo for the e-service
-- Reachability	Means for communication
---- Internet	Public internet
---- Other means	Other communication means
2- E-service user	User of the e-service
-- User identification	Identification of the user of e-service
--- Public services	Need no identification of the user
--- Directed services	Need the user to be identified indirectly
----- Semi personalized	Usability of not secured means for identification
--- Restricted services	Need for a securely identified user
------- Outside IS initiation	Identification of the user outside the scope of IS
------- Inside IS initiation	Identification of the user inside the scope of IS
--------- Fully personalized	Usability of secured means for identification
-- User role	Possible option of user roles for the e-service
--- Individual (customer)	Customer of the e-service
--- Agent	Agent that represents the customer of the e-service
--- Organizational representative	Organization that has obligation for customer e-service

Table 1. (*continued*)

3- Case handling	E-service process handling
---- Manual case processes	Manual input of data and/or decision (human-to-system interaction)
------ Interactive forms	Interactive on-line forms (info and decision)
------ Non-interactive forms	Forms downloaded, filled and uploaded or sent by e-mail (info and decision)
------ e-Approval	Internal approval of data and/or decision electronically
---- Automated case processes	Automatic case handling
---- e-Notification	Notification about the progress of the e-service
4- Document handling	Automatic handling of the document
-- Application	An application for the service (service contract)
---- e-Application	Usability of electronic application
---- Attachments	Electronic documents can be attached
-- Other documents	Other document for the service
---- e-Document	Usability of other electronic document
-- e-Authentication	Electronic authentication of the document
5- E-payment	Electronic payment of service
-- Internet banking	Direct e-Payment through internet banking
-- Other e-Payment method	Direct e-Payment through other means
6- Integration of services	Integration of services and agencies (system-to-system interaction)
---- Joint information services	Joint web production
------ e-Identification	Electronic identification service through third party
------ e-Signature	Electronic signature service through third party
------ e-Payment	Electronic payment service through third party
------ Other e-service	Other electronic service through third party
---- Info or decision	External info or decision provision required
------ e-Restriction	Electronic restriction of e-service
------ e-Approval of decision	External electronic approval of e-service
---- Database access	Database access in information gathering
------ Registers	Electronic data exchange with registers
------ Other electronic data sources	Electronic data exchange with other data sources
---- Transparency	Transparency in processes of several independent decisions
7- Post-service activities	E-service completion activities
-- Manual or not automated processes	Not automated activities
---- e-Request	Request for human interaction (system-to-human interaction)
-- e-Delivery	Electronic delivery of e-service results
---- e-Certificate	Electronic certificate can be formed and downloaded
---- e-Invoice	Electronic invoice can be formed and downloaded
---- Other results e-delivery	Electronic delivery of other results of e-service
8- Real world effect	Consequence of invoking the e-service
---- Information return	Response to the request for that information
---- Change of shared state	A change of shared state of defined entity

3 Conclusions and Future Work

We constructed and presented the list of evaluation criteria for e-service assessment and comparison in this paper. The basis for criteria construction was Reference Model (RM) for Service-oriented Architecture [9], the models presented in the papers [5] and [10]. The evaluation criteria can be used for self-evaluation benchmarking of e-services, in assessment and comparison of different e-services in a country or in different countries, or in assessment and comparison of the same type of e-services in different countries. The e-service assessment as a tool could promote development of the governance of the virtual enterprise - collaborative e-government.

Future works that are planned are focused on the validation of presented criteria in practical testing on real existing e-services and the systems that provide these services.

References

1. Smarter, Faster, Better eGovernment. 8th eGovernment Benchmark Measurement (2009), http://ec.europa.eu/information_society/eeurope/i2010/docs/benchmarking/egov_benchmark_2009.pdf
2. E-Government Survey, United Nations (2008), http://www2.unpan.org/egovkb/global_reports/10report.htm#sa
3. Electronic Service Delivery, including Internet use by Commonwealth Government Agencies, Australian National Auditing Office, Canberra, Australia (1999)
4. The 24/7 Agency: Criteria for 24/7 Agencies in the Networked Public Administration, Statskontoret 2000:41, Sweden (2000)
5. Layne, K., Lee, J.: Developing fully functional E-government: A four stage model. Government Information Quarterly 18, 122–136 (2001)
6. Hiller, J., Belanger, F.: Privacy strategies for electronic government. PricewaterhouseCoopers, Arlington (2001)
7. Persson, A., Goldkuhl, G.: Stage-models for public e-services - investigating conceptual foundations. Accepted to the 2nd Scandinavian Workshop on e-Government, Copenhagen (2005)
8. IBM Business Consulting Services. How e-government are you? e-government in France: State of play and perspectives (2003), http://www-935.ibm.com/services/id/igs/pdf/g510-3552-00-esr-e-government.pdf
9. Reference Model for SOA, Version 1.0, OASIS Standard (2006), http://docs.oasis-open.org/soa-rm/v1.0/soa-rm.pdf
10. Ostasius, E., Petraviciute, Z.: Modeling e-services in public sector – INFORMACIJOS MOKSLAI (to be published in 2010), http://www.leidykla.eu/en/journals/information-sciences/, http://e-stud.vgtu.lt/files/dest/13822/im2010.pdf

Pro-Active Service Entity Framework for a Better Mapping between Business and Software

Tiago Cardoso and Luis M. Camarinha-Matos

Universidade Nova de Lisboa, Faculty of Sciences and Technology,
Campus de Caparica, 2829-516 Monte Caparica, Portugal
{tomfc,cam}@uninova.pt

Abstract. The service concept is widely used in distinct research and application areas. Particularly in Collaborative Networks, Service Orientation represents a main trend in the development of support platforms. Nevertheless, a literature review shows that it does not gather a common understanding, namely from the software and business perspectives. This paper proposes a conceptual framework aiming at contributing to make these two perspectives come closer, through a refinement of the Service concept itself and the usage of Pro-Activeness.

Keywords: Pro-Active Service Entity, Web-Service, Multi-Agent System.

1 Motivation

Service Orientation in Collaborative Networks, as well as the service concept itself, although quite popular nowadays, have not reached a consensus definition particularly when used from two different perspectives – business and software. In fact, although considerable progress has occurred in last decades in SOA, there is a gap between the way a business entity sees the services it is able to provide to customers and the counterpart proposed by the used software, in terms of systems or components created to represent such services and / or automate (part of) their provision. In other words, while the value creation towards customer satisfaction is the focus from a business perspective,, the remote procedure calling and "black box" encapsulation are key points from the software perspective.

The same gap in the notions of service exists in the case of a Virtual Organization Breeding Environment or Professional Virtual Community, from now on referred to as a Collaborative Business Ecosystem (CBE). The way a CBE member sees the services it is willing to provide to the network is distinct from the available software approaches.

This paper proposes a conceptual framework inspired on Web-Services, but adding elements of pro-activeness and social ability. The main objective is to provide a single construct – the Pro-Active Service Entity – that represents the services that a business entity (service provider) can provide and behave in an auto-initiative manner towards finding new Business Opportunities, on one hand, and improving the chances such services have to be selected among competitors, on the other hand.

The intention is to reduce the distance between business and software services, with particular focus on overcoming some limitations of the Web-Service approach. Although other factors also contribute to this distance, they are out of the scope of this

L.M. Camarinha-Matos et al. (Eds.): PRO-VE 2010, IFIP AICT 336, pp. 451–460, 2010.

paper. Some examples may include the management of the resources, other than computational resources, needed for the services - from the business side they are mandatory whilst neglected from the software side.

Web-Service Approach Limitations. Service Oriented Computing provided major improvements in terms of modularity and interoperability for ICT systems, namely in the case of Web-Services. Through the usage of SOAP, WSDL, UDDI and related standards, it became possible to publish Web-Services and register them in catalogues, so that clients can find and call them. Typically, enterprises create Web-Services and register them in catalogues. Then, a client may query the catalogues and retrieve lists with matching instances. Finally, the client chooses a Web-Service from a list and calls it.

In fact, the adoption of Web-Services improved the way Information Systems can be integrated. The main reasons for this improvement are based on the adoption of standards that are (expected to be) independent of the provider's environment or development platform. This fact facilitates the development of value-added services by composition of simpler services provided by different members of the collaborative network. Nevertheless, although this approach is enough in many scenarios, a number of limitations can also be identified:

1. Functional restriction - The concept does not directly cope with other non-functional elements that an entity can provide to a client, like the provision of some business process model or some multimedia content, for example. In other words, a business service may require not only some functionality (software services) but other elements such as intelligent content.
2. Web-Services are "passive" entities - Providers may publish and register them, making their functionality available for clients to discover and call, but these constructs stay still waiting for the clients' initiative. In other words, they don't perform any action in order to attract clients or promote their functionality.
3. Difficult selection process from clients' perspective - if the list provided by a catalogue has a large number of items, a problem arises on how to make a selection.
4. Limitation of the selection process from the providers' perspective – in the same case of large number of matching available Web-Services, the providers face a problem on how to improve the chances that their Web-Services have to be selected.
5. Catalogues may become out-of-date - there are scenarios where Web-Services change their availability frequently. In such scenarios, the information catalogues have may easily become out of date.
6. No aggregation – Web-Services created better conditions for software composition purposes. A workflow definition can support a composition of Web-Services, in order to achieve a higher level goal, or a higher abstraction level functionality, that may itself become a Web-Service, as well. However, having one of these higher level Web-Services composed of several simpler services, each one from a distinct provider, is much more "expensive" than having the same number of services provided by fewer providers. In other words, under similar circumstances it could be desirable to select two services from the same provider, instead of two distinct providers, which could lead to higher costs related to the agreement reaching processes. The aggregation of distinct services from the same provider within a single construct would improve this possibility. Another reason is the reduction of the dilution of responsibilities.

2 Suggested Approach

Main Concepts. The proposed Pro-Active Service Entity Framework is based on a refinement of the service concept, including distinct categories of (technical) services a Collaborative Business Ecosystem (CBE) member can provide. First, the "functional category" of services, similar to Web-Services, corresponds to the cases where CBE members make some procedures available through the network for clients to call. Some examples can be considered, like the launching of a manufacturing process of some products in a given industry, a reservation of a hotel room in the tourism sector, or some order submission for buying a specific book or DVD. Second, the "intelligent content" service category (i-content), corresponding to the cases where a CBE member can provide some information content associated with specific manipulation operations tailored to "present" this content in the desired form, such as, for instance, a business process model or some manufacturing description for the case of a given industry, or some multimedia cultural content on a given city, for the case of the tourism sector. Furthermore, the framework shall be open so that more service categories can be identified.

The main objective of this proposal is the creation of constructs that represent the services a CBE member is able to provide to the network in an auto-initiative / pro-active basis. In the case of functional category, mechanisms like remote function call, input and output parameters, as well as result information are the focus information for representation purposes whilst for the case of intelligent content the focus may be on semantic information about the included content or information about the "presentation" format. The auto-initiative / pro-activeness property can be considered as a brokerage role for the construct, towards better business success for the represented services. Two initial objectives were identified for this representation: 1 - finding new business opportunities where the services may be included as contributing components; 2 – improving the chances the services have to be selected among competitors. Finally, the entire framework assumes the specification of reference ontology for each CBE. This common ontology is a mandatory factor for the interaction between distinct services, namely for service composition purposes.

Let us now introduce the main concepts of the framework:

Definition 1 - **Service**: is a construct materializing the value an entity can provide to a customer, which can be represented by a tuple S=(SR, C, D, RO), where:
- SR – a reference to the actual (technical) service, enabling the functional call or the i-content provision launch;
- C – the category of the service;
- D – the detailed description of the service. Depending on the specific Service and Category, this description may include format or semantic specifications, for the case of an i-content service; or input parameters and results' information, for the case of a functional service.
- RO - the reference ontology.

In order to aggregate distinct services provided by the same CBE member under a single construct the Service Entity concept is defined as follows [1]:

Definition 2 - **Service Entity**: is a construct characterizing a CBE member from the service provision perspective. A tuple SE= (CR, AT, SS), where:

- CR – reference to the CBE member represented by the service entity;
- AT = $\{attr_i \mid i \in N\}$ - the Set of Attributes of the corresponding CBE member;
- SS = $\{s_i \mid i \in N\}$ - the Set of Services the represented CBE member can provide.

A preliminary notion of Service Entity was first introduced by Franco et al. in [3]. Our model extends the original notion in two directions: (i) inclusion of different categories of services, while Franco's definition is limited to the functional services;(ii) inclusion of proactiveness, while Franco's entities are passive. In order to provide the mentioned pro-activeness behavior, the Pro-Active Service Entity concept is introduced. This construct includes the SE corresponding to a CBE member with all the services this construct will represent. Furthermore, the construct includes a set of base functions used for representation purposes. In order to materialize such representation, the Behavior Specification concept is introduced, specifying the behavioral characteristics, namely what exactly it should do. The two concepts are defined as follows:

Definition 3 - **Behavior Specification**: is a functional configuration of a flow of actions. A tuple BS = (D, PREC, POSC, TM, BWS), where:
- D - a description including the aim of the BS;
- PREC –Pre-Conditions - verified before the behavior is triggered;
- POSC - Pos-Conditions - verified to assess the behavior success;
- TM - Triggering Mechanism - timings, frequency and data-flow conditions specifying the execution launch;
- BWS - Behavior Workflow Specification – specification of the base functions that are used within the behavior, their input parameters and their execution flow graph.

Definition 4 - **Pro-Active Service Entity**: is a construct representing a CBE member focusing on the promotion of its service. A tuple PSE = (SE, AT, BS), where:

- SE – Reference to the represented and promoted Service Entity,
- AT = $\{at_i \mid i \in N\}$ - a set of the "base functions" aiming representation purposes that can be performed by the PSE in the defined behaviors.
- BS = $\{bs_i \mid i \in N\}$ - a set of Behavior Specifications - that identify the triggering mechanisms, the timings, the frequency and the workflow of each behavior.

Finally, within a CBE the concept of Pro-Active Service Park is introduced as a virtual market place where the PSEs register themselves and Clients or Brokers post their needs, the Business Opportunities (BOs). This concept, aligned with the Service Park concept defined in [2], is a space that brings together all the PSEs to a pre-configured place fostering faster consortium establishment, whenever a new need / BO is specified and the collaboration between distinct CBE members is needed to fulfill it. This component also includes performance measurement and certification mechanisms, introducing the notion of conspicuity for the registered PSEs.

Definition 5 – **Pro-Active Service Park** – is an architecture implementation of a CN members' market-like infrastructure. A tuple PSE-Park = (PS, BO, PM, CR, BF), where:

- PS = {pse_i | i ∈ N} - set of registered PSEs;
- BO = {bo_i | i ∈ N} - set of specified needs / BOs;
- PM = {$pm_{i,j}$ |(∀ $pm_{i,j}$ ∃ pse_i ∈ PS ∧ ∃ bo_j ∈ BO} - set of Performance Measurement Information for each PSE used in every BO (historic data).
- CR = {cse_i | (∀ cse_i ∃ pse_i ∈ PS)} - set with certification information on PSEs.
- BF = {f_1, f_2, f_3, f_4} - 4 built-in functionality, where:

f_1 (PSE Registration) - enabling distinct PSEs to register themselves;
f_2 (BO Posting) - enabling brokers to post their needs - the Business Opportunities;
f_3 (Performance Measurement) - providing PSE performance measurement mechanisms, as well as enabling brokers to grade their performance, in order to increase the information on every registered PSE. As a result, more accurate data becomes available to support future CBE members' service selection process.
f_4 (Certification) - based on PM info, a PSE-Park can certify some PSE's quality on request, introducing the notion of conspicuity associated with a PSE.

Fig. 1 represents the relationships between the 5 concepts in a UML diagram:

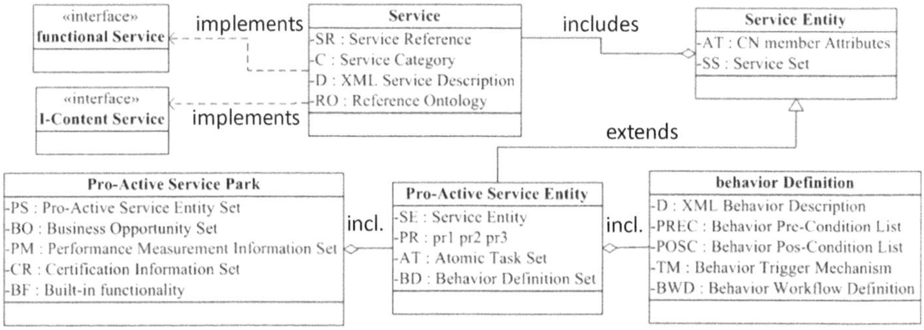

Fig. 1. Relationships among PSE Framework concepts

Inspiring Contributions. The proposed Pro-Active Service Entity is inspired by three main contributing research areas: Web-Services, Multi-Agent Systems and Blackboard Systems. Fig. 2 shows the main contributions that each one gave to the framework.

The Web-Services, as the main inspiration area, have evolved through three main phases that can be identified by the keywords: Publish, Register / Find and Compose. Publish, when the concept was presented and used by any entity wanting to publish some procedure towards reaching potential worldwide clients. As time shown, the access to these worldwide potential clients could not become effective, since they were not notified and could not find the published services. At that time, UDDI and WSDL were proposed and Services could register themselves in catalogues, in order to be found. Eventually, the creation of Value-Added-Services, made through composition of other Web-Services was the advent of the third generation, resorting to mechanisms like Workflow and technologies like BPEL4WS. Other initiatives like OSGi provided the technological support for dynamic composition [7, 9]. The Web-Service Eventing introduced a protocol that allows Web-Services to subscribe to or accept subscriptions for event notification messages [8]. Finally, the notion of Service Entities [3] introduced the aggregation of distinct Web-Services. In fact, the Web-Services area is an inspiring baseline because it aims at providing a standard interoperability mechanism; being platform independent, and thus can wrap services from a CBE member.

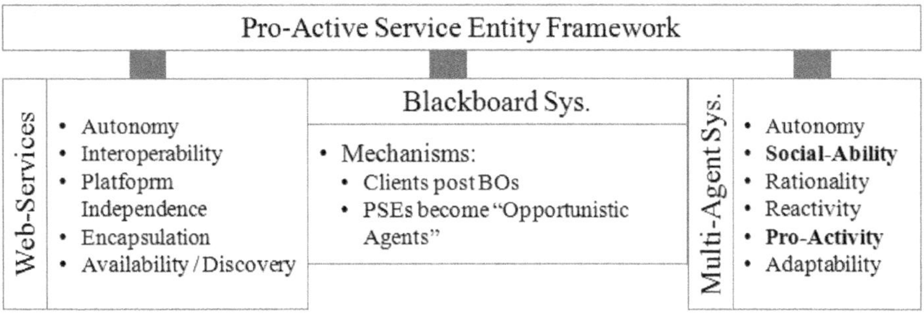

Fig. 2. Inspiring Contributions

The Multi-Agent Systems (MAS) area "represents a promising approach to both model and implement the complex supporting infrastructures required for virtual enterprises and related emerging organizations" [5]. This approach has four important characteristics, as identified by Wooldridge [6]: autonomy, reactivity, social-ability and pro-activeness. First, agents can operate without a direct human intervention. Second, agents perceive the environment surrounding them and can react to it. Third, they can interact with peers / other agents, towards common goals. Fourth, agents do not simply respond to their environment "triggers" but they can take the action initiative, towards the goal they pursue. These MAS characteristics are base inspiring characteristics for the PSE concept, namely the pro-activeness that is used for the PSE to look for new Business Opportunities in an auto-initiative basis.

Finally, the bidding mechanisms introduced in the Blackboard Systems inspired the proposals a PSE makes when bidding for a given BO.

3 Logical Architecture

Multi-level Modelling Approach. The implementation of the Pro-Active Service Entity Framework leads to three abstraction layers, as represented in Fig. 3. At the lower layer - the Actors Space, there are the CBE members - Free-Lancers, Enterprises, or other Organizations. At the middle layer - the Service Space, there are the Pro-Active Service Entities, representing the Services CBE members can provide. Finally, at the top, there are the Integrated Services indirectly corresponding to consortia created as a response to Business Opportunities. This multi-layered modeling approach has some advantages: 1) Services - instead of modeling only functional Services a CBE member is able to provide, other categories of components can also be considered, as for example some welding process documentation; 2) Aggregation - distinct Services from a CBE member are modeled within a single construct - this can be useful in a composition process, in order to decrease consortia dimension, based on the inclusion of partners that can provide more than one needed Service; 3) Pro-Activeness – PSEs may find interesting BOs, prepare bids and submit them in an auto-initiative basis.

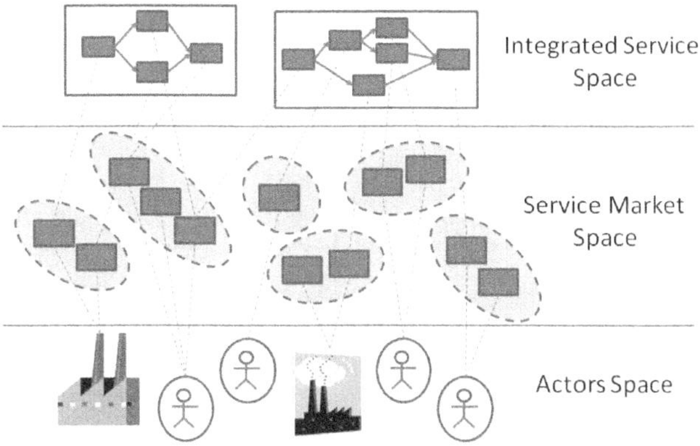

Fig. 3. Three Abstraction Levels / Layers

Actors, Roles and Mechanisms. The design and development of the ICT system framework needed to support the defined concepts requires the identification of the Actors, their main Roles, and needed Mechanisms. Five actors were identified:

- CBE members - the providers of the services,
- Clients - making high-level specifications of the needs / BOs,
- Brokers - responsible to prepare proposals for clients' needs and to select the Services that best fit these needs,
- Pro-Active Service Park Administrator, and
- Pro-Active Service Entity - although not a human actor, PSEs are considered like actors, given their pro-activeness.

The identified roles and the corresponding mechanisms are:

- PSE-Park Administration - providing Monitoring tasks and Managing Performance Information,
- Performance Measurement - providing the needed mechanisms to assess the performance of Services, consortia, as well as client's satisfaction,
- Accounting - providing the payment mechanisms corresponding to the single and consortium Services' provision,
- Contract Management - providing the legal consortium contractual support,
- Service Integration - providing the Service composition mechanisms,
- Workflow Engine - providing the Service execution mechanisms,
- Assistants to both CBE members, Clients and Brokers,
- SE Representation – the PSE role. Mechanisms: PSE-Park registration, blackboard check and service match, and bids management.

4 Service Composition Process

The framework usage process is divided into 5 temporal phases, as illustrated in Fig. 4.

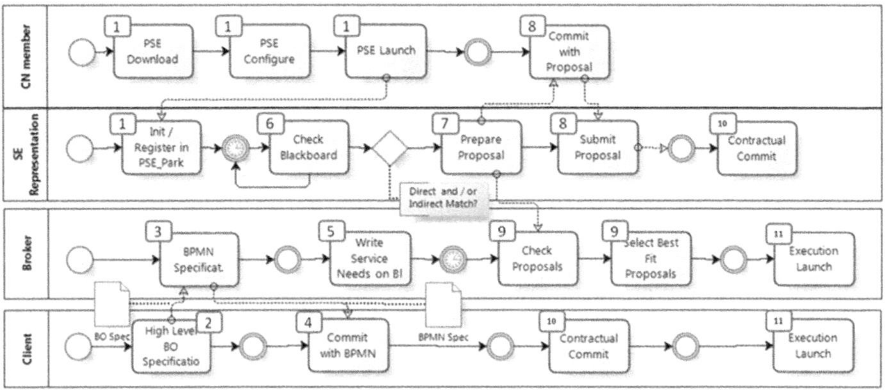

Fig. 4. Framework usage phases

I - Configuration Phase

1. **PSE Configuration** - first a CBE member downloads a PSE template and configures it. This includes setting up the Services to be represented by such PSE and the fulfillment of information concerning the provider – the CBE member. Afterwards, the PSE has to be launched so it registers itself in a pre-defined PSE-Park associated to the CBE. After this step, the PSE starts looking for Business Opportunities.

II - Business Opportunity Specification Phase

2. **Client Needs Specification** - Through the Client Assistant, a high level specification of needs can be made starting a new Business Opportunity.
3. **Broker details Business Needs** - Based on the high level Business Opportunity specified by the client, the Broker creates a Business Process Model (BPM), through the Service Integrator Module, detailing required Services to accomplish the specified needs. The BPM does not have to be complete, but the Core Services have to be defined in order for that BPM to be able to start an execution.
4. **Client BPM Commit** - When the BPM specification is ready (not necessarily complete), the Client is requested to commit with that BPM.
5. **Broker writes needs on Blackboard** - After the Client Commits with the BPM, the Broker posts the specific Service needs in the Blackboard of the PSE-Park.

III - PSE Proposals Phase

6. **PSE check for Business Need** - The PSE looks for Business Opportunities on the PSE-Park's Blackboard towards two possibilities of matching:

a. **Direct** - a Business Need matches exactly one of the Services the PSE represents;

b. **Indirect** – following the notion that the needs for a service A may represent a need of some other Service B, the Base Ontology has a service association registration that is used to check if any of the represented Services indirectly matches the specified needs. In other words, if the clients that request service A usually need also the provision of Service B, the PSE may propose the provision of B, in an auto-initiative basis, whenever a need for A is specified (a kind of recommendation engine)..

7. **PSE prepares Proposal** - both in the direct and indirect cases.
8. **Provider Commits to the Proposal** - PSEs can be configured to send the proposals automatically or ask for the provider to complete / review it before submission.

IV - Service Selection / Negotiation Phase

9. **Broker checks Proposals** –the Broker checks the received proposals and selects the ones that best fit the needs or goes through a negotiation process with some.
10. **Contractual Commitment** - Both the Client and the Providers have to commit with each other through a contract generated for that purpose.

V - Execution Phase

11. **BPM Launch** - After the BPM has all the providers selected, at least for the Core Services, it is possible to launch it. This trigger is made by the Client, in the first place and the Broker, in a second place. After that, the Workflow Engine is responsible for asking the provision of each Service at the right time.

* **Edition at Runtime** - at anytime during the execution phase, the Broker can complete or change the BPM, rolling back:

- to phase II - when the BPM did not get complete before starting execution. In this case, the Broker has to complete it, and eventually, change some Services;
- to phase III / IV - when some providers haven't been selected yet or there is some ongoing negotiation process.

5 Implementation Approach, Conclusions and Future Work

Three possible approaches were identified for the implementation of the proof of concept prototype, based on the main contributing research areas:

1. Develop the whole system from scratch, including all the multi-threaded mechanisms in order to create independent and autonomous PSEs, as well as all the message exchange mechanisms;
2. Build the framework on top of an existing MAS middleware solution;
3. Build the framework on top of an existing Web-Services middleware solution.

The selection made was on the integration between option 2 and 3, through the usage of the Web-Service Integration Gateway (WSIG), defined by FIPA, because it is a user-friendly bridge already existing between the two worlds – MAS and SOA. This gateway is thus extended in order to cope with the defined conceptual framework.

The specific platform on which the prototype system is developed is JADE, which was chosen because it is supported by an active research community, it offers an easy development approach, and three of its specific design choices make a good match with the Pro-Active Service Entity Framework concepts [4]: 1) an agent is autonomous and pro-active; 2) agents are loosely coupled, meaning that the communication is asynchronous and no strict temporal dependency exists between message senders and receivers; 3) the system is peer-to-peer, meaning that each agent is uniquely identified by the AgentIdentifier, as defined by FIPA. The ongoing development is providing the proof of the defined concepts through a Web-based prototype infrastructure built on top of the JADE platform. In terms of practical validation, the proposed framework is being applied to a collaborative network (PVC like) of senior professionals that want to remain professional active after retirement.

The proposed Pro-Active Service Entity Framework targets a contribution to the reduction of the distance between the perspectives of business and the software counterparts, in terms of the systems that represent the Services CBE members can provide. The driving forces for the creation of the framework were the enumerated limitations of web-services, namely their "passive" approach and the isolation of distinct Web-Services from the same provider. With the PSE concept, the services a CBE member can provide have a single "ambassador" construct, pursuing business objectives for them, instead of waiting for a client initiative.

Another tacit improvement introduced is that the proposals a broker receive have the guarantee to be up to date, whilst the lists gathered from service catalogues may be outdated. On the other hand, the restriction of the application of the framework to a group of CBE members, within a Pro-Active Service Park is not a limitation as long as we are in a CBE context, and thus the needed baseline for the adoption of a compatible software approach and adoption of a common ontology.

As near future work, the legal / contractual perspectives, the recommendation engine, and the accounting mechanisms need further developments in order to support "on the fly" contractual arrangements, needed for some specific scenarios. The creation of a library of most commonly used Pro-Active Service Entity templates is also an objective for the near future.

Acknowledgements. This work was supported in part by the Portuguese Foundation for Science and Technology (FCT) (CTS multiannual funding) through the PIDDAC Program funds.

References

1. Cardoso, T., Camarinha-Matos, L.: Pro-Active Asset Entities in Collaborative Networks. In: Camarinha-Matos, L., Pereira, P., Ribeiro, L. (eds.) Emerging Trends in Technological Innovation (2010)
2. Petrie, C., Bussler, C.: The Myth of Open Web Services - The Rise of the Service Parks. In: Petrie, C. (ed.) IEEE Internet Computing (2008)
3. Franco, R.D., Bas, Á.O., Esteban, F.L.: Modelling extended manufacturing processes with service oriented entities. Service Business 3, 31–50 (2008)
4. Bellifemine, F., Giovanni, C., Greenwood, D.: Developing Multi-Agent Systems with JADE, ch. 3. John Wikey & Sons, Lda (2007)
5. Camarinha-Matos, L.: Multi-Agent Systems in Virtual enterprises. In: Internat. Conf. on AI, Simul. and Plan. in High Autonomy Syst. (AIS 2002), pp. 27–36. AIS Publications (2002)
6. Wooldridge, M.: Agent-based computing. Interoperable Communications Network (1998)
7. OSGi Service Platform Release 4 Version 4.2 Core Specification, http://www.osgi.org
8. Web Services Eventing (WS-Eventing), W3C Member Submission March 15 (2006)
9. Jammes, F., Smit, H.: Service Oriented Paradigms in Industrial Automation. In: Internat. Multi-Conference Parallel and Distributed Computing and Networks (2005)

Engineering of Service Oriented Collaborative Network

Nesrine Elhabib, Xavier Boucher, and Sophie Peillon

Ecole des Mines de Saint Etienne
158 cours fauriel, centre G2I
42023 Saint Etienne, France
{elhabib,boucher,peillon}@emse.fr

Abstract. This paper presents an engineering approach of product/service oriented value creation chains. When configuring product/service productive networks, a high variability in alternative scenarios have to be considered due to flexibility levers introduced by the service oriented approach. To cope with the difficulty of scenario selection a 2 stages engineering approach is proposed. The first stage is developed in this paper, aiming at a general analysis of alternative scenarios: a network model and an evaluation system for scenario comparison are explained and discussed.

Keywords: Service oriented enterprise, Collaborative networks analysis, Collaboration scenario, Engineering methodology.

1 Introduction

In the paradigm of service-oriented enterprises, the dynamic configuration of value-creation chains is addressed by a networking approach of Business Service (BS) supplied by several companies acting as service providers. In relation with the functional-economy model [1], we will consider that these value creation chains deliver integrated product-service systems (PSS) which mix tangible products with intangible services [2]. New enterprise engineering models are required to support the configuration of such a service-oriented network. Notably, the objective is to fully integrate the concept of service at the business level, and cope with the new degree of agility induced by the service approach [6]. This paper addresses this issue.

Several authors have already contributed to the engineering of service-oriented value-creation chains. Nicola Morelli [3] suggests an engineering method based on 3 levels: (1) mapping of the actors involved and of their interactions; (2) analysis of the logical and physical connections between the different stages and components of the system; (3) analysis of possible scenarios and uses. The main contribution of this work lies in showing how the components of the organizational system influence the PSS delivered. Tomohiko Sakao et al. [4] put forward a new "service-engineering" method, which takes into account the customer satisfaction and aims at designing sustainable product-services. The authors introduce the concept of receiver state parameters RSPs used to support the design of the PSS model, with their computer application (« Service Explorer »). Nevertheless, they have not really address the design of the productive system which provides the PSS.

L.M. Camarinha-Matos et al. (Eds.): PRO-VE 2010, IFIP AICT 336, pp. 461–468, 2010.

The engineering of PSS value-creation chains should contain a comparative analysis of alternative PSS delivery scenarios. Several papers discuss indicators systems in this perspective. Jian-Hia Yang [5] proposes an approach based on balanced scorecard adapted to PSS delivery. While, Zeng Sen and al. [6] suggest an assessment methodology with several steps including simulation and optimization mechanisms. However, these papers are in line with a detailed engineering approach, and thus require very accurate data to correctly evaluate scenarios. More general works suggest an overall evaluation, such as MacDonald [7] who tries to assess the "value-in-use" of the product-service, or Omann [8] who assesses the sustainability of a PSS. But this kind of assessment only focuses on PSS supplied, without any real evaluation of the organizational delivery system.

Our paper presents an engineering method to construct Business Service Networks which meet specific customer needs. A conceptual framework is provided for this approach, and briefly illustrated by an "academic" case study. In section 2 an overview of the engineering method is given. Then, a structural model of service-oriented enterprise networks is specified. In section 4, an indicator system is discussed allowing the assessment of alternative organizational scenarios. Finally, the positioning of the approach and concluding remarks are provided.

2 Overview of the Approach

2.1 An Engineering Method Based on Two Models

The first objective of our approach is to manage, directly at the business level, the interoperability among the partners of the value creation chain. Consequently, the concept of "Business Service" is central to the method. The combination of BS generates a high number of alternative scenarios, induced by demand variability (e.g. distinct service level) or by solution flexibility (e.g. alternative providers). This engineering approach can provide a decision support to analyze and select suitable configurations (i.e. scenarios) of the PSS delivery system.

Another objective of our approach is to integrate the requirements of the "Functional Economy" Business Model [1]. This concept has been developed in economic sciences as a model of value creation for PSS, which integrates sustainable development objectives. Thus, as a base-hypothesis, we introduce sustainable development decision criteria into the engineering approach for the productive system. The system of indicators will be explained more deeply in section 4.

Our network engineering approach proposed hereafter is composed of two principal stages: both a structural and dynamic analysis, each of which requires a distinct model to further develop decision aids.

- The structural or static analysis of the network: defines a structural mapping of the organizational network, corresponding to a scenario of customer needs satisfaction. Several alternative solutions and their corresponding networks are possible, and the model compares the different networks, through a strategic analysis of organizational configurations, corresponding to a step of general design of the network.

- The dynamic composition for Business Service (BS) is based on the modeling and analysis of BS interconnectivity, flows exchanges and a temporal chain of events. This dynamic model can analyze the dynamic performances of the service delivery processes, taking into account working parameters, constraints and uncertainty along the PSS life-cycle. This model requires much more accurate information on the BS Network at the design stage.

Next, the structural model of the productive network will be presented.

2.2 Case Study

The service-oriented approach can manage and compare various organizational scenarios induced by the high uncertainty on the client behavior but also due to the flexibility of networks according to the principles of Business Services composition. To illustrate this notion of scenario we consider an example of a vehicle repair service (with a single damaged part). We deal with three typical scenarios, with different service levels and customer participation:

- *Scenario 1*: the damaged part is completely replaced by an identical piece by the garage. This scenario includes the purchase of a substitute part and the disposal of damaged part. The customer can borrow a vehicle until the repair is effectuated.
- *Scenario 2*: the damaged piece is repaired by the garage. Again, the customer can borrow a vehicle for the duration.
- *Scenario 3*: garage facilities are provided to customers, where they will repair their vehicle. Replacement parts can be bought and diverse tools rented.

These 3 generic scenarios can lead to many 'sub-scenarios', related to various business services offerings. The structural and static analysis model and dynamic composition of SM are intended to provide decision support for analyzing and selecting scenarios.

3 Static and Structural Model to Analyze Productive Network Scenarios

The static and structural analysis (1st step of the engineering approach) provides a comparative assessment of different scenarios, as part of a general design phase. A structural model of the network (Figure 1 and Annex) is proposed, to organize all relevant information for the subsequent assessment procedure (developed in 4). Each scenario corresponds to a network of organizations of business services (BS). Each BS encapsulates business activities and competencies. This model (Figure 1) is based on 3 key principles:

1. Organizational entities of the production system. To meet the needs of structural analysis, the network is represented by 3 organizational entities: a "Business services", "Interface" between BS, and «Infrastructure components". In a service approach, Infrastructure acts supports production processes performed by business services.

2. Considering the life cycle. Consistent with the service approach, we position the organizational entities within the life cycle of a PSS. Business services of each scenario are distributed throughout the full life cycle. Each scenario can be differentiated by covering more or less stages of the life cycle.

3. Three distinct functional layers. In reference to the separation of Back and Front Office plus Infrastructure, we consider a production oriented service system consisting of these 3 distinct functional layers [9], [10] that mobilize different competencies: a "User management" function for managing customer relationships through a "service agreement" process, a "PSS providing" function that includes the production process of PSS and the "Infrastructure" function which supports to the other functions.

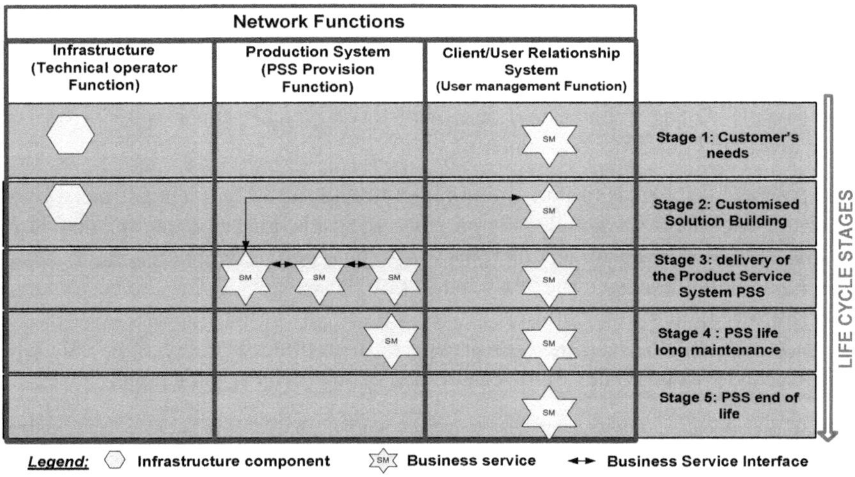

Fig. 1. Static and structural Model of the productive network

This structural model is associated with a logic process diagram providing a general description of the PSS production steps. The diagram consists of a series of activities or sub processes. The main process that ensures the expected PSS delivery can be associated to secondary processes indirectly involved (e.g., substitution part manufacturing in scenario 1 of the example) which contribute to the adaptability to the different levels of service required. The application of the model to this case study is presented in the annex.

4 Comparative Analysis of the SPOS

4.1 Definitions Points of Views for Assessment as Well as Generic Indicators

To specify the evaluation system, we start by translating the evaluation objectives into various assessment viewpoints, represented by the 3 axes in Figure X. The definition of these perspectives follows 3 principles:

- Necessity to take into account the different aspects of sustainable development: economic, societal and environmental assessments.

- Represent the actors' intentions. In our context, there are two main stakeholders are involved in service delivery: the productive network and the customer. Moreover, since our approach lies in the deployment of sustainable development, we propose to consider a third actor the "Territorial actor"[1].

- Opportunities and risks are evaluated at a rather strategic level of engineering of the production system via standard methods of strategic analysis as the SWOT method.

These principles generate 3 evaluation axis (axes "Sustainable development", "intentionality", "strategic factor") defining the generic evaluation structure of Figure 2.

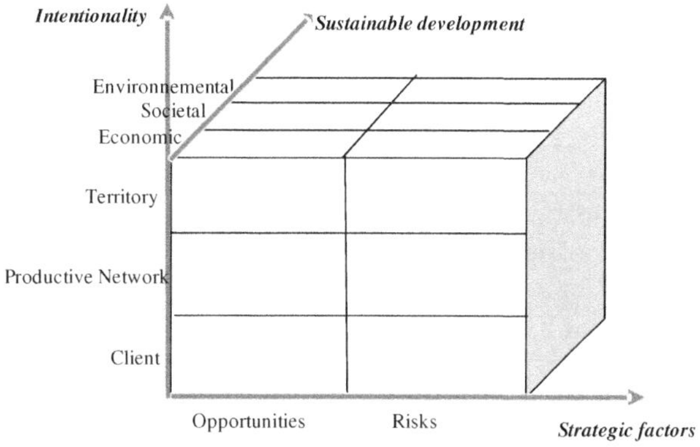

Fig. 2. Generic Evaluation Structure

This evaluation framework is very broad, and according to the specific case considered, all views are not systematically necessary. This framework is therefore a generic grid that guides the construction of indicators but should be adapted to any specific network considered. During this transition from the generic to the particular, we systematically maintain all facets of "Intentionality" and "Strategic factors" axes. However, the 3 facets of the axes "Sustainable Development" are not necessarily represented, as illustrated below for the case study presented in Section 3.

The analysis of the case study, only define 6 generic indicators specified in Table1:

- For the case study, the environmental dimension for the "Territorial" actor is illustrated by "Territorial risks" assessment. Given the strategic level of the analysis, environmental impact is only assessed at the level of the territory, and not analyzed more in detail for the other stakeholders. However, the application of the evaluation factor analysis specified in 4.2 will identify detailed risk factors contributing to the overall "Territorial risks".

- The societal dimension is represented through the points of the client standpoint (with the indicators "Potential of value creation" and "Risk of inadapted answer") and of the territorial actor (Indicator "Potential of territorial value creation"). In this case, there is a convergence of the societal and economic evaluations: the 2 indicators of

[1] The 'territory 'represents the territorial environment of the service oriented enterprise network, including economic, socio-human and ecological dimensions.

value creation simultaneously evaluate a societal preoccupation and an economic dimension. There is little need to separate the 2 evaluations in this example.

Since this evaluation a aforementioned is situated at a strategic analysis level. The economic dimension is formalised by value creation indicators, and not by cost-oriented evaluation. In fact, a cost evaluation would require a more detailed analysis of the productive processes which will be developed in the 2nd step of the engineering approach (dynamic evaluation).

Table 1. Generic indicators for the case study

	« Territorial» Actor	Actor « network »	Actor « client »
Opportunities	Territorial value creation	Value creation for the network	Value creation for the client
Risks	Territorial risks	Organisational risks for the network	Risks of inadapted answer

After having defined the dimensions and generic indicators of the evaluation systems, a qualitative analysis of evaluation factors is developed in the following section.

4.2 Qualitative Analysis of Evaluation Factors

This analysis will detail and formalise the generic indicators. 3 key concepts are used to build the qualitative description of the evaluation factors (fig. 3):

- *Aggregated indicators*: represent the risks and opportunities for the 3 actors of the intentionality axis. 2 aggregated indicator levels are distinguished: the *generic indicators* identified in table 1 are evaluated by aggregation of more *contextualized indicators* depending on each case study.
- *Explicative factors* represent all the pertinent factors to be considered for the evaluation of aggregated indicators. This factors can be linked one with another by a qualitative link of "influence relationship". They can be associated to qualitative or quantitative metrics.
- *Performance drivers*: they represent the concrete levers of the service-oriented enterprise network which have an influence on the explicative factors and, consequently, on the aggregated indicators. In this approach, the drivers are the structural components (Business services, BS Interfaces, Infrastructure components) of the 3 organisational levels of the service oriented network.

Based on these key concepts, the qualitative analysis can build qualitative diagrams of influence relationships among performance drivers, explicative factors and aggregated indicators. These influence diagrams are necessary to cope with the complexity of performance factors considered, before further formalising a quantitative metric. For the vehicle repair case study, the 6 indicators of table 1 have to be analysed. Figure 3 shows an example with the generic indicator "Territorial value creation".

Figure 3 demonstrates that the generic indicator is first devided into 3 contextualized indicators which formalized the vision of the territorial actor : « Employment development », « Development of territorial competences », « Development of territorial attractivity ». The contextualized indicators are further elaborated by a network of explicative factors, linked to drivers constituted by the structural components of the enterprise network. These structural components are described in the model of section 3. For each scenario, the characteristics of the Business Services, BS interfaces and infrastructure components will have an impact of the explicative factors, making possible a comparative analysis of the scenarios.

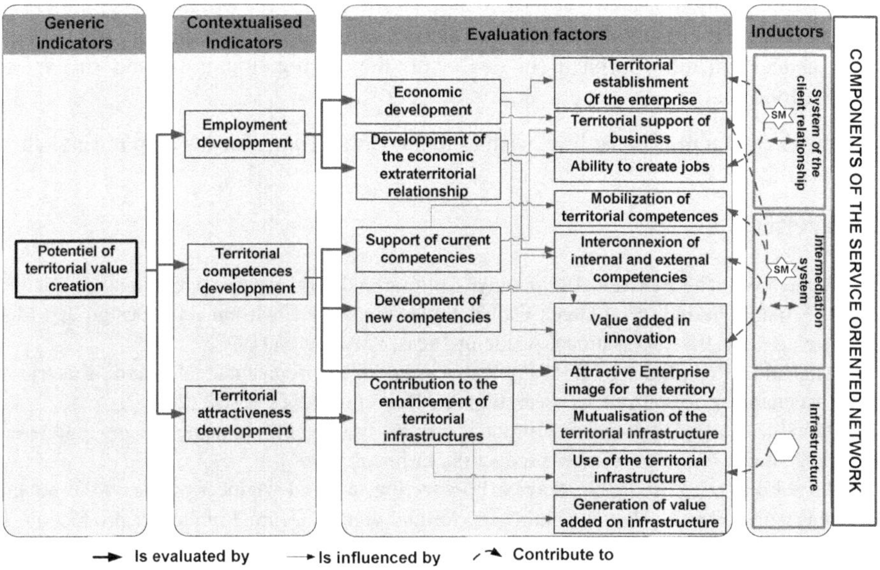

Fig. 3. Example of qualitative diagram of evaluation factors

5 Positioning of This Approach and Conclusion

Among the existing work we have targeted three specific approaches to the modeling of service-oriented production systems. Y. Shimomura [11] proposes a study of service-oriented manufacturing process based on state variables to represent the user. Nicolas Maussang [12] presented a PSS design method where models of service delivery scenarios are integrated within the design processes and tools. Third, Balin [13] has suggested a process-oriented simulation method for optimizing the quality of service-oriented production systems. Although complementary and using different formalisms (state agent models, design methodology, production system simulation), it should be noted that all these articles focus on the sequence of dynamic activities necessary to deliver services, in order to evaluate the quality of service. The approach developed here is complementary as we do not represent the dynamic process, but we only seek to represent the organizational structure of the service-oriented production systems: the distribution of actors and services across all layers and the functional interactions among these actors. Thus, in this first stage of general design of the production system, we aim to assess the relative contribution of alternative solutions to the organizational value creation expected by the client. This is an assessment of the quality of the structure organizational set up and not directly on the quality of service received.

Our next step will consist in building the quantitative metrics for comparative evaluation of scenarios. To answer the need of structural and static analysis of the networks, the optimisation or dynamic simulation methods generally used to evaluate service oriented systems (e.g [6], [12], [13]) are not relevant. For this static evaluation, we are going to use two complementary formalisms: the Fuzzy sub-set theory (to take in charge the coupling among qualitative and quantitative factors) and a multi-criteria decision aid approach (to deal with the aggregation issue and the actor's points of view).

Acknowledgement. The authors wish to thank Chris Yukna for his help in English.

References

1. Stahel, W.: The Functional Economy: Cultural and Organizational Change. In: Richard, D.J. (ed.) The Industrial Green Game: Implications for Environmental Design and Management, pp. 91–100. National Academy Press, Washington (1997)
2. Michelini, R.C., Razzoli, R.P.: Product-service for environmental safeguard: a metrics to sustainability. Resources, Conservation and Recycling 42(1), 83–98 (2004)
3. Morelli, N.: Developping new product service system (PSS): methodologies and operational tools. Journal of cleaner production, Denmark (2006)
4. Tomohiko, S., Yoshiki, S.: Service Engineering: a novel engineering discipline for producers to increase value combining service and product. Journal of cleaner production, Japan (2006)
5. Yang, J.-H.: A balanced performance measurement scorecard approach for product service system. In: International Conference on Business Intelligence and Financial Engineering, China (2009)
6. Zeng, S., et al.: Service-oriented Business Process Modeling and Performance Evaluation based on AHP and Simulation. In: IEEE International Conference on e-Business Engineering (2007)
7. MacDonald, E.K., Martinez, V., Wilson, H.: Towards the Assessment of the Value-in-Use of Product-Service Systems: a Review. In: Performance Management Association Conference, New Zealand (2009)
8. Omann, I.: A Multicriteria tool for Evaluating the Impacts of Product Service Systems on Sustainable Development: An application in Austrian companies. Sustainable Europe Research Institute, SERI Working Papers, n°5 (2007)
9. Tannery, F.: Internal report of the regional project SPOS. ENSMSE, France (October 2009)
10. Zarifian, P., Gadrey, J.: l'émergence d'un modèle de service: enjeux et réalités (2002)
11. Shimomura, Y., et al.: Service engineering-Methods and Tools for Effective PSS Development. In: Introduction to Product/Service-system Design. Springer, Heidelberg (2009)
12. Maussang, N.: Méthodologie de conception pour les systèmes produits-services, Institut polytechnique de Grenoble (2008)
13. Balin, S.: Amélioration de processus de production de services par la simulation, Université Paris Dauphine (2007)

Towards a Reference Architecture for a Collaborative Intelligent Transport System Infrastructure

A. Luis Osório[1,2], Hamideh Afsarmanesh[2], and Luis M. Camarinha-Matos[3]

[1] Instituto Superior de Engenharia de Lisboa (ISEL), Portugal
aosorio@deetc.isel.pt
[2] University of Amsterdam (UvA), Netherlands
h.afsarmanesh@uva.nl
[3] Faculdade de Ciências e Tecnologia, Universidade Nova de Lisboa, Portugal
cam@uninova.pt

Abstract. The intelligent transport systems, which aim at providing smarter transport infrastructures and sustainable mobility, are deeply grounded on the Information and Communication Technologies. Current trends in the development of integrated complex systems, such as integrated road/highway concessions management, require new strategies to match business processes to the underlying technology. New road management policies, supported on new user-payer models, and increasing concerns about traffic safety, establish requirements for a new family of emergent business services. Offering the driver the possibility to extend current tolling business service contracts to make possible the access to public transport systems, parking areas, subscription to innovative insurance service, etc., all covered by a single contract, is a promising strategy to promote sustainable and safe mobility. Nevertheless, this new wave of emergent business services requires high interoperability among a diversity of (heterogeneous) technology systems considering both vehicle and road infrastructures. This paper discusses an approach to the required ICT-based intelligent infrastructure based on a collaborative network of stakeholders as contributors to the business service offering.

Keywords: Intelligent Transport Systems; Reference Architecture; Service Oriented Architectures; Collaborative Networks.

1 Introduction

The intelligent transport systems (ITS) area has its origins in the need to introduce advanced ICT support to the transport infrastructures, empowering sustainable transport policies. A first reference in this area was the formation of a group in the USA in mid 1990s, involving public transportation authorities, universities, and representatives from the private sector to propose a strategy for what was first as named Intelligent Vehicle Highway Systems (IVHS) and later as Intelligent Transportation Systems [1]. Similar dynamics were simultaneously happening in Europe and in Japan. In Europe, the programme Prometheus, established in 1986, aimed to contribute to the reduction of road accidents and to improve traffic efficiency by adopting new information and

L.M. Camarinha-Matos et al. (Eds.): PRO-VE 2010, IFIP AICT 336, pp. 469–477, 2010.

communication technologies [2]. In Japan a research committee RACS (Road/ Automobile Communication System) was established in 1984, followed by a three years project (1986-1989) to develop vehicle/ground digital communication. In 1987 a new project, the AMTICS (Advanced Mobile Traffic Information and Communication System) [3] was initiated. These initial synergies between transport experts and the information and communication technologies have been evolving leading to a multidisciplinary collaboration. The ITS community used to involve mainly the participation of civil engineers as experts on the processes managed in this application domain. The progressive introduction of new technologies based on electronics, communication or information management, and computing in transportation scenarios, raised the need for collaboration with computer engineering experts. As systems become more complex, only through a multi-disciplinary collaboration it is possible to achieve truly intelligent transport systems. In line with this trend, this paper proposes a strategy to address ITS by establishing a multi-layer infrastructure able to support the participation of such multidisciplinary competencies. The proposed approach is supported on the experience at Brisa motorway management company and generalizes the developed open service oriented infrastructure (ITSIBus) supporting the extension of tolling system to payment of additional services (automatic payment in parking lots and in gas stations using motorway tolling service subscription) [4].

As a base assumption, we consider that business services in this sector tend to be offered by more than one organization, leading to: i) integrated services for users (drivers, or movers in general); and ii) an increased possibility for reutilization of technological systems being at the road level or as information systems supporting the involved companies. Most of the current approaches in ITS still have a focus on specific aspects of communication or business oriented issues. In this paper we argue about the need for a holistic vision. The paper offers thus a contribution to a discussion about how to establish a reference architecture where the involved experts can identify their core contributions and at the same time understand how they fit in the overall picture (integrated collaborative solutions).

2 Towards an Intelligent Infrastructure Architecture

Systems currently used in the transport sector are not developed under a cooperation perspective. Nevertheless, the service oriented paradigm is emerging as a key contribution from the ICT area to establish a grid of autonomous computational components. If developed for the cooperation, those components are able to "participate" as components of more advanced solutions. However, a long way is still ahead in order to overcome the limitations of current technologies and development strategies so that we can achieve a really agile cooperative space able to support business services for users (persons) as compositions of autonomous computational systems (computational services). Existing systems for tolling, telematics or traffic management are computational/sensorial systems that were developed under a "closed approach" and based on low level communication standards. As a consequence, the application business logic is tightly coupled with the physical road side systems (dedicated short range communication/road side equipment - DSRC/RSE, traffic counters, Free-flows, etc.).

For instance, in the case of the infrastructure of the Portuguese highway operator Brisa, the DSRC/RSE system needs a service adapter to harmonize the plug-ability of systems from two distinct suppliers (Q-free and Kapsch), this because such systems are not ready for the cooperation. The road side equipments implement an application layer out of any normalization process, which requires the development of adaptors in order to integrate such road systems. The question is: why not embed such service adapters into the DSRC/RSE, offering a higher level language to make possible a dynamic pluggability of road systems to the community of autonomous computational entities in this domain, which potentially come from different suppliers and are developed (implemented) in a diversity of technologies (tailored for internal requirements)?

The possibility of technology interoperation in order to support a diversity of services is discussed by [5] in the context of the GNSS (GPS based) tolling, mandatory for tracks in Germany. The authors raise the possibility of promoting co-usage of in-vehicle technology modules considering the sharing of a GPS module, which is already embedded from the manufacturing stage in a significant number of vehicles, to support both navigation and tolling services. This cooperative perspective among technology modules or systems needs to cope with responsibility and liability issues. As multiple system/component providers might contribute to different services with the associated business risks, a clear framework needs to be defined. Moreover, while there are traffic systems that have a local impact, as the case of signal traffic lights and motorway ramp meter systems, according [6] "*many intelligent transportation systems are subject to network effect and scale challenges, thus requiring extensive system coordination - often needed at the national level - to deploy and integrate ITS systems*", what requires innovative networked strategies both at technical and business levels.

Therefore, the challenges of more integrated business services call for novel architectural solutions, both at the technological and at the business levels. Regarding technology, there is a need to evolve to cooperative systems, as communities of autonomous computational entities able to participate in compositions or assemblies. On the other hand there is a need for a new approach to establish a business services modeling language filling the gap both between the information and communication technology space and the processes space.

The proposal of a collaboration ITS intelligent infrastructure is derived from the need to structure *de facto* collaborative business models, which are based on the participation of a number of stakeholders (see Fig. 1). The running examples of such collaborations mostly follow a traditional ad-hoc data exchange, using manly the file transfer paradigm, although there are some trends to evolve to service oriented architectures, as the case of the Brisa's ITSIBus [4]. When involving richer information exchange, open business and technical frameworks are lacking. This leads to the need for a layer where computational services defined in a technology independent manner are able to answer business services requirements. The list of business services, as they are being discussed in the intelligent infrastructures work group (IIWG), a European Commission funded project coordinated by ERTICO, is considered to help positioning the proposed discussion. Such list groups business services in: i) travel information services; ii) traffic management services; iii) freight and logistics services; and iv) other services. The travel information services are organized as: pre-trip travel information; ii) on-trip travel information; iii) in-car incident warning; and iv) co-modal travel information.

Considering as an example of a travel information service the "in-car incident warning", we can imagine a European citizen traveling around Europe on holidays and somewhere in a highway in another country, his "dream" is to be confident that if an accident happens the on-board-computer, the OBU or its nomadic device warns him about the imminent danger. This requires in fact that a sensor in the vehicle involved in the accident broadcasts an alarm message, or eventually, some video sensor detects the incident and presents a message in variable message panels through the traffic coordination centre for the drivers approaching the dangerous zone.

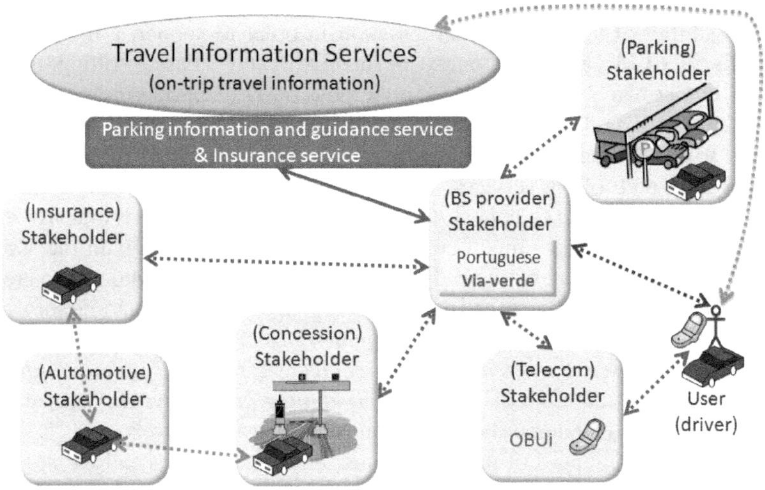

Fig. 1. Network of stakeholders offering business services based on a single contract

Considering the above scenario, there is a need to establish an agreement among the different stakeholders to establish a uniform approach on how to interact with drivers, with road coordination centers, national or European emergency mechanisms associated to the eCall initiative and why not, emergency services like rescue and medical institutions to get prepared in advance for the case they are activated by responsible authorities. If considered a pro-active coordinated system, all the interested entities (stakeholders with their own ICT infrastructures) might be involved at the same time, offering an increased and coordinated response capability. However, if the on-board system responsible for the generation of eCall emergency message does not work or gives the wrong coordinates and the vehicle is not rescued, there is a need to identify the responsibility [5].

Let us consider another example, the "parking information and guidance service", which can be classified as a "on-trip travel information" and a "travel information services" from the proposed list of IIWG, one might consider that some vehicle system or a group of cooperative systems (an OBU with DSRC+GSM/GPRS+GPS paired with nomadic device or, if the automotive industry embeds these functions in the cars as an enhanced on-board computer with its native HMI) is responsible to interact with the business service subscriber (the driver or someone on behalf of him/her). Nevertheless, the implementation of a service like this raises other challenges: the parking lots need to be prepared to collaborate with such business service. This needs for preparedness challenges not only the physical sensors infrastructure and the parking management system but also the information system of the involved parking stakeholders. Beyond free space detection and identification there is a complex business relation among the involved stakeholders that needs to be developed and coordinated.

Our hypothesis is to consider a kind of collaboration infrastructure not staying at the level of physical sensors or systems, as typical in other ITS approaches, but rather at a higher level, considering a number of logical resources able to be used to construct such proposed services involving more than one stakeholder in the majority of the cases. This configures the need to establish a collaborative network [7], [8] where the participating stakeholders need to be prepared to join business oriented associations of organizations (a kind of virtual organizations breeding environment) offering services to users and logistics in the context of mobility. The basic communication and data exchange centered approaches are not able to model the complex relationships among technical systems on both vehicle and road side systems and back-office (stakeholder's information systems). New technology patterns are necessary to cope with the technological platforms contributing to different services (the above mentioned co-usage [5]) and at the same time support collaboration and responsibility management based on a network of independent participating companies under some agreed business model.

3 Collaboration-Oriented Road Mobility Infrastructure

The proposed collaboration-oriented road mobility infrastructure (CORMI), Fig. 2, aims at establishing "bridges" among the infrastructures of different stakeholders and

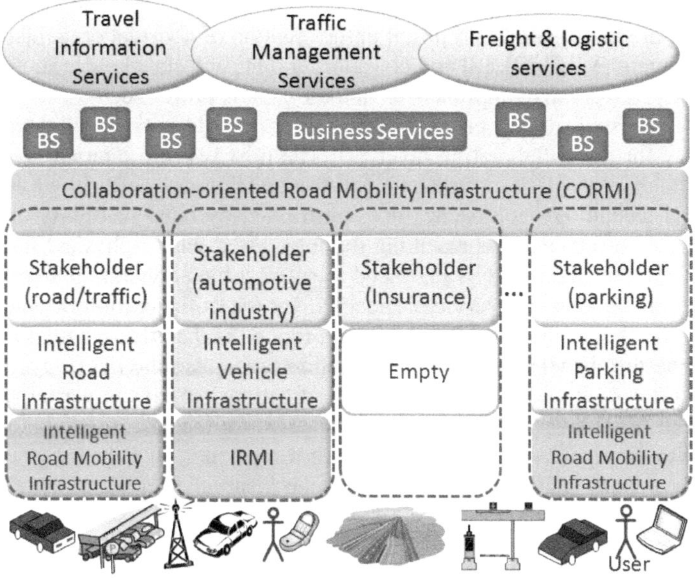

Fig. 2. A strategy to address mobility intelligent infrastructures

the moving entities (vehicles, people associated to nomadic devices). Independently, if these are vehicles or nomadic devices they should be seen as resources participating in the composition of the already mentioned business services.

In this context, it is important to see the automotive industry not as a direct contributor to the business services but rather as an organization that influences the technology and business patterns in relation how to structure such collaborative networks.

The collaboration-oriented infrastructure is responsible to provide a collaborative space where services are offered, making transparent to users the complex relations among the supporting stakeholders. While expected to share common features to other application domains, the proposal is to define specialized interfaces tailored to the transport application domain. Those shared features might be related to coordination, security, distributed information management, directory services, and authentication and authoring, common to collaborative networks in different application domains.

Therefore, the CORMI layer aims to model resources necessary to answer the business services requirements. As an example, if some analytical activity (application) associated to a business service requires to access the last two transactions in tolling and parking for a specific subscriber, these two services if defined on a technology independent approach should hide the access to specific software services implementations of the participating stakeholders who are involved in providing the required information. This approach raises a number of issues: i) where are the (computational) services running, if they are part of the information system of the business service provider or part of the information technology systems of the participating stakeholders; ii) the emerging collaborative business models generate a number of collaborative business processes with the participation of diverse stakeholders that somehow will be committed to support its coordinated and reliable execution; and iii) auditability, certification, security concerns and operational risks establishing a responsibility and market fairness framework need to be settled. To give a clearer picture about what should be the strategy for the stakeholder's organization considering a kind of preparedness state as proposed in the creation of a virtual organizations breeding environment (VBE) [7], [8] and considering that each stakeholder should maintain its autonomy, a federative approach, as in the Fig. 3, is proposed.

CORMI is responsible to promote an open services definition and shared information models for the collaboration layer [9]. The next two are internal layers specific for each stakeholder. They contribute for the collaborative efforts while following process and technology approaches not constrained by interoperability and cooperation issues. A lower layer, representing the interaction with a physical infrastructure, is implemented by stakeholders that need to support the cooperation among vehicles. This layer implements the services specified by the collaboration-oriented mobility infrastructure, thus constituting for what we propose as the effective intelligent mobility infrastructure (IRMI). Like the collaboration layer, also the IRMI layer specifies a common infrastructure (following open specifications) to all the participating stakeholders. The IRMI layer might not be implemented for the case a stakeholder does not interact with a vehicle, which is shown as an Empty box in Fig. 2. For instance, an insurance company participating on offering an insurance service to a vehicle driver based on his driving behavior, which is obtained through a specialized on-board-unit (OBU) connected to the vehicle CAN bus to access sensor data, does not need to implement the IRMI layer considering it accesses vehicle information through the other collaborative network participants (those managing road infrastructures).

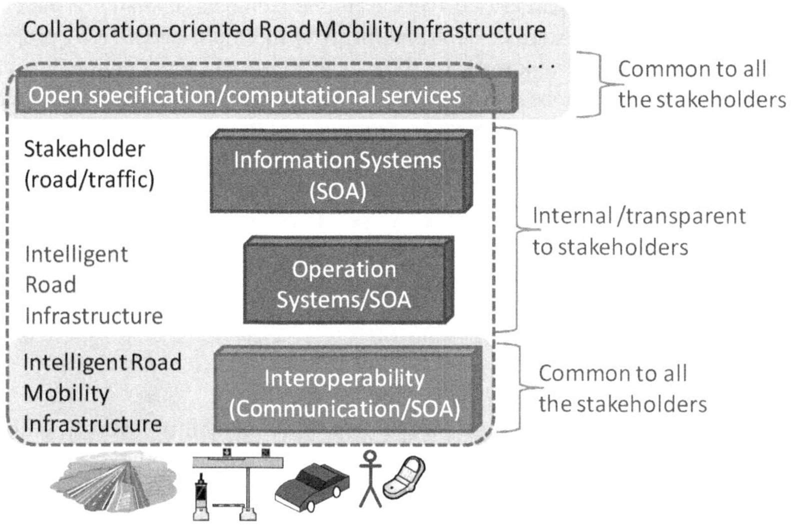

Fig. 3. The proposed architecture for a participating stakeholder

4 Related Work

Communication and interoperability issues have received most research attention in the intelligent transport systems area. Projects like CVIS, Safespot, Coopers, COMe-Safety and FRAME [10] are examples of European Research projects focused mainly on communication and basic cooperative systems while Pre-Drive C2X project extends the discussions to the backend infrastructure [11]. Particularly this project proposes an integration strategy based on a Vehicle Integration Platform and a Backend Integration Manager able to associate vehicles as moving services to services in the backend. While considering security as a key issue, the promised reference platform lacks the establishment of an open, technology independent language, able to support the cooperation between vehicle services and road side infrastructure services considering that the vehicle "crosses the space" of a diversity of stakeholders (collaborative network members).

The European Telecommunications Standards Institute (ETSI) has a technical committee for Intelligent Transport, responsible for the development of ICT technical standards and specifications for transport infrastructures, vehicles and users [12]. Nevertheless, a broader and multidisciplinary approach is needed by including other research perspectives like the distributed information systems and collaborative network organizations. As an example, the ETSI ITS reference architecture while including concepts like ITS road side station, central ITS station, operational support ITS station, and vehicle ITS station, connected through a diversity of networks (ITS Ad Hoc networks, ITS road side infrastructure network, generic access network and internet) connected to specialized routers, does not address the necessary collaboration among stakeholders to make transparent to drivers/users the technical diversity of the crossed road infrastructures [13]. Another contribution from the multi-agents area proposes a collaborative multi-agent framework for ITS focused on wireless communication between vehicles and the infrastructure without considering the situation where the vehicle is in a diversity of stakeholder´s infrastructures and how their information systems coordinate the offered services [14]. Furthermore, most of the discussions involving the communication between road side systems and central coordination information systems are based on specific data driven messaging protocols, lacking an open service oriented approach as a strategy to establish generalized collaboration among heterogeneous, multi-supplier technology systems.

5 Conclusions

A strategy based on two technology independent interoperability layers at collaborative network stakeholder level is proposed and discussed. A collaboration-oriented road mobility infrastructure layer establishes the basis for a network of stakeholders to collaborate on offering services for vehicle drivers. This layer aims to establish a technology independent specification able to be developed by each stakeholder following its processes and technology culture. An intelligent road mobility infrastructure layer is proposed for the stakeholders that have to provide connectivity to the vehicle. This road side level infrastructure is somehow an implementation of the collaboration counterpart as services accessible at physical level are also accessed on a stakeholder peer basis. This means that an insurance company holding subscribers for some insurance service will access insurance vehicle services through such intelligent road mobility infrastructure (while the vehicle might be located at different stakeholder´s infrastructure). Beyond this minimal interoperability specification, the stakeholders managing road infrastructures also maintain their specific infrastructure. A parking lot is an example of a stakeholder that beyond the specific parking infrastructure implements a number of services, those established by the IRMI.

The proposed strategy establishes a disruptive approach in comparison with the classical ITS architectures considering the proposed shift from a communication to a network collaborative centered approach. Associated to the adoption of service oriented architecture where coordination among autonomous computational services superimposes communication concerns, is the way to deal with emergent ITS business service challenges offered in a collaborative network organization.

Acknowledgements

This work was partially supported by BRISA Innovation and Technology company, through a research and development project. Special acknowledgments to Mr. Rui Camolino from APCAP, the Portuguese Association of Motorway and Bridges Concessionaires and co-chair of Intelligent Infrastructures Work Group (IIWG) of eSafety forum EU initiative.

References

[1] Sussman, J.M.: Its: A short history and a perspective on the future. Transportation Quarterly (Special Issue on the occasion of the 75th Anniversary of the Eno Foundation), 115–125 (December 1996)
[2] Williams, M.: Prometheus - the European Research Programme for optimising the road transport system in Europe. In: IEE Colloquium on Driver Information (December 1998)
[3] Takaba, S.: Japanese projects on automobile information and communication systems—things aimed at and obtained in 20 years' experiences, vol. 2, pp. 233–240 (October 1991)
[4] Osório, A.L., Camarinha-Matos, L.M., Gomes, J.S.: A Collaborative Network Case Study: The Extended "ViaVerde" Toll Payment System. In: Collaborative Networks and Their Breeding Environments, pp. 559–568. Springer, US (2005)
[5] Springer, J., Freyer, K.-G.: Service Modelling and Engineering in the Telematics Industry – The View from the Perspective of a Toll Service Provider. In: Industrial Engineering and Ergonomics, pp. 151–163. Springer, Heidelberg (2009)
[6] Ezell, S.: Explaining international it application leadership: Intelligent transportation systems. The Information Technology and Innovation Foundation (ITIF), Tech. Rep. (2010)
[7] Camarinha-Matos, L.M., Afsarmanesh, H., Ollus, M.: ECOLEAD And CNO Base Concepts. In: Methods and Tools for Collaborative Networked Organizations, pp. 3–32. Springer, US (May 2008)
[8] Afsarmanesh, H., Camarinha-Matos, L.M.: A Framework for Management of Virtual Organization Breeding Environments. In: Collaborative Networks and Their Breeding Environments, vol. 186, pp. 35–48. Springer, US (2005)
[9] Osorio, A.L., Afsarmanesh, H., Camarinha-Matos, L.M.: Open Services Ecosystem supporting Collaborative Networks. In: 9th IFIP International Conference on Information Technology for Balanced Automation Systems (BASYS 2010). Springer, Heidelberg (2010)
[10] Jesty, P.H., Bossom, R.A.P.: Using the frame architecture for planning integrated intelligent transport systems. In: EATIS - Euro American Conference on Telematics and Information Systems (2009)
[11] Bechler, M., Bohnert, T.M., Cosenza, A.F.S., Gerlach, M., Seeberger, D.: Evolving the European its architecture for car-to-x communication. In: 16th ITS World Congress and Exhibition, Stockholm, Sweden (September 2009)
[12] Hess, S., Segarra, G., Evensen, K., Festag, A., Weber, T., Cadzow, S., Arndt, M., Wiles, A.: Towards standards for sustainable ITS in Europe. In: 16th ITS World Congress and Exhibition, Stockholm, Sweden (September 2009)
[13] Segarra, G.: Road co-operative systems — societal and business values. In: 2009 9th International Conference on Intelligent Transport Systems Telecommunications (ITST), pp. 610–615 (2009)
[14] Liu, X., Fang, Z., Qu, G., Yang, H., Pan, T.: A framework of agent-based collaborative intelligent transport system. In: Shen, W., Yong, J., Yang, Y., Barthès, J.-P.A., Luo, J. (eds.) CSCWD 2007. LNCS, vol. 5236, pp. 424–428. Springer, Heidelberg (2008)

Using Event B to Specify QoS in ODP Enterprise Language

Hafid Belhaj, Youssef Balouki, Mohamed Bouhdadi, and Said El Hajji

Department of Mathematics & Computer Science,
Faculty of science, Med V University
BP 1014 RP, 4. Av Ibn Batouta - Agdal – Rabat, Morocco
belfid@yahoo.fr, baloukiy@yahoo.fr, bouhdadi@fsr.ac.ma,
elhajji@fsr.ac.ma

Abstract. The ODP enterprise viewpoint focuses on the roles and policies on the enterprise that the system is meant to support. QoS-ODP management is now an important research topic for many universities, institutes and industrial organizations. Several approaches are being used in the field of the formalization of QoS-ODP. The use of formal methods in the design process of ODP systems is explicitly required. In this paper, we explore the benefits provided by using the proof construction approach to define the protocol of negotiating QoS requirements when the enterprise objects perform roles constrained by policies. In this context, we investigate the support for the specification of Quality of Service (QoS) in Event-B when modelling open distributed System in the enterprise viewpoint.

Keywords: RM-ODP, Enterprise Language, Trader function, QOS requirements, event B, RODIN platform.

1 Introduction

RM-ODP [1] provides a framework within which support of distribution, networking and portability can be integrated. It defines a framework comprising five viewpoints provide a basis for the specification of ODP systems. In this paper we treat the need of formal notation of ODP viewpoint languages. The languages Z, SDL, LOTOS, and Esterel are used in RM-ODP architectural semantics part [1] for the specification of ODP concepts. However, no formal method is likely to be suitable for specifying every aspect of an ODP system.

Elsewhere, we used the meta-modelling approach [4], [5] to define syntax of a sub-language for the ODP QoS-aware enterprise viewpoint specifications. We defined a UML/OCL meta-model semantics for structural constraints on ODP enterprise language [6]. We also used the same meta-modelling and denotational approaches for behavioral concepts in the foundations part and in the enterprise language [7]. Furthermore, for modelling ODP systems correctly by construction, the current testing techniques are not widely accepted and especially for the enterprise viewpoint specifications. In this paper, we use the event-B [8], [9] formalism as our formal framework for developing distributed systems. Hence we can benefit from the useful formalism

L.M. Camarinha-Matos et al. (Eds.): PRO-VE 2010, IFIP AICT 336, pp. 478–485, 2010.

for reasoning about distributed systems given by refinement techniques and from the tool support in B [10], [11], [13], [15]. In this context, we developed the QoS negotiation process using trader function with event B. The Rodin Platform for Event-B provides effective support for refinement and mathematical proof. [10], [14]

The paper is organized as follows. Section 2 presents trader function in the enterprise viewpoint. Section 3 describes and specifies the process of negotiation QoS in ODP enterprise view point by using trader function. In Section 4, we use event B as refinement support to specify this process of negotiation. Section 5 presents the Rodin platform as tool of proving initial and refinement models. A conclusion ends the paper.

2 Trader Function in the Enterprise Viewpoint

The ODP functions [12] are required to support ODP systems. RM-ODP defines three repository functions: Type Repository, Relocator and the trader function [12]. The ODP Trader provides "a dating service for objects"; its purpose is to support dynamic binding by allowing services to be discovered at run-time.

In the enterprise viewpoint, the objectives, the functional requirements, and the policy statements that govern the activities of a trading enterprise are identified. A trader is the centre of a community established for the purpose of trading. The trading activities of the community are service exports and service imports, and are governed by a trading policy of the trader. The community consists of members (objects) that have roles such as: trader, exporter, importer, trading administrator and trading policy maker. Members of the trading community are obliged to obey Policy statements (rules). Some important rules are for Trader Quality of Service requirements. The specification of an enterprise requirement has consequences in the other viewpoints.

3 QoS in the Enterprise Specification

One of the items identified in the work developed by ISO/ITU-T regarding QoS [2], [3] in ODP is the need for a QoS language capable of representing all the QoS information related to all viewpoints specification ODP system. This is the concrete QoS problem this paper focuses on. It presents a QoS language that is expressed by event B in order to take advantage of the support tools such as Rodin platform.[10]

The QoS statements in the enterprise specification are those that relate to objectives, responsibilities and policies of the ODP system in its environment. In general, these statements express QoS requirements, which are taken to include requirements on the system from the outside world, as well as the guarantees or claims its designers make in order to meet the user requirements. QoS requirements are associated with enterprise objectives, responsibilities and policies. These will correspond to requirements expressed on the enterprise objects and their interactions.

3.1 The QoS Enterprise Object Model

We illustrate how trader function is used to specify QoS when modelling an open distributed system in the enterprise viewpoint. The Quality of service may be specified in a contract or measured and reported after the event (Fig 1).

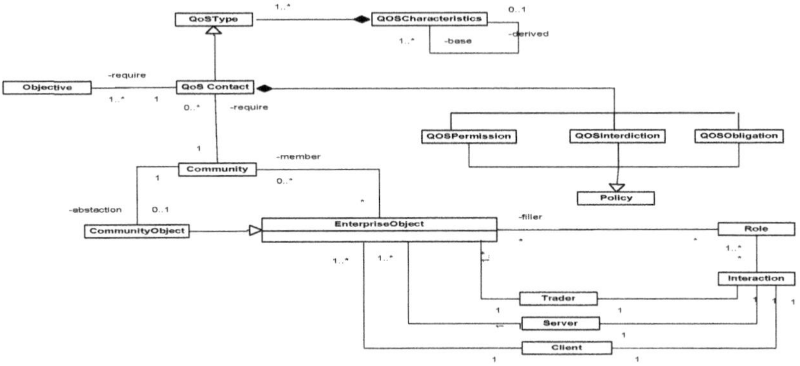

Fig. 1. Modelling QoS by trader function enterprise viewpoint

In this QoS enterprise object model, QoS management activities are driven by a trader object that is responsible to obey the system policies that are in force on objects interactions while filling roles for responding user requirements.

3.2 Single Parameter QoS Negotiation

The concept of QoS negotiation between enterprise objects includes the trader object between them. In this paper we focus on single parameter negotiation:

1) The client (the peer initiating communication) proposes a value P to the trader.
2) The Trader user could refuse the request but, if accepted, could select a new value P' that is not better than the one proposed by the Server, P '<= P.
3) The Server could refuse the request. Instead, when the Server accepts the request, could select a new V value that is not better than the initial value proposed by the client, namely V<= P'. The Server gives this value to the Trader.
5) The Server leaves the V value unchanged.
6) The selected value, V, is returned to the client and it is the value of agreement.

This mechanism is illustrated in Figure 2.

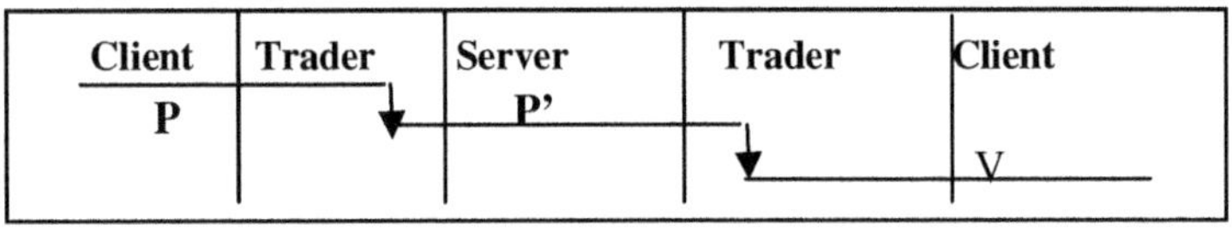

Fig. 2. QoS single parameter negotiation

4 Specifying QoS Negotiation with Event B

4.1 Requirement Document

The requirement document consists in explaining what kind of believe each enterprise object may have at the end of the protocol:

The system is negotiating QoS between enterprise objects	FUN-1

Then we explain what a successively negotiation means:

The final QoS value is published by trader object	FUN-2

We also explain what a proposed QoS:

The initial QoS value is proposed by client object	FUN-3

We describe now what both client and server may believe at the end of the negotiation protocol:

Client and server might either believe if the QoS value is conformably negotiated or failed	FUN-4

We relate the beliefs of both the client and the server:

When the QoS value is published by trader, the client and server believe that the QoS value has been negotiated successively. Otherwise, they believe that negotiation failed.	FUN-5

We explain that it is possible that the client refuse:

However, if the client refuse QoS value, the negotiation is aborted	FUN-6

4.2 Refinement Strategy

In this section, we present our strategy for constructing the QoS single parameter negotiation protocol. This will be done by means of an initial model followed by three refinements.

a) The initial model set up the scene by taking account of requirements FUN-1 to FUN-3. It essentially presents the protocol as done in one shot.
b) In the first refinement, we take care of the remaining requirements FUN-4 to FUN-6 in an abstract way. The QoS is approved step by step, but we are still abstract in that both client and server can have a direct access to the state of the other.
c) In the second refinements, we introduce the trader between client and server so that each of them only reacts to the content of trader messages: it cannot look directly at the value of its partner as was the case in the previous refinements. For these messages, we introduce the trader between client and server (as negotiator). we also introduce the timers in both participants.

4.2.1 Initial Model

Our initial model contains a partial specification of the QoS single parameter negotiation protocol. It deals with requirements FUN-1, FUN-2 and FUN-3. The protocol is executed in one shot.

4.2.1.1 The State

The state is made of the set or real positive numbers IR+ to represent the set of QoS values. The maximum QoS value allowed by server object is denoted by a constant positive value Vserver_max. the QoS values wanted by the client object is expressed by a constant positive value P. These values are defined in axm0_1 and axm0_2.

Sets: IR$^+$	**Constants:** Vserver_max P	**Axm0_1 :** Vserver_max Є IR+ **Axm0_2:** P Є IR+

The negotiated and the final QoS values are variables typed in invariants inv0_1, inv0_2, inv0_3, inv0_4, and inv0_5.

variables : Vnegoc Vfinal	**Inv0_1** : Vnegoc Є IR$^+$ **Inv0_2** : Vnegoc ≤ Vserver_max **Inv0_3** : Vfinal Є IR$^+$ **Inv0_4** : Vfinal ≤ Vserver_max **Inv0_5** : Vfinal ≤ P

4.2.1.2 The Events

The initial value of Vnegoc is P. the final value of the protocol is non-deterministically defined by event QoSspnp, that explained that Vfinal value becomes Vnegoc.

Init : Vnegoc := P Vfinal := 0	**QoSspnp** Vfinal :| Vfinal = Vnegoc

4.2.2 First Refinement

The role of this refinement is to specify the final value of the status of client and server as defined in requirements FUN-4 to FUN-6. We shall also see how the QoS value is negotiated step by step between client object and server object.

4.2.2.1 The State

In this first refinement, we introduce the concept of status. For this, we introduce a carrier set named STATUS. It is made of three distinct elements: propose, accept and refuse as shown below.

Sets: STATUS **Constants**: Propose Accept Refuse	**Axm1_1**: STATUS ={Propose,Accept, Refuse} **Axm1_2** : Propose ≠ Accept **Axm1_3** : Propose ≠ Refuse **Axm1_4** : Accept ≠ Refuse **Axm1_5** : Vserver Є IR$^+$ **Axm1_6** : Vserver ≤ Vserver_max

We introduce the status variables c_st and s_st of the client object and server one respectively. Such variables are member of the STATUS.

variable: c_st s_st Vnegoc Vfinal	**Inv1_1** : c_st Є STATUS **Inv1_2** : s_st Є STATUS **Inv1_3** : c_st = Accept ⇔ P ≥ Vserver **Inv1_4** : s_st = Accept ==> c_st =

Requirement FUN-5 is formalized in inv1_4 where it said that the client accept when the server does.

4.2.2.2 The Events

In this refinements, we introduce many new events : Client_accept, Client_refuse, Server_accept and Server_refuse. The events Client_accept and Server_refuse are still very abstract because in the first one, the client is aware of the status of the server and in the second one the server is aware of the status of the client. This is clearly not possible and will be implemented correctly in the next refinement.

```
Client_accept
When
  c_st = Propose
  s_st = Accept
Then c_st := Accept
     Vfinal :=Vserver
End
```

```
Client_refuse
When
s_st = Propose
Then
 c_st := Refuse
End End
```

```
Server_accept
When
 s_st = Propose
Then
  s_st := Accept
End
```

```
Server_refuse
When
  s_st = Propose
  c_st = Refuse
Then
    s_st := Refuse
 End
```

This is clearly a convenient abstraction but not a final implementation. In fact, this direct access will be removed in the next refinement.

```
Init :   Vnegoc := P
         Vfinal  := 0
         c_st := Propose
         s_st := Propose
```

```
QoSspnp
   When    c_st ≠ Propose
           s_st ≠ Propose
   Then    skip    End
```

The refinement of event QoSspnp must refine its abstraction, which is a non-deterministic event.

4.2.3 Second Refinement

In this refinement, the trader will enter into the scene by cooperating with client and server objects in order to negotiate the QoS value. In fact, the client will not access any more directly the server value as was the case of the previous refinement, this will be done by the trader. We then introduce this trader which is situated between client and server.

4.2.3.1 The State

The state is first enlarged with a constant QoS trader value :Vtrader denoted by the axioms axm2_1 and axm2_2 and a Boolean variable Publish indicated implicitly by inv2_1.

```
Sets:  B
```

```
Constants: Vtrader
           True
           False
           Max_timer
```

```
Axm2_1:   Vtrader Є IR+
Axm2_2:   Vtrader ≤ Vserver_max
Axm2_3:   B={True, False}
Axm2_4:   Max_timer Є  IN
```

```
variables: Publish
           c_timer
           s_timer
```

```
Inv2_1: Publish Є B
Inv2_2: Publish=True ==> Vtrader ≤ Vserver
Inv2_3: c_timer  Є 0 .. Max_timer
Inv2_4: s_timer  Є 0 .. Max_timer
Inv2_5: c_timer = Max_timer + 1 ⇔ c_st = Refuse
Inv2_6: s_timer = Max_timer + 1 ⇔ s_st = Refuse
```

4.2.3.2 The Events

The initialization event is extended in a straightforward fashion as indicated below. The Boolean value publish is set to False at the beginning so that the only two events which can be fired are the ones described next.

```
Init :  Vnegoc := P
        Vfinal := 0
        c_st := Propose
        s_st := Propose
        Publish := False
        C_timer := 0
        S_timer := 0
```

```
Client_accept
When   c_st = Propose
  Publish = True
  c_timer ≤ Max_timer
Then   c_st := Accept
       Vfinal := Vserver
End
```

```
Client_refuse
When c_st = Propose
  Publish = False
  C_timer > Max_timer
Then   c_st := Refuse
End
```

```
Server_accept: When s_st = Propose
               Publish = True
               s_timer ≤ Max_timer
               Then s_st:= Accept   End
```

```
Server_refus:  When  s_st = Propose
               Publish = False
               s_timer > Max_timer
             Then   s_st := Refuse  End
```

5 Conclusion and Perspectives

RM ODP is intended to create an international standard for the design and realization of open distributed systems. The use of formal methods in the design process of ODP systems is explicitly required. In this article the use of the Formal Description Techniques event B is investigated and evaluated. We presented our approach for developing distributed system in Event B. we proposed a visualization of, and guidance for, event B refinement using trader enterprise viewpoint function for negotiating QoS requirements between enterprise objects. Moreover, in order to verify our final model, the refinements models are integrated with the Event B platform developed by the RODIN.

As for future work, we are going to generalize our approach to other methods of reaching QoS agreements in ODP systems in particular using event-B in the design process of ODP systems.

References

1. ISO/IEC: Basic Reference Model of Open Distributed Processing-Parts1,2, 3 and 4, ISO/IEC CD 10746 (1994)
2. ISO/IEC TR 13243 – Information technology – Quality of service –Guide to methods and Mechanisms (November 1999)
3. ITU-T Recommendation G.1000 - Communications quality of service: a framework and Definitions (November 2001)
4. Bouhdadi, M., et al.: A UML-Based Meta-language for the QoS-aware Enterprise Specification of Open Distributed Systems. IFIP Series, vol. 85, pp. 255–264. Springer, Heidelberg (2002)
5. Bouhdadi, M., Balouki, Y.: Semantics of Behavioral Concepts for Open Virtual Enterprises. Lecture Notes in Electrical Engineering, vol. 27, pp. 275–286. Springer, Heidelberg (2009)

6. Balouki, Y., Belhaj, H., et al.: Event B for ODP Enterprise Behavioral Concepts Specification. In: Proceedings of the World Congress on Engineering, WCE 2009, London, U.K., July 1-3. Lecture Notes in Engineering and Computer Science, vol. I, pp. 784–788. Newswood Limited (2009)
7. Balouki, Y., Bouhdadi, M.: Using BPEL for Behavioral Concepts in ODP Enterprise Language, Virtual Enterprises and Collaborative Networks. IFIP, vol. 283, pp. 221–232. Springer, Heidelberg (2008)
8. Abrial, J.-R.: The B-Book: Assigning programs to meanings. Cambridge University Press, Cambridge (1996)
9. Abrial, J.-R.: Extending B without changing it (for developing distributed systems). In: Habrias, H. (ed.) First B Conference (November 1996)
10. Event-B and the Rodin Platform, `http://www.event-b.org/`
11. Joochim, T., Snook, C., Poppleton, M., Gravell, A.: Timing Diagrams Requirements Modelling Using Event-B Formal Methods. In: IASTED International Conference on Software Engineering (SE 2010), Innsbruck, Austria, February 16-18 (2010)
12. ISO/IEC: The ODP Trading Function, ISO/IEC JTC1/SC21 (1995)
13. Butler, M.J., Hallerstede, S.: The Rodin Formal Modelling tool. In: BCS-FACS Christmas 2007 Meeting Formal methods in Industry, London (2007)
14. Abrial, J.-R.: Tutorial - Case study of a complete reactive system in Event-B: A mechanical press controller. In: Proc. 5th International Symposium on Formal Methods (FM 2008), Turku, Finland (2008)
15. Cansell, D., Méry, D., Rehm, J.: Time Constraint Patterns for Event B Development. In: Proc. Formal Specification and Development in B, 7th International Conf. of B (B 2007), Besancon, France, pp. 140–154 (2007)

Towards a Modeling Framework for Service-Oriented Digital Ecosystems

Rubén Darío Franco, Angel Ortiz,
Pedro Gómez-Gasquet, and Rosa Navarro Varela

Research Centre on Production Management and Engineering,
Universidad Politécnica de Valencia
Edificio 8B, Acceso L, Planta 2
46022 Valencia, Spain
dfranco@cigip.upv.es

Abstract. Reference modeling for collaborative networks has been identified as a key topic in consolidating this new scientific discipline. Earlier contributions on this field have provided a solid initial framework and they are considered starting points for this work. Based on two well-known approaches, the CIMOSA and ARCON modeling frameworks, what this work proposes is a set of modeling constructs for CNO modeling under a service-orientation perspective. Service Entities are incorporated as a third approach that may be considered if service ecosystems are being modeled.

Keywords: Collaborative Networks Reference Modeling, Service Ecosystems, Service Oriented Architectures.

1 Introduction

Considered as a commonly-agreed framework for understanding the significant concepts, entities, and relationships of some domain, Reference Modeling in the Collaborative Networks domain has been identified as a research topic that needs to be further developed [1].

Reference models are intended to provide a conceptual basis on top of which systems designers and implementers may build robust solutions for specific domains.

The main goal of this paper is to provide an initial set of modeling constructs for CNO modeling if service-orientation is being also considered.

The work has been structured in four sections. Besides this introduction, Section 2 reviews three complementary approaches that will be adopted, are introduced. Section 3 describes the approach and, finally, Section 4 briefly discusses the need, expected contribution and further research steps.

2 CNO Reference Modeling

Developing reference models is a complex task which requires a lot of effort. Actually, most well-recognized initiatives come from heavily-contributed large research

L.M. Camarinha-Matos et al. (Eds.): PRO-VE 2010, IFIP AICT 336, pp. 486–493, 2010.

projects. Both the AMICE [2] and ECOLEAD [3] consortiums involved several worldwide partners in developing CIMOSA and ARCON proposals, respectively. Being considered inspirational sources of this work, next sections will briefly describe both initiatives in order to better focus the contribution.

2.1 ARCON Reference Modeling Framework

In [4] a comprehensive modeling framework is introduced. A Reference Modeling Framework for Collaborative Networks (ARCON) is the result of developing a slid conceptual base intended to support different modeling levels ranging from General Representations of CNO up to detailed and concrete manifestations as Professional Virtual Communities or Virtual Labs.

Based on information collected from previous initiatives and developments of ECOLEAD project, proponents combine three main dimensions which are supposed to cover CNO (specifically its manifestations) modeling needs.

As it was mentioned earlier, developing a reference model for a specific domain may involve several people and take several years to reach its mature stage. Actually, in [], authors argue that ARCON represents just a first step in that direction and more research contributions will be needed.

What this work is providing is just a minor step in that way. Specifically, in Section 3, a set of building blocks is provided for each modeling intent layer (GR, SM and IM) but this proposal is only considering the CNO modeling from its Endogenous perspective.

2.2 CIMOSA Building Blocks for CIM Modeling

The Open Systems Architecture for CIM (Computer Integrated Manufacturing), initiative carried out by the AMICE consortium, perhaps it may be considered one of the most influential works of the Enterprise Engineering body of knowledge.

Initially conceived as an open architecture for manufacturing systems, its main concepts have influenced many other works. Specifically, the Virtual Enterprise Reference Architecture (VERAM) [5] and more recently ARCON, included implicit or explicit references to some of its underlying concepts.

The CIMOSA modeling framework is also characterized by three dimensions:

- **Genericity dimension**: related to the degree or particularization of created models. It goes from generic building blocks, intended for general purpose models, to specific company-wide ones.
- **Modeling dimension**: provides modeling support from a systemic perspective, going from requirements up to the description of system implementation.
- **View dimension**: this dimension provides users with different perspectives intended to model near-orthogonal abstractions of the system being modeled.

In terms of building blocks, a comprehensive list has been provided. Main CIMOSA building blocks are detailed in [6].

2.3 Service Entities for CNO Reference Modeling

Service Entities paradigm has been proposed as a complementary approach of Virtual Breeding Environments (VBE) and Virtual Organizations (VO) management practices and they are considered a key component of the next generation of VBE Management Systems [6].

In their simplest form, Service Entities represent abstracted specifications of actual entities existing in some specific domain, in terms of its attributes and methods (business services) needed to define their behavior. In [7], has been discussed how SE may be used to support CNO reference modeling, mainly from their Functional, Structural and Informational perspectives.

3 A Modeling Framework for Service-Oriented Digital Ecosystems

Based on the above mentioned approaches, next sections will describe a three-layered approach for the identification of the main building blocks in CNO reference modeling. First, a description of building blocks for CNO General Representation is introduced. This layer considers generic building blocks that may be used to describe many CNO manifestations.

Next, Specific Modeling (SM) building blocks are introduced. Most of constructs are derived from GR layer and, complementarily, two service-oriented specific ones are given:

- **Digital business service interface**: which is intended to support the definition of business services that CNO members may need to define in order to properly support CNO service-orientation approach
- **Abstract Service Entity**: this construct will be used to represent actors (i.e. resources) of the CNO which will be providing such business service interfaces.

At the Implementation level, main contribution includes two related constructs which can be used to describe their implementation details: **Web Services** and **Concrete Service Entity**.

3.1 General Representation (GR) Modeling Constructs

General Representation modeling constructs are intended to provide a common understanding framework for modeling generic descriptions and requirements of collaborative networks despite their nature and specific class.

Figure 1 provides an overview of main constructs and their relationships. Complementarily, Table 1 includes a brief description of such constructs. Previous contributions are *indicated.*

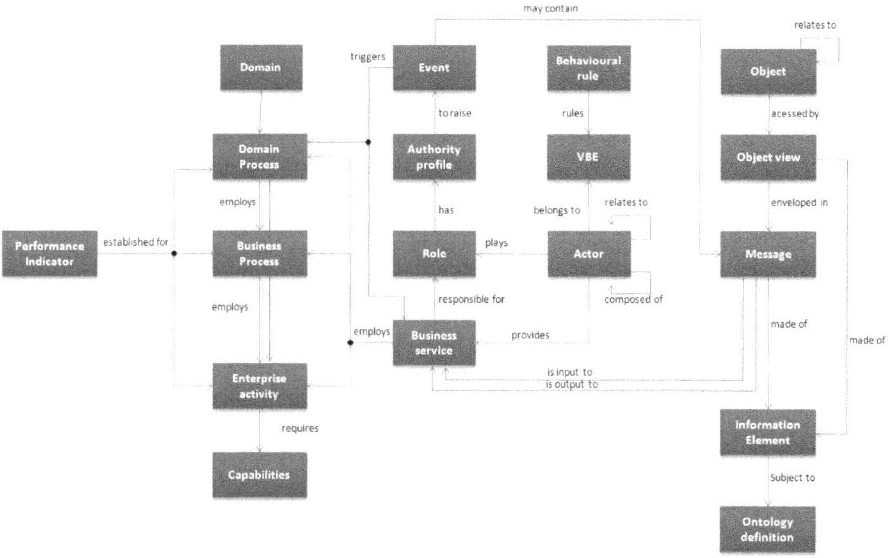

Fig. 1. CNO General Representation building blocks

Table 1. Main modeling constructs for CNO General Representation (GR)

Construct	Description	Dimension
Domain	Defines the functional areas subject to system analysis and implementation.	*Functional*
Domain processes	DPs are stand-alone processes triggered by nothing but Events and producing defined end results. They encapsulate a well-defined set of (network) functionality and behavior.	*Functional*
Business processes	BPs are user-defined sub-processes of Domain Processes defining pieces of network behavior. They are made of other Business Processes and/or Enterprise Activities.	*Functional*
Enterprise activities	Define the network functionality as elementary tasks defined by their inputs, their outputs, their function and their required capabilities.	*Functional*
Events	Describe real-world happenings, timers or requests to do something in the network. They activate the processing of the DP (and possibly the BP) of the network.	*Functional*
Performance indicator	Performance Indicators are related to specific DP, BP or EA of the network and their definition includes both target goals and constrained limits.	**Functional**
Business service	A business service represents a "business interface" that any member of the network makes available to third parties by means of an interface specification	**Functional**
Actor	Each individual network member (or candidate). They may represent organizations, individuals, systems or machines being able to provide business services.	**Organization**
Role	Roles are played by actors and, depending on the network type, they may assume several roles along their life-cycle.	**Organization**

Table 1. *(continued)*

Construct	Description	Dimension
VBE	Virtual Breeding Environments represent containers where specific CNO instances may be launched and where actors belong to.	Organization
Behavioral rule	Behavioral rules constrain in the sense that is described in E4 ARCON's perspective.	**Organization**
Object	Describe generalised entities (or objects) of the network which can thought as a whole.	*Information*
Message	Represent the basic exchange mechanism used for processes activation and events generation.	**Information**
Information elements	Describe elementary, i.e. atomic, pieces of information as perceived by users.	*Information*
Ontology definition	Express constraints on Information Elements to ensure their consistency.	**Information**

3.2 Specific Modeling (SM) Constructs

Specific Modeling Constructs refer to a set of building blocks that can be used to model specific types of CNO. Their specification will serve as base for modeling specific types of CNO and they may be based on currently available GR building blocks.

Figure 2 shows the constructs of this layer and their main relationships. Complementarily, Table 2 includes a brief description of them where previous contributions are *highlighted*.

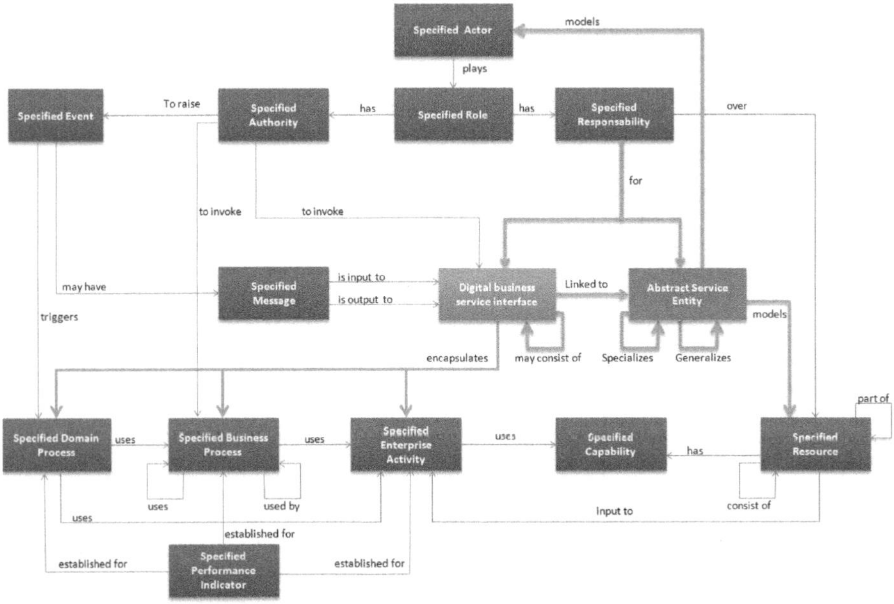

Fig. 2. CNO Specific Modeling building blocks

Table 2. Modeling constructs for CNO Specific Modeling (SM)

Construct	Description	Dimension
Specified Domain Process	Formal specifications of Domain Processes.	*Functional*
Specified Business Process	Formally defined specifications of Collaborative Business Processes. They are defined by their triggering condition and Process Behaviour	*Functional*
Specified Enterprise Activity	Specification of Enterprise Activities defined by their Inputs, Control, Resources, Outputs and Resources.	*Functional*
Specified Performance Indicator	Formal definition of Performance Indicators linked to operational processes and resources.	**Functional**
Digital business service interface	Linked to GR-Business Services, they represent the formal definition of a business service interface (mainly in terms of inputs, outputs and expected functionality) that will be provided by means of digital networks.	**Functional**
Abstract Service Entity	Representing a type of Actor, they provide functional capabilities by means of their abstract digital service definitions.	**Organization**
Specified Message	Formal definition of messages to be exchanged inside the network when DP and BP are executed.	**Functional**
Specified Event	Formally defined specifications of both external and internal Events	*Functional*
Specified Resource	They provide the specified Capabilities which meet or exceed the required Capabilities defined at the GR definition level	*Resource*
Specified Capability	Provided by specified Resources, meet or exceed the required Capabilities defined at the GR Modeling Level	*Resource*
Specified Responsibility	Formally defined engineering responsibilities for the creation, and maintenance of specific modeling activities	*Organization*
Specified Actor	Formal identification of entities involved in the CNO. At this modeling level they only are identified as classes or types.	**Organization**
Specified Role	Directly linked to actors, a role is assumed by one or more actors, depending on network specific constrains.	**Organization**
Specified Authority	are formally assigned engineering responsibilities for the creation, and maintenance of specific modeling activities	*Organization*

3.3 Implementation Modeling (IM) Constructs

Implementation Modeling Constructs refer to a set of building blocks that can be used to model specific instances of specific CNO models. They may be based on currently available SM building blocks. Figure 3 shows the constructs of this layer and their main relationships. Complementarily, Table 3 includes a brief description of them where previous contributions are *highlighted*.

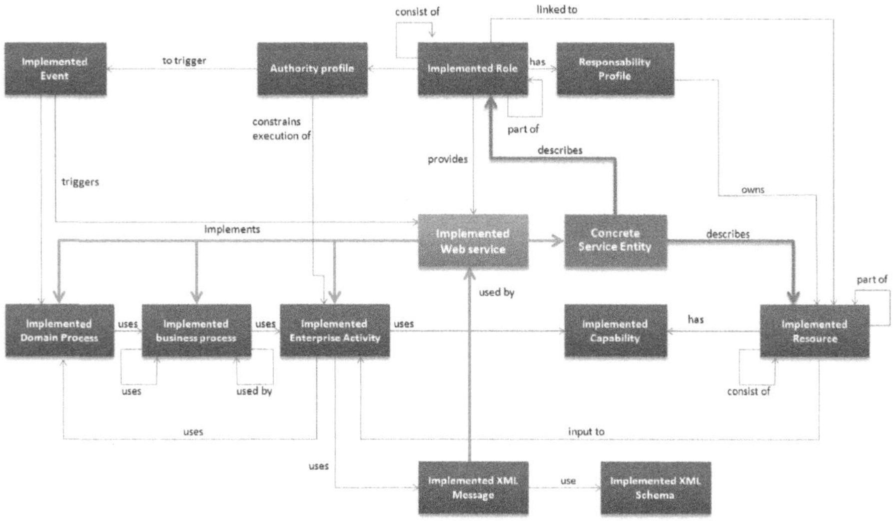

Fig. 3. CNO Implementation Modeling building blocks

Table 3. Modeling constructs for CNO Implementation Modeling (IM)

Construct	Description	Dimension
Implemented Domain Process	Describe the implemented Domain behavior	*Functional*
Implemented business process	Describe the implemented flow of control for a part of a DP.	*Functional*
Implemented Enterprise Activity	Describe the implemented functionality and indicate resources needed to execute it.	*Functional*
Implemented Event	Describe how enterprise events initiate action by the physical system of the enterprise	*Functional*
Implemented Resource	Describe resources which are derived from Specified Resources.	*Resource*
Implemented Capability	Describe capabilities which are provided by Implemented Resources and which comply with Specified Capabilities defined at the Design Specification Modelling Level.	*Resource*
Implemented authority profile	Define engineering and operational responsibilities	*Organization*
Implemented role	CNO Specific roles that may be assumed by Implemented resources and Concrete Service Entities	**Organization**
Implemented responsibility profile	Assign engineering and operational responsibilities	*Organization*

Table 3. (*continued*)

Construct	Description	Dimension
Web service	Implemented digital business service interface which constitutes the expected digital functionality provided by them	**Information**
Implemented XML Message	Describe XML-based messages that are going to be used for CNO information sharing and coordination mechanism.	**Information**
Implemented XML Schema	Describe implemented XML-schemas that will be used to validate messages and ontological validation.	**Information**
Concrete Service Entity	Actual instances of Abstract Services Entities linked to implemented resources and able to provide their expected capabilities	**Organization**

4 Brief Discussion

Reference modeling in the Collaborative Networks domain has been identified as a key research topic that needs to be further addressed.

Earlier contributions in this field have provided solid initial foundations and this work has introduced a first attempt to provide a set of modeling constructs for CNO, based on three converging research streams: the CIMOSA Modeling Framework, ARCON Modeling Framework and Service Entities approach.

As a result, an overall framework has been made available for systems architects and developers.

We are aware that developing this kind of models requires deep research community consensus. Cause of that, next research steps will include its submission to public bodies as the Society for Collaborative Networks (SOCOLNET) for further enrichment and validation.

References

1. Camarinha-Matos, L., Afsarmanesh, H.: Towards a reference model for Collaborative Networked Organizations. In: Proceedings of BASYS 2006. Information Technology for Balanced Manufacturing Systems. Springer, Heidelberg (2006)
2. AMICE Consortium, `http://cimosa.cnt.pl/Docs/Primer/primer2.htm`
3. ECOLEAD Project (2009)
4. Camarinha-Matos, L., Afsarmanesh, H.: Collaborative Networks: Reference Modeling. Springer, Heidelberg (2008)
5. VERAM. Virtual Enterprise Reference Architecture and Methodology, `http://cic.vtt.fi/projects/globemen/book/01_zwegers2.pdf`
6. Franco, R.D., Ortiz Bas, A., Lario, F.: Modeling extended manufacturing processes with service-oriented entities. Service Business 3(1) (March 2009)
7. Franco, R.D., Ortiz Bas, A., Prats, G., Navarro Varela, R.: Supporting Structural and Functional Collaborative Networked Organizations Modeling with Service Entities. In: Leveraging Knowledge for Innovation in Collaborative Networks, pp. 547–554. Springer, Heidelberg (2009)

Application of the EKD Process Model to Support the Coordination of Collaborative Networks in the Civil Construction Sector

Flávia Vancim Frachone Neves and Fábio Müller Guerrini

São Carlos Engineering School (USP) – Production Engineering Department
Trabalhador Sãocarlense Avenue, nº 400, Zip Code 13566-590 São Carlos, Brazil
frachone@sc.usp.br, guerrini@sc.usp.br

Abstract. The civil construction industry has an operation way similar to virtual organizations, but in not structuralized form, leaving to provide competitive advantages. For in such a way, the paper will propose, through analytical research and case studies and based on EKD (Enterprise Knowledge Development) methodology, the Process Model to support the coordination of collaborative networks in the civil construction sector. This model will analyze each process and information flow contained in the business, that is, describes in a structuralized form the organizational activities, so that promoting better understanding of how the processes could be done to support companies of civil construction sector.

Keywords: Collaborative Networks, Civil Construction, EKD Process Model.

1 Introduction

Under a general background, [1] and [2] defends that the civil construction industry occupies strategically position in the generation of jobs, mainly of low qualification, and that it starts to demonstrate continuous effort for process improvement with the use of partnerships among companies. On the other hand [3], [4], [5], [6], [7] and [8] displays that it has low degree of innovation, communication, confidence, coordinate cooperation, the culture steel conservative and the majority of the works, as [9] affirms, are organized in unique projects.

A success partnership does not occur itself. For [10], [11] and [8] affirms that develop shared relationship reliable, equality or benefits, communication accomplishes and competent management, is difficult and these are critical factors. Therefore, is possible to affirm that the construction partnership is surrounded of high risks and profits. The main factor for partnership in the construction projects is, according to [1], the benefit to share the risk among the parts. With bigger projects, a unique firm could not obtain all necessary resources. Already through the partnership, the construction companies can combine resources and abilities.

Due to the advantages cited above, this paper proposes, based on EKD (Enterprise Knowledge Development) methodology, the Process Model to support the coordination of collaborative networks in the civil construction sector.

L.M. Camarinha-Matos et al. (Eds.): PRO-VE 2010, IFIP AICT 336, pp. 494–500, 2010.

2 Research Method

In accordance with [12], the organizational modeling methodology EKD (Enterprise Knowledge Development) provides to the involved ones in the project to have more analytical organization optics and its components as a whole, through the organizational modeling. The EKD composition, continuing in accordance with [12], through the use of the EKD, a clear and not ambiguous description can be promoted of how the organization functions; which the requirements and reasons for change; which alternatives must be created to find these requirements and which criteria and arguments for evaluation of these alternatives. Also, some of the most important benefits offered by EKD, which: better understand the business; facilitate the organizational learning and communication and assist the agreement of the organization processes.

Ahead of the displayed context, and to fulfill with the research goal it will be presented a qualitative analysis of the organizational aspects of virtual nets among civil construction partners. The used method will be given by means of approach bibliographical research, searching a problem from theoretical references, of qualitative character, propitiating bigger proximity of the researcher with the problems studied beyond the analysis of the searched context, and exploratory, giving correlations between study objects to collaborative with future research. The analytical research, in accordance with [13], prevents the duplicity of knowledge and, it gets theoretical recital for the work development. The empirical study was divided on phases. The first one, evidence collection, was composed of documents of four construction workmanships, of two Brazilian constructions companies both acting in national level, and interviews with their managers. These numbers of cases, in accordance with [14] and [13], supply convincing base for an initial set of proposals.

The second phase, chaining of the collected data, was composed based on after data collected and refined, some information had to be confirmed, with its respective ones interviewed, in order to cure eventual doubts of the researchers and, therefore, to chain the collected and observed evidences, to give pursuing to the following and final stage, which was Modeling the Process Model. Once the data collected, refined, validated and chained, the model considered was shaped.

The interviewed ones were responsible for workmanships management. The research was made under the analytical clipping of virtual nets, in elapsing of seven months, year of 2009. Inside of this context, the general questions that the studies had been considered to enclose corresponded to clarify: why is necessary modeling the processes of virtual nets among civil construction partners; what organizational levels should be suggested to be involved in the network among civil construction partners; and which are the detailing levels that the model should reach to solve the necessities and to correspond to the expectations of the studied economic sector.

3 Data Analysis

During six months were analyzed four civil construction workmanships of two Brazilian constructors, and interviewed the responsible for workmanships management through meetings and, later, at a distance (using the Internet as communication way).

This process was made using half-structuralized questionnaire, which was divided in three stages, as mentioned subsequently.

On first stage, companies characterization, it is import to remember that both companies have a familiar structure, acts in national levels, and the interviewed ones where workmanships managers. The companies analyzed will be called here: "Company A" and "Company B".

Specifically about Company A, founded at year of 1966, could be observed that it generates about a thousand jobs and acts in different types of workmanships, like: houses and residential buildings of high standard; educational, commercial and industrial buildings. In addiction, the high professionals are stimulated to improve the knowledge through partnership with academic institutions.

From Company B, founded at year of 1996, could be observed that it generates about two hundred and sixty five jobs and acts in different types of workmanships, like: houses and residential buildings of high standard; intelligent houses (all spaces using the high technology); commercial buildings and logistical condominiums. Besides the workmanships employees have extra benefits, extended to his family, that stimulate them to keep satisfy in company. In the same way, the high employees (engineering, managers, directors for example) where stimulated to improve their knowledge through specializations in academic institutions.

On second stage, companies operation's way, during the interview's meetings could be observed that both companies studied had the same characteristics in operation's ways, as observed subsequently.

The partnership use to be more frequently, and for long time, among company and workmanship's projectors. In this case, is more difficult to change the partners due to the fact that the work executed from them has a high level of costs and specificities. Also, it is important to say that the companies used to be afraid to test new workmanship's projectors and besides, do not stimulate the intercommunication among these partners.

With suppliers (materials or services), the partnership use to has a short period, due to the fact that companies are more receptive to test new suppliers until they gains confidence in definitive. While this, it is usual happens problems of not fulfillment of stated periods, inferior quality of materials and services, among other things. Such occurrences are not registered, consequently do not exist performance registers of any supplier partner.

Beyond the use of tools/software as publishers of text and spread sheets, do not have another tool/software for aid to the management of the workmanships used by the company. Also, time and money are usually wasted due to the unfamiliarity of the partners and absence of register of its respective behaviors, by the companies, in elapsing of the workmanship where they participate.

Finally on third stage, workmanship analysis, the four workmanships analyzed where: a logistic condominium (finished); a high level residence building (almost finished); and two commercial buildings (one in planning phase and another under initial construction phase).

From the Logistic Condominium could be noted that the company made the workmanship in another State and because of this, they had a high level of difficulty in found partners. This brought some problems to the workmanship like: delay of the stipulated time to build, due to the time wasted in found the partners; changing some partners in the middle of the construction phase due to the low qualification of them; waste of materials and a constant changing's financial chronograms.

The High Level Residence Building had problems related to task's delay. Besides, the initial projects did not match with the task's executions, due to the lack of communication among projectors. But, it is important to remember that workmanships like this had the special characteristic that the final clients possess a level of decision in construction's final phase, contributing to delay the conclusion.

The other two workmanships, the commercials buildings at initial phases: one of them, in the planning phase, was having problems because the city hall's licenses were taking a long time to be approved and the operational partners were been paid without executing the service. This mistake was occurring due to the lack of initial planning of time and in having alternatives actions in case of occur unexpected actions like this. The other commercial building, in initial phase of construction, had problems just related to the difficulty of founding some specific suppliers to execute some specific construction's services in some phases.

Due to these facts, this article will propose, in the next section, a Process Model based on EKD methodology as a first step to support the coordination of cooperation networks among civil construction partners.

4 Result – The Process Model

Considering the analytical view made by the authors, this section will propose the Process Model, figure 1, in order to help companies to coordinate its partnerships through the workmanships phases.

As can be noted subsequently, from figure 1, the process of evaluate possibility of new workmanship (Process 1) began with a possibility of new workmanships possibilities (Inf. 0). This process signalized the possibility to invest (Inf. 1), which starts the next process of defining the workmanship broker (Process 2). With this paper defined (Inf. 2), starts the bureaucratic/strategic procedures (Process 3), which makes all workmanship planning (Inf. 3). That refers to approving workmanship's licenses in the City Hall (Process 3.1), analyze and choose the workmanship's projectors (Process 3.2) and suppliers (Process 3.3). At the same time, it's important to remember that projectors must congregate (Process 3.2.1) to know each other project (Inf. 3.2.1). Concomitantly the chronograms (activities, time and cost) must be defined (Process 3.4).

When projectors and suppliers are founded (Inf. 3.2 and 3.3 respectively), it's time to elaborate/review the contract (Process 4) in order to have the workmanship's clauses signed (Inf. 4).

With the licenses approved (Inf. 3.1), suppliers founded (Inf. 3.3), contract signed (Inf. 4) and projectors knowing each other (Inf. 3.2.1), the workmanship can be executed/reconfigured (Process 5).

With goals reached (Inf. 5), the workmanship is finished (Process 6) and the performance of all partners are measured (Inf. 6).

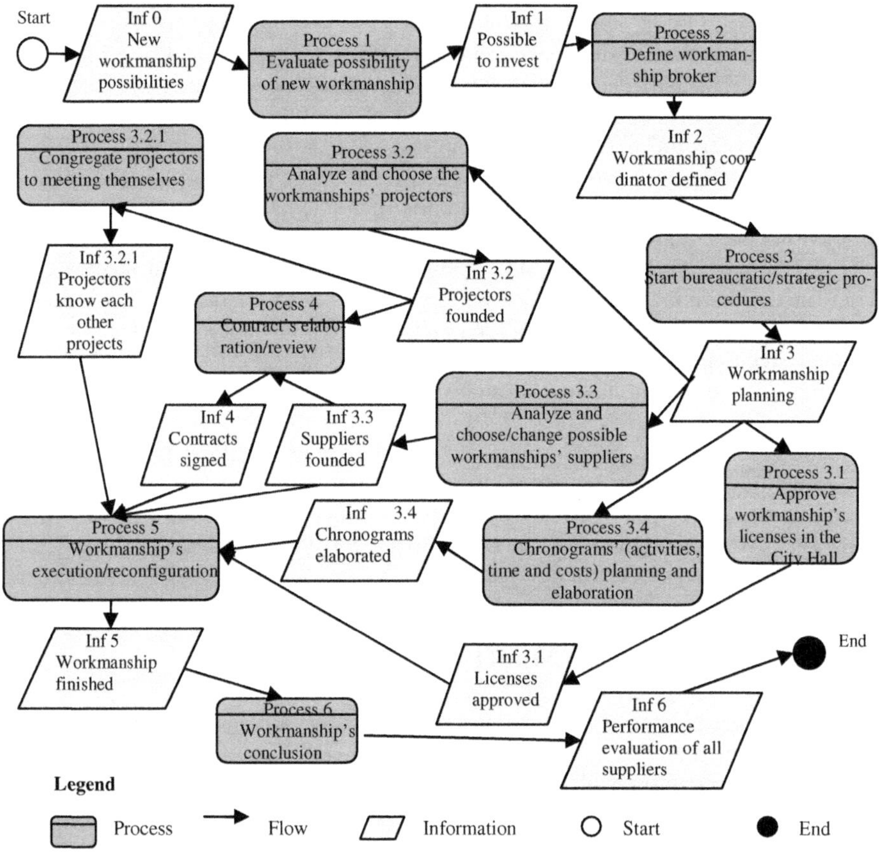

Fig. 1. The Process Model to Coordinate Networks among Workmanships Partners

As referenced by [15], [6], [16] and [17], is necessary that the companies keep in permanent change and improvement. Also, competitiveness make companies constantly look for new advantages opportunities. These proposals had delimitated Process 1 (Evaluate possibility of new workmanship).

Once the market opportunities detected, next step is select a workmanship broker, that defines the resources, capabilities and abilities necessary to execute the workmanship. On this context [18] affirm that broker manages the dynamic net, also serving as facilitator, coordinator and moderator among partners. Due to the importance of this actor, the Process 2 (Define workmanship broker) was defined.

With the workmanship facilitator defined, the company, as mentioned by [17], must carry through the procedures that must be followed. This refers to Process 3 (Start bureaucratic/strategic procedures) and consequently Process 3.1 (Approve workmanship's licenses in the City Hall).

Concomitantly, it's necessary to verify witch partners are apt or not to participate in the workmanship. The main factor for partnership in the construction projects is, according to [1], the benefit to share risk and focus on core competencies. Based on this, Process 3.2 (Analyze and choose the workmanships' projectors) and Process 3.3 (Analyze and choose/change possible workmanships' suppliers) where defined.

As [10] approach that the involved parts in the construction partnership must meet before workmanship execution, and argue the specific procedures of the Project, like Process 3.2.1 (Congregate projectors to meeting themselves) demonstrate. After this phase, creates the teams of cooperation and development of the business relationship. Additionally, so that this partnership is formed, it is necessary that all partners understand the goals clearly.

As [8] affirms, construction partnership is surrounded of high risks and profits. Therefore, and after choosing partners, it's crucial to define and register partnership clauses that will guarantee the fulfillment of the agreement. This important factor defined the Process 4 (Contract's elaboration/review).

When the bureaucratic procedures are done and partners defined, the workmanship is operated. On this phase, as cited by [19], the workmanship are playing the business processes in order to reach the common goals established. In addiction, there are cases where some partners must be replaced or reconfigured. This motivated the Process 5 (Workmanship's execution/reconfiguration).

Steal in accordance with [19], once the workmanship's goals are reached, the project is finalized and partnership dissolution. This motivated the Process 6 (Workmanship's conclusion).

5 Conclusion

Treating on the Brazilian civil construction industry, could be detached the changes resistance and conservative culture. On this way, the article considered the adoption of the modeling methodology EKD, due its facility in understanding the functioning of the business stimulating the involvement and active participation of all stakeholders. Beyond this, develops a business process description.

Also, it's important to point out that the chosen method independent of specific tool for development. This becomes the proposal highly viable, a time that drastic investments in tools for orientation of the coordination of the organization are not well accepted for the investors. In addiction, the EKD methodology allows stakeholders to easily visualize which organizational changes are necessary to be carried through in order to take care of the goals stipulated. Also, the Process Model proposed by this article, the methodology propitiates the necessary steps and alternative ways to execute some strategy. On this case, it refers to which process must be executed/done to coordinate a network among workmanships partners.

Moreover, it's important to remember that the actions of evaluating the partners makes possible to the directors and decision makers having the necessary information to support the process of chosen partners in future workmanships, based on his past behavior, what probably will increase the partners' commitment with the company due to the fact that they have interest in continuing working. Finally, and continuing with suggestible future research, it must be empathized that: the lacks of communication on workmanships' planning phase presents unsustainable actions that, consequently, damage, even so, our ecosystem. This occurs due to the fact that this lacks of communication causes, among other things, waste of material on workmanships' execution that is discarded on City Halls Garbage and not recycled. So, another possible future research must also treat the question of sustainability in workmanships.

References

1. Black, C., Akintoye, A., Fitzgerald, E.: An Analysis of Success Factors and Benefits of Partnering in Construction. International Journal of Projects Management 18, 423–434 (2000)
2. Lima, C., Stephens, J., Böhms, M.: The BCXML: Supporting Ecommerce and Knowledge Management in the Construction Industry. In: Itcon 2003, vol. 8 (2003)
3. Brightman, J.R., Eden, C., Heijden, K.V.D., Langford, D.A.: The Development of the Construction Alternative Futures Explorer. Automation in Construction 8, 613–623 (1999)
4. Wilson, I., Harvey, S., Vankeisbelck, R., Kazi, A.S.: Enabling the Construction Virtual Enterprise: the OSMOS Approach 2001, vol. 6 (2001), `http://www.itcon.org/2001/8` (consulted on December, 01,2005)
5. Cheng, E.W.L., Li, H.: Construction Partnering Process and Associated Critical Success Factors: Quantitative Investigation. Journal of Management in Engineering, 194–201 (October 2002)
6. Chan, A.P.C., Chan, D.W.M., Chiang, Y.R., Tang, B.S., Chan, E.H.W., Ho, K.S.K.: Exploring Critical Success Factors for Partnering in Construction Projects. Journal of Construction Engineering and Management, 188–197 (March/April 2004)
7. Holmen, E., Pedersen, A.C., Torvatn, T.: Building relationships for technological innovation. Journal of Business Research 58, 1240–1250 (2005)
8. Wong, P.S.P., Cheung, S.O., Ho, P.K.M.: Contractor as Trust in Construction Partnering – Prisoner's Dilemma Perspective. Journal of Construction and Management, 1045–1053 (October 2005)
9. Zarli, A., Richaud, O.: Requirements and Technology Integration for It- Based Business-Oriented Frameworks in Building and Construction. In: Itcon 1999, vol. 4 (1999)
10. Glagola, C.R., Sheedy, W.M.: Partnering on Defense Contracts. Journal of Construction Engineering and Management, 127–138 (March-April 2002)
11. Rahman, M., Kumaraswamy, M.: Relational Selection for Collaborative Working Arrangements. Journal of Construction Engineering and Management, 1087–1097 (October 2005)
12. Bubenko, J.Á., Brash, D., Stirna, J.: EKD User Guide. Department of Computer and Systems Sciences. Royal Institute of Technology, Stockholm (1998)
13. Yin, R.K.: Case Study Research: Design and Methods, 3rd edn. Sage Publications, Inc., California (2003)
14. Herriot, R.E., Firestone, W.A.: Multisite qualitative policy research: optimizing description and generalizability. Educational Research 12, 14–19 (1983)
15. Belusi, F., Arcangeli, F.: A Typology of Networks: Flexible and Evolutionary Firms. Research Policy 27, 415–428 (1998)
16. Matthews, J.: The rise of the virtual company. Supply Management 9, 15 (2004)
17. Jones, O.: Managing public-private partnerships: the enactment of a business venture. Technovation 25, 587–597 (2005)
18. Manring, S.L., Moore, S.B.: Creating and Managing a Virtual Inter-Organizational Learning Network for Greener Production: a conceptual model and case study. Journal of Cleaner Production, 1–9 (2006)
19. Camarinha-Matos, L., Afsarmanesh, H.: Infrastructures for Virtual Enterprises - Network Industrial Enterprises. In: Working Conference for Virtual Enterprises (PRO-VE) (October 1999)

Lightweight Process Modeling for Virtual Enterprise Process Collaboration

Lai Xu[1], Paul de Vrieze[1], Keith Phalp[1],
Sheridan Jeary[1], and Peng Liang[2]

[1] Software Systems Research Centre, Bournemouth University, UK
{lxu,pdvrieze,kphalp,sjeary}@bournemouth.ac.uk
[2] State Key Lab. of Software Engineering, Wuhan University, China
liangp@sklse.org

Abstract. Mashup is a new web 2.0 technology for data aggregation applications, combining data from different sources to create valuable information. The uses of mashups are often more data related than process related. In this paper, we explore the differences between data-oriented mashups and process-oriented enterprise mashups and consider how process mashups can be used for virtual enterprise collaboration. We highlight the modeling of end users' process mashup applications from both a control flow and a data flow perspective. Based on our analyses, a lightweight process modeling approach is proposed for process enterprise mashup applications. Our approach, illustrated by reference to an example personal collaborative activity, will support collaboration among users with different levels of modeling skills and expertise in a virtual enterprise environment.

Keywords: Lightweight business process modeling, Business process modeling, Virtual enterprise process collaboration, Process-oriented mashups, Web 2.0.

1 Introduction

The internet lies at the core of a connected world, acting as a conduit for the exchange of information, allowing tasks to be processed collaboratively, and enabling the formation of communities amongst users with similar interests. An Internet interconnected world has increased both business and personal efficiency and performance. On-line mashups have the capability to combine data with (possibly external) functionality to create and produce useful outputs. The term "mashup" implies easy, fast integration, usually made possible by access to open APIs and data sources to produce results that the data owners did not originally envisage.

As the business environment changes rapidly the ability set up a collaborative business process in a virtual enterprise is desirable. Collaborative business processes are increasingly driven by business agility, adaptability, and flexibility, particularly in a virtual enterprise environment. There is increased pressure to build enterprise applications quickly in order to respond to situational needs of the business.

Service-orientation allows a way of thinking of business process management in terms of computational infrastructures, services, service-based development and outcomes

L.M. Camarinha-Matos et al. (Eds.): PRO-VE 2010, IFIP AICT 336, pp. 501–508, 2010.

of those services [1]. Service-oriented architecture (SOA) is a significant computing paradigm and is being embraced by organizations worldwide as the key to business agility. Web 2.0 technologies such as AJAX enable efficient user interactions for successful service discovery, selection, adaptation, invocation and service construction. SOA and Web 2.0 technologies also balance automatic integration of services and human interactions, separating content from presentation in the delivery of the service. Another Web technology, such as Web services, implements functionality using pre-designed building blocks. Integrating SOA, Web 2.0 technologies and Web services into a service-oriented application connects business processes in a horizontal fashion.

We propose a process-oriented enterprise mashup [2], [3], and [4], which allows a user to specify their needs, find related web resources, and eventually execute the resulting process for rapidly building collaborative business process in a virtual enterprise. The first step is to allow business users who have no professional modeling skills to model business processes. Thus, lightweight process modeling for process-oriented mashups aims to be a step towards the enablement of business process modeling to an end user group in a virtual enterprise. The finished business process models provide the basis for process automation.

1.1 Related Work

Well established business process modeling languages like Petri net, Event Process Chains (EPC), Business Process Modeling Notation (BPMN), or Business Process Execution Language (BPEL) require major training efforts and thus are only accepted by certain groups of people. Our work aims to enable the end-user and introduces an intuitive and guided way to model business processes. One facet which this work addresses is the context awareness aspect of business process models to achieve reusability and consistency. Due to page limitation, we are not going details such as how to implement context-awareness modeling principle.

Papers [5] and [6] propose a new modeling approach based on proclets, performatives and channels. A proclet represents only one aspect or one element of a whole business process using Petri net style notations. Our lightweight process language can also be used to describe a proclets or used as a requirements acquisition tool to describe a part of a whole process.

Our previous work [2], [3], and [4], has identified key issues in the implementation and use of a lightweight business process modeling environment. One of the key issues is in supporting end-user process modeling. Papers [7] and [8] discuss lightweight business process modeling issues only from a control flow perspective. In this paper, we examine the capabilities that need to be added to data-oriented mashups to enable the implementation of process-oriented enterprise mashups. We first identify the modeling requirements of lightweight process applications in Section 2 and introduce the modeling principles for process-oriented mashup applications in Section 3. This is followed by discussion of details of process modeling related with both a control flow and a data-flow perspectives in Section 4 and Section 5 respectively. A personal collaborative activity is used to demonstrate our modeling method in Section 6.

2 Lightweight Business Process Modeling Requirements

Lightweight process modeling is a combination of techniques that seek to lower the barrier to entry for users who need to apply some process modeling to their current task. The approach involves fostering a participative style of modeling and providing a forum for community of experts. However to enable a user to participate in lightweight process modeling and execute the process models there are a number of technical requirements.

The fist requirement is to provide executable process models. A process-oriented enterprise mashup should allow a user to specify and automate business tasks and activities. Hence, the lightweight business process modeling language must be executable. The modeling language needs to provide logic information which is associated with precise semantics that can be used to automatically validate and simulate business processes.

The second requirement is providing easy access to the modeling environment for end users and to ensure business users buy-in there needs to be a focus on usability. This comprises both simplicity of the approach and a low foot-print for the solution ("zero install"). Ideally, users can model processes using simplified notations in a Web 2.0 environment and draw up on modeling best practices.

Actively participation is the third requirement for supporting lightweight process modeling. Combine both structured and unstructured information and publish them as a single point of reference to the organization, such as blogs or wiki. A process wiki allows the community to participate in discussions, and to provide comments or ratings in relation to process proposals. Process documents can be generated for offline reading and dissemination.

The process editor should provide an intuitive user interface. Furthermore, it needs to ensure the user is given advanced guidance during the modeling activities. Errors, misspelling and inconsistencies should be avoided from the beginning.

3 Lightweight Business Process Modeling Principles

Following the summary of the requirements for lightweight business process modeling, it is possible to detail our four modeling principles for process-oriented enterprise mashups. The first principle is to minimize the need to design from scratch. For many end users, it is difficult to start to create a model from scratch and it is easier to design a process model based on an existing example. Learning by examples style is common in a community environment where pre-design, highly reusable process models and templates can be selected. These existing models can also serve as a learning model or a base for end users to create a new process model.

The second principle relates to context awareness. The names of activities and tasks involved in a process model should be unified. The context-driver principle allows identification, storage, and representation of a business process artifact only once. A business process is instantiated depending on specific context categories (e.g., business process, industry, country, business role, etc.).

The third principle involves the concept of reusability. We adopt eight control flow patterns from workflow patterns. Details can be found in Section 4. Process patterns, process templates, process fragments, reference models, best-practice models, and further example models are provided in association with the process modeling language; these are all reusable.

Finally, the fourth principle is the community. A web-based community environment provides recommendations, ranking, accompanied by commenting on process models and templates. These process templates will initially be related to usage in the early stages of development, but we expect them to be both significantly improved and expanded within the community environment.

In the following sections, we focus on control-flow and data-flow design for lightweight process modeling.

4 Control Flow Modeling for Process-Oriented Mashups

In order to simplify business process modeling, models must be highly reusable, giving process flexibility and minimizing designs made from scratch. There is wide agreement that patterns can both accelerate the process of designing a solution and reduce modeling time [9]. Patterns enable participants of a community to communicate more effectively, with greater conciseness and less ambiguity [10], [11]. A pattern is an abstraction from a concrete form which keeps recurring in specific non-arbitrary contexts [12]. The use of patterns is a proven practice in the context of programming, as shown by the impact made by the design patterns of Gamma et al. [13] as well as various other patterns.

We have adopted eight symbols from BPMN. Because BPMN has been well accepted by business users [14] and our research is focused on the design of an executable process modeling language not on the design of notations. This minimum number of notation means a user will have minimized learning efforts. Research shows that the average subset of BPMN used in process models consists of just nine different symbols [14]. Notation pool and lanes are dropped because they are used for expressing process collaborations. In the lightweight process modeling process collaboration can be expressed from an individual business partner perspective and an integrated view will be generated by the process editor. We have further adapted the notation for multiple instance business processes. The symbols adopted are presented in Fig. 1 Adopted Symbols from BPMN.

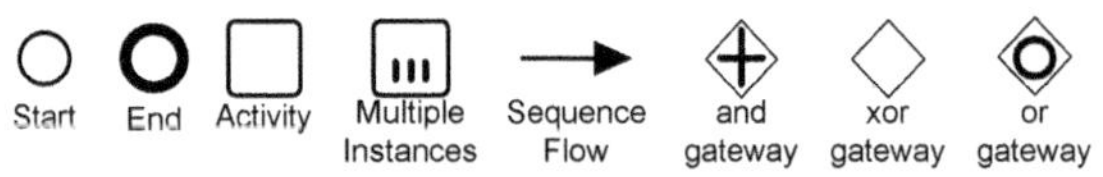

Fig. 1. Adopted Symbols from BPMN

We have also used the eight most frequently used workflow patterns (see Fig. 2) from [15] as our process patterns. The patterns can be captured within most common business process models and have a well-defined formal foundation.

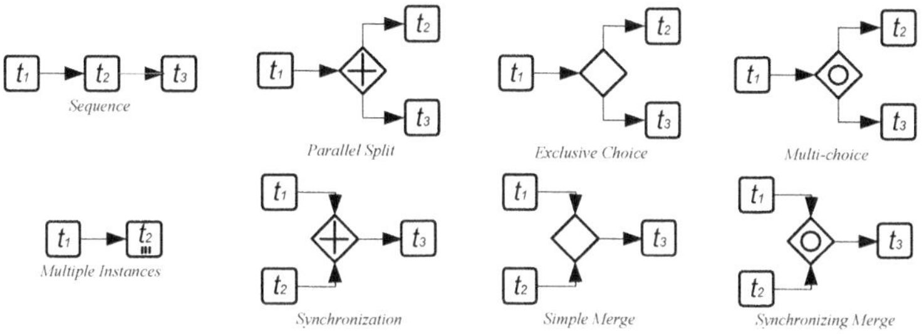

Fig. 2. Basic Process Patterns

These workflow patterns from [15] are however too fine-grained and have insufficiently information on the context and results to represent a reusable solution. Therefore, we introduce process templates that are different combinations of process patterns. The processes represented by a process template are sound. Certain process templates can be enriched with the information that they are valid for different domains, i.e. business context.

Using patterns, the soundness of process models can be guaranteed in certain ways [16]. The patterns can further be used to develop domain-specific process templates. Following context-aware modeling principles, it is possible to adapt the best fitting process artifacts during selections e.g., a user can fill in context information such as particular industry, location, and process name; a specific process template will appear to the users accordingly.

5 Data Flow Modeling for Process-Oriented Mashups

Data flow patterns aim to capture the various ways in which data is represented and utilized within processes. Russell et.al. present 40 data-related patterns for process-aware information systems [17] which are divided into four distinct groups: data visibility, data interaction, data transfer and data-based routing. Data visibility relates to the extent and manner in which data elements can be viewed by the various activities of a process. Data interaction focuses on the manner in which data is communicated between active elements within a workflow. Data transfer considers the means by which the actual transfer of data elements occurs between activities or sub-processes and describes the various mechanisms by which data elements can be passed across the interface of an activity or sub-process. Data-based routing characterizes the manner in which data elements can influence the operation of other aspects of the workflow, particularly from a control flow perspective.

See [18] for a discussion on data integration related issues of the current mashup tools. Data flow operators to be performed on either the structure of the data, or on the data itself. Data is generated and updated using different data refresh plans, such as pull and push strategies. The pull strategy is based on frequent and repetitive requests from the client; there are two ways to handle pull interval. In a global strategy, this will be set for the whole application. But in the local strategy, each data source is given its own refresh interval. In the push strategy, the client does not send requests but is required register with the server.

According to the definition of the data flow patterns in [17], the data operators and data refresh strategies in data-oriented mashups only cover data transfer, data interaction, and data routing. Data visibility is not covered by data-oriented mashups. The most popular data operators in the current data-oriented mashups are ``Union", ``Join", ``Sort" and ``Filter". A comparison of IBM mashup tool, Yahoo Pipes, Microsoft popfly and Google mashup editor is presented in [8].

From the business process application perspective, all data flow operators can be implemented using data transfer web services. In a process-oriented enterprise mashup, the data flow operators are not limited by the mashup providers. Collecting a library of web services which can support different data operators is useful and powerful for end users.

We have chosen 13 out of 40 dataflow patterns, i.e., three dataflow patterns for data visibility, five patterns for data interaction, three patterns for data transfer mechanisms, and two patterns for data-based routing. Multi-instance patterns are selected, which BPEL does not support. These 13 dataflow patterns provide an expressive power for the lightweight language. We do not expect that end users will be able to understand them completely when they first start to complete a mashup. However, we expect that they will be easily learned from existing process templates, reference models, and other process fragments.

6 Model Personal Collaborative Activity

To illustrate our idea we have modeled a personal collaborative activity that is often associated with social networks. A user named Lorraine uses data from three social websites to build her personal preferences about music, recipes, and book collections, as shown in Figure 3. Lorraine subscribes to RSS feeds from a popular music review website. She is only interested in piano pieces from Mozart. If any information in the

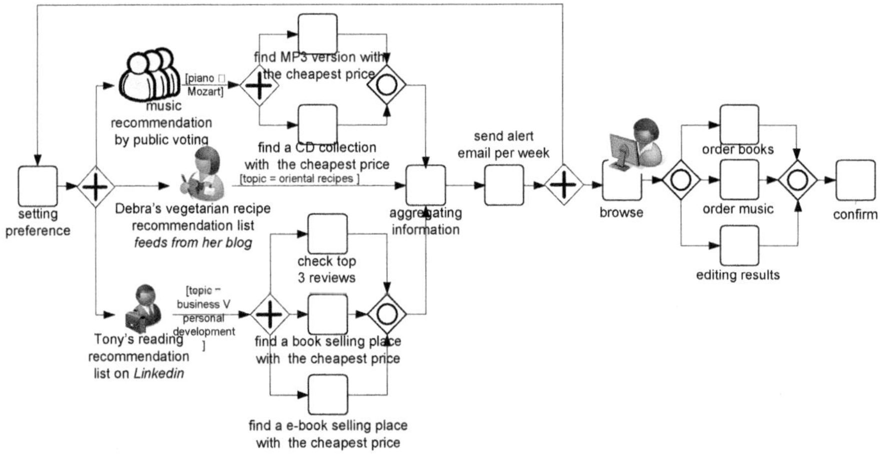

Fig. 3. Personal Collaborative Activity Scenario

feed is related Mozart's music, two web services are used to find the cheapest MP3 version and CD version from the Web. Lorraine also collects oriental vegetarian recipes from Debra's blog. Finally, she follows Tony's reading recommendation list on Linked-In. The topics of all books recommended by Tony on business or personal development will be selected. After receiving these book titles, Lorraine wants to read the top three reviews and find the cheapest price for the paperbacks, as well as any e-book versions.

All information related with music, recipes and books will be aggregated in the process. An alert email is sent to Lorraine every week. After Lorraine reads the aggregated information, she can decide whether to order books, music or save the results. She can also further trace the orders, etc.

7 Conclusions

Web-based technologies not only impact our communication patterns, but also provide opportunities to bring information and knowledge to our daily activities. Process composition in a process-oriented mashup provides an agile approach to adapting to changing business environments for virtual enterprises. This paper has presented the new concept of a process-oriented mashup. A lightweight process modeling method is provided for modeling the needs of a process-oriented enterprise mashup. The current version of the lightweight business process modeling language has eight graphical symbols and eight control flow patterns. A range of executable process templates are in used and development is continuing. Thirteen dataflow patterns have been chosen to support the current needs of perimeter enterprise applications. The primary evaluation of the lightweight process model method and language can be found from [7], [8].

Finally, we would like to emphasize that process-oriented mashups will not completely replace core business process management systems. Process-oriented mashup applications address different needs and are built for just a handful of users, applications that are used for only a few weeks or months, or situational applications that address a small piece of functionality. Process-mashups can serve users with different modeling skills for collaboration within a virtual enterprise environment.

Acknowledgement

The authors would like to thank the EU SOA4All and FAST projects. Part of work by Dr. Lai Xu and Dr. Paul de Vrieze was performed at the SAP Research, Switzerland.

References

1. Papazoglou, M.P., Georgakopoulos, D.: Service-oriented Computing. Communications of the ACM 46(10), 24–28 (2003)
2. de Vrieze, P., Xu, L., Bouguettayay, A., Yang, J., Chen, J.: Process-oriented Enterprise Mahsups. In: 2009 Workshops at the Grid and Pervasive Computing Conference 2009 Workshops at the Grid and Pervasive Computing Conference (2009)
3. de Vrieze, P., Xu, L., Xie, L.: Situational Enterprise Services. Encyclopedia of E-Business Development and Management in the Digital Economy. Idea Group Publishing (accepted)

4. Xie, L., de Vrieze, P., Xu, L.: When Social Software Meets Business Process Management. In: 2009 International Conference on Computer Sciences and Convergence Information Technology (ICCIT 2009), Seoul, Korea, November 24-26 (2009)
5. van der Aalst, W.M.P., Barthelmess, P., Ellis, C.A., Wainer, J.: Workflow Modeling using Proclets. In: Scheuermann, P., Etzion, O. (eds.) CoopIS 2000. LNCS, vol. 1901, pp. 198–209. Springer, Heidelberg (2000)
6. van der Aalst, W.M.P., Barthelmess, P., Ellis, C.A., Wainer, J.: Proclets: A Framework for Lightweight Interacting Workflow Processes. International Journal of Cooperative Information Systems 10(4), 443–482 (2001)
7. Xie, L., Xu, L., de Vrieze, P.: Lightweight Business Process Modelling. In: 2010 International Conference on E-Business and E-Government (ICEE 2010), Guangzhou, China, May 7-9 (2010)
8. Xie, L., Xu, L., de Vrieze, P.: Process Modelling in Process-oriented Enterprise Mashups. In: 2010 The 2nd IEEE International Conference on Information management and engineering (IEEE ICIME 2010), Chengdu, China, April 16-18 (2010)
9. Medicke, J., McDavid, D.: Patterns for Business Process Modeling. Business Integration Journal 1, 32–35 (2004)
10. Buschmann, F., Henney, K., Schmidt, D.C.: Past, Present, and Future Trends in Software Patterns. IEEE Software 24(7/8), 31–37 (2007)
11. Tran, H.N., Coulette, B., Dong, B.T.: Broadening the Use of Process Patterns for Modeling Processes. In: Proc. SEKE, Knowledge Systems Institute Graduate Schools, pp. 57–62 (2007)
12. Riehle, D., Zullighoven, H.: Understanding and using patterns in software development. Theory and Practice of Object Systems 2(1), 3–13 (1996)
13. Gamma, E., Helm, R., Johnson, R., Vlissides, J.: Design Patterns Elements of Reusable Object-Oriented Software. Addison-Wesley Publishing Company, Reading (1995)
14. zur Muehlen, M.: How much BPMN do you need? BPM Research, http://www.bpm-research.com/2008/03/03/how-much-bpmn-do-you-need/
15. van der Aalst, W.M.P., ter Hofstede, A.H.M., Kiepuszewski, B., Barros, A.P.: Workflow Patterns. Distributed and Parallel Databases 14(3), 5–51 (2003)
16. Gschwind, T., Koehler, J., Wong, J.: Applying Patterns during Business Process Modeling. In: Dumas, M., Reichert, M., Shan, M.-C. (eds.) BPM 2008. LNCS, vol. 5240, pp. 4–19. Springer, Heidelberg (2008)
17. Russell, N., ter Hofstede, A.H.M., Edmond, D., van der Aalst, W.M.P.: Workflow Data Patterns. QUT Technical report, FIT-TR-2004-01, Queensland University of Technology, Brisbane (2004)
18. Di Lorenzo, G., Hacid, H., Paik, H.-y., Benatallah, B.: Data Integration in Mashups SIGMOD Record (2009)

Integration of the Supplier Capacity for Choosing the Less Risky Schedule within an Uncertain Environment

Romain Guillaume[1,2], Caroline Thierry[1], and Bernard Grabot[2]

[1] Université de Toulouse IRIT / UTM 5, Allées A. Machado, 31058 Toulouse Cedex 1, France
guillaum@irit.fr, thierry@univ-tlse2
[2] Université de Toulouse INPT / LGP / ENIT 47 Av. d'Azereix, BP 1629 65016 Tarbes Cedex, France
benard@enit.fr

Abstract. This communication addresses the integration of the supplier capacity in the procurement planning process of a customer within a supply chain. Since this supply chain evolves within an uncertain environment, uncertainties may be due to an ill-known demand (prevision) and to the customer production system (scraps, imprecise processing time...). Thus, we propose a collaborative process where the customer aims at taking the less risked decision. The integration of the supplier capacity in the gross requirement enables to assess the risk of back order so that the feasibility of the requirement plan. It then enables the customer to make the decisions which limit this risk.

Keywords: Planning, Decision under uncertainty, Possibility theory, Supply chain.

1 Introduction

Nowadays, companies are not competing as independent entities but as a part of collaborative supply chains. The uncertainty on the demand creates risk in the supply chain as backordering, obsolete inventory due to the bullwhip effect. To reduces this risque to different approche exist the collaboration between customer and suplier or the integration of the uncertainty into the planning process.

The collaborative processes mainly aim at reducing the supply risk [1]. The coordination of the supply chain can be realized by two different ways: the vertical and horizontal approach. The vertical is a centralized decision making which synchronize the supply chain (common way to coordinate within companies). The horizontal approach is referred to the collaborative planning (supply chain of independent entities) [2]. The industrial collaborative process has been standardized for implementing cooperation between retailers and manufactures. This process is called "Collaborative Planning, Forecasting and Replenishment" (CPFR®) [3].

These techniques aim at creating short and reactive decision loops between customers and suppliers in order to cope with the growing uncertainty on demand forecasting, due to the shortening of the product life cycle and to customers' versatility.

L.M. Camarinha-Matos et al. (Eds.): PRO-VE 2010, IFIP AICT 336, pp. 509–516, 2010.

Within these supply chains, the collaborative processes are usually characterised by a set of point-to-point (customer / supplier) relationships with partial information sharing [1].

More precisely, a procurement plan, or several procurement plans, are built and propagated through the supply chain. Taking into account the uncertainty of the demand in the planning processes itself can be another solution for making more "informed decisions" [4][5][6]. And then integrate the uncertainty into the cooperative planning processes with the suppliers, what we propose in this article.

Within this context, this communication focuses on the integration of imperfection on the customer's gross requirements, taking into account his knowledge on the capacity of the suppliers, with the final goal to cope with an uncertain environment (linked to demand, scraps, processing time...)...

The theory of possibility and the theory of fuzzy sets [7][8] are often used to model the uncertainty when historical data can hardly be obtained or are obsolete [9][10][11]. Different models have been used to represent the imperfection on the requirements. [6] represents the imprecision on the quantity by a trapezoidal fuzzy number; [5] integrates the uncertainty on the order and the imprecision on the quantity to compute the demand.

In a previous work (see [12]), we consider the uncertainty on the order itself, so that the imprecision and the uncertainty on the quantity and on the date. Moreover, the dependencies between the requirements are considered (see [4]) to compute a gross requirement, modelled by a graph. This graph has possibility levels on arcs and fuzzy quantities on nodes.

In this communication, we propose a method to integrate the supplier capacity before choosing the final procurement plan and the associated production sequence. This method is composed of three steps: 1) design of the graph which represents all possible gross requirements (section 2), 2) computation of the level of feasibility of each node (section 3), 3) choice of the final schedule (section 4).

2 Gross Requirement

In this section is first introduced the model of requirements and dependencies, followed by the method to design a graph representing these possible requirements.

2.1 Model of Requirements

We consider that the customer has a make-to-Order production. In this context, the requirements of components are expressed by a quantity for a date which can be both imperfect (uncertain and/or imprecise). Moreover, the requirement itself can be uncertain (i.e. may be cancelled). Possibility theory is suggested to represent these imperfections. The requirement is thus composed by two sets of fuzzy sets: the first one represents the imperfect quantities and the uncertainty on the requirement, whereas the second one represents the imperfectly known date. For instance, Figure 1 represents an imperfect requirement (this model is developed in [12] and [13]).

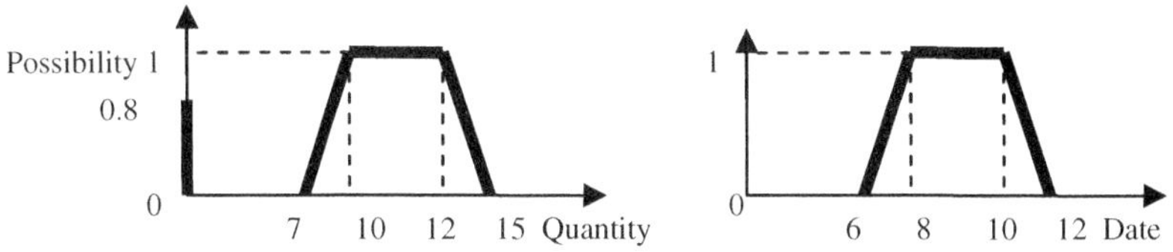

Fig. 1. Uncertain requirement (quantity equal at zero possible) with an imprecision on the quantity and an uncertainty and imprecision on the date

Dependencies often exist between requirements. These dependencies are linked to constraints linked to the bills of materials or to the resources (assembly lines) (see [10]). The first kind of dependency (denoted "quantity dependencies") exists if the required component appears at different levels in the bill of material of the same final product (see Figure 2).

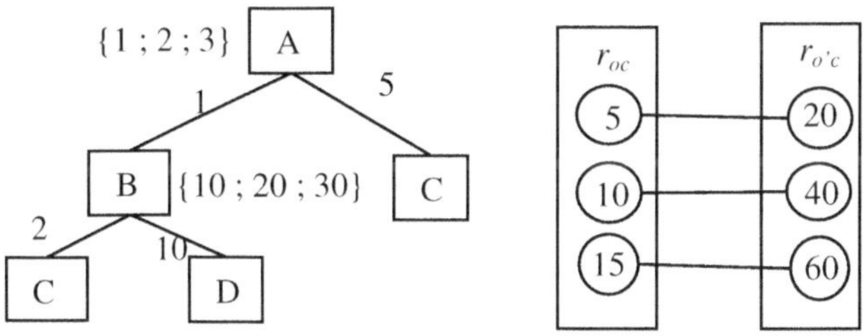

Fig. 2. Quantity dependencies; the requirement is linked with the requirement $r_{o'c}$ by the component B. The possible quantities of r_{oc} are linked with the possible quantities of $r_{o'c}$. When r_{oc} is equal at 5 then $r_{o'c}$ is equal to 20 (similarly, 10 with 40 and 15 with 60).

On the other hand, requirements processed on the same assembly line can be linked by "precedence dependencies" (see Figure 3).

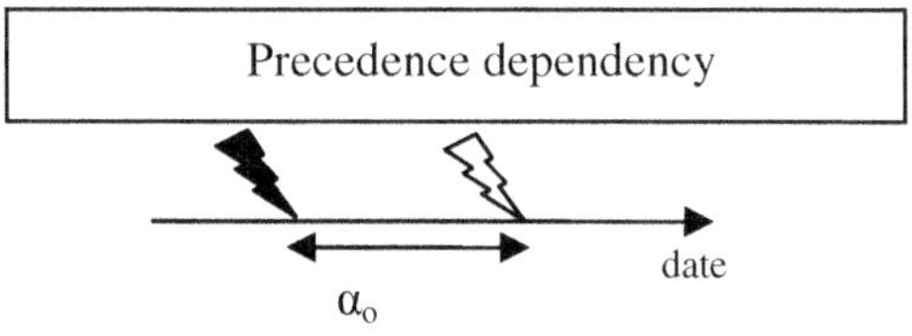

Fig. 3. Illustration of a "precedence dependency" between two requirements: the requirement r_o (black) and the requirement $r_{o'}$ (white)

Moreover, the customer may consider some feasible sequences evaluated with a level of preference (see Figure 4).

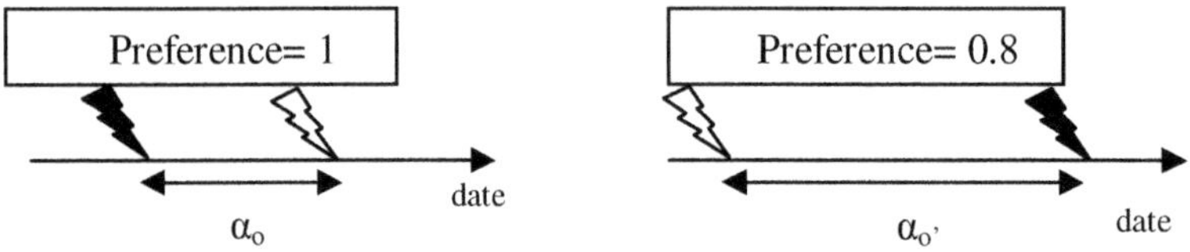

Fig. 4. Possible sequences, between two requirements: requirement r_o (black) and requirement $r_{o'}$ (white)

2.2 Gross Requirement Model

Since the supplier is supposed to perform a Make-to-Stock production, he has to compute gross requirement expressed as quantities by period from requirements expressed as quantities for date (due to make to his order production) in order to build a requirement planning.

From the information on the requirements, the dependencies and the levels of preference between two decisions, a graph which represents the gross requirements can be built. The method to design this graph is explicitly explained in [4]: the nodes (t,c_t) of the graph represent the possible quantities (represented by a trapezoidal fuzzy number) for each given period) (see Figure 5). The arcs $(t, ,c_t , c_{t+1})$ of the graph are valued by a set of characteristics $A_{t,c_t,c_{t+1}}$: a possibility level and the preference linked to a given quantity for period t and a given quantity for period $t+1$. So, the graph (see Figure 6) takes into account the imperfections on the requirements, the dependencies between requirements and the preferences on the chosen sequences.

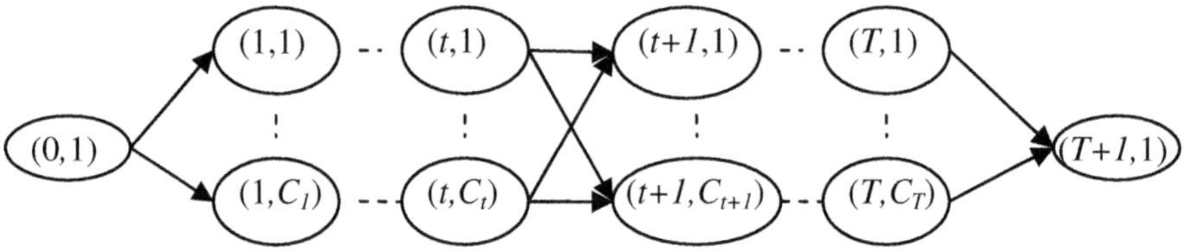

Fig. 5. Representation of gross requirements

Notations:

t: period with $t \in [1,T]$

c_t: index of fuzzy gross required quantity of period t with $c_t \in [1,C_t]$

s: index of the sequence with $s \in [1,S]$

k_s: index on the choice of sequence s with $k_s \in [1,K_s]$

$\tilde{D}_{t,c_t}$: fuzzy gross required quantity on node (t,c_t)

$A_{c_t,c_{t+1},t}$: set of characteristics of the arc (t,c_t, c_{t+1}) linking the node (t,c_t) with the node $(t+1,c_{t+1})$

$w_{c_t,c_{t+1},t}$: possibility level of the arc linking the node (t,c_t) with the node $(t+1,c_{t+1})$

μ_{s,k_s} : preference level of a sequence s for the choice k_s

The set $A_{c_t,c_{t+1},t}$ is defined by $A_{c_t,c_{t+1},t} = \{w_{c_t,c_{t+1},t}; \mu_{1,k_1}; \ldots; \mu_{S,k_S}\}$.

3 Computation of Feasibility Level

This section addresses the computation of the feasibility of the graph by considering the delivering constraints of the supplier. These constraints are ill-known. The delivering capacity of the supplier can be transmitted by the supplier himself. The customer may also have his own knowledge on these constraints (in this study we focus on the computation of the level of feasibility and not on the problem of confidentiality of data and degree of collaboration between the customer and the supplier). The supply constraints are modeled by triangular fuzzy number (see Figure 7). To compute the level of feasibility of the gross requirements, the inventories or backorders are considered. Thus, we evaluate the necessity to satisfy the gross requirements with the possible delivered quantity (production plus inventories minus backorders).

Notations:

input data:

$\tilde{C}_t$: maximum supply capacity of the period t

$\tilde{D}_{t,c_t}$: gross required quantity (t,c_t)

$w_{c_t,c_{t+1},t}$: possibility level of the arc linking the node (t,c_t) with the node $(t+1,c_{t+1})$

Dependent parameters:

$\tilde{I}'_{t,c_t}$: possible inventory which can be positive or negative, for the node (t,c_t)

$\tilde{I}_{t,c_t}$: inventory of the node (t,c_t)

$\tilde{B}_{t,c_t}$: backorders of the node (t,c_t)

Ouput data:

$\Phi_{t,i}$: level of feasibility of the gross required quantity (t,c_t)

The fuzzy numbers $\tilde{F}$ are expressed as quadruplets $(a_F; b_F; c_F; d_F)$. The level of feasibility is computed using algorithm 1. The possible inventory level of the previous nodes is firstly computed, then the feasibility of the nodes is assessed and the critical general fuzzy inventory is deduced. Finally, the fuzzy inventory and the fuzzy backorder levels are estimated.

Algorithm 1. Computation of feasibility level

Input: Graph $G = <V, A>$, and fuzzy supplier Capacity $\tilde{C}_t$;

Output: level of feasibility of each node Φ_{t,c_t};

For each t **do**

For each note (t,c_t) **do**

For each $c_{t-1} \big| w_{c_{t-1},c_t,t-1} \neq 0$ **do**

//computation of the possible inventory level of the previous nodes//

If $\tilde{B}_{t-1,c_{t-1}} = 0$

Then $\tilde{I}'_{t,c_t,c_{t-1}} = \tilde{I}_{t-1,c_{t-1}} (+) \tilde{C}_t (-) \tilde{D}_{t,c_t}$;

Else $\tilde{I}'_{t,c_t,c_{t-1}} = \tilde{C}_t (-) \tilde{B}_{t-1,c_{t-1}} (-) \tilde{D}_{t,c_t}$;

End if

End for each

//computation of the feasibility of the nodes//

$$\Phi_{t,c_t} = \min_{c_{t-1}}(\Phi_{t,c_t,c_{t-1}}) = \min_{c_{t-1} \big| w_{c_{t-1},c_t,t-1} \neq 0} \left(\left(1 - \mathrm{N}\left(\tilde{I}'_{t,c_t,c_{t-1}} \geq 0\right)\right) \times w_{c_{t-1},c_t} \right);$$

//computation of the critical fuzzy general inventory level//

$$\tilde{I}'_{t,c_t} = \tilde{I}'_{t,c_t,c_{t-1}} \big| \Phi_{t,c_t} = \Phi_{t,c_t,c_{t-1}};$$

//computation of the fuzzy inventory and fuzzy backorder levels//

$$\tilde{I}_{t,c_t} = \begin{Bmatrix} a_{\tilde{I}_{t,c_t}} = \max(0; a_{\tilde{I}'_{t,c_t}}); b_{\tilde{I}_{t,c_t}} = \max(0; b_{\tilde{I}'_{t,c_t}}) \\ c_{\tilde{I}_{t,c_t}} = \max(0; c_{\tilde{I}'_{t,c_t}}); d_{\tilde{I}_{t,c_t}} = \max(0; d_{\tilde{I}'_{t,c_t}}) \end{Bmatrix};$$

$$\tilde{B}_{t,c_t} = \begin{Bmatrix} a_{\tilde{B}_{t,c_t}} = \max(0; -a_{\tilde{I}'_{t,c_t}}); b_{\tilde{B}_{t,c_t}} = \max(0; -b_{\tilde{I}'_{t,c_t}}) \\ c_{\tilde{B}_{t,c_t}} = \max(0; -c_{\tilde{I}'_{t,c_t}}); d_{\tilde{B}_{t,c_t}} = \max(0; -d_{\tilde{I}'_{t,c_t}}) \end{Bmatrix};$$

End for each

End for each

Return Φ_{t,c_t};

4 Choice of the Manufacturing Sequence

From the feasibility level and the knowledge on the manufacturing sequences, the "risk" r_{s,k_s} linked to the choice k_s for the sequence s (equation (1)) is computed. The choice K_s is made, which maximizes the preference level in the set of the less "risky" decisions (equation (2)).

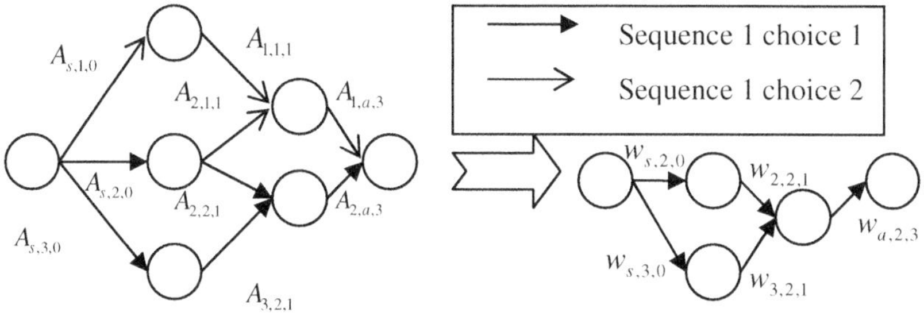

Fig. 6. Representation of graph before and after the integration of supplier capacity. The graph has two possible choices for one sequence (left graph). The decision is taken and the resulting graph is on the right side of the figure (choice 1 has been selected).

The preferences between two sequences are considered as less important than the "risk". Therefore, the preferences are used for the choice between two sequences of equivalent risk. After making all the choices on the sequences, the graph is reduced. The characteristics of the arcs (t, ,c_t , c_{t+1}) $A_{t,c_t,c_{t+1}}$ are reduced to the possibility level $w_{c_t,c_{t+1},t}$. Figure 7 shows an example of graph before and after decision. In the initial graph (before the decision), there are two possible choices for one sequence. After the decision (choice 1), the resulted graph is obtained.

$$r_{s,k} = \max_{t,c_t \,|\, \mu_{s,k_s} \in A_{c_{t-1},c_t,t-1}} (1-\Phi_{t,c_t}). \tag{1}$$

$$K_s = k_s \Big|_{\max_{k_s \,|\, r_{s,k_s} = \min_{k_s}(r_{s,k_s})} (\mu_{s,k_s})}. \tag{2}$$

5 Conclusion

In this paper, a model of gross requirement plan which takes into account the imperfections on the requirements, the dependencies between requirements and the possible manufacturing sequences has been presented and the Delivering capacity of the supplier. A method allowing to compute the feasibility of each sequence, then to choose a sequence has been proposed. This method allows the customer to choose the less risky sequence in terms of backorder.

In collaborative process the customer and the supplier could negotiate on the delivering capacity, the risk level and a price. In fact, if the risk of the optimal solution is too high the customer can ask the supplier to propose a other delivering constrains (of course with a cost).

Acknowledgments. This study has been performed with the support of Région Midi-Pyrénées and of the University of Toulouse.

References

1. Galasso, F., Mercé, C., Grabot, B.: Decision support for supply chain planning under uncertainty. In: 12th IFAC International Symposium Information Control Problems in Manufacturing (INCOM), St-Etienne, France, pp. 233–238 (2006)
2. Dudek, G.: Collaborative planning in Supply Chains. Lecture notes in economics and mathematical systems, pp. 533 (2004)
3. Ireland, R., Crum, C.: Supply chain Collaboration: how to implement CPFR® and other best collaborative practices. Integrated Business Management series and APICS (2005)
4. Guillaume, R., Thierry, C., Grabot, B.: Integration of ill-known requirements with dependencies into a gross requirement plan. In: 8ème ENIM IFAC Conférence Internationale de Modélisation et Simulation, Hammamet, Tunisia, May 10-12 (2010)
5. Grabot, B., Geneste, L., Reynoso Castillo, G., Vérot, S.: Integration of uncertain and imprecise orders in the MRP method. Journal of Intelligent Manufacturing 16(2), 215–234 (2005)
6. Fargier, H., Thierry, C.: The use of Possibilistic Decision Theory in Manufacturing, Planning and Control: Recent Results in Fuzzy Master Production Scheduling. In: Slowinski, R., Hapke, M. (eds.). Studies in fuzziness and soft computing, vol. 36, pp. 45–59. Springer, Heidelberg (2000)
7. Zadeh, L.A.: Fuzzy sets as a basis for a theory of possibility. Fuzzy Sets and Systems 1, 3–28 (1978)
8. Dubois, D., Prade, H.: Possibility Theory. Plenum Press, New York (1988)
9. Peidro, D., Mula, J., Poler, R., Verdegay, J.L.: Fuzzy optimization for supply chain planning under supply, demand and process uncertainties. Fuzzy Sets and Systems 160(18), 2640–2657 (2009)
10. Lan, Y.F., Liu, Y.K., Sun, G.J.: Modeling fuzzy multi-period production planning and sourcing problem with credibility service levels. Journal of Computational and Applied Mathematics 231(1), 208–221 (2009)
11. Aliev, R.A., Fazlollahi, B., Guirimov, B.G., Aliev, R.R.: Fuzzy-genetic approach to aggregate production–distribution planning in supply chain management. Information Sciences 177(20), 4241–4255 (2007)
12. Guillaume, R., Thierry, C., Grabot, B.: Intégration de besoins en composants mal connus dans un plan. In: 8ème Congrès International de Génie Industriel (CIGI 2009), Bagnères de Bigorre, France, June 10-12 (2009a)
13. Guillaume, R., Thierry, C., Grabot, B.: Integration of ill-known requirement into a plan. In: 39th International Conference on Computer and Industrial Engineering (CIE39), Troyes, France, July 6-8 (2009b)

The Impact of Inter-organizational Social Capital in Collaborative Networks Competitiveness: An Empirical Analysis

Janaina Macke[1], Rolando Vargas Vallejos[2], Kadígia Faccin[3], and Denise Genari[4]

[1] TSO – Social Theory Research Group, University of Caxias do Sul,
R. Francisco Getúlio Vargas, 1130,
95020-972 Caxias do Sul, RS, Brazil
jmacke@terra.com.br
[2] rolandovvallejos@hotmail.com
[3] kadigia@msn.com
[4] denisegenari@hotmail.com

Abstract. With the social context of collaborative networks becoming increasingly important, research has broadened the traditional concept of competitiveness to include and emphasize 'soft' elements, like social capital. The social capital concept can be attained in two different contexts: intra and inter-groups. The objective of this study is to identify inter-organizational social capital elements and the relationship with collaborative network competitiveness. We intend to provide answers to these questions: (i) what are the elements that explain inter-organizational social capital? (ii) how are these elements related to competitiveness? (iii) what organizational characteristics facilitate social capital formation? A survey was conducted in the enterprises from the Brazilian Wine Industry Cluster. The data were analyzed using factorial analysis and bivariate correlations. The results point out three social capital factors that correspond to the social capital dimensions found in literature: structural, relational and cognitive. The research shows that the correlations among social capital dimensions and competitiveness are strong and significant, specially the structural and relational dimensions. Finally, implications for research and managerial practice were discussed.

Keywords: inter-organizational social capital, collaborative networks, competitiveness, Brazilian Wine Industry Cluster.

1 Introduction

Collaborative networks are organizational forms based on the collaboration between its members, according to a specific shared goal.

A collaborative network organization (CNO) is a form of emerging organizational setting that involves mutual engagement of participants to solve a problem together, which implies mutual trust, and therefore takes time, effort and dedication. A CNO can be created from a regional grouping of companies that already have a longstanding relationship and a cultural history [1].

L.M. Camarinha-Matos et al. (Eds.): PRO-VE 2010, IFIP AICT 336, pp. 517–526, 2010.

The associative capacity depends on the degree that communities, groups and businesses share norms and values and are prepared to subordinate individual interests to those of larger groups. From these shared values trust emerges [2].

Collaborative networks organizations are structured primarily to make a favorable position against the competition. Therefore, internal resources presented in the group should be valued because they can become the source of competitive advantages [3], [4], [5], [6].

The resource-based view assumes that the most important variables are, in general, those that are less measurable and identifiable. We can see this statement in the case of social capital elements and the measurement difficulties. Moreover, internal resources become a source of competitive advantage when they have unique historical conditions, thus they are rare and difficult to imitate [7].

In this sense, social capital becomes a strongly competitive resource, enhancing the individual and collective capacity through the collaborative practices. Like the other forms of capital, it is productive, making possible the achievement of goals that would be unattainable without its existence becoming a public good [8], [9].

The present study aims to identify inter-organizational social capital elements and the relationship with collaborative network competitiveness. We intend to provide answers to these questions: (i) what are the elements that explain inter-organizational social capital? (ii) how are these elements related to competitiveness? (iii) what organizational characteristics facilitate social capital formation?

2 Theoretical Background

The social capital produces socio-cultural goods, in the form of emotions, feelings and relationships [10]. Social capital is the "sum of the actual and potential resources embedded within, available through and derived from the network of relationship possessed by an individual or social unit". The interaction between the agents of the network is what gives shape to relationships [11].

Many links form a dense network [12], with unique relational features [11], which positively affect the economic results and business competitive advantage [13], [14], [15]. When there is trust – the most important social capital element -, there is an expansion of horizontal contacts and consequently, business relationships [11]. The network formation involves interaction with a large number of people [7].

High levels of social capital enable better use of development opportunities [8], due to increased information that facilitate the action [16], [17].

Thus, confidence, stability, durability of relationships and the network density are key elements to high levels of trust and cooperation. These qualities also influence the clarity and visibility of mutual obligations [8], [11], [16].

In the study of Social Capital and its importance in the creation of intellectual capital, Nahapiet and Ghoshal [11] proposed three Social Capital dimensions, which are: structural, relational and cognitive. In the structural dimension of Social Capital we analyzed: the presence or not of relationships between the actors, the configuration or morphology of the network, describing the standards of connections, through variables as density, connectivity network configuration, stability and ties.

The relational dimension describes the kind of personal relationship, developed through a history of interactions [12]. This concept focuses on aspects that influence the behaviors, like respect and friendship, which are going to decide on sociability, acceptance and prestige. Two actors can occupy similar positions in a network, however if their emotional and personal attitudes differ, their actions will be different in many aspects; therefore it is related to a behavioral component, which is revealed through facets as trust and distrust [17], [8], [18], norms [8], [16], obligations and expectations [16], [12] participation and diversity tolerance [11]. The third dimension of Social Capital, cognitive, refers to the resources that emanate shared visions, interpretations and systems of meaning, mainly codes and narratives, shared values and other cultural elements. Some authors affirm that this dimension is not being explored in the literature [11].

The social capital level presented in a network, facilitates member's access to opportunities and initiatives for collaborative action. Therefore, social capital can be considered the basic resource for a competitive strategy based on cooperation [7]. For the social capital flow among organizations, the presence of four main conditions is necessary such as time, interaction, interdependence and closure [11].

A collaborative network can be more competitive and have greater success when investing in two key elements that are: organizational culture and people (relationships). Firms within a network have a greater number of alliances and thus become more able to remain competitive and to introduce a complex repertoire of actions which aim competitiveness improvement [19].

3 Methodological Aspects

In order to evaluate inter-organizational social capital and its relations with competitiveness, we chose the survey technique of collecting data.

We made an extensive theoretical investigation from the literature of the most important studies on social capital [20], [11], 21], collaborative networks and competitiveness [22], [15]. After a meta-analysis phase, we started to build variables that could take part in an inter-organizational social capital survey, in the network context.

The final instrument version contains 66 variables divided into 3 blocks: i) social capital variables; ii) competitiveness variables and iii) control variables (number of employees, time dedicated to network activities, motivation to participate in the network, company revenue, length of association, gender, age, and educational level.

All items were measured using a five-point Likert scale (1=strongly disagree; 5=strongly agree). Before formal survey, we conducted semi-structured interviews with three experts in collaborative networks and social capital theory to validate our scale items. We also ran a pre-test with ten respondents.

A survey was conducted in the enterprises from the Brazilian Wine Industry Cluster (directors as respondents). The data were analyzed using factorial analysis and bivariate correlations.

4 Results: Context and Discussion

One of the most prosperous Brazilian states, Rio Grande do Sul is known especially for its grain, wine production, cattle, agribusiness, and for its considerable industrial output. The main products exported by Rio Grande do Sul are shoes, tobacco, automobiles, grains, beef, leather, and chemical products.

The Serra Gaúcha, The Gaucho Highlands, is the mountainous region in the northeastern portion of Rio Grande do Sul state in southern Brazil. The wine cluster production of Serra Gaúcha is responsible for 80% of the national production.

Brazil occupies the 17th position in the ranking of wine producers in the world. Figured as the fifth largest producer of the southern hemisphere, which includes countries of more recent production, exceeded only by Argentina, Australia, South Africa and Chile [23].

The number of wine companies in Rio Grande do Sul increased from 439 in 2001 to 682 companies in 2006, according to data from IBRAVIN (Brazilian Institute of Wine). Of the total 1.35 million tons of grapes produced in 2007 in the country, 705 thousand tones came from Rio Grande do Sul soil. The chain of grape and wine, represents an important part of the state's economy. It is estimated to exceed R$ 1 billion Brazilian *reais* (US$ 625 million dollars) [24].

The Brazilian wine industry is going through some difficulties. In addition to the unfavorable world stage with the intensification of global competition where wine producing countries implement aggressive strategic actions, there are internal adverse conditions in Brazil: (i) low consumption of wine per-capita (1.8 l/pp) compared to Argentina and Uruguay (30 l/pp); (ii) there is a lack in the culture: moderate drinking wine with meals; (iii) high incidence of taxes (42% of the price), in Argentina and Chile remains at half of that [23].

However, some private and even government agencies stimulate the formation of collaborative networks in southern Brasil. Serra Gaúcha became the region where the formation of networks was eased up by the culture and the history of immigration bringing to light the culture of mutual assistance and cooperation for the local development. In addition to the networks of cooperation in this emerging industry, other agents form the basis for sustaining the wine industry such as higher education institutions and government agencies.

4.1 An Inter-organizational Social Capital Instrument

The data were submitted to factor analysis using PCA (Principal Component Analysis), with varimax rotation and treatment pairwise (considered all valid observations of each variable) for the missing data. The index of Kaiser-Meyer-Olkin (KMO) adequacy of the sample was 0.848 and the Bartlett's Test of Sphericity - (significant to 0.000) indicated the factorability of data.

The results of factor analysis suggested that social capital is shown by three factors, with 67.36% of total variance explained. The Cronbach´s Alpha for this scale was 0.928, that represents a very good range for an exploratory study [25]. It is possible to conclude that the items in each dimension of the construct are suitable for measuring the social capital in collaborative networks context (Table 1).

Table 1. Inter-Organizational Social Capital Items and Results from the Brazilian Wine Industry Cluster

Factor		Items	Loading	Mean
Relational	0,919 *	8 - Even if my opinion is contrary to most other members of the network, I feel comfortable to discuss it.	0.801	3.65
		12- The differences within the group do not affect the network.	0.790	3.32
		15 - Within the network, the members think and act in accordance with the interests of all.	0.697	3.31
		14 - When I need help, I can count on other members of the network.	0.642	3.23
		21 - Within the network there are several opportunities to exchange information.	0.621	3.13
		18 - In the formal activities of the network, I do feel part of a group.	0.600	3.63
		6 - The similarities between participants facilitate the dynamics of the network.	0.567	3.26
		11 – I identify with the members of the network.	0.532	3.65
		10 - The members of the network always seek to work together through ideas, resources and information.	0.487	3.51
Structural	0,923 *	13 - Problems of human resource development and training in my company are often discussed in meetings of the network.	0.806	2.40
		26- I have contact with members of the network at least once a week.	0.784	2.86
		22 - I consider the members of the network my friends.	0.705	3.71
		24 - If I need some information for a decision, I know where to find on the network.	0.656	3.18
		2 - The members of the network always share information with others.	0.638	3.38
		27 - The network organizes group activities with our partners: training, trade shows and events in general in the local community.	0.612	3.26
		5 - There are no barriers to communication between my company and network partners in the exchange of professional knowledge.	0.588	3.48
		25 - The network is connected to other entities, as other networks of businesses, unions, government agencies, among others.	0.584	3.74
		4 - I participate in the network because I agree with the purpose for which it was created.	0.561	3.93
Cognitive	0,705 *	16 - Most members of the network participate on events proposed (meetings, exhibitions, lectures, seminars, trips, etc.).	0.766	3.53
		3 - The objective of the network is also clear to those not participating in the network.	0.755	2.85
		1 - Most members know and agree with the objective of the network.	0.568	3.74

Table 2. Competitiveness Items and Results from the Brazilian Wine Industry Cluster

Factor		Items	Loading	Mean
Organizational Assets	0,905 *	43 - My company was able to provide higher quality products and customer service after entering the network.	0.783	3.39
		36 - The network is very important to carry my business on.	0.772	3.26
		37 - When a problem occurs within the network, the members work together to solve it.	0.766	3.43
		35 - My company acquired valuable contacts in participating in the network.	0.751	3.36
		32 - If there is a conflict between members of the network, I offer to mediate.	0.732	3.32
		34 - I feel motivated to participate in the network.	0.674	3.38
		42 - The leadership of the Network respects the views of all	0.622	3.56
Endogenous Resources Appropriation	0,885 *	46 –The network promotes regional events related to products and services offered by the members.	0.859	3.18
		47 -The network contributes to the improvement of socio-cultural issues related to members, relatives and the local community.	0.821	3.08
		48 –The network promotes awareness campaigns on environmental conservation.	0.661	3.31
		41 - If there is a problem in the company of one of the members, others work to solve it	0.658	2.67
		40 - The members of the network are encouraged to propose ideas for change	0.553	3.34
		45 –The network promotes actions that aim to enhance the tourism in the region.	0.547	3.77
Networking	0,778 *	33 - Within the network there are different types of skills such as technical, managerial and social competences	0.725	3.69
		31 - I also have contact with members of the network outside the formal activities of the same.	0.575	3.63
		39 - The members are responsible for bringing new business opportunities to the network.	0.564	3.38
		38 - The activities of the network are aligned with the main objective	0.542	3.54

As one contribution of this study, Table 1 shows the variables from final solution (as they appear in the questionnaire), in order to provide an inter-organizational social capital instrument.

By analyzing the emerged factors, we observed that they represent the dimensions of social capital theory: structural, relational and cognitive. The meaning of each factor can be inferred from the content.

In the case of Brazilian Wine Cluster, the social capital is represented mainly by the relational dimension, which explains 25.60% of the total variance. The structural dimension represents 25.28% and, finally, the cognitive dimension, explains 16.48% of the total variance.

The results call attention to the fact that the levels of social capital variables are very similar, ranging from 2.40 to 3.74. Similarly, average factors were close: for the cognitive dimension, 3.37, for the structural dimension, 3.33 and for the relational, 3.41.

We concluded that there is a high level of social capital in the cluster and a general balance among the three dimensions. In this perspective, we argued that the institutional structure of the network was effectively a conductor of the creation in social capital in the cluster, as discussed below.

4.2 A Network Competitiveness Instrument

Statistical analysis for competitiveness produced three factors that summarize the original set of observed variables. Together, the three factors explain 67.994% of the total variance.

As the measurement of capital, the responses of the indicator of competitiveness were also submitted to factorial analysis (PCA) with varimax rotation and pairwise treatment for the missing data. The index of Kaiser-Meyer-Olkin (KMO) adequacy of the sample was 0.868 and the Bartlett's Test of Sphericity - (significant to 0.000) indicated the factorability of data.

In the case of the Brazilian Wine Cluster, the competitiveness is represented mainly by the organizational assets, which explains 29.47% of the total variance. The endogenous resources appropriation represents 22.64% and, finally, the networking, explains 15.88% of the total variance. The total explained variance of the construct was, therefore, 67.99% (Table 2).

After building the scales of social capital and competitiveness to measure these constructs in the case of the wine cluster, we sought to examine whether there were significant relationships between the social capital level in a network and its competitiveness.

The Relational social capital showed the higher correlation with Endogenous Resources Appropriation, as well as Cognitive social capital. This indicates that a better use of local characteristics comes from the existence of ties among network participants. In the context of wine cluster many values are linked to the community, which may explain why correlation is also strongly associated with cognitive dimension (Table 3).

Table 3. Social Capital and Competitiveness Relations in the Brazilian Wine Industry Cluster

Factors	Relational social capital	Structured social capital	Cognitive social capital
Organizational Assets	0.796**	0.860**	0.460**
Endogenous Resource Appropriation	0.741**	0.736**	0.516**
Networking	0.692**	0.743**	0.396**

**. Correlation is significant at the 0.01 level.

The Structural social capital provides the largest structural variations found in the dimension of Organizational Assets. It can be inferred that the network configuration determines the improvement of its competitiveness.

These results confirm the initial thesis that social capital is closely linked to the competitiveness improvement and the resource-based view defends that resources clearly provide competitive opportunities and high returns. In other words, the results show that social capital is indeed a kind of capital.

In addition, we observe that all three dimensions of social capital (cognitive, structural and relational) are based on information sharing as a mediator for use of resources that generate improvement in competitiveness.

Finally, the results support the theoretical arguments that the benefit of information is one of the key benefits of social capital, that information sharing contributes to business performance, and that different dimensions of social capital have different levels of influence on company performance.

5 Final Considerations and Future Research

The CNs have inter-organizational foundation as an example for the elimination of barriers created by the environment and/or other organizations, leading to an extensive network of collaboration among enterprises. In this case, a network can be understood as an organizational structure in which members that have dimensional, structural and financial limitations, cannot ensure the necessary conditions for survival and development alone.

Some convergent features within the members of a network are: i) the existence of more than two companies that, even collaborating with one another, remain independent, ii) the development of collective efficiency to obtain competitive advantages and overcome weaknesses and individual limitations, iii) the establishment of long-term relationship, iv) the openness to new participants who will contribute to reach the group goals. The network is usually linked to the freedom that individuals and/or organizations have to enter or leave the group, but makes possible to establish restrictions with the agreement of all members.

In order to represent the model that shows the social capital importance to competitiveness in CNs context, we adopted the idea of the intellectual capital mechanism, as Nahapiet and Ghoshal [11] used for the social capital and knowledge construction. The concept fits because this mechanism represents a continuous and dynamic process of combination and knowledge exchange (Figure 1).

The combination contributes to social capital creation through incremental changes and development of existing resources or radical changes and the combination of disconnected elements. Thus social capital can be promoted by radical or incremental resource combinations. The exchange process occurs when the parties involved have experience of joint activities, i.e., when individuals have lived the experience of working together as a team. We point out four conditions to the combination and to the exchange process: (i) the opportunity to make the combination or exchange; (ii) the worthwhile interactions; (iii) the motivation (receptivity to learning and new knowledge creation); and (iv) the combination capabilities (capacity to combine information or experience) [11].

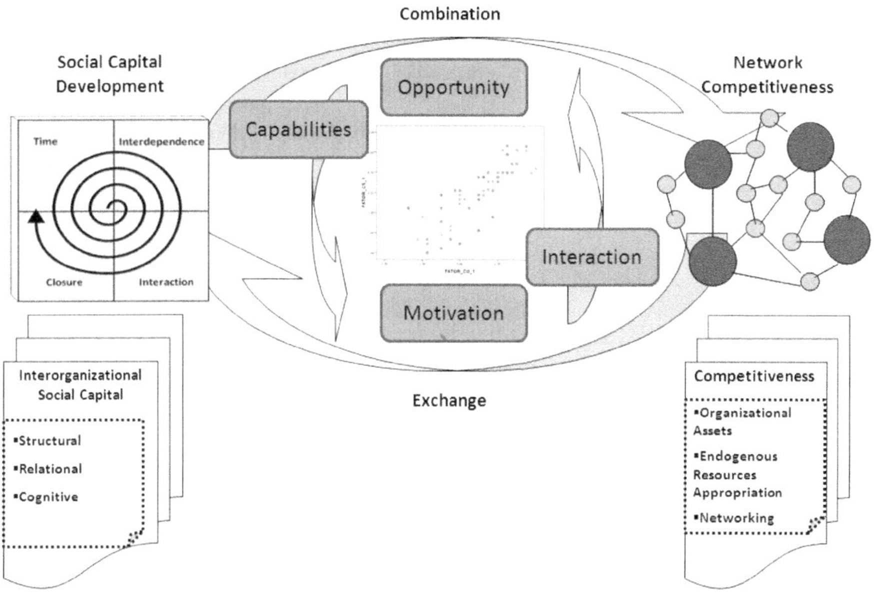

Fig. 1. Inter-organizational Social Capital and Competitiveness Model in Collaborative Networks Context

Finally, the importance of assessing social capital in collaborative networks can be summarized as: (i) high level of social trust and strong reciprocity norms, reduce the transaction costs; (ii) social networks attenuate the risks, allowing that their members engage more in innovations; (iii) social networks facilitate the fast information dissemination and with this, they reduce the asymmetries; and (iv) social networks allow that its members solve their collective problems easily.

Acknowledgments. This work is being supported by the University of Caxias do Sul (Universidade de Caxias do Sul - UCS), the Faculty of Technology TECBRASIL (Faculdade de Tecnologia TECBRASIL - FTec, and the National Counsel for Scientific and Technological Development (Conselho Nacional de Desenvolvimento Científico e Tecnológico - CNPq). We would also like to thank three unknown reviewers and our English teacher, Jane Dai-Prá.

References

1. Camarinha-Matos, L.M., Afsarmanesh, H.: The Virtual Enterprise Concept. In: Infrastructures for Virtual Enterprises: Networking Industrial Enterprises. Kluwer Academic Publishers, Boston (1999)
2. Fukuyama, F.: Trust: the social creation virtues and the creation of prosperity. Free Press, New York (1995)
3. Prahalad, C.K., Hamel, G.: The Core Competence of the corporation. Harward Business Review 68, 79–91 (1990)

4. Barney, J.: Firm resources and sustained competitive advantage. Journal of Management, Greenwich 17(1), 99–120 (1991)
5. Penrose, E.T.: The Theory of the Growth of the Firm. Oxford University Press, New York (1995)
6. Wernerfelt, B.: A Resource-based view of the firm. Strategic Management Journal 5, 171–180 (1984)
7. Macke, J., Sarate, J.A.R., Vallejos, R.V.: Collective Competence and Social Capital Analysis in Collaborative Networks. Journal of Systemics, Cybernetics and Informatics 8, 18–23 (2010)
8. Putnam, R.D., Leonardi, R., Nanetti, R.Y.: Making Democracy Work: civic traditions in modern Italy. Princeton University Press, Princeton (1993)
9. Arregle, J., Hitt, M.A., Sirmon, D., Very, P.: The Development of Organizational Social Capital: Attributes of Family Firms. Journal of Management Studies 44(1), 73–95 (2007)
10. Robison, L., Flora, J.: The Social Capital Paradigm: Bridging Across Disciplines. American Agricultural Economics Association 85(5), 1187–1193 (2003)
11. Nahapiet, J., Ghoshal, S.: Social capital, intellectual capital and the organizational advantage. Academy of Management Review 23(2), 242–266 (1998)
12. Granovetter, M.S.: The strength of weak ties. American Journal of Sociology 78, 1360–1380 (1973)
13. Sequeira, J.M., Rasheed, A.: Start-up and Growth of immigrant small businesses: the impact f social and human capital. Journal of Development Entrepreneurship 11(4), 357–375 (2006)
14. Watson, G.W., Papamarcos, S.: Social capital and organizational commitment. Journal of Business and Psychology 16(4), 537–552 (2002)
15. Wu, W.: Dimensions of Social Capital and Firm Competitiveness Improvement: The Mediating Role of Information Sharing. Journal of Management Studies 45(1), 122–146 (2008)
16. Coleman, J.S.: Capital in the creation of Human Capital. American Journal of Sociology 94, 95–120 (1988)
17. Fukuyama, F.: The great disruption: human nature and the reconstitution of social order. Profile Books, London (1999)
18. Putnam, R.D.: Bowling Alone: the collapse and revival of American community. Simon & Schuster Paperbacks, New York (2000)
19. Vallejos, R.V., Macke, J., Olea, P.M., Toss, E.D.: Collaborative Networks and Social Capital: a theoretical and practical convergence. In: Camarinha-Matos, L.M., Picard, W. (eds.) Pervasive Collaborative Networks, pp. 43–52. Springer, Boston (2008)
20. Woolcock, M.: Social capital for social policy: lessons from international research and policy. In: Policy Research Conferation, Otawa (2005)
21. Onyx, J., Bullen, P.: Measuring Social Capital in Five Communities. The Journal of Applied Behavioral Science 36(1), 23–42 (2000)
22. Su, K., Lee, Y., Tsai, Y.: The paradigm of knowledge acquisition and social capital in engineering education: empirical research from Taiwanese universities. World Transactions on Engineering and Technology Education 4(1), 93–98 (2005)
23. Feinsterseifert, J.E.: The Emerging Brazilian Wine Industry. International Journal of Wine Business Research 19(3), 187–216 (2007)
24. IBRAVIN, Instituto Brasileiro do Vinho, Cadastro Vinícola, IBRAVIN/MAPA/SAA-RS, Bento Gonçalves, `http://www.ibravin.org.br/index.php#tomada_preco`
25. Hair, J.F., Babin, B., Money, A.H., Samoul, P.: Essentials of Business Research Methods. Leyh Publishing, LLC (2003)

Measuring and Evaluating Communication Intensities in Collaborative Networks

Jens Eschenbächer[1], Novica Zarvić[2], Oliver Thomas[2], and Klaus-Dieter Thoben[1]

[1] BIBA – Bremer Institut für Produktion und Logistik GmbH, Hochschulring 20, 28359 Bremen, Germany
{esc,tho}@biba.uni-bremen.de
[2] Universität Osnabrück, Fachgebiet Informationsmanagement und Wirtschaftsinformatik, Katharinenstr. 3, 49069 Osnabrück, Germany
{novica.zarvic,oliver.thomas}@uni-osnabrueck.de

Abstract. Companies that are actively participating in a collaborative network (CN) need to show a high level of cooperation ability and willingness. The concept of cooperation contains various aspects that need to be considered, like e.g. communication, resource exchange, or cross-organisational processes. These aspects should become permanent subjects of analysis during the operational phase of the CN. The article at hand considers one of these aspects, namely the communication aspect. Our approach is based on a combination of fundamental concepts stemming from the Media-Richness-Theory (MRT) and Graph-Theory. It enables the analyser to firstly measure and then evaluate communication intensities in CNs. We present our approach by means of an example and discuss possible application areas and extensions.

Keywords: Communication intensity, collaborative networks, cooperation.

1 Introduction

Today, globalisation and also the tendency towards decreasing in-house production force many companies to cooperate within Collaborative Networks (CNs) [1-3]. The concept of cooperation is defined as the collaboration of systems or the merging of activities. In order to measure this concept, all aspects that can have an influence on cooperation must be taken into account. In networks of manufacturers the exchange of resources is of fundamental relevance, whereas for service networks outsourcing and offshoring of work are dominating aspects [4]. Both the exchange of resources and the external allocation of tasks are dependent on high-quality communication between the partners in the CN and are therefore crucial for the success of the network. Therefore communication must be seen as an indispensable aspect, because it does not only support but it enables cooperation. Because of this importance, the article focuses solely on the communication aspect in cooperation and provides a systematic approach for measuring and evaluating communication in CNs.

The paper is structured as follows. Section 2 gives an introduction about relevant elements that need to be considered when performing a collaborative network analysis. Then, in section 3, we present the building blocks of our approach and provide the

L.M. Camarinha-Matos et al. (Eds.): PRO-VE 2010, IFIP AICT 336, pp. 527–536, 2010.

reader with important background information on the MRT (Media Richness Theory) [5-7]. Thereby we enrich MRT with an evaluation scheme that delivers values to be used in network graphs. Then we present in section 4 our approach on the basis of a case study. The approach itself is straightforward applicable and represents – next to resource exchanges and external task allocations – one important building block of a holistic method that is able to measure and evaluate cooperation. Finally, in section 5 we summarise our findings, discuss possible future research for extending our approach and conclude the article.

2 Elements of Collaborative Network Analysis

Firstly, a method to measure and evaluate communication in CNs must be developed. According to Wührer [8], there are four crucial elements that a so-called network analysis must incorporate. These four elements, also shown in Fig. 1, are (a) type of entity, (b) type of relationship, (c) content of relationship, and (d) level of analysis.

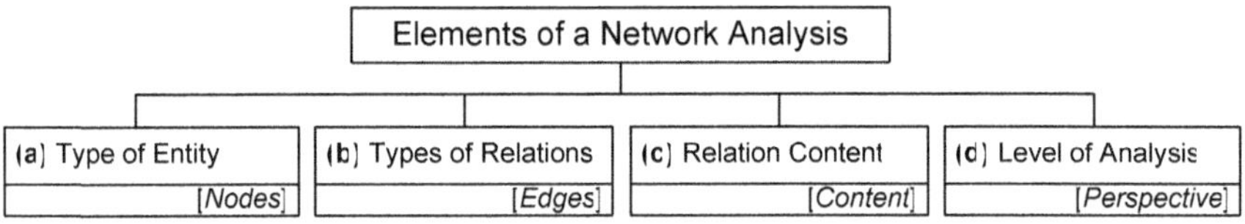

Fig. 1. Essential Elements of the Collaborative Network Analysis (cf. [8])

When looking at a CN from a graph-theoretical perspective, the *type of entity* (a) is usually represented by nodes in the graph. Every node stands for an actor of the network and could represent entities such as companies, departments within those companies, and individuals. The second element, *types of relationships* (b), describes the relationships between the nodes, which are visualised by means of edges between nodes. The *content of relationship* (c) describes the instantiation of edges, delivering content and values to the type of relationship under consideration. Finally, the *level of analysis* (d) deals with the perspective that is chosen for the examination. Nodes and edges in the graph may be analysed separately, before the attention is directed at specific pair- relationships on the next level of analysis.

3 A Reference Model for Measuring and Evaluating the Communication Aspect

3.1 ICT-Systems

First results in research underline the high importance of designing ICT (information and communication technology) infrastructures [9-11]. This section briefly introduces ICT-systems that are treated by the following investigation, where some basic ideas of Weber [12] are adopted. The term information system (IS) comprises the computer-assisted processing and presentation of information and their functional as well as data-technical integration. The focus is though mainly on the integration and interoperability of existing information systems available for communication in and between companies. The benefit of these systems particularly depends on two distinct components: the data-structure that determines what sort of data may be computed on one side and the functional component as the actual processing-instance on the other side. Within the framework of the communication system concept, the emphasis lays on communication and is understood as information exchange. Lockermann et al. define a communication system as an exchange-oriented IS [13]. Meanwhile some authors try to develop a formal ontology for IS which have received some attention [14]. In the 80ies, the development of new telecommunication technologies led to the investigation on how these techniques could be used for handling diverse office tasks [15]. The telecommunication technologies did not continue to center exclusively on the mere information processing, but put communication itself into the spotlight. Upcoming terms like "office communication system" demonstrate this change of paradigms. Objects of interest were mainly the information flow, the communication partner, the throughput time of interactions, and finally the communication costs. In this context, IS were viewed as black boxes, while the attention was turned to both the processes and the media of communication. Key aspects of research were among others Workflow- and Groupware Systems as well as the multimedia-based communication support of distributed collaborative processes. Figure 2 shows a selection of ICT-Systems. The four-field matrix makes obvious that some ICT-Systems can be positively classified as IS, whereas others clearly are part of the group of communication systems. Besides ICT-systems, the matrix additionally discriminates between storage and output media. Criteria for the differentiation are interaction possibilities on one hand, and electronic reusability on the other hand.

From a theoretical viewpoint, there are many different approaches on how ICT-systems can be utilized effectively in collaborations. For example, Reichwald et al. [16] discussed the MRT, in which complexity is perceived as the driver of selection.

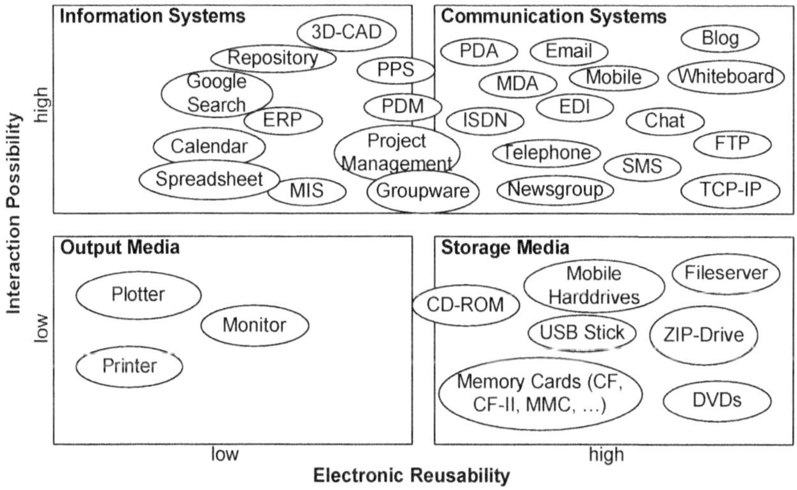

Fig. 2. Characterisation of a Selection of ICT-Systems

3.2 Theoretical Approaches for Creating Communication Processes

Some German researchers have discussed heavily theoretical approaches that support communication processes in ICT environments [17-19]. These led to diverse and even conflicting results. In this section we will not focus on this debate, but rather use one theoretical perspective, which is MRT [20, 21]. Whenever face-to-face communication is not possible, media support is required. This comes true whenever the communication partners cannot be at the same place at the same time. Fortunately, the broad spectrum of communication-supporting media ranging from the classical letter or fax to telephones and video-conferences allows users to overcome barriers of space and time and is still growing constantly.

Principally, the users have alternatives to choose from. This simple fact has got a considerable impact on the success of communication processes, because the media choice strongly influences interaction. The communication research tries to track down such connections. One field of communication research concentrates on the factors in media choice, namely, the reasons why people tend to use certain media in specific communication situations. Another central field, namely the media impact, examines the effects of media usage on the success of communication processes. Numerous empirical studies have dealt with these questions and produced many surprising insights [16]. At large, three classes of influence factors that determine the selection and utilisation of media are distinguished in literature:

- According to the *MRT*, objective attributes of the medium regarding the analog and digital communication content dominate the decision (Is the medium rich or lean?).
- The *theory of subjective media acceptance* assumes that the individual way of working and preferences for certain communication types determines the media choice (Does the medium support one's own preferences concerning speed, comfort, etc.?).
- The *social influence approach* argues that the media acceptance of the communication partners' (social) environment predetermines the media selection (Which medium does my interaction partner prefer?).

None of these theories is capable of explaining all forms and reasons of media decision, and even combined, they leave many questions unanswered. Nevertheless, recent research makes one thing very clear. New telecommunication media may not be considered suitable for the overcoming of borders in time and space just because of their technical potentials. Only if further influence factors and dependencies are taken into account, concrete behavior may be explained properly, like for instance, why high-cost and time-consuming personal communication (face-to-face) is often still preferred in business despite of the wide availability of telephone and other media. The most ostensive depiction for explaining such phenomena is offered by the MRT. It states that technical and non-technical communication forms have distinct transmission capacities regarding both analog and digital information and consequently can be classified as richer or leaner communication [22]. Correspondingly, face-to-face communication in personal contact is a rich communication form. It offers a multitude of so-called parallel communication channels like speech, tone, gesture, facial expression, etc., allows for direct feedback, responses, and a rich spectrum of possible expression, as well as the intermediation and observation of mood and emotion. In contrast, the mere exchange of documents, for example by fax, represents a lean communication with a very low degree of media-richness.

3.3 Applying MRT to the Communication Aspect in CNs

Our approach is based on the MRT, which we extended by an evaluation scheme as shown in figure 3. We do so for being able later on to instantiate the edges in our network analysis with values (cf. section 2). In practice, the MRT is discussed controversially, but in our view, it constitutes a rather useful approach for the differentiation of communication processes. Acting on the assumption that the effectiveness of communication depends on the communication medium used, a direct and personal communication is defined to be most effective, while the group of unaddressed documents bears the lowest effectiveness. Because the effectiveness of communication also expresses the used media's communication intensity [23], the extended media-richness concept appears to be an appropriate reference model for the measurement and evaluation of the aspect to be investigated. Communication as such usually includes only one sender and one receiver. However, in business relationships communication cannot be unidirectional, but in most cases implies reactions and answers. The evaluation scores have been allocated to the medium type by considering the medium effectiveness. This means that the more effective the communication medium in MRT, the higher the evaluation score.

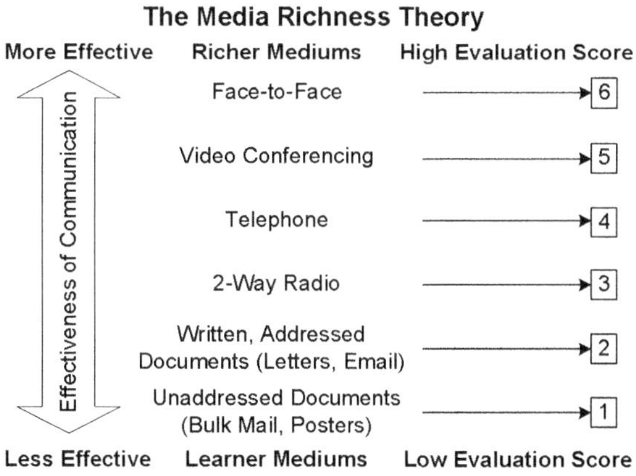

Fig. 3. Evaluation Scheme on basis of the MRT

4 Presentation of the Methodology: A Case Study

The measurement of organizational communication has been a research subject for many years [24]. Nevertheless today more research is needed to understand the exploding number of communication processes in organizations. Consequently our approach for measuring and evaluating communication shall now be illustrated with the help of a concrete case study. The developed methodology consists of five steps (cf. Figure 4) that will be explained in this section. The first step presumes the knowledge of the company network's structure. In accordance with *types of entities* (a) and *types of relationships* (b) introduced within the framework of the collaborative network analysis, such a structure consists graph-theoretically of nodes and edges, where nodes symbolize the companies and edges the relationships (here in terms of the communication aspect as communication channels) within the network. In a second step, the existing interaction types within the network are identified and assigned to the respective edges. This step describes the element *relationship content* (c) of the network analysis. We discriminate the following interaction types [25-29]:

1. Material-related interactions
2. Juridical interactions
3. Financial interactions
4. Human resource interactions
5. ICT interactions

The third step is the alignment of the graph with so-called bidirectional multi-edges, which means that each edge (step 1) is duplicated and aligned in order to mirror both interaction directions in the communication of the respective companies. In the next step, the interaction type to be examined must be determined.

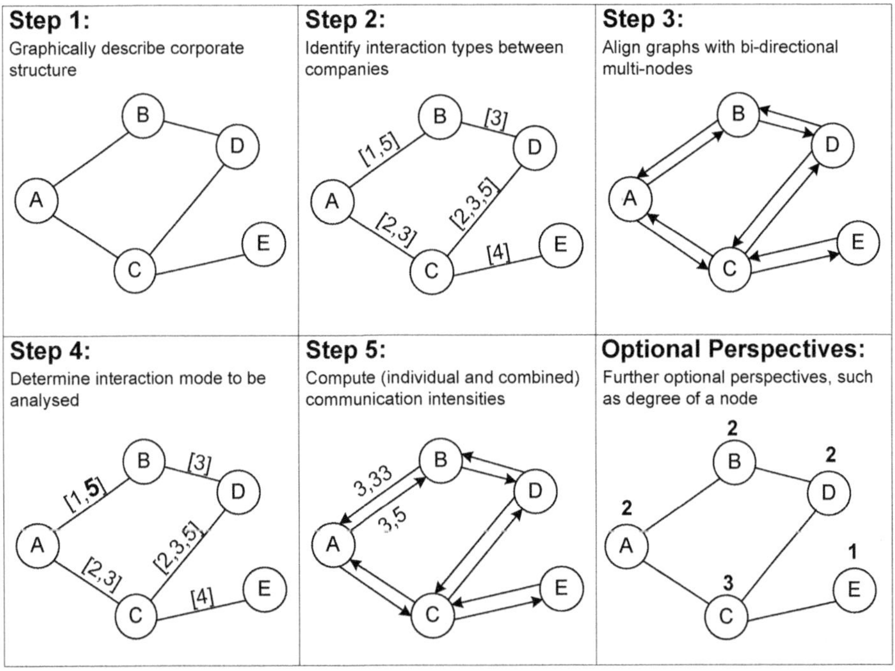

Fig. 4. Methodology for the Measurement and Evaluation of Communication

In our case study, we analyse the ICT-interaction type (interaction type 5) in more detail. At this point, we exemplarily focus on the communication aspect of this interaction type.

Business Case Description. The challenge of this case study is the development of a car driver assisting system that heavily improves driving safety. It is based on the idea to design and implement touch screen functionalities for applications in cars. The innovation to be developed displays essential information like velocity, navigation data, and the control panel directly upon the surface of the windshield and therewith within the driver's field of view. The driver controls the display with his finger tips and may conduct such adjustments at the make-believe distance of the menu elements. This simple mechanism avoids the eye adjustment in the case that the driver switches its eye focus and attention from "infinite distance" (observation of the road) to "2-foot" (usual distance to the front panel) and back. This bears the advantage that the driver hasn't got to turn his eyes from the road anymore - a tremendous safety advance. The information is additionally presented on the front panel. The front seat passenger could furthermore enjoy from entertainment functions like a movie player without distracting the driver.

Application of the Methodology. In the above described business case – within the phase of the innovation project – a communication exchange between two suppliers in the CN appears, where supplier A needs to know the project management competency from supplier B. This represents a realistic example of a typical communication exchange within the project [30]. An excerpt of a communication between supplier A and supplier B is represented by means of a communication transcript on the left (Fig. 5a) and message flows in a BPMN-like model on the right (Fig. 5b). Every outbound message is evaluated on basis of the evaluation scheme from figure 3 and consequently given a certain value. These values are finally summed up and divided by the total number of outbound communication. The results shown in step 5 reveal a communication intensity of 3.5 for supplier A and slightly lower value for supplier B (3.33). These thoughts are in line with the initially introduced collaborative network analysis element *level of analysis* (d). On the subsequent level, namely the aggregated level of pair-relationships, we receive a mean value of 3,415 for the communication intensity of suppliers A and B. Our simple approach towards the measurement and evaluation of communication in collaborative business networks is concluded by the fifth step.

It should be noted here that suppliers sometimes tend to hold back important information among each other, because of competitive reasons and the like. Such behaviour could lead to distortions and mistakes. It is therefore expected that the need for social presence is much higher in such cooperations than inside a single company, which in turn requires a richer medium for achieving high communication intensity. This is, of course, also subject to the task to be achieved. Nevertheless, inter-personal and inter-organisational trust issues, but also inter-cultural cooperations, are representing a particular characteristic of CNs, where effective communication can help to overcome hindrances.

Certainly, additional examination of further graph-theoretical attributes is possible and might add valuable insights [31]. One possible extra-perspective would be the degree of nodes. This perspective shows how many other nodes a node is connected with, that is, how many participants a member has interactions or communication with. This is of major importance, if the communication of an entire company and CN respectively is to be examined.

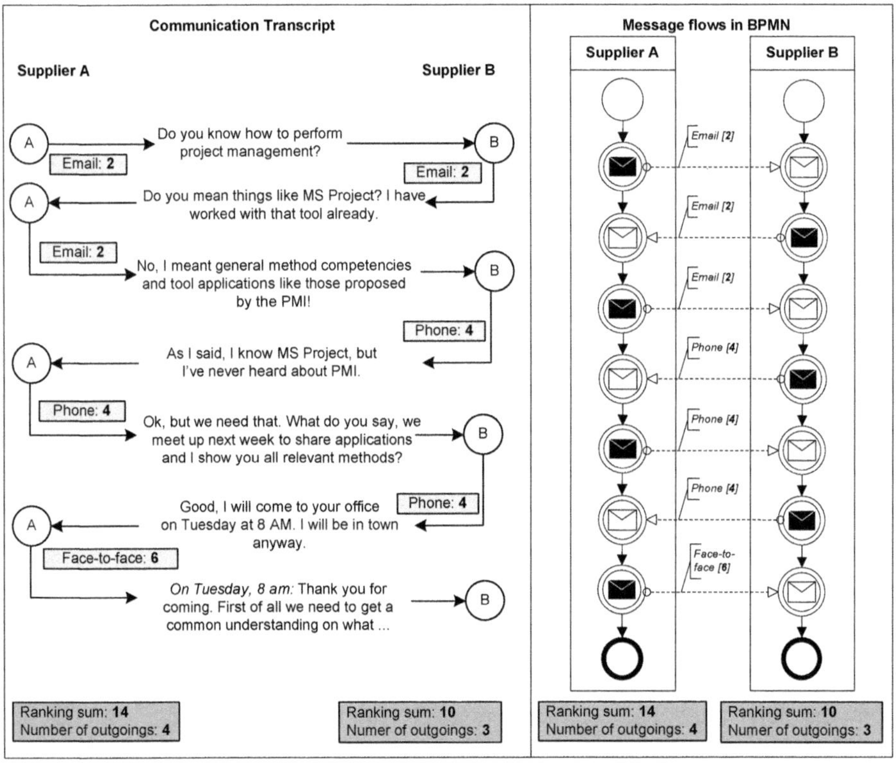

Fig. 5. a) Communication Transcript, and b) BPMN-like representation of communication

5 Results and Conclusions

The measurement and evaluation of communication intensities in CNs poses a major problem in practice. Especially the spatial distribution and the particular form of inter-organisational cooperation remain obstacles. In this context, approaches of the tele-cooperation help understand and pinpoint the challenges of communication. The introduced graph-theoretical approach explains a model that facilitates a simple measurement of communication-intensities in five steps [30]. Overall, the approach might appear at first a bit simplistic, but it represents a combination of fundamental elements that are coming from two different and distinct theories. Secondly, it is straightforward applicable and delivers fast material for discussion inside CNs. And thirdly, it represents just an extensible building block of the envisioned cooperation measurement, which still needs some extensions like for instance semi-automation of creating and evaluating the communication transcripts or the handling of multiple inbound and outbound messages and their dependencies from different partners in the CN. As mentioned above, the objectives of measuring and evaluating cooperation in CNs also include further aspects like resource exchange or external allocation of tasks over and above communication. This is why this article only shows a first concept that indeed includes the communication intensities, but must be expanded by more attributes. The assumptions of MRT have been intensively discussed in theory, and, due to broad experience in inter-organisational cooperations, the authors are certain that they can be validated in practice as well. Nevertheless, facing the multitude of new forms and instruments of communication [33], there is a great need for further research.

References

1. Ahuja, G.: Collaboration Networks, Structural Holes, and Innovation: A Longitu-dinal Study. Administrative Science Quarterly 45(3), 425–455 (2000)
2. Camarinha-Matos, L., Afsarmanesh, H.: Collaborative networks: a new scientific discipline. Journal of Intelligent Manufacturing 16, 439–452 (2005)
3. Newman, M.E.J.: The structure of scientific collaboration networks. PNAS 98(2), 404–409 (2001)
4. Lacity, M.C., Willcocks, L.: Global Information Technology Outsourcing: In Search of Business Advantage. John Wiley & Sons, Inc., Chichester (2000)
5. University of Twente: Media Richness Theory, Accessed at: `http://www.tcw.utwente.nl/theorieenoverzicht/Theory%20clusters/Mass%20Media/Media_Richness_Theory.doc/`
6. Dennis, A.R., Kinney, S.T.: Testing the Media Richness Theory in the New Media: The Effect of Cues, Feedback and Task Equivocality. Information Systems Research 9(3), 256–274 (1998)
7. El-Shinnawy, M., Lynne Markus, M.: The poverty of media richness theory: explaining people's choice of electronic mail vs. voice mail. Int. J. Human-Computer Studies 46(4), 443–467 (1997)
8. Wührer, G.: Internationale Allianz- und Kooperationsfähigkeit österreichischer Unternehmen: Beiträge zum Gestaltansatz als Beschreibungs- und Erklärungskonzept. Linz Trauner (1995)
9. Proakis, J.G., Masoud, S.: Communication Systems Engineering. Prent Hall, Englewood Cliffs (2002)
10. Roberts, J.: From Know-how to Show-how? Questioning the Role of Information and Communication Technologies in Knowledge Transfer. Technology Analysis and Strategic Management 12(4), 429–443 (2000)
11. Lankhorst, M., et al.: Enterprise Architecture at Work: Modelling, Communication and Analysis, 2nd edn. Springer, Berlin (August 2009)
12. Weber, F.: Formale Interaktionsanalyse - Ein Beitrag zur systematischen Gestaltung von Informations- und Kommunikationsstrukturen im Concurrent Enterprise durch die Berücksichtigung von Informationseigenschaften, Dissertation, Universität Bremen, Bremer Schriften zur Betriebstechnik und Arbeitswissenschaft, vol. 61. Verlag Mainz (2009)
13. Lockermann, P., Krueger, G., Krumm, H.: Telekommunikation und Datenhaltung. Carl-Hanser Verlag, München (1993)

14. Guarino, N.: Formal Ontology and Information systems. In: Cuarino, N. (ed.) Proc. of FOIS 1998, Trento, Italy, June 6-8, pp. 3–15. IOS Press, Amsterdam (1998)
15. Krcmar, H.: Informationsmanagement, 4. Auflage. Springer, Berlin (2006)
16. Reichwald, R., Möslein, K., Sachbacher, H., Englberger, H., Oldenburg, S.: Telekooperation: Verteilte Arbeits- und Organisationsformen. Springer, Berlin (1998)
17. Stadlbauer, F.: Zwischenbetriebliche Anwendungsintegration - IT Management in Unternehmensnetzwerken, Dissertation, Universität München, Wiesbaden, Deutscher Universitäts-Verlag (2007)
18. Wittenberg, S.: Gestaltung interner Märkte in Unternehmensnetzwerken, Dissertation, LMU München, Lohmar Köln, Josel Eul Verlag (2006)
19. van's Gravesande, B.S.: Internetbasierte Anwendungen in der F&E-Kooperation: Eine empirische Analyse basierend auf der Adaptive Structuration Theory, Dissertation, Universität Witten-Herdecke, Wiesbaden. Deutscher Univ.-Verlag (2006)
20. Daft, R.L., Lengel, R.H.: Organizational information requirements, media richness and structural design. Management Science 32(5), 554–571 (1986)
21. Trevino, L., Lengel, R.H., Bodensteiner, W., Gerloff, E., Muir, N.: The richness imperative and cognitive style: The role of individual differences in media choice behavior. Management Communication Quarterly 4(2), 176–197 (1990)
22. Zack, M.H.: Interactivity and Communication Mode Choice in Ongoing Management Groups. Information Systems Research 4(3), 207–239 (1993)
23. Dawes, P.L.: Communication Intensity in Large Scale Organizational High Technology Purchasing Decisions. Business-to-Business Marketing 3(3), 3–38 (1996)
24. Roberts, K.H., O'Reilly, C.A.: Measuring organizational communication. Journal of Applied Psychology 59(3), 321–326 (1974)
25. Weber, D.: Strategische Planung im Unternehmensnetzwerk am Beispiel industrieller Dienstleistungen im Industrieanlagenbau Elektronikfertigung. Dissertation, Technische Universität Braunschweig. Shaker Verlag, Aachen (2005)
26. Liebhart, U.-E.: Strategische Kooperationsnetzwerke: Entwicklung, Gestaltung und Steuerung. Dissertation, Universität Klagenfurt. Deutscher Universitäts-Verlag (2002)
27. Preece, J., Rogers, Y., Sharp, H.: Interaction Design: Beyond Human-Computer Interaction. John Wiley, Chichester (2002)
28. Madhok, A., Tallman, S.B.: Resources, Transactions and Rents: Managing Value Through Interfirm Collaborative Relationships. Organization Science, Special Issue: Managing Partnerships and Strategic Alliances 9(3), 326–339 (1998)
29. Eschenbächer, J.: Gestaltung von Innovationsprozessen in Virtuellen Organisationen durch Kooperationsorientierte Netzwerkanalyse, Dissertation, Universität Bremen, Bremer Schriften zur Betriebstechnik und Arbeitswissenschaft. Band 64. Verlag Mainz (2009)
30. Zarvić, N., Eschenbächer, J., Thoben, K.-D.: Messen und Bewerten von Kommunikationsintensitäten in Unternehmensnetzwerken. Information Management und Consulting 24(4), 19–24 (2009)
31. Zarvić, N.: Considering Structural Properties of Inter-organizational Network Fragments during Business-IT Alignment, TR-CTIT-08-12, Centre for Telematics and Information Technology, University of Twente (2008) ISSN 1381-3625
32. O'Brien, G.: The measurement of cooperation. Organizational Behavior & Human Performance 3(4), 427–439 (1968)
33. Watson-Manheim, M.B., Bélanger, F.: Communication Media Repertoires: Dealing with the Multiplicity of Media Choices. MIS Quarterly 31(2), 267–293 (2007)

Generic Mechanisms for Coordinating Operations and Sharing Financial Benefits in Collaborative Logistics

Jean-François Audy[1], Sophie D'Amours[1], Nadia Lehoux[1], and Mikael Rönnqvist[2]

[1] Laval University, Quebec City, Quebec, G1K 7P4, Canada
[2] Norwegian School of Economics and Business Administration, Helleveien 30, NO-5045 Bergen, Norway
Jean-Francois.Audy@cirrelt.ca, Sophie.DAmours@gmc.ulaval.ca, Nadia.Lehoux@gmc.ulaval.ca, Mikael.Ronnqvist@nhh.no

Abstract. Collaborative logistics is increasingly emerging as a new opportunity for cost reduction through internal and cross chains coordination. This paper presents different coordination mechanisms to support collaborative logistics. These mechanisms are differentiated by their planning function, their sharing approach and the information, decision and financial flows. Often, the logistics planning is run first, and secondly, the sharing is set on the basis of the plan. However, recently, new approaches have been proposed where both the logistics plan and the sharing are optimized simultaneously. Constraints on the financial flows also introduce specificities to the coordination mechanisms and these are described and discussed. Finally, the proposed coordination mechanisms are used to describe a series of research and applied projects in which collaborative logistics has been implemented.

Keywords: Coordination mechanism, Collaborative planning in logistics and transportation, Benefit sharing approach, Game Theory, Operations Research.

1 Introduction

In this paper, we propose five generic coordination mechanisms for logistics activities in a coalition. These mechanisms aim to help managers design their collaboration schemes. They define generic approaches to support how the collaborating units can share information, plan their activities jointly or sequentially, and share the financial benefit of the collaboration.

Logistics activities provide many opportunities for collaboration between companies. This collaboration aims to reduce the cost of executing the logistics activities, improve service, enhance capacities as well as protect the environment and mitigate climate change (Simchi-Levi et al., 1999). Collaboration occurs when two or more autonomous and self-interested *business units* form a *coalition* and exchange or share resources (including information) with the goal of making decisions or undertaking activities that will generate benefits that they cannot (or only partially) generate individually. Collaboration can occur among business units belonging to the same supply chain (i.e. vertical collaboration) or to different ones (i.e. horizontal collaboration), in competition or not. Information exchange to reduce the bullwhip effect is a typical

L.M. Camarinha-Matos et al. (Eds.): PRO-VE 2010, IFIP AICT 336, pp. 537–544, 2010.

example of vertical collaboration between business units located at different echelons in the same supply chain, while group purchasing organizations are a typical example of horizontal collaboration among buyers belonging to different business units. The level of collaboration can range from information exchange, joint planning, joint execution, to strategic alliance (e.g. co-evolution) (Frayret et al., 2003).

Frayret et al. (2004) propose a classification scheme of the various coordination mechanisms of manufacturing activities in a distributed manufacturing system. One class of coordination mechanism, designated as 'coordination by plan' (from March and Simon, 1958), involves the establishment of predefined plans to coordinate a priori interdependent activities under the responsibility of autonomous and self-interested business units.

This class is subdivided into three subclasses of mechanism: (i) 'direct supervision with plan', (ii) 'mediation with plan' and (iii) 'joint plan establishment'. The first two subclasses use a third party to perform the coordination. In subclass (i), the third party performs a centralized planning of all business units' activities and each business unit must follow the centralized plan. In subclass (ii), each business unit performs a first planning of their own activities and then the third party performs an integration of these individual plans into one coherent-centralized plan that each business unit must follow. Such integration involves modifications to the individual plans that are possible through the mediation between the third party and each business unit. In subclass (ii), the third party acts as a support (i.e. non-coercive) for the coordination rather than a supervisor (i.e. coercive) as in subclass (i). In the third subclass (iii), with mutual adjustments between them, the business units perform joint planning of their activities to agree on a centralized plan that each company will follow.

By addressing financial issues within these mechanisms, we can tailor some of them to coordinate interdependent (vertical collaboration) or similar (horizontal collaboration) logistics activities on which a coalition of business units aim to collaborate. These financial issues include a number of questions such as:

(a) How should the potential financial benefit of the coordination of the logistics activities among a set of collaborating business units be computed?

(b) How should the potential financial benefit be shared among the collaborating business units?

We address both questions (a) and (b) in the following Sections 2 and 3, respectively. The latter also describes the five generic coordination mechanisms proposed in this paper.

2 How to Compute the Potential Benefit of the Coordination

In several case studies involving collaboration in logistics, question (a) is addressed with optimization problems, and Operations Research (OR) methods are used to solve them, see e.g. Cruijssen et al. (2005), Forsberg et al. (2005), Palander and Väätäinen (2005), le Blanc et al. (2007), Cruijssen et al. (2007), Ergun et al (2007), Krajewska et al. (2007), Agarwal and Ergun (2008a,b), Lehoux et al. (2008), Özener and Ergun (2008), Lehoux et al. (2009), Marier et al. (2009) and Frisk et al. (2010). The solution of one optimization problem corresponds to the predefined plan on which is based the coordination mechanisms within the class 'coordination by plan'. The financial benefit for an optimization problem with a minimization objective generally refers to a savings, whereas with a maximization objective, the benefit refers to a profit. In logistics, most optimization problems have a minimization objective. Thus for the potential financial benefit of the collaboration, we will refer to a savings except when we mention it as a profit. In many of the previously mentioned case studies, the savings are defined according to hypothesis 1: the savings are the difference between the sum of the cost of each stand-alone solution (i.e. logistics activities planning of each business unit alone) and the cost of the common solution (i.e. logistics activities planning of all business units together).

In the literature, there exist many optimization problems and OR methods for the planning of the logistics activities for one business unit (i.e. stand-alone solution). Modifications to such problems and OR methods could be required in a context of collaboration in which the planning of the logistics activities is for several autonomous and self-interested business units (i.e. common solution). For example, Forsberg et al. (2005) report, in their case study of raw material exchange between two companies, some additional constraints to their allocation model according to a different exchange scenario (e.g. a limit on the total volume that could be exchanged between the companies). By adding constraints to the common optimization problem, such modifications usually reduce the potential savings of the collaboration. In a case study of raw material exchange on a monthly basis between three companies, Lehoux et al. (2009) report that each company must remain the main supplier (specified minimum percentage, for example, 50%) for its own mills and raw material exchange must be pair-wise equal (i.e. a company must supply each collaborator with the equivalent volume received from this collaborator). These two modifications (or constraints in the optimization problem) decrease by 1-2% the potential savings of each month, which are in the range of 5-20%. Moreover, as we will explain in subsections 3.3 and 3.4, such modifications could also be directly linked to question (b).

Modifications to the individual optimization problem of some companies can also be required. With the previously mentioned hypothesis 1, the solution value of the individual optimization problem of one specific company represents its expected stand-alone cost. Consequently, to obtain a realistic value, the individual optimization problem should be representative of the stand-alone logistics or transportation approach of each company. For instance, if a low volume shipping company A uses only less-than-truckload (LTL) carriers, while a high volume shipping company B uses only full-truckload (FT) carriers, the individual optimization problem of each company must be adapted to fit such different cost functions. Otherwise, if in the individual optimization problem of both companies, allow the use of LTL carriers only, the stand-alone cost of company B will be overestimated since with high shipping volume, the use of FT carriers is cheaper than the use of LTL carriers.

3 How to Share the Potential Benefit of the Coordination

When question (b) is addressed in the previously mentioned case studies involving collaboration in logistics, different sharing approaches are employed. Furthermore, they can be grouped into five generic coordination mechanisms (CM), as illustrated in Figure 1. In other words, these five generic coordination mechanisms result of a categorization exercise based on several sharing approaches discussed in the literature and used in various cases studies involving collaborative logistics. Each mechanism includes at least two collaborating business units (only two business units are illustrated to keep Figure 1 simple) having logistics activities (e.g. transportation) to be coordinated by a plan and their own resources (e.g. carriers) available to achieve the plan. Even though collaborating business units may share different resources such as warehouses, this possibility is not illustrated to keep Figure 1 simple. Also, designated as a 'Planning function', the latter represents the step in the mechanism where the predefined plan is established according to the sharing approach of the generic mechanism. Such a planning function could be performed by a third party (as in the previously mentioned subclasses (i) and (ii)) or with a joint planning process between the collaborating units (as in subclass (iii)). Finally, the information, decision and financial flows in each mechanism are illustrated (the flows numbering respects the chronological sequence of the mechanism). The following subsections describe each proposed coordination mechanism.

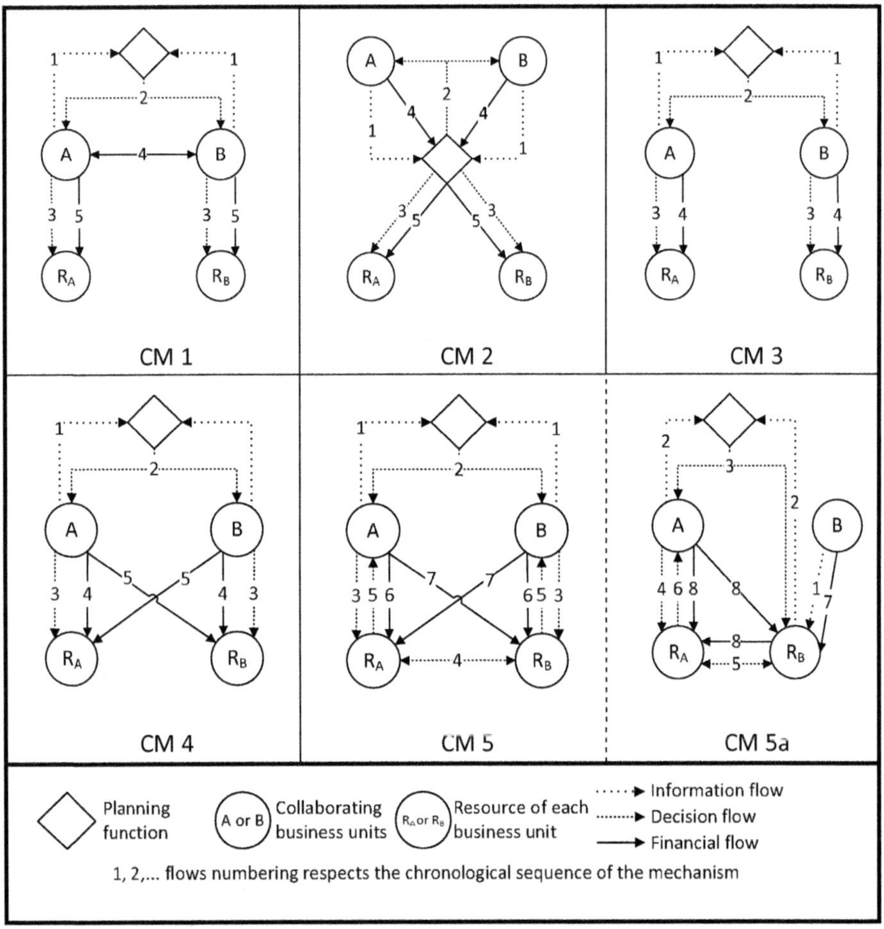

Fig. 1. Generic coordination mechanisms for the logistics activities

3.1 Coordination Mechanism 1 (CM 1)

In this mechanism, the planning function solves the optimization problem in order to achieve maximum savings and then, the benefit sharing is addressed with a financial flow between the business units. Such a financial flow is based on a predefined incentive rule such as pricing agreements or quantity discount. A detailed review of these incentives can be found in Cachon (2003). Lehoux et al. (2009) present a case study using coordination mechanism 1. The case study involves bilateral collaboration between a paper producer and a wholesaler. To establish the collaborative approach providing the greatest savings for the coalition as well as for both companies, the paper producer must share part of its transportation savings (i.e. incentive rule) with the wholesaler.

3.2 Coordination Mechanism 2 (CM 2)

In this mechanism, the planning function solves the optimization problem in order to achieve maximum savings and then, the benefit sharing is addressed with a sharing principle based on an economic model (i.e. cost allocation method) such as the Shapley value, the nucleolus and the separable and non-separable costs. Such economic models, generally based on cooperative game theory, effect an allocation of the total cost of the common-solution among the companies. These fractions paid by each company are then used to pay each resource. A survey on these models can be found in Tijs and Driessen (1986) and in Young (1985, 1994). Case studies using coordination mechanism 2 include e.g. Frisk et al. (2010) and Audy et al. (2009) for collaboration in transportation activities.

3.3 Coordination Mechanism 3 (CM 3)

In this mechanism, the planning function solves the optimization problem in order to achieve maximum savings, with respect to an additional constraint related to the benefit sharing. The optimization problem decides that certain activities belonging to a business unit are accomplished by its own resource and others are accomplished by the resource of the second business unit. Such decisions lead to the generation of two plans, one for each company. Since there is no financial flow between the business units or between the business unit and the resource belonging to the other business unit, the cost of the plan of each business unit must be, at the least, less than the cost of their stand-alone plan. Such a condition (or a more restrictive one) related to benefit sharing could be expressed by a constraint in the optimization problem.

In their case study involving three companies performing raw material pair-wise exchange, Lehoux et al. (2009) report the use of this mechanism. These companies previously agree with the sharing principle behind the Equal Profit Method (from Frisk et al., 2010), an economic model that aims to find a stable allocation such that the maximum difference in relative savings between all pairs of two collaborating companies is minimized. Thus, to come up with three plans resulting in a benefit sharing that the companies could agree on, a new constraint has been added to the optimization problem. The new constraint states that each pair of companies must have the same relative savings.

3.4 Coordination Mechanism 4 (CM 4)

In this mechanism, the planning function simultaneously addresses the resolution of the optimization problem and the benefit sharing. For each activity, the optimization problem fixes a cost to be paid for its completion by a specific resource. The fixing of the cost takes into account the cost incurred by the resource to realize the activity and the revenue associated to the activity. For all their activities, each company pays this cost to their resource or to that of the other company, according to which resource has been chosen in the plan. Thus, the benefit sharing is addressed with the financial flow between each company and the resource of the other company. In Agarwal and Ergun (2008a), coordination mechanism 4 is used by sea container carriers sharing the loading capacity of their ships to deliver their respective customers' shipments. Other collaborative logistics case studies or examples using coordination mechanism 4 include e.g. Agarwal and Ergun (2008b) and Agarwal et al. (2009).

3.5 Coordination Mechanism 5 (CM 5)

In this mechanism, the planning function partially solves the optimization problem (or a relaxation (i.e. more simplified version) of the optimization problem) and provides its partial plan to each business unit. Firstly, each business unit assigns its activities to its own resource, but also provides the partial plan. Such a partial plan includes a list of potential collaboration opportunities, if any, for each activity. That means that such opportunities may appear within the activities assigned to one resource, but also between activities assigned to different resources. Given these latter potential collaboration opportunities, it is then up to the two resources to decide together to collaborate or not, and if they collaborate, to decide together which resource will carry out the activities (i.e. flow 4). Since the resources are paid only for each activity they accomplish (i.e. flows 6 and 7), the decisions they made in flow 4 fix the benefit sharing.

Mechanism 5 is based on a generalization of the mechanism used in the case study in Eriksson and Rönnqvist (2003), which is illustrated in CM 5a. In this case study, the potential collaboration opportunities are back-hauling tours existing among the transportation activities of two forest companies. Moreover, this collaboration is realized through the carrier (i.e. the resource) of the second company (i.e. business unit).

4 Conclusion

This paper proposes five generic coordination mechanisms for logistics activities in a coalition. These mechanisms are differentiated by their planning function, their sharing approach and the information, decision and financial flows. Some mechanisms perform their logistics planning first and then their sharing on the basis of the complete (mechanisms 1 and 2) or the partial (mechanism 5) plan while others perform both simultaneously (mechanisms 3 and 4). Proposed recently in the literature, these latter mechanisms guarantee that a logistics plan satisfying the sharing conditions of the coalition will be obtained.

To our knowledge this is the first attempt to characterize generic coordination mechanism building on the integration of the planning function, the information sharing as well as financial benefit sharing.

Acknowledgments. The authors acknowledge the financial support of the Natural Sciences and Engineering Research Council of Canada and the private and public partners of the FORAC Research Consortium.

References

1. Agarwal, R., Ergun, Ö.: Network design and allocation mechanisms for carrier alliances in liner shipping. Under revision for Operations Research (2008a)
2. Agarwal, R., Ergun, Ö.: Mechanism design for a multicommodity flow game in service network alliances. Operations Research Letters 36(5), 520–524 (2008b)
3. Agarwal, R., Ergun, O., Houghtalen, L., Ozener, O.O.: Collaboration in cargo transportation. In: Chaovalitwongse, W., Furman, K.C., Pardalos, P.M. (eds.) Optimization and Logistics Challenges in the Enterprise. Springer Optimization and its Applications, vol. 30, pp. 373–409. Springer, New York (2009)
4. Audy, J.-F., D'Amours, S., Rousseau, L.-M.: Cost allocation in the establishment of a collaborative transportation agreement – An application in the furniture industry. Forthcoming in Journal of the Operational Research Society (2009)
5. Cachon, G.P.: Supply Chain Coordination with Contracts. In: Kok, A.G., Graves, S.C. (eds.) Handbooks in Operations Research and Management Science, vol. 11, pp. 229–339. Elsevier, Netherlands (2003)
6. Cruijssen, F., Borm, P., Fleuren, H., Hamers, H.: Insinking: a methodology to exploit synergy in transport. CentER Discussion Paper 2005-121, Tilburg University, Netherlands (2005)
7. Cruijssen, F., Bräysy, O., Dullaeert, W., Fleuren, H., Salomon, M.: Joint route planning under varying market conditions. International Journal of Physical Distribution and Logistics Management 37(4), 287–304 (2007)
8. Ergun, O., Kuyzu, G., Savelsbergh, M.: Reducing truckload transportation costs through collaboration. Transportation Science 41(2), 206–221 (2007)
9. Eriksson, J., Rönnqvist, M.: Transportation and route planning: Åkarweb - a web-based planning system. In: 2nd Forest Engineering Conference, pp. 48–57, Skogforsk, Sweden (2003)
10. Forsberg, M., Frisk, M., Rönnqvist, M.: FlowOpt: a decision support tool for strategic and tactical transportation planning in forestry. International Journal of Forest Engineering 16(2), 101–114 (2005)
11. Frayret, J.-M., D'Amours, F., D'Amours, S.: Collaboration et outils collaboratifs pour la PME Manufacturière [Collaboration and collaborative tools for manufacturing SMEs]. CEFRIO Technical Report, Canada (2003)
12. Frayret, J.-M., D'Amours, S., Montreuil, B.: Co-ordination and control in distributed and agent-based manufacturing systems. Production Planning and Control 15(1), 1–13 (2004)
13. Frisk, M., Jörnsten, K., Göthe-Lundgren, M., Rönnqvist, M.: Cost allocation in collaborative forest transportation. European Journal of Operational Research 205(2), 448–458 (2010)
14. Krajewska, M.A., Kopfer, H., Laporte, G., Ropke, S., Zaccour, G.: Horizontal cooperation among freight carriers: request allocation and profit sharing. Journal of the Operational Research Society 59(11), 1483–1491 (2007)
15. le Blanc, H.M., Cruijssen, F., Fleuren, H.A., de Koster, M.B.M.: Factory gate pricing: an analysis of the Dutch retail distribution. European Journal of Operational Research 174(3), 1950–1967 (2007)

16. Lehoux, N., D'Amours, S., Langevin, A.: Collaboration and decision models for a two-echelon supply chain: a case study in the pulp and paper industry. Journal of Operations and Logistics 2(4), VII.1–VII.17 (2009)
17. Lehoux, N., Audy, J.-F., D'Amours, S., Rönnqvist, M.: Issues and experiences in logistics collaboration. In: Camarinha-Matos, L., Paraskakis, I., Afsarmanesh, H. (eds.) 10th IFIP Working Conference on Virtual Enterprises, vol. 307, pp. 69–77. Springer, Berlin (2009)
18. March, J.G., Simon, H.A.: Organizations. John Wiley & Sons, New York (1958)
19. Marier, P., Gaudreault, J., D'Amours, S.: Network collaboration and optimization: chip supply in an integrated pulp and paper company. In: 14th Annual International Conference on Industrial Engineering Theory, Applications & Practice, United-States, pp. 18–21 (2009)
20. Özener, O.Ö., Ergun, Ö.: Allocating costs in a collaborative transportation procurement network. Transportation Science 42(2), 146–165 (2008)
21. Palander, T., Väätäinen, J.: Impacts of interenterprise collaboration and backhauling on wood procurement in Finland. Scandinavian Journal of Forest Research 20(2), 177–183 (2005)
22. Simchi-Levi, D., Kaminsky, P., Simchi-Levi, E.: Designing and managing the supply chain: concepts, strategies and cases. McGraw-Hill, United-States (1999)
23. Tijs, S.H., Driessen, T.S.H.: Game theory and cost allocation problems. Management Science 32(8), 1015–1058 (1986)
24. Young, H.P.: Cost allocation: methods, principles, applications. Elsevier, Netherlands (1985)
25. Young, H.P.: Cost allocation. In: Aumann, R.J., Hart, S. (eds.) Handbook of Game Theory with Economic Applications, vol. 2, pp. 1193–1235. Elsevier, Amsterdam (1994)

Managing Performance to Align the Participants of Collaborative Networks: Case Studies Results

Roberto da Piedade Francisco, Américo Azevedo, and João Bastos

INESC Porto & Faculdade de Engenharia da Universidade do Porto,
Rua Doutor Roberto Frias S/N
4200-465 Porto, Portugal
{roberto.piedade,ala,joao.bastos}@fe.up.pt

Abstract. The paper underlines the interest of using a performance management system applied to monitor the strategy effectiveness and the interoperation's performance in the collaborative networks (CN). The aim with this study is to verify if a performance management system helps decision-makers reach the alignment among participants in a collaborative network. It is expected that this work provides an adequate tool for supporting quick decisions to meet the feasible and desirable improvements in inter-organisational processes. A framework (CNPMS) is also presented, having been developed to support the dynamic performance management, which was applied in case studies of two Brazilian collaborative networks.

Keywords: Collaborative Networks, Alignment, Performance Management.

1 Introduction

Nowadays organisations recognize that a tight interaction and coordination among participants of their business chain, or emergent opportunities, motivates them to act in Collaborative Networks (CN), and furthermore it is a crucial strategy to reach continuous competitiveness and to reduce business uncertainty. Therefore, this new model involves the interoperation of different organisational systems that must be integrated and orchestrated in order to provide effectiveness, bringing a suitable performance. Then, this new vision requires technology and infrastructure support, management tools and appropriate performance measurement solutions that can ensure the alignment expected regarding the strategic objectives pertaining to business among the participants in a business networked environment.

Then, this paper intends to highlight some aspects regarding performance management seeking to achieve the alignment of participants in collaborative networks. Thus, this document is organized as follows: the second section presents definitions and explanations on alignment in CNs. In the third section, an overview of the performance management is provided. Then, the fourth section addresses the results of some case studies, including the explanation of the Collaborative Network Performance Management System (CNPMS); finally, some conclusions are presented in fifth section.

L.M. Camarinha-Matos et al. (Eds.): PRO-VE 2010, IFIP AICT 336, pp. 545–552, 2010.

2 Alignment in Collaborative Networks

Collaborative networks are the interaction among entities geographically separated with distinct competencies, and sometimes distinct interests, that intend to cooperate in order to reach common goals, symbiotically in the same breeding environment [1]. This new paradigm emerged as a powerful mechanism to achieve competitiveness, excellence and agility in the turbulent market conditions. To define "collaborative network", Camarinha-Matos & Afsarmanesh [2] argue that this term is often confused with cooperation and thus state there are other types of interactions between firms, such as coordination and networking. These interactions are defined as:

- Networking. It constitutes the interactions of communication and exchange of information between groups of organizations for their own use. This can occur even if there are no common goals among the participants.
- Coordinated Networking. Keeping premise that there are no specific common goals, the coordination of information sharing may involve the alignment of activities so that it is possible to achieve more effective results.
- Cooperation. The division of specific activities between participants. Exchange of information and redirection of activities occurs as in previous settings, but it includes the sharing of resources to achieve feasible and desirable goals.
- Collaboration. It occurs when the partners work together to plan, implement and evaluate inter-organizational processes providing the grounds for share information and resources to achieve common goals and to strengthen the each one's capacities. Acting under a single identity, it that risks, resources and responsibilities are shared, so that the benefits can be achieved.

Therefore, an interaction can occur in a simple cooperation between organizations or to advance to a level where there is coordination of inter-organizational processes that exploit information and communication among them. On the other hand, there can be cooperation where responsibilities on the inter-organizational processes and respective resources are shared, or cooperation that can advance to an even higher level with an agreement on the common strategic objectives, i.e., collaboration.

In this context, Saiz, Rodríguez & Bas [3] argue that companies operating in CNs can maximize the participants' capabilities, once combined to achieve the strategic objectives to meet customer needs for integrated and efficient solutions. So, the alignment is very important in formulating the strategy mainly on the adjustment of systems and key processes, as well as the decision-making system [5]. Although it has other connotations, the term "alignment" can be defined as a proper or desirable coordination or relation of components [4]. However, in the management scope, it can be properly considered as a situation where strategies, organizational structures, stakeholders, stockholders, and whatever participant or process in a business environment are strictly combined under a set of roles to reach specific objectives and goals. Align the main activities of the organization around a generic strategy improves communication with customers, employees and shareholders, considering the business environment, strategies and resources established.

The alignment can be referred to as taking the following perspectives into consideration: strategic alignment, organizational alignment, operational alignment and team alignment. However, the main focus of this work does not concern about the alignment of teams or about the operational alignment. Instead, it focuses on achieving strategic alignment in a collaborative network supported by the organizational alignment. In this context, some factors should be considered in the organizational structure to bring organizational alignment, such as: project size, duration, the organization's experience in managing projects, the philosophy of the company's upper management regarding project management, the physical location of the project, available resources, and specific project aspects [6].

We argue that there are three moments of decision-making that can affect more significantly the strategic alignment, such as: partner selection, agreement and performance management. To achieve the alignment, these moments should be properly planned during the CN's implementation. Moreover, there are different fitting levels according to each moment of the CN life-cycle, which must be addressed since the selection of partners, in the agreement, and until the start-up (figure 1). After that, due to results not yet known whether that will happen during the runtime, it is expected that the measurement and performance management system helps improve the alignment. If the performance is instantiated, the decision-makers can improve the inter-organisational processes and the customer solutions. At this moment, the strategic alignment should be achieved even if there are some setbacks.

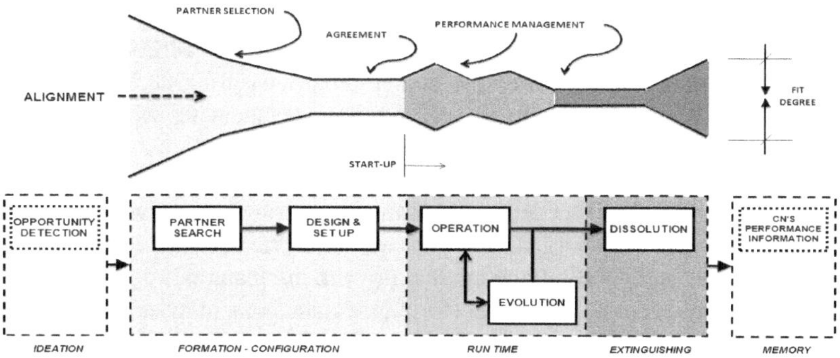

Fig. 1. Alignment through the CN life-cycle

Then, the alignment requires a measure, even if it is subjective, to instantiate the degree of alignment (fit degree) that occurs in the three moments mentioned above. The proposal is to use five degrees of alignment, such as: highest, high, medium, low, and lowest. This evaluation process can be obtained through fieldwork in the CN, application of questionnaires to the participants or/and stakeholders, collaborative meetings for the review of inter-organizational processes where procedures are established for continuous improvement, and also results from the view of the board.

However, another approach is being developed to improve this alignment evaluation form in order to fill possible gaps originated from the personal and subjective evaluations. It is based on Fuzzy Logic and intends to use the result of strategic key performance indicators (KPI) set by decision-makers and turn them into qualitative assessments of compliance with the targets. Thus, through the rankings of each participant make possible to obtain the "fit degree" of the CN as a whole. If the Fit Degree measure is considered by participants as an important factor, both in CN configuration and in subsequent improvements, this may mean that, in these decision-making moments, it is possible has a CN's management processes more effective.

3 Managing Performance

In a collaborative network, the decision-makers seek to improve the performance of inter-organisational processes in order to fulfill the CN's purposes. They must use systems of performance management and measurement derived from its strategies and capabilities [7]. The main principle is to integrate the goals with strategies and thus reach a better definition of the processes, their performance and their relationship with the internal and external clients.

In fact, in order to improve the management of collaborative networks, a dynamic performance management system (PMS) should be considered in order to build an interactive and aligned framework. This should support the collaborative networks in a simple and consistent manner to support decisions based on performance.

For organisations to manage this new model effectively, it is important to understand how to implement effective systems that can integrate and align inter-operational performance. The use of a PMS helps organisations provide instances of performance, contribute to decision-making, and lead to the alignment of all participants in the defined strategic direction [8]. For an organization to make an effective use of the performance measurement outcomes, it should be able to make the transition from measurement to management. According to Evans, Roth & Sturm [8], a performance measurement system is considered a subset of a PMS due the evolution of the concepts. Also, Busi & Bititci [9] contend that measuring performance is only one practical and technical support to performance management, which is a broader approach to treat performance and its implications.

In this context, Amaratunga & Baldry [10] state that performance management is using information from performance measurement to trigger positive changes in the systems and processes of the organization, as well as in the organizational culture, and to define objectives and goals, allocating and prioritizing features.

Nowadays, there is some specific performance management systems used in CNs, each one consisting of gathering some concepts in order to build a framework that can support decision-makers so that they can achieve the specific purposes or strategies, and identify new challenges.

The strategic alignment helps provide consistency and efficiency to the interrelationships among the CN's participants. However, to achieve organizational alignment, each one of them, must provide contributions (operation efficiency) to the CN. Then, it becomes desirable to achieve sustainable gains from the synergy conquered in collaborative processes. This can occur if a performance management system, acting as a tool, can transform the strategies into action through the alignment once happening in the relevant and critical activities [1].

Nevertheless, defining an appropriate set of categories of performance measures that meet the requirements of a particular network represents a critical step towards the establishment of an effective PMS. So, the question is "how can a performance management system make it possible to reach, or support, the strategic alignment in the CN?" The proposal is to manage performance through a collaborative network performance management system (CNPMS) that strictly depends on the alignment degree occurring in the specific moments of the CN life-cycle. Therefore, it is necessary to know how to define, configure and implement an effective CNPMS in order to support the CN decision-makers.

4 Results of Case Studies

The exploratory case studies reviewed in this paper deal with the practical application of the CNPMS framework [11], and its support methodologies, considering the propositions of Afsarmanesh, Marik & Camarinha-Matos [12] to classify the network topology. In Case 1, a temporary partnership established to explore short-term market opportunities is addressed, and, in Case 2, a dynamic project-based partnership without a dominant partner is addressed.

4.1 Approaches and Methodologies

The framework CNPMS proposed by Azevedo & Francisco [11] was developed using the Case Study Research (CSR) in order to drive the research method and the Soft System Methodology (SSM) to set and reset performance indicators [13]. It is based on two main layers: data and information, and functionality. The first one concerns the data acquisition and management repository, which intends to provide reliable information based on trust, competences (skill level), experience and know-how through the historical performance of the participants. Thus, it is possible to save time in the Partner Search phase (Figure 2).

The second layer consists of three performance functionalities, such as 1) network performance that supports the CN phases Design & Set-up and Evolution, using performance benchmarking, and outlines the performance targets that will be adapted and improved during processes improvement; 2) real-time performance to instantiate the inter-organisational performance. In the Operation phase, the static and dynamic indicators applied in real time in order to solve emerging problems and to make improvements (Evolution phase) are validated; and 3) performance evaluation in order to understand in the Dissolution phase, whether the CN has achieved its objectives and set the memory performance, and has also learned from the analysis itself by creating a repository of information about the performance generated by participants at each stage of the life-cycle.

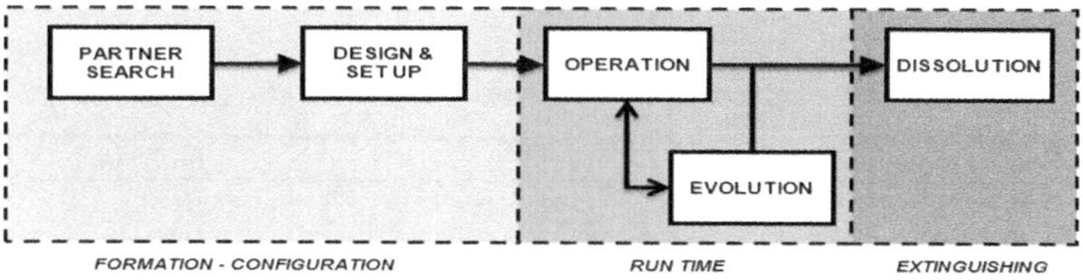

Fig. 2. Collaborative network life-cycle

The referred framework intends to motivate organizations to monitor the strategy effectiveness and the interoperation's performance of collaborative networks, i.e., to continuously monitor the intra- and inter-organisational performance. Therefore, some steps must be followed so that it is possible to manage the CNPMS, such as: defining strategies and inter-operations, and performance management skills; undertaking effective analysis about the benefits for each participant; choosing a set of indicators for the CNPMS; checking alignment (fit degree) in the specified moments; monitoring the performance targets and checking whether it fits with those originally proposed; reconfiguring processes of inter-operations in the event of poor performance; and checking if the previous intentions are still valid.

4.2 Case Studies

Some case studies were observed as part of a PhD program, and thus partial results obtained during the practical application of the model CNPMS [11] in some Brazilian collaborative networks are presented as follow.

Case Study 1. LogVale Logistics, a small company that provides logistics operations, seeking solutions to reduce the client's business cost. Initially, in the year 2007, a cooperation project was formed with a motorcycle dealership and both agreed to consider a collaborative network acting as a temporary partnership that would be established in order to explore market opportunities on the short term [12]. Soon after, they included three more business management consulting and ICT services firms.

On the strategic planning of this CN, the basic issues to consider had to do with trust and management of inter-operational processes. In the beginning, the application of the CNPMS model was not so easy because there were some difficulties concerning computer systems interoperability, different management backgrounds, low collaborative partnerships experience, and so on.

Then, the alignment measurement (table 1) helped the decision-makers to implement actions towards to better manage the inter-operational processes. At the partner selection moment, the alignment was interpreted only by the two initial participants. When this occurs, the first goal that is to know the participants' skills were compromised because there was a lost opportunity to improve the alignment of the other participants to the main objectives and goals. In the following moment, the agreement, reviewed inter-operational procedures were presented and the goals properly defined inducing the partners, once questioned, to conclude that they were highly aligned. Therefore, during the run time, many meetings were carried out to measure strategic alignment considering that defined KPIs were provided trustworthy information that allows decision-making improvements.

Table 1. LogVale Logistics case results

Decision-making moments	Form	Fit Degree
Partner Selection	*Board view*	*High*
Agreement	*Questionnarie*	*High*
Performance management	*Critical analysis*	*Medium*

The Fit Degree measurement can properly induce, at least, the visualization of processes or/and participants with poor performance allowing then correct timely wrong actions.

In 2008, the CN became extinct because the initial intentions were no longer the same, although the initial partners continued their trade. When the contributions of the partners responsible for consulting and ICT are integrated in the inter-operations, they no longer have an active participation in the project.

Case Study 2. Pet shop retailers network, a small Brazilian collaborative network that congregates participants interested in achieving benefits through the joint formulation of strategies and operations in a regional market. This CN was created within the Empreender Project, sponsored by the Brazilian Support Service to Micro and Small Enterprises (SEBRAE). It is an initiative to increase entrepreneurship actions of the micro and small companies so that they can benefit from the synergy among competitors within the same branch business. It seeks to address common problems with regard to common suppliers, logistics services, marketing, asset security, employee training, among others, which can be contracted through aligned strategies. It intends to reduce costs, increase bargaining power with suppliers. In conclusion, they work together towards an increase in competitiveness.

This collaboration group includes about twenty participants. This group acts as a dynamic project-based partnership without one dominant participant [12]. SEBRAE has expertise in business management and provides resources to support planning activities, consulting in marketing issues, among others, pointing the way forward.

Then (table 2), in the partner selection moment, only the roles imposed by the Executive Direction of the Commercial and Industrial Association of the Region Garavelo (ACIRG), an association that congregates and encourages small retailers of this region to collaborate, were take in account. So, when asked about the alignment on the goals to pursue, the participants had significant differences in terms of the concepts and competencies appearing three different groups with distinct concerns. Once questioned, the partners concluded that they were not aligned with the strategies proposed. In the following moment, the agreement, the reviewed strategic planning was presented in many sessions by consultants promoting with this action the balance of different proposals and narrowed the alignment on the strategic objectives. It was noted that problems related to trust have been solved and, once questioned, partners concluded that they were satisfactorily aligned with the new goals. Furthermore, during the run time many activities were jointly carried out by the participants, such as: marketing campaigns, purchases, training sessions, outsourced services, among others. Then, in an evaluation meeting, the participants concluded that there was a medium alignment degree and they would need for more time to reach alignment because due the different perceptions, or specificities.

Table 2. Pet shop retailers case results

Decision-making moments	Form	Fit Degree
Partner Selection	*Questionnarie*	*Low*
Agreement	*2 Questionnaires*	*High*
Performance management	*Critical analysis*	*Medium*

Measuring the Degree Fit induced at least that the perception that significant differences among participants can disrupt the necessary alignment to improve effectiveness in the inter-organisational processes.

The network continues to exist today, but still more external support is required to improve the alignment because many partners still have a deficit in knowledge management. However, individual performance has improved and there was an increase in the business experience of each participant.

5 Conclusions

In fact, performance management systems are yet an important management decision support tool that represents a crucial requirement to assure effective inter-organisational processes. Thus, the collaborative network (CN) may decide on the performance results of these processes. Nevertheless, the results of the alignment measurements are important to relay the concept to participants, highlighting the need for alignment along the life-cycle of the CN.

The performance management system must support quick decisions for the changes required in the CN's strategy, and also for possible and feasible improvements in the interoperable processes.

This approach believes that performance management is a tool to align the participants of CNs once this condition is detected by the partners involved.

References

1. Chituc, C.M., Azevedo, A.L.: Multi-Perspective Challenges on Collaborative Networks Business Environment. In: Camarinha-Matos, L.M., Afsarmanesh, H. (eds.) Collaborative Networks and their Breeding Environments, pp. 25–32. Springer, Boston (2005)
2. Camarinha-Matos, L.M., Afsarmanesh, H. (eds.): Collaborative Networks: Reference Modeling. Springer, New York (2008)
3. Saiz, J.J.A., Rodríguez, R.R., Bas, A.O.: A Performance Measurement System for Virtual and Extended Enterprises. In: Camarinha-Matos, L.M., Afsarmanesh, H. (eds.) Collaborative Networks and their Breeding Environments, pp. 285–292. Springer, Boston (2005)
4. Thefreedictionary.com, `http://www.thefreedictionary.com/alignment` (10/02/2010)
5. Kathuria, R., Joshi, M.P., Porth, S.J.: Organizational Alignment and Performance: Past, Present and Future. Management Decision. Emerald 45(3), 504–517 (2007)
6. Shimizu, T., Carvalho, M.M., Laurindo, F.J.B.: Strategic Alignment Process and Decision Support Systems: Theory and Case Studies. IRM, Hershey (2006)
7. Kaplan, R.S., Norton, D.P.: The Balanced Scorecard – Measures that Drive Performance. Harvard Business Review, 71–79 (January-February 1992)
8. Evans, S., Roth, N., Sturm, F.: Performance Measurement and Added Value of Networks. In: A Research Agenda for Emerging Business Models. Kluwer, Norwel (2004)
9. Busi, M., Bititci, U.S.: Collaborative Performance Management: Present Gaps and Future Research. International Journal of Productivity and Performance Management 55(1), 7–25 (2006)
10. Amaratunga, D., Baldry, D.: Moving from performance measurement to performance management. Facilities. Emerald 20(5-6) (2002)
11. Azevedo, A.L., Francisco, R.P.: Dynamic Performance Management in Business Networks Environment. In: Cunha, P.F., Maropoulos, P.G. (eds.) Digital Enterprises Technology, pp. 401–408. Springer, New York (2007)
12. Afsarmanesh, H., Marik, V., Camarinha-Matos, L.M.: Challenges of Collaborative Networks in Europe. In: Camarinha-Matos, L.M., Afsarmanesh, H. (eds.) A Research Agenda for Emerging Business Models. Springer, New York (2004)
13. Francisco, R.P., Azevedo, A.: An SSM-Based Approach to Implement a Dynamic Performance Management System. In: Camarinha-Matos, L.M., Paraskakis, I., Afsarmanesh, H. (eds.) Leveraging Knowledge for Innovation in Collaborative Networks. Springer, Berlin (2009)

Collaborative Assessment of Potential Value Generation in Development Projects

Ingo Westphal[1], Jens Eschenbächer[2], and Donatella Vedovato[3]

[1] BIBA – Bremer Institut für Produktion und Logistik GmbH, Hochschulring 20, 28359 Bremen, Germany
win@biba.uni-bremen.de
[2] BIBA
esc@biba.uni-bremen.de
[3] Venice International University, 30122 Venezia, Italy
donatella.vedovato@univiu.org

Abstract. Today development projects, in particular the development of complex products, are in many cases no task of a single company anymore. They usually require the active involvement of suppliers and sometimes even of customers. Since all involved partners have to invest time and money in the development activities it has to be ensured that the new product generates concrete value for the potential customers so that there is an adequate return on investment. One challenge is to assess the potential value generation in the early development phases when only a few basic specifications are available. This challenge becomes even bigger when contributions of different partners and customers are required. In this paper the assessment of potential value generation is regarded as a collaborative process and it is analyzed which collaboration capabilities are required in this process. The objective of the paper is to suggest an approach for a collaborative assessment of potential value generation in early development phases that considers the requirements upon collaboration capabilities of the different involved partners. In research and development projects this should provide input for the question if the project activities are on the right path to a positive return on investment. The suggested approach was tested in a research project on intelligent cargo solutions with different pilot scenarios.

Keywords: Collaborative process, assessment, value proposition, collaboration capability.

1 Introduction

Development work is an investment. Only if the output of this work generates adequate value for its customers there is a chance for a positive return on investment. For example, it is not enough that a new software-tool provides "fancy" new features. It is important that these features reduce, facilitate, accelerate or qualitatively improve the customer's work so that he can reduce cost or generate higher revenues. The value is determined by the difference between those benefits and the liabilities, in particular the price, the implementation costs, and the maintenance costs [1]. Only in case of a

L.M. Camarinha-Matos et al. (Eds.): PRO-VE 2010, IFIP AICT 336, pp. 553–560, 2010.

positive value the costumer would be willing to buy the new tool and implement it. So, in addition to the potential market volume (number of potential customers) a concrete value proposition is an essential prerequisite for market success of newly developed products [1], [2], [3], [4], [5].

To increase the likelihood of a positive return on investment it is necessary to compare the expected development cost with the potential market volume and the benefits the customers could obtain from the new product. This should already be done in the early development phases to avoid that resources are used for concepts that do not fulfill the requirements for market success. Therefore the project has to gain a sound understanding of the mechanisms of value generation for potential customers. However, this is difficult when only very rough specifications are available (e.g. in the early development phases) and there are only few or no experiences from existing products in particular for highly innovative products that should be "pushed" into the market. This difficulty is even amplified if the new product is developed for very dynamic markets since there is no time for extensive analysis after a first rough specification of the product.

In many development projects the initiating companies involve other partners, in particular suppliers, research institutes and costumers, for additional competencies, resources and experiences. Due to the uncertainties and the required creativity this involvement is usually no standard customer-suppliers relationship with precisely defined deliverables and payments. Rather it can be regarded as collaboration [6] where the partners contribute to a common goal in a more or less non-hierarchic way. Thus, there is a need for a collaborative process to assess the potential value generation on the side of potential customers (also called "customer value" [2]). The general approach in this paper to accomplish this objective is to identify a suitable existing approach for assessing customer value and adapt it if necessary for a collaborative process in the early development phases. In the second step the required collaboration structure and corresponding interactions for this process will be described. Finally it will be analyzed what requirements upon the collaboration capabilities are caused by the suggested process. The considerations are based on the practical application in a research project on intelligent cargo solution with different pilot scenarios.

2 Assessment of Potential Value Generation on Customer Side

As described above the objective of the assessment process is to enable a rough estimation of the value that the potential customer could obtain from the new solution. The customer value is determined by the gained benefits minus the liabilities the customer has to take for applying the solution. Taking the example of new intelligent cargo solutions the benefit could be reduced labor costs due to a higher degree of automation. On the liability side the price for hard- and software as well as the implementation costs, e.g. for setting up the system and creating interfaces to existing systems, have to be regarded. The question is how to come to a conclusion regarding the benefits and their significance? The following aspects have to be taken into consideration:

- The assessment will start in the very early phases of the development project with many uncertainties. So there is only a low level of specification available for the future product. In addition the effort of the assessment has to be low since it is not sure that the development will produce a return on investment.

- Most likely there will be a parallelism of the assessment and the ongoing development work to ensure short development cycles. Consequently it will be necessary to update the assessment according to the progress of development (dynamic process).
- If the project is dealing with very innovative ideas there is usually a gap between these ideas and the practical user problems. In some cases entire processes become obsolete and are replaced by new ones.
- The new product can often be used in different application domains. This means that several specific mechanisms of value generation in different application scenarios have to be considered. In addition it is necessary to make results comparable to draw generic conclusions that are also adequate for other application scenarios.
- The involved partners are generally independent, so they cannot be "forced" to contribute (beyond contractual obligations, if there is a contract at all). So it is necessary to convince partners and to reach consensus and common agreements.

Regarding these conditions it has to be analyzed if there are already suitable approaches to assess value generation on the customer side.

Since the objective is to do this assessment in the early development phases it was analyzed first if there are approaches in the corresponding models for development processes that are provided by research in particular for ICT solutions. Some well known examples for these process models are the Stage Gate approach [7] the so called "Waterfall Model" [8], the Spiral Model [9], the V-Model [10] or IBM's Rational Unified Process – RUP [11], or the Microsoft Solution Framework [12]. However, although some of these models, e.g. the Stage Gate approach or the Microsoft Solution Framework, mention explicitly the business aspect and the fulfillment of customers' requirements, there is no concrete suggestion for the assessment of value proposition.

Another research domain that is engaged in considerations on customer value and could be a source for assessment approaches is the domain of business models. A business model represents a way to express the logic of how a company is earning money [13] and value proposition is regarded as a key element of a business model [4], [3], [5]. Business Models (or Business Plans) are usually prepared when a new business should be established and investors have to be informed about the quality of the business. So they consider the customer value in a very early stage. In addition they consider in most cases all relevant application domains to demonstrate the market potential. However, business models are usually built upon a clearly specified future product and an assumed price for this product, while they take a more generic view on the customer value generation (it is assumed that the customer has a need for this product). These approaches for business models do not provide a method to analyze the potential value generation.

A more specific view on the value generation is provided by approaches for so called "Business Cases" (sometimes also called project charters) [14], [15], [16].

They are usually used inside an organization to convince the potential sponsors to support a defined improvement project, e.g. the implementation of RFID readers in a warehouse. Most approaches for business cases describe the problem / opportunity for improvements, the project scope, the approach for solutions, objectives regarding the improvements, and the relation between costs and benefits. This provides the necessary information to the sponsors. An approach that describes the mechanisms of value generation in a causal chain from changing process parameters to business effects is provided by Kapadia et al. [17]. The basic idea is to analyze which process parameters can be controlled directly by the organization (Process X) and then evaluate the impact that certain changes in the process parameters have on the overall process performance (Process Y as a function of Process X) and finally on the costs and revenues (Business Y).

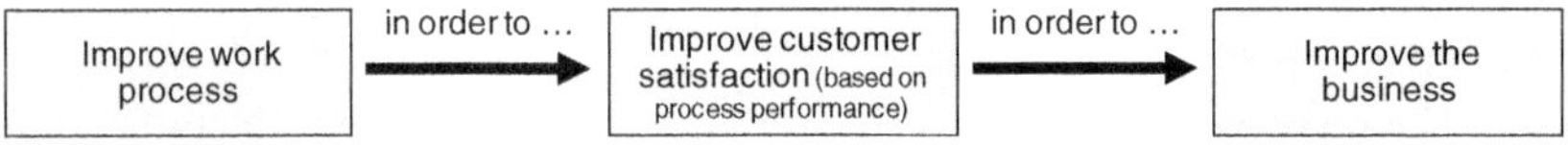

Fig. 1. Causal chain from improving process work to business effects [16]

Since these types of business cases are very specific for a particular company / organization they generally do not provide generic conclusions for the value generation in a whole application domain or even in different application domains. In addition, business cases are often not driven by innovation. They are looking for the best solution for a certain problem / improvement opportunity instead of looking for potential application opportunities for new innovative solutions. Summarized this means that a business case approach could provide a good understanding of the mechanisms of value generation on the customer side. In particular the approach of Kapadia et al. describes this mechanism in a structured way. However, it is necessary to go beyond the level of a single company / organization to enable an assessment that is sufficient for a development project. Therefore the business case approach should be combined with a business model view that considers different groups or types of customers in different application domains. Exemplary business cases at different pilot customers from the most relevant application scenarios will lead to general conclusions regarding the potential generation of customer value. For the development of innovative products it is important to identify customers that are market leader and ahead in their field. Hippel [18] suggested an approach to identify those so called Lead Users.

3 Methodological Approach for Collaborative Value Assessment

The assessment of the customer value that a new product can generate requires a relation between the capabilities of the product and a business case on the customer's side. This relationship is illustrated in the picture below (Figure 2).

On the customer's side the value generation is described according to the business case approach from Kapadia et al. It is assumed that the application of the new product has an impact on certain parameters of a customer's process, e.g. the acceleration of process steps. This should have a positive impact on the overall process performance that is received by the end customers or stakeholders, e.g. an improved on-time delivery. The improved process performance should lead to less cost, e.g. fewer penalties due to late delivery, or increased revenues from satisfied customers.

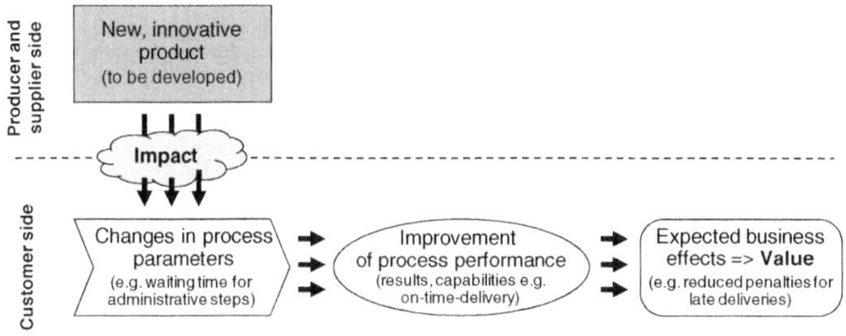

Fig. 2. Link between the product to be developed and the business case

It is important to look at the entire chain from product capabilities to business effect, since there is no value in changing certain process parameters if this does not lead to a significant business effect. If for example a product can increase the frequency of providing tracking and tracing information during a transport but the final customer does not need such detailed information and there is also no cost reduction, then there is no real value in this product capability. It is essential to analyze if the new product has an impact on current problems of the customer (cost, time, quality) or if the product can support fundamentally new processes with new revenues. Therefore, one of the first steps is to ask typical customers in the different application domains if they can see rooms for improvement in their processes regarding the new solution or if there are even already identified problems ("where are we losing money") that could be addressed by it. Based on these first ideas the whole causal chain from impact on process parameters to business effects has to be described and analyzed to assess if the potential value is relevant.

One challenge in this analysis is the specification of the new product that is needed to assess its potential impact on process parameters. Therefore it is important to achieve a rough first understanding of the product's future capabilities already in the very early development phases. Probably the considerations on the business cases will provide a feedback to the development work when additional requirements upon the new product become apparent.

The described analysis has to be done not only for one business case but for several business cases in different application domains. This provides an input for the assessment of the overall potential that is required for the business model. The different analyses are shown in the lower part of Figure 3.

How to get the necessary information to do this analysis? The producer has usually not such a deep understanding of the processes on the customers' side. In addition, at least for complex innovative products he needs information from his suppliers to draw up a first rough specification. Sometimes the suppliers even need information about customer requirements upon the new product to provide their input for the specification. So the assessment requires the involvement of different partners. Since these partners are generally independent and have not yet a hierarchic relationship the assessment can be regarded as a collaboration subject (or a collaboration opportunity). The producer, his suppliers and the selected pilot customers build up a Collaborative Network Organization (CNO) [6] as shown in the graphic below (Figure 3).

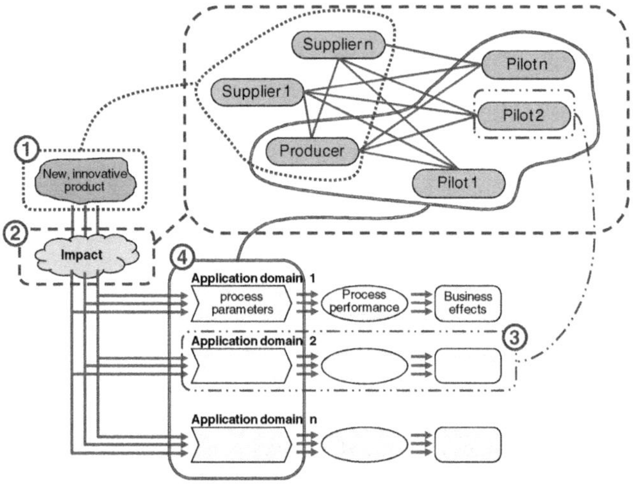

Fig. 3. Collaboration to assess potential value generation for different business cases

As a starting point (collaboration #1 in Figure 3) the new product has to be specified by the producer in collaboration with his suppliers since the capabilities of new solutions in most cases also depend on the development work of the suppliers. The assessment of the potential impacts requires coordinated contributions from all partners (#2). Based on the first specifications the pilot customers come up with first ideas for process improvements that can be achieved by applying the new solution. The developing partners have to check if the assumptions of the customers fit and if their requirements could be fulfilled by the new solution. Thus there are feed-back cycles to verify the application scenarios. The particular business cases are mainly drawn up by the corresponding pilot customer (#3). All pilots together can support the producer to generalize results to come to conclusions that are not only pilot-specific (#4).

4 Practical Application and Required Collaboration Capabilities

The suggested assessment approach was applied in the EURIDICE research project on Intelligent Cargo Solutions that support the interaction of individual cargo items with other cargo items and the surrounding environment. The objective is to improve the logistic performance of in the daily business of operators and industrial users [see www.euridice-project.eu]. The project, funded by the EU, is a collaboration of different companies that are developing technical solutions, research institutes, and pilot customers from different application domains. The single steps that were used to identify the mechanisms of value generation and corresponding assessment criteria at the different partners were already described in an earlier paper [19]. Here the focus should be directed towards the aspect of collaboration of the different partners. The required collaboration capability is analyzed according to different aspects of collaboration performance [20], in particular communication, reliability, promptness/speed, flexibility as well as elements of commitment like trust building and information sharing.

First, all partners need a strong ***ability to communicate***, since it is important that the pilot customers understand the potential capabilities of the new product to identify relations to their own processes. On the other side, it is also important for the developers to understand the mechanism of value generation on the customers' side to obtain input for further improvement of the development. Finally it is important to reach a common understanding regarding the assessment criteria and performance indicators to obtain results that are usable for a general assessment.

Flexibility, reliability and ***promptness/speed*** are other important collaboration capabilities that are required. Development is usually a time-critical work with a lot of uncertainties and there are strong dependencies between different activities. Therefore it is important that the partners can react flexible on changes (e.g. adaption to new product functionalities) and provide their contribution in a short time according to deadlines.

The coordinator of this collaboration must be capable of ***trust building***, since the all partners provide confidential data (technical approaches, internal processes and problems), in particular have other business relations or act as competitors in the market. Only if the partners trust each other they will be effective in ***information sharing***, which means that relevant information is provided to the other partners without delay. An important capability for the identification of the impact that the solution could have on the process parameters is to ***give impulses***. Only if new ideas are triggered and generated, the development will produce innovative solutions with a high potential. Other aspects like decision synchronization, problem solving, sharing benefits, cost and risks are less important in this early phase, since the objective is just to provide a rough assessment of the potential value proposition. All this is required for understanding of the future mechanisms of value generation and for avoiding unnecessary work.

5 Conclusions

The practical application has shown that it is important for the development of new products to understand if and how the customers could gain a specific value from the product. The suggested method provides a guideline for the involved partners to do a first rough assessment of the potential value assessment and it becomes obvious that some functions of the new solutions have a much higher potential for cost reductions and new revenues than others in different application domains. However, the method requires intensive collaboration between the partners. Therefore it has to be assessed if there are partners that can provide the required collaboration capabilities before this method is chosen. The suggested method is designed for the assessment of specific functional capabilities that have an impact on processes. For non-functional features, like prestige, the potential value has to be assessed in a different way. Further research is required for a methodological approach to determine profiles of collaboration requirements in a case specific way and train the partners on this process.

References

1. Yang, K., El Haik, B.S.: Design for Six Sigma - A Roadmap for Product Development, pp. 58–61. McGraw-Hill, New York (2003)
2. Woodruff, R.B.: Customer value: The next source for competitive advantage. Journal of the Academy of Marketing Science 25(2), 139–153 (1997)
3. Mahadevan, B.: Business models for Internet-based e-Commerce: An anatomy. California Management Review 42(4), 55–69 (2000)
4. Afuah, A., Tucci, C.L.: Internet business models and strategies: Text and cases, p. 45. McGraw-Hill Irwin, Boston (2001)
5. Elliot, S.: Research model and theoretical implications. In: Elliot, S. (ed.) Electronic Commerce: B2C strategies and models, pp. 291–325. John Wiley, Chichester (2002)
6. Camarinha-Matos, L.M., Afsarmanesh, H.: Collaborative Networks: Reference Modeling, pp. 52–56. Springer, New York (2008)
7. Cooper, R.G.: Stage-Gate Systems: A New Tool for Managing New Products. Business Horizons, 44–54 (May-June 1990)
8. Royce, W.W.: Managing the Development of Large Software Systems. In: Proceedings 9th Conference on Software Engineering, pp. 328–338. IEEE Computer Society, Los Alamitos (1987); Reprinted from Proceedings, IEEE WESCON, pp. 1–9 (1970)
9. Boehm, B.: A Spiral Model of Software Development and Enhancement. Computer 21(5), 61–72 (1988)
10. IABG: The V-Model Development Standard for IT-Systems of the Federal Republic of Germany (1997), `http://www.v-modell.iabg.de`
11. Rational Software Corporation: Rational Unified Process - Best Practices for Software Development Teams. White Paper. Cupertino, USA (1998)
12. Versteegen, G. (ed.), Dietrich, M., Reckert, H., Salomon, K.: Risikomanagement in IT-Projekten, p. 198. Springer, Heidelberg (2003)
13. Osterwalder, A.: The business model ontology – a proposition in a design science approach. PhD Thesis, University of Lausanne, p. 15 (2004)
14. Harmon, P.: Business Process Change – A guide for business Managers and BPM and Six Sigma Professionals. Morgan Kaufman Publishers, Burlington (2007)
15. CTG, Center for Technology in Government: Making Smart IT Choices: Understanding Value and Risk in Government IT Investments (2003), `http://www.ctg.albany.edu`
16. Toutenburg, H., Knöfel, P.: Six Sigma - Methoden und Statistik für die Praxis. Springer, Heidelberg (2008)
17. Kapadia, M.M., Hemanth, S., Sharda, B.: Six Sigma: The Critical Link between Process Improvements and Business Results. American Society for Quality (2003)
18. von Hippel, E.: Lead Users: A Source of novel product concepts. Management Science 32(7), 791–805 (1986)
19. Westphal, I., Vedovato, D., Kalaboukas, K., Bolic, T.: Business Case Driven Assessment of Effects Gained by Intelligent Cargo Objects. In: Cunningham, P., Cunningham, M. (eds.) eChallenges e-2009 Conference Proceedings, IIMC (2009)
20. Westphal, I., Thoben, K.-D., Seifert, M.: Managing collaboration performance to govern virtual organizations. Journal of Intelligent Manufacturing (2008), doi:10.1007/s10845-008-0182-5

A Collaborative Decision Support Method to Design Performance Evaluation Systems in CNOs

Rui Pinto Ferreira[2] and António Lucas Soares[1,2]

[1] INESC Porto, Campus da FEUP, Rua Dr. Roberto Frias, 378, 4200-465 Porto, Portugal
[2] DEI, FEUP, University of Porto, Rua Dr. Roberto Frias, sn 4200-465 Porto, Portugal
rui@omegadata.pt, asoares@inescporto.pt

Abstract. This paper describes an approach to the design of performance management models in collaborative networks, from a constructivist approach. The general approach is outlined and the part concerning a multi-criteria decision support method is explained. The paper finishes with an illustration of a scenario for test and validation of the method.

Keywords: Performance management; collaborative networks; constructivism.

1 Introduction

The complexity of network evaluation arises from at least four problems mentioned by [1]: (i) the choice of appropriate evaluation criteria and indicators; (ii) network evaluation should be approached on different levels of analysis; (iii) network structural properties may involve outcomes that are also potential inputs in network processes; and (iv) there are multiple stakeholders involved who will have multiple interests. Managing collaborative networks of organizations (CNO) clearly involves a set of multi-criteria problems. In particular, understanding what are the objectives of the individual members of the network as well as the global network objectives, for the different types of collaborative structures, is an important research topic. It is difficult to prove the advantages of CNOs, but according to [2], the ability to measure the performance of a collaborative network as a whole, as well as the individual performance of each of its members, could represent an important boosting element for the wide acceptance of the paradigm. The collective construction of the performance evaluation (or more broadly, management) model, for a given situation and timeframe is, at least, as important as the use of the performance management system. In this paper, an approach to the design of network performance information models is described. The *pmColNet*[1] approach adopts a constructivist perspective, providing the methodological and IT tools for the joint development of contextual and situational models fostering collaboration and negotiation. The paper focus on the multi-criteria decision support method for the negotiated agreement of the model.

---

[1] This paper describes results of the pmColNet project funded by the Fundação para a Ciência e Tecnologia under the contract PTDC/GES/71482/2006.

L.M. Camarinha-Matos et al. (Eds.): PRO-VE 2010, IFIP AICT 336, pp. 561–568, 2010.

2 The *pmColNet* Approach

Nowadays, we assist three major transformations in performance measurement: (i) "from performance measurement to performance management"; (ii) "from individual to collaborative performance measurement"; and (iii) "from lagging to leading performance management". Performance management is then defined as: “the use of performance measurement information to effect positive change in organizational culture, systems and processes, by helping to set agreed-upon performance goals, allocating and prioritising resources, informing managers to either confirm or change current policy or programme directions to meet those goals, and sharing results of performance in pursuing those goals”.

A supporting performance management system would include the following key elements [3]: (i) a structured methodology to design the performance measurement system; (ii) a structured management-process for using performance measurement information to help make decisions, set performance goals, allocate resources, inform management, and report success; (iii) a set of requirements specifications of the necessary electronic tools for data gathering, processing and analysis; (iv) theoretical guidelines on how to manage through measures (performance management systems are used to apply the information and knowledge arising from performance measurement systems); and (v) a review process to ensure that measures are constantly updated to reflect changes in strategy and/or market conditions.

The *pmColNet* approach addresses the point (i) of the above requirements, as applied to CNOs, by providing models and methods to: (i) develop and manage conceptualizations (models) of performance management systems, both individually and in collaboration through information and knowledge management tools and (ii) negotiate a network performance information model through a multi-criteria decision support method. The fundamental premise in *pmColNet* is that the socio-economic environment in which CNOs operate changes increasingly faster, meaning that CNOs need to constantly adapt to their specific contexts. This results in manifestations of CNOs that either result in an increasing rate of formation/dissolution (joint projects, partnerships, virtual enterprises, etc.) or, when operating in a more long-term, need to reassess goals and objectives more often. Consequently, CNOs performance models are required to be designed/adapted more frequently than before, be it when a new short-term oriented CNO is formed or when a long-term oriented one recognizes the need to reassess the existing performance model.

Roughly speaking, and from an information and knowledge management point of view[2], the *pmColNet* approach has two moments (see figure 1): firstly the elaboration of an individual *i* (the organization as member of the network) performance information model and secondly the negotiation and synthesis of a shared network N performance information model. Both moments require the adequate tools to support the individual and collective processes of domain conceptualization, information organisation and retrieval. A reference performance information model (*R_PInfoModel*) was developed, aimed at being used as a structured "catalogue" of perspectives, criteria and indicators to be selected for a performance management information model. From the reference model, each network member *i* derives its own performance

---

[2] This part of the *pmColNet* approach is only outlined here.

information model (*i_PInfoModel*). The final network performance information model (*N_PInfoModel*), for a given time frame and network composition and structure, is a subset of the reference model and is achieved by negotiation under multi-criteria decision support method described in section 3. The *r_PInfoModel* considers aspects such as network typology, stakeholders, the framework (objectives/tasks/periods and ranges of evaluation time), evaluation levels, perspectives, criteria, sub-criteria and indicators.

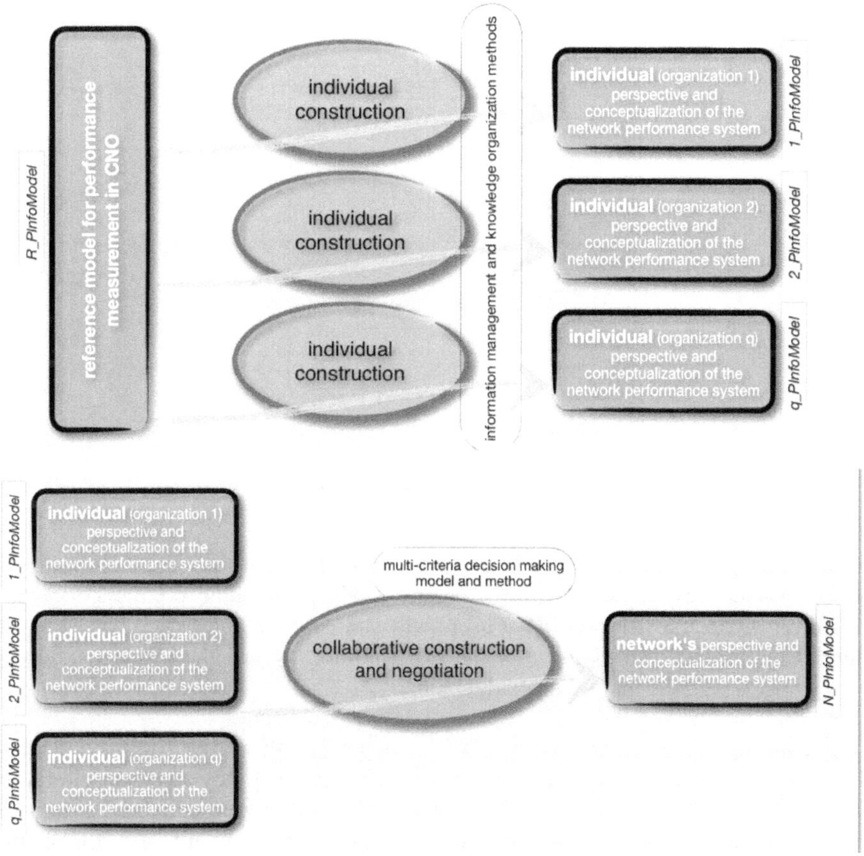

Fig. 1. The *pmColNet* approach

3 The pmColNet Collaborative Decision Support Method

The multi-criteria decision support model and method is at the core of the collaborative construction and negotiation phase of the *pmColNet* approach. In the beginning of this phase each of the members of the collaborative network should have conceptualised their individual view of the performance management information model. In the following paragraphs the fundamental components of the method are described.

HPFA. *pmColnet* decision-support model is structured along a very simple Hierarchical Framework for Performance Analysis (HFPA) (see figure 2). Criteria are forms of aggregation; they represent a common feature within different indicators. Within a specific perspective, a performance element is an indicator or a criterion or an objective. But, within two different perspectives, an element can be an objective for perspective A and an indicator for perspective B. In real life applications, hierarchical performance elements classification is sometimes subjective, that's why it follows a specific perspective. A perspective is just a specific materialisation, for a given situation, of the hierarchical performance elements.

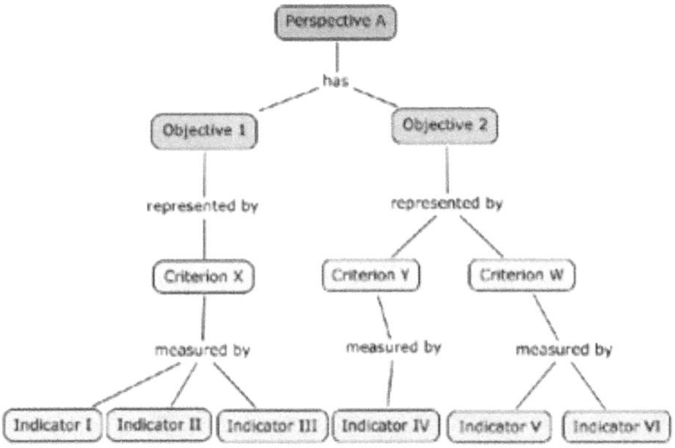

Fig. 2. HPFA used in the *pmColNet* approach

Visual pairwise judgment. Multi-criteria decision making is based on comparing different alternatives. pmColNet will use a visual rule to attain preference intensity, based on MCGDSS [4]. *pmColNet* users will simply click and drag a bar, starting at "Equal importance", dropping it at the exact point they feel the visual relation correctly manifests their importance judgement.

Aggregating preferences. Partners will rank HFPA alternatives using a 5 degree visual judgment. Using eigenvectors of the reciprocal matrices obtained, alternatives will be ranked. Nevertheless, final decision will ultimately be delivered with a final partner meeting, where interaction and negotiation will prevail over the method. *pmColNet* will promote vote power definition and negotiation. If this feature is not used, partners will be considered as having equal vote power.

The decision support method is outlined in table 1. The method is designed with a special emphasis in partner interaction and "decision overriding". This means that *pmColNet* results, as indicating in a certain way, or using certain performance elements may be contradicted by network members applying any different method at any phase. *pmColNet* has the ability to incorporate this "manual" network decision and carry on to the next phase. In fact, every network decision will be supported by the structured *pmColNet* suggestion and by an unstructured partner's meeting, where the partners can freely discuss and achieve a different path of the structured proposal. The

Analytic Hierarchy Process (AHP) is the multiple criteria decision support method used in the *pmColNet* approach. The method has some limitations, but they are minimised in our approach. Rank reversal problems can be minimized, because in a real network analysis partners will include only the relevant alternatives. Each alternative will be at least relevant for one particular network partner. Reducing the amplitude of the scale, for instance by using 1 to 5, over 1 to 9, inconsistency problems are also reduced. Because all the network partners are experts in the particular situation, 1 to 5 scale is perfectly adapted. Despite of the proposed pairwise verbal judgements, which are common to AHP, Macbeth or even Electre methods, and the prescriptive results, *pmColNet* definitely focus on interaction and commitment agreement, accordingly with its constructivist perspective. In other words, the prescriptive results regarding objectives, criteria and indicators should never be taken as final, but as a starting point for discussion.

Table 1. Steps of the *pmColNet* multi-criteria decision support model

Description	Method/characteristics
Phase A – Contextualisation I. Initial setup II. Partner's individual performance model III. Network typology IV. Defining vote power	Web form/ PROMETHEE GDSS framework; Tree structure; Private folders; HFPA; Commitment level
Phase B – Partner's proposals	HFPA
Phase C – Measuring preference intensity	Visual pairwise judgment; AHP; Veto threshold
Phase D – Negotiating and achieving a commitment package I. Network global commitment level II. Defining failure and success III. Levels of analysis IV. Performance relationships V. Index construction	Weighted Arithmetic Mean; Index construction
Phase E – Monitoring performance I. Normalising indicators and achieving a dashboard/ tableau de bord II. Ideal performance – TOPSIS III. Relationship between individual and network performance model	Normalisation; Topsis

4 A Scenario for Test and Validation

Two detailed scenarios were setup to demonstrate and validate the pmColNet approach. The first one deals with a CNO aimed at building a logistic planning information system and the second with an industry cluster with several strategic cooperative agreements, to collectively design, produce and distribute their textile goods. In this section some relevant aspects of the former are described.

Three organisations will start this year a new collaborative project: a Business School (BS); a Technology SME (SME); and an Industry Association (ASSOC). These three organisations are used to collaborate in past projects and have achieved their objectives in a satisfactory way. Nevertheless, in spite of the institutional trust they deposit in each other, they wish to improve their collaborative network efficiency, starting to monitor their performance through the *pmColNet* system.

Phase A - I, II, III and IV (see table 1)
In the initial phase of the method, each network member estimates the effort allocated to the network activities. They also build an individual performance evaluation model (individual HPFA) using the *r_PInfoModel* and the pmColNet collaborative modelling tool. The commitment level of the member towards the network is also defined at this stage (e.g., % allocated research hours or % of allocated investment). Type of inter-organisational governance: strategic cooperative agreements - "contractual business networks based on joint multi-party strategic control, with the partners collaborating over key strategic decisions and sharing responsibilities for performance outcomes." [5].

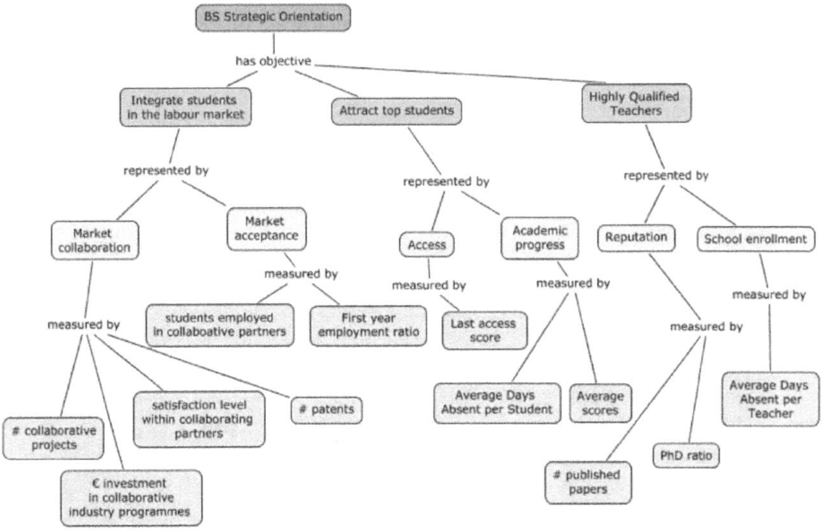

Fig. 3. Scenario #1: BS individual HFPA (*i_PInfoModel*)

Type of network regarding its objective: Technological/functional synergies network - a network of organisations that collaborate to obtain functional synergies in support chain value areas: such as R&D, marketing and logistics [6]. Network main objective: As said before, the project final objective is building a logistic planning information system adapted to the scenario industry. All partners agreed on that.

Phase B - Partner's proposals (see table 1)

A partner can propose several different alternatives for each of the network main objectives. If he does so, he must evaluate the several alternatives obtaining an ordered list according to its preferences and using the visual pairwise judgments and aggregation methods mentioned before. Each HFPA's element may have a description field and indicators must have additional scaling description, so that every partner correctly understands the proposal.

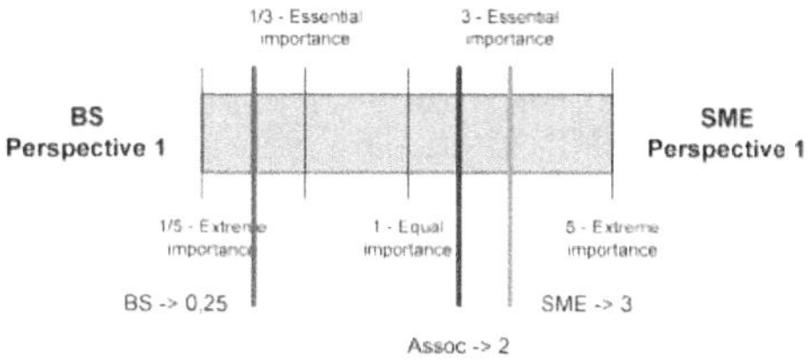

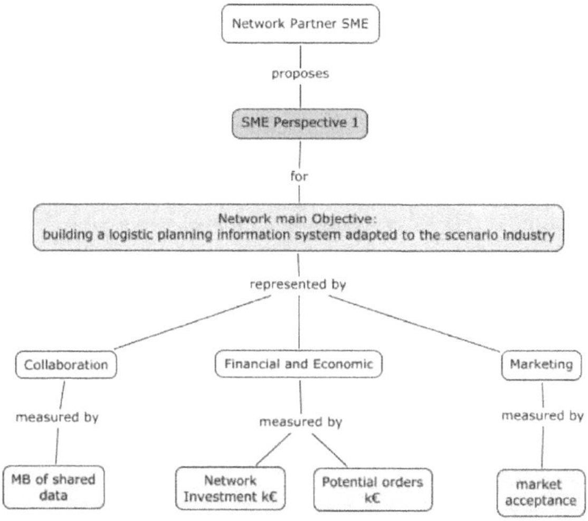

Fig. 4. Scenario #1: SME network HFPA proposal and pairwise judgement

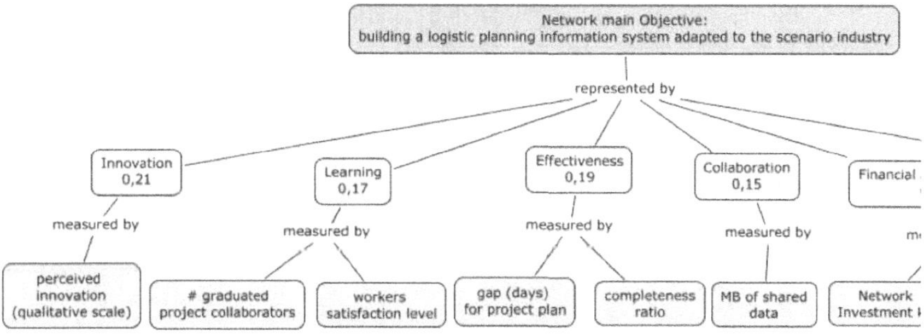

Fig. 5. Scenario#1 extract of the network HFPA (*N_PInfoModel*) showing the final global priorities for a distribution of vote power of BS=0.50, SME=0.17 and ASSOC=0.33

Phase C - Measuring preference intensity (see table 1)
Each partner evaluates the different HFPA on a pairwise visual judgement (see figure 4 for an example of measuring preferences). Applying the AHP methodology and the defined vote power, the ASSOC HFPA was out of the veto threshold and therefore was excluded from the final network performance model. Next, partners evaluate criteria of the two winning perspectives, once again applying visual pairwise judgements and AHP. The final result is depicted in the form of a concept map in figure 5 (network HFPA).

5 Conclusions and Further Work

pmColNet is an innovative approach to the collaborative design of network performance models in CNOs, combining information&knowledge management techniques with multi-criteria decision analysis ones. In this paper, a partial account of the later was presented, focusing on the steps necessary to achieve an agreed network performance model. From an epistemological perspective, the approach here presented can be considered as constructivist. Agreements regarding the network performance models are collectively built through concept maps explicitation and interpretation and through relational multi-criteria methods. Further work will involve the ability to store past network context, HFPA and results. This would enable for new networks to be advised for similar HFPA regarding its contextualisation: "similar networks have chosen this criteria: ..."

References

1. Sydow, J., Milward, H.B.: Reviewing the Evaluation Perspective: On Criteria, Occasions, Procedures, and Practices, `http://papers.ssrn.com/sol3/papers.cfm?abstract_id=1605177` (visited in 10/3/2010)
2. Camarinha-Matos, L.M., Abreu, A.: Performance indicators for collaborative networks based on collaboration benefits. Production Planning and Control 18(7), 592–609 (2007)
3. Busi, M., Bititci, U.S.: Collaborative performance management: present gaps and future research. International Journal of Productivity and Performance Management 55(1), 7–25 (2006)
4. Zahir, S., Dobing, B.: Designing a web-based multi-criteria group support system (MCGSS). Journal of Computer Information Systems 42(4), 50–60 (2002)
5. Todeva, E., Knoke, D.: Strategic alliances and models of collaboration. Management Decision 43(1), 123–148 (2005)
6. Carneiro, L., et al.: Redes Colaborativas de Elevado Desempenho no norte de Portugal. Public Report. INESC Porto (2007)

A Privacy Enhancing Architecture for Collaborative Working Environments

Jasone Astorga, Purificacion Saiz, Eduardo Jacob, and Jon Matias

University of the Basque Country
Faculty of Engineering. Alameda de Urquijo s/n. 48013 – Bilbao
{jasone.astorga,puri.saiz,Eduardo.jacob,jon.matias}@ehu.es

Abstract. Recent widespread deployment of different types of sensors and detectors has opened the door to a new way of understanding collaborative applications. The use of such devices allows information to be collected, used and disclosed on a massive scale and under very different conditions from which we are currently familiar with. Despite the huge potential of these collaborative environments, privacy is one of their most criticized aspects and probably the greatest barrier to their long-term success. To address this problem, we present a privacy-enhancing security model specifically tailored to the characteristics of ubiquitous and heterogeneous environments consisting of low capacity devices. This security model is based on the Kerberos symmetric key protocol which has been modified and extended to avoid using timestamps and to accomplish the authorization process. Finally, we present a validation of our proposal using an automated tool and we show a real world deployment use case.

Keywords: Kerberos, Centralized Authorization, Privacy, Sensors.

1 Introduction

Companies and organizations have traditionally promoted collaboration as a way of improving their processes and ultimately saving time and money. Frequently, the used collaborative tools rely on distributed applications in which different devices and software modules interact with each other. The resulting collaborative environments often integrate mobile devices such as PDAs or laptops to provide users with ubiquitous access to the system, but also sensors and other low capacity devices, which are used to collect data or provide real-time information. This gives place to a new trend of smart environments, mainly characterized by their invisibility and pervasiveness. Despite their huge potential value, these kinds of environments must still deal with some key challenges, being privacy one of the most important ones. In fact, this type of system dreadfully raises the level of the challenge to protect end-users' privacy, mainly due to the unprecedented data collection coverage, the invisibility of the collection process, the amount of data collected and the envisioned system connectivity. In this regard, we understand the concept of privacy as defined by Westin as "the claim of individuals, groups or institutions to determine for themselves when, how, and to what extent information about them is communicated to others" [1].

L.M. Camarinha-Matos et al. (Eds.): PRO-VE 2010, IFIP AICT 336, pp. 569–576, 2010.

The aim of our work is to develop an infrastructure that allows the construction of privacy-aware collaborative applications integrating low capacity devices. With this purpose, we have developed a security model which allows the enforcement of different privacy enhancing mechanisms such as authentication and authorization of remote parties and secrecy of private data. In order to address the authentication issue, this model relies on the standard Kerberos [2] protocol. However, we propose a modification of this protocol so that it also provides authorization functionalities. Additionally, after a successful authentication and authorization step, communicating parties share a secret key which can be used to implement additional functionalities such as ensuring the integrity and confidentiality of the transmitted data.

2 Collaborative System Architecture

The considered collaborative application model is based on a layered architecture that follows the principles of an Open Service Oriented Architecture (OSOA). This multi-layer architecture relies on decoupled building blocks that deal with different aggregation levels of business functionality, namely *core services,* which provide specific functionalities, and higher lever *software collaborative tools*. As shown in Fig. 1, the core services are defined as reusable software modules that implement very diverse basic or core functionalities, while the software collaborative tools are defined at a layer above. Thus, they can exploit one or more core services to offer aggregated functionalities.

Given the distributed and dynamic nature of the envisioned collaborative applications, such a system cannot be conceived without reliable mechanisms to ensure certainty in peer identification, to restrict data dissemination to the desired entities, and to guarantee the secrecy and integrity of these communications. Although these are common security tasks, a new level of difficulty appears when it comes to dealing with highly dynamic and radically unpredictable elements and interactions.

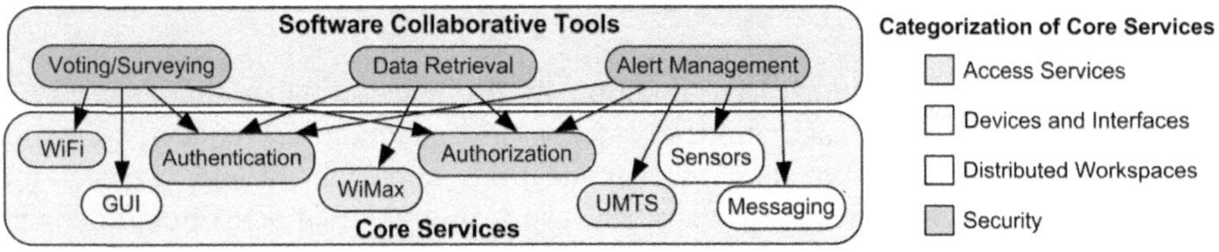

Fig. 1. Examples of collaborative applications based on the layered architecture model

2.1 Privacy and Security Concerns

Privacy and *security* are very closely related concepts. *Privacy* implies the possession of some kind of information and the subsequent terms and conditions by which it may be used, retained and disclosed to others, while *security* is often used to describe the capability of a technical system to protect and maintain the privacy of the information circulating within that system. Therefore, privacy breaches can occur when a system is not secure and leaks information to unauthorized parties.

From the data exchange point of view, building a privacy-aware collaborative architecture entails the implementation of security mechanisms to provide authentication and authorization of remote peers as well as to ensure the integrity and confidentiality of the transmitted information. This invariably results in the utilization of cryptographic algorithms, which are by nature highly resource consuming. However, typical small information gathering devices are mainly characterized for having small batteries and limited processing and storage capacity. Thus traditional security mechanisms are not directly applicable to these environments; and more specifically the use of asymmetric cryptographic algorithms is not preferable as they are more resource intensive than symmetric key algorithms [3].

From the logical point of view, one of the key concepts of the collaborative architecture introduced above is that the core services must be neutral and independent from the higher level applications that make use of them. As a result, it is not feasible for the core services to maintain and manage identity and authorization related information regarding all the remote parties they may interact with. Additionally, trust relationships among the same core services may vary from one collaborative application to another. For these reasons, a centralized management of identity and access rights related information is essential to ensure the simplicity and scalability of the system.

3 Proposed Solution

The aim of our work is to provide the above introduced architecture with mechanisms to ensure that the communications between the different entities that compose the collaborative applications are authenticated, authorized and protected from eavesdropping and modification by third parties. To that end, we have designed a security protocol which deals with the two major constraints of the considered environments: (1) the resource limitations of the involved devices make it necessary to keep the communication overhead as well as the computation power to a minimum, and (2) the dynamic nature of the collaborative applications makes a centralized management of authentication and authorization processes preferable.

Following these design principles, we have developed a lightweight security model based on the use of symmetric key cryptography, and more specifically, on the Kerberos authentication protocol. However, we have enhanced this protocol so that apart from authenticating the identities of the requesting entities, it also verifies their access rights. This way, all the information regarding identities and rights is maintained in a centralized location, where it can be easily accessed and updated by a system administrator. Additionally, the actual authentication and authorization processes are executed out of the basic components, relieving these entities of time and computation power consuming tasks, such as exhaustive searches, etc. Regarding the previously introduced distributed architecture, the security modules are integrated into it as core services, supporting this way, different higher level collaborative applications.

A detailed description of the underlying cryptographic mechanisms of this privacy enhancing model is beyond the scope of this paper; readers desiring a thorough review of these mechanisms are referred to [4].

3.1 Why a Kerberos-Based Approach

Kerberos [2] is a time-tested, widely-deployed system that provides authentication and the establishment of secure channels in open networks. As it is a well-known protocol, it will not be explained in detail here, but it is worth reminding some of its terminology and basic operation concepts, as they will be used later in this paper.

Each client or service is known as a *principal* in Kerberos, and each principal is characterized by owning a secret key known only by the principal itself and the Kerberos Key Distribution Center (KDC). The Kerberos authentication mechanism is based on the use of *tickets*. A *ticket* is a capability distributed by the Kerberos KDC that contains a proof of the identity of the principal that requested it. The tickets are encrypted so that only the entities for which they are intended are able to decrypt them. Therefore, each client that wants to authenticate to a server will present a ticket issued by the Kerberos KDC for that service.

Some of the benefits of Kerberos that make it a suitable technology for our approach are that it prevents the transmission of passwords over the network and makes use of a centralized user account administration. However, Kerberos also presents some constraints that make its deployment difficult: it requires synchronization between the participants and it lacks an authorization service.

3.2 Related Work

Most of the work carried out so far regarding security in sensor networks [5], [6] focuses on protecting the communications among these devices at the physical or MAC layer, but they are not suitable to manage security at the application level.

On the other hand, there have been numerous efforts to add authorization support to Kerberos, being the most remarkable ones SESAME [7], IDfusion [8], an implementation based on restricted proxies [9] and Microsoft's implementation of Kerberos [10]. We have studied all these protocols and concluded that they all present different drawbacks which make them unsuitable for the environments considered in this work, being the most remarkable ones the use of public key technology in different steps and the lack of a centralized management of authorization information.

3.3 The Time Synchronization Issue

Kerberos makes use of timestamps as a way of proving the freshness of the messages, and thus avoiding reply attacks. One major drawback of using timestamps is that it requires synchronization among all the interacting entities. However it also presents some desirable properties, such as statelessness, which is extremely valuable from the scalability point of view.

In order to avoid the necessity for synchronized clocks, we propose a *nonce*-based implementation of Kerberos, which basically uses the *authtime* field of the Kerberos tickets and protocol messages to include a nonce value. To provide the participating entities with a mechanism to check the validity of these nonce values, we have introduced the concept of a *Nonce Validation Service (NVS)*. The NVS is a new service that resides in the Kerberos Key Distribution Center (KDC), together with the Authentication Server (AS) and the Ticket Granting Server (TGS). As a result, the developed system becomes stateful, but it has the advantage that the state-related information is only maintained in the KDC and not in the end nodes, minimizing this way its impact on the system's scalability.

3.4 The Authorization Issue

The architecture of the proposed security protocol is shown in Fig. 2, which deviates from the conventional Kerberos protocol essentially in the introduction of two new information stores and the extension of the protocol with two new messages. Regarding the new information stores, one is used by the NVS to store the nonce values associated to each ticket, and the other contains information regarding access control restrictions, based on a role-based access control (RBAC) model.

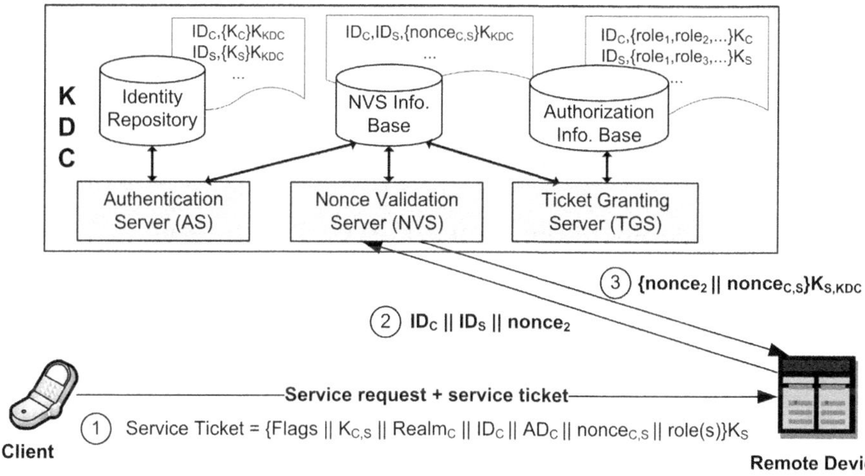

Fig. 2. Basic architecture and message exchanges of the proposed security protocol

Kerberos provides a user with the necessary credentials to access a service in two steps: first, it authenticates the user and provides him with the necessary elements to establish secure and authenticated communications with the KDC. Then, it generates specific credentials for each service the user wants to communicate with. It is before the second step where the authorization rules are enforced, limiting this way the generation of authentication credentials to legitimate authorized users. That is, whenever the KDC receives a request for a Service Ticket, before generating it, it verifies if the requesting principal owns the necessary rights to access the desired end service. With this purpose, the KDC queries its local authorization base and compares the roles with access right to the service with the roles that can be undertaken by the user. If a match is found, the user is determined to be authorized to access the desired service and the requested Service Ticket is generated, embedding in its authorization payload field the role undertaken by the client.

When a resource provider receives a new service request accompanied by a Service Ticket, it has to validate the content and the format of the received ticket. The validity of this ticket asserts that the identity claimed by the client is true and also that the client is authorized to access the given service. Therefore, the resource providers rely on the Kerberos KDC for both authentication of remote users and control of unauthorized accesses. The validation of a Service Ticket consists basically of three steps. First the ticket must be successfully decrypted with the service principal's secret key. Second, the validity of the nonce value contained in the ticket must be checked against the Kerberos KDC, for which a new request/response message pair has been introduced in Kerberos to allow querying the NVS, as shown in Fig. 2. Third, it must be guaranteed that the received Service Ticket contains a role identifier embedded in its authorization payload field.

Finally, it must be noted that the generation of a Service Ticket involves some resource consumption: bandwidth consumption, as the ticket must be transmitted from the KDC to the requesting entity and then from this entity, to the desired end server; and CPU consumption, mainly in the resource provider, as it has to decrypt the received Service Ticket and perform the validation of the incoming request. All these processes become a waste of resources when it can be determined beforehand that in the end the service will not be provided because the user is not authorized to access it. Therefore, limiting the generation of Service Tickets to legitimate requests reduces the network load, as well as the data processing performed by the service principals.

4 Formal Validation of the Proposed Security Protocol

As security protocols are notoriously difficult to design and extremely error-prone, new security approaches must be validated before deployment. Taking into account that with informal reasoning it is hard to consider all possible actions that an adversary may perform to breach security, formal verification has proved to be an essential tool in the verification of security protocols. The tool we have used to analyze our protocol has been AVISPA: Automated Validation of Internet Security Protocols and Applications [11]. This tool relies on the HLPSL (High Level Protocol Specification Language) protocol for the formal specification of the security protocol to be assessed and it integrates with four different back-ends, which perform the actual analysis of the protocol. All back-ends assume perfect cryptography, that is, an attacker cannot solve encryption without the knowledge of the whole key. Additionally, the communication channels are based on a Dolev-Yao intruder model, which means that the attacker has basically full control over the channel.

An essential part of the HLPSL description are the *security goals*, as the security analysis is performed against these goals and the results indicate whether the protocol meets them or not. AVISPA provides templates for two of the most frequently used security goals: *authentication* and *secrecy*. Among the properties that a security protocol may satisfy we have defined the following as critical to ensure our protocol's reliability and modelled them accordingly:

- *Authentication*: the protocol should be able to check and provide guarantees about the identity of any component of the system. This property is modelled by the *authentication_on* and *weak_authentication_on* security goals.
- *Access control*: the protocol should avoid the unauthorized use of resources or access to data. This feature is assessed by checking that every Service Ticket contains at least one role_ID in its authorization payload field and by enforcing the *secrecy_of* security goal on this field.

- *Data confidentiality and data integrity*: the protocol should provide protection against the disclosure and modification of the data during a communication. These features are validated by enforcing the *secrecy_of* security goal on all the exchanged secret or session keys.

One crucial aspect of a security validation is the initial knowledge allocated to the intruder. In this sense, first we have validated the protocol by implementing a single session and allowing the intruder to play the role of each legitimate agent. Then we have evaluated the case in which two parallel sessions of the protocol are executed, and in one of them, one of the legitimate agents is playing a role for which it is not intended to. AVISPA does not report about any attack in any of the cases.

5 Architecture Deployment in a Real Environment

The security model introduced in this paper has been developed and implemented under the scope of the C@R project, an Integrated Project under the 6th Framework Programme. The aim of C@R (A Collaborative Platform for Working and Living in Rural Areas) is to promote collaborative environments in rural areas in order to enable their development and permit their integration in the information society. To achieve this goal, a novel architecture for the composition of collaborative applications has been developed, in which the introduced security model has been integrated. Then, this architecture has been validated following a Living Lab methodology [12]. As a specific example, the Cudillero Living Lab [13] has implemented a use case with the objective of obtaining a quality hallmark with origin certificates for hake catches.

To implement this use case both fishermen and fishing boats should be equipped with different types of sensors providing information about location, temperature, humidity, etc. Regarding the origin certification of the catches, location information is a critical piece of data. Nevertheless, this information is also highly sensitive, as fishermen are not willing to reveal their fisheries to potential competitors, and thus in normal conditions it must be kept secret and only available to entitled parties. However, this fact changes dramatically when an emergency situation arises. In this case location information must be automatically disclosed to emergency services and also to any other boat nearby. Therefore, the deployed security model must be able to deal with the dynamic and real-time management of access rights.

6 Conclusions

The aim of this paper has been to draw attention to the privacy needs that must be addressed so that the deployment of dynamically built collaborative applications is feasible in environments involving low capacity devices. For this purpose, the basic characteristics of the targeted application scenarios have been studied, identifying the privacy and security issues affecting them. These issues have led to the high-level requirements of (1) a lightweight cryptographic solution and (2) a centralized management of authentication and authorization related information.

The introduced security model meets these requirements allowing the different entities that compose a collaborative application to establish trust relationships for the secure exchange of data. Although our model provides the necessary cryptographic material to protect these data, it does not specify whether they should be protected or not, or in which manner. This will in fact depend on the specific collaborative application above and on the critical nature of the transmitted information.

References

1. Westin, A.F.: Privacy and Feedom. Atheneum, New York (1967)
2. Neuman, C., Hartman, S., Raeburn, K.: The Kerberos network authentication service, v5 (2005), http://www.ietf.org/rfc/rfc4120.txt
3. Ruangchaijatupon, N., Krishnamurthy, P.: Encryption and power consumption in wireless LANs. In: 3rd IEEE Workshop on Wireless LANs, Newton, Massachusetts (2001)
4. Astorga, J., Matias, J., Saiz, P., Jacob, E.: Security for Heterogeneous and Ubiquitous Environments Consisting of Resource-Limited Devices: An Approach to Authorization Using Kerberos. LNICST, vol. 42, pp. 65–76. Springer, Heidelberg (2010)
5. Perrig, A., Szewczyk, R., Tygar, J.D., Wen, V., Culler, D.E.: SPINS: security protocols for sensor networks. ACM Wireless Networks 8(5), 521–534 (2002)
6. Karlof, C., Sastry, N., Wagner, D.: TinySec: A Link Layer Security Architecture for Wireless Sensor Networks. In: 2nd International Conference on Embedded Networked Sensor Systems (SenSys 2004), Baltimore, MD, USA (2004)
7. Kaijser, P., Parker, T., Pinkas, D.: SESAME: the solution to security for open distributed systems. Computer Communications 17(7), 501–518 (1994)
8. Wettstein, G.H., Grosen, J.: IDfusion, an open-architecture for Kerberos based authorization. In: AFS and Kerberos Best Practices Workshop, Michigan (2006)
9. Neuman, C.: Proxy-based authorization and accounting for distributed systems. In: 13th International Conference on Distributed Computing Systems, Pittsburgh, pp. 283–291 (1993)
10. Walla, M.: Kerberos explained, issue of Windows 2000 Advantage magazine (2000), http://technet.microsoft.com/en-us/library/bb742516.aspx
11. AVISPA: Automated Validation of Internet Security Protocols and Applications. FET Open Project IST-2001-39252 (2003), http://www.avispa-project.org
12. Schumacher, J., Feurstein, K.: Living labs – a new multi-stakeholder approach to user integration. In: 3rd International Conference on Interoperability of Enterprise Systems and Applications (I-ESA 2007), Funchal, Portugal (2007)
13. Valenzuela, M., Sierra de Miguel, A., Navarro, M.M.: A Living Lab for Stimulating Innovation in the Fishery Sector in Spain. In: Schaffers, H., García, J., Navarro, M., Merz, C. (eds.) Living Labs for Rural Development. Results from the C@R Integrated Project, pp. 83–104. TRAGSA, Madrid (2010)

Collaborative Design System for Supporting Dynamic Virtual Enterprises

Michele Germani, Marco Mandolini, Maura Mengoni, and Margherita Peruzzini

Polytechnic University of Marche, Department of Mechanics, via Brecce Bianche, 60131 Ancona, Italy
{m.mengoni,m.germani,m.peruzzini}@univpm.it

Abstract. Collaborative design provides creative design solutions and improves product quality as well as enriches participants' knowledge. Nevertheless, design and supply chain integration in product development processes is not a trivial task. The complex scenario of the dynamic extended enterprise triggers research toward the development of an innovative co-design platform to support multidisciplinary workgroups. Starting from the definition of a new design process model, the proposed approach is based on the formalization of the distributed knowledge in terms of interaction rules and representational models.

Keywords: collaborative design, virtual teamwork, agile organizations.

1 Introduction

Product development implies two main challenges: multidisciplinary team work and extended enterprise. As product design requires the integration of several specific domain solutions, multiple competences need to be involved in the design cycle, each performing their own task, converging on the same goal. Due to the different expertise, individual knowledge and background, communication problems can emerge. This means a continuous adaptation of the adopted design tools and methods for achieving the best solution in the estimated time. As a consequence, unforeseeable iterations increase, decision-making activities become more and more critical and time to market stretches. The creation of virtual teamwork extends product development, not only in terms of multisite enterprise, but mainly in methodological terms:

1. The typical cognitive design model is rearranged. Individual work is reduced while collective work is extended [1];
2. The whole design knowledge is dispersed along the product development chain. It is differently formalized according to the design stage and to the participants skill and adopted tools. It is mainly organized according to the project it is related to instead of the product structure;
3. Interaction styles and communication modes change according to synchronous and asynchronous collaboration. Supporting platforms should fit in with different collaborative dimensions needs.

L.M. Camarinha-Matos et al. (Eds.): PRO-VE 2010, IFIP AICT 336, pp. 577–584, 2010.

In order to overcome all mentioned problems, supporting tools should stimulate collective creativity, facilitate communication, manage product models evolution, monitor the whole process and reconfigure it according to the unpredictable scenario that continuously changes during the project development. In this complex context, this paper proposes a knowledge-based approach that allows defining a process model able to manage all concurrent aspects in co-design. This model extends traditional processes by introducing more strategic decision-making activities involving design teams. It aims at overcoming the distinction between the leader company and its supply chain by managing collective acceptance and the legitimacy of rules and by using role-playing for collaboratively develops new projects. The developed model is then implemented by a web-based co-design platform that integrates different organizational structures, supports novel modes of interaction and creates a CAD-based environment for elaborating product models.

2 Research Background: Distributed Knowledge Management

Among all kinds of industrial cooperation, design and supply chain collaboration is one of the most complex. As time to market needs to be decreased and synchronous collaboration requires the involvement of multiple partners, face-to-face collaboration is progressively replaced by a computer mediated one [2].

Another important issue regards with knowledge management across design cycle, among teamwork members, inside different organizations. Byrne, Brandt and Port [3] definition of Virtual Enterprise (VE) points out three crucial aspects in virtual teamwork: 1) the importance of integrating different independent organizational structures, 2) the role of information management and 3) the concept of temporary, that is reconfigurable according to the different project tasks, product development stages and team members. VE problems can be faced by adopting a process view enabling the creation of inter-enterprises business collaboration while keeping autonomy of participating enterprises [4]. Supporting systems focus more on managing internal and external processes instead of investigate how the distributed knowledge can be formalized through the flow of activities and the mechanisms of collective problem solving. In the last years, several researches have been oriented to the management of dynamic workflows by developing advanced frameworks to support exception handling [5]. All proposed architectures remain at an academic level and requires strong implementation efforts for defining rules reconfiguring workflow models. Inter-organizations efficiency depends mainly on the strategic management of information and on the adopted methodologies to support networking. This statement is more evident by analyzing current limitations of available Communication Information Technologies. Current PLM implementations are strongly document-oriented, have a structured and not much customizable data model and suffer from inter-enterprise integration difficulties [6]. Open-source web-based platforms allow establishing communities of practice and harnessing the knowledge gained by individuals [7] by providing web portals to sharing documents and applications [8]. Main problems regard with: 1) the organization of data according to the specific project, to the specific stage of product development and partners involved in, 2) the legitimacy of adopted rules and 3) the policy of data exchange authorizations.

The starting point to create integrated platforms to support virtual teamwork is the analysis of the distributed knowledge across the virtual teamwork and the definition of a new process model fitting in with the challenges of the extended enterprise [9]. As product design is heavily based on know-how gained from personal experience, the introduction of design teamwork makes complex knowledge capturing, formalization, storing, reuse, sharing and dissemination in distributed environments [10]. Enabling factors include: the use of common representational modalities and the integration of different design tools; the adoption of procedures shared by all participants; the management of responsibilities across the CPD; teamwork participants attitude, just-in-time expertise matching and timing of communication.

Both tacit and explicit knowledge can be related to the product and to the process. While product knowledge depends on the product model used to represent the different design aspects, the improvement of teamwork performance requires a robust analysis of process-related knowledge in order to formalize it across the distributed team context. Process information can be formalized within Workflow Management Systems (WfMS) using JECA (Justification, Event, Condition, Action) rules. They examine a set of conditions on the occurrence of events, and determine what actions need to be taken. Main implementation problems occur when the event has not been foreseen during the process analysis. In this case, Case Based Reasoning Algorithms (CBR) can be used to find a solution to unexpected events. They are able to search similar cases inside a proper database, to order them according to the similarity between the actual case and the historical ones and to adopt the right actions.

3 The Approach: Collaboration Modes

The adopted approach can be summed-up into three steps:

1. Analysis of traditional product development processes and identification of the main drawbacks during collaboration;
2. Identification of new interaction modes in the extended enterprise and their integration into a process model that includes additional collective activities, new ways of participants engagement, different team working styles;
3. Implementation of the identified process model into a web-based co-design platform able to efficiently support virtual teamwork by providing an integrated tool to manage both process and product knowledge.

The investigation of inner and outer connections in the extended enterprise has been carried out within 21 companies (5 Large and 16 Small and Medium), involved in the CO-ENV project (www.coenv.it), funded by the Italian Minister of Economic Development. The project aims at developing innovative co-design supporting tools.

The study shows that although collaborative activities are often carried out, contacts with the design and supply chains are switched on and off only by the leader company. Suppliers just appear as external actors attending the leader company process without really influencing it. Data transfer is generally carried out by the support of shared workspaces (e.g. ftp server) and traditional communication means, but only in one-way direction without exploiting the mutual opportunities to improve product and process knowledge. On the contrary, real team working requires a continuous stream of activities to achieve a coherent product design, as well as crosswise information management. The well known communication modes based on 1- to-1, 1-to-many and many-to-many patterns are not able to represent virtual teamwork (Fig. 1a). It is necessary to include the different identified relationships between the leader company and its design and supply chain. The network-based proposed model (Fig. 1b) considers the deployment of individual and collective work during interactions (Fig. 1c).

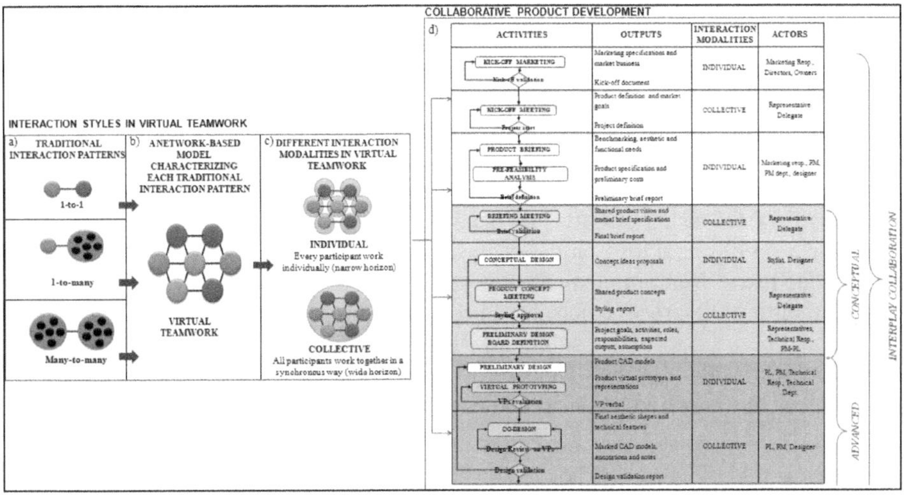

Fig. 1. The network-based model proposed to represent interaction styles in virtual teamwork created to support CPD

It is based on a network, where each node communicates with the other ones in both exclusive and mutual way, depending on the type of activity, on the design stage requirements and hence, on the adopted interaction pattern. In the network-based model, colours represent the 'specific gravity' of each actor carrying out individual and collective activities. When participants are separately working, their horizon is quite narrow and limited to those aspects they need to see in that particular moment to perform their own task (Fig. 1c at the top). In that case, traditional interaction modes fit in with collaboration needs. Otherwise, decision-making activities require knowledge sharing, individual work evaluation and specific solutions matching. A common space should be provided to activate the team network and make individual horizons in contact to extend the single viewpoints into the whole product perspective (Fig 1c, at the bottom). Figure 1d illustrates the proposed network model applied to conceptual design, advanced design and interplay collaboration stages. It highlights those activities whose interaction modality changes according to the design stage and the involved participants. The proposed representation aims at pointing out expected output, role-playing, interaction modes and collaborative dimensions. The lasts change according to the process phase, the participating actors, the exchanged information, the ways of communication, the type of relationship (mutual or direct).

4 The Co-design Platform

In order to support the identified collaboration modes, a co-design platform has been developed. It supports product and process knowledge by creating 1) a structured repository of documents arranged according to the project they are related to, 2) project templates for supporting team members' communication and data exchange, 3) a collaboration area for collaboratively interacting on virtual prototypes enriched with attributes and annotations stored and retrieved from/to the databases and finally, 4) an activity-based workflow area for managing information flow across team members. The last is linked with an external module for dynamically configuring the implemented workflows according to the collaborative process targets (efficiency, timesaving, costs, etc.) and shared rules.

The platform architecture adopts a client-server approach and consists of three main modules through which data coherently flows (Fig.2).

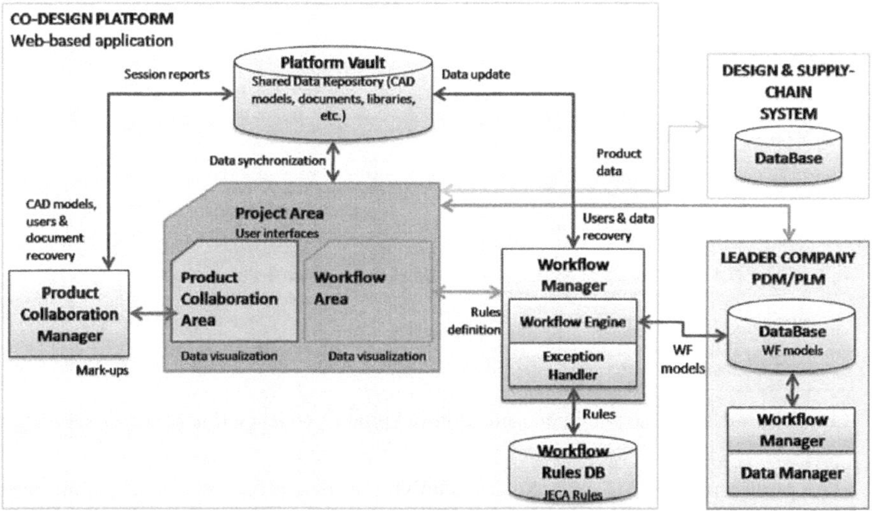

Fig. 2. The proposed co-design platform architecture

The project area represents the main interface for each participating actor. It is a project-based web platform supported by a collaborative portal server and a common vault. The project area consists of the collaborative and the workflows areas. All project have their own areas where similar and customized functionalities are implemented. The product collaboration manager allows collaborating on shared product models according to differentiated accesses for each team role. Both synchronous and asynchronous collaboration can be carried out. Data can be directly accessed through the collaboration area in the corresponding project space. Information is collected in and retrieved from the documents vault organized according to the different projects carried out by different teams. This collaborative portal server enables the management of role-playing, the easy identification of project progress, of achieved results and of employed resources. Finally, the workflow manager allows both designing and instantiating CPD workflows enacting distributed design tasks and supporting their dynamic management according to the implemented knowledge-based rules stored into the JECA rules DB. The workflow manager is directly accessible by the workflow area in the relative project space. It consists of a workflow engine to implement the proposed collaborative model and of an exception handler to automatically support workflow problem-solving (e.g. desertion of a partner, dismissal, changes in executive jobs, times delays, costs variation, product's requirements changes).

The system framework has been implemented by integrating the different modules within a web-based collaborative portal server based on Microsoft Office Sharepoint Server 2007 to have comprehensive content management and enterprise search, to accelerate shared business processes, to control users and to facilitate information-sharing across boundaries for better business insight (Fig.3).

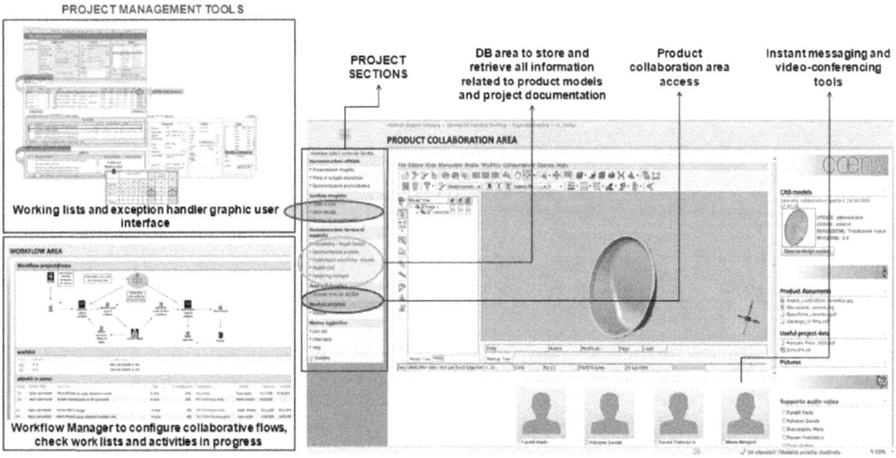

Fig. 3. Co-design platform implementation and product collaboration area user interface

The platform vault is a SQL Server database storing a list of websites (templates), each representing a project area. For each project, documents are collected and structured. The project page is structured by different sections: official project documents, technical information, obtained results, supporting adding resources, collaboration manager, project management tools. The last section provides the access to the workflow manager, to the exception handler, to the project plan, partners roles and responsibilities. The product collaboration area consists of a user interface that is directly visible from the project web-page, and of a project manager. The manager represents the real engine of the co-design tool. It integrates different commercial software packages: a collaborative CAD-based tool (AutoVue by Oracle), an instant messaging and communication tool (Skype), a video-conferencing area to support tele-presence and a DB area to automatically collect and retrieves information related to the product model under investigation. The workflow area consists of a graphical user interface and of a workflow manager. The workflow manager consists of a workflow designer (softFlow) and a plug-in software for handling exceptions. The area can be accessed by the relative project area, as well as by the collaboration area. Some ad hoc applications have been also implemented to satisfy system requirements:

1. a set of dedicated website pages as templates has been created in order to support users in populating each project area according to the specific collaboration tasks.
2. a plug-in software has been developed to integrate the chosen WfMS (softFlow by Metisof) and the co-design platform. It enables the access to the WfMS from the project area and hence, to enact distributed design tasks;
3. a novel module to dynamic handle unpredictable events occurred during WfMS runtime.

In an operational way, once a new project is initiated in the CO-ENV platform by adopting a web page template, the leader company implements both the whole CPD and its sub-flows related to the collective activities carried out with the design and supply chain partners. To each teamwork member is assigned a role in the project and a set of activities in the specific workflows where he/she acts. At this point, each participant can control his/her own work list by directly accessing the project collaboration area. The system administrator can use the Exception Handler module to manage the unexpected events occurring during each collaborative workflow runtime. It enables firstly the identification and classification of the type of the occurring event, secondly the recognition of the best solution to the exception and thirdly, the reconfiguration of the related workflow to improve the whole process efficiency. All mentioned functions are carried out thanks to the information stored in the JECA rules DB and by the implemented CBR algorithms. They operate in case of no rules finding by searching similar historical cases to the occurred unexpected event. They order all retrieved cases by JECA rules according to a set of particular attributes, such as the activity actor, the workflow typology, the failure reason, etc. In order to compare each of them, a similarity multilevel structure has been identified (e.g. the organization chart can be used for determining the similarity level of the activity actor attribute). The search result is the most similar case to a previous one and the corresponding rule for problem-solving. The platform can itself instantiate the new reconfigured workflow or ask the administrator to modify the rule solution in order to better fit with the specific occurring event. In the second case, a new rule and event connection are created and automatically stored in the JECA rules DB. As a consequence the system knowledge increases.

5 Conclusions

Competitiveness highly depends on the ability of industrial companies to efficiently cooperate, communicate and collaborate in order to innovate processes and products and face everyday design challenges. This paper is a step forwards the implementation of a proper co-design platform for supporting virtual teamwork. A knowledge-based approach has been adopted to define the main modules features and relative functionalities. Experimentations are carrying out in four different projects involving multiple partners of the COEVN consortium. All projects aim at developing new products. Preliminary results showed advantages in terms of team member engagement, reduced time to market, better control of project goals and expectations and decrease of design errors and iterations.

Future work will be focused on a better integration of all modules, on the objective measurement of the achieved experimental results, on the collection of more test cases to enrich JECA rules DB.

Acknowledgments

The research reported in this paper was supported by the Italian Ministry of Economic Development and the COENV R&D consortium

References

1. Bryan-Kinns, N., Healey, P.G.T., Leach, J.: Exploring Mutual Engagement in Creative Collaborations. In: Proceedings of the International Conference on Creativity and Cognition, Washington, USA. ACM Press, New York (2007)
2. Yang, M.C., Jin, Y.: An Examination of Team Effectiveness in Distributed and Co-located Engineering Teams. International Journal of Engineering Education 24(2), 400–408 (2008)
3. Byrne, J.A., Brandt, R., Port, O.: The virtual corporation. The company of the future will be ultimate in adaptability. Business Week 36, 36–40 (1993)
4. Jiang, P., Xinyu, S., Qiu, H., Gao, L., Li, P.: A Web services and process-view combined approach for process management of collaborative product development. Computer in Industry 60, 416–427 (2009)
5. Mourão, H., Antunes, P.: Supporting Effective Unexpected Exceptions Handling in Workflow Management Systems. In: Proceedings of the ACM symposium on Applied computing, Seoul – Korea, pp. 1242–1249 (2007)
6. Aziz, H., Gao, J., Maropoulos, P., Cheung, W.M.: Open standard, open source and peer-to-peer tools and methods for collaborative product development. Computer in Industry 56, 260–271 (2005)
7. Pollalis, Y.A., Dimitriou, N.K.: Knowledge management in virtual enterprises: A systemic multimethodology towards the strategic use of information. International Journal of Information Management 28, 305–321 (2008)
8. He, F., Han, S.: A method and tool for human-human interaction and instant collaboration in CSCW-based CAD. Computers in Industry 57, 740–751 (2006)
9. Krehmer, H., Eckstein, R., Lauer, W., Roelofsen, J., Stober, C., Troll, A., Weber, N., Zapf, J.: Coping with multidisciplinary product development – a process model approach. In: Proceedings of ICED 2009, Standford, CA, USA, August 24-27 (2009)
10. Wallace, K.: Capturing, storing and retrieving design knowledge in a distributed environment. In: Proceedings of the Ninth International Conference on Computer Supported Work in Design, Coventry University, UK, May 24-26 (2005)

Towards Controlling the Acceptance Factors for a Collaborative Platform in Engineering Design

Ardavan Dargahi[1], Franck Pourroy[2], and Frédéric Wurtz[1]

[1] G2Elab laboratory, 961, rue Houille Blanche BP 46 -38402
St Martin d'Hères Cedex, France
[2] G-scop laboratory, 6 avenue Félix Viallet - 38031 Grenoble
Cedex 1, France
{Ardavan.Dargahi,frederic.wurtz}@g2elab.grenoble-inp.fr,
Franck.Pourroy@g-scop.inpg.fr

Abstract. This paper might serve as a guide to take step towards a better acceptance of computer-based Knowledge management (KM) tools in institutional setting. At first time, it investigates a set of factors with different origins which are proved to have an effect on usage decision. Secondly, we set a list of candidate factor which are supposed to influence future users of a collaborative KM platform (Dimocode). At the end, we develop a methodology to take into account the selected factors and master their positive or negative impacts. The contents of this paper would be an appropriate framework in the way of Knowledge management systems (KMS) deployment.

Keywords: acceptance factors, collaborative, platforms, engineering design.

1 Introduction: The Controversial Success of KMS

Engineers involved in a design process use and create a large amount of technical knowledge during their daily work. Managing this knowledge is claimed to be a way of improving the efficiency of these engineering design activities by fostering knowledge formalization and sharing [1].

Collaborative platforms are often presented as a relevant support for knowledge management activities. They rely on information repositories and provide users with different means of interaction, either with the documents or with other users. Based on the assumption that intensive collaboration between engineers will support knowledge sharing, some research works report successful implementations of such collaborative platforms in the engineering design domain [2]. However, even if the idea of these platforms seems to be attractive and useful to the users, some research works rise into question the relevance of IT systems for applications such as knowledge management or organisational memory systems [3]. The main challenges IT is facing with regarding the potential success of such systems are discussed both in terms of technical challenges and organisational ones [4] and despite their importance, the latter seem to be often underestimated, leading to disappointing results.

L.M. Camarinha-Matos et al. (Eds.): PRO-VE 2010, IFIP AICT 336, pp. 585–592, 2010.

The issue of identifying and overcoming these organisational challenges is at the heart of our concern, as we are working on the development and the implementation of a new collaborative platform. This platform, namely DIMOCODE, will be dedicated to the sharing of calculation models of electrical components between design engineers and calculation experts. In addition to the sharing of the models' documents, DIMOCODE is also meant to support a knowledge network, thus giving more value to these calculation models. In this paper, we try to identify which factors will play a particular role in the acceptance of a collaborative platform, and which animation policy should be engaged in order to ensure a successful deployment.

The following section gives an overview of the state of the art regarding the acceptance factors of knowledge management systems (KMS). The forthcoming DIMOCODE collaborative platform is then briefly presented in section 3. Finally, section 4 draws some propositions regarding the main acceptance factors of the platform and the technological and organizational leverage for action related with those factors.

2 Acceptance Factors in the Literature

The degree in which individuals interact with a system, is seen as the key point in successful implementation of a KMS [5] and [6]. Nevertheless, many studies in the literature report failures in KMS deployment due to their underutilisation by individuals [7] and [8]. That is why, knowing how to foster the employees to use such devices and to embrace them in their daily work practices remains a major concern in the institutional setting [9]. Since the 70s studies on factors likely to affect human intention to use a system, this issue appears to be a crucial research field needed to promote KMS adoption in organisations [8]. Given that one can deal with a KMS either to feed it with his narratives or to seek suitable information, both knowledge sharing and knowledge seeking situations have been tried to be taken into account in our acceptance factors analysis.

A synthesis of several theoretical models of KMS usage suggested by different studies [10] and [7], has highlighted a fourfold dimension to what can be assigned each of the acceptance factors. These four dimensions are: *1) Organisational context*: some authors argue that the organisational settings, in which teams are embedded, can play an outstanding role on how a technology is framed and enacted [8] and [11]. *2) Tool:* many papers account for the perceived characteristics of the system itself as determinant for an effective KMS usage. 3) *Users:* the intrinsic characteristics of potential users are also highlighted [7] as another dimensions of KMS acceptance 4) Task: the nature of task which is supposed to be assisted by KM tool could alter the form of information exchange, thus that makes it harder or easier contrariwise [7]. This classification approach yields to consider four main classes of factors respectively called: organizational factors, system related factors, user related factors and task related factors. A second way has been also derived from our literature review to classify the causal factors might be separating them depending on their inhibitory or stimulating effects on KMS usage behavior into two categories. Table 1 combines both the fourfold dimension and effect-based classification visions by connecting to each category a set of deterrent (italic) and incentive (normal) factors. Each of the factors only comes with a very short description but the related bibliographical references can help those who are seeking to know more about them.

Table 1. KMS acceptance factors in the literature

Factor	Short description	References
Organisational factors		
Cooperative culture	An organisational culture conductive to knowledge sharing causes the employees to recognize the benefits of knowledge sharing behavior.	[12], [11], [9]
Reciprocity	Knowledge providers share their experiences when there will be a great chance of returning from others.	[9], [13], [14]
Episodic change	Under a high rate of episodic context change, people are reluctant to adopt a sharing behavior.	[11],[17]
Resource availability	A sufficient amount of time and a fast access can multiply the interactions with implemented system.	[8], [9]
Psychological safety	Legitimates the errors in well-intentioned actions	[11], [15]
Pro-sharing norms	The rules of teamwork are meant to enhance and facilitate the knowledge sharing climate.	[6], [10]
Generalised trust	The members are more inclined to share their skills with those who are trustworthy and whom they believe in their skills and goodwill.	[10],[13],[15]
Supervisory control	Feeling monitored by a superior can improve the willingness of people to make use of KMS irrespective of their contribution interest.	[13],[15]
Organisational reward	Moral or material incentives are sometimes proved to promote KMS usage.	[6],[8],[10], [12],[14]
User-related factors		
Image of self	The information contributed to KMS could bring a good reputation to his author.	[10],[11],[14]
Self-confidence	Perceived conviction in his abilities to face and solve the problems may foster the contribution.	[5],[9],[10]
Altruism	Satisfaction due to benefit another from one's experience and skills.	[10]
Loss of power	Reluctance to disseminate his knowledge using KMS fear of losing the resulting superiority.	[10]
Identification	Commitment to membership in the virtual communities of the KMS.	[7],[9],[10], [12]
System-related factors		
Contribution cost	The amount of time and energy required to contribute.	[9],[10],[13], [14],[15]
Research cost	The expense of time and energy to find sought information in knowledge base.	[9],[14]

Table 1. *(continued)*

Perceived usefulness	Quality of contents, task-technology-fit and awareness of potential benefits	[7], [9]
Ease of use	Easier is a software to manipulate, more it will be used.	[5],[6],[8],[9]
Task-related factors		
Task interdependence	When there is an obligation to share resources and expertise with others in order to achieve his aim.	[6],[10]
Task Tacitness	The proportion of tacit knowledge upon explicit one, needed to perform a task using KM tool.	[6],[9]

However, we believe the factors distribution into a fourfold dimension as suggested by the table.1 gives rise to an issue in the sense that certain factors, whatever deterrent or incentive they are, own a multidimensional nature and could correlate at the same time with more than a single dimension. For instance, we assume that spreading a cooperative culture between staff, having organizational conditions conductive to cooperation will not only be sufficient; but individual intrinsic characteristic might also largely determine the adoption of such a behavior. This type of assumptions led us to draw the model form Fig.1 taking into account the multidimensionality property of factors. This model will serve to define some requirements of the Dimocode platform which is now briefly presented.

3 What Is the DIMOCODE Platform?

With the DIMOCODE platform, we are interested by the problematic of capitalization and reuse of numerical models for the simulation and optimization of energetic system designed by engineers. We call energetic systems, systems like cars, buildings, or planes, it means systems that uses electric, mechanical, or hydraulic energy. For the simulation, and the optimization of those systems, engineers use physical and mathematical models in order to compute the characteristics of those systems: consumed energy, efficiency, weight, cost...

We made the hypothesis that the knowledge around those physical and mathematical models is composed of two aspects: *1)* Explicit knowledge: the file containing the models with their physical and mathematical equations, with the associated documentation explaining the assumptions, the limits of use, …*2)* Implicit or tacit knowledge: this is the skill developed by the expert who has developed the model.

So the goal of the DIMOCODE platform is to capitalize all the explicit knowledge and to provide experts and users of model with the opportunity to exchange their knowledge by having possibilities to work in a collaborative way around those models.

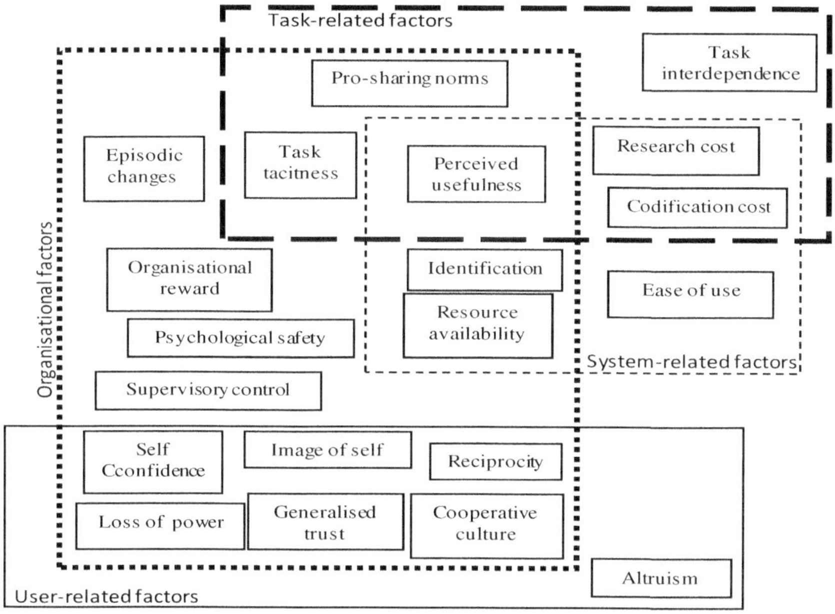

Fig. 1. The multidimensional nature of acceptance factors

The explicit knowledge can be stored and exchanged thanks to the possibility of creating a workspace for each model. In this workspace, the expert who has developed the model can expose all the files containing the equations and all the information and documentation for his models.

In order to offer a possibility to exchange the implicit or tacit knowledge, some functionalities have been implemented like:

- In the workspace of each model, there is a forum that allows users of models to ask question to the expert who has developed the model: this is a semi-formal way in order to offer the possibility to made explicit some knowledge aspects which are not clear, or simply not explained
- Experts can also work together around their model, with their simulation and optimization simulation tool, by using virtual meeting rooms in the platform: the idea is here to have the possibility to work together at the same moment on the same problem using the model.

In addition to the model workspace and its associated interaction facilities, the platform is also meant to support communities of practices around the simulation of energetic systems. Thus, it comes with a community workspace in which users have the opportunity to structure a community in order to share their knowledge around a specific practice. One can for example organise online (or offline) events, share documents or stories, define projects. The issue is now to define technical and organizational requirement in order to insure a successful deployment of the platform.

4 Technological and Organizational Requirements for the Dimocode Platform

It comes from section 2 that many factors may influence the behavior of individuals who contribute to KMS. The approach which was followed in order to take account of these factors for the specification requirement of Dimocode is now presented in three different steps: selecting primary factors, defining strategies in order to manage these factors, and defining leverage for action related with these strategies. The latter will lead us to define both technological and organizational requirements.

4.1 Selecting Primary Factors

From the initial set of factors listed in section 2, a selection of primary ones is proposed, based on the specific aims and context of Dimocode.

Dimocode is an open platform, transverse to existing organizations (laboratories, companies...) whose future users are members of. The organizational context in which they work is so quite varied. Moreover, being external and independent from these organizations, Dimocode's capacity of action on these organizational contexts is very limited. This led us to remove from our selection those of the factors that are mainly related with the organizational context. Nevertheless, it is to be considered that the Dimocode platform will also come with some kind of organization which overlaps with those sometimes highly structured and hierarchical of companies. As an example, it could be proposed to introduce within Dimocode an economic reward system for the contributors, regardless of the local policies of companies. For the particular case of this factor of organizational reward, the choice has yet been made to remove it from the selection, due to some issues in predicting its effect [8]. Again, this characteristic of being independent from already existing organizations led us to remove from our selection those of the factors that are mainly related with the task of the users inside their company. Coming from the outside makes it difficult to have leverage on the purely task related factors.

Finally, a finer evaluation of the relevance of each of the remaining factors, which is not developed in this paper, led us to focus on the list of ten primary factors which are: Reciprocity, Resource availability, Psychological safety, Pro-sharing norms, Generalised trust, Image of self, Altruism, Identification, Contribution cost, Research cost, Perceived usefulness, and Ease of use.

At this stage of the method, the grid of factors form Fig.1 also proved to be a very useful tool in order to increase both our understanding of the global context of the platform to be developed, and our awareness of threats and opportunities.

4.2 Defining the Main Strategies

Because of the plausible role of the retained factors in using a KMS, controlling for their positive or negative effect is perceived as being a priority in the goal of insuring a dynamic life for the DIMOCODE platform and reaching a mass usage of it. In this way, once the primary factors have been selected, the second step of the approach was to associate each of them with one or more strategies in order either to develop its positive effect or to limit the negative one (see Table 2 for an example).

4.3 Identifying Leverage for Action

To support the defined strategies, we have looked for the levers of action making it possible to put into action and materialise them. The levers of action connected to each factor are considered to be able to act on the impact of primary factors and moderate it and are essentially composed of some platform animation policies and/or some features already built into the last version of the Dimocode platform. Table.2 gives an example of a strategy associated with *Image of self* and the corresponding levers of action.

Table 2. Strategies and levers of action for moderating the effect of retained acceptance factors

Factor	Strategy	Leverage for action	
		Organisational	Technical
Image of self	Making the contributors visible	Identification of most relevant contributions	Publication on news pages of the communities
		Organizing invited online conferences from the expert	Visio-conference facilities

5 Conclusion

Despite collaborative platforms are meant to be a good means for sharing the technical knowledge between engineers, the deployment of such systems often leads to disappointing results, mainly due to a poor contribution level from the users. The paper deals with the case of the future Dimocode platform, which will be dedicated towards the sharing of simulation models for energetic systems.

Based on a literature survey, 20 acceptance factors have been identified and it was suggested a four-dimensional classification to structure these factors, The proposed classification accounts for the multidimensional nature of a large part of these factors, and made it possible to select the most relevant of the factors for the Dimocode context. Finally, a strategy and related leverage for action were associated to each of these primary factors, leading to a more complete set of requirements for the Dimocode platform.

This approach on the Dimocode platform might be considered as the preliminary draft of a more general method to account for acceptance factors in KMS requirement specification.

Among the limitations of this work, one has to consider that the multidimensional nature of some of the factors still has to be consolidated. Another point of importance is the Generalised influence between some of the acceptance factors which was not discussed in this paper.

References

1. Gardoni, M., Dudezert, A.: Valuing Knowledge Management Impact on Engineering Design Activities. In: The Design Society, International Conference on Engineering Design, Melbourne (2005)

2. Beylier, C., Pourroy, F., Villeneuve, F.: A collaboration-centered approach to manage engineering knowledge: a case study of an engineering SME. Journal of Engineering Design 20(6), 523–542 (2009)
3. El Louadi, M., Tounsi, I.: Do Organizational Memory and Information Technology Interact to Affect Organizational Information Needs and Provision? The International Journal of Knowledge Management 4(4), 21–39 (2008)
4. Atwood, M.: Organizational Memory Systems: Challenges for Information Technology. In: Hawaii International Conference on System Sciences (HICSS 2002), vol. 4, pp. 104–112 (2002)
5. Turner, A., Money, W.: Assessing knowledge management system user acceptance with the technology acceptance model. International Journal of Knowledge Management 1(1), 8–26 (2005)
6. Kankanhalli, A., Tan, C.Y.B., Wei, K.K.: Understanding Seeking From Electronic Knowledge Repositories: An Empirical Study. Journal of the American Society For Information Science and Technology 56(11), 1156–1166 (2005)
7. Lin, T.C., Huang, C.C.: Understanding knowledge management system usage antecedents: An integration of social cognitive theory and task technology fit. Information Management 45(6), 410–417 (2008)
8. Bourdon, I., Vitari, C., Ravarini, A.: The key success factors of Knowledge management systems: a proposed explanatory model. In: Proceeding of 8th colloquium of AIM conference, pp. 1–11 (2003) (in French)
9. Goodman, P.S., Darr, E.D.: Computer-aided systems and communities: Mechanisms for organizational learning in distributed environments. MIS Quarterly 22(4), 417–440 (1998)
10. Kankanhalli, A., Tan, C.Y.B., Wei, K.K.: Contributing Knowledge to Electronic Knowledge: An Empirical Investicatio. MIS Quarterly 29(1), 113–143 (2005)
11. Bernard, J.-G.: A typology of knowledge management system use by teams. In: 39th International Conference on System Sciences (IEEE), Hawaii, pp. 155–164 (2006)
12. Leidner, D., Alavi, M., Kayworth, T.: The role of culture in knowledge management: A case study of two global _rms. International Journal of e-Collaboration 2(1), 17–40 (2006)
13. King, W.R., Marks Jr., P.V.: Motivating knowledge sharing through knowledge management systems. Omega 36(2), 131–146 (2008)
14. Lynne Markus, M.: Toward a Theory of knowledge Reuse: Types of Knowledge Reuse Situation and Factors in Reuse Success. Journal of Management Information Systems 18(1), 57–93 (2001)
15. Beylier, C., Pourroy, F., Villeneuve, F.: Implementation of a light knowledge sharing tool in engineering design. In: International Conference on Engineering Design (ICED 2007), Paris (2007)

Learning Collaboration Moderator Services: Supporting Knowledge Based Collaboration

A.K. Choudhary, J.A. Harding, R. Swarnkar, B.P. Das, and R.I. Young

Wolfson School of Mechanical and Manufacturing Engineering
Loughborough University, Loughborough, Leicestershire, LE11 3TU
United Kingdom
{a.k.choudhary,j.a.harding,r.swarnkar}@lboro.ac.uk
{b.p.das,r.i.young}@lboro.ac.uk

Abstract. Collaboration Moderator Services (CMS) as an evolution of earlier Moderator research has emerged to address the issues relating to knowledge based collaboration by providing a set of functionalities such as raising awareness of business opportunities, problems areas, conflicts, change in the item of interests and lessons learned from collaboration. This paper presents a framework for learning CMS within the context of SYNERGY project. It has been shown that knowledge miners of CMS can be used to learn from the databases of the collaborative networked organizations (CNO) and semi-automatically update the CMS Knowledge Base. A case study from construction project has been used to show that the knowledge miner of CMS can "learn" by extracting various kinds of knowledge from Post Project Reports (PPRs) using different text mining techniques. The discovered knowledge in the form of rules relates to improving the processes, identifying recurring problems, good and bad practices, improving customer relationships and enhancing the coordination between members of CNO.

Keywords: Collaborative Networked Organization, Collaboration Moderator Services, Knowledge Discovery, Text Mining, Virtual Organization and PPRs.

1 Introduction

Recent organizational trends show an increase in the formation of collaborative networked organizations (CNO) to improve competitive advantage, and provide world class excellence and flexibility to address dynamic and turbulent market conditions. Collaboration of various forms can increase profits by improving chances to capture valuable business opportunities, address market demands and share resources and competences in very competitive and rapidly changing environments[1,2]. Effective knowledge sharing between the members of a CNO is core to the success of the CNO. A critical aspect of effective knowledge sharing within Virtual Organizations (VOs) is the identification of the most appropriate knowledge for reuse or exploitation in a particular context combined with the most efficient tools and mechanisms for its identification, sharing or transfer [3]. In any collaborative activity, an individual partner

L.M. Camarinha-Matos et al. (Eds.): PRO-VE 2010, IFIP AICT 336, pp. 593–600, 2010.

will at times make decisions that may affect (perhaps unintentionally), some or all of the other collaboration partners; each member therefore needs to be aware of other's needs as well as their own. The problem is complicated in most situations because of the fact that the members are not even aware of the extent of the effect that their actions can cause. Therefore, a collaboration support system needs a mechanism for checking the occurrence of these sorts of activities and, where necessary, raising awareness of the conflicts detected and situations of interest that occur. Therefore tools and methods are needed to support knowledge sharing through the increasing awareness of possible consequences of actions and other partner's needs during collaboration [4].

Collaboration Moderator Service as an advancement of earlier Moderator research [5-9] to extend the boundaries of the application of moderator technology to support the knowledge based collaboration of individual enterprise, VO and Collaboration Pool (CPool) by raising awareness of business opportunities, problem areas and embedding learning elements. The CMS is one of the services provided by the SYNERGY (FP-7 funded project) system to support knowledge based collaboration [4]. However, the functioning of Collaboration Moderator Service is limited by the knowledge it has about the team members, VOs and CNO. Knowledge acquisition, learning and updating of knowledge are the major challenges for a CMS implementation [7, 10]. These researches shows how a CMS can continuously learn from the operational/past project databases of the company and semi-automatically update the knowledge relating to members of a CPool in CMS-Knowledge base.

2 Collaboration Moderator Services and Its Architecture

The main objective of the CMS is to support individual partners (as well as the collaboration as a whole) by raising awareness of issues affecting any of a partner's registered items of interest and in cases where problems may be occurring, to raise awareness of which partners may be affected and how. Before CMS can support a user, CMS must acquire knowledge about that user and how the moderation activities for the user need to be carried out. When a change to an item of interest, or another event is detected, the CMS needs to access knowledge from CMS Database. This knowledge is stored in CMS Knowledge base (CMS KB) and is accessed when an event with potential to affect an item of interest occurs [10].

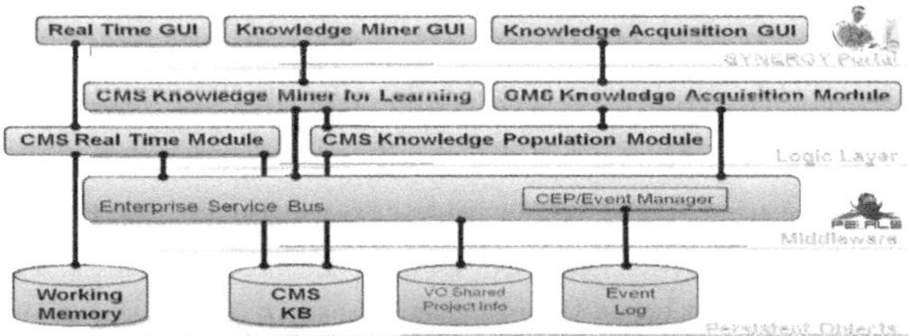

Fig. 1. CMS modules and repositories

2.1 CMS Architecture Component

Figure 1 shows the different modules of the CMS at different layers with various types of repositories. These are briefly discussed as follows; however a detailed discussion is presented in [11]. One of the major tasks for the CMS throughout the VO life cycle is knowledge acquisition. The CMS requires knowledge about each and every one of its subscribers. Knowledge about how CMS can support the subscriber, e.g. knowledge of things that are important to the subscriber or member, "items of interest", etc are held as CMS knowledge in the CMS KB. The **Knowledge Acquisition Module** (KAM) of CMS should be able to capture the information from the user using a simple interface and store it in the knowledge base (KB) of the CMS as shown in figure 2. The KAM should provide the users with facilities to access review and modify the knowledge whenever needed.

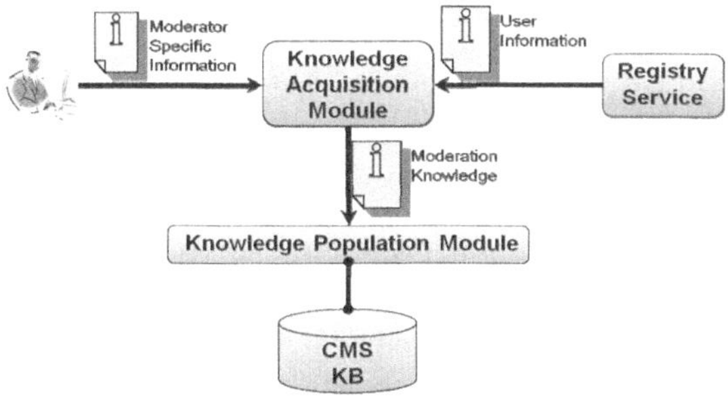

Fig. 2. CMS–KAM retrieving information and populating the knowledge base

The **CMS Knowledge Population Module** (KPM) is there to create, populate, update and delete the expert modules for the subscribed members. The knowledge captured from the user is fed to the KPM which stores them as persistent objects in the CMS KB. The KAM utilises the KPM to manage (create, access, change, delete etc) persistent CMS knowledge within its knowledge base as shown in Figure 2.

The role of **CMS Real Time Module** is to monitor the flow of subscribed events which relate to a user's "item of interest" and analyse with the help of the CMS knowledge base if there are any possible conflicts or problems, or any changes or occurrences that a subscriber should be made aware of. When a likely event is detected, the second step is to assess the situation. This step includes retrieving knowledge and additional information from repositories and other services. If the CMS then determines that a problem has arisen, a conflict has been caused or any object of user's interest has been changed, it communicates this to the user in the third step and raises his / her awareness of the situation or current activities which may be relevant to their work or contributions to the VO (or CPool).

The purpose of the **CMS Knowledge Miner for Learning** (KML) is to perform mining activities on the log of events (or other suitable data sources) to extract meaningful information and knowledge for updating the expert modules and CMS-KB. On the request of the user, this module should perform data mining for knowledge discovery on available data from various sources and present the user with the results. At the same time, the user is presented with options to update the knowledge base with the extracted knowledge. After verification from the user, the CMS knowledge base is updated with the help of KPM. To demonstrate the concept, the following section discusses construction project based collaborative networks and post project reports and thereafter it has been shown that how KML can be used to extract knowledge to semi-automatically update CMS-KB with the help of KPM.

3 Construction Project Based Collaborative Network and PPR

The construction industry is very diverse and faces widely fluctuating demand cycles, project specific product demands and uncertain production conditions. A construction project based collaborative network (CPCN) may contain many SME firms, contractors, subcontractors, material and equipment suppliers, engineering and design teams and consulting firms [12]. Collaboration between the various entities of the CPCN is temporary and may vary from project to project. The lifecycle of a virtual organization is limited to its particular project. PPRs of construction projects are one of the most important and common approaches to capture knowledge and lessons learned from the lifecycle of a CPCN. They provide opportunities for the project partners to share discuss and explain their experiences through face-to-face, facilitated interactions before a project is closed and the VO is dissolved. PPRs therefore allow multi-disciplinary teams to critique a project to determine both positive and negative aspects, potentially capturing tacit knowledge as learning points to improve the planning, execution and design of VO for upcoming construction projects [12].

PPRs are a rich source of data and information for organisations - if organisations have the time and resources to analyse them. Too often these reports are stored, unread by many who could benefit from them. If these reports were analysed collectively, they may expose important knowledge and experiences which have perhaps been repeated across a number of projects. However, most companies due to lack of resources to thoroughly examine these PPRs, leading to missed opportunities to learn from past projects. This research attempts to capture hidden knowledge from PPRs using the CMS-Knowledge Miners. Knowledge Miners uses techniques of knowledge discovery in text (KDT) and text Mining (TM) approaches to uncover patterns, associations, and trends in text based unstructured PPR reports. The application of KDT and TM methods on PPRs can extract useful knowledge relating to good or bad practices, process performance, avoid reinventing solutions, and re-use lessons learned on previous projects etc [12]. Identified knowledge can then be verified by the user before updating the expert modules (EM) in the CMS-Knowledge base.

In the remainder of this paper, a knowledge miner of a CMS is implemented on the PPR based database as part of a knowledge acquisition process to extract explicit knowledge from the PPR based database, so that it can be used to (1) equip the expert module with knowledge which was previously only available to the project team members by reading the PPRs and (2) update the content of an expert module as soon as a project finishes. The ultimate aim is to show how a CMS-knowledge miner can be used to extract useful knowledge for semi-automatic update of CMS knowledge base.

4 Knowledge Miners for Learning from PPRs: A Case Study

As shown in figure 3, multiple projects at different stages of their lifecycle can co-exist simultaneously in a collaboration pool. Hence, any company can participate in several VOs involving different stakeholders. Inevitably, during the life cycle of a VO, problems will arise due to conflicting decisions. In such situations, an intelligent software tool such as CMS might be used as a special manager to proactively raise the awareness of potential opportunities and problem areas based on registered "items of interest" that might affect the team members. The CMS-KB needs to be populated with knowledge about each of the team members and things that are important to each of them. For example, the main contracting company is interested in a number of key knowledge areas that have been identified as important to the success/failure of the project. In order to perform the moderation activity, CMS must be able to identify when events occur which affect any of these key knowledge areas and therefore the expert module within CMS-KB representing the main contractor must contain knowledge related to these knowledge areas. PolyAnalyst 5.0 software system has been used in this research as an instance of a CMS-Knowledge Miner. It applies techniques such as text analysis, link analysis and text OLAP to discovery variety of useful knowledge from PPR database. A brief overview of these techniques is presented in [13]. Once the knowledge is discovered, it is presented to the user for verification and knowledge can then be updated in the appropriate expert modules using the KAM interface. The whole process of knowledge discovery works in several stages including understanding the problem domain, process, identification of data source and its type, data cleaning, data transformation, data selection, data mining, pattern evaluation and knowledge representation. A CMS-Knowledge Miner is equipped with several modules to perform these functionalities at each stage of knowledge discovery as required.

4.1 A Case Study from Construction Industry

This example is based on PPR documentation from a construction company relating to 40 projects over the three years. The reports are quite long, typically 15- 25 pages, and analysis has been carried out with an aim to discover useful knowledge to improve decision making in future projects and reduce mistakes by identifying patterns of good or bad practices. An iterative methodology was therefore designed for this research.

1. Discussions with domain experts to determine key knowledge areas and types of knowledge which should be found and Ontology development.
2. KDT and TM using the PPR reports
3. Evaluation of the TM results by domain expert.
4. Representation of knowledge and update of items of interest in the EMs.

Ontology development: An ontology is developed so that particular types of knowledge can be targeted for knowledge discovery in the PPRs. An ontology based approach can also deal with semantic issues and issues of multilingualism.

Data Preparation Module performs the pre-processing tasks to transform the textual data into a form suitable for the application of algorithms. It includes transformation of data, data cleaning and other pre-processing tasks.

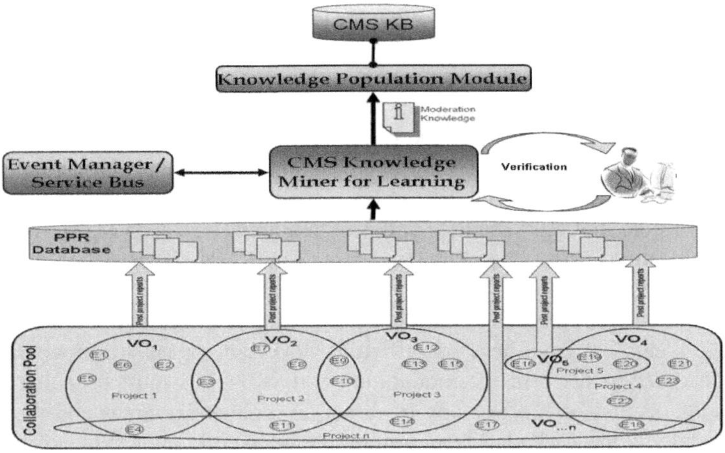

Fig. 3. Functioning of CMS-Knowledge Miner for Learning

Text Mining Module: involves the application of various algorithms to extract patterns, trends and discover useful knowledge as illustrated below.

Text Analysis (TA): provides the morphological and semantic analysis of unstructured textual PPR reports in a database format. TA extracts and counts the most important words and word combinations from the textual PPR reports, and stores terms-rules for tokenizing database records with pattern of encountered terms. Domain expertise may be needed to determine the relevancy and importance of combinations of terms identified in this manner. TA can be used to highlight the commonly used words in various areas of PPRs such as planning, estimation, errors or mistakes, quality, health and safety, defects and many more using visualization techniques like Link Analysis. They can then be captured as "item of interest" in the EM so that the moderator can make the partner aware of potential problems that may arise when they occur in future projects.

Link Analysis: reveals and visually represents complex patterns of correlations between various keywords that exist in the textual data. Figure 4 shows an example of the application of LA on the PPRs. LA has been applied on the ontology developed for the VO. The strength of the link shows the correlation between keywords or phrases. Exploration of these links provides the user with a set of knowledge where one keyword or phrase has effect on the other. Figure 4 shows the linkages between finance and time, i.e. various attributes of "Time" are linked with attributes of "finance". This knowledge can then be transferred in the form of IF-THEN rules by the user and added to the EMs manually for further use by Moderators. For example, let us consider 2 "item of interest" such as design change and accident. The knowledge can be represented as follows:

IF "there is a change in design" THEN "alert the contracting company for possible loss" AND "negotiate with designing team for redesign".

IF "accident happens" THEN "alert the contracting company for extension of project".

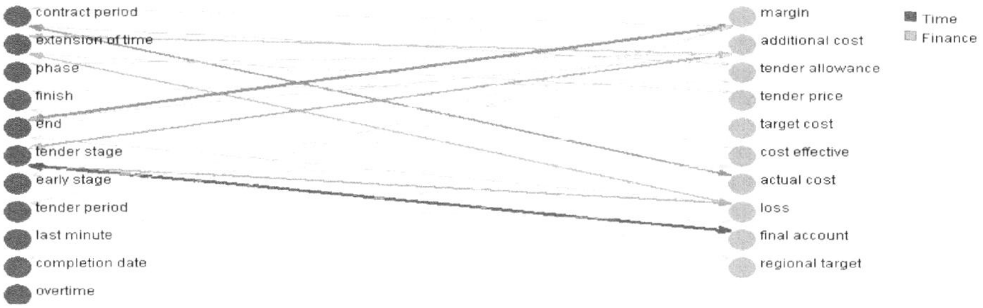

Fig. 4. Linkages between attributes of finance and time

However, a limitation of LA is that it only relates two keywords at a time. To overcome this, the next section discusses the use of a dimensional matrix or Text Online Analytical Process (OLAP).

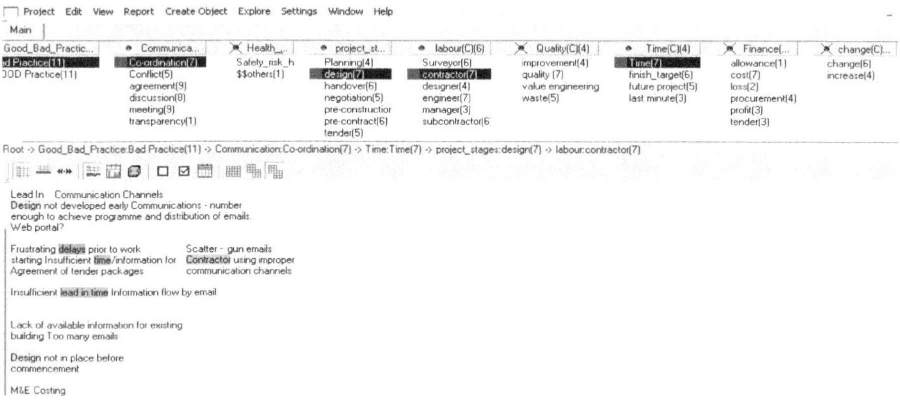

Fig. 5. Dimensional Matrix representing key knowledge areas

Text OLAP (Dimension Matrices): uses the OLAP - On-Line Analytical Processing feature which provides the user with the capability of performing multi-dimensional analysis of the data. Each column consists of different cells where each cell (block) represents the key word(s)/rules to be searched within the PPR Reports. For example, the first column represents Good_Bad_practices consisting of good practice and bad practice keywords. Here bad practice consists of a rule IF(the PPR report contains bad practice words such as poor, bad, slow, delay, late, wrong or worse) THEN (include that PPR report). However, these bad practice words alone are not sufficient to extract knowledge therefore they need to be combined with several other keywords. As shown in Figure 5, the bad practice keywords are combined with several other keywords such as coordination which comes under the communication column, delay which comes under TIME column, design which comes under project stage column, and contractor which comes under labour column. Finally, a set of reports have been identified which contain knowledge relating to these keywords. In this manner, it can be seen that CMS knowledge can be derived from PPRs based on the domain expertise using Text OLAP.

5 Conclusion

Collaboration Moderator Service has been developed to support knowledge based collaboration of individual enterprise, VO and Collaboration Pool (CPool) by raising awareness of business opportunities, problem areas and embedding learning elements. Functioning of a CMS is limited to the knowledge it has about the team members. This paper presents a framework for CMS to enable them to continuously learn from the operational databases of the company and semi-automatically update the corresponding expert module in CMS-KB using CMS-Knowledge Miners for learning. An example has been presented and emphasis has been placed on how a variety of knowledge can be extracted from PPRs using a variety of techniques from TM. This knowledge can then be verified by the domain experts and considered for addition or update of an expert module in CMS-KB.

References

1. Camarinha-Matos, L.M., Afsarmanesh, H.: Collaborative Networked Organization: A research agenda for emerging business models. Springer, Heidelberg (2004)
2. Camarinha-Matos, L.M., Afsarmanesh, H.: Collaborative networks: a new scientific discipline. Journal of Intelligent Manufacturing 16(4), 439–452 (2005)
3. Camarinha-Matos, L.M., Afsarmanesh, H., Ollus, M. (eds.): Methods and Tools for Collaborative Networked Organizations, pp. 257–274. Springer, New York
4. SYNERGY Project (2008), `http://www.synergy-ist.eu/` (Last accessed March 30 2010)
5. Harding, J.A., Popplewell, K.: Driving concurrency in a distributed concurrent engineering project team: a specification for an Engineering Moderator. International Journal of Production Research 34(3), 841 (1996)
6. Harding, J.A., Popplewell, K., Cook, D.: Manufacturing system engineering moderator: an aid for multidiscipline project teams. Int. J. of Prod. Research 41(9), 1973 (2003)
7. Harding, J.A., Popplewell, K., Lin, H.K.: A generation of moderators from single product to global E-supply. In: Putnik, G.D., Cunha, M.M. (eds.) Knowledge and Technology Management in Virtual Organizations: Issues, Trends, Opportunities and Solutions, ch. 5. IGI Publishing, Portugal (2007)
8. Lin, H.K., Harding, J.A., Shahbaz, M.: Manufacturing system engineering ontology for semantic interoperability across extended project teams. Int. J. of Prod. Research 42(24), 5099–5118 (2003)
9. Lin, H.K., Harding, J.A., Teoh, P.C.: An inter-enterprise semantic web system to support information autonomy and conflict moderation. Proc. Inst. Mech. Eng. Pt. B: J. Eng. Manuf. 219, 903–911 (2005)
10. Das, B., Harding, J., Swarnkar, R.: Knowledge Modelling Requirements of Collaboration Moderator. Internal report D3.1, Wolfson School of mechanical and manufacturing engineering, Loughborough University (2009)
11. SYNERGY, D7.1, Conceptual Architecture of SYNERGY Integrated System (2009), `http://www.synergy-ist.eu/docs/SYNERGYD7.1FINALSUBMITTED.pdf`
12. Choudhary, A.K., Oluikpe, P.I., Harding, J.A., Carrillo, P.M.: The needs and benefits of Text Mining applications on Post-Project Reviews. Computers in Industry 60(9), 728–740 (2009)
13. Feldman, R.: Text Mining Handbook: Advanced Approaches in Analyzing Unstructured Data. Cambridge University Press, Cambridge (2006)

A High Level Architecture for Personalized Learning in Collaborative Networks

Hamideh Afsarmanesh and Jafar Tanha

Informatics Institute, University of Amsterdam, Science Park 107,
1098 XG, Amsterdam, The Netherlands
h.afsarmanesh@uva.nl, j.tanha@uva.nl

Abstract. In Collaborative Network (CN) environments, creation of *collective understanding* about both the aimed outcome and the procedure for achieving it by its members is the antecedent to any successful co-working and co-development. While a part of the common CN knowledge is pre-existing to its establishment, once the collaboration activities begin the emergent knowledge also needs to be commonly understood within this environment. Creating such commonality in understanding is however quite challenging. This paper suggests a bottom-up approach to reach collective understanding by all individuals involved in these networks, namely by the staff involved at all organizations which participate in the CN. The proposed approach is founded on the idea of *learning-together* by the CN members to reach their collective understanding. In this approach, the domain/application experts in the CN act as the instructors and content providers, and assist with the modeling/remolding of the *education domain for the CN environment*. Considering that the individuals involved in the CN are highly diverse and have different backgrounds, their learning requirements are also highly varied. Aiming to reach common understanding in CNs, this paper first addresses the main challenges in this area of learning; it then presents the related state-of-the-art and proposes a high level architecture for *personalized learning* of the members in collaborative networks.

Keywords: Personalized learning, Learning Ontology, Learning Style, Cognitive State, Swarm Intelligence.

1 Introduction

While beneficial to all CNs, creation of collective understanding is particularly important for the long term strategic CNs, e.g. the Virtual organizations Breeding Environments (VBEs), in which effective collaboration among its members are the base for innovation as well as improving the efficiency of the joint production of competitive goods and services. Nevertheless, considering the nature and representative characteristics of the VBEs, being *a strategic alliance of organizations that covers wide variety of needed expertise within one sector or domain*, its member organizations and their staff are highly diverse. For instance, each individual in the VBE, while is an expert in one specialty area (e.g. logistics, marketing, assembly, etc. in the manufacturing domain), may have little or no knowledge about other specialties in the VBE, or about the general knowledge of different collaboration models or existing support systems for it.

L.M. Camarinha-Matos et al. (Eds.): PRO-VE 2010, IFIP AICT 336, pp. 601–608, 2010.

Therefore every individual in the VBE has a different set of requirements for learning the pre-existing knowledge in this environment.

The base pre-existing knowledge common to all collaboration networks is currently addressed by: (1) the reference models defined for different kinds of CNs, e.g. applying the ARCON model (Afsarmanesh & Camarinha-Matos, 2008), as well as (2) the base set of functionality supporting CN's management, e.g. the set of subsystems supporting the management of members' competency and trust, etc. in– the Virtual organizations Breeding Environments (VBEs) (Afsarmanesh, et. al., 2009). Finding the best learning materials as well as the near optimal learning path are the dreams of every learner, and these wishes are also shared by the learners in the CN environment. But unlike other learning environments, such as schools, which are typically characterized as individualistic and/or competitive learning environments (Johnson & Johnson, 1999), learning within the CN environments needs to be a cooperative learning environment, due to the common goal shared by all learners in this environment, as needed to together achieve a bigger and more competitive mass in the market/society. Combining this specific required characteristic in the CNs with the wide diversity among the individuals in the CNs, creates yet another new challenge in this area. However, within a group representing the same competency/role/position in the CN, e.g. design engineers, financial planners etc. the individuals have closer backgrounds, terminology, etc. than between such groups. Therefore, when it comes to the target area of learning inside the CNs, further tailoring of the learning materials and the learning paths is also required according to specific learning characteristics of each group. This requires also addressing and modeling the personality, trait, or culture of the groups in regards to learning, which distinctly identifies one group against another. Considering both the vast amounts of potential materials on every subject, and the large number methods for learning, developing a personalized learning approach is promising.

In a face-to-face classroom, the instructor teaches a course simply using a textbook and a fix syllabus that covers the course in sequence. Instructors usually design a conventional learning path based on their personal understanding of what "good teaching" means as a result of their teaching experience. Learners then have to all follow a fixed list of contents. In such a case, since learners have minimal options among which to choose, their individual interests and preferences are generally ignored (Chen, liu, & Chang, 2006). An alternative perspective was introduced for learning in the last decade, the aim of which was to provide personalized learning and find learning path customized to each learner, based on his/her preferences, requirements, learning style, and other determining characteristics.

Each learner has a specific Learning Style and a distinct Cognitive State and that LOs also have their own different Styles and Levels, etc. Ideally, when the learner has a request for learning, an automatic personalized learning system can generate the needed material and the guideline on what to study and in which order. This system careful considers his/her background knowledge and preferences etc. in order to identify the LOs whose specifications, better fit the learner's attributes, and provides the suitable learning path that best matches the learner style and considering the successful paths followed in the group to which the learner belongs. The problem which is explained above is primarily an optimization problem. The paper proposes the application of the Swarm intelligence method for solving this optimization problem, and finding suitable LOs and learning paths based on the specific collaboration among the learners and the group experiences.

The rest of this paper addresses the problem area of personalized learning in collaborative networks and its challenges and proposes a high level architecture to personalize the learning within collaborative networks.

2 Related Research

One line of research in this area is focused on personalized learning and finding suitable learning paths for learners. Some researches apply reasoning and semantic web techniques for personalized learning and recommendation of LOs, while others apply the optimization algorithms to find the best learning path and optimal solution. Other researches have also applied the multi agent system and intelligent tutoring to personalize learning. This paper however, due to the lack of space, addresses a few related researches, focused only on the first two main mentioned Approaches.

2.1 Personalized Learning Based on Reasoning and Semantic Web

PASER is proposed in (Kontopoulos et. al., 2008), and presents a system for automatically synthesizing curricula, applying the AI planning and semantic web methods. This system is based on the learner's profile, preferences, needs, and abilities to dynamically construct the learning path. However, this research does not adequately address personalized learning based on the learner's attributes and it also does not consider the features of LOs. In relation to our proposed approach, this research addresses the use of machine learning techniques for planning of the learning, but does not address any optimization algorithm. Also the proposed system does not indicate how this system is validated.

The research in (Gaeta et. al., 2009) describes methodologies and techniques for supporting a community of experts in modeling educational domains through the management of educational ontologies, namely through the e-learning ontologies and exploiting them in order to define and execute personalized learning experiences blended with learning activities. While the focus on the editor is strong, the issue of personalized learning is not sufficiently addressed by this research. Namely, it considers that identification of the learning path is simply done through a pre-existing graph, and does not address the detailed characteristics of the LOs, learners, or group experiences.

Research presented in (Chi, 2009) addresses a knowledge-intensive approach to create a general sequencing knowledge base for e-learning. This approach includes two components, including: (1) an ontology which is used to represent abstract views of content-sequencing and educational contents, and (2) a set of semantic rules that are used to represent relationships between individuals. However, this research does not adequately address the learners and LOs attribute. It mainly introduces a knowledge base system which based on its previously learnt knowledge suggests a learning path. Therefore its suggested learning path does not consider the set of features that we introduce in our proposed approach.

2.2 Personalized Learning Based on Optimization Algorithm

In (Chu et. al., 2009) the PC2PSO (personalized e-course composition based on Particle Swarm Optimization) is introduced for personalized learning, focused on four specific factors as its objective function. In their approach, Particle Swarm Optimization (PSO) method is used to find the near optimal solution, while almost entirely covering the above four objective functions. It is also discussed that when an e-course authoring tool is based on the proposed approach, the PC2PSO system facilitates instructors in selecting suitable e-learning materials from a mass repository. The issue of personalized e-course composition is however not sufficiently addressed by this research, because individual learner attributes is ignored. This research primarily aims to assist the instructor in finding suitable education material for suggesting to learners.

The research in (Wang & Huang, 2008) proposes an extended approach based on the ant colony optimization, which is rooted in a recent Meta-heuristic algorithm for discovering the on-line learning patterns along an adaptive learning path. This research emphasizes the relationship between the learners' learning style and the leaning objects, in order to achieve an adaptive learning plan for each learner. However, the optimization algorithm introduced in this research does not consider the learner's cognitive state, and searching the LO is basically done within the static repository that sometimes is updated manually by instructors.

In (Lin et. al., 2009) an automatic course generation system is introduced for organizing the existing LOs in a repository. It applies a kind of swarm intelligence techniques namely, the Particle Swarm Optimization (PSO). The purpose of their research is to find solutions to the problem of how to assist instructors re-organize well-structured teaching materials, utilizing existing repository of LOs. The suggested optimization algorithm in this research however does not consider the attributes of the learners and the LOs. This approach also only performs the search in a static repository and without consideration of resources accessible through the Internet.

In (Yang & Wu, 2009) an attribute-based ant colony system is proposed for recommending the adaptation of learning objects for learners. It introduces an extended ant colony system based on the Kolb's learning style model (Kolb, 1974). The proposed system is used to construct a search mechanism for finding a suitable learning object. In this system fitting learner to the related learning object is achieved considering the learner's learning style and his/her domain knowledge, and also the LO's style and complexity level. In combinatorial optimization problems usually one important aspect is to find the adequate condition for stopping the iterative execution of the algorithm (due to time complexity issues). The approach suggested in this research however requires in some cases to comprehensively search all the nodes in the search space, which due to time complexity problems is not possible, without introducing any meta-heuristic technique to address this challenge. Also the search for LOs in this approach is done manually by the instructors. The proposed system needs to be validated in real environments.

3 A High Level Architecture for Personalized Learning

The comprehensive architecture proposed in this paper applies both of the above approaches for different purposes, and aims to identify and take into consideration the main determining features that influence personalized learning.

In the first step, we characterize the main features of the learners and the learning objects. The main features a learner include: (1) Learning style, (2) cognitive state, and (3) learning goals. Correspondingly, the important features identifying and describing a learning object include: (1) style, (2) level, and (3) educational objectives. These six features cover the most important aspects related to the problem area of personalized learning. Fig. 1 represents our proposed high level architecture, showing the main required modules for a personalized learning system and their primary interactions. The architecture represents a number of repositories storing different information about the learners, LOs, and the groups in the environment. One of these repositories deals with the LOs. A learning object is a resource, usually digital and web-based, that can be used and re-used to support the learning in the environment (IEEE-LOM). Each learning object has a Style (e.g. animation, text, diagram, and so on), a Complexity Level (e.g. very easy, easy, and etc.), and an educational objectives (addressing the subject it covers). For example in the VBE, the repository of LOs includes information related to the VBE management system functionalities (Afsarmanesh et. al. 2009). The individuals involved in a VBE need to learn about these general aspects, but at different levels of details depending on their role and tasks in the VBE. As a result, careful construction of the LOs' repository in collaborative networks is important and necessary for its effective operation, as explained in the Introduction section.

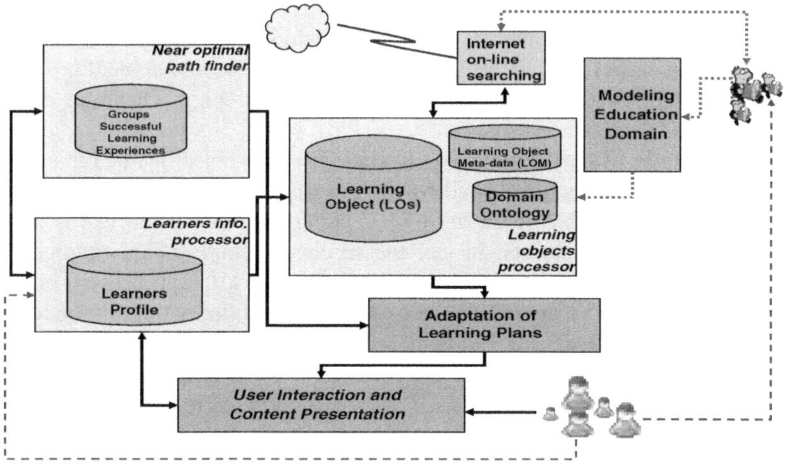

Fig. 1. A high level architecture for personalized learning in collaborative networks

Learning Object Metadata (LOM) is a data model, usually encoded in XML and RDF (IEEE, 2002 & IMS, 2004), and is used to describe a learning object and similar digital resources that support learning. The purpose of LOM is to support the reusability of learning objects, to aid discoverability, and to facilitate their interoperability, usually in the context of online learning. In our approach the LOs are indexed by LOM in order to let the system know about their attributes and how they can be used. Therefore, the LOM repository is another important component in this architecture. Each LOM describes: (1) a list of explained concepts, (2) property of each concepts and its special value, and (3) a list of learning objects in the repository.

A third repository in the architecture is an ontology, which represents all Domain Concepts (DC) and their inter-relationships. As such, a DC is any concept belonging to the described educational domain and is possibly explained by several LOs.

The repository of the learners profile consists of the user's information, such as his/her cognitive state, learning goals, and learning style (Kolb, 1974 and Felder & Silverman, 1988). The last repository contains information which is gathered for each group in the CN, during the operation of its learning system. Namely, this repository collects and records the information about the paths followed in any successful learning experience by any member of each group. The content of this repository is very important for further adaptation of the learning plan for the individuals in each group.

The **learner model** in this system is composed of learner's Cognitive State, Learning style, and learning goals. Cognitive state represents the current knowledge of the learner on the specific topic which he/she tries to learn. Each learner also has a preferred method for learning, which is called the learning style (Felder 1988). Meanwhile, each education has an objective; similarly each learner also has his/her learning goals.

The **Modeling of Educational domain** is a module in the architecture to assist the instructors and content providers to set up the learning domain for the CNs. For instance, through this domain, the instructors can create relationships between the ontology and LOMs. Through this module also a metadata is associated to one or more learning objects that exist in the LOs repository. Instructors and content providers in a specific domain construct the domain concepts in the ontology. Then they create relation between LOs and concepts.

The **Near Optimal path finder** tries to find for each subject learned in each group, the successful learning path followed by the most number of learners who passed the test on that subject. So based on the past experiences, the system learns to suggest better paths for future requests. In fact the feedback reports of the learners in each group on each subject, which is included in their profile, will be processed in the background by this path finder to provide the successful path information for the repository.

The **Adaptation of learning Plans** module try to find the best learning path for the learner from a group in the CN who tries to learn a subject. Imagine the learner submits a list of Target subjects to study. Given the Target C as input, the planning model builds a list of LOs which satisfy all the Target C's DCs, taking into account the learner's cognitive state, learning style, and learning goals. In this model also all restrictions and attributes of the LOs are considered. The module looks at all these attributes as aspects within an optimization problem. In our approach applying the Swarm intelligence techniques such as the Particle Swarm Intelligence (Kennedy, 1995) or Ant colony system (Dorigo, M., 1992) are foreseen to serve as the best methods for finding the near optimal solutions.

The **User Interaction and Content Presentation** module is the interface through which both the user specifies his/her request, and the system presents to user the learning path and the list of LOs, as a response to his/her request. In fact presentation of a response to the user consists of a relevant list of LOs delivered to the learner, while addressing all her/his learning requirements.

The leaner interacts with the system for personalized learning. According to the Fig. 1, users submit their request, and then based on their current knowledge on the subject and/or domain that they need to learn, the system identifies and presents a list of LOs together with a learning path. In time, the profile of each learner is updated with the feedback from the learners test results. Also learners participate in evaluating the subject they learned, through commenting on the LOs, as well as other aspect related to the performance of the system. This feedback will be then processed by the content providers and instructors.

4 Further Challenges in Personalized Learning

As was indicated in the description of the high level architecture of Figure 1, there are a number of challenges that need to be addressed for personalized learning in CNs. Below these challenges are further addressed.

An important part of the personalized learning is how to deal with the learners' model. In this model recognizing the current knowledge of the learner in relation to the domain/subject which he/she tries to learn is challenging, because the identification and evaluation of the level of human knowledge is complex. Each learner has a different learning goals and different preference for the learning style. But, similar to above, identification and formulation of both the preferred learning style and the learning goals of the learners are challenging. .

Another important feature of the personalized learning is how to identify the list of learning objects that best match the learners' requirements. On one hand, there are learners' aims and profile, and on the other hand there exist a large number of LOs addressing the subject in question. Developing the suitable technique to fit these two aspects and finding the near optimal solution is challenging. Similarly identification of the near optimal path for the learner requires its input from the results of mining all past successful learning experiences in different groups.

Another challenge in this architecture is how to deal with expanding the learning objects available in the system with the LOs that can be found on the web, namely how to search for LOs on the Internet. For instance if a subject requested by a learner is not sufficiently addressed in the existing repositories, then identifying the set of criteria to be used for searching/mining new suitable LOs on the Internet, and primarily based on the learner's profile, is challenging.

The architecture also represent collecting feedbacks from the learners. Voluntary input from learners about learning materials (indicated by the dashed arrow on the right hand side of Figure 1) helps the instructors to improve the Ontology, LOM, and LOs. With the results of learners' on the subject (indicated by the dashed arrow on the left hand side of Figure 1), the cognitive states of the learners in their profiles will be updated, and near optimal learning paths for future learners will be adjusted.

5 Conclusion

E-leaning, on-line, and web-based tutoring systems supporting the learning process is a promising approach in creation of collective understanding on pre-existing knowledge in CNs. In collaborative networks, such as in VBEs, the involved individuals are not typical learners in academic environments, and therefore it is even more important to make the learning time/cost effective. The personalized learning approach suggested in this paper aims to carefully apply both the learner's and the environment's characteristics into the customization of the most suitable reduced list of LOs, as well as the near optimal learning path for each learner individually. The paper addresses this problem area, its key conceptual challenges, and proposes a high level architecture to personalize the learning within CNs. This bottom-up approach represents the first step required for building the CN's common terminology and later on the ontology of the environment, as subjects of forthcoming papers.

References

Afsarmanesh, H., Camarinha-Matos, L.M.: The ARCON modeling framework. In: Collaborative networks: reference modeling, pp. 67–82. Springer, New York (2008) ISBN: 978-0-387-79425-9

Afsarmanesh, H., Camarinha-Matos, L.M., Msanjila, S.S.: On Management of 2nd Generation Virtual Organizations Breeding Environments. Journal of Annual Reviews in Control 33(2), 209–219 (2009)

Chen, C.-M., Liu, C.-Y., Chang, M.-H.: Personalized curriculum sequencing utilizing modified item response theory for web-based instruction. Expert Systems with Applications 30(2), 378–396 (2006)

Chi, Y.-L.: Ontology-based curriculum content sequencing system with semantic rules. Expert Systems with Applications 36, 7838–7847 (2009)

Chu, C.-P., Chang, Y.-C., Tsai, C.-C.: PC2PSO: personalized e-course composition based on Particle Swarm Optimization. Appl. Intell. (2009), doi:10.1007/s10489-009-0186-7

Dorigo, M.: Optimization, learning and natural algorithms, PhD thesis, Politecnico di Milano, Italy (1992)

Felder, R.M., Silverman, L.K.: Learning and teaching styles in engineering education. Engineering Education 78(7), 674–681 (1988)

Gaeta, M., Orciuoli, F., Ritrovato, P.: Advanced ontology management system for personalised e-Learning. Knowledge-Based Systems 22, 292–301 (2009)

IEEE, Standard for learning object metadata: http://ltsc.ieee.org/wg12

IMS, Learning Resource Meta-data Information Model Version 1.2.2, IMS Global Learning Consortium (2004), http://www.imsglobal.org/

Johnson, D.W., Johnson, R.T.: Learning Together and Alone: Coopeartive, Competitive, and Individualistic Learning. Allyn & Bacon, Boston (1999)

Kennedy, J., Eberhart, R.: Particle swarm optimization. In: Proceedings of IEEE international conference on neural networks, vol. 4, pp. 1942–1948 (1995)

Kolb, D.A.: Learning style inventory technical. McBer & Co., Boston (1974)

Kontopoulos, E., Vrakas, D., Kokkoras, F., Bassiliades, N., Vlahavas, I.: An ontology-based planning system for e-course generation. Expert Systems with Applications 35, 398–406 (2008)

Lin, Y.-T., Cheng, S.-C., Yang, J.-T., Huang, Y.-M.: An Automatic Course Generation System for Organizing Existent Learning Objects Using Particle Swarm Optimization. In: Chang, M., Kuo, R., Kinshuk, Chen, G.-D., Hirose, M. (eds.) Learning by Playing. Game-based Education System Design and Development. LNCS, vol. 5670, pp. 565–570. Springer, Heidelberg (2009)

Wang, T.-I., Wang, K.-T., Huang, Y.-M.: Using a style-based ant colony system for adaptive learning. Expert Systems with Applications 34, 2449–2464 (2008)

Yang, Y.-J., Wu, C.: An attribute-based ant colony system for adaptive learning object recommendation. Expert Systems with Applications 36, 3034–3047 (2009)

Non-hierarchical Collaboration in Dynamic Business Communities

A.H.M. Shamsuzzoha[1], Timo Kankaanpaa[1], Petri Helo[1], Luis Maia Carneiro[2], Ricardo Almeida[2], and Rosanna Fornasiero[3]

[1] University of Vaasa, Finland
[2] INESC Porto, Portugal
[3] CNR-ITIA, Italy
ahsh@uwasa.fi

Abstract. A business community where communication can be streamlined, information shared and trust can be built can be considered as a collaborative network promoting SMEs long term sustainability by assuring quick response, fast time to market, differentiated offerings and competitive prices. This collaboration could be orchestrated both in hierarchical and non-hierarchical forms depending on the firms size, capacity and objectives. In this research, we have considered non-hierarchical networking among firms, especially for small and medium sized enterprises (SMEs), where the basic requirements are related with choosing appropriate business partners, building trust and sharing valuable information among them. In order to articulate the concept of this non-hierarchical collaboration, six pilot SMEs were analyzed and a methodological approach to manage these environments is proposed. A generic overview of different variables or factors necessary to build such business collaboration are presented and discussed critically in this study.

Keywords: Business community, non-hierarchical collaboration, business competition, virtual organization, case study.

1 Introduction

In order to achieve competitive advantage, non-hierarchical collaboration among firms has nowadays become very important, especially for SMEs. This type of collaboration is considered as a key issue to cope with markets demands and stay competitive in the market segment through the sharing of competencies and resources among SMEs [1]. Firms need to improve their competences significantly through new business models, up-to-date strategies, technological capabilities and processes with a view to be successful in the market. In such business environment, firms are increasingly restructuring their internal operations, information systems, production processes and collaboration strategies with other firms in complex value chains, business ecosystems, which extend globally [2]. These collaborative business networks are complex entities, where proper understanding for designing, implementing and managing is needed, with a view to business success and for better decision making [3]. This collaboration provides value creation processes for firms in terms of developing

L.M. Camarinha-Matos et al. (Eds.): PRO-VE 2010, IFIP AICT 336, pp. 609–618, 2010.

Virtual Organization Breeding Environment (VBE) or Virtual Organization (VO), which are the long term and short term strategic alliances respectively with specific opportunities/goals [4, 5].

Business collaboration can be both hierarchical and non-hierarchical based on the objectives, requirements and the controlling power of the participating partners. In hierarchical collaboration, firms are generally connected following a vertical type of information exchange, where the collaborations are considered as rigid and with strong control on each other. Whereas, in non-hierarchical collaboration, firms are connected with each other in a horizontal power sharing where firms enjoy similar level of controlling on each other. This non-hierarchical collaboration is more flexible and operates in a more agile way than hierarchical ones. Mostly, SMEs collaborates hierarchically with big firms, whereas they collaborate with each other non-hierarchically. Large firms usually use economics of size as their competitive advantage, supported by large market channels, whereas small firms collaborate to compete in terms of flexibility and focus on totally different market segments than their larger competitors. The key problem is that in hierarchical networks, larger companies control the whole process and keep most of the added value, forcing SMEs frequently to compete based on price.

In literature various approaches/methodologies are initiated to provide for collaborative business networks. Afsarmanesh and Camarinha-Matos [6] defined a collaborative framework ARCON (A Reference model for COllaborative Networks) mainly for enterprise modeling that provides a comprehensive environment for modeling a variety of collaboration forms, namely VBE, VO, Professional Virtual Community, and Virtual Team. Romeo et al [7] developed VBE instantiation methodology with the views to identify the required components and functionalities necessary during the successful creation of a breeding environment for achieving the collaborative goals. Paszkiewicz and Picard [8] proposed a collaborative methodology within ECOLEAD project referred as Virtual Organization Breeding Methodology (VOBM) that defines the structure of VBE and VO architectures in a service-oriented environment, as well as an architecture development method for virtual organizations (ADM4VO). A meta-methodology concept articulated by Noran [9] can be defined as a method on how to produce methods for various collaborative networked organizations (CNOs) or CNO types whereas; Hoffner et al. [10] proposed a concept of typed domain, which helps establish successful relationships between partner organizations and simplify the negotiation between potential partners.

The growing rate of networking among SMEs reflects a catch-up of technology that considers as one of the competitive advantages for them. Mytelka [11] states that a firm's competitiveness may be in fact determined more by its external network than its size. In less hierarchical collaboration SMEs overcome their economic of size and find the proper market niche, especially in complex products with low volume and high variety. Those products are frequently engineer-to-order (ETO) and/or assemble-to-order (ATO) products and the manufacturing of such products is basically project based. These products are highly customer-oriented and individually tailored according to customers' own preferences and choices. To cope with such challenges in product development, firms adopt external support in a form of non-hierarchical collaboration to exchange valuable information and resources between each other to fulfill market demands and earn more revenue. Isolation nowadays kills firms, especially for SMEs which affects negatively over them in terms of innovation and prosperity.

2 Research Methodology

In this research, it was adopted a case study approach with the view to understand the formation of non-hierarchical collaboration among SMEs. Various data was collected from six companies belonging to three case networks in different industrial sectors namely, textile and apparel, footwear and machine tools. Two companies from each industrial sector were identified and selected based on their product offerings, market shares, annual turnovers and number of employees. All the companies were leaders in their corresponding market segments and in small/medium sized in terms of revenue earnings. The objectives of these multiple case study were to elaborate and positioning of non-hierarchical collaboration trends among different business communities and investigate the suitability and/or applicability of this methodology.

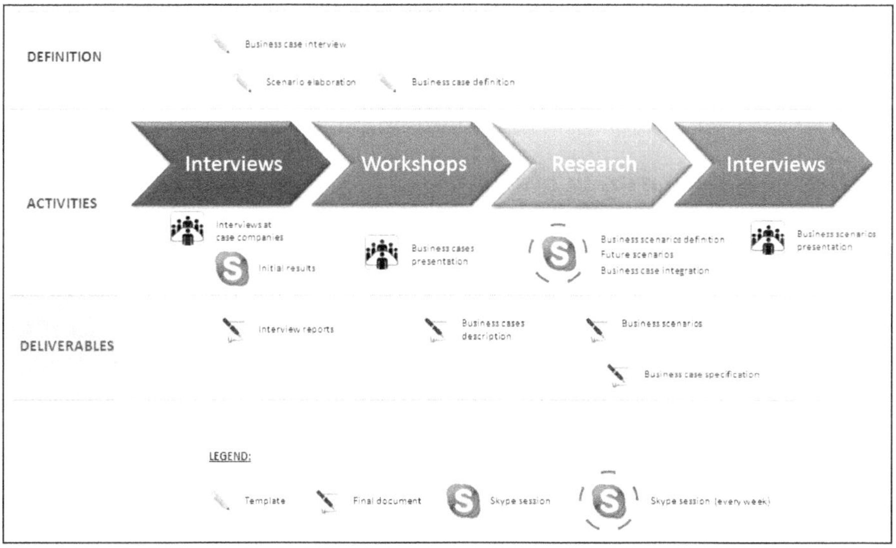

Fig. 1. Business case definition workflow

The study was conducted through structured interviews with management personnel of the case companies in order to collect and compare the available information such as; their current products, existing market shares, available resources, potential partners and their selection criteria, networking practices and specific business constraints, technologies implemented and constraints. Three specific steps were adopted to conduct this study such as: **Definition** (creation of templates to be used on interviews and questionnaires), **Activities** (activities and tasks performed to achieve the desired findings) and **Deliverables** (documents produced by researcher and business partners.) Figure 1 presents the three internal stages as described.

The *definition* stage included the creation of templates and definition of workflows for a complete data acquisition. The templates for the business case interview questionnaires were followed as guidelines for each case company and can be presented as follows:

(a) Background information (Business objectives; Market targets; Products; Major customers; Major suppliers/partners);
(b) Current major production processes and supply network strategies;
(c) Current status and practices of collaboration or networking;
(d) Future needs for collaboration and associated supporting tools, regarding Business methodology, Business processes, IT decision support tools.

The *activities* phase included all the methods used to analyze and gather data (based on the previous templates defined). Applying a constant abstraction on the data provided, a deep study has been made to match the first "common" needs for the six companies and a brainstorm (with all partners) was organized, resulting on a workshop. The result of this meeting was a full description of the business cases and acted as a starting-point to a deep benchmark research about current scenarios on other companies and a first study of possible business scenarios (which could fulfil business companies' needs). A new set of interviews was performed with the business case's managers to specify relevant business scenarios. The *deliverables* phase concerns all the documents produced related to the previous stage.

3 Business Scenarios in SMEs

The objective of defining future business scenarios is to analyze activities that can create higher value for the potential customers and provide increased competitiveness for SMEs. In non-hierarchical networks, it is therefore needed to offer high value products and services through direct involvement of partners, both up and downstream in the value chain, including customers, suppliers, distributors, etc. For such non-hierarchical collaboration environment, SMEs could pursue product and service innovation, offer high value products and services, to enlarge their value chains and decision power related to production and delivery. In any business scenario trade-off between many different dimensions like flexibility, time, cost and quality across the entire value chain has to be taken into consideration when defining how to implement these networks.

Before implementing multiple business scenarios such as expansion of market segments, achieving cost competitiveness, quality, manufacturability, production timing, supply chain flexibility etc for collaboration in non-hierarchical networks, SMEs have to identify and prioritize the most valuable and important scenarios for target implementations. They need to examine these multiple scenarios before approaching any form of networking strategy. Both the benefits and obstacles to implement those business scenarios in SMEs need to be identified. Three major disciplines that use business scenarios are strategic management, human-computer interaction and software and systems engineering with a view to deal with description of current and future realities [12]. In this research, we studied the approach of six European SMEs belonging to 3 industrial sectors, in order to define business scenarios for collaboration in non-hierarchical networks which are displayed in Table 1 [13].

During this research most important categories of network lifecycle have been defined as: Build (which includes scenarios for companies with common business goals and are supported by a common ICT platform for sharing information and getting known to each other), Qualify (including scenarios for qualification of partners in the community), Form (including scenarios during which specific partnerships are created for a business opportunity), Operate (which include scenarios for design /production implementation), dissolve. The scenarios identifies with the companies have been classified according to the networking phase to which they belong. The first four scenarios include the establishment of the business community (Virtual Organization Breeding Environment), inviting companies into building the community and scenarios 5, and 6 qualifying the potential partners of the community. Scenarios 7, 8, 9, and 10 are grouped together to form the VO with a view to achieve design, engineering and communication systems among partners, while scenarios 11, 12, 13, 14, 15, 16, and 17 are involved in the operational phase of the virtual organization. Scenario 18 outlines the dissolution mechanism of the virtual organizations when certain missions of the business community's are fulfilled within specific time limit.

Table 1. Generic business scenarios of the six case companies

Scenario no.	Description of the scenario	Networking Phase
1	A company wants to participate in a business community	Build
2	A community member invites a company to participate in the business community	Build
3	Selection of potential partners for a new business line	Build
4	Knowledge sharing within the network	Build
5	Qualification of potential partners for a new business line	Qualify
6	Select partners for a specific market opportunity	Qualify
7	Design a new collection (catalogue)	Form
8	Developing market research	Form
9	Standardize communication with customers	Form
10	All processes of the company are concentrated in one and only very simple ICT tool	Form
11	Improve operations plan for an order	Operate
12	Monitoring operations	Operate
13	Reaction to an unexpected event	Operate
14	Evaluating the network performance	Operate
15	Adjusting production capacity to meet expected demand	Operate
16	Creating a global production schedule for an order	Operate
17	Subcontracting	Operate
18	Network dissolution	Dissolve

There are also several scenarios related with knowledge transfer and trust building. The result from different market research, community as business promoter, standardizing communication and technical workshops require commitment and interaction from the partners and link the partners closely together. It's expected a strong commitment and trust among business partners to fulfill various scenarios which are beneficial to fulfill their business targets. The practice of planning business scenarios encourages SMEs to envision plausible future prospects and consider how to take advantage of opportunities and avoid potential threats.

4 Business Partners and Non-hierarchical Collaboration

4.1 Potentials for Business Partners

Manufacturing firms especially SMEs are forced to cooperate even sometimes with their core competitor in order to faster access to new business opportunities and new markets. With the views for successful production planning and achieving certain business objectives, SMEs need specific support to find the right partners (according with several criteria) as well as their qualification as future business partners. Business partners can be defined as a commercial entity with which another commercial entity has some form or collaboration or alliance. Partners can overcome business challenges: attain business goals, access resources (expertise, know-how etc.), which are generally outside the scope of a single firm. Through partnering SMEs achieve global presence, reduce risks, gain cost benefit, increase the utilization of assets, allows achieving economies of scale, etc [14].

Crowley and Karim [15] proposed co-operative partnership using diagrams indicating permeable boundaries and indicating a cell-like organization. They conceptualized that partnerships involved four dimensions: (i) adversarial (perceived by the involved parties as a win/lose situation and leading to more formal litigation); (ii) guarded adversarial (relationships that strictly adhere to and are interpreted by the contracts); (iii) informal partners (understand and cooperate with parties with fewer disputes) and (iv) project partners (equal partners working co-operatively to pursue a common set of goals). Angulo et al. [14] presented a simple but operational model for selecting the potential partners, where the partners are selected from a Virtual Enterprise Breeding Environment. Bittencourt and Rabelo [16] proposed an Analytic Hierarchy Process (AHP) method considering SCOR model as the base metrics to the selection process of the most suitable enterprises (partners) in a given business opportunity.

In long term partnerships, SMEs commitment is important to exchange detailed and reliable information about product, capacity, demand and orders with customers and suppliers, improving planning and control processes and material flow and evolving to full collaboration within a network. A critical evaluation among partners are therefore required before proceed any kind of collaboration with each other in order to achieve several business goals. Several important critical factors for partnerships are needed to be analysed to match the common requirements among partners. What came out from the analysis with the companies in the project research is that: selection process of business partners is not an easy task but a thorough understanding of the potential partners' business information is required.

4.2 Critical Success Factors of Partnerships

Business collaboration is the most innovative development in delivering a project efficiently. It provides a sound basis for achieving a win-win situation among partners. The fundamental principles of partnering are trust, commitment, communication, respect, and equality. It includes the appropriate consideration of the interest of all parties involves in the collaboration process at every level and aiming to build trust among the parties involved in a contract. In business collaboration, there needs to evaluate critical success factor among potential partners in order to achieve specific business goals.

Critical success factors of non-hierarchical collaboration can be defined as those factors that determine the success or failure of a firm. These factors are measured by comparing the value of several predefined variables (noticed or unnoticed) in successful and unsuccessful partnerships. General measures of success in partnerships (satisfaction and sales volume in the relationship) can be stated as communication quality and participation, conflict resolution techniques, coordination and trust and a partnership attributes of commitment [17].

According to the results of the business process analysis hold on during this research, the key success factors for non-hierarchical collaborative business networks can be summarized as follows.

- Development of trust between participants in the business community
- Development of change management programs to reduce the natural reaction to change from internal personnel, at different levels of the organization
- Well defined, clear and formalized roles for all partner companies
- Formalized and standard collaboration process
- Availability of shared knowledge, competencies and experiences with partner companies
- Human resources with the required technical skills and collaboration experience
- Shared values between the companies in the business community
- Enough financial resources for the defined strategic objectives
- The ICT support tools to be made availability to use by the companies at different levels involved

As a result, the development of regional or sectorial Business Communities, where trust can be built and communication streamlined will be critical for the fast and efficient creation of these business networks. There needs to be special care when considering the success factors as the success or failure of any kind of collaboration mostly depends on the outcomes of these factors. These factors or variables vary from one collaborative network to another network depending on its main objectives.

5 Empirical Study: Business Cases

The companies of the case studies produce complex and/or customized products, with low volumes and high product varieties in their production processes. Complexity can be given by different factors such as: in the case of machine tools the product itself is very complex and requires the collaboration of many different factors for many months; in case of footwear and apparel companies the complexity is given by the variability of the product to be managed concurrently, every season each company can produce/manage 3-400 different product models which needs to be designed, industrialized and produced in a collaborative way. The descriptions of the case companies are summarized in Table 2 in terms of country, business field, number of employees and annual turnover.

Table 2. Business information of the six case companies

Company	Country	Business field	Number of employees	Turnover
Case A	Portugal	Textile and apparel	800	50M€
Case B	Portugal	Textile and apparel	23	5M€
Case C	Italy	Footwear	10	0.5M€
Case D	Italy	Footwear	35	8.5M€
Case E	Spain	Machine tool	6	1.8M€
Case F	Spain	Machine tool	150	23 M€

During Business Scenarios analysis hold with the six case companies and comparing the results of the analysis with the most important collaborative models in literature, it is observed that companies are laggings of proper tools or methodologies to select, establish and communicate among potential partners in their business communities. There are also misconceptions and confusions for selecting potential partners and in the definition of the type of collaboration they can establish for their business success. For complex products manufacturing it is especially important the integration between design and partner selection. Building trust among potential partners seems the highest level of concern for this collaboration. There are also fears of confidentiality of information flow among partners and type of collaboration they are looking for.

In such business environments, it looks very comfortable for the companies to build up non-hierarchical collaboration, where companies could support each other in a horizontal relationship rather than vertical dependency as in hierarchical network. In such non-hierarchical relationships, case companies could share their resources, valuable information and value added activities among them in order to be benefited in the market place. This trust building influences them for potential innovation in their product development processes and capture new market shares for business expansion. From this study, it is noticed that although the case companies have some collaboration with other business networks it doesn't exist any IT based tools or methodologies to track the real-time information, which could ensure the safety and confidentially of valued information exchange among partners.

When in the need to create a specific Virtual Organization within a Business Community, most common way to communicate with their partners is done by phone calls, faxes or emails. Phone discussions are used for non-formal tacit knowledge exchange. Written emails are more formal to finalize the discussion started in phone. Both methods have the lack of sharing the agreed decisions inside the companies or even with other partners in the same virtual organization, also by the unstructured data result provided by these types of communication. Therefore, the research has started in defining a standard procedure for knowledge sharing for the case companies involved in collaborative networks. Some possible ways to improve collaboration in non-hierarchical networks can be: to standardize the communication roles using RASCI-model. Another way to share the discussion would be to share a pin-code for the information and every partner who has the pin-code could access to the available information.

6 Results and Discussions

To cope with turbulent business environment and meet customers' demands efficiently and effectively, there is no ways to be collaborative among SMEs rather than stay isolated from the business community. This collaboration is very much influential for SMEs, which are especially forced to produce products with different degrees of complexity such as textile and apparel, footwear, machines tools etc., creating higher product varieties, lower or unstable demand volumes. Business collaboration can contribute by developing production methods and new product features through exchanging valuable information among partnering companies. This methodology might attract SMEs for future developments in design for collaboration (DFC).

Exchanging emails and phone discussions are not enough for SMEs to collaborate. They should exchange documents using more controlled processes and adapt methodologies to share knowledge with trustable partners. The networking partners need social business solutions that are easy to use but still include the confidentiality aspect needed for business transactions. However, during the scenario collection process it has become obvious that the SMEs are acting in an ad-hoc world. The reason to prioritise an order might be for one partner the cash pre-payment and for the other the low season capacity level. The culture for sharing is not mature and the SMEs should get positive results that the collaboration gives more than takes. There is also need to enable not sharing critical knowledge, currently the partners are not sharing the information about the customer and price.

The research points out the high importance of promoting dynamic business communities as an enabler for the fast and efficient response to market opportunities. Various business scenarios that might be useful guidelines for SMEs in a non-hierarchical collaboration are presented. This structuring might be a valuable support for SMEs in a methodological approach and ICT-solution for guiding the network formation and partner qualification through sharing information among each other. This approach opens the platform for sharing required data in order to establish the collaborative network. The research presented in this paper provides specific support to find the right partners as well as their qualifications as future business communities. The project will develop tools for SMEs to select and qualify partners, build and collaborate within business community and enable online communication.

Acknowledgement

The authors would like to acknowledge the co-funding of the European Commission within NMP priority of the Seventh RTD Framework Programme (2007-13) for the Net-Challenge project (Innovative Networks of SMEs for Complex Products Manufacturing), Ref. CP-FP 229287-2.The authors also extend their thanks to the anonymous reviewers for their helpful comments and support.

References

1. Camarinha-Matos, L.M., Afsarmanesh, H., Ollus, M.: Ecolead and CNO Base Concepts. In: Methods and Tools for Collaborative Networked Organizations. Springer Science+ Business Media, LLC, Heidelberg (2008)

2. Myers, J.: Future Value Systems: Next Generation Economic Growth Engines & Manufacturing. In: Proceedings of the IMS Vision Forum 2006, Seoul, Korea, pp. 30–47 (2006)
3. Camarinha-Matos, L.M., Afsarmanesh, H.: A Comprehensive Modeling Framework for Collaborative Networked Organizations. J. Intell. Manuf. 18, 529–542 (2007)
4. Romeo, D., Galeano, N., Molina, A.: Virtual Organization Breeding Environments Value System and Its Elements. J. Intell. Manuf. 21, 267–286 (2010)
5. Romeo, D., Molina, A.: VO Breeding Environments & Virtual Organizations Integral Business Process Management Framework. Information System Frontiers (ISF) 11, 569–597 (2009)
6. Afsarmanesh, H., Camarinha-Matos, L.M.: The ARCON modeling framework. In: Collaborative networks: Reference modeling, pp. 67–82. Springer, New York (2008)
7. Romero, D., Galeano, N., Molina, A.: A Virtual Breeding Environment Reference Model and Its Instantiation Methodology. In: Camarinha-Matos, L.H., Picard, W. (eds.) Pervasive Collaborative Networks, pp. 15–24. Springer, Boston (2008)
8. Paszkiewicz, Z., Picard, W.: Modeling Virtual Organization Architecture with the Virtual Organization Breeding Methodology. In: Leveraging Knowledge for Innovation in Collaborative Networks, vol. 307, pp. 187–196. Springer, Boston (2009)
9. Noran, O.: Towards a meta-Methodology for Collaborative Networked Organizations. In: Virtual Enterprises and Collaborative Networks, vol. 149, pp. 71–78. Springer, Boston (2004)
10. Hoffner, Y., Field, S., Facciorusso, C.: The Typed Domain- a Recipe for Creating Virtual Enterprises. In: Virtual Enterprises and Collaborative Networks, vol. 149, pp. 53–62. Springer, Boston (2004)
11. Mytelka, L.: Crisis, Technological Change and the Strategic Alliance. In: Mytelka, L. (ed.) Strategic Partnerships and the World Economy, pp. 7–34. Pinter, London (1991)
12. Jarke, M., Bui, T.B., Carroll, J.M.: Scenario Management: An Interdisciplinary Approach. Require. Engng. 3, 155–173 (1998)
13. Carneiro, L., Kankaanpää, T., Almeido, R., Ferreira, P., Loichate, M., Pecina, M., Fornasiero, R., Zaniacomi, A., Chiodi, A., Rymaszewska, A.: Specification of Business Cases. Delivery D1.2. NetChallenge Project (2009)
14. Angulo, P.S., Martin, J.J.B.: Design and Implementation of a Multi-agent Framework for the Selection of Partners in Dynamic VEs. In: Leveraging Knowledge for Innovation in Collaborative Networks, vol. 307, pp. 341–348. Springer, Boston (2009)
15. Crowley, L.G., Karim, A.: Conceptual Model of Partnering. J. Mgmt. Engng., ASCE 11, 33–39 (1995)
16. Bittencourt, F., Rabelo, R.J.: A Systematic Approach for VE Partners Selection Using the SCOR Model and the AHP Method. In: Collaborative Networks and Their Breeding Environments, vol. 186, pp. 99–108 (2005)
17. Mohr, J., Spekman, R.: Characteristics of Partnership Success: Partnership Attributes, Communication Behavior, and Conflict Resolution Techniques. Strate. Mgmt. J. 15, 135–152 (1994)

Knowledge Representation in Virtual Teams: A Perspective Approach for Synthetic Worlds

Giacomo Fiumara[1], Dario Maggiorini[2], Alessandro Provetti[1,3], and Laura A. Ripamonti[2]

[1] Dip. di Fisica, Sezione d'Informatica. Università degli Studi di Messina
V.le F. Stagno d'Alcontres 31, I-98166 Messina, Italy
{gfiumara,ale}@unime.it
[2] Dip. d'Informatica e Comunicazione, Università degli Studi di Milano
Via Comelico, 39, I-20135, Milan, Italy
{dario,ripamonti}@dico.unimi.it
[3] Oxford-Man Institute, University of Oxford
Eagle House, Walton Well Rd., Oxford OX2 6ED, UK

Abstract. Thanks to ICT, new organizational forms are emerging that keep the pace of an increasingly demanding competitive environment. Among them, Virtual Enterprises (VEs) and Virtual Teams (VTs) represent two challenging organizational forms from the point of view of effective management.

An open issue in VEs/VTs is the social and economical sustainability of knowledge sharing in virtual environments, which is often underestimated. We address it from the point of view of "virtual worlds" and developed a prototypal solution that facilitates the cooperative building/sharing of knowledge representation.

Keywords: Virtual worlds, Virtual teams, Ontologies, Folksonomies.

1 Introduction

Barriers against effective integration among people belonging to different organizational functions/organizations are a well known phenomenon, whose complexity grows with the degree of virtualization of the organization: this problem becomes particularly relevant when "virtual enterprises" (VEs) and/or "virtual teams" (VTs) are involved. Barriers to integration proceed from socio-cultural misalignment among people belonging to different organizational environments, and they could be classified into five main classes (*personality*, *cultural*, *language*, *organizational* and *physical* barriers [1]). Integration among different organizational units has been often addressed through the integration of information systems, achieved through the use of appropriate software applications. Anyway, this approach leads to failure in many cases, since it solves only part of the problem [2]: good interaction among different functions/people can be achieved only when a good (social) interaction pattern is established among all the actors involved. This means that not only data and information systems should be integrated, but also – and perhaps mainly – social systems and social networks. This issue could be looked at as a problem of *sustainability*, For the purpose of this work, we adopt a description of sustainability which puts sustainable

L.M. Camarinha-Matos et al. (Eds.): PRO-VE 2010, IFIP AICT 336, pp. 619–625, 2010.

systems at the intersection of *social*, *economic* and *environmental* sustainability. In particular, we will put the accent on the interplay between the first two subtypes of sustainability (nevertheless, we underline that virtual organizations may positively impact on the environmental problems due, e.g., to a lesser need for trips and physical meetings [3]). The *economic* sustainability of an effective VE/VT is intertwined with its *social* (from the perspective of its members) sustainability. In particular, we claim that the problem of social sustainability can be tackled through the lenses of a *semiotic* ladder [4], which offers us a key to understand how to unfold integration into its different components (*physical, empiric, syntactic, semantic, pragmatic* and *social*), as shown in Fig.1.

This paper is based on the theoretical assumptions derived in [26], that highlight how a sound and appropriate support to the higher levels of the semiotic ladder could be achieved through a perspective approach – rooted into both the socio-semantic web [5] and the pragmatic web [6] paradigms – which couples formal and social interaction in virtual worlds. In particular, Multi User Virtual Environments (MUVEs) are considered suitable environments for supplying *digital habitats* to VEs/VTs which are sustainable both from a social and economic point of view. The idea is to combine the social capabilities of the current web2.0 applications with those of the semantic web in representing, managing, and retrieving explicit knowledge, within an immersive virtual world which extends and augments the actual one.

Building on these bases, we describe the characteristics of a prototypal implementation of a tool for creating three-dimensional representations of knowledge in virtual worlds (see also [7]).

2 Three Paradigms for Sharing Knowledge and Social Interaction

We can define a VT as "*a temporary arrangement of individuals belonging to different organizations and cultures, possessing different functional backgrounds, and working across different time zones on a common task*" ([7], p. 61). This definition well describes how VTs are structured, nevertheless it is worth noting that the key factor for the existence of VTs is the possibility to rely on an effective communication system, based on digital technologies. This aspect has been too long underestimated, perhaps also due to the fact that digital-based infrastructures are more and more perceived as *commodities*, forgetting the increasingly relevant social implications of their use. And, as a consequence, forgetting that effective interaction among different organizational units must rely upon *communication* and not only on the mere *sharing of data and information.*

To exploit effectively the opportunities offered by ICTs as enabler of integration, it is of fundamental importance to understand how ICTs can support communication, social interaction and knowledge generation and sharing among people, also and mainly when they become the principal (if not the only) means of interaction among the actors of the organization. Form this standpoint, three different paradigms have different pros and contras, as shown in Fig. 1 (for an exhaustive discussion on this topic, see: [3]):

- *Semantic Web* (SW) offers powerful tools for managing and retrieving explicit knowledge (i.e., ontologies, semantic search tools, etc.), while underestimates the aspects linked to social interaction and tacit knowledge management. Moreover, knowledge representations cannot be modified, updated or integrated with the degree of agility and flexibility needed by virtual organizations. This paradigm could be used to address at most the semantic level of the semiotic ladder.

- *Web2.0* (and *Pragmatic web* – [6]) is the expression of the social use of the web. Through tools for sharing knowledge and information on a social basis (e.g., social tagging and folksonomies), it adds agility, flexibility, and portability to knowledge representations. Anyway, it has a number of drawbacks; such as the lacking of semantic tools for searching, the impossibility to create complex knowledge maps, etc. Moreover, the web2.0 is a mesh-up of different technologies, information sources, web sites, etc., thus lacking one specific point of aggregation able to become the "environment" for building relations supporting integration. Again, this paradigm is unable to support effectively enough the last two levels of the semiotic ladder, while – compared to SW – it could enhance the support to the semantic level.
- *Multi User Virtual Environments (MUVEs)* are exceptional for augmenting actual lives of their users [8]. They support effectively the extension of people actual social networks and they can be moulded into places that may become synthetic loci for sharing tacit knowledge and expertise (see, e.g. the SUN OpenWonderland Project). MUVEs can be exploited as synthetic environments for supporting the higher levels of the semiotic ladder (pragmatic and social world), hence they can be of help in lowering certain integration barriers. Unfortunately, at the moment, even the more developed MUVEs (i.e., Second Life – SL) are quite lacking from the point of view of formalized systems for collecting, sharing, retrieving and reusing knowledge (even in its explicit form). Again this approach alone is not enough.

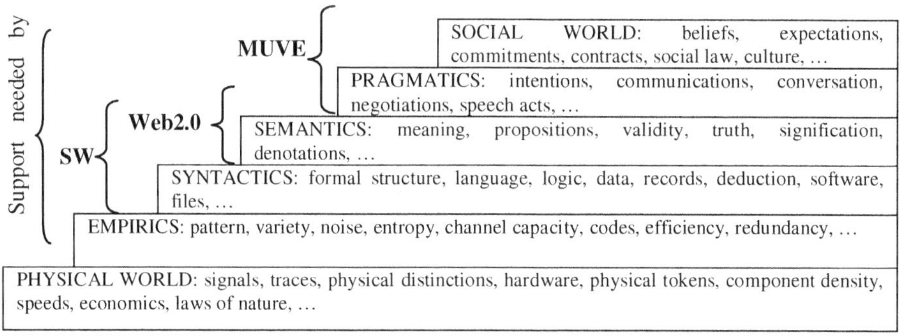

Fig. 1. Support offered by SW, Web2.0 and MUVEs to the "semiotic ladder"

Hence, none of these paradigms – *when adopted alone* – seems to be a solution good enough to address effectively the problem of integration.

3 Towards Collaboratively Built, Shared, 3D Representations of Knowledge

Since its appearance, SL attracted the attention of researchers and practitioners, and several have been the experiments aiming at coupling virtual environments with semantic web applications running on external web servers [9], [10], [11], [12], [13], and [14]; anyway, none of them seems to put the accent on the fundamental importance of the social factor in the process of sharing knowledge. On the other hand, several organizations (e.g., IBM, SUN, Northrop Grumman Corporation, etc.) are experiencing with SL as an environment for team building, but without coupling it with any semantic software application.

3.1 Representing Knowledge in a MUVE

In our project, we have designed and implemented a software application that brings into the virtual world the organization of a *folksonomy*, intended as a keywords-deployed user annotation. The folksonomy is located outside SL and represented in the standard RDF notation (thus maximizing flexibility and accessibility by non-human agents), but it can be updated also by users (avatars and/or agents) from within SL. Hence, our solution blurs the distinction between consulting/annotating objects inside and outside SL and the distinction between user and agent annotations. The application is potentially available to all authorized avatars approaching its 3D representation. The conceptual representation can evolve through collaborative concepts' annotation and updating, thus making a shared semantic to emerge. From a strictly technical point of view, the long-term goal of our project is the creation of a knowledge base within SL that is accessible both to human users (through their avatars) and software applications. Our knowledge base will support automated access, selection, and consultation of the objects appearing on one or more specified SL loci.

3.2 Composition of the Knowledge Base: The SCOT Ontology

A Knowledge Base (KB) can be seen as a set of formulae that express information (knowledge) about an object or a resource which is to be described. By now, almost all semantics annotations on the web are expressed by means of RDF (Resource Description Framework). At the very bare, the attributes of a resource are described by means of properties which in turn are described within ontologies, which are publicly available through the web.

In order to describe the composition of declarative languages used in our application, we have adopted the SCOT (Semantic Cloud of Tags) ontology [15], [16]. We briefly recall the properties of the SCOT ontology that were used more frequently in our application:

- `TagCloud`. This class describes the main repository of the tagging activity, namely the cloud of tags. All other properties derive from this one.
- `HasTag`. This property describes the set of tags associated to an object. This property belongs to another ontology, namely SIOC (Semantically-Interlinked Online Communities).
- `Tag`. This class describes the single tag belonging to a cloud of tags. It is a string used to identify a specified resource.
- `OwnAFrequency` is a RDF DataTypeProperty used to describe the absolute frequency of occurrences of a tag; fore in detail, the total number of times the specified tag containing this property has been associated to an object.

These properties have a hierarchical structure: TagCloud contains HasTag which in turn contains Tag, which contains OwnAFrequency.

3.3 Taxonomies and Folksonomies

A taxonomy defines both a hierarchical classification of concepts and the complex of ideas and rules with which object are classified. The taxonomic model seems to be in contrast with the folksonomic model, as in the former there is a well-founded rule to bind concepts while in the latter there is no rule at all. In this application we created a hybrid model which exploits hierarchical features of taxonomic model and the lack of rules of folksonomic model. In short, we created a folksonomy organized as a taxonomy. The only relationship established between concepts is that of inheritance between a concept and its ancestor. Since no other relationship is expresses, not even ordering among siblings to a common ancestor, the tree format is natural and sufficiently expressive. Of course, the scalability of this model is somewhat limited since the tagging of all conceivable concepts would produce a graph rather than a tree. Nevertheless, the goal of the model is the creation of a topic map, with an arbitrary depth, derived from a single concept.

3.4 Bridging the Gap between 3D Conceptual Maps and Web-Based Folksonomies

The main result of the application is a KB with semantic models. The KB resides in a RDF native repository, and is reachable by the application within SL and/or HTTP protocols and/or plain TCP/IP connections. The database, being multi-protocol, allows for the content to be usable in different contexts, assuring the stability and availability of data from within different applications developed in environments different from SL. An high-level architecture of our application is depicted in Fig. 2. Our application works as follows: associated to the 3D objects in SL there are scripts coded in LSL, the scripting language available in SL. When an avatar interacts with any of them one of the following actions takes place: a query to the RDF repository located outside SL, a tagging action of a resource, or the representation of the KB. Queries coded in SPARQL, the RDF query language, can be submitted from avatars as well as from users in the real world.

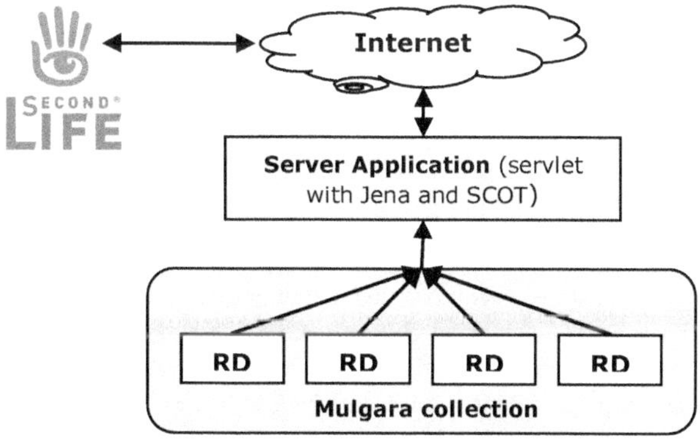

Fig. 2. Schema of the application

The same tool allows to build multi-level topic maps. Topic maps can cover great lengths (w.r.t. Second Life virtual land), and may be composed by a large number of 3D objects; hence, the client application must be activated in locations where suitable resources are available. In order to preserve performances of the hosting server, topic maps undergo an automatic self-destruction after a timeout. The prototype of our application has been tested for a period of three months against a varying number of avatars. The response time and the scalability seem encouraging, even if estimating the performances of this application is not easy, as they depend on various factors. Among these factors the most relevant are the degree of network congestion, the load on servers, the number of 3D objects to manage, and the complexity of the submitted query.

4 Conclusions and Future Development

The virtualization of teams/organizations may negatively affect the quality of interaction and knowledge sharing among individuals, thus generating problems of socio-economical sustainability. VEs/VTs may exploit opportunities offered by ICT (that should be considered a critical success factor) as enablers of social interaction and knowledge sharing to partially overcome those constraints. To achieve this goal, it is necessary to deploy solutions able to build trust and empathy, improve and develop social relations, increase opportunities to interact, reflect interdependencies of tasks, formalize knowledge representation, bridge long distances, and create (in)formal meeting places. The major part of these requirements could be addressed through a socio-technical approach, aimed at designing solutions and applications able to foster knowledge sharing into digital social environments. At the moment the principal approaches to this problem (i.e., SW, Web2.0) are too focused on one or another of the problem's facets, lacking a holistic vision. In particular, they lack in supporting effectively online (synthetic) extension of people identity and relations, as well as the creation of synthetic "places" where social networks can live and evolve. These latter aspects of synthetic life can instead flourish in synthetic worlds (MUVEs), which are unable to offer a convincing solution for managing knowledge in a formalized way. To overcome those limits, we have presented a perspective approach that intersects SW, Web2.0 and MUVEs, aiming at providing tools for sharing knowledge in a synthetic social environment.

References

1. Vandevelde, A., Van Dierdonck, R.: Managing the design-manufacturing interface. International Journal of Operations & Production Management 23(11), 1326–1348 (2003)
2. Tan, A., Kondoz, A.M.: Barriers to virtual collaboration. In: CHI 2008 Extended Abstracts on Human Factors in Computing Systems, CHI 2008, Florence, Italy, April 5-10, pp. 2045–2052. ACM, New York (2008), http://doi.acm.org/10.1145/1358628.1358636
3. Ripamonti, L.A., Peraboni, C.: Managing the Design-Manufacturing Interface in VEs through MUVEs: a perspective approach. In: Putnik, G. (ed.) International Journal of Computer Integrated Manufacturing, Special issue: "Semiotics based integrated manufacturing". Taylor & Francis, Abington (forthcoming, 2010) ISSN: 0951-192X

4. Stamper, R.K.: Signs, information, norms and systems. In: Holmqvist, B., et al. (eds.) Signs at work. De Gruyter, Berlin (1996)
5. Cahier, J.P., Zacklad, M.: Socio-Semantic Web applications: towards a methodology based on the Theory of the Communities of Action. In: COOP 2004 Workshop on Knowledge Interaction and Knowledge Management (2004)
6. Schoop, M., de Moor, A., Dietz, J.L.G.: The Pragmatic Web: a Manifesto. Communication of the ACM 49(5), 75–76 (2006)
7. Kahai, S.S., Carroll, E., Jestice, R.: Team Collaboration in Virtual Worlds. The Data Base for advances in Information Systems 28(4) (November 2007)
8. Boellstorff, T.: Coming of Age in Second Life. An Anthropologist Explores the Virtually Human. Princeton University Press, Princeton (2008)
9. Bogdanovych, A., Rodriguez, J.A., Simoff, S.J., Sierra, A.C.C.: Developing virtual heritage applications as normative multiagent systems. In: AOSE. LNCS. Springer, Heidelberg (2009)
10. Galanis, D., Karakatsiotis, G., Lampouras, G., Androutsopoulos, I.: Naturalowl: Generating texts from OWL ontologies in Protégé and in Second Life. In: 18th European Conference on Artificial Intelligence (2008)
11. Galanis, D., Karakatsiotis, G., Lampouras, G., Androutsopoulos, I.: An open-source natural language generator for OWL ontologies and its use in Protegé and Second Life. In: EACL (Demos), pp. 17–20. The Association for Computer Linguistics (2009)
12. Kleinermann, F., Troyer, O.D., Creelle, C., Pellens, B.: Adding semantic annotations, navigation paths and tour guides to existing virtual environments. In: Wyeld, T.G., Kenderdine, S., Docherty, M. (eds.) VSMM 2007. LNCS, vol. 4820, pp. 100–111. Springer, Heidelberg (2008)
13. Schneider, M., Kratzer, F., Mainzer, K.: SEMSL: Tagging and data linking for Second Life. In: 7th International Semantic Web Conference - ISWC 2008 (2008), http://data.semanticweb.org/conference/iswc/2008/paper/poster_demo/76 (Retrieved 2010-03-26)
14. Oberlander, J., Karakatsiotis, G., Isard, A., Androutsopoulos, I., Unit, D.C.: Building an adaptive museum gallery in second life (2008), http://nlp.cs.aueb.gr/pubs/mw2008_preprint.pdf (Retrieved 2010-03-26)
15. Kim, H.L., Passant, A., Breslin, J., Scerri, S., Decker, S.: Review and Alignmnet of Tag Ontologies for Semantically-Linked Data in Collaborative Tagging Spaces. In: Proceedings of the 2nd International Conference on Semantic Computing, San Francisco, USA (2008)
16. Kim, H.L., Scerri, S., Breslin, J., Decker, S., Kim, H.G.: The State of the Art in Tag Ontologies: A Semantic Model for Tagging and Folksonomies. In: Proceedings of the Int. Conference on Dublin Core and Metadata Applications, Berlin, Germany (2008)

Eigenvector Centrality Based on Shared Research Topics in a Scientific Community

Antonio P. Volpentesta and Alberto M. Felicetti

Department of Electronics, Computer Science and Systems,
University of Calabria
via P. Bucci, 42\C, 87036 Rende (CS), Italy
{volpentesta,afelicetti}@deis.unical.it

Abstract. In this paper we propose a weighted multi-hypergraph as logical structure to model relationships between researchers and interest groups that join them on the base of shared research topics in a given scientific community. The well known concept of eingenvector centrality for graphs is extended to weighted multi-hypergraphs and we present a model instantiation for centrality analysis in the Pro-VE scientific community.

Keywords: Eigenvector centrality, scientific community, weighted multi-hypergraph.

1 Introduction and Backgrounds

Scientific communities are commonly defined as networks of scientists, researchers and professionals who aim to produce, in a collaborative way, new knowledge within a specific domain or issue-area. However, in many cases, collaboration in scientific environments is restricted, and occurs among a small number of people working in the same group, ignoring in some cases the existence of other researchers who are working on similar projects [1].

Moreover, a scientific community is generally characterized by different research topics and contributions that come from a variety of disciplines and backgrounds. In this context, it might be useful to have an idea of the importance of the different research topics and researchers who work on them within a scientific community.

This has led many scholars to study the concept of centrality in a collaboration network of scientists. As matter of fact, network centrality is a concept widely discussed in literature, especially in social network studies [2], and in general, it refers to the importance of a position within a network.

Several authors have studied the "importance" of a node in a network; according to different approaches, they introduce different measures of centrality, As stated by Freeman [3], "there is certainly no unanimity on exactly what centrality is or on its conceptual foundations, and there is very little agreement on the proper procedure for its measurement". In literature different centrality measures are presented. Closeness centrality and Graph centrality [4] are based on the distances with the rest of nodes, while Betweenness centrality and Stress centrality [3] emphasize the medium mediating between a pair of nodes. Another centrality measure that is often used in network

L.M. Camarinha-Matos et al. (Eds.): PRO-VE 2010, IFIP AICT 336, pp. 626–633, 2010.

analysis is eigenvector centrality [5], called also "rank prestige" [2]. Eigenvector centrality analysis is based on the idea that a node is "more central" if it is in relation with nodes that are themselves central, so the centrality of a node does not only depend on the *number* of its adjacent nodes, but also on their value of centrality.

The usage of centrality measures are particularly interesting in the study of networks formed by researchers belonging to a scientific community [6]. These studies use models based primarily on graph structures, constructed on the basis on the author-topic relationship and, more in general, on the analysis of papers' contents. However, in several cases, models based on graphs do not provide a suitable representation of complex relationships, for instance supra-dyadic relations. The use of more general logical structure as hypergraphs [7] seems to be more appropriate in these situations. Few attempts have been made to utilize hypergraphs in modeling a social network [8], and, more specifically, a scientific community network [9]. However, in our opinion, weighted multi-hypergraphs are the appropriate structures to represent multiple and weighted relationships.

In this paper we propose a model based on a weighted multi-hypergraph to represent relationships between researchers and research interests, grouping researchers with common interests. Moreover, in order to measure the importance of researchers and research topics in a scientific community ,we extend the eigenvector centrality notion to this general logical structure and we present an algorithmic approach. Lastly, we describe a first application of the model to the Pro-Ve community, a scientific community that aims to promote research and production of new knowledge on Collaborative Networks.

2 Eigenvector Centrality for Weighted Multi-hypergraphs

A multi-hypergraph is a generalization of a multi-graph, in which edges, called hyperedges, may connect any positive number of vertices [7]. Formally, a multi-hypergraph $\mathcal{H}$ is a pair ($\mathcal{V}$, $\mathcal{E}$) where $\mathcal{V} = \{v_1,\ldots, v_m\}$ is a set of vertices, $\mathcal{E} = \{E_1,\ldots, E_n\}$ is a multi-set of nonempty subsets of $\mathcal{V}$, called hyperedges. Because $\mathcal{E}$ is a multiset, an hyperedge may appear more than once in $\mathcal{E}$. A vertex-hyperedge weighted multi-hypergraph is one in which each couple vertex-hyperedge (v_i,E_j), such that $v_i \subset E_j$, is assigned a positive weight.

We use $w_{ij} \in R_+$ to denote the weight given to (v_i,E_j) and refer to $W=(w_{ij})$, where $w_{ij}= 0$ if $v_i \notin E_j$, as a vertex-hyperedge weighted incidence matrix for $\mathcal{H}$. Notice that W is the classical vertex-hyperedge incidence matrix for $\mathcal{H}$ when $w_{ij}= 0$ or 1.

In order to study the centrality of vertices and hyperedges in ($\mathcal{H}$, W) we make the well known *mutually reinforcing relationship* assumption [10]: *an important hyperedge is a hyperedge whose elements are important vertices; an important vertex is a vertex that belongs to many important hyperedges.*

Numerically, it is natural to express the mutually reinforcing relationship between hyperedges and vertices as follows:

Let x_i be the 'importance' of vertex v_i and let y_j be the 'importance' of hyperedge E_j.

The simplest formulation of the mutually reinforcing relationship assumption is given by these equations:

$$x_i = c_1 \sum_{j=1}^{n} w_{ij}\, y_j \,, \qquad \text{for i} = 1,\dots,\text{m}. \tag{1}$$

where the constant of proportionality, c_1>0, is independent of i.

$$y_j = c_2 \sum_{i=1}^{m} w_{ij}\, x_i \,, \qquad \text{for j} = 1,\dots,\text{n}. \tag{2}$$

where the constant of proportionality, c_2>0, is independent of j.

In matrix notation with x= $(x_1,x_2,\dots,x_m)$ and y= $(y_1,y_2,\dots,y_n)$ this yields

$$WW^t x = \lambda x, \qquad W^t W y = \lambda y, \qquad \text{where } \lambda = c_1 c_2. \tag{3}$$

Standards results of linear algebra[1] lead to state that (3) is a solvable system of equations. More precisely, a solution is given by setting $\lambda=\lambda^*$, the dominant W^tW's eigenvalue (that is equal to the dominant eigenvalue of of WW^t), $x=x^*$, a nonnegative eigenvector of WW^t in the eigenspace associated with λ^*, $y=y^*$, a nonnegative eigenvector of W^tW in the eigenspace associated with λ^*. We call a normalization of x* an *eigenvector-centrality measure* of the vertices in ($\mathcal{H}$, W) and a normalization of y* an *eigenvector-centrality measure* of the hyperedges in ($\mathcal{H}$, W).

If W is the vertex-hyperedge incidence matrix of an hypergraph, the equations (3) are the well known ones that arise when studying eigenvector centrality in hypergraphs, [8]. This means that the notion of eigenvector-centrality we introduced for a weighted multi-hypergraph is the natural extension of the well known one for an hypergraph. Moreover, we can use an adaptation of the Hits (Hyperlink-Induced Topics Search) algorithm, proposed by Kleinberg, [10], in order to calculate eigenvector-centrality of vertices and hyperedges in ($\mathcal{H}$, W).

In the algorithm we have used the sum-norm to range nodes and hyperedge according to their proportion of the centrality within a vertex-hyperedge weighted multi-hypergraph. The effect that different normalization have on the interpretation of eigenvector-centrality within a graph is investigated in [11].

3 The Weighted Multi-hypergraph Model

In order to study the centrality of researchers and research topics in a scientific community, we propose a model whose underlying logical structure is a vertex-hyperedge weighted multi-hypergraph. The components of the model are:

- **D** = $\{d_1,\dots, d_p\}$ an ordered set of documents (scientific papers);
- **T** = $\{t_1,\dots, t_m\}$an ordered set of research interests (research topics);
- **R** =$\{r_1,\dots, r_n\}$ an ordered set of researchers (authors), members of a scientific community;

---

[1] WW^t and W^tW share minimum(m,n) eigenvalues; these eigenvalues are all ≥0; due to the theorem of Perron–Frobenius, there exists an eigenvector of the maximal eigenvalue with only nonnegative entries, [15].

- **A** $\in \mathbb{R}^{m \times p}$ a binary matrix that represents the relationships between authors and documents produced by them, i.e.: $a_{ik} = 1$, if researcher r_i is one of the authors of document d_k, otherwise $a_{ik} = 0$.
- **B** $\in \mathbb{R}^{p \times n}$ a nonnegative matrix that gives a measure of how much documents are devoted to research topics. More precisely, the generic entry b_{kj}, measures the portion of the document d_k that deals with research topic t_j and it's required that $0 \le b_{kj} \le 1$, for any j, k, and $\sum_j b_{kj} = 1$, for any k.
- **C** = $(c_1, c_2, \ldots, c_p)$ a positive vector, where the generic entry c_k represents a measure of the popularity [2] of d_k in the scientific community.

We introduce the multi-hypergraph $\mathcal{H}$ $(\mathcal{R}, \mathcal{E})$, where:

$\mathcal{R} = \mathbf{R} = \{r_1, \ldots, r_n\}$;
$\mathcal{E} = \{E_1, \ldots, E_n\}$;, with $E_j = E(t_j) = E(tj) = \{r_i \in \mathbf{R}: \exists$ k such that $a_{ik} = 1$ and $b_{kj} > 0\}$.

By assuming that research interests of any researcher r_i are manifested on documents whose r_i is an author, E_j represents an interest group on a research topic t_j; in other words E_j is the subset of **R** consisting of all researchers that share the research topic t_j. Of course, a researcher may belong to many interest groups and many interest groups may be constituted by the same subset of researchers (this is the reason why $\mathcal{H}$ is a multi-hypergraph). The relationship between researchers and interest groups may be derived through a semantic analysis of the documents' content.

In order to assign a weight[3] to any couple researcher-interest group (r_i, E_j), we make the following assumptions and settings:

- The content of a document is due in equal measure to all its authors. More precisely, the fraction a_{ik}/h_k, where h_k is the number of authors of d_k, measures the document portion that is attributed to r_i and the research topics of d_k are also research interests of its authors.
- The number $b_{kj} \cdot c_k$ measures the contribution given by the research topic t_j to the popularity of the document d_k.
- The number $(a_{ik}/h_k) \cdot (b_{kj} \cdot c_k)$ measures the contribution given by the portion of d_k, dealing with t_j and attributed to r_i, to the popularity of d_k.

According to these assumptions and settings, we propose to estimate the weight associated to the couple (r_i, t_j), as follows:

$$w_{ij} = \sum_{k=1}^{p} (a_{ik}/h_k) \cdot (b_{kj} \cdot c_k)$$

In order to calculate eigenvector-centrality of researchers and research topics in a scientific community, we may consider the weighted multi-hypergraph $(\mathcal{H}, W)$,

[2] Researches in bibliometrics have long been concerned with the concept of popularity (or importance or impact) of individual scientific papers and journals and they have provided quantitative estimates based on the use of citations. The most well-known measure in this field is Garfield's impact factor, [13].

[3] Some authors explain the meaning of a weight in terms of strength of endorsement within a community, [10].

where W=(w_{ij}), i=1,…m and j=1,…n, is the matrix that represents the weighted relationships between researchers and research topics. We observe that the characteristic matrix associated with W is the incidence matrix of $\mathcal{H}$.

Example

Let us consider the following instantiations of the model components:

D = $\{d_1, d_2, d_3\}$; T = $\{t_1, t_2, t_3, t_4\}$; R = $\{r_1, r_2, r_3, r_4, r_5\}$; C =(1,2,3);

A	d_1	d_2	d_3
r_1	1	0	0
r_2	1	1	0
r_3	0	1	0
r_4	0	1	1
r_5	0	0	1

B	t_1	t_2	t_3	t_4
d_1	3/4	1/4	0	0
d_2	0	0	1	0
d_3	1/4	1/4	0	1/1

We have: $h_k = \frac{1}{\sum_i a_{ik}}$ k=1,2,3, i.e. $(h_1, h_2, h_3) = (2, 3, 2)$;

The multi-hypergraph $\mathcal{H}$ has the following vertex-hyperedge incidence matrix and graphical representation:

E	t_1	t_2	t_3	t_4
r_1	1	1	0	0
r_2	1	1	1	0
r_3	0	0	1	0
r_4	1	1	1	1
r_5	1	1	0	1

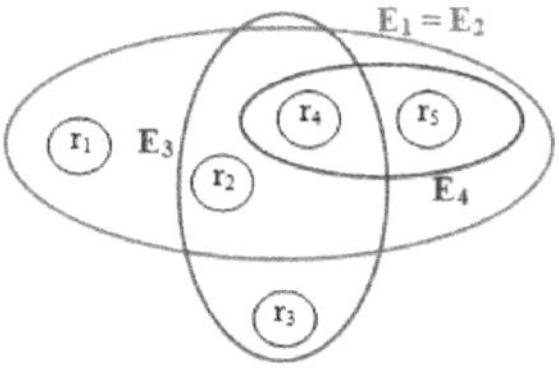

and the matrix W is the following:

W	t_1	t_2	t_3	t_4
r_1	3/8	1/8	0	0
r_2	3/8	1/8	2/3	0
r_3	0	0	2/3	0
r_4	3/8	3/8	2/3	3/4
r_5	3/8	3/8	0	3/4

Through the application of an adaptation of HITS Algoritm to W, we obtain the eigenvector-centrality of researchers and research topics:

x =(0,0656; 0,1966; 0,1309; 0,3689; 0,2379)
y =(0,2165; 0,1729; 0,3082; 0,3024)

4 A Model Instantiation for the Pro-Ve Community

The Pro-VE community is a scientific community that aims to promote research and production of new knowledge on Collaborative Networks (shortly, CN). PRO-VE conferences offer researchers and practitioners opportunities to meet together, present and discuss both latest research developments and industrial practice case studies.

In what follows we briefly describe the instantiations of the model components as well the path taken to them. In order to instantiate the sets **D**, **R** and the matrix **A**, we have considered scientific papers presented at Pro-Ve conferences. More specifically, **D** consists of all selected papers that were published in the books of the last five Pro-Ve conferences (2005-2009), [14], **R** is the set of those researchers who appeared as an author of at least one scientific article published in such books and **A** represents their authorship relation to their Pro-Ve papers.

In order to instantiate **T**, we have modeled a research topic t_j in the Pro-Ve community as a triple $t_j = (OF, DA, \mathrm{ES})$, where:

- OF is the set of CN Organizational Forms. OF is a flat set whose elements are substantially derived from the classification provided in [15];
- DA is the set of Dimensional Aspects of a CN. DA is a flat set whose elements are substantially derived from the reference model described in [16], and widely accepted in the Pro-Ve community;
- ES is the set of the economic sectors, each one encompassing real business environments, where CN models, mechanisms, methodologies, principles and supporting tools are instantiated and implemented. According to the well known four-sector hypothesis, ES consists of primary, secondary, tertiary and quaternary sector and a "dummy" element denoting that no real world application is addressed by the research.

In other words a research topic is characterized by a dimensional aspect of a CN organizational form and possibly a case study or an application in primary industry, manufacturing, industrial services or intellectual services, (see the following table):

Table 1. Instances of research topics components

ORGANIZATIONAL FORMS	Collaborative Network (*), Supply chain, Virtual Government, Virtual Enterprise, Virtual Organization, Extended Enterprise, Virtual team, Human breeding environments (communities), Organizational Breeding Environments (VBE), Industry Cluster, Industrial District, Business Ecosystem, Collaborative Virtual Lab, Disaster rescue Net, Innovation networks.
DIMENSIONAL ASPECTS	Actors/relationships, Roles, Hardware / software resources, Human resources, Information / knowledge resources, Ontology resources, Processes, Auxiliary processes, Methodologies, Prescriptive behavior, Obligatory behavior, Constraints and conditions, Contracts and cooperation agreements, Meta dimension (**), External view (***)
ECONOMIC SECTORS	No real world application, Primary Economic Sector (****), Secondary Economic Sector (****), Tertiary Economic Sector (****), Quaternary Economic Sector (****).

(*) The focus is on general forms of CN rather than on specific organizational forms.
(**) This dimension addresses to the analysis of principles, models and theories applicable and useful for modeling Structural, Componential, Functional and Behavioral dimension of CN.
(***) This dimension deals with exogenous interactions with CN surrounding environment, such as Market (customers, competitors, other CNs) and/or Society (third party institutions, Governments, No Profit Organizations).
(****)Primary sector (i.e.): Agriculture, Fishing, Forestry, etc...
Secondary sector (i.e.): Automotive, Construction, Electronics, Mechanical, Textile, etc...
Tertiary sector (i.e.): Industrial Services, Commerce, Transportation, Hospitality, Maintenance, etc..
Quaternary sector (i.e.): Banking, Consulting, Education, Government Services, Healthcare, etc...

The instantiation of the matrix **B** has been obtained through a collaborative process of semantic analysis of Pro-Ve papers' content. Such a process, widely described in [17], is collaboratively performed by a team of experts that are supported by an automatic paper indexing tool. It is aimed to associate one or more instantiation of the triple (OF, DA, ES) to any Pro-VE paper and it essentially consists of the following interrelated steps:

- Making the list of research topics.
- Developing a structured set of concepts for any research topic.

- Extracting a set of keywords from any paper.
- Associating paper's keywords to concepts.

By assuming an equi-distribution of the content of a paper among its research topics, the matrix **B** has been instantiated as follows: $b_{kj} = 1$, if is a research topic of the k-th paper, otherwise $b_{kj} = 0$. Lastly, any entry c_k of C is instantiated at x_k+1 , where x_k is the number of documents in D that cite d_k.

5 Conclusions and Future Works

The presented work is a proposal aimed to determine eigenvector centrality in scientific community, starting from research publications. From a theoretical point of view, the model we have introduced can be further exploited by extending other well known concepts of centrality (e.g. closeness or betweenness centrality) to weighted multi-hypergraphs. From a practical point of view, we have presented a model instantiation that allows us to study eingenvector centrality in the Pro-Ve community. This work is still in implementation phase (we are collecting and validating data derived from a semantic analysis of Pro-Ve papers) and one of the future steps is its completion in order to provide measurements and statistucal analysis of the centrality of researcher and research topics within the Pro-Ve community.

References

1. Rodrigues, S., Oliveira, J., Moreira de Souza, J.: Competence mining for virtual scientific community creation. Int. J. Web Based Communities 1(1), 90–102 (2004)
2. Wasserman, S., Faust, K.: Social Network Analysis: Methods and Applications. Cambridge University Press, Cambridge (1994)
3. Freeman, L.C.: A set of measures of centrality based on betweenness. Sociometry 40, 35–41 (1977)
4. Sabidussi, G.: The centrality index of a graph. Psychometirka 31, 581–603 (1966)
5. Bonacich, P.: Factoring and weighting approaches to clique identification. Journal of Mathematical Sociology 2, 113–120 (1972)
6. Newman, M.E.J.: Scientific collaboration networks. II. Shortest paths, weighted networks, and centrality. Physical Review E 64 (2001)
7. Berge, C.: Graphs and Hypergraphs. Elsevier, Amsterdam (1973)
8. Bonacich, P., Holdren, A.C., Johnston, M.: Hyper-edges and multidimensional centrality. Social Networks 26, 189–203 (2004)
9. Estrada, E., Rodríguez-Velázquez, J.A.: Subgraph centrality and clustering in complex hyper-networks. Physica A 364, 581–594 (2006)
10. Kleinberg, J.: Authoritative sources in a hyperlinked environment. Journal of the ACM 46(5), 604–632 (1999)
11. Ruhnau, B.: Eigenvector-centrality: a node-centrality? Social Networks 22, 357–365 (2000)
12. Golub, G., Van Loan, C.F.: Matrix Computations. J. Hopkins University Press (1989)
13. Garfield, E.: Citation analysis as a tool in journal evaluation. Science 178, 471–479 (1972)

14. Camarinha-Matos, L.M., et al. (eds.): Pro-VE 2005. IFIP, vol. 185, Pro-VE 2006. IFIP, vol. 224, Pro-VE 2007. IFIP, vol. 243, Pro-VE 2008. IFIP, vol. 283, Pro-VE 2009. IFIP, vol. 307. Springer, Heidelberg
15. Camarinha-Matos, L.M., Afsarmanesh, H.: Collaborative Networks: Value Creation in a Knowledge Society. In: Knowledge Enterprise. IFIP, vol. 207, pp. 26–40. Springer, Heidelberg (2006)
16. Romero, D., Galeano, N., Molina, A.: A Virtual Breeding Environment reference model and its instantiation methodology. In: Camarinha-Matos, L.M., Picard, W. (eds.) Pervasive Collaborative Networks. Springer, Heidelberg (2008)
17. Volpentesta, A.P., Ammirato, S., Felicetti, A.M.: Competence mapping through analysing research papers of a scientific community, Technical Report, DEIS-Unical (2010)

Security Awareness in Virtual Communities: The Case of Non-collocated Academic Research Collaborations

Adam Marks[1] and Yacine Rezgui[2]

[1] Department of Business Administration, World Wide Embry-Riddle Aeronautical University
Marksa@erau.edu
[2] School of Engineering, Cardiff University, Queen's Buildings, The Parade, Cardiff CF24 3AA, Wales, UK
RezguiY@cardiff.ac.uk

Abstract. Internationalization of research is reflected in the distributed nature of research communities. Research has a strong collaborative dimension. It is often carried out by non-collocated individuals and teams in the context of national / international funded programs, institutionally led projects, or simply self-motivated initiatives. Universities form a strong and influential component of these virtual research communities. Advances in information and communication technologies (ICT), including the Internet, have helped sustain these virtual research communities. However, despite the strategic nature of research, there exist various levels of awareness about the security risk factor linked with virtual collaboration. This study examines the security awareness of academics and researchers across higher education institutions with a focus on three different academic settings. The paper suggests that a security awareness program aimed at academics should be initiated across universities to pave the way to security aware research collaborative communities.

Keywords: Virtual Collaboration, Research Community, Security Awareness.

1 Introduction

Universities are among the least Information Systems (IS) secured environments [2]. Only a fraction of universities provide security and conduct awareness training [15]. Colleges and universities are targeted for cyber attacks for two main reasons; first, is the vast amount of computing power they posses; and second, is the open access they provide to their constituents [9]. In addition, universities have a considerable amount of confidential and strategic information that makes them prone to IS security threats [11]. Most IS managers tend to focus more on technical security solutions such as firewalls, routers, and intrusion detection software; but much less on hazards caused by end users' lack of awareness [11]. And, while in general information security awareness is acknowledged, the number of studies that consider it in depth is limited. This may be attributed to (a) the non-technical nature of security awareness [17] and / or (b) its scope, as it falls outside the traditional engineering and hard computer science domains [8]. Never the less, organizations with strong technical security

L.M. Camarinha-Matos et al. (Eds.): PRO-VE 2010, IFIP AICT 336, pp. 634–641, 2010.

countermeasures, may still fail to protect their information systems. The human factor is considered the weakest link in the IS security chain [14].

In any given network in today's connected globe, the level of one user's IS security awareness may have a direct impact on the level of IS security exposure of all directly or indirectly connected users within that network. Information technology and the Internet have helped create non-collocated communities. Academic and research-based groupings form an important and influential component of these virtual collaborative research communities. However, despite the strategic nature of research (some of which subject to Intellectual Property Rights), there exist various levels of awareness about the security risk factor linked with virtual collaboration.

This study examines the IS security awareness levels of academics / researchers across different higher education institutions. The paper is structured into five sections. Following this introduction, the research methodology that underpins the research and relevant related work are summarized. Fieldwork results are then presented, followed by a discussion of the main findings. The paper concludes with key recommendations and directions for future research.

2 Methodology

The purpose of this study is to explore the levels of information systems security awareness of the virtual community of academic researchers who collaborate across different higher education institutions and environments.

The authors have used their own collaboration, extended to their institution and national academic environment, as the focus of this research. The first author used to be a member of staff of Zayed University in the UAE, prior to returning to the US as an academic member of Embry-Riddle Aeronautical University. The second author has during this period worked in two academic institutions in the UK, namely Salford University and Cardiff University. The focus of the research spans a duration of 4 years during which the two academics have collaborated across their respective institutions. Therefore, this study focuses on three academic environments in the UK, UAE, and the US and addresses the following main research question: *Are higher education research communities aware of the security challenges involved with virtual collaborative working that underpins academic research?*

An interpretive philosophical stance is adopted to conduct the research. The selected case study institutions not only exist in different environments, but also exhibit varying levels of security awareness and maturity while presenting some notable differences in their higher education vision, procedures and processes. To ensure consistency and validity of findings, multiple sources of data are gathered through the use of four main instruments: Interview, Questionnaire, Documentation, and Observation. The field work in Zayed University, Salford University, and Embry-Riddle University targeted research academics in different schools. This involved gathering 36 questionnaire responses and 10 interviews in the context of Zayed, 22 questionnaire responses and 10 interviews have been obtained in Salford, and 24 questionnaire responses and 8 interviews in Embry-Riddle University. Additional data was captured in the mode of direct observation [3] throughout the entire study. To measure the levels of users IS security awareness; the sources of data of this study targeted the following 10 themes: (a) User's IS security awareness of available and accessible IS systems, and their intended use; (b) User's IS security awareness of existing IS security policies, standards, and guidelines; (c) User's IS security awareness of existing IS security laws and legislation; (d) User's IS security awareness of available IS staff and personnel; (e) User's IS security awareness of possible IS security threats and concerns; (f) User's IS security awareness of possible IS security solutions; (g) User's IS security awareness of available IS security training session and materials; (h) User's IS security awareness of available IS security documents and help material; (i) User's IS security awareness and perception of the value of university data; (j) User's IS security awareness and perception of their role in university's IS security. The chosen 10 themes were selected from a variety of prior IS security awareness studies [6], [9], [15], [16], and [17].

3 Related Work

Information security awareness is concerned with creating and maintaining security-positive behavior [13]. According to the Information Security Forum [10], information security awareness can be defined as (a) the degree to which every user understands the importance of information security, (b) the appropriate level of information security to the organization, (c) users' security responsibility, and (d) users' behaviors and acts. Reference [17] defines information security awareness as the state where users in an organization are aware of, and ideally committed their security mission defined by the organization's end-user security guidelines. Information security awareness may cover a range of topics, including: password construction, password management, authentication, Internet usage, telephone fraud, physical e-mail usage and security, private information, virus protection and detection, PC security, software licensing, backups, building access, social engineering, identity theft and home office security [1].

The majority of today's IS attacks are not concerned with only circumventing the authentication process of an individual or an organization; they are more inclined to access confidential information. This has resulted in IS threats like phishing, identity theft, and social engineering [7]. While technical solutions are with no doubt necessary to address IS security problems, the consideration of humans, and more generally human factors, is equally important [1], [7]. The effective implementation and use of IS security awareness practices can lead to improved security for organizations. Reference [5] suggests that in order to avoid IS security breaches, organizations should provide users with IS security awareness training programs. The training program should cover areas like social engineering, password protection, and heightened physical security alertness. Reference [12] takes a step further by suggesting that organizations should implement a continuous security awareness training programs as part of the corporate asset protection program. But while information security is a key organizational goal and users have a responsibility to maintain this goal, it is important to understand that the implementation of an information security awareness program does not warrant that all users within the organization will understand their roles and responsibilities when it comes to information security [4]. Perhaps, this is why reference [16] recommends a combination of measures to increase users IS security awareness. Reference [16] suggests that organizations use IS security awareness training, campaigning, and reward and punishment to establish an effective IS security awareness program. Reference [6] believes that Continuous reinforcement of proper IS security practices is needed to remind individuals of their role in information security. Both [1] and [13] recommend that a systematic approach to measure the effect of a security awareness program should be implemented to evaluate the contribution and the return on investment of such programs [13].

4 Field Work

This section provides a summary of relevant fieldwork data across the three selected academic environments extended to their regional and national context. This is structured according to the above listed driving themes that underpin the research.

- **User's IS security awareness of available and accessible IS systems and their intended use:** The data evidence gathered for this category portrays that the examined institutions have a comparable IS infrastructure in terms of software, hardware, and network resources. The majority of academic researchers examined were aware of available IS resources. 87% of Zayed University respondents, 92% of University of Salford respondents, and 89% of Embry-Riddle University respondents referred to the availability of email, Internet, Intranet, extranet, IP telephony, wireless connectivity, course delivery, and administration applications, e-library system, and electronic databases. Most respondents were also aware of the intended use of these services.
- **User's IS security awareness of existing IS security policies, standards, and guidelines:** The examined institutions varied considerably in this category. Zayed University did not have any IS security policies, standards, or guidelines in place, while University of Salford and Embry-Riddle did. In terms of awareness, 74% of the respondents in Zayed University could not confirm the existence or the lack thereof of IS security policies, standards, and guidelines. Only 16% of the respondents in Zayed were able to confirm that no policies exist. 76% of the examined respondents in Salford, and 68% were able to reference existing universities' IS security policies, standard, and procedures.
- **User's IS security awareness of existing IS security laws and legislation:** In 2006, the UAE government issued two laws to combat electronic trading and cyber crimes. All respondents in Zayed University were not aware of existing IS legislation. 64% of the respondents in Salford referred to the Computer Misuse Act and the Data Protection Act. 90% of the users learned about the two acts through the Information Services Division, while the remaining 10% were informed through other resources. Similarly, 41% of the respondents in Embry-Riddle referenced the Data Protection Act and the Computer Misuse Act, the Digital Millennium Copy Right Act, and the Electronic Communication Privacy Act. 74% of the respondents were informed of many of these laws through the Information Technology Department web site.
- **User's IS security awareness of available IS staff and personnel:** 32% of respondents in Zayed University were able to identify whom and how to contact in case of IT-security related problem or question. 65% of the respondents in

Salford, and 76% of the respondents in Embry Riddle referred to the IT department web site for contact information of IT support staff. While the IT department in Zayed University maintained a web page for the university, it did not maintain a web page for the department with the exception of the hardware and software Help Desk.

- **User's IS security awareness of possible IS security threats and concerns:** Respondents in Salford and Embry-Riddle scored higher than their counterparts in Zayed in terms of awareness of IS security threats. 74% of IS users in Salford and 82% in Embry-Riddle respondents were able to identify several possible IS security threats including denial of service attack, social engineering, shoulder surfing, and email spam, compared to 41% in Zayed University. Many of which had an IS background.
- **User's IS security awareness of possible IS security solutions:** Respondents in Salford and Embry-Riddle University also scored higher than their counterparts in Zayed in terms of awareness of IS security solutions. 80% of IS users in Salford and 84% of respondents were familiar with security solutions such as data back up procedures, virus protection, and password change rules, compared to 46% of the respondents in Zayed University.
- **User's IS security awareness of available IS security training session and materials:** Although the Information Services Division in Zayed University offers periodical training session in Microsoft Office applications, it did not offer a single IS security training since the university inception in 1998. Naturally, none of the respondents were aware of any IS security training sessions. Respondents at Salford are required to attend an IS security training session as part of their orientation (Faculty, staff, and students). In addition to the mandatory session, the IS security coordinator offers periodical sessions throughout the academic year. In the Embry-Riddle University, IS security training is also part of the induction program for both faculty and students. Training materials are also available online.
- **User's IS security awareness of available IS security documents and help material:** Similar to the training category, respondents in Zayed University were not aware of IS security documents and help material mainly due to non-availability. 54% of the respondents at Salford, and 67% of respondents at Embry-Riddle University were able to locate key IS security documents and help materials.
- **User's IS security awareness and perception of the value of university data:** 46% of the respondents in Zayed University viewed university data as valuable and worthy of protection, while 54% viewed the university data as "of no interest to hackers". Many of these came from academics with less computer/IS background. 96% of the respondents in the University of Salford, and 88% Embry-Riddle University viewed university data as valuable, private, confidential, and worthy of protection.
- **User's IS security awareness and perception of his/her role in university's IS security:** In this last category, 88% of the respondents in Zayed University believed that they have a role in IS security, 65% of which could not define it. They also believed that the full responsibility of IS security falls on the shoulder of the Information Service Division. Surprisingly, many of these are IS users

who had some sort of IS background, tend to take for granted and fully trust their institution in implementing security policies. On the other hand, the remaining 13%, was mainly academics from computer science and information technology disciplines who viewed their role as "first line of defense" to university IS security. 96% of the respondents in the UK university of Salford, and 86% of respondents from Embry Riddle viewed their role in the overall IS security cycle as important. More than 70% in both cases viewed the protection of their PC password and data as the main goals.

5 Discussion

The findings of this study indicate a considerable difference between the level of IS security awareness of academic researchers in the UAE and those of academic researchers in the UK and the US. The level of IS security awareness of academic researchers in each environment correlated with the level of IS security awareness supporting tools utilized in that environment as shown in table (1) and figure (1). Respondents in the University of Salford and Embry-Riddle University appeared more aware of IS security-related matters than their counter parts in Zayed University. The higher level of IS security awareness in the case of the UK and the US can mainly be attributed to the existence of IS security awareness supporting tools and activities. The IS security function in the examined institutions in the UK and the US appeared more supported, coordinated, regulated, and centralized than that in the UAE. The majority of academic researchers in Zayed University were not aware of possible IS security threats and their role in defending against them. They were not aware of whom to reach in case of an IS security problem, and they were not aware of proper policies, standards, and guidelines that should govern their access and use of IS systems. It should be noted that (a) Academics from areas other than computer science and information systems exhibited a lower level of security awareness than academics with a computing background, (b) users with a computer science background tend to take for granted and fully trust their institution in implementing security policies which may result in overlooking basic security threats, and (c) academics tend to work from home, or while on the move (including conference venues, hotels, etc…) which makes them prone to wireless network security threats.

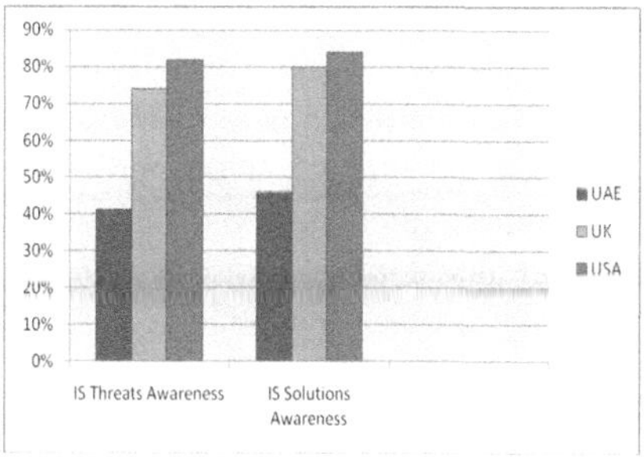

Fig. 1. User's IS Security Awareness

Table 1. Used IS Security Tools

Case Study	IS Security Policies	IS security Training	IS security Documentation
UAE	X	X	X
UK	√	√	√
USA	√	√	√

The low-perceived value of IS security and the data stored by the examined institution in the UAE is a natural result of the lack of emphasis shown by the university management; which is visible through: (a) Lack of IS security training, (b) Lack of IS security policies, (c) Lack of IS security coordination. Inversely, the higher level of IS security awareness in the examined institutions in the UK and the US can be attributed to the university emphasis and commitment to IS security awareness, by: (a) Establishment, communication, and enforcement of IS security training programs, (b) Establishment, communication, and enforcement of IS security policies; (c) Establishment of a coordinated IS security function. While understanding that no single practice described will work everywhere, from the findings of this study, and in correlation with [14] and [16], the authors believe that the following steps have the potential to increase the level of IS security awareness, and consequently the level of IS security awareness in UAE and more generally academic institutions in developing economies: (a) Establishment and communication of IS security policies and procedures to academic members of staff; (b) Campaign and advertise IS security awareness best practices and IS security training sessions and materials; (c) Train academic members on IS security best practices to increase their awareness; (d) Reward secure academic collaborations and identify / disseminate ill security practices; and (e) Conduct continuous evaluation and readjustment.

6 Conclusion

The paper explores if higher education research communities are aware of the security challenges related to the virtual collaborative working that underpins academic research. The examined institutions are believed to be a typical representation of higher education institutions within the selected communities.

The findings of this study indicate that although the examined institutions presented a similar IS infrastructure, and employed similar IS security technical measures, the level of IS security awareness varied considerably. This variance can be directly attributed to the level of IS security awareness supporting tools and activities utilized by the institution. The study indicates that the level of IS security awareness correlated with the availability and enforcement of IS security awareness supporting tools such as training, policies, documents, and coordination. The low level of IS security awareness of academic researchers in the case of the UAE, and more generally academic institutions from developing countries, constitute a higher level of possible risk of IS security threats to other academic researchers from developed countries who undertake joint collaborative research. Developing countries tend to have a large underground market for illegal software [18] and an increased number of unaware users who can easily become easy targets to criminals and hackers.

The main research question that underpins the paper deserves further and more in-depth exploration using larger samples of academic users across institutions, while using larger collaborative academic networks or communities as case studies. This constitutes ongoing research to be reported by the authors in future publications.

References

[1] Rezgui, Y., Marks, A.: Information security awareness in higher education: An exploratory study. Computers and Security 27(7-8) (2008)

[2] Updegrove, D., Gordon, W.: Computers and Network Security in Higher Education, EDUCAUSE (2003)

[3] Yin, R.K.: Applications of case study research. Sage, London (2003)

[4] Albrechtsen, E., Hovden, J.: The information security digital divide between information security managers and users. Computers & Security (2009)

[5] Bray, T.J.: Security actions during reduction in workforce efforts: what to do when downsizing. Information systems security (2002)

[6] Cooper, M.: Information Security Training- Lessons Learned Along the Trail. In: Proceedings of the 36th annual ACM SIGUCCS conference on User services conference (2009)

[7] Dlimini, M., Eloff, J., Eloff, M.: Information security: The moving target. Computers & Security (2008)

[8] Dunlop, C., Kling, R.: Social Relationship in Electronic Commerce. In: Dunlop, C., Kling, R. (eds.) Introduction in Computerization and Controversy- Value Conflicts and Social change. Academic Press, New York (1992)

[9] EDUCAUSE: Center for Applied Research: Information Technology Security: Governance, strategy, and practice in Higher Education (2003)

[10] ISF- International Security Forum. The Forum's Standard of Good Practice for IS security, `http://www.isfsecuritystandard.com/index_ie.htm` (Cited May 18, 2006)

[11] Katz, F.H.: The Effect of a University Information Security Survey on Instructing Methods in Information Security. In: Proceedings of the 2nd annual conference on Information security curriculum development (2005)

[12] Kovacich, G.: Information system security Officer's Guide: Establishing and Managing an Information Protection Program. Butterworth-Heinemann, USA (1998)

[13] Kruger, H.A., Kearney, W.D.: A prototype for assessing information security awareness. Computers & Security 25(1), 289–296 (2006)

[14] Mitnick, K.D., Simon, W.L.: The Art of Deception: Controlling the Human Element of Security. Wiley, Indianapolis (2002)

[15] North, M., Roy, G., North, S.: Computer Security Ethics Awareness in University Environments: A Challenge for Management of Information Systems (2006)

[16] Puhakainen, P.: A Design Theory for Information Security Awareness (2006)

[17] Siponen, M.T., A Conceptual Foundation for Organizational Information Security awareness. Information Management & Computer Security (2000)

[18] Joseph, M.: IT in the Middle East: Overview. In: Proceedings of the 7th conference on Information technology education (2006)

Inter-Organizational Information System Architecture: A Service-Oriented Approach

Mohammad Kazem Haki and Maia Wentland Forte

Faculty of Business and Economics, Institute of Information Systems,
University of Lausanne, Switzerland
{kazem.haki,mwf}@unil.ch

Abstract. The strategic value of Inter-Organizational Information System (IOIS), regarded as an automated information system shared by two or more companies, highly depends on its architecture to support agile business needs. The main requirements of this architecture for supporting business agility are *flexibility and scalability*, *interoperability and integration* as well as *process-centric architecture and continuous business process improvement*. We claim that the service-oriented architecture (SOA) approach, the latest in a long series of attempts in software engineering, is the best for meeting these requirements. In this paper, after investigating the compatibility of SOA features with IOISs requirements, we propose a service-oriented IOIS architecture composed of business service, application and integration layers.

Keywords: Inter-Organizational Information Systems (IOISs), Service-Oriented Architecture (SOA), Business Agility.

1 Introduction

Inter-organizational systems are information and communication technology-based systems that deal with Business-to-Business supply chain interactions. Transcending legal enterprise boundaries [16], they are considered as one of the major critical success factors for getting a real time response to the continuous changes of the market. When mobilized properly, they can bring the organization a significant competitive advantage. The role IT plays in these systems, called Inter-Organizational Information Systems (IOISs), is strategic. Hence, the introduction of new IT technologies opens new architectural avenues. IT is currently moving from object-orientation to service-oriented computing, now considering services as fundamental elements for application development [27]. Thus Service-Oriented Architecture (SOA) is becoming the fundamental approach for developing the next generation of IOISs. Regardless of the trend, compatibility between the SOA specifications and the IOISs requirements leads to service-oriented IOISs.

In this paper we will propose a service oriented IOISs architecture that provides a solution meeting the requirements of IOISs. After examining these requirements, based on the literature, we will propose a classification highlighting the potential of using SOA. We will then describe the characteristics of SOA and prove the compatibility of

L.M. Camarinha-Matos et al. (Eds.): PRO-VE 2010, IFIP AICT 336, pp. 642–652, 2010.

its capabilities and features with IOIS requirements. Based on this demonstration, we will conclude by proposing a top-down three layers service-oriented architecture for IOISs.

2 Requirements of IOISs

Inter-organizational information systems (IOISs) date back to 1966, when Kaufman raised awareness on information systems that operated across organizational boundaries [13]. IOISs, defined by [5] as "an automated information system shared by two or more companies", aims at facilitating the creation, storage, transformation and transmission of information that transcends legal enterprise boundaries [12, 16]. Indeed the use, by two or more organizations, of a one and same system is considered necessary and sufficient to qualify it as inter-organizational [7].

An IOIS differs from an internal, distributed information system in that it allows information to be sent across organizational boundaries. Access to stored data and applications programs is obviously shared to varying degrees depending on the participants' specific contexts [12]. When compared to internal IS, IOISs following characteristics have been identified by [29]: 1) they require partners which are willing, able and ready to cooperate 2) standards play a key role (e.g. data communications protocols, company policies), 3) third parties are often involved such as software-service providers, partners for supporting inter-organizational business processes, etc., 4) the work must be synchronized among partners 5) technical aspects are less important than the new electronic relationships involved i.e. the importance of electronic business models and 6) efforts cannot be secretive, i.e. IOIS requires more openness especially when industry standards are adopted.

Looked at from a operational point of view, IOISs lead to real-time interaction, higher transaction accuracy, more efficient and quicker payments, rapid response, reduced search costs, reduction in inventory and tighter links to customers. These benefits enable all parties to have high operational efficiency and capability, explaining why more and more corporations tend to adopt IOIS in order to gain competitive advantages [12, 21].

In the literature of IOISs different buzzwords have appeared reflecting the main characteristics of IOISs. Among those, one can cite extranet, EDI (Electronic Data Exchange), Internet EDI, B2B e-commerce, e-SCM (Supply Chain Management), etc. In effect, IOISs covers all the spectrum from simple EDI systems for exchanging data such as purchase orders to more complex transactions such as shared technical databases. Depending on the characteristics of each IOIS, the implementation needs to take into account some specifics. Hereafter, we mention the result of some studies in this regard we consider as pertinent for our purpose.

Critical Success Factors (CSF) of IOISs:

[21] mentioned seven CSFs regrouped within three clusters:

1. Decision motivation: 1) strong motivation is essential to gain and thereby guarantee partners' commitment 2) shared motivation and vision is essential;
2. Implementation process: 3) cross-organizational implementation team is necessary 4) high integration with internal information systems is indispensable 5) inter-organizational business process re-engineering could be needed;

3. Infrastructure conditions: 6) advanced legacy information system and infrastructure should be taken care of 7) shared industry standard should exist.

These CSFs show the technical and non-technical requirements for implementing IOISs.

IOISs requirements from an integration perspective:
On one hand, integration contributes to exchanging data so as to unify software components and streamline business processes. On the other hand, tight integration of IS in different companies may well reduce flexibility and agility of these organizations.

[30] studied the integration requirements of an IOIS from a two dimensions perspective determining some criteria for each, as follows:

1. Intensity of integration: scope of integration, type of integration
2. Flexibility of integration: scope of standard usage, types of and compliance with standards

Features of dynamic inter-organizational business processes:
[28] introduced the concept of "dynamic inter-organizational business processes". It entails a continuous building and dismantling of partnerships, which is the key difference between dynamic and static inter-organizational business processes, which have existed since the 1960s and have been based on technologies such as EDI. This study introduces six requirements of dynamic inter-organizational business processes as bellow:

1. Process Autonomy: capability of autonomously defining and executing business processes
2. Flexibility: dynamic inter-organizational business processes are subject to more changes than static inter-organizational business processes
3. Scalability: provides quick support for adding business processes or for increasing significantly the instances of an already existing business process
4. Service Autarchy: capability of independently associating the services needed to support business processes or sub-processes
5. Service Extensibility and Integration: new services must be continually integrated due to changes in the business processes
6. Asynchronous Service Evolution: with dynamic inter-organizational business processes, services evolve independently

In synthesis and according to the above, we can conclude that the crucial requirements needed to successfully implement an IOISs are:
1) From the IT point of view:

- *Flexibility and scalability*, i.e. the capability of plugging-in and unplugging software/business components based on market needs as well as
- *Interoperability and integration*, creating a unified whole by interconnecting different systems or components.

2) From the business point of view: *process-centric architecture and continuous business process improvement,* i.e. the capability of executing all type of business processes based on a universal standard.

It appears that these requirements are the same of those of business agility, a concept that extends adaptability and flexibility to include speed and scalability [2], and a term applied to the capability of an organization to react to unanticipated market change and rapid transformation of business processes [10]. This translates into the fact that the strategic value of IOIS for partners mostly depends on the alignment between IOIS specifications and capabilities with the requirement of business agility.

3 Compatibility of SOA Features with IOIS Requirements

The service-oriented architecture (SOA) approach is the latest in a long series of attempts in software engineering in trying to foster the reuse of software components [19]. SOA is an enterprise architecture that advocates loosely coupled and reusable systems. It has evolved from component-based development to distributed internet architectures as a new abstraction layer allowing internal and external systems to interact using common standards and protocols [4].

In a SOA, the business and technical processes are implemented as services. Each service represents a certain functionality that maps explicitly to a step in a business process. In this context, a service is a software component that can be reused by another software component or accessed via a standard-based interface over the network [22].

Technically, the main components of SOA are: service directory, service provider and service requester (see Figure 1). Some of the most important standards related to these components are:

- SOAP (Simple Object Access Protocol) (www.w3.org/TR/SOAP12): defines a mechanism for the communication with Web services over the Internet. It specifies the format of messages that are exchanged between the service requestor, the service provider, and the service directory.
- WSDL (Web Services Description Language) (www.w3.org/TR/WSDL.html): defines the structure and the contents of the service directory. Two related pieces of this standard are: 1) service types which are typically standardized by standards and 2) actual business information.
- UDDI (Universal Description, Discovery, and Integration) (www.uddi.org): provides the capability to describe a Web service, without the need to have it formally standardized. A WSDL description of a Web service provides all information needed to actually invoke it [19].

The fundamental features of SOA are: (1 it is based on services that can be readily integrated, (2 it is based on standards, (3 it is available on multiple platforms, (4 it provides self-contained (hence, loosely coupled) services, and (5 it incorporates and presupposes a contract that specifies the functionalities offered and at the same time, guarantees that they are replicable [1, 23].

A close examine of SOA special features and characteristics shows that they are fully compatible with the special requirements of IOISs listed above.

Furthermore, [22] illustrates the SOA potential benefits to IOISs as follows: loosely coupled applications and location transparency, application connectivity and interoperability, alignment of IT around the needs of the business, enhanced reuse of existing assets and applications, process-centric architecture, parallel and independent development, better scalability and graceful evolutionary changes, reduced costs of application development and integration, easier maintenance and reduced vendor lock-ins. In turn, [9] claims that from a technical point of view, SOA provides flexible and cost-effective solutions through interoperability, reusability and composability between loosely coupled services, while from a business point of view, SOA is an architectural strategy that helps achieve enterprise resource integration and organizational agility.

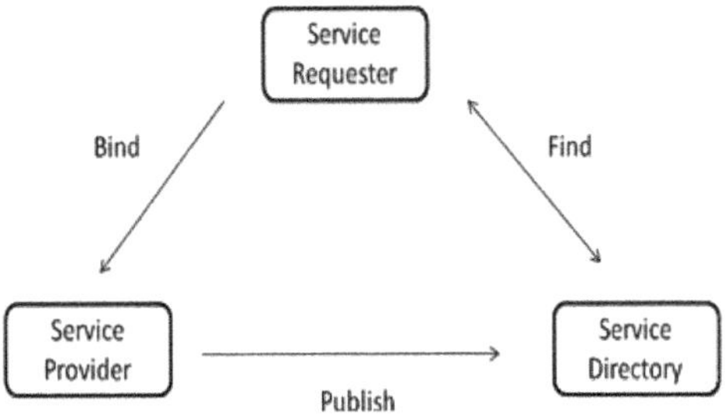

Fig. 1. Components of SOA

The SOA has been chosen as it allows for increased flexibility and scalability in comparison to traditional software engineering techniques [11].

SOA, web services and Web-based technology platforms provide best hope at IT level and provide reasonable solutions for reaching technical interoperability [8] allowing different distributed services to run on a variety of software platforms and hardware architectures. In effect, service composition enables scalability from small to more complex, distributed applications. Also, the SOA has the potential to address application integration issues by opening up the functionality with standardized, interoperable interfaces. Since services may be offered by different participants and communicated via the Web, they provide a distributed computing infrastructure for both intra- and inter-enterprise application integration and collaboration [26]. In terms of integration with legacy systems, SOA facilitates aligning existing IT infrastructure and systems to achieve end-to-end enterprise connectivity by removing redundancies, generating unified collaboration tools, and streamlining IT processes [3].

Last but not least, for process-centric architecture and continuous business process improvement, SOA allows a clear representation of the process flows identified by the order of the components used in a particular business service—and provides business users with an ideal environment for monitoring business operations. The process is decomposed into a series of steps, each representing a business service. In effect, each service or component functions as a sub-application. These sub-applications are chained together to create a process flow capable of satisfying the business need. This granularity lets processes leverage and reuse each sub-application throughout the organization [6].

Accordingly, SOA contributes flexibility and scalability [9, 11, 21, 24], interoperability and integration [8, 9, 21, 24] and process-centric architecture [6, 21] to the architecture of the IOISs in order to cover all the requirements of this kind of information systems. This demonstrates that SOA is today be one of the best architecture for developing IOISs, leading us to propose a SO-based architecture for IOISs that should be capable for developing a seamless IOIS for supporting agile businesses needs. The architecture of service-oriented IOISs, consequently takes advantage of all the benefits and advantages of the SOA - as the latest approach in software engineering trend-. In comparison with SOA, Model-Driven Architecture (MDA) brings another perspective which is not an alternative approach to SOA because these two approaches enable and complete each other [17, 25, 31].

4 Service Oriented-Based Architecture for IOIS

Based on the excellent fit between SOA features and IOISs requirements, we propose a three layer architecture for IOISs. Ours is a top-down architecture span from business to IT infrastructure in order to support business requirements. As the two others are designed based on it, the business service layer is the most important layer of the proposed architecture. Composite applications, constituting the second layer, need to be identified for supporting business services throughout the organization as well as services between organizations. As the lowest layer, integration between applications by utilizing service-oriented standards will be investigated (see Figure 2).

The Business service Layer. The business architecture is the vital part and the first architectural layer of an IOIS that impacts other architectural layers. In this layer we have to decompose business processes in order to determine business services. When applying the service-oriented paradigm to enterprise computing, the functionality is encapsulated as a service, either as a simple or composite one [27].

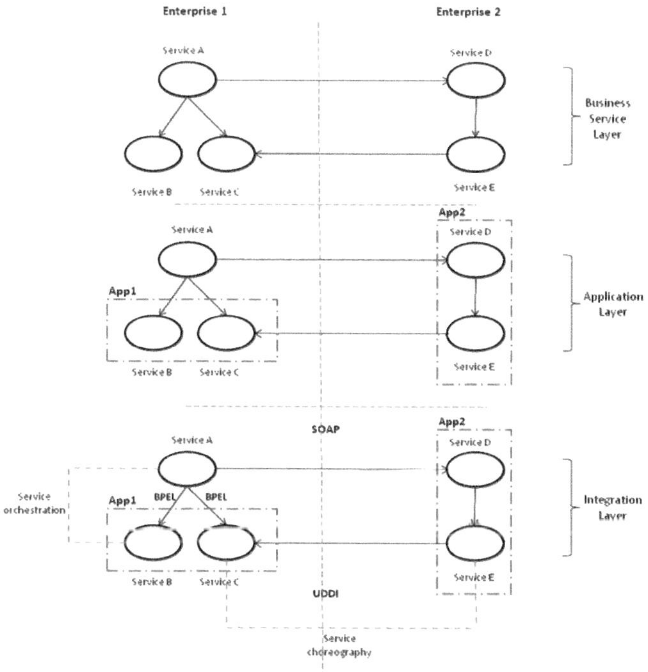

Fig. 2. The proposed Service-Oriented IOIS Architecture

A business process is composed of a series of continuous actions or operations that are performed upon a commodity. It is usually initiated by a customer. It must provide results directly to a customer, who may be internal or external to the company [18]. We have observed three common patterns for studying business process: 1) *Organizational level* consists of strategic level, tactical level and operational level [18], 2) *Interaction* consists of peer-to-peer/ conversational structure and hierarchical structure [14, 19], 3) *Value chain* consists of primary and support business processes [24]. According to the requirements of agile businesses, that also describe the requirements of developing an IOIS, the componentization of the business using the SOA is not far.

In this regard, we should identify the functionality of each business process, the so-called aspect. Every business process can feature several aspects: 1) the functional aspect which describes how a business process is composed of sub-processes 2) the control aspect which describes how activities are executed dependent on the result or completion of other activities 3) the organizational aspect in which the relation between the business process and the organization structure is established and 4) the operational aspect which describes external services to be used during the process. These aspects are the atomic part of business processes and contain only one functionality and shape the representation element of each business process [28]. Therefore, for following service-oriented logic in IOIS architecture, we need to use a tool or standard for converting business processes into business services.

BPEL4WS is a technology that defines a business process as a set of service invocations [6]. It is a service orchestration and choreography language which fulfills the need for modeling all the above mentioned business process patterns. By using this language, we can define application and infrastructure services directly based upon business services.

Application Layer. We propose a composite approach for defining applications. In other word, we have combined different services for determining application services. A composite application is created by a set of interconnected and specialized services. The specialization information contains both parameterization and connection information. Parameterization information adapts the service to the individual needs of the composite application. The connection information contains information about the connection of the service with other services within the context of the composite application [28].

In effect, composite applications are similar to Component Based Software (CBS) focusing on building large software systems by integrating previously build software components. A composite application has three different layers:

- User interface layer: the different forms and functions are presented to the user
- Choreography layer: defines the correct order of calling services in the composite application
- Service layer: represents service to composite application [20].

We use BPEL4WS because it fully supports this compositional approach. BPEL4WS's composition functionality described by [14] as following: enable flexible integration, offering choreography as a web service, support for multiple composition patterns and support for lifecycle management. It is currently the preferred standard for performing web service composition [27].

Integration Layer. After determining composite applications, in the integration layer we will identify the environment in which application services supports all the business services.

The relationship between services in composite applications could be inter or intra-organizational. Hence the information about existing services is stored in a service registry based on UDDI. For each representation element of the business processes, an appropriate service has to be found. In most cases, there is no perfect fit; therefore, the search has to include services which can be properly adapted. Furthermore one service may fit well with several representation elements. This information is returned in the form of WSDL files and by using XML-based interface. These XML-based messages do exchange between services by using SOAP. Service orchestration and choreography within organization and between organization and its stakeholders is handled by BPEL4WS [20, 28]. Apart from the application integration, some other integration considerations are the end-user interface, the application connectivity, the process integration, the information integration and a build-to-integrate development model [6].

We could classify different integration standards based on the layer of integration. Figure 3 illustrates the related standards of every integration layer [15].

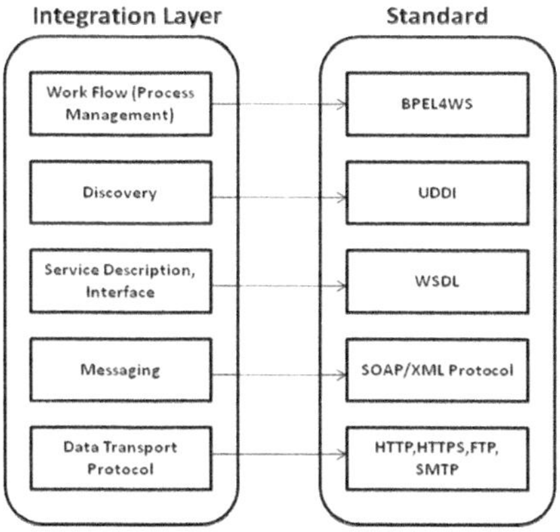

Fig. 3. Integration standards

5 Conclusion

Inter-Organizational Information Systems (IOISs), a cross-organizational automated information system, allows sharing an information system between several companies thus facilitating the creation, storage, transformation and transmission of information. Based on the literature in this field, we have demonstrated that an IOIS is capable of 1) plugging-in and unplugging software/business components (flexibility and scalability), 2) interconnecting different systems or components (interoperability and integration) and 3) executing all types of business processes based on a universal standard (process-centric architecture and continuous business process improvement).

The strategic effects of IT on IOISs on one hand, and the introduction of the service-oriented architecture in software engineering on the other hand, led us to study the compatibility of SOA's features and capabilities with the requirements of an IOIS. In SOA, the business and technical processes are implemented as services; a service being a software component that can be reused by another software component or accessed via a standard-based interface over the network. We determined that SOA provides flexible and cost-effective solutions through interoperability, reusability and composability between loosely coupled services. We discussed the fact that it also helps achieve enterprise resource integration and organizational agility based on interoperability and addresses application integration issues by opening up the functionality with standardized, interoperable interfaces. We finally showed that SOA is a process-centric architecture because it decomposes business processes into business services, each business service functioning as a sub-application.

After making sure there is a real compatibility between the IOISs requirements and the SOA's features, we have proposed a top-down service-oriented architecture for IOISs composed of a three layers architecture: 1) business service layer that consists of decomposing business processes in order to determine business services, 2) application layer that consists of combining different services for determining application services 3) integration layer that consists of identifying the environment in which application services supports all the business services. In order to fully support the compositional approach for defining and integrating application services of our three layers model, we recommend BPEL4WS as an orchestration and choreography language in the business service layer.

As a next step, we will examine the combination of the artifacts of this architecture with the building blocks of Enterprise Architecture (EA) in order to follow this approach from strategic level of the company and inter-organizational business processes with business partners. We will also investigate this approach from the Business Process Management (BPM) perspective for supporting inter-organizational BPM systems and work-flow management systems.

References

1. Baskerville, B., Cavallari, M., Hjort-Madsen, K., Pries-Heje, J., Sorrentino, M., Virili, F.: Extensible Architectures: The Strategic Value of Service Oriented Architecture in Banking. In: Proceeding of European Conference on Information Systems, ECIS (2005)
2. Baskerville, R.: Business Agility and Information Technology Diffusion. IFIP Advances in Information and Communication Technology, vol. 180, Atlanta, Georgia (2005)
3. Bieberstein, N., Bose, S., Walker, L., Lynch, A.: Impact of Service-Oriented Architecture on Enterprise Systems, Organizational Structure and Individuals. IBM Systems Journal 44(4) (2005)
4. Brahe, S.: BPM on top of SOA: Experiences from the Financial Industry. In: Alonso, G., Dadam, P., Rosemann, M. (eds.) BPM 2007. LNCS, vol. 4714, pp. 96–111. Springer, Heidelberg (2007)
5. Cash, J.I., Knsynski, B.R.: IS Redraws Competitive Boundaries. Harvard Business Review, 134–142 (March-April 1985)
6. Channabasavaiah, K., Holley, K.: Migration to a Service-Oriented Architecture. IBM Software Group (2004)

7. Chatterjee, D., Ravichandran, T.: Inter-organizational Information Systems Research: A Critical Review and an Integrative Framework. In: Proceedings of the 37th Hawaii International Conference on System Sciences, USA (2004)
8. Chen, D., Doumeingts, G., Vernadat, F.: Architectures for enterprise integration and interoperability: Past, present and future. Computers in Industry 59, 647–659 (2008)
9. Chen, H.M.: Towards Service Engineering: Service Orientation and Business-IT Alignment. In: Proceedings of the 41st Hawaii Int. Conference on System Sciences (2008)
10. El-Ghareeb, H.A.M.: Aligning Service Oriented Architecture and Business Process Management Systems to Achieve Business Agility. Requirements Network Group (RQNG) (January 2009)
11. Hanemann, A., et al.: PerfSONAR: A Service Oriented Architecture for Multi-domain Network Monitoring. In: Benatallah, B., Casati, F., Traverso, P. (eds.) ICSOC 2005. LNCS, vol. 3826, pp. 241–254. Springer, Heidelberg (2005)
12. Johnston, H.R., Vitale, M.R.: Creating Competitive Advantage with Interorganizational Information Systems. MIS Quarterly (June 1988)
13. Kaufman, F.: Data systems that cross company boundaries. Harvard Business Review (January-February 1966)
14. Khalaf, R., Mukhi, N., Weerawarana, S.: Service-Oriented Composition in BPEL4WS. In: Proceeding of the twelfth international World Wide Web conference, WWW 2003, Budapest, Hungry (May 2003)
15. Koshutanski, H., Massacci, F.: An Access Control Framework for Business Processes for Web Services. In: Proc. 2003 ACM workshop on XML security, Virginia, USA, pp. 15–24 (2003)
16. Kumar, K., Dissel, H.G.V.: Sustainable Collaboration: Managing Conflict and Cooperation in Interorganizational Systems. MIS Quarterly (September 1996)
17. Kumaran, S., Bishop, P., Chao, T., Dhoolia, P., Jain, P., Jaluka, R., Ludwig, H., Moyer, A., Nigam, A.: Using a Model Driven Transformational Approach and Service-Oriented Architecture for Serving Delivery Management. IBM Systems J. 46(3), 513–529 (2007)
18. Kung, M.T., Zhang, Y.Z.: Analysis of Business Process Models in Enterprise Web Services. International Journal of E-Business Research 4(2), 69–87 (2008)
19. Leymann, F., Roller, D., Schmidt, M.T.: Web services and business process management. IBM Systems Journal 41(2) (2002)
20. Liegl, P.: The Strategic Impact of Service Oriented Architecture. In: Proceedings of the 14th Annual IEEE International Conference and Workshops on the Engineering of Computer-Based Systems (ECBS 2007), Tucson, AZ (2007)
21. Lu, X.H., Huang, L.H., Heng, M.S.H.: Critical success factors of inter-organizational information systems—A case study of Cisco and Xiao Tong in China. Information & Management 43, 395–408 (2006)
22. Mahmood, Z.: Service Oriented Architecture: Potential Benefits and Challenges. In: Proceedings of the 11th WSEAS International Conference on COMPUTERS, Agios Nikolaos, Crete Island, Greece, July 26-28 (2007)
23. Meredith, L.G., Bjorg, S.: Contracts and Types. Com. of the ACM 46(10), 41–47 (2003)
24. Porter, M.: Changing Patterns of International Competition. California Management Review XXVIII(2), 9–40 (Winter 1986)
25. Radhakrishnan, R., Wookey, M.: Model Driven Architecture Enabling Service Oriented Architecture. Sun Micro Systems (March 2004)
26. Raghupathi, W., Kesh, S.: Interoperable Electronic Health Records Design: Towards a Service-Oriented Architecture. e-Service Journal 5(3), 39–57 (2007)

27. Rosenberg, F., Dustdar, S.: Business Rules Integration in BPEL:A Service-Oriented Approach. In: Proceedings of the Seventh IEEE International Conference on E-Commerce Technology, Washington, DC, USA, pp. 476–479 (2005)
28. Schmidt, R.: Web Services Based Architectures to Support Dynamic Inter-organizational Business Processes. In: Jeckle, M. (LJ) Zhang, L.-J. (eds.) ICWS-Europe 2003. LNCS, vol. 2853, pp. 123–136. Springer, Heidelberg (2003)
29. Sprague, R.H., McNulin, B.C.: Information System Management in Practice. Prentice Hall, Englewood Cliffs (1993)
30. Stelzer, D., Fischer, D., Nirsberger, I.: A Framework for Assessing Inter-Organizational Integration of Business Information Systems. Int J. Interoperability in Business Information Systems 2(2), 9–20 (2006)
31. Torkaman Rahmani, A., Rafe, V., Sedighian, S., Abbaspour, A.: An MDA-Based Modeling and Design of Service Oriented Architecture. In: Alexandrov, V.N., van Albada, G.D., Sloot, P.M.A., Dongarra, J. (eds.) ICCS 2006. LNCS, vol. 3993, pp. 578–585. Springer, Heidelberg (2006)

Factors Affecting RFId Adoption in a Vertical Supply Chain: The Case of the Silk Industry in Italy

Cristina Quetti[2] and Federico Pigni[1]

[1,2] Università Carlo Cattaneo – LIUC, Lab#ID, Italy
cquetti@liuc.it, fpigni@liuc.it

Abstract. RFId adoption process is receiving a lot of attention in literature; studies assessing its potentials in supply chains are now well documented. Despite this rising interest, the diffusion pattern of RFId systems in the vertical supply chains has been only scarcely addressed and theoretical contributions explaining dynamics and drivers are still missing. This study shows that the Diffusion of Innovation Theory can be effectively used to explore these questions in a vertical SC. However, three major considerations emerged: 1) the factors influencing, facilitating or inhibiting the adoption process change over time and during the adoption process; 2) facilitators such as business associations play an important role in the supply chains composed of SMEs; 3) the position of adopters within the SC greatly influences the diffusion process.

Keywords: Interorganizational Systems, RFId, Diffusion of Innovation Theory, supply chain.

1 Introduction

The increasing complexity and turbulence of markets are notably shaping a fiercely competitive business environment. Besides, worldwide mobility of labor and capital are extending companies' value chains, increasing the difficulties in managing business processes [1]. Information and communication technologies (ICT) provide the needed support to enable the collaboration among trading partners to face this new competitive context. Radio Frequency Identification systems (RFId) gained attention both from researchers and practitioners, as an interesting emerging technology capable of enabling cross-company information flows integration. However, supply chain–SC wide RFId system implementations are scarcely documented; the adoption process, in particular, is lacking the necessary understanding of patterns and dynamics when refereed to the inter-organizational context [2]. With this paper, we aim at filling this gap exploring the main factors driving RFId adoption across a vertical SC, assuming that these factors represent the rationale behind the diffusion of RFId systems, thus influencing and eventually predicting the intent to adopt. To answer this research question we first review past conceptual and empirical research on IOS adoption. Then we propose an explorative model, based on the Diffusion of Innovation Theory (DoI) and through qualitative methods, we seek confirmation of the validity of the main constructs through seven case studies.

L.M. Camarinha-Matos et al. (Eds.): PRO-VE 2010, IFIP AICT 336, pp. 653–663, 2010.

2 Literature Review

The literature dealing with inter-organizational system (IOS) adoption is vast. IOS adoption is an organizational-level decision that has to be considered in an inter-organizational perspective, where synchronization and alignment between an organization and its trading partners become significant [3]. Most of the past studies adopted the DoI [4] to outline the attributes of an individual new technology and tools that drive its adoption[5-9]. RFId adoption studies have been built on the base of these previous findings and have only been examined recently. In comparison to former researches, they put a greater emphasis on the assessment of the interdependencies. This is particularly true as RFId systems affect information sharing at several levels (operational, tactical and strategic) and are capable of supporting different SC collaboration practices. In a recent article, [10] integrated the models proposed by [11] [9] and adapted them to explore adoption in RFId context. Another stream of research on RFId adoption focuses on the assessment of the potential benefits [12-14] and business performance of RFId applications [15], exploring the business value and drivers influencing the investment decision [16] [17-18]. Finally, other studies investigate RFId adoption on the base of specific case studies [19-21].

Despite these studies tried to frame the complexity of the inter-organizational adoption process, they focused on the assessment of the diffusion pattern on the horizontal dimension, comparing similar companies within the same industry, or framing the problem in an aggregated manner. This simple fact underlines an important emerging issue: the diffusion pattern of RFId systems in the vertical SC has been only scarcely addressed; theoretical contributions on the topic are still missing noteworthy in the understanding of its dynamics and drivers. In the following section, we present a model, structured on the DoI theory, to study the adoption drivers of RFId systems across a vertical SC.

3 Framework

Based on the findings of previous IOS adoption studies, three elements - external environment, organizational readiness, perceived benefits- were identified as the main drivers of adoption [3, 9-10]. In addition to these elements, we propose to include "supply chain readiness" as a new driver to account for the forces influencing SC dynamics for RFId adoption defined on the base of the studies by [22] [10] [23].

Thus the proposed model is composed of four main factors influencing RFId adoption: the external environment, the organizational readiness, the perceived benefits and SC readiness. The following section will detail in succession each factor and the hypothesis tested. In the tables we describe each factor, detailing its sub-constructs. This work is the result of a literature analysis covering all the studies published in the main IS journals and conferences on RFId adoption. Among these, we selected and proposed those factors which are supposed to be relevant drivers for adoption decision for enterprises belonging to the same SC.

3.1 External Environment

External environment covers all pressures coming from the different forces shaping the business environment of the SC. Usually, political, economics, sociological and technological dynamics can affect companies' competitiveness and performances.

The external environment is composed of strategic and institutional drivers.

Strategic factor

Strategic factors encompass market dynamics and deals with those forces that in a SC stimulate a better market positioning through enhancement based on IT (in this case RFId) adoption and exploitation. We propose four main sub-constructs shaping this factor; we state the name of the sub-construct, its short description and reference.

Table 1. Strategic factors

H1-1	**Technology Maturity**	[4, 10, 19, 23-24]
H1-2	**Competitive Pressure**	[3, 8-10, 19, 24-31]
H1-3	**Industry**	[10, 19, 25, 32]
H1-4	**Emulation Effect**	[10, 24, 33]

Institutional factors

Enterprises can be persuaded to adopt RFId systems pressed by socio-political forces. Regulatory institutions, trade and industry associations, laws and regulations can effectively influence adoption's decisions [34]. We identified four sub-construct capable of influencing the RFId adoption process as detailed in the table below:

Table 2. Institutional factors

H1-5	**Normative**	[10-11, 33, 35]
H1-6	**Incentives**	[2, 10]
H1-7	**Supervisor**	[33]
H1-8	**Privacy**	[36][27]

3.2 Organization Readiness

Organizational readiness refers to the internal resources that a company could commit to supporting RFId adoption. Studies on EDI outlined that financial and technological resources are the main adoption drivers [9]. However, managerial drivers were found significant in influencing the process [8] [10]A lack of internal resources even in a single company, could limit RFId potential for the entire SC.

Financial resources

Financial resources consist of the monetary resources the organization can commit to covering RFId investment and costs.

Table 3. Financial resources

H2-1	**Financial resources**	[3, 9-10, 19, 22, 24, 35, 37]

Technological factors

Technological factors concern the implicit characteristics of the RFId system (such as complexity and compatibility), the infrastructural dimension and refer to the development and usage of the inter-organizational technology [9].

Table 4. Technological factors

H2-2	**Complexity**	[3-6, 8-9, 11, 24-25, 31, 33].
H2-3	**Compatibility**	[3-6, 8-9, 11, 24-25, 31, 33, 38]
H2-4	**IS infrastructure**	[3-6, 8-9, 11, 24-25, 31, 33, 38-39]

Top management support and company size

Top management support and company size are fundamental characteristic of an organization, which could favor or thwart RFId adoption. Its support is required to facilitate change during transition phases and for project sponsorship. Company size is often related to the actual availability of resources: larger companies could easily commit in comparison to smaller ones to innovative projects.

Table 5. Organizational factors

H2-5	**Top Management**	[3, 8-10, 19, 25, 31-35, 40-43]
H2-6	**Company Size**	[8, 23, 31, 37, 44-45]

3.3 Perceived Benefits

The perception of the potential benefits has been traditionally considered one of the main drivers behind IOS adoption. In the scope of RFId inter-organizational adoption, perceived benefits plays a relevant role, too. In a vertical SC, benefits usually are related to business process effectiveness and efficiency improvements, which in turns could generate operational performance gains and bullwhip effect reduction.

Table 6. Perceived benefits/costs

H3	**Perceived benefits /Costs**	[3, 7-10, 12-13, 15, 19, 25, 31, 35, 40, 46-47]

3.4 Supply Chain Readiness

RFId technology has a great potential in supporting interorganizational collaboration, information sharing and material flow coordination in the SC.

Moreover, adoption decisions in vertical supply chains are largely influenced by the dynamics emerging among trading partners.

Factors describing SC readiness are illustrated in the table below.

Table 7. Supply chain readiness factors

H4-1	**Bargaining Power**	[3, 8-10, 13, 19, 38, 46, 48-52]
H4-2	**Initiators**	[33, 35]
H4-3	**Trust**	[3, 33, 35, 38, 43, 46, 49-51, 53]
H4-4	**Partner ICT readiness**	[3, 24, 32, 35, 43]
H4-5	**IO Dependencies**	[38, 43, 51, 54]

4 Methodology

The aim of this work is to identify and explore the adoption drivers outlined in the model in the context of a vertical SC. The explorative case study methodology was found appropriate, investigating "a contemporary phenomenon within its real-life context, especially when the boundaries between phenomenon and context are not clearly evident", [55] a typical occurrence in studies dealing with inter-organizational issues. The study focused on a SC operating in the silk-textile Italian cluster of Como. Textile industry was identified a good candidate for the study as it shows a great potential and interest for RFId technology as it fits their needs to improve product traceability along the SC and to certify products' origin thus safeguarding the "Made in Italy" distinctive value. The analyzed SC is composed of seven SMEs each specialized in a specific process: weaving, purge, dyeing, printing, finishing and tailoring of high quality women dresses. The figure below illustrates the positioning of the companies interviewed along the Sc (names and the stage they act):

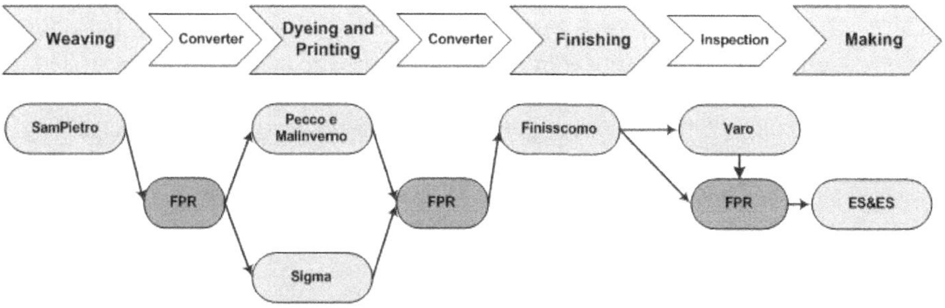

Fig. 1. The vertical supply chain

These companies performed a feasibility study and a tested in a pilot project the opportunity to implement RFId technology in their supply chain. They decided to apply RFId tags on the fabrics manufactured by Sampietro and to preserve them until the end of the chain. The information regarding the fabric are shared in real time thanks to the memory of the RFId tags and through a web service.

Data were gathered through in depth semi-structured interviews of executives and CIO across the seven organizations. Responded bias was avoided by involving multiple respondents in each organization. All direct interviews were performed between June and July 2008 and took place at companies' premises. Usually, interviews lasted 2-3 hours. The interviews were supported by a questionnaire developed on the base of the proposed model; they were recorded and then summarized. The interviews, then, provided the qualitative background to adopt an "interpretative" approach in this explorative study.

5 Results

External Environment
Concerning strategic factors and H1-1, technology maturity was not found to be a relevant inhibitor of RFId adoption. RFId vendors resulted capable of providing proper solutions to meet SC actors' needs, contrary to [10] findings.

Consistent with H1-2, our results show that competitive pressure strongly influences companies belonging to the same SC in adopting the new technology. In particular, companies confirmed that they are aiming at creating a sustainable competitive advantage leveraging RFId traceability potential. FPR owner: *"competitive environment forces us towards the research of new technologies capable of supporting item traceability, recording weaves history along the entire SC and demonstrating the Italian origin of the product. That's why we decided to adopt RFId systems";* Pecco e Malinverno TM:"*in this downturn time, we are seeking innovations to enhance company's agility and counter Asian competitors; A SC wide RFId implementation fits our needs"*. According to Henderson and Vankatramam [56], RFId is a tool for strategy execution influencing internal IS infrastructure and process (internal), in order to fit the objective of ensuring fabrics origin and enhance SC relationship for a effective collaborative activity planning and a better customer transparency.

H1-3 was confirmed, too. We found that the presence of existing RFId "closed loop" implementation within the industry, actually positively influenced the propensity *for* adoption of other actors within the SC (existing experiences demonstrated the ability of tags to survive to several aggressive industrial processes as the printing, purge or pressing). On the contrary, H1-4, investigating contagion, was found not applicable as SC wide implementations within the industry were still missing.

The Normative institutional element, H1-5, despite significant in other contexts, resulted poorly relevant as Italian regulation leaves to manufacturers the choice to voluntary adhere or propose a traceability system.

Interestingly, confirming H1-6, revealed that the presence of a "supervisor" facilitate, and in several situations actually permitted, cross-company adoption. The project champion from UNICO (Confindustria Como, the local business association) responsible for overseeing the adoption process, guaranteeing and controlling the fairness of the implementation was decisive. The Top Management of Pecco and Malinverno commented: "*supervisor persuaded our participation in the project and his presence confirmed its importance*".

Moreover, the involvement of a University Lab in the project effectively supported RFId knowledge transfer and eased the process: university researchers led the feasibility study and took care of the supporting activities towards SC participants.

Incentives favored RFId inter-organizational adoption confirming H1-7. The public incentives provided by Lombardy Region convinced hesitating partners by covering half of investment costs: companies were at the same time reducing their expenses and "reassured" of the political relevance of the innovation effort. Contrary to common understanding, but consistent with studies on RFId implementations supporting B2B transaction, H1-8 was not confirmed. Privacy was considered relevant only for those goods impacting directly the consumer.

Organizational readiness

The weight of Financial resources in influencing RFId adoption were found less relevant to adoption than expected. We are not supporting that the financial capability of companies to commit to the investment is irrelevant, but it did not impact the SC favoring or inhibiting adoption. This result confirms [39] study in which they demonstrated that RFId adoption is not strictly determined by the sheer amount of financial resources, but by the investment expectations. Actually we found that ROI can show only a window of investment returns: other index, such as KPI, can measure an early return on the RFId investment. Respondents generally confirmed that RFId complexity was low (H2-2) requiring only incremental process improvements.

H2-3, compatibility, was found capable of affecting RFId adoption. Those companies that already had an identification system in place (such as a barcode one) showed less compatibility problems in integrating and adapting their systems with those of other companies. Scarce IS infrastructure was found to be a inhibitor factor for RFId adoption, confirming H2-4. Sigma TM: "*our company has not the expertise to support cross-company RFId implementation*".

TM support (H2-5) was indicated as fundamental by all the companies interviewed and in several occasion suggested to be critical for achieving project goals. Firm size, H2-6, was effectively influencing RFId adoption.

Cost/Benefits

The distribution of cost and the appropriability of the generated benefits were found significant for the adoption process along the analyzed SC (H3). Benefits, as much as costs, were not evenly distributed among participants, as already assessed in previous studies [13]. In particular, we found that companies at the edge of the downstream of the supply chain experienced more advantages related to the information sharing enabled by the RFId system, than the other companies; implementation expenditures resulted similar along the SC and largely dependent on the existing IS infrastructure.

SC Readiness

Bargaining power of partners, H 4-1, resulted decisive in persuading companies to participate to the system and was mainly exerted through recommendations [9].

Trust among trading partners, (H 4-2) built on top of a solid relationship and a recognized competence, was effectively contributing to the success of the adoption process; Pecco and Malinverno TM commented: "*FPR owner visit our plants three times per week. We trust him and we thing that tools like RFId technology, capable of enabling information sharing, would help our collaboration*".

The presence of an initiator, was confirmed to favor adoption (H 4-3). FPR owner, whose company is positioned at the center of the SC, after perceiving the business opportunity for an RFId based SC traceability system, actively involved other companies in the project. Its first effort, he told us, was frustrated by partners' low ICT readiness, thus confirming that in a SC the companies with low ICT can slow down both the process and hinder the benefits emerging from the project (H 4-4).

Surprisingly, H 4-5, SC dependencies were found less significant than other factors in favoring RFId adoption. In particular, in the analyzed SC companies have stable relationship, factors like the bargaining power of the partner, or the trust among them resulted to drive more the adoption process than more institutionalized contracts.

6 Conclusions and Discussion

Consistently with our expectation, we found that external environment, organization readiness, cost/benefits sharing and SC readiness are the all driving factors of RFId adoption even in a vertical SC. However, in this context only of the several factors identified were found significant.

Our findings suggest that competitive pressure strongly influence managers' adoption decision [19]. The chance to improve competitiveness through RFId items traceability drove the initiator (FPR) to assess the feasibility of RFId, involving other companies in the SC. However, companies presenting low technological compatibility and inadequate IS infrastructures nearly stopped the project (Sigma and Finisscomo); companies were after encouraged, mainly from the incentive, to align their technological level to that of their partners [3-4, 9-10, 19].

Other decision elements, underlying a life cycle for the decision making process of the RFId adoption, appeared later in the project: those companies showing good organizational readiness based their decision on the evaluation of cost/benefits (Sampietro, FPR, Pecco e Malinverno, Varo and ES&ES). This assessment discouraged the company located on the upstream of the supply chain (Sampietro), which decided, in a first time, to give up the project as implementation costs were not balanced by corresponding benefits (they were supposed to tag items) [13]. Only agreeing on a "fair" division of costs, supported by a compensation of tag costs and application, had the project running. This suggest that the position of a company within the supply chain is a strong determinant of adoption, thus partially hindering DoI application in this context. The presences of a supervisor and the availability of financial incentives were confirmed as strong facilitator of adoption [33]. Without a supervisor, not only the implementation would have failed, but also some of the partners would not have committed the resources for the feasibility study. Moreover, the supervisor – the business association – acted as a guarantor of the stakes of all the parties involved and of adoption fairness. The bargaining power of certain actors was actively used, suggesting it as a critical factor of adoption. FPR recommended [9] Sigma and Finisscomo to participate to RFId, although these companies were reluctant. The existing trust between FPR and Pecco e Malinverno and based on competences [49] enabled the cross-company adoption, as both companies saw the RFId project as a chance to enhance collaboration.

In conclusion, this study effectively supports the use of the DoI Theory to study the diffusion of RFId in a the specific context of vertical supply chains, an aspect still unexplored in literature. However, several observation should be noted. Firstly, despite the majority of factors were found significant, their relevance changed in time. The more the project progressed, the factors influencing, facilitating or inhibiting the adoption process changed their importance and companies changed their mind as soon as actions were taken to correct the emerging deadlocks. Moreover, even when all members of the SC decide to adopt the RFId system, and that performance gains have been demonstrated the real commitment of companies and their TM is needed to enact collaboration and information sharing.

References

1. Friedman, T.L.: The World is flat: A Brief History of the Twenty-first Century. Farrar, Straus and Giroux, New York (2005)
2. Kauffman, R.J., Curtin, J., Riggins, F.J.: Making the most out of RFId technology: a research agenda for the study of the adoption, usage and impact of RFId. Management Science 40(8) (2005)
3. Chwelos, P., Benbasat, I., Dexter, A.S.: Empirical Test of an EDI Adoption Model. Information System Research 13(3), 304–321 (2001)
4. Rogers, E.M.: Diffusion of innovations, 5th edn. Free Press, New York (2003)
5. Cooper, R.B., Zmud, R.W.: Information technology Implementation Research: a Technological Diffusion Approach. Mgt. Sc. 36(2), 123–139 (1990)
6. Moore, G.C., Benbasat, I.: Development of an instrument to measure the perceptions of adopting an information technology innovation. Information Systems Research 2(3), 192–222 (1991)
7. O'Callaghan, Kaufmann, Konsynski: Adoption correlates and share effects of electronic data interchange systems in marketing channels. Journal of Marketing 4, 45–56 (1992)
8. Premkumar, G., Ramamurthy, K.: The role of Interorganizational and Organizational factors on decision mode of adoption of Interorganizational Systems. Decision Science 26, 75–86 (1995)
9. Iacovou, C.L., Benbasat, I., Dexter, A.S.: Electronic data interchange and small organizations: Adoption and impact of technology. MIS Quarterly 19(4), 465–485 (1995)
10. Sharma, A., Citurs, A., Konsynski, B.: Strategic and Institutional Perspectives in the Adoption and Early Integration of Radio Frequency Identification (RFID). In: Proceeding the 40th Hawaii International Conference on System Science, Hawaii, USA. IEEE, Los Alamitos (2007)
11. Teo, H.H., Wei, K.K., Benbasat, I.: Predicting Intension to Adopt Interorganizational Linkages: An Institutional Perspective. MIS Quarterly 27(1) (2003)
12. Baars, H., et al.: Profiling benefits of RFId applications. In: Americas Conference on Information System, AMCIS 2008 (2008)
13. Bensel, P., et al.: Cost-Benefit in cross-company RFId application: a case study approach. In: International conference of Information System, Paris, France (2008)
14. Pigni, F., Ugazio, E.: Measuring RFId Benefits in Supply Chains. In: Proceedings of the Fifteenth Americas Conference on Information Systems, San Francisco, California (2009)
15. Gille, D., Strüker, J.: Into the Unknown: Measuring the Business Performance of RFID Applications. In: Proceedings of the 16th European Conference on Information Systems, Galway, Ireland (2008)
16. Becker, J., et al.: Calculating the Process Driven Business Value of RFID Investments - A Causal Model for the Measurement of RFID Technologies in Supply Chain Logistics. In: Proceedings of the Fourteenth Americas Conference on Information Systems, Toronto, ON, Canada (2008)

17. Ivantysynova, L., Ziekow, H., Gunther, O.: A guide to Asses Cost and Benefits for RFId Investments in Manufacturing. In: Proceeding of ICIS 2007 Workshop on E-business, Montreal, Canada (2007)
18. Tellkamp, C.: The impact of Auto-ID technology on process performance - RFID in the FMCG supply chain. Dissertation of University of St.Gallen, Graduate school of business Administration (2006)
19. Krasnova, H., Wezer, L., Ivantysynova, L.: Adoption in the Automotive Industry. In: Americas Conference of Information System, AMCIS (2008)
20. Tewary, A., Kosalge, P., Motwani, J.: Piloting RFID in an Aerospace and Defense Supply Chain. In: Proceedings of the Fourteenth Americas Conference on Information Systems, Toronto, ON, Canada (2008)
21. Loebbecke, C., Huyskens, C.: Towards Standardizing Success: RFID in Fashion Retailing. In: BLED Proceedings, Bled, Slovenia (2006)
22. Ranganathan, C., Jha, J.: Adoption of RFID Technology: An Exploratory Examination from Supplier's Perspective. In: Proceedings of the Eleventh Americas Conference on Information Systems, Maha, NE, USA (2005)
23. Madlberger, M.A.: A Model of Antecedents of RFID Adoption Intention in the Supply Chain. In: Proceedings of the 42nd Hawaii International Conference on System Sciences (2009)
24. Fichman, R.G.: Going beyond the dominant paradigm for information technology innovation research: Emerging concepts and methods. Journal of the Association for Information Systems 5(8), 314–355 (2004)
25. Brown, I., Russel, J.: Radio Frequency Identification Technology: An exploratory Study on Adoption in the South African Retail Sector. International Journal of Information Management 27(4), 250–265 (2007)
26. Chau, P.Y.K., Tam, K.Y.: Factors Affecting the Adoption of Open Systems: An Exploratory Study. MIS Quarterly 21(1), 1–24 (1997)
27. Chin, W.W., Johnson, N., Schwarz, A.: A fast Approach to Measuring Technology Acceptance and Other Constructs. MIS Quarterly 32(4), 687–703 (2008)
28. Davis, F.D.: Perceived Usefulness, Perceived Ease of Use, and User Acceptance of Information Technology. MIS Quarterly 13(3), 319–340 (1989)
29. Mithas, et al.: How Strategic Posture and Competitive Environment Influence Firms' IT Investments: Theory and Evidence. In: Proceedings of the 30th International Conference on Information Systems (2009)
30. Porter, M.E., Millar, V.E.: How information gives you competitive advantage. Harvard Business Review (1985)
31. Seymour, L., Porter, E.L., Willuweit, L.: RFID Adoption into the Container Supply Chain: Proposing a framework. In: Proceedings of the 6th Annual ISOnEworld Conference, Las Vegas, NV (2007)
32. Morrel, M., Ezingeard, J.N.: Revisiting adoption factors of inter-organizational information systems in SMEs. Logistics Information Management 15(1), 46–57 (2002)
33. Karahanna, E., Straub, D.W., Chervany, N.L.: Information technology adoption across time: A cross-sectional comparison of pre-adoption and post-adoption beliefs. MIS Quarterly 23(2), 183–213 (1999)
34. Goswami, S., Teo, H.H., Chan, C.: Decision-Maker Mindfulness in IT Adoption: The Role of Informed Culture and Individual Personality. In: AMCIS (2009)
35. Robey, D., Im, G., Jonathan, D.W.: Theoretical foundations of empirical research on interorganizational systems: assessing past contributions and guiding future directions. Journal of the Association for Information Systems 9(9), 497–518 (2008)

36. Brown, M., Patadua, S., Dua, S., Meyers, M.: Comptia RFId plus passport. McGraw-Hill, New York (2007)
37. Lee, J.H., Kim, C.O.: Multi-agent systems applications in manufacturing systems and supply chain management: a review paper. International Journal of Production Research 46(1), 233–265 (2008)
38. Saunders, C., Hart, S.: Elettronic Data Interchange Across Organizational Boundaries: Building a theory of motivation and implementation. In: Administrative Sciences Association of Canada Twenty First Annual Conference, Lake Luise, Alberta, Canada (1992)
39. Whitaker, J., Mithas, S., Krishnan, M.S.: A Field Study of RFID Deployment and Return Expectations. Production and Operations Management 16(5), 599–612 (2007)
40. Byrnes, J.L.S., Shapiro, R.D.: Intercompany operating ties: unlocking the Value In Channel Restructuring. Sloan Management Review 32, 15–18 (1991)
41. Klonglan, G.E., Coward, E.W.: The Concept of Symbolic Adoption: A Suggested Interpretation. Rural Sociology 35(1), 77–83 (1970)
42. Kunnathur, A.S., Vaithianathan, S.: RFID Adoption: An Exploratory Study of Issues and Concerns. In: 2008 AMCIS Proceeding (2008)
43. Mentzer, J.T.: Fundamentals of Supply Chain Management. Sage Publications, Inc., Thousand Oaks (2004)
44. Patterson, K.A., Grimm, C.M., Corsi, T.M.: Adopting new technologies for Supply Chain. Logistics and Transportation Review 39(2), 95–121 (2003)
45. Crum, M.R., Premkumar, G., Ramamurthy, K.: An assessment of motor carrier adoption, use, and satisfaction with EDI. Transportation Journal 35(4), 44–57 (1996)
46. Madlberger, M., Roztocki, N.: Digital Cross-Organizational Collaboration: Towards a Preliminary Framework. In: Proceeding of the Fifteenth Americas Conference on Information Systems, San Francisco, CA (2009)
47. Pfeiffer: The Diffusion of Electronic Data Interchange. Springer, N.Y. (1992)
48. Carter, J.R., Slaight, T.H., Blascovich, J.: Technology collaboration, supply chain design. Supply Chain Management Review (2007)
49. Ghosh, A., Fedorowicz, J.: Governance Mechanisms for Coordination and Information Sharing in Supply Chains: The Role of Trust. In: AMCIS Proceeding (2005)
50. Hart, P., Saunders, C.S.: Power and Trust: Critical factors in the adoption and use of electronic data interchange. Organizational Science 8(1), 23–42 (1997)
51. Klein, R., Rai, A.: Interfirm strategic information flows in logistic supply chain relationship. MIS Quarterly 33(4), 735–762 (2009)
52. Son, J., et al.: Understanding the Development of IOS-Based Trading Partner Relationships: A Structural Model and its Empirical Validation. Journal of Organizational Computing and Electronic Commerce 18(1), 34–60 (2008)
53. Rai, A., et al.: Firm performance impacts of digitally enabled supply chain integration capabilities. Mis Quarterly 30(2), 225–246 (2006)
54. Schaefermeyer, M., Rosenkranz, C.: Inhibiting Factors for Adopting Enterprise Systems in Networks of Small and Medium-Sized Enterprises – An Exploratory Case Study. In: AMCIS (2008)
55. Yin, R.K.: Case Study Research. In: Design and Methods, 3rd edn. Sage Publications, California (2003)
56. Henderson, J.C., Vankatramam, N.: Strategic Alignment: leveraging Information Technologies for transforming organizations. IBM System Journal 32(1), 472–484 (1993)

Value Creation in Collaborative Networks: The Case of RFiD Implementation

Carine Dominguez[1,*], Blandine Ageron[2], and Gilles Neubert[3]

[1] Carine Dominguez, University Jean Monnet, Coactis laboratory, 6 rue basse des rives 42023 Saint-Etienne, France
carine.dominguez@univ-st-etienne.fr
[2] Blandine Ageron, Université de Grenoble, CERAG laboratory, IUT Valence, Rue Barthelemy de Laffemas, 26000 Valence, France
[3] Gilles Neubert, LIESP Laboratory, Saint-Etienne Business School, 51-53 Cours Fauriel, 42009 Saint Etienne, France

Abstract. In this article, we question the way CNs are built around the implementation of RFiD in a supply chain and what are the value creation logics among these CNs. We address three main questions: the way and types of CNs in a RFiD implementation project, the nature of the aggregator and value creation of each actor during the different phases of the project and finally the interconnections between CNs in the value creation logic. We provide answers to theses questions based on a case study that describes the implementation of the RFiD innovative technology in a jewellery supply chain.

Keywords: collaborative networks, supply chain, RFiD, value generator, value creation.

1 Introduction

There are different forms of collaborative networks. In this article, we question the way CNs are built dynamically around the implementation of RFiD in a supply chain and what are the value creation logics among these CNs.

To do so, we observe the dynamic construction of three types of collaborative networks (CNs) that emerge with the implementation of RFiD in jewellery products. At each phase of the RFiD project, we aim at understanding the value generator (investment in the collaboration) and value creation (gains) of each actor. We also question the interconnections of value creation between different CNs based on the fact the RFiD impact studies to date largely focus on a single firm setting. This leads to characterise the specificity of collaboration of each network and the type of value created in this project. We finally open the discussion on the appropriate models that could describe how to create value in RFiD supply chain projects via the different RFiD CNs.

---

* Corresponding author.

L.M. Camarinha-Matos et al. (Eds.): PRO-VE 2010, IFIP AICT 336, pp. 664–671, 2010.

1.1 Inter-organizational Information Systems Supporting Collaborative Networks

[5] define a collaborative network (CN) is constituted by a variety of entities (organizations and people) that are largely autonomous, geographically distributed, and heterogeneous in terms of their: operating environment, culture, social capital and goals. Nevertheless these entities collaborate to better achieve common or compatible goals, and whose interactions are supported by inter-organizational information systems. Different forms of collaborative network organizations (CNOs) can be distinguished in the literature [6] from temporary networks that are goal-oriented (virtual organizations and teams, dynamic supply chains, virtual government) to more long-term strategic networks (virtual organization breeding environment, clusters, business ecosystems, supply chains, districts) that remain relatively stable with a clear definition of members' roles along the value chain.

Supply chains are specific CNOs defined as a network of organizations interlinking suppliers, manufacturers and distributors in the different processes and activities that produce value in the form of products and services delivered to end customer [7].

Given the dynamic and often temporary nature of CNs, it is important to understand their life cycle that can be describe into five main steps [6]: creation, operation, evolution, dissolution and metamorphosis.

Traditionally, the main inter organizational information systems supporting products in the supply chain are bar codes linked to EDI [14]. One of the key requirements of temporary CN is to develop a generic Information System to control the interoperability of the participating organizations, distributed, heterogeneous and concurrent systems for the purpose of accessing and sharing the necessary data and resources. Because temporary CNs are short terms alliances, formed to address fast-changing opportunities, they should be connected to the IS of the long-term CN via "plug-and-play" options [1]. RFiD technology is emerging in order to improve process efficiency, notably by reducing daily receipts and inventories [26].

1.2 Collaborative Networks around RFiD in a Supply Chain

Supply chain collaboration implies that the chain members become involved in coordinating activities that span boundaries of their organizations in order to fulfil end users needs [2]. According to [24], the intensity of collaboration depends on the following impact horizons: Short-term, medium-term or long-term.

Collaboration between supply chain partners has been covered extensively in the strategic management literature ([2]; [15]; [11]; [3]). Several research surveys have shown that improvement of inter-enterprise processes is one of the major issues in Supply Chain Management [4]. [13] have recognised that the application of information technology in the supply chain management has become one of a major issue of both managers and researchers, as Information technology improve the performance of both individual firm and supply chain as a whole. Information technology plays major role in various supply chain collaboration practices as it enables and integrates information exchanges between supply chain partners. In this context, EDI, Internet, standards and others technologies have been developed in order to support increasing exchanges. By the same time, new collaborative practices emerge between supply chain partners, such as Vendor/Supplier management inventory, Collaborative Planning, Forecasting and Replenishment (CPFR). And as the volume of information exchanged and the intensity of interactions between partners further increased, there has been an amplified requirement towards an adequate underlying technology infrastructure. In order to cope with these new collaboration practices, new ways of information exchanges have emerged [23].

The recent industry report CGI [10] emphasizes the new collaborative processes that will be empowered through the use of RFID. The emergence of these new technologies revolutionize many of the supply chain operations by reducing costs, improving service levels, etc [26].

1.3 Value Creation in RFiD Collaborative Networks

Different value generators have been highlighted in the literature. [22] propose main value generators in CNs that are good indicators of the metric of the collaboration: physical and financial assets, human, organizational and relational capital.

Finally, there are both tangible and intangible types of benefits that can be reached with RFiD in a manufacturing process [16]. The main benefits are production planning, process optimization, IT management, improving quality and customer service, increasing reputation and improving inter organizational collaboration.

RFID provides multiple benefits for the supply-chain. It can add value along the entire supply-chain and related logistical operations and business relationships for more effective business process design. It provides a means of tracking supplier items from supplier through the distribution network to the point of consumption. The possibilities of RFID let its use in the supply-chain somewhat transformational ([20]; [9]) have identified the four main processes that can be directly affected by RFID.

Finally, the logic of value creation in these networks included different layers. While the layers may embrace sequential activity chains, other co-producing value creation activities will also take place in parallel, further enhancing value creation at the network level [1]. The notion of value creation is central to strategic management theory and includes value not only in supply and IS flows but also on knowledge sharing, learning and innovation [17] in what can be labelled strategic supplier networks. Firms acting in different value constellations [21] are characterized by social embeddedness [12], governance mechanism and the development of a sense of trust and reciprocity.

2 The Case Study Analysis

The majority of research on RFiD projects has focused on quantitative methodologies and there are very few case studies focusing on the description of the complexity of RFID implementation project in a supply chain such as those developed by [18] and [19]. We conducted a single case study with 15 semi-structured interviews, to reach an in-depth and insight understanding into this contemporary phenomenon [27].

Our case study was performed with one of the main French retailer. The choice of this case study is largely explained by the fact that:

- The company is a pioneer in the implementation of the RFID technology and no research has been done in France.
- The jewellery supply chain with RFID has never been studied before.

2.1 Actors Involved in the RFID Project and Chronological Steps

We can present three main CNs in this project (Fig.1).

- **The Product Collaborative Network (PCN):** the more stable CN that deals with supplying Casino's stores (POS) with jewellery products. Different actors are part of this CN: suppliers of jewels, the logistics service provider (LSP), Casino's 80 Stores called "Boutique Or".
- **The Information System Collaborative Network (ISCN):** the network that is in charge of the evolution and maintenance of Casino' IS linked with the jewellery supply chain. Different actors are part of this CN: Casino's CIO (Information Systems Department) and the Information System Service Provider (ISSP)
- **The RFiD Collaborative Network (RFiD CN):** it is the temporary network that is build with the RFiD project. Different actors are part of this CN: the label supplier, the printer pupplier: this company proposes printing machines to encode and print the RFiD tags inside the LSP warehouse, the reader supplier and the tag supplier.

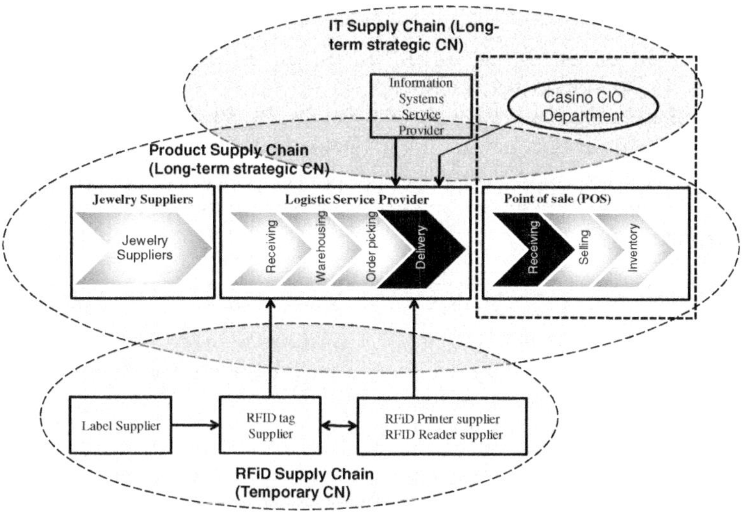

Fig. 1. Temporary and long-term collaborative networks value creation linked with the RFiD project

How had these CNs been built over time? Different logics explain the configuration of these networks. The PCN was the initial and historical one: Casino was working with its LSP to supply jewellery products for many years with bar codes. It is interesting to come back to the main criteria that explain the shaping of theses CNs.

To do so, let us enter into more details in the description of the phase 1 "seeking opportunities" step 4 (See 3.2.1) and the phase 2 "pilot project and validation" step 7 (See 3.2.2). First, the choice of the ISSP in the IS CN can be surprising as the retailer Casino decided to choose a very small-sized firm with high expertise in IS. Among the different criteria to select an ISSP, the fact that the company that was selected had been working in the past, and for many years, with the LSP brought trust in the relationship. Trust build in the PCN was spread out in the IS CN. Second, the shaping of the RFiD CN did not follow the same logic. Casino sent an invitation to tender to different companies positioned in the RFiD market. Two main RFiD tag suppliers were selected in the final short list and the one that was finally chosen proposed the lower global cost. After that, the RFiD tag supplier managed to convince Casino to work with its own CNS, hence connecting the Label supplier and the RFiD printer and reader supplier.

2.2 The Case Study Analysis

In order to analyse the value creation logic in the RFiD project, we use the framework of [9] that we adapt and complete to illustrate our case study. Fosso and Wamba's framework, specifically developed for RFID projects, is composed of a sequence of three main phases that describe a RFID project implementation: opportunities seeking, pilot project and validation and RFID project deployment. In the following section, we will present only phase 1 : Opportunity seeking; phases 2 : Pilot project and validation and phase 3: RFID project development will be discussed later during the session.

2.2.1 Phase 1: Opportunities Seeking

This initial phase deals with the opportunities to implement the RFID project in a specific value chain. It is composed of six steps. In the table below, we describe for each phase what actors were involved, what did they do, what type of value they invest in the CN called value generator [22] and the value created (gains) for each actor in the different CNs.

Phase 1: Opportunities seeking	Actors and CNs involved	Value generator (investment in the collaboration)	Value creation (gains)
Step1: Primary motivation (Why?)	- IS CN: IT consultancy company came and propose its services to Casino CIT - IS CN (Operation): Casino CIT sees the project as an opportunity to develop an innovative technology and gain visibility inside the company		- IS CN (CIO): Scanning the environment and IT opportunities in business (Organizational) - CIO: IS innovation (Organizational)
Step2: Analysis of the product value chain (What and Why?)	- IS CN (Operation): *CIO was searching for products disconnected to the main Casino's IS to lower risks in case of project failure	- IS CN (CIO): minimize risks linked to the main IS Infrastructure (Physical)	- PCN (Casino POS) identification of jewellery products as best suited to test RFiD (Organizational)

Step3: Identification of the critical activities (Which?)	- PCN (Operation): LSP in cooperation with CIT study the productivity and cost gains in different processes and finally hold receiving and inventories	- PCN: LSP and Casino POS (Human)	- PCN (Casino POS): identification of SC activity improvement opportunities (Organizational)
Step4: Mapping of the network of firms supporting the PVC (Who and with Whom?)	- IS CN (Evolution): CIO Casino - IS RFiD (Creation): CIO	- IS CN (CIO): identification of RFiD competencies in the market: Information Systems LSP, Label Supplier, RFiD Tag supplier (Human)	- IS CN (CIO): RFiD market knowledge (Human)
Step5: Mapping of intra-organizational processes for the identified opportunities (How within organization?)	- IS CN (Evolution): CIO Casino - PCN (Evolution): the jewellery supply chain foresees potential changes in its processes with the introduction of RFiD	- IS CN (Evolution): CIO Casino is looking for complementary competencies - PCN:LSP: process modifications to adapt to Casino POS demand (Organizational)	-ISCN (CIO): competencies identification: make of buy decision - PCN (Casino POS) identification of SC process improvement opportunities (Organizational)
Step6: Mapping of inter-organizational processes for the identified opportunities (How between organization?)	- ISCN (Evolution): CIO Casino	- ISCN (CIO): competencies identification (make or buy decision)	- ISCN (CIO): add complementary IS resources outside the core IS infrastructure (Relational)

2.2.2 Phase 2: Pilot Project and Validation

The objective of this second phase is to develop a pilot project in order to validate the feasibility of the RFID implementation. The goal is to identify the business opportunities that could come from this new technology and to propose process and IT reconfiguration to fit with RFID. It is made of four steps.

2.2.3 Phase 3: RFID Project Deployment

The last phase concerns the validation of the pilot project and the deployments of the technology on the whole supply chain.

3 Discussion

The main results of the case study analysis are the following:

- During the project, different CNs are built or broken: the RFiD CN is built upon the project itself, the choice of Casino to externalize the IS part of the project to an ISSP initiated a long-term ISCN working in cooperation with the PCN.
- Some CNs are stable (ISCN and PCN) whereas others are temporary [6], formed only during the project opportunities seeking and pilot project. The project deployment phase transforms a temporary collaboration between the RFiD CN and the IS CN/PCNs mainly based on an innovative project to a business relationship between the Tag Supplier and Casino.

- The RFiD Temporary CN only invested during the Phases 1 and 2 of the project (Human, Organizational, Physical) and captured value in the last Phase 3 of the project (Brand and Relational above all). Hence, the temporary RFiD CN largely participated to increase the value of the stable CNs
- Value creation (gains) is largely oriented in a CN logic rather than in an individual logic based on criteria such as size and power. For instance, the ISSP, which is a small company, that is working with CIO in the ISCN reinforced its business relationship with Casino (Relational value) and managed to build a long-term ISCN with CIO, owing to its past business relationships with LSP.

The configuration of temporary and long-term strategic CNs are based on collaborative characteristics such as personal and historical relationships (the information system service provider get used to work with the LSP, the RFiD tag supplier knows personally some CIO department managers) [12], trust and partners competencies. Moreover, the innovative capacity of all the stakeholders of the collaborative network and their willingness to explore new opportunities are important enablers of these configurations. The RFiD technology engenders organizational change and process optimization ([20]; [9]). The RFiD technology also generates intangible benefits [16] but these seem not the same as in manufacturing processes. Knowledge and innovation capacities [17] seem to be the main gains for stakeholders participating in a supply chain temporary CNs. This hypothesis had to be developed in further research through a comparison case-study research design.

References

1. Bolton, R., Dewey, A., Horstmann, P.: Requirements for Plug and Play, Information Infrastructure Frameworks and Architectures to Enable Virtual Enterprises. In: Proceedings of SPIE 1996, pp. 2–19 (1996)
2. Bowersox, D.J.: The strategic benefits of logistics alliances. Harvard Business Review 68(4), 36–43 (1990)
3. Bowersox, D.J., Closs, D.J., Keller, S.B.: How supply chain competency leads to business success. Supply Chain Management Review 4(4), 70–78 (2000)
4. Boyson, S., Corsi, T.M., Dresner, M.E., Harrington, L.H.: Logistics and the Extended Enterprise: Benchmarks and Best Practices for the Manufacturing Professional. Wiley, New York (1999)
5. Camarinha-Matos, L.M., Afsarmanesh, H.: Collaborative networks: a new scientific discipline. Journal of Intelligent Manufacturing 6, 439–452 (2005)
6. Camarinha-Matos, L.M., Afsarmanesh, H., Galeano, N., Molina, A.: Collaborative networked organizations - concepts and practice in manufacturing enterprises. Computers and Industrial Engineering 57(1), 46–60 (2009)
7. Christopher, M.L.: Logistics and supply chain management. Pitman Publishing, London (1992)
8. Czajkowski, K., Fitzgerald, S., Foster, I., Kesselman, C.: Grid Information Services for Distributed Resource Sharing. In: 10th IEEE International Symposium on High Performance Distributed Computing, pp. 181–184. IEEE Press, New York (2001)
9. Fosso Wamba, S., Lefebvre, L.A., Lefebvre, E.: Integrating RFID Technology and EPC Network into a B2B retail supply chain: a step toward intelligent business processes. Journal of Technology Management and Innovation 2(2), 114–124

10. GCI, EPC: A Shared Vision for Transforming Business Processes, Global Commerce Initiative (2005), http://www.gci-net.org
11. Gilmour, P.: Benchmarking supply chain operations. International Journal of Physical Distribution & Logistics Management 29(4), 283–290 (1999)
12. Gulati, R.: Does familiarity breed trust? The implications of repeated ties for contractual choice in alliances. Academy of Management Journal 38, 85–112 (1995)
13. Gunasekaran, A., Ngai, E.W.T.: Information systems in supply chain integration and management. European Journal of Operational Research 159(2), 269–295 (2004)
14. Holland, C.: Cooperative supply chain management: the impact of inter-organizational information systems 4(2), 117–133 (1995)
15. Hanman, S.: Benchmarking your firm's performance with best practice. International Journal of Logistics Management 8(2), 1–18 (1997)
16. Ivantysynova, L., Klafft, M., Ziekow, H., Günther, O., Kara, S.: RFiD in manufacturing: the investment decision. In: Pacific Asia Conference on Information Systems, PACIS (2009), http://aisel.aisnet.org/pacis2009/41
17. Kogut, B.: The Network as Knowledge: Generative Rules and the Emergence of Structure. Strategic Management Journal 21(3), 405–425 (2000)
18. Loebbecke, C.: Piloting RFID along the supply chain: a case analysis. Electronic Markets 17(1), 29–37 (2007)
19. Loebbecke, C.: Use of innovative content integration information technology at the point of sale. European Journal of Information Systems 16, 228–236 (2008)
20. Niedermann, F., Mathieu, R.G., Morley, R., Kwon, I.W.: Examining RFiD in Supply Chain Management. Communications of the ACM 50(7), 92–101 (2007)
21. Norman, N., Ramirez, R.: From value chain to value constellation: designing interactive strategy. Harvard Business Review 71, 65–77 (1993)
22. Parung, J., Bititci, U.: A metric for collaborative networks. Business Process Management Journal 14(5), 654–674 (2008)
23. Pramatari, K.: Collaborative supply chain practices and evolving technical approaches. Supply Chain Management: An International Journal 12(3), 210–220 (2007)
24. Simatupang, T.M., Sridharan, R.: The collaborative supply chain: a scheme for information sharing and incentive alignment. International Journal of Logistics Management 13(2), 257–274 (2002)
25. Tzeng, S.F., Chen, W.H., Pai, F.Y.: Evaluating the business value of RFiD: Evidence from five case studies. International Journal of Economics 112, 601–613 (2007)
26. Veeramani, D., Tang, J., Gutierrez, A.: A framework for assessing the value of RFID implementation by Tier-one suppliers to major retailers. Journal of Theoretical and Applied Electronic Commerce Research 3(1), 55–70 (2008)
27. Yin, R.K.: Case Study Research: Design and Method. Sage Publication, Thousand Oaks (2003)

Supporting Software Services' Trustworthiness in Collaborative Networks

Maiara Heil Cancian[1], Ricardo J. Rabelo[1], and Christiane Gresse von Wangenheim[2]

[1] Department of Automation and Systems - Federal University of Santa Catarina, Brazil
[2] Department of Computer Science - Federal University of Santa Catarina, Brazil
{maiara,rabelo}@das.ufsc.br, gresse@inf.ufsc.br

Abstract. Collaborative Networks realization fundamentally relies on the need of *collaboration* among involved partners. From the supporting ICT infrastructures point of view, an increasing movement has been observed in direction of the development of applications based on the Service Oriented Architecture paradigm as a way to maximize reuse, to minimize integration efforts and to augment processes' adaptability. The underlying motivation of this paper is the possibility of CN members to enlarge their collaboration sharing software services. This means allowing that available services can be accessed by any member so enlarging and reinforcing collaboration while development and hosting costs are decreased. This paper presents an approach, in the form of a reference guide and based on Software-as-a-Service (SaaS) model, that helps both CN clients to be more confident when accessing services from CN members, and to CN members to have a support on how their services should be properly developed and made available to CN clients.

Keywords: Software-as-a-Service; trustworthiness; Quality reference guide.

1 Introduction

The adoption of the Collaborative Networks (CN) paradigm by organizations imposes enormous pressure on the companies´ competitive matrix, affecting their market positioning in terms of general quality, diversity and innovation of processes and products, prices, delivery dates, and level of relationship with suppliers and customers.

CN realization relies, however, on three essential pre-conditions. The first one is that it requires *collaboration* among involved partners. The second one is the existence of *trust*, considering that partners shall trust to one another (at variable levels). The third pre-condition is the *digital transactions*, i.e. most of the activities carried out within a CN should be made via computer networks [1]. The ultimate goal is to enable networked organizations to agilely define and set up relations with other organizations as well as to be adaptive according to the business environment conditions and current organizations' autonomy levels [2]. This requires, therefore, very high effectiveness and trustworthiness in businesses and collaborations.

From the ICT point of view, a number of approaches have been proposed to cope with those requirements in terms of supporting ICT infrastructures devoted to CNs [1]. The most relevant aspect is the shift from traditional monolithic software packages and

L.M. Camarinha-Matos et al. (Eds.): PRO-VE 2010, IFIP AICT 336, pp. 672–684, 2010.

licenses to Service Oriented Architecture (SOA) and Utility paradigms [3]. SOA can be generally defined as an architectural paradigm for components of a system and interactions between them, where its functions are viewed as software modules called *services* [4]. *Utility* associates the idea that a service should be somehow permanently available, discoverable and usable anytime, anywhere, like electricity.

The underlying motivation of this paper is the possibility of CN members - VBE, VE, VO, PVC[1] members and other type of companies, as logistics operators and software providers - to enlarge their collaboration towards a full-fledged, fully interoperable and transparent collaboration "cloud". Several works have been developed having this future CN scenario in mind, such as virtual machining [5], knowledge search and sharing over CN's information repositories [6], virtual shop-floor [7] and CN supporting ICT infrastructures [1]. This paper intends to contribute within this wider collaborative scenario towards sharing *software services*, i.e. to see services under the Utility paradigm point of view.

The relevance of this issue is related to the fact that, in practice, CN members who have SOA-based solutions keep the involved services (typically implemented using web-services technology) in their local silos. This means that the SOA potential in terms of reuse could be extended and highly increased if such silos could be shared among CN members, i.e. if all services could be accessed by any member so enlarging and reinforcing collaboration while development and hosting costs are decreased. This seems particularly relevant as CN members are mostly composed of MSMEs[2], without many conditions to maintain IT infrastructures and costly staff. In other words, this means that CN members can be both clients and service providers [1].

Providing this level of CN collaboration bumps, however, into plenty of obstacles, of several levels of complexity. One problem refers to the access mode and business models that can be aligned to this collaborative scenario [8]. In the SOA context, SaaS (*Software-as-a-Service*) [9, 10] has arisen as one of the most prominent models. Using SaaS, clients (i.e. CN members) can flexibly build their services portfolio according to their needs [11]. Services are accessed remotely, upon request, paid-per-use, based on contractual rules specified in SLAs (*Service Level Agreement*) [12, 13] for hosting, managing, providing access to them following QoS levels, no matter where the services providers are and how services have been deployed [10]. This model seems suitable to accommodate CN intrinsic specificities, namely members' independence, autonomy and heterogeneity, especially when they also act as service providers. A second problem comes as a consequence of this envisaged collaboration scenario: how trusting in a certain service whose CN member (provider) is not necessarily known or whose service quality is not trustworthy. Therefore, clients must feel confident to access and to use a given service as it is going to be used or integrated into their composite SOA applications, so they want to minimize the risk of a crash in the system due to the lack in the service's quality. The problem is that there are not very concrete guidelines and practices about how to develop highly reusable services under the SaaS business and architectural models. Existing quality reference models are huge and complex hence far from been easily adopted by MSMEs.

---

[1] VBE (Virtual Organization Breeding Environment), VE (Virtual Enterprises), VO (Virtual Organization), PVC (Professional Virtual Communities).

[2] MSME – Micro, Small and Medium Enterprises.

This is the underlying research question of this paper. Based on software engineering theories and quality models, this ongoing work approaches the problem of service trustworthiness in a qualitative and partially exploratory way, proposing a reference guide devoted to software services for SaaS model in way CN members can be more confident in sharing services among them. The research hypothesis is that a reference guide can act as an extremely useful enabler to support that envisaged collaboration at software services level. CN providers can be assisted on how to better develop and make available their services on one hand, and clients can be assisted on how to evaluate services trustworthiness on the other hand.

This paper is organized as following. Section 1 has motivated the issue of services trustworthiness. Section 2 gives an overview on the researches about trustworthiness. Section 3 resumes the methodology used to devise the proposed guide. Section 4 presents the preliminary version of the Reference Guide for SaaS applications. Section 5 provides an assessment of the work and some conclusions.

2 A Revision on Software Trustworthiness and Quality

Trustworthiness in loosely coupled computational systems – which is the case of SOA/SaaS – has received great attention in the last recent years [14]. Actually, there is neither a largely adopted definition for it nor for the best way to manage it [15].

A current view of trustworthiness defines it as a measurable property with different entities at different levels. In the software services context, the concept of trustworthiness is extended to include a view of a mechanism for the realization and maintenance of the service quality and its interactions [14]. Trustworthiness can be determined based on some information, like personal experiences, observations, recommendations and global reputation [15].

In some works, the concepts of trustworthiness and reputation seem similar. Trustworthiness is gained by the act of meeting policies, code of ethics, rights and agreed promises [16]. Reputation is gained throughout the time, based on the general service performance and on users' evaluations [17]. Malik and Bouguettaya [18] mention that the reputation of web-services-based systems depends on the information received to establish trustworthiness between unknown participants. This work also includes the assessment of reputations of newly deployed web services, which is an important matter in SOA environments, as historical information is not always available. This work presented a hierarchical ontology, but does not present any technique for the verification of this reputation.

Msanjila and Afsarmanesh [19] approaches the automation of processes related to the trustworthiness level assessment in CNs. They formalized an analytical model and developed a system to evaluate the trustworthiness level of CN members [20]. As it focused on companies, it does not offer comprehensive support to software services.

Supporters of 'SOA architecture as Global Information Grid' (GIG), 'Department of Defense' (DoD) and the 'Intelligence Community' (IC) state that there is an explicit relation among security, flexibility and cost when trustworthiness is the focus [12]. They developed a trustworthiness management architecture based on their experiences, predicting a unified management of the specification and interpretation of the security policies, credentials e relationships. This architecture is however very directed to the GIG specific model, hard to use by other companies, besides not providing supporting methodologies for its implementation. Grandison e Sloman [21] present a work related to trustworthiness in web applications based on a research on available methods and tools, such as *PolicyMaker* e *KeyNote*. However, the scope of this work does not cover software services, but Internet pages only, in order to control their content.

Within the software arena, the most considered and recognized way to get trustworthiness is via certifications [21]. Nowadays, there are institutions that certify the software development process of companies applying some reference models, such as ISO/IEC 15504 [22], CMMI Development [23], MPS.br [24]. There are also some initiatives in terms of reference models devoted to services, but they provide a different contextualization when SaaS is considered. In these models (e.g. ITIL [25], CMMI for Services [26] and the Capacity Models for outsourcing [27, 28]), service is understood just as an outsource or a post-sales provision (such as *helpdesk*, for instance).

Progress Software and its partners have jointly developed a SOA Maturity Model (SOA-MM), which is based on CMMI and ISO standards [29, 30]. It provides IT decision makers with a framework for benchmarking the strategic value of their SOA implementation. Based on CMMI, IBM has also developed a maturity model for SOA, called SIMM - Service Integration Maturity Model, composed of six levels of capability [23, 31]. This model includes elements that impact services' maturity, namely: coupling, standards usage, service identification, business models, goals, and metrics that need to be supported by services, technologies, governance and infrastructure. However, it is very generic and do not present any support for SaaS.

CobiT (Control Objectives for Information and related Technology) is another reference work [17]. It is a framework of best practices directed to the management of information technology with the focus on governance. This framework is platform independent as well as is not bound to any business model [32]. Despite of its large acceptance by companies, it has no specific recommendations for SaaS scenarios.

In fact, there are many other works which deal with software trustworthiness and quality in the literature. This overview tried to highlight the ones considered as the most relevant for the scope of this paper. As a conclusion of this revision, it was realized that there is no quality reference models for software services devoted to SaaS. Most of models cope with the traditional software acquisition model and even the ones related to SOA are still too generic. As such, they are models that cannot be readily applied by CN members towards the envisaged collaborative scenario. Yet, there are not models which take the particularities of the CN environment (i.e. a "club" of actors who are, per definition, willing to collaborate and to share assets) into account.

Building a totally new reference quality model for SaaS from scratch and that can comprise CN features is evidently too complex. In this sense, the approach was considering consolidated existing practices (like CMMI and ISO' practices) and adapting them to the context of SaaS and CN. Next section describes the methodology in general.

3 Methodology for the Reference Guide development

This chapter resumes the methodology used to devise the proposed guide development. The detailed description of the methodology can be found in Cancian et al 2010 [33].

The first general step of the methodology was related to know which requirements were necessary to be assessed from CN services providers regarding trustworthiness when CN clients would be playing the role of a SaaS client. A research was performed to gather information related to services and processes' quality criteria that should be analyzed or required from services providers.

A group of 280 professionals from the software services area were duly selected, from different countries, from academia / R&D and from companies. This step was carried out by using a free tool called *LimeSurvey* [34], which allows the creation of researches with several questionnaires. The research was available in the Internet during 60 days and 84 answers were received. A list of 25 criteria has been identified at the end. A formal description was assigned to each quality criteria, normalizing the different definitions and scope given by the different interviewed based on formal definitions existing in the reference literature. After this, quality requirements were grouped into three categories (as suggested in [35, 36]) with the aim of facilitating their understanding and awareness about their scope of use:

- *Organization* requirements: requirements that the organization must have anyway no matter the product or process dealt with;
- *Product* requirements: requirements to allow a verification in the product (i.e. the service itself) as a whole;
- *Process* requirements: requirements needed to follow in terms of services design and implementation.

The professionals were also asked about the importance - Essential, Very Important, Important or Unnecessary - of each criterion when looking at SaaS scenario. Figures 1 to 3 show the final compilation of the results, per category.

ITEM	QUALITY CRITERIA RELATED TO THE PRODUCT OCCURRENCES			
	Essential	Very important	Not critical	Unnecessary
Accessibility	59.26%	25.93%	14.81%	null
Reliability	58.02%	37.04%	3.70%	1.23%
Performance	27.16%	58.02%	13.58%	1.23%
Availability	33.33%	41.98%	19.75%	4.94%
Scalability	20.99%	50.62%	27.16%	1.23%
Integrity	69.14%	25.93%	4.94%	null
Interoperability	27.16%	51.85%	19.75%	1.23%
Robustness	29.63%	48.15%	20.99%	1.23%

Fig. 1. Quality requirements related to Product

The answers were further and deeply discussed and assessed by three PMP (Project Management Professional) specialists on software services. The occurrences classified as "essential" and "very important" were considered as relevant criteria for SaaS (i.e. included in the guide) when their sum were above 75%. This average was considered as representative based on the experience of those PMPs.

At this stage of the methodology the goal was to have a list of requirements considered relevant to be considered by both clients and providers when dealing with SaaS. Next stage was then related to identifying which processes and practices from software quality reference models that CN members should apply to indeed prepare themselves to adopt SaaS. A mapping was done in order to make this analysis.

ITEM	QUALITY CRITERIA RELATED TO THE ORGANIZATION OCCURRENCES			
	Essential	Very important	Not critical	Unnecessary
Infrastructure capability	32.10%	59.26%	7.41%	1.23%
Technically competent employees	29.63%	37.04%	33.33%	null
Prevision of continuity of service	29.63%	41.98%	23.46%	4.94%
Technically competent in business	22.22%	50.62%	25.93%	1.23%
Utilization of standards	35.80%	41.98%	19.75%	2.47%
Governance	complement	complement	complement	complement
Reputation	complement	complement	complement	complement

Fig. 2. Quality requirements related to Organization

ITEM	QUALITY CRITERIA RELATED TO THE PROCESS OCCURRENCES			
	Essential	Very important	Not critical	Unnecessary
Acquisition	34.57%	48.15%	17.28%	null
Change control	22.22%	56.79%	19.75%	1.23%
Quality control on software process	38.27%	45.68%	16.05%	null
Version control	30.86%	48.15%	19.75%	1.23%
Development and requirement management	48.15%	35.80%	16.05%	null
Maintenance	29.63%	45.68%	22.22%	2.47%
Certification of process quality	6.17%	37.04%	45.68%	11.11%
Security (of sent and stored data)	54.32%	38.27%	7.41%	null
Help desk	19.75%	49.38%	29.63%	1.23%
Tests	30.86%	54.32%	13.58%	1.23%

Fig. 3. Quality requirements related to Process

QFD was used (*Quality Function Deployment*) as the supporting methodology for this mapping (requirements against models' practices). QFD considers the point of views of the clients and of the organization, according to the technological needs [37-39]. The mapping was performed by those same three PMP specialists on software process improvement. An example (on *accessibility*) of this is given below.

After a very comprehensive analysis it was observed that ISO/IEC 15504 copes with most of the elicited requirements. Other processes more directed related to 'services' came from CMMI and CobiT due to the governance requirement.

Next step was to identify the relevance of each models' process, i.e. which processes are indeed important to be considered in a SaaS scenario. Those PMP specialists went through every single process and they classified each process as Essential ("E"), Very important: ("V"), Important ("I"), Weakly important ("W"), and Unnecessary ("U"). Let´s take the Accessibility quality criterion (see Figure 1) as an example. Accessibility within ISO/IEC 15504 is dealt by a number of processes, e.g. acquisition. According to this model, there are five issues (subprocesses) that should be observed within acquisition: acquisition preparation, supplier selection, contract agreement, supplier monitoring, and customer acceptance. In theory, targeting traditional business models, the acquisition process is very relevant and the reference models indicate a number of practices to support all of them. However, looking at SaaS perspective, it is observed that while e.g. *supplier selection* subprocess is not critical (i.e. is it unnecessary), the *contract agreement* subprocess is seen as essential regarding the importance of SLAs. Another example is the *infrastructure* subprocess (within the *resource and infrastructure* process), which is considered as essential. It is because a SaaS-driven service should naturally be available permanently and with a very high-level of performance as it tends to be accessed intensively and by several CN members, perhaps even simultaneously.

The subprocesses classified as "V" and "I" were also considered relevant for being considered by CN SaaS providers. For example, the subprocess *software requirements analysis* (within the *engineer* process) was classified as "I". As such, the practices associated to it should be applied as well (see Table 1 as an example of a subset of practices for this subprocess).

This all means that a CN member that wants to share its software services under the SaaS model should apply the recommended model's practices that are associated to each subprocess that has been classified as E, V or I as a way to "prove" to clients that it supports the subprocesses according to the norm. In this way, CN clients will be more confident to access the given service / provider as there would be a "guarantee" that the subprocesses would had been properly implemented.

As the final result of this mapping a correlation matrix was created. It contains the relevance identification of all elicited quality criteria against every subprocess[3].

4 Preliminary Reference Guide

The ultimate but general goal of a reference guide is to serve as a quick and easy source of information to users [40]. In this case, it serves as a guide to help both CN

[3] The complete matrix is available at `www.gsigma.ufsc.br/~cancian/msc/mapping.pdf`

clients to have a more solid basis on how to select services from CN providers, and to CN providers to know which quality requirements (from the elaborated list) should be supported, besides which practices should be used for each process.

The Reference Guide can be either visualized on-line or be downloaded[4]. Figure 4 shows an excerpt of the guide. The Guide is composed of quality requirements and of best practices suggested for each requirement. For each best practice, it was suggested a level of importance according to its relevance: (i) Essential; (ii) Very important; (iii) Important; (iv) Weakly important; or (v) Unnecessary. For the Guide utilization, one should implement the best practices suggested for each requirement. The set of requirements with their descriptions can be found at label "Quality Requirements"

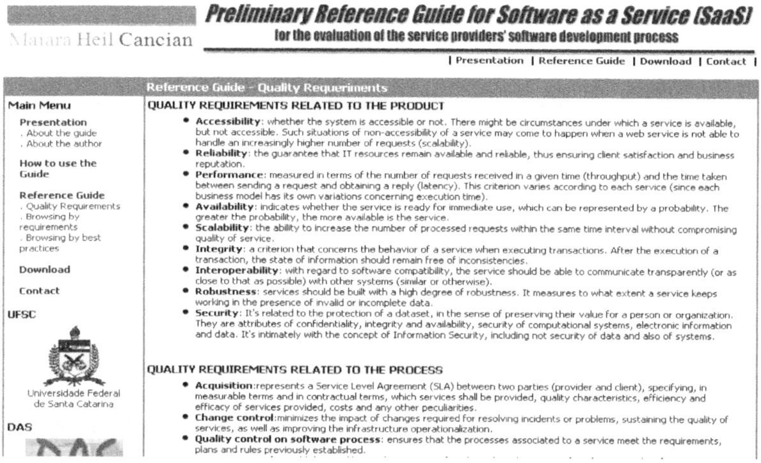

Fig. 4. Elicited SaaS software quality requirements

The Guide offers two options for browsing over requirements and their best practices:

- Browsing by requirements: requirements are grouped by their classification. Clicking on the classification, requirements for that classification are shown (figure 5);
- Browsing by processes: best practices' titles are shown firstly. Clicking on the given practice, the respective requirements are shown.

Table 1 presents a partial view of the description of a process' practice. This exemplifies the Requirements elicitation. The information of this practice are: Process ID, Process Name, Process Purpose, Process Outcomes, Base Practices.

[4] The complete Reference Guide is available at
`http://www.gsigma.ufsc.br/~cancian/guide`

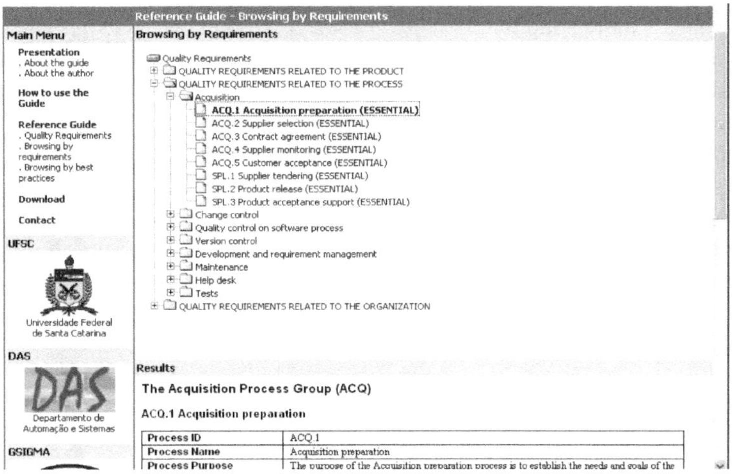

Fig. 5. Navigation through Requirements

Table 1. Eng.1 Requirements Elicitation Description

Process ID	**ENG.1**
Process Name	**Requirements elicitation**
Process Purpose	Requirements elicitation process aims to gather, process, and track evolving customer needs and requirements throughout the life of the product and/or service so as to establish a requirements baseline that serves as the basis for defining the needed work products. Requirements elicitation may be performed by the acquirer or the developer of the system.
Process Outcomes	As a result of successful implementation of Requirements elicitation process: 1) continuing communication with the customer is established; 2) agreed customer requirements are defined and baseline; 3) a change mechanism is established to evaluate and incorporate changes to customer requirements into the baseline requirements based on changing customer needs; 4) …
Base Practices	**ENG.1.BP1: Obtain customer requirements and requests.** Obtain and define customer requirements and requests through direct and continuous solicitation of customer and users. NOTE 1: Requirements may also be obtained through review of customer business proposals, target operating and hardware environment, and other documents bearing on customer requirements. **ENG.1.BP2: Understand customer expectations.** Ensure that both supplier and customer understand each requirement in the same way. Review with customers their requirements and requests to better understand their needs and expectations and to check the feasibility and appropriateness of their requirements. [Outcome: 6] NOTE 2: Environmental, legal and other constraints that may be external to the customer need to be considered. **ENG.1.BP3: Agree on requirements.** Obtain agreement across teams on the customer requirements, obtaining the appropriate sign-offs by representatives of all teams and other parties contractually bound to work to these requirements. [Outcome: 2] **ENG.1.BP4: ...**

5 Final Considerations

This work has presented an approach on how services' trustworthiness in SOA-based SaaS applications can be supported within a CN. This approach is represented by a reference guide, which is seen as a list of quality criteria to be used by CN members (services clients and providers) when sharing services, no matter their size or CN type.

The elaboration of the guide has followed a methodology, which was fundamentally grounded on the rationale of existing and best-of-breed quality reference models of software engineering. However, the guide cannot be seen as definitive. SaaS in an emergent area and there is not very solid reference theoretical foundations about it yet. In spite of this, it is believed that the guide has a structure that can be applied as an useful instrument to assess CN members services' trustworthiness, keeping their autonomy and heterogeneity while collaboration among them is enlarged.

The guide integrates some reference models and best practices into a more specialized, single, relatively simple and free-of-access model. This is important as long as small companies have tremendous difficulties to go through each (huge) reference model and to evaluate which one is better aligned to their strategy. Therefore, from the exploratory perspective of this research, it can be said that a guide like that has the potential to solve the "theoretical" part of the problem, which refers to how CN members – the guide's clients and beneficiaries – can be more confident when sharing their services. It is important to point out that a guide should be seen as *a* common instrument, among many others (e.g. security, infrastructures, service discovery, etc.), necessary to support the envisaged collaborative scenario.

However, from the applied perspective of this research, a guide like this, even being simpler and devoted to SaaS, is not easy to implement in practice as it impacts companies at several levels. As such, the usage of a guide may be not so feasible for CN members regarding their usual small size and limitations. As a consequence, CN members might rather prefer maintaining their services in their isolated silos or even developing their services without sharing purposes as a possible attitude regarding that development of software services are not their core business.

On the other hand, the own VBE can adopt an institutional position creating a task-force or hiring a specialized company to help members in implementing the guide in all members in way to also share costs. This kind of joint or shareable activities is a common practice in VBEs. As a matter of fact, this can be considered as one additional preparedness level for a member getting into a VBE. Moreover, companies can make some profit out of this since the access to their services (considering that they would have to maintain them anyway) would be on-demand and paid-per-use. Yet, strategic benefits can be a good argument for the guide adoption as companies can become more agile and feel better prepared to enter in a new VO as new required software services may be, in fact, available at the VBE. This would prevent them from new services development or acquisition, in opposite to the case without any sharing. Therefore, this "new" collaboration *bus* can add some value to CN members' business.

From the SOA perspective, a guide like this can also be a powerful mechanism for helping in services discovery and SLA establishment.

Future short-term improvements in the guide include the definition of more detailed practices to cope with SaaS for every single criterion as well as the creation of different capacity levels (e.g. A, B and C) allowing a better assessment by CN members. After this, a more solid and larger validation of the guide intends to be carried out using methodologies like IEEE [41] in way its accuracy, completeness and consistency can be better evaluated. Finally, new more CN-related criteria may be added to the guide, such as 'collaboration frequency', for instance.

Acknowledgments

This work has been partially supported by the Brazilian agencies CAPES and CNPq.

References

[1] Rabelo, R.: Advanced Collaborative Business ICT Infrastructures. In: Methods and Tools for Collaborative Networked Organizations, pp. 337–370. Springer (2008)

[2] Camarinha-Matos, L., Afsarmanesh, H.: The Emerging Discipline of Collaborative Networks. In: Virtual Enterprises and Collaborative Network, pp. 3–16. Springer (2004)

[3] NESSI, _Strategic_Research_Agenda, Framing the future of the Service Oriented Economy. Version 2006-2-13 - Revision 3.1 (2006), `http://www.nessi-europe.com/documents/NESSI_SRA_VOL_1_20060213.pdf`, 2006: ICT for Enterprise Networking, `http://cordis.europa.eu/ist/directorate_d/en_intro.htm`

[4] Singh, M.P., Huhns, M.N.: Service-Oriented Computing Semantics, Processes, Agents. John Wiley & Sons, Ltd., Chichester (2004)

[5] de Souza Jr., J.L.N., et al.: An Internet-oriented Management and Control System in a Distributed Manufacturing Environment. International Journal of Manufacturing Research 5, 5–25 (2009)

[6] Tramontin Jr., R.J., Rabelo, R.J., Chirab, H.: Customizing Knowledge Search in CNOs through Context-based Query Expansion. Production Planning & Control 21(2), 229–246 (2010)

[7] Ribeiro, L., Barata, J., Colombo, A.: Supporting agile supply chains using a service-oriented shop floor. Eng. Application Artificial Intelligence 22(6), 950–960 (2009)

[8] Borst, I., et al.: Technical Report D62.2 ICT-I Business Models (2005), `http://www.ecolead.org`

[9] Candan, K.S., et al.: Frontiers in Information and Software as Services. In: IEEE 25th International Conference on Data Engineering, ICDE 2009, pp. 1761–1768 (2009)

[10] Ma, D.: The Business Model of "Software-As-A-Service". In: IEEE International Conference on Services Computing, SCC 2007, pp. 701–702 (2007)

[11] Tsai, W.T.: Service-oriented system engineering: a new paradigm. In: IEEE International Workshop on Service-Oriented System Engineering, SOSE 2005, pp. 3–6 (2005)

[12] Eliadis, H., Rand, A.: Setting Expectations In SaaS: The Importance of the Service Level Agreement to SaaS Providers and Consumers. In SIIA Software as a Service Working Group: Software & Information Industry Association (2007)

[13] Cancian, M.H., Rabelo, R.J., Wangenheim, C.G.v.: A proposal for elaborating SLAs for Software-as-a-Service (SaaS). In: 8th International Information and Telecommunication Technologies Symposium (2009) (in Portuguese)

[14] Terzis, S.: Trust Management. Guest Editor's Introduction - The many faces of trust (2009), `http://www.computer.org/portal/web/computingnow/archive/april2009`

[15] Bhargava, B., et al.: The pudding of trust. IEEE Intelligent Systems 19(5), 74–88 (2004)

[16] Blaze, M., et al.: Dynamic Trust Manag. Computer 42(2), 44–52 (2009)

[17] ISACA: Serving IT Governance Professionals - COBIT Control Objectives for Information and related Technology (2008), `http://www.isaca.org/Template.cfm?Section=COBIT6&Template=/TaggedPage/TaggedPageDisplay.cfm&TPLID=55&ContentID=31519` (10/12/2008)

[18] Malik, Z., Bouguettaya, A.: Reputation Bootstrapping for Trust Establishment among Web Services. IEEE Internet Computing 13(1), 40–47 (2009)
[19] Msanjila, S.S., Afsarmanesh, H.: Automating Trust Assessment for Configuration of Temporary Partnerships. In: Innovation in Manufacturing Networks, pp. 95–104 (2008)
[20] Msanjila, S.S., Afsarmanesh, H.: HICI: An Approach for Identifying Trust Elements The case of technological trust perspective in VBEs. In: The Second International Conference on Availability, Reliability and Security, ARES 2007, pp. 757–764 (2007)
[21] Grandison, T., Sloman, M.: A Survey of Trust in Internet Applications. IEEE Communications Surveys and Tutorials 3(4) (2001)
[22] ISO/IEC: International Organization for Standardization and International Electrotechnical Commission, ISO/IEC 15504-5: Information Technology - Process Assessment, in Part 5: An exemplar Process Assessment Model, Genebra (2006)
[23] Team, C.P.: CMMI for Development (CMMI-DEV). Technical Report CMU/SEI-2006-TR-008, V. 1.2, Carnegie Mellon University / Software Engineering Institute (2006)
[24] Softex, Associação para Promoção da Excelência do Software Brasileiro, MPS.BR – Guia Geral, versão 1.2, Editor (2007), http://www.softex.br/mpsbr/_guias/default.asp
[25] Taylor, S.: ITIL Service Management Practices - V3 Qualification scheme, Editor, p. 31 (2007), http://www.itil-officialsite.com/Qualifications/Examiners/SharonTaylor.asp
[26] Team, C.P.: CMMI for Services (CMMI-SVC). Technical Report CMU/SEI- PA 15213-3890, Carnegie Mellon University / Software Engineering Institute, Pittsburgh (2008)
[27] Hefley, W.E., Loesche, E.A.: The eSCM-CL v1.1: Model Overview The eSourcing Capability Model for Client Organizations. In: Mellon, C. (ed.), Carnegie Mellon University (2006)
[28] Hyder, E.B., Heston, K.M., Paulk, M.C.: The eSCM-SP v2.01: Model Overview The eSourcing Capability Model for Service Providers. In: Mellon, C. (ed.) Carnegie Mellon University (2006), http://www.ae-scm.fr/bibliotheque-escm/eSourcing%20Capability%20Models%20Overview.pdf
[29] Sonic: Progress Software Corporation, A new Service Oriented Architecture (SOA) Maturity Model, Bedford, MA 01730 USA, p. 27 (2007)
[30] Josuttis, N.M.: SOA in practice. O'Reilly, Sebastopol (2008)
[31] Arsanjani, A., Holley, K.: Increase flexibility with the Service Integration Maturity Model, SIMM (2005), http://www.ibm.com/developerworks/webservices/library/ws-soa-simm/
[32] Sahibudin, S., Sharifi, M., Ayat, M.: Combining ITIL, COBIT and ISO/IEC 27002 in Order to Design a Comprehensive IT Framework in Organizations. In: Second Asia International Conference on Modeling & Simulation, AICMS 2008, pp. 749–753 (2008)
[33] Cancian, M.H., et al.: Discovering Software Process and Product Quality Criteria in Software as a Service. In: The 11th International Conference on Product Focused Software Development and Process Improvement (PROFES 2010), Limerick, Ireland (2010)
[34] LimeSurvey. The open source survey application 2008, http://www.limesurvey.org/ (cited 02/04/2008)
[35] Nightingale, P.: The product-process-organisation relationship in complex development projects. Research Policy 9(7), 913–930 (2000)
[36] Noël, F.: A product-process-organisation integrative model for collaborative design. In: Innovation in Life Cycle Engineering and Sustainable Development, pp. 407–418 (2006)

[37] Liu, X., et al.: QFD application in software process management and improvement based on CMM. SIGSOFT Software Engineering Notes 30(4), 1–6 (2005)
[38] Richardson, I.: Quality Function Deployment - A Software Process tool? In: Third Annual International QFD Symposium 1997, Linkoping, Sweden, pp. 58–66 (1997)
[39] Herzwurm, G., Schockert, S., Pietsch, W.: QFD for Customer-Focused Requirements Engineering. In: Proceedings of the 11th IEEE International Conference on Requirements Engineering. IEEE Computer Society, Los Alamitos (2003)
[40] Steehouder, M., van der Meij, H.: Designing and evaluating procedural instructions with four components model. In: Professional Communic. Conference, pp. 797–801 (2005)
[41] IEEE, S.: IEEE Recommended Practice for Software Requirements Specifications. The Institute of Electrical and Electronics Engineers, New York, NY (1998)

Supporting Software Services Discovery and Sharing in Collaborative Networks

Alexandre Perin-Souza and Ricardo J. Rabelo

Department of Automation and Systems - Federal University of Santa Catarina, Brazil
{perin,rabelo}@das.ufsc.br

Abstract. Collaborative Networks (CN) realization fundamentally relies on the need of *collaboration* among involved partners. CN members who have SOA-based solutions keep the involved web-services at their local silos. This means that the CN potential in terms collaboration could be enlarged and reinforced if such silos could be opened up and shared among CN members, so decreasing development and hosting costs. This is particularly relevant as CN members are mostly composed of small companies. This paper presents a result of an exploratory research, proposing a model for dynamic service discovery based on Software-as-a-Service business model, which considers not only services' functional requirements, but also the requested QoS and business processes' context. A prototype has been developed to show the concepts. A preliminary assessment from the ICT and CN perspectives is given in the end.

Keywords: BPM; SOA; Web Service Discovery; QoS; Business Process.

1 Introduction

Market dynamics has been imposing many challenges to organizations nowadays in order to adapt themselves and hence to be agile. Agility should be tackled under several perspectives. In this context, the adoption of the Collaborative Networks (CN) paradigm by organizations has been considered one of the most promising strategies. Its ultimate goal is to enable networked organizations to agilely define and set up relations with other organizations as well as to be adaptive according to the business environment conditions and current organizations' autonomy levels [1]. This requires, however, more effectiveness, flexibility and collaboration in businesses.

From the ICT perspective, such requirements have demanded more advanced infrastructures [2]. A number of prominent ICT approaches have been proposed in this sense. The most impacting ones are SOA (Service Oriented Architecture) and Utility paradigms [3]. SOA can be generally defined as an architectural paradigm for components of a system and interactions between them, where its functions are viewed as software modules called *services* [4]. *Utility* associates the idea that a service should be discoverable and usable anytime, anywhere, like electricity.

The problem is that, in practice, CN members who have SOA-based solutions keep the involved services (typically implemented using web-services technology) in their local silos. This means that the SOA potential in terms of reuse could be

L.M. Camarinha-Matos et al. (Eds.): PRO-VE 2010, IFIP AICT 336, pp. 685–696, 2010.

extended and highly increased if such silos could be shared among CN members, i.e. if all services could be accessed by any member so enlarging and reinforcing collaboration while development and hosting costs are decreased. This seems particularly relevant as CN members are mostly composed of MSMEs[1], without many conditions to maintain IT infrastructures and costly staff. In this sense, CN members could be both clients and service providers [2].

This is the underlying motivation of this paper. CN members - VBE, VE, VO, PVC[2] members and other type of companies (e.g. logistics operators and software providers) have the potential to enlarge their collaboration via an interoperable and transparent collaboration "cloud". Several works have been developed having this future CN scenario in mind, such as virtual machining [5], knowledge search and sharing over CN's information repositories [6], virtual shop-floor [7] and CN ICT infrastructures [2]. This paper intends to contribute within this wider collaborative scenario seeing services under the Utility paradigm point of view, proposing a supporting model for software services discovery when partners share their services.

Supporting this scenario requires coping with many issues, of different levels of complexity. One of the issues refers to the access mode and business models that can be aligned to this collaborative scenario [8]. In the SOA context, SaaS (*Software-as-a-Service*) [9] has arisen as one of the most powerful models. Using SaaS, clients (i.e. CN members) can flexibly build and adapt their services portfolio according to their needs [10] instead of getting held to single vendors of monolithic software packages whose full set of functionalities are often few used/accessed. With SaaS, services are accessed remotely, upon request, paid-per-use, based on contractual rules specified in SLAs (*Service Level Agreement*) [11] for hosting, managing, providing access to them following QoS (*Quality of Service*) levels, no matter where the services providers are and how services have been deployed [12]. This seems suitable to CN members due to their intrinsic independence, autonomy, large geographic distribution and heterogeneity. A second issue refers to the discovery of services that are shareable, and this is what this paper is more about.

In this services discovery scenario, client and provider perspectives should be taken into account. From the CN clients' side this means how expressing the desired service as well as how finding, selecting and binding services to their composite SOA-based applications. From the CN providers' side, this means how publishing and making their services available. Besides that, CN clients must feel confident to access not only a given functionally-compliant service, but ideally to the most suitable service regarding the current computing environment (in terms of required QoS) in use and business process' context.

Therefore, this paper presents an ongoing work, corresponding to an exploratory, applied and essentially qualitative research, which aims at contributing to answer the following research question: how to support those two mentioned issues considering CN characteristics in way to leverage web services discovery and sharing ? In this sense, a strongly ICT standards-based model that supports dynamic services discovery over largely distributed CN services providers is proposed. It considers SaaS architectural

---

[1] MSME – Micro, Small and Medium Enterprises.

[2] VBE (Virtual Organization Breeding Environment), VE (Virtual Enterprises), VO (Virtual Organization), PVC (Professional Virtual Communities).

model, dealing with not only services' functional requirements, but also the requested QoS and business processes' context.

The paper is organized as follows. Section 1has framed the problem and the tackled scenario of services discovery and sharing among CN members. Section 2 summarizes the main concepts and literature overview on services discovery. Section 3 presents the proposed model and section 4 presents a software prototype. Section 5 discusses about the preliminary results. Some conclusions are presented in section 6.

2 Basic Literature Overview

The problem of web services discovery involves many complex issues, such as: i) technological heterogeneity and low level of interoperability; ii) ambiguity of concepts due to differences of domain applications; and iii) limitations in the technologies used to design services [13]. There are plenty of works and visions on services discovery in the literature. The review here presented encompasses only the considered most relevant works for the purpose of this paper.

Two basic strategies resume the works on service discovery presented in the literature: static and dynamic discovery. There are a number of advantages and disadvantages in both. In the static way services are discovered at design time and they are immediately associated / bind to the given SOA application. However, the previously chosen service can be not available when the service is invoked. The main advantage of the dynamic approach is the possibility of replacing services by others or of choosing the most appropriate one, on-the-fly. However, this strategy usually presents higher discovery time (as all discovery actions should be done at execution time) and demands more sophisticated levels of intelligence from the discovery algorithm. This intelligence can be in the form of criteria relaxation [14] or other techniques such as classification systems, providers' reputation, costs negotiation and quality of service development process [15].

Existing models and approaches for services discovery can be grouped into four dimensions: *information retrieval, architecture, QoS* and *standards* [11]. In general terms, in the information retrieval dimension the focus has been put on semantics in way to provide greater precision in the services selection [14] [16]. In the architectural dimension, works have focused on aspects such scalability, security, availability, etc. [17]. In the QoS dimension there are three basic fields of research [18] [19]. The first one refers to the definition of attributes and metrics for QoS. The second one involves the establishment of more comprehensive and robust frameworks to represent, select, verify and maintain QoS attributes. The third field involves the development of *ad hoc* strategies to solve specific cases involving QoS. In the standards dimension, the initiatives have focused on interoperability (in heterogeneous environments). ICT standards like UDDI [20], SOAP [21], WSDL [22] have been intensively used.

The problem is that the envisaged collaborative scenario requires a more holistic and comprehensive view about services discovery. Besides requiring a joint view of those four dimensions, other dimensions not tackled in any of the reviewed works are also necessary, namely the consideration of the business level. In spite of the very high complexity all this represents and challenges that have to be faced, this proposed model intends to contribute to this.

3 Proposed Model

3.1 Essential Rationale

The essential proposal's rationale is fundamentally related to a tighter integration between BPM and SOA as a way to enhance services discovery quality. Actually, the combination of BPM (Business Process Management) [23,24] and SOA [25] has been considered as the current state-of-the-art approach to improve the quality of integration and alignment of business and IT [26].

Very roughly, it can be said that BPM allows managers to express business processes' rules whereas SOA acts as the link with the IT level. In spite of the availability of several BPM and SOA software solutions in the market, the complete integration of them is a tremendous challenge in practice regarding the required organization and IT changes for a company. One issue of this challenge refers to the problem of web services composition, whose ultimate goal is to bind services (i.e. to compose the SOA-based application) for the involved business processes (BP).

State of practice on BPM&SOA integration shows that companies use to make the composition in a fixed, not much assisted and hard-coded way, i.e. once managers specify the processes (at BPM level) the IT engineers bind them with existing (or to be developed) web services. The execution is further carried out via e.g. BPEL (Business Process Execution Language) tools [27]. Moreover, most managers use to make that specification without considering already available business process models standards, such as UBL (Universal Business Language) [28] or RosettaNet [29], which has the potential to mitigate semantics interoperability problems when integrating (SOA) applications. However, even when this is considered, its usage gets normally restricted to the process modeling moment (business level), and not extended and passed to the SOA layer (IT level). This means, for instance, that BPs' context is lost for further services discovery purposes. If on one hand this conventional way somehow works in the companies, on the other hand it prevents them from being more flexible and agile in their business. Each new process or modification requires reprogramming and rebinding, which is usually costly and time consuming, especially for CN members, whose core business does not use to be web services development. Even so, companies are responsible for managing this asset as well as for handling the involved services' QoS.

Another problem refers to this perspective of allowing largely distributed and heterogeneous CN members (including small software providers) to share their services under the SaaS (Software-as-a-Service) [9]. This scenario can be particularly interesting for CN members as one of the ways they can somehow outsource their TI needs. Besides that, this scenario provides the potential for choosing (even on-the-fly) the most adequate service for the current BP's requirements (from the functional and non-functional points of view, including different web services' costs) and computing environment a given CN manager is in.

3.2 Issues to tackle

Coping with all the requirements involved in the envisaged collaborative scenario of services discovery and sharing is extremely complex and also involves several challenges at business and IT levels [30].

In the proposed model for services discovery within a CN scenario, there are five basic issues to be considered: *i) what to express; ii) how to express the desired service; iii) who expresses the desired service; iv) who evaluates and how discovery results are evaluated; and v) when expressing and searching*.

The first point refers to which information should be expressed to specify the desired service for the given BP. In the proposed model, this involves: i) functional aspects (service's name and operations); ii) inputs and outputs; iii) expected QoS values; and iv) BP's context.

The second point refers to services expression including the components and the relationship between them. Natural language, formal or dedicated languages are examples of how to do this. The proposed model adopts ontology. They create a uniform vocabulary to be used by the discovery mechanisms, besides improving discovery process accuracy and precision.

The third point refers to who informs the desired service. Traditionally, the SOA application designer is the one who explicitly specifies the details of the desired service. Considering the role of BPM systems in this work, four ways might be considered: Automatic (A), Strongly Based on Designer (SBD), Semi-Automatic (SA) and Assisted (As). In the Automatic way (A), the discovery task is left to the BPM environment. It automatically identifies needs, makes changes in the expression and determines which service will be selected and be bind to a given BP. This process occurs without designer intervention. In the SBD way is somehow the opposite case, where the designer is the responsible for indicating the required service and for evaluating and deciding about the most adequate service to be selected. The designer interacts with the BPM environment intensively. In the SA way is a hybrid way. The BPM does the whole process but asks to the designer for some constraint relaxation in the case no expected service is found out. In the Assisted (As) way, there is a closer interaction between BPM environment and designer. The designer specifies service's requirements whereas BPM environment informs the BP's context. The evaluation of the discovery result is jointly performed.

The fourth point involves determining who evaluates the discovery results and how this evaluation occurs (assisted, without designer participation, etc). Four situations are considered: i) more than one 'perfect' service (i.e. there is full compliance between desire and outcome), which means having the need for ranking and selecting the most appropriate service; ii) just one perfect service; iii) none service; iv) one partial service (any 'perfect' service); and v) more than one partial services.

The fifth point refers to at which moment the activities of identifying the BP, its requirements, etc. as well as the results evaluation will be carried out by of the discovery actions. This point is detailed in the next section.

3.3 Operation

A key aspect in the proposed model is a change in the way the problem of dynamic services discovery have traditionally been seen. In this work, the problem is split into two phases: design phase and running phase (Figure 1). The essential rationale of this separation is trying to prevent CN managers from handling IT issues as much as possible. In this sense, at BPM level, it is considered that they are very familiarized with business rules and can specify how business processes should be executed. On the other hand, at the running time, they shouldn't get too much worried about the services discovery and this should be essentially left to the SOA environment / discovery system to do it.

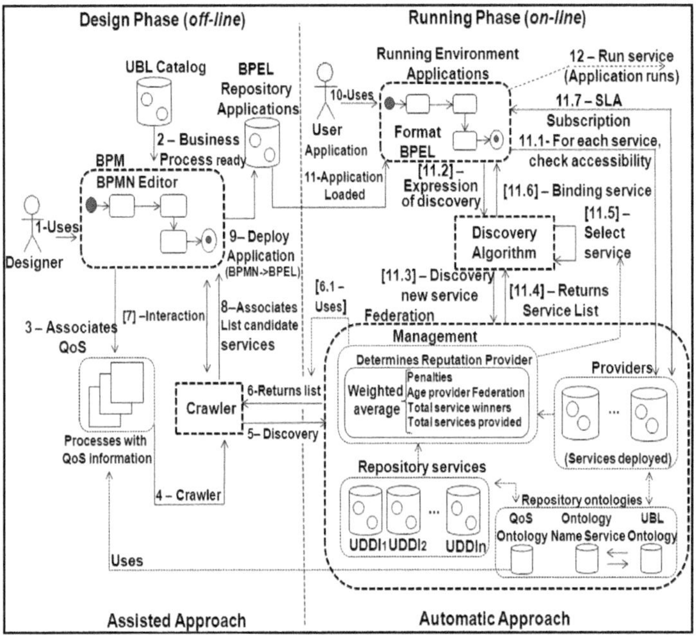

Fig. 1. Overview of the Model operation

The first phase basically refers to the specification of the SOA application to be built, including capturing the given BP's context and indication of the required QoS, which are crucial elements for a more proper discovery (left side of Figure 1). This is done off-line and CN managers are assisted by the composition environment (see section 3.2 - third point). Initially, the (s)he uses a BPM environment for composing applications (step 1) - also showed in Figure 2 - which offers the access to a standard *BPs catalog* (step 2). This catalog, an additional element of the model, comprises all the business processes of UBL standard (the one chosen in this exploratory work), meaning that all composite applications will be compliant with a standard or with a specialization of it. Yet, it is possible to identify and to capture the BP's context. This speeds up the application design and provides greater semantic richness to the discovery since services (from the several CN providers) are published taking a UBL standard ontology into account.

In step 3, CN manager together with an IT technician assign QoS attributes for each BP's activity. A QoS ontology (Figure 1 right / bottom) is used for this, and it is also used by the CN providers when publishing their services. The search expression is then assembled. The expression is structured as a 3-tuple: the wanted web service W = (F,O,Q), where F represents the set of functional requirements (i.e. the required functionalities), O represents the BP's ontology, and Q the non-functional requirements (i.e. QoS). As an example, let´s take the UBL general process related to *purchasing*. According to the UBL ontology, *ordering* is one of its subprocesses. *Ordering* has some I/O to be respected in terms of number of arguments and types. The other sublist refers to QoS, where some values are assigned to the several attributes comprised in the QoS ontology (e.g. *response time*).

An internal crawler service is activated (step 4) having the search expression as input. The crawler begins searching (step 5) for services in the CN members' services repositories with the aim of bringing a list of possible services that matches the subprocess requirements. It is also important to mention that the crawler acts in "background", i.e. that list is retuned at design time, and not at the running time. The underlying strategy is to decrease the whole discovery time, avoiding an exhaustive search when the composite SOA application would be in execution.

A list of services is returned (step 6). This list is ranked according to the CN providers' reputation (step 6.1 - historical, penalties, etc). As mentioned in the previous section, a 'perfect' matching may be not occurs, and the crawler should handle this (step 7). If the list contains just one service, it is already settled to the subprocess. If the list is empty, the crawler asks for a requirements relaxation for a new search, or leaves the option (or risk) of keeping the same requirements and doing the search at running time. If the list has more than one service, they are stored as XML files for further treatment at execution time (see below). In step 8, still at the design phase, this list of candidate services is passed to the BPM environment. The SOA application is then composed, it is converted to BPEL [27] format and gets available in stand-by to run (step 9).

It is important to clarify one aspect related to the used ontologies and the matching. Actually, the use of ontologies is a strategy to face semantics interoperability problems when consumers go for a discovery and providers publish their services. UBL and QoS ontologies (previously populated) act as a common / agreed set of terminologies and concepts used to express the BPs and QoS. This makes possible that the matching in the discovery can be "syntactic", via a comparison of the same (semantic) terms used in the adopted ontologies.

The second phase of the model – the on-line phase – starts when the CN manager or collaborator wants to execute a given application (that one previously composed). At this time, it is relatively transparent to him that it is a SOA-based application. He navigates through the process / BPEL repository and chooses which application he wants to run (steps 10 and 11, Figure 1 right side). A runtime task checks if the preselected web services are actually available (step 12), invoking the selected ones in the case they are ok. Otherwise the second one from the list will be picked up, and so forth. In the case none of them are available then the whole discovery activity is triggered again, with a new possible list, etc. Once everything is settled for a given service, the respective SLA (Service Level Agreement) is dynamically generated (step 11.7) and integrated into the BPM environment, as proposed in [31]. Thus, and helped by a BPEL engine, the desired composite SOA application (e.g. the *purchasing* application in this case) is ready to run, with the most appropriate services (step 12).

This proposed model has a set of assumptions. Two of them are important to be highlighted. The first assumption is what we call 1:1 relation. This means that the composition model is prepared to find and to compose 1 service for each 1 BP's subprocess activity. Taking the same example used along the paper and according to

UBL ontology, *purchasing* process is composed of a set of subprocesses e.g. *ordering*. Therefore, the model will understand that a discovery action (considering functional, QoS and context requirements) will be carried out aiming at finding a sort of possible web services for *ordering* but only one (1) web service will execute it. In other words, this assumes that services providers would have implemented one (1) service per subprocess (eventually they can have different versions, associated or not to different business models, depending on the client). The second assumption is that the so-called CN manager and IT technician are expected to be experienced persons, who understand company's processes and rules (and UBL ontology) as well as have the 'feeling' about suitable QoS metrics (and ontology) for the SOA application that is going to be built up.

4 Implementation and Preliminary Assessment

In order to evaluate and to compare the value added of the proposed model against the so called traditional model (i.e. without consideration of QoS and contexts), two prototypes have been implemented.

About the UBL ontology, it was based on the UBL standard specification and was expressed in BPMN (Business Process Modeling Notation). The catalog was built on top of this, as a plugin of IBM WebSphere BPM suite. About the QoS ontology, it was conceived based on a high-level ontology [32] and QoS definitions from two other works [33, 34]. Both ontologies were modeled using Protégé tool. It is assume that CN members / VBE share such ontologies.

Web services repositories were implemented based on the UDDI 3.0 specifications, using *bindingTemplate* elements [20] to save QoS aspects.

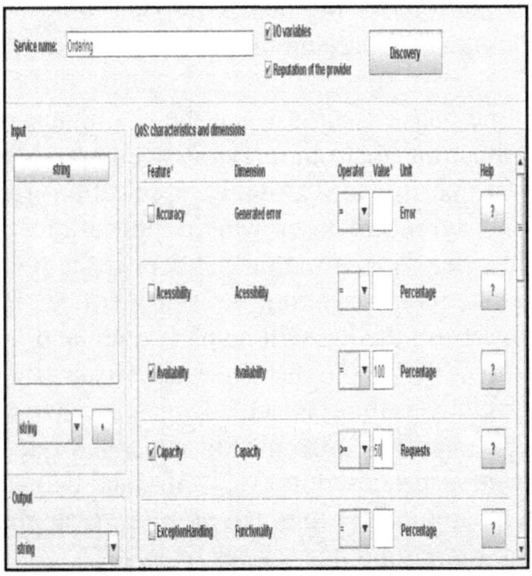

Fig. 2a. Interface for service discovery

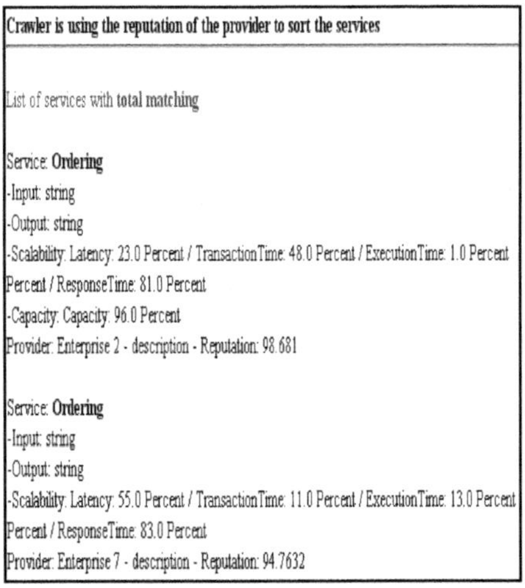

Fig. 2b. Example of discovery results

Figure 2a shows one of the several interfaces of the proposed model's environment. It is the main one through which a CN client indicates which service is requested (using the UBL ontology; in this case, the *ordering* service) as well as the expected QoS values (using QoS ontology). Figure 2b shows a result of the discovery. For each desired service, the system presents the list of 'perfect matching' services (see section 3.3 / step 6) with their name ("ordering", which is related to the UBL *purchasing* process' context), the CN providers' identification and the QoS values they support.

A hypothetical scenario was created in order to preliminary test the model. It assumes the existence of 10 CN providers offering 100 web services in total. All registries and providers were deployed and placed in a local network. QoS values were randomly assigned to them. These services are related to the *purchasing* UBL process, which in turn has four subprocesses: *Ordering, Sourcing, Payment and Billing.* 25 similar (UBL compliant) services were equally developed for each of these subprocesses and randomly deployed over the providers. UBL and QoS ontologies were used for services publishing.

Three search queries were idealized to try to make a preliminary evaluation of the model's approach (Figure 3). The first query was composed of four discoveries, one for each of those four subprocesses. This query did not take into account QoS information, i.e. it only dealt with functional requirements, which corresponds more or less to the traditional scenario of discovery. After a search 100 services (25 per subprocess) have returned as all registered services were semantically compliant with those subprocesses terminology and functional requirements. In the second query QoS information was added to the search expression. The number of returned services (8) was evidently lower than in the first query. This represents the result of the QoS filtering, meaning that only 8 services (out of 25) actually had 'perfect matching' and hence are potentially suitable for the given process. A complementary filtering that can be used is the consideration of the service / providers reputation.. The third query tried to explore a more "realistic" scenario, which considers not only 'perfect' services but also services with partial (QoS and/or functional requirements) matching. As a result of the search the returned list of services (12) was numerically greater than

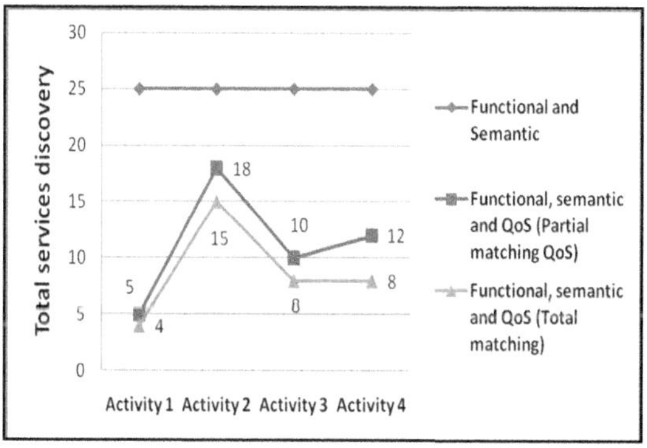

Fig. 3. Result of the queries 1, 2 and 3

the second query. Now the designer's job would be more difficult. If in the second case his job would be selecting the best service based on the reputation ranking (as all services had matched everything), in this third case a more careful analysis should be done. This means that the designer should go through each of possibility to see the eventual need for requirements relaxation (see section 3 step 7).

In terms of global performance, the discovery process itself (i.e. not considering the design time where the designer manipulates the catalog, assigns QoS, etc.) was executed in seconds. However, this is evidently biased to the fact that all UDDIs and services were deployed in a local network. In a real scenario of largely distributed CN providers and members in general, network latency (besides reliability) is a must to be considered. In terms of computational efficiency, the current version of dynamic discovery and the crawler algorithms have an efficiency of linear time $O(n)$.

5 Conclusions

This paper has presented an ongoing and exploratory work on dynamic services discovery. It copes with some characteristics of CN as well as with current trends in integration of business and IT levels, namely considering BPM and SOA paradigms.

The proposed model is strongly grounded on standards, at all tackled levels. It facilitates interoperation and mitigates problems for a larger acceptance of more advanced concepts – BPM and SOA in the case – by CN members.

Compared to the state-of-the-art, this model adds value when brings BPM closer to IT/SOA level, applying standards, allowing more adequate and dynamic services selection when considering BP's context and QoS, and providing an advanced and sustainable business model (SaaS) for services sharing among CN members.

The model is currently instantiated with UBL open standard, although it is prepared to deal with other equivalent ones, such as RosettaNet or some future initiative that can formalize CN-related business processes. It is foreseen that plenty of small software companies and CN members over the world will be engaged in offering and using standard-compliant services under the SaaS model in the near future. A model like the proposed one can be a good starting point for tacking this so challenging scenario.

From the exploratory perspective of this research, it can be said that the proposed model has the potential to solve the "theoretical" part of the problem (based on the chosen approach), which refers to how CN members can share their web services and hence can enlarge their collaboration and reinforce trust building. This can give suitable conditions for a more agile adaptation in the members' business processes, in particular when they need to cope with specific business opportunities forming a virtual organization.

However, from the applied perspective of this research, a model like that cannot be seen as the solution for all issues involved in services discovery and services sharing among CN members. For example, SaaS in an emergent area and there is not solid theoretical foundations about it yet. Trust, adequate ICT infrastructures, security, cultural changes, BP (re)organization, among many other aspects, are examples of additional and complex issues that should be dealt with. In spite of this, it is believed that this model has a structure that can be used as a starting and useful instrument to allow a wider collaboration among CN members, preserving their independence, autonomy and heterogeneity.

The problem related to CN members services' quality and trustworthiness can be talked by means of applying reference guidelines for SaaS development, such as proposed in [35].

On the other hand, the own VBE (which involved CN members would come from) can adopt an institutional position stimulating CN members to share their services. In the future, companies can even make some profit out of this since the access to their services (considering that they would have to maintain them anyway) would be on-demand and paid-per-use. Yet, strategic benefits can be a good argument for its adoption as CN members can become more agile and feel better prepared to enter in a new VO as new required software services may be, in fact, available, preventing them from new services development or acquisition, in opposite to the case without any sharing.

References

1. Camarinha-Matos, L.M., Afsarmanesh, H.: Collaborative Networked Organizations: a Research Agenda for Emerging Business Models. Kluwer Academic Publishers, Dordrecht (2004)
2. Rabelo, R.J.: Advanced Collaborative Business ICT Infrastructures. In: Methods and Tools for Collaborative Networked Organizations, pp. 337–370. Springer, Heidelberg (2008)
3. NESSI Strategic Research Agenda - Framing the future of the Service Oriented Economy. Version 2006-2-13 (2006), http://www.nessi-europe.com/documents/NESSI_SRA_VOL_1_20060213.pdf, ICT for Enterprise Networking, http://www.cordis.europa.eu/ist/directorate_d/en_intro.htm
4. Singh, M., Huhns, M.: Service Oriented Computing. Wiley, Chichester (2005)
5. de_Souza_Jr., J.L.N., et al.: An Internet-oriented Management and Control System in a Distributed Manufacturing Environment. International Journal of Manufacturing Research 5, 5–25 (2009)
6. Tramontin Jr., R.J., Rabelo, R.J., Chirab, H.: Customizing Knowledge Search in CNOs through Context-based Query Expansion. Production Planning & Control 21(2), 229–246 (2010)
7. Ribeiro, L., Barata, J., Colombo, A.: Supporting agile supply chains using a service-oriented shop floor. Engineering Application Artificial Intelligence (2009)
8. Borst, I., et al.: Technical Report (Deliverable) D62.2 ICT-I Business Models, http://www.ve-forum.org/default.asp?P=284
9. Software & Information Industry Association (SIIA). Software as a Service: Strategic Backgrounder (2001), http://www.siia.net/estore/ssb-01.pdf
10. Tsai, W.T.: Service-oriented system engineering: a new paradigm. In: IEEE International Workshop on Service-Oriented System Engineering, SOSE 2005, pp. 3–6 (2005)
11. IBM-WSLA. Web Service Level Agreement (WSLA) Language Specification. V 1.0 (2003), http://www.research.ibm.com/wsla/WSLASpecV1-20030128.pdf
12. Ma, D.: The Business Model of Software-As-A-Service. In: IEEE International Conference on Services Computing, SCC 2007, pp. 701–706 (2007)
13. Garofalakis, J., et al.: Contemporary Web Service Discovery Mechanisms. Journal of Web Engineering 5(3), 265–290 (2006)

14. Kokash, N.: Web Service Discovery With Implicit QoS Filtering. In: Proceedings of the IBM PhD Student Symposium (2005)
15. Mello, E.R., Fraga, J.S., Wangham, M.S.: Using a trust model for the composition of Web Services. In: Brazilian Symposium on Computer Networks (2009) (in Portuguese)
16. Kourtesis, D., et al.: Web Service Discovery in a Semantically Extended UDDI Registry: The Case of Fusion. IFIP International Federation for Information Processing, The Foundation of Collaborative Networks, vol. 243, pp. 547–554. Springer, Boston (2007)
17. Lamparter, S., Anupriya, A., Studer, R., Grimm, S.: Preference-based Selection of Highly Configurable Web Services. Alberta, Canada (2007)
18. Ran, S.: A Model for Web Services Discovery With QoS. Journal SIGecom Exch. 1(1) (2003)
19. Wang, X., et al.: A QoS-aware Selection Model for Semantic Web Services. In: Dan, A., Lamersdorf, W. (eds.) ICSOC 2006. LNCS, vol. 4294, pp. 390–401. Springer, Heidelberg (2006)
20. OASIS. UDDI Specific. V 3.0.2 (2004)
21. W3C. SOAP Specification. V. 1.2 (2007)
22. W3C. Web Services Description Language Specification. V 2.0(2007)
23. ORACLE. State of the Business Process Management Market. An Oracle White Paper (2008), http://www.oracle.com/technologies/bpm/docs/state-of-bpm-market-whitepaper.pdf
24. BPMINSTITUTE. State of Business Process Management (2006), http://www.bpminstitute.org
25. W3C. Web Services Architecture (2004), http://www.w3.org/TR/2004/NOTE-ws-arch-20040211
26. Kamoun, F.: A Roadmap Towards the Convergence of Business Process Management and Service Oriented Architecture. Ubiquity Journal 8(14), 1–8 (2007)
27. OASIS. Web Service Business Process Execution Language V 2.0 (2007), http://docs.oasis-open.org/wsbpel/2.0/OS/wsbpel-v2.0-OS.html
28. OASIS. Universal Business Language V2.0 (2006), http://docs.oasis-open.org/ubl/os-UBL-2.0/UBL-2.0.html
29. ROSETTANET. Business Process Specific (PIP) (2008)
30. Dorn, J., Grün, C., Werthner, H., Zapletal, M.: From business to software: a B2B survey. In: Information Systems and E-Business Management, vol. 7, pp. 123–142. Springer, Heidelberg (2009)
31. Cancian, M.H., Rabelo, R.J., Wangenheim, C.G.V.: An approach for the generation of SLAs for Software-as-a-Service. In: 8th I2TS Int. Conference, Florianopolis, Brasil (2009) (in Portuguese)
32. Tondello, G.F.: Sematic Specification of QoS: the QoS-MO Ontology. M.Sc. Thesis, Federal University of Santa Catarina (2008) (in Portuguese)
33. OMG (Object Management Group). UML Profile for Modeling QoS and FT Characteristics and Mechan. Specification, v1.0 (2006)
34. W3C. QoS for Web Services: Requirements and Possible Approaches (2003), http://www.w3c.or.kr/kr-office/TR/2003/ws-qos/
35. Cancian, M.H., Rabelo, R.J., Wangenhein, C.G.: Supporting Software Services' Trustworthiness in Collaborative Networks. To be presented in 11th IFIP Working Conference on Virtual Enterprises, Saint Etienne (2010)

Methodology for Prior Evaluation of Interoperability

Mamadou Camara, Yves Ducq, and Remy Dupas

University of Bordeaux, IMS, CNRS 5218
351 cours de la Libération, 33405 Talence cedex, France
{mamadou.camara,yves.ducq,remy.dupas}@ims-bordeaux.fr

Abstract. Interoperability is the ability of two or more systems or components to exchange information and use the exchanged information without special effort on either system. This paper attempts to propose a framework for evaluating and improving interoperability in each one of partners collaborating in a supply chain. The definition of the framework is based on three important hypotheses. The first hypothesis supposes the existence of interoperation activities which correspond with the part of business processes representing efforts for interoperability. The second one is the definition of Key Performance Indicators (KPIs) as aggregation of time, cost and quality performance for interoperation activities and also for actual business activities. The third one proposes to analyze impact of interoperability investments on enterprise objectives in two steps: the first step is the evaluation of the impact of interoperability solutions in KPIs; the second step analyzes the impact of improving KPIs in the achievement of enterprise's operational, tactical and strategic objectives. A methodology for prior evaluation of interoperability and improvement based on this framework is also proposed. The goal of this methodology is the validation of interoperability solutions to be implemented.

Keywords: Enterprise Interoperability, Interoperability Measurement, Business Process Modeling, Business Activity Monitoring, Business Process Simulation.

1 Introduction

Interoperability is the ability of two or more systems or components to exchange information and use the exchanged information without special effort on either system [1]. Approaches developed in the literature to measure and improve interoperability can be categorized into qualitative and quantitative models. Qualitative models propose interoperability evaluation methods based on maturity models. Quantitative models use indicators to measure interoperability characteristics like time, cost and quality of interoperation. The main limitation of these approaches is that they are partial because the considered interoperability is disconnected from enterprise objectives. In this study, the goal is to propose a quantitative methodology for interoperability evaluation and improvement. For this, it is necessary to evaluate how interoperability investments participate to the achievement of enterprise objectives. A framework is proposed as a foundation to address this issue. This framework is based on the physical and the decisional systems of the GRAI conceptual reference model [2]. The framework is composed of three complementary and connected layers: the

L.M. Camarinha-Matos et al. (Eds.): PRO-VE 2010, IFIP AICT 336, pp. 697–704, 2010.

interoperability investments layer, the operational interoperability impact layer, and the tactical and strategic interoperability impact layer.

The paper is structured in six sections. Section two presents the state of the art of *Performance Measurement System* and Causal Performance Measurement Models. Section three introduces interoperability measurement methods existing in the literature. Section four describes framework. The structured methodology is described step by step in the fifth section. To finish, a short example is given in section six.

2 Performance Measurement System and Causal Performance Measurement Models

To evaluate interoperability we must connect it with enterprise objectives. For that purpose, we need, in the one hand, a Performance Measurement System to define performance indicators. In the other hand, we need a Causal Performance Measurement Models to analyze causation between indicators in the Performance Measurement System. A performance measurement system is a set of strategic objectives and performance metrics applied throughout the entire enterprise [3]. If we consider the literature, there are a lot of methods to define performance indicators or more generally performance measurement system starting from enterprise strategy or from customer satisfaction. Balanced Scorecard [4] or the Performance Prism [5] or QMPMS [6] define the indicators focusing only to the strategic level. The definition of objectives in coherence with performance indicators and decision variables, and its extension to all levels are the main reasons why we've chosen to work with ECOGRAI. According to Kasperskaya [7], causal performance measurement models were substituted for traditional performance measurement systems, because they enable not only to measure and control but, also guide the companies' performance. Balanced Scorecard strategy map [8], Action-profit linkage (APL) [9] and the graph of decomposition [10] belongs to the most important existing causal performance measurement models. For the methodology for interoperability evaluation a causal performance measurement model will be defined using elements from these three models.

3 Interoperability Measurement

This section presents the literature of qualitative and quantitative measurement of interoperability. The INTEROP framework is used first to give some basic definition of concepts related to interoperability. It provides three explicitly defined interoperability dimensions to allow defining interoperability: interoperability barriers, interoperability concerns and interoperability approaches [11]. Barriers are incompatibilities of various kinds and at various enterprise levels. The incompatibilities obstruct the sharing of information and prevent from exchanging services. Interoperability concerns represent the various enterprise levels where interoperations can take place: Data, Services, Process and Business [11]. Interoperability approaches are basic ways to remove barriers: integrated approach, unified approach and federated approach [11].Solutions for interoperability remove barriers at a particular enterprise level (concerns), through a specific interoperability approach [12]. The solutions are then respectively related to the three dimensions.

Interoperability models that have proposed interoperability measures can be classified into qualitative and quantitative models. Mostly, qualitative models are designed as a mean of attaching a label or maturity level to a specific type of interoperability [13]. Each maturity level of a qualitative model is equivalent to an interoperability sophistication degree [14]. Levels of Conceptual Interoperability Model [14], System of Systems Interoperability (SoSI) Model [15] and Organizational Interoperability Agility Models (OIAM) [16] can be cited as qualitative models based on maturity levels.

Quantitative models are approaches that have numerical measures of interoperability characteristics [17], [13], [18], [19], [20], [21]. The measurement of interoperability is done in operational phase of the collaboration between two enterprises and allows them quantifying their interoperability and being able to improve it. Some equivalence can be noted between interoperability measures defined in the literature:

- Quality of exchange [19] and connectivity [17].
- Time of interoperation [19], data latency [17] and cycle time [20]
- Reliability [20] and conformity [19]

In our opinion, time, cost and quality are limited number of measures which encompasses all other types of interoperability efforts. Measuring interoperability with these three characteristics is an interesting option that we want to develop in this study.

4 Interoperability Evaluation Framework

This work proposes a framework for evaluating interoperability in each one of partners collaborating in a supply chain (Fig. 1). The framework should enable an understanding of how interoperability influences the achievement of enterprise objectives. The framework is partly inspired by the Lebreton, et al.'s [20] IIAM, but it is organized according to the GRAI conceptual reference model. The framework is composed of three layers: the interoperability investments layer, the direct (operational) impact layer and the tactical and strategic impact layer. The interoperability investments layer is aimed to study relations between elements located in the structural level of the physical system of the GRAI conceptual reference model. Theses elements are interoperability barriers, solutions for interoperability, internal or collaboration business processes and the business and interoperation activities they contain (Fig. **1**). The main hypothesis of our model is that business processes can be broken up into business activities and interoperation activities. Business activities are those which create value in business process. Interoperation activities are non-value-added activities representing efforts for the interoperability of information exchanges between partners. Solutions for interoperability eliminate interoperation activities by deleting interoperability barriers. This is the way internal or collaboration business processes are transformed by solutions for interoperability.

The direct (or operation) interoperability impact layer is composed of two sub-layers. Its first sub-layer measures the interoperability impact on the operational level of the physical system of the GRAI conceptual reference model. This sub-layer contains business indicators, interoperation indicators and key performance indicators. Interoperation indicators are defined on interoperation activities and business indicators defined on business activities. Key performance indicators (KPI) are considered as aggregations of business and interoperation indicators of all activities of a business process in order to measure the performance of the latter. In the general case, this aggregation corresponds to the summation of indicators values of all activities. Interoperation indicators, business indicators and key performance indicators (KPI) are all of three types: Average Elapsed Duration, Average Cost and Percentage of Failure. These measures are first quantifications of the operational impact of interoperability investments on business processes in terms of performance. The second sub-layer is composed of decision centers of the operational level of the decisional system of GRAI conceptual reference model. It enables to measure the impact of interoperability in terms of achievement of objectives of the operational level. Some operational objectives are directly related to process key indicators while the others only indirectly.

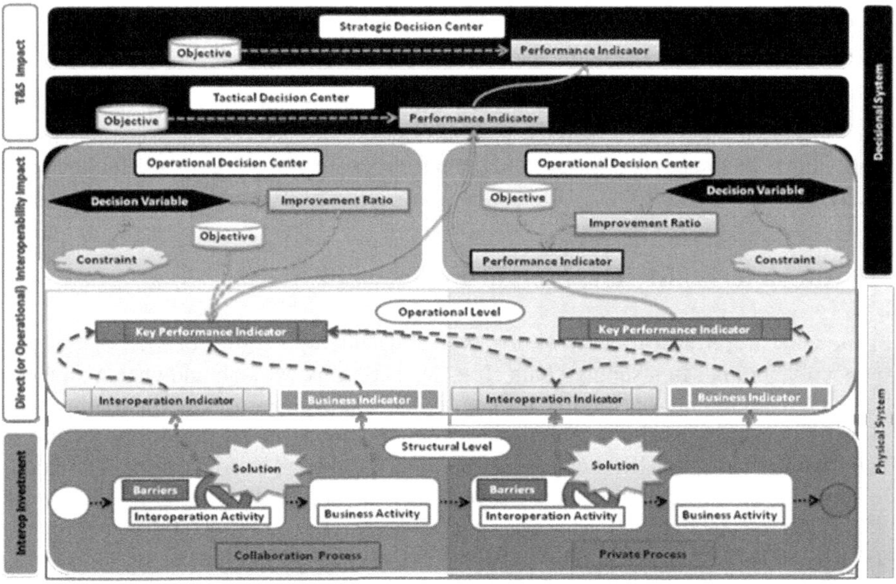

Fig. 1. Interoperability Impact Evaluation Framework

In the first category, the objectives are measured by operational performance indicators that are equivalent to key performance indicators because they are defined as process cost, time or quality (left side Fig. 1). In the second case, performance indicators are not defined as measures of time, cost and quality of business processes (right side Fig. 1). They can be related for example to equipments used or peoples working on physical level. Objectives are not directly related to key performance indicators in this situation. The tactical and strategic impact layer uses the tactical and strategic performance indicators of the GRAI decisional system to evaluate impact of interoperability investments on high level objectives (Fig. 1). The framework is founded upon a performance measurement system and a causal performance measurement model. Indicators in the performance measurement system are grouped in four components: process

KPIs, operational performance indicators (O_PI), tactical performance indicators (T_PI) and strategic performance indicators (S_PI).The causal performance measurement model links together indicators of the four components, and materializes relation between the layers of our framework. It establishes how interoperability impact at operational level translates into benefits at tactical and strategic levels.

5 Methodology for Interoperability Evaluation and Improvement

The methodology that we propose aims to evaluate the interoperability and its impact in a supply chain. It is based on the interoperability evaluation framework. The methodology provides prior evaluation of interoperability in order to validate solutions for interoperability to be implemented on the basis of their capacity to improve the achievement of enterprise objectives. This prior evaluation takes place during "As-is" and "To-be" situation of the project. "As-is" situation describes how activities (physical system) and decisions (decisional system) are actually performed in the supply chain. "To-be" situation represents the transformations of the "As-is" situation expected as a result of the implementation of solutions for interoperability. Steps in the methodology can be grouped in three blocks: Learning, Design and Validation. The learning builds a causal performance measurement model linking together process KPIs to performance indicators of the different levels in the decisional system (Fig. 2.). As all the variables of our causal performance measurement model are continuous, the task of predicting performance indicators from process KPIs is a numerical prediction. Our model is built with regression analysis because, according to Han, et al. [22 p. 24] it is the most often used statistical methodology for numerical prediction. The learning block builds also the

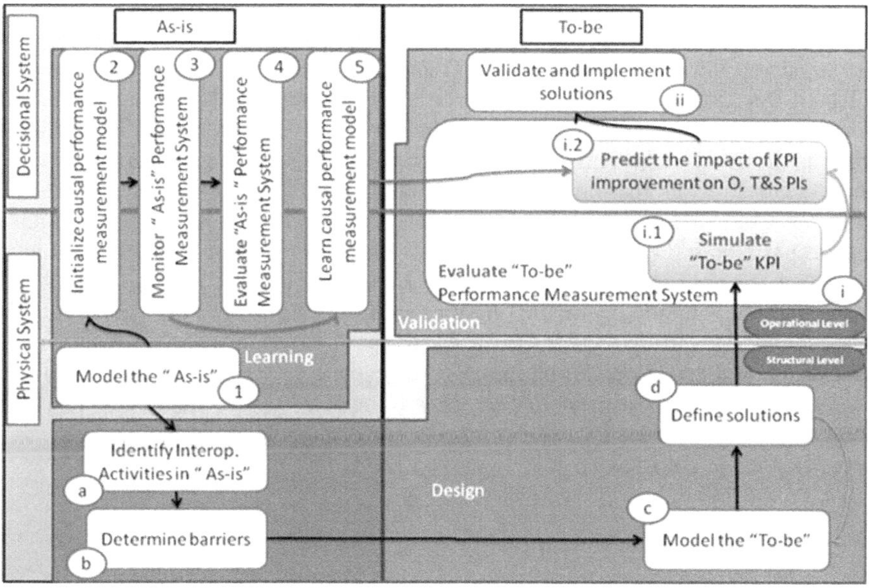

Fig. 2. Interoperability impact evaluation

"As-is" performance measurement system which represents averages of measures collected in the "As-is" situation. The Design block is aimed to find transformations needed in physical and decisional systems to solve problems related to interoperability (Fig. 2.). The validation block is aimed to validate solutions for interoperability by evaluating their improvement capacity. The first task is the evaluation of the "To-be" performance measurement system which is released in two stages (i Fig. 2.).

First the *"To-be" KPIs are estimated a prior by simulation of the "To-be" process model* (i.1 Fig. 2.). The impact of the KPI improvement on operational, tactical and strategic performance indicators is predicted using the causal performance measurement model built in the learning block (i.2 Fig. 2.). The comparison between the "As-is" and the "To-be" performance measurement systems represents the improvement capacity. The validation of solutions for interoperability is the second task of this block (ii Fig. 2.) and it is based on the results of this comparison.

6 Application of the Methodology

The example used to illustrate the applicability of our methodology is about a supply chain where an interoperability investment is undertaken to improve the quality of the collaboration. Partners involved in this collaboration are: the customer (an e-commerce company), the stockist, the customs declarant and the customs. The first element of our example is a "As-is" *goods entry* (collaboration) process in which all the four partners participate. To get the "To-be" *goods entry* process model, it suffices to take the model of "As-is" process and remove its interoperation activities. Influence relations between the variables of the causal performance measurement model were established by managers. The process KPIs component of the Performance Measurement System contains only the Computerization time measure. The *Computerization time* represents the delay between the moment when the *customer* places his order for goods entry and the moment when the *Stockist* informs him that goods entry is closed and the *Material Accounting is updated.* It is in the same time the Average Elapsed Duration of the *goods entry process and* an operational performance indicator for the objective "satisfy demand" of the *goods entry* decision center. The customers can run the goods output process and sell goods only once the goods are registered in the system. For this reason managers hypothesize that there is a causal relationship between Computerization time variable (process KPIs), and number of outputs of pallets per month (O_PI), number of outputs of boxes per month (O_PI) and number of outputs of units per month (O_PI). The Handling Turnover (T_PI) receives influence from theses three operational performance indicators. An improvement in Handling Turnover will drive an increase Handling Turnover in relation to staff (T_PI) and Sales turnover (T_PI). Both the Price of logistic services (S_PI) and Total turnover compared to department cost (S_PI) are impacted by the Handling Turnover in relation to staff (S_PI). The Sales turnover indicator belongs to the customer while others belong to the stockist.

7 Conclusion

This study aimed to provide the means for evaluating the interoperability and its impact on enterprises in a supply chain. We have proposed an analytical framework that introduces concepts related to interoperability and establishes their relations. The core element of this framework is the causal relationship between process key performance indicators and the objectives of partners, at all decisional levels. A structured methodology has been also proposed to perform the priori evaluation of interoperability. This methodology is organized around the validation and implementation solutions for interoperability. The use of business process models to locate interoperation activities and interoperability barriers and to measure performance is an important contribution of the methodology. That enables quantifying interoperation indicators with existing simulation and monitoring tools used in business process management.

In future work, the methodology can be completed with a posterior evaluation which would take place once improved business processes have been implemented using solutions for interoperability. Posterior evaluation would build "Implemented" Performance Measurement System and compare it with the one of the "As-is" situation in order to measure real benefits of interoperability investments.

Acknowledgement

This work was done in the frame of ASICOM (*Architecture de Système d'information Interopérable pour les industries du Commerce*), a project labeled by the *"Pole de Compétitivité"* PICOM of the region *Nord-Pas-de Calais (Lille)* in France and funded by the FUI (*Fonds Unifié Interministériel*). The Goal of the ASICOM project is to allow e-commerce companies to be connected at low cost, in short time and with flexibility to their partners and to the custom administration, using an interoperable information system. Examples used to illustrate the applicability of our methodology are taken from this project.

References

1. Access, Committee on Cataloging: Description &. Task Force on Metadata (2000)
2. Doumeingts, Guy. The GRAI Methodology (2004)
3. ManageMentor, Harvard. Performance Measurement Systems, `http://www.sema.org/`. [Online] 1.0.1120 .9999 .1.0 .1 .5/16/2007 12:17:49 PM (2007), `http://www.sema.org/hmm10/performance_measurement/what_is_a_performance_measurement_system.html`
4. Kaplan, R.S., Norton, D.P.: The Balanced Scorecard: Translating Strategy Into Action. Harvard Business School Press, Boston (1996)
5. Neely, A., Adams, C., Kennerley, M.: The Performance Prism: The Scorecard for Measuring and Managing Business Success. Edition Prentice Hall (2002)
6. Bititci, U.S., Suwignjo, P., Carrie, A.S.: Strategy management through quantitative modelling of performance measurement systems. International Journal of Production Economics 69 (2001)
7. Kasperskaya, Y.: Essays on Causal Performance Measurement Models. Universitat Pompeu Fabra (2007)
8. Kaplan, R.S., Norton, D.P.: Strategy maps: converting intangible assets into tangible outcomes. Harvard Business Press, Boston (2004)
9. Epstein, M.J., Westbrook, R.A.: Linking Actions to Profits in Strategic Decision Making. Mit Sloan Management Review (2001)

10. Ducq, Y., Vallespir, B., Doumeingts, G.: Coherence analysis methods for production systems by performance aggregation. Int. J. Production Economics (2001)
11. Chen, D., Doumeingts, G., Vernadat, F.: Architectures for enterprise integration and interoperability: Past, present and future. Computers in Industry (2008A)
12. Naudet, Y., et al.: Towards a systemic formalisation of interoperability. s.l.: Computers in Industry (2010)
13. Ford, T., et al.: The Interoperability Score. In: CSER 2007 (2007)
14. Tolk, A., Muguira, J.: The Levels of Conceptual Interoperability Model. In: The 2003 Fall Simulation Interoperability Workshop (2003)
15. Morris, E., et al.: System of Systems Interoperability (SOSI): Final Report. The Software Engineering Institute (2004)
16. Kingston, G., Fewell, S., Richer, W.: An Organizational Interoperability Agility Model. In: The 10th Command and Control Research and Technology Symposium, CCRTS (2005)
17. Kasunic, M., Anderson, W.: Measuring Systems Interoperability: Challenges and Opportunities. Software Engineering Measurement and Analysis Initiative (2004)
18. Ford, T., et al.: A Survey on Interoperability Measurement. In: 12th International Command and Control Research and Technology Symposium (2007B)
19. Chen, D., Vallespir, B., Daclin, N.: An Approach for Enterprise Interoperability Measurement. In: MoDISE EUS 2008 (2008B)
20. Lebreton, B., Legner, C.: Interoperability Impact Assessment Model: An Overview. In: Enterprise Interoperability II: New Challenges and Approaches, pp. 725–728. Springer, London (2007)
21. Grandin-Dubost, M., et al.: Using IIAM to Assess Interoperability Investments: A Case Study. In: Enterprise Interoperability II. New Challenges and Approaches, pp. 119–123. Springer, London (2007)
22. Han, J., Kamber, M.: Data Mining: Concepts and Techniques. Morgan Kaufmann Series in Data Management Systems (2001)

Semantic Reconciliation in Interoperability Management through Model-Driven Approach

Frédérick Bénaben[1], Nicolas Boissel-Dallier[1,2], Jean-Pierre Lorré[2], and Hervé Pingaud[1]

[1] Mines Albi – Université de Toulouse, France
[2] Petals Link – EBM WebSourcing
{frederick.benaben,nicolas.boissel-dallier}@mines-albi.fr,
herve.pingaud@mines-albi.fr
{nicolas.boissel-dallier,jean-pierre.lorre}@petalslink.com

Abstract. The MISE Project (Mediation Information System Engineering) aims at providing virtual enterprises with a Mediation Information System (MIS) in charge of supporting interoperability in a collaborative network. MISE proposes an overall MIS design method according to a model-driven approach, based on model transformations. This MIS is in charge of (i) information management, (ii) services sharing and (iii) behavior orchestration. Semantic issues are accompanying those objectives: How to deal with information reconciliation? How to ensure the matching between business activities and technical services? How to identify workflow among business process? This article aims first, at defining these semantic gaps along the whole MISE approach. The second part of this article presents how some specific solutions have been found in the specific context of crisis management (French funded project ISyCri). Finally, the current and future works concerning semantic reconciliation (in a generic non « 1 to 1 » context) will be introduced.

Keywords: interoperability, semantic reconciliation, model-driven engineering, information system.

1 Introduction

Collaborative networks support large diversity of collaboration forms, including virtual enterprises [1]. Virtual enterprises and the associated collaborative network are strongly dependent from their ability to manage collaboration and to assume the involved interoperability functions: *information exchange*, *activities coordination* and *processes orchestration*. Furthermore, Information Systems (IS) and computed systems are assuming both the roles of interface of organizations (external and internal exchanges) and functional engine of organizations (driving processes and business activities). Therefore, the previously listed interoperability functions must be supported by these IS. A collaborative network must consequently be able to provide one homogeneous IS, dealing with all the potentially heterogeneous IS of its components (partners of the collaborative network).

The MISE project (Mediation Information System Engineering), presented in [2] and [3], aims at defining a model-driven design approach of a MIS (Mediation

L.M. Camarinha-Matos et al. (Eds.): PRO-VE 2010, IFIP AICT 336, pp. 705–712, 2010.

Information System), in charge of interoperability functions. This MIS could be considered as a third-part based on Service-Oriented Architecture (SOA) principles, allowing existing IS to work fluently altogether, according to a common behavior, without any special effort. This goal is fully compliant with the definition of interoperability given in [4] and [5]. The MIS design framework defined in MISE, dealing with business requirements and logical considerations in order to deploy a technical mediation solution should necessarily succeed in the business-to-technical alignment: the abstract solution (proposed at the business and/or logical level) must be precisely implemented by the concrete solution (deployed at the technological level). The semantic attributes must be appropriately defined at the abstract level and rigorously taken into account at the concrete level.

Following the previous considerations, the main objective of this article is to present the semantic issues embedded into the MISE project, according to two horizontal levels: *abstract* (business/logical) and *concrete* (technology) among three vertical layers: *informational* (information vs. data), *functional* (activity vs. service) and *behavioral* (process vs. workflow).

The second section of this article introduces the MISE project and the associated general principles. The third section identifies semantics issues. The fourth section presents specific solutions that have been used in the French funded project based on MISE results (ISyCri – Interoperability of Systems in Crisis situations). The fifth section outlines perspectives and current work to deal with these semantic issues.

2 Overview of MISE Project

The following global presentation of the MISE project will be based on three main parts: (i) overall big picture of the design approach, (ii) model transformation principles and (iii) presentation of each step of the design approach.

2.1 Overall Big Picture of the Design Approach

This design approach might be seen as a dive into abstraction layers. Consequently it is based on model-driven engineering and on the associated model transformation concepts [6]. The general principle is therefore structured into three steps:

1. Gathering a structured knowledge on the considered collaboration (partners, roles, goals, services, data, etc.) in order to instantiate a specific ontology. By applying deduction rules on this knowledge, a collaborative process model is deduced (as described in [7]). This is the CIM level (Computation Independent Model), corresponding to the business layer.
2. The knowledge embedded in this collaborative process is then used through model transformation mechanisms in order to propose a MIS structure (as described in [8]) at the PIM level (Platform Independent Model), corresponding to the logical layer.
3. Finally, a technical model of the MIS is build, based on the knowledge embedded in the PIM and on the technological target platform, which is an ESB (Enterprise Service Bus) at the PSM level (Platform Specific Model), corresponding to the technological layer.

The two first steps concern the abstract level while the third step is dedicated to the concrete level (which is a useful point considering the semantic issues to come). The following picture illustrates this global MDE design approach:

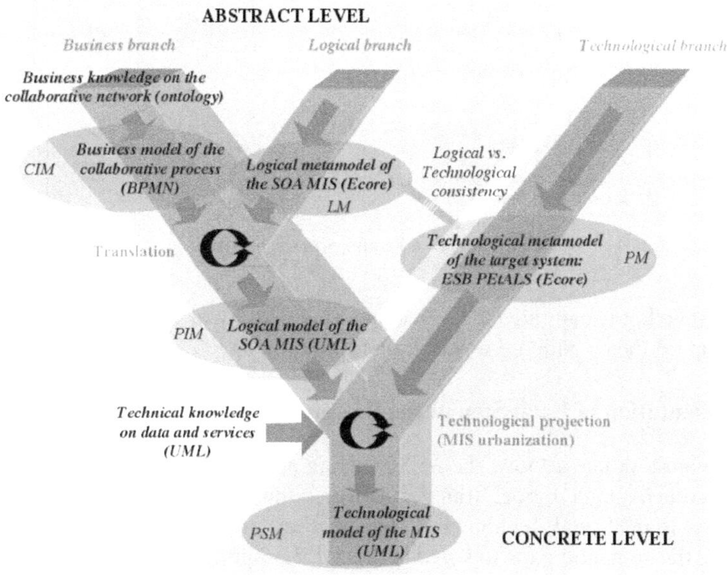

Fig. 1. "Big Picture" of the MISE design approach

Before detailing this MDE approach, we will focus on the required theoretical elements concerning model transformation principles.

2.2 Model Transformation Principle

Considering our model-driven issue, the first crucial point of the presented approach is model transformation. This issue concerns each of the three previously presented steps (business / logical / technical). A source model is used (built according to a source metamodel (MM)) to obtain a target model (respecting a target MM). The key point is that the source MM shares part of its concepts with the target MM. Note that the two spaces, source and target, have to be partially overlapping in order to allow model-morphism. As a consequence, the source model embeds a shared part and a specific part. The shared part provides the extracted knowledge, which may be used for the model transformation, while the specific part should be saved as capitalized knowledge in order not to be lost. Then, mapping rules (built according to the overlapping conceptual area of MMs) can be applied onto the extracted knowledge in order to provide the transformed knowledge. That transformed knowledge and an additional knowledge (to fill the lack of knowledge concerning the non-shared part of concepts into the target MM) may be finally used to create the shared part and the specific part of the target model. The general theoretical framework of all these model transformations may be synthesized as follow:

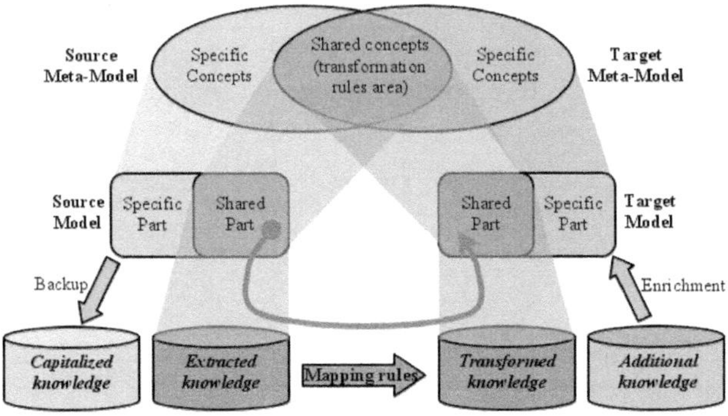

Fig. 2. Model transformation principle

Note that both, capitalized knowledge and additional knowledge may be empty depending on the considered model transformation case.

2.3 Presentation of Each Step of the Design Approach

On a semantic point of view, the MISE design approach includes two levels (abstract and concrete). On a model transformation point of view, it includes three steps (business, logical and technical). This section presents these steps in order to introduce the semantic gaps to solve in the MISE approach (see [3] for more details).

- Business step (*Abstract level*): The objective is to transform a characterization of the collaborative situation into the business model of a collaborative process. According to section 2.2, the *source model* is a network characterization, based on a network ontology (respecting a network MM which is the *source MM*). The *additional knowledge* is a repository of business activities, containing all the available functions of partners. As detailed in [9], this repository may be the Process Hand Book (see [10]). The *target MM* is the collaborative process MM described in [7], while the *mapping rules* may therefore be the ones fully described in [8]. There is no specific *capitalized knowledge* in this model transformation step. The obtained *target model* is finally a collaborative process model, dedicated to support dynamically the described collaborative situation.
- Logical step (*Abstract level*): The objective is to transform a business model of a collaborative process into the model of the logical structure of the MIS. According to section 2.2, the *source model* is the previously obtained collaborative process model, based on the collaborative process MM (which is the *source MM*). There is no specific *additional knowledge*, which shows that this model transformation is still at the abstract level. The *target MM* (SOA UML MM) and the *mapping rules* are fully described in [7]. There is no specific *capitalized knowledge* in this model transformation step. The obtained *target model* is finally a SOA logical UML model, dedicated to present the logical architecture of the MIS in charge of supporting the collaborative situation.

- Technical step (*Concrete level*): The objective is to transform the model of the logical structure of the MIS into the technical model of the MIS (usable for an ESB deployment). According to section 2.2, the *source model* is the previously obtained SOA logical UML model, based on the SOA architecture MM (which is the *source MM*). The *additional knowledge* contains all the technical elements concerning services and data (knowledge embedded into WSDL files). The *target MM* is the UML technical architecture of the MIS. The *mapping rules* are described in [3]. There is no specific *capitalized knowledge* in this model transformation. The obtained *target model* is a UML model, describing the technical structure of the MIS (based on the deployment of an ESB).

The following section will focus on the semantic issues of the MIS design. In such a design schema, strongly based on model-transformation principles, the semantic gaps are clearly linked to the additional knowledge. Actually, this knowledge brings new elements that have to be identified and correlated to the existing knowledge and the target MM in order to be appropriately integrated in the target model.

3 Semantic Issues in MISE Project

According to the previous section, the main semantics gaps might be, first at the business model design step and second at the transition between logical and technical MIS models (two steps where additional knowledge is included). The first semantic issue will not be considered in this article, as it is more a matter of transition between problem description and potential solution. The second semantic issue is more interesting due to the fact that it is a transition between abstract level and concrete level, aiming at finding technical elements to implement strictly logical components. Therefore, the global semantic framework of the MISE project is the following:

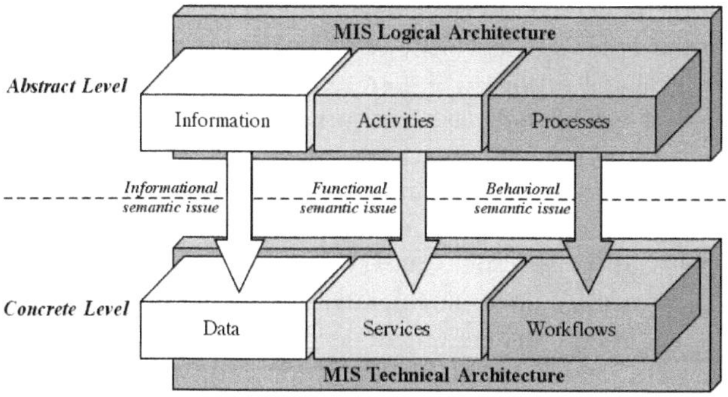

Fig. 3. Semantic framework of the MISE project

There are clearly three semantic issues, which, once solved, may allow to connect relevantly abstract level to concrete level: informational issue, functional issue and behavioral issue. These issues may be formulated as follows: How to deal with information reconciliation? How to ensure the matching between business activities and technical services? How to obtain workflow from business process? The first two questions deals with many-to-many issues. The objective is to map a set of business activities (respectively information) with a set of technical services (respectively data) during the model transformation (in order to define a technical way to implement precisely a theoretical solution). Furthermore, information are linked to activities (activities deal with information as inputs or outputs for example) and data are linked to services (similarly, services deal with data). The third question is more a problem of translation due to the fact that process defines the way activities and information should behave while workflow does the same with services and data.

4 Specific Semantic Treatment in ISyCri Project

The ISyCri project is a French funded project (ANR/06/CSOSG) dealing with *Interoperability of Information Systems in Crisis situations*. It is mainly focus on providing a crisis management cell with a MIS dedicated to ensure the collaboration between partners of the crisis cell (while these partners are assuming the collaboration with their people on site through their personal and specific channels). To reach that goal, the previous semantic issues had to be solved, in the crisis management context.

We will first explain the functional issue as far as it may be considered as the core-part, essential to understand both the informational issue and the behavioral issue. The solution adopted to deal with that key semantic issue is quite rough but well adapted to the considered field: The *added knowledge* of the business step is based on a repository of *technical services*. This is a strong short-cut to avoid semantic problems at the functional levels but it is quite realistic as far as, for partners of a crisis management cell, technical service are actually factual representation of business activities. For example, if policemen are able to establish on the crisis site a security perimeter (business activity), and if the MIS, orchestrating the collaborative workflow inside the crisis management cell, aims at starting that action, then, the MIS should call a service of the policemen IS (technical service) which will inform the policemen delegate inside the crisis management cell that it is time to establish the security perimeter. This technical service will therefore be a kind of interface, requesting the business activity of establishing a security perimeter. Schematically, in this case, instead of trying to match business activities with technical services, the chosen way oblige to select business activities among technical services. The matching is not necessary anymore. This direct way to deal with the functional semantic issue is mainly compliant with the specific context of crisis management (due to the previous consideration on proximity of technical services with business activities) but would not be adapted to other domains where the semantic distance between technical services and business activities would be more consequent.

As for the informational issue, first a part of the required matching is done through the previous mechanism as far as selecting business activities among a repository of technical services implies also to select inputs and outputs of this business activities. Furthermore, another principle is also in charge of that informational semantic reconciliation: Mediation services (inside the MIS) are in charge of translation and matching between data. If one output information of one business activity is conceptually an input of another business activity, it is necessary that the output of the corresponding technical service is correctly interpreted and used as the input of the following corresponding technical service. Therefore, some static matching tables have been built, according to the specific considered field. Mediation services have also been built in order to be able to read these tables and to use them in order to transform outputs of technical services into required inputs of other technical services:

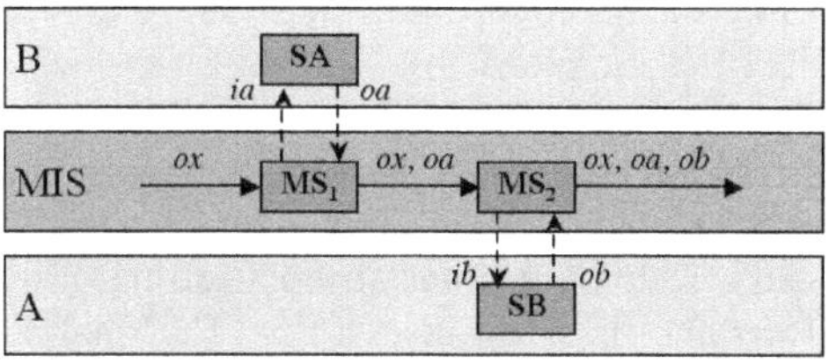

Where mediation services MS_1 and MS_2 know, thanks to matching tables, that:
$ox = (ox_1, ox_2, ox_3)$
$ia = ox_1 + ox_3$ (built by MS_1)
$oa = (oa_1, oa_2)$ (result from SA)
$ib = ox_2 - oa_1$ (built by MS_2)
and are able to provide services with the required elements

Fig. 4. Mediation services principle

The informational semantic issue is then managed by the ability of mediation services to use pre-established semantic matching tables. Similarly to the functional solution, this is a result specifically dedicated to crisis management context. As a critical point, the design of matching tables should be automatically managed by knowledge management tools. Currently it is a manual work, thanks to the fact that, in crisis management situation, the existing emergency plans define formally the information required for each activity and where they can be found.

Finally, concerning the behavioral issue, there is no real semantic reconciliation due to the fact that the workflow design is based on a BPEL transformation tool, which proposes a BPEL file, orchestrating technical services and data (already semantically consolidated by the management of informational and functional issue). The behavioral issue is managed through the syntactic mapping (BPEL generation) and the preceding semantic reconciliations (informational and functional).

5 Semantic Issues in MISE: Perspectives and Current Work

Semantic issues have been identified and defined in MIS design context. Furthermore, some specific ways to solve these issues have been presented in the particular field of crisis management. In this case, we consider that semantic distance between business activities and technical service is small enough to select activities directly into a technical service repository. We also created static matching tables for the mediation service. This approach is only available with a few static services. These solutions are not satisfying for a general context. That is why we are currently working on semantic reconciliation in MISE.

In one hand, we aim to match business activities and technical services, considering granularity differences between abstract and concrete levels. It involves an "n-to-m" matching during the logical to technical transformation and ontology matching of concepts from different levels. In the other hand, we aim to enable on the fly data adaptation with automatic add of transformation services when necessary, in order to avoid manual matching. Service and data reconciliations require three phases:

(i) knowledge modeling of technical and collaboration domain concepts, (ii) incorporating semantics into business and technical models thanks to existing or new standards, (iii) using semantic information to match services or messages. It is a major challenge in MIS design to find semantic correspondences between business activities and real web services as well as to configure messages transformations on the fly using semantic matchmakers.

In order to generalize its use to any collaboration network, our work focuses on existing standards such as SAWSDL, OWL-S, WSMO or WSMO-Lite which support efficiently development of Semantic Web Services [11]. Some of these standards allow semantic description of internal service behavior (e.g. internal process of orchestration service). On the other hand, by describing semantically business activities (through business ontologies), we plan to infer abstract profile of technical service (or set of services) able to assume these business roles. The final semantic reconciliation between services and abstract profile of inferred (set of) service(s) will bridge the gap between abstract and technical layers, through an "n-to-m" matching.

References

1. Camarinha-Matos, L.M., Picard, W.: Foreword. In: 5th IFIP International Conference on Virtual Enterprises (Pro-VE), vol. 283, pp. xv–xvi. Springer, Poznan (2008)
2. Benaben, F., Pingaud, H.: The MISE project: a first experience in Mediation Information System Engineering. In: 5th Italian Chapter of AIS (ITAIS), Paris (2008)
3. Benaben, F., Wenxin, M., Truptil, S., Lorre, J.-P., Pingaud, H.: Information Systems design for emerging ecosystems. In: 4th IEEE International Conference on Digital Ecosystems and Technologies, Dubai (2010)
4. Konstantas, D., Bourrieres, J.-P., Leonard, M., Boudjlida, N.: Preface. In: 1st International Conference on Interoperability of Enterprise Software and Applications (InterOp-ESA), pp. v–vi. Springer, Genova (2005)
5. Pingaud, H.: Prospective de recherches en interoperabilite: vers un art de la mediation. In: Plenary Lecture, 8th International Congress on Industrial Engineering (CIGI), Tarbes (2009)
6. OMG, MDA Guide Version 1.0.1, omg/2003-06-01 (2003)
7. Touzi, J., Bénaben, F., Pingaud, H., Lorré, J.-P.: A Model-Driven approach for Collaborative Service-Oriented Architecture design. International Journal of Production Economics 121(1), 5–20 (2009)
8. Rajsiri, V., Lorré, J.-P., Bénaben, F., Pingaud, H.: Knowledge-based system for collaborative process specification. Computers in Industry 61(2), 161–175 (2009)
9. Rajsiri, V., Lorré, J.-P., Bénaben, F., Pingaud, H.: Collaborative process definition using an ontolohy-based approach. In: 5th IFIP International Conference on Virtual Enterprises (Pro-VE), vol. 283, pp. 205–212. Springer, Poznan (2008)
10. Malone, T.W., Crowston, K., Herman, G.A.: Organizing business knowledge. In: The MIT Process Handbook, chs. 1, 3 (2003) ISBN 0-262-13429-2
11. Lausen, L., Lara, R., Polleres, A., de Bruijn, J., Roman, D.: Description: Semantic Annotation for Web Services, Semantic Web Services: Concepts, Technologies and Applications, pp. 179–209. Springer, Heidelberg (2008)

Security, Privacy and Interoperability in Heterogeneous Systems

Jian Zhong, Peter Bertok, and Zahir Tari

Computer Science and Information Technology, RMIT University, Melbourne, Victoria, Australia
{jian.zhong,peter.bertok,zahir.tari}@rmit.edu.au

Abstract. Partners in VOs can share large amount of data. Sharing of individual data items is straightforward, but sharing components of complex data structures stored in heterogeneous systems is often a challenge. Sharing is typically governed by rules and policies that need to be translated into access right / privilege control and data granularity control. Simultaneous control of privileges and data granularity across different organizations is a difficult task, and most traditional approaches, such role-based access control can become prohibitively complex in such scenarios. We propose a scheme for concurrent control of subject privileges and object granularity. It includes participants, duties and operations, and generates security labels that describe security features. To facilitate interoperability between heterogeneous systems, the labels also carry information about the data model, including dynamic hierarchy description. The model supports subject activity control over objects with variable data access granularity. It encompasses the advantages of existing role based and label based control. First, an abstract subject privilege control model is built, and the mathematical relationships between privileges in the label system are defined. Second, an abstract object dynamic granularity model is produced and the mathematical relationship between granularity levels is established. At last, a pair-wise privacy label system is provided as an integrated information protection mechanism, where relationships between subject activities and privileges are described for actual access control. A formal verification of the proposed method has also been performed.

Keywords: Interoperability, heterogeneous systems, security & privacy.

1 Introduction

Diverse organizations, governments and individuals share vast amount of information. Since information sharing can potentially harm certain parties, it is typically governed by roles and policies that support subject privilege control and data granularity control [1]. Both methods have been well studied on their own, and typically they are enforced by role-based access mechanisms and label based approaches respectively.

The increasing complexity of data, combined with the growing number and diversity of users who must access it, highlighted the limitations of traditional role based privilege control. One of the main problems is that with existing approaches the deployment of data granularity control becomes difficult when the majority of users are

L.M. Camarinha-Matos et al. (Eds.): PRO-VE 2010, IFIP AICT 336, pp. 713–721, 2010.

unique, i.e. when a role is assigned to a single user only. The solution requires two issues to be addressed simultaneously: (i) when accessing a whole object, which activities are available for each granular data component, and (ii) with numerous unique users, how to realize dynamic granular data access level control. We look at these issues from three perspectives. Namely, when there are many *unique users*, no advantage can be gained by grouping them into roles or generalizing access rights according to rules [2], because user privileges may vary greatly even within the same group. Secondly, traditional management focuses on subject-based *granular privilege control*; however, for sharing private data, object-based granular privilege control needs to be considered. Thirdly, classical RBAC does not support multi-domain / *cross-domain application* in a straightforward manner.

In this paper, we propose a practical solution to integrate sophisticated access control into a request-based pair-wise privilege control model. The proposed system has three modules: one for parameterized 3D subject granular privilege control, one for object-based dynamic granular data control and one for privilege refinement. The model also utilizes the advantages of existing role-based and label-based control. The major contributions are the following.

- Enhanced subject-based granular privilege control to support unique subjects with diverse privileges as well as reduced privilege assignment (PA) computation complexity and role storage consumption.
- Object-based granular data privilege control that supports dynamic granular data access and object cross-domain sharing. An embedded special request component makes the private and sensitive data sharing more flexible and easier to be customized.
- Cooperation between subject-based and object-based control encompasses the advantages of existing role based and label based control, raises the efficiency of privilege assignment and lowers the cost.

The rest of this paper is organized as follows. First we provide general background about the foundations of cooperation between user privilege granularity control and object dynamic granular data level control. This is followed by details of the proposed method, its implementation and testing. Then a section discusses the advantages and disadvantages of the proposed system, before the paper is concluded.

2 Related Work

A number of papers have looked at unique users with diverse privileges. By involving context tables, one solution supports fine-grained privileges and variable subject requests [3]. Another approach handles complex roles with diverse privileges by using an additional condition list [4]. In a third approach the traditional concept of 'role' is replaced by a new parameterized model, which not only supports unique users better but also reduces storage consumption compared to traditional role-based approaches [5]. These solutions add different modules to extend privileges and support user diversity, but unfortunately also result in decreased efficiency, as the unique users may come and go continuously. In addition, in [5] role models are difficult to build before the users lodge their requests. As opposed to these solutions, the proposed method builds an enhanced model that can directly assign privileges to subjects by request, priority check and privilege refinement. The storage requirements decrease when diverse roles don't need to be stored on the subject server. Moreover, the delicate modules and components offer efficient privilege assignment.

For collaboration control, connecting subject-based and object-based privilege control was considered by some approaches [6, 3]. However, the former solution [6] does not address granular data control, while the latter one, non-independent object based privilege control, limits dual control performance [3]. In the proposed solution, the use of the same hierarchical model for subject-based and object-based privilege control improves the efficiency of granular data control. In addition, an independent object controller offers high performance and supports special-condition control.

For multi-domain applications the use of role-mapping tables was proposed [7]. However, practical issues, such as role switching and data granularity may deteriorate the performance, as the building of mapping tables for all roaming roles and data will not only consume considerable storage space but also lower the efficiency of privilege assignment. Dissimilar to this approach, a dynamic hierarchy component employed by our proposed method caters for data roaming without high management costs.

3 Proposed Method

The proposed pair-wise privilege control scheme contains three parts, namely the privacy-label based subject granular privilege control (PSPC) module, the privacy-label based object granular data control (PODC) module and the collaboration control module as shown in fig. 1. Due to space limitations, only the hierarchical PSPC component, the dynamic hierarchical control component in the PODC module and privilege refinement are described here.

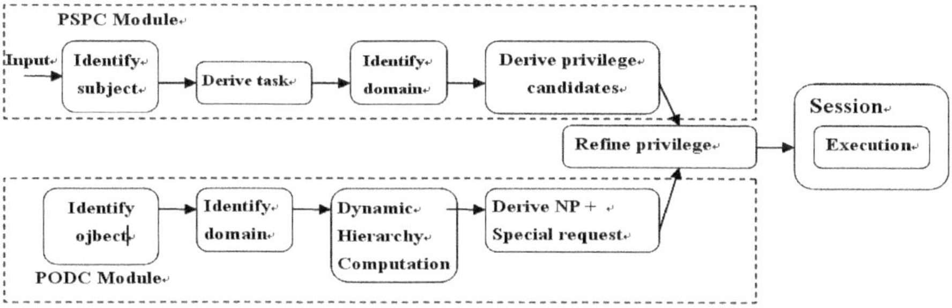

Fig. 1. Pair-wise Privilege Control Model

Basic concepts and definitions are given as follows. Given a set of subjects *S*, a set of objects *O*, each object has a set of granular data $O_x = \{OGD_i \mid i = 1, 2, \cdots, n\}$, where n is the number of granular data items. Each subject has a set of activities $SA = \{SA_i \mid i = 1, 2, \cdots, n\}$, where n is the number of subject activities. A set of *Subject Activity Level*, represented by $SL = \{\Omega(SA)_i \mid i = 1, 2, \cdots, n\}$ denotes the activity priority on the required object, where n is the number of subject activity levels and operation Ω(SA) denotes a subset of SA. Subject Grade denotes the subject's overall privacy priority, and is represented by SG. A set of Subject Sub-grades $SSG_x = \{\Omega(SL)_i \mid i = 1, 2, \cdots, n\}$ denotes the access priority for each granular data item of an object, where x denotes a certain sub-grade and n is the number of activity levels included in the sub-grade. The set of Negative Permissions is $NP = \{NP_i \mid i = 1, 2, \cdots, n\}$, where n is the number of negative permissions. A permission $P_x = \{(D_i, Boolean)\}$ can be accepted or denied, as indicated by the Boolean.

Hierarchical PSPC defines the control of subject granular privileges.

Rule 1: *Subject Activities* on the same *Subject Activity Level* are mutually exclusive, so only one will be activated in any one session. However, if they are on different levels, these activities can operate in the same session in parallel.

Rule 2: *Subject Activity Level* in a *Subject Sub-Grade* must be different from other activity levels in the same subject grade.

Rule 3: Different *Subject Sub-Grades* are controlled independently.

Basically, after a request has been lodged to a subject server, the subject is to be associated with an overall privacy priority, also called main subject access grade and represented by *Subject Grade* (*SG*). The *SG* usually consists of a set of *SSG*s that are associated with granular data items of the required object. Each *SSG* is composed of a set of *SL*s, which indicates the priority and correlation between different *SA*s. *SA*s included in the *SL* are the activities that can be executed over the object.

The *Dynamic Hierarchy* component has two main functions: hierarchy assignment (HA) and condition assignment (CA). When data is roaming, the original privacy priority control may not be able to work properly. Fig. 3 shows the concept of HA applied mapping.

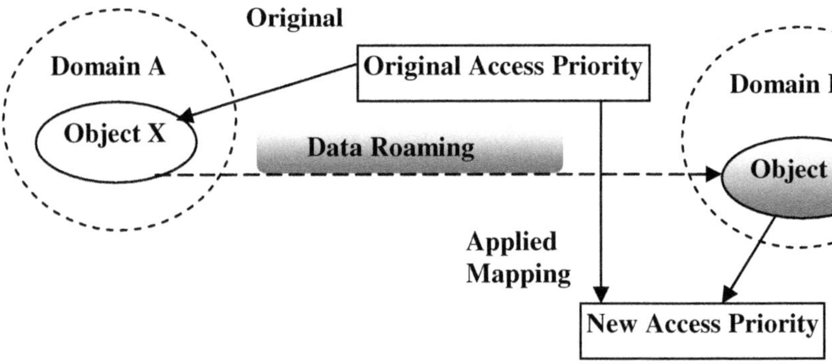

Fig. 2. Hierarchy Assignment (HA)

In fig. 2, Access Priority is represented by the object grade (*OG)* including object subgrades (*OSG*s). When object X (including granular data) is created, it is processed by the original object server in domain A, where the original access priority is a non-absolute classification value. If such data is required for roaming, the original object server will first assign a *basic sub-grade* (*BSG*) to one or more granular data parts. Then, all other data parts can be assigned proper grades by referring to *BSG* at the original object server. When the data is roaming to domain B, the object server in domain B will first map BSG to a basic applied grade (*BAG*) based on the data sharing environment and sharing requirements. Then, the system maps the original granular data sub-grades to applied grades relative to the *BSG*. The PODC control frame merely defines any negative permission (NP) for each granular data where necessary, which states what cannot be done over each granular data. Any special request on granular data is supported by Condition Assignment (CA).

The Privilege Refinement (*RE*) function computes proper permissions for the subject request. The left side of fig. 3 describes the first step of permission computing, which produces the overall permission of an access. If the subject's grade is equal to or higher than the 'object prohibited' grade, authorization will be given, otherwise access will be denied. $S_iPL.S_iG$ denotes the Subject Grade of Subject *i*; OPL.OG denotes object overall grade. The algorithm for sub-grade computing is given in the right side of fig. 3. The process compares all the subject sub-grades to all object granular data grades respectively, where → denotes 'move to the next'. The notations of permission symbols and extended *SL* operations are as follows.

Notion 1: (Positive Permission Operation =Γ) $S_iSG_x = \Gamma^{SA_j} OSG_y$ denotes that subject *i* is allowed to perform activity *j* on the object's granular data *y* in operation *x*.

Notion 2: (Negative Permission Operation !Γ) $S_iSG_x !\Gamma^{SA_j} OSG_y$ denotes that subject *i* is not allowed to perform activity *j* on the object's granular data *y* in operation *x*.

Notion 3: (Activity and Process Level Θ)

$S_iL_x\Theta^{\rightarrow}S_iL_y$ for subject *i* and a granular data of the object, level *y* must be processed after level *x*.

$S_iL_x\Theta^{\leftarrow}S_iL_y$ for subject *i* and a granular data of the object, level *y* must be processed before level *x*.

$S_iL_x\Theta^{\leftrightarrow}S_iL_y$ for subject *i* and a granular data of the object, level *y* and level *x* are mutually exclusive, which means only one of the levels will be processed.

$S_iL_x\Theta^{\updownarrow}S_iL_y$ for subject *i* and a granular data of the object, level *y* and level *x* can be processed simultaneously.

```
function Compare (subject i 's grade, object grade)
    (sg = SiPL.SiG)→(og = OPL.OG)
    if sg ≥ og do
        Si =Γ O
        move Next Process
    else
        Si !Γ O
        end
    end if
```

```
function Compare (all subject subgrades, all object granular data grades)
    for all x such that 1 ≤ x ≤ m do
        if SiSGx ≥ OSGx then
            SiSGx =Γ OSGx
        else
            SiSGx !Γ OSGx
        end if
    end for
    move Next Process
```

Fig. 3. Grade Computing and Sub-grade Computing

The left side of fig. 4 describes the algorithm of computing the relationship between each pair of levels. The computing logic will go through each pair of levels and output results. The right side of fig. 4 shows activity execution based on the results of three algorithms: the two in fig.3 and the one in the left side of fig.4.

The proposed scheme has been verified by Failures-Divergence Refinement (FDR) [8], a model verification tool based on Communicating Sequential Processes (CSP) state machines, and was implemented in JAVA.

4 Example

In this paper, we assume that data sharing is taking place without malicious attacks such as identity forgery, object forgery or dishonest subjects. For sake of simplicity we show only one object (O) with 3 pieces of granular data (OSG_x, $1 \leq x \leq 3$) and three independent subjects (S_A, S_B, S_C). We also assume that there are 8 different subject activities in the subject activity set (SB): *read* (b_r), *edit* (b_e), *add* (b_a), *delete* (b_d), *comment* (b_c), *declare* (b_{dc}), *replicate* (b_{re}) and *manage* (b_m). Also, both subjects S_A and S_B have direct access to the object and S_B has the 'manage' permission. S_C can access the object through S_B. Thus, we have $S_AG \geq OG$, $S_BG \geq OG$, $S_CG < OG$. We also assign the sub-grade sets $S_ASG = \{S_ASG_1, S_ASG_2, S_ASG_3\}$, $S_BSG = \{S_BSG_1, S_BSG_2, S_BSG_3\}$, $S_CSG = \{S_CSG_1, S_CSG_2, S_CSG_3\}$, where $S_ASG_1 \geq OSG_1$, $S_ASG_2 \geq OSG_2$, $S_ASG_3 < OSG_3$, $S_BSG_1 \geq OSG_1$, $S_BSG_2 \geq OSG_2$, $S_BSG_3 \geq OSG_3$. The logical relationship between the subjects and the object are shown in fig. 5.

```
function Compare (SiL)
  for all x such that 1 ≤ x ≤ m do
    for all y such that 1 ≤ y ≤ n do
     if Θ→ then
      SiLy.precondition(SiLx)
      continue
     else if Θ← then
      SiLx.precondition(SiLy)
      continue
     else if Θ↔ then
      select SiLx or SiLy
      selection
      continue
     else if Θ↕ then
      continue
      else continue
     end if
    end for
  end for
```

```
function execution (SiB)
  Compare (subject i 's grade, object grade)
  Compare (all subject sub-grades,
    all object granular data grades)
    Compare (SiL)
    for all x such that 1 ≤ x ≤ m parallel do
      select executing activity
      if selection is in negative permission list
then
          activity denied
          continue
      end if
      if precondition = true then
          select precondition activity or abort
          execute selection
          continue
      end if
      if mutually exclusive = true then
          select one of the mutually exclusive
    activities or abort
          execute selection
          continue
      end if
          execute selection
   end for
```

Fig. 4. Level Computing and Activity Execution

5 Discussion

In the proposed method, privileges are allocated to a subject request in the automatically executing refinement process, or manually for special requests. The PSPC module supports fine-grained, diverse granular privileges for numerous unique subjects, and generates privacy labels in accordance with the request of the subject and its privacy level. Consequently, it can effectively reduce the consumption of computation and storage resources. The dynamic hierarchy component of the PODC improves cross-domain data roaming, and can cater for different data sharing environments without redeploying all modules and components. This reduces the cost and processing overhead of subject reorganization.

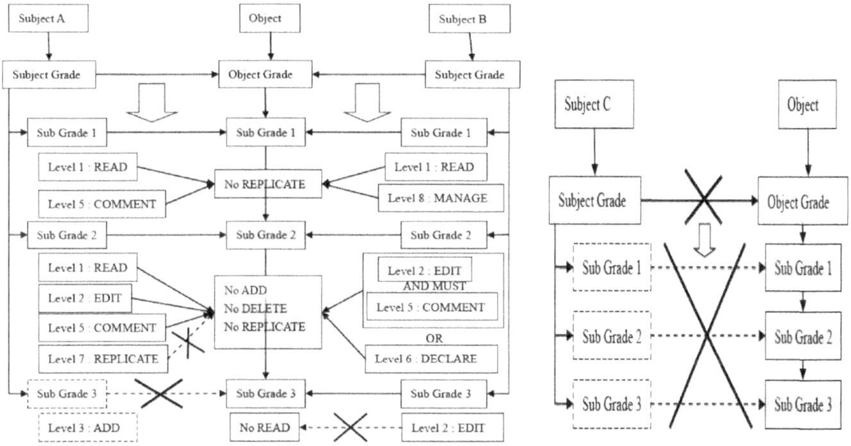

Fig. 5. Instantiation and Scenario

The unique subject issue mentioned in the introduction can be modelled mathematically [2]. Assuming that adding a target system causes 1/10 of the existing roles to be replaced by 10 roles each and the first system has 20 roles, the progressive explosion in roles is shown on the left side of fig. 6. It reveals that 10 systems push the total number of roles up to 6500. In practical deployments, hundreds of systems managed in a traditional role-based manner will aggravate the problem.

By involving granular subject privileges, the improvement is shown in the right side of fig. 6. We assumed that each subject submits two requests that contain three activities for each granular data, at every time unit.

From the figure it can be seen that with a fixed number of domains, a traditional role-based system consumes around 400% more resources in terms of space than our request-based system. The difference increases with the number of domains. The advantages of our approach are easily noticeable in the case of routine business events, such as changing the responsibilities of a single employee or extending the function of a department. They require the adjustment of the role model, and the ongoing nature

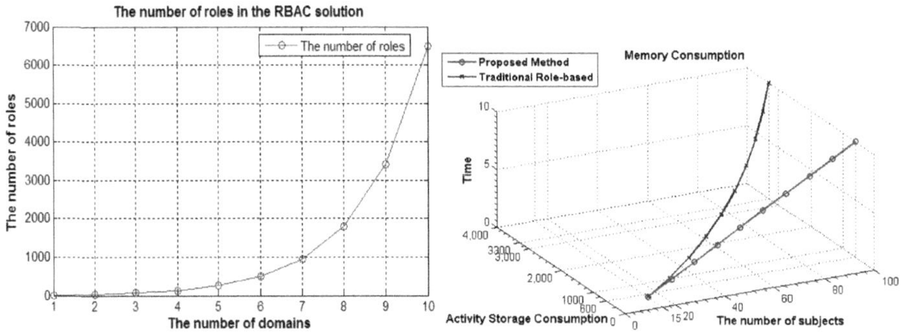

Fig. 6. System-Role Model and Memory Consumption

of such events may necessitate the employment of a team of expert staff for role maintenance. Cross-system or cross-field reorganization is also constrained in such systems .Adding and removing subject activities are cumbersome tasks of role model maintenance. In the proposed system, subject activities can be added or removed according to system needs in a fairly straightforward manner.

On the other hand, when many subjects share similar privilege sets, traditional role-based approaches perform better.

6 Conclusion

This paper proposed an approach to combined subject granular privilege control and object dynamic granular access level control. The characteristics of the proposed model are as follows.

- The model can be implemented in various scenarios where private and sensitive data sharing is practical. Its memory requirements are moderate even with a large number of unique subjects when compared to traditional role-based methods. Easy handling of frequently changing privileges along with reduced computation complexity are also advantages of our model over existing solutions.
- Dynamic granular data privilege control is also supported by the proposed model; which allows the handling of object roaming and subject privileges in a compatible manner.
- Using the concept of applied mapping, the method supports data roaming between different domains.

References

1. Zhang, L., Brodsky, A., Swarup, V., Jajodia, S.: A Framework for Maximizing Utility of Sanitized Documents Based on Meta-labeling. In: IEEE International Workshop on Policies for Distributed Systems and Networks, pp. 181–188 (2008)
2. Hitachi ID Systems, Inc.: Beyond Roles: A Practical Approach to Enterprise User Provisioning, http://www.idsynch.com/docs/beyond-roles.html (access in August 2009)

3. He, Q., Anton, A.I.: A Framework for Modelling Privacy Requirements in Role Engineering. Department of Computer Science, North Carolina State University, Raleigh, NC 27695-8207, USA
4. Li, X., Naeem, N.A., Kemme, B.: Fine-Granularity Access Control in 3-tier Laboratory Information Systems. In: The Proceedings of the 9th International Database Engineering & Application Symposium, IDEAS 2005 (2005)
5. Abdallah, A.E., Khayat, E.J.: A Formal Model for Parameterized Role-based Access Control. Research Institute for Computing, London South Bank University, U.K. (2005)
6. Acevedo, M.T., Fillingham, D., Nicolettos, J.L.: Enterprise Security Application of Partition Rule Based Access Control (PRBAC). In: Proceedings of the 6th Workshop on Enabling Technologies on Infrastructure for Collaborative Enterprises, pp. 285–292
7. Martino, L.D., Ni, Q., Lin, D., Bertino, E.: Multi-domain and Privacy-aware Role Based Access Control in eHealth. Computer Science. Purdue University, USA (2008)
8. Goldsmith, M.: FDR2 User's Manual Version 2.82. Formal System (Europe) Ltd.

From BPMN 2.0 to the Setting-Up on an ESB – Application to an Interoperability Problem

Y. Lemrabet, D. Clin, M. Bigand, and J.-P. Bourey

Univ Lille Nord de France, F-59000 Lille, France
Laboratoire de Modélisation et de Management des Organisations,
Ecole Centrale de Lille, BP48
59651 Villeneuve d'Ascq cedex, France
Youness.Lemrabet@centraliens-lille.org,
{David.Clin,Michel.Bigand,Jean-Pierre.Bourey}@ec-lille.fr

Abstract. To solve interoperability problem from semantic level, we propose to contribute to orchestration of the business processes to implement a mediation based on Enterprise Service Bus (ESB). We show how to take advantage of the forthcoming version of *Business Process Modeling Notation 2.0* (BPMN 2.0) of the *Object Management Group (*OMG) within the framework of a *Services Oriented Architecture (*SOA) development. This new version of BPMN is characterized by the addition of the notion of private/public process, choreography and conversation which are essential components of SOA architecture. We propose a model driven approach using an intermediate BPMN 2.0 model stemming from the high-level Modeling of the business processes defined from the industrial partner's requirements, to implement the solution on an ESB. The results, within a project whose objective is to allow the *Small and Medium Enterprises* (SME) to benefit from a collaborative interoperable architecture, allows the definition of domain process interfaces.

Keywords: Model Driven Interoperability, ESB, BPMN2.0, SOA.

1 Introduction

Each firm needs to bring its *Information System* (IS) into line with its business processes in order to improve its efficiency, its reliability and to rationalize its development's costs.

Moreover, the rapid evolution of technology means that enterprises need to advance ever faster, and they must establish collaborative networks, such as Extended and Virtual Enterprises, so as to be able to take advantage of their core competences and to look for others that they do not have [1]. So, enterprises have to fit their functions and processes with each other's in order to improve their competitiveness and to take advantage of new market opportunities; it is an interoperability problem whose issue is to save time and to make the exchanges reliable.

L.M. Camarinha-Matos et al. (Eds.): PRO-VE 2010, IFIP AICT 336, pp. 722–729, 2010.

Both Business Process and Enterprise Modeling techniques and methods have been successfully used by enterprises to integrate their information and manufacturing systems throughout the last few decades. More recently, European research programs, like Athena and InterOp[1], have been developed to improve the companies' interoperability.

Traditionally, researches on Interoperability tend to focus on one aspect of interoperability: (i) businesses; (ii) processes; (iii) services; and (iv) data interoperability. But in order to develop a practical solution for enterprise, interoperability problem should be addressed from both organizational and technical viewpoints. Businesses and processes interoperability are considered mainly at the organizational level, whereas services and data interoperability require focus on (information) technology issues [2]. In this paper, we are interested in solving the interoperability problem within the framework of the ASICOM[2] project.

ASICOM project will provide SMEs in both trade and logistics sectors with a pragmatic and generic approach to set up more rapidly simplified interoperable and adaptable solutions for improving communication with their partners (dematerialization).

The ASICOM project aims to support the development and realization of systems based on four SMEs requirements. The first requirement was the use of open-source solutions and frameworks to reduce the costs for SMEs. The second one was the respect of standards to facilitate the interoperability and communication at both the modeling and the technical levels, including the semantics aspects. The third one was the capacity of solutions to be deployed in a heterogeneous environment to improve communicability between exiting information systems already implemented in the SMEs. The last requirement was the agility of the proposed approach: indeed, due to the constant evolution of the technology, of the Customs regulations, of the trade partnerships it is needed to keep traces between the business level and the *Information Technology* (IT) level.

In order to meet these requirements, the following decisions have been made:

- A model driven approach was chosen. This kind of approach based on separation of concerns, modeling techniques and model transformations makes it possible to build models at different abstraction levels (from Business to IT) and to establish links between these representations.
- To meet the second requirement, standard notations and languages such as BPMN[3], *Business Process Execution Language* (BPEL)[4], *Unified Modeling Language* (UML)[5], *eXtended Markup Language* (XML)[6], and *Web Service Description Language* (WSDL)[7] … were selected.
- A SOA based solution was preferred in order to make easier the integration of heterogeneous existing systems. It also encourages reusability thanks to the service approach.

---

[1] http://interop-vlab.eu
[2] French acronym for Architecture of Interoperable Information System for Trade Industry.
[3] http://www.omg.org/spec/BPMN/2.0
[4] http://docs.oasis-open.org/wsbpel/2.0/OS/wsbpel-v2.0-OS.pdf
[5] http://www.omg.org/spec/UML/2.2/
[6] http://www.w3.org/TR/2008/REC-xml-20081126/
[7] http://www.w3.org/TR/2008/REC-xml-20081126/

- The open-source Petals ESB from the Petals SOA Suite[8] was chosen to implement the proposed service oriented approach. Some elements of comparison with other historical integration platforms are given in section 3.4.

The paper is structured as follows: the first section describes the context of the study and identifies the challenges addressed by the ASICOM project. The second section outlines the methodological and technical solution developed in the project. Finally the third section presents the industrial use cases wherein the developed technologies are tested and demonstrated.

2 Methodological and Technical Aspects

2.1 Model Driven Interoperability

Solving interoperability problems not only at the code level but also starting from a higher level of abstraction is a challenge that was one of the objectives proposed by InterOP NoE, and more precisely by Task Group 2 (TG2), in order to search for solutions to achieve interoperability following a model-driven approach.

The aim of TG2 has been to analyze and propose guidelines and methods that can help to solve the interoperability problems of *Enterprise Software Applications* (ESA) starting out from the enterprise models level and using an approach based on *Model Driven Architecture* (MDA) [3]. This method is called *Model Driven Interoperability* (MDI) [4]. The work of TG2 first focused on the models and transformations to be performed at the *Computation Independent Model* (CIM) level from the theoretical point of view. At this level the GRAI method was chosen as means to capture the enterprise models at the highest level of abstraction and BPMN (for business process view) and UML (business data view) were selected to play an interface role between enterprise models and IT models. To address the feasibility of its proposal, TG2 has tested it with transformation tools [4].

2.2 BPMN 2.0

BPMN is an OMG specification providing a notation for modeling business processes. The initial objective of BPMN was to give a picture of the business processes that can be shared between the different stakeholders, and that can be transformed in an execution language in order to be executed (on a workflow tool or using an ESB orchestration tool for example). It can be used by the business analysts who create the initial drafts of the processes, by the technical developers in charge of the implementation of the technology that will perform those processes, and finally, by the business people who will manage and monitor those processes.

The new version, BPMN2.0 which adoption is planned by end of June 2010, proposes numerous improvements of the previous version among them:

- Of course, the resolution of previous version's inconsistencies and ambiguities;
- A better formalization of the execution semantics for all BPMN elements;

[8] http://www.petalslink.com/societe/societe-metiers

- A mapping of a subset of BPMN model to an execution language of BPM Systems (WS-BPEL 2.0);
- A definition of new diagrams: Conversation Diagram, Choreography Diagram...

These two last points are very important evolution in the framework of a SOA-based development. Indeed private and public processes are useful to give the specification of what is visible or not from other participants. Moreover a Conversation Diagram which provides a "bird's eye" perspective is composed of a set of pools, represented as "black" boxes, exchanging messages grouped into a Conversation. A Conversation will ultimately be executed through an orchestration Process. In contrast to orchestration Choreography Diagram provides a multi-party perspective of a Conversation and therefore it focuses rather on information exchange (Messages) between participants. It makes it possible to derive the Process interfaces of each participant's process. As it will be presented in the following sections, a choreography Diagram gives a well adapted specification of what will be executed within an ESB orchestration engine.

2.3 Service Oriented Architecture

Service oriented architecture (SOA) is a way of organizing and understanding organizations, communities and systems to maximize agility and scale, it is also seen as an enabling factor for enterprise interoperability. SOA is not a technology nor a software solution but an architectural and organizational approach. The choice of technologies and tools is secondary [5].

Service oriented architecture is a paradigm that utilizes services as fundamental elements to develop applications [6], it place the service concept as the primary mean to achieve enterprise strategic objectives [7]. Not only Service is considered as the unit construction of system, but also each service is reusable, shared and loosely-coupled with the other services.

From the technical perspective SOA services can be considered as "functions" that are accessible across a network via well-defined interface and to implement technical services we need an SOA integration platform.

2.4 SOA Integration Platform: ESB

Integration platform must allow an independent mechanism to integrate disparate systems to ASICOM. SOA integration platform is the technical part of SOA that enable interoperability. Thus it must provide the capability to mediate, transform, route and transport service request from the service consumer to the service provider.

The application integration concept is nothing new. We have been dealing with this mechanism since we have had to connect more than two business systems. Several technical solutions have been proposed to address the problem of integration: *Extract Transform Load* (ETL), Middleware, *Enterprise Application Integration* (EAI), *Enterprise Service Bus* (ESB. The ASICOM platform must allow several participants with different ITs to communicate with each others. But traditional middleware provides only a point-to-point solution between systems.

ETLs are used to integrate data from multiple sources and integrating this data into a central warehouse. These tools are not a real time process; They operate in a Batch mode, so they are not adapted to our needs. Moreover they don't support the mechanisms used to manipulate services (example: orchestration, etc.).

EAI reached its peak in the 1990s [8]. This technology was a response to the demand of enterprises that need to share their data and process without having sweeping changes to their applications and data. With EAI all integration is done in a hub, for each system it is enough to provide and maintain only one adapter to the hub instead of a specific adapter for each of the systems with which it communicates [9]. The downside of EAI is twofold. First EAIs products are proprietary and expensive. Second they are not based around standards.

An ESB is an architectural pattern of middleware that enable standards-based integration between applications and services. It's provides a broad set of capabilities. Firstly it's decoupling the interactions between the customers and the providers: services are accessible independently of implementation and location, they may be accessed by the service consumer in the same way. Secondly it's allows services to be exposed consistently across multiple communication protocols like *Simple Object Access Protocol* (SOAP)[9], *Simple Mail Transfer Protocol* (SMTP) [10], etc. Other functionalities are supported through the ESB such as transformation with XSLT[10], routing and security.

3 Application to ASICOM

Several service composition approaches have been proposed to address the problem of interoperability but none of them cover all the aspects of the interoperability. The majority of the approaches mainly focuses on the services and processes design. A major business opportunity and research challenge is to delivering executable services from models to the end-users [2].

In this section we combine the benefits of different approaches (Praxem Institute[11], SOMA[12]) to provide a method with a collection of comprehensive techniques for the model driven engineering of service-oriented landscapes. The ASICOM project focuses more precisely on relations with Customs to facilitate procedures such as on-line clearance of goods, payment of customs duty, and management of bonded warehouses…

3.1 ASICOM Model from BPMN 1.2 and BPMN2.0

The example we introduce describes the process of discharging the end of the Community transit procedure used for external Community transit document named *T1*[13]. The process is triggered by the goods arrival at the stockist (See figure 1).

In this orchestration the central process (ASICOM process) takes control of the involved partners and coordinates the execution of different operations. The involved partners do not need to know that they are taking part in a higher level business process. Only the central coordinator of the orchestration is aware of this goal.

---

[9] http://www.w3.org/TR/2000/NOTE-SOAP-20000508/

[10] http://www.w3.org/TR/xslt

[11] http://www.praxeme.org/DocumentsGeneraux/Praxime-LivreBlanc_v2.SLB02.pdf

[12] http://www.ibm.com/developerworks/library/ws-soa-design1

[13] http://ec.europa.eu/taxation_customs/resources/documents/customs/procedural_aspects/transit/common_community/transit_manual_en.pdf

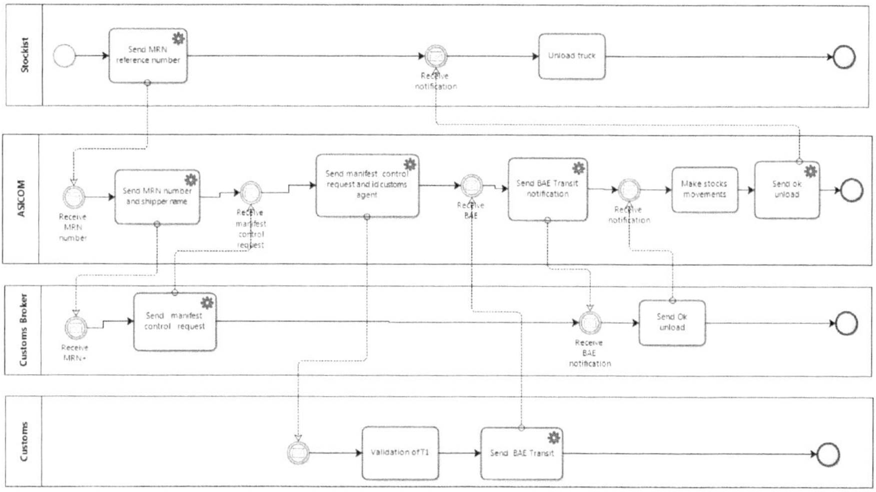

Fig. 1. Discharge T1 when goods arrive to the stockist orchestration diagram (BPMN 1.2)

Among its new features, BPMN 2.0 introduces choreography diagrams. Choreography process differs in purpose and behavior from an orchestration process. It focuses only on the exchange of information between the Participants (figure 2).

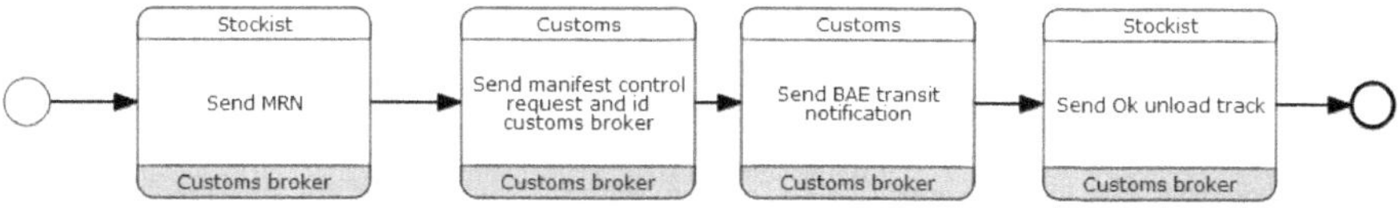

Fig. 2. Discharge T1 when goods arrive to the stockist choreography diagram (BPMN 2.0)

3.2 Deployment onto Petals ESB

BPMN specifications explicitly suggest BPEL to be used for the execution of business process. So after the description of the BPMN we refine it with the implementation details using BPEL. Then we use the orchestrations diagram to create the BPEL process (The BPMN 2.0 specifications precise that implementation is not expected to support directly Choreography Modeling elements).

In this scenario partners are represented by Web services, which have been developed without any transformation. The BPEL Process receives a request from the stockist. To fulfill it, the process invokes the involved Web services of the customs broker and customs sequentially and then responds to the original caller (figure 3).

We have chosen an Enterprise Service Bus to support the ASICOM SOA infrastructure. ESBs are the latest Middleware technology so they well integrate the principles of SOA. They provide an infrastructure that removes the direct connection dependency between service consumers and providers. We have opted for Petals ESB, owned by the Petals Link open source SOA solutions provider.

Fig. 3. Discharge T1 when goods arrive to the stockist BPEL diagram

The BPEL process is packaged in a Service Assembly component and deployed into Petals ESB, which uses the BPEL Service Engine component to run the BPEL process. The figure 4 shows the target architecture of the ASICOM platform that supports the execution of business process.

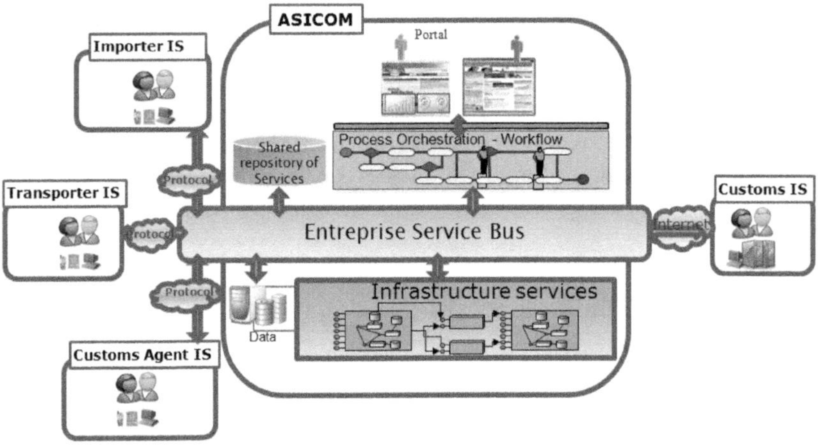

Fig. 4. ASICOM platform Architecture

4 Conclusion

The proposed method is a top-down realization of SOA based on a model driven approach. It uses BPMN at business level to describe the semantics of processes; then a mediation pool is added that can be transformed into a choreography diagram and that allows the highlighting of the partners services. Besides the BPMN process is refined with the implementation details using BPEL. And finally the BPEL is packaged and deployed as a BPEL Service Assembly on the Petals ESB. BPMN2.0 interest is to give more synthetic and so readable diagrams.

Our current works concern models transformations and the emerging standard SoaML [11] to support the activities of service modeling and the central aspects of SOA. SOA will be used to expose reusable services from the ASICOM infrastructure applications, and BPM technology will be used to consume those services by combining them together as steps in a business process. The proposed method is being currently implemented within the SMEs context of ASICOM and is not limited to SMEs nor to trade industry. We are also applying it within aeronautics domain to solve interoperability problems between a manufacturer and its subcontractors for the design of aircraft parts.

Acknowledgements. This work was partially funded by the ASICOM project. This project started in April 2008 was approved by two French poles of competitiveness: PICOM[14] in Trade Industries domain and Nov@log[15] in Logistics domain.

References

1. Tae-Young, K., Sunjae, L., Kwangsoo, K., Cheol-Han, K.: A modeling framework for agile and interoperable virtual enterprises. Comput. Ind. 57(3) (2006)
2. Rodrigo, M.P., Eduardo, S., Marten, V.S., Dick, A.C.Q., Luís, F.P.: Enterprise Interoperability with SOA: a Survey of Service Composition Approaches (2008)
3. OMG. : MDA Guide Version 1.0.1 (2003), http://www.omg.org/docs/omg/03-06-01.pdf
4. Bourey, J.-P., Grangel, R., Doumeingts, G., Berre, A.: INTEROP NoE: DTG2.2: Report on Model Interoperability (2006), http://interop-vlab.eu/ei_public_deliverables/interop-noe-deliverables/tg2-model-driven-interoperability
5. Marks, E., Bell, M.: Service-Oriented Architecture: A planning and Implementation Guide for Business and Technology, 375 p. Wiley Editions, Chichester (2006)
6. Kim, H.-k.: Modeling of Distributed Systems with SOA & MDA. IAENG International Journal of Computer Science, IJCS 35(4), 35-4-10 (2008), http://www.iaeng.org/IJCS/issues_v35/issue_4/IJCS_35_4_10.pdf
7. Eloudrhiri, S., Halin, P., Monti, V.: Urbanisation et SOA Vers une Entreprise Agile version 1, Centre de compétences TIC, Walloon Region, Belgium (2008)
8. Davies, J., Schorow, D., Ray, S., Rieber, D.: The Definitive Guide to SOA: Oracle Service Bus, 2nd edn. Apress (2008)
9. Josuttis, N.M.: Josuttis.: SOA in Practice the Art of Distributed System Design. O'Reilly, Sebastopol (2007)
10. Postel, J.B.: RFC821 - Simple Mail Transfer Protoco Information Sciences Institute University of Southern California 4676 Admiralty Way Marina del Rey, California 90291 (213), pp. 822–1511 (1982)
11. SoaML, Service oriented architecture Modeling Language (SoaML) – Specification for the UML Profile and Metamodel for Services (UPMS). Revised Submission, OMG document: ad/2008-11-01 (2008), http://www.omg.org/docs/ad/08-11-01.pdf

[14] http://www.picom.fr/

[15] http://www.novalog.eu/index.asp

Use of Ontology for Solving Interoperability Problems between Enterprises

Hui Liu[1,2], Anne-Françoise, Cutting-Decelle[1,2], and Jean-Pierre Bourey[1,2]

[1] Univ Lille Nord de France, F-59000 Lille, France
[2] LM2O, Ecole Centrale de Lille
Cité Scientifique – BP 48 – 59651 Villeneuve d'Ascq Cedex
{hui.liu,anne-francoise.cutting-decelle}@ec-lille.fr,
jean-pierre.bourey@ec-lille.fr

Abstract. When trying to solve interoperability problems between enterprises, the semantic issues are important. To date, they are more and more focused on ontology. This paper presents how to use ontology in the PBMEI method, aimed at solving enterprise interoperability problems in modelling environment. During the elaboration of PBMEI, the necessary ontology information is explicitly specified. Because of two different uses of ontologies, this paper proposes two variants of PBMEI. Finally, this paper concludes with the content of the ontologies required in PBMEI. The ontologies in the PBMEI method PBMEI for an application case are being studied.

Keywords: Ontology, collaborative process, interoperability process, transformation.

1 Introduction

How to bring together the distributed and heterogeneous information systems of enterprises and make them collaborate with each other to achieve a certain business objective is known as the enterprise interoperability [1] problem. To solve this kind of problem, data heterogeneity must be considered from two aspects: structural/schematic heterogeneity and semantic heterogeneity. Structural heterogeneity may be caused by type conflicts, labeling conflicts, aggregation conflicts, and generalization conflicts occurring in different databases/information systems [3]. This kind of heterogeneity can be solved by various techniques, such as XML, SOAP, EAI, ESB/SOA among others; semantic heterogeneity may come from naming conflicts, scaling and unit conflicts and confounding conflicts in different systems [3]. To overcome the problem of semantic heterogeneity, ontologies and semantics-based technologies can play a key role [4, 5]. How to use ontology in integration systems to achieve semantic interoperability is studied in [5] from four main criteria: role/architecture of ontology, ontology representation [8, 9], use of mapping [10] and ontology engineering [11], and furthermore in [7], semantic interoperability is discussed in more detail from the point of view of ontology mapping in three aspects: mapping discovery, mapping representation and reasoning with mapping. However all the above researches deal with the way of using ontology during the integration process, but how to use ontology in the modelling

L.M. Camarinha-Matos et al. (Eds.): PRO-VE 2010, IFIP AICT 336, pp. 730–737, 2010.

phase of an integration system, especially for enterprise interoperability remains a problem. This problem will be discussed here based on the method we proposed in [6].

The proposed method in [6] aims at solving the enterprise interoperability problem. It starts from modelling collaboration requirements between enterprises with collaborative process[1] and after several steps of transformation, it ends up with executable interoperability processes, such providing a method for the modelling environment. In [6], the use of ontology has not been discussed. This paper will discuss how to use ontology in our proposed method to solve enterprise interoperability problem.

So far the method proposed in [6] has been enhanced and it will be elaborated in Section 2. According to different uses of ontologies in our method, the proposed method has two variants, which are discussed in Section 3. Section 4 concludes with the content of ontologies.

2 Process-Based Method for Enterprise Interoperability

In order to solve enterprise interoperability problem, a "Process-Based Method for Enterprise Interoperability" (PBMEI) is proposed in the paper and illustrated in Fig. 1. In PBMEI, business requirements about enterprise interoperability are represented in collaborative processes among which the enterprises involved. Through the analysis of the development mode of information systems [15], the limitation of workflows [16] and the advantages of web services (WS) [17], our method focuses on service-related process specification languages to describe collaborative processes; for example BPMN [13]. The collaborative process will finally be achieved through interoperability processes which are described in executable process specification languages. Our method is process-based and it also makes relevant enterprises more responsive to changing collaboration requirements. PBMEI is described in detail in the following sections.

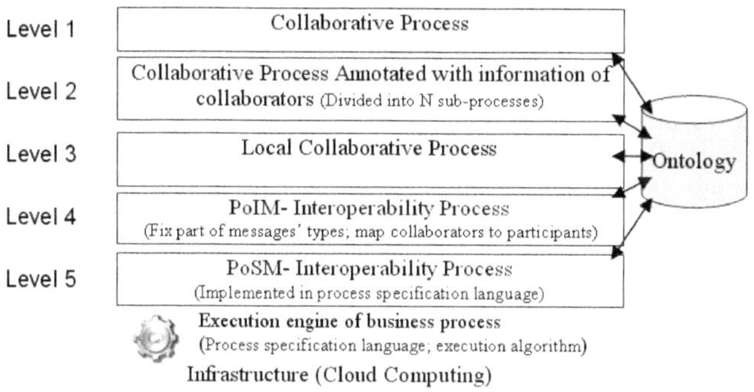

Fig. 1. Process-Based Method for Enterprise Interoperability

At the first level, collaborative process must be defined from two aspects: business flow and data/message flow, which is inspired by [2]. According to [2], US Army proposed an expansion of the system architecture into three further sub-architectures:

---

[1] The definitions about collaborative process, interoperability process, collaborator, participant, cooperator, internal process, coordination process, cooperation process can be found in [6].

software architecture, data architecture and network architecture. Software architecture defines the functionality of each module, data architecture is related to data definition, and network architecture is related to software deployment requirement. Furthermore, all business requirements must be mapped onto a certain system architecture to be implemented. The collaborative process is one kind of business requirements, so collaborative process must also be mapped onto the above three sub-architectures, that is to say a collaborative process must have some aspects that can be mapped onto the above three sub-architectures. However, the network sub-architecture is determined by concrete business requirements and related to the whole system, so this paper will consider this problem from the overall point of view, not in collaborative processes. Finally the collaborative process will be constructed from two aspects: functionality and data. The business flow describes the functionality of the collaborative process and the data flow describes the data exchanged in the process.

At the second level, the collaborative process will be annotated with collaborators' information, i.e., all the activities in the process must be charged by one collaborator. This task depends on an ontology. When searching the relevant collaborators for a certain activity, the ontology will be inspected to determine which collaborator can do such activity. If several candidates are selected, the target candidate will be selected according to the collaboration policy/requirements, or according to predefined conditions, such as QoS, trust rank/belief value etc. So the ontology must contain the necessary information about all the collaborators (for example, collaborator's name, historical information about service running, responsibility, etc). Once annotated with the information of collaborators, the collaborative process will be transformed into a set of collaborative sub-processes as long as it follows a given transformation method.

At the third level, the collaborative processes (including the generated collaborative sub-processes) will be transformed into local collaborative processes by each collaborator. During this transformation, the business terminologies will be transformed from global to local terminologies and the process specification language will also be transformed from global to local if necessary.

At the fourth level "PoIM" (**Pro**tocol **I**ndependent **M**odel), messages type in collaborative process must be determined according to messages context (messages sender and receiver, and relevant business context). Some messages type information may also be partially declared in the collaboration requirement. The above two cases of message type determination are ontology-based. This ontology must contain the definitions of business messages which have some context specifications.

After the determination of the type of messages, collaborators in a collaborative process will be mapped onto participants. The key of the mapping focuses on an activity functionality and context. After the mapping from collaborator to participant, the collaborator's information in the process must also be kept, since such information has a semantics that is not included in participants, for example, several roles of collaborators, whose semantics cannot be represented by the participant roles. The above tasks also rely on ontology. And because a participant is an element of the system architecture, the ontology must also contain the information about each collaborator's system architecture. At last, after messages' types are fixed and the mapping from collaborators to participants is done, collaborative processes become interoperability processes.

At the fifth level "PoSM" (**Pro**tocol **S**pecific **M**odel), the interoperability process will be implemented in an executable process specification language, and all the message transport protocols will be explicitly specified.

According to this description, PBMEI closely depends on ontology and SOA and it also has one precondition: interoperability process totally depends on the original functions of each collaborator's information system. Of course PBMEI also relies on the process execution engine and a given infrastructure, such as cloud computing infrastructure [18, 19].

3 Two Variants of PBMEI

In [6], collaborative business processes are divided into three types: internal process, coordination process, and cooperation process. As internal process and coordination process can be easy to implement with the help of WS-Business Process Execution Language or workflow model, this paper focuses on cooperation process in PBMEI.

When using PBMEI to solve interoperability problems, the first problem we meet is the following: who will create the cooperation process and in which style? In practice, if there is a core cooperator, the cooperation (collaborative) process is created by the core cooperator who will not negotiate with any other cooperator; if there is no core cooperator, the cooperation (collaborative) process is created through the negotiation of all the cooperators. When applying PBMEI to the above two cases, two variants of PBMEI are generated -- they are described below.

3.1 Process-Based Method for Collaboration without Core Cooperator

If the collaborative process has no core cooperator, PBMEI becomes the following variant, see Fig. 2. The first and second levels and the transformation between them are global and depend on the global ontology; the third, fourth and fifth levels and the transformations related to them are done locally by each separate collaborator, depending on the local ontology. Once all the collaborators have generated their own interoperability process, they can execute it through an identical execution algorithm.

The global ontology is created, managed and accessed by all cooperators, and it includes the common sense necessary when the collaborators negotiate with each other to create a collaborative process. The global ontology will also provide the syntax and the semantics of the collaborative processes. The business expressions of all elements of a collaborative process must also respect the definitions in the global ontology. The global ontology must also contain the collaborators' information needed when the collaborative process is annotated.

Each cooperator creates and manages its own local ontology which can be accessed by the other cooperators under a certain condition. The local ontology contains all the information about the enterprise architecture for a corresponding collaborator. It includes three basic ontologies: business ontology, model ontology and network ontology. Business ontology contains all the terminology related to local business requirements. Model ontology contains all the models (architecture models and data models) corresponding to the different software development phases. Network ontology contains the information about software deployment.

Of course, there must be mappings between the global ontology and the local ontologies for all collaborators and such mappings will be used by each collaborator to transform the collaborative process into their own collaborative process. The mapping between the global and local ontology will be stored and maintained in the corresponding local ontology for each cooperator.

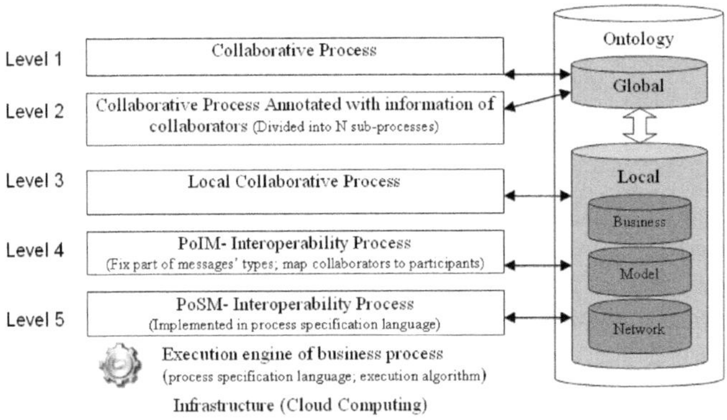

Fig. 2. Process-Based method for collaboration without core cooperator

3.2 Process-Based Method for Collaboration with Core Cooperator

If a collaborative process in PBMEI has a core cooperator, once the core cooperator generates the process, it transforms the process into executable interoperability processes and then deliver them to its collaborators. The other collaborators will then transform the received processes into processes which are expressed in their own languages and based on their own local ontologies.

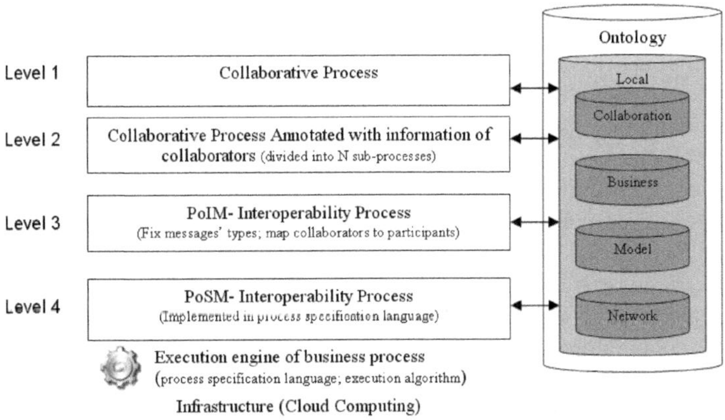

Fig. 3. Process-Based method for collaboration with core cooperator

Since the collaborative process is created by the core cooperator, the process is only based on the core collaborator's local ontology, and there is no need to transform the global collaborative process into local collaborative process: this is why the variant depicted in Fig. 3 does not have the level "Local collaborative process".

Note that besides the business ontology, model ontology and network ontology, the ontology of the core cooperator also contains the collaboration ontology which offers information about the other collaborators and their services.

4 Content of the Ontologies in PBMEI

As Section 2 proposes suggestions about the content of the ontologies in PBMEI, and Section 3 provides the categories of ontologies in PBMEI, this section will present the content of each ontology: see Table 1. Fig. 4 shows an example of the global ontology in PBMEI, as created using Protégé v3.4.3[20].

Table 1 shows mappings between global/collaboration ontology and business ontology, between business and model ontology and between model and network ontology. These mappings must be maintained and managed and they will be used during the transformation of business processes. The above mappings between ontologies of

Table 1. Content and mapping of ontologies in PBMEI

Ontology		Content	Mapping
Global		• information about all the collaborators: name, business roles, and postal address, email address, network address, offered business services, published web services and related statistical information about their offered services (e.g., QoS, trust rank), etc • common business object model • specification language for collaborative processes and business policies • collaborative process, collaboration policies	
Local	Collaboration	• information about all the collaborators: name, business roles, and postal address, email address, network address, offered business services, published web services and related statistical information about their offered services (e.g., QoS, trust rank), etc • information about services published by other collaborators • collaborative process, collaboration policies	
	Business	• all business concepts in its own domain and relationships • local business policies • local collaborative process • organizational information	Mapping to/ from global ontology; Mapping to model ontology;
	Model	• formal descriptions of business concepts, their relationships • formal descriptions of business rules and technical rules • formal descriptions at different levels about the architecture of an enterprise information system • formal descriptions about all physical components of enterprise software systems • Interoperability processes at "PoIM" and "PoSM" levels	Mapping to business ontology; Mapping to network ontology;
	Network	• deployment information of all software components in an enterprise information system	Mapping to model ontology

a collaborator are vertical, but there are also the horizontal mappings between ontologies of different collaborators, and such mappings will be used in the second variant of PBMEI, which will be presented in another paper.

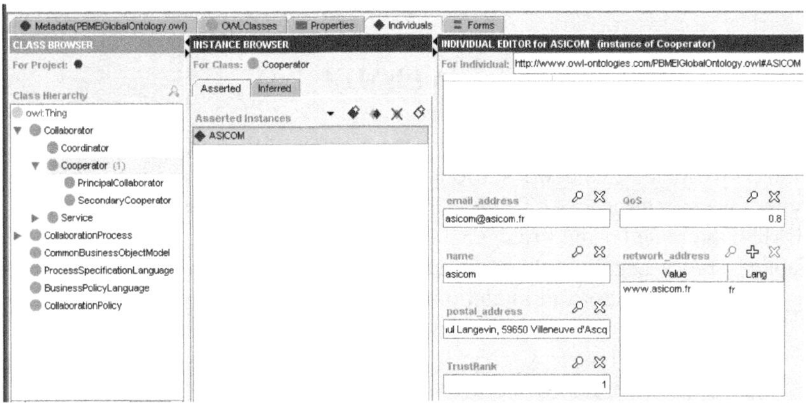

Fig. 4. Example of the Global Ontology in PBMEI

According to Table 1, the ontology contains information about collaboration, business, model and deployment. In fact, the data storage in the ontology can be real or virtual. This means that data can be directly stored in the ontology, or they can also be stored in remote professional servers : in that case the ontology only stores the ontology-based description of remote data, for example, business rules can be stored in Business Rule Management System (BRMS) [14]. Theontology only contains ontology-based description of business rules.

5 Conclusion

This paper presents some initial developments about the PBMEI method which uses ontology in modelling environment to solve enterprise interoperability problems. This method also makes collaborators in collaborative process easily adaptable to collaboration requirement changes. After analyzing the dependent information in PBMEI and its two variants, the global ontology, local ontology, business ontology, model ontology and network ontology are introduced and a first overview of their contents is proposed, thus building the foundation for further research on the way of using PBMEI in a concrete application case.

The proposed PBMEI method is ontology-based, process-based and model-driven [12] and it is also ontology-language-independent. However there are still many research points to be done in the future, for example, how to validate whether a collaborative process is based on a designated ontology or how to support process transformation according to horizontal ontology mappings between collaborators.

References

1. Chen, D., Doumeingts, G.: European Initiatives to develop interoperability of enterprise applications - basic concepts, framework and roadmap. Journal of Annual reviews in Control 27(3), 151–160 (2003)
2. Hamilton, J.A.: A practical application of enterprise architecture for interoperability. In: ISE 2003 (2003) ISBN: 1-56555-270-9
3. Goh, C.H.: Representing and Reasoning about Semantic Conflicts in Heterogeneous Information Sources. Phd, MIT (1997)
4. Uschold, M., Grüninger, M.: Ontologies and semantics for seamless connectivity. SIGMOD Record 33(3) (2004)
5. Wache, H.: Ontology-Based integration of information, a survey of existing approaches. In: Workshop on ontologies and information sharing, IJCAI (2001)
6. Liu, H., Bourey, J.-P.: Transformation from a Collaborative Process to Multiple Interoperability Processes. In: I-ESA Conference, Coventry (2010)
7. Noy, N.: Semantic Integration: A Survey of Ontology-based Approaches. Sigmod Record, Special Issue on Semantic Integration (2004)
8. Corcho, O., Gómez-Pérez, A.: Evaluating knowledge representation and reasoning capabilities of ontology specification languages. In: Proceedings of the ECAI 2000 Workshop on Applications of Ontologies and Problem-Solving Methods, Berlin (2000)
9. Horrocks, I., Patel-Schneider, P.F., van Harmelen, F.: From SHIQ and RDF to OWL: The Making of a Web Ontology Language. J. of Web Semantics 1(1), 7–26 (2003)
10. Kalfoglou, Y., Schorlemmer, M.: Ontology mapping: the state of the art. The Knowledge Engineering Review 18(1), 1–31 (2003)
11. Gómez-Pérez, A., Fernández-López, M., Corcho, O.: Ontological Engineering. Springer, Berlin (2004)
12. Bourey, J.-P., Grangel Seguer, R., Doumeingts, G., Berre, A.-J.: Deliverable DTG2.3 Report on Model-Driven Interoperability (2007), `http://interop-vlab.eu/ei_public_deliverables/interop-noe-deliverables/dap-domain-architecture-and-platforms/D91/`
13. OMG:Business Process Model and Notation (2009), `http://www.omg.org/spec/BPMN/1.2/`
14. Graham, I.: Service Oriented Business Rules Management Systems (2005), `http://www.trireme.com/whitepapers/Business%20rules/Trireme_Report_Service_Oriented_Business_Rules_Management_Systems_Ver2b.pdf`
15. Dumas, M., van der Aalst, W.M.P., ter Hofstede, A.H.M.: Process-Aware Information Systems: Bridging People and Software through Process Technology. Wiley & Sons, Chichester (2005)
16. van der Aalst, W.M.P., Benatallah, B., Casati, F., Curbera, F., Verbeek, E.: Business process management: Where business processes and web services meet. Data Knowl. Eng. 61(1), 1–5 (2007)
17. Alonso, G., Casati, F., Kuno, H., Machiraju, V.: Web Services Concepts, Architectures and Applications. Springer, Berlin (2004)
18. Chappell, D.: Introducing the Azure services platform. DavidChappell & Associates (2008), `http://download.microsoft.com/download/e/4/3/e43bb484-3b52-4fa8-a9f9-ec60a32954bc/Azure_Services_Platform.docx`
19. Rimal, B.P., Choi, E., Lumb, I.: A Taxonomy and Survey of Cloud Computing Systems. In: Fifth International Joint Conference on INC, IMS and IDC 2009, NCM 2009, pp. 44–51, 25–27 (2009)
20. Protégé, `http://protege.stanford.edu/`

Building an Informal Ontology to Support Collaborative Network Operation: A Case Study

Carla Pereira[1,2], Cristóvão Sousa[1,2], and António Lucas Soares[1,3]

[1] INESC Porto, Campus da FEUP, Rua Dr. Roberto Frias, 378, 4200-465 Porto, Portugal
[2] DEI, FEUP, University of Porto, Rua Dr. Roberto Frias, sn 4200-465 Porto, Portugal
[3] ESTGF-IPP, Apartado 205 4610 - 156 Felgueiras, Portugal
csp@inescporto.pt, cpsousa@inescporto.pt, asoares@inescporto.pt

Abstract. Looking at collaborative networks of organizations as social-technical systems, information and knowledge sharing implies sharing a set of common conceptual structures across organizations. Through this paper, we describe a case study on how to construct meaningful collective conceptualizations by means of a new approach based on conceptual blending theory.

Keywords: conceptualization, ontology development, meaning construction, collaborative networks.

1 Introduction

The early phases of setting up information and knowledge management architectures for inter-organizational teams (e.g., large scale international R&D or systems engineering projects) are complex and problematic mainly due to the actor's heterogeneous professional and cultural backgrounds. The big challenge stands on the proper definition, in short-term, of the concepts and relations, which are the basis of the information and knowledge architecture to be common to the collaborative network. Like this, considering a common conceptualization of a given reality as the cornerstone for information and knowledge sharing among a network of social actors, the core problem is how to create suitable socio-technical tools to support the collaborative process of creating semantic artifacts to be operationalized in some short-term business opportunity.

Sharing information and knowledge implies sharing a set of conceptual structures between network partners. They need to negotiate a common vocabulary, meaning of concepts and their relations, to develop the information organization system. The problems raised by information and knowledge sharing in the context of collaborative networks have been researched in the last decade (and is still being researched) in the so-called Ontology Engineering community. After a deep analysis of the state-of-the-art in this area one can conclude that the current underpinnings of ontology engineering are not enough for the future challenges of building semantic artifacts, i.e., the current underpinnings of ontology engineering do not give an appropriate answer to the new challenges raised by the every time larger need of collective construction of meaning. Even though the most used definition of ontology [1] "An ontology is a formal, explicit

L.M. Camarinha-Matos et al. (Eds.): PRO-VE 2010, IFIP AICT 336, pp. 738–745, 2010.

specification of a shared conceptualization", underlines the collaborative construction of conceptualizations in the scientific context, it is established that: "While different degrees of formalizations have been well investigated and are now found in various ontology-based technologies, the notion of a shared conceptualization is neither well-explored, nor well-understood, nor well-supported by most ontology engineering tools" [2]. Our view is that ontology engineering needs a "socio-cognitive turn" in order to generate tools that are really effective in copying the complex, unstructured, and highly situational contexts that characterize a great deal of information and knowledge sharing in businesses collaboration. This line of research is therefore directed towards the application of cognitive semantic results in the creation of artifacts acting as socio-technical devices supporting the view that meaning socially constructed through collaboration and negotiation. The first line of this research work deals with the application and extension of the Conceptual Blending Theory (CBT) [3] to the realm of collaborative semantic tools. The practical application of our approach is to support the co-construction of semantic artifacts by groups of social actors placed in organizational contexts interacting towards a set of common objectives. We propose a new method to support de collaborative construction of semantic artifacts with special focus in the initial phase of the process, the conceptualization phase (to obtain a detailed description of the CBT based method, see [4, 5]).

In this paper, are described the usage of the method in the scope of a large European project, AC/DC[1], showing the main results and lessons learnt with this case study.

2 Application Case: Building a Project Informal Ontology

This experiment was carried out within a trans-national (European) project, AC+DC project, in the area of industrial (automotive) engineering. In this project, a consortium of major European car manufacturers, suppliers, and research institutes develop the "dynamic supply chain collaboration" concept that changes the conventional automotive terms of delivery to a highly reactive "5-Day-capable" system that radically cuts down inventories in the supply network. This is a huge and complex project, as it involves 19 partners, from 7 countries and 9 tasks grouped in 3 work packages. One of the work packages aims at building an ontology to be used in several tasks of the project. The general goal of the AC+DC ontology is to facilitate a common and precise understanding of the concepts used by all partners in the several project activities. The resulting common vocabulary should match standardized terms of automotive production domain and the particular concepts on development in the project. The ontology development task started initially without a supporting methodology or even a clear vision of the ontology goals and scope. Without the concern of clarifying the general goal of the ontology, and without discussion of this with the partners, began its development. The first obstacle comes at this very early stage, where to start and how to start? The first version of the ontology was presented. Comprised data models which included concepts, relations, properties and data types. Basically, the first version was based on a software application data model related to the planning and

[1] http://www.acdc-project.org/public/

production scheduling. The terms contained in the above example, were made available to other members in the form of a "Protégé Project". This version came out from expert domain partners with lack of knowledge in the development of ontologies. They were not aware about the real purpose of "Protégé", as well as its limitations and capabilities. Therefore, the result was not as it was intended initially. Moreover, when creating the ontology, the process itself was lame and neither truly collaborative nor guided by basic collaborative rules, essential to support the process. The Protégé files were exchanged by e-mail to all partners, which, by their turn, could reply some comments on the ontology. The participation was weak; probably due the lack of knowledge of the Protégé software and its associated notation, which constituted a barrier, making the process, move forward without the contributions of all.

Within this context, the authors took the opportunity to set-up an action-research project aiming at, from the one side, to help the project to develop its ontology and, on the other side, to create knowledge about the collaborative construction of ontologies by designing and undertaking a set of experiments. From the preliminary analysis of the problem, jointly with the project team, the following general requirements were derived: (1) the goals and scope of the ontology should be clearly stated, even if not completely detailed; this is of utmost importance to guide the conceptualization process; (2) there is a clear need for a method and tools to support the conceptualization process; only with such a support a collaborative process is feasible; (3) There is a need to use tools and techniques that can be used by all involved regardless of their training. Initially the emphasis should not be in formal aspects related to the ontology codification. The concern should focus on the informal knowledge representation that will constitute the ontology; and (4) the possibility of reusing other ontologies should be evaluated. For example, the analysis of models created in the project ILIPT[2] shows that the results can be used to prepare the initial proposal for a shared conceptualization.

Hereupon, the authors attempted to see whether it would be possible to reuse existing ontologies in supply chain management domains. From the studied ontologies, [8] and [9] were based on SCOR model; others such as [13] are focused inside organizations but not among them; and The United Nations Standard Products and Services Code which provides an open, global multi-sector standard for efficient, accurate classification of products and services. These ontologies cover very specific subdomains making them difficult to reuse. There are also several upper-level ontologies which are too abstract to be applied in particular situations. Since collaboration concepts behind supply chains and their requirements could be fundamentally different, there is no standard ontology, which would be detailed enough to be applicable in every practical case.

In this experimental phase four tools were used to support the collaborative conceptualization process. For the joint construction of a conceptual representation, Concept Maps supported by CmapTools[3] and Semantic Media Wiki[4](SMW) were used. CmapTools was used essentially to support the frame definition, preliminary proposal and input spaces creation [4, 5]. The blend services and negotiation process was assured by SMW. An integration service between CmapTools and SMW was developed

[2] http://www.ilipt.org/public/

[3] http://CMAP.ihmc.us/conceptmap.html

[4] http://semantic-mediawiki.org/wiki/Semantic_MediaWiki

allowing the discussion of input spaces and the annotation of concepts within each input space, gathering information to run the blend. To support the blend spaces creation, together with CmapTools features and SMW, the text mining tool, TermExtractor[5], capable to extract relevant terms in the interest domain, by submitting an archive of domain-related documents in any format was used. IATE was used, occasionally, to search for the correct correspondent terms chosen to name a concept, in several languages, according to a specific domain.

The application case scenario was identified and some preliminary studies made, leading to the following experiment context: Four teams from four different organizations (geographically dispersed) participated in the domain conceptualization. Two of those teams (Team1 and Team2), from two different organizations (Org1 and Org2), were domain experts from academic and professional areas respectively; another team (Team3) from another organization (Org3) was composed by experts in information and knowledge management and in collaborative networks; the fourth team (Team4) from another organization (Org4), beyond their academic expertise in the specific domain, has a reasonable understanding about ontologies. The experiment started to be more formally structure, firstly by establishing the roles of each actor: 1) Contributor: all team members should play this role contributing for the improvement and enlargement of the current version of the AC+DC conceptualization. The contributor responsibilities are to make inputs to the shared conceptualization by proposing and discussing concepts and relationships; 2) Facilitator: responsible by facilitating the discussion/negotiation around the conceptualization. Teams 2, 3 and 4 were assigned the role of contributor; team 1 was assigned the role of facilitator. The first step, the context frame definition, was accomplished in the initial formal meeting and helped to define the context, goal and mission of the ontology development task, as well as the scope and boundaries of the conceptualization. It was then decided that initially the ontology would contribute to a common understanding of the concepts used and needed by all partners in the various project activities, their goals may be expanded in the next iterations of the process. Thus, considering the original purpose it was decided that the ontology should in the first instance, reorganize itself around the main concept in developing the project, "Dynamic Supply Loops" (DSL), this being his main focus. Along with the capture, organization and justification for each term inherent to DSL, it would be necessary to identify concepts, common in the automotive production field and supply chain management, to be able to explain and contextualize the new concepts. With the main focus in the dynamic supply chain collaboration concept, more precisely in the DSL concepts, the team created an initial shared conceptualization guided by the following focus question: "what processes, activities and information are involved in the DSL network planning model, allowing collaboration in entire supply chain in feedback loops?" The resulting conceptualization was presented in a concept map, defining the scope and boundaries of the conceptualization process, i.e., this result together with the goals initially defined for the ontology constituted the "context frame". Afterwards, the conceptualization of the several process and activities was initiated, which means detailing the DSL. The first process to be treated was the "Production Planning Process". After the construction of the first concept map (the preliminary proposal, see figure 1), an object was created in SMW in

[5] http://lcl2.uniroma1.it/TermExtractor

order to aggregate ideas and propositions about the Production Planning Process. Thus, all the teams in the project were able to extend the first shared domain conceptualization, contributing with their own inputs (changes that were made in the input spaces (on CmapTools or SMW) and which were published. All members could see the other member's inputs. The creation of new inputs by each team's domain expertise come from the results from TermExtractor tool document analysis, other documents produced by the several project work packages, the logistics area of SAP dictionary[6], the terms and glossary about supply chain management proposed by [10] and, most important of all, by the conceptual structures identification in the experts mind when they interact with the other member's proposals.

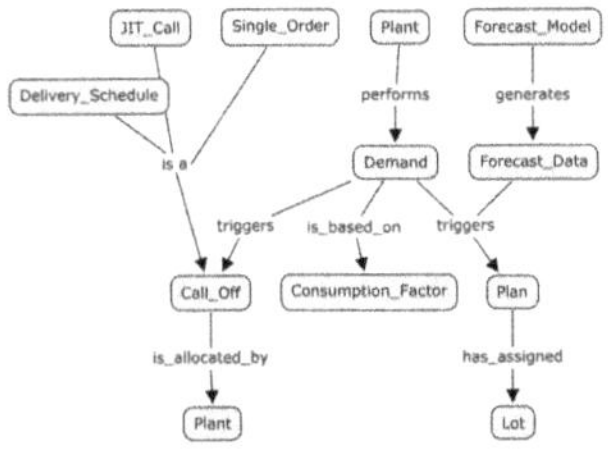

Preliminary proposal (Production Planning Process)

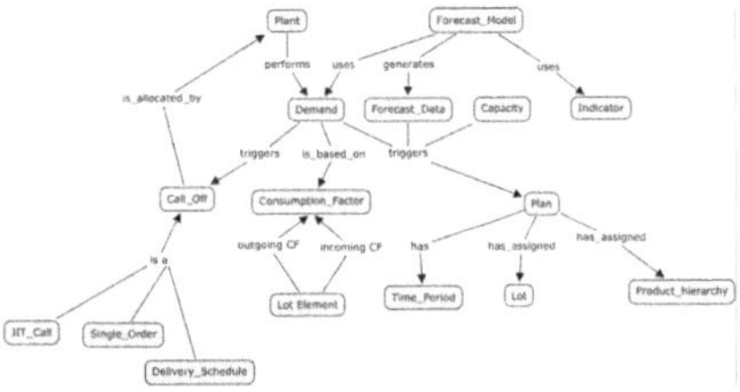

Partner conceptualization proposal (example of an input space)

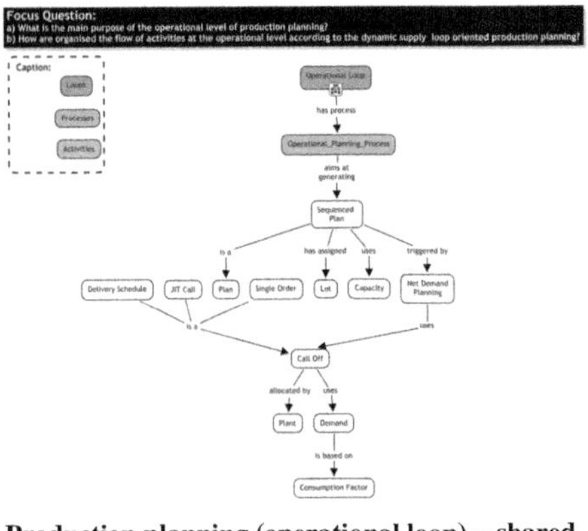

Production planning (operational loop) – shared conceptualization

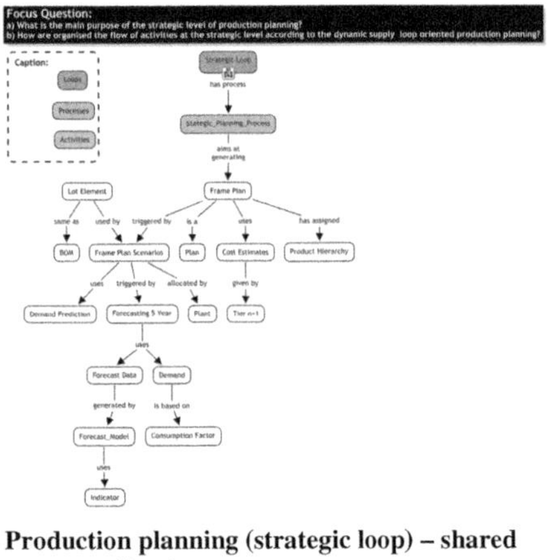

Production planning (strategic loop) – shared conceptualization

Fig. 1. Excerpt of the concept maps created during the collaborative conceptualization process

The discussion is initiated using the functionalities of SMW. Following the end of a discussion, the approved (consensual) concepts, can be imported directly to the CmapTools Client instance of each organization, updating the personal map in focus. An excerpt of the final shared conceptualization achieved is presented in figure 1.

[6] http://help.sap.com/saphelp_46c/helpdata/En/35/2cd77bd7705394e10000009b387c12/frameset.htm

Technically, all this process is supported by the CmapTools and Semantic Media Wiki. CmapTools aggregates in the server all the input spaces, therefore users are able to publish them in SMW. With TermExtractor the enrichment of the current conceptualization by the discovery of new terms and the supported validation of the existing ones was achieved. All the input spaces have the same conceptual structure and the person in charge for coordinating the process performs the upload of the final (consensual) map into the server. The concept maps present in the CmapServer, comprise the generic space.

2.1 Main Observations and Recommendations

The trend towards the development of formal models early in the process, it is confirmed to be a bad principle, leading to poor results and demanding an excessive concern by the participants with the formal semantics restrictions (e.g., starting development using tools such as Protégé). At the beginning, becomes essential for participants to be focused on the task of building the conceptual model in an environment without constraints, trying to express they knowledge about the domain. The lack of prior analysis and knowledge of methods and tools to support the collaborative construction of a conceptualization, result in an inadequate selection of them. For example, the type of players in the process, knowledge areas and technologies and techniques proposed, are factors that may be decisive for the success of the overall process. There was a high receptiveness regarding the use of concept maps as visual representation technique. This experience showed that conceptual maps are a suitable tool to be used during the collaborative conceptualization process, because in this phase "completeness is more important neatness and rigor" [11]. From our observation and from the interviews, we concluded that discussing the problem using a domain-specific vocabulary supported by a visually oriented, easy to use, informal tool, effective results could be achieved in a relatively short time. Our goal is to allow that the users could start informally, the construction of a (non-computational) "knowledge base" without having to commit to a particular knowledge representation, and without having to translate their know-how into any particular knowledge representation format. After the informal knowledge is built up, its structure may become more obvious. Thus, users could then begin to gradually coerce the concept maps to conform to the formal semantic system.

In the following paragraph we share some lessons learnt with this experiment. (1) *Initial social and cultural analysis:* the social and cultural analysis of the various partners, although brief, is necessary to design the process. For example, the decision by a process with rules and procedures more or less rigid may depend on the type and number of players in the process; (2) *Appropriate definition of the context frame and road map*: The starting point of this case study shows clearly the importance of these tasks. After the initial definition of the context frame and road map, is equally important that in the previous specified time periods, go backwards and review the following questions: What do we have? What do we want? and How to get there? These questions allow the team to evaluate the forces and weaknesses of current situation; (3) *Rules to organize the process and motivate the participation:* The evaluation showed that the majority of users were passive in their participation. Automatic notifications of all teams whenever changes exist, version control and definition of a time frame in which the proposals can be discussed are fundamental to better organize the process, and motivate the participants. Therefore, if no one present suggestions during the time period defined, it means that agreement exists. Every time there's a change in any discussion item within the process, users should be informed and invited to comment the new proposals. All these procedures must be agreed initially. Should be defined, also initially, a strategy that will lead the negotiation process. The use of workflow mechanisms allow us to manage the process and maintain the control of the various conceptualization proposals that are created. (4) *Always try to reduce the complexity of the process*: The collaborative process of conceptualization is really complex because of the high number of areas, processes and activities, among others. One way to deal with this is to follow some rules such as [12]; (5) *Project generated documentation as an enabler:* The continuous production of project documentation is a way to validate and improve the conceptualization. On the other hand, the consensual conceptual structure, agreed so far, should be used in the production of new deliverables in order to standardize the contents of each deliverable. By this reason it's easy to share and understand the meaning of the concepts in the domain; (6) *First version of the conceptualization*: the necessity of the preliminary proposal was identified in the first experiment. Even with only the high-level concepts, this first version proved to be, a good way to focus the discussion and guide the process; (7) *The existence of a negotiation space (blend space):* The existence of a blend space provided more reliability, collaboration and agility to the process of conceptualization. This was due to the fact that the inputs for blend were based on project produced documentation, as well as other important resources selected by the domain experts. This resulted in a high level of acceptance of the proposals. (8) *Carefully selection of the information resources used as inputs in the blend space:* The results obtained in the blend depend directly on the information sources used. The blend results can be accepted with more or less support, according to the provided inputs during its creation.

The work performed under the project AC/DC triggered the attention of the remaining project partners, especially the leader, Continental Teves AG for the process and its benefits in creating semantic artifacts. Continental is a growing organization and recently acquired other companies. One of the biggest challenges that Continental has faced has been the implementation of their processes and knowledge sharing associated with the operationalization of them. Continental faced this process based on concept maps as a simple way to provide information about their processes and for sharing how they are to be implemented. The technological framework (SemSys4CCM platform, presented in [4]) inherent to the experience carried out under this project, also served as a inspiration for Continental to start its new approach to knowledge sharing, which reveals the satisfaction of the project leader with the procedures used during the informal ontology building.

3 Conclusions and Further Work

It is important to refer that the correct understanding of this paper implies the reading of [4, 5], the limitation on the number of pages required to leave the background some important issues, but already published and can be found in the mentioned papers. The approach advocated in this paper proposes a shift in the process of creation of semantic artifacts from a "semantic artifact engineering" perspective to an "actor-artifact co-evolution" one. Socio-semantics is the scientific umbrella to this approach, which is also inspired in cognitive semantics and networking social theories (see [6, 7]). The case studies accomplished allowed us to design the architecture of a collaborative environment architecture that will support all steps of the method (see [4]). Future work involves: (1) considering the conceptualization as a social process, to explore the socio-semantic framework aiming at specifying mechanisms to support the social activity involved in the shared meaning creation; (2) Apply social network analysis to study the influence of social relationships within the meaning negotiation process; (3) conclusion of the SemSys4CCM platform development; (4) Enrichment of the input spaces and blend space using knowledge of terminology and computational linguistic areas; and (5) extend the CBT based method to support the development of multilingual conceptualizations.

References

1. Gruber, T.R.: A Translation Approach to Portable Ontology Specifications. Knowledge Acquisition 5(2), 199–221 (1993)
2. Staab, S.: On understanding the collaborative construction of conceptualisations. In: International and Interdisciplinary Conference "Processing Text-Technological Resources" at the Center for Interdisciplinary Research, Bielefeld University, March 13-15 (2008)
3. Fauconnier, G., Turner, M.: Conceptual Integration Networks. Published in Cognitive Science 22(2), 133–187 (1998)
4. Pereira, C., Sousa, C., Soares, A.: A socio-semantic approach to collaborative domain conceptualization. In: Meersman, R., Herrero, P., Dillon, T. (eds.) OTM 2009 Workshops. LNCS, vol. 5872, pp. 524–533. Springer, Heidelberg (2009)
5. Pereira, C., Sousa, C., Soares, A.: Short-Term Semantic Consensus: Towards Agile Ontology Specification for Collaborative Networks. In: Leveraging Knowledge for Innovation in Collaborative Networks. IFIP Advances in Inf. and Com. Technology. Springer, Boston (2009)
6. Evans, V., Green, M.: Cognitive Linguistics: an introduction. Edinburgh University Press, Edinburgh (2006)
7. Cahier, J.-P., Zaher, L.H., Leboeuf, J.-P., Guittard, C.: Experimentation of a socially constructed "Topic Map" by the OSS community. In: Proc. of the IJCAI 2005 workshop on KMOM, Edimbourg (2005)
8. Ureten, S., Ilter, H.K.: Supply Chain Management Ontology: Towards an Ontology-Based SCM Model. In: Proc. of the Fourth Int. Logistics and Supply Chain Management Congress (2006)
9. Fayez, M., Rabelo, L., Mollaghasemi, M.: Ontologies for Supply Chain Simulation Modeling. In: Proc. of the 2005 Winter Simulation Conference (2005)
10. Vitasek, K.: Supply Chain Management, Terms and Glossary (2008)
11. Kremer, R.: Concept Mapping: Informal to Formal. Appeared in Proceedings of the International Conference on Conceptual Structures, University of Maryland (1994)
12. Gómez-Gauchía, H., et al.: Two-layered approach to knowledge representation using conceptual maps and description logics. In: Concept Maps: Theory, Methodology, Technology, Proc. of the First Int. Conf. on Concept Mapping (2004)
13. Maier, A., Schnurr, H.-P., Sure, Y.: Ontology-Based Information Integration in the Automotive Industry. In: Fensel, D., Sycara, K., Mylopoulos, J. (eds.) ISWC 2003. LNCS, vol. 2870, pp. 897–912. Springer, Heidelberg (2003)

Towards Business Ontologies Matching for Inter-Enterprise Collaboration Platform in a Lean Manufacturing Strategy

Ahlem Zayati[1], Lilia Sidhom[2], Youakim Badr[3], Frédérique Biennier[3], and Mohamed Moalla[4]

[1] INSA de Lyon - Laboratoire LIESP - F69621 Villeurbanne Cédex, France & Faculté des Sciences de Tunis, Laboratoire LIP2
ahlem.zayati@insa-lyon.fr
[2] INSA de Lyon - Laboratoire AMPER - F69621 Villeurbanne Cédex, France
lilia.sidhom@insa-lyon.fr
[3] INSA de Lyon - Laboratoire LIESP - F69621 Villeurbanne Cédex, France
{frederique.biennier,youakim.badr}@insa-lyon.fr
[4] Faculté des Sciences de Tunis, Laboratoire LIP2, Tunisie
mohamed.moalla@fst.rnu.tn

Abstract. The Lean Manufacturing strategy aims at developing the enterprise value chain concept. The Lean makes extensive use of new organizational strategies such as business refocusing and development strategies for inter-enterprise collaboration. These reorganizations involve agility to deal with structural changes supported by communication technologies. However, the multiplicity of enterprise IT leads to complicate the inter-enterprise collaboration. However, the Services-Oriented Architecture provides flexibility and openness to enterprise Information System thanks to the "service" notion but fails to deal with business semantic mediation between partners involved in the collaboration. To meet these issues, this paper focuses on a semantic Enterprise Services Bus (ESB) which is a Service-Oriented Architecture middleware to define a business ontology-based matching and provide business and technological alignment to homogenize the information exchanged in the whole collaboration network. This paper also focuses on the technical implementation of the semantic ESB.

Keywords: Virtual Enterprise, Service Oriented Architecture (SOA), Enterprise Interoperability Business Ontologies & Industrial Service.

1 Introduction

The economic context evolution leads to extending supply chains and inter-enterprise collaboration strategies. It fosters the development a global value chain which transcends beyond individual organizations to be applied to the entire supply chains and collaborative networks. The Lean Manufacturing strategy involves the extensive use of new organizational strategies in addition to the business refocusing strategy. It proceeds from the customer demands and defines the enterprise value, and then it

L.M. Camarinha-Matos et al. (Eds.): PRO-VE 2010, IFIP AICT 336, pp. 746–754, 2010.

streamlines processes, eradicates wastefulness and improves enterprise interoperability [13]. The inter-enterprise collaborations involve agility and call for a coherent Information System (IS). However, advances in enterprise technologies tend to increase and lead to complicate the inter-enterprise collaboration. However, legacy enterprise IS is not consistent and presents a lack of interoperability. In this context, the Service-Oriented Architecture (SOA) deals with technical inconsistencies and provides flexibility and openness through the "service" notion. However SOA turns out to be a solution for ensuring a technological interoperability and fails deal with business semantic mediation between all the parts of the collaboration.

To meet these issues, we introduce a collaborative platform in order to create extended and global value chains. Therefore we propose to adopt the alignment between enterprise IS and its business strategy to ensure flexibility and reactivity. We particularly pay attention to ensure interoperability within the collaboration network at different levels namely conceptual, organizational and technological.

The remaining of the paper is organized as follow: In section 2, we present the context and the state of the art. Section 3 introduces our contribution and section 4 depicts the conclusion.

2 Context and State of the Art

An efficient economic activity aims at increasing production output and relying on optimal consumption of services and goods. It tends to use available resources to maximize the production by taking into account the cost factor [13]. To meet this issue, collaboration strategies emerge to provide flexibility of resources usage and production efficiency. In addition, the Lean Manufacturing strategy aims to extend the enterprise value chain to a global value of virtual enterprise [13]. It involves the emergence of an inter-enterprise collaboration strategy which is based on collaborative processes composed as dynamic choreography of services according to customer requirements. As result, inter-enterprise collaboration urges open, agile and interoperable information system. Some works introduce perspectives of inter-enterprise collaboration as "4C-model" [5] which provides a collective business processes and activities for collaborative context considering the capacities of resources, the product cost and the validity of distributed information. However the basis of a Lean strategy is to eliminate wastefulness. That is why this approach is not appropriated to such production strategy because authors don't emphasize the monitoring and supervision of production processes.

In general, the enterprise IS has to deal with the following interoperability levels [3]:

- **Business Level:** refers to the global enterprise organization harmonisation
- **Process Level:** concerns processes interaction according to the enterprise specific needs.
- **Service Level:** identifies, composes and creates common functions for enterprise applications taking into account semantic and syntactic aspects.
- **Data Level:** refers to data models in a collaborative work and a conceptual schema organization.

However, enterprise existent IS outlines some interoperability problems as outlined by [4]:

- **Conceptual problem** concerns semantic and syntactic presentation of high level information modelling.
- **Technological problem** is related to the inconsistency of information technologies.
- **Organizational problem** is associated to authority and responsibility definitions of work conditions.

To face the technological interoperability problem, the SOA implements IS components in a loosely coupled approach [7] in order to interconnect distributed IS components. The Enterprise Service Bus (ESB) is a SOA middleware which enables service integration and distributed communication services, and provides access to multiple heterogeneous applications [16]. The SOA can implement a collaborative platform but it fulfils only a syntactic mediation and improves technological interoperability. The ESB does not take into account semantic mediation and organizational interoperability. The ontology can deal with semantic mediation. It refers to the shared understanding of some domain of interest which may be used as a unifying framework to solve a semantic problem and provides a semantic interoperability when acting as a communication medium. The mediation part is used to process messages mechanism through the middleware and enables modifying, transforming, routing messages to be delivered according to some conditional logic in the mediation [6]. ARPA I3 architecture [11] can deal with semantic mediation. It distinguishes three interesting service classes among five: coordination services (discovery, invocation), semantic transformation services (ontology translation, process integration) and adaptation services (event managing, form conversion). ARPA I3 meets semantic mediation but does not emphasize business and monitoring services but does not consider organizational interoperability. To overcome this limit, one can consider the Enterprise Ontology (EO) and ISA S-95 to deal with organizational interoperability. First, the EO presents enterprise organization. Then, ISA S-95 standard depicts the product lifecycle when introducing production models and performance. It contains most of the general terms relating to an enterprise such as sales, activities, strategies and can serve as the basis for a shared understanding of an organization [12]. This ontology is conceptually divided into different sections as Meta-Ontology, Activities and Processes, Organization, Strategy and Marketing and presents a global view of the organization as well as an integration support which brings flexibility and coherent communication between different enterprise views [15]. ISA S-95 is the international standard for the integration of enterprise and control systems through the development of automated interfaces between enterprise and control systems [1] fitting mostly interfaces between enterprise and production control systems by specifying which information should be exchanged between ERP and MES systems. Therefore ISA S-95 can define pivot ontology. To overcome organizational interoperability problem, we purpose to take into account the Enterprise Ontology and ISA S-95 standard as pivot business ontologies. Therefore, we propose to develop ISA pivot ontology and then to match EO and ISA S-95. We mainly distinguish two matching mechanisms:

- **The elementary matching** can be performed as a non-logical matching based on text similarity measurement or path-length based similarity of concepts and as logical matching based on deductive approach
- **The hybrid** matching is a combination of logical and non-logical matching mechanism [2].

The YASA4WSDL matchmaker supports multiple ontologies to annotate semantically services. It relies upon elementary matching with exploiting a logic-based approach. It extends SAWSDL, a basic type of annotation (the model reference and the schema mapping) for enhancing expressiveness of service description. As seen previously different works are done in this interoperability field but they lack of interpreting the different levels. Our goal is to couple the business and technological levels to set a "Lean" middleware to support enterprise interoperability.

3 A Collaborative Platform Based on a Semantic ESB

The inter-enterprise collaboration has to take into account both business and technological interoperability constraints and requires an alignment between enterprise technologies and its business strategy to ensure flexibility and reactivity. Thus implies that the industrial and technological contexts have to be integrated in the organisation to support organisational and technological interoperability in the same time. This involves adding semantic annotation to capture the business related to knowledge and integrating them with the technological level. To fit this goal, we propose a Lean ESB (see Fig. 1) extending the classical ESB middleware with business semantic management to support inter-business area mediation and business alignment [14].

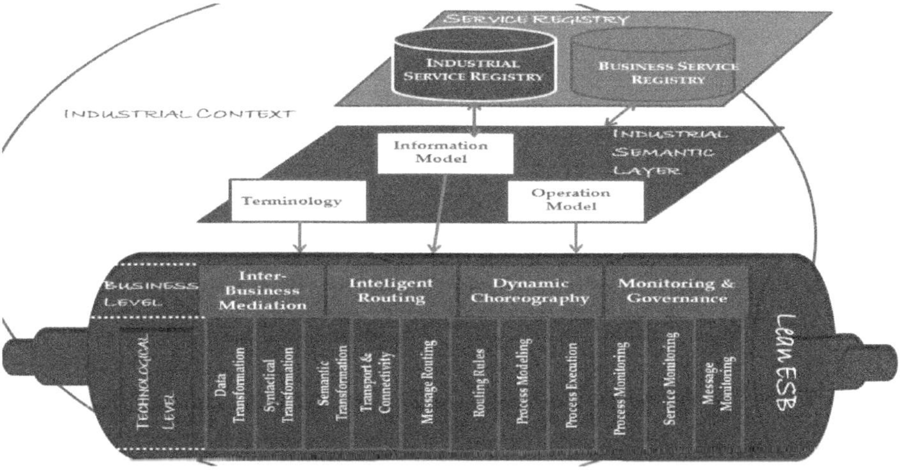

Fig. 1. The Collaborative Platform Global Organization

The semantic layer is related to business modules as well as industrial service registries [15]. The work presented here focuses on defining a single industrial registry which contains the matching of all industrial constraints such as production definition, organizational entities, physical processes, product definition, etc.

3.1 Business Semantic Integration

The purposed Semantic ESB aims to define a single industrial services registry which contains the matching results of all industrial constraints such as production definitions, organizational entities, physical processes, product definitions etc Industrial services chains are organized through a selection process which takes into account functional industrial service properties (i.e. product, material constraints, rules management) and non-functional industrial service properties (i.e. quality constraints, security and process maturity). Constraints related to functional and non-functional properties are defined in terms of Service Level Agreements (SLA) [15]. The industrial service annotation refers to ISA S-95 semantics as illustrated in Fig 2.

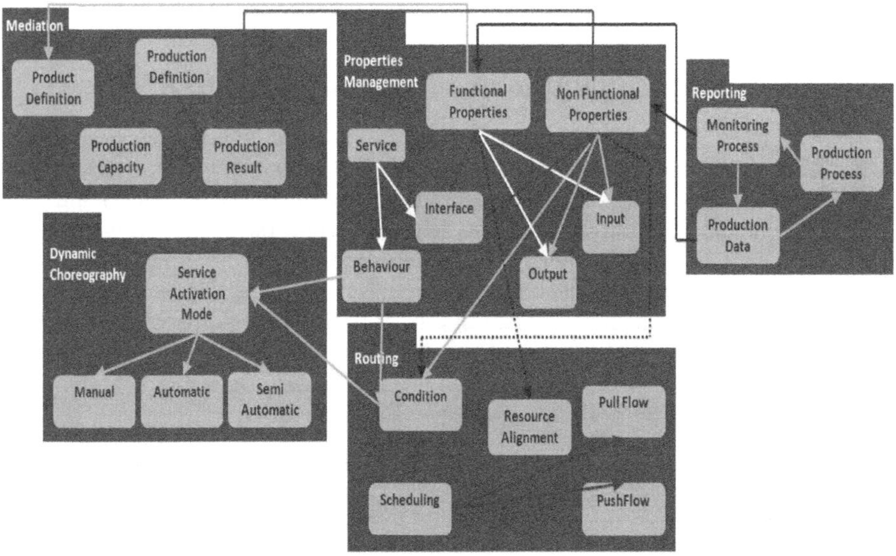

Fig. 2. The Industrial Service Model

In fact, the ISA S-95 standard enables the integration of production management and control systems (see Fig 3a, b, c) as it gathers different models (production definition, production schedule, production performance, production capacity and maintenance models).

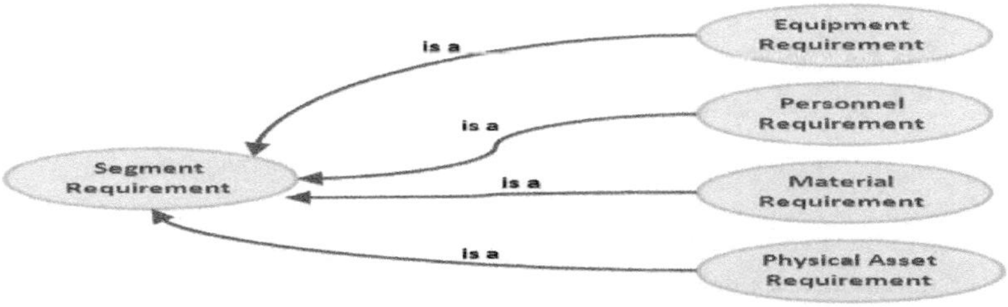

Fig. 3(a). The ISA S-95 Ontology – Production Tools

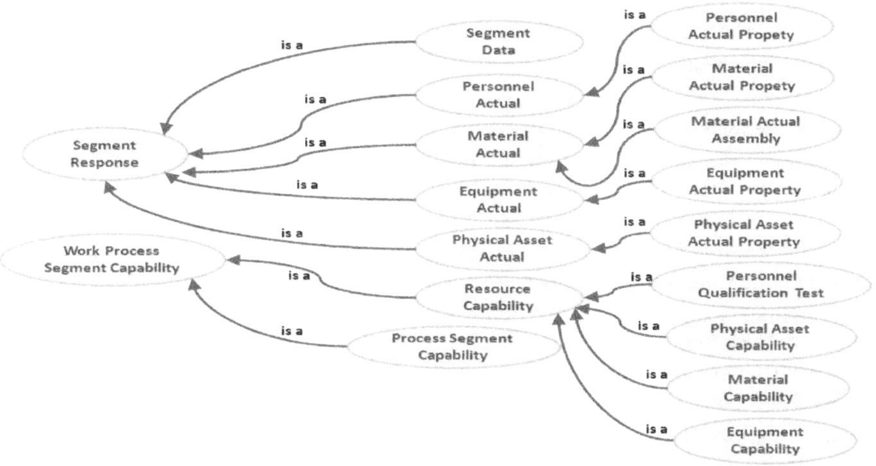

Fig. 3(b). The ISA S-95 Ontology – Resource Detail

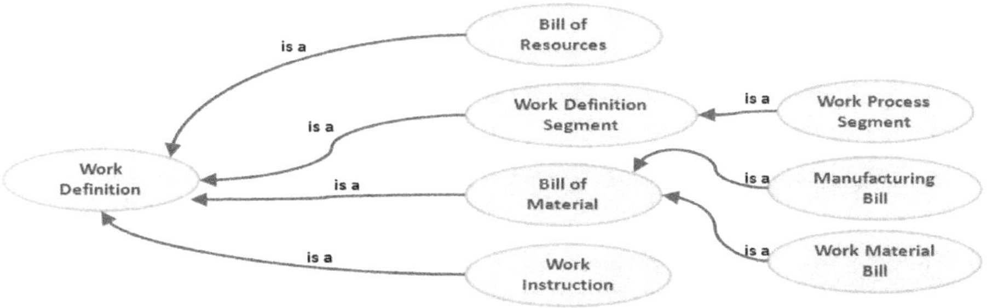

Fig. 3(c). The ISA S-95 Ontology – Operative scale

This is why we adopt it to develop the pivot ontology. Each industrial service description respecting ISA S-95 ontology is set as semantic annotations. As we have to mix technological and domain related annotations, we use YASA4WSDL to integrate these two kinds of annotations. The technological ontology refers to service semantics (input, output, operation, behaviour) whereas the domain ontology refers to the business interpretation of these data (Fig. 4). In the case of a Production Execution for example, we define industrial services according to the ISA S-95 ontology: When receiving a customer order, a message will be delivered to the workshop including product specifications, delivery delay, and requested quantities of finished products. It is defined as a "Work Request". Although, the ISA S-95 ontology provides a full definition of the production concepts, it does not meet the interoperability problems between the production management and organization and the production control. This is why the organizational ontology EO must be integrated.

3.2 Industrial Services Composition and Orchestration

Collaboration strategy hinges on a set of collaborative processes. In a Lean Manufacturing strategy, collaborative processes are dynamically composed by services choreography according to customer demands. Therefore, semantically annotated services are selected to compose "just in time" processes. To fit inter-business area interoperability, the business choreography includes a routing part to set business matching thanks to our ISA S-95 ontology and then uses this transformed service in the service chain. The ISA and EO ontologies matching provide an end-to-end business and technological interoperability mixing service and business annotations (see Fig. 4).

According to our previous example, "Customer Order" and "Product Features" define production processes and production scheduling. The EO ontology defines "Features of Product" and "Strategic Plan" which assist production process definition and business strategy. The "Organizational Entities" define resources which take a part in business processes. Therefore, YASA4WSDL improves a schema-based mapping among the two business ontologies in order to define industrial services orchestration.

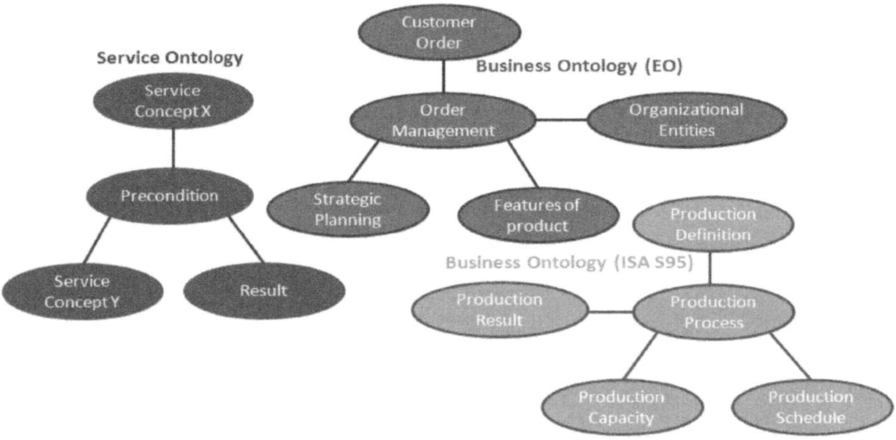

*<operation name="customerOrderManagement"
serviceConcept="&ServiceOntology#precondition&ServiceOntology#result"
productionSchedule="&BusinessOntology#customerOrder&BusinessOntology#featuresofProduct&BusinessOntology#ProductionDefinition&BusinessOntology#productionCapacity"
organizationalEntities="&BusinessOntology#orderManagement&BusinessOntology#featureofProduction&BusinessOntology#productionProcess&BusinessOntology#productionSchedule"
productionResult="BusinessOntology#customerOrder&BusinessOntology#managementOrder&BusinessOntology#productionDefinition">*

Fig. 4. Service Ontology and Domain Ontology (Business Pivot Ontology)

Lastly, this business choreography launches the industrial monitoring process when a service is triggered. This monitoring process governs the industrial service quality and concurrently monitors production processes. Then performance indicators are different from those saved in a regular situation, the monitoring process detects a production failure. In this case, the routing process tunes resource and service allocation so that production process will not fail.

4 Conclusion

In this paper, we proposed an industrial service middleware based on a semantic ESB infrastructure and on a dedicated industrial service registry. This middleware rests on a pivot business ontology (built from EO and ISA S-95 ontologies) to improve technological and business alignment. Industrial services are annotated according to different business ontologies before being "translated" in a pivot form (based on EO and ISA S95 ontologies) thanks to the YASA4WSDL framework.

Our prototype extends the SemEUsE semantic ESB [8] band uses the open source Dragon [9] framework to store and retrieve services with respect to their semantically defined functional and non-functional properties.

Acknowledgement

This work is supported partly by the ANR SemEUsE Project under grant 2007, TecLog 018 and by the Rhone-Alpes Area Council via the Cluster GOSPI SimSyProd project.

References

1. ANSI/ISA: Enterprise Control System Integration - Part I: Models and Terminology for Enterprise-Control System Integration (2007)
2. Chabeb, Y., Tata, S.: Yet Another Semantic Annotation for WSDL (YASA4WSDL). In: Proceedings of the IADIS WWW/Internet 2008 Conference, pp. 437–441 (2008)
3. Chen, D.: Enterprise Interoperability Framework. In: Workshop on Enterprise Modelling and Ontologies for Interoperability, EMOI-INTEROP (2006)
4. Daclin, N., et al.: Evaluation de l'Interopérabilité Organisationnelle et Managériale des Systèmes Industriels: le projet Carioner, CEROM – MTO (2008)
5. Ermilova, E., Afsarmanesh, H.: Competency Modelling Targeted on Promotion of Organizations towards VO Involvement. IFIP, vol. 283, pp. 3–14 (2008)
6. IBM WebSphere Developer Technical Journal: A practical introduction to message mediation – Part 1, http://www.ibm.com/developerworks/websphere/
7. Khoshafian, S.: Service Oriented Enterprise. Auerbach Publications, Taylor & Francis Group (2007)
8. Petals White Paper, http://petals.ow2.org/docs/PEtALS-Architecture-3-07-09.pdf
9. SEmEUse Project, http://www.semeuse.org/architecture.html
10. Schmidt, M.T., Hutchinson, B., Lambros, P., Phippen, R.: The Enterprise Service Bus: Making Service Oriented Architecture Real. IBM System Journals, 781–797 (2005)
11. Touzi, J., Bénaben, F., Pingaud, H.: Model transformation of collaborative business process into mediation information system. In: IFAC World Congress 2008 (2008), http://tc.ifac-control.org/5/3/activities/tc5-3-sessions-at-wc2008/c24-presentations/SeoulJTFBHP.pdf

12. Uschold, M., Gruninger, M.: ONTOLOGIES: Principles, Methods and Applications. Knowledge Engineering Review 11(2) (1996)
13. Womack, J., Jones, D.: Système Lean, Penser l'entreprise au plus juste, 2nd edn. (2005)
14. Zayati, A., Sliman, L., Biennier, F., Badr, Y., Moalla, M.: Framework de Bus de Services de Data Mining pour un Système d'Information Industriel. In: SETIT 2009-IEEE (2009) ISBN 978-9973-0-0122-1
15. Zayati, A., Biennier, F., Badr, Y., Moalla, M.: Towards Lean Service Bus Architecture for Industrial Integration Infrastructure and Pull Manufacturing Strategies. Journal of Intelligent Manufacturing no. 10845, ISSN 0956-5515
16. Zhao, Y.Z., Zhang, J.B., Zhuang, L.Q., Zhang, D.H.: Service-Oriented Architecture and Technologies for Automating Integration of Manufacturing Systems and Services. In: ETFA 2005, pp. 349–355 (2005)

An Educational Game in Collaborative Logistics

Sophie D'Amours[1] and Mikael Rönnqvist[2]

[1] Université Laval, Québec City, Québec, G1V 0A6, Canada
[2] Norwegian School of Economics and Business Administration, Helleveien 30, NO-5045 Bergen, Norway
Sophie.DAmours@cirrelt.ca, Mikael.Ronnqvist@nhh.no

Abstract. We describe an educational game in collaborative logistics. The game is based on an award winning application in cost allocation in forest transportation. The purpose of the game is to get an understanding of negotiation, coalition building and cost/profit sharing when the players have different power and hold different levels of information. The game is played with each player representing a single company. The objective of the game is to find an efficient plan and to share the benefits of the collaboration. We outline the game and discuss experiences from running the game in several countries and with students registered in business schools, engineering and forestry faculties.

Keywords: Collaborative Logistics, Cost sharing, Cooperative game, Logistics.

1 Introduction

In order to beat the competition, access new markets and respect operational, social and environmental constraints, enterprises establish more and more collaborations with many other business entities. Furthermore, with costs and information sharing, organizations have the opportunity to optimize their logistics activities. However, each enterprise has its own objectives and typically makes its own planning decisions to maximize individual profit. Therefore, it becomes crucial to determine how business entities will work together, the value of the collaboration and how to share the benefits. In order to illustrate the behavior when companies are faced with the task of sharing information and agree on sharing of benefits, we have developed an educational game. The game is based on an industrial case described in Frisk *et al.* (2010). This article won the EURO Management Science Strategic Innovation Price 2007. The game is easy to understand and can be used in many logistics or quantitative courses and for many different students. We have used it for Master students at business schools, engineering schools and professionals in transportation planning. In addition, we have used it in several countries including Sweden, Norway, Canada, France and Chile.

A popular and well used educational game is the "beer distribution game" (beer game) developed at MIT (Sterman, 1989). It is a simulation game to illustrate the impact of the bullwhip effect in supply chains. It serves to identify best practices in supply chain management. There are also electronic versions of the game, see e.g. Simchi-Levi et al. (2003). The beer game has also been adopted and implemented for

L.M. Camarinha-Matos et al. (Eds.): PRO-VE 2010, IFIP AICT 336, pp. 755–764, 2010.

different sectors, for example, the FORAC Research Consortium had developed an online version for the forest industry. The importance and positive effect to use business games as teaching tools in Management Science (MS) and Operations Research (OR) courses are discussed in Griffin (2007) and Ben-Zvi and Carton (2007). It is argued that business games are an effective way to engage students in MS/OR topics. It provides an understanding of the real problem and the practical situation faced by the companies or organizations where the problems exist. There exist games for several industrial sectors. Recently, Talluri (2009) described a game for teaching revenue management and Allon and Mieghem (2010) described one for supply chain sourcing. A general list of on-line simulation games is described in Wood (2007).

In this paper, we describe how the game can be played and report on some general observations. A lecture where the game is played is divided into four parts. In the first part, the background of the case study and setting of the game is introduced. In the second and third part, the game is played in two runs. In the first run, a restricted game is played, where the number of participants in the collaboration is limited. In the second run, any collaboration is allowed. In the last fourth part, the results and experiences of the real case study is described and discussed. The outline of the paper is as follows. In Section 2, we describe the case study used in the game. In Section 3, we describe some material used to play the game. In Section 4, we describe experiences from running the game in different settings. We end with some concluding remarks.

2 Case Study

The data used in this paper has been taken from a study done by the Forestry Research Institute of Sweden for eight participating forest companies. These companies operate in the southern part of Sweden as shown in Figure 1. The green area is the location of supply areas and the stars are industries. In total there are 898 harvest areas and 101 industries. The total number of products (or assortments) is 39. A product is a log with specific combination of species, diameter, length and quality. Demand is either expressed as a volume per product or as a volume of a mix of products (there are 12 possible products mix).

In our case we consider the problem of coordinating fiber procurement and transportation for several companies. It is common that transport costs can be decreased if companies use wood bartering. However, this is difficult as planners do not want to reveal supply, demand and cost information to competitors. In practice, this is solved by deciding on wood bartering of specific volumes. Today, this is typically done in an ad-hoc manner and is mostly dependent on personal relations. In Figure 2, we illustrate the potential benefits of wood bartering when two companies are involved. Here, we have four mills at two companies (two mills each) together with a set of supply points for each company. On the left hand side, each company operates by itself. The transportation distances are relatively long as compared to the right side where all supply and demand points are used by both companies. Since the overall cost is more or less proportional to the distance, it is clear that the solution to the right side with collaboration is much better than the left side without collaboration.

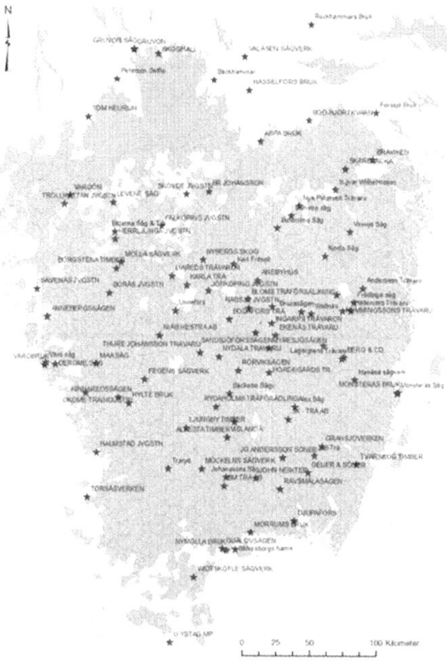

Fig. 1. Illustration of geographical area where the companies operate in southern Sweden

Fig. 2. Illustration of wood bartering between two companies. In the left part, two companies (indicated in blue and red) work with their own supply and demand. In the right part, the companies treat their supply and demand as common.

The data to support the case study is taken from transportation files reporting on activities carried out during one typical month. It involves all transports from the eight companies and includes information on time, from/to nodes, volume and product. The level of activities varies within the companies. Table 1 shows the volume transported and the proportion over the total transported volume for each of the companies. It is clear that company 2 is much larger than company 8. This aspect and its consequences will be very clear in the game.

Table 1. Monthly volumes (cubic meters) for each of the eight companies

Company	Volume	Proportion
Company 1	77361	8.76%
Company 2	301660	34.16%
Company 3	94769	10.73%
Company 4	44509	5.04%
Company 5	232103	26.29%
Company 6	89318	10.12%
Company 7	36786	4.17%
Company 8	6446	0.73%

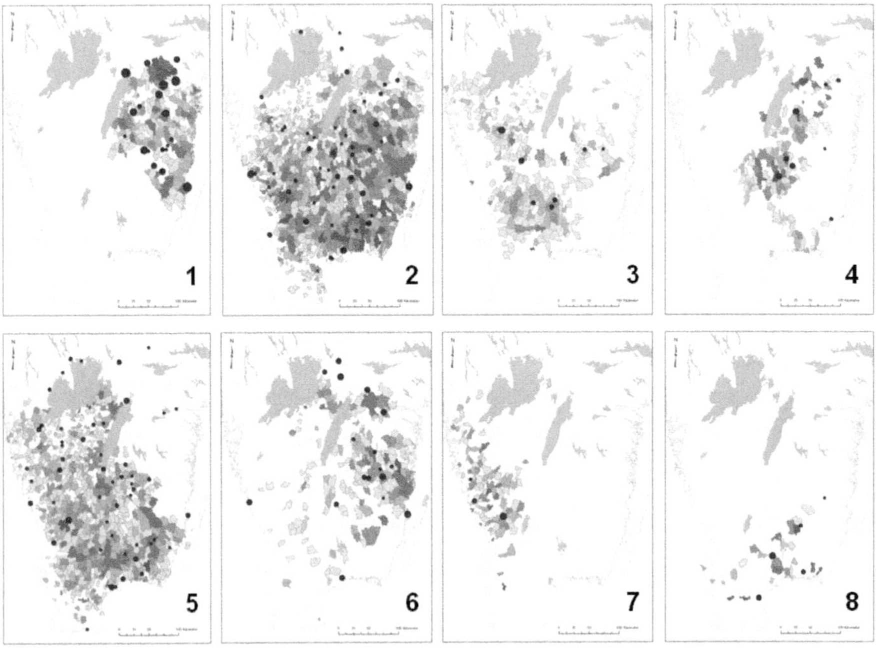

Fig. 3. Supply areas (indicated with green) and demand points or mills (indicated with red circles) for the companies

The companies operate in southern Sweden and cover different geographical areas; see Figure 2 where the green areas show the supply areas and the red circles denote the industries. Some companies cover the entire region (e.g. company 2) and others only a part (e.g. company 1). A good coverage, i.e. they work in the same region, between two companies indicates high potential for savings. For example, if companies 2 and 5 collaborate the cost savings can be large. At the same time, if companies 1 and 5 collaborate the cost savings would be small.

From the case study, we had detailed information on all transports made by the eight companies. With this information, we can compute the optimal cost for each company as well as the cost if all eight companies work together. In addition, we can also compute the cost of all possible coalitions. There are 245 (2^8-1-8) coalitions possible. The new transportation costs were computed with the system FlowOpt (Forsberg et al. 2005). This is a decision support system which includes a Geographical Information System, the Swedish road database NVDB and optimization routines to solve the OR models. The transportation planning problem is to decide how to transport logs from supply to demand point. The transportation can be done directly or indirectly through terminals. Moreover, there are several transportation modes including trucks, trains and ships. In Table 2, we provide information of the actual cost of the transportation activities, the cost when transportation is optimized within the company and finally, the cost when all companies are working together. The total saving when all companies are working together is 8.6%. In the game, we use only the optimized values as the companies may have different efficiency in their own planning.

Table 2. Real and optimized costs associated with each company and when all work together. All cost units are given in kSEK (thousand of Swedish kronor).

Company	Cost - real	Cost - opt	Cost - all
Company 1	3,894	3,778	
Company 2	15,757	14,859	
Company 3	4,828	4,742	
Company 4	2,103	2,067	
Company 5	10,704	10,340	
Company 6	5,084	4,959	
Company 7	1,934	1,884	
Company 8	333	333	
Companies 1-8			39,253
Total	44,637	42,963	39,253

3 Game

The game can be played in two versions. The first version include four companies and the second all eight companies. In the version with four companies more information is provided to the players. Most important is the actual costs of the all possible coalitions. Both versions of the game are played during a lecture of 2-3 hours. In a standard class, there will be a set of groups of four students. The information provided for the students in version 1 is given below.

The purpose of this collaboration game is to establish an agreement in how four companies should organize themselves and divide the overall cost and the potential savings. Each company has a supply and demand for a set of products in balance, see Figure 4, and the cost arises when the supply is transported to the demand locations. Each company can work individually and has a specific transportation cost. The costs are found by using an optimization model which minimizes the cost given supply and demand. A summary of the companies when they are working individually during one month is given in Table 3.

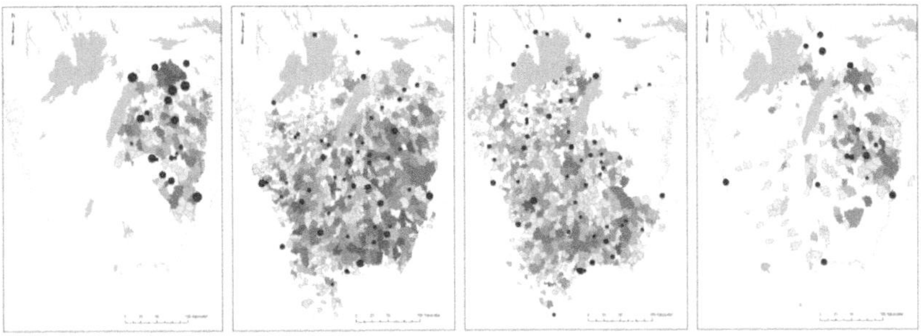

Fig. 4. Maps describing each of the four companies C1 – C2 – C3 – C5. Green areas describe supply areas and red circles industries with demand.

Table 3. Summary of the four companies and their transportation volume, transportation cost and average transportation distance

Company	*Volume*	*Individual cost*	*Average distance*
Company 1	*77,300 m^3*	*3,780 (kSEK)*	*70,3 km*
Company 2	*301,300 m^3*	*14,860 (kSEK)*	*56,8 km*
Company 3	*232,100 m^3*	*10,340 (kSEK)*	*68,5 km*
Company 5	*89,300 m^3*	*4,960 (kSEK)*	*68,5 km*
Total	*700,000 m^3*	*33,940 (kSEK)*	-----

The companies can form one or several coalitions (a set of companies working together). If they work in a coalition, they simply treat their supply and demand as common, and can find a solution that lowers the overall transportation cost. For example, if companies C1 and C2 work individually, the overall cost is 3,780 (C1) + 14,860 (C2) = 18,640 kSEK. However, if they work together, the cost is 18,300 kSEK which represent a saving of 340 kSEK (18,640-18,300). One question is how these 340 kSEK should be divided between the two companies C1 and C2. There are many possible coalitions and Table 4 summarizes their costs and savings. The improvement in the table is given as percentage i.e. savings divided by the the aggregated individual cost. For example, the improvement for coalition (C1+C2+C3) is computed as 1,270/28,980=4.38%.

Table 4. Summary of possible coalitions sand their cost if they work together, summed individual cost, saving and improvement

Coalition	*Cost (kSEK) (collaboration)*	*Cost (kSEK) (individual)*	*Saving (kSEK)*
C1 + C2	*18,300*	*18,640*	*340*
C1 + C3	*14,000*	*14,120*	*120*
C1 + C5	*8,510*	*8,740*	*230*
C2 + C3	*24,210*	*25,200*	*990*
C2 + C5	*19,040*	*19,820*	*780*
C3 + C5	*15,060*	*15,300*	*240*
C1+C2+C3	*27,710*	*28,980*	*1,270*
C1+C2+C5	*22,490*	*23,600*	*1,110*
C1+C3+C5	*18,580*	*19,080*	*500*
C2+C3+C5	*28,400*	*30,160*	*1,760*
C1+C2+C3+C5	*32,000*	*33,940*	*1,940*

Assignments

In the collaboration game, each group consists of four players. Each player is responsible for one company. The objective for each player is to improve its own cost/profit as much as possible. The task is to discuss and agree which companies should work together (if any). In part A only two companies can work together. In part B any coalition structure is possible. For example, all companies can work together, no companies work together, any group of two or three companies can work together. Each company can only participate in one coalition (in both part A and part B). Given the agreed coalitions in the two parts, how should the overall savings be divided among the participating companies?

Once the first part is played, we have a discussion on how the participant made their decisions, their thinking and their bargaining power. We also discuss the different results (displayed for groups) that the students have agreed on. This discussion is often interesting and provides a good basis for the second part.

The information provided for the students in version 2 is different. Each company has information about its total cost together with the information about collaborating with one other company. There is no information on collaborating with three or several companies. In this version, it is more important to find agreements without knowing the real benefits. Below in Table 5, we provide the information for one company. Version 2 also has two parts. In the first part, coalitions of at most two companies should be found. This is more difficult, as compared to version 1, as there are many more alternatives. Also, here it is very clear that companies 2 and 5 have much higher negotiation power. In the second part, any coalition and principle for sharing the benefit is to be found. At the end, the real benefits of the agreed coalitions are provided to the agreed groups and they need to split the savings according to the agreed principles.

Table 5. Costs and savings (kSEK) when company 1 works together with a second (2-8) company

Company	Company	Cost (separate)	Cost (together)	Saving
1	2	18,640	18,300	340
1	3	8,520	8,490	30
1	4	5,840	5,770	70
1	5	14,120	14,000	120
1	6	8,740	8,510	230
1	7	5,660	5,660	0
1	8	4,110	4,100	10

Once the game is played, we follow up with what happened in the real case and what sharing mechanisms were tested and used. We introduce the students to basic game theory including the core conditions, efficient allocation and individual rationality concepts. We then go through well known methods such as the Shapley value, the shadow price approach, the nucleolus approach. We also show results when using a simple "volume" based allocation method which often is the one used in practice. Finally, we present the retained approach named the equal profit method. These are described in the paper and there is also a powerpoint presentation that is used to describe models, methods and results.

4 Experiences

We have been playing this game with students, business people and researchers in France, Sweden, Norway, Chile and Canada. All information (PDF documents, Excel sheets and ppt presentation) is provided by the authors. We first developed version 2 of the game where 8 players are provided with the company information and on the impact of partnering with another company. For example, company 1, knows its cost, average transportation distance and the geographical location of its catchment areas and industries. Company 1 also knows the potential benefit of pairing with company 2, 3, 4, 5, 6, 7 and 8 respectively. It does not know the benefit of being part of a larger coalition. This was for us the replication of the real case as there are eight companies involved in the real case. We however found that the players with the smallest companies where rapidly put aside. The only way they could really be heard by the others was to join their force even though they did not have any incentive at first sight. Only once, as a "larger" player, would the others start discussing with them. This was difficult for the student to realize; very few participants saw the potential of this strategy and were capable of using its power into the negotiation process.

Running the game in different countries permitted us to capture cultural differences. These observations cannot be generalized but are interesting to discuss here as they illustrate strategies in dealing with the case. North Americans tend to build their coalition one by one, this is in opposition to Scandinavians who typically start with the grant coalition and rarely eliminate a company from the grant coalition. Participants from France and Chile have used mixed strategies mainly based on the relations – pairing with their friends. In Chile, one group decided to eliminate the smallest company and gave the player the responsibility of mediating the grand coalition. These are only some examples of how the participants approach the challenges of this game and again no generalization is possible. In this game the players focus more on coalition building than on designing the sharing mechanism.

We then developed version 1 of the game. This version is dealing with only four companies and provides more information. Each player knows the potential benefit of paring with one, two and three company. The players are rapidly challenged by the fact that no equilibrium exists and that they need to negotiate an incentive to get the maximum out of the grant coalition (four companies). The discussions are easier to manage than in version 2 of the game as only four players are involved in each group. The players focus more on sharing mechanism than on coalition building. We have also developed an Excel sheet for this version to illustrate the results and characteristics of the most common sharing principles.

5 Conclusions

Collaboration in supply chain is raising interest from the academic and industrial communities. It is seen as a new approach to increase the value created through better cross-chains coordination. However, most agree on the fact that establishing efficient and sustainable collaborations requires highly skilled and competent people. This is why we developed this game.

Business games are often used for developing complex competences. This is the case of this game as the participants are integrating advanced knowledge on game theory as well as developing their negotiation skills.

To be efficient, business games need to be simple and meaningful. The game proposed is focusing on two aspects of collaboration in logistics: coalition building and sharing mechanism. It is simple to explain and to run. Moreover, the game builds on a real industrial case providing a meaningful background in terms of the data (e.g. maps, costs, distances and volumes) and human behaviors. It also shows that the theories learned through the exercise are relevant to students.

References

1. Allon, G., Van Mieghem, J.A.: The Mexico-China Sourcing Game: Teaching Global Dual Sourcing. INFORMS Trans. of Ed. 10(3), 105–112 (2010)
2. Ben-Zvi, T., Carton, T.C.: From Rhetoric to Reality: Business games as Educational Tools. INFORMS Trans. of Ed. 8(1), 10–18 (2007)
3. Forsberg, M., Frisk, M., Rönnqvist, M.: FlowOpt – a decision support tool for strategic and tactical transportation planning in forestry. Int. J. of For. Eng. 16, 101–114 (2005)
4. Frisk, M., Göthe-Lundgren, M., Jörnsten, K., Rönnqvist, M.: Cost allocation in collaborative forest transportation. Eur. J. of Oper. Res. 205, 448–458 (2010)
5. Griffin, P.: The Use of Classroom Games in Management Science and Operations Research. INFORMS Trans. of Ed. 8(1), 1–2 (2007)
6. Simchi-Levi, D., Kaminsky, P., Simchi-Levi, E.: Designing and Managing the Supply Chain, 2nd edn. Irwin/McGraw-Hill, New York (2003)

7. Sniedovich, M.: OR/MS Games: 1. A Neglected Educational Resource. INFORMS Trans. of Ed. 2(3), 86–95 (2002)
8. Sterman, J.: Modeling managerial behaviour: Misperceptions of feedback in a dynamic decision making experiment. Man. Sci. 35(3), 321–339 (1989)
9. Talluri, K.: The Customer Valuations Game as a Basis for Teaching Revenue Management. INFORMS Trans. Ed. 9(3), 117–123 (2009)
10. Wood, S.C.: Online Games to Teach Operations. INFORMS Trans. Ed. 8(1), 3–9 (2007)

Extending Networks of Collaboration to Multi-market Oligopolies

Pascal Billand[1,*], Christophe Bravard[1], Subhadip Chakrabarti[2], and Sudipta Sarangi[3]

[1] Pascal Billand, University Jean Monnet, Gate Lyon-Saint-Etienne,
6 rue basse des rives 42023 Saint-Etienne, France
pascal.billand@univ-s-etienne.fr
[2] Subhadip Chakrabarti, School of Management and Economics, Queen's University Belfast,
Northern Ireland, United Kingdom
[3] Sudipta Sarangi, Department of Economics, Louisiana State University,
Baton Rouge, LA 70803, USA

Abstract. In this article, we extend the Goyal and Joshi's model (2003) of network of collaboration in oligopoly to multi-market situations. We examine the incentive of firms to form links and the architectures of the resulting networks in this setting. We also present some results on efficient networks.

Keywords: collaborative networks, multimarket oligopolies.

1 Introduction

Research collaborations among firms take a variety of forms, such as joint ventures, technology sharing or joint R&D, and can play a prominent role in economic performance (Hagedoorn, 2006). These collaborations are often bilateral and non exclusive, and form a network of collaborative links between firms. Goyal and Joshi (GJ, 2003) develop a model of network formation between firms which compete on one market in order to predict the architectures of the networks that should emerge and examine to what extent these networks are socially efficient. Now it is often the case that firms compete in few markets. In a seminal paper, Bullow et al. (1985) examine how the introduction of multimarket competition can produce quite unexpected results. In this paper, we ask what happens to equilibrium and efficient networks when we introduce multimarket competition in the GJ's model of formation of collaborative networks. We assume for purposes of simplicity, a heterogeneous product market, with linear demand curves and quadratic cost functions, where multimarket competitors can form quality products enhancing collaborative links on one market. Concerning equilibrium networks it turns out that as in GJ (2003), equilibrium networks have a dominant group architecture, i.e. a group of firms are linked to each other while other firms have no links at all. We show that this result follows from the fact that our collaborative multimarket game qualifies as playing the field games (Goyal and Joshi, 2006), with payoff function satisfying convexity in own links as well as the strategic substitutes property with regard to quantities. However, using Bullow et al. (1985)

[*] Corresponding author.

L.M. Camarinha-Matos et al. (Eds.): PRO-VE 2010, IFIP AICT 336, pp. 765–772, 2010.

analysis, we show that contrary to the model of GJ (2003) there exist situations where competitors do not form collaborative links in order to increase the quality of their products even if these links have no costs. This result follows from the fact that there are joint diseconomies across markets and goods produced by competing firms are strategic substitutes. It illustrates how the intermarket effect plays a key role in the incentive of firms to collaborate.

With regard to efficient networks, though we cannot arrive at a precise characterization of these networks, we can derive some interesting properties of such networks and restrict the set of networks that are efficient into a small group. More precisely, for four firms or more, efficient networks have only one component (or one group). Moreover in an efficient network the diameter of the component is very low, since the geodesic distance between two connected firms in the component cannot exceed two.

The rest of the paper proceeds as follows. Section 2 introduces the model and discusses the notation and terminology. Section 3 examines equilibrium networks, while Sections 4 deals with efficient networks[1]. Section 5 concludes.

2 The Framework

2.1 The Multi-market Cournot Model

Suppose there are n firms indexed by i = 1, 2,..., n (where n > 2) that compete a la Cournot in two inter-related markets A and B. We denote by q_i and Q_i the quantities sold by firm i on markets A and B respectively, and by p_i and P_i the prices of firm i's products on these markets. Focusing on the most interesting case, we suppose that competitors' products are strategic substitutes and there are diseconomies of scope across markets. More specifically, demand in markets A and B for firm i are respectively given by

$$p_i = \alpha_i - q_i - \sum_{j \neq i} q_j, \quad P_i = \beta_i - Q_i - \sum_{j \neq i} Q_j$$

And the cost function of a firm i is given by

$$C_i(q_i, Q_i) = \frac{1}{2}(q_i + Q_i)^2$$

2.2 Quality Improving Links and Collaborative Networks

We assume that firms can improve the quality of their products via collaborative links in market A. More specifically, we suppose that if a firm has formed k links, then we have

$$\alpha_i = \gamma_0 + \gamma \cdot k,$$

with $\gamma_0, \gamma \in IR_+$.

[1] The detailed proofs of the results can be found in a complete version of the paper at the following address: http://portail.univ-st-etienne.fr/bienvenue/recherche/working-papers-creuset-2010-285615.kjsp?RH=0611171526yr.

It is reasonable to assume that $\gamma_0 > \gamma$. For reasons that will be clear later, we assume γ_0 is sufficiently large compared to γ, namely,

$$\gamma_0 > \left(\frac{(n-1)^2}{2}\right) \cdot \gamma$$

A collaborative network g is a list of pairs of firms who are linked to each other. For simplicity, we denote the link between i and j (where $i \neq j$) by ij, so $ij \in g$ indicates that i and j are linked in the network g.

Let g^N be the set of all subsets of N of size 2. The network g^N is referred to as the complete network. The set $G = \{g \subset g^N\}$ denotes the set of all possible networks on N. A network in which there are no links is called an empty network and is denoted by g^0. We let g + ij denote the network formed by adding the link ij to the network g, and g - ij denote the network formed by deleting the link ij from the network g. A network profits function $\pi_I : G \to R_+$ assigns some profits to firm i by virtue of being part of a network. Let $\pi = (\pi_1, \pi_1, \ldots, \pi_n)$ denote the vector of profits functions. Then π combined with N defines a network game.

A firm i's neighborhood $N_i(g)$ is given by $\{j \in N \setminus \{i\} \mid ij \in g\}$ and its cardinality is given by $\eta_i(g) = |Ni(g)|$. $\eta_i(g)$ is called the degree of firm i in network g. We also define N(g) as the set of firms that have at least one link. Let $\eta(g) = \#N(g)$ with the convention that if $N(g) = \emptyset$, we let $\eta(g) = 1$.

We define as $L_i(g) = \{ij \in g\}$ the set of links in which firm i is involved. Let $\lambda(g) = 1/2(\sum\eta_i(g))$ be the total number of links in a network g.

For any $h \subset g$, let g - h denotes the network formed by deleting the set of links h from the network g. Similarly, for $h \subset g^N \setminus g$, g + h denotes the network formed by adding the link set h to the network g. Moreover we define $g_{-i} = g \setminus Li(g)$ the resulting network once we remove firm i and all his links from the network g. A network g is regular if each firm has the same number of links. A path in g connecting i and j is a set of distinct firms $\{i_1, i_2, \ldots, i_p)$, with $p > 2$, such that $i_1 = i$, $i_p = j$, and $\{i_1i_2, i_2i_3, \ldots, i_{p-1}i_p\} \in g$. We refer to the number of links on this path, here p - 1, as the length of the path. We say i and j are connected to each other if a path exists between them and they are disconnected otherwise. The number of links on the shortest path between two distinct firms i and j is called the geodesic distance between i and j. The network $g' \subset g$ is a component of g if $N(g') \geq 2$ and for all $i \in N(g')$ and $j \in N(g')$, $i \neq j$, there exists a path in g' connecting i and j and for any $i \in N(g')$ and $j \in N(g)$, $ij \in g$ implies $ij \in g'$. In other words, a component is simply a maximally connected subnetwork of g. We denote the set of network components of the network g by C(g). The set of firms that are not connected in the network g are connected in the set of (fully) disconnected firms in g denoted by

$$N_0(g) = N \setminus N(g) = \{i \in N \ \ | N_i(g) = \emptyset\}$$

Such firms are known as singletons. A component $g' \subset g$ is complete if for all distinct i $j \in N(g')$, $ij \in g$. A component $g' \subset g$ is regular if for all distinct i, $j \in N(g')$, $\eta_i(g) = \eta_j(g)$. The dominant group architecture g^k is characterized by one complete non-singleton component with $k > 2$ firms and n - k singletons.

2.3 Equilibrium and Efficient Networks

A network g is a pairwise equilibrium network with regard to a profile of profits functions $\pi = (\pi_1, \pi_2, \ldots, \pi_n)$ if

(a) for all i and $h \subset L_i$ (g), $\pi_i(g) > \pi_i(g - h)$, and
(b) for all i and ij $\notin$ g, if π_i (g + ij) > π_i(g) then π_j (g + ij) < π_j(g).

For any network g, and $h \subset g^N \setminus g$, we denote the marginal benefit of link formation by $\Delta\pi_i(g, h) = \pi_i(g + h) - \pi_i(g)$. Obviously, for a pairwise equilibrium network, $\Delta\pi_i$ (g–h, h) > 0 for all $h \subset Li$ (g), and for all ij $\notin$ g, if $\Delta\pi_i(g, ij) > 0$, then $\Delta\pi_j(g, ij) < 0$.

Next, we define efficient networks. Consider a welfare function W given by sum of payoffs of all the firms, i.e. $W(g) = \sum_{i\in N}\pi_i(g)$. A network g' is efficient if it maximizes the welfare function, that is W(g') > W(g) for all g ≠ g'. For any network g, and $h \subset g^N \setminus g$, we denote the marginal change in welfare as a result of link formation by $\Delta W(g, h) = W(g + h) - W(g)$.

3 Characterization of Equilibrium Networks

While the payoff functions are quite complicated, this game has features that were analyzed by Goyal and Joshi (2006). We will devote some space to reproducing their definitions and terminology.

Definition 1. A network game is called playing the field game if the payoff of firm i is a function of her degree, $\eta_i(g)$, and the total number of links formed by the other firms, $\lambda(g_{-i})$, namely,

$$\pi_i(g) = \Phi(\eta_i(g), \lambda(g_{-i})).$$

Definition 2. The payoff function Φ is convex in its own links if the marginal returns Φ(k + 1, l) - Φ(k,l) is strictly increasing in k.

Definition 3. Suppose l' > l. The payoff function Φ satisfies the strategic substitutes property if Φ(k + 1,l') - Φ(k,l') < Φ(k + 1,l) - Φ(k,l).

The next lemma is a reproduction of Proposition 3.1 of Goyal and Joshi (2006).

Lemma 1. For a playing the field game, if the payoff function satisfies convexity in own links and the strategic substitutes property, then a pairwise equilibrium network always exists. Furthermore, a pairwise equilibrium network is either complete or empty or has the dominant group architecture.

It is easy to check that the collaborative multimarket game qualifies as playing the field game. Furthermore, the payoff function satisfies convexity in own links as well as the strategic substitutes property. In fact, if we define

$$\Delta(k,l) = \Phi(k+1,l) - \Phi(k,l),$$

then we have

$$\frac{\partial\Delta(k,l)}{\partial k} = \frac{2\gamma^2(11n^4 + 44n^3 - 6n^2 - 100n + 83)}{18(1+n)^2(3+n)^2} > 0$$

and

$$\frac{\partial\Delta(k,l)}{\partial l} = \frac{2\gamma^2(22n^3 + 102n^2 + 66n - 158)}{18(1+n)^2(3+n)^2} < 0$$

Therefore, applying Lemma 1, we get the following corollary.

Corollary 1. The pairwise equilibrium network is either complete or empty or has a dominant group architecture.

Few remarks are in order here.

Remark 1. There are some surprising implications of this result. In the one-market Cournot model of GJ (2003), the dominant group architecture emerges if there are substantial link formation costs. Hence, introducing competition in additional markets has the same effect as introducing link formation costs.

Remark 2. It is easy to show using BGK (1985) analysis that the empty network can be a pairwise equilibrium network when costs of forming links are null. The intuition behind this fact is as follows: the formation of a link by firms i and j in market A enhances the quality of their product in this market and leads these firms to produce more for this market. Due to joint diseconomies across markets this reduces marginal profitability for these firms associated with a unit of production in market B and induces these firms to reduce their quantities on this market. Because of strategic substitutability, rival firms will increase their quantities on market B and this induces certainly a loss in market B, and possibly an overall loss for firms i and j.

Remark 3. When the cost function exhibits economies of scope, there is no tension across markets anymore, that is the formation of a link by firms i and j in market A leads these firms to enhance the quantities produced on both markets at equilibrium.

As a result the profits of these firms increase. It follows that when costs of forming links are null, the complete network is always the only equilibrium network. Thus we obtain the same result as in the Goyal and Joshi model where firms compete on one market only.

4 Characterization of Efficient Networks

In this section, we shall discuss efficient networks. While we do not obtain an exact characterization of efficient networks, we can identify certain properties of such networks. Consider the welfare effect of link formation between two arbitrary firms i and k in a network g. This effect is given by

$$\Delta W(g,ik)=k'\left(\alpha_i+\alpha_K-\frac{\tau'}{n}\sum_{l\pm i,k}\alpha_l+\Lambda'\right)-2c$$

where τ' > 0, k' > 0, and Λ' are constants independent of network structure. τ' has an upper bound less than 11 (at n = 2, its value is 10.79) and is strictly decreasing in n. It has a lower bound of 2 and converges asymptotically to 2. It is important to note that at n = 4, τ' = 3.5. For the discussion that follows, let us assume n ≥ 3.

Lemma 2. (i) For any network g and firm i such that ik, im ∉ g and $\eta_m(g) > \eta_k(g)$, ΔW(g + ik, im) > ΔW(g, ik), (ii) If $\eta_m(g) = \eta_k(g)$, but n ≥ 4, ΔW(g + ik, im) > ΔW(g, ik) as well.

Proof. (i) Starting from an arbitrary network g with ik, im ∉ g. Suppose firm i and k form a link. The increase in welfare is proportional to:

$$\frac{\Delta W(g,ik)}{k'}=2\gamma_0+\gamma(\eta_i(g)+\eta_k(g))$$

$$-\frac{\tau'}{n}\left((n-2)\gamma_0+\gamma\sum_{l\pm i,k,m}\eta_l(g)+\gamma\eta_m(g)\right)+\Lambda'-\frac{2c}{k'}$$

Suppose then that firms i and m form a link. The increase in social welfare is proportional to

$$\frac{\Delta W(g+ik,im)}{k'}=\frac{\Delta W(g,ik)}{k'}+\gamma\left(2+\left(1+\frac{\tau'}{n}\right)(\eta_m(g)-\eta_k(g)-1)\right)$$

Now, since $\eta_m(g) \geq \eta_k(g) + 1$, this expression is positive, completing the proof.

(ii) We have

$$\frac{\Delta W(g+ik,im)}{k'}=\frac{\Delta W(g,ik)}{k'}+\gamma\left(1-\frac{\tau'}{n}\right)$$

Since τ' = 3.5 for n = 4, τ'/n < 1. Furthermore, τ' and hence τ'/n are strictly decreasing in n, therefore τ'/n < 1 for all n > 4. Hence it follows that in all cases we have

$$\frac{\Delta W(g+ik,im)}{k'}>\frac{\Delta W(g,ik)}{k'}$$

The following lemma plays a key role in the results that follow.

Lemma 3. For any efficient network g, if ij ∈ g and ik ∉ g, then $\eta_j(g) \geq \eta_k(g)$. If n ≥ 4, then $\eta_j(g) > \eta_k(g)$.

Proof. Suppose there exists an efficient network g and ij ∈ g and ik ∉ g. Then, ΔW(g - ij, ij) > 0. Suppose, towards a contradiction, $\eta_k(g) > \eta_j(g)$. This implies by

Lemma 2 that $\Delta W(g, ik) > 0$ contradicting that g is efficient. Hence, for all k such that $ik \notin g$, $\eta_k(g) <= \eta_j(g)$.

Next let $\eta_j(g) = \eta_k(g)$ and $n \geq 4$. Again, $\Delta W(g, ik) > \Delta W(g - ij, ij) > 0$ which contradicts that g is efficient. Therefore, $\eta_k(g) < \eta_j(g)$.

The proposition below sets forth properties that characterize efficient networks.

Proposition 1. (i) If $n \geq 4$, then the efficient network cannot consist of more than one component, (ii) the geodesic distance between any two connected firms in a efficient network is less than or equal to 2.

Proof. (i) Suppose $h_1, h_2 \in C(g)$ where g is an efficient network and $ij \in h_1$ and $kl \in h_2$. Now, i is linked to j and not to k which implies using Lemma 3, $\eta_j(g) > \eta_k(g)$. But l is linked to k but not to j which implies $\eta_k(g) > \eta_j(g)$. Hence, we arrive at a contradiction.

(ii) Take two firms i and j such that i and j belong to N(h) where $h \in C(g)$. Hence, a path exists between i and j. Suppose the shortest path is $\{i_1i_2, i_2i_3, \ldots, i_{p-1}i_p\}$, where $i_1 = i$ and $i_p = j$, and $p \geq 4$. i_1 is linked to i_2, but i_1 is not linked to i_3; i_2 is linked to i_3 but i_3 is not linked to i_2. Hence, from Lemma 3, we get both $\eta_{i2}(g) > \eta_{i3}(g)$ and $\eta_{i3}(g) > \eta_{i2}(g)$. A contradiction.

Remark. It is noteworthy that pairwise equilibrium and efficient architectures do not coincide. Indeed, among non empty and non complete networks, while only networks with a complete component can be pairwise equilibrium, this is no longer true for efficient networks. Thus by contrast with pairwise equilibrium networks, in efficient networks firms who have formed links can be very asymmetric. Think for instance to a network where the component has a star architecture, that is one firm, say i has formed links with all other firms of the component while the latter have formed links only with firm i.

5 Conclusion

The dynamics of multi-market oligopolies first discussed in Bulow et al. (1985) can upset many results, which would hold in isolated oligopoly markets. Here we take the situation of collaborative link formation among Cournot oligopolists. The results that a complete network materializes in equilibrium when costs of links are null, no longer holds once we introduce multimarket competition. With positive link formation costs efficient networks have the very interesting feature that they consist of only one component with a very low diameter. An exact characterization of efficient networks in our framework, or more broadly in playing the field games, is an open question.

References

1. Bulow, J.I., Geanakopolos, J.D., Klemperer, P.D.: Multimarket Oligopoly: Strategic Substitutes and Complements. The Journal of Political Economy (1985)
2. Bernheim, B.D., Whinston, M.D.: Multimarket Contact and Collusive Behavior. Rand Journal of Economics 21, 1–26 (1996)

3. Billand, P., Bravard, C., Chakrabarti, S., Sarangi, S.: Corporate Espionage, Working Paper (2010)
4. Dixit, A.: A Model of Duopoly Suggesting a Theory of Entry Barriers. Bell Journal of Economics 10, 20–32 (1979)
5. Chakrabarti, S., Haller, H.: An Analysis of Advertising Wars, Manchester School (2010) (forthcoming)
6. Goyal, G., Joshi, S.: Networks of Collaboration in Oligopoly. Games and Economic Behavior 43, 57–85 (2003)
7. Goyal, G., Joshi, S.: Unequal Connections. International Journal of Game Theory 34, 319–349 (2006)
8. Jackson, M., Wolinsky, A.: A Strategic Model of Social and Economic Networks. Journal of Economic Theory 71, 44–74 (1996)
9. Vives, X.: Oligopoly Pricing: Old Ideas and New Tools. The MIT Press, Cambridge (1999)

The Application of Incentive Mechanisms for the Participation of Enterprises in Collaborative Networks from an Economic Perspective

Hendrik Jähn

Chemnitz University of Technology, Dept. of Economic Sciences, Thüringer Weg 7
09126 Chemnitz, Germany
hendrik.jaehn@wirtschaft.tu-chemnitz.de

Abstract. This contribution is to be assigned to the operative production management of collaborative networks. By the application of incentive mechanisms, a competitive and effective management of production processes allows sustainable success. Incentives are relevant for all stages of a network lifecycle. In this paper, the problem is discussed that enterprises from a pool of cooperation-willing enterprises do not take part in a certain value-added process, even though it would be possible from the technical point of view and would also be economically reasonable. As a reason for this behavior, the utility calculus of an enterprise plays a decisive role. To convince these enterprises to collaborate in a value-added process, primarily incentive mechanisms are to be applied. In the following, this topic is taken on and is discussed extensively by means of two concrete examples. In this connection, a concrete calculation model both for the amount of incentives and the profit share is introduced.

Keywords: Collaborative network, incentive mechanisms, operative network management, sustainable success.

1 Motivation

The implementation of value-added processes within networked production structures has strongly gained in importance. Integral advantages are a high degree of flexibility, sustainability and cost saving potential. However, not in every case value-added processes may be realized by collaboration although this would be reasonable from an economic perspective. So, the effort of an enterprise to cooperate primarily depends on the economic advantageousness of a project, i.e. when the utility can be maximized or a benefit can be achieved respectively. A project is, however, only reasonable if the overall benefit of the network is maximized or if a benefit results. In certain cases, enterprises do maximize their benefit without cooperation although participation is desirable if seen as a whole. Reasons for not cooperating may principally be found in a shortage of production capacity or missing financial attractiveness of an order. In these cases, the network management has the possibility to interfere in a regulating way. To achieve a sustainable outcome, incentive mechanisms can be applied to a certain degree for selected enterprises.

L.M. Camarinha-Matos et al. (Eds.): PRO-VE 2010, IFIP AICT 336, pp. 773–780, 2010.

2 Incentives in an Economic Environment

The application of incentives in an economic environment is possible in various ways and for numerous situations. In relation to the analysis of principal-agent-relations [1] within the frame of the principal-agent-theory [2], [3], incentives can be applied as a possible solution approach for problems classes representing hidden action and hidden information. Here, the whole enterprise network represents the principal; the involved enterprises are the agents. In this context, incentives serve as alignment of interests between principal and agent after conclusion of a contract. At this point, a reduction or removal respectively of the moral hazard on the agent's side is achieved. Within the frame of the principal-agent-theory, these actions are tendentially agent-related. Here, incentive systems represent the combination of several single incentives. In this context, incentives also stand for a suitable measure for an alignment of interests of the agent to those of the principal [4].

In this context, incentives are understood as a situational condition, which is supposed to motivate the economic agents due to their individual needs, i.e. utility structure for a performance for the purpose of the principal. By means of incentives, agents are influenced to perform actions in the intensity desired by the principal (management) [5]. Incentive systems represent the sum of all working conditions designed purposely enforcing certain behavior patterns and reducing the probability of the occurrence of undesirable behavior patterns. Behavior patterns are made stronger by the application of positive incentives in form of rewards taken as an example. Undesirable behavior can be reduced by negative incentives in form of sanction mechanisms [4]. From that results the so-called "motivation problem", which in its core statement says that an individual needs an incentive to produce a certain performance or to omit an action as long as this has no connection to the individual utility maximization [6]. By means of incentives, it is aspired to suppress self-interested behavior of agents and to adjust their behavior to the aims of the principal. However, this method does not lead to the fact that an agent does not maximize its individual utility, but it is rather attempted to bring the agent to actions by directed incentives for which, by maximizing of his individual utility, also the utility of the principal is maximized. In this connection, one also speaks of incentive compatibility [4]. This procedure can be summarized by the terms interest alignment or interest harmonization. In addition to these rather generally formulated functions of incentive systems, incentives can also be divided into single part functions [7]:

- Activation function: stimulation of motivation and cognitive abilities,
- Controlling function: influence of the agents' behavior,
- Information function: agents get signals regarding desirable behavior,
- Selection function: principals get information about agents' performance and
- Coordination function: coordination of single actions of agents.

To ensure that these functions are fulfilled as good as possible, incentive systems shall meet different requirements. On the one hand, incentives need to be economically justifiable. Also the application of incentive mechanisms is only reasonable if the costs caused by the incentive system are lower than resulting (additional) earnings. These costs result from the measures conducted for the incentive system and also the administrative costs.

3 Incentive Design with insufficient Production Capacity

To be able to guarantee and quantify incentives, reasons for this need to be identified. So, not taking part in a value-added process may for an individual enterprise be the best alternative, but not necessarily for the whole network. This would be the case if a core competency is missing in the value-added chain to be able to perform a service in a collaborative network. In such a case the "missing" enterprise needs to be guaranteed suitable incentives for participating. In the following it is assumed that an enterprise does not cooperate due to insufficient production capacity (machine or personnel). Here incentives need to be paid for supplying additional capacities.

There are several approaches to solve this problem. One was is to compensate the additional costs for the enterprise supplying additional capacities. The starting point is that an enterprise is not able to fulfill the respective requirements within the given time frame on the basis of a request of the network. As a reason for this it is assumed that insufficient production capacities lead to this decision. Although a possible completion date can be stated within the frame of the tender preparation, this should however be oriented at the desired date of the customer or, in case the customer does not give a desired date, the date should be within a reasonable time span for the fulfillment of an order. At this point, it must be decided whether the enterprise being the only one offering the demanded core competence can be made giving a (realistic) offer. A practicable solution would be, taken as an example, to create suitable capacities by replanning. This option marks the starting point for the following considerations.

It is assumed that a certain enterprise aspires to be able to give an offer by suitable replanning. The costs accruing by replanning are difficult to quantify, which however is indispensable for the calculation of the incentives. Personnel costs resulting from the replanning taken as an example may be included in the costs of replanning. Additional costs resulting from overtime, nightshifts or weekend work can be included as well. Furthermore, costs accruing from delayed delivery caused by other replanned orders have to be calculated. These additional accruing costs need to be refunded to the affected enterprise, which can be interpreted as an incentive payment. Here, the affected enterprise has to raise a part of the incentive amount by itself. This is explained by the fact that the respective enterprise is entitled to get a share in profit when taking part in the value-added process, which would not be obtained when not participating.

Guaranteeing incentive payments is based on the assumption that all enterprises aspire individual utility maximization. So, it is always first goal to cooperate in a value-added process as long as benefit (profit) can be obtained. For the case that a customer order cannot be realized due to missing enterprises, no benefit can be achieved. As a general rule, abandoning the participation in a value-added process by an enterprise has high probability if the missed benefit is lower than additional costs. These include replanning costs or further costs for capacity expansion. The latter kind of costs includes costs for the purchasing or leasing of a machine, but also additional personnel costs like overtime payments or rewards for working on holidays or at the weekend. Such costs have to be taken into account for consideration of total costs for the calculation of possible incentives.

4 Incentive Design for Lacking Financial Rewarding of an Order

4.1 Description of the Situation

The financial aspect of an order is primarily represented by the profit to be gained for an enterprise. So the focus is laid on approaches for calculating enterprise-related profit shares g_i. For this purpose various approaches have been developed [8] and are available. As a precondition, knowledge concerning the entire distributable profit G is essential. If no quote can be submitted for the concrete enquiry of a customer in the network from the network's side, this situation is unsatisfactory for all involved parties. Therefore, an alternative solution needs to be found.

In the present case, it is assumed that the enterprise(s), which need(s) to be engaged for the considered value-added process possess(es) sufficient production capacity. So, the missing financial profitability of the order can be considered to be the only reason for the rejection. Therefore, it is the aim to convince the respective enterprises (here it is assumed that only one enterprise i^* is concerned) regarding participation in the value-added process by means of suitable incentives. To be able to make a decision for or against an incentive payment, various results connected to the guaranteeing or omission of incentives, need to be analyzed and compared.

Based on the situation that the single shares of profit g_i were determined within the frame of an algorithm for determining the profit G, but no agreement could be found with enterprise i^* regarding profit g_{i*} and therefore it was not possible to submit a quote for a customer enquiry, suitable incentives need to be guaranteed. Quantification of these incentives is described in the following. For this purpose, an algorithm for the calculation of profit and incentive payments within networked production structures is introduced.

Assuring a minimal profit for an enterprise represents a material incentive on the network's side. This incentive is guaranteed in cases if an enterprise rejects participation due to lacking profitability, although the respective core competency is urgently needed to be able to implement the value-added process in the network. This situation always occurs when the share of profit of an enterprise is lower than the expectation of profit (minimal profit) according to the model for distribution of profit. So, a guaranteed minimal profit is a security incentive.

4.2 Calculation of the Individual Share of Profit of an Enterprise

Assumptions. The calculation of the cash flows in the network may be conducted for a comprehensive model regarding the distribution of profit when applying a suitable calculation approach. For the modeling of this approach regarding determining participation incentives, the following five assumptions apply representing the general conditions for the application of incentive mechanisms:

a) guaranteed incentive payments are paid by integration into the process of distribution of profits,
b) each enterprise receives an individual share of profit g_i, which depends on the part in total costs and also consists of a fixed part,
c) all incentive and profit payments (a_i or g_i respectively) resulting from the concrete value-added process have to be financed from the realized network profit G of the considered value-added process,

d) the model for distribution of profit can be modified by agreements about minimal profit shares between network and the single enterprises; the minimal profit share of an enterprise g_i^{min} has to be guaranteed by the regular share of profit and if necessary by an incentive payment.

Modeling. Consecutively the modeling of the calculation approach is introduced. This calculation approach can then be applied if a finite number of enterprises take part in the value-added process, but only one enterprise receives incentive payments.

Condition 1: The sum of the profit share of the enterprises g_i results from the gained or distributable network profit G less all guaranteed incentive payments a_i. This side condition implies that the guaranteed incentive payments a_i in the present model are financed from profit G.

Condition 2: The second condition contains the calculation regulation for the share of profit of enterprises g_i. In the present case, a two-component-approach is applied with a distribution parameter according to [8]. The profit share consists of a fixed and a variable part. Both parts are calculated according to the respective formulas.

Condition 3: The guaranteed minimal profit of an enterprise g_i^{min} consists of the individual realized share of profit of this enterprise g_i and an incentive payment being possibly guaranteed to enterprise a_i. In addition, a difference variable u_i is introduced. Its function is to represent a potential difference between the individual share of profit g_i and the guaranteed minimal profit g_i^{min}. This can occur if the individual share of profit is higher than the guaranteed minimal profit because no incentive payment is necessary. Therefore, variable u_i makes sure that the equation condition is valid also in such cases. Each enterprise represents a specific u_i.

Condition 4: This condition is based on the third condition. So, variable u_i is only applied for cases in which no incentive payment a_i is guaranteed to the respective enterprise. This results in the fact that in this case u_i gets a value of not equal to zero if the incentive payment a_i equals zero and vice versa. Therefore, the product from difference variable u_i and incentive payment a_i has to be zero in each case.

Additional conditions: For completion of the modeling several more model conditions need to be determined. This also contains the respective definition and co domains of the variables. So, non-negativity conditions for the total profit G, the incentive payments a_i, the individual share of profit g_i, the guaranteed individual minimal profits g_i^{min}, the individual costs c_i and the difference variable u_i have to be introduced. Furthermore, it has to be stated that the weighting parameter α shall be between 0 and 1, as the incentive is supposed to be applied independently. Finally, the number of enterprises in the network n has to be defined.

Calculation Approach. In the following, the previously described calculation approach is presented formally. For this modeling, it needs to be noted that only a selected model for distribution of profit according to condition 2 is applied. The calculation approach consists of four equations and three unknown variables a_i , g_i , u_i. This constellation makes an unproblematic solving of the task possible. However, the complexity of the model increases with a rising number of enterprises taking part in the value-added process, as then n+3 equations need to be solved with n+2 unknown variables.

Condition 1: $$\sum_{i=1}^{n} g_i = G - \sum_{j=1}^{n} a_i$$

Condition 2: $$g_i = \alpha \cdot \frac{\sum_{j=1}^{n} g_i}{n} + (1-\alpha) \cdot \frac{c_i}{\sum_{j=1}^{n} c_i} \cdot \sum_{j=1}^{n} g_i$$

Condition 3: $$g_i^{min} = g_i + a_i - u_i$$

Condition 4: $$a_i \cdot u_i = 0$$

Fig. 1. Calculation model for incentives

Example. The calculation approach introduced in the section before can be applied for cases, in which a finite number of enterprises *n* takes part in a value-added process and only one enterprise receives a financial incentive. Having a number of three enterprises in the network, when taken as an example and only one enterprise receiving an incentive, the following six equations result including five unknown variables a_i, g_1, g_2, g_3, u_i.

(1) $$\sum_{j=1}^{n} g_i = G - a_1$$

(2) $$g_1 = \alpha \cdot \frac{\sum_{j=1}^{n} g_i}{n} + (1\text{-}\alpha) \cdot \frac{c_1}{\sum_{j=1}^{n} c_i} \cdot \sum_{j=1}^{n} g_i$$

(3) $$g_2 = \alpha \cdot \frac{\sum_{j=1}^{n} g_i}{n} + (1\text{-}\alpha) \cdot \frac{c_2}{\sum_{j=1}^{n} c_i} \cdot \sum_{j=1}^{n} g_i$$

(4) $$g_3 = \alpha \cdot \frac{\sum_{j=1}^{n} g_i}{n} + (1\text{-}\alpha) \cdot \frac{c_3}{\sum_{j=1}^{n} c_i} \cdot \sum_{j=1}^{n} g_i$$

(5) $$g_1^{min} = g_1 + a_1 - u_1$$

(6) $$a_1 \cdot u_1 = 0$$

Fig. 2. Calculation model for incentives for three network participants

In the following a quick solution finding is demonstrated. Here enterprise 1 was assumed to receive incentive payments. Consideration of this condition in the model leads to the result that the difference variable u_l is zero. It follows:

$$(6) \quad a_1 \cdot u_1 = 0 \qquad a_1 \neq 0 \rightarrow u_1 = 0$$

$$(5) \quad g_1^{min} = g_1 + a_1$$

After that, the formula for a calculation of the profit share has to be created.

$$(1) \quad \sum_{j=1}^{n} g_i = G - a_1$$

$$(2) \quad g_1 = \alpha \cdot \frac{\sum_{j=1}^{n} g_i}{n} + (1\text{-}\alpha) \cdot \frac{c_1}{\sum_{j=1}^{n} c_i} \cdot \sum_{j=1}^{n} g_i$$

$$(1) \text{ in } (2) \rightarrow (2'){:} \quad g_1 = \alpha \cdot \frac{G-a_1}{n} + (1\text{-}\alpha) \cdot \frac{c_1}{\sum_{j=1}^{n} c_i} \cdot (G - a_1)$$

Then, equation (2´) can be included in equation (5).

$$(2') \text{ in } (5) \rightarrow (5'){:} \quad g_1^{min} = \alpha \cdot \frac{G-a_1}{n} + (1\text{-}\alpha) \cdot \frac{c_1}{\sum_{j=1}^{n} c_i} \cdot (G - a_1) + a_1$$

For calculation of the amount of incentive payment a_l, equation (5´) has to be transposed to a_l. To facilitate this process, the following two substitutions are conducted:

$$(1 - \alpha) = \beta$$

$$\frac{c_1}{\sum_{i=1}^{n} c_i} = m_1$$

So, transposition from equation (5´) to a_l can be realized as follows:

$$g_1^{min} = \alpha \cdot \frac{G-a_1}{n} + \beta \cdot m_1 \cdot (G - a_1) + a_1$$

$$g_1^{min} = a_1 + (G - a_1) \cdot (\tfrac{\alpha}{n} + \beta \cdot m_1)$$

$$g_1^{min} = a_1 + G \cdot (\tfrac{\alpha}{n} + \beta \cdot m_1) - a_1 \cdot (\tfrac{\alpha}{n} + \beta \cdot m_1)$$

$$g_1^{min} - G \cdot (\tfrac{\alpha}{n} + \beta \cdot m_1) = a_1 - a_1 \cdot (\tfrac{\alpha}{n} + \beta \cdot m_1)$$

$$g_1^{min} - G \cdot (\tfrac{\alpha}{n} + \beta \cdot m_1) = a_1 \cdot (1 - (\tfrac{\alpha}{n} + \beta \cdot m_1))$$

$$a_1 = \frac{g_1^{min} - G\cdot(\frac{\alpha}{n} + \beta\cdot m_1)}{1 - (\frac{\alpha}{n} + \beta\cdot m_1)}$$

$$a_1 = \frac{G\cdot(\frac{\alpha}{n} + \beta\cdot m_1) - g_1^{min}}{\frac{\alpha}{n} + \beta\cdot m_1 - 1}$$

Finally, the variables inserted by substitution can be replaced by the original terms again. The following formula results from that and by means of it, the amount of the incentive payment to enterprises 1 can be calculated:

$$a_1 = \frac{G \cdot (\frac{\alpha}{n} + (1-\alpha) \cdot \frac{c_1}{\sum_{j=1}^{n} c_i}) - g_1^{min}}{\frac{\alpha}{n} + (1-\alpha) \cdot \frac{c_1}{\sum_{j=1}^{n} c_i} - 1}$$

In addition to the realized individual share of profit g_l, enterprise 1 receives an incentive payment a_l. Consecutively the remaining profit shares can be calculated by means of equations (2), (3) and (4). Finally, all necessary values can be calculated.

5 Conclusions

In the previous sections, it has been proven that the implementation of incentive mechanisms is an effective and promising instrument of the operative network controlling. For this purpose the maximization of the profit both for the network (principal) and for the single enterprises (agents) is realized by guaranteeing financial incentives. Possible criteria for the assessment of a contractual behavior of the enterprises are comparisons between target and actual performance when considering various performance parameters [9]. The provision of service according to the contractual duty has an essential importance for the network as these criteria have a considerable influence on customer satisfaction and decide on the continuance and sustainable success. Because of its structure the model is applicable for an unlimited number of network participants. In case a different approach for profit distribution is considered, the affected side conditions need to be modified.

References

1. Ross, S.A.: The Economic Theory of Agency: The Principal's Problem. American Economic Review 63, 134–139 (1973)
2. Furubotn, E.G., Richter, R.: Institutions and Economic Theory: The Contribution of the New Institutional Economics, 2nd edn. University of Michigan Press, Ann Arbor (2005)
3. Laffont, J.J., Martimort, D.: The Theory of Incentives – The Principal-Agent-Model. Princeton University Press, Princeton (2002)
4. Picot, A., Dietl, H., Franck, E.: Organisation - Eine ökonomische Perspektive, 4th edn. Schäffer-Poeschel, Stuttgart (2005)
5. Macho-Stadler, I., Pérez-Castrillo, D.: An Introduction to the Economics of Information – Incentives and Contracts, 2nd edn. Oxford University Press, Oxford (2001)
6. Milgrom, P., Roberts, J.: Economics, Organization and Management. Prentice Hall, Englewood Cliffs (1992)
7. Winter, S.: Prinzipien der Gestaltung von Managementanreizsystemen. Gabler, Wiesbaden (2002)
8. Jähn, H., Fischer, M., Teich, T.: Distribution of Network generated Profit by considering individual Profit Expectations. In: Camarinha-Matos, L.M., et al. (eds.) Establishing the Foundation of Collaborative Networks, pp. 337–344. Springer, New York (2007)
9. Jähn, H.: Value-added process-related performance analysis of enterprises acting in cooperative production structures. Production Planning & Control 20, 178–190 (2009)

Author Index

GPSR Compliance

The European Union's (EU) General Product Safety Regulation (GPSR) is a set of rules that requires consumer products to be safe and our obligations to ensure this.

If you have any concerns about our products, you can contact us on ProductSafety@springernature.com

In case Publisher is established outside the EU, the EU authorized representative is:

Springer Nature Customer Service Center GmbH
Europaplatz 3
69115 Heidelberg, Germany

Batch number: 10837184

Printed by Printforce, the Netherlands